Dictionary of the Bible and Western Culture

DICTIONARY OF THE BIBLE AND WESTERN CULTURE

Edited by

Mary Ann Beavis
Michael J. Gilmour

SHEFFIELD PHOENIX PRESS

2017

Copyright © 2012, 2017 Sheffield Phoenix Press
First published in hardback, 2012
First published in paperback, 2017
Published by Sheffield Phoenix Press
Department of Biblical Studies, University of Sheffield
45 Victoria Street, Sheffield S3 7QB

www.sheffieldphoenix.com

All rights reserved.
No part of this publication may be reproduced or transmitted in any form or by any means, electronic or mechanical, including photocopying, recording or any information storage or retrieval system, without the publishers' permission in writing.

A CIP catalogue record for this book
is available from the British Library

Typeset by the HK Scriptorium
Printed by Lightning Source

ISBN 978-1-907534-79-9 (hardback)
ISBN 978-1-910928-33-2 (paperback)

Contents

PREFACE	vii
RECOMMENDED READING	ix
ABBREVIATIONS	xi
CONTRIBUTORS	xiii
DICTIONARY OF THE BIBLE AND WESTERN CULTURE	1

Preface

'All writers learn from the dead', according to Margaret Atwood. Indeed, 'the dead control the past, they control the stories, and also certain kinds of truth ... so if you are going to indulge in narration, you'll have to deal, sooner or later, with those from previous layers of time'. Similarly, her fellow Canadian novelist Robert Kroetsch understands writing as dialogue with earlier texts: 'Perhaps the generative moment of my young writer's life came when I realized I had not two *pages* to write upon but rather two *margins* to write in. I could write alongside, with and against, the blackly printed page of our inheritance'.[1] Those reading in the humanities—literature, history, philosophy, religion, law, film studies, language, music, art history, cultural studies—learn quickly that intellectual developments and artistic productions do not occur in a vacuum. They inherit much from the dead, regardless of the subject. Atwood presents the situation as a challenge, reminding us of the need to be aware of those earlier voices. Kroetsch views it as an opportunity to engage those precursors, to embrace and challenge them, 'with and against'.

Readers also discover before long that the Bible is one particularly influential 'layer' of narration. Artists and thinkers from Augustine to *Avatar* write in its margins, telling their own stories alongside that ancient bundle of tales. For many readers, however, the Bible is as remote as *Avatar*'s moon Pandora and its language as incomprehensible as Pandora's Na'vi. This dictionary aims to assist those needing basic, easily accessible information about the Jewish and Christian Scriptures. Whereas more technical dictionaries, encyclopaedias, and commentaries offer the kinds of analyses necessary for in-depth research, our intent is more modest, providing an easy-to-use quick reference for those needing to track down information on characters, phrases, places, and concepts originating in the Bible.

Since we have in mind readers without the specialization of formal biblical studies, and even those not familiar with the Bible's basic content, our presentation is twofold in approach. Entries begin with discussion of biblical terms in their original settings, and then illustrate occasions when those terms reappear in later cultural artefacts. Said differently, though the emphasis falls on definition and context, we are concerned also with the reception of the Bible in later Western artistic and intellectual expression. The instances of reception noted are representative, not exhaustive. Although we have attempted to achieve balance in each entry, the nature of some topics necessitates that matters of historical context are more

---

1. Margaret Atwood, *Negotiating with the Dead: A Writer on Writing* (Cambridge: Cambridge University Press, 2002), 178; Robert Kroetsch, *A Likely Story: The Writing Life* (Red Deer: Red Deer College Press, 1995), 96.

prominent, whereas in others, reception history dominates. The short bibliography below suggests resources to pursue the latter line of inquiry further.

Contributors represent a broad cross-section of scholarship that is diverse geographically, methodologically, theologically, and to a lesser degree, in disciplinary focus. (Most work in religious and/or biblical studies, representing a wide array of institutions.) The opinions expressed on matters of history and literature, and particular interpretations advocated are, needless to say, equally diverse. As in all academic disciplines, scholars do not always agree. As editors, we accept this range of opinion, eclectic as it is, as one of the volume's merits. We did not impose any rigid expectations on individual contributors with respect to content, even when our own opinions varied, something that occurs often.

In his preface to *A Dictionary of the English Language* (1755), the lexicographer Samuel Johnson states the obvious: 'A large work is difficult because it is large, even though all its parts might singly be performed with facility'. We find this remark rather humbling, and it certainly puts our editorial duties in some perspective. Whereas Dr Johnson's dictionary includes more than forty-two thousand terms, ours includes a little more than one thousand. Whereas he prepared his volume on his own—'with little assistance of the learned, and without any patronage of the great', as he put it—we enjoyed the assistance of more than two hundred scholars who generously contributed to this project, including a great deal of proofreading help from Scott Daniel Dunbar. But Dr Johnson we are not, and even though our project is modest in scope next to his, and even with the help of so many, we still confess 'A large work is difficult because it is large'. Our goal of providing a relatively uniform 'voice' for all entries will inevitably fall short, and no doubt the omission of certain topics will surprise some readers, just as the inclusion of others will strike others as odd. Yet for all that, there is much here to explore and discover, and we trust that flipping through these pages will prove illuminating not only as an introduction to biblical literature but also as a demonstration of its persistent contributions to our cultural heritage.

Mary Ann Beavis
Michael J. Gilmour

Recommended Reading

Alter, Robert. *Canon and Creativity: Modern Writing and the Authority of Scripture.* New Haven and London: Yale University Press, 2000.

Culbertson, Philip, and Elaine Wainwright, eds. *The Bible in/and Popular Culture: A Creative Encounter.* Semeia Studies. Atlanta: SBL, 2010.

Dyas, Dee and Esther Hughes. *The Bible in Western Culture: The Student's Guide.* London and New York: Routledge, 2005.

Frye, Northrop and Jay MacPherson. *Biblical and Classical Myths: The Mythological Framework of Western Culture.* Toronto/Buffalo/London: University of Toronto Press, 2004.

Ginzberg, Louis. *Legends of the Bible.* Old Saybrook, CT: Konecky & Konecky, 1956.

Jeffrey, David L. *A Dictionary of Biblical Tradition in English Literature.* Grand Rapids, MI: William B. Eerdmans Publishing, 1992.

Klauck, Hans-Josef et al. *Encyclopedia of the Bible and its Reception.* Multiple volumes. Berlin: Walter de Gruyter, 2009- .

Kugel, James L. *The Bible As It Was.* Cambridge, MA/London: Belknap Press, 1997.

Lieb, Michael, Emma Mason, Christopher Rowland, and Jonathan Roberts, eds. *The Oxford Handbook of Reception History of the Bible.* Oxford University Press, 2011.

Manser, Martin H. *The Facts on File Dictionary of Biblical and Classical Allusions.* New York: Checkmark Books, 2003.

Metzger, Bruce M. and Michael D. Coogan, eds. *The Oxford Companion to the Bible.* New York/Oxford: Oxford University Press, 1993.

Roncace, Mark, and Patrick Gray, eds. *Teaching the Bible Through Popular Culture and the Arts.* Society of Biblical Literature Resources for Biblical Study 53. Atlanta: Society of Biblical Literature.

Ryken, Leland, Jim Wilhoit, Tremper Longman, III, Douglas Penney and Daniel G. Reid, eds. *Dictionary of Biblical Imagery.* Downers Grove, IL: InterVarsity Press, 1998.

Sawyer, John F.A. *A Concise Dictionary of the Bible and its Reception.* Louisville, KY: Westminster John Knox, 2009.

Schippe, Cullen and Chuck Stetson. *The Bible and its Influence.* New York and Fairfax, VA: BLP Publishing, 2006.

Abbreviations

Hebrew Bible / Old Testament

Gen.	Genesis
Exod.	Exodus
Lev.	Leviticus
Num.	Numbers
Deut.	Deuteronomy
Josh.	Joshua
Judg.	Judges
Ruth	Ruth
1–2 Sam.	1–2 Samuel
1–2 Kgs	1–2 Kings
1–2 Chron.	1–2 Chronicles
Ezra	Ezra
Neh.	Nehemiah
Est.	Esther
Job	Job
Ps., Pss.	Psalm, Psalms
Prov.	Proverbs
Eccl.	Ecclesiastes (Qoheleth)
Song	Song of Songs (Song of Solomon, Canticles)
Isa.	Isaiah
Jer.	Jeremiah
Lam.	Lamentations
Ezek.	Ezekiel
Dan.	Daniel
Hos.	Hosea
Joel	Joel
Amos	Amos
Obad.	Obadiah
Jonah	Jonah
Mic.	Micah
Nah.	Nahum
Hab.	Habakkuk
Zeph.	Zephaniah
Hag.	Haggai
Zech.	Zechariah
Mal.	Malachi

New Testament

Matt.	Matthew
Mark	Mark
Luke	Luke
John	John
Acts	Acts
Rom.	Romans
1–2 Cor.	1 Corinthians
Gal.	Galatians
Eph.	Ephesians
Phil.	Philippians
Col.	Colossians
1–2 Thess.	1–2 Thessalonians
1–2 Tim.	1–2 Timothy
Tit.	Titus
Phlm.	Philemon
Heb.	Hebrews
Jas	James
1–2 Pet.	1–2 Peter
1–2–3 John	1–2–3 John
Jude	Jude
Rev.	Revelation

Apocrypha and Septuagint

Bar.	Baruch
Add. Dan.	Additions to Daniel
Pr. Azar.	Prayer of Azariah
Bel	Bel and the Dragon
Song Three	Song of the Three Men
Sus.	Susanna
1–2 Esd.	1–2 Esdras
Add. Est.	Additions to Esther
Ep. Jer.	Epistle of Jeremiah
Jdt.	Judith
1–2 Macc.	1–2 Maccabees
Pr. Man.	Prayer of Manasseh
Ps. 151	Psalm 151
Sir.	Sirach (Ecclesiasticus)
Tob.	Tobit
Wis.	Wisdom of Solomon

Other Ancient Writings

3–4 Macc.	3–4 Maccabees

Abbreviations

Other

b.	born	HB	Hebrew Bible
		KJV	King James Version
b.	born	LXX	Septuagint (the Greek OT)
c.	circa, about	MS(S)	Manuscript(s)
ch(s).	chapter(s)	MT	Masoretic Text
d.	died	NT	New Testament
ET	English translation	*OED*	*Oxford English Dictionary*
frag.	fragment	OT	Old Testament

Contributors

AB	**Amber Beasock** Barton College	AW-J	**Arthur Walker-Jones** University of Winnipeg
AB-E	**Amanda Bahr-Evola** Southern Illinois University	AWP	**Andrew W. Pitts** McMaster Divinity College
ABP	**Andrew B. Perrin** McMaster University	BA	**Bill Anderson** Concordia University College of Alberta
AC	**Amy Cummins** University of Texas Pan American	BCB	**Ben C. Blackwell** Durham University
ACF	**Alison C. Fleming** Winston-Salem State University	BCW	**Brandon C. Wason** Emory University
ACKW	**Andy Chi Kit Wong** PGA College and Theological Seminary	BDGD	**Brenton D. G. Dickieson** University of Prince Edward Island
ACW	**Andrew C. Whitmore** The Catholic University of America	BFR	**Bryan F. Rivers** Université de Saint-Boniface
		BJL	**Bradley J. Longard** Acadia University
AD	**Alex Damm** Independent	BMS	**Beth M. Stovell** St. Thomas University
AdamR	**Adam Reinherz** University of Cambridge	BR	**Bill Richards** College of Emmanuel & St Chad
AG-M	**Alexandra Gruca-Macaulay** Saint Paul University	BRD	**Brian R. Doak** George Fox University
AHC	**Alan H. Cadwallader** Australian Catholic University	BRO	**Benjamin R. Overcash** Macquarie University
AHK	**August H. Konkel** Providence University College and Theological Seminary (Canada)	BVH	**Bracy V. Hill II** Baylor University
AJW	**Andrew J. Waskey** Dalton State College, Morton Memorial Presbyterian Church	BW	**Byron Wheaton** Emmanuel Bible College
		CAE	**Christian A. Eberhart** Lutheran Theological Seminary
AK-H	**Agnes Kramer-Hamstra** McMaster University	CAM	**Calogero A. Miceli** Concordia University, Montreal
AM	**Andrew Martens** ACTS Seminary, Trinity Western University	CBZ	**Christopher B. Zeichmann** University of Toronto
		CC	**Christina Clever** Ruhr-University Bochum
AR	**Andy Reimer** St. Mary's University College	CCB	**Chad C. Brewer** Westminster Seminary California
AS	**Adam Stewart** University of Waterloo	CD	**Cécile Deslandes** Independent
ASYL	**Anna Suk Yee Lee** McMaster Divinity College		

Contributors

CDR	Christopher D. Rodkey, Lebanon Valley College	DLS	David L. Smith, Westmount Baptist Church
CEM	Charles Edward Meeks, University of Toronto	DM	Daniel Maoz, Vice President, Canadian Society for Jewish Studies
CF	Christopher Francis, Barton College	DMac	David MacLachlan, Atlantic School of Theology
CG	Chaviva Galatz, New York University	DN	Dana Nichols, Gainesville State College
CHB	Clayton H. Bench, University of Alberta	DomR	Domenic Ruso, Wycliffe College
CLH	Chelica L. Hiltunen, McMaster University	DP	Daniel Pyke, Acadia University
CRJH	Christopher R. J. Holmes, University of Otago	DR	Delio Ruiz, SCJ, Catholic Biblical Association of the Philippines
CSS	Carl S. Sweatman, University of Gloucestershire	DRB	Derek R. Brown, University of Edinburgh
CZ	Christopher Zoccali, University of Wales Lampeter	DS	Drew Strait, University of Chicago Divinity School
DAB	David A. Bergen, University of Calgary	DunR	Duncan Reid, Wycliffe College
DAS	David A. Skelton, Abilene Christian University	DWB	Drew W. Billings, McGill University
DavS	Davide Sciarabba, Andrews University	EAG	Elizabeth A. Goodine, Loyola University New Orleans
DB	Denis Bekkering, University of Waterloo	ÉB	Éric Bellavance, McGill University
DC	Daniel Chaloner, Independent	ED	Elizabeth Danna, Independent
DCT	David C. Tollerton, Bangor University	EG	Elaine Guillemin, Independent
DD	Darry Dinnell, McGill University	EH	Edward Ho, McMaster Divinity College
DDC	Dries De Crom, Katholieke Universiteit Leuven	EID	Elaine I. Daigle, Acadia University
DEB	David E. Briones, Durham University	EJW	Erin J. Wright, Aarhus University
DG	Deane Galbraith, University of Otago	EM	Eric Montgomery, McMaster University
DHJ	David H. Johnson, Providence University College and Theological Seminary (Canada)	ET	Eliot Tofa, University of Swaziland
DIS	David I. Shaw, Abilene Christian University	EV	Elke Verbeke, Katholieke Universiteit Leuven
DJHB	David J. H. Beldman, University of Bristol	EW	Ellen White, Assumption College
DJP	Darrell J. Pursiful, Mercer University, Smyth & Helwys Publishing	FVG	Franz Volker Greifenhagen, Luther College, University of Regina
DL	Dorothy Lee, Trinity College Theological School, MCD University of Divinity	GDB	Graeme D. Bird, Gordon College

Contributors

GJF	Glen J. Fairen University of Alberta	JHK	Jeremy H. Kidwell University of Edinburgh
GJSK	Grace Ji-Sun Kim Moravian Theological Seminary	JIM	Jesse Ian Myers Milltown Institute
GK	Grenville Kent Wesley Institute	JKG	John K. Goodrich Durham University
GM	Garry Merritt Gainesville State College	JKS	John K. Stafford St. John's College, University of Manitoba
GO	Gordon Oeste Heritage Theological Seminary	JL	Jason Lecureux University of Gloucestershire
GOA	Gabriel O. Alalade University of Toronto	JLZ	Jonathan L. Zecher Durham University
HDZ	H. Daniel Zacharias Acadia Divinity College	JMB	J. Matthew Barnes Fuller Seminary
HK	Hiram Kümper Bielefeld University	JMK	Jonathan M. Kiel Southern Baptist Theological Seminary
HL	Helen Leneman Independent	JNR	Joshua N. Rhone George Fox Evangelical Seminary, Mt. Union Wesleyan Church
HM	Heather Macumber St. Michael's College	JoL	John Lee Midwestern Baptist Theological Seminary
HP	Harold Penner Independent	JP	James Petitfils University of California Los Angeles
IDW	Ian Douglas Wilson University of Alberta		
IHH	Ian H. Henderson McGill University	JPD-W	Janice P. De-Whyte McMaster Divinity College
IK	Isaac Kalimi University of Chicago	JR	Joseph Royal University of Western Ontario
JAL	Jonathan A. Linebaugh Durham University	JRH	James R. Hamrick Trinity Western University
J-AS	Joyce-Ann Spinney Acadia University	JRHa	James R. Harrison Sydney College of Divinity
JBT	J. Brian Tucker Moody Theological Seminary	JRM	John R. Markley University of Edinburgh
JBW	J. Blair Wilgus Hope International University	JRW	Joyce Rilett Wood St. Michael's College, University of Toronto
JC	Justin Corfield Geelong Grammar School	JS	Joshua Scott Princeton Theological Seminary
JCh	Jennifer Chaloner Independent	JSW	Jane S. Webster Barton College
JCP	John C. Poirier Kingswell Theological Seminary	JWB	James W. Barker Luther College
JDB	John D. Barry Editor-in-Chief of *Bible Study Magazine*; Publisher for Logos Bible Software	JZ	Jennifer Zilm McMaster University
JDR	John David Rausch, Jr. West Texas A&M University	KAM	Kimberly A. Miller University of the Cumberlands
JerP	Jeremy Penner McMaster University	KaS	Karl Shuve University of Edinburgh
JFW	Joshua F. Walker Reformed Theological Seminary		

Contributors

KB	Kit Barker Sydney Missionary and Bible College		MD	Marc Debanné École de Théologie Évangélique de Montréal / Université de Sudbury
KCM	Kelly C. MacPhail McGill University		MDM	Mark D. Mathews Durham University
KDH	Kevin Douglas Hill Durham University		MFL	Matthew Forrest Lowe McMaster Divinity College
KDP	Kyle D. Potter Georgetown College		MH	Margaret Hebron Trinity Western University
KFM	Kelvin F. Mutter McMaster Divinity College		MHH	Marina H. Hofman University of Toronto
KJL-P	Kara J. Lyons-Pardue Princeton Theological Seminary		MiraM	Mira Morgenstern The City College of New York
KJV	Katherine J. Veach Claremont Graduate University		MiWH	Michael Warren Helfield York University
KK	Karen Klassen Acadia University		MJG	Michael J. Gilmour Providence University College (Canada)
KrS	Krzysztof Sonek Ecole Biblique (Jerusalem)		MJL	Michael J. Lakey Ripon College Cuddesdon (Oxford, UK)
KS	Kevin Scull University of California Los Angeles		MKWS	Michael K. W. Suh Duke Divinity School
KT	Kari Tolppanen Master's College and Seminary		MLC	Mary L. Coloe Australian Catholic University
LB	Lee Beach McMaster Divinity College		MLG	Maxine L. Grossman University of Maryland
LM	Luca Marulli Adventist University of France		MLW	Matthew L. Walsh McMaster University
LV	Lily Vuong Valdosta State University		MM	Maria Mayo Vanderbilt University
MA	Matthew Arbo University of Edinburgh		MN	Michael Naylor Columbia International University
MAC	Matthew A. Collins University of Chester		MP	Matthew Pfiffner Trinity Western University
MALB	Mary Ann L. Beavis St. Thomas More College, University of Saskatchewan		MRA	Matthew R. Anderson Concordia University (Montreal)
MalouSI	Ma. Marilou S. Ibita Katholieke Universiteit Leuven		MSW	Mark S. Wheller University of Alberta
MaM	Mallory Magelli Barton College		MW	Meredith Warren McGill University
MAP	Mark Anthony Phelps Independent		MWB	Michael W. Boyce Booth University College
MaricelSI	Ma. Maricel S. Ibita Katholieke Universiteit Leuven		MWH	Mark W. Hamilton Abilene Christian University
MattH	Matt Hauger Duke Divinity School		MWM	Matthew W. Mitchell Canisius College
MB	Mark Batluck University of Edinburgh		MWP	Michael W. Pahl Cedarville University
MBS	Mark B. Stephens Wesley Institute			
MBW	Melton B. Winstead Southern Evangelical Seminary			

NTB	Nicholas Thomas Bott Stanford University; Palo Alto University	RKM	Renee Kwan Monkman University of Toronto
NCL	Nancy C. Lee Elmhurst College	RL	Russell Lawson Bacone College
NDL	Nathaniel D. Lollar Brandeis University	RLM	R. Lee McLeod, CJ Asbury Theological Seminary
NH	Norman Habel Flinders University, South Australia	RRJ	Roy R. Jeal Booth University College
NKB	Nathan K. Bennett Claremont Graduate University	SAA	Sean A. Adams University of Edinburgh
NKG	Nijay K. Gupta Durham University	SB	Sandra Beardsall St. Andrew's College
NRP	Neil R. Parker United Church of Canada	SDD	Scott Daniel Dunbar Independent
PDSP	Preston D. S. Parsons The Parish of St. Mary Magdalene, Anglican Diocese of Rupert's Land	SEP	Stanley E. Porter McMaster Divinity College
		SL	Simon Lasair St. Thomas More College
		SNW	Steven N. Waller University of Tennessee
PEN	Paul E. Norrod Asbury Theological Seminary	SP	Seth Pollinger Southeastern Baptist Theological Seminary
PGM	Patrick George McCullough University of California, Los Angeles	SPR	Sara Parks Ricker McGill University
PJS	Peter J. Schuurman University of Waterloo	SS	Shayna Sheinfeld McGill University
PKH	P. Kelly Hernández Princeton Theological Seminary	STS	Sarah Toombs Smith University of Texas Medical Branch
PMF	Philip Michael Forness Princeton Theological Seminary	SV	Sylvain Vachon Acadia University
PRW	Paul R. Wilson Independent Scholar	SW	Simon Woodman Bloomsbury Central Baptist Church
PT	Peter Trudinger Flinders University		
RAHC	Rosemary A. H. Canavan MDC University of Divinity	ShW	Shawn White University of Edinburgh
RB	Roberto Badenas Adventist University of France	SWF	Shawn W. Flynn St. Mark's College
RC	Robyn Cadwallader Flinders University	TÅ	Tobias Ålöw Gothenburg University
RF-C	Raúl Fernández-Calienes St. Thomas University School of Law	TAB	Timothy Andrew Beech Horizon College and Seminary
		TJV	Timothy J. Vermande Art Institute of Indianapolis, and Secretary of the United Methodist Association of Ministers with Disabilities
RFH	Randall Holm Providence University College (Canada)		
RicL	Richard Last University of Toronto	TM	Tyler Mayfield Union Theological Seminary
RJK	Ralph J. Korner McMaster University	TP	Tim Perry Laurentian University Canada
RJM	Robert J. Merecz University of Edinburgh		

Contributors

TR	**Tiberius Rata** Grace College and Theological Seminary	**WJL**	**William John Lyons** University of Bristol
TSM	**T. Scott Manor** University of Edinburgh	**WJP**	**Wendy J. Porter** McMaster Divinity College
VSB	**Vicky S. Balabanski** Flinders University	**YR**	**Yosil Rosenzweig** Senior Rabbi, Congregation Beth Israel (Kitchener, Ontario, Canada)
WAS	**W. Andrew Smith** University of Edinburgh	**ZAC**	**Zeba A. Crook** Carleton University
WB	**Wayne Baxter** Heritage College & Seminary		
WDS	**W. Derek Suderman** Conrad Grebel University College, University of Waterloo		

A

A day is like a thousand years. The phrase 'a day is like a thousand years' comes from a passage found in the letters (epistles) of the NT, 2 Pet. 3.8: 'do not ignore this one fact, beloved, that with the Lord one day is like a thousand years, and a thousand years are like one day'. Most agree this alludes to Ps. 90.4: 'For a thousand years in your sight are like yesterday when it is past, or like a watch in the night'.

The NT often reflects a widespread expectation that the 'Second Coming' of Jesus would occur quickly, and some believed that it would occur during the lifetime of those who had been witnesses to the life of Jesus. As this generation began to die, a variety of challenges occurred to the faith of those awaiting Christ's return. In response, 2 Pet. 3.8 advises believers not to listen to scoffers, for the divine perspective is not the same as the human perspective. The writer advises patience and faith in the promise of return, no matter how long it might take.

Some Christians use this passage to interpret other portions of the Bible. For instance, some use it to claim that the 'days' of creation in Genesis are not literal twenty-four hour periods, thereby attempting to reconcile the account with scientific findings. Others combine it with the seven days of creation to posit that the created order will exist for 7,000 years. These readers generally anticipate that the last 1,000 years will be the millennium, a period of divine rule, introduced with the return of Jesus. Some combine this with the dating scheme of Archbishop James Ussher (1581–1656) in *Annales Veteris Testamenti, a prima mundi origine deducti* (1650), which places creation in 4004 BCE. As the year 2000 approached, some who embraced such readings of the Bible suspected the Second Coming was at hand. When the year 2000 came and went, some recalculated the timeline to accommodate the lunar year and other factors, resulting in new predictions ranging from 2004 to 2057 CE.

Psalm 90 is the basis of a hymn by Isaac Watts, 'O God, our Help in Ages Past', which was sung at the funeral of Sir Winston Churchill and those of countless other people. Similar phrases are found in the sacred books of other religions. The Hindu *Bhagavad-Gita* (8.17) states that the spiritually aware know that the divine Brahma's day lasts a thousand ordinary eras. The Qur'an (22.47; see also 32.5), states that one day in Allah's sight is equal to a thousand years in human time. A variety of songs use a variation of the phrase as a simile for patience and hope in spiritual life, and some, less religious, as a symbol of long-lasting love: Matthew West, 'A Few More Days'; Rosanne Cash, '44 Stories'; Sting, 'A Thousand Years'; The Gathering, 'Every Day Is like A Thousand Years'.

See also PETER, EPISTLES OF; MILLENNIUM; NUMBERS, SYMBOLISM OF; PAROUSIA; SECOND COMING [TJV]

Aaron. A descendent of Levi and the son of Amram (Exod. 6.14-27), Aaron is best known as Moses's older brother (Exod. 4.14). The meaning of his name is uncertain, although it could be derived from Egyptian. He first appears on the scene when God calls Moses to deliver the children of Israel from the Egyptian oppression (Exod. 3–12). He marries Elisheba and they have four sons: Nadab, Abihu, Eleazar, and Ithamar (Exod. 6.23). Aaron serves as Moses's spokesperson both in front of the elders of Israel (Exod. 4.30) and in front of Pharaoh (Exod. 7.2). Along with his two sons Nadab and Abihu, and along with Moses and 70 elders, Aaron is chosen by God to behold God's glory and to feast together before Moses's ascent to the mountain of God where he will receive the Ten Commandments (Exod. 24.1-11). Aaron displays weakness when he listens to the pleas of the people and manufactures a golden calf when Moses tarries on the mountain (Exod. 32). In spite of this, God chooses Aaron and his sons to serve as priests in the tabernacle (Exod. 28; 40.13-16; Lev. 8). Even though he becomes the first high priest, he is not allowed to enter the promised land, but rather dies and is buried on Mount Hor (Num. 20.23-28). The NT presents Elizabeth, the mother of John the Baptist, as a direct descendant of Aaron (Luke 1.5). The writer of Hebrews also mentions Aaron when talking about the priestly ministry of Jesus (Heb. 5.5; 7.11).

In his 'Adoration of the Golden Calf', the Renaissance artist Lucas van Leyden paints Aaron as leading the rebellion. In the Romantic period, James Tissot portrays Aaron and Moses calling the locust plague on the Egyptians.

See also MOSES; PENTATEUCH; PRIEST; HIGH PRIEST [TR]

Abaddon. Abaddon derives from a verb form with the primary meaning of 'perish'. In the HB, the verb frequently refers to divine judgment, often in a context of judgment or military warfare. In wisdom literature, those who act wickedly will perish (Ps. 1.6;

Job 4.9; Prov. 11.10). The concept of destruction extends to a place of destruction, in particular the place of damnation or the underworld. In Hebrew it is found parallel to Sheol, the abode of the dead (Prov. 15.11; 27.20). Once it is parallel with grave (Ps. 88.11).

We find the noun Abaddon three times in Job, a wisdom writing of the Persian period. In a creation context, the writer describes the place of the dead as exposed before God (Job 26.6). In defending the record of his life, Job avers unwavering loyalty to his wife and family, because dispersion of the family is a fire worthy of Abaddon (31.12). In an ode to wisdom, Job searches for a place where he might find wisdom; the poem contains a refrain declaring wisdom cannot be found within the world of humans (28.12-14; 20-22). In this refrain, the limits of the universe are named from the heights to the depths. Abaddon, death, and the deep, the chaotic pre-creation 'waters' that must be conquered, are all found as personified terms; all declare that wisdom cannot be found with them.

In the literature found at Qumran (the Dead Sea Scrolls), Abaddon is the hellish home of Belial in 1QH 3(11) 16, 19, 32. The 'pit' and 'abyss' open and fulminate out billows, arrows, and the 'spirits of the asp' (5[13].27) against hardened hypocrites, leaving them with no hope. The destruction emanating from the pit is interpreted as deceptive influences, especially false teaching, affecting unbelievers, but not those truly loyal to God (2[10].12-34; 4[12].5-22). Angels of destruction from the pit inflict the most sorrowful chagrin and most bitter misfortune as allies of the spirits of perversity and darkness (1QS 3.13–4.14).

In the NT Apocalypse, the name of the angel who controls the realm of the demons is Abaddon and Apollyon (Rev. 9.11). The latter term is Greek for 'Destroyer' (the present participle of the Greek verb for destroy). There may be an allusion to the god Apollo, sometimes called 'Tormentor' by the Romans (Suetonius, *Augustus* 70). Abaddon is either the devil himself or an evil representative of the devil.

In the Talmud, Abaddon appears as the second of the seven names of Gehenna (*'Erub.* 19a); the proof verse is Ps. 88.11. The *Midrash Konen* makes Abaddon the actual second department of Gehenna.

See also GEHENNA; HELL; SATAN; SHEOL [AHK]

Abba. The term *abba* is Aramaic for 'father', which was the common language of Palestine during the time of Jesus. Originally, *abba* was derived from the language of toddlers and suggested an intimacy akin to our English word 'papa' or 'daddy'. However, even before the time of Jesus, adult sons and daughters also began calling their fathers *abba*, meaning something like 'dear father'. It is in this fashion that the NT uses *abba*, as both a term of familiarity and respect. It does not use *abba* with the sense of 'daddy'.

References to God as father (*ab*, 'father'; *abi*, 'my father') in the HB and in Jewish literature of the Second Temple period (e.g., Sirach, Wisdom of Solomon, 1QH) are *statements about* God as father. There are no *direct addresses to* God as father within individual prayers, as is the case in the NT. The only unambiguous pre-Christian Palestinian example of God being addressed as father in prayer is found in a Dead Sea scroll dubbed the 4QApocryphon of Joseph (4Q372 1). However, Joseph uses only *abi* ('my father') therein, rather than the more intimate *abba* ('dear father').

Jesus addresses God as father. However, since the language of the Gospels is Koiné Greek, these authors usually translate the Aramaic *abba* Jesus uses with the equivalent, *patēr* (e.g., Luke 11.2-4, the Lord's Prayer). There are three places, though, where the actual Aramaic word *abba* remains. In Mark 14.36, we find *abba* and *patēr* side by side when Jesus prays in the Garden of Gethsemane. In Romans 8 and Galatians 4, the apostle Paul describes how God's children received the Spirit of adoption. It is out of this new familial relationship with God the Father that 'we cry…' (Rom. 8.15), and 'the Spirit cries…' (Gal. 4.6), '*abba patēr*'.

Throughout the centuries, the Church has sought *abba*-like intimacy with God the Father. Western authors have spurred on untold millions in this quest. Some of the enduring classics from France include *The Imitation of Christ* by Thomas à Kempis (c. 1380–1471), which is one of the most widely translated books in Christian literature, and *The Practice of the Presence of God* by Brother Lawrence (1614–1691), which describes how one's everyday activities can become worshipful service of God. In the British Commonwealth, one could highlight works by the South African Andrew Murray (1828–1917) whose devotional classics, such as *Abide in Christ* and *With Christ in the School of Prayer*, emphasize the need for a rich, personal devotional life. The classic devotional *My Utmost for his Highest* by Scottish minister Oswald Chambers (1874–1917) also remains popular.

Since the 1960s, worship music in the Western world has significantly increased its focus on intimacy with the Godhead. This musical wave parallels the rise of the Charismatic movement. Key names in the North American scene include Bill and Gloria Gaither (e.g., 'Because He Lives'); the Maranatha! Music label, inspired during the Jesus Movement of the 1970s; John Wimber of The Vineyard (e.g., 'Spirit Song'), and his later Canadian counterparts Brian Doerksen (e.g., 'Faithful Father') and Andy Park (e.g., 'In the Secret'); Hosanna / Integrity Music worship leaders such as Paul Baloche, Ron Kenoly, and Don Moen; and Chris Tomlin (e.g., 'Indescribable'). Key names in the British Commonwealth include Graham Kendrick, Matt Redman (e.g., 'Heart of Worship'), Stuart Townend (e.g., 'How Deep the Father's Love for Us') (UK); and Darlene Zschech ('Shout to the Lord') (Australia).

See also FATHER; WORSHIP; MUSIC [RJK]

Abel. This character is often referred to as the 'brother of Cain' or the second son of Adam and Eve (Gen. 4.2a). The biblical text does not explain the meaning of the name 'Hevel'. Usually, it is related to the Hebrew noun *hevel* = steam, breath (Isa. 57.13; Ps. 144.4; Job 7.16), which might allude to the short life of Abel who was murdered by Cain.

Cain was a farmer and Abel a shepherd (Gen. 4.2b) and both brought an offering to the Lord. Cain brought an offering of the fruit of the land (not necessarily 'worthless fruit', *Gen. R.* 22.8), and Abel brought of 'the firstlings of his flock, their fat portions'. The Lord had respect for Abel rather than for Cain. Cain became furious and his jealousy led him to kill Abel when they were in the field far away from their parents (4.3-8). Genesis 4.8 is an abbreviated text that does not explain what Cain said to Abel before killing him (cf. 1 Chron. 21.27; 2 Chron. 1.2-3; 13.10). Accordingly, the Septuagint and the rabbis filled in the gap: 'let us go out into the plain' (*Gen. R.* 22.16). God's words 'Listen, your brother's blood is crying out to me from the ground' (Gen. 4.10) refers to the blood of innocent Abel which was crying for justice because he himself, who was killed suddenly, could not cry for justice (as did, e.g., Zechariah; 2 Chron. 24.22).

In postbiblical literature, Abel became the symbol of an innocent who is murdered for no reason. According to *1 En.* 22.5-8, 'the spirit which had left Abel... (continues to) sue him until all of (Cain's) seed is exterminated from the face of the earth, and his seed has disintegrated from among the seed of the people'. In Matt. 23.35 (// Luke 11.50-51), ascribed to Jesus saying, 'So that upon you (= Jews) may come all the innocent blood shed on the earth, from the blood of innocent Abel to the blood of Zechariah … whom you murdered'. The Gospels refer here to Zechariah who was stoned by command of Joash of Judah in the Temple courtyard (2 Chron. 24.20-22), and thus indicate the first and last murders of innocent people as documented in some first-century collections of Scripture (i.e., Genesis to Chronicles). By these words, Jesus indicates he was not the only one of God's messengers killed by those unwilling to hear the prophet's message. Though Cain was not a Jew, the Jews were assigned blame for the murder of Abel, and they were certain to be punished also for Abel's blood. Some Christian commentators were aware of this problem, still they attempted to Judaize Cain or somehow to relate him to Jews. Hebrews 11.4 regards Abel as the first righteous believer in God. The story of Cain and Abel often influences later fiction and art, as is the case with John Steinbeck's *East of Eden* (1952).

Bibliography. Kalimi, I. *The Retelling of Chronicles in Jewish Tradition and Literature: A Historical Journey*. Winona Lake, IN: Eisenbrauns, 2009. Thatcher, T. 'Cain and Abel in Early Christian Memory: A Case Study in 'The Use of the Old Testament in the New'.' *CBQ* 72 (2010) 732-51.

See also CAIN; JESUS OF NAZARETH; JOASH; ZECHARIAH [IK]

Abigail. Abigail (meaning, 'my father is joy') was a woman in Judah who wisely placated David when her husband, the wealthy farmer Nabal, insulted him. In the narrative of David's rise to kingship, David and his 600 followers are on the run from King Saul. Nabal (meaning, 'fool', 'wineskin, bladder', in Hebrew, though it may come from another language) insults David's messengers and refuses to repay him for security duty. David, already depressed due to the recent death of his supporter Samuel the prophet, is stung and demoralized by Nabal's insult, exclaiming, 'Surely it was in vain that I protected all that this fellow has … he has returned me evil [Hebrew *ra*] for good' (1 Sam. 15.21). David marches 400 men to attack and kill all Nabal's men (the Hebrew literally says 'everyone who pisses on the wall' vv. 23, 34).

A servant tells Abigail of Nabal's rudeness, so she sends gifts of food, and sets out personally to meet David. In the Bible's longest female speech, Abigail shows respect, apologizes, offers food to his men, reminds David of God's promise of kingship, rebuilds his hope, visualizes his positive future, and persuades him to avoid revenge and the bloodguilt it would bring, urging that 'evil [*ra*] shall not be found in you so long as you live'. David thanks God for Abigail's good sense, and decides he will leave vengeance to God.

Abigail goes home to find her husband drunk. In the morning, Nabal is apparently urinating (Hebrew: 'while the wine was going out of Nabal / bladder', characterizing him as a walking wineskin). His wife tells him that armed men had come to the house the previous night. Nabal falls down with heart problems and later dies, a target of poetic justice with a comedic touch: David wanted to kill all the men, which would have unjustly victimized innocent men including the servant who had spoken up for him, yet God's vengeance falls only on the guilty man, the 'wall-pisser' himself. David thanks God for having 'kept back his servant [David] from evil (*ra*)' and 'returned the evildoing (*ra*) of Nabal upon his own head' (1 Sam. 25.39). David's view on theodicy seems to be that God solves the problem of evil through justice to the guilty and grace to the repentant. Abigail then marries David, becoming his second wife (1 Sam. 25.43) and adding her wealth and political connections to his cause. She bears his second son, variously named Chileab (2 Sam. 3.3) or Daniel (1 Chron. 3.1), though he does not figure in the accounts of later struggles among David's sons' to inherit his throne.

Feminist scholarship has variously seen Abigail as the stereotypical modest wife constructed by the patriarchy, or as a subversive, a survivor, and a strong political operator. The name Abigail is still popular. David also had a sister (or perhaps half-sister) named Abigal (2 Sam. 17.25) or Abigail (1 Chron. 2.16-17).

Recommended reading. Alter, Robert. *The David Story: A Translation with Commentary of 1 and 2 Samuel*. New York: Norton, 1999. Brenner, Athalya. *The Israelite Woman: Social Role and Literary Type in Biblical Narrative*. Sheffield: Sheffield Academic Press, 1985.

See also DAVID; NABAL [GK]

Abimelech (Hebrew, *'abimelek*). The name Abimelech refers to several biblical figures. In Gen. 20.1-18, Abraham and his wife Sarah settle in the Philistine area of Gerar. Abraham passes Sarah off as his sister, and unknowingly Abimelech, king of Gerar, takes her for himself, though he does not sleep with her. Consequently, the women in Abimelech's household can no longer have children (20.17-18). When God reveals Abimelech's error to him, Abimelech makes reparations to Abraham and Sarah (20.14-15). In Gen. 21.22-34, Abraham and Abimelech make a non-aggression treaty that includes water rights to a well dug in the wilderness of Beersheba. The early church father Origen (*Homilies on Genesis* 6.2) interprets Abimelech's restraint regarding Sarah allegorically, suggesting that Abimelech represents the world-wise person who knows something of God and godly ethics, yet is not a fully committed God-follower.

The experiences of Isaac, Abraham's son, mirror those of his father with Abimelech, king of Gerar. He too settles near Gerar and fears for his life, also passing off his wife Rebekah as his sister (Gen. 26.1-11), before Abimelech discovers otherwise. Abimelech sends Isaac away, but Isaac's growing wealth, which includes water rights to numerous wells, serves as a point of contention between Isaac's servants and the servants of Abimelech. Abimelech and Isaac resolve the issue by negotiating a treaty, also in the area of Beersheba (26.31-33).

The name Abimelech also appears in the superscription of Psalm 34 in reference to a Philistine king during the time of David. The repeated use of the name Abimelech for Philistine kings may suggest that Abimelech (meaning 'my father is king' or 'father of the king') served as a generic title for Philistine kings.

Abimelech is also the name of one of the seventy sons of Gideon (also known as Jerubbaal) in the period of the Judges (Judg. 8.31; 9.1-57; 10.1). Abimelech is the son of Gideon and his concubine from Shechem, who persuades his mother's kinfolk to support his bid for kingship in the city of Shechem, becoming the first Israelite king. After receiving the endorsement of the Shechemites, Abimelech secures his kingship by slaughtering his seventy brothers upon one stone (Judg. 9.5). One brother, Jotham, survives and through a fable warns of mutual destruction if Abimelech's coronation proceeds (Judg. 9.7-21). His words go unheeded, and the people of Shechem soon rebel against Abimelech, pledging allegiance to a rogue named Gaal. Abimelech subsequently attacks and destroys Shechem and all the Shechemites (including his family) before he himself is mortally wounded when a woman drops a millstone on his head at the tower of Thebez. Judges 9 then interprets this mutual destruction as the hand of God (9.56-57). The writer of 2 Samuel uses Abimelech as an example of someone who (foolishly) wandered too close to a city wall during battle (11.21).

The Puritan John Milton (1608–1674) saw in Abimelech's abuse of power and death at the hand of a woman a warrant for individuals to resist tyranny (*Defence of the People of England*, 1651). Abimelech's brutality, noted French Deist Voltaire (1694–1778), compared well with that of any modern king (*Bible enfin expliquée*, 1776). Jewish theologian Martin Buber suggested Jotham's fable was 'the strongest anti-monarchical poem of world literature' (*The Kingship of God*, 1967).

Recommended reading. Boogaart, T.A. 'Stone for Stone: Retribution in the Story of Abimelech and Shechem'. *Journal for the Study of the Old Testament* 32 (1985) 45-56.

See also ABRAHAM; GIDEON; KINGSHIP; PHILISTINES [GO]

Abishag. Abishag the Shunammite is a beautiful young woman who appears in the first two chapters of 1 Kings. We first hear of her in 1 Kgs 1.3-4. The servants of David send Abishag to care for the ailing king. Abishag keeps David warm in bed and ministers to him in other matters but the Bible makes it clear the two do not engage in sex together. We hear Abishag's name again after David's death, when one of his sons Adonijah asks for Solomon's permission to marry Abishag (2.16-18). What motivates this request remains elusive, but King Solomon seems to view this as an ambitious political move (2.19-22) and has his half-brother Adonijah put to death (2.24-25).

The Bible, then, provides very limited information regarding Abishag. Other than her odd relationship with David and a brief comment on her beauty, we know next to nothing about her. However, this paucity of information helped fuel the imagination of later readers. For instance, rabbinic literature explains that David did not marry Abishag because the king already had the maximum number of wives and he did not want to divorce one of them to make room for the young virgin (*b. Sanh.* 22a). In this same passage we find an explanation of why Solomon's execution of his brother over Abishag was a sensible decision (*b. Sanh.* 22a). The name of Abishag appears in later poetry as well, such as Byron's *Don Juan*, Rainer Maria Riike's 'Abishag', Stephen Duck's 'The Shunamite', and Robert Frost's 'Provide, Provide'. Abishag is also a popular subject for painters (e.g., Richard Earlom's *Bathsheba Leading Abishag to David*).

Though a minor character whose name is mentioned only a few times in the Bible, Abishag sometimes plays a much more important role in contemporary motion pictures that retell the stories of David and Solomon. For example, Abishag has a greatly expanded role in the story presented in *Solomon and Sheba* (1959) and *Solomon* (1997), including plots such as how she died and how Adonijah fell in love with her. In the original soundtrack of *Solomon and Sheba*, one of the tracks is titled 'Death of Abishag [*Morte di Abishag*]', indicating the greatly amplified significance of this character in the movie.

The story of David and Abishag the Shunammite also inspired a practice coined as Shunamitism, which involves an old man sleeping with a young virgin in hope of physical rejuvenation. This is, of course, no longer an acceptable practice in modern societies but some physicians used to consider Shunamitism an effective treatment of aging. For example, the English philosopher/scientist Francis Bacon and the English physician Thomas Sydenham in the seventeenth century, and the Dutch medical professor Hermann Boerhaave and the German physician Christoph Wilhelm Hufeland in the eighteenth century approved and/or recommended Shunamitism to their patients.

Recommended reading. Gunn, D.M. *The Story of King David: Genre and Interpretation* JSOTSup, 6. Sheffield: JSOT Press, 1978.

See also KINGS, BOOKS OF; DAVID; SOLOMON [ACKW]

Abraham. The story of Abraham the patriarch begins in Gen. 11.27 and it appears under the heading, 'These are the generations of Terah'. Abraham, the son of Terah, is introduced to the Bible reader as Abram. Abram means 'exalted father', but God changes his name into Abraham, 'father of a multitude' (Gen. 17.5). Abraham is a person of faith. When God tells Abraham to leave his family and his country to go to a place that God will later reveal to him, Abraham obeys. Along with the command, God also gives Abraham the promise of a great name, a great people, and a great land (Gen. 12, 15, 17). He lives a semi-nomadic life, and his wanderings take him from Ur to Shechem, Bethel, the Negeb, and even Egypt. Though God promises Abraham and his wife Sarah an heir (Gen. 15.4-5), Abraham does not wait but instead has a son through his wife's Egyptian maiden, Hagar (Gen. 16.1-16). Eventually, Sarah gives birth to the promised child, Isaac. Abraham passes the greatest test of his life when he is willing to sacrifice this son of promise (Gen. 22). After Sarah's death, Abraham marries Keturah, with whom he will have six more children (Gen. 25.2). Yahweh is often identified as the God of Abraham, Isaac, and Jacob (e.g., Exod. 3.15; Luke 20.37; Acts 3.13).

Abraham is very much present in the NT as well. He is part of Jesus' genealogy (Matt. 1.1, 2, 17), and Jesus tells his audience that Abraham will be a fixture in heaven and at the heavenly banquet (Matt. 8.11; Luke 16.19-31). The apostle Paul makes many allusions to Abraham. In Romans, Paul writes of Abraham's faith (Rom. 4.1-12). In his letter to the Galatian churches, Paul affirms that those who believe are descendants of Abraham (Gal. 3). The writer of Hebrews makes many allusions to Abraham, but most importantly, Abraham appears in the so-called Hall of Faith (Heb. 11.8, 17).

Abraham plays an important role not only in Judaism and Christianity but also in Islam. His name appears almost two hundred times in the Qur'an where he is presented as a prophet sent by God. According to the Qur'an, Abraham built a temple for God at Mecca.

Western artists captured various scenes from Abraham's life in their paintings especially during the Renaissance period. Pieter Lastman, a student of Rembrandt, painted *Abraham on the way to Canaan*, while Caravaggio, Rembrandt, and Tiepolo used their imagination to envision the near-sacrifice of Isaac described in Genesis 22.

See also AQEDAH; COVENANT; GENESIS, BOOK OF; GOD; ISAAC; KETURAH; LOT; PATRIARCHS AND MATRIARCHS [TR]

Absalom. Absalom was the third son of David. His mother was Maacah, the daughter of Talmai, the king of Geshur. The elements of 'father' (*ab*) and 'peace' or 'recompense' (*shalom*) in his name could not provide more irony for his choices in life and relationship with his father. His story dominates the section of the Bible known to scholars as the Succession Narrative (2 Sam. 13–1 Kgs 2), in which the successor to David is revealed. Absalom appears in the story after half brother Amnon rapes his full sister Tamar (2 Sam. 13.1-19). Absalom took her into his personal estate. Women who were not virgins could command little or no bride wealth upon marriage; princesses who were not virgins could not be exchanged for diplomatic marriages. Absalom's motive for killing Amnon, the first born of David, may involve more more than simple revenge (killing an Israelite for the crime of rape is unparalleled in the HB). The murder left him next in line to the throne. After the death of Amnon (2 Sam. 13.28-29), Absalom fled to the court of Talmai where he remained in exile for three years. Joab's machinations eventually ensure David's reconciliation to Absalom (2 Sam. 14).

Absalom was ambitious, however, and plotted to usurp his father's rule. He went to Hebron, David's original capital, and sent messengers throughout the tribes to raise support for a campaign against his father. David fled Jerusalem for the wilderness, from which his army will be better suited to defeat the forces of Absalom. Absalom then entered Jerusalem and publicly defiled David's remaining concubines, an act proclaiming he was replacing his father as king (16.20-23).

The mission of Hushai the Archite (and the priests and their sons) ultimately sent Absalom to his doom. His decision to follow the deliberately bad advice of Hushai lead to a decisive battle. The story of his death by the hand of Joab is part of another literary unit, referred to by scholars as the Davidic Apology (1 Sam. 18–2 Sam. 24). It is a collection of stories (starting with the expulsion of David by Saul) in which violent acts surrounding David are shown to be circumstances which he could not avoid (such as Saul and Jonathon's deaths). The death of Absalom is an event which appears rather unseemly at first glance, involving the killing of the king's son to secure political power. However, in the course of the Apology, it is clear that David loved his son and gave explicit orders that he should not be hurt. Yet again, the bad guy is Joab, not David (cf. 2 Sam. 3.6-39).

See also DAVID; JOAB [MAP]

Achan. Achan, the son of Carmi from the tribe of Judah, brought trouble on the Israelites after they entered the promised land under the leadership of Joshua. Contrary to God's instructions, given through Joshua, Achan took 'devoted things' that were supposed to be destroyed during the conquest of Jericho (Josh. 7.1). Because of this sin, the Israelites lost a battle against the small fortress of Ai. Although Achan confessed his sin after he was found out (7.20-21), he and his family were stoned in the Valley of Achor (7.25-26). The phrase 'Achan's sin' appears on occasion, referring to greed or a hidden crime.

See also JOSHUA; JOSHUA, BOOK OF; FALL OF JERICHO, THE [TR]

Acts of the Apostles, the. The Book of Acts is the fifth book in the NT, located between the Gospels and the Pauline letters. It was written by the author of the third Gospel, traditionally attributed to St Luke. This book commences with the ascension of Jesus into heaven after the resurrection, and his promise of the coming Holy Spirit (Acts 1.1-11). The arrival of the Spirit occurred during Pentecost, an occasion marked by a number of miraculous signs as the Apostle Peter addressed the crowds, and many 'welcomed his message' (Acts 2.41). Following this, there are a number of stories about miracles performed by the believers and growing tensions between the Christians and the Jewish authorities. The latter culminate with the stoning of Stephen on the authority of Saul, later renamed Paul (Acts 6–7). Saul the persecutor of Jesus' followers encountered the risen Jesus himself while on the road to Damascus. He becomes an ardent Christian (Acts 9.1-19) and his proclamation of the gospel around the north Mediterranean comprises much of the later chapters of Acts.

After the story of Saul/Paul's encounter with Jesus, the scene shifts to Peter and the conversion of Cornelius and his household (Acts 10). Up until this time, Luke's presentation of the church was comprised largely of Jewish people. With the conversion of Cornelius and his family, the story shifts to the spread of the gospel among the gentiles. The second half of the Book of Acts focuses on Paul's missionary journeys in which he takes his message through Asia Minor, Greece and finally in Rome. Throughout Paul's journeys, he encountered opposition and eventually Paul is arrested as an agitator. Acts ends with Paul arriving in Rome as a prisoner, though the book ends without reporting the outcome of his trial. The Book of Acts is the second half of Luke's Gospel, therefore forming a two-part work outlining the major events of Jesus' life (Luke) and the early church's activities soon after the resurrection (Acts), with particular focus on the Apostles Peter and Paul.

The Book of Acts plays a dominant role in the house/home church models that have developed in the late twentieth and early twenty-first centuries. This movement looks to the example of early Christian gatherings in Acts, which met in the homes of believers. Typically resistant to meeting in large church buildings, this movement involves the formation of small intimate groups of Christians that help meet the specific needs of its members without the high overhead of a church building. This movement is particularly prominent in countries where Christianity is heavily persecuted or illegal, because it is more inconspicuous and easier to hide from the authorities.

Recommended reading. Fitzmyer, Joseph A. *The Acts of the Apostles: A New Translation and Commentary.* Anchor Bible, 31. New York: Doubleday, 1998. Pervo, Richard I. *Acts.* Hermeneia. Minneapolis: Fortress Press, 2008. Peterson, David. *The Acts of the Apostles.* Pillar New Testament Commentary. Grand Rapids: Eerdmans, 2009.

See also CHURCH; DAMASCUS ROAD; GENTILES; SYNOPTIC GOSPELS; LUKE, GOSPEL OF; PAUL, THE APOSTLE; PENTECOST; PETER, THE APOSTLE [SAA]

Adam. The Hebrew word *adam* can be a generic term for 'humankind' or refer to a particular 'human being' (of either sex). There are only five verses in the Bible where *adam* is clearly the proper name of the archetypical male whose creation is mentioned in Gen. 1 and 2, and whose sin and expulsion from the Garden of Eden is recounted in Gen. 3. According to Gen. 5.5, Adam lived 930 years, a symbolic number emphasizing his great vitality as a primeval patriarch that creates the impression that he and his descendants lived in a very distant past. The etymology of the word *adam* is uncertain, but there is an obvious wordplay between the terms *adam*, *adamah* ('ground', 'soil'), *adom* ('red'), and *dam* ('blood').

Among interpreters of Adam's story, the Apostle Paul stands out. He draws on the narrative of Adam's disobedience in Gen. 3 and develops a rather pessimistic view of human character in Rom. 5, interpreting Adam's failure as the cause of sin and death experienced by the human race. However, the New Adam, Jesus Christ, brings justification and life to all humanity. Augustine of Hippo (354–430) elaborates on this teaching, and transforms it into the doctrine of original sin. Some Talmudic rabbis (fifth century) argued Adam was a hermaphrodite, based on Gen. 1.27, and only afterwards did God create the first woman. Maimonides (1135–1204 CE) maintained Adam's defining feature was his intellect, explaining Adam's sin as a substituting of physical pleasures for the contemplation of intellectual truths.

Visual representations of Adam in European art abound, often portraying him with his wife Eve. The earliest examples are Christian frescos at Naples (second century), Dura-Europos (third century), and the Junius Bassus sarcophagus in Rome (fourth century). However, the best-known depiction of Adam is Michelangelo's *Creation of Adam* (1512), found on the ceiling of the Sistine Chapel in the Vatican. George Handel contrasts Adam and Christ in the *Messiah* (1741) when he alternates a plaintive lament with a triumphant song, both based on 1 Cor. 15.21-22. Joseph Haydn devotes part of his oratorio *The Creation* (1798) to the happy hours the first pair spent in Eden.

Adam appears in many works of literature, and one of the oldest is the twelfth-century Anglo-

Norman play *Jeu d'Adam*. Shakespeare refers to the Adam tradition in a humorous way in *Much Ado about Nothing* (1598). In *Paradise Lost* (1667), John Milton depicts Adam as both a heroic and sinful character, who hopes for future redemption brought by Christ. Milton's masterpiece was later illustrated by William Blake (1808), and his expressive watercolors remain a powerful commentary on Milton's work and an expression of Blake's vision of humanity. Some writers have tried to fill gaps in the biblical narrative about Adam, and Mark Twain's short story *Extracts from Adam's Diary* (1904) is one of the cleverest literary attempts to do it.

In popular culture, the figure of Adam is often linked to the theme of sin. Bob Marley in his reggae song 'Adam and Eve' admits the first couple sinned, but he wants to know why that happened. In contrast, Red Hot Chili Peppers' 'Shallow Be thy Game' is an iconoclastic manifesto rejecting the idea of original sin traditionally associated with Adam. Finally, in *Simpsons Bible Stories* (*The Simpsons*, tenth season, 1999), Adam is portrayed as a simpleton who protests against the expulsion from Eden by saying 'God is love, right?'

Recommended reading. Capoa, Chiara de. *Old Testament Figures in Art*. Los Angeles: J. Paul Getty Museum, 2003. Westermann, Claus. *Genesis 1–11: A Commentary*. Trans. J.J. Scullion. Minneapolis: Augsburg, 1984.

See also ADAM'S RIB; CREATION; EVE; FINGER OF GOD; GARDEN OF EDEN; NAMING OF THE ANIMALS

[KRS]

Adam's rib. The Hebrew word *tsela* ('side', 'rib') appears in the Bible in different contexts. In Gen. 2.21-22 it refers to the creation of the first woman from the first man's side, or, as most translators suggest, his rib. Since most read the Hebrew *ha-adam* ('the man' in Gen. 2.21-22) as a proper name, the phrase *Adam's rib* entered popular parlance. Although the original meaning of this striking imagery is no longer accessible to us, the image fits well other ancient Near Eastern stories about the origin of humankind. It conveys the truth that man and woman belong together and share the same human nature but, at the same time, they are different in terms of physical appearance. Theologians of the first century speculated on the relationship between man and woman in the light of this biblical image. For Philo of Alexandria, the image proves the inferiority of women (see *QG* 1.27), whereas for Paul the Apostle (1 Cor. 11.12), it speaks of their equality.

Ephrem the Syrian, a fourth-century Christian theologian, contrasts the 'bareness' of Adam's rib with the beautiful appearance of the first woman, and thus emphasizes God's creative powers. For the next generation of theologians, notably Augustine of Hippo (354–430) and Jerome (347–420), the story of the woman's creation out of the man's rib is a symbol foreshadowing the union of Christ and his Church. Talmudic (see *Yevamot* 61b) and medieval Jewish interpreters (e.g., Nahmanides, thirteenth century) go in a different direction: they underline the close relationship between the man and the woman, and see in the biblical imagery the beginning of the institution of marriage.

The most famous example of the visual representation of Eve's creation from Adam's rib is Michelangelo's fresco painted on the ceiling of the Sistine Chapel (1512). Adam's deep sleep contrasts sharply with Eve's joy and surprise when she looks at her Creator depicted as an old man and symbolizing the archetypal matchmaker. In literature, Chaucer interprets the biblical image of the woman's creation in terms of mutual love and compatibility between both sexes ('The Parson's Tale' in *The Canterbury Tales*, fourteenth century).

In modern popular culture, *Adam's Rib* (1949) is a romantic comedy featuring Katharine Hepburn and Spencer Tracy, which, according to the American Film Institute, was voted the seventh best film in the romantic comedy category. The film illustrates the never-ending tension between the two sexes, and points out the issue of women's inequality.

Recommended reading. Capoa, Chiara de. *Old Testament Figures in Art*. Los Angeles: J. Paul Getty Museum, 2003. Westermann, Claus. *Genesis 1–11: A Commentary*. Trans. J.J. Scullion. Minneapolis: Augsburg, 1984.

See also ADAM; BONE OF MY BONE; EVE [KRS]

Adoption. From the Greek *hyiothesia*, the term adoption appears in four Pauline verses: Rom. 8.15, 23; 9.4; Gal. 4.5; Eph. 1.5. Though specific adoption language does not appear before the NT, several OT passages mention the fatherhood of God with both Israel (e.g., Deut. 32.5-6; Isa. 63.8, 16; Mal. 1.6; 2.10) and specific leaders identified as children (e.g., 2 Sam. 7.14; Ps. 2.7; 89). The Bible portrays individuals as adopted, though without the explicit language in the text (e.g., Moses by Pharaoh's daughter, and possibly Jesus by Joseph).

Brief mentions of adoption occur in catalogues of God's blessing in Eph. 1 and Rom. 9. In Rom. 8 and Gal. 4, Paul incorporates adoption language into larger soteriological discourses. The Romans passage focuses on the physical and ontological aspects of the freedom enjoyed by those adopted, as it explores being conformed to Christ's image through suffering and glory. Liberation is also the focus in Galatians but the primary concern here is the Law rather than death as in Romans. In both passages, Paul mentions the 'Abba, Father' cry in association with the Spirit's work (cf. Luke 22.42).

There is debate whether Paul has in mind Jewish or Greco-Roman adoption when he writes. Even though there is no specific mention of adoption in Jewish writings, the concept of sonship as a signifier of God's eternal redemption appears regularly in intertestamental literature. With passages like 2 Sam. 7.14 and Ps. 89, some draw a correlation between adoption of the Messiah and of believers (cf. Rom. 1.4 and 8.15, 23). Others argue that adoption refers to a second Exodus, based on the slavery and freedom antithesis. On the other hand, adoption is familiar in Greek and Roman society, with legal instructions regulating its practice. However, the majority of documented Greco-Roman adoptions occur only at the highest levels of society, particularly in the imperial household (e.g., Hadrian by Trajan) to maintain family political control.

Adoption holds a central position for Greek patristic theologians' soteriological model of deification. In particular, these theologians note that believers are called 'gods' based on the association of sonship and implied immortality in Ps. 82.6 (81.6 LXX; cf. John 10.33-36). In later theological debates, adoptionism is also a description of a type of Christology where Jesus is a normal human until divinized at his baptism or at some other point.

The western practice of adoption probably stems more from our inheritance of Greco-Roman culture than from the Bible. Thus, numerous accounts of adopted children occur in literature, such as in *Anne of Green Gables* by Lucy Maud Montgomery or *Ben Hur* by Lew Wallace, but these are not specifically associated with biblical notions of adoption. With no explicit narrative accounts of adoption in the Bible, adoption does not find regular representation in religious art. One may, however, see an example of Moses's experience in Paolo Veronese's painting *Moses Found*.

Recommended reading. Scott, James M. *Adoption as Sons of God*. WUNT 2/48. Tübingen: Mohr–Siebeck, 1992.

See also SALVATION; ABBA [BCB]

Adultery. The unabridged *OED* offers the following definition of *adultery*: 'voluntary sexual intercourse of a married person with one of the opposite sex, whether unmarried, or married to another (the former case being technically *single*, the latter *double adultery*'. OT writers employ the Hebrew verb *na'aph* and cognates to denote adultery, whereas those of the NT use *moicheuolaomai* and cognates. In the Bible, the term adultery can also indicate unchaste behavior generally.

Mosaic Law strictly prohibited adulterous intercourse (Exod. 20.14; Lev. 18.20; Deut. 5.18; John 8.2-5) and both offenders incurred the death penalty (Lev. 20.10; Deut. 22.22, cf. 23-24; Ezek. 18.11-13; 22.11; Mal. 3.5). Sexual intercourse with the concubine of another man did not constitute a capital offence but a misdemeanor: atonement required a guilt offering (Lev. 19.22). However, the sexual exploitation of Jacob's concubine by his son Reuben was deemed to have been incest rather than adultery (Gen. 35.22; 49.3-4; 1 Chron. 5.1).

The NT writers also proscribe adultery (e.g.,1 Thess. 4.1-8; cf. 1 Cor. 6.15-20). Interestingly, a man might divorce his wife on grounds other than sexual impropriety on her part, but should he remarry he commits adultery (Matt. 19.1-9), and should she remarry she and her subsequent husband commit adultery (Matt. 5.31-32; cf. the stricter ruling in Mark 10.11-12). Jesus characterizes lust as adultery 'in one's heart' (Matt. 5.28).

Ancient Near Eastern societies understood marriage as covenant so adultery was not primarily considered moral depravity, but rather violation of the husband's right of sole position of his wife and the guarantee that his children were his. Later the word adultery found figurative application to Israel's apostasy in the prophets (e.g., Hos. 1.2; 2.1-23). Israel's 'adulteries' are said to have separated her and God. Elsewhere God resolves to divorce his 'adulterous wife' (Jer. 3.8-9). Likewise, NT writers employ the metaphor of adultery in connection with religious unfaithfulness (see Matt. 12.39-40; Mark 8.38; Rev. 2.20-22). Early Christian post-NT writers also proscribed *adultery*, but some applied the label to any marriages of which they disapproved. Thus Athenagorus of Athens maintains the indissolubility of marriage even by death. He denigrates second marriage as 'cloaked *adultery*' (*contra* Paul, see Rom. 7.1-3).

Mediaeval authors upheld the Church's teaching. Geoffrey Chaucer explained the location of the commandment against adultery in the Decalogue: sandwiched between those against theft and murder, adultery constitutes the greatest of each—theft of the body and murder of the one-flesh spousal union.

There is much less consensus among Modernist authors. D.H. Lawrence's short story 'Two Blue Birds' reflects ambivalence toward adultery; the sterile relationship with her husband provided the backdrop for the wife's extra-marital affairs. However, the opening couplet of Ezra Pound's satire on the poor role modelling of the two mother figures in his poem 'The Patterns' presupposes rejection of adultery.

The treatment of adultery in modern entertainment is decidedly more casual but nonetheless, Western jurisprudence continues to reflect biblical mores. Adultery constitutes incontestable grounds for divorce.

Recommended reading. Baumann, Gerlinde. *Love and Violence: Marriage as Metaphor for the Relationship between YHWH and Israel in the Prophetic Books*. Trans. Linda M. Maloney. Collegeville, MN: Liturgical Press, 2003.

See also BATHSHEBA; COVENANT; DIVORCE; HOSEA, BOOK OF; IMMORALITY; MARRIAGE [NRP]

Agapē. One of four Greek words for love, *agapē* was originally (in the classical Greek period) a somewhat colorless word used for affection and compassion, and covering a wide range of possible positive treatments of people. The NT writers, however, took the word over and filled it with content denoting self-sacrificing, willful, unconditional love as found in God. It combines the meaning of two Hebrew words, *'āhēb* (love) and *hesed* (loving kindness, mercy). It is God's preeminent attribute. First John 4.8 and 16 tell us, 'God is love'. From God's active love flow many of his other attributes: grace (2 Cor. 8.9); mercy (Hos. 1.6); patience (Judg. 2.11-12); goodness, faithfulness, and knowledge.

This doctrine of God is the distinctive gift of the Christian faith (although Sir John Templeton argues that *agapē* love itself may be found in eight different world religions). Because we love, we know that we have passed from death to life (1 John 3.14). If we love Christ, we will obey his commandments (John 14.15). If we refuse to forgive those who have offended us, it is a sign that we are empty of God's love (1 John 2.9-11). *Agapē* is as much an act of the will as an emotion; we are called on to love our enemies (Matt. 5.44).

One should not make the mistake of thinking that the above meaning is the only one in use, even by the Gospel writers. It may denote a willful love of aspects opposed to the divine. For example, in 2 Tim. 4.10, Paul writes that Demas has deserted him, because he loved (*agapao*) the world. In recent times, *agapē* has been taken over as the name of Christian bookstores and Christian churches, singles ministries, missions, and so forth. It has even been the name of a 1983 song album from Popol Vuh, including the title song, 'Love–Love' by Florian Fricke. In modern Greece, the word is similar to our use of 'love', such as *s'agapo*, 'I love you' (much as the French would say, '*Je t'aime*').

Recommended reading. Lewis, C.S. *The Four Loves*. Glasgow: Collins, 1960.

See also LOVE [DLS]

Aggadah, Aggadot. Judaism balances two traditions, an oral tradition and a written tradition, blended together to complement each other as well as to address better both cognitive and emotional aspects of human existence. Within Judaism's oral tradition, another two-fold expression exists, that of halakhah and of aggadah. Halakhah literally means 'the walk', and refers to legal rulings that determine the extent and boundaries of obedience to God within daily life. Aggadah refers to stories that relate biblical text to contemporary life in a highly creative and imaginative manner. In terms of halakhah, faith is an inner commitment that obligates a person to think, speak, and act in accordance with Jewish religious tradition. In terms of aggadah, faith is an expression that takes on as many faces as there are situations in a person's life. Many ancient writings preserved by Judaism contain aggadic narratives; many more collections are entirely composed of aggadot (pl. for 'aggadah'). The content of these collections has been identified as myth, legend, fanciful story, and inventive discourse. Those who prefer to read the Lord of the Rings or Harry Potter rather than Robert's Rules of Order would have a natural affinity toward the aggadot over the halakhot. This is the case in Judaism as well. Whereas the halakhot have maintained how Jews should live before God throughout history, the aggadot have provided the entertainment to keep Jews interested in the path they are to walk. Aggadah also provides practical advice on why it is important to struggle to maintain faith in contemporary society. If the halakhot are the bricks of the structure of Judaism, then the mortar that holds together the structure and gives it form is the aggadot. There are many excellent publications of sayings from ancient collections of aggadic midrash preserved over the centuries.

The early rabbis took everyday events and the people that they knew by name and generated lessons from their lives by reinventing their stories in manners of expression that have come to apply to future generations in lands well beyond their own. But far different and removed is the world in which we live today. Ours is an integrative and integrated world, a world that I like to describe as both polyvocalic and polyperspectival. Unquestionably we live in an age where imagination serves technology. Great minds are enlisted to engage in thinking through how scientific advancement and technological invention can best benefit and serve humankind in the widest possible manner. It can equally be said, however, that we live in an age where technology serves imagination. Some of the most creative minds spend endless amounts of time exploring how new discoveries in media technology can provide hours of entertainment and restful diversion for the public at large. 3D glasses, magic eye images, creation of entire fantasy worlds (whether Middle Earth or Narnia or Hogwarts School of Witchcraft and Wizzardry) all remain more deeply imbedded in the mind of those who have read the literature after they have added to this book-knowledge the more comprehensive sensory experience gained by participating in the sights and sounds of the modern movie theatre.

Recommended reading. Maoz, Daniel. *Aggadic Midrash. I. Sample Reader*. Lewiston, NY: Mellen Press, 2012. Schwartz, Howard. *Tree of Souls: The Mythology of Judaism*. New York: Oxford University Press, 2004.

See also HAGGADAH [DM]

Agony in the garden. Jesus is described in the Synoptic Gospels as suffering emotional anguish prior to his arrest and trial. The title 'agony in the garden' is a mingled phrase, as it is only the Gospel of John that describes it as a garden (and mentions little else), and only Luke who uses the word agony (*agonia*). Mark indicates that Jesus was 'distressed and agitated' (14.33) and Matthew states that he was 'grieved and agitated' (26.37). Although agony may denote the idea of physical pain to modern readers, the Greek words used to describe Jesus' state are all in reference to emotional or mental anxiety. The emphasis and contrast between Jesus' great anxiety in a tranquil setting is reflected in Giovanni Bellini's painting *The Agony in the Garden*.

Luke alone adds two notable features to the scene in the garden: the appearance of an angel to strengthen Jesus, and Jesus sweating 'like great drops of blood falling down on the ground' (22.44), from which the figurative expression 'sweating blood' originates. Luke 22.43-44 is absent from a number of early manuscripts. This and other factors have led many modern scholars to argue that it is a later scribal insertion of an early tradition (the tradition is inserted after Matt. 26.39 in some manuscripts). What the sweating of blood signifies is unclear: (1) it may be that the sweat simply *fell like* blood, not that it was actually blood; (2) perhaps Jesus suffered from Hematidrosis, a rare condition of sweating blood because of extreme stress; (3) it is a theological and symbolic anticipation of Jesus' imminent crucifixion; or (4) it signified the close tie his agony has with his crucifixion in order to integrate it into the atoning work of the cross.

The aspect of the Gospel narratives which highlight most strongly Jesus' agony is the given motive and words of his prayer in the garden. The Gospel of Mark says, 'he threw himself on the ground and prayed that, if it were possible, the hour might pass from him' (14.35). All three synoptic Gospels record some words of his prayer, asking the Father to remove 'this cup' of upcoming suffering from him, while also resigning his fate to the will of God—a portion of which is echoed in U2's song 'Falling At Your Feet'. The cup as a metaphor for suffering is a common one used elsewhere in the Gospels (Matt. 20.22-23; Mark 10.38-39; John 18.11) and the HB (Pss 11.6; 75.8; Isa. 51.17, 22; Jer. 25.15, 17, 28; Lam. 4.21; Ezek. 23.31-33; Hab. 2.16). The historical core of this story is not heavily disputed, as it portrays a very human Jesus fearing for his life— a story not likely to be invented by the early church. The typology of fear but resignation to God's will inspired Christian martyrs through persecution during the early centuries, and likely lies behind the scene from Mel Gibson's *Braveheart* when William Wallace, alone and in his cell, confesses his fear and prays for strength before his execution.

Recommended reading. Green, Joel B. 'Jesus on the Mount of Olives (Luke 22.39-46): Tradition and Theology'. *Journal for the Study of the New Testament* 9 (1986) 29-47.

See also GARDEN OF GETHSEMANE; PRAYER; TRIAL OF JESUS; JUDAS ISCARIOT [HDZ]

Ahab, king of Israel. The meaning of this Hebrew name is 'father's brother', with the sense 'just like the father'. Ahab ruled over the Northern Kingdom of Israel for 22 years (c. 875–853 BCE). He succeeded his father Omri, who was a founder of a new dynasty and who moved the capital of the state to the newly built town of Samaria.

The biblical portrayal of Ahab is not univocal. On the one hand, he is presented as the one who 'did evil in the sight of the LORD more than all who were before him' (1 Kgs 16.30) and who built a temple for Baal (1 Kgs 16.32). On the other, he consulted prophets of Yahweh (1 Kgs 20.13-14, 22, 28; 1 Kgs 22.8) and gave his children Yahwistic names (Ahaziah and Jehoram). Most of all, however, the biblical record depicts Ahab as a victim of his wife Jezebel. It was she who urged him to do evil (1 Kgs 21.25) and who made him a new hallmark of the evilness of Israel. Ahab's ease of falling under other's influence is vivid in the Books of Kings, which present Ahab as a very passive person who fulfils Jezebel's, Elijah's, and others' commands.

A very different picture of the king emerges from the analysis of ancient inscriptions. Shalmaneser III mentions Ahab as a leader of the coalition of twelve kings opposing the armies of the Assyrian empire (the Israelite king supplied more than half of all the chariots of coalition forces). In spite of Shalmaneser's claim to be victorious, the events following the battle at Qarqar (853 BCE) testify to the contrary. The latter fact, as well as the marriage with a Phoenician princess, the coalition with Jehosphaphat, and the domination of Moab (as mentioned in Mesha Stele) prove Ahab to be a very effective player on the international scene. The biblical narrator who focuses on the religious aspect of Ahab's reign, however, downplays this. This aspect makes him the most wicked king in Israel who on at least three occasions had to be confronted by the prophet Elijah.

After his death, Ahab functions in the Bible as a symbol of evilness and destruction in Israel (cf. 2 Kgs 21.3, 13; Mic. 6.16). Probably due to his acceptance and promotion of Baalism in the Northern Kingdom, the dynasty founded by Omri is called in the Bible by Ahab's name, even though the OT typically names dynasties after their founders.

Ahab is a character not as commonly alluded to in art and literature as his wife Jezebel. However, reference to him (as well as his main opponent, Elijah) can be found in Herman Merville's novel *Moby Dick*. One of the novel's central characters is Ahab, captain of the whaling ship *Pequod*. His obsession to kill Moby-Dick dooms his ship and its crew. Only Ishmael survives to tell the story. There is also a minor reference to Ahab in James Joyce's *Ulysses*, in which Stephen Dedalus is compared to the Israelite king. Among other works that allude to biblical Ahab are Mark Twain's *The Innocents Abroad* and John W. de Forest's poems 'Elijah's Curse' and 'The Death of Ahab'.

Recommended reading. Walsh, Jerome T. *Ahab: The Construction of the King*. Interfaces. Collegeville, MN: Liturgical Press, 2006. Waldman, Nahum M. 'Ahab in Bible and Talmud'. *Judaism* 37 (1988) 41-47.

See also JEZEBEL; ELIJAH; BAAL; OMRI [RJM]

Ahithophel. The meaning of the name 'Ahithophel' (Heb. *'Ahitopel*) is uncertain, though it may derive from *'ah* ('brother') and *topel* ('foolishness'), thus 'brother of foolishness'. Interestingly, in later Syriac his name becomes an adjective meaning 'traitor' (Syr. *'ahitōpēlājā*), which is appropriate in light of the man's story.

In 2 Samuel, Ahithophel the Gilonite is King David's counsellor (2 Sam. 15.12; also 1 Chron. 27.33), whose advice was held in high esteem by all: 'Now in those days the counsel that Ahithophel gave was as if one consulted the oracle of God' (2 Sam. 16.23). When Absalom revolted against his father King David, Ahithophel chose to side with Absalom (15.12; 16.15), and when the king heard this, he prayed that Ahithophel's counsel would be turned into foolishness (15.31). He also asked Hushai the Archite to pretend to defect to Absalom, so as to counter Ahithophel's advice (15.32-37). Though Absalom heeded Ahithophel's suggestion to defile the king's concubines (16.20-22; cf. 12.11-12), Hushai convinced him not to follow Ahithophel's recommendation to pursue David immediately (17.1-14). This delay allowed David and his followers opportunity to re-group (18.1-8). Ahithophel, realizing that the rebellion would now fail, returned to Giloh and hanged himself (17.23).

A comparison of 2 Sam. 11.3 and 23.34 may suggest that Ahithophel was the grandfather of Bathsheba. If so, the means by which David acquired her in marriage (2 Sam. 11) may provide Ahithophel's motive for betraying the king. One might conceivably read his treachery into Pss 41.9 and 55.12-14. Furthermore, there are significant overlaps with Judas's betrayal of Jesus in the Gospels (e.g., David/Jesus crossing the Kidron [2 Sam. 15.23; John 18.1]; David/Jesus praying for deliverance on the Mount of Olives [2 Sam. 15.30-31; Matt. 26.30-46]; Ahithophel/Judas hanging himself [2 Sam. 17.23; Matt. 27.5]).

In rabbinic tradition, Ahithophel is confirmed as the grandfather of Bathsheba (*Sanh.* 69b) and associated with Balaam as one of 'the two great sages of the world who, failing to show gratitude to God for their wisdom, perished in dishonor' (*Num. Rab.* 22). Having misread the astrological signs, he believed that he would become king and so joined Absalom, planning later to take the throne for himself (*Sanh.* 101b). Previous clashes between Ahithophel and David are mentioned (*Num. Rab.* 4.20; *Sukkah* 53a-b) and it is said that he will have no share in the world to come (*Sanh.* 11.1). Moses Isserles, in his work *Torat ha-'Olah* (1659), also reports a tradition that Socrates learnt from Ahithophel.

Ahithophel appears in later literature as 'a conventional tag for traitor, wicked politician, and suicide' (Carver 27). For example, in 'The Parson's Tale' from Geoffrey Chaucer's *The Canterbury Tales* (fourteenth century), Ahithophel is associated with giving wicked and deceptive counsel (10.635-40), which is intriguing since, in 2 Sam. 15–17, his advice is always sound, albeit not always heeded. Nathanael Carpenter's *Achitophel: or, The Picture of a Wicked Politician* (1627) likewise uses the image of Ahithophel to describe treacherous counselors. In John Dryden's political satire *Absalom and Achitophel* (1681), the biblical story is employed as an allegory for the attempted rebellion that year by the Duke of Monmouth (illegitimate son of Charles II) and the Earl of Shaftesbury (the 'Achitophel' of the poem, who receives most of the blame).

Recommended reading. Bodner, Keith, Yitzhak Berger, and Matthew A. Collins. 'Ahithophel'. In *Encyclopedia of the Bible and its Reception*, I. Ed. H.-J. Klauck, et al. Pp. 663-66. Berlin/New York: De Gruyter, 2009. Carver, Larry. 'Ahithophel'. In *A Dictionary of Biblical Tradition in English Literature*. Ed. David L. Jeffrey. Pp. 27-28. Grand Rapids: Eerdmans, 1992.

See also ABSALOM; DAVID [MAC]

Allegory. From the Greek *allo* ('other') and *agoreuein* ('to speak publicly'), it is a literary device that means, 'to say one thing and mean another'. Its earliest use appears to date to the sixth century BCE, when certain Greek philosophers began to interpret the Homeric epics (the *Illiad* and the *Odyssey*) as allegories, according to which the gods represented either the natural elements or psychological dispositions. They did so likely to defend against accusations by other philosophers that Homer spoke impiously about the gods. The earliest extant example of the systematic allegorization of the Homeric epics is the Stoic philosopher Heraclitus's *Homeric Problems*, which he composed in the first century CE.

It is around this time that Hellenized (i.e., Greek-speaking) Jews in Alexandria, most notably Philo (c. 20 BCE–50 CE), began applying the allegorical method of interpretation to the HB to demonstrate that it did not contradict contemporary philosophical and cosmological doctrines. For example, stories that depicted God as becoming violently angry violated the Stoic virtue of *apatheia*—the stilling of the emotions—and so could not be read as literal descriptions of God's disposition.

The allegorical interpretation of the HB passed into early Christianity through Hellenistic Judaism. The term 'allegory' appears once in the NT, in Gal. 4.24, where Paul employs it in its verbal form (*allegoreuein*). Paul tells his readers in Galatia that the narrative in Genesis which relates the birth of Abraham's sons Ishmael and Isaac to Hagar, his slave, and Sara, his wife, was given as 'an allegory' (Gal. 4.24). Subsequent generations of Christians turned increasingly to allegorical interpretation of the HB as a way of explaining perceived discontinuities between the 'Old' and 'New' Testaments. An early example of this is the pseudepigraphic *Epistle of Barnabas*, which interprets the cultic proscriptions of the HB as representations of Christ and Christian virtues. The most important theorist of allegorical biblical interpretation was the third-century theologian Origen of Alexandria, who developed a theory of three 'senses' in Scripture.

In the fourth century, a debate arose in the Eastern Empire over the appropriateness of allegorical readings of Scripture. The detractors were largely bishops in Western Syria, and they preferred instead the use of *theoria* ('discernment') to refer to non-literal interpretations, if one were to be given in addition to the *historia* ('history'). Allegory, however, remained the most popular method of interpretation in the West through to the end of the medieval period, during which time it acquired a more technical meaning as one of the four senses of Scripture—historical, allegorical (ecclesiological interpretation), anagogical (eschatological interpretation), and tropological (moral interpretation)—which John Cassian (c. 360–433) first enumerated. The Reformers, notably Luther and Calvin, ended the hegemony of allegory in the West by privileging of the *sensus litteralis* (Lat. 'literal sense') of Scripture.

Allegorical interpretation should be distinguished from allegorical composition, which is the intentional writing of a text as an allegory. The earliest Christian example is the *Psychomachia* ('Soul-War') of Prudentius (348–ca. 410), which relates the battle of the soul against the vices. The genre of allegorical composition remained popular amongst Protestants. John Bunyan (1628–1688) wrote the *Pilgrim's Progress* about the journey of a man named 'Christian', which enjoyed great success. In the modern period, perhaps the most well-known allegory is George Orwell's (1903–1950) *Animal Farm*, a dystopian critique of Stalinism.

Recommended reading. Dawson, David. *Allegorical Readers and Cultural Revision in Ancient Alexandria*. Berkeley: University of California Press, 1992. Young, Frances. *Biblical Exegesis and the Formation of Christian Culture*. Peabody, MA: Hendrickson, 2002.

See also BIBLE; TYPOLOGY [KAS]

Alpha and Omega. The terms 'alpha' and 'omega' refer to the first and last letters of the Greek alphabet, respectively. In Revelation, the phrase 'Alpha and Omega' occurs three times and is a title used for both Jesus and God. Two occurrences (1.8; 21.8) are self-designations of God, and Jesus uses it of himself in 22.13. Most English translations, rather than rendering it into some comparable expression using the English alphabet (such as 'I am the 'A' and the 'Z') retain the expression of the Greek alphabet.

The phrase occurs alongside the parallel expressions 'first and the last' (1.17; 2.8; 22.13) and 'beginning and the end' (21.6; 22.13). As a set of titles, it appears that imagery from Isa. 44.6 (cf. also Isa. 41.4; 43.10; 48.12) lies behind these terms. Within its context in Isaiah, this imagery depicts God as the one true God who is sovereign over all things, including the gods of the nations, which are mere idols (see Isa. 44.9-20).

In addition to these thematic connections with Isaiah, some suggest the imagery draws from Greco-Roman magical contexts. Within the Greek magical papyri, interest in the divine name could be expressed through the combination of vowels. Alpha and omega were significant due to their status as the first and last vowels in the Greek alphabet. Although these texts come from a later time, it may be that they contain traditions present in the first century. The form *IAW* (*iota*, *alpha*, *omega*) appears to be significant as well due to its usage in Greek as a form of the divine name. It has been suggested that the connection of Jesus with this expression may have resulted from an exegesis of these three letters as 'Jesus (is the) alpha (and) omega', with the initial *iota* corresponding to the first letter of the name 'Jesus' in Greek.

In light of these contexts, it appears likely that the title was utilized in Revelation as an expression of lordship over all things. The application of this title to Jesus in 22.13 should be seen as an expression of the high Christology reflected throughout the book.

Within the contemporary secular context, the use of the expression 'A to Z' is often found in advertisements. Although not reflecting particular influence from Revelation, this similar expression noting totality may be found in modern usage. The expression may also be found in literary and cinematic works. In Charlotte Brontë's *Jane Eyre* (1847), Rochester refers to Jane as his 'alpha and omega'. In the film *Beneath the Planet of the Apes* (1970), an atomic bomb features the symbolism of 'alpha and omega'. The expression has found most significant influence, however, as a Christian symbol. Within early Christian art, the Greek letters 'alpha' and 'omega' could be incorporated with other Christian symbols, such as the cross and the *chi-rho* (a symbol formed from the first two letters of 'Christ' in Greek). The phrase has also appeared in a number of Christian hymns, including 'Love Divine, All Loves Excelling' and 'Of the Father's Love Begotten'.

Recommended reading. Aune, David E. 'The Apocalypse of John and Greco-Roman Revelatory Magic'. *New Testament Studies* 33 (1987) 481-501. Bauckham, Richard. *The Theology of the Book of Revelation*. New Testament Theology. Cambridge: Cambridge University Press, 1993.

See also CHRIST, TITLES OF; REVELATION, BOOK OF [MN]

Altar. An altar is a place of sacrifice. In most religions, an altar is as characteristic a feature of a sanctuary as a temple. Priests usually have the particular task of caring for the altar. The English term is derived from Latin *altare* (meaning altar), and this Latin term is probably related to *adolere* (to burn). Thus, an altar is specifically the place where a sacrifice is offered to God through burning. The first altar mentioned in the HB was spontaneously erected by Noah after the flood (Gen. 8.20). Noah sacrificed some of the animals there, which implies that he slaughtered and burnt them. God perceived Noah's sacrifice by smelling the smoke rising up from the altar (Gen. 8.21).

The oldest HB regulation on altars is found in the altar law (Exod. 20.24-25). It defines two types: (1) an altar of earth, consisting either of earth heaped up or a simple hole in the ground in which a fire would be lit. (2) An altar of unwrought stone without steps. The tabernacle (the portable sanctuary made by Israel) featured two different altars: (1) The 'altar of burnt offering', made of wood and copper, was located in the courtyard in front of the tabernacle entrance (Exod. 27.1-8; 38.1-7; 40.29). Animals or cereal offerings were sacrificed to God on this altar (Lev. 1–7). The actual offering occurred while the sacrifice was burnt in the altar fire that was never to extinguish (Lev. 6.12 ET). This altar was sometimes called God's 'table' (Ezek. 41.22; Mal. 1.7). (2) Made of wood and gold, the 'altar of incense' stood inside the tabernacle tent (Exod. 30.1-10; 37.25-28; 40.26). Incense prepared from special ingredients was burnt upon it (Exod. 30.34-38; 37.29; 40.27). The four corners of both altars featured horns (Exod. 27.2; 30.2) symbolizing the presence and strength of Israel's God. All altars had to be consecrated before they could be used for worship (Exod. 29.12, 36-37; 30.10; Lev. 8.15; Ezek. 43.18-27). It is unclear what type of altar was located in front of Solomon's temple in Jerusalem. 2 Chronicles 4.1 mentions a bronze altar, but relates only its dimensions. According to 1 Kgs 8.64, however, 'the king consecrated the middle of the court that was in front of the house of the Lord', referring to a simple elevation of the ground where large quantities of sacrifices could be offered. The postexilic altar is described as a large stone structure with rims (Ezek. 43.13-17).

The NT contains only few allusions to altars. In the Sermon on the Mount, Jesus suggested that reconciliation with one's neighbor should be sought before offering a sacrifice at the altar (Matt. 5.23-24). Jesus furthermore challenged the opinion of scribes and Pharisees that an oath sworn by the altar was invalid (Matt. 23.18-22). The author of Hebrews mentions both the main altar (7.13) and the incense altar (9.4) in a depiction of Christ as the new high priest and ultimate sacrifice. Most NT references to altars occur in the Revelation of John (6.9; 8.3, 5; 9.13; 11.1; 14.18; 16.7) which contains visions of God enthroned in a heavenly sanctuary.

Today, the flat-topped furniture at the center of most Christian churches is called 'altar' because the Lord's Supper, interpreted as the sacrifice of Jesus, is celebrated there. Beyond religious contexts of the English speaking western culture, the word 'altar' is not frequently employed. By contrast, in German and French the equivalent of the idiom 'to sacrifice something on the altar of…' can be used to express the willingness of giving up something in order to achieve a higher goal.

Recommended reading. Eberhart, Christian. 'A Neglected Feature of Sacrifice in the Hebrew Bible'. *Harvard Theological Review* 97 (2004) 485-93. Hayward, Robert. *The Jewish Temple*. London/New York: Routledge, 1996.

See also FIRE; LORD'S SUPPER; OFFERING; SACRIFICE [CAE]

Amen. The Hebrew word *amen* derives from the verbal root *mn* ('to be firm, trustworthy, or safe'). The term typically affirms a preceding curse or declaration as valid (i.e. 'Surely!' or 'So be it!'). 'Amen' thus frequently appears as the formulaic response to liturgical doxologies (cf. Ps. 41.13; 1 Chron. 16.36).

Greek biblical documents employ 'Amen' in similar fashion and form. NT usages of 'Amen' echo the word's OT sense. Like their Hebrew forebears, both Paul (cf. Rom. 9.33-36; Phil. 4.20) and the early Christian gatherings (cf. 1 Cor. 14.16) end doxologies with 'Amen'. Revelation's description of Christ as 'the Amen, the faithful and true witness' (3.14) may be a reference to Isa. 65.16, which describes the LORD as 'the God of Amen'. In fact, the Christian gospels contain the NT's only truly unique use of 'Amen'. Jesus frequently affirms the reliability of his *own* words by introducing them with the phrase 'Amen, I say to you…' (e.g., Matt. 5.18). The Septuagint occasionally transliterates the word into Greek (*amēn*). This tradition—preserving the Hebrew word in a new language—has continued throughout the history of the Christian church and resulted in the English word 'Amen'.

Jewish and Christian worship liturgies inherited 'Amen' from scripture. The Talmud soberly discusses the proper and improper ways of speaking the 'Amen', used to close doxologies and blessings. Christians generally conclude not only doxological declarations, but all personal and corporate prayer with 'Amen'.

Christian congregations that encourage spontaneous congregational response (e.g., churches in the revivalist traditions) often feature an 'Amen corner'. The term refers to those congregants who shout 'Amen' to express agreement with the preacher or singer. Frequently, the preacher will elicit this response by ending an important declaration by asking, 'Can I get an 'Amen'?' James Baldwin's play *The Amen Corner* (1968) references this preacher–congregation interplay and pries at the complex relationships between pastor, family, and congregation in the context of a Harlem church.

The popular gospel song 'Amen, Amen' also emerged from the African American church. A recording of this tune ('Amen, Brother', recorded in 1969 by the soul band The Winstons) has found new life in the sample-based music scene. Musicians from a wide variety of electronic-based genres (e.g., hip-hop, hardcore rap) have extracted a six-second drum solo from the piece (the 'Amen break') and rewoven it into their works.

Generally, 'Amen' in contemporary Western culture functions in ways similar to its biblical usage. Even in everyday conversations, 'Amen' or 'Amen to that' can (as in the biblical doxologies) assert strong agreement. The word can also bring something significant to a close (as in prayer). Cole Porter's 1935 song 'Just One of Those Things' ends a relationship with 'Goodbye, dear, and amen'. Similarly, the 1983 finale of the popular television series M*A*S*H, was titled 'Goodbye, Farewell, and Amen'.

See also DOXOLOGY; PRAYER [MATTH]

Amorites. The *ha'emori* are inhabitants of the land of Canaan, living near the Dead Sea and in the Transjordan. They are descendants of Noah's younger son Ham, through his fourth son Canaan (see Gen. 10.15-16; 1 Chron. 1.13-14). When God promises the land to Abraham's descendants, he adds, 'they shall come back here in the fourth generation; for the iniquity of the amorites is not yet complete' (Gen. 15.16), thus anticipating the conquests under Joshua.

At the time of the Exodus the Amorites were inhabitants of the Land of Canaan along with the Hittites and Hivites (Exod. 13.5). When the Hebrews sought innocent passage through the land of a group of Amorites led by their king Sihon of Heshbon, he refused the request. Marching against the Hebrews, he was destroyed at the Battle of Jahaz (Num. 21.21-31). This victory was followed by the destruction Amorites led by Og of Bashan (Num. 21.33-35). At a later time, representatives of the Amorite city of Gibeon fooled the Israelites into making an alliance with them (Josh. 9), thus obligating Joshua to protect their interets when threatened (Josh. 10.6-14).

The numerous Amorites gods became temptations to apostate idolatry for many Israelites. During the time of the divided monarchy, King Ahab used Amorite religion to strengthen his power as the king of the Northern Kingdom (1 Kgs 21.26). King Manasseh followed the same policy (2 Kgs 21.11). Ezekiel (16.3-45) claimed poetically that the Southern Kingdom of Judea had had an Amorite for a father as the only way to explain Israelite spiritually faithlessness to God. Memory of the Amorites was used as a standard for evil. Deuteronomy 3.11 and Amos 2.9 describe the Amorites as very tall and strong because they were supposedly descended from the ancient Rephaim (giants).

Historically the information about the Amorites is limited. Much of current knowledge of the Amorites has come from 20,000 clay tablets found at Mari (Mari Letters) on the Euphrates River. They were named by an Akkadian word, 'Amurru' which meant 'westerner'. The term was applied to scattered tribes of Semitic nomads who were west to Mesopotamia who came from the Arabian Desert. Syria-Palestine was called the land of the Amorites by Akkadians.

Following the collapse of the Sumerian Third Dynasty of Ur (c. 1950 BCE), Amorites came to dominate the southern Mesopotamian region. The most famous of the Amorites was Hammurabi the Great (c. 1728–1686 BCE), king of the First Dynasty in Babylon. His laws antedated the laws in the Pentateuch.

See also BALAAM; BASHAN; GIBEONITE; JOSHUA; JOSHUA, BOOK OF; OG OF BASHAN; TWELVE TRIBES OF ISRAEL [AJW]

Amos, Book of. The book of Amos is one the twelve so-called minor prophets. The main protagonist in the book is a putatively eighth-century BCE prophet named Amos, who lived in the southern part of Israel but was called by God to travel to the northern parts of the country and speak words of judgment against various nations and, more specifically, against northern Israel. One of the primary themes of the book is a stark condemnation of what the prophet Amos considered to be illicit places of worship at cultic sites in the cities of Bethel and Dan, followed by assurances that God would punish the wealthy and corrupt worshippers at these locations.

Perhaps the most famous passage in the book is Amos 5.21-24, where the prophet expresses God's stark disapproval of the people's religious practices and commands: 'let justice roll down like waters, and righteousness like an everflowing stream'. This condemnation of Israelite cultic behavior in favor of practicing social justice is a motif found elsewhere in the HB's prophetic corpus, most prominently in Isa. 1.10-17; Jer. 7.21-23; Hos. 6.6; and Mic. 6.6-8. Moreover, in all of these passages, including Amos 5.25 ('Did you bring to me sacrifices and offerings the forty years in the wilderness, O house of Israel?'), the various prophetic authors raise a question that has continued to interest interpreters up to the present day, namely, whether Israel's God ceased to desire animal sacrifice at some point, or even whether God had commanded such sacrifices in the first place (i.e., seemingly in contradiction to the books of Exodus and Leviticus).

In the Christian NT, the Book of Amos is explicitly quoted on two occasions (though there are many other indirect allusions to the book). In Acts 7.42-43, the martyr Stephen quotes Amos 5.25-27 as a condemnation of the Israelite people's infidelity to God. In Acts 15.16-17, James (probably the brother of Jesus and leader of the Jerusalem church) quotes an enigmatic prophecy from Amos 9.11-12 in support of accepting Gentiles into the new Christian faith: 'After this I will return, and I will rebuild the dwelling of David, which has fallen; from its ruins I will rebuild it, and I will set it up, so that all other peoples may seek the Lord—even all the Gentiles over whom my name has been called' (note that the NT authors here are quoting the Greek Septuagint version of Amos 9.11-12 and not the Hebrew, which does not contain any reference to 'Gentiles'). Medieval Jewish commentators typically saw the raising of the fallen dwelling as referring to a future messianic era, while others saw the references to the booth in terms of the destroyed/rebuilt Temple.

The phrase in Amos 5.24, 'let justice roll down', has become a popular slogan for racial, social, and economic egalitarianism movements throughout the late nineteenth and twentieth centuries, particularly in the American Civil Rights movement of the 1960s and beyond. For example, in his famous 'I Have a Dream' speech in 1963, Dr Martin Luther King, Jr proclaimed, 'No, no, we are not satisfied, and we will not be satisfied until justice rolls down like waters and righteousness like a mighty stream'. Again, in a 1965 article in *The Nation* entitled 'Let Justice Roll Down', King invoked Amos directly as a call for revolutionary change, and another pioneering American Christian social activist, John M. Perkins, entitled his 1976 autobiography *Let Justice Roll Down*.

See also Cows of Bashan; PROPHETS; SACRIFICE

[BRD]

Ananias and Sapphira. According to Acts, the early Christians were in the habit of selling their possessions and giving the proceeds to the church leaders who in turn ensured the needs of every member of the community were met (Acts 4.32-37). Ananias, not to be confused with the high priest of the same name in Acts 23.2, was a member of the Christian community who sold a piece of property. With his wife Sapphira's knowledge, Ananias donated only a portion of the proceeds to the communal treasury. Upon receiving this partial gift, however, the Apostle Peter exposed the deceit: 'Ananias, why has Satan filled your heart to lie to the Holy Spirit and to keep back part of the proceeds of the land? While it remained unsold, did it not remain your own? And after it was sold, were not the proceeds at your disposal? How is it that you have contrived this deed in your heart? You did not lie to us but to God' (Acts 5.3-4). After hearing these words Ananias 'fell down and died' (Acts 5.5). Three hours later, Sapphira appeared on the scene only to repeat her husband's lie and thus to suffer the same fate (Acts 5.7-10).

Within the Christian theological tradition, this graphic incident has been the source of much debate about the justice of God and the security of salvation. For Patristic interpreters, the severity of the punishment was an indication that the sin of Ananias and Sapphira was not just greed and lying, but idolatry (valuing material things above God, see e.g., Jerome, *Ep.* 14.5). This sort of interpretative tradition reflects a reading that sees the death of Ananias and Sapphira as consequence of divine retribution. It is therefore not surprising that allusions to this story have appeared repeatedly within the Western literary and artistic traditions in reference to divine judgment. A representative example of this allusive use can be seen in Melville's novel *Billy Budd*. After Budd kills the untrustworthy Claggart, Captain Vere approvingly calls it 'the divine judgment of Ananias'. The artistic depictions of this event almost unanimously highlight the theme of judgment from above by the upward looking stares of Ananias and Sapphira. Raphael's *The Death of Ananias* (1515–1516) is particularly graphic in the way it portrays the event as a spectacle of sorts, with the crowd gazing at the centralized Ananias who alone is gazing heavenward. In addition to the motif of divine judgment, Ruskin, in *Sesame and Lilies*, focuses on the paradigmatic character of Ananias's sin: 'most of us think not of what we are to do, but of what we are to get…the sin of Ananias.…We want to keep back part of the price'.

Recommended reading. Fitzmyer, Joseph A. *The Acts of the Apostles: A New Translation and Commentary*. Anchor Bible, 31. New York, Doubleday, 1998. Pervo, Richard I. *Acts*. Hermeneia. Minneapolis: Fortress Press, 2008. Peterson, David. *The Acts of the Apostles*. Pillar

New Testament Commentary. Grand Rapids: Eerdmans, 2009.

[JAL]

Anathema. This word derives from a Greek term meaning something devoted or accursed, and is the root word of the *anathematizo* 'laying a curse'. It was translated in the Septuagint (third century BCE) from the Hebrew word *herem* (meaning 'set aside'). It is used in Lev. 27.28; Num. 21.3; Josh. 6.17-18, 7.12-13; Judg. 1.17; 1 Chron. 2.7; and Zech. 14.11. In examining its usage in the Septuagint, it has two meanings: a thing that is devoted to God and a thing that is to be destroyed. Anathema is understood by the hellenistic Jewish philosopher Philo of Alexandria (20 BCE—50 CE) to mean a dedication or an offering to God like first fruits of harvest, which are offered up for destruction. It is used in the NT in Gal. 1.8; Rom. 9.3; 1 Cor. 12.3; 16.22; and Acts 23.14 with the meaning of bodily harm (as in Acts 23.14) and separation (as in Rom. 9.3). Interestingly, in Acts, anathema is connected with taking an oath where if the oath was not honored, then a curse would take effect.

In the early Church, anathema took on a technical meaning that was synonymous with *excommunication* that is being forced to separate from the Church. By the eleventh century CE, the word was associated with the major curse of total excommunication from all Christian religious rights, which also meant the real possibility of exclusion from Heaven.

In medieval literature, Chaucer's (c. 1343–1400) *The Canterbury Tales* has echoes of anathema in the tales of the 'Wife of Bath' and the 'Friar'. In contemporary literature, Scott Westerfeld uses the idea of anathema in his novel *Peeps* where a parasite causes people to become vampires with an 'anathema effect' to sunlight and crucifixes. In 2002, Detective Comics showcased a grotesque villainess called Anathema who fought against the Justice League of America (i.e., Superman, Batman, and Wonder Woman as well as many others) and almost defeated them. Finally, the death metal band Anathema has songs detailing the disastrous effects of separation from a true love, as in 'A Natural Disaster' which includes the phrase, 'It's been a long cold winter without you'.

Anathema does not have a single definition and can be understood as something or someone set aside, excommunicated or accursed. These varied uses can be seen throughout history from ancient to modern times.

See also ACHAN; CHURCH; ACTS, BOOK OF [MSW]

Ancient of Days. From the Aramaic words *'atiq* (advanced or ancient) and *yomaya* (period of time/day). The term Ancient of Days, often translated as the Ancient One, appears three times in Dan. 7 to describe the divine judge in Daniel's vision of the last days. Most agree this divine judge is no one else but Yahweh the God of Israel. The language of Dan. 7, which includes clothing as white as snow and hair like wool, is a clear influence on the writing of John the Seer (see Rev. 1.14).

The expression Ancient of Days is a descriptive term that suggests sovereignty rather than length of living. A similar description is found in the Ugaritic epic of Aqhat where the chief Canaanite god was referred to as 'the king, father of years'. Also used in different religions to describe God, the term transcends theologies and dictates more of an Eastern understanding of a supernatural being outside time.

Though there is no such description as a white beard in Daniel's vision, artworks depicting the Ancient of Days usually show him as an old man with long white beard and white hair. A famous artwork that follows this interpretation is the Ancient of Days watercolor relief by William Blake in 1794. In the relief, one sees an old man kneeling on one knee with what looks like a compass in his hands, and himself somewhat wrapped in the Sun. This artwork was also the cover illustration for Blake's collection of poem called *Europe, a Prophecy* (1794). In contemporary culture, different authors and musicians have used Blake's painting *Ancient of Days* in different forms. The American funk band Slave, popular in the 70s and 80s had Blake's artwork on the cover of the 1978 *The Concept* album. The expression usually appears in songs as a name for God. Gospel artists like Ron Kenoly (*Lift Him Up*, 1994) have songs titled 'Ancient of Days'. In the popular hymn composed by Walter Smith 'Immortal Invisible', the term was one of the numerous ones used in describing God. There is also a popular hymn called 'Ancient of Days' composed by the first Episcopal bishop of Albany New York, William Doane (1832–1913).

Due to the description given of the divine judge in Daniel's vision of this Ancient One, many characterization of this divine being in contemporary culture usually reflects an old man with long white beard. In *The Simpsons* episode 'Homer the Heretic' (1994), the God that appeared to Homer in his dream was an old man with long beard. Movies like *Bruce Almighty* differ from this stereotype, but still use the concept of an old man.

While there are no specific references to the Ancient of Days in the NT, the description given in Rev. 4.9 is strikingly similar to the language of Dan. 7.

See also SON OF MAN; YAHWEH [GOA]

Andrew. All four NT Gospels include Andrew among the first followers of Jesus. In Matthew (4.18-22) and Mark (1.16-20), Jesus calls Andrew and his brother, Simon Peter as they are fishing in the Sea of Galilee. In Luke, Andrew appears when Jesus chooses the twelve he will name apostles; again, he is referred to as Peter's brother (Luke 5.12-16; also Matt. 10.1-4). Early in the Gospel of John, Andrew is a follower of John the Baptist. When John calls Jesus 'the Lamb of God', Andrew begins to follow Jesus. He tells his brother Simon, 'We have found the Messiah!' and then takes him to meet Jesus (John 1.35-42), so becoming the first person in John's Gospel to identify Jesus as the 'Anointed One'. In the other gospels, it is not Andrew but Peter who first confesses Jesus in this way.

Andrew otherwise plays a small role in the NT Gospel narratives. In Mark, he is one of the four disciples who ask Jesus privately when the destruction of the Temple will occur (Mark 13.3). In John, he introduces Jesus to a boy with five loaves and two fish that will go on to feed 'about five thousand' people (John 6.1-14). He helps Philip tell Jesus that 'some Greeks' wish to see him (John 12.20-26), and he appears early in Acts in a list of the eleven apostles (Acts 1.13).

Eusebius of Caesarea, in his fourth-century *The History of the Church*, mentions Andrew once, noting that in the scattering of the apostles, 'tradition tells us' that Andrew 'was chosen' for Scythia (southern Russia and the Caucasus). Eusebius had rejected as heretical the *Acts of Andrew* (*Acta Andreae*)—a text, likely from the mid-second century, which survives only in pieces, and comprises a series of adventures related to the apostle. In the *Acts*, Andrew travels throughout Greece and Asia Minor. He founds churches, ordains bishops, and performs extravagant miracles, including halting an attacking army with the sign of the cross. At Patras, Greece, the Proconsul Aegeates orders Andrew's crucifixion for having converted, among others, Aegeates' wife Maximilla. Andrew preaches three days from the cross before dying. Another, perhaps earlier version of text, the *Acts of Andrew and Matthias in the City of the Cannibals*, describes more adventures and miracles.

The popularity of the *Acts* led eastern Christians to revere Andrew as an eastern counterpart to Peter. The Greek Church named him the *Protokletos* (First Called). The tradition developed that Andrew had been executed on an x-shaped, or 'saltire' cross. In the eighth century, some of Andrew's relics (remains) were transported to Scotland, perhaps in an attempt by the Roman church to counter the popularity of the indigenous Celtic saints. There Andrew gave his name to a cathedral town, a university, and eventually a historic golf course. His saltire cross appears on the Scottish flag. (The saltire form also figures in the battle flag of the American Confederate army, although its creators claimed it was not intended to represent St Andrew.) Andrew's feast day, November 30, was designated a Scottish bank holiday in 2006.

Andrew's legacy endures: he is the Patron Saint of Greece, Romania, Russia, Scotland, and Constantinople; and of mariners, fishers, and rope makers. He represents, in iconography and legend, a tough, woolly fisherman who fearlessly responds to the call of Jesus, and carries his robust faith to the ends of the earth. He suggests a rugged masculine Christianity, perhaps in distinction to his refined and ethereal Roman brother, Peter. Andrew thus exudes a working class appeal that subtly subverts western cultural and religious domination.

Recommended reading. MacDonald, Dennis Ronald. *The Acts of Andrew and The Acts of Andrew and Matthias in the City of the Cannibals*. Atlanta: Scholars Press, 1990.

See also DISCIPLE; TWELVE DISCIPLES, THE; PETER, THE APOSTLE [SB]

Angel. The Greek word *aggelos* means 'messenger'. The Hebrew equivalent is *mal'ak*. In the HB, these beings have a complicated nature and often are indistinguishable from God. They have typically been considered the lowest level of the divine council but recent scholarship demonstrates a more complicated and vital role for these divine characters. The literature of Second Temple Judaism gives a significantly larger role to angels and allows them to develop as characters with individual identities. In the Christian Testament, the role of angels as messengers is more pronounced.

In post-biblical Judaic traditions, the concept of archangels developed with particular significance granted to Michael, Gabriel, and Metatron. Yet, despite this belief in the personality of certain angelic figures there is also a strand of tradition that does not allow for angelic free will and sees these beings as merely an extension of the deity. Maimonides, in the middle ages, claimed that biblical references to angels were only one way of explaining natural phenomenon in a world that did not fully understand its environment and therefore should be understood metaphorically. The idea that each person has a guardian angel arose very early in church history and was followed by St Jerome, Peter the Lombard, and St Ambrose.

The Church of Jesus Christ of Latter Day Saints was founded after Joseph Smith encountered an angel, and the *Book of Mormon* was written due to further angelic visitation. They also identity the angel Michael with Adam and the angel Gabriel with Noah. Angels provide ample subject matter for the modern media as well. Television shows such as *Touched by an Angel* are popular due to their depiction of traditional presentations of angelic life. The television show *Supernatural* took on the topic of angels in the second season in an episode entitled 'Houses of the Holy', where the marginalized of society start killing hidden criminals because angels tell them to do it. On the flip side, the popular film *Dogma* with Matt Damon and Ben Affleck took a satirical look at religion through the lens of two angels who have found themselves trapped out of heaven. A more romanticized notion of angels can be found in Nicholas Cage and Meg Ryan's movie *City of Angels*.

Recommended reading. Meier, Samuel. *Messengers in the Ancient Semitic World*. Atlanta: Scholars Press, 1988. Sullivan, Kevin. *Wrestling with Angels: A Study of the Relationship between Angels and Humans in Ancient Jewish literature and the New Testament*. Leiden: Brill, 2004.

See also BALAAM; DIVINE COUNCIL, THE; ELOHIM; GOD; LOT; SWORD; YAHWEH [EW]

Animals, Symbolism of. In the beginning, God created animals and brought them to Adam for naming (Gen. 2.19-20). The serpent plays a large role in the Fall (Gen. 3) when he entices Eve to eat the forbidden fruit; thereafter Satan is often likened to a snake or serpent (Rev. 12.9). God commands Noah to take two of every animal onto the Ark, to perpetuate postdiluvian life (Gen. 6.19-20).

Like birds, animals are put in categories: clean and unclean. Leviticus 11 explains the distinctions: clean beasts have divided hooves and chew cud; sea creatures must have both fins and scales. Many animals are used for sacrifice: bulls, rams (Exod. 29.1), lambs (Exod. 29.38), pigeons, turtledoves (Lev. 1.14), sheep, goats (Lev. 1.10), and calves (Mic. 6.6). Exodus 8–10 describes plagues of frogs, gnats, flies, and locusts.

The 'golden calf' was made by Aaron and worshiped by the Israelites until Moses intervened (Exod. 32.1-20). Modern references are made to worshiping false idols, with the 'golden calf' symbolizing material goods (see e.g., Charles Dickens's *Martin Chuzzlewit*). The 'fatted calf' was prepared to celebrate the return of the Prodigal Son (Luke 15.11-32). This phrase is used to imply a lavish welcome by Chaucer, William Shakespeare, Eugene O'Neill, and Thomas Wolfe.

Predators—lions, bears, wolves, foxes, and leopards—inspire fear. Lions are strong and powerful, but also menacing. Both Christ (Rev. 5.5) and Satan (1 Pet. 5.8) are likened to lions. The phrase 'lion in the streets' (Prov. 26.13) refers to an excuse for avoiding something unpleasant. Daniel is thrown into the lion's den, but is saved by his faith (Dan. 6.17-25). Isaiah foretells a peaceful future when 'The Wolf shall live with the lamb, the leopard shall lie down with the kid; the calf and the lion and the fatling together' (Isa. 11.6). Shelley, Blake, and Henry James cite this prophecy in their written works.

Jesus said: 'I am sending you out like sheep into the midst of wolves; so be wise as serpents, and innocent as doves' (Matt. 10.16). Literary references to these animals are later found in the works of Melville, Huxley and Maugham. The sly, bold and opportunistic wolf 'in sheep's clothing' is mentioned in Matt. 7.15, as well as in Aesop's fable. The fairy tale Little Red Riding Hood reworks the idea.

References to horses are usually in a military context (e.g., Deut. 20.1), or seen as a symbol of strength or wealth (e.g., Rev. 18.12-13). The colloquialism 'death on a pale horse' derives from the description of the Four Horsemen of the Apocalypse in Revelation 6.

Christ is called the Lamb of God in John 1.29, and later in Melville's *Billy Budd* and Joyce's *Ulysses*. He is also the good shepherd (John 10.14) and calls followers his flock (Luke 12.32). A prophecy (Matt. 25.31-33) speaks of him dividing the sheep (good souls) from goats (wicked). The parable of the lost sheep (Matt. 18.12-14) is referred to in the first chapter of Twain's *Huckleberry Finn*. The modern term scapegoat derives from the distribution of goats for sacrifice in Lev. 16.7-10.

Associating animals with concepts or virtues carries over into the modern world, with references that evoke biblical symbolism. For instance, much as

Herod is named a 'fox' (Luke 13.32) and the Pharisees and Sadducees called 'vipers' (Matt. 3.7), politicians debating war today are designated 'hawks' or 'doves'.

Recommended reading. Goodard, Burton L. *Animals and Birds of the Bible*. Mulberry, IN: Sovereign Grace Publishers, 2007. Cansdale, G.S. *All the Animals of the Bible Lands*. Grand Rapids, MI: Zondervan, 1970.

See also BIRDS, SYMBOLISM OF; GOLDEN CALF; LAMB OF GOD; NAMING OF THE ANIMALS; SCAPEGOAT; SHEEP; WISE AS SERPENTS [ACF]

Anna. The cameo appearance of Anna the Prophetess at the Presentation of the infant Jesus in the Temple (Luke 2.36-8) is a masterpiece of concentrated symbolism and thematic irony.

Anna, whose name means 'grace', is the daughter of Phanuel ('Face of God'), of the tribe of Asher' ('happy') (v. 36). This cluster of genealogical cues symbolically emphasizes her role which is, through grace, to bring happiness by proclaiming the birth of the Messiah 'to all who were looking for the redemption of Jerusalem' (v. 38).

Thematically and structurally Anna is one of several disadvantaged individuals in the opening of Luke's gospel who are recipients of God's grace: Elizabeth, the mother of John the Baptist, who is barren and advanced in years (Luke 1.7, 36); Zechariah, her elderly husband; the Virgin Mary; the shepherds (2.8-20); and Simeon who, the text implies, is also elderly (2.29).

Anna is one of only a handful of biblical women specifically identified as Prophetesses, and thus she would have been associated, in the minds of Jewish readers, with her OT precursors: Miriam, Deborah and Huldah. As an elderly widow Anna was potentially vulnerable and disadvantaged; yet, along with the shepherds, another socially marginalized group, Anna can be viewed as one of the first evangelists. She stands in ironic juxtaposition to Zechariah, a priest, and father of John the Baptist, who is struck dumb by the angel, in the Temple, because of his lack of faith (1.20), whereas Anna, also in the Temple, enthusiastically proclaims the good news of the Messiah's birth. The ministry of the shepherds, Anna, and later the disciples, illustrates the shift of power away from the religious institution of the Temple and its priests, into the hands of the common people under the inspiration of the Holy Spirit.

Luke's depiction of Anna has further political dimensions, given the multi-cultural, polytheistic context of her time, especially in Israel which, under the pro-Roman King Herod, saw the building of many temples to pagan gods, including one to Caesar. In the classical, pre-Christian world, the temple priestess was the major vehicle of communication between the pagan gods and their worshippers. Anna is the Christian counterpart to the pagan priestesses and their oracles; she never leaves the Temple (v. 37), implicitly speaks in the power of the Holy Spirit, and reveals the presence of the Messiah. Like her OT predecessors, Anna the Prophetess proclaims the true God of Israel in the face of pagan enemies and deities.

Gregory of Nyssa and other commentators interpret Anna typologically. According to such readings, Simeon is the symbolic personification of the Law while Anna is the symbolic personification of Grace, or sometimes the Prophets. Both coexist in the Temple but, with the birth and arrival of the Messiah, the Law (Simeon) is fulfilled, and Grace (Anna) begins its prophetic ministry of revealing the incarnate presence of Jesus in the world.

The depiction of Anna combines several literary archetypes: the wise old woman who possesses secret knowledge which will reveal the identity of the true king (Jesus), and thus threaten the illegitimate and corrupt usurper (Herod); the priestess/oracle/soothsayer; and the pious widow.

Anna is regarded as a Saint by the Roman Catholic and Eastern Orthodox Churches and figures frequently in icons, murals and paintings, including a striking rendition by Rembrandt.

Recommended reading. Estrada, Nelson P. 'Praise for Promises Fulfilled: A Study of the Significance of the Anna the Prophetess Pericope'. *Asian Journal of Pentecostal Studies* 2 (1999) 5-18.

See also INFANCY NARRATIVES; LUKE, GOSPEL OF [BFR]

Annunciation. The term refers to the angel Gabriel's announcement to the Virgin Mary that she would conceive and give birth to a child who would be called Son of God. This story is found only in Luke 1.26-38. Scholars have long debated whether this story is based on an older source, and to what extent the writer crafted or re-crafted this story. Luke's account has general affinities with miraculous birth stories in the HB. Early Greek and Latin Christian writers, however, would highlight the most distinctive feature of this story, namely Mary's virginal status. This takes on theological significance in later Christian theology.

The stories of miraculous divine intervention to ensure a child of promise (at times complete with divine announcements) can be found in Gen. 17 (Sarah/Isaac), Gen. 16 (Hagar/Ishmael), Gen. 25 (Rebekah/Esau and Jacob), Gen. 29.31–30.24 (Leah and Rachel/Simeon and Joseph), Judg. 13.2-7 (Manoah's wife/Samson), and 1 Sam. 1.1-20 (Hannah/Samuel). The announcement of Samson's birth provides the best HB parallel for the Lukan annunciation story, complete with an awe-inspiring angel. In Luke, the announcement to Mary is juxtaposed with the previous announcement by Gabriel to the priest Zechariah that his aged wife would give birth to John the Baptist (Luke 1.5-20; cf. Gabriel and Dan. 8.16-27, 9.21-27). The similarities of the two only serve to heighten the difference in response by Mary and Zechariah to the angelic announcement—acceptance versus doubt.

As Christianity developed in the Greco-Roman world, so did Mary's role, including receiving the title of *theotokos* ('God-bearer' or 'Mother of God'). Couple this with the general scarcity of material about her in the biblical text and it is not surprising that the annunciation is ubiquitous in Christian art of all varieties. Nearly every significant Medieval and Renaissance painter tackled the subject. Representing the annunciation became a means of declaring the doctrine of the perpetual virginity of Mary. Many representations include a lily, often in Gabriel's hand, a symbol of Mary's purity.

Perhaps the greatest influence of Luke's annunciation account is its role in birthing the 'Hail Mary' or *Ave Maria* prayer. Gabriel's words in Luke 1.28, 'Greetings, favored one, the Lord is with you' via Jerome's Latin translation create the opening words of 'Hail Mary, full of grace, the Lord is with thee'. This is then coupled with Elizabeth's greeting to Mary in Luke 1.42 ('Blessed are you among women, and blessed is the fruit of your womb'). This prayer plays a central role within Catholic piety, most notably in the Rosary prayer method in which it is repeated in sets of ten for a total of 150 times. Several famous musicians have set the text of the *Ave Maria* to music, including the well-known version created by Charles Gounod in 1859 based on J. S. Bach's C major Prelude. One is hard pressed to name a major composer before the twentieth century who has not worked with the *Ave Maria* text. The *Angelus* prayer, often associated with the ringing of church bells at 6 am, noon, and 6 pm, is also based on Luke's annunciation text. The Christian feast or celebration of the Annunciation is observed on March 25, exactly nine months before Christmas.

See also GABRIEL, THE ANGEL; MARY, MOTHER OF JESUS; CHRISTMAS [AR]

Anoint. To anoint a person was common in ancient cultures both for medicinal and ritualistic purposes. The word *anoint* in the OT (Hebrew, *mashach*) and NT (Greek, *eleipho, aleipho*, and *murizo*) have largely the same meanings, referring to the anointing of a person's body because they are ill, dead, elevated to kingship, or sanctified by God.

Among ancient cultures, oil was a commonplace medicine for skin conditions, wounds, and moods. In Isa. 1.6, oil softens bruises and sores; David in Ps. 109.18, implies that oil soothes the pains of joints. Priests were anointed with oil (Exod. 29.21), as were holy implements (Exod. 30.25-27). Prophets and priests also anointed kings; for example the prophet Samuel anointed King Saul (1 Sam. 10.1) as well as David (1 Sam. 16.13). When Samuel anointed David, 'the Spirit of the Lord came mightily upon David'. David refused to hurt Saul when he had him in his power, as he was also God's anointed (1 Sam. 24.6), and his person was therefore sacrosanct.

Anointing with oil figures prominently in the NT as well. Jas 5.14, describes how the sick are anointed with oil in a religious act calling upon God's help. Jesus commanded his disciples to go about the countryside ridding people of unclean spirits and healing by anointing the sick with oil (Mark 6.13). Dead bodies were also anointed; Mary Magdalene, Mary the mother of James, and Salome brought spices to anoint the body of Jesus in the tomb (Mark 16.1). A young woman, perhaps Mary Magdalene, anointed Jesus with pure nard, an expensive ointment, when he was still alive as an act, according to Luke (7.36), of love, or according to Mark (14.8) and John (12.7), anticipating his death, anointing his body as if for burial. According to the author of Acts (10.38), Jesus has been anointed by the Holy Spirit. Indeed the Greek translation of the Hebrew anointed one, *Christos*, became a title, almost like a surname, for Jesus of Nazareth, the anointed one of God.

For centuries after the death of Jesus, European kings were anointed in their consecration to power, as if they were living messiahs, ruling for Christ. The Christian church adopted christening oil, chrism, to anoint new Christians, either the baptized or the confirmed. One of the sacraments of the church, Holy Unction, is the act of anointing the sick and dying with holy oil. Anointing with oil among Christians today is symbolic of anointing with the Holy Spirit. Artists have repeatedly portrayed the anointing of David, Christ, and kings. An example is *The Anointing of Jesus* by William Hole (1906).

See also OIL; CHRIST [RL]

Antichrist. The word antichrist (*antichristos* in Greek) is used by only one author in the Bible, the writer of the NT letters called 1 and 2 John (2.18, 22; 4.3; 2 John 1.7). He warns his readers that the antichrist is already in the world and that many 'antichrists' have already appeared (2.22). This phenomenon is for him a sign of the 'last hour' (2.18). He also gives a definition in this letter of the title antichrist by relating the name to any 'spirit' (literally) which denies that Jesus is the anointed one or Messiah (*christos*) or that Jesus is 'of God' (4.3).

Paul also refers to a figure that plays a role similar to that of an antichrist in his second letter to the Thessalonians (2.3-4). He speaks about a figure whose appearance will precede the coming of the Lord Jesus (cf. 1 Thess. 4.13-18). Although Paul does not reveal his sources, his descriptions of the man of lawlessness and the opposition to God are reminiscent of apocalyptic thinking seen elsewhere in the Bible especially in Mark 13.14-37 and Rev. 13. Other examples of those opposing God and his people are found in Ezek. 38–39 and Dan. 7.21-27; 9.24-27; 11.

The expectation of tribulation and the appearance of great evil ahead of God's final victory, or associated with the end of the world, is common in apocalyptic literature, ancient and modern. Jesus speaks to the disciples about events in the last days preceding his coming again in the 'little apocalypse' in Mark (13.13). In his description of an antichrist figure in Rev. 13, this author depicts a beast who arises from the earth and mimics the Lamb but in behavior oppresses the elect and inspires the nations to commit idolatry (13.11-15). He labels this beast with the number 666 which is said to be 'the number of a person' (13.18). It is this symbol which has exercised the imagination of readers as much as any other passage in the Bible.

The concept and symbols of the antichrist appear often through history as a way of denouncing one's enemies or opponents both inside and outside of Christianity. Various individuals and nations have been assigned this status from the Pope in the time of the Reformation to Hitler in the last century. The large number and variation of suggestions for the identity of the antichrist should warn us about how malleable this symbol is in anyone's hands.

Recommended reading. Kirsch, Jonathan. *A History of the End of the World*. HarperCollins: New York, 2006. Peterson, Simon. *A Brief History of the End of the World*. London: Constable & Robinson, 2006. Wainwright, Arthur. *Mysterious Apocalypse*. Nashville, TN: Abingdon Press, 1993.

See also APOCALYPSE, APOCALYPTIC; BEAST; FALSE PROPHET [DMAC]

Antioch. The city of Antioch in Syria (now Antakya, in Turkey) was founded by Seleucus Nicator in 300 BCE, and was named in memory of his father Antiochus, king of Syria. The great wealth of the Seleucid Empire meant that Antioch was briefly a rival of Rome in the third century BCE, and there were people from Antioch who competed in the ancient Greek Olympics. However, the city declined although it played an important part in the early history of Christianity, being mentioned nineteen times in the Acts of the Apostles, once in Galatians, and once in 2 Timothy. Indeed, in Acts 11.26, it is noted that the followers of Jesus were first called 'Christians' in the city. The other references are largely to seeking converts from the city, and it is clear from Acts that Antioch was on one of the main trade routes through the region. In 341 CE, it was the location of the Council of Antioch, which sought to replace the Nicene theology with Arianism. This led to the appointment of a Patriarch of Antioch, long regarded as a very senior position in the Christian Church. Six saints: Eusthathius, Ignatius, Lucian, Margaret, Meletius and Pelagia, are associated with the city.

The city was destroyed by the Persians in 538 CE, rebuilt by the Byzantine Emperor Justinian, and then captured by the Saracens in 638. It was its connections with early Christianity that led the armies of the First Crusade to capture it in 1098 (when St George was seen helping them). Tom Harper, in his novel about the First Crusade (*Siege of Heaven*, 2006) describes Antioch as plague-ridden, and there are also many legends which surround the discovery in Antioch of what was believed to have been the 'Holy Lance', a relic said to be the lance that pierced the side of Jesus during the crucifixion. Subsequently, the Crusaders established the Principality of Antioch that they maintained until 1268 when the city was sacked by the Marmluks. Antioch inspired Sir Arthur Sullivan to compose *The Martyr of Antioch* in 1880. From the break-up of the Ottoman

Empire after World War I, until 1939, the French held the city as part of what became known as the Protectorate of Hatay.

See also ACTS OF THE APOSTLES, THE; PAUL THE APOSTLE [JC]

Antiochus IV Epiphanes. Antiochus IV Epiphanes (c. 215–164 BCE), born Mithridates, was the eighth ruler of the Seleucid Empire and ruled between 175 and 164. After the death of Alexander the Great in 323 BCE, and after years of fighting in wars of the *Diadochi* (Greek for 'successors'), Alexander's territory was divided into four main kingdoms: the Ptolemaic dynasty in Egypt; the Seleucid dynasty in Syria and Mesopotamia; the Antigonid dynasty in Macedon and central Greece; and the Attalid dynasty in Anatolia.

Having ascended to the throne upon the assassination of his brother Seleucus IV Philopator, Antiochus IV looked to expand his territory. Although he had originally captured Egypt in 170, Antiochus led a second attack on Egypt and sent a fleet to capture Cyprus in 168 to reclaim those territories. Before reaching Alexandria, however, his path was blocked by a Roman army who demanded that Antiochus withdraw his armies from Egypt. Antiochus said he would discuss it with his council, whereupon the Roman envoy drew a line in the sand around him and said, 'Before you cross this circle I want you to give me a reply for the Roman Senate'. Rome would declare war if the king stepped out of the circle without committing to leave Egypt immediately. Weighing his options, Antiochus wisely decided to withdraw. This incident may lie behind the expression 'draw a line in the sand'.

Arguably the most notorious act of Antiochus IV was his capture of Jerusalem and the sacking and desecration of the temple (1 Macc. 1.20-24). While Antiochus was busy in Egypt, a riot broke out in Jerusalem and on his return from Egypt, he attacked Jerusalem, restored Menalaus, his appointed high priest, and executed the dissidents responsible for the unrest. To strengthen his hold over the Jerusalem and the Jewish people, Antiochus decided to Hellenize the Jews by ordering the worship of Zeus as the supreme god. This was anathema to the Jews and when they refused, Antiochus sent an army to enforce his decree (167 BCE). According to Josephus, upon seizing Jerusalem his soldiers entered the Jewish Temple and slaughtered a pig on the altar (an animal considered unclean by Jews). They then attempted to force the Jewish men to eat the pig meat (*War* 1.34). When the men refused, the soldiers mutilated the men's bodies before burning them alive on the altar of the Lord.

The goal of Antiochus IV was to force assimilation of the Jews by Hellenizing their religion, which was an extreme provocation to the faithful. The Jews broke into a full-scale rebellion led by the Maccabees, who defeated Antiochus's armies, leading to the reclamation of the Temple and the first celebration of Chanukah (the Feast of Lights), and the establishment of a short-lived period of Jewish independence (1 Macc. 4.59). This further undermined the Seleucid regime in Judea and provided the Romans with opportunities to ally with the Jews (1 Macc. 12.1).

Recommended reading. Shipley, Graham. *The Greek World after Alexander 323–30 BC*. London: Routledge, 2000.

See also EGYPT; HIGH PRIEST; JERUSALEM; JUDEA; MACCABEES, THE; MACCABEES, BOOKS OF; TEMPLE, ISRAEL'S [SAA]

Apocalypse, Apocalyptic. The words apocalypse and apocalyptic come from the one Greek word, *apokalypsis*, meaning an uncovering or disclosure and in this sense a revelation. *Apocalypsis* is the first word in the Book of Revelation, appearing in the phrase 'the revelation of Jesus Christ' (Rev. 1.1). For this reason, some refer to this book as the Apocalypse. The word also indicates an extensive body of biblical and extra-biblical apocalyptic writings. The apocalyptic movement grew out of the ancient Israelite prophetic traditions. The apocalyptic writers took the prophetic message, applied it to the world stage, and included not just the actions and fate of Israel but now the nations, and even the whole creation.

Eventually, the apocalyptic writers' developed the use of heavenly imagery, symbols, and numbers and worked with visions and dreams all purporting to be inspired by God or a heavenly source (such as a notable or a righteous person long dead). They often wrote under an assumed name, a device intended to enhance the authority of the document with its readers. John the Seer, who wrote Revelation, is an exception to this convention (Rev. 1.9). The word apocalyptic in biblical studies is now used to refer to a whole collection of Jewish and Christian writings from approximately 200 BCE to 200 CE. Apocalyptic writings occasionally describe the close of the present age, scenes of judgment, and the beginning of God's reign on earth. Often the suffering of God's people provides the context for much of ancient apocalyptic literature (see e.g., 1–2 Macc, with the Book of Daniel). The use of numerology, angels and devils (possibly reflecting the early influence of Zoroastrianism), and many Israelite symbols characterize this literature as well. Revelation, the last book of the Bible, is considered by many to be the quintessential apocalyptic work. Jesus also uses apocalyptic imagery in the Olivet Discourse, found in Mark 13 and parallels.

The modern use of the word apocalyptic often conjures up world changing events and can refer to a decisive one that reveals or uncovers portents of the immanent end of history or even the often-dark depths of the human heart. In the film *Apocalypse Now* (1979), army agent Benjamin Willard travels through Cambodia's jungles to take out a rogue army officer in a journey loosely based on Joseph Conrad's novel, *Heart of Darkness*. In *Apocalypto*, by Mel Gibson, the final scenes introduce the revelation or uncovering event in the arrival of Europeans, which signals the end of the Mayan world. C.S. Lewis's *The Final Battle* in his Narnia series is an interesting attempt to capture apocalyptic themes in a children's story.

Recommended reading. Russell, D.S. *Prophecy and the Apocalyptic Dream*. Peabody,, MA: Hendrickson, 1994. Witherington, III, Ben. *Revelation*. Cambridge: Cambridge University Press, 2003. Pearson, Simon. *A Brief History of the End of the World*. London: Constable & Robinson, 2006.

See also ANTICHRIST; ARMAGEDDON; BEAST
[DMAC]

Apocrypha, Deuterocanonicals and Intertestamentals. The term Intertestamentals refers to the extensive body of Jewish literature not part of the Jewish HB/Christian OT that emerged approximately between the end of the Babylonian Exile and the NT era. This broad term includes the Apocrypha—included alongside the OT in many Christian Bibles, based on the Septuagint and Vulgate—and many books called pseudepigrapha because usually attributed to some biblical hero. Occasionally the NT writers draw on these noncanonical writings (e.g., Jude 6, 9, 14).

Martin Luther and the other Reformers, noting that the apocryphal books had never been in the HB, excluded them from the canon. However, the Anglican Church, the Roman Catholic Church and Eastern Orthodox Churches accept varying numbers of the apocryphal books as canonical. Roman Catholics call these works Deuterocanonical to distinguish these writings from the HB/OT.

The number of apocryphal books varies depending on whether they are considered independent or as part of another book. They include: Tobit, Judith, Wisdom of Solomon, Ecclesiasticus (The Wisdom of Jesus, Son of Sirach), Baruch, 1 and 2 Esdras, Epistle of Jeremiah, 1–2 Maccabees, the Prayer of Manasseh, an addition to Esther, the Song of the Hebrew Children (including the Prayer of Azariah or Abenodab), Susanna, and, Bel and the Dragon. The latter three are additions to the Book of Daniel.

Pseudepigrapha are the works written in a biblical style and ascribed to some historically ideal Jewish person. They were actually written anonymously in order to gain authority for their message. Included among these extra-canonical books are 1–2 Enoch, the Testament of the Twelve Patriarchs, the Testament of Moses, the Assumption of Moses, and many others. Some of the books of the Apocrypha, such as Baruch, are also pseudepigraphical.

Examples of the cultural impact of the Apocrypha and Pseudepigrapha includes the claim that Christopher Columbus used 2 Esd. 6.42 to risk sailing the Atlantic. The Roman Catholic Church's introits for Quasimodo Sunday and for its traditional Requiem are based upon 2 Esd. 2.36-37 and 2.34-35 respectively. Themes in Susanna are familiar to readers and viewers of courtroom dramas. The book is referred to in Shakespeare's *The Merchant of Venice* by Shylock. The bath scene in Susanna influenced various artists (e.g., Tintoretto's *Susanna Bathing*, 1555). Wallace Steven's 'Peter Quince at the Clavier' refers to it as well. The Apocryphal Bel and the Dragon is an example of the locked room mystery. In 1941 James Agee used Sir. 44.1 for his work 'Let Us Now Praise Famous Men' about Alabama sharecroppers.

Recommended reading. Charlesworth, James H. . *The Old Testament Pseudepigrapha: Apocalyptic Literatuand Testaments*. 2 vols. New York: Doubleday, 1983. Kee, Howard Clark. *Cambridge Annotated Study Apocrypha*. Cambridge: Cambridge University Press, 1994.

See also BEL AND THE DRAGON; TOBIT, BOOK OF; SUSANNA; ESTHER, ADDITIONS TO; PSEUDEPIGRAPHA
[AJW]

Apollos. Apollos (a shortened form of Apollonius) was an Alexandrian Jew mentioned in Acts 18.24-28; 1 Cor. 1.12; 3.1-9, 21-23; and Tit. 3.13. He is described as eloquent (that is, skilled in Greek rhetoric), well versed in the Jewish Scriptures, and 'boiling over with the spirit'—a reference either to his enthusiasm or to his being filled with God's Spirit. Largely on the strength of his notable eloquence, Martin Luther (and some modern scholars) proposed that he might be the author of Hebrews, a book known for its refined Greek style.

According to Acts 18, Apollos arrived in Ephesus shortly after Paul's departure at the end of his second missionary venture. Luke presents him as a Christian disciple ('instructed in the Way of the Lord', v. 25) who nevertheless was deficient in his understanding, as he knew 'only the baptism of John [the Baptist]'. These sparse details have inspired much speculation about Apollos's religious orientation. Was he an orthodox Christian although lacking in either knowledge or apostolic credentials? Was he a heterodox Christian? Were his beliefs more in line with other followers of John the Baptist such as those Paul encountered in Acts 19.1-7?

The most one can say with certainty is that he was a follower of Jesus, originally adhering to a pre-Pauline type of Christianity. Acts 18.28 suggests that, before his meeting with Priscilla and Aquila, Apollos didn't yet know how to demonstrate from Scripture that 'the Messiah is Jesus'. This is the most straightforward interpretation of Apollos's progress from an 'accurate' to a 'more accurate' understanding of 'the Way of God' (Acts 18.26).

Apollos then set off to minister in Corinth with the backing of the Ephesian church. What Paul says of Apollos in 1 Corinthians harmonizes well with Acts. Both sources agree that Apollos arrived in Corinth after Paul had established a church there (Acts 18.27; 1 Cor. 3.6), and both agree that he was an eloquent speaker (Acts 18.24). Paul acknowledges his own lack of eloquence in 1 Cor. 1.18-25; 2.1-5, perhaps a contributing factor in the apparent rivalry in Corinth between supporters of Paul and of Apollos (1 Cor. 1.12). To quell this rivalry, Paul insists that he and Apollos are fellow servants of God (1 Cor. 3.5-15; 4.6-7). They are not competing against each other.

Later tradition states that Apollos, weary of the divisions at Corinth, spent some time on Crete (see Tit. 3.13). When the conflict was resolved, it is said he returned to the Corinthian church and became its bishop. Other sources say he became bishop of Caesarea.

The Orthodox Church commemorates Apollos on December 8 along with Sosthenes, Tychicus, and Epaphroditus—all companions of Paul. Lutheran churches also often include him in their calendars of saints and observances.

Recommended reading. Beatrice, Pier Franco. 'Apollos of Alexandria and the Origins of the Jewish-Christian Baptist Encratism'. *Aufstieg und Niedergang der römischen Welt* II.26.2. Pp. 1232-75. Berlin: de Gruyter, 1995. Hartin, Patrick J. *Apollos: Paul's Partner or Rival?* Collegeville, MN: Michael Glazier, 2009.

See also HEBREWS, EPISTLE TO THE; JOHN THE BAPTIST; PRISCILLA AND AQUILA [DJP]

Apollyon. Apollyon is the Greek version of the Hebrew name Abaddon, meaning destruction (cf. Job 26.6; Ps. 88.11; Prov. 15.11). The name echoes the Greco-Roman deity Apollo, with whom the Roman emperor Nero believed himself to have a special affinity. In Rev. 9.11, Apollyon is identified as the angel of the bottomless pit, and as king of the destructive army of locusts, which emerge from the bottomless pit to torture those who have not been marked with the seal of God. This symbolic depiction of Nero at the head of a vast military machine terrorizing the world forms part of Revelation's socio-political critique of Rome. It is possible that, rather than emerging from the pit with the locusts, Apollyon should be identified with the fallen star that receives the key to open the bottomless pit and thus calls the locusts forth into the world (Rev. 9.1).

Interpreters down the centuries have sought to identify Apollyon with other scriptural characters. Some have seen him as a fallen angel, Antichrist or as Satan himself. The Jehovah's Witnesses identify him as Jesus Christ. The image of the satanic destroyer named Apollyon has featured in Western culture in numerous guises. From Christian's fight with the 'foul fiend' Apollyon in John Bunyan's allegorical story *Pilgrim's Progress*, to Milton's epic poem *Paradise Lost*, to the name of a twentieth-century heavy metal band, Apollyon has come to denote satanic destruction on a global scale.

Recommended reading. Boxall, Ian. *The Revelation of St John*. Black's New Testament Commentaries. London: Continuum, 2006. Kovacs, Judith L., and Christopher Rowland. *Revelation*. Blackwell Bible Commentaries. Oxford: Blackwell, 2004. Woodman, Simon. *The Book of Revelation*. SCM Core Text. London: SCM Press, 2008.

See also ANTICHRIST; NERO; REVELATION, BOOK OF; SATAN; WORMWOOD [SW]

Apostasy. The term derives from the Greek *apostasia*, to 'stand back from, repudiate' what one has accepted or confessed. Associated NT language is much broader: 'to fall from grace, fall out, to be disqualified'. The dangerous possibility of apostasy, having once begun the Christian faith journey, is a recurring NT theme. For instance, Jesus warned that such blasphemy against the Holy Spirit could not be forgiven (Matt. 12.31-32). Hebrews 6.4-6 reiterates this warning. If people fall away from the living faith, they cannot repent a second time, for Jesus cannot be crucified afresh.

The intense persecutions of believers in the early centuries netted many who denied Christ and renounced their allegiance to him. Later, when Christianity became the state religion, they sought re-entry to the church, igniting a series of conflicts with those who had remained faithful. The Donatists were separatist Roman Catholics who believed that all who had been unfaithful in any way to the church during the persecutions were damned for eternity and should be denied the sacraments. Augustine, Bishop of Hippo in North Africa, brought an end to such thinking through his writings and through aggressive action against these purists.

Since the Protestant Reformation, arguments over apostasy have been between the followers of John Calvin—who hold that once one is saved, one is forever safe from eternal loss no matter what happens—and the followers of his disciple Jacobus Arminius, who believe that personal freedom, even to apostatize, remains a possibility for every Christian. Though condemned by the Reformed Church at the Synod of Dort in 1618–1619, this free will theology spread to other religious communions. The first Baptists were Arminians, although a much greater portion of those who followed were Calvinists. Other Arminian groups include Mennonites, Methodists, and most Holiness churches.

The concept of apostasy is not unique to Christianity. In some traditions, the penalties for rejecting tenets of religious belief are dire. This is particularly so in contexts where one of these religions is both the dominant and state faith. One famous example of the extreme penalty is the *fatwah* issued by the Ayatollah Khomeini of Iran (and confirmed by his successor Ayatollah Khameini) against British Indian author Salman Rushdie in 1989 for blasphemy against Islam in the publication of his 1988 book *The Satanic Verses*, which alleged that Muhammed, in an earlier version of the Qur'an, allowed for prayers to three pagan Meccan goddesses. This death sentence has never been revoked.

Any violent action against a person who has left a religion for any reason whatsoever contravenes Article 18 of the Universal Declaration of Human Rights which allows people the freedom to change their religious views or affiliations in public or in private, individually or in community.

Recommended reading. Claybrook, Frederick W., Jr. *Once Saved, Always Saved? A New Testament Study of Apostasy*. Lanham, MD: University Press of America, 2003.

See also BLASPHEMY; GRACE; JUDGMENT [DLS]

Apostle. From the Greek *apostolos*, the term literally means 'one sent out', but in context, apostles are special messengers or envoys. The non-biblical use has surprisingly few occurrences, but is consistently associated with naval dispatches and embassies. In the Greek translation of the HB the noun is used only once (1 Kgs 14.6), but the verb and its cognates regularly describe special, often prophetic, commissions (2 Kgs 2.2; Isa. 6.8; Jer. 1.7; Ezek. 2.3). The term can also carry this general sense in the NT. Jesus, for instance, affirmed that the one who sends a messenger (*apostolos*) is superior to his delegate (John 13.16). Paul also refers to Epaphroditus and other unnamed messengers to the Macedonian churches as 'apostles' (Phil. 2.25; 2 Cor. 8.23).

In the NT 'apostle' most often refers to individuals of extraordinary status sent from God. In this sense, Jesus was appropriately labeled an 'apostle and high priest' (Heb. 3.1). According to Luke's Gospel, the group known as the Twelve Apostles originated at Jesus' commission of his closest followers (Luke 6.13). In Mark's account, the Twelve were appointed by Jesus 'to be with him, to be sent out (*apostelein*) to proclaim the message, and to have authority to cast out demons' (Mark 3.14-15). Jesus implies that he chose exactly twelve so that they might represent the twelve tribes of Israel (Matt. 19.28; cf. Rev. 21.12-14). These original twelve included: Simon Peter, his brother Andrew, James and John (the sons of Zebedee), Philip, Bartholomew, Thomas, Matthew, James (the son of Alphaeus), Thaddaeus, Simon the Cananean, and Judas Iscariot. Matthias succeeded Judas following the latter's betrayal and death (Acts 1.15-26). Several other early Christian ministers were also regarded as apostles, most significantly Paul (1 Cor. 15.9), Barnabas (Acts 14.14), James, the brother of Jesus (Gal. 1.19; 1 Cor. 9.5), and Andronicus and Junia (Rom. 16.7). Although NT apostleship resembles the office of prophet, the NT authors distinguished between the two (1 Cor. 12.28-29; Eph. 4.11; 2 Pet. 3.2). Paul implies that apostleship was limited to those who had personally witnessed the resurrected Jesus (1 Cor. 9.1).

The modern relevance of apostleship differs between major sects of Christendom. According to Roman Catholic dogma, the authority of the Apostle Peter is perpetually succeeded to the Pope. Some strands of Protestant Evangelicalism (e.g., Pentecostalism) apply the title to itinerant evangelists, as seen in Robert Duvall's 1997 film *The Apostle*. The Church of Jesus Christ of Latter Day Saints also retains the title for members of their ecclesial hierarchy.

Apostleship appears in numerous aspects of modern art and culture. Many paintings underscore the historical and theological significance of the apostles, particularly those from the Renaissance such as da Vinci's *The Last Supper* and Rembrandt's *Self Portrait of the Apostle St Paul*. Edward Elgar's Opus 49, *The Apostles*, was intended to convey the ministerial experiences of The Twelve. The first dozen of eighteen spindle-shaped towers of Barcelona's *La sagrada família* cathedral similarly represent the apostles. In what became the world's first animated feature film, Quirini Cristiani ironically applied the title *El Apóstol* (1917) to his satire of Argentinean President Hipólito Yrigoyen. Geologically, the Twelve Apostles is a collection of offshore limestone stacks in Port Campbell National Park, Australia.

Recommended reading. Agnew, Francis H. 'The Origin of the NT Apostle-Concept: A Review of Research'. *Journal of Biblical Literature* 105 (1986) 75-96.

See also PROPHETS; SPIRITUAL GIFTS; TWELVE DISCIPLES, THE [JKG]

Apple. Several English translations of the OT refer to finding God's favor as being 'in the apple of his eye' (Deut. 32.10; Ps. 17.8; Prov. 7.2; Zech. 2.8; Sir. 17.22), although the corresponding words in both Greek (*kore*) and Hebrew (*ishon*) do not literally refer to the fruit as we know it, but rather to the 'pupil of the eye'. In the same way, literature and art refer to the 'fruit' (lit.) that Adam and Eve eat in the Garden of Eden (Gen. 3.6) as an 'apple'. Early Christian art in the catacombs and on sarcophagi depict apples as symbols of the Fall, and later as symbols of redemption when used with the Second Adam—Jesus—and Mary. Renaissance artists blended elements of Greek mythology into biblical scenes, incorporating images of the golden apples of Atalanta, or the apple awarded to Aphrodite by Paris. See, for example Albrecht Altdorfer's *The Fall of Man* (1535), Tintoretto's *Adam and Eve* (1550), and Giuseppe Arcimboldo's *Eve and the Apple with Counterpart* (1578). In literature, 'apple' was often used as a generic word for 'fruit' in Old English. The Latin noun meaning 'apple' (*malus*) bears a striking resemblance to the adjective *malus* ('evil') and is easily co-identified when juxtaposed in the passage referring to the fruit of the Tree of Good and *Evil*. See for example *Paradise Lost* by John Milton. The prominent cartilage in the front of a man's neck is called an Adam's apple, suggesting the apple (i.e., sin) caught in his throat. Because of its association with the 'forbidden fruit'—another term not found in the Bible—the apple has been associated with irresistibly seductive items; the apple thus gives its image to sex shops and the logo of *Desperate Housewives*, a popular weekly soap opera exposing the sex-lives of suburban women. Because of the apple's association with (the tree of) knowledge, it also lends its image to computers and teachers, although the allusion may also be to Sir Isaac Newton. The phrase 'bad apple' refers to immoral people.

See also GARDEN OF EDEN; FALL, THE; ADAM AND EVE [JSW]

Aqedah. Aqedah (or Akedah), which means 'binding' in Hebrew, is the title given by rabbis to the story of the near-sacrifice of Isaac first found in Gen. 22. In this passage, Abraham receives a command from God to offer his son Isaac as a sacrifice on a mountain in the land of Moriah. Abraham then takes Isaac to the designated mountain and sets up an altar for the sacrifice. Immediately before the bloodshed, however, an angel appears and interrupts the offering. As a reward for Abraham's obedience, God reiterates his profound promises for Abraham and his descendants, that they will greatly multiply and inherit the promised land.

This story leaves behind a few ambiguities for its audience. Why does God want to test Abraham? How old is Isaac? What father would agree to kill his beloved son, even for the sake of piety? Early interpretations of this story tried to fill these lacunae. For instance, some Jewish texts explain that the one who is held responsible for this whole incident is not God, but a devil as in *Jubilees* (17.16) or some jealous angels as in *Biblical Antiquities* (32.2). Possibly as an attempt to downplay the violent tone of the story, Isaac is aged 15 in *Jubilees* (17.15), 25 in Josephus's *Jewish Antiquities* (1.227), and 37 in *Targum Pseudo-Jonathan* of Gen. 22.1, so the sacrifice does not involve a child victim. In fact, according to some Jewish texts, Isaac even gives explicit consent to be slaughtered (e.g., *Pirqe R. El.* 31). The Aqedah is also of great interest for Christians, as the author of the *Epistle of Barnabas* and several other prominent figures of the early Church such as Irenaeus, Tertullian, Clement, and Origen understood the salvation of Jesus in the light of the sacrifice of Isaac.

The Aqedah continues to be a lasting icon in Western civilization, but contrary to the early Jewish attempts to downplay the violence of the story, representations that are more recent tend to highlight the agony and/or hesitation of the characters involved. In paintings, for example, we often see Abraham grab Isaac's hair from behind (e.g., Empoli, 1590) or cover Isaac's eyes in an aggressive manner (e.g., Rembrandt, 1634), and the diminutive Isaac scream in discomfort (e.g., Caravaggio, 1601–1602). In his *Fear and Trembling* (1843), Søren Kierkegaard also emphasizes on the absurd nature of the sacrifice to underscore the point that Abraham is a knight of faith. Wilfred Owen, a famous poet in World War I, in 'The Parable of the Old Man and the Young' even alters the story's ending to have Abraham kill Isaac despite an angel's intervention: 'But the old man would not so, but slew his son'.

In popular culture, the Aqedah features in music and movies, the best-known example being Bob Dylan's song 'Highway 61 Revisited' from the album of the same name (1965), which *Rolling Stone* crowned the fourth greatest album of all time. The biblical story also figures in Andrei Tarkovsky's Swedish film *Offret* (1986), a Grand Prix winner at the Cannes Film Festival that retells the Aqedah in the fictional setting of a World War III.

Recommended reading. Chilton, B.D. *Abraham's Curse: The Roots of Violence in Judaism, Christianity, and Islam*. New York: Doubleday, 2008. Kessler, E. *Bound by the Bible: Jews, Christians and the Sacrifice of Isaac*. New York: Cambridge University Press, 2004. Levenson, J.D. *Death and Resurrection of the Beloved Son: The Transformation of Child Sacrifice in Judaism and Christianity*. New Haven: Yale University Press, 1993.

See also ABRAHAM; ISAAC; GENESIS, BOOK OF

[ACKW]

Aramaic language. An ancient Semitic language closely related to Hebrew that is acknowledged as one of the languages spoken by Jesus. Aramaic, in its many dialects, has been spoken in the Levant since the ninth century BCE and is still spoken in parts of the Middle East and elsewhere. Aramaic uses a twenty-two character alphabet and utilizes a square script. For classification purposes it is divided into five principal periods: Old Aramaic (925–700 BCE); Official Aramaic (700–200 BCE); Middle Aramaic (200 BCE–200 CE); Late Aramaic (200–1200 CE); and Modern Aramaic.

The language originated among the Arameans living in Northern Syria, who are believed to be among the ancestors of Abraham. When the Assyrians conquered the Arameans, Aramean scribes within the empire worked to keep Aramaic alive. Aramaic continued to be utilized and eventually succeeded the Akkadian language, the language of Assyria and Babylonia, as the official language of the Persian Empire. The Aramaic language was spread extensively and ancient inscriptions in Aramaic have been found over a large area extending from Egypt to China. However, with the spread of Islam, Arabic eventually replaced Aramaic as the *lingua franca* of the Middle East.

At the time of the siege of Jerusalem in 701 BCE, Hebrew was the everyday language of the Jews and Aramaic was the language used in official transactions with Assyria. However, the situation reversed itself upon the Jews return from the Exile. Aramaic became the vernacular language of the Jews and Hebrew was used in official proceedings and in the schools. The transition from Hebrew to Aramaic was virtually seemless since they are both Semitic languages and close cognates.

The Aramaic language is vital to biblical studies due to its role as a major spoken language during the emergence of Christianity and rabbinic Judaism. Two ancient translations of the OT are composed in Aramaic, the Syriac Peshitta and the Jewish Targums, as well as other significant literary works of Syriac Christianity. Certain OT texts were written in Aramaic (Dan. 2.4b-7.28; Ezra 4.8-6.18, 7.12-26; Gen. 31.47; and Jer. 10.11) and instances of Aramaic phrases and words, such as Golgotha, are found in the NT (Mark 5.41; 7.34; 15.34; Matt. 27.46; 1 Cor. 16.22; Rev. 22.20). Two of the earliest collections of biblical studies in rabbinic Judaism, the Babylonian and the Palestinian Talmud, are written in dialects of Aramaic. Aramaic remained common throughout the first century CE as evidenced by many surviving inscriptions and documents, such as the Dead Sea Scrolls.

Aramaic is a tremendously important language for both Christians and Jews and is classified as an endangered language. Several dialects of Aramaic are still in use in parts of Syria, Turkey, Iran, and Iraq and there are efforts underway in these areas to preserve the language for future generations.

Recommended reading. Fitzmyer, Joseph A. 'The Aramaic Language and the Study of the New Testament'. *Journal of Biblical Literature* 99 (1980) 5-21. Kaufman, Stephen A. 'Aramaic'. In *The Semitic Languages*. Ed. Robert Hetzron. Pp. 117-30. London: Routledge, 2005.

See also ASSYRIA; DEAD SEA SCROLLS; *ELOI, ELOI, LAMA SABACHTHANI?*; GOLGOTHA; HEBREW LANGUAGE; LANGUAGES OF THE BIBLE; PERSIA [AB-E]

Ararat. Probably from the Assyrian *Urartu*, this is the name of a mountain or region mentioned four times in the HB. In 2 Kgs 19.37 and Isa. 37.38, Adrammelech and Sharezer are said to have fled into the land of Ararat. Jeremiah 51.27, however, refers to Ararat as a kingdom. Even so, Ararat is mainly associated with the so-called flood story. In Gen. 8.4, the mountains of Ararat are mentioned as the place where the ark rested at the end of the flood. For centuries, many have searched for some physical remains of the ark on Mount Ararat. This is likely motivated by a longing for physical proof of the historical correctness of the biblical account and the conviction that the ark would be the only material link to the pre-flood era. Hippolytus of Rome stated that certain relics of the wood of the ark still lie on the top of the mountain. He, however, refers to the mountain as Mount Kardu.

Ararat is said to be a mountain in the Greek Tobit (Tob 1.21) as well. *Jubilees* mentions the mountains of Ararat and specifies that the ark came to rest on one of the peaks, called Lubar. Like Josephus in his *Antiquities*, the Latin Vulgate does not speak about Ararat, but states that the ark rested on the mountains of Armenia. In the Qur'an, the mountain is called Mount Judi (Sura 11.44).

Mount Ararat is also related to the legend of the ten thousand martyrs as presented in Vittore Carpaccio's *Martyrdom of the Ten Thousand of Mount Ararat* (Oil on canvas, 1515, Venice). The painting tells the story of Roman soldiers who were converted to Christianity by the voice of an angel and were instructed on Mount Ararat. After an unsuccessful attempt to stone them to death, a Roman emperor ordered their crucifixion on the mountain.

Nestorian Christians built the so-called *Cloister of the Ark* on the summit of Mount Ararat. It was destroyed in the eighth century CE, and replaced by a Muslim mosque, allegedly built with wood from the ark. Armenian priests still have a conical head covering that, by its shape, reminds of and expresses their longing for Mount Ararat, their holy mountain. Nowadays, the mountain is situated in Turkish territory, close to the Armenian border. In popular culture, the troublesome relationship between Armenians and Turks and the story of the Armenian Genocide are told in Atom Egoyan's movie *Ararat* (2002).

See also NOAH'S ARK; GENESIS, BOOK OF; FLOOD [EV]

Areopagus. From the Greek *Areios pagos*, 'Ares' rock,' the Areopagus is a hill north-west of the Acropolis at Athens, Greece, as well as the name of the ancient council that convened there. In ancient times, the Areopagus council seems to have been an exclusively aristocratic body of advisors to early monarchs and magistrates. Membership was automatic for those having occupied a public office. In this sense, the Areopagus may be favorably compared to the Roman Senate. In the classical period, the Areopagus had surrendered most of its prerogatives to the *boule* or general council of citizens, following democratic reforms by Solon (c. 600 BCE) and Ephialtes (562/1 BCE). It retained some legislative and juridical functions, most notably the jurisdiction over cases of homicide. During the fifth century BCE, the Athenian orator Isocrates sponsored the reinstatement of the Areopagus as an important political body in his *Areopagiticus*, with little apparent effect. The Areopagus's continued existence is attested throughout the Hellenistic and Roman periods, up until the fourth century CE. The present-day Court of Cassation of the Hellenic Republic of Greece was also named Areopagus upon its founding in 1834.

The juridical role of the Areopagus in classical Athenian civilization is reflected in Aeschylus's play *Eumenides*, the finale to his Oresteian trilogy (458 BCE). Orestes is tried for murdering both his mother Clytaemnestra and her lover Aegisthus, and acquitted by equality of votes. According to Acts 17.16-34, the apostle Paul addressed the Areopagus during his sojourn in Athens. In a famous speech, he identified the Christian God with 'the unknown god' whose statue he had found in the city. Several listeners, including some members of the Areopagus, became followers of Christ afterwards. An unknown Christian writer of the fifth–sixth century CE authored a corpus of mystical writings under the pseudonym of Dionysius the Areopagite, one of Paul's reputed converts. Both Paul's speech before the Areopagus and Isocrates' pamphlet inspired John Milton's *Areopagitica* (1644), one of the most influential essays in defense of press freedom.

Recommended reading. Wallace, R.W. *The Areopagos Council, to 307 BC*. Baltimore: Johns Hopkins University Press, 1989.

See also PAUL, THE APOSTLE [DDC]

Ark of the Covenant. After the Lord rescued the Israelites from slavery in Egypt, he commanded them through Moses to make an Ark. He specified the materials, the size, the decorations, as well as the manner in which it is to be carried. It was made of acacia wood overlaid with gold, with four gold rings, two on each side, for the two poles which were used to carry the Ark. On top of the Ark were two cherubim, one on each end, with their wings extending toward each other. The place between them was called the mercy seat, and this was where God met with his people: 'There I will meet with you and from above the mercy seat, from between the two cherubim that are on the ark of the covenant, I will deliver to you all my commands for the Israelites' (Exod. 25.22). The Ark, then, was where the Lord dwelt among his people. The Israelites carried the Ark with them while they wandered through the desert. When they camped, they pitched the tabernacle, a tent structure used for worship. The Ark resided inside the tabernacle, behind the altar.

The Israelites would sometimes take the Ark into battle with them, believing it to guarantee victory. This was not the case, however, as proved by the Ark's capture by enemies in 1 Sam. 4. The moral of the story is that faithfulness to God, not the physical presence of the Ark, is what matters. God proved his power by ensuring the Ark's return to Holy Land through supernatural means (see 1 Sam. 5). The Ark remained on the fringe of Israelite worship until David brought it to Jerusalem (2 Sam. 6). This required two attempts, as during the first one a man named Uzzah died because he touched the ark. Once the Temple was built in Solomon's reign, the Ark was placed inside. As the Ark represented the presence of God with his people, it was the center of worship, though it could only be accessed by the high priest once a year on the Day of Atonement. Inside the Ark were the stone tablets of the Ten Commandments, Aaron's staff, and a jar of manna.

Speculations on the ultimate fate or current whereabouts of the Ark are rife. They range from its destruction during the razing of the Hebrew Temple in 70 CE to its present-day survival in Ethiopia. Some believe the Knights Templar removed the Ark from the Holy Land during the medieval crusades. The Ark continues to have a firm grasp on the western imagination, as witnessed in the numerous appearances it makes in modern culture. The television series *Xena: Warrior Princess* featured the ark of the covenant in the episode 'The Royal Couple of Thieves' in which Xena saves the Ark from the clutches of an evil warlord. The video games 'Halo 2' and 'Assassin's Creed' both feature the Ark, though in 'Halo 2' it is a weapon that could destroy all life on earth. The idea of the Ark as a weapon is evoked in what is perhaps the most famous modern cultural use of the Ark, the movie *Indiana Jones and the Raiders of the Lost Ark*, starring Harrison Ford. In this film, Indiana Jones tries to find the Ark before the Nazis, who want to use it as a weapon. When it is opened, the Ark kills all who look at it.

See also MERCY SEAT; TEN COMMANDMENTS; AARON; CHERUBIM AND SERAPHIM; TABERNACLE; DAY OF ATONEMENT, THE [JCH]

Armageddon. This term derives from two Hebrew words and means, literally, the Mountain of Megiddo (*Har Magedon*) and is used only once in the Bible (Rev. 16.16). References to the town of Megiddo in northern Israel appear in the HB several times (Josh. 17.11; Judg. 1.27 etc.) and battles are fought near Megiddo (Judg. 5.19) but there is no mention of a mountain. Strategically the town of Meggido oversees a crossroads point in the Middle East (2 Kg 23.29) and overlooks a vast plain (2 Chron. 35.22). The symbolic importance of this place begins with the death of the beloved and faithful king Josiah who foolishly goes out to fight against Neco, the king of Egypt, even against the warnings of the Egyptian king on behalf of God (2 Kgs 23.29; 2 Chron. 12.12). Josiah is subsequently killed on the plain of Meggido. The town is associated with great mourning in the prophet Zechariah (12.11) and this king of Israel is remembered for his delusion and foolishness in the intertestamental book 1 Esdras (1.32; second century BCE).

In the Book of Revelation, Harmagedon signifies the place where all the armies of the earth will gather for the last great battle against God (16.16). Other ancient enemies of God are named as Gog and Magog (20.8; taken from Ezek. 38–39). The preparations for battle at this site begin with the activity of three unclean spirits, which are released in the sixth bowl and delude the kings of the earth into gathering their armies for battle against God, although no battle engagement actually takes place. John may well be working here more with the association of a mountain (an important symbol in apocalyptic writings, as in e.g., Rev. 6.15-16; 16.20; Isa. 14.9-17) and the place of Megiddo as a symbolic site, rather than with an actual historical event or place. Again, he describes a delusion pursued by the kings of the earth marshalled against God Almighty. The theme of deception, by self or demonic spirits, may also be a clue as to why John includes the strange activity of Jesus' threat to steal people's clothes (in a battle scene!) rather than taking up a sword to slay anyone in his vision of the sixth bowl (16.15, 12-16). Could he be saying that this action of exposing the truth and foolishness of any or all battles, including an 'Armageddon', is the divine role here?

Today the name of Armageddon has the symbolic value of a final battle, which may or may not be perceived as ushering in the last days. The film, *Armageddon* (1998) is an example of how the name signifies a cataclysmic event, which apparently has little to do with the Bible or God's intervention in history. The crisis emerges as an asteroid the size of Texas approaches the earth on a collision course. To avert the disaster a group of drillers with the help of NASA and a nuclear bomb land on the asteroid, break it apart and deflect it past the earth.

Recommended reading. Harrington, Wilfred J. *Revelation*. Sacra Pagina, 16. Collegeville, MN: Liturgical Press, 1993. Kirsch, Jonathan. *A History of the End of the World*. New York: HarperCollins, 2006. Pearson, Simon. *A Brief History of the End of the World*. London: Constable & Robinson, 2006.

See also APOCALYPSE, APOCALYPTIC; BEAST; FALSE PROPHET [DMAC]

Armor of God. The exhortation to 'put on the Armor of God' is found in Eph. 6.11-17. The passage envisions readers putting on specific pieces of military-type armor for their protection in a fierce battle. They are to put on the belt of truth, the breastplate of righteousness, shoes that make them ready for the gospel of peace, the shield of faith, the helmet of salvation and to take up the sword of the Spirit. The pieces of armor, which look at first like standard Roman infantry equipment, are given metaphorical definitions because they are gospel implements, to be used to fight a gospel battle 'not against flesh and blood, but against the rulers, against the authorities, against the world rulers (cosmocrats) of this darkness, against the spiritual beings of evil' (Eph. 6.12). Christians are called to stand firmly against the enemy. The armor imagery and the exhortation reflect descriptions found in Isa. 11.5; 52.7; 59.17; 49.2; and Wis. 5.18-20. Many interpreters view the enemy as evil spiritual, cosmic or demonic forces under the control of the Devil. The passage may refer, however, to evil *human* political forces, also viewed as being under the Devil's control, that place social and religious pressures on believers.

The imagery of putting on armor is powerful because putting on clothing signals a change in identity and behavior. Christians are also directed to 'put on the Lord Jesus Christ' (Rom. 13.14) and to be clothed with the new person, i.e., with Christ (Col. 3.10; Eph. 4.24). They have a new identity defined by Christ himself. Now in Eph. 6, Christians are seen in a military role where a particular enemy must be faced and resisted. This language is reminiscent of ancient Mediterranean battle speeches employed to rally troops for fighting. It was also common to speak of life as a battle where people face not only ordinary difficulties, but must also fight against evil passions, desires and temptations. Soldiers must plan to win battles, to defeat the enemy and be visibly victorious. This theme was a common feature of Roman statuary in Asia Minor, the destination of the Letter to the Ephesians, for example in the images on the Altar of Pergamon.

The armor of God has always been a popular topic for sermons and church teaching. Its graphic nature allows it to be used to great emotional effect, giving people a sense of strength and righteous power over legitimate enemies. The armor and the battle have been the subject of many hymns, for example 'Soldiers of Christ Arise' (Charles Wesley). It is frequently the subject of popular artistic works. The action film *Armour of God* (1994) portrays an adventurer who searches for the five pieces of armor described in the biblical text. Many popular level publications have been produced to describe 'spiritual warfare' and encourage Christians to engage in it.

Recommended reading. Neufeld, Thomas R. Yoder. *Put on the Armour of God*. Sheffield: Sheffield Academic Press, 1997. Talbert, Charles H. *Ephesians and Colossians*. Grand Rapids, MI: Baker, 2007.

See also PAUL, THE APOSTLE; EPHESIANS, EPISTLE TO [RRJ]

Artemis (Latin *Diana*) is the virgin goddess of hunting and the moon. The temple of Artemis at Ephesus was considered one of the Seven Wonders of the ancient world. Worshippers came from far and wide to honor Artemis as an aspect of the Great Mother, a fertility goddess of Asia Minor. The cult's typical iconography is encountered from the sixth century BCE until well into the Roman era, attesting to its widespread popularity. Images of the Ephesian Artemis are instantly recognizable by the many tear-shaped objects hanging from her chest. Traditionally viewed as a multitude of breasts, these droplets have been identified as votive offerings (probably bulls' testicles) strung around the statue's neck.

The popularity of the cult seems to have been a hindrance to the initial spread of Christianity in Asia Minor, as recounted in Acts 19.23-41. Throughout the Middle Ages, Artemis of Ephesus was known to the west only through the biblical account, and contemporary representations of her were non-existent. Not until the sixteenth century saw the recovery of archeological remains of the cult, did the Ephesian Artemis become a common topic in literature and the figurative arts. She is portrayed among the sixteenth-century statues adorning the gardens of the Villa d'Este at Tivoli, Italy, as well as on the ceiling fresco of the *Stanza della Segnatura* in the Vatican. Diana of Ephesus and her temple appear on stage in the fifth act of Shakespeare's *Pericles, Prince of Tyre* (between 1603 and 1608).

Whereas the 'classical' Artemis was portrayed as a hunting goddess or as a symbol of chastity, Artemis of Ephesus became a symbol of fertility, nature, and natural order. As such her image entered into the highly symbolical debate on the 'imitation of nature' in the theory of art. She is, for instance, prominent in pieces inspired on the death of Rafaele Sanzio (1483–1520), the Italian painter whose epitaph in the Pantheon (Rome, Italy) credits him with a near-victory over his teacher, Nature. Authors and printers in revolutionary France adopted her as an image of political order and innate rationality, echoing the ideals of enlightenment. As Mother Nature, she is portrayed in the frontispiece of many seventeenth- to nineteenth-century works on biology, including Carl Linnaeus's *Fauna svecica* (1746).

Recommended reading. Strelan, R. *Paul, Artemis and the Jews in Ephesus*. Berlin: de Gruyter, 1996.

See also PAUL, THE APOSTLE [DDEC]

Ascension. In the context of biblical literature, the term ascension refers to an individual who does not experience death but is instead taken to heaven when alive. The stories of Elijah (2 Kgs 2.11) and Enoch (Gen. 5.22-24) are examples of this phenomenon. Most often, the term applies to Jesus' return to heaven as described by Luke in Acts 1.1-11. Forty days after the resurrection, surrounded by the eleven apostles (Judas was dead by this time [Acts 1.15-26]), Jesus gave his followers some final words of instruction and then 'was lifted up, and a cloud took him out of their sight' (Acts 1.9).

The story of Jesus' Ascension is often debated. For instance, around 180 CE. Bishop Irenaeus wrote in *Against Heresies* that Gnostics maintained differing views about the Ascension, and long after the Council of Nicea enshrined the doctrine in creedal form, competing viewpoints remain. In more recent years, the Jesus Seminar rejected the doctrine, suggesting it is an invention of the early Christian community. Debates aside, the ideas that undergird the doctrine of Ascension have found their way into popular culture. The word is frequently employed in works of science fiction to describe the process by which a character comes to exist in a more enlightened state. The science fiction television show *Stargate* employs the term ascension to describe the process by which one becomes a spiritual, body-less entity on a higher plane of existence. In *The X-Files*, the word is the title for the October 24, 1994 episode that dealt with the kidnapping of FBI agent Dana Scully by a self-proclaimed alien abductee.

Recommended reading. Walton, Steve. '"The heavens opened": Cosmological and Theological Transformation in Luke and Acts'. In *Cosmology and New Testament Theology*. Ed. Jonathan T. Pennington and Sean M. McDonough. Pp. Pages 60-73. New York: T. & T. Clark, 2008.

See also ACTS OF THE APOSTLES, THE; CHRIST; HEAVEN [JNR]

Asenath. Asenath is introduced in Gen. 41.45 when Pharoah gives her in marriage to Joseph. She is daughter of Potiphera (Pentephres in LXX) and priest of On, given to Joseph as he is commissioned steward of the land of Egypt. The only other reference to her in the Bible occurs in Gen. 41.50-52, that records she gave birth to two sons, Manasseh and Ephraim. In addition to these brief biblical references, there is a Hellenistic romance story about Joseph and Asenath, likely contemporaneous with the NT. This story deals with marriage and conversion dramatically illustrated through the changing of clothes and name as Asenath mourns her loss of kin and adopts Joseph's faith.

Asenath's name means 'holy of Anat', which connects her to the Egyptian goddess Neith, also known as 'Queen of Heaven'. Royal women often called themselves after the goddess of Neith, a goddess of weaving and the domestic arts, protector of women, and a guardian of marriage.

When given to Joseph in marriage, Asenath leaves her parents and their gods and is disowned, orphaned. She laments her loss but embraces God as her father. She receives a new name, which means 'City of Refuge'.

This crossing of natural boundaries by marriage is a familiar theme in contemporary storytelling, as in the *Star Wars* trilogy, in which Anakin Skywalker falls in love with Queen Amidala of Naboo, and *The Lord of the Rings*, in which Aragorn falls in love with Arwen. As the brief mention of Asenath in Genesis and the later apocryphal story about her illustrate, this is an ancient story.

See also JOSEPH SON OF JACOB [RAHC]

Asherah (Ashtoreth). Asherah is a Canaanite deity and the consort of El, the chief God of the Canaanite pantheon. There are depictions of her in Egyptian, Hittite, Philistine, and Arabic records. She is the mother of the 70 gods, including Ba'al, Astarte, and Anat, of the Ugaritic divine council. There is some indication that Asherah was also a part of the Israelite cult. There are references to the worship of Asherah throughout Israel in the Deuteronomistic history, particularly in the books of Deuteronomy and Kings. The worship of Asherah is often linked to the worship of Ba'al and is predominantly negative. However, the assessment of Asherah is not as simple because the HB makes reference to the deity, her cult, and her cultic symbol, usually thought to be a pole or a tree, but it is not always clear which element is being referred to by the biblical author. Asherah and Eve share the epitaph of 'mother of all living'.

Two inscriptions (one from Khirbet El-Qom and the other from Kuntillet 'Ajrud) found in the 1970s mention Asherah alongside Yahweh, the head of the divine council of the HB. Since these discoveries, scholars have been debating whether or not Asherah was considered to be the wife of Yahweh in Israelite popular religion. Some believe that Asherah was the precursor to Shekhina in the Talmudic tradition and in Gnostic Judaism. It has also been suggested that the Menorah was originally designed as a stylized Asherah tree and that this is the last remaining element of her cultic worship, even though it has lost any connection to its origins.

In contemporary culture, Asherah is depicted in a variety of ways. Neal Stephenson uses her as inspiration for the negative power depicted in the sci-fi novel *Snow Crash*. In contrast, Asherah in the video game *Mortal Combat* is a positive divine character who has to escape hell. In another video game, *Fire Emblem: Path of Radiance*, she is a globally dominant goddess and the ultimate power in the game. In the novels by Anita Diamant (*The Red Tent*) and Jacqueline Carey (*Kushiel's Chosen*), the worship of Asherah plays a role in the plot.

Various movements have been created to 'recover' the worship of Asherah. Organizations such as Asherah International incorporate ideas of divine feminism, kabbalah, tantric meditation, and ritual dance as a means of worshiping this goddess. Asherah poles have been erected in several California nightclubs such as the Octopus Bar.

Recommended reading. Day, John. 'Asherah in the Hebrew Bible and Northwest Semitic Literature'. *Journal of Biblical Literature* 105 (1986) 385-409. Emerton, J.A. 'Yahweh and his Asherah': The Goddess or her Symbol?' *Vetus Testamentum* 49 (1999) 315-38. Hadley, Judith M. *The Cult of Asherah in Ancient Israel and Judah: Evidence for a Hebrew Goddess*. Cambridge: Cambridge University Press, 2000.

See also BAAL; CANAAN, CANAANITES; KINGS, BOOKS OF; YAHWEH; DIVINE COUNCIL, THE [EW]

Ashes to ashes, dust to dust. This term is based on the biblical descriptions of death: 'Dust thou art, and unto dust thou shalt return' (Gen. 3.19 KJV); 'I will bring thee to ashes upon the earth in sight of all them that behold thee' (Exod. 28.18 KJV). The phrase is used in Anglican burial services when the vicar notes that the person is returning 'Earth to earth, ashes to ashes, dust to dust'. The three phrases seem to represent the Trinity.

The expression appears in literature, as in the writings of the Elizabethan sea dog Sir Walter Raleigh (1554–1618) who notes in his famous poem that 'our youth, our joys, our all we have, pays us nothing but earth and dust'. The term is also the title of various books, films, and plays. The most famous instance of the latter is undoubtedly the 1996 play by the English playwright and winner of the 2005 Nobel Prize for Literature, Harold Pinter. It centers on two characters 'in their forties' whose relationship to each other is ill defined. The other bestseller with the title *Ashes to Ashes* is quite different. It is Richard Kluger's history of the cigarette industry, subtitled *America's Hundred-Year Cigarette War, the Public Health, and the Unabashed Triumph of Philip Morris*. Published in 1996, it won the Pulitzer Prize and the front cover was illustrated with a burning cigarette, the analogy being the link between cigarette smoking and death.

In television, an episode of *Star Trek: Voyager* had that title, as did an episode of *CSI: Miami*. There was also a British television series that involved a British police officer travelling in time back from 2008 to 1981. In terms of music, there have been songs by David Bowie and Woody Guthrie. The phrase is also the title of a Wayne Gerard Trotman film that focuses on martial arts in London.

See also DEATH [JC]

Asmodeus. In the apocryphal/deuterocanonical book of Tobit (c. 200 BCE), Asmodeus is the demon who killed Sarah's seven husbands, each on their wedding night (3.8). With the aid of the angel Raphael, Tobias marries Sarah and, on the wedding night, burns the liver and heart of a fish in order to create an odor that drives Asmodeus away (6.1–8.3). The demon is followed to Egypt by Raphael, who then 'bound him there hand and foot' (8.3).

The name 'Asmodeus' (Greek *Asmodaios*; cf. Hebrew *'shmd'y*) may derive from the Avestan *aēshma-daēuua* ('demon of wrath'), thus suggesting some relation to the Zoroastrian demon, Aēshma. The Hebrew form (*'shmd'y*) may also reflect an attempt to associate him with the Hebrew term *shmd*, meaning 'to destroy'.

Asmodeus does not appear elsewhere in the Bible (though cf. Mark 12.20-22). One of the Aramaic copies of Tobit found among the Qumran Dead Sea Scrolls, however, adds that the demon was in love with Sarah (4QpapTob^a ar 6.15 [frag. 14 I, 4]). In rabbinic tradition, Asmodeus (Ashmodai) is said to have been forced to help Solomon with the construction of the Temple (*b. Git.* 68; cf. *Num. Rab.* 11.3). Once released, he sent Solomon into exile and established himself as king, until eventually Solomon returned to reclaim his throne. He is described as 'king of demons' in *b. Pesah.* 110a.

In the *Testament of Solomon* (first to fourth century CE), Solomon summons a series of demons, including Asmodeus. Similarities are attested with both Tobit and the rabbinic tradition; Asmodeus is said to be opposed by the angel Raphael and subdued by burning the innards of a fish. The latter revelation is used to subjugate him and ensure his assistance with the construction of the Temple (*T. Sol.* 5). His previous association with lust and sexuality (e.g., Vulgate Tob 6.17; 4QpapTob^a ar) is reinforced here in connection with marital disharmony and adultery (*T. Sol.* 5.7-8).

Asmodeus reappears in demonological works, including Johann Weyer's *Pseudomonarchia Daemonum* (1577), where he is described as breathing fire, having the heads of a bull, a man, and a ram, a serpent's tail, and sitting atop a dragon. A nineteenth-century statue from Rennes-le-Château church (France), however, portrays him as humanoid with horns, red skin, bat-like wings, and a pointed beard. He is mentioned in John Milton's *Paradise Lost* (1667; 4.167-71; cf. 6.365), and appears as a fallen angel in John Dryden's play, *The State of Innocence* (1674). In Collin de Plancy's *Dictionnaire Infernal* (1818), he is associated with the serpent of Gen. 3.1-15 (cf. the adder, Asmodeus, in Brian Jacques's novel *Redwall* [1986]), while in Alain-René Le Sage's novel, *Le diable boiteux* (1707), and Christoph Wieland's poem, 'Oberon' (1780), he is identified with Cupid, the god of love. Johann Wolfgang von Goethe's *Faust II* (1832), however, depicts Asmodeus as predominantly a destroyer of relationships (vv. 5378-80), reminiscent of *T. Sol.* 5.7-8.

More recently, Asmodeus is attested in films (e.g., Shane Abbess's *Gabriel* [2007]), computer games (e.g., *Gabriel Knight III* [Sierra, 1999]), fiction (e.g., Richard Harland's *Heaven and Earth* trilogy [2000–2003]), and Japanese anime (e.g., *Rental Magica* [Itsuro Kawasaki, 2007–2008]). Furthermore, a song, 'Asmodeus' (1985; Nasty Savage), contains lyrics which draw heavily upon the rabbinic tradition, the *Testament of Solomon*, and Weyer (1577).

Recommended reading. Collins, Matthew A. 'Asmodeus: Reception History'. In *Encyclopedia of the Bible and its Reception*, II. Ed. H.-J. Klauck, *et al.* Pp. 1046-49. Berlin/New York: De Gruyter, 2009.

See also ANGEL; DEMON; RAPHAEL, THE ANGEL [MAC]

Assyria. The Assyrian heartland is located in the northern reaches of modern Iraq along the Tigris. The region is first noted during the dynasty founded by Sargon of Agade, the world's first empire (c. 2234–2193 BCE). A colony of Assyrian merchants living at Kultepe (in modern Turkey) left an archive of documents in the nineteenth century written in the Akkadian dialect known as Old Assyrian. Assyria was subsumed by Hammurapi of Babylon in the middle of the eighteenth century.

The El Amarna letters reveal an Assyria which claimed (over the counterclaims of the Babylonian king) to be independent and worthy to be considered a peer of the major states of the day. During this era, the Middle Assyrian laws were produced.

The Assyrians went through cyclical periods of expansion and decline until the advent of the reign of Tiglath-Pileser III (745–727). His reign is the beginning of the period known as the Neo-Assyrian empire, lasting until 609. The empire would encompass Egypt, eastern Asia Minor, the Caucasus, the northern reaches of the Persian Gulf, and all points in between. The Assyrians employed overwhelming numbers, relentless attack, unbridled brutality, and sophisticated psychological warfare (Isa. 36; 37.8-13) in the course of conquest.

Assyrian kings went on annual campaigns, starting with Ashurnasirpal III (883–859). Wayward vassal kingdoms were destroyed and incorporated into the empire, and new vassals were created on the periphery. The Assyrians did not just simply kill, but they sent messages. Rebellious vassals kings were often flayed alive, with their skin displayed upon the city wall. Piles of heads, hands, penises, and full corpses were left by city gates.

Tiglath-Pileser III (745–727) tried to rule by creating a single society, Greater Assyria. To achieve this end, conquered peoples were transplanted into a number of areas, divided into small enough groups to pose no political or military problems, settled among people who did not have the same language or culture. Thus, the common language and culture of these population centers would be Assyrian. This was the fate of the northern kingdom of Israel, as the population of Samaria and the region were resettled in the Habur Valley and villages east of Assyria proper in Media (modern Iran). Those from Babylon, Cuthah, Avva, Hamath, and Sepharvaim were settled in the former kingdom (2 Kgs 7.5-6, 24-41). The resulting population of this ethnic mixing were the Samaritans, who were despised and avoided in the NT by Jews of unmixed backgrounds (e.g., John 4.8; 8.48).

It is hardly surprising to see the hatred with which the biblical writers viewed the Assyrians. It is Jonah's hatred of the Assyrians that drives him to hop on a ship bound for the extreme west (Tarshish, in modern Spain), rather than go east to Ninevah. His fear that the people would repent, rather than get the nastiest judgment imaginable from God, drove this flight (4.1-2). The prophecy of Nahum is concerned with the coming judgment on Assyria, that the nation will face its own 'scatterer' (2.1). Babylon accomplished this scattering by 609.

Recommended reading. Saggs, H.W.F. *The Might That Was Assyria*. London: Sidgwick & Jackson, 1984. Soden, W. van. *The Ancient Orient: An Introduction to the Study of the Ancient Near East*. Trans. D.G. Schley. Grand Rapids, MI: Eerdmans, 1994.

See also BABYLON [MAP]

Athaliah. Athaliah was a queen of Judah. Her name in Hebrew means 'Yahweh has declared his eminence'. There is an ambiguity about the identity of her father. According to 2 Kgs 8.26 and 2 Chron. 22.2 she was a daughter of Omri but according to 2 Kgs 8.18 and 2 Chron. 21.6 it was Ahab who was her father. One explanation argues she was a daughter of Omri but grew up as an orphan in Ahab's court, which explains the title 'daughter of Ahab'.

The narrator of 2 Chron. 22.3 depicts Athaliah as an evil influence on her son Ahaziah, king of Judah. After the death of her son, she killed all of Ahaziah's male descendants (i.e., her grandchildren) except for a year old baby Joash, who was hidden from her. Athaliah then reigned as sole ruler over Judah for six years (c. 841–835 BCE) until Jehoiada, a priest, supported by the army, organized a putsch during which Joash was proclaimed a new king. Athaliah was not able to stop it and was put to death. Though not directly stated in the Bible, Athaliah is often credited for building Baal's temple in Jerusalem. The cultic place was destroyed soon after her death (2 Kgs 11.18).

Athaliah occasionally appears in western art forms as a symbol of the cruel usurper. Her story was an inspiration for Jean Racine's 1691 play *Athalie*, which most likely stood behind George F. Handel's oratorio entitled *Athalia*.

See also JOASH; JEHOIADA [RJM]

Atonement. The term atonement (or 'expiation', 'propitiation') generally conveys human salvation in its broadest sense. It presupposes that the profane human realm is separate from the divine sphere which is holy. Immediate contact is impossible, therefore special efforts are necessary to unite God and humans. Dealing with human salvation, the concept of atonement is found in Judaism and is central for Christian doctrines and theology. However, it is a complex concept that scholars have defined in controversial ways.

According to the HB, the Israelites were separate from God due to their sins and impurities. Besides being considered a personal burden, such sins and impurities were also understood to defile the sanctuary where God resided (Lev. 15.31; 16.16). How could these sins be forgiven, and how could the sanctuary be purified so that God would not abandon it? The answer to both problems was atonement (Hebrew root *kpr*). The Septuagint translated this term with a range of equivalents denoting sanctification/purification, forgiveness of sins, substitution, or release from liabilities.

The key institution to achieve atonement was sacrifice. During certain sacrificial rituals, animal blood was applied to various parts of the sanctuary (Lev. 4; 16.14-19). Furthermore, certain parts of the sacrifice (Lev. 2.2, 9; 3.3-5, 9-11; 4.8-10, 19-20; etc.) or the sacrifice in its entirety (Lev. 1.9, 13, 17) were burnt on the main altar. How did these different ritual acts atone? In the context of a sacrifice, blood represents the animal's life (Lev. 17.11); therefore atonement was actually achieved through life. Blood purified humans (Lev. 8.23-24, 30; 14.14) or the sanctuary (Lev. 8.15; 16.16, 19, 20) from sin and impurities. On the other hand, the sacrifice was actually offered to God when burnt on the altar. This act pleased God who then granted forgiveness or blessings to humans (Exod. 20.24; Lev. 1.4, 9; 4.31; 16.24-25; see also Num. 16.46-47 ET). Thus both blood application and burning rite contributed towards atonement—it is a frequent modern misunderstanding that blood rites alone or animal slaughter effected atonement in sacrificial rituals. Atonement is, moreover, mentioned in HB texts not dealing with ritual sacrifices where it describes appeasement between humans (Gen. 32.20 ET; Prov. 16.14), sin-removal (Lev. 16.10; Prov. 16.6), reparation payments (Exod. 30.15; Num. 31.50), or purification through retaliation (2 Sam. 21.1-9).

The term atonement occurs less frequently in the NT. Christ is sometimes called 'atonement' (Greek *hilasmos*) for sins (1 John 2.2; 4.10; see also Heb. 2.17) or '(place of) atonement (Greek *hilaterion*) by his blood' (Rom. 3.25). This image conveys, analogous to atonement in the HB cult, that Christ's blood purifies those who come into contact with it. Jesus himself refers to this tradition when calling the Eucharistical wine 'my blood of the covenant' (Mark 14.24): the sins of whoever drinks from this cup are purged. Overall the NT presents salvation in Christ with multi-faceted resourcefulness; atonement is but one of many images, alongside redemption (Rom. 3.24; Eph. 1.7), reconciliation (Rom. 5.10-11; 11.15; 2 Cor. 5.18-20), Christ's substitutionary death (John 11.50-52; Rom. 5.6, 8; 14.15; 1 Cor. 15.3), and so on.

Today some scholars limit their usage of the term atonement to occurrences of the Hebrew root *kpr* while many other (Christian) scholars tend to employ this term as a comprehensive category for all concepts articulating Christ as savior, regardless of whether they are derived from the temple cult and regardless of actual occurrences of the term 'to atone'. In Christian church history, various atonement theories about salvation in Jesus have been developed. Some of these have focused on various biblical concepts, others have featured new paradigms, e.g., that Jesus provided satisfaction to God (by Anselm of Canterbury). Yet many of these tended to overemphasize the death of Christ or depicted God as vengeful and unjust for requiring the punishment of an innocent person.

In western secular culture, the word atonement usually occurs in juridical contexts where it expresses punishment and reparation after crimes. This is conveyed in Ian McEwan's novel *Atonement* (movie adaptation, 2007): a man faces wrongful charges of having assaulted his fiancée's younger sister; later this sister tries to 'atone' for the injustice.

Recommended reading. Eberhart, Christian A. 'Atonement. II. New Testament'. In *Encyclopedia of the Bible and its Reception*, vol. 3. Ed. Hans-Josef Klauck, et al. Berlin/New York: Walter de Gruyter, 2011, 32-42. Eberhart, Christian. 'A Neglected Feature of Sacrifice in the Hebrew Bible'. *Harvard Theological Review* 97 (2004) 485-93. Finlan, Stephen. *Problems with Atonement: The Origins of, and Controversy about, the Atonement Doctrine*. Collegeville, MN: Liturgical Press, 2005.

See also BLOOD; LORD'S SUPPER; SACRIFICE [CAE]

Augustus, Caesar Octavianus. Augustus (63 BCE– 14 CE) was born Gaius Octavius Thurinus. Prior to 27 BCE he was known as Gaius Julius Caesar Octavianus. When he was quite young, Augustus lived with his grandmother (and Julius Caesar's sister) Julia Caesaris but it was not until he was 16, when he made it across hostile territory to reach Caesar's camp, that he caught the Emperor's attention. Following this, Julius Caesar took particular interest in Augustus's development, adopting him in 44 BCE.

Octavius came into power after Caesar's assassination on March 15, 44 BCE. IN 43 BCE, Octavian joined forces with Mark Antony and Marcus Aemilius Lepidus in a military dictatorship known as the Second Triumvirate. As a Triumvir, Octavian effectually ruled Rome and most of its provinces as an autocrat, seizing consular power and having himself perpetually re-elected. The Triumvirate was eventually torn apart by the competing ambitions of its rulers; Lepidus was driven into exile, and Antony committed suicide following his defeat at the Battle of Actium by the armies of Octavian in 31 BCE. Following this, Augustus became the first emperor of the Roman Empire and ruled from 27 BCE until his death in 14 CE.

As Emperor, Augustus was particularly concerned with the expansion of the Empire and during his reign the size of the provincial empire doubled. The need for conquest stemmed from Augustus's political strategy and his ever-increasing need for prestige. In light of this high level of military activity, the security of the Empire rested on maintaining the loyalty of the solders, which required excessively large sums of money. The taxation system at the time was generally inefficient, which led to Augustus implementing large-scale changes. Augustus's reforms and censuses (see Luke 2.1) created new provinces and imposed consistent, direct taxation from Rome, instead of exacting varying, intermittent, and somewhat arbitrary tributes from local provinces. This reform greatly increased Rome's net revenue from its territorial acquisitions, stabilized its monetary flow, and regularized the financial relationship between Rome and the provinces.

One of the most memorable contributions of Augustus was his building projects in the heart of Rome. Claiming 'I found Rome of clay; I leave it to you of marble', Augustus contributed to the beautification of Rome—a solid indicator of his success. Although too lengthy to recount here, Augustus's deeds and works can be found in his *Res Gestae*. On August 19, 14 CE, Augustus died while visiting the place of his father's death, and Tiberius, his stepson, was named his heir. Augustus's famous last words were, 'Did you like the performance?', referring to the play-acting and regal authority that he had put on as emperor. Upon his death and burial in Rome, the Senate declared Augustus a god.

Although not widely represented in modern culture, the character of Caesar Augustus is portrayed in the TV shows *Ancient Rome: The Rise and Fall of an Empire* (2006) and *Rome* (2005). Similarly, Augustus is the primary character in a number of fictional works, such as *Augustus* by Allan Massie and *Augustus*, by John Williams.

Recommended reading. Everitt, Anthony. *Augustus: The Life of Rome's First Emperor*. New York: Random House, 2006. Severy, Beth. *Augustus and the Family at the Birth of the Roman Empire*. London: Routledge, 2003.

See also EMPEROR; JUDEA; ROME [SAA]

Azariah, Prayer of. The Prayer of Azariah is one of the Deuterocanonical books found only in the Catholic and Eastern Orthodox versions of the Bible. It was the prayer of Azariah (Abednego) while he and his friends were in the fiery furnace. Azariah, a Hebrew name meaning, 'Yahu/Jehovah has helped', was one of the three Hebrew boys who refused to bow down to the golden statue erected by King Nebuchadnezzar (see Dan. 3). The king commanded them to be thrown into the fiery furnace for this disobedience, but they were protected from harm by an angel.

Though the Hebrew–Aramaic version does not have this text, the Greek translation of the HB inserts this prayer, along with the Song of the Three Young Jews, in between Dan. 3.23 and Dan. 3.24. It is mostly a prayer of penitence, praise and deliverance. The prayer spans twenty one verses, followed by the narration of the king's servants stoking the furnace and descriptions of the Chaldeans near the furnace being burnt to death.

Due to the obscure nature of the text, not much reference is made to the prayer in contemporary culture. Catholics and Eastern Orthodox churches use this prayer in their liturgies. Essentially a prayer of deliverance, not much is debated about its content though there is contention regarding its originality and authorship.

See also SONG OF THE THREE JEWS; DANIEL, BOOK OF; SHADRACH, MESHACH, AND ABEDNEGO [GOA]

B

Baal. *Ba'al* is either the proper name of a deity known throughout the ancient world or the common noun in Hebrew and other Semitic languages for 'owner, lord, or husband'. It sometimes occurs in the plural as 'the baals' (*habb'alim*; Judg. 2.11; 10.6) as objects of worship. Baal was a well-known warrior-storm deity in Syria-Palestine and specifically associated with Ugarit (Ras Shamra), an ancient city north of Israel (1440–1185 BCE). In Ugaritic literature Baal fights for kingship by defeating the sea god Yamm, wins kingship, has a palace built and then fights and looses to the god of death, Mot. Baal eventually returns from the underworld to defeat death. As a storm god, his death and rising are metaphors for the cycle of the rain, important to ancient agricultural societies.

Baal's relevance for HB study is both his role in the Bible as a god and his likeness to Yahweh. Like Baal, Yahweh battles with the sea (Exod. 18.1-15) and is often depicted as controlling the storm (Exod. 19.16). The close association between the two is partly due to the writers of the HB attempting to supplant popular Baalism of their time for Yahwehism (Judg. 2.11; 1 Sam. 7.41; 12.10; 1 Kgs 18).

Baal also surfaces in the NT as the demonic figure Beelzebub (Mark 3.23) and is given the etymology 'lord of demons', although in Hebrew it meant 'lord of the fly' (2 Kgs 1.2-16), which was an intentionally corrupted form of the original Ugaritic 'the high one, Lord of the earth'.

Representations of both Jesus and God carry the image of the storm god in literature and art. In Michelangelo's *The Last Judgment* (1534–1541 CE), Jesus the judge comes riding on the clouds, a common image of the storm god Baal on his divine chariot. Romantic literature continued to represent Baal like imagery in God the Father who is also associated with the storm and situated on a cloud in William Blake's famous image of God sending a bolt from heaven (*The Ancient of Days*, 1794). John Milton, referring to the sin of Israel, speaks of Baal in *Paradise Regained* (3.414-17) claiming Baal as one of the gods Jesus overcomes in 'On the Morning of Christ's Nativity' (l. 197). As a result of Jesus's birth, Baal flees his temple and presumably loses his power. Further, Beelzebub is classified as Satan's chief advisor in John Milton's *Paradise Lost* (1667). Despite the common negative portrayals of Baal, there is a more rare sympathetic portrait of Baal in Lord Byron's *Sardanapalus* (1821).

Baal is also reinvented in the recent science fiction television series, *Stargate SG-1* (1997–2007). Baal is represented as the fiercest of the Goa'uld system-lords (based on Egyptian gods). *Stargate*'s Baal is possibly historically accurate since he tries to gain power over all the gods; likewise there have been scholarly debates whether Baal was challenging the role of El as the head god of the Ugaritic divine council.

Contemporary expressions have maintained some original associations of Baal but ignored his contributions as a restorer of order and whose rains result in a bountiful harvest. It seems the writers of the HB have successfully transferred the positive attributes of Baal onto Yahweh leaving little left for Baal. Thus, contemporary representations have been influenced by biblical writings, only presenting Baal as an angry, fierce, demonic figure.

Recommended reading. Smith, Mark S. *The Early History of God: Yahweh and Other Deities in Ancient Israel*. San Francisco: Harper & Row, 1990.

See also BEELZEBUB/BEELZEBUL; CANAAN, CANAANITES; CHARIOT; DEITY; DEMON; MOUNT CARMEL; YAHWEH [SWF]

Babel, Tower of. The name of the biblical city Babel is a play on the Hebrew words *Babel* (Babylon) and *balal* (to confuse). The story may have been inspired by the famous Babylonian ziggurat (temple tower) Etemenanki. The city and its tower are described in a brief narrative in Gen. 11.1-9, which tells the story of humankind moving from a nomadic group who share one language to a scattered people who live in cities and represent different ethnic, linguistic, and territorial groups. The narrative itself describes the building of a city and a tower 'with its top in the heavens' (11.4). Upon observing this, God is displeased and subsequently confuses their language 'so they will not understand one another's speech' (11.7). He then scatters them 'over the face of all the earth' (11.8).

The story has traditionally been read as a condemnation of human pride. Modern scholarship has pointed out, however, that pride is nowhere mentioned in the text; the source of God's displeasure rather seems to be the homogeneity of the human race. Thus, the intent of the narrative is most likely to explain the human plan for homogeneity in conflict with the divine plan for diversity.

Although not mentioned in the text, the building of the tower has been associated with Nimrod (Gen.

10.8-12; 1 Chron. 1.10; Mic. 5.6). Nimrod's presence in the HB is rather limited, but post-biblical tradition has accorded him a more prominent place as a powerful ruler and city-builder.

The story is rich in metaphor and image and, as such, it is pervasive in Western culture. Among the most iconic images of the tower are those of Dutch painter Pieter Bruegel and Flemish painter Abel Grimmer (1563 and 1604 CE, respectively.) Author William Golding draws thematic parallels in his 1964 novel *The Spire*, a story of a man who undertakes the building of a large cathedral spire. English writer A.S. Byatt makes explicit reference in the title of her 1996 novel *Babel Tower*. In Douglas Adams's *The Hitchhiker's Guide to the Galaxy*, small leech-like creatures called 'Babel fish' function as universal translators. The 2007 film *Babel* alludes to the biblical story in its title and themes of cultural and linguistic barriers. Prominent classical composers have drawn inspiration from the story, most notably Igor Stravinsky's *Babel* (1944).

See also BABYLON; GENESIS, BOOK OF; NIMROD
[JR]

Babylon. The city of Babylon was located on the banks of the Tigris on the great alluvial plain in what is modern Iraq. It came to prominence in the eighteenth century BCE, in the wake of the Amorite migrations into Mesopotamia. The Amorite king of Babylon, Hammurapi, conquered a number of other confederations to become the sole ruler of an empire stretching from the Persia Gulf to modern Syria. This era is known as the Old Babylonian Period (1800–1600). His dynasty lasted until the Hittite raid of c. 1595. A people known as the Kassites (Indo-Aryans from modern Iran) then ruled from Babylon until c. 1200. Their kingdom included area as far north as Assyria, though their hold on the region was tenuous, as is witnessed in the correspondence of the Kassite kings with the Egyptian pharaohs found in the El Amarna texts.

The Amarna texts were written in Middle Babylonian, a dialect of Akkadian, which was the lingua franca of the ancient Near East. To learn Middle Babylonian, scribes all over the region would practice by copying texts (practice copies have been found, including in Israel). Thus, Babylonian myths were well known throughout the ancient Near East. Genesis 1 responds to the Babylonian creation epic, the *Enuma Elish*, asserting that Yahweh alone created the universe by fiat (not by the titanic struggle between gods of the Babylonian myth) and that celestial bodies were created by Yahweh for human usage.

After the collapse of Kassite rule, a period with little documentation ensued, until the resurgence of Assyria in the ninth century. Babylon was dominated by the Assyrians until the end of the seventh century when it rebeled, destroying Ninevah in 612 and obliterating what remained of Assyrian forces in 609. This era is known as the Neo-Babylonian empire, which lasted until the Persians conquered Babylon in 539. The pinnacle of the empire in terms of geographic and economic extent was reached under Nebuchadnezzar, the second ruler of the dynasty (605–562).

Nebuchadnezzar conquered Judah in 587, destroying the temple and the walls of Jerusalem. The Babylonians chose to separate the elite of conquered regions from the rest of the population and settle them near the center of the empire. There were three separate Judean exiles, in the years 597 (2 Kgs 24.6-17), 586 (Jer. 39–40.6), and 585 (Jer. 40.7–41.18), which ensured the elite would not have a power base from which to rebel. However, these resettled elite were allowed to engage in economic activity with those left at home, and the tended to do well. Indeed, at the end of Babylonian rule (539), much of the exiled Israelite community remained in Babylon. This community was the leading academic center of the Jewish world, producing what became the authoritative HB and the highly regarded Talmud collection. The exile and ultimate diaspora of the population led to the development of Judaism, with the creation of the synagogue and the de-emphasis of Temple worship. Despite this outcome, the pain of separation from the land for that first generation is poignantly captured in Ps. 137.

The portrayal of Nebuchadnezzar in Daniel has long been recognized by scholars as more consistent with the behavior of the last ruler of the empire, Nabonidus (556–539). He spent ten years of his rule in Tema (553–543), a city in modern Saudi Arabia. His son, Belshazzar, was established as coregent, reflected in Dan. 5.

Recommended reading. Bottero, J. *Mesopotamia: Writing, Reasoning, and the Gods*. Chicago: University of Chicago Press, 1995. Oates, J. *Babylon*. London: Thames & Hudson, 1986.

See also NEBUCHADNEZZAR; ASSYRIA [MAP]

Babylonian Captivity, the. Also known as the Babylonian Exile, it is one of the major turning points in Judah's history. It is the term given to the forced removal of the Judeans by King Nebuchadnezzar of Babylon. In a series of deportations beginning in 597 BCE, many of the nobles and artisans of Jerusalem were taken away into captivity. The cause for the deportation stemmed from a long history of political rebellions by the Judeans against their Babylonian overlords. For centuries, the southern kingdom of Judah had been in a vassal relationship, first with the Assyrians and then the Babylonians. The final rebellion by Zedekiah in 587 BCE precipitated the destruction of the temple and city of Jerusalem by Nebuchadnezzar. The Babylonian Captivity also had a very important theological impact on Judah. In an effort to explain the exile, both the biblical historians and prophets argued that it was God who orchestrated the destruction of Jerusalem and the temple as punishment for the nation's unfaithfulness. The notion that the Temple in Jerusalem had been destroyed by a foreign army jeopardized the nation's faith in the power of their own God. Not only had the nation lost its land and Temple, but their faith in the power of God was shaken as it appeared that a Babylonian god like Marduk was more powerful. However, it was during the exile that much of the HB was written and compiled, and also where important Jewish customs such synagogue worship, circumcision and Sabbath observance were instituted.

The pain and suffering of the exilic community are remembered in Ps. 137, which recounts the difficulty of singing a song while captive in a foreign land. This concept has proven popular with modern songwriters. In the 1970s the reggae group Boney M released their song 'Rivers of Babylon' based on Ps. 137 that began, 'By the rivers of Babylon / there we sat / sat and wept / as we thought of Zion'. Different versions of the song have been released by Bob Marley, Sublime, and Sinéad O'Connor. With a much more somber tone, Leonard Cohen revisited Ps. 137 in his own song called 'By the Rivers Dark'.

The memory of Israel's exile in Babylon has resonated with many different communities throughout history. In the Middle Ages, the movement of the Catholic Church from Rome to Avignon, France for almost seventy years is remembered as the Babylonian Captivity of the Papacy. It lasted from 1309–1377 and its name was derived from the fact that the prophet Jeremiah had predicted that the Babylonian Captivity of Judah would last seventy years. A second community that has naturally identified itself with the Babylonian Captivity was the Jews following the Holocaust of the Second World War. In his famous book, *Night*, Elie Wiesel likens the 587 BCE crisis to that of the Jewish communities who were forced to leave their homes and were deported to ghettos and concentration camps. As mentioned above, the song 'Rivers of Babylon' became popularized by reggae groups but also became the anthem of the Rastafarian movement who saw themselves as exiled from their homeland in Africa. One final community that has identified with the Judean exiles are modern day Tibetans whose land was invaded and annexed by the People's Republic of China in 1949–1951. The Dalai Lama himself has drawn this comparison as he and his people still live in exile around the world.

Recommended reading. Brueggemann, Walter. *Hopeful Imagination: Prophetic Voice in Exile*. Philadelphia: Fortress Press, 1986. Smith-Christopher, Daniel L. *A Biblical Theology of Exile*. Minneapolis: Fortress Press, 2002.

See also NEBUCHADNEZZAR; BABYLON; RIVERS OF BABYLON [HM]

Balaam. Balaam is one of the most intriguing and confusing individuals in the Bible, appearing at times humble and heroic, at other times a failure. The HB first mentions Balaam when the Israelites arrive to the Transjordan, as they approached the promised land. Balak, the king of Moab, was understandably concerned about the Israelites' presence on his border after their victories over Sihon and Og (Num. 22), so he sent for the prophet Balaam from Pethor (likely the Pitru on the upper Euphrates in modern Syria) in hopes he would curse them (Num. 22.6). Yahweh refused to allow Balaam to go with the first embassy of Moabite and Midianite leaders, but he received permission from Yahweh to go with the second embassy. He cautioned them that his blessing and cursing could not be purchased, insisting instead that he could only bless those Yahweh blesses, and curse those Yahweh curses. It is perplexing to hear that a Syrian prophet did the bidding of the Israelite God.

The most memorable part of Balaam's story was his encounter with an angel of Yahweh while riding his jenny. In contradistinction to his third and fourth oracles (Num. 24), which suggest he is a man who sees clearly and recognizes the vision of the *shadday* (the Almighty), in this episode it takes a talking donkey to get his attention (Num. 22.1-35). It is the donkey, not the seer, who sees the sword-wielding angel of Yahweh. The anger of Yahweh and his angel are inexplicable by lack of context here, though one must assume Balaam had somehow lost focus on his job of telling only the truth in the name of Yahweh (see 2 Pet. 2.15 and Jude 11 for commentary on Balaam's failure).

Num. 31.8 recounts that Balaam was killed in Midian, as the Israelites avenged themselves for the incident at Baal Peor, in which the Israelites were led astray sexually and religiously by the women of Moab and Midian (Num. 25). Numbers 31 does not explicitly say that Balaam himself was involved in the events at Baal Peor, though Rev. 2.14 suggests a connection.

Recommended reading. Levine, B. *Numbers 21–36.* Anchor Bible, 4A. New York: Doubleday, 2000. Moore, M.S. *The Balaam Traditions.* Society of Biblical Literature Dissertation Series, 113. Atlanta: Society of Biblical Literature, 1990.

See also ANGEL; NUMBERS, BOOK OF; SWORD

[MAP]

Balm of Gilead. The Balm of Gilead is a resin used in healing. Scholars debate what plant produced the Balm of Gilead. Candidates are the Styrax tree (*Styrax officinalis*); a species of poplar (such as *Populus candicans*); resin produced from the Arabian tree *Commiphora gileadensis*, known as the Balsam of Mecca; or *Balsamodendron gileadense*, a relative of the tree that produces myrrh. The OT contains three passages referring to the resin. In Gen. 37.25, Joseph's brothers sell him to 'Ishmaelites coming from Gilead, with their camels bearing gum, balm, and myrrh'. Balm, like gum and myrrh, was the healing resin. The other two passages referring to the resin both come from Jeremiah. In 8.22, Jeremiah laments the abandonment of the Jews by God because of their transgressions, and cries out: 'Is there no balm in Gilead? Is there no physician there?' Later, however, in 46.11, Jeremiah taunts the Egyptians who are feeling the wrath of God: 'Go up to Gilead, and take balm, O virgin daughter of Egypt! In vain you have used many medicines; there is no healing for you'. Balm of Gilead was perhaps used to cover wounds, to anoint the sick and dead, and, taken internally, to help an upset stomach.

The Balm of Gilead has had many references in popular culture over the centuries. It is referred to as a healing medicine in Edgar Allan Poe's *The Raven.* A traditional hymn by Washington Glass, which became an African spiritual, includes these lines: 'There is balm in Gilead, / To make the wounded hole; / There's power enough in heaven, / To cure a sin-sick soul'. American playwright Lanford Wilson published the play *Balm in Gilead* in 1965 about the down and out in New York. The singer Ricki Lee Jones put out the album *Balm in Gilead* in 2009.

See also OIL; ANOINT; PHYSICIAN; JEREMIAH, BOOK OF

[RL]

Banquet. The term derives from the Hebrew *mishteh* (banquet/feast) and *marzēah* (sumptuous banquet given as part of the mourning rite), and the Greek *dochēn* (banquet/feast). In the ancient world, the banquet was far more than simply an extraordinary meal. Although food and drink were essential staples at such gatherings, banquets also served a variety of socio-cultural and political functions and purposes. In Hebrew culture, banquets were an integral part of the mourning rite used to mourn the dead and console the living (see Jer. 16.5-9). Banquets were also venues for personal and religious celebrations, expressions of love and generous hospitality, or scenes of sensuous excesses (see Song 2.3-5; Amos 6.4-7; Luke 14.12-24; 15.22-32; Jude 12). Within the highly charged political world of the Persian court, Queen Esther used the banquet as the means to gain the political favor of her husband King Ahasuerus (Hebrew, or Xerxes in Greek), and the exposure and demise of her arch-enemy, Haman (see Est. 5–7.10).

In Greco-Roman society, banquets were considered both a pleasure and an art. The master host was adept at creating an atmosphere where guests could engage in stimulating conversation, discuss political or business matters, flatter one another, exchange humorous jibes with each other and enjoy eating and drinking, often to excess. Guests were expected to be active and engaging participants in banquet activities. Much of this activity, depending on the occasion, took place beyond the actual banqueting room. Testimony to the excesses of revelry and blasphemy at such gatherings is found in the accounts of the ancient Greek historians Herodotus and Xenophon. In the Roman context, guests at a marriage banquet (*cena*) were obligated to bring gifts and make crude jokes about the physical appearance and characteristics of the bride and groom. Such a feast was usually held at breakfast time and was paid for by the groom.

Within the OT and NT there are frequent references to banquets held in a variety of settings for a number of different reasons. The banquet held by the Babylonian king Belshazzar and recorded in Dan. 5 provides an account of how royal banquets were conducted in the Babylonian court. In Matt. 14.1-12, Herod's birthday banquet provides the backdrop for the beheading of John the Baptist. Revelation 19.9, uses the apocalyptic imagery of 'the wedding supper of the Lamb' to express and emphasize the intimate relationship between God and his people. Each of these references speaks to the socio-cultural centrality of the banquet in the ancient world.

Although the form has certainly changed significantly, our wedding and funeral receptions, graduation celebrations, Christmas, retirement and birthday parties still share some similarities with ancient banquets. Western popular culture is filled with images in magazines, on television and in film that promote the party lifestyle and good times with family and friends with plenty of food and drink. Our banquet-like gatherings and celebrations remain an important theme or sub-theme in feature films such as *My Big Fat Greek Wedding*, *Father of the Bride*, *The Wind and the Lion* and *Babette's Feast*.

Recommended reading. Finley, M.I. (ed.). *The Portable Greek Historians*. New York: Penguin, 1959. King, Philip J., and Lawrence E. Stager. *Life in Biblical Israel*. Louisville and London: Westminster John Knox Press, 2001.

See also FEASTS [PRW]

Baptism. From the Greek *baptizo* (to immerse or submerge), baptism refers to the ritual ablution that facilitates entry into Christian community. In Jewish tradition, the Torah mandates cleansing by water as a means of restoring ritual purity. Leviticus 8.6 depicts Moses washing Aaron and his sons with water during their consecration to the priesthood, rendering them pure for cultic service. Bathing was also prescribed for those ritually polluted (e.g., Lev. 15.16-18; Num. 19.11-13). In Palestine during the first century CE, proselytes to Judaism underwent ritual immersion as part of their entry into the covenant community.

The Gospel of Mark introduces the itinerant preacher John, who baptizes people in the Jordan River. Mark 1.4 states that John administered 'a baptism of repentance for the forgiveness of sins', a ceremonial cleansing of the human error that kept Jews from fulfilling their obligations to God. Among those baptized by John is Jesus, who after surfacing from the river is anointed by God's spirit in the form of a dove and proclaimed to be the Son of God by a heavenly voice (Mark 1.9-11).

The resurrected Jesus orders his disciples to baptize those entering the community of faith 'in the name of the Father and of the Son and of the Holy Spirit' (Matt. 28.19). Paul linked baptism with the death and resurrection of Jesus, asserting that those who rose from the water had become 'dead to sin and alive to God in Christ Jesus' (Rom. 6.11). The role of baptism in the removal of sin was further emphasized by Augustine, whose belief in original sin contributed to infant baptism becoming the norm by the fifth century CE. Many groups descending from the sixteenth-century CE European Anabaptist movement deny the validity of infant baptism, stressing that entry into Christian community must be accompanied by a rational choice that children are unable to make.

Jesus' baptism has been a popular theme in Christian art. The ceiling mosaic of the *Baptistery of the Arians* in Ravenna, Italy, dating to the late fifth century CE, presents a nude Jesus standing in the Jordan River up to his waist. This mirrored the experience of the initiate in the baptismal pool below, who was to be fully immersed in sacred water. In contrast, the Spanish painter El Greco's *Baptism of Christ*, from the early seventeenth century CE, features Jesus kneeling on the Jordan riverside, surrounded by angels in robes of brilliant color, as John pours water onto his head from a shell, referencing the baptism by sprinkling (aspersion) of the period.

Riverside baptisms featuring white-robed participants are commonplace in North American film and television. In the Coen brother's *O Brother Where Art Thou?* (2000), Delmar O'Donnell rushes to join a baptism ceremony at a Mississippi river. Joyously emerging from the water, Delmar tells his fellow convicts: 'The preacher said all my sins is warshed away, including that Piggly Wiggly I knocked over in Yazoo'. A 1995 episode of *The Simpsons* features devout neighbors Ned and Maude Flanders rushing the Simpson children to the Springfield River after learning that they had not been baptized. As Ned pours the first drop of water onto young Bart's head, Homer Simpson appears and pushes his son out of the way, causing himself to be hit by the water, which burns his scalp.

Recommended reading. Ferguson, Everett. *Baptism in the Early Church: History, Theology and Liturgy in the First Five Centuries*. Grand Rapids, MI: Eerdmans, 2009. Cramer, Peter. *Baptism and Change in the Early Middle Ages*. New York: Cambridge University Press, 1993.

See also JOHN, THE BAPTIST; WATER; DOVE; CONVERSION; BORN AGAIN [DB]

Barabbas. Barabbas is a minor biblical figure known exclusively from the four NT Gospels (Matt. 27.15-26; Mark 15.6-15; Luke 23.18-25; John

18.39-40). The name is a patronymic, meaning 'son of the father', derived from the Aramaic *bar-'abba'*.

According to the Gospels, Pilate was accustomed to releasing one prisoner for the Jerusalem crowd during Passover, an institution for which there is no other attestation in classical literature. In accordance with this tradition, after the trial of Jesus the assembled crowd is given the choice to release either Barabbas, a revolutionary who was involved in a murder, or Jesus, the one who is called Christ (Matt. 27.17) and the King of the Jews (Mark 15.9; cf. John 18.39). Both figures are 'sons of the father', one by name and the other as the true son of God, the Father. The crowd, who represents a sub-group of Judeans that have been influenced by the chief priests (Mark 15.10-11; cf. Matt. 27.20) and the elders (Matt. 27.20), cries out for the release of Barabbas, instructing the compliant Pilate to crucify Jesus. Barabbas's function in the Gospels is to serve as a foil for Jesus. His use of violence to achieve revolution is contrasted by Jesus' method of ushering in God's dominion by non-violence, humility, and suffering.

Barabbas is sparingly referred to by Western artists, as might be expected of a marginal biblical character. One of the more famous references is from Samuel Crossman's Good Friday hymn, 'My Song Is Love Unknown' (1664), which reads, 'A murderer they save; the Prince of Life they slay'.

Pär Lagerkvist's novel, *Barabbas* (1950), is probably the most significant artistic representation of Barabbas. It won the author the Nobel Prize in Literature in 1951. The novel follows Barabbas's journey after Jesus' crucifixion. Throughout, he struggles with the guilt that Christ, a man that he knew to be innocent, was crucified in his place. His defiant attitude towards Christ, caused by an inability to understand Jesus' teaching, finally gives way to a struggling faith. Barabbas is eventually crucified in Rome, mistaken as a Christian after Nero's fire, but Lagerkvist's notoriously ambiguous prose in the penultimate sentence leaves the status of Barabbas's faith while on the cross open for interpretation. Lagerkvist's was not the first novel to cast Barabbas in a leading role. Marie Corelli's *Barabbas: A Dream of the World's Tragedy* was published in 1893, but was bestowed minimal critical acclaim. Lagerkvist's novel was adapted by Christopher Fry into a screenplay and in 1961 *Barabbas* the film, directed by Richard Fleischer and staring Anthony Quinn, was released. That same year also saw the release of Nicholas Ray's film, *King of Kings*, wherein Barabbas plays a key role. He is depicted as a principled freedom fighter engaging the Romans in guerrilla warfare. After being released by Pilate, he witnesses Jesus' crucifixion and questions why someone he never knew should die in his place. As he leaves the scene, the viewer wonders what impact this experience might have on Barabbas's life.

In 2000, Barabbas was afforded an interesting interpretation in a British television mini-series directed by Norman Stone, which consisted of eight fifteen-minute narratives by marginal characters from the Gospels. Years after his days as a rebel and revolutionary, Barabbas is portrayed to dismiss Jesus as a 'loser', but to be obsessed with both the meaning of his encounter with Jesus and also with Jesus the man.

Recommended reading. Jenkins, Bill. 'Barabbas in Literature and Film'. *Journal of Religion and Society* 11 (2009). No pages. Online: http://moses.creighton.edu/JRS/2009/2009-5.html. Scoobie, Irene. 'Contrasting Characters in "Barabbas."' *Scandinavian Studies* 32 (1960) 212-20.

[RICL]

Barnabas. Barnabas appears as one of the significant leaders of the Jesus movement in the Acts of the Apostles and in some letters in the Pauline corpus. A native of Cyprus but also a Levite with landholdings in Jerusalem (Acts 4.36-37), and probably a foundation member of the church in Antioch, he is most remembered as a supporter and companion of Paul of Tarsus (Acts 13.2). Yet a fracture occurred in preparations for their second missionary journey over the presence of an assistant, John Mark, who had prematurely absented himself from the first mission (Acts 15.36-41). Paul's letter to the Galatians hints at a different tension in their relationship, involving disputes over dietary requirements and other scruples affecting Jewish and Gentile Christians (Gal. 2.13). The deutero-canonical letter to the Colossians probably suggests that the strain between these key leaders was ultimately overcome (Col. 4.10). Barnabas's name has been appropriated as the author of the NT letter to the Hebrews (by Tertullian), of a second-century letter, and a fifteenth-century Moslem apologetic work, the *Gospel of Barnabas*, which presented an Islamic view of Jesus. He has also been claimed as the founder of the Cypriot church and as first bishop of Milan.

Joseph Barnabas was remembered as an encourager or advocate. The interpretation of the name Barnabas as 'son of encouragement' is based on the portrayal of his facilitating role in the spread of the early Jesus movement beyond Jerusalem and an explanatory note given in the book of Acts (Acts 4.36). Acts relates Barnabas's mediating role in gaining acceptance for Paul amongst a church suspicious about one who had been their violent persecutor (Acts 9.26-27), his ambassadorial role from the Jerusalem church to the church at Antioch where Gentiles were beginning to join the expanding Christian community, his representation of the interests of the Antioch Gentiles at the Council of Jerusalem, and his almsgiving through sale of property for the benefit of the Christian community. In language reminiscent of contemporary honorific monuments, Barnabas is described as 'a good man', to which is added 'full of the Holy Spirit and of faith' (Acts 11.24).

The etymology of the name is probably 'son of a prophet'. This connects him with one of the major emphases of the Antioch church (Acts 13.1). Barnabas's leadership carried into the first missionary journey where, until the encounter with the proconsul, Sergius Paulus, he is consistently named first in the pairing with Saul/Paul (Acts 13.2-13). Even when at Lystra, Barnabas is the acclaimed by the Lycaonians as Zeus, head of the Greek pantheon of gods, whereas Paul is linked with the gods' messenger, Hermes (Acts 14.8-18). Both Barnabas and Paul are named 'apostles' (Acts 14.4), a designation with which Paul concurs (Gal. 2.9; 1 Cor. 9.5-6).

Literary, cinematic and musical works that recognize the role of the wise, reliable supporter in the career of a more illustrious figure are working with a typology that is exemplified in Barnabas. The name continues to be claimed by those groups and institutions that propound a ministry of support, encouragement, and advocacy.

Recommended reading. Brown, R.E., and J.P. Meier. *Antioch and Rome: New Testament Cradles of Catholic Christianity.* New York: Paulist Press,1983. Kollmann, B. *Joseph Barnabas: His Life and Legacy.* Collegeville, MN: Liturgical Press, 2004.

See also ANTIOCH; PAUL, THE APOSTLE; COUNCIL, JERUSALEM; ACTS OF THE APOSTLES, THE

[AHC]

Bartholomew. The name Bartholomew likely derives from the Aramaic translation of a Greek name: Bar (= son of) Tolmay (= Ptolemy). Bartholomew appears in every synoptic list of Jesus' twelve disciples (Matt. 10.3; Mark 3.18; Luke 6.14; Acts 1.13). Yet, in the NT, Bartholomew never acts or speaks. Fittingly, in Leonardo DaVinci's famous painting of the last supper, Bartholomew is standing on the far left, at the end of the table far from Jesus.

In the Synoptic Gospels, Bartholomew is always listed together with Philip; in the Gospel of John, however, Bartholomew is never mentioned, and instead it is Nathanael who appears with Philip. For this reason, some claim Nathanael and Bartholomew are in fact the same person, though there is no solid evidence to support this. The assumption, however, is reflected in the Catholic 'Prayer to Saint Bartholomew the Apostle': 'O Glorious Saint Bartholomew, Jesus called you a person without guile'. Of course, it is Nathanael that Jesus describes as guileless (John 1.47).

Local traditions from Asia Minor, Ethiopia, India, and Armenia all attribute to Bartholomew the spread of Christianity to those places; in India it is even claimed that he left a copy of the Gospel of Matthew for them (Eusebius, *Hist. Eccl.* 5.10.3). He is the patron saint of Armenia, and that is where legends of his death are based, that he was flayed alive and crucified upside-down. He is also the patron saint of tanners, leatherworkers, trappers, plasterers, cobblers, and bookbinders.

There is even a *Gospel of Bartholomew*, mentioned (and condemned) in Jerome's preface to his commentary on the Gospel of Matthew, though little is known about it. More is known about a later, possibly related work entitled *The Questions of Bartholomew.* This fifth-century text, probably originating in Egypt, contains a series of 'interviews'. Bartholomew learns from Jesus how he ascended into heaven, and what that was like; he learns from Mary how she came to carry the son of God, but she is interrupted just as she is about to describe the actual conception of Jesus; he learns from the devil the sorts of punishments that await the wicked; and he sees hell.

In *The Last Judgment*, painted onto the walls of the Vatican's Sistene Chapel, Bartholomew is depicted holding a knife in one hand and his own flayed skin in the other; the face on the skin Bartholomew holds is Michelangelo's own face. The imagery recalls Bartholomew's martyrdom, derived from Armenian traditions. Through the middle ages, relics played a great role in the cult of St Bartholomew, and healing and medicine were associated with the relics often enough that today medical centers often carry the name of St Bartholomew, especially in Great Britain. Prayers to Bartholomew are said to ward off nervous diseases, neurological disorders, and twitching.

Francis Bacon's utopian novel, *The New Atlantis* (1626) has the people of a mythical land, Bensalem, discover a letter written by Bartholomew, along with the NT and HB, in the original Ark floating off their shore. In this way, the people discover the revelation of God. Somewhat less pious a depiction is found in Christopher Moore's satirical novel *Lamb: The Gospel according to Biff, Christ's Childhood Pal* (2002). Moore's Bartholomew is a Greek cynic who settles in Nazareth, living the typically counter-cultural lifestyle of the cynic, to great humorous effect.

See also LORD'S SUPPER; NATHANAEL; PHILIP; TWELVE DISCIPLES, THE [ZAC]

Bartimaeus. The blind beggar Bartimaeus (Mark 10.46) stands out in Mark's Gospel because this writer does not usually name those who are healed. However, this is also a story about discipleship. Bartimaeus is sitting by the road when he hears Jesus leaving Jericho. He cries out to him and when Jesus calls, Bartimaeus throws off his cloak and approaches the miracle worker. This simple gesture is revealing. Presumably as a beggar, this cloak was his only possession. In 10.28, Peter says they (the disciples) left everything to be with Jesus yet in 10.32, those who followed him were afraid. Bartimaeus shows courage in calling out to Jesus, even doing it again when the crowd reprimands him. Throwing off the cloak also indicates his willingness to leave behind the 'old' and embrace the 'new,' something symbolically significant in Mark's Gospel, suggested by the many references to garments in this text (see 2.21; 5.25-30; 6.56; 9.3; 11.7-8; 13.16; 15.20-29).

The story about Bartimaeus appears only in Mark's account. Matthew has a healing of two blind men (20.29-34) leaving Jericho but neither one is named. Luke also has a healing of a blind man (18.35-43) but it is on the way into Jericho. How these stories relate, if at all, is unclear. The themes of (literal) blindness and (spiritual) vision are utilized in contemporary culture. For instance, the movie *Blindness* (2008), based on the novel of that name by José Saramago (Portugese original, 1995), uses an epidemic of blindness to examine humanity's potential for depravity and mercy. In this story, only one person has use of their physical eyes: 'the only thing more terrifying than blindness', she says, 'is being the only one who can see'.

See also BLINDNESS; EYE [RAHC]

Baruch, Book of. The Bible identifies at least three people named Baruch. The Baruch who was an officer in the court of King Zedekiah and friend and secretary of Jeremiah the Prophet was a member of a prominent family; he was the son of Neriah and the brother of Seraiah, chief chamberlain to King Sedecias. Jeremiah directed him to write his prophecies and to read them to the people (Jer. 32.12; 36.4; 51.59). After the Fall of Jerusalem, nothing is known for sure of his life. He probably was forced to go to Egypt with Jeremiah, although one tradition says that he went to Babylon and died there twelve years later.

The Book of Baruch is a pseudepigraphon from the intertestament period and is included in the Apocrypha. It is in a biblical style and falsely purports to have been written by Baruch, the scribe, at the request of Jeremiah the prophet (Jer. 36.4-8). The words in the book are alleged to be the words of Jeremiah that were burned by King Jehoiakim of Judah. The only extant copies of Baruch are in Greek, though linguistic features suggest that it was originally written in Hebrew. Some scholars believe that the translation may have been made a little over an hundred years before the birth of Jesus by the grandson of Ben Sira who, according to the Prologue of The Wisdom of Jesus Son of Sirach (Ecclesiasticus), translated his grandfather's teachings.

Baruch identifies Belshazzar as the son of Nebuchadnezzar rather than as the son of Nabonidus as does Dan. 5.2-18. Scholars believe this shows that Baruch postdates Daniel possibly as late as 150 BCE when the rule of the Maccabees had disappointed many. Baruch was offered as hope for divine intervention. Others see it as a collection of material produced as late as 50 BCE.

Baruch does not have any apocalyptic features like the Book of Daniel. Instead it is closer to the Judaic wisdom tradition that developed in the Hellenistic period, which linked itself to the Torah (Bar. 4.1-4). Baruch is sometimes referred to as 1 Baruch to distinguish it from at least three other pseudepigraphical works—*2, 3, and 4 Baruch*. In the Vulgate, the Epistle of Jeremiah is added as chapter 6.

Baruch is partially prose and partially poetry. The first two sections (1.1-3.8) are in prose and the third and fourth sections (3.9-5.9) are in poetry. It contains a letter (1.1-14), a prayer-sermon (1.15–3.8), a hymn (3.9–4.4; 'The Zion Poem') and a lament (4.5–5.9) similar to Lamentations. Some scholars believe that Baruch was reworked until as late as the Fall of Jerusalem during the Jewish Revolt (67–70 CE). While it has a theme of exile and return, these are metaphors of repentance rather than historical because it is a late apocryphal book.

Clement of Alexandria (c. 150–ca. 215) was one of the first Christian philosophers. He quoted Bar. 3.16-19 in his 'Paean for Wisdom'. Thomas Aquinas (1225–1274) interpreted Baruch 3.38, 37, which says that afterwards he (God's wisdom) was seen on earth and conversed with people, to be a reference to Christ. This interpretation was followed in 1965 by the Second Vatican Council which was issued by Pope Paul VI as the 'Dogmatic Constitution on Divine Revelation—*Dei Verbum*' on November 18, 1965, following approval by the assembled bishops. It was one of the Council's most important documents.

Recommended reading. Kee, Howard Clark. *Cambridge Annotated Study Apocrypha*. Cambridge: Cambridge University Press, 1994. Wright, J. Edward. *Baruch ben Neriah: From Biblical Scribe to Apocalyptic Seer*. Columbia, SC: University of South Carolina Press, 2003.

See also JEREMIAH; JEREMIAH, BOOK OF; APOCRYPHA, DEUTEROCANONICALS AND INTERTESTAMENTALS

[AJW]

Bathsheba. The meaning of her name is uncertain though daughter of Sheba, or daughter of abundance, from the Hebrew *bat* (daughter) and *sheba* (Sheba or abundance), is possible. She is daughter of Eliam and wife of Uriah the Hittite, and later on wife of King David and the mother of King Solomon (cf. Matt. 1.6-7).

In 2 Sam. 11, King David sees Bathsheba, then wife of Uriah, bathing and he desires her. The ensuing adultery results in pregnancy, and David has Uriah killed so that he can marry the widowed Bathsheba. Although their child died, they had another, Solomon, who eventually becomes king. Her three other children are Shimea, Shobab, and Nathan.

In the biblical story, Bathsheba's character is suppressed, and David receives full blame for Uriah's murder. No hint is given of Bathsheba's feelings, nor does she speak directly about the death of their child. However, toward the end of David's life, Bathsheba emerges as a strong woman with considerable political acumen. Through her efforts, her son Solomon succeeds David on the throne of Israel.

In much medieval art, Bathsheba represents the perils of carnal appetite. Her bathing is often a subject of European art from the fourteenth to the eighteenth centuries. Her nude body is depicted by Memling (1440–1494), Lindtmayer the Younger (1532–1605?), Van Haarlem (1562–1638), Heinrich Fueger (1751–1818), Rembrandt (1606–1669), and Rubens (1577–1640), among others. Rembrandt also portrays her with a letter from David (1654). Other themes include Bathsheba asking David for Solomon's succession (Strozzi, 1581–1644) and Bathsheba at David's deathbed (Rudolf von Ems, fourteenth century).

In ancient and medieval literature, Bathsheba is a secondary character in the story of David. Jewish legends embroider the story and portray Bathsheba in various ways; as a prize carelessly thrown away by David who must then endure a painful period of waiting to possess her; as the cause of David's fall from grace; as a prophetic woman who knew Solomon would be the wisest of men; as an angry mother who wanted to kill Solomon; as a fearful widow, pregnant with David's child who begs him to keep her crime a secret lest she be put to death as an adulteress. Many medieval plays focused on David rather than Bathsheba but the fourteenth-century Cornish biblical drama *Ordinalia*, has Bathsheba urging David to kill Uriah, then weeping as Uriah dies. Hans Sachs (1556) gives full dramatic treatment to the story and even attributes the rape of Tamar and Absalom's rebellion to David's sin with Bathsheba. In sixteenth-century baroque literature, the story of Bathsheba appears more frequently, often with a focus on David's erotic conflicts. Nineteenth-century authors A.G. Meissner, E. von Harmann, and W. Gaedke focus on David's passion for Bathsheba, and his guilt and penance. Thomas Harding's *Far From the Madding Crowd* (1874) treats Bathsheba by association as Bathsheba Everdene grows through suffering into a wise woman. Some twentieth-century authors try to lessen David's guilt by introducing evil counselors who tempt David, or by treating Uriah's marriage as one coerced or even unconsummated, as in W. Winne, *David und Bathshua* (1903). Modern French literature includes M. Payot's *Bethsabee* (1905), and André Spire's *Abishag*. American author Mark van Doren's *The People of the World* (1964) contains a poem on Bathsheba.

Musical interpretations include Nicola Porpora's oratorio *Davide e Bersabea* (1743), and an oratorio-opera, *Le Roi David* by Honegger (1921). In film, Darryl F. Zanuc's movie *David and Bathsheba* (1951) is an epic love story starring Susan Hayward as Bathsheba. Other adaptations include Bruce Beresford's *King David* (1985) and Robert Markowitz' *David* (1997).

See also ADULTERY; DAVID; SOLOMON; URIAH

[EG]

Beast. The term beast (in Hebrew, *hayyah*; in Greek, *therion*,) in the Bible may signify any animal other than humans. The word can be used of domesticated (Gen. 1.24 etc.) or of wild animals (Exod. 23.11; Ps. 147.9 etc). In Israelite law there is a distinction between clean and unclean animals (see Lev. 11). Beasts of various kinds can also represent both good and bad people such as one's enemies (Ps. 74.19; Jer. 12.9). Paul refers to his encounters with some troublemakers as a struggle with beasts (1 Cor. 15.32). Jesus also used sheep to represent his followers and their oppressors or opponents as 'wolves' (Matt. 7.15; 10.16). His parable of the sheep and goats depicts the nations of the world at the time of judgment (Matt. 25.31-46). Beasts or animals can also describe nations or empires in apocalyptic writings, as in Dan. 7.

One of the best-known representations of a beast as embodying bad or evil appears in Rev. 13. As the author develops his vision of the forces that oppose God and the Lamb (Jesus Christ) in chaps. 13–20, he portrays the great Dragon (the Devil or Satan, among other titles [12.9]) as conjuring up two beasts to give him assistance, one from the earth and one from the sea (12.17; 13.1, 11). Both creatures are bizarre in appearance and combine aspects of a leopard, a bear, and a lion, with horns and several heads. The second beast imitates the Lamb (13.11; 5.6) and joins the Devil and the other beast in the business of blasphemy, deception, and intimidation of the followers of God (13.1-2, 11).

This second beast is also identified as the famous '666' (13.18) which is 'the number of a person'. In the ancient Greek and Hebrew languages, the letters of the alphabet were assigned numeric values. In this way, an ancient name could be translated into a number and vice versa. Attempts to apply this number to individuals through history abound. The most plausible solution for this puzzle is the identification of the Emperor Nero as the 'man' referred to by the number. John calls for wisdom in reckoning this number (13.17), however, and each age has offered its own solutions. The symbolic use of this number also points us to the activities of the Beast more than to a literal rendering of its name.

In the sixteenth century, Luther named the Pope as the Beast. Thomas Müntzer, in turn, labeled Martin Luther as the Beast because of his collusion with earthly princes. Today, a bear can represent a nation such as Russia or be a metaphor for a downturn in the stock market (the bull signifies an upswing). Songwriters can use the word to describe their personal struggles such as Johnny Cash's 'The Beast in Me'. In the film *The Omen* (1976, 2006) a child is identified as the son of the devil and the fulfillment of Rev. 13.18 (especially in the 2006 remake), although neither the Devil nor a beast sires a child in Revelation.

See also NAMING OF THE ANIMALS; ANIMALS, SYMBOLISM OF; 666 [DMAC]

Beatitudes, the. The Beatitudes, a fixed set of 'blessing' statements, are a favorite portion of the NT, found at the beginning of Matthew's account of Jesus' Sermon on the Mount (Matt. 5.3-12), and in a shorter form in Luke's Sermon on the Plain (Luke 6.20-23). A beatitude is a literary form widely represented in both ancient Greek and Jewish literature. The term 'beatitude' comes from the Vulgate translation of the Greek *makarios* (in the plural in the Matthean and Lukan beatitudes) with the Latin *beatus*.

The ancient forms of the beatitude vary considerably, and the NT reflects this diversity. There are over forty beatitudes in the NT, including those in Matt. 5.3-12 and Luke 6.20-23. Major forms are those with a blessing followed by a participial ('who') statement (similar to some of the Jewish forms), a conditional statement followed by a blessing statement, and the Beatitudes proper, with a blessing followed by a causal statement, in either the second or third person. There are nine beatitudes in Matthew's Sermon on the Mount, and four beatitudes in Luke's Sermon on the Plain. Matthew and Luke appear to share four similar beatitudes, while Matthew also has five additional ones. The ones that Matthew and Luke share include: blessed are the poor, blessed are those who hunger, blessed are those who weep/mourn, and blessed are those who are persecuted. Many scholars believe that these four beatitudes derive from a common earlier source, although their differences lead other scholars to see them as either developing independently of each other or reflecting the editorial interests of their Gospel authors. In any case, most scholars see the beatitudes as ultimately originating with the words of Jesus.

Matthew also includes the following five beatitudes: blessed are the gentle or meek, blessed are the merciful, blessed are the pure in heart, blessed are the peacemakers, and blessed are those who are persecuted (a second persecution beatitude). Besides the fact that Matthew includes five more Beatitudes, there are a number of other differences between those found in Matthew and Luke. Matthew's are written in the third person ('blessed are the poor in spirit, for theirs is the kingdom of heaven', NASB), while Luke's are in the second person ('blessed are the poor, for yours is the kingdom of God', NASB). But both are in the plural. The beatitudes in Matthew sometimes modify the particular trait that it specifies, as in 'blessed are the poor in spirit', rather than Luke's simple, unmodified use of 'poor'. There is also a difference in the ordering of the beatitudes, with the second and third of the four common beatitudes reversed.

Matthew's beatitudes have fuller, spiritually based meanings than Luke's, describing ideal readers as 'the poor [plural] in spirit', 'those who hunger and thirst for righteousness', and 'those persecuted for the sake of righteousness'. Luke's beatitudes, on the other hand, are simpler, more straightforward, and fewer in number. This might indicate they are closer to an original oral gospel source used by both Matthew and Luke. Others believe that Luke's beatitudes address the physical needs of people, while Matthew's transform and expand upon the same beatitudes by incorporating a spiritual sense.

Recommended reading. Guelich, Robert A. *The Sermon on the Mount: A Foundation for Understanding*. Waco, TX: Word, 1982.

See also JESUS OF NAZARETH; SERMON ON THE MOUNT [SEP]

Beelzebub/Beelzebul. The Greek term *Beelzeboub* derives from the Hebrew *Baal* (lord) and *zebūb* (fly). Baalzebub was a god worshiped by the Philistines in the city of Ekron (2 Kgs 1.2). Baalzebub was most likely a local variation of Baal, the Canaanite storm god. The name means 'lord of the flies', and suggests that Canaanites sought relief from infectious insects. As Judaism moved toward monotheism, earlier deities were conflated into the one main oppositional entity: Satan. According to the *Testament of Solomon* 6.2, Solomon summons Beelzeboul, the prince of demons, and learns that he is one of the fallen angels. In the NT, both Jesus and his opponents use the name Beelzebul to describe the chief of demons; in order to undermine his authority, the scribes and Pharisees accuse Jesus of casting out demons 'by Beelzebul' (Matt. 12.24, 27, cf. 10.25; Mark 3.22; Luke 11.15-19). Jesus retorts, 'If Satan casts out Satan, he is divided against himself' (Matt. 12.26). Their logic is faulty. The names Beelzebul and Satan are used interchangeably. The Greek name 'Beelzebul' was changed to 'Beelzebub' in the Syriac and Latin Vulgate; this substitution continued into the King James Version. Only recently have translations restored the original Greek form of Beelzebul.

In *Paradise Lost* (1667), John Milton describes Beelzebub as a fallen angel who serves as Satan's lieutenant. In *The Pilgrim's Progress* (1678), John Bunyan names one of the devil's companions Beelzebub. In the award-winning allegorical novel *Lord of the Flies* (1954), William Golding describes a group of young British boys who descend into savagery when they are stranded on a deserted island; 'The Lord of the Flies', a severed pig's head impaled on a stick, symbolizes the presence of evil on the island and within the boys themselves.

In *Dictionnaire Infernal* (1863), Collin de Plancy illustrates Beelzebub as a large fly with a skull and crossbones on both of his wings. The Black Metal band *Beelzebul* uses Satan and demons as their lyrical themes. In the movie *Constantine* (2005), a horror film that exposes evil forces in the world, insects take the form of a demon; in one scene, a fly comes out of a man's eye to indicate he is possessed. In the tradition of *Jesus Christ Superstar*, *Fallen Angel* (2006) describes the fall of Lucifer and one of his sidekicks, Beelzebub. Mel Gibson's *The Passion of the Christ* (2004) moves the Beelzebul conflict story of Jesus and the Pharisees to the trial before the high priest; there, Jesus is accused of casting out devils with the help of 'devils', a more familiar word than Beelzebul.

See also SATAN; LUCIFER [AB]

Behemoth. The only reference to this huge creature is in Job 40.15-24. The Hebrew term *behemoth* resembles the Greek *dinosaurian*, meaning 'terrible lizard', which of course gives us the modern term 'dinosaur'. Scholars variously identify the beast mentioned in Job as a hippopotamus, a water buffalo, or an elephant. The description could possibly fit these animals, but other options are readily available, especially since the phrase 'It is the first of the great acts of God' (Job 40.19; 'He *is* the chief of the ways of God' [KJV]) could hardly be adequately explained as an elephant or hippo.

Behemoth is found in common parlance today as something that is very huge or gargantuan. A contemporary heavy metal band goes by the name Behemoth. The term often appears in films involving large monsters or dinosaurs, such as *Jurassic Park*.

See also JOB, BOOK OF; ANIMALS, SYMBOLISM OF [MBW]

Bel and the Dragon. This short story is an addition to the Book of Daniel in the Septuagint and Theodotion, likely composed between the third and first century BCE.

Bel and the Dragon contains two independent but connected narratives of Daniel in the court of Cyrus, king of the Persians. In the first story (Dan. 14.1-22), Daniel proves to Cyrus that Bel is merely 'clay inside and bronze outside' not a living god. By scattering ash around the temple to reveal footprints, Daniel shows that the priests and their families return to Bel's temple by a secret passage and that they, not Bel, eat the offerings of food and drink. As a result of this deception the priests and their families are put to death and Cyrus gives Daniel the idol of Bel to be destroyed. In the second story (14.31-42 [Catholic editions]), Daniel again refuses to worship a false god, this time a dragon, not an idol. He asks the king's permission to slay the dragon without sword or club, which he does by making cakes of pitch, fat and hair (*trichas*) that cause the dragon to burst open when eaten. As a result of this slaying and destruction of Bel, the Babylonians demand Daniel, saying to the king: 'Hand [him] over to us, or else we will kill you and your household' (Dan. 14.29). In a variant of Dan. 6, they throw him into a den of lions, where he remains unharmed and is fed by the prophet Habakkuk who is miraculously transported from Judea by the angel of the Lord (Dan. 14.31-39). These stories may have circulated independently before being included as the fourteenth chapter of Daniel.

Daniel's refusal to compromise his traditions and faith by worshiping false gods connects Bel and the Dragon with Dan. 3 and 6 thematically. Structurally Bel and the Dragon resembles Dan. 3 and 6, Susanna, and Gen. 37–50: the hero falls from his position of honor, has his life threatened, and is vindicated and restored to his former role. There are also obvious, and likely intentional, parallels between Daniel's killing of the dragon and the battle of the god Marduk and the dragon Tiamat described in Babylonian mythology.

While Bel and the Dragon has been represented visually in art (notably by Stephan Kessler and Maerten van Hemmskerck) its most lasting influence is, along with the story of Susanna, as a prototype of the modern detective story. Although the genre was not formalized until the late 1800s by writers like Edgar Allan Poe, Charles Dickens, Wilkie Collins, and Sir Arthur Conan Doyle, many of the characteristics of detective fiction and the literary detective can be traced to these ancient narratives. The Bel narrative, in particular, describes 'a locked room mystery', a common plot device of classic detective fiction. For instance, in 'The Adventure of the Golden Pince-Nez', Sherlock Holmes, like Daniel, uses ashes on the ground to reveal the secret hiding place of a murderer in a variation on the locked-room plot.

Bel and the Dragon also figures prominently in Barbara Kingsolver's *The Poisonwood Bible* (1998) both as a favorite story of the fundamentalist Baptist missionary, Nathan Price, and a thematic subtext of the novel. Daniel's unwillingness to participate in and antagonism towards the 'foreign' culture of the Babylonians reflects Price's own inflexible adherence to American ideals and practices while serving as a missionary in Africa.

See also DANIEL; DANIEL, BOOK OF; SUSANNA; SEPTUAGINT; APOCRYPHA, DEUTEROCANONICALS AND INTERTESTAMENTALS; SEPTUAGINT [MWB]

Belial. 'Belial' (often synonymous 'Beliar') is a semi-divine and/or Satan-like figure found throughout the Bible, the Apocrypha, Pseudepigrapha but particularly the Dead Sea Scrolls. While the etymology of 'Belial' is uncertain, scholars have commonly translated the word as a noun denoting someone as 'worthless' or 'without worth' (Judg. 19.22). Regardless of the literal meaning, however, when Belial is rendered as a mythic figure, he is consistently cast within a dualistic framework in which he sits at the 'negative pole' opposite to the 'positive' position of God (*Jubilees* 1.20) or Christ (2 Cor. 6.15). Indeed, Belial's primary function seems to be that of a kind of pejorative mythical figurehead used to demonize specific groups or behaviors as self-evidently 'evil' and as such beyond the pale according to the position of the author(s) of the text.

For example, in the *Damascus Document*, the current negative state of the world is a result of it having fallen under the influence of 'Belial [who] is unrestrained in Israel' (Geniza A. 4.13; see also 1QS 1.17-18). According to *The War Scroll*, this age will end in an apocalyptic conflict in which the 'the Sons of Light' will attack 'the Sons of Darkness, the army of Belial; the troops of Edom, Moab, the sons of Ammon, the [Amalekites], Philistia, and the troops of the Kittim of Asshur. Supporting them are those who have violated the covenant' (1QM 1.1-2). At the end of the battle, 'the great hand of God shall overcome [Belial and al]l the angels of his domination, and all the men of [his forces shall be destroyed forever]' (1QM 1.10-15).

However, Belial is not only a demonic 'outsider' or a god of 'foreigners'. As part of the dualistic framework in which he is used, he encapsulates those who do not hold to the 'proper' Judaism. Indeed, it seems that Belial was at times understood as an agent or 'spirit' sent by God. For example, the *Damascus Document* states that 'the verdict on all members of the covenant who do not hold firm to [God's] laws: they are condemned to destruction by Belial. That is the day on which God shall judge' (Geniza A. 8.1-3; see also Geniza A. 1.1-2).

While Belial is relatively scarce or ambiguous in the biblical text, and tends to be more fully 'fleshed out' in lesser known sources, his oppositional nature nonetheless still makes appearances in more modern and contemporary contexts. For example, Belial can be found in such diverse sources as Milton's *Paradise Lost* (Book One, 490-92; Book Two, 110-12); Victor Hugo's *The Toilers of the Sea* (1866); the *Satanic Bible* (1969), as one of the four chief demons; the films *Nosferatu* (1922) and *The Exorcism of Emily Rose* (2005); Philip K. Dick's science fiction trilogy *VALIS* (1978–1981); and even as one of the adversarial non-player characters in the role playing game, *In nomine* (1997).

Recommended reading. Charlesworth, James, H (ed.). *The Hebrew Bible and Qumran: The Bible and the Dead Sea Scrolls*. Richland Hills, TX: BIBAL Press, 2000. Steudel, Annette. 'God and Belial'. In L. Schiffman, E. Tov and J. VanderKam (eds.). *The Dead Sea Scrolls Fifty Years after their Discovery*. Pp. 332-40. Jerusalem: Israel Exploration Society, 2000.

See also LUCIFER; SATAN [GJF]

Beloved Disciple. The 'Beloved Disciple' is a character who appears in the Gospel of John. Five times (13.23; 19.26; 20.2; 21.7; 21.20) the narrator refers to this figure as the disciple whom Jesus used to love (the verbs are in the imperfect tense). The Gospel of John does not use the same verb for love each time (once using *phileō* instead of *agapaō*), and this character is just as often referred to as the 'other disciple'. Thus, use of the phrase 'Beloved Disciple' as a title gives an impression of consistency that does not actually exist in the Fourth Gospel.

This character is never named, and so his (her?) identity has been a long-standing source of debate. Theories include Lazarus, whom Jesus raised from the dead; John Mark; a mysterious Jerusalem disciple connected to the high priest; an unnamed female disciple; John the son of Zebedee; or a disciple of John. Some scholars doubt there was ever a beloved disciple at all, arguing instead that this follower of Jesus is a symbolic figure created by the author. For reasons not entirely self-evident, the early Church (Irenaeus, Polycrates) concluded that the beloved disciple was John the son of Zebedee.

This nameless disciple has a special place in John's narrative. He sits next to Jesus at the last supper (13.23-24), and appears even to sit between Jesus and Peter, who in the Synoptic Gospels is the chief of the disciples. At the crucifixion, Jesus looks down from the cross at his mother Mary and the Beloved Disciple, and instructs the two of them to care for one another as mother and son (19.26-27). This disciple was also the first to reach the empty tomb, ahead of Peter (20.4-5). John 21.24 appears to indicate that the Beloved Disciple's teachings are the source for the Fourth Gospel, giving it an eyewitness authority.

In Leonardo DaVinci's painting of the last supper, the Beloved Disciple sits beside Jesus. His soft (feminine?) appearance in the painting led Dan Brown (*The DaVinci Code*) to speculate that 'the beloved disciple' was actually Mary Magdalene (as Jesus' wife). Evangelical novelist Walter Wangerin has written a novel of Jesus' life that is narrated by the Beloved Disciple. True to form, the disciple is not named, and explains how Mary the Mother of Jesus was a source of much authentic information about Jesus. In this way, this novel is consistent with traditional Christianity's deep regard for the Gospel of John.

Recommended reading. Brown, Raymond E. *The Community of the Beloved Disciple*. London: Chapman, 1979. Reinhartz, Adele. *Befriending the Beloved Disciple: A Jewish Reading of the Gospel of John*. New York: Continuum, 2001. Wangerin, Walter, Jr. *Jesus: A Novel*. Grand Rapids, MI: Zondervan, 2005.

See also LORD'S SUPPER; JOHN, GOSPEL OF; TWELVE DISCIPLES, THE [ZAC]

Beloved Physician. Luke is described as 'the beloved physician' in Col. 4.14. Based on Eusebius's claim, this may be the same person who wrote the Gospel of Luke and the Acts of the Apostles. He is mentioned as a travelling companion of Paul in 2 Tim. 4.11 and Phlm. 24. According to the 'we' passages in Acts (sections using the first person; see Acts 16.10-16; 20.5-15; 21.1-18; 27.1–28.16), Luke was occasionally with Paul. However, Luke is not included in Paul's listing of his Jewish co-workers (Col. 4.9-11) and thus may have been Greek. Many scholars, however, doubt these conclusions and question whether we can determine with any specificity whether Luke was Greek, or a physician, or even the author of Luke–Acts. The King James Version of the Bible is responsible for bringing the expression, 'The Beloved Physician' into the English language and many modern translations of the Bible maintain this distinctive phrase. It is a translation of two Greek nouns: *iatros* meaning 'physician', and *agapētos* meaning 'beloved'. The Greek word *iatros* could describe one who sought to cure ailments and is understood as a profession by Strabo 10.5.6. Luke, therefore, could have been a person of some means, though *iatros* could also indicate that he was a slave or a freedman who had been educated to be a personal physician (Diog. Laert. 6.30). The descriptor 'beloved' would not have normally been used for physicians during the imperial period. Romans, such as Pliny (*N. H.* 29.11), distrusted them, while Cicero (*De. off.* 1.42.151) thought medicine was an honorable profession for those of a lower social status. Marcus Aurelius used a phrase slightly related to 'The Beloved Physician' in describing Galen as the 'first among doctors and unique among philosophers' (M. Aur. *Med.* 14.660). The use of the term 'beloved' indicates one who is valued, prized, and dear. It asserts a close relationship between the parties involved, and may specify the way in which Luke practised medicine in comparison to other imperial era physicians (see Galen *Meth. medendi* 1.1).

St Luke is considered the patron saint of physicians and surgeons, and his Feast Day is celebrated on October 18. Because of his connection with this phrase, it has been frequently used in literature. Edgar Allan Poe wrote a poem entitled 'The Beloved Physician' around 1847 for Marie Shew, the nurse who cared for him in the midst of his physical problems. Often, memoirs of heroic doctors include 'The Beloved Physician' in their title. This genre of literature was quite popular in the nineteenth century and continues to be used to describe the life of important physicians, for example *The Beloved Physician: A Memoir of Peter Murray*, written by Robert Balgarnie in 1864. Frank G. Slaughter, in 1951, combined his interests in medicine and the biblical world in his imaginative retelling of Luke's life, *The Road to Bithynia: A Novel of Luke, the Beloved Physician*. Al and Joanna Lacy, in 2006, published the historical novel *Beloved Physician*, which describes American frontier life and the way a heroic Christian physician navigates the challenges of the medical profession and his Christian faith.

Contemporary use of the term continues for physicians who show skill, empathy, spirituality, and compassion in the carrying out of their duties. Science fiction fans often use the variant phrase, 'The Beloved Doctor', to refer to the enigmatic but brilliant Time Lord from the planet Gallifrey in the long-running BBC television program *Doctor Who*.

Recommended reading. Ferngren, Gary B. *Medicine and Health Care in Early Christianity*. Baltimore: Johns Hopkins University Press, 2009.

See also LUKE, GOSPEL OF; PAUL, THE APOSTLE; KING JAMES VERSION (KJV) [JBT]

Belshazzar. A personal name which means 'Bel protect the king'. The only other person with a similar name in the Bible is Daniel, also known as Belteshazzar. Belshazzar, however, was the son of Nabonidus, and grandson of Nebuchadnezzar II (605–562 BCE) the Babylonian king. According to the biblical records, he was the last king of Babylon. Though the biblical account records him as the son of Nebuchadnezzar (Dan. 5.2, 18-22), extra-biblical sources confirm he was not the son, but the grandson of Nebuchadnezzar. A regent in his father's stead, Belshazzar's story appears in Dan. 5. Other references to him were only as historical placements for Daniel's vision (Dan. 7.1; 8.1).

Belshazzar was known as the king who threw a feast for a thousand of his lords, and defiled the temple vessels taken from Jerusalem (Dan. 5). While the feast was going on, and under the influence of wine, Belshazzar drank from the vessels, along with his wives, concubines, and lords, praising the gods of gold, silver, and iron. While this was going on, a hand mysteriously appeared on the wall and wrote, 'MENE, MENE, TEKEL, PARSIN', which is translated literally as 'Numbered, numbered, weighed and divided' (Dan. 5.24-27).

No one was able to translate the meaning of the words, but someone remembered Daniel had a reputation for solving such problems. When Daniel was summoned, and after rejecting the offer of gifts made by the king, he interpreted the words as: 'MENE, God has numbered the days of your kingdom and brought it to an end; TEKEL, you have been weighed on the scales and found wanting; PERES, your kingdom is divided and given to the Medes and Persians'. That same night, the prophecy was fulfilled and the Chaldean King Belshazzar was killed (Dan. 5.30).

There are several depictions of Belshazzar's feast in artworks. Two famous ones include Rembrandt and John Martin's paintings both titled *Belshazzar's Feast*. The Dutch painter Rembrandt (1606–1669) painted his *Belshazzar's Feast* in 1635, which is quite detailed in its depiction of the surprise on the king's face and that of the Queen. The English painter John Martin (1789–1854) also painted *Belshazzar's Feast* in 1821.

There are several references to Belshazzar's feast in contemporary culture, especially in the English language. Idiomatic expressions such as 'the writing on the wall' and 'you have been weighed and found wanting' are both references to the judgment pronounced on Belshazzar during the feast. The first expression is generally a prediction of doom. Rufus Sewell's character Adhemar in the movie, *A Knight's Tale*, used a similar expression to speak of Heath Ledger's character: 'You have been weighed, you have been measured and you have been found wanting'.

Emily Dickinson's poem 'Belshazzar had a Letter' brought this strange biblical story to life: 'Belshazzar had a letter, / He never had but one; / Belshazzar's correspondent / Concluded and begun / In that immortal copy / The conscience of us all / Can read without its glasses / On revelation's wall'. Belshazzar's feast is mostly used to symbolize the uncertainties that surround our lives and positions in this world.

See also DANIEL; DANIEL, BOOK OF; HANDWRITING ON THE WALL; NEBUCHADNEZZAR; SHADRACH, MESHACH, AND ABEDNEGO [GOA]

Benjamin. From the Hebrew *Binyamin* (son of my right hand). The last of Jacob's twelve children and the only child born in Palestine, Benjamin—born on the journey his family made from Padan Aram to Canaan—was originally named Ben-oni (son of my affliction) by his mother Rachel before she died in childbirth. Jacob immediately renamed him Benjamin, referring to the right hand as a symbol of power and fortune. No more is written of Benjamin until the account of his journey to Egypt with his brothers where they meet Joseph, a brother sold into slavery earlier in his life. Soon after a reunion of brothers and father, Jacob on his deathbed offered a blessing describing Benjamin as 'a ravenous wolf, in the morning devouring the prey, and at evening dividing the spoil' (Gen. 49.27). In the Book of Joshua, as the territory is divided among the twelve tribes, Benjamin inherits a commercially and militarily strategic position, which borders the Jordan River and includes Jericho and Jerusalem. Thus, the tribe of Benjamin becomes an important group, whose skills in archery are much praised throughout the HB.

Modern cultural references to Benjamin abound, and they appear in a variety of media, from video games and toys, to literary works and motion pictures, to musical groups. In the *Final Fantasy Mystic Quest* video game, for instance, the protagonist is a character named Benjamin who—with swords, axes, bombs, and claws—must reunify his fictional world, a task reminiscent of the battles waged in and among the twelve tribes of Israel. And Ty, Inc., designer and manufacturer of stuffed toys, released a Beanie Baby named Benjamin that sports a red, white, and blue top hat and bowtie. While the toy is undoubtedly an allusion to Benjamin Franklin, the American Founding Father was likely named after the biblical figure since he was his father's youngest son born to his father's second wife.

In 1929, Mississippi novelist William Faulkner released a stream-of-consciousness novel titled *The Sound and the Fury*, which includes a mentally challenged youngest son originally named Maury. Due to his disability, he is a source of shame and grief for his family, especially his mother who insists on changing his name to Benjamin. Just as the Benjaminites rarely live up to their progenitor's reputation, so too does Faulkner's Benjamin fail to live up to his mother's expectations. English writer and journalist George Orwell's famous allegorical novella entitled *Animal Farm: A Fairy Story* (1945) contains a skeptical donkey named Benjamin who is both literate and wise. His mantra in the book is 'Life will go on as it has always gone on—that is, badly'.

On the big screen, *The Curious Case of Benjamin Button* (2008) tells the fantastical story of an infant who is born old and grows younger rather than older. Like the biblical Benjamin, Benjamin Button's mother dies in childbirth, and there is also an ironic allusion to 'the child of his old age' (Gen. 44.20). Perhaps the most famous musical group to bear the name of Benjamin is 'Breaking Benjamin', an American post-grunge rock band whose lead singer is Benjamin Burnley. However, 'Tribe of Benjamin', the backing musicians for urban church/jazz artist Ben Tankard, is a more direct popular music reference to the biblical Benjamin. This progenitor of one of the original twelve tribes of Israel, therefore, maintains a healthy cultural presence even today.

See also JOSEPH, SON OF JACOB; JACOB; RACHEL; GENESIS, BOOK OF [DN]

Bethany. Bethany ('house of unripe figs') was a village east of Jerusalem on the Jericho road. Located on the lower slopes of the Mount of Olives (Mark 11.1; Luke 19.29), Bethany was about three kilometres from Jerusalem (John 11.18). Today the village is called by its Arabic name, el-Azariyeh (Lazarus).

Jesus visited Bethany on several occasions (Matt. 21.17; Mark 11.11), and was a visitor at the home of Lazarus, Mary, and Martha (Luke 10.38-42; John 12.1-8). When Lazarus became ill, Mary and Martha sent word to Jesus to come and heal him but Lazarus was already dead and buried for four days by the time he arrived. He then went to the grave site and wept, prayed, called for the tomb to be opened, and commanded Lazarus to come out, thus raising him from the dead (John 11.1-44).

On another occasion Jesus visited Simon the Leper in Bethany where he was anointed with costly perfume by an unnamed woman (Matt. 26.6-13; Mark 14.3-9; Luke 7.36-50). Bethany was also the starting point for Jesus' Triumphal Entry into Jerusalem (Mark 11.1-11; Luke 19.29-38), and the place where he blessed his disciples before his Ascension (Luke 24.50).

In the 400s CE, a church was built on the traditional site of Lazarus's tomb. Archeological investigations indicate an earlier church was destroyed by an earthquake. This church was modified periodically until the 1950s when a new church was built on the foundations. The church in Bethany has many tombs cut into the rock of its foundation. One of these is rather elaborate and considered by some to be Lazarus's tomb. Not to be confused with the village of Bethany is 'Bethany Beyond the Jordan', which was where Jesus was baptized by John the Baptist (John 1.28). The exact location of this site is disputed.

The events that occurred at Bethany informed various works of literature, including Rudyard Kipling's 'The Sons of Martha' (1907), G.K. Chesterton's 'The Convert', Henry Coleman's 'On Lazarus Raised from the Death', Alfred, Lord Tennyson's *In Memoriam A. H. H.*, and Sylvia Plath's 'Lady Lazarus'.

Recommended reading. Elser, Philip F., and Ronald A. Piper. *Lazarus Mary and Martha: Social Scientific Approaches to the Gospel of John.* Minneapolis: Augsburg Fortress Press, 2006.

See also MARY AND MARTHA OF BETHANY; LAZARUS OF BETHANY [AJW]

Bethel. From the Hebrew *bet* (house) and *el* (God), the biblical town of Bethel was important mainly for two reasons. First, it had a prominent and easily accessible location. It was just north of a major road that ran east to west from the Mediterranean Sea to the Jordan River, and nineteenth kilometres north of Jerusalem, on the road running north to south from Shechem, through Jerusalem, to Hebron.

More important than location was Bethel's cultic significance. The first mention of the town is in Gen. 12.8 when Abram first entered the land of Canaan. He built an altar between Bethel and Ai and lived here before and after a famine forced him to Egypt.

Bethel was given its name by Jacob. In Gen. 28.10-22, Jacob had a dream in which he saw angels ascending and descending a ladder into the sky and God spoke to him, affirming the covenant he had first made with Abram. Convinced God's presence was in this place, Jacob named the location Bethel, meaning 'House of God'. When Jacob returned from his years working for Laban (Gen. 29–31), he returned to Bethel, built an altar, and God again reaffirmed the covenant with him (Gen. 35.1-15)

It seems there was always a remnant of faithful prophets residing at Bethel (Judg. 20.18; 2 Kgs 2.3) as well as those loyal to the royal court of the northern king (1 Kgs 12.31-33; Amos 7.10-17). Such was the significance of the town that the ark of the covenant was kept there for a time (Judg. 20.27).

The cultic popularity of Bethel may have diminished with the choice of Jerusalem for both palace and temple but this was reversed when the kingdom was divided. To prevent the Israelites from travelling back to Judah to offer sacrifices in Jerusalem, northern King Jeroboam I made two gold calves and placed one in the far northern town of Dan and the other in southern Bethel (1 Kgs 12.25-33).

The NT makes no mention of Bethel, and the city died near the end of the Byzantine period. Most scholars identify Tell-Beitin as ancient Bethel and archaeological excavations took place at this site several times between 1934 and 1960.

The significance of 'the house of God' lives on still today. Beth-el is a common name for Jewish synagogues and temples. It is also a popular name for cities, towns, churches within various denominations, as well as religiously affiliated schools and groups, most often in North America. Additionally, in each country where the Jehovah's Witnesses are present there is a branch office referred to as Bethel with their workers referred to as Bethel families.

See also ARK OF THE COVENANT; COVENANT; JACOB; JACOB'S LADDER [JBW]

Bethesda. Bethesda is the name of a pool near the 'sheep-gate' in Jerusalem. In the biblical literature, it is referred to only in John 5.2. Several textual uncertainties concerning the name of the pool, however, make the reference difficult. There are three main possible names, each with its own strengths and weaknesses. (1) 'Bethsaida' is found in some manuscripts, but is suspect due to assimilation (cf. John 1.44; 12.21). (2) 'Bethzatha' is also found in the manuscripts and reflected in the NRSV and JEB, though it may be a mere variant of 'Bezetha', the name which Josephus gives to the Northern extension of Jerusalem (Josephus, *JW* 5.4.2). (3) The manuscript tradition also supports the spelling 'Bethesda', which is reflected in the KJV and the NIV. Some have suggested, however, that this name is also suspect as a scribal change. In the end, 'Bethzatha' and 'Bethesda' are the two most plausible original names of the pool in John 5.2. The pool itself was probably a double pool and was surrounded by four porticos plus another in the middle.

In John 5, Jesus heals a paralytic on the Sabbath at the pool of Bethesda. When asked if he wants to be healed, the man tells Jesus that he is unable to enter the pool when its water is stirred up, which is either a reference to the notion that the first person to enter would be healed, or to the dubious textual variant (John 5.4) which suggests that an angel (Raphael, according to tradition) would 'trouble' the water before any entered it. The former is more likely, though the latter has spawned several intriguing references in later literature and tradition. Instead of taking the man to the pool, Jesus commands him to 'stand up, take your mat and walk', and in doing so heals the man and incites the anger of 'the Jews' since it was the Sabbath.

As with many of the healing scenes in the Gospels, Jesus' healing of the man at the pool of Bethesda is the subject several artistic paintings, including Bartolomé Estaban Murillo's *Christ healing the Paralytic at the Pool of Bethesda* (1667–70) and William Hogarth's *The Pool of Bethesda* (1736–37), which he gave to St Bartholomew's Hospital in London. The tradition of the angelic touch is depicted in works such as James Tissot's *La Piscine Probatique ou de Bethesda* (1886–94) and Robert Bateman's *The Pool of Bethesda* (1877).

Several significant literary allusions to the pool of Bethesda are also noteworthy. For example, the Puritan minister Cotton Mather tellingly entitled his medical guide, which considered the relationship of faith, illness, and repentance, 'The Angel of Bethesda' (1724, though it remained unpublished in Mather's lifetime). In a poem entitled 'Nocturne at Bethesda' (1927), the African-American poet Arna Bontemps poignantly laments the absence of the angel's presence from the pool, and thus also its dormant healing power: 'Bethesda sleeps / The ancient pool that healed / A host of bearded Jews does not awake'. So although the story of the healing of the man at the Pool of Bethesda as told in the Gospel of John is a remarkable story in itself, it is the apocryphal description of the angel 'troubling' the water that remains the most common focus of later allusions to the narrative in John's Gospel.

See also JOHN, GOSPEL OF; SABBATH; RAPHAEL, THE ANGEL [DRB]

Bethlehem. Bethlehem is a village in the hill country of Judah (Judea during the Roman period) located approximately ten kilometers south of Jerusalem. The Hebrew name *Beit Lehem* means 'house of bread'. Another village called Bethlehem was located in the ancient tribal territory of Zebulun (Josh. 19.15). Bethlehem is most famous as the birthplace of Jesus (Matt. 2.1-5; Luke 2.1-15), but references to it extend far back into Israelite history. It is adjacent to the burial site for Rachel (Gen. 35.19), is the location of the story of Ruth and Boaz (Ruth 1.1–2.4; 4.11-22) and the ancestral home of the house of David (1 Sam. 17.12; Luke 2.4; John 7.43). According to the prophet Micah (5.2-5), Bethlehem was to be the birthplace of the ruler of Israel who would bring peace and security to a restored Israel. The Gospel of Matthew recites these verses as a reference to the birthplace of Jesus Christ (Matt. 2.3-6).

Bethlehem has always been important in western culture, particularly figuring in annual Christmas narrations and pageants. Most people are familiar with the Christmas carol 'O Little Town of Bethlehem' (1868). Bethlehem is featured in various medieval mystery plays and literary descriptions of the nativity of Jesus (e.g., *Piers Plowman*, c. 1360–1387). Poets such as Emily Dickinson ('They Have Not Chosen Me'), John Milton ('On the Meaning of Christ's Nativity'), and Gerard Manley Hopkins ('The Blessed Virgin Compared to the Air We Breath') have made focused references to Bethlehem. Novelists such as James Joyce (*Ulysses*) and John Updike (*The Centaur*) have set Bethlehem significantly in their stories. Bethlehem has been the actual location of visual art for many centuries with the architecture, paintings, mosaics and decorative features of the Church of the Nativity (sixth century, rebuilt over a fourth-century church), particularly the grotto under the church which many have thought to be the actual birthplace of Jesus. Well known paintings by Pieter the Elder Bruegel (*The Numbering at Bethlehem*, 1566), Leonaert

Bramer (*Journey of the Three Magi to Bethlehem*, 1638–1640) and Edward Burne-Jones (*The Star of Bethlehem*, 1887) and many others are displayed in museums. There is long tradition from the thirteenth century onward in Italy of constructing elaborate nativity scenes called *presepio*.

Bethlehem was the home of St Jerome from about 386 CE and the location where he did much of his work translating the Bible into Latin (the Latin Vulgate). The St Mary Bethlehem Hospital in south London was one of the oldest psychiatric institutions in the world. The word 'bedlam', meaning uproar and confusion, is derived from a corrupted pronunciation of the hospital's name.

See also DAVID; MATTHEW, GOSPEL OF; INFANCY NARRATIVES; CHRISTMAS; BREAD [RRJ]

Bethsaida. Bethsaida is a place mentioned several times in the Gospels (Matt. 11.21; Mark 6.45; 8.22; Luke 9.10; 10.13; John 1.44; 12.21). Jesus performed two of his best-known miracles (the healing of a blind man; the feeding of the five thousand) near Bethsaida. Because many there rejected Jesus' message, he pronounced judgment over it along with two other cities, Capernaum and Chorazin. These three Galilean cities formed a triangle where Jesus' ministry concentrated. His three disciples—Peter, Andrew, and Philip—were from Bethsaida.

Josephus Flavius (37–ca. 100 CE), a Jewish historian, also mentions Bethsaida several times in his writings (*Ant.* 18.28, 108; *J.W.* 2.168; 3.57, 515; *Life* 1.398, 399). According to Josephus, Herod Philip (ruled in 4–34 CE), the tetrarch of Gualanitis, elevated Bethsaida's status from village to city and renamed it after Augustus's wife (or daughter) Julias. Herod Philip was buried in the city. During the First Jewish War of 66–73 CE, the rebels led by Josephus and the Roman army clashed near Bethsaida. There are also references to Bethsaida in Roman (Pliny, *Nat.* 5.71; Ptolemy, *Geog.* 5.15.3), rabbinic, and Christian pilgrimage literature.

The precise location of Bethsaida is disputed. Theories include Et-Tell, an ancient ruin located on the eastern bank of the Jordan River, about three kilometres to the north of the shore of the Sea of Galilee. It was one of the largest cities bordering the Sea, with dimensions of 400 x 200 meters and covering twenty acres. Since 1987, Israeli archaeologist Rami Arav has led excavations on the site, which now officially identified as Bethsaida by the Israeli government. Some scholars, however, question the identification, arguing that it is located too far from the Sea of Galilee to be a fishing center (Bethsaida, *Bet Zayyada*, means 'house of fisherman' in Hebrew) and it is located on the eastern rather than on the western side of the Jordan, contradicting the statement of John 12.21 where the city is located in Galilee. Arav and others' response to this criticism has been that geological evidence suggests that earthquakes and deposits from the Jordan have changed the topography, altering the course of the river and causing the shore of the Sea to recede south. Another theory suggests Tel el-Araj is the likely site, a small ruin on the shore of the Sea of Galilee, east of the Jordan. Based on a small random probe conducted at the site in 1987, Arav concluded that the site could not be ancient Bethsaida because the remains are from the Byzantine period or later. A later survey conducted by Y. Stepansky in 1990, however, revealed remains from both the Early Roman and Later Roman periods.

Jesus' miracle of the feeding of the five thousand near Bethsaida has been depicted in paintings by many great artists, including Bartolomé Esteban Murillo (c. 1618–1682), Francisco Goya (1746–1828), and Bernardo Strozzi (c. 1581–1644).

Recommended reading. Arav, Rami. 'Bethsaida'. Pages 145-66 in *Jesus and Achaeology*. Ed. James H. Charlesworth. Grand Rapids, MI: Eerdmans, 2006. Rainer, Anson F. and R. Steven Notley (eds.). 'The Search for Bethsaida'. Pages 356-59 in *The Sacred Bridge: Carta's Atlas of the Biblical World*. Carta: Jerusalem, 2006.

See also GALILEE; FISH, FISHER, FISHING; TWELVE DISCIPLES, THE [KT]

Beulah. Beulah is a Hebrew word meaning 'married', sometimes applied symbolically to Israel signifying the future prosperity of the land of Israel: 'You shall not be termed Forsaken and your land shall no more be termed Desolate, but you shall be called My Delight Is in Her and your land Married [Beulah]' (Isa. 62.4)

Beulah is one of the anticipated new names given to the redeemed after the return from the Babylonian Captivity because Jerusalem—and by extension, Israel—will be 're-married' to God. It signifies Yahweh's wife. This image is rare in the OT but found in Hos. 2.26, 19; Jer. 2.2; and Ezek. 16.32.

The image of the land of Israel as married extends beyond the return from exile and foresees a Messianic age of fertility. The Lord will be the *ba'al*, 'Husband', who brings fruitfulness based upon righteousness (see Isa. 62.1-2; Deut. 28.1-14). She,

Israel, will be like a 'weak' but beloved woman who is cleansed and restored to her Lord.

The theme of God married to his people appears in the NT as well, where writers present Jesus Christ as the bridegroom and the church as his bride (Eph. 5.23-27; Rev. 21.1, 9, with reference to New Jerusalem).

The image of Beulah, while used sparingly in the Bible, reappears in later literature, hymnody, and songs. In *Pilgrim's Progress*, John Bunyan describes it as a place of rest where pilgrims pause before crossing over the River of Death. William Blake saw it as a land which was virtually paradise, but it was still lacking because even there John Milton was not able to experiences total artistic freedom. For Blake, Beulah was a place in which sexual love can bring again Eden's bliss. It was a place of flowers ('Four Zoas') and a land of beautiful maidens ('Jerusalem').

In gospel music Beulah is a synonym for Heaven. Edgar Page Stites (1836–1921) wrote 'Beulah Land' (1875), with its chorus depicting the singer as looking away from earth to heavenly Beulah. C. Austin Miles wrote 'Dwelling in Beulah Land', with its hymn tune 'Beulah Land', which describes the far away land of Beulah. The chorus is in the first person and those who sing it describe themselves as living in a mountain paradise where they can drink from an ever-lasting fountain under cloudless skies. In 1973, Squire Parsons wrote 'Sweet Beulah Land'. It was recorded in 1979 and rapidly became a hit being sung by the Gaither Homecoming Choir, the Chuck Wagon, and others.

Charles Ingles, a character in 'Little House on the Prairie', parodied the hymn tune 'Beulah Land' in his song 'Dakota Land', to express the frustration of pioneers wanting to settle the prairie. The movie *Beulah Land* starring Lesley Ann Warren, Eddie Albert, Hope Lange, Meredith Baxter and others was issued in 1980 and again in 1985. It was based on the novels of Lonnie Coleman and tells the story of the rise and fall of an aristocratic family of the Old South.

Recommended reading. Andersen, T. David. 'Renaming and Wedding Imagery in Isaiah 62'. *Biblica* 67 (1986) 75-80. Rothenbusch, Esther. 'Is Not This the Land of Beulah?' The Search for the Holy Spirit in American Gospel Hymns'. *Review and Expositor* 94 (1997) 53-77.

See also BRIDE; BRIDEGROOM; EXILE; JERUSALEM; MARRIAGE [AJW]

Bible. The Bible is most commonly seen as a 'holy book'. Its synonym 'scripture' simply means 'sacred writing'. Most religions in the world have sacred writings. In that sense, a Bible is not necessarily unique. For instance, Hinduism has the *Vedas*, Buddhism the *Tripitaka*, Islam the Qur'an, and Mormonism the *Book of Mormon*. The Jewish holy books (the Hebrew Bible or Tanak) are written in Hebrew and Aramaic and the content corresponds to the Christian Old Testament though with a different arrangement of the books. The HB was translated into Greek (the LXX or Septuagint), a collection which includes additional writings.

The Christian Bible is divided into two major sections, the OT (Genesis–Malachi), and the NT (Matthew–Revelation), written in Greek. These writings are the work of many different authors employing several literary genres (e.g., historical narrative, poetry, wisdom, epistolary, and apocalyptic). In Western culture, the Bible's influence is immeasurable, informing legal and ethical values (e.g., the Ten Commandments) as well as the arts and popular culture. Examples of the Bible's influence on film, for instance, are legion: *The Ten Commandments* (Cecil DeMille, 1956); *Shawshank Redemption* (Frank Darabont, 1994); *The Unforgiven* (Clint Eastwood, 1992); *The Passion of the Christ* (Mel Gibson, 2004); *Angels and Demons* (Ron Howard, 2009); and *The Book of Eli* (Albert Hughes, Allen Hughes, 2010), to name but a few. In literature, biblical themes and storylines appear in such works as C.S. Lewis's *The Chronicles of Narnia*, John Milton's *Paradise Lost*, Daniel Defoe's *Robinson Crusoe*, and John Bunyan's *Pilgrim's Progress*.

See also TANAK; OLD TESTAMENT; NEW TESTAMENT; SCRIPTURES; SEPTUAGINT; CANON [MBW]

Biblical archaeology. There are as many definitions for the discipline of biblical archaeology as there are scholars digging in the ground, and the differences between them are often only slight. Biblical archaeology most broadly applies to a study of the material culture of the land of Israel within its biblical context, covering a chronology that spans from c. 3000 BCE—first century CE (the Early Bronze Age to the Roman period). The discipline examines the cultural contexts of the land of Canaan, the kingdoms of Israel and Judah, the city of Jerusalem, and a number of other locations and peoples described in the HB. In addition, there is growing interest in the archaeology of the NT, and the possibility of shedding light on Jerusalem and the Galilee of Jesus' time.

The history of biblical archaeology is nearly as interesting as the subject of its study. Its roots can be traced to individual explorers and adventurers, who travelled to the 'Holy Land' to recover and reconstruct the ancient biblical landscape for faithful patrons in America and Britain. Throughout the nineteenth century, for example, Edward Robinson famously toured the land of Palestine with Bedouin guides, in order to identify cities that appear in the HB. The father of the modern discipline, however, is William F. Albright. Under Albright, biblical archaeology was adopted into the mainstream of academia by the mid twentieth century.

Albright conceived biblical archaeology as a subfield of biblical studies, for the purpose of explaining and clarifying the historical world of Scripture. The discipline was intended to verify the historicity of the stories that appear in the Bible, and took the text as its starting point. Thus, Albright and his students assumed that the artefacts in the ground could corroborate the historical accounts in biblical texts. Since the 1970s, however, sweeping changes in the field have altered how the study of biblical archaeology is conceived. A growing number of scholars no longer see biblical archaeology as a subfield of biblical studies, but as a separate discipline with shared interests. For many the goal of biblical archaeology should no longer be to verify the historicity of the Bible, but simply to study the history of cultures that informed and produced the text. In fact, biblical archaeologists sometimes conclude that the material remains cast doubt on the veracity of various biblical accounts. Reflecting this change in the field, there has even been discussion of abandoning the designation 'biblical archaeology' for Syro-Palestinian archaeology.

No matter the name, biblical archaeology continues to capture the imagination of academics and laymen alike. It is not uncommon that archaeological finds make a big splash in popular media as well as scholarly journals. The controversy surrounding the discovery of the so-called James Ossuary—a burial box that purported to have held the remains of Jesus' brother—and the subsequent investigation by the Israel Antiquities Authority is just one recent example. As long as the Bible captures the imagination, the enthusiasm for biblical archaeology to contextualize and, for some, even reconstruct the biblical past will remain.

Recommended reading. Meyers, Eric M. *The Oxford Encyclopedia of Archeology in the Near East*. 5 vols. Oxford: Oxford University Press, 1997. Moreland, Milton C. (ed.). *Between Text and Artifact*. Atlanta: Society of Biblical Literature, 2003. Reed, Jonathan L. *The HarperCollins Visual Guide to the New Testament*. New York: HarperCollins Publishers, 2007.

See also ISRAEL; ROMAN EMPIRE [NKB]

Bilhah and Zilpah. Bilhah and Zilpah are both concubines of Jacob. Both women were given by Laban to his daughters: Bilhah was the servant of Rachel, and Zilpah was the servant of Leah. Four of the twelve sons of Jacob are born to these two women: Dan and Naphtali are the sons of Bilhah, and Gad and Asher are the sons of Zilpah. The giving of a maidservant to one's husband in order to have claim to her children (see Gen. 30.5-7) was a common practice in the Ancient Near East. In the Founding Families narratives, Sarah does this with Hagar, believing that she is past the ability to bare children. Children are an important means for women to achieve status. Rachel, who like Sarah believes herself to be barren, gives Bilhah to Jacob in order to be built up through her. Leah, who believes she is finished having children after giving birth to four sons, responds by giving Zilpah to Jacob in an effort to out do her sister. Both women are wrong in their assessments of themselves. Bilhah is also known for her affair with Reuben (Gen. 35.22), the oldest son of Leah, and this is the reason that he loses the rights of the firstborn. Based on the references to this incident in *Jubilees* 33 and *The Testament of Reuben* 3, it may be Bilhah was asleep or even passed out drunk when Reuben had sex with her and therefore, she is not blamed by Jacob.

Canadian novelist Margaret Atwood took her inspiration for the *Handmaid's Tale*, the 1985 Governor General's Award winner, from the lives of these women; however, instead of setting her novel in history, she places the ideology of the past into a fictional future. These women are actual characters in Anita Diamant's *The Red Tent* (1997). In her fictional retelling of the life of Dinah, Leah's daughter who is raped in the biblical text, Diamant envisions Bilhah and Zilpah as younger half-sisters of Leah and Rachel.

Recommended reading. Kugel, James. *Traditions of the Bible: A Guide to the Bible as It Was at the Start of the Common Era*. Cambridge, MA: Harvard University Press, 1998.

See also GENESIS, BOOK OF; RACHEL; LEAH; LABAN; JACOB; TWELVE TRIBES OF ISRAEL; SARAH; HAGAR; BIRTH [EW]

Birds, Symbolism of. There are over 300 references to birds in the Bible, starting with their creation on the fifth day (Gen. 1.20-22). While many times they are named specifically—as diverse as the cock, owl, pelican, dove, sparrow, ostrich, turtledove, eagle, raven and peacock—the majority of mentions refer to birds in general. They are described as messengers, sacrifices and food sources. Discussions of birds that are clean as opposed to unclean (birds of prey) may be found in Lev. 11.13-19 and Deut. 14.11-20. Likewise, birds have both positive and negative associations, symbolizing destruction as well as resurrection and peace. There are few mentions to bird song, but the lack of birds and their singing is noted as a sign of desolation in Jer. 4.25 and 9.9. Birds of prey (i.e., the raven, owl and pelican) are noted in Isa. 34.11 and Zeph. 2.14 as those who will reside in devastated lands. More positively, the protection of God is repeatedly equated to a bird watching over his nest and covering young with his wings (Exod. 32.11; Ps. 17.8; Isa. 31.5). Hosea 11.11 describes Israel's return from exile like that of migratory birds.

Ravens are cited primarily as messengers; one is sent from the ark of Noah (Gen. 8.7) and ravens brought food to Elijah in the desert (1 Kgs 17.2-6). Instructions for offering a turtledove or pigeon as a sacrifice are given in Lev. 1.14-17. They are mentioned repeatedly in this context (e.g., Num. 6.10), and specifically at the Presentation of Christ in the Temple (Luke 2.24). Jesus employed birds as metaphors on many occasions. He used the image of the sparrow to warn his disciples against becoming disheartened when facing persecution (Matt. 10.28-31; Luke 12.6-7). He also used the cock to note Peter's denial, saying 'Truly I tell you, this day, this very night, before the cock crows twice, you will deny me three times' (Mark 14.30). The dove comes to symbolize peace, resulting from its return to Noah's ark with an olive branch (Gen. 8.8-12), as well as purity and innocence, in its connection to the Baptism of Jesus when 'he saw the Spirit of God descending like a dove and alighting on him' (Matt. 3.16). In paintings of the Baptism the Holy Spirit is often visualized as a dove.

The pelican is among those birds cited as 'detestable' for eating (Lev. 11.13-19; Deut. 14.12-18), but later comes to symbolize the sacrifice of Christ on the Cross, as the female pelican will peck at her breast to draw blood to feed her young. The Hymns of Thomas Aquinas speak of the pelican in this sense, and artistic images of the crucifixion from the late Middle Ages and Renaissance periods sometimes include a pelican for this reason. The prophets see the eagle as one of the four beasts (Dan. 7.3-7; Ezek. 10.14) and it becomes a symbol for St John the Evangelist. The majestic peacock is associated with the riches of Solomon (1 Kgs 10.22; 2 Chron. 9.21). It comes to symbolize immortality and resurrection due to the legend that its flesh does not rot. The peacock also figures in Greek mythology and Indian folktales. The mythical phoenix is similarly associated with resurrection imagery, as the bird self-immolates and then is reborn from the ashes.

Recommended reading. Goddard, Burton L. *Animals and Birds of the Bible*. Mulberry, IN: Sovereign Grace Publishers, 2007. Stratton-Porter, Gene. *Birds of the Bible*. Whitefish, MT: Kessinger Publishing, 2006.

See also ANIMALS, SYMBOLISM OF; COCK; DOVE; SPARROW'S FALL [ACF]

Birth. Giving birth to a child (Hebrew *yeled*) is a common event in the Bible. Reflecting predominantly male authorship and a patriarchal culture, the HB's chief concern in discussing birth is the production of male heirs. The importance of producing heirs and continuing the father's lineage (his 'name') lies behind such traditions as levirate marriage (Deut. 25.5-6), and the use of 'handmaids' (slave-girls) to produce children in certain narratives in Genesis (e.g., Hagar and Abraham, Bilhah and Jacob). The ability to bear children is viewed as a sign of blessing, while childlessness is also viewed as God's doing, whether for punishment or for reasons unknown (Gen. 30.1-2; Deut. 7.12-14; 1 Sam. 1.5-6). This is related to God's more general control over the fertility of land and people (e.g., the fruit of 'the womb', 'livestock' and 'ground' are all listed together in Deut. 28).

The Pentateuch emphasizes the firstborn male's status. Whether human or animal, the firstborn (who 'opens the womb') belongs to God (Exod. 13; Num. 3.11-14). Stories of remarkable/miraculous conceptions and births appear throughout the HB, such as Sarah giving birth at an advanced age (Gen. 17). Similar stories about individuals with a special destiny being born to otherwise childless women include Samson's mother (Judg. 13) and Hannah (1 Sam. 1), with both Samson and Samuel being in turn dedicated to God's service.

In the NT, there are three narratives of a miraculous conception and birth following the patterns of the Jewish Bible. Both Matthew and Luke present angelic announcements of the birth of Jesus. Luke also includes an account of John the Baptist's birth that echoes those of Samson and Samuel closely.

Like some OT precursors, an angel announces John's birth ahead of time, to parents beyond childbearing years, which foreshadows the boy's special destiny (Luke 1.7-25). The stories about Jesus' birth also follow themes from the Jewish Bible, but augment God's role by removing any need for a human father. Individual elements from these stories, such as Gabriel's visit to Mary (Luke 1.26-38), the Magi following the star (Matt. 2.1-11), and angels encountering shepherds (Luke 2.8) are familiar in artwork and popular culture from medieval to modern times, particularly during the church feasts of the Annunciation and Epiphany. Christmas pageants are commonplace, of course. The text of Luke 2.8-16 famously serves as the climax to the television special *A Charlie Brown Christmas* (1965).

Metaphorical uses of birth imagery in the NT also draw heavily on the HB. In 1 Cor. 15, Paul uses the Pentateuch's term 'first fruits' to describe the resurrection of Jesus, and in Rom. 8.19-23 he describes the signs of the Day of Resurrection as comparable to the onset of labor pains. Revelation describes Jesus as the 'firstborn of the dead' (Rev. 1.5), while Rev. 12 contains celestial imagery of a woman giving birth (often read as a Marian reference and frequently depicted by artists as varied as Albrecht Dürer and William Blake). Famously, John 3.1-10 contains a play on the Greek words *anōthen* ('again' or 'from above') and *pneuma* ('wind' or 'Spirit'). Nicodemus hears Jesus saying that one must be 'born again', and be 'born of the wind', when Jesus says that one must be born 'from above', and 'of the Spirit'. Contemporary reference to Protestant evangelicals as 'born-again Christians' finds its language in this passage.

Recommended reading. Stol, M. *Birth in Babylonia and the Bible: Its Mediterranean Setting*. Groningen: Styx/Brill, 2000.

See also Womb [MWM]

Blasphemy. Blasphemy means to speak evil words against God, gods, religion, sacred beliefs, or other defamations of divine matters. Besides injuring the reputation of another, or showing contempt or lack of reverence for God or something sacred, the term can also mean falsely claiming divine attributes by either word or deed. King Herod was struck by an angel of the Lord because he allowed supplicants from Tyre and Sidon to give him divine honors (Acts 12.20-23). In the OT, the Hebrew term for blasphemy is the expression, *aqab shem 'Adonai*, to despise or to 'curse the name of the Lord' (Isa. 52.5). It is the same as 'reviling' (Ezek. 35.12) or 'cursing '(Lev. 24.11) God or sacred things. Blasphemy could also be a deed (Ezek. 20.27) such as dealing treacherously with the Lord or by practicing idolatry (Isa. 65.7). The OT sanctioned the death penalty for blasphemy of the divine Name. The whole community was to perform the stoning (Lev. 24.16). To avoid committing blasphemy, a practice developed among Jews to avoid saying the sacred Tetragrammaton (YHWH) altogether, using the names Adonai or Elohim in its place.

Jesus was accused of blasphemy on several occasions during his ministry because he claimed to have the authority to forgive sins (Matt. 9.3; Luke 5.21); and claimed to be the Christ and the Son of God (Matt. 26.63-65; Mark 14.61-64; John 10.29, 36). He was convicted by the Sanhedrin of blasphemy on the presumption that his claim to be the Son of Man was a false claim to divinity (Mark 14.64).

The NT considers reviling Jesus as blasphemous (Matt. 27.39; Mark 15.29; Luke 22.65). In addition, opposition to the gospel is blasphemous, as is mocking, reviling, or slandering religious authorities who are representatives of Christ (Acts 13.45; 18.6; 2 Pet. 2.10-12; Jude 8-11). Blasphemy against the Holy Spirit is the 'unforgivable sin' (Mark 3.28-30 etc.). Exactly what it is has not been clear to most biblical interpreters. Common interpretations of the sin of blaspheming the Holy Spirit say it is either continual unrepentance, or, that it was the claim of Jesus' enemies that his miracles were from a satanic rather than a divine source of power.

Blasphemy has been used to convict and judicially murder unpopular people. The first Christian martyr, Stephen, was stoned for blasphemy against God and Moses (Acts 6.11). The charge of impiety, which is similar to blasphemy, was used in Athens to condemn the philosophers Anaxagoras (banished), Socrates (executed), Aristotle (fled) and the Sophist Protagoras (fled). In recent decades Salman Rushdie, cartoonists, film makers and others have been attacked in the West for blasphemy against Islam.

In 1951 the United Sates Supreme Court decided in the case of *Burstyn v. Wilson*, (343 US 495) that the Italian movie *The Miracle* was protected by the First Amendment even if considered by Roman Catholics to be sacrilegious. Since then popular culture or 'art' has been allowed freedom of expression that the Puritans and others would have found to be blasphemous.

Recommended reading. Cabantous, Alain. *Blasphemy: Impious Speech in the West from the Seventeenth* to the Nineteenth Century. New York: Columbia University Press, 2001. Levy, Leonard W. *Blasphemy: Verbal Offense against the Sacred, from Moses to Salman Rushdie.* Chapel Hill, NC: University of North Carolina Press, 1993. Nash, David. *Blasphemy in the Christian World: A History.* New York: Oxford University Press, 2007.

See also HOLY SPIRIT; HOLY, HOLINESS [AJW]

Blessing, Blessed. What do you think about when you hear the word 'blessing?' Some might recall their religious upbringing in the Catholic Church, where the priest would trace the shape of the cross on the foreheads of parishioners and piously state, 'Bless you, my child'. Others may recount the time when they enjoyed a delicious steak dinner with their extended family and someone shouted, 'Who wants to say the blessing?' Still others may want to forget the day when one of their co-workers obtained the promotion everyone wanted and joyously hollered, 'What a blessing!'

These contemporary illustrations demonstrate how Western culture has drastically modified the sense of the terms 'blessing' and 'blessed' as they appear in biblical literature. In the HB, a 'blessing' (*berakhah*) generally denotes God's bestowal of material goods, happiness, peace, and security upon humanity (Gen. 26.14; 28.3-4; Num. 6.22-27; Deut. 7.12-16; Judg. 1.15; Ps. 5.11-12; 133.3; Prov. 10.22). Recipients of such gifts were considered 'blessed' by God (Gen. 24.31; 2 Sam. 26.25). Conversely, people 'blessed' (*barak*) God, reciprocating thanks through hymns and prayers for the benefactions received (Gen. 24.26-27; Neh. 9.5), and invoked God to 'bless' others, which operates as a performative utterance (i.e., speech act) that brings good upon another person (1 Sam. 25.14; 2 Sam. 14.22; 1 Chron. 18.10).

In the NT, the use of 'blessing' (*eulogia*) and 'blessed' (*eulogeo*) are analogous to the HB. Jesus 'blessed' the loaves and fish for the multitudes (Mark 6.41), the disciples at his ascension (Luke 24.50-51), and the Passover meal (Matt. 26.26). Similarly, Paul 'blessed' the 'cup of blessing' when celebrating the Lord's supper (1 Cor. 10.16), and regularly employed these terms to portray the human response of praising and thanking God for his manifold 'blessings' in Christ (2 Cor. 1.3-4; Eph. 1.3; Gal. 3.9, 14). Moreover, people 'blessed' God through prayer and other acts of worship (Luke 1.64; 2.28; 24.53; Rom. 1.25; 1 Cor. 14.16; Jas 3.9; Rev. 5.12, 13; 7.12), and they also entreated God to pour out his 'blessing' on others (Luke 2.34).

Recommended reading. Mitchell, Christopher W. *The Meaning of BRK 'To Bless' in the Old Testament.* Atlanta: Scholars Press, 1987. Westermann, Claus. *Blessing in the Bible and the Life of the Church.* Philadelphia: Fortress Press, 1977.

See also EUCHARIST; PRAYER [DEB]

Blindness. Blindness in the OT (Hebrew *'ivvârôwn*) and the NT (Greek *pōrōsis*) is both a physical and a moral condition. The physically blind are unfortunates who have lost or never had their sight due to personal or human sin. The morally blind are close-minded people who refuse to the see the truth, the presence of God before them.

In the OT, the blind (Hebrew *'ivvêr*) are due consideration and help—it is a sin and against the law not to help (Lev. 19.14). Blindness is a consequences of disobedience (Deut. 28.28), yet blindness might befall a good and charitable man as well (Tob 2.10). Healing the blind is a messianic sign in the OT. Isaiah (6.9) is sent by God to proclaim to the morally blind: 'see and see, but do not perceive'. He predicts (35.5) that 'the eyes of the blind shall be opened'.

In the NT, a good part of Jesus' healing ministry involves bringing sight to the physically blind (Greek, *tuphlos*). In Mark 8, at Bethsaida, Jesus heals a blind man by spitting into his eyes and putting his hands on him; Jesus asks him what he can see, and the man replies that he sees men who look like trees walking; then Jesus again puts his hands on the man, who looks intently, and his vision becomes clear. After healing the man, Jesus orders him to tell no one. In John 9, Jesus brings sight to a man born blind. In this extraordinary story, Jesus tells his disciples that the man is not blind because of sin but rather as an opportunity to show God's glory. He makes a clay paste from his own spittle mixed with earth, anoints the man's eyes with the clay, and tells the man to go wash his eyes in the pool of Siloam. When the man does this, he can see. People notice that the blind man who daily begged is now completely different and can see. They take the man to the Pharisees, who question the man, assuming that the blind man had been and continues to be a sinner. They also assume the one who healed him on the Sabbath is a sinner as well. The lengthy exchange between the Pharisees and the man with new sight reveals that the Pharisees are blind to the reality of the Messiah living among them. The man, however, meets Jesus again and 'sees' that he is the Messiah. The NT also describes the morally and spiritually blind, as in Matt. 13.13, where Jesus tells his disciples 'I speak to them in parables, because seeing they do not see'.

In art, images range from El Greco's *Christ Healing the Blind Man* to Carl Bloch's *Jesus Heals the Blind Man (Bartimaeus)* to the modern *Healing of the Blind Man* by the French artist Corrine Vonaesch.

Recommended reading. Rosner, Fred. *Encyclopedia of Medicine in the Bible and the Talmud.* Lanham, MD: Jason Aronson, 2000.

See also EYE; DEAFNESS [RL]

Blood. In all Ancient Near Eastern cultures, blood was recognized as a principal life force due to the general observations that it is shed at childbirth and that its injury-related loss is fatal. The Hebrew language makes this connection manifest through the similarity of the terms *dam* (blood) and *adam* (human being, humanity, man). As that which represents life, blood was considered to belong to God, the giver of life; hence blood was sacred. In later texts the word 'blood', often in conjunction with 'flesh', could be used as a metaphor to mean 'mortal life' (Sir. 14.18; 17.31; Matt. 16.17; attested also in the Talmud). In other biblical texts, however, it refers specifically to the shedding of blood (i.e., killing and bloodguilt; the guilt incurred by bloodshed, often implying the death of innocent people; Gen. 9.6; Num. 35.33; Hos. 12.14 ET; Matt. 23.30; Luke 11.51).

In the HB, the idea that blood belongs to God is probably the reason for the prohibitions of blood consumption (Gen. 9.4; Deut. 12.23). The term 'blood' occurs frequently in texts on Passover and sacrifice. These rituals required specific techniques of animal slaughter to assure that most of the blood was drained from the animal. The HB then describes that this blood had to be applied to doorposts, to the sanctuary, or to humans. How did these blood rites function? The HB provides an explicit rationale for the meaning of blood in sacrifices: 'For the life of the flesh is in the blood; and I [God] have given it to you for the altar in order to atone for your lives; because it is the blood that atones through life' (Lev. 17.11). As a vital force, sacrificial blood effected atonement by cleansing the sanctuary (Lev. 8.15; 16.16, 19-20) or humans (Lev. 8.23-24, 30; 14.14). During the first Passover the blood of lambs was applied to the doors of the Israelites' houses (Exod. 12.7). As a sign of life it protected the Israelites from the fatal strike of the 'destroyer' (Exod. 12.13, 23). Since life belongs to God, the priests had to pour out sacrificial blood at the base of the 'altar of burnt offering' (Lev. 1.5; 3.2; 4.7) in order to return it. Likewise the blood of game was to be poured out and covered with earth (Lev. 17.13). Because of its sacredness, sacrificial blood was used to consecrate priests (Lev. 8.23-24, 30) for service at Israel's sanctuary.

The atoning power of blood is a frequent image in NT christological concepts: forgiveness of human sins is achieved through the purifying power of Christ's blood (Rom. 3.25; 1 Pet. 1.2; 1 John 1.7; Rev. 7.14). In the Lord's Supper, the cup of wine represents Christ's 'blood of the covenant' (Mark 14.24), which consecrates the Christian community. Yet the term blood does not always reference ritual atonement; in other contexts it designates the death of Christ that brings redemption or peace for humans (Rom. 5.9; Col. 1.20).

Since medieval times, the Roman Catholic and some Anglican churches have claimed that priests turn the Eucharistic wine into the actual blood of Jesus through the words of institution (transubstantiation), while Reformed churches have taught that the wine merely symbolizes Christ's blood.

Recommended reading. Eberhart, Christian A. 'The 'Passion' of Gibson: Evaluating a Recent Interpretation of Christ's Suffering and Death in Light of the New Testament'. *Consensus* 30/1 (2005) 37-74.

See also ATONEMENT; BLOOD OF THE LAMB; LORD'S SUPPER; SACRIFICE [CAE]

Blood of the Lamb. The phrase derives from the Greek *haima* (blood) and *arnion* (lamb), and occurs twice in the Book of Revelation (7.14; 12.11), where the lamb represents Christ. In 7.14 the people of God have 'washed their robes and made them white in the blood of the Lamb', signifying their salvation. In 12.11, the Devil is conquered by the blood of the Lamb. This echoes themes from the OT, in particular the sacrifice of lambs for the mending broken relationships (Num. 6.12), and the blood associated with sacrifices of purification (Lev. 4.1-6.7, 6.24–7.10). These two themes, blood and lamb, come together in the story of the Passover. In Exod. 12, a lamb is sacrificed, and the blood of the lamb is put on the door posts and lintels of the house. The blood of the lamb acts as a sign to God to 'pass over', and save the occupants from the plagues sent to Egypt.

NT references to Jesus as lamb retains the themes of sacrifice, vicarious offering, the repairing of relationships, and the giving of life (Rom. 3.25; 1 Cor. 5.7-8; 1 Pet. 1.19; Heb. 9.12-14, 26, 28; 1 John 2.2; 4.10; Rev. 5.6). In John in particular, the Passover lamb forms the symbolic background for the crucifixion. In John 1.29 Jesus is called 'the Lamb of God who takes away the sin of the world' by John the Baptist, and the Passover lambs are sacrificed at the same time as Jesus is crucified (19.14). For John the death of Jesus is a reenactment of God's redemption of Israel and their release from captivity. This association between the crucifixion and Passover is seen in the twelfth century Mosan iconographic tradition, exemplified in Nicholas of Verdun's *Klosterneuberg Ambo*, which shows Aaron painting a T (signifying the cross) in the blood of the Passover lamb on the door lintel.

The Eucharistic motif, arising from Jesus' words at the last supper identifying the wine was his blood (Matt. 26.28, Mark 14.24, Luke 22.20), is shown in the *Klosterneuberg Ambo* as well. At the foot of the avenging angel is a lamb shedding blood into a Eucharistic cup. This image is also found in Jan and Hubert van Eyck's 1432 altarpiece *The Adoration of the Mystic Lamb*, known also as the *Ghent Altarpiece*. At the centre of the bottom panel is a lamb standing on a Eucharistic altar, whose blood is pouring into a cup. Men, women, priests, angels, and bishops, all worshiping the Lamb, surround the altar.

The associations made between the crucifixion of Jesus, the blood of the lamb, and the Eucharist, are clear in Mathias Grünewald's 1515 altarpiece *The Crucifixion*. It shows a lamb with a cross shedding blood into a Eucharistic cup, at the feet of John the Baptist. The whole scene takes place at the foot of the cross, where Jesus is shedding blood from the same place on his breast as the lamb.

In the late nineteenth century, the blood of the Lamb became a central point of devotion in Evangelical Pietist worship, and is the subject of a number of American revival hymns such as Elisha Hoffman's 'Are You Washed in the Blood?' This tradition of American Protestant hymnody associates the washing of Rev. 7.14 with baptism, and emphasizes the salvation of the individual. These hymns influenced American songwriters of the twentieth century like Tom Waits whose 'Down There by the Train', a song popularized by Johnny Cash, is about forgiveness for past misdeeds, and a place 'down there where the train goes slow' 'where the sinners can be washed in the blood of the lamb'.

[PDSP]

Boanerges. The etymology of this term is uncertain. This word is found only once in the Bible and is probably an altered Greek transliteration of a composite Aramaic or Hebrew word meaning 'sons of commotion, anger, or quake'. According to Mark 3.17, Jesus gave this nickname to two of his disciples, John and James, the sons of Zebedee. In the same passage this awkward word (for a non-Jewish audience) is explained by the evangelist as meaning 'Sons of Thunder', maybe in the attempt to provide a somewhat free translation. Thunders, both in Jewish and Greco-Roman culture, were associated with display of divine power (Yahweh or Zeus).

Since John and James are depicted in the Gospels as both overly zealous and somewhat able to cast fire from heaven (cf. Mark 9.38-41; Luke 9.51-54), *boanērges* has been understood as an epithet describing their impetuosity as well as their zeal. Consequently, the term is usually employed figuratively to refer to loud, fiery preachers, as, for example, in *The Christian Soldier* by Thomas Watson (1669). The idea of power associated with this exotic word also made it an ideal name for a 1922 Brough Superior motorcycle model (the 'Boa', for *boanērges*).

As James R. Harris (*Boanerges*, 1913) has showed, the tradition surrounding the sons of Zebedee (regarded later as 'twins') as 'sons of thunder' has often been readily adopted by populations reached by Christian missionaries. For instance, some Peruvians used to look the birth of twins as an impious occurrence which required a penance, and had the habit of calling one of the newborns 'child of the lightening'. However, with their adoption of the Christian faith, they replaced that name with 'Santiago' (James). Moreover, even in recent times, the Danes who regard the fossil sea-urchins as thunderstones still call them *sebedaei, sepadeje,* or even *sebedee*-stones.

The Church of Jesus Christ of Latter-day Saints (Mormons) holds that John, brother of James, is to be identified with the 'beloved disciple' of the Gospel of John (13.23; 19.26; 20.2; 21.7; 21.20). John allegedly asks Jesus for immortality to carry the task of bringing souls to him. Jesus consents to his request and transforms him in a 'flaming fire and a ministering angel' (*Doctrine and Covenants*, 7).

The violent thunders-and-fire imagery associated with gospel proclamation makes *boanērges* a preferred name for musical groups willing to convey a Christian message in non-conventional, mostly stigmatized musical genres, such as heavy metal (i.e., a band called Boanerges from Argentina), rap, and R'n'B (i.e., a band called Boanerges from France). The double connotation of a positive and negative connection with the thunder (power as opportunity and curse) is also portrayed in such films as *Highlander* (1986), and in the various literary and filmic renderings of the novel *Frankenstein, or The Modern Prometheus* by Mary Shelley (1818).

Recommended reading. Rook, John T. '"Boanerges, sons of thunder" (Mk 3:17)'. *Journal of Biblical Literature* 100 (1981) 94-95. Buth, Randall. 'Mark 3:17 Boneregem and Popular Etymology'. *Journal for the Study of the New Testament* 10 (1981) 29-33.

See also TWELVE DISCIPLES, THE [LM]

Boat. The key terms in the Bible are the Greek *ploion* (boat) and *naus* (ship), and the Hebrew *tebah* (boat) and *'oniyah* (ship). The boat as a symbol is found in the HB and is often associated with Noah's Ark in Genesis (Gen. 6.1-9), where the Ark is a vessel that saves humanity, and later is understood by Philo of Alexandria (20 BCE–50 CE), a Hellenistic Jewish Philosopher, as the image of the body and soul moving toward blessedness. Other references in the OT to boats can be found in Wis. 14.5-7, where the boat takes on a corporate aspect, and Jon 1.4-16, which describes the consequences of disobeying God. A reference to boat found in the non-biblical pseudepigraphal *Testament of Naphtali* (6.1-10) uses boat/ship to indicate the Twelve Tribes of Israel.

There is a great deal of ancient boat symbolism associated with body, souls, and death. The boat as a Jewish symbol in the Greco-Roman period was understood as a psycho-pomp, that is a vehicle that assists the souls of the dead to the afterlife, an idea influenced by Ancient Egyptian mythology. Carved boats during this time period are found in tombs as shown in 1 Macc. 13.27-29, which explains that Simon built a tomb for his father and brothers and included 'carved ships, so that they could be seen by all who sail the sea'. Furthermore, the boat/ship symbol was heavily influenced by Greco-Roman culture, particularly Homer's *Odyssey* and Virgil's *Aeneid*, which present images suggesting the boat/ship as a state, an individual's soul, or the world. As one of the earliest Christian symbols, it symbolizes the Church, as a corporate symbol, with Christ as the helmsman and where the mast represents the Cross. This understanding is developed from the Synoptic Gospels where the 'Stilling of the Storm' and 'Walking on Water' stories describe the disciples in the boat with Christ (see Mark 4.35; 6.45-53; Matt. 8.23-27; 14.22-33; Luke 8.22-25) where the underlying message is faith in Christ. In other words, the boat is a vessel that houses Christians during 'stormy' times. Furthermore, the concept of the boat as a soul which is guided by Christ toward Heaven is picked up by later Christian writers.

Boats/ships as settings are found in classical Western literature like Herman Melville's *Moby-Dick* (1851) which has strong parallels with the Book of Jonah, as well as contemporary literature such as in Yann Martel's fictional novel *Life of Pi* (2001) in which the characters of the story are stranded on a lifeboat. W.B. Yeats's poem 'Sailing To Byzantium' picks up a lot of the boat symbolism especially as it pertains to a person's soul moving toward eternity. Similarly, Alfred, Lord Tennyson's poem, 'Crossing the Bar' (1889) depicts the narrator acting as a boat, as he 'sets out to sea' hoping to see 'my Pilot face to face'.

Recommended reading. Danielou, Jean. *Primitive Christian Symbols*. Trans. Donald Attwater. London: Burns & Oates, 1964.

See also NOAH'S ARK [MSW]

Boaz. Boaz was a rich and reputable Jew from Bethlehem of Judah and a relative of Elimelech, Naomi's husband (Ruth 2.1). Following the law of levirate marriage, Boaz married Ruth, and she thus became an ancestor of Israel's King David (Ruth 2–4) and Jesus Christ (Matt. 1.5; Luke 3.32). The great Renaissance artist Michelangelo painted Boaz on the famous Italian Sistine Chapel, while the Louvre hosts Nicolas Poussin's 'Summer' canvas which depicts Boaz and Ruth in the field. Boaz was the name of the north bronze pillar placed at the entrance of Solomon's temple (1 Kgs 7.21-22; 2 Chron. 3.15-17).

See also RUTH, BOOK OF; LEVIRATE MARRIAGE; TEMPLE, ISRAEL'S [TR]

Body. As the principal Greek term for the body (*sōma*) has no single Hebrew or Aramaic cognate, analysis of biblical 'body' terminology is not straightforward. The Septuagint (LXX) is a helpful guide in this regard. The LXX uses *sōma* to render a complex of overlapping terms, the usages of which fall into several categories: 'flesh' (e.g., *bāśār* Lev. 15.19); 'bodies' of animals, human beings or cherubim (e.g., *gâviyah* Ezek. 1.11; *gĕšēm* Dan. 3.27; *shâ'er* Prov. 5.11); and '*dead* bodies' (e.g., *peger* Gen. 15.11; *nâbelah* Deut. 21.23; *gâviyah* 1 Sam. 31.10; *gûpâ* 1 Chron. 10.12).

Hebrew body language generally denotes the person as a psychosomatic totality (e.g., Prov. 11.17), although this is not a decisive criterion for a biblical anthropology. In the Pentateuch, bodies are occasions of ceremonial purity and impurity and important sites of ritual performance. An emission from the body (Lev. 15.16, 19) renders a person ceremonially unclean, as does contact with a corpse. In such cases, bodily ablutions are involved in the act of purification (Num. 19.8). The Levitical code (Lev. 19.28) prohibits certain socio-symbolic uses of the body (cutting and tattooing), although the male body is also the bearer of the covenant mark of circumcision.

NT uses of *sōma* cover a similar range of senses. *Sōma* can denote a living (Mark 14.8), dead (Luke 23.55), and resurrected (John 2.21; Acts 9.40) body. Notions of bodily purity continue (e.g., 1 Cor. 6.18) even after the Christian community ceases to enforce circumcision and purification rituals. Especially in Paul, *sōma* rarely denotes the material constitution of the body; this notion is more often covered by the expression 'flesh (*sarx*) and blood (*haima*)' (Eph. 6.12; Heb. 2.14). Partly, this terminological distinction derives from a belief that the body that is resurrected is raised to a transformed physicality—a *sōma* that is not 'flesh and blood'. This opposition is encapsulated in Paul's description of the resurrected body as a *sōma pneumatikon*, a 'spiritual body' (1 Cor. 15.44).

Wider culture has long used the body as a powerful social and religious symbol. Vedic, Orphic and Norse mythologies each describe primordial reality in terms of a body from which the gods and the cosmos derive (e.g., Ymir in *Vafthrudnismal* 21). Like today, ancient political thinkers also used the body as a metaphor for society (the *body* politic). Central to this are ideas of mutual dependence and cooperation, notions that underpin an ideology of conformity (cf. Livy, *Ab Urbe Condita* 2.32). The social body and the cosmic body are probably implied in the extended metaphor of the Church as 'body of Christ' (1 Cor. 12.12-31).

One of the most notable representations of the human body is da Vinci's *Vitruvian Man* (c. 1487), a male nude that illustrates the geometry of the body. Other notable works include Michelangelo's iconic statue *David* (1504), and his *Creation of Adam* (c. 1511). Of the many depictions of Christ's body, Rubens's dark and meditative *Descent from the Cross* (c. 1612–1614) is particularly moving. In terms of female bodies, René Magritte's disturbing work *The Rape* (1934) strikingly superimposes a female torso onto a woman's head. In this, and several of his other works, the artist anticipates later feminist critique of the hegemony at work in stereotypically male attitudes to the female form.

Recommended reading. Gundry, R.H. *Sōma in Biblical Theology*. Cambridge: Cambridge University Press, 1976.

See also BODY OF CHRIST; HEAD [MJL]

Body of Christ. The 'body of Christ' is an important subcategory of uses of the Greek word *sōma* in the NT. There are several senses or applications of the expression—literal, metaphorical and eucharistic.

References to the literal *sōma* of Christ in the NT predominate in the Gospels. As might be expected, statements regarding Christ's literal body occur mainly in the passion narratives (e.g., Matt. 27.59; John 19.38). In the Pauline corpus, this sense usually occurs in relation to Christ's death and its effects (Rom. 7.4; Eph. 2.16; Col. 1.22), although the epithet 'the body of his glory' (Phil. 3.21) manifestly denotes Christ's body after resurrection.

'Body of Christ' is also an important Pauline metaphor for the Church. It takes two forms, in both cases the unity of Christ and the Christian community being emphasized. The first form figuratively denotes the Church vis-à-vis itself and its members (Rom. 12.5; 1 Cor. 12.27). Using somatic terminology in this manner was common in antiquity. Its purpose was frequently paraenetic (ethical) (e.g., Livy, *Ab Urbe Condita* 2.32), since describing a community as a 'body' underpins an ethos of cooperation, concord and harmony. The second form of the metaphor is not specifically paraenetic but can also be expressive and declaratory. It denotes the Church as it relates to Christ (Col. 1.18, 22; Eph. 1.23), who is correspondingly designated 'head' (*kephalē*). The notion of Christ the 'head' as source of the body's direction and growth (Eph. 4.15-16) goes beyond simple identification; it uses ancient beliefs regarding the physiological function of the head to signal the Church's dependence upon Christ.

Of the different senses of 'body of Christ', it is likely that eucharistic references have generated both the widest cultural influence and the greatest contention. These references relate to what are termed the words of institution, attributed to Jesus at his last Passover meal ('*this* is my body'; Matt. 26.26; Mark 14.22; Luke 22.19). Paul provides the earliest extant testimony regarding these statements (1 Cor. 11.23-25) and his argument suggests that he understands there to be a close affinity between the literal, metaphorical and Eucharistic senses of 'body of Christ'. Present-day Christians remain in disagreement regarding the nature of the Eucharistic rite. Roman Catholics and Eastern Orthodox churches understand from Jesus' words that the substance of the consecrated bread changes during the sacrament. Protestant churches eschew this view, but lack consensus regarding whether Christ's body becomes literally, spiritually or symbolically present alongside the bread.

The eucharistic liturgy has been an important impetus for Western cultural productivity. Indeed, the Western musical tradition was greatly influenced by the liturgy of the Mass, and this has occasioned several works of great beauty. Of these, Tallis's *Mass for Four Voices* (sixteenth century), Mozart's *Requiem*, K.626 (1791), and Fauré's, *Requiem*, Op.48 (1890) stand out. The most famous visual artwork is probably da Vinci's *Last Supper* (c. 1495–98). This painting is notable for denoting the moment at which Jesus predicts his betrayal. Visual allusions are also detectable in subsequent artworks and cinematographic media. In terms of popular culture, it appears in Dan Brown's conspiracy novel *The Da Vinci Code* (2003) and the Ron Howard film (2006) based upon it.

Recommended reading. Martin, D.B. *The Corinthian Body*. New Haven: Yale University Press, 1995. Wedderburn, A.J.M. 'The Body of Christ and Related Concepts in 1 Corinthians'. *Scottish Journal of Theology* 24 (1971) 74-96.

See also BODY; CHRIST; HEAD [MJL]

Bone of my bones. This Hebrew idiomatic expression (*etsem meatsamay*) occurs in Gen. 2.23 as part of a longer rhythmic and poetic phrase 'this at last is bone of my bones and flesh of my flesh' uttered by the first man when he saw the first woman created from his rib. In general, biblical writers emphasize both unity and diversity of both sexes. However, 'bone of my bones' in the mouth of the man is a powerful statement of the fundamental correspondence existing between man and woman. A similar expression appears several times in the Bible in the form of 'my bone and my flesh', and usually signifies the ties of kinship. Only in Job 2.5 is the expression 'his bone and his flesh' used in a literal and narrow sense, referring to Job's body.

For Ephrem the Syrian, a fourth-century Christian theologian, the fact that the woman is 'bone of the man's bones' emphasizes her special place in the created world as well as a unique relationship with the man. One generation later, Ambrose of Milan (340–397 CE) interprets this image as a confirmation of the same physical nature shared by man and woman. In addition, Ambrose reads the passage from Genesis in the light of the NT (see Eph. 5.30), and states that all Christians are, likewise, members of Christ's body and bones of his bones.

Interestingly, some fifth-century Jewish commentators who refer to the image of 'bone of my bones' place the emphasis on the woman's features that make her different from the man. She should be humble, modest, and restrained (see *Genesis Rabbah* 18). Furthermore, her intellect matures more quickly and she has more understanding than the man (see *Niddah* 45b).

The motif of 'bone of my bones' often appears in European literature and is used either in the context of the institution of marriage or to explain the parent–child relationship. Thus the former is exemplified by Charlotte Brontë's novel *Jane Eyre* (1847) and William Faulkner's *The Wild Palms* (1939), whereas a good modern example of the latter is Sylvia Wilkinson's novel *Bone of My Bones* (1982), which explores the vicissitudes of female adolescence.

Recommended reading. Westermann, Claus. *Genesis 1–11: A Commentary*. Trans. J.J. Scullion. Minneapolis: Augsburg, 1984. Wilkinson, Sylvia. *Bone of My Bones*. New York: Putnam, 1982.

See also ADAM; ADAM'S RIB; EVE [KRS]

Book. The term translates the Greek *biblion* and Hebrew *sefer*. Though one often encounters the notion of books of the Bible, the concept of a book, as we know it is somewhat misleading in reference to the ancient biblical texts. Books in antiquity generally took the form of scrolls. Scrolls were formed by joining sheets of papyrus or animal skin end to end, in long rolls that generally reached a length of 20 to 30 feet. Perusing through such scrolls would have seemed a clumsy process to modern readers, as it required both hands, one for unrolling a new section and the other for rolling up the section already read. What are referred to now as the different books of the HB were often written on different scrolls. The NT describes a reading of one such scroll: 'He [Jesus] stood up to read, and the scroll of the prophet Isaiah was given to him. He unrolled the scroll and found the place where it was written…' (Luke 4.16-17). Some scholars have even suggested that it was the length of an easily handled scroll that determined the divisions in the Pentateuch.

In the Roman period, Christians began to replace the more traditional scrolls of the HB with the codex, a Roman invention. A codex is a collection of sheets, either of papyrus or animal skin (later of parchment or vellum), fastened together at the back, often with a protective cover. Thus the codex more resembles our modern conception of a book. A single codex might include both Septuagint and NT texts, with writing on both sides of a single sheet. The Christians eventually came to refer to OT and NT texts as *ta biblia* (the plural of *biblion*), from which the English word 'Bible' is derived.

The HB and NT occasionally refer to books, some of which we have, and others we do not. For example, Num. 21.14 mentions the Book of the Wars of the Lord, and 2 Sam. 1.18 refers to the Book of Jashar. Both citations suggest books that contained historical information, possibly used in the production of the canonical texts, which no longer survive. In 2 Tim. 1.13, Paul asks Timothy to bring the books (*ta biblia*) he had left behind. In this case, the author is most likely referring to the books of the HB.

Recommended reading. Herbert, Edward D., and Emanuel Tov (eds.). *The Bible as Book: The Hebrew Bible and the Judean Desert Discoveries*. New Castle, DE; Oak Knoll Press, 2002. McKendrick, Scot, and Olaith O'Sullivan (eds.). *The Bible as Book: The Transmission of the Greek Text*. London: British Library, 2003. Robters, Colin H., and T.C. Skeat. *The Birth of the Codex*. London: Oxford University Press, 1983.

See also SCROLL [NKB]

Book of the Law. Deuteronomy is 'the book of the law' upon which King Josiah based his religious reforms (622 BCE). The historian of 2 Kgs 22–23 pictures a cleansing of temple worship that conforms with the legislation of Deuteronomy (2 Kgs 23.4-6, 14 = Deut. 12.2-3; 2 Kgs 23.24 = Deut. 18.10-12). Deuteronomy, composed of *this law* or *the words* of Moses, was said to have been expounded and written by him and, after disappearing for centuries, was found in the library of the Jerusalem temple (Deut. 1.1-5; 31.9, 24-26; 2 Kgs 22.8, 11). The king's obligation to write 'a copy of *this* law in a book' (Deut. 17.18) anticipates the story of the discovery of *Deuteronomy* during Josiah's reign. The book of the law presupposes a written culture (Deut. 28.58, 61; 30.10; 31.24). 'The curses written in this book' (Deut. 29.20, 26) are the curses enumerated in Deuteronomy (Deut. 27.15-26; 28.15-69).

Deuteronomy's collection of laws (Deut. 12–26) reflects a developed society with local law courts, a higher judicial authority, judges and officers that are analogous to the structure of modern legal institutions (Deut. 16.18-20; 17.8-13; 19.17-18; 21.2; 25.1-3). The concept of 'justice' or 'righteousness' is the critical perspective behind the laws of Deuteronomy (Deut. 1.16; 4.8; 6.25; 16.18-20; 24.17; 25.15; 32.4; 33.21), but Western culture adopted instead the Enlightenment's intention, 'equality of all before the law' as the basis of its legislation, a principle often at odds with history. In eighteenth and nineteenth-century England, for instance, the poor could be incarcerated in debtors' prisons or workhouses until death, a central theme in Charles Dickens's novels (e.g., *Oliver Twist* 1837–1839; *Little Dorrit* 1855–1857). Defaulting Israelite debtors could become slaves, but biblical civil law stipulated their freedom and release from debt in the seventh year (Deut. 15; Exod. 21). By contrast African-American slavery (1776–1865) was a coercive, inherited legal institution, justified by theories of racial inferiority, in which blacks permanently suffered the loss of their freedom for the benefit of America's economy.

Deuteronomy's idea of justice as an ethical concept is expressed in its law regarding the cities of refuge, the setting aside of nine cities or sanctuary towns for guilty persons seeking refuge from blood vengeance, to serve as places of protection and accountability for crimes committed (Deut. 4.41-43; 19.1-13; Exod. 21.12-14; Num. 35.6-34; Josh. 20). The problem envisaged is that avengers, consumed with rage, might kill the person who is guilty of manslaughter. The right of asylum established in antiquity continued through the medieval ages down to the early modern period. Unlike ancient legal systems (Hebrew, Greek, Roman, Teutonic), Western culture developed a repressive system of punishment, while simultaneously discarding former models of compensation, resolution and restoration. Punitive crime control did not prevent mob violence. Between 1886 and 1935 some 6000 people in the United States became victims of lynch mobs, the topic of German director Fritz Lang's American film called *Fury* (1936). Finding inspiration in Deuteronomy's philosophy of justice, Dutch criminologist Herman Bianchi (*Justice as Sanctuary*, 1994) reintroduces the institution of sanctuaries as an integral part of our legal system, serving as places of refuge and negotiation for violent and nonviolent crimes, where criminal procedure concludes with conflict resolution instead of punishment.

Recommended reading. Levinson, Bernard M. *'The Right Chorale': Studies in Biblical Law and Interpretation*. Tübingen: Mohr Siebeck, 2008. Rideau, Wilbert. *In the Place of Justice: A Story of Punishment and Deliverance*. New York: Knopf, 2010.

See also DEUTERONOMY, BOOK OF; JOSIAH; SLAVE [JRW]

Book of Life. Also described as God's book (Exod. 32.32-33; cf. Ps. 56.8; Dan. 7.10; *1 En.* 47.3), the book of the living (Ps. 69.28; the 'book of the living' mentioned in the 1999 film, *The Mummy* is pure fiction), the Lamb's book of life (Rev. 21.27; cf. 13.8), and possibly the book of remembrance (Mal. 3.16), the reference can be found across a range of writings, both canonical and non-canonical, as well as early Christian theologians. In each case, the meaning is virtually the same: a divine record of either righteous deeds or righteous persons (or both), which will be used for determining who will be blessed by God (cf. Dan. 7.10; *2 En.* 52.15; 53.2; *Ascen. Is.* 9.22).

Some texts suggest that the blessing relates to the present life (Exod. 32.32-33; Ps. 68.28; Isa. 4.3) while later texts refer to the blessing of eternal life with God (Dan. 12.1; *1 En.* 47.3; 104.1; 108.7; Phil. 4.3; Rev. 3.5; 13.8; 17.8; 20.12, 15; 21.27; cf. Hippolytus, *Scholia on Daniel* 12.2; Irenaeus, *Haer.* 5.2; Augustine, *Civ.* 20.15, 16). Conversely, those not found in this book are condemned to eternal separation from God (*1 En.* 108.3; cf. *Jub.* 36.10). The writer of *Jubilees* contrasts the book of life with the book of death. The righteous appear in the former, the wicked in the latter, and all receive their blessing or curse in the present world and the world to come (see *Jub.* 30.20-22).

For some, those who are righteous in this life are included in the book of life (Herm. *Vis.* 1.3; Ps.-Clem, *First Epistle on Virginity* 6; cf. Tertullian, *Scorp.* 12). This view accords with the Christian idea that faith in the ways of God results in a person having a place in heaven. For others, those who are included in the book are guaranteed a righteous status in life (Hippolytus, *Antichr.* 2.37). This latter view gave way to ideas of divine predestination where those in the book of life are those specifically chosen by God before creation. The *Summa Theologica* of Thomas Aquinas contains one of the longest treatments on this connection, one that became a key feature for later Reformation theology. Moreover, the link between the two ideas and the original notion of a divine record consulted at the final judgment became central topics in the sermons of famous American preachers such as Jonathan Edwards, John Wesley and Charles Spurgeon.

Recent books employ 'book of life' for self-help purposes in order to focus on how people can cultivate a meaningful existence during their lifetime. Upton Sinclair (1922), Jiddu Krishnamurti (1995), Kevin J. Todeschi (1998) and Michael Sharp (2004) are just a few examples of this usage. Others appropriate the phrase for scientific purposes, such as Lily Kay's summary on the development of the genetic code (2000), Barbara Rothman's concerns with genetic research for mapping human traits, growth and personality (2001), or even Stephen Jay Gould's attempt to detail the origin and progression of creation (2001). Others have given the phrase a more generic nuance for describing what it means to be alive in the world, or what we can learn about life from others. Katrine Stewart encourages people to create their own life-lessons via journaling (2000) and Eve Claxton draws insight from famous individuals in history (2005). The focus of the modern use *vis-à-vis* the ancient is obviously quite different.

See also CHILDREN OF GOD [CSS]

Booths, Feast of (Succot). The Festival of Booths (Hebrew *Succot*) was the most joyful and probably the oldest of Israel's three pilgrimage festivals (Passover, Weeks/Pentecost, and Booths). It probably developed from an early agricultural festival celebrating the ingathering of the summer crops of grapes and olives as well as beseeching God to send the autumn rains. In the OT, it has various names: 'Tabernacles' (Lev. 23.34); 'ingathering' (Exod. 23.16); 'the feast of the Lord' (Lev. 23.39), and simply 'the Feast' (1Kgs 8.2).

The festival began five days after the Day of Atonement and lasted for seven days, with the addition of a special eighth day of observance. During these days, the pilgrim slept and ate within a specially constructed booth originally made of myrtle, willow, and palm branches (Neh. 8.13-18). These booths recalled Israel's Exodus wanderings in the wilderness when they lived in temporary shelters, and the people remembered God's protective care for them in providing the cloud, the manna, and water. The booths probably derived from an agricultural practice of building shelters in their fields during autumn to protect the olive and grape harvest. The word 'succot' means 'protection', and whatever the historical origins, the feast became a memorial of God's protective care and presence during the wilderness. After the Exile (582–537 BCE), the festival developed further. In celebrating the ingathering of the harvest the people of Israel looked ahead to the end time ingathering of all the nations to worship in Jerusalem (Zech. 14.16-19; Isa. 2.2-4; 56.6-8).

Each morning of the festival a procession of priests filed down to the Pool of Siloam to draw a flagon of water, which was carried back to the Temple. During the procession, pilgrims sang special Psalms (Pss 113–118) and carried myrtle, willow and palm branches (the *lulab*) in the right hand, and a citron representing the harvest produce, in the left. On reaching the altar, the priest carrying the golden water-flagon circled the altar then poured a libation of water and wine. On the seventh day, the priests circled the altar seven times.

Each night in the Court of the Women four huge Menorahs (seven-branched candlesticks) were set up, lighting the entire Temple area. Under these lights, the people danced and sang the Psalms of Ascent (Pss 120–134). Before sunrise each morning, the priests processed to the East gate of the Temple looking towards Mount Olives. At the moment of sunrise they turned their backs to the rising sun, faced the Temple and said, 'Our fathers who were in this place turned with their backs toward the Temple of the LORD and their faces toward the east, and they worshiped the sun toward the east (Ezek. 8.16). 'But as to us, our eyes are to the Lord' (*m. Sukk.* 5.4). In John 7–8, the three rituals of this feast involving water, light and a faith affirmation are given a new interpretation in the person of Jesus.

Recommended reading. Yee, G.A. *Jewish Feasts and the Gospel of John*. Wilmington, DE: Michael Glazier, 1989. Ulfgard, H. *Feast and Future: Revelation 7:9-17 and the Feast of Tabernacles*. Stockholm: Almqvist & Wiksell, 1989.

See also FESTIVALS [MLC]

Born again. The phrase 'born again' originates in John 3, which depicts Jesus in conversation with the Pharisee Nicodemus, a 'leader of the Jews' (John 3.1) and 'teacher of Israel' (John 3.10). Jesus informs Nicodemus that 'no one can see the kingdom of God without being born from above' (John 3.3). The Greek *gennao anothen*, translated in the NRSV as 'born from above', and perhaps pointing to a heavenly birth, has alternately been translated as 'born anew', or the more popular 'born again'. Nicodemus appears to understand Jesus as referring to a physical birth, as he asks how it is possible for a person to return to their mother's womb to be born a second time (John 3.4).

Jesus' reply to Nicodemus that 'no one can enter the kingdom of God without being born of water and Spirit' (John 3.5) symbolically describes the process of becoming a follower of Jesus. One was 'born of water' by emerging from the waters of baptism, the central ritual of admission to the new community. Baptism moved the initiate from social groups bonded by a shared 'flesh', in particular the Jewish covenant community descended from Abraham that both Jesus and Nicodemus belonged to, into a group composed of members from varied backgrounds united by the divine 'spirit' (John 3.6).

Beginning in the 1960s, the phrase 'born again' gained currency with evangelical Christian groups, and came to be used as a descriptor for Christians who had undergone a particularly notable, and often unexpected, conversion to Christianity. In North America, significant media attention was focused on public figures who turned their backs on lives of highly publicized debauchery to become 'born again Christians'. Fabled rock musician Bob Dylan, who in 1966 decreed 'everybody must get stoned', briefly identified as a born again Christian in the late 1970s. To the consternation of many fans, Dylan conveyed his newfound convictions through a series of Christian-themed songs, including 'In the Garden', from the 1980 album *Saved*: 'Nicodemus came at night so he wouldn't be seen by men / Saying, 'Master, tell me why a man must be born again?''

'Born again' has become a generalized phrasal prefix used to describe a seemingly endless variety of personal renewals or regenerations; from 'born again virgins' claiming a return to sexual innocence in a spiritual sense, to 'born again conservatives' who shed their previously held liberal values. The phrase is also employed in a standalone fashion, as in the song 'Airbag' on Radiohead's album *OK Computer* (1997), which describes feelings of new life in the aftermath of an automobile accident: 'In the next world war, in a jack knifed juggernaut, I am born again / In the neon sign, scrolling up and down, I am born again'.

Recommended reading. Colson, Charles W. *Born Again*. New York: Bantam Books, 1977.

See also NICODEMUS [DB]

Brass serpent. The expression translates the Hebrew words *nahas* (serpent/snake) and *nechosheth* (bronze/brass). A symbolic image of God's sovereignty and grace, the brass serpent was a bronze replica of poisonous snakes that plagued the Israelites during their journey to the promised land (Num. 21.4-9). Built by Moses at God's behest, the brass serpent was a medium of healing those who were bitten by the poisonous snakes. By looking up at the bronze serpent/snake on the pole, they were healed.

It was also used as a cultic symbol and worshiped for centuries after the Exodus from Egypt. Destroyed by King Hezekiah during his religious reforms (2 Kgs 18.4), the brass serpent up until that time was known as Nehushtan and was worshiped alongside other idols like the Asherah. No other reference was made to the brass serpent in the HB. However, the use of a bronze serpent was not unique to the Israelites as there were several bronze serpents uncovered from pre-Israelite Palestinian cities that date back to the Late Bronze Age.

Jesus made the only reference to it in the NT during Nicodemus's nocturnal visit. Two verses before the often quoted John 3.16, Jesus explained his mission as one of healing the world, by predicting his death on the cross and comparing it to the brass serpent that was raised in the wilderness (John 3.14-15). Even though contested, its symbolism as a healing medium remains today, mostly among medical practitioners.

The origin of the usage of the image of a snake on a rod among medical practitioners and organisations is not always clear. Some associate the origin to the rod of Asclepius, the Greek god of medicine. In ancient Greek religion, Asclepius was the son of Apollo, and was known as 'the Healer'. Iconography associated with Asclepius shows him holding a rod/staff with a snake entwined around it. Hippocrates who is considered the father of Western medicine was thought to have been a worshipper of Asclepius (specific reference to Asclepius was made in the original Hippocratic Oath). Following this reasoning, it is possible that the use of the icon in the medical field owes its origin to this ancient Greek god. On the other hand, it can also be argued that Moses's brazen serpent predates the rod of Asclepius and as such, it is the origin for the usage in a Western world heavily influenced by Christianity.

Often confused with the Caduceus (a herald's staff with two serpent and wings found commonly on the crest of the United States Army medical corps), the image of the brass serpent or the rod of Asclepius remains a symbol of healing and healers. Many medical organisations like the Canadian Forces Medical Services and the American Medical Association use the icon in their logos and crests.

Depicted in several artworks, the brass serpent is an image that has invited different theological arguments, speculations, and interpretations. Some of the well-known depictions of the brass serpent include Michelangelo Buonarotti's fresco of Moses raising the brass serpent (1508), painted on the ceiling of the Sistine chapel, and William Blake's watercolor painting of the same scenery (1805) hanging in the Museum of Fine Arts in Boston. Some scholars have argued that Blake's use of the serpent was basically as a symbol of Moral Law, rather than following the intent of the biblical authority.

See also ASHERAH (ASHTORETH); GOLDEN CALF; SERPENT/SNAKE, THE [GOA]

Bread. The Hebrew term *lehem* means 'bread' or 'solid food', and is found nearly 300 times in the OT. The Greek *artos* means 'wheatbread', a term appearing nearly 100 times in the NT. Biblical texts do not extensively describe the production and eating of bread, as it was so commonplace. Physical bread is understood to be a gift from God in the OT because its production depends heavily on environmental conditions (e.g., Deut. 28.5).

Because of bread's ubiquity in human and biblical contexts, the word's metaphorical meanings stress the fundamental role bread performs in human life, including to earn a living (2 Thess. 3.12), the word of God (Isa. 55.2), the necessity of God (Deut. 8.3), and Jesus as the 'Bread of Life' (John 6). Bread also may refer to the wrath of God, as the 'bread of adversity' (Isa. 30.20) or the 'bread of tears' (Ps. 80.5). The physical dependency on bread for life also relates to the spiritual dependency on God for 'everlasting life' (John 6.47).

The use of the term in popular culture reinforces the vital function of bread in human society. 'Making dough' and 'getting bread' and 'bread winning' are phrases referring to earning a living, making money. Hundreds of Jewish and Christian non-profit organizations that feed the poor use 'bread' in their title in order to highlight their essential, life-sustaining role. Images of 'The Last Supper' consistently show only bread at the table where Jesus and the disciples ate, epitomized in Leonardo da Vinci's rendering of the scene. Depictions of Jesus feeding the 5,000 with loaves of bread and fish also reinforce the association of Jesus with bread. Bread's most prominent role in Western culture is its use in sacred rituals in the Jewish and Christian faiths. The Feast of Unleavened Bread, a thanksgiving for the grain harvest, gave way to the celebration of Passover, which recalls the Jewish deliverance from Egypt. The Christian sacrament of the Eucharist, or Holy Communion, reenacts the Last Supper when Jesus broke bread (his body) and blessed wine (his blood) and gave it to the disciples (Matt. 26.26-28; Mark 14.22-25; Luke 22.14-20; 1 Cor. 11.23-26).

See also FEAST OF UNLEAVENED BREAD; PASSOVER; LORD'S SUPPER; BREAD OF LIFE [CF]

Bread of Life. This phrase translates the Greek *ho artos tēs zōēs*. In the Gospel of John, Jesus uses the metaphor 'Bread of Life' to describe himself and his work (6.35). The context is instructive because the metaphor follows the well-known story of Jesus feeding 5000 people. After that meal, his disciples gathered twelve baskets of leftovers, demonstrating that everyone ate their fill. However, the crowd returns the next day and prods Jesus to perform the miracle a second time because they were hungry again (implied in John 6.26). He then teaches them not to work for food that perishes (6.27) but to seek spiritual food, a discourse that reaches its dramatic high point in Jesus' famous claim, 'I am the bread of life. Whoever comes to me will never be hungry, and whoever believes in me will never be thirsty' (6.35).

Bread was vitally important to the Middle Eastern cultures of the day and was a dietary staple for Palestinian Jews. Jesus argues that he is superior to literal bread because he is the source of eternal, spiritual life, whereas temporal, literal bread can only sustain physical life for a short time. Jesus is the living bread that gives life to deadened souls. Jesus' self identification as the Bread of Life further foreshadows the role of bread—symbolizing the broken body of Christ that brings salvation—in the Last Supper and the subsequent Sacrament of the Eucharist. It is also worth nothing that Jesus was born in Bethlehem (from the Hebrew, *Bayth Lekhem*), which means the House of Bread.

This significant phrase also numbers among the seven 'I am' statements employed in the Gospel of John to reveal aspects of the person and work of Jesus. These seven statements are called 'predicate 'I am' statements', because predicate nouns, which grammatically describe the speaker, follow the 'I am' clauses. These seven statements compliment other groups of sevens in the Gospel of John, namely the seven miracles and the seven discourses.

When the image of the Bread of Life is taken up in literature, it is often through its connection to the bread and wine of the Sacrament of the Eucharist, as in Dylan Thomas's 'This Bread I Break' (1936) or George Herbert's 'The Sacrifice' and 'Holy Communion' (1633). The Bread of Life provides the subject of Edward Taylor's poem, 'Meditation Eight' (1684), which pictures the human soul after being expelled from the Garden of Eden as a starving bird that is only revived when the Bread of Life is sent to it from heaven. The phrase is also the English title of *Sagan af brauddinu dýra* (1987), a memoir written by Icelandic Nobel Prize winner Halldor Laxness.

Recommended reading. Culpepper, Alan (ed.). *Critical Readings of John 6*. New York: Brill, 1997.

See also BREAD; EUCHARIST; FEEDING OF THE FIVE THOUSAND; I AM; LOAVES AND FISHES; MANNA

[KCM]

Bread upon the waters. Ecclesiastes 11.1-2 states, 'Send out your bread upon the waters, for after many days you will get it back. Divide your means seven ways, or even eight, for you do not know what disaster may happen on earth'. A literal interpretation of this saying makes little sense, as bread scattered upon water disintegrates in a matter of minutes. Interpreters therefore have proposed a number of figurative meanings.

Traditionally, the saying has often been taken as a reference to almsgiving. Give to charity, this interpretation says, and it will come back to you. Following this line of thought, the New Living Translation paraphrases v. 1: 'Give generously, for your gifts will return to you later'. Several Southern gospel songs feature the imagery of 'bread upon the waters', usually as a reference to the hope that the believer's faithfulness will eventually be rewarded. The same sentiment appears in Prov. 19.17: 'Whoever is kind to the poor lends to the LORD, and will be repaid in full'.

In keeping with the broader context in vv. 4-6, another interpretation is that commercial activity is in view. The terms 'sending' and 'upon the face of the waters' suggest international trade. The same language describes ambassadors traveling by sea in Isa. 18.2. Proverbs 31.14 speaks of 'bread' in a commercial context. This reading highlights the element of the unknown in v. 2 and urges readers to plan for the future—either to dare to take a financial risk or to diversify one's investments. A modern equivalent might be, 'Don't put all your eggs in one basket'.

Another possibility is to read this proverb in light of the ancient process for making beer, which involved creating a cake made from malted barley or wheat. Beer-makers would place this bread in water, where it would eventually form a sweet liquid called a wort. After a few days, yeast would be added, and the carbohydrates would begin turning into alcohol and carbon dioxide. Thus, beer making literally involved casting bread upon water and then waiting for fermentation to take place. In this light, perhaps Eccl. 11.1-2 is the ancient Hebrew equivalent of *carpe diem* (seize the day). Make beer and share it with your friends, the author advises, because the future is uncertain.

'Bread upon the Water' is the name of a song by Dr Hook and the Medicine Show (words by Shel

Silverstein). Here, however, Ecclesiastes's positive advice becomes a warning. In the song, the 'bread upon the water' is a lover's infidelity, which, the speaker warns, will eventually be repaid.

Recommended reading. Homan, Michael M. 'Beer Production by Throwing Bread into Water: A New Interpretation of Qoh. xi 1-2'. *Vetus Testamentum* 52 (2002) 275-78. Horne, Milton P. *Proverbs–Ecclesiastes*. Smyth & Helwys Bible Commentary. Macon, GA: Smyth & Helwys, 2003.

See also BREAD; ECCLESIASTES, BOOK OF [DJP]

Bride. The Hebrew *kallah* (bride, daughter-in-law) often expresses the covenant relationship of God to Israel. Israel herself is the Lord's bride (Isa. 62.5). The Lord cared for Israel until she was 'old enough for love', then entered into a covenant with her 'and you became mine' (Ezek. 16.8-9). Commentators often interpret bridal imagery in Ps. 45 and Song of Songs as references to Israel, and the prophets occasionally describe Israel as a faithless woman whose idolatry is compared to adultery (e.g., Jer. 3.8; Ezek. 16.32). God promises to forgive his people (Hos. 3.1) and renew his covenant (Isa. 54.9-10).

Paul compares the covenant to a marriage producing 'children of promise' (Gal. 4.28). He presents them 'as a chaste virgin' to Christ (2 Cor. 11.2). Since the church is Christ's bride, she should be dead in affections to the world (Rom. 7.1-6). Husbands should imitate Christ, who suffered to make his bride holy, so as 'to present her to himself ... without stain or wrinkle or any other blemish, but holy and blameless' (Eph. 5.27). Paul calls this analogy (bride is to bridegroom as church is to Christ) 'a great mystery' (Eph. 5.32). The image of church as Christ's Bride reaches its apogee in Rev. 21 and 22 where, adorned with every virtue, she beckons from the new Jerusalem: 'the Spirit and the bride say, Come' (Rev. 22.17). It forms the last, triumphal image of the Christian canon.

Teachers throughout the church's history employed bridal imagery to represent a range of key theological ideas, including the people of God collectively, the individual soul, and Mary. Mystical literature on the espousement of the soul appears in the teachings of Mechtild of Magdeburg, John of the Cross, and Teresa of Avila, among others. Katherine of Alexandria was a popular subject for paintings depicting this union (e.g., in the work of Fra Angelico, Correggio, Raphael, and Titian). The idea of the Church as Bride of Christ, reflecting an ironic counterpoint to earthly lovers, shows up in various writers, including Dante, Chaucer, and Spenser.

Recommended reading. Huber, Lynn R. *Like a Bride Adorned: Reading Metaphor in John's Apocalypse*. Emory Studies in Early Christianity. New York: T. & T. Clark International, 2007. McIlraith, Donal A. *The Reciprocal Love between Christ and the Church in the Apocalypse*. Rome: Columban Fathers, 1989.

See also ADULTERY; BRIDEGROOM, FRIEND OF THE [STS]

Bridegroom, Friend of the. In the Fourth Gospel, John the Baptist refers to himself as the 'friend of the bridegroom' (John 3.29), what today we might call 'the best man'. In NT times, marriage was an arrangement entered into by two families involving a formal betrothal with the wedding following at least a year later. In these arrangements the friend of the bridegroom had a major role.

When negotiating a marriage, the two fathers did not deal directly with each other but through deputies, including the bridegroom's friend, probably to avoid any loss of honor if the negotiations broke down. The two deputies negotiated the bride's dowry, which the bridegroom would pay and which would revert to the wife in case of divorce. When consent was reached, then the deputies and the fathers drank together as a sign of agreement. The betrothal was a very formal and binding agreement that could only be broken by divorce or death. The deputies drew up the marriage contract which was signed by the two fathers and then given to the bridegroom's friend. Because the bridegroom's friend played such a critical role in the negotiations there were ancient laws preventing the 'friend' ever marrying the intended bride even if the proposal was turned down.

The procession of the young woman from her father's house to the home of the bridegroom, usually arrived late in the day for the wedding ceremony, which was always in the evening. Sometimes the groom would lead the bride, and sometimes his 'friend.' The most solemn moment came when the bride entered into the home of the bridegroom. Often the bridegroom would travel in his own procession, arriving some hours later in the evening. The bridegroom's friend then led him into the bridal chamber and it seems that he awaited the call of the bridegroom to fetch the nuptial sheet to testify to the virginity of the bride.

In the creation story in Gen. 2, God is considered to have had the role of the friend of the bridegroom when, following the creation of Eve, God brings her to Adam. In the NT, some of these customs lie behind the parable of the ten maidens (Matt. 25.1-13). In the Gospel of John, Jesus' role as the bridegroom is implied in the Wedding at Cana when the head steward goes to the bridegroom to congratulate him on producing good wine late in the festivities (John 2.9-10). This would indicate that the bridegroom has the task of providing wine, and, in this case, it is Jesus who has provided the good wine. Thus this Gospel presents Jesus as the bridegroom and John the Baptist as the bridegroom's friend.

Recommended reading. Collins, J.J. 'Marriage, Divorce and Family in Second Temple Judaism'. In *Families in Ancient Israel*. Ed. C. Meyers. Pp. 104-62. Louisville, KY: Westminster John Knox, 1997. Satlow, F.P. *Jewish Marriage in Antiquity*. Princeton: Princeton University Press, 2001. Yamauchi, E.M. 'Cultural Aspects of Marriage in the Ancient World'. *Bibliotheca sacra* 135 (1978) 241-52.

See also JOHN, GOSPEL OF; BRIDE [MLC]

Brothers of the Lord. From the response of audiences in Mark 6.3, Matt. 13.55, and Luke 4.22, it is apparent that those in the early church knew Jesus' brothers and sisters. The brothers of Jesus named in the NT are James, Judas, Simon, and Joses. The NT letters attributed to Jude and James are often considered compositions by Jesus' brothers. Paul, in Gal. 1.19, mentions James the Lord's brother as someone he visited when in Jerusalem. Some debate Jesus' relationship to these so-called siblings, suggesting the Greek term *adelphos* can mean other things. Were they Jesus' immediate family members or part of his extended family? Saint Jerome suggested the 'brothers' of Jesus were in reality his cousins. The theory likely emerged to uphold the Catholic teaching of Mary's perpetual virginity. Contrary to Jerome, Epiphanius subscribes to the view that the brothers of the Lord were in fact his half-brothers (i.e., sons to Joseph's first wife). The Epiphanian view was widely accepted in the early church and is supported in an apocryphal writing called the *Protoevangelion*. In 9.1 of that work, we read that Joseph took a young wife called Mary at an advanced age.

[ET]

Bruised reed. This expression comes from Isa. 42.3: 'A bruised reed (*qane razuz*) he will not break, and a dimly burning wick he will not quench'. The Hebrew word for reed (*qane*) is generally applied to several kinds of grasses with jointed, hollow stems that grow along the banks of streams. They are mainly used for thatching and roofing. Reeds are very strong when they are kept intact, but become quite weak once they have been bruised. For this reason, they are considered worthless and are discarded. A bruised reed is more easily smashed than straightened, and a smouldering wick can be more easily blown out than fanned into a flame.

This image is part of a long description of the mission of the Servant of the Lord, or Suffering Servant (Isa. 40–66), a prophetic figure interpreted in several ways. For some it refers to the people of Israel and for others, the coming Messiah, who would show mercy, grace, and compassion to the outcasts of society. Some NT writers borrowed Isaiah's language for their descriptions of Jesus of Nazareth (e.g., Matt. 12.18-21).

Under the title *The Bruised Reed*, Richard Sibbes (1577–1635) wrote one of the most influential Puritan books in history for spiritual help and comfort. As an image suggesting gentleness toward those that are weak and vulnerable, the idea of treating a bruised reed gently appears often. One well-known example is the story of Anne Sullivan (1866–1936) and the education of Helen Keller (1880–1968), the first deaf and blind person to earn a Bachelor of Arts degree. This story became known worldwide through the play and film *The Miracle Worker* (1962). Another remarkable example is Mother Theresa (1910–1997), who ministered to the dying in Calcutta for over forty-five years, and founded the Missionaries of Charity. In a similar way, the Salvation Army focuses its mission on extending help and compassion to the outcast and meeting human needs in God's name 'without discrimination'.

The theme of compassion for the bruised reed touches us all. The unexpected results of trust, love and courage among despised, handicapped or abused people, has inspired moving films based on real stories of helpless cases who were given a second chance, such as *Midnight Express* (1978), *The Elephant Man* (1980), *Champions* (1984), *My Left Foot* (1989), *Schindler's List* (1993), *The Piano* (1993), *A Beautiful Mind* (2001), *Seabiscuit* (2003), *The Chorus* (2004), or *Invictus* (2009), based on the life of Nelson Mandela.

See also SUFFERING SERVANT [RB]

Burning bush. This phrase appears in a story about Moses. While on Mount Horeb, he saw a bush burning without being consumed (Exod. 3.1-6). This paradoxical event was a theophany during which Israel's God revealed the divine name to Moses and appointed him to lead the Israelites from Egypt into the promised land (Exod. 3.7-22). Theophanistic manifestations accompanied by fire (or clouds and smoke) are common in the HB, where God also appears in a pillar of fire (Exod. 13.21-22), speaks 'out of the fire' when proclaiming the covenant (Deut. 4.12), or executes punishment through consuming fire (Num. 16.35; Zech. 13.9). The Hebrew word for bush (*seneh*) designates brambles. In biblical texts it always refers to the theophany in the burning bush. Some scholars have thus suggested that this word might be a mistaken interpretation of the word 'Sinai', the mountain in the desert where God encountered all of Israel after the exodus from Egypt (Exod. 19.1-9; 24.1-11). It is, however, more likely that the Hebrew word *seneh* is a conscious pun using similarly sounding words, both of which refer to the sites of God's appearance.

The NT contains a few references to the burning bush which are coupled with allusions to God's self-revelation (Mark 12.26; Luke 20.37; Acts 7.30-35). In recent centuries, the image of the burning bush has become a frequent symbol of Protestant identity in various Reformed and Presbyterian Churches; the fire signifies the presence of God while the enduring bush that does not burn indicates perseverance in the face of religious persecution.

Recommended reading. Durham, John I. *Exodus*. Word Biblical Commentary, 3. Waco, TX: Word Books, 1987. Freedman, David N. 'The Burning Bush'. *Biblica* 50 (1969) 245-46.

See also FIRE; MOSES; SINAI, MOUNT [CAE]

C

Caiaphas. Caiaphas was the Jewish high priest between 18 and 37 CE. He was appointed by the Romans, and a participant in Jesus' trial after his arrest in the Garden of Gethsemane (Matt. 26.57-68; John 18.12-14, 19-24). Caiaphas also had a part in the trial of Peter and John described in Acts 4.1-22 (note especially vv. 5-6). Caiaphas appears in several artistic accounts of the events of passion week. For instance, he is a character in Charles Dunscomb's *Bond and the Free* (1955) and, with the first name 'Joseph', Taylor Caldwell's and Jess Stearn's *I Judas* (1977). When Dennis Potter's play *Son of Man* was first performed as a BBC1 television play on April 16, 1969, Bernard Hepton played Caiaphas. In film, Rudolph Schildkraut appeared as Caiaphas in *The King of Kings*, a silent film from 1927. Anthony Quinn played the character in *Jesus of Nazareth* (1977) and Mattia Sbragia in Mel Gibson's *The Passion of Christ* (2004). He was also played by Dob Gunton in *Judas* (2004) and by Kai Cofer in *The Life and the Passion of Christ* (2005).

Recommended reading. Brownrigg, Ronald. *Who's Who in the New Testament*. New York: Oxford University Press, 1993.

See also TRIAL OF JESUS; CHIEF PRIESTS [JC]

Cain. Cain was Adam and Eve's firstborn son, usually remembered for killing his young brother Abel (Gen. 4.1-16). This makes Cain not only the first human being born (Adam was made from the dust of the ground, and Eve from his rib [Gen. 2.7, 21]), but also the first murderer. When Cain brought 'the fruit of the ground' as an offering, the LORD had 'no regard' whereas Abel's offering of 'the firstlings of his flock' earned the LORD's 'regard'. This angered Cain who then committed fratricide. The account provided in Genesis includes the well-know reply Cain gives to the LORD when asked about the whereabouts of his brother: 'I do not know; am I my brother's keeper?' (4.9). Cain then learns the blood of his murdered brother cries out from the ground, and he is forced to wander because the ground is cursed to him: 'When you till the ground, it will no longer yield to you its strength; you will be a fugitive and a wanderer on the earth' (Gen. 4.12). This story is also the source of the expression 'mark of Cain'. The LORD puts this mark on him to assure him 'that no one who came upon him would kill him' (Gen. 4.15). Banished from the presence of the Lord, Cain went to the land of Nod, east of Eden, where he took a wife. Their son was named Enoch, as was the city Cain built (Gen. 4.16-19). His descendants to the sixth generation are described in Gen. 4.18-24.

The NT Book of Hebrews (11.4) cites Abel as a model of faith unlike Cain. John 3.12 warns Christians not to be like Cain who was from the evil one and Jude 11 denounces those who are seeking to pervert the faith once delivered to the saints as people like Cain. Lord Byron dramatized the story of Cain and Abel in his poem 'Cain'. William Blake wrote 'The Ghost of Abel' in direct reply to Lord Byron. It addresses the revenge, atonement, forgiveness, and self-annihilation present in the Cain and Abel story. Siegfried Sasson's *Ancient History* portrays Adam grieving over his lost sons. John Steinbeck's novel, *East of Eden* (1952) refers to the land of Nod to which Cain went. The novel, set in the Salinas Valley of California, retells the story of Cain in dramatic ways. It was made into movie in 1955.

Recommended reading. Schillman, Gabe. *Cain and Abel*. Fredrick, MD: Publishamerica, 2009. Collins, Wilkie. *The Legacy of Cain*. Stroud, Glos.: Sutton, 1993.

See also ABEL; ADAM; DEATH; EVE; SIN [AJW]

Caleb. Caleb (meaning 'dog') was a faithful Israelite spy and, in old age, a fearless head of the tribe of Judah who led the conquest of Canaan. When Moses first attempted to lead Israel into their 'promised land' after the Exodus, he chose twelve spies—one from each tribe—to examine the land (Num. 13.1-20). Ten came back demoralized by giant enemies and well-fortified cities, and publicly reported that invasion was impossible (Num. 13.27-28). This started a mutiny. Two spies, Caleb son of Jephunneh and Joshua son of Nun, tried to encourage Israel (Num. 13.30) but the depressed rabble ignored them and even threatened their lives. God initially stated an intention to destroy Israel completely, but Moses asked for mercy. Then God said Israel would wander the desert for forty years until that rebellious generation died, but Joshua and Caleb 'had a different spirit'. God promised Caleb's descendants would possess that land (Num. 14.24).

Forty-five years later, the 85-year-old Caleb was now tribal leader of Judah. When the conquest of Canaan began, he asked Joshua, now the national leader, for the right to attack a hilly region in the southern Negev desert, which was known to be occupied by giants. Caleb said he was still as strong as ever, and that God had promised him victory

(Josh. 14.6-15). After successfully taking the city of Hebron, he offered his daughter Achsah (perhaps from *akas*, meaning handcuffs, tinkling jewelry) to whoever could capture the city of Kiriath-sepher. A young man named Othniel (meaning, 'the force of God') won the city and the girl.

As the couple settled in the newly occupied land, Othniel urged Achsah to use a daughter's charm and ask Caleb for good property. Yet this proved unnecessary. When Caleb saw Achsah arrive, he asked her what she wanted. She asked for a well-irrigated portion of land and her father generously complied (Josh. 15.15-19 = Judg. 1.12-15).

That general region was later referred to as the Negeb of Caleb (1 Sam. 30.14). Its exact location is unknown, though it is possibly South of Hebron, where Caleb's descendant Nabal later lived (1 Sam. 25.2-3). Hebron was later given to the priestly tribe of Levi for a city of refuge, although Caleb's clan owned the surrounding district (Josh. 21.10-12; 1 Chron. 6.56). Perhaps ironically, Caleb was likely descended from Edomites, namely Kenaz (Gen. 36.15), the founder of a tribe of Kenazites who were mentioned among the peoples whose land Abraham's descendants would take (Gen. 15.19).

The name Caleb became popular after the Protestant Reformation, and Puritans brought it to America in the seventeenth century. It means dog, a term which can be pejorative (2 Kgs 8.13), yet the Hebrew spelling (or Masoretic pointing) of the name *kaleb* distances it from the usual word for a dog, *keleb*, and suggests faithfulness and strength.

The Bible also mentions one Caleb son of Hezron, also called Chelubai (1 Chron. 2.9, 18, 42). His descendants include Hur, Aaron's associate while Moses was away in Sinai, and Bezalel, the master craftsman whose work adorned the tabernacle and its furnishings (Exod. 31.2-11; 35.30-35; 1 Chron. 2.18-20). Some have identified Caleb son of Hezron with Caleb son of Jephunneh because both had a daughter named Achsah (1 Chron. 2.49), but this would create difficulties with chronology and other surrounding names. It may be a case of inherited names.

Recommended reading. Hawk, L. Daniel. *Joshua.* Collegeville, MN: Liturgical Press, 2000. Howard, David M., Jr. *Joshua.* Nashville, TN: Broadman and Holman Publishers, 1998.

See also JOSHUA; NUMBERS, BOOK OF [GK]

Calvary. The description of the place outside the walls of Jerusalem where Jesus was crucified, Calvary is only used once in the Bible (Luke 23.33), with Matthew, Mark and John referring to it as Golgotha. As all four Gospels also refer to it as the 'place of the Skull' (or in the case of Luke, 'the place which is called The Skull'), there is no doubting that Calvary was another name for Golgotha.

The name Calvary appears often outside of Israel. The town of Kalvarija in Lithuania was named after this biblical site—the ruins of a thirteenth-century castle shows that it dates back to medieval times. In neighboring Poland, the towns of Gora Kalwaria and Kalwaria Zebrzydowska also take their name from Calvary. A number of cemeteries around the world have also incorporated the name, as one located in Queens, New York, one of the oldest in the United States. Calvary appears in some hymns such as 'At Calvary' by William Newell.

There is also the Calvary Clover, a flower said to have sprung up on the tracks made by Pontius Pilate as he approached the cross. There is also a heraldic symbol known as the Cross Calvary, a Latin Cross mounted on three steps.

See also GOLGOTHA [JC]

Camel through a needle's eye. 'Again I tell you, it is easier for a camel to go through the eye of a needle than for someone who is rich to enter the kingdom of Heaven' (Matt. 19.24). Jesus uses this well-known phrase after encountering a rich man unwilling to leave his fortune behind to follow him. It is recorded in the other Synoptic Gospels (Mark 10.25, Luke 18.25) and similar phrases are found in extra-biblical literature.

Unsurprisingly, interpretations of the saying normally try to soften its strict literal reading. In the Middle Ages, the phrase was thought to refer to an invitation to join Christ in the trials of his Passion. Reformer John Calvin thought the phrase was a gloss and that 'camel' ought to read 'rope', given that the words sound similar in Aramaic, Jesus' native tongue. Finally, and most commonly, it has been taught for centuries that there was a low gate through the walls of Jerusalem which a Camel would have to stoop down to pass through, insinuating that the rich likewise must stoop to pass through heaven's gates. However, there appears to be no evidence such a gate existed outside of the story itself. The Talmudic phrase 'who can make an elephant pass through the eye of a needle' seems to make it likely that Jesus said and meant camel (rather than rope) and that it was a hyperbolic phrase designed to demonstrate the impossibility of obedience to

God without God's help. This point is underlined by Jesus' response to the apostle's astonishment at this teaching: 'For mortals it is impossible, but for God all things are possible' (Matt. 19.26). The Qur'an contains a similar saying: 'until the camel goeth through the needle's eye' (Sura 7.40). Here it is illustrative of the impossible, used in the same way we might say, 'when pigs fly'.

The phrase is often used in literature and popular culture as shorthand for the perennial issues between the rich and the poor. Other times it is used to describe the perceived difficulty in relating to God. Shakespeare's *Richard II* ponders the difficulty in reconciling Christ's invitation with the teaching that, 'It is as hard to come as for a camel / to thread the postern of a small needle's eye'. Robert Browning's 'The Pied Piper of Hamelin' uses the teaching to underscore the fable's own message. The citizens of Hamelin after cheating the Piper are reminded of 'A text which says that heaven's gate / Opes to the rich at as easy rate / As the Needle's Eye takes a Camel in'. Czech playwright František Langer's most successful piece was a comedy about lower class life entitled '...through the eye of a needle'. It was translated and produced on Broadway in 1929 and a Czech film was shot in 1936.

The Song 'Eye of the Needle' by Divine Comedy off their 2001 album *Regeneration* highlights the discontinuity between prosperous Western Christians and Christ's teaching. Congregants drive cars that are 'shiny and German / Distinctly at odds with the theme of the sermon' and during communion 'squeezing themselves through the eye of the needle'. The visual absurdity of a camel threading itself through a needle has meant that the image is sometimes used to comic effect, especially in political cartoons.

See also KINGDOM OF GOD (KINGDOM OF HEAVEN); RICH FOOL, PARABLE OF THE [JIM]

Cana. Cana is a town in Galilee the precise location of which is unknown. The only explicit evidence of its geography is the notice that Jesus 'went down' from Cana to Capernaum (John 2.12). Traditionally, Cana has dubiously been associated with Kefr Kenna, north of Nazareth. Other possibilities include 'Ain Qâna and the more likely possibility of Khirbet Qâna, both of which are within close proximity to Nazareth. Today, Khirbet Qâna is still locally referred to as 'Cana of Galilee', and recent archaeological discoveries of first-century artefacts have further strengthened the view that Khirbet Qâna is the probable location of the biblical Cana.

In the NT, Cana is mentioned only in the Gospel of John, and it is a place of great significance. Cana is best known as the place where, prior to his public ministry, Jesus performed his first miracle of turning water into wine after the wine provided by the bridegroom had run out (John 2.1-11). Cana is also the home of the disciple Nathaniel (21.2) and the place where Jesus performed his second miracle, or 'sign', by healing an official's son who was dying in Capernaum. Many scholars suggest that Cana comes from the Hebrew *qaneh* ('reed'); *qaneh* is mentioned in the Book of Joshua (19.28) as a place belonging to the tribe of Asher. Yet early Christian writers such as Origen (*Comm. Jo.* 13.62) and later Epiphanius (*Haer.* 51.30.10) held that Cana means 'the bride'. Thus, Cana is difficult to pinpoint both geographically and etymologically.

Because the miracle of the wine does not feature in the Synoptic Gospels, other scholars have questioned the historical veracity of this story, suggesting the miracle at Cana is intended to be an allegory. Interpreted allegorically, the lack of wine may be seen in OT terms as a spiritual famine that is replaced by the death and resurrection of Jesus. Other scholars have suggested that when Jesus changed the water into wine, it was symbolic of transubstantiation, the belief that the substance of the Eucharistic bread and wine are transformed into the substance of Christ's body and blood. Some NT critics suggest that Jesus' miracles at Cana derive from an earlier, albeit lost, 'signs source' that is embedded within the Gospel of John.

Modern understandings of Cana are varied. Although the town of Cana itself is an infrequent reference, Jesus' first miracle that occurred there is used in a variety of contexts. Some have interpreted Jesus' miracle of the wine at Cana as divine permission for the consumption of alcohol by Christians. Others suggest that the attendance of Jesus at the wedding in Cana is evidence that Jesus endorsed the sacrament of marriage. In western popular culture, Cana and the significance of the events recorded there can be found in various media. For example, television shows such as *King of the Hill* and *South Park* disparagingly portray Jesus' miracle as a clever magic trick, comedian Steve Harvey has incorporated Jesus' first miracle into his show, and the Dave Matthews Band uses Jesus' miracle at Cana metaphorically in their song 'Water into Wine'.

Recommended reading. Kopp, C. *The Holy Places of the Gospels*. Trans. Ronald Walls. New York: Herder & Herder, 1963. Richardson, P. 'What Has Cana to Do with Capernaum?' *New Testament Studies* 48 (2002) 314-31.

See also MIRACLES; SIGN; WEDDING AT CANA
[TSM]

Canaan, Canaanites. The Canaanites were a group of Semitic peoples who during the Bronze Age occupied what is today Jordan, Israel, Lebanon and Syria. In Israelite times, the Canaanites lived in Palestine west of the Jordan (Gen. 10.15-19; Josh. 5.1; 11.3). The Canaanites were well known as traders in cloth and wool products dyed in red-purple (Isa. 23.8; Prov. 31.10-25; 2 Chron. 2.7). Since 1929, our knowledge of Canaanite religion and culture improved, thanks to thousands of literary, ritual and administrative texts recovered from the libraries of ancient Ugarit (c. 1550–1200 BCE), a flourishing seaport on the North Syrian coast, now called Ras Shamra. The most important series of mythological texts, *The Epic of Baal*, narrate the conflicts between gods and goddesses (El, Baal, Yamm, Mot, Anat, Asherah). The Ugaritic parallels show that Canaanites and Israelites shared a common culture and that Canaanite imagery is dominant in historical and prophetic texts, as well as in the poetry of the Psalms and wisdom writings (e.g., Exod. 15; Judg. 5; Pss 29, 82, 93–99; Hos. 2; 6; Job 7.12). The Canaanites are best known in contexts involving the Israelites entrance to the promised land. Before Israel could possess the land 'flowing with milk and honey', they were required to drive the Canaanites out, with divine assistance (Josh. 3.10, etc.).

The conquest of the Canaanites is anticipated in earlier biblical narratives. According to Gen. 9.18, Noah's son Ham was the father of Canaan. Because Ham was guilty of an impropriety, Noah cursed Canaan and his descendants (9.25). The Israelites eventually settled in the land of Canaan, though they never fully dispossessed those original inhabitants or eliminated Baal worship (e.g., Gen. 12.6b-7; 13.7b; 24.37; Num. 13.29; 14.39-45; Josh. 16.10; 17.12-13; 24; Judg. 1; 2.2-3, 11-13; 9.4; 2 Sam. 24.5-7; 1 Kgs 18). Noah's curse on Canaan in Gen. 9.25 foreshadows a persistent diatribe against the Canaanites, prohibiting treaties and marriages with them, and condemning the adoption of their religious and sexual practices (e.g., Deut. 7.2-5, 25-26; 12.2-4; 13.7-19; 23.17-18; 1 Kgs 12.28-33; 2 Kgs 23).

Exegetes have long struggled with the story of Noah's curse because Ham was the obvious sinner and the curse on Ham's son appears unjustified. Partly in response to this ambiguity, the sixteenth and seventeenth centuries witnessed the gradual disappearance of the curse of Canaan in biblical commentaries and dictionaries. The Coverdale Bible (1535) introduces Gen. 9: 'Noe is dronken, Ham uncoverth him, and getteth his curse'. Other Bibles translated the curse on Canaan (Gen. 9.25) but omitted chapter introductions referring to him (e.g., Martin Luther's Bible, 1534; Geneva Bible, 1560; Bishop's Bible, 1568; Douay–Rheims Bible, 1582/1609–1610). The authorized King James Version (1611) discussed Canaan in its commentary on Gen. 9, but could not prevent Canaan's marginalization. This subtle removal or minimizing of Canaan's role in the story was instrumental in shifting Noah's curse toward Ham and his African descendants in some interpretations of the passage. This had terrible consequences. Turning the curse of Canaan into the curse of Ham provided a 'biblical' rationale for the African slave trade, serving to justify the monstrous idea that black Africans were Ham's cursed descendants, doomed to perpetual bondage.

Recommended reading. Whitford, David, M. *The Curse of Ham in the Early Modern Era: The Bible and the Justifications for Slavery.* Burlington, VT: Ashgate, 2009.

See also HAM; JAPHETH; JOSHUA; JOSHUA, BOOK OF; SHEM
[JRW]

Canaanite (Syrophoenician) woman, the. The Gospel of Mark's story of the Syrophoenician woman (Mark 7.24-30) is paralleled in Matthew's Gospel with that of the Canaanite woman (Matt. 15.21-28). Matthew's story has long controlled the history of interpretation. The 'Sunday of the Canaanitess' is a fixed day in the Orthodox liturgical calendar and is celebrated with an accent on the transition of the gospel from its Jewish roots into Gentile reception.

The story features a woman of foreign ethnicity and without embedding in a male guardian. She approaches the Jewish healer, Jesus of Nazareth, seeking the healing of her possessed daughter, only to receive a strong rebuff. However, she refuses to accept the rejection and delivers an answer that is praised as an example of great faith in Matthew's telling and as a healing word in Mark's Gospel. The conclusion of both stories emphasizes the restoration of the daughter.

By naming the woman as Canaanite, Matthew's version evokes the long traditions of enmity with Jews. Her presence testifies against the thorough execution of the Joshua pogrom on the earlier inhabitants of the land (Josh. 11.20), and her liturgical language in her plea to Jesus ('Have mercy on me,

Lord, son of David') lays claim to the temple worship from which her race is banned (Zech. 14.21). Her answer to Jesus' ethnocentric rebuttal wrings the breakthrough of healing for foreign women by the exercise of faith (cf. Matt. 8.5-13) and is taken as indicating the breakthrough of the early Jesus movement into Gentile acceptance and even as the model of humble, acquiescent piety, especially in earlier interpretations.

By contrast, the Markan story accents the triumph of the word, not the faith, of a woman—'for saying that' (v. 29). The contest between the words of Jesus and the words of the woman has dominated the history of interpretation in the last two centuries. A barely hidden apologetic exoneration for Jesus' harsh words has been sought through postulating a humorous or ironic by-play, the non-committed use of a Jewish proverb antipathetic to dogs, the pedagogical cultivation of the woman's faith or the development of the historical Jesus' awareness of his mission. Conversely, especially among feminist and two-thirds-world interpreters, the word of the woman has been prized as the voice of women in the shaping of the gospel, as the vanguard of the Gentile mission, as the resistance of a dominated group against a colonizing master, as a preservation of the integrity of local culture, as a shaper of the Christian message, and even as a Cynic philosopher's wit that subverts conventional perspectives.

Usually overlooked is the importance of the Syrophoenician daughter, who not only repeatedly anchors the flow of the narrative and exchange of dialogue but who provides the culminating point of the story. The household of two women, mother and daughter, becomes the final repudiation of any patriarchal necessity for the appropriation of the gospel (cf. Mark 10.30 with the omission of 'fathers' in the household of the reign of God). More significantly, this aspect of the story lays the foundation for the dramatic privileging of children in and for the reign of God (Mark 9.36-37; 10.13-16).

Recommended reading. Cadwallader, A. *Beyond the Word of a Woman: Recovering the Bodies of the Syrophoenician Women*. Adelaide: ATF Press, 2008. Schüssler Fiorenza, E. *But She Said: Feminist Practices of Biblical Interpretation*. Boston: Beacon Press, 1992. Jackson, G. *'Have Mercy on Me': The Story of the Canaaanite Woman in Matthew 15.21-28*. London and New York: Sheffield Academic Press, 2002.

See also WOMAN; GENTILES; CANAAN, CANAANITES; MARK, GOSPEL OF; MATTHEW, GOSPEL OF; CHILD

[AHC]

Candle. The term candle, referring to long cylinders made of wax or tallow with a cloth cord in the center for a wick, is used in the King James Version (and a few other versions) where 'lamp' or 'light' should be use. This translation is inaccurate because candles were unknown in the centuries in which the OT was written. While it is possible that they could have been available in NT times, it is unlikely that they had any common use. The method of lighting used in the Ancient Middle East was oil lamps.

The Bible does not give a specific description of the form or material of 'lamps' so it usually assumed that they are the ones typically found by archeologists. The invention of oil lamps was a great advance in human technology. The oil lamps had two main parts: a container for the oil and a place for the wick. The oil was usually olive oil which would soak the fabric (usually linen) used as a wick and then burn, giving off light. Salt added to the wick gave a brighter flame.

The tabernacle had a single lampstand made of gold onto which lamps were placed. Solomon's temple had ten golden lampstands (1 Kgs 7.49) with multiple branches for holding the lamps. After the Temple was restored by Nehemiah, it used a single lampstand. However, after the Temple was looted several times the multi-branch lampstand was adopted. This is apparently the lampstand that is identified as a menorah in 1 Maccabees and seen in Rome on the Arch of Titus. The Book of Revelation describes seven golden lampstands that are of the original single lamp style. Symbolically Revelation extends the vision of Zachariah of two lampstands that suggest two trees beside the lampstand.

In the parable of the Ten Virgins (Matt. 25.1) the Wise Virgins trim their wicks, the foolish ones did not, symbolizing disobedience to Christ. Among symbolic uses, the lamp represents the Word of God (Ps. 119.105), salvation (Isa. 62.1), God's guidance (2 Sam. 22.29; Ps. 18.22; Prov. 6.23), wise rulers (2 Sam. 21.17; John 5.35), life (Job 21.17), and Christ as the light of the world (John 8.12).

Recommended reading. Dowley, Tim. *Living in Bible Times*. Grand Rapids, MI: Lion Hudson, 2008. Smith, R.H. *Biblical Archaeologist* 27 (1964) 1-31, 101-24.

See also LIGHT UNDER A BUSHEL; MACCABEES, BOOKS OF; OLIVE, OLIVE BRANCH; OIL; PARABLE; TABERNACLE; TEMPLE; TREE OF LIFE; WISE AND FOOLISH VIRGINS

[AJW]

Canon. The word canon refers to an authoritative guide to a particular subject. Various churches have recognized many kinds of canon lists, such as a canon of saints or a canon of ethical or ecclesiastical laws. In biblical studies, canon refers to a list of ancient books that has been recognized by the church as its authoritative guide to its beliefs and practices. The books were considered ancient because they supposedly had the authorization of prophets or apostles. The books were recognized through liturgical and ecclesiastical usage in Christian churches in widespread geographical locations. The books were adopted because they bore the rule of faith (*regula fidei*).

The major branches of the Christian church have inherited differing lists of books considered to be Holy Scripture. The differences are mainly in what is called the First or Old Testament (OT). Catholic and Orthodox churches inherited the First Testament books generally found in the Septuagint (LXX), which is a Christian adoption of mostly Jewish Scriptures translated into Greek and some Jewish Scriptures composed in Greek. That the LXX is a Christian adaptation can be seen in some early manuscripts that include specifically Christian content such as 'The Song of Mary the *Theotikos*' from Luke 1. Protestant churches chose the Jewish Scriptures that are in Hebrew. The Protestant First Testament is essentially the same as the HB, although the books are arranged according to the Septuagint and have Septuagintal names.

The canon of NT books of almost all Christian churches is the same. In the time immediately after the death of Jesus (and probably even before), his Jewish followers regarded the Jewish Bible to be authoritative, but they also thought of the teachings of Jesus as authoritative alongside the written Jewish texts. Almost immediately, due to the teaching of Jesus concerning his apostles, the church regarded the teaching of the apostles, both in oral and written forms, as the 'rule of faith'. The teachings of Jesus and the apostles formed the New Covenant 'canon' set beside the Old Covenant canon. As the apostles passed off the scene, their writings came to be recognized as authoritative and thus as canonical, to be used in the worship services of the church, in the recognition of orthodoxy and heresy, and as a means of encountering Jesus through the work of the Holy Spirit. So the NT canon is believed to have authority because it bears the teaching of Jesus, which he delivered to his apostles, and which they in turn passed on to succeeding generations of Christians through their writings. The list of canonical books was finalized under the emperor Constantine in the fourth century, but the process of canonization began in the time of the apostles. The story of the canonization of Jewish and Christian scriptures is the story of a quest for authority.

The historical-critical method virtually ignores the canonical status of biblical books in the process of interpretation. For this method, the origin of the books is crucial. On the other hand, approaching biblical books as a part of a divinely inspired canon creates an interpretive context, linking passages across historical and geographical proximities. Thus, for example, the Gospel of John can say Moses wrote about Jesus (John 5.46). Christian theology is based on such intertextual readings. Canonically based intertextual readings were common in Jewish interpretation as evidenced in the Mishnah, Talmuds, and Midrashim. This is clearly how the early Christians read the Jewish Scriptures and composed the Scriptures of the New Covenant.

Recommended reading. McDonald, Lee Martin. *The Biblical Canon: Its Origin, Transmission, and Authority*. Peabody, MA: Hendricksen, 2007.

See also OLD TESTAMENT; NEW TESTAMENT [DHJ]

Catholic Epistles. As many as twenty-one out of twenty-seven NT books are 'letters'. Thirteen of these are attributed to Paul, and one (the anonymous Hebrews), though best defined as a sermon, includes epistolary qualities (see Heb. 13.22-25). The remaining seven 'letters' are variously labelled 'Catholic' or 'General' epistles. In modern Bibles, they appear as a group in the penultimate position, prior to Revelation: James, 1–2 Peter, 1–2–3 John, and Jude.

While this arrangement appears to come from the Vulgate, a fourth-century CE Latin translation of the Bible, variations in order exist among early copies of the NT and other Christian writings. Hence the grouping of the seven was not self evident from the outset but resulted from the lengthy NT canonization process during which time the term 'catholic' was applied to individual letters. In the fourth century, Eusebius (an early church historian) and then Athanasius (bishop of Alexandria) used the term catholic to designate the group. The significance of the designation is not entirely clear, though it serves to differentiate these books from Paul's letters and captures a shared quality of most of them, namely their address to non-specific audiences (2–3 John are obvious exceptions).

While the Catholic Epistles generally receive less attention than the Gospels and Paul's writings, recent scholarly trends are working to redress the imbalance. Disputes are ongoing over such matters as authorship and time of writing, literary relations, structural and rhetorical features, and social setting. While some scholars reject the homogeneity of the group, others detect an intrinsic thematic unity with James as the representative head. One strikingly common element is the direct connection of the ostensible authors to the historical Jesus. Whereas Jude and James are seemingly blood relatives (brothers), Peter and John were key players among his twelve disciples. The latter three are called 'pillars' of the church by Paul (Gal. 2.9) and play an important role in the early chapters of Acts.

If the authorship designations are authentic, the Catholic Epistles are important contributions from those close to the historical Jesus. More often, these writings are considered pseudonymous, at least in part, representing ecclesiastical interests of the late first or early second century (1–2–3 John are actually anonymous, though traditionally attributed to the disciple John). Their perspective is often seen as providing a contrast to Paul who himself had no direct contact with the earthly Jesus.

Individual motifs echoed in contemporary culture include the fallen angels of Jude 6 (cf. Gen. 6.1) in the movie *Blade Runner*, as well as dualistic notions of alien worlds in combat, detectable for example in 1 John, in the movie *The Matrix*. Matters of perennial interest such as politics, slavery, marriage, and innocent suffering are the subject matter of 1 Pet. 2.11–4.19. Saint Peter, the ostensible author of this letter, enjoys iconic status in the Roman Catholic Church as the original 'Pope' whose burial site is below the famous basilica in Rome. In popular culture, he stands guard at heaven's gates.

Recommended reading. Harner, Philip B. *What are They Saying about the Catholic Epistles?* New York: Paulist Press, 2004.

See also CANON; JAMES, EPISTLE OF; PETER, EPISTLES OF; JOHN, EPISTLES OF; JUDE, EPISTLE OF   [DUNR]

Cattle. Animals appear frequently in the Bible which is not surprising given their presence as a regular part of daily life. This is certainly the case with cattle, which are mentioned hundreds of times in a variety of ways, both literally and metaphorically. For instance, Jabal is described as the ancestor of those who have livestock (Gen. 4.20). The possession of cattle often denotes wealth, which is true of Abram (Gen. 13.2), the Reubenites and Gadites (Num. 32.1). God himself is described as the owner of 'cattle on a thousand hills' (Ps. 50.50). Cattle are involved in many Levitical instructions, including instructions regarding sacrifice (see Lev. 1–9; Heb. 9.12-19). They are slaughtered for special meals (Gen. 18.8; Judg. 6.25-28; Matt. 22.4; Luke 15.23-24) and given as gifts to cement covenantal promises (Gen. 21.27). Some Torah regulations emphasize the wellbeing of domesticated animals. A straying animal was to be returned to safety (Exod. 23.4; Deut. 22.1), a fallen animal was not to be ignored, but rather helped to its feet (Deut. 22.4), and while treading grain, an ox was not to be muzzled as this would prevent it from eating while working (Deut. 25.4; cf. 1 Cor. 9.9; 1 Tim. 5.18). Furthermore, the commands regarding Sabbath observance extend to cattle (Exod. 20.10; 23.12; Deut. 5.14).

Animals also function as symbols and metaphors in visions, dreams, and prophecy. Joseph interprets the lean cows in Pharaoh's dream as indicators of famine (Gen. 41.26-36), Amos describes the unjustly wealthy Samaritan noblewomen as the fat cows of Bashan (Amos 4.1), and Jeremiah describes Egypt as a 'beautiful heifer' (Jer. 46.20), perhaps to indicate both wealth and helplessness (cf. 46.15). Other striking symbolic uses of cattle appear in Ezek. 1.10 and Rev. 4.7.

Several contemporary writers have drawn attention to the moral vision regarding just treatment of animals (in the OT especially), in order to criticize the harsh commoditization and treatment of creatures which has resulted from the relatively recent industrialization of horticulture. In contrast to the actual context in which cattle often now live, idealized pastoral representations continue to persist in cultural representation. Cattle are a central part of the creche (or nativity) and the Christmas carol 'Magnum Mysterium' marvels at 'the great mystery ... that animals should see the new-born Lord'.

Recommended reading. Borowski, Oded. *Every Living Thing: Daily Use of Animals in Ancient Israel*. Walnut Creek, CA: AltaMira Press, 1998.

See also AMOS; ANIMALS, SYMBOLISM OF; COWS OF BASHAN; NAMING OF THE ANIMALS   [JHK]

Chaldeans. The Chaldeans were residents of Chaldea or the swampy lower Tigris and Euphrates River delta. The Bible's first reference to the Chaldeans is Gen. 11.28. Haran the son of Terah died in 'Ur of the Chaldeans'. Gen. 11.31 says that Terah left Ur of the Chaldeans with his son Abram and the rest of his family. There is one reference to the Chaldeans in the NT (Acts 7.4) and eighty in the OT (in Genesis, 2 Kings, 2 Chronicles, Ezra, Nehemiah, Job, Isaiah, Jeremiah, Ezekiel and Daniel).

Some scholars believe that the Chaldeans originated in the mountains of Kurdistan, others that they were inhabitants of Urartu (Ararat in Armenia), and others suggest they were one of the Cushite tribes that lived on the alluvial plain of Mesopotamia. These maintain the remains of their language are close to Galla, which was the ancient language of Ethiopia. The Chaldeans were called Kaldu by the Assyrians, Kasdu by the Babylonians and Kasddim in Hebrew. They were associated with the city of Kaluadha. They were first mentioned in the Assyrian chronicles of King Ashurnasirpal II (884/3–859 BCE). In 850, the Assyrian king Shalmaneser III raided to the Persian Gulf, which he called the 'Sea of Kaldu'.

In 721 BCE, Sargon II ascended the Assyrian throne and was immediately faced with the seizure of the Babylonian throne by Merodach-apla-iddina II (biblical Merodach-Baladan, Isa. 39.1) ruler of the Bit-Uakin district of Babylonia. In 711, Merodach-Baladan sent a delegation to visit King Hezekiah of Judah in order to invite him to join a Babylonian (Chaldean) led confederacy (2 Kgs 20.12-19; Isa. 39.1-8). Merodach-Baladan was forced to flee in 710 as the Assyrians retook the region. In 625, Nabopolassar, a governor in Babylonia took the throne of Babylonia with widespread approval. Allied with the Medes and Scythians he destroyed the Assyrian Empire. His kingdom was then called the New Babylonian Empire or the Chaldean Empire. The Chaldean Empire continued to expand under Nabopolassar and his son Nebuchadnezzar (who looted and burned Jerusalem in 586 and then deported its people). After Nebuchadnezzar the Chaldeans declined rapidly and were conquered by the Persians under Cyrus the Great in 539. The terms Babylonian and Chaldean became virtually synonymous during the Chaldean Empire. The biblical term Chaldean eventually came to mean anyone from the region of Babylon (Jer. 21.4, 9; 35.11; 51.4, 54; Ezek. 16.29).

Ancient Greek writers such as Herodotus and Strabo described the Chaldean priests as magicians as did St Athanasius in *De incarnatione* (48–51). The *Chaldean Oracles* can be traced to a Hellenistic commentary on sources believed to have originated in Chaldea (Babylon). The scholastics and some Reformation commentators used them as symbols of idolatry.

Recommended reading. Woolley, Leonard. *Ur of the Chaldees: A Record of Seven Years of Excavation*. New York: W.W. Norton, 1965.

See also BABYLON; ASSYRIA [AJW]

Chariot. A chariot is a lightweight, two-wheeled, horse-drawn vehicle. An outgrowth of earlier four-wheeled ox- or ass-drawn carts, the first chariots were prestige vehicles (see Gen. 41.43; 50.9) that only later came to be used militarily.

The chariot's battlefield potential came to be fully realized only after the Sack of Babylon by Murshili I (1531 BCE [Low Chronology]). In the HB, the prophet Samuel warned the Israelites that, if they went through with their plans to acquire a king, he would 'take your sons and appoint them to his chariots and to be his horsemen, and to run before his chariots' (1 Sam. 8.11). Fielding a chariot force required great expenditures, not only to build the chariots (and likely to import the raw materials) but also to train the horses and both train and equip the chariot warriors. Thus, chariot forces were a major factor separating prosperous, 'civilized' kingdoms from 'barbarians'. The classic chariot team consisted of a chariot pulled by two horses and manned by two warriors: a driver and an archer. Hittite chariot teams also had a shield-bearer, and apparently spears were the weapon of choice rather than the composite bow.

During the Late Bronze Age, chariotry was central to the ancient armies of Egypt, Hatti, Syria, Mesopotamia, Greece, and India. Infantry served mainly in support positions: guarding the camp, escorting chariots on the march, and so on. Obviously, this form of combat was only effective on the alluvial plains; rough terrain rendered chariots largely ineffective. This form of warfare is reflected in the crossing of the Red Sea (Exod. 14), famously depicted in Cecil B. DeMille's *The Ten Commandments*.

With the end of the Bronze Age, new infantry tactics and equipment led to the demise of the great chariot armies. Infantry supplanted the chariot's former preeminence, and chariots were ultimately replaced even in support roles by mounted cavalry some time after c. 900 BCE. When chariots were used after that, it was usually to transport officers to and from the battlefield (see 1 Kgs 22.34; 2 Kgs 23.30). Coming full circle, the chariot was once again a prestige vehicle with limited military applications. Chariots mainly enter modern consciousness as racing vehicles, as in *Ben Hur*, the Beach Boys' 'Fun Fun Fun', and, obliquely, the pod races in *Star Wars: The Phantom Menace*.

In the biblical narratives, chariots are depicted both as non-military and as military vehicles—as either 'limousines' or 'tanks'—depending upon the era being represented. When used symbolically, chariots are usually associated with warfare or military might (Ps. 20.7; Ezek. 23.24; Joel 2.5; Rev. 9.9).

God is sometimes depicted riding a chariot. Ezekiel 1.4-26 describes God's 'throne chariot', a four-wheeled vehicle driven by four supernatural creatures (cf. Ezek. 10). This is perhaps reminiscent of 'the golden chariot of the cherubim' in 1 Chron. 28.18 and other passages in which God is mounted upon cherubim (Ps. 18.10). At any rate, Ezekiel's vision is the basis for Hellenistic-era esoteric speculations that eventually gave rise to Merkabah (literally, 'chariot') mysticism within Judaism. The African American spiritual 'Swing Low, Sweet Chariot' anticipates such a vehicle transporting one's soul to heaven.

According to the biblical writers, God also has an angelic chariot force at his disposal, as in 2 Kgs 6.17 and Ps. 68.17. Second Kings 2.11-12 describes how a fiery chariot separated Elijah from Elisha as the former was taken up to heaven in a whirlwind.

Recommended reading. Drews, Robert. *The Coming of the Greeks*. Princeton: Princeton University Press, 1988. Drews, Robert. *The End of the Bronze Age*. Princeton: Princeton University Press, 1993.

See also CHERUBIM AND SERAPHIM [DJP]

Cherubim and Seraphim. The term Cherubim appears 91 times in the HB and they function as guardians of the divine throne and the sacred tree. Based on the iconography, they parallel the sphinx in Egyptian traditions. The term Seraphim appears 7 times in the HB (Num. 21.6, 8; Deut. 8.15; Is 6.2, 6; 14.29; 30.6). The term comes from the Hebrew verb 'to burn' and that has led to the understanding of the Seraphim as fiery serpents with human attributes that praise Yahweh and engage in acts of purification. The role of the Seraphim expands in Second Temple literature. In the hierarchy of angels, Pseudo-Dionysius places Cherubim on the second level of importance and during the middle ages the Seraphim were considered the highest order (the angelic choir).

The Cherubim and Seraphim were depicted by Andrea Mantegna in 1460 in a painting entitled *Madonna and Child with the Cherubim and Seraphim*. These characters have been a vivid source of inspiration for many artists throughout art history.

In 1926, the Cherubim and Seraphim movement was begun in Nigeria under the leadership of Moses Orimolade Tunolase. The name is said to have been divinely inspired over the course of two years but these characters do not feature prominently in the theology of the movement. It now has 28 churches in 5 divisions, including North America. These names have been used in popular titles that have little to do with the actual character. An example of this is the Inspector Morse episode 'Cherubim and Seraphim' that aired in 1992.

See also CHERUBIM AND SERAPHIM; ANGEL; DIVINE COUNCIL, THE; YAHWEH; ASHERAH (ASHTORETH) [EW]

Chief priests. According to the NT, the *archiereis* or 'chief priests' were members of a Jewish sect or group called the Sadducees (Acts 4.6). Priesthood was hereditary in Judaism, and thus the chief priests would have come from high priestly families, descending from Levi. The primary role of the priests was to act as mediator between the Jewish people and God. Thus, their primary duties would have involved ritual sacrifice and the running of the temple. The leader of the priesthood was called the *archiereus*, or high priest; during Jesus' ministry this was Caiaphas, although his father-in-law Annas is also named in some Gospel accounts.

Since the NT is our only source of information about the historical relationship between the chief priests and Jesus, only one side of the story has been preserved, and it provides us very little general information about the chief priests. It is clear from the Jesus narratives, however, that the chief priests were certainly considered among the primary antagonists of the early Christian movement, and that they were in opposition to both Jesus' teaching and to the later preaching of the resurrection by Jesus' followers.

Appearing in all four Gospel accounts, as well as Acts, the chief priests are all but directly blamed for the death of Jesus; they are consistently portrayed as instrumental in the plot to kill Jesus, as well as the handing of him over to Pilate to be condemned to death. In Acts, we learn that it is on the chief priests' authority that Jesus' followers are to be imprisoned (Acts 9.14), however in all accounts the chief priests rarely act alone, and are usually cited as working together with other Jewish authorities, including the scribes, the elders of the community, the council, and the Pharisees.

The chief priests have often been portrayed in biblical art, and not surprisingly in a negative light. One painting, by the French artist James Tissot (1836–1902) bears the colorful title *The Evil Council of Caiaphas*, which rather accurately describes how Caiaphas and the chief priests have been consistently portrayed for nearly two millennia. Popular scenes to be illustrated include depictions of Jesus before the Sanhedrin, and the payment of Judas. In most paintings, however, it is Caiaphas (sometimes with Annas) who is obviously the central antagonist, with the chief priests or council as an anonymous mob often placed behind or off to the side of him. An exception is found in depictions of the council conspiring against Jesus, however, in which all subjects are as a rule equally incriminated. An example of this is another painting by Tissot—*The Chief Priests Take Counsel Together*—in which the chief priests are portrayed in the foreground in luxurious attire and lavish temple surroundings, creating a stark contrast to the commoners (possibly followers of Jesus) who are conservatively shown in the middle ground.

Portrayals of the chief priests in films are as a rule no different from their painted counterparts. One particularly striking depiction, however, appears in the Andrew Lloyd Webber musical *Jesus Christ Superstar* (1973). In the film, Caiaphas and council scrutinize Jesus and his followers from atop makeshift scaffolding in flapping black robes, not unlike a flock of carrion crows. While actually somewhat sympathetic to Jesus, who Caiaphas admits is 'cool', they give the argument that Jesus and his followers are dangerous for the Jews, being under Roman rule. To their credit, the other members of the council at least exchange unsettled looks before joining in the chorus led by Caiaphas: 'so like John before him, this Jesus must die!'

See also PRIEST; CAIAPHAS [EJW]

Child. This term translates the Hebrew *bat* (daughter), *bēn* (son, grandchild), *na'ar* (little boy, infant), *yeled* (boy), or *yaldah* (girl); from the Greek, *brephos* (unborn child, infant), *pais* (a very small child, servant), *paidion* (child below the puberty stage), *teknon* (child), or *teknion/paidarion* (little child). 'Child' is a relational term between the children (small or grown-up) and their living/non-living parents. It is evident in the genealogy, traced through the male line of descent (Num. 1.1-46; Luke 3.23-38; some mention daughters, see Gen. 5), underscoring God's covenant with the people through Abraham, Isaac, and Israel/Jacob as well as King David (Matt. 1.1-17).

A child is a divine blessing (Gen. 1.28). Women endeavor to give birth to at least one (Gen. 29–30, 1 Sam. 1–2). Some children are born twins (Gen. 25.21-28). In the Bible, children relate to parents in an interdependent cycle. They become the adults who take care of the past generation and continue the future of the extended family as a people in covenant with God. This is underscored in the circumcision of the boy-child (Gen. 17.10-14).

Children need nurturance (Ruth 4.16; 1 Tim. 5.10). They are also educated by the community in their covenantal relationship with God and their responsibility with one another (Deut. 11.19; Ps. 78.5). They must honor their parents (Exod. 20.12). Brought up by the women in their tender age within the domestic sphere, they gradually partake of everyday tasks (Jer. 7.18). In puberty, they begin to assume gender-specific work (1 Sam. 16.11). Biblically, children at play is rarely mentioned (Gen. 21.9; Matt. 11.16-17) but it is one of the images of the messianic times (Isa. 11.8; Zech. 8.5). Children's value is not only functional but also rooted in their relationship with the Creator even from the womb (Ps. 139.13-14). They should not grow independent from God (Hos. 11.3).

Children need deliverance from illness (Mark 7.24-30; Matt. 15.21-28), slavery (2 Kgs 4.1-7), and death caused by sickness (2 Kgs 4.18-37; Mark 5.21-43). They also need protection from ill-will, which is the case with Moses and Jesus, and their contemporaries (Exod. 1.15-22; Matt. 2). God stops Abraham from sacrificing his son Isaac (Gen. 22; see also Mic. 6.6-8).

In the NT, Jesus appears in the Gospels as a baby, and briefly as an adolescent (Matt. 1–2; Luke 1–2). He later blesses children (Mark 10.13-16; Luke 18.15-17). A child shares his five barley loaves and two fish before Jesus could feed the multitude (John 6.1-13). Regardless of age, Jesus refers to his disciples (John 13.33) and older people as children (Luke 19.9; Matt. 9.2; Mark 5.34). Children feature in Jesus' parables (Matt. 21.28-32; Luke 15.11-32) and sayings (Mark 13.12; Matt. 10.21). He underlines the children's teachability as a model for Christian life (Matt. 18.2-4; Luke 9.46-48). Some NT epistles writers developed the childhood theme to underline their relationship with their communities and to solicit their obedience (1 Thess. 2.7-11; 1 Cor. 4.14; 2 Cor. 6.13; 1 Pet. 1.14; 3 John 4).

The image of the child is important in Western culture. Artworks abound concerning the life of the child Jesus, particularly in scenes when he appears with the Madonna. Depiction of children in danger like the *Aqedah* and the Massacre of the Innocents are also well-known subjects. In contemporary society, children's choirs, like the Vienna Boys Choir, are famous. In the 1989 United Nations' Convention of the Rights of the Child, the full range of children's human rights—civil, political, cultural, social, and economic—are enumerated.

See also JESUS, CHILDHOOD OF; ISRAEL, CHILDREN OF; SON OF GOD [MALOUSI]

Children of God. The relationship between God and his chosen people is often described in the Bible in terms of a parent-child relationship. This metaphor is in fact not unique to the Bible; the conception of divine parenthood was common throughout the ancient Near East, as is evidenced in the great number of personal names with the form 'god/goddess X is my father/mother.'

In the HB, the phrase 'children of God' (*bene Elohim*) is most often an exclusive expression designating Israel as a people. In Deut. 14.1-2, the Israelites are said to be God's children because God 'has chosen [them] out of all the peoples on the earth to be his people, his treasured possession'. God is said to have compassion on his children (Ps. 103.13), but he also disciplines them when they rebel (Ezek. 20.21). NT authors expand this motif, extending the right to become God's children (*tekna theou; huioi theou*) to everyone (John 1.12; Rom. 8.14; 1 John 5.1). The Apostle Paul emphasizes this point: 'For in Christ Jesus you are all children of God through faith … There is no longer Jew nor Greek, there is no longer slave nor free, there is no longer male nor female' (Gal. 3.26-28). The author of 1 John contrasts children of God with children of the devil: the former do not sin, while the latter 'do not do what is right' and 'do not love their brothers and sisters' (3.8-10). In the Beatitudes, Jesus proclaims that peacemakers will be blessed as children of God (Matt. 5.9).

In contemporary culture, the idea of 'children of God' appears frequently as a theme in human rights and social justice movements. In his famous 'I Have a Dream' speech, Martin Luther King, Jr envisages 'that day when all of God's children, black men and white men, Jews and Gentiles, Protestants and Catholics, will be able to join hands and sing in the words of the old Negro spiritual: 'Free at last! Free at last! Thank God Almighty, we are free at last!' The hit charity single, 'We Are the World' (1985), composed by Michael Jackson and Lionel Richie, also employs this motif: 'We are all a part of / God's great big family / And the truth, you know love is all we need'.

Not all twentieth-century applications of this idea have been for humanitarian causes. A popular science fiction novel entitled *Children of God* (1998) by New York Times Best Selling Author Mary Doria Russell explores the themes of cultural misunderstandings and the problems of evil and suffering. 'The Children of God' was also the name of a new religious movement that emerged in the late 1960s, although it was later renamed 'The Family'. The movement, which derived from American fundamentalist Christianity adapted to the youth counter-culture of the 1960s, has aroused major criticism and antagonism as a result of its aberrant sexual practices.

The phrase 'children of God', both in the Bible and in contemporary culture, evokes images of innocence, dependence, protection, affection, and above all relatedness. It is an expression which no doubt for many reflects a future hope for peace, security, and contentment.

See also ABBA; ADOPTION; CHILD; FAMILY; FIRSTBORN; HEIR; ISRAEL, CHILDREN OF; SONS OF GOD

[BRO]

Children of Israel. The children of Israel are the physical descendants of the patriarch Jacob, whose name was changed to Israel in Gen. 32.28 (see 2 Kgs 17.34). In Gen. 35.10-11, Jacob's name change is mentioned again, but this time it is promised that 'a nation and a company of nations shall come from you'. The phrase children of Israel only occurs six times in the NRSV (1 Kgs 6.13; Isa. 17.3, 9; Tob 13.3; Sir. 51.12; Rom. 9.27). However, this obscures the fact that the same Hebrew or Greek phrase underlies the translation into other English expressions (e.g., Israelites [Exod. 1.12; Heb. 11.22], sons of Israel [Exod. 1.1], and people of Israel [Jer. 39.32; Rev. 2.14]). Thus 'Children of Israel' is a key self-referential term used by the descendants of Jacob in the HB. The phrase involves insider language and describes those who have been chosen by God. It indicates a focus on covenantal identity for those who are part of the people of God through Jacob/Israel. Other terms for this group include 'the Hebrews', an expression sometimes used in Exod. 1.22 (but see Phil. 3.5), and 'the Jews', a term that develops later and connects the people to the land of Judea (Ezra 6.14; Neh. 1.2; 1 Cor. 1.22).

Contemporary appropriation of the phrase children of Israel is widespread. Many within Christianity consider the church to have replaced ethnic Israel as God's chosen people (Gal. 6.16). The reference to the 'People of Israel' in Rev. 7.4 appears to indicate that the church has become the spiritual Israel (see also Rom. 9.6-7; 11.17-21). However, Rom. 11.29 asserts that 'the gifts and calling of God are irrevocable'. Paul argues in Rom. 9–11 that God's covenant relationship with Israel has not ended (cf. Rom. 9.6; 1 Cor. 7.17-24).

Many within the contemporary nation of Israel, however, use this term to connect their current political existence with the biblical nation. In the Israeli–Palestinian conflict, this claim is quite contested. In 1998, Laurel Holliday published a book entitled, *Children of Israel, Children of Palestine: Our Own True Stories*, which provides a collection of stories from actual 'children of Israel' who were raised in the midst of the Arab-Israeli conflict. The phrase is most notably associated, in cinematic history, with the Cecil B. DeMille's 1956 Oscar-winning movie, *The Ten Commandments*. This movie brought the story of the children of Israel to life in a way that continues to impact contemporary popular culture. In 2009, the television show *Lost*, in an episode entitled 'Follow the Leader', contained numerous allusions to the plight of the children of Israel as presented in DeMille's movie. This is nothing new; imperialistic and liberationist readings of the exodus and identification with the children of Israel were appropriated during the American Revolution and the Civil War. This raises an important issue concerning the legitimacy and implications of a group's use of this term to re-inscribe the biblical narrative into their own story. Although the phrase 'children of Israel' continues to be drawn on to describe oppressed groups, this should not diminish the continued significance of the actual 'children of Israel', especially in a post-Shoah environment.

Recommended reading. Harvey, Graham. *The True Israel: Uses of the Names Jew, Hebrew, and Israel in Ancient Jewish and Early Christian Literature*. Boston: Brill, 2001.

See also JEW/JUDAISM; ISRAEL [JBT]

Children of light. In Eph. 5.8, the children of light describes those who follow Christ: 'For once you were darkness, but now in the Lord you are light. Live as children of light'. In 1 Thess. 5.5, Paul expands the description, 'you are all children of light and children of the day'. Luke 16.8 employs the phrase 'children of light' in contrast to 'the children of this age'. John 12.36 urges becoming 'children of light' as a goal of Christian belief. This brief survey indicates that 'children of light' in its biblical context refers to Christian disciples (see also Ignatius, *Phld* 2.1). This specific phrase does not occur in the HB but is used in the Dead Sea Scrolls, where it describes those who are members of the community in Qumran as 'the sons of light' (1QS 1.9; 2.16; 3.13, 24, 25; 1QM 1.1, 3, 9, 11, 13). In contrast, those outside the community, who are also the enemies of God, are referred to as 'the sons of darkness' (1QS 1.10; 1QM 1.1, 7, 10). *1 En.* 108.11-12 describes those who shall be called by God as those who are 'born of light' and will be placed 'upon the throne of his [God's] honor', because of 'their faithfulness'. The phrase 'children of light' describes those who were rightly related to the God of Israel (cf. Isa. 9.2; Matt. 4.16). The light/dark binary draws from standard imagery in the Ancient Near East, in which darkness describes that which is oppressive and dominating, while light represents relief from subjugation. The Semitic idiom, 'son of...' is used to characterize the quality that is in view so 'child of light' emphasizes the subject's purity, or more likely one who is enlightened spiritually.

The followers of George Fox (1624–1691 CE) were referred to as 'Children of Light', though now they are described as 'The Society of Friends', or alternately 'The Quakers'. This may have arisen because of Fox's teaching that the light of Christ was within humankind. Reinhold Niebuhr, in 1949, wrote *The Children of Light and the Children of Darkness*, in which he calls 'the children of light' to be as wise in virtue and goodness as 'the children of the darkness' are in evil and wickedness. Thus, he builds on the explicit contrast in the biblical imagery and applies the teaching of Jesus from Luke 16.1-8 in a contemporary context. Niebuhr, however, understands that those in the light do not always act as such. Robert Stone's 1992 novel, *Children of Light*, explores the difficulty of living out the social implications of 1 Thess. 5.5. Stone concludes that it is much easier to live as children of darkness, described in his novel as a life of betrayal, drug addiction, and alcoholism. 'Children of Light' continues to be a live metaphor that evokes images of good and evil, while contemporary use of this term often considers the challenges in living up to the standard inherent in being called 'Children of Light'.

Recommended reading. Koester, Craig R. *Symbolism in the Fourth Gospel: Meaning, Mystery, Community*. Minneapolis: Fortress Press, 2003. Niebuhr, Reinhold. *The Children of Light and the Children of Darkness: A Vindication of Democracy and a Critique of its Traditional Defense*. New York: C. Scribner's Sons, 1949.

See also DARKNESS; JOHN, GOSPEL OF; DEAD SEA SCROLLS [JBT]

Chosen People, the. As the oldest of the three Abrahamic faiths, Judaism differs from other belief systems because it does not consider itself a religion but a covenant and a contracted arrangement between God and those he chose to act as a beacon of light and morality in dark times.

Two pivotal events in Jewish history factor significantly into this relationship. First, the exodus from Egypt (Exod. 1–14) testifies to Jews persecuted by an Egyptian Pharaoh who would not allow Moses and the Jews to leave Egypt to go to the promised land. According to the Torah account, God sent ten plagues to the Egyptians and the Israelites were spared. They marked their doors with lamb's blood to signify their faith. This led to the exodus from Egypt; Passover is celebrated every year to commemorate this significant event. Second, the Revelations on Mount Sinai resulted in the passing of the ten commandments from God to the chosen people through Moses (Exod. 19–20).

Choosing is a major theme in Jewish history, from God choosing Abraham and Sarah to progenerate a great nation (Gen. 12, 15, 17), through God choosing Moses to lead that same people out of Egypt (Exod. 12–15) into a land God chose for them (Num. 34.2-12), to God choosing a line of kings including David and Solomon (1 Sam. 13.14; 1 Kgs 2.13-15) to bear the sceptre of God's kingdom on earth (2 Sam. 7.11-13).

With reference to God's choice of Moses, Judaism has much to say about God's reasons for that choice. Moshe Rabbeinu (Moses our teacher) was chosen as the instrument of divine redemption. Three scenes portray Moses mingling among people: in the first Moshe sees an Egyptian striking an Israelite, and he gets involved; then he sees two Israelites arguing, and again Moses gets involved; finally, after he fled Egypt, Moses sees the daughters of Jethro attempting to water their sheep at a well and other shepherds forced them away—once again, Moses got involved (Exod. 12.11-20). God chose Moses as a vessel of freedom because he could not bear to see injustice. Whether it was Gentile versus Jew, or Jew versus Jew, or Gentile versus Gentile—Moses got involved; he interfered and tried to correct the situation, even if it led to his own harm. This was Moses's great virtue, and for this he was chosen to become the father of all prophets.

Western culture has latched onto the idea of Jews as God's chosen (1 Chron. 16.13), sometimes for better and sometimes for worse. William Norman Ewer's ubiquitous couplet, 'How odd of God / To choose the Jews', perhaps penned in neutrality, has elicited not a few attempts to 'correct' any application of anti-Semitism including Leo Roston's 'Not odd of God / Goyim annoy 'im' and 'But not so odd / Of those who choose / A Jewish God / Yet spurn the Jews' (attributed to Ogden Nash and also to Cecil Brown). Perhaps the most popular Jewish response to any non-Jewish address of God's choice can be found in the Broadway play, *Fiddler on the Roof*, where Tevye dialogues with God about this very subject: 'We are y*our chosen people. But, once in a while*, can't *You choose someone else*?'

Recommended reading. Gurkan, S. Leyla. *The Jews as a Chosen People: Tradition and Transformation*. New York: Routledge, 2008. Jacobs, Jill. *There Shall Be No Needy: Pursuing Social Justice through Jewish Law and Tradition*. Woodstock, VT: Jewish Lights Publishing, 2009.

See also JEW, JUDAISM; CHILDREN OF ISRAEL   [YR]

Christ. In the Bible, the terms Christ and Messiah are intimately connected. Both terms refer to an 'anointed one', as in a king who is anointed to his position of leadership or a priest anointed to perform his role (Lev. 4.3, 5). The Greek term *christos* is used in the Greek Septuagint to translate the Hebrew *mashiakh*, or Messiah. Saul is 'anointed' as the first king of Israel (1 Sam. 9.16; 10.1; cf. 1 Sam. 26.9), but tradition favors his successor, David, who becomes the quintessential 'anointed one' in the OT. God promises to secure David's kingship forever (2 Sam. 7.12-13; cf. Ps. 89).

In the period of the Second Temple, the term Messiah plays an important function in Jewish imagination. Though variety exists, messianic expectations from the period are typically of a Davidic military leader who will free the Jewish people from foreign occupation and restore Israel (e.g., Psalms of Solomon 17). The Dead Sea Scrolls reveal an expectation of two Messiahs, one militaristic and the other priestly. Jesus is not the only important historical figure to be named the Messiah. It is applied to the non-Israelite King Cyrus of Persia (Isa. 45.1), and later, Rabbi Akiba names the leader of the Bar Kokhba Revolt (132–35 CE) as Messiah.

Identifying Jesus of Nazareth as Christ, his early followers link Jesus with the Davidic promise (e.g., Matt. 1.6; Luke 3.31). The Gospels contain much confusion about what sort of Messiah Jesus represents. After Jesus conveys his understanding of being 'anointed' (see Luke 4.16-30), John the Baptist questions Jesus: 'Are you the one who is to come, or are we to wait for another?' (Luke 7.20). Depictions of Jesus' execution show similar confusion. The Romans execute Jesus in the style of a treasonous insurrectionist. Jesus is mockingly robed as a 'king' and a sign displayed above him reads 'King of the Jews'.

In their efforts to study Jesus of Nazareth, modern scholars have often made a distinction between the 'Jesus of history' and the 'Christ of faith'. David Friedrich Strauss's German work, *Life of Jesus Critically Examined* (1835) marks an important milestone in this regard. Perhaps foreshadowing its broad impact, its English translation (1846) is the first published work of nineteenth-century British novelist, George Eliot.

Varying understandings of the Christ has had profound impact in political thought, philosophy, artistic expression, and popular imagination. In music, perhaps the most vivid artistic expression of the term Christ or Messiah is George Frideric Handel's oratorio entitled *Messiah* (1741), a portion of which is perennially featured in Christmas concerts. The 'Hallelujah' chorus within this piece emphasizes the kingship of Jesus with God: 'the kingdom of this world is become the kingdom of our Lord and of his Christ, and he shall reign for ever and ever'.

In literature and film, 'Christ-figure' typically refers to a self-sacrificial character (symbolic of Jesus' crucifixion and its related atonement theology). Many consider Gandalf the Grey plays such a role within J.R.R. Tolkein's *The Lord of the Rings* trilogy (1954–1955). The originally equivalent term Messiah, on the other hand, typically carries a less 'sacrificial' meaning in contemporary language. A 'messianic figure', for instance, often refers to a highly charismatic leader with a large following.

Recommended reading. Fredriksen, Paula. *From Jesus to Christ: The Origins of the New Testament Images of Christ*. 2nd edn. New Haven: Yale University Press, 2000. Mowinckel, Sigmund. *He That Cometh: The Messiah Concept in the Old Testament and Later Judaism*. Grand Rapids, MI: Eerdmans, 2005.

See also ATONEMENT; CHRIST FIGURE; CROSS, CRUCIFIXION OF CHRIST; JESUS OF NAZARETH [PGM]

Christ figure. The word Christ stems from the Greek *christos* (anointed one), which was used as a title for Jesus and not a proper name. A Christ Figure is a literary technique employed by authors to associate their character with the biblical figure of Jesus. These characteristics are not associated with any one Gospel in particular, but constitute a blend of the various descriptions, actions, and rhetoric of Jesus from all of the canonical and non-canonical works. Though Christ Figures are often represented as martyrs who sacrifice themselves for others or for a greater cause, they also exhibit any number of the following traits: ability to perform miracles, ability to heal others, guidance by a spiritual father, virginal birth, or an ability to resurrect from death. Unfortunately, the term is used loosely and oftentimes a protagonist is labelled a Christ Figure by the fact that they showcase one or two minor resemblances with Jesus. There are no specific guidelines for labelling a character as a Christ Figure nor does it matter whether or not the author intended for such a connection to be made.

In literary works, Christ Figures are not uncommon. In J.R.R. Tolkien's *The Lord of the Rings*, the wizard, Gandalf, is often considered a Christ Figure because various allusions to Jesus: he exhibits remarkable powers, gathers and leads a group of followers, saves others through his death, rises from the dead, and returns to his followers. These same attributes appear in the film versions of *The Lord of the Rings,* directed by Peter Jackson.

Films with interesting Christ Figures among their characters include *Jesus de Montréal*, *Hero*, *The Butterfly Effect*, *Star Wars*, *The Lion King*, and *The Wrestler*. In Denys Arcand's *Jesus de Montréal*, the protagonist is an obvious Christ Figure since he is literally playing the role of Jesus in a staged passion play. In *The Wrestler*, directed by Darren Aronofsky, Randy Robinson sacrifices himself for a crowd at the end of the film.

Recommended reading. Baugh, Lloyd. *Imagining the Divine: Jesus and Christ Figures in Film*. Kansas City: Novalis, 2002. Kozlovic, Anton Karl. 'The Structural Characteristics of the Cinematic Christ-Figure' *Journal of Religion and Popular Culture* 8 (2004), http:www.usask.ca/relst/jrpc/.

See also JESUS OF NAZARETH; CHRIST [CAM]

Christmas. Christmas is the feast or celebration of the Nativity (birth of Christ), the story of which is recounted in the Gospels of Matthew (1.18–2.12) and Luke (1.5–2.21). It falls every year on December 25. Scholars are uncertain when the first Nativity celebration was held, but it is unlikely to have been much before the early fourth century CE. There is also much debate concerning how early Christians arrived at a date of December 25. From the late second century onwards, Christians began making attempts to date the birth of Christ. Clement of Alexandria reports several different dates that have been suggested, all occurring in the period from March to May in our calendar.

The earliest reference we have linking December 25 to the birth of Christ is in the *Chronograph* of Furius Dionysius Philocalus, which was compiled at Rome in 354 CE. By this time Christmas appears to have become the starting-point of the liturgical year and a major feast in the West. It was not until the end of the fourth century, however, that the churches of the East adopted December 25 as the feast of the Nativity, which they had been celebrating on January 6. After this point, January 6 became the feast of the Epiphany, which commemorated the visit of the Magi to the infant Jesus. The modern song 'The Twelve Days of Christmas' refers to the period between Christmas and Epiphany.

There are two leading theories about why December 25 became the date of Christmas. The most popular view is that early Christians appropriated an existing pagan celebration, the 'Birthday of the Unconquered Sun', which occurred on December 25. This festival marked the winter solstice, the point at which the days began to grow longer. There is also evidence, however, that early Christians believed that Jesus was conceived and died on the same day of the year. In the West, the crucifixion was believed to have occurred on March 25. If Jesus were conceived on this date, he would have been born on December 25.

Christmas remained a major feast in the Western Church until the end of the Middle Ages. Many of the Protestant Reformers, however, considered the observance of liturgical feasts to be a negative part of Roman Catholicism, and as a result Christmas was no longer celebrated in certain parts of Western Europe. In the modern period, Christmas has become an increasingly secularized holiday, associated with giving gifts, singing carols, showing generosity towards the poor, family togetherness, and generally spreading good cheer. These virtues are extolled in many Christmas specials and movies, such as *Rudolph the Red-Nosed Reindeer*, *The Grinch Who Stole Christmas*, *Frosty the Snowman*, *It's a Wonderful Life*, and *Elf*. Many of these elements of Christmas celebration can be traced to Victorian England, and they are exemplified in the novella *A Christmas Carol* (1843) by Charles Dickens. The most recognizable figure associated with the modern holiday is Santa Claus (St Nicholas). St Nicholas of Myra was a bishop in the late fourth century, known for his generosity towards the poor. In Belgium and the Netherlands, his feast day, December 6, became associated with the giving of presents. Although originally depicted in bishop's robes, in the nineteenth century St Nicholas merged with the English 'Father Christmas', a jolly green-robed bearded man, to create the figure now recognizable as Santa Claus.

Recommended reading. Kelly, Joseph F. *The Origins of Christmas*. Collegeville, MN: Liturgical Press, 1996. Roll, Susan K. *Toward the Origins of Christmas*. Kampen: Kok Pharos, 1995.

See also INFANCY NARRATIVES; MAGI; VIRGIN/VIRGIN BIRTH　　　　　　　　　　　　　　　　[KAS]

Chronicles, Book of. The Book of Chronicles, or 1 and 2 Chronicles, are late biblical historical writings that describe the history of Israel—particularly Judah and the House of David—from the earliest times until Cyrus's Decree (538 BCE). Roughly half of it has parallel material in the earlier biblical writings, namely Torah, Joshua, Samuel, Kings, Psalms, Ruth, and Ezra–Nehemiah, and it includes numerous genealogical and geographical lists (e.g., 1 Chron. 1–9). Chronicles is one of the largest books in the HB, and it ends the Jewish canon. The Rabbis ascribed it to Ezra and Nehemiah, though most likely it originated in Jerusalem, the work of a Levite, approximately 400–375 BCE.

The Chronicler evaluates the past in light of contemporary events and theological concerns: he emphasizes the implementations of the priestly codex (P); the Temple, its services and service-givers; and the continuity of Judah's tribes as the true Israelites who survived until his era. He encourages Diaspora Jews to move to Jerusalem and Judah.

Immediate personal reward and punishment is one of the core theological principles of Chronicles. Reliance on the Lord and obedience to his commandments results in victory, peace, and prosperity. In contrast, disobeying and neglecting the Lord's word and his Temple leads to war, disaster, and defeat. The heavenly promise to give the kingdom to David and his descendants is eternal so the very existence of the Northern Kingdom indicates rebellion against the Lord. The Temple and royal city Jerusalem was captured by 'all Israel', and so it represents the nation's true center.

Chronicles is one of the least popular and least studied books in the Scriptures. It was translated relatively late into Greek and Aramaic, and the Syriac translation of the Bible, as it existed in the third century CE, lacked Chronicles altogether. Despite Jerome's well-known comment about the book ('Chronicles is condensed to such an extent and so well abridged, that whoever claims to know Scriptures without having knowledge of Chronicles, would make himself a laughingstock'), Chronicles was almost completely neglected in Christianity. It was excluded from Scriptural studies of some communities. Hugh of Saint-Cher states that the Jews were generous towards Chronicles by including it in the Writings, while its appropriate place should be among the Apocrypha. Chronicles received a better reception in the Jewish tradition and literature. Verses from the book were integrated into the Jewish liturgy, and *Zohar*, used in the artistic works in the synagogues of Dura-Europos and En-gedi, and in disputations with Christians. There are several medieval commentaries on Chronicles. Nevertheless, some negative opinions exist as well. Spinoza, for one, wished that Chronicles would be excluded from the canon. In the last decades there is increasing scholarly interest in Chronicles.

Recommended reading. Kalimi, I. *The Reshaping of Ancient Israelite History in Chronicles*. Winona Lake, IN: Eisenbrauns, 2005. Kalimi, I. *An Ancient Israelite Historian.* Assen: Van Gorcum, 2005. Kalimi, I. *The Retelling of Chronicles in Jewish Tradition and Literature: A Historical Journey.* Winona Lake, IN: Eisenbrauns, 2009. Klein, R.W. *1 Chronicles: A Commentary*. Hermeneia. Minneapolis: Fortress Press, 2006.

See also SAMUEL, BOOKS OF; KINGS, BOOKS OF

[IK]

Church. The term church is the usual translation of the Greek *ekklēsia* in the NT. This translation is problematic because there are marked differences between the first-century *ekklēsia* and contemporary notions of what constitutes church. Prior to the first century, *ekklēsia* referred to the principal assembly of the democracy of Athens in its golden age 480–404 BCE, so its meaning derives from being an assembly of people and not a building.

Ekklēsia occurs 115 times in the NT, always referring to a gathering of people. In the undisputed Pauline letters, it occurs 44 times with a further 21 mentions in the deutero-Pauline and 3 more in the Pastoral Letters. In the NT, *ekklēsia* denotes the assembly of Christ or the community of Jesus' followers as distinct from the Jewish gathering or synagogue that adheres to the Old Covenant. There are some occasions when *ekklēsia* refers to a general assembly, as in Acts 19.32 and 1 Cor. 14.19, where 'synagogue' is used in relation to the gathering of Christ's disciples. The distinction between *ekklēsia* and synagogue was not as rigidly observed in the Septuagint (LXX) where *ekklēsia* is used as the equivalent of the Hebrew *qahal*, meaning the entire community of the children of Israel. *Ekklēsia* comes to describe the New Covenant, the assembly of Christ, and is used in the Pauline corpus to refer to both the local assemblies in house churches, assemblies of the whole church in a region, and for the universal church. The NT also refers to the gathering of Christians in homes as a primary place of worship. For instance, Paul sends greetings to Prisca and Aquila, and 'also the church in their house' (Rom. 16.3, 5).

Increasingly through history and particularly from the time of Constantine and the building of basilicas, 'church' came to mean the building rather than the assembly. From the ornate to the austere, the buildings dot the landscapes of the Christian world. More recently, communities are reclaiming their identity as an assembly with some denominations choosing to locate again in houses following the ancient tradition.

Recommended reading. Gehring, Roger W. *House Church and Mission: The Importance of Household Structures in Early Christianity.* Peabody, MA: Hendrickson Publishers, 2004. Trainor, Michael F. *The Quest for Home: The Household in Mark's Community*. Collegeville, MN: Liturgical Press, 2001. White, L. Michael. *The Social Origins of Christian Architecture: Building God's House in the Roman World.* 2 vols. Harvard Theological Studies 42, 43. Valley Forge, PA: Trinity Press International, 1990.

See also HOUSE

[RAHC]

Circumcision. The term comes from the Hebrew verb *mûl* and the Greek verb *peritemnō*. In Gen. 17, God instructs Abraham to be circumcised as a sign of the covenant and Abraham obeys, ultimately circumcising his sons Ishmael and Isaac also. Descendants of Abraham's family would undergo circumcision on the eighth day, including Jesus but circumcision was not unique to Israel, since other countries in the area, such as Egypt, made use of it. 'Circumcision of the heart' appears in the HB several times (e.g., Deut. 10.6; Jer. 4.4) and seems to mean that the one whose heart is circumcised will be more fully devoted to God. Both of these sets of meanings—literal and symbolic—are also present in subsequent Jewish literature (Apocrypha, Pseudepigrapha, the writings of Josephus, Philo, and the rabbis), and in the NT as well. Circumcision became so identifiable with those who followed the God of Israel that they were sometimes known simply as 'the circumcised', as in Rom. 3.30. During the Greek and Roman occupations of Palestine some Jews attempted to assimilate into the reigning culture by abandoning some of their ancestral practices, even including the removal of 'the marks of circumcision', as reported in 1 Macc. 1.15. In the earliest church the circumcision of Gentile coverts became a major point of controversy, as evidenced in Acts 15 and Gal. 2. Paul rails against those who compel Gentiles to be circumcised in Gal. 6.12-15, since for Paul the cross has relativized circumcision. Paul also associates circumcision with the Law in Rom. 2.25 and Gal. 5.3 and seems to view it as a demarcation of Jewish identity.

Augustine (*De civ. Dei* 15.16–16.27) sees circumcision as a sign of spiritual regeneration that has been superseded by faith in God and God's grace. Likewise, Jerome argues (*Comm. in Genesim* 3.1) that Gentiles are not required to be circumcised and that instead they undergo a 'spiritual circumcision'. Luther's position on the matter is similar ('On the Councils and the Church') and he argues that 'the articles of faith' are preeminent to circumcision. Calvin contends that baptism has taken the place of circumcision as an initiatory right (*Institues* 4.16.3).

In English literature circumcision is seldom a central theme but it does appear periodically. One example is in Shakespeare's *Othello* (5.2.354-56) where the protagonist says that he struck a 'circumcised dog'. Milton has a poem entitled 'Upon the Circumcision' in which he compares circumcision with the crucifixion, since both were ultimate signs of obedience, and he influenced other poets such as Christopher Harvey and Robert Herrick to view it in similar ways.

More recently, circumcision continues to be a topic of interest in the West. Even though the number of males circumcised has decreased dramatically in Europe and is declining in the United States as well, the topic appears in popular media on occasion. For example, in an episode of *Sex and the City*, Charlotte is uncomfortable with the fact that the man she is dating is uncircumcised, which helps him decide to have the procedure done. On the show *Friends*, Joey auditions for a play in which the director wants an uncircumcised actor to appear nude. In an effort to win the role, Joey attempts to make himself appear to be uncircumcised by using various items such as silly putty and lunchmeat. In an episode of *Seinfeld*, Jerry winces while holding a baby who is about to be circumcised and as a result Jerry's finger is 'circumcised' instead.

See also GENTILE; JEW, JUDAISM [JMB]

Cities of refuge. The cities of refuge were six literal cities given by God to his people (Num. 35.6-28; Deut. 4.41-43; see also Deut. 19.2-13; Josh. 20.7-9). Cities of refuge were made available for people to flee for protection after they accidently killed someone (manslaughter). Perpetrators involved in premeditated murder were not allowed into the cities. Only those who accidently killed someone could flee there. The rationale for traveling to a city of refuge was the fear of retaliation by the deceased's family. The guilty party could escape to one of the six cities, rush inside, grab the 'horns of the altar' (goat or cow horns were attached to the top four corners of stone altars), and cry for mercy to the high priest. The villain would have to live in this city until such time as he went to trial or until the high priest died.

The concept of refuge can be seen embedded in western culture. The American penal system adapts this concept when it offers a much lesser penalty for 'manslaughter' as opposed to that of 'premeditated murder'. Music shows the influence of 'refuge' with phrasing in songs such as Guns N' Roses' 'Sweet Child O' Mine' (1987), and the Red Hot Chili Peppers' 'Under the Bridge' (1992). Phrases in this song show that the writer's city (Los Angeles) was his friend, confidant, fortress, safe haven. Arch Nicholson directed *Fortress* (1985), which offers a cave as a refuge for a teacher and her school kids against abductors. The refuge concept can also be seen in *The Road* (2009, John Hillcoat, director), and *I Am Legend* (2007, Francis Lawrence, director).

The concept of refuge is found in literature as well, as in *Cities of Refuge* by the Canadian Michael Helm (McClellan & Stewart, 2010). The Bible itself transfers it into theological terms. Before the establishing of the cities in Numbers, Noah's ark was a refuge for Noah, his family, and representative animals that saved them from the wrath of God. The promised land given to the Israelites was itself a place of refuge from nomadic life, warring neighbors, and destitution (the land was 'flowing with milk and honey'). In NT literature, Jesus is seen as a refuge from temptation, the world system, the hatred of Satan (1 Pet. 5.8), and the Judgment of God upon his enemies.

The Psalmist looked to God as his city of refuge. He used the imagery of rocks, crags, mountains, caves, etc. as places of refuge from enemies. In one such instance, he wrote of God: 'my rock and my fortress, my stronghold and my deliverer, my shield, in whom I take refuge, who subdues the peoples under me' (Ps. 144.2). Seventeenth-century British author John Donne also viewed God as his refuge in 'A Hymn to God the Father'.

Local fire departments throughout America double as 'safe havens' for children. This refuge is for any child who feels threatened by strangers or abusive family members. They can run into any fire department that displays safe haven signs and find refuge. An international organization (ICORN) exists for providing a degree of refuge for the freedom of expression for international writers who have been censored or even targeted by governments.

See also SANCTUARY; NUMBERS, BOOK OF; BOOK OF THE LAW [MBW]

Cleansing of the Temple. Every Gospel records Jesus' actions in the Temple when he disrupts the buying and selling of sacrificial animals and overturns the tables of the moneychangers (Matt. 21.12-13; Mark 11.15-19; Luke 19.45-48; John 2.14-16). The Synoptic Gospels place this action at the end of Jesus' ministry, which is then linked to his trial and crucifixion. The Gospel of John places this event at the beginning of a three year ministry. The synoptic chronology is more likely to be accurate on this point with John's placement reflecting his theological purpose in presenting Jesus as the Temple. While it is clear that Jesus carried out some disruptive action in the Temple, scholars differ about the extent and possible meaning of this. The four Gospel writers record the event differently and with their own interpretations.

According to Jewish sources, the moneychangers were not a desecration of the Temple, and it is possible that the larger animals were also permitted in the outer court since at Festival times the purity laws were relaxed *(m. Hagigah* 3.6-7). The presence of animals and moneychangers helped the pilgrims who came to Jerusalem for Passover. A month before this event, Passover tables were erected in the Temple to collect the half-shekel Temple tax *(m. Shekalim* 1.3) since this was a time when Jews from many lands would come to Jerusalem. This tax paid for the upkeep of the Temple and its rituals. Since this tax could not be paid with Roman coins which offended Jewish law with the image of the emperor, the coins were exchanged for coins from Tyre which had no 'graven image'. Pilgrims could change their money, pay their Temple-tax and buy an animal for sacrifice. The moneychangers and animals therefore were part of Israel's system of worship and not a corruption. Jesus' action was not so much a cleansing as a prophetic, symbolic action. It was common for OT prophets to criticize worship when rituals did not involve authentic covenantal living (e.g., Amos 5.21-24; Jer. 7.1-7). These prophetic critiques were a call to covenant renewal. Jesus' actions need to be understood historically against this prophetic tradition.

In 70 CE, following a brief Jewish uprising, Roman armies destroyed the Temple and all the Gospels were written after this event. From this retrospective position, Jesus' Temple action could be remembered and reinterpreted. For Mark the Temple is to be 'a place of prayer for all the nations' (11.17). Matthew presents it as a claim of Jesus' messianic authority. John offers the most explicit link between the destruction of the Temple and Jesus' action. Following the action Jesus speaks about the destruction and raising of the Temple (2.19) and the narrator adds an interpretive comment that Jesus meant the Temple of his body (2.21). The Dead Sea Scrolls show that some Jews at this time linked a Davidic Messiah with the task of building a new Temple (4Q174). Mark (14.58) and Matthew (26.61) record this saying about the destruction of the Temple during Jesus' trial as part of the charges against him.

Recommended reading. Coloe, M.L. *God Dwells with Us: Temple Symbolism in the Fourth Gospel*. Collegeville, MN: Liturgical Press, 2001.

See also JESUS OF NAZARETH; NAZARENE; TEMPLE, ISRAEL'S [MLC]

Coat of many colors. From the Hebrew *ketonet* (coat, tunic) and *passim* (the etymology of which is uncertain), 'coat of many colors' (Gen. 37.3, KJV) is a translation of the Greek, not the Hebrew. The LXX scribes may not have understood the Hebrew word for sleeves, or they interpreted it for their culture, and so they translated it into Greek as *poikilon* (colorful, multicolored, and variegated). The early translators of the English Bible (as early as Wycliffe, c. 1385) did not understand the word either, and so relied upon the much older Greek translation, resulting in the widespread belief that it was a multicolored tunic. With a better understanding of the Hebrew word, it is now thought to be a long coat or more literally, a coat that went to the hands and the feet.

Its first appearance is in Gen. 37.3. Jacob, one of the OT Patriarchs, presented this coat to his beloved son Joseph. This gift widened the rift that existed between Joseph and his brothers. It is not explained why this tunic in itself is so special, however, it symbolized to his brothers the exalted status of Joseph with his father. That and other factors, led Joseph's brothers to plot his death. When the perfect opportunity came upon them to get rid of him permanently, his brothers stripped him of his coat, thus signalling Joseph's fall from favor and his journey to hardships (Gen. 37.23). His brothers decided at the last minute to sell him to a caravan of Ishmaelites, who were passing by, for twenty pieces of silver. They then dipped the coat in goat's blood to convince their father that a wild animal had eaten him.

The Hebrew phrase makes its last appearance in 2 Sam. 13.18, 'a garment of divers colors' (KJV), where it is explained as 'the kind of garment the virgin daughters of the king wore'. This garment belonged to Tamar, one of King David's daughters. Amnon, her half-brother, had just raped her and had put her outside his room. Tamar, in terrible distress, threw ashes on her head and tore her special robe. The narrator then informs his audience about what kind of robe she was wearing, which was the *kethoneth passim*, the long robe with sleeves.

Ford Madox Brown, who was an English painter of moral and historical subjects, painted in 1867 a scene depicting Joseph's brothers deceiving their father concerning his death by presenting the blood-stained coat to him. Shoshannah Brombacher, a modern day painter, painted *Joseph Receives his Coat of Many Colours* in 2008. It is a very vibrant painting depicting Joseph with his robe, along with his parents and brothers.

In contemporary culture, the musical *Joseph and the Amazing Technicolor Dreamcoat* is based on the account of Joseph, from his staged death to his reconciliation with his brothers. The cast sings 'Joseph's Coat' in Act 1, which mentions Jacob's favoritism, his sons' jealousy toward their brother Joseph, and describes the various colors of the coat. Dolly Parton sang 'Coat of Many Colors' in 1971, which Shania Twain later covered: 'As she (her mother) sewed, she told a story / From the Bible, she had read / About a coat of many colors / Joseph wore'.

See also JOSEPH, SON OF JACOB [EID]

Cock. This bird had a significant reputation in the Ancient Near East, most notably because of its ability to foretell the coming dawn. Thus, the Cock was often associated with such themes as creation, light, diligence, and wisdom. It was dedicated to a number of deities spanning from Greece to Persia: Apollo and Mithra, Greek and Persian sun gods, Mercury, the Greek god of trade, and Athena, the Greek goddess of work. The Cock's lascivious character also made it a significant symbol in Greco-Roman fertility cults, often representing ithyphallic gods. The mythic symbolism of the Cock was quickly adopted in Christianity. Most notably, the Cock became a symbol of divine wisdom heralding the coming of Christ.

The special ability of the Cock to foresee events influenced scriptural interpretation, hence the rare word in Job 38.36 *sekwi* (from the verb *skh* 'to look [out]', 'to foresee',) was translated as 'cock' (*gallo*) in the Latin Vulgate ('Who gives the cock its understanding?'). Those with prophetic ability have at times been compared with the Cock. In his thirteenth-century CE discussion of ecclesiastical symbolism, *Rationale divinorum officium*, William Durandus writes that the cock on church spires is like a preacher who can foresee the coming Day of Judgment, and that the preacher's crow summons all from their slumber to repent, convert, and keep watch for Christ's return.

The Cock also came to symbolize Christ. The apocryphal *Book of the Cock* (c. sixth century CE), still used in the Ethiopic Church, records that at the Last Supper, Akrosenna, the wife of Simon the Pharisee, brought out a roasted cock which Jesus resurrected, foreshadowing his own resurrection. The theme of the resurrected Cock is also found in various other apocryphal texts like *Acts of Pilate*, and became a popular tradition in medieval Christian legends in the west. The analogy between the Cock and Christ is also found in early Christian hymnography. The hymn of St Ambrose (340–397 CE), 'Maker of all, Eternal King' (*Aeterne rerum Conditor*) states: 'The bird, the messenger of dawn, Sings out the light is near, And Christ, the rouser of our minds, Now calls us back to life'. Another good example is Prudentius's (348–413 CE) hymn, 'The Winged Herald of the Day' (*Ales diei nuntius*). In Chaucer's 'Nun's Priest's Tale', a fox named 'newe Scariot', a reference to Judas, betrays the protagonist cock, Chauntecleer, who is often regarded a Christ-type.

The time of the cock-crow was predictable and functioned as a nocturnal clock. The ancient Romans designated the hours from midnight to 3 am, *gallicinium* ('cockcrow'), as part of a four-fold night watch: evening, midnight, cockcrow, and dawn. This system was eventually adopted in ancient Palestine (see Mark 13.35 [*alektorophōnia*]; *m. Yoma* 1.8 [*qri'at haggeber*]). These hours quickly developed into a canonical time of prayer in the early Christian church (cf. Mark 13.35; *Apostolic Consti-*

tutions VIII, iv, 34) and came to be associated with eschatological vigil.

Recommended reading. Baird, Lorrayne. 'Christus Gallinaceus: A Chaucerian Enigma; or the Cock as Symbol of Christ in the Middle Ages'. *Studies in Iconography* 9 (1983) 19-30. Leclercq, Henri. 'Coq'. In *Dictionnaire d'archéologic chrétienne et de liturgie*. Ed. Fernand Cabrol and Henri LeClercq. Vol. III, cols. 2886-2905. Paris: Letouzey & Ané, 1955. Piovanelli, Pierluigi. 'Exploring the Ethiopic *Book of the Cock*: An Apocryphal Passion Gospel from Late Antiquity'. *Harvard Theological Review* 96 (2003) 427-54.

See also ANIMALS, SYMBOLISM OF [JERP]

Colossians, Epistle to the. Colossians presents itself as a letter from Paul 'to the saints and faithful brothers and sisters in Colossae', that is, to the church in the city of Colossae. The letter congratulates these 'saints' for their faith and love (1.4), and informs them that Paul prays they will be filled with the knowledge of God's will so that they may lead lives worthy of the Lord (1.9-10). There is a lengthy moral and behavioral exhortation (2.16–4.6). While its exact nature is disputed by biblical scholars, Colossians addresses a false teaching, probably related to Jewish Torah and traditional requirements, that demanded that the Colossian believers observe a variety of regulations (2.4, 16-23). Colossians claims that although obedience to regulations appears wise, it does not make people more holy and the regulations should be ignored. The letter argues that God through the actions of Jesus Christ has provided complete redemption (1.13-20; 2.9-15). Believers should look only to Christ. Many scholars are of the view that Colossians was not written by Paul. Its literary affinities are in many ways closer to Ephesians than to other letters in the Pauline Corpus.

Colossians is not often quoted directly in literature or represented in artistic works, but there are allusions to the letter's language and ideas in various places. Colossians is often classified as a 'prison epistle' on the belief that Paul was imprisoned in Rome when it was written. Rembrandt's famous *St Paul in Prison* reflects this view. A line from Ben Jonson's (1572–1637) poem 'A Hymn on the Nativity of My Savior' ('The Word, which heaven and earth did make') might draw on Col. 1.15-20. The title of Tolstoy's *The Power of Darkness* alludes to Col. 1.13. More recently, the popular film *The Da Vinci Code* (2006) offers the argument that things may not need to be either human or divine, but that the human is divine. This might allude to christological notions found in Colossians (1.15-16, 19; 2.9). The traditional roles for men (husbands), women (wives) and children seen in the domestic code (3.18–4.1) seems to be reinforced by such things as the song 'Tradition' in the musical and film *Fiddler on the Roof* (1971). Popular images and thinking about ancient (and more recent) slavery are aroused by the discussion of the roles of slaves and masters in Col. 3.22–4.1, drawing the mind to recall such films as *Spartacus* (1960) and the institution of African slavery in the sixteenth to nineteenth centuries.

Some phrases from Colossians occasionally appear in popular usage, including 'set your minds on things that are above' (3.2), 'the image of the invisible God' (1.15; cf. Gen. 1.26; *Imago Dei*), 'the firstborn from the dead' (1.18), and 'principalities and powers' (rulers and authorities, 1.16; 2.15). The letter to the Ephesians employs some of the same ideas and phraseology.

Recommended reading. Hay, David M. *Colossians*. ANTC. Nashville, TN: Abingdon Press, 2000. Walsh, Brian J., and Sylvia C. Keesmaat. *Colossians Remixed: Subverting the Empire*. Downers Grove, IL: InterVarsity Press, 2004.

See also PAUL, THE APOSTLE; EPISTLE; EPHESIANS, LETTER TO THE [RRJ]

Colors, Symbolism of. The Bible contains many references to color, primarily used to describe nature: blue for sky and water, green for plants, and so on. A spectrum of colors—a rainbow—is seen after the flood as a sign of hope (Gen. 9.12-17). The breastplate of the high priest is set with a colorful array of gemstones (Exod. 28.15-21). One of the most vivid colored objects of the OT (at least in the KJV translation) is the so-called 'coat of many colors' given by Jacob to son Joseph, incurring the wrath and envy of his brothers (Gen. 37.3). This is the foundation of many modern literary works, prominently Andrew Lloyd Webber's Broadway musical *Joseph and the Amazing Technicolor Dreamcoat*.

White is a symbol of purity, innocence, righteousness, joy and redemption: 'Purge me with hyssop, and I shall be clean; wash me, and I shall be whiter than snow' (Ps. 51.7). Many other objects are described as being white, including garments (Dan. 7.9), animals (Gen. 30.35), and manna (Exod. 16.31). Christ wears white at the Transfiguration (Matt. 17.2), as seen in Raphael's 1520 painting. The references in Revelation are abundant, ranging from the robes of the Elders (Rev. 4.4) to the throne of judgment (Rev. 20.11); from angels (Rev. 15.6) to the horses ridden by the redeemed (Rev. 6.2). Here white may be seen as a symbol of victory. White is contrasted to red with regard to sin (Isa. 1.18). The 2002 film *White Oleander* is characterized by contrasting the positive and negative aspects of white.

Black is connected to sin and death, and used to describe the barren earth left by the plague of locusts (Exod. 10.15), and in many instances, dark and threatening skies (1 Kgs 18.45; Jer. 4.8; Joel 2.2; Mic. 3.6). At the opening of the third seal the sun turns black (Rev. 6.12). Gold, a precious and hard metal, symbolizes divinity and even immortality (Exod. 28.36; Ps. 21.3). The Golden Calf (Exod. 32.4) is symbol of idolatry. It is mentioned in songs by Bob Dylan ('Gates of Eden') and The Hooters ('All you Zombies').

Red is the color of blood, and therefore associated with sacrifice, particularly that of Christ. Toni Morrison's novel *Beloved* contains extensive biblical references and relies heavily on symbolism of the color red. Stephen Crane's *Red Badge of Courage* specifically evokes the red of a bloodied bandage. The Whore of Babylon is described as 'sitting on a scarlet beast ... clothed in purple and scarlet' (Rev. 17.3-4). Hawthorne's novel *The Scarlet Letter* repeats this symbolism for his adulterous protagonist, Hester, described as 'a scarlet woman, and a worthy type of her of Babylon'. Purple is a color created from a precious dye, used (with blue and crimson) for the temple linens (Exod. 26.1) and worn by those with high rank in the Bible (Judg. 8.26; Est. 8.15; Prov. 31.22; Dan. 5.16). The robe placed on Jesus was also purple (Mark 15.17, 20), and thereafter associated with royalty. The rock musician Prince played with this idea for his 1984 album and film *Purple Rain*.

Green is a common descriptor of natural forms. Green pastures are referred to in Ps. 23.2, reflecting God's care for his people; a 1936 film of the same name reworked this theme. The fourteenth-century romance *Sir Gawain and the Green Knight* contained various allusions to this color as characterizing both youth and its passing.

Recommended reading. Ottmann, Klaus (ed.). *Color Symbolism*. Putnam, CT: Spring Publications, 2005. Pastoureau, Michel. *Blue: The History of a Color*. Princeton: Princeton University Press, 2001.

See also COAT OF MANY COLORS; GOLD; GOLDEN CALF; GREEN PASTURES; WHORE OF BABYLON [ACF]

Communion. Communion is one of the names for the Lord's Supper, also referred to as the Eucharist and the Breaking of Bread (see Matt. 26.26-29; Mark 14.22-25; Luke 22.14-23; 1 Cor. 11.23-26). The also also has a broader sense related to notions of community. The NT uses the Greek word *koinonia*. Rarely used in secular Greek before it was taken up by Paul, it means sharing things in common.

Paul uses *koinonia* in 1 Cor. 10 where he is giving pastoral advice to the Corinthians about temptations to idolatry. In v. 16, Paul writes that the cup and the bread of communion are shared. However, if they participate in eating food offered to idols in idolatrous practices that are then in communion with something other than Christ. Paul's argument is an ethical one as well as a spiritual one, that says that Christians cannot drink of the cup of Christ and also the cup of idols. Nor may Christians join with pagans in eating at their idolatrous feasts. In 2 Cor. 6.14, Paul urges his readers to avoid entangling relations with non-believers. He asks, 'what fellowship is there between light and darkness?' He continues and asks what do believers share (*koinonia*) with unbelievers?

Communion is also used in 2 Cor. 13.13 by Paul in what is sometime called the Apostolic Benediction: 'The grace of the Lord Jesus Christ, the love of God and the communion of the Holy Spirit be with all of you'.

There are many poems, hymns and other works in English literature that celebrate the mystery of corporate fellowship believers find in Communion. Poems include 'Holy Communion' by William Cullan Bryant (1794–1878) and 'The Bugler's First Communion' (1918) by Gerard Manley Hopkins (1844–1889). Among the hymns are 'I Am His and He Is Mine', 'Nearer, My God to Thee', 'Blest Be the Tie That Binds', and 'There Is a Fountain Filled with Blood'.

Recommended reading. Barron, Robert E. *Eucharist*. Maryknoll, NY: Orbis Books, 2008. Marshall, I. Howard. *Last Supper and Lord's Supper*. Grand Rapids, MI: Eerdmans, 1980.

See also EUCHARIST; LORD'S SUPPER; SACRAMENTS; UPPER ROOM [AJW]

Conversion. Most are surprised to learn that there is no word for 'conversion' in the Bible. The terms we find there are exclusively metaphorical. The Greek verb *metanoeō* is typically translated as 'to repent', but it refers literally to 'a change of mind'. In the HB, the notion of conversion is expressed by the term *shuv*, literally, 'to turn', as in 'to turn away from the wrong path and turn towards the correct path'.

In the context of the Bible, the term apples most famously to Paul the Apostle. Though Paul is piously referred to as a Christian convert, scholars disagree on whether the term suits; is Paul a convert to a new religion or a Jewish believer in Jesus? Paul never uses the term Christian of himself; indeed, the term did not even exist in his lifetime. Others, such as Krister Stendahl, encourage us to consider whether it is better to think of Paul's experience on the model of the call of the prophet in the HB (see, for example, Paul's own language in Gal. 1.15).

Paul says little about his first encounter with Jesus in his letters so Christians typically turn to the Acts of the Apostles for details, often not realising that each of Luke's three descriptions of Paul's conversion (Acts 9, 22, 26) are different! Although many passages in Paul's letters might allude to his conversion experience, there is widest agreement that the following passages refer to that event: Gal. 1.11-17; Phil. 3.4b-11; 1 Cor. 9.1; 1 Cor. 9.16-17; 1 Cor. 15.8-10.

In modern scholarship, there has been intense interest in the phenomenon of conversion and in Paul's conversion in particular. In keeping with the individualistic and introspective perspective of modern Western people, our understanding of conversion has been psychological; emotional, tumultuous, and cataclysmic are typical terms we use to express the depth of a conversion experience. Recent scholarship, however, has questioned whether such categories are relevant to ancient Mediterranean cultures that were outward looking and community minded.

Conversion is a common motif in Christian art and Paul's story is a favorite subject. Caravaggio captures the scene in Acts 9 in a work called *The Conversion on the Way to Damascus* (1601). Michelangelo's *The Conversion of Saul* (c. 1542–1545) is a panoramic, showing the heavens with God and many angels sending the blinding light down upon Paul who is on the ground.

Luke's narratives of Paul's conversion have been so influential in Western culture that the phrase 'Damascus Road' or 'Damascus Road experience' refers to an unexpected change of heart, and appears in popular media everywhere (headlines, television, and radio talk shows). There has been speculation that the song 'Blinded by the Light', written by Bruce Springsteen (1973) but made popular by Manfred Mann's Earth Band (1979) takes its title from the conversion narratives of Paul, but this is debatable.

Recommended reading. Crook, Zeba A. *Reconceptualising Conversion: Patronage, Loyalty, and Conversion in the Religions of the Ancient Mediterranean*. Berlin: Walter de Gruyter, 2004. Segal, Alan. *Paul the Convert: The Apostolate and Apostasy of Saul the Pharisee*. New Haven: Yale University Press, 1990.

See also ACTS OF THE APOSTLES, THE; DAMASCUS ROAD; PAUL, THE APOSTLE; SCALES FELL FROM HIS EYES [ZAC]

Corinthians, Epistles to the. First and Second Corinthians belong to the Pauline letter corpus and fall between Romans and Galatians in the NT canon. Modern scholarship unanimously affirms the authorial authenticity of the letters, placing them among the seven 'undisputed letters' of Paul. Both epistles were written to the church in the Roman colony of Corinth, Greece. Paul first visited Corinth in c. 51/52 CE (Acts 18) and sent 1 Corinthians from Ephesus (1 Cor. 16.8) in c. 54/55 CE. Second Corinthians is notoriously difficult to date, primarily because most modern scholars believe the letter in its canonical form is the compilation of several shorter epistles delivered on separate occasions. This theory is disputed, however, and no consensus currently exists.

First Corinthians responds to certain doctrinal and ethical inquiries of the Corinthians, as is evident by the frequently cited introductory formula, 'Now concerning . . '. (*peri de*; 1 Cor. 7.1, 25; 8.1; 12.1; 16.1, 12). The major themes of the letter include boasting, wisdom, leadership, church discipline, sex, food, the Eucharist, spiritual gifts, resurrection, the Jerusalem collection, and the visit of Apollos. How these themes relate to one another has been the subject of many rhetorical studies. It has recently been argued that 1 Corinthians is a sample of deliberative rhetoric. In other words, throughout 1 Corinthians Paul is exhorting the church to conform to a particular pattern of thought and behavior. That pattern is expressed in the letter's thesis statement: 'Now I appeal to you, brothers and sisters, by the name of our Lord Jesus Christ, that all of you be in agreement and that there be no divisions among you, but that you be united in the same mind and the same purpose' (1 Cor. 1.10). All of the individual pieces of the letter then support Paul's exhortation to ecclesial unity.

Second Corinthians, while being far more disjointed than its predecessor, is perhaps the most candid and intimate of Paul's letters, demonstrating his great vulnerability and deep reflection upon his apostolic position. While it is easily observed that critics of Paul loomed somewhere in the background of 1 Corinthians, by the time Paul wrote 2 Corinthians an anti-Pauline party had clearly invaded the church and spread their critical evaluation of him throughout the congregation (2 Cor. 10.10), leaving some Corinthians to question Paul's apostolic legitimacy. However, according to Paul, 'such boasters are false apostles, deceitful workers, disguising themselves as apostles of Christ' (2 Cor. 11.13). Paul defended his apostleship not by pointing to his great personal achievements, but his afflictions and weaknesses (2 Cor. 4.6-12; 6.4-10; 11.23-28; 12.7b-10). The letter also contains Paul's most elaborate treatise on Christian charity (2 Cor. 8–9).

Two motifs from the Corinthian epistles continually resurface in Western culture. The first is Paul's treatment of the superiority of love (1 Cor. 13.1-8a). Perhaps the most quoted text in modern wedding ceremonies, this pericope continues to speak powerfully about how and how not to love one another. The second theme is Paul's mysterious 'thorn in the flesh' (2 Cor. 12.7). The original referent of the phrase has puzzled scholars for centuries, yet its ambiguity has allowed people suffering from all kinds of ailments and afflictions to borrow the phrase when referring to their individual struggle.

See also EPISTLE; NEW TESTAMENT; PAUL, THE APOSTLE [JKG]

Council, Jerusalem. According to the Acts of the Apostles and Galatians, there was a meeting of churches at Jerusalem, the headquarters of the primitive church. Generally, this meeting is dated around 48 CE. The gathering of churches was prompted by the judaizing controversy, meaning that some ultra-conservative Jewish Christians (Judaizers) insisted that Gentile converts be circumcised and keep the Mosaic Law in order to be part of the church. Paul and Barnabas quarreled with them and the church at Antioch had to refer the matter to the parent church in Jerusalem. A council of churches was convened and after fierce debate, a resolution passed. Gentile Christians were free not to observe the Mosaic laws but were encouraged to eschew those acts that may create friction with strict Jews: eating meat offered to idols; eating meat with blood; and sexual immorality. The historicity of the Jerusalem council is often challenged because even though there are various similarities between the accounts in Gal. 2.1-10 and Acts 15.1-32, there are striking differences.

The council of Jerusalem could be compared to the periodic meeting of World Council of Churches in Geneva, Switzerland. At these meetings the body deliberates on issues of shared concern such as poverty, HIV and AIDS, human rights and democracy, child abuse, sustainable development, to mention only a few.

See also ACTS OF THE APOSTLES, THE [ET]

Covenant. In Hebrew epic, Yahweh makes a covenant or cuts a treaty (*karat berit*) at Sinai with Moses and Israel to drive out the nations (Exod. 34.10-12, 14, 24, 27). Moses is a king in relation to a divine king, and this idea of covenant is modeled on treaties of the Neo-Assyrian Empire in which a great king like Esarhaddon makes a treaty with a vassal ruler and his people. Subsequent writings mostly refuted the idea that God can be bound by a treaty to protect Israel. One historian affirms the validity of the Mosaic covenant but argues that ongoing occupation of the land depends on unswerving dedication by Davidic kings to the law of centralization (Deut. 12; 2 Kgs 18.22). Another author sets aside the Sinai covenant and binds God to an everlasting covenant in which he promises Noah to preserve the earth from flood (Gen. 9) and guarantees Abraham the whole land of Canaan (Gen. 17). Yet another writer replaces the treaty at Sinai with God's disclosure of binding laws on Israel (Exod. 21–23 *passim*). One of the exilic historians also obligates Israel by interpreting the Sinai covenant as being synonymous with the law, making Moses its mediator, and adding legal policy (Exod. 20.2-26; Deut. 5).

The idea of covenant acquires new meaning in different historical contexts. Calvin the Protestant Reformer argues for an inviolable covenant with Jesus as mediator between Jews and Gentiles in place of the old covenant which was not inscribed upon the hearts of men (Jer. 31.31-33). Calvin's insistence that God's covenant gives Israel priority is upheld by theologian Karl Barth in an Advent sermon he delivered at Bonn on Romans 15 (*Theologische Existenz Heute*, 1933), in opposition to Nazism and the national aspirations of the German Christian Movement. God initially made his covenant 'with and only with this people'. His covenant was not broken (cf. Jer. 31.32) but was revealed for Israel and for Gentiles as 'a covenant of grace for sinners' who 'can only live by God's mercy'. The terrifying reality of Auschwitz made it impossible for Elie Wiesel to participate in the camp's New Year liturgies (*Rosh Hashanah*) in which God is proclaimed King and praised for remembering his covenant with Israel (*Night*, 1969). Wiesel claims the Holocaust inaugurated a type of anti-Sinai, in which the covenant is between Israel and death. The prophet Isaiah ridiculed the covenant as a pact with death because the citizens of Jerusalem erroneously believed that God would deliver them from the Assyrians, unaware that covenant requires justice as its foundation (Isa. 28.14-19). For Wiesel God is the unreliable partner in the covenant. His novel *The Town Beyond the Wall* (1964) ends with a legend in which a man says to God, 'You be man, and I will be God. For only one second'. After the change neither God nor man was ever the same. Philosopher Emil Fackenheim asserts that Jews must not abandon the covenant: 'We shall keep it alive and be its witnesses'. Otherwise, Jews 'hand Hitler posthumous victories'.

Recommended reading. Berenbaum, Michael. *The Vision of the Void: Theological Reflections on the Works of Elie Wiesel*. Middletown, CT: Wesleyan University Press, 1979. Fackenheim, Emil L. *God's Presence in History: Jewish Affirmations and Philosophical Reflections*. New York: New York University Press, 1970. Peckham, Brian. *History and Prophecy: The Development of Late Judean Literary Traditions*. New York: Doubleday, 1993.

See also BOOK OF THE LAW; ISRAEL; LAW; MOSES

[JRW]

Cows of Bashan. Amos composed a cycle of poetry in which he addresses the wealthy women of the city of Samaria as 'the cows of Bashan' (4.1). Each woman speaks to her husband, then in unison, 'Bring, and let us drink'. Amos denounces the women for initiating drinking parties or symposia feasts which impose oppressive fines on the destitute (2.8; 6.4-7). He speaks to the men and prophesies coming days of war. Then he tells the wives they will be deported with fishhooks (4.2). God addresses the females as fugitives going out through breaches in the walls of the city, comparing them metaphorically to a herd of cows stampeding through a hole in a fence (4.3). The women are called cows because of their positive association with *Bashan*, a mountainous northern area, east of the Jordan River, famous for its cattle, sheep and goats (Deut. 32.14; Ezek. 39.18). Their men are 'bulls' because they give them themselves horns (Amos 6.13). The 'strong bulls of Bashan' (Ps. 22.12) owe their strength to the fertile grazing land of *Bashan* (Mic. 7.14; Jer. 50.19). Thus 'cows and bulls of Bashan' are flattering images of virility and fertility. Recent inscriptional evidence found at Kuntillet 'Ajrud represents Yahweh as a bull and his consort Asherah as a cow (Exod. 32; Deut. 9; 1 Kgs 12; 2 Kgs 10.29, 17.16, 21.7, 23.4; Hos. 8.5-6; 10.5; 13.2; Ps. 106.19; Neh. 9.18). By applying animal imagery to the women and men of Samaria, Amos is perhaps mocking the ruling elite as goddesses and gods.

The expression Cows of Bashan has found rather limited representation in Western culture. However, two are worthy of mention. Sculptor Alex Hallmark has fashioned a number of works based on characters from the OT, including one entitled *Amos and the Cows of Bashan*, and John Herbert Kaufman wrote a two-act play with musical accompaniment called *The Cows of Bashan* (1984). As a metaphor for a woman thought to possess attributes normally associated with female members of the bovine species, the word cow has found its way into everyday English parlance. A derogatory epithet the OED offers the following definition: 'Applied to a coarse or degraded woman. Also, loosely, any woman, used especially as a coarse form of address'. Here the word cow does not denote what Amos would have intended—he does not ridicule his female readership for being obese or overfed. Indeed one errs to attribute this sense in Amos 4.1. The narrator's address to the disagreeable cook, referred to as a cow, in George Orwell's novel *Down and out in Paris and London* (1933) conveys the modern sense aptly. Feminist spokesperson Germaine Greer also cites a disparaging riddle in reference to Paul McCartney's late wife in the initial recordings of the band Wings: 'What do you call a cow with wings? Linda McCartney'. Her vocal performances were allegedly off-key.

Recommended reading. Coggins, Richard J. *Joel and Amos*. New Century Bible Commentary. Sheffield: Sheffield Academic Press, 2000. Greer, Germaine. 'Germaine Greer: Pop Bitch'. *The Independent* (May 21, 2006). Rilett Wood, Joyce. *Amos in Song and Book Culture*. JSOTSup, 337. Sheffield: Sheffield Academic Press, 2002.

See also ANIMALS, SYMBOLISM OF; ASHERAH (ASHTORETH); AMOS, BOOK OF; CATTLE; GOLDEN CALF; YAHWEH

[NRP AND JRW]

Creation, Creator. Although the biblical account of creation (Gen. 1–3) is not the oldest such story, it forcefully distances itself from its Mesopotamian and Egyptian counterparts by its monotheistic declaration of a universal creator who orders and rules the cosmos through the authority of the spoken word. Genesis, in fact, combines two independent creation stories. Their canonical form suggests they were intentionally placed alongside one another in order to emphasize complimentary aspects of both creator and creation.

The first story (Gen. 1.1–2.4a) makes a liturgical statement about God's creation of an orderly universe out of the primordial chaos. The first three days present a general ordering of creation (the separation of light from darkness, the separation of the waters above from the waters below to create the atmosphere, and the separation of dry land from water). The next three days of creation parallel the first by populating these spheres (the placing of the sun and heavenly lights, the placing of the aerial and aquatic creatures in their respective domains, and the population of the dry land with all ground-dwelling creatures, including humanity). This principle of order eventually comes to underscore many aspects of Hebrew life and thought. God created the world with a sense of order; those who live in accordance with that order align themselves with the creator and thus find his favor. Those who violate the order of creation position themselves in opposition to God and reintroduce chaos to the world. After completing the work of creation in six days, God spent the seventh day resting from his labors—a paradigm that underscores the origins and importance of Sabbath observation for all those created in the image of God.

The second story (Gen. 2.4b–3.24) moves from universal to local canvas by making statements about the intimate and purposeful creation of humanity, the place of humanity within God's creation, and whether humanity would choose to live in accordance with God's created order. In this respect, the tragic events of disobedience in the narrative are paradigmatic of the human struggle to navigate ambiguity and alienation in their relationships with God, others human, and the whole of creation.

The theme of creation reappears explicitly in a number of biblical texts including Proverbs, which denotes wisdom as the first order of creation and the means by which God created (3.19-20; 8.22-36; cf. John 1.1-5). Job appeals to the act of creation in order to juxtapose human finitude alongside God's unfathomability (38.4-11). A number of the Psalms highlight God's creation as evidence of his sovereignty, majesty, and glory (8.1-9; 19.1-6).

A variety of extra-biblical texts also offer a substantive recasting of the creation story including *Jubilees*, which expands upon the priestly aspects of the Genesis narrative by including additional legal material on Sabbath observation, purification after childbirth, and sacrifice (2.1–3.31). *Sibylline Oracles* 1 creatively interweaves the Genesis creation story within the context of a Greco-Roman mytho-historical framework, and the first chapter of Josephus's *Antiquities* combines, paraphrases, and nuances the two biblical accounts in order to create a smooth-flowing narrative.

In recent years, the message of the biblical creation account has often been overshadowed by the imposition of modernist statements of scientific theory and pseudo-science onto this foundational biblical text. These concerns, however, were certainly foreign to the biblical writer, and to pursue them is to ignore the bevy of theological statements latent within Genesis.

Recommended reading. Anderson, Bernhard W. *From Creation to New Creation*. Minneapolis: Fortress Press, 1994. Cassuto, Umberto. *A Commentary on the Book of Genesis*. Trans. Israel Abrahams. Vol. 1, pp. 7-177. Jerusalem: Magnes Press, 1961.

See also FINGER OF GOD; GOD [TAB]

Cross, Crucifixion of Christ. At its height, the Roman Empire was a vast civilization which exuded its influence over a number of conquered nations. Due to the fact that the Roman Empire was so expansive, it was difficult to ensure order and maintain compliance by the different regions. As a result, the Roman elite adopted a lethal form of punishment that was so cruel that it was feared by all people. Although the Romans were not the first to practice the punishment of crucifixion, which was developed by the Carthaginians and utilized by the Persians and Alexander the Great, their use of the technique is best known.

The actual act of crucifying a person involves nailing or hanging a person to a tree or to timbers in the shape of a T or X. Although there are references to the use of nails in the act of crucifixion, most notably Jesus (although not explicit in the NT, see John 20.25; *Gospel of Peter* 6.20), some crucifixion victims were attached to a cross by tying their arms and legs to the wood. Regardless of the nature of the cross, or how that person was attached, after the person was raised up on the cross the crucifixion of a person continued until that person died, usually from suffocation.

This is merely the act of crucifixion; however, the entire process is much more involved and degrading. The whole process of crucifixion was designed to humiliate the victim and maximize the amount of shame and suffering that person incurred. Regardless of whether the person was still living or dead, this type of public exposure stripped the victim of their last vestiges of honor, leaving them entirely shamed. In the ancient sources, one thing associated with crucifixion and punishment of crimes is a torture list. Crucifixion did not occur by itself, but was accompanied by a number of other physical and emotional punishments that compounded the shame and pain.

Easily the most famous incidence of crucifixion is the story about Jesus reported in the Gospels (Matt. 27.32-44; Mark 15.21-32; Luke 23.26-43; John 19.17-27). In evaluating these crucifixion narratives, it is clear that his execution by the Romans follows the typical procedure for killing a person this way. Similarly, the mocking and flogging that preceded Jesus' death (Matt. 27.27-31) also resembles crucifixion narratives found in other sources.

The cross eventually became an important Christian symbol. In the first centuries after Jesus' death, the cross was still feared as emblematic of the highest form of torture and so the cross is relatively rare in Christian iconography. The majority of Christians preferred the *Ichthus*, or fish symbol. However, after Constantine's famous dream in which he saw a heavenly cross, it gradually became the dominate symbol of Christianity.

When looking for the use of the cross and crucifixion in modern culture, it is clear that Christians and the church are the primary utilizers of this motif. Although a number of movies tell the story of the passion narrative, the most recent and arguably one of the best received in North America is Mel Gibson's *The Passion of the Christ* (2004). In addition to this, the theme of crucifixion has been the subject of many novels, including the religious-fiction *Crucifixion Trilogy* by Sam Sheldon.

Recommended reading. Adams, Sean A. 'Crucifixion in the Ancient World: A Response to L.L. Welborn'. In *Paul's World*. Ed. Stanley E. Porter. Pp. 111-29. Leiden: Brill, 2008.

See also JESUS OF NAZARETH; ROMAN EMPIRE; TRIAL OF JESUS [SAA]

Crown of thorns. In common usage, 'Crown of Thorns' refers to something that causes great suffering, an image originating in biblical passages related to Jesus. When Jesus is sentenced to death in the Gospels, he is first mocked by the Roman soldiers and forced to wear a purple robe and a crown made of thorns. This event is recorded in three of the four canonical Gospels (Matt. 27.29; Mark 15.17; John 19.2, 5).

In art, Jesus is often depicted wearing the Crown of Thorns while carrying his cross and during his crucifixion. These depictions are known as *Ecce Homo* scenes, which derive from Latin words literally translated as 'behold the man'. Such representations in art began around the ninth and tenth centuries and continue today. Perhaps the most famous contemporary portrait of this scene is Lovis Corinth's painting *Ecce Homo* from 1925, which offers, from the perspective of the crowd, Jesus tied up with a soldier at one side and Pontius Pilate on the other.

The Crown of Thorns may also refer to a relic some believe is still in existence. As early as the beginning of the fifth century, St Paulinus of Nola wrote that along with the cross and the pillar of Jesus, the Crown of Thorns is a relic held in admiration. As to its location, in the sixth century Antoninus of Piacenza believed the relic of the Crown of Thorns was displayed in a church on Mount Sion. Today, a portion of the Crown of Thorns is preserved in the upper room in Sainte Chapelle, Paris, France.

As a literary device, the Crown of Thorns highlights the title attributed to Jesus during the Passion scene when he is referred to as the King of the Jews. The crown acts as a symbol of this kingship. Though the characters who surround Jesus mock him by placing the crown on his head, they inadvertently emphasize his role in the narrative.

In film, the Crown of Thorns has been employed as a symbol for relating a character to Jesus, thus creating a Christ Figure. The 1989 film *Dead Poets Society* directed by Peter Weir, depicts one of the protagonists Neil Perry committing suicide with his father's revolver. During this scene, he is barechested and wears a Crown of Thorns similar to the popular depictions of Jesus.

Recommended reading. Nickell, Joe. *Relics of the Christ*. Lexington, KY: University Press of Kentucky, 2007.

See also CHRIST FIGURE; ECCE HOMO; JESUS OF NAZARETH [CAM]

Cup. The term indicates various types of drinking vessels used in daily life and in both the personal celebrations and religious rituals of people living in the Ancient Near East and throughout the Greco-Roman world. In the OT, the Hebrew word most commonly used is *kōsôt* (drinking cup-bowl) while in the NT the Koine Greek word *potērion* (cup) is most often utilized.

Cups were essential and valued objects in the ancient world. Those of lower social rank used cups made of clay, and they often consumed their daily drink with a straw made from a reed or grain stalk. The wealthy, who were usually members of the ruling class, used cups made of gold, silver, or glass. A cupbearer like Nehemiah, who served the Persian King Artaxerxes, held a position that gave its holder significant responsibility, political influence, and personal prestige. Such an individual was required to test the king's food and drink for poison, and when asked, offer advice to the monarch (see Neh. 1.11–2.6).

Cups also came in various shapes and sizes. Beautifully decorated bowls, sieve-spouted jugs, elaborate goblets, and horn-shaped vessels (known as rhytons) were some of the cup-styles used in the ancient world. Such vessels could depict animals, such as the ram, horse or bull, or supernatural creatures or deities. Cups used in the royal courts were often engraved with inscriptions.

Many biblical references to cups point to their social, symbolic and spiritual roles and purposes. The connection between a cup and its contents is emphasized throughout the OT and NT. The overflowing cup of Ps. 23.5 refers to the metaphor of Yahweh as the gracious and generous host. The 'cup of his wrath' in Isa. 51.17 is also a metaphor used to compare the experience of God's judgment to the experience of becoming drunk where one (usually a nation) loses control and becomes disoriented and confused. In the NT, 'the cup' (of suffering) in the Garden of Gethsemene, the 'cup of blessing', the 'cup of thanksgiving' and the 'cup of the Lord' illustrate the many levels of meaning associated with the use of 'the cup' in the Lord's Supper (see 1 Cor. 10.14-22; Luke 22.14-18).

Perhaps the most famous cup in Western cultural mythology is 'The Holy Grail', the drinking vessel used by Jesus at the Last Supper. The quest to find this relic formed a key element in the legendary adventures of King Arthur and his Knights of the Round Table. Western interest in 'The Holy Grail' continues to the present. Books and films, such as Dan Brown's best-selling novel, *The Da Vinci Code* (2003) and the subsequent blockbuster feature film in 2006 testify to our enduring fascination with this western cultural icon. Undoubtedly, one of the most popular films about the Holy Grail is the 1975 satirical comedy entitled *Monty Python and the Holy Grail*. This film remains a cult classic. In 2000, for example, readers of *Total Film Magazine* voted *Monty Python and the Holy Grail* the fifth greatest comedy film of all time.

Recommended reading. King, Philip J., and Lawrence E. Stager. *Life in Biblical Israel*. Louisville and London: Westminster John Knox Press, 2001. Wilkins, John M., and Shaun Hill. *Food in the Ancient World*. Malden, Oxon.: Blackwell Publishing, 2006. Fleming, Stuart J. *Vinum: The Story of Roman Wine*. Warminster, Wilts.: Piccari Press, 2001.

See also WINE; EUCHARIST [PRW]

Cyrus II (the Great). Cyrus II (Hebrew/Aramaic, *kores*), ruled 559–530 BCE, founding the Persian Empire. Under Cyrus, Persia transformed from being a small kingdom—possibly subservient to Media—to becoming more expansive than any prior empire. He conquered nearly all of the Ancient Near East (except Egypt), including Assyria (547) and Babylon (539).

As exemplified in the so-called 'Cyrus Cylinder' and his decree found in Ezra 1.2-4 (cf. also 2 Chron. 36.22-23), Cyrus permitted his subjects to worship local deities, like Marduk and Yahweh. The Cyrus Cylinder suggests that Cyrus was summoned by Marduk in defeating Nabonidus and restoring worship of the Babylonian god. Likewise, after conquering Babylon he allowed the Jews to return home and reestablish proper worship of their god. This strategy effectively secured the loyalty of the people-groups he conquered, and has resulted in a consistently positive portrayal of Cyrus by his contemporaries and later writers. The Book of Isaiah even describes Cyrus, a non-Jew, messianically (*mashiah*, 'anointed one', Isa. 45.1).

Cyrus's approach involved propaganda, functioning for the greater purpose of maintaining peace throughout the empire. The text on the Cyrus Cylinder suggests that he desired to be perceived as benevolent by his subjects, even though he sometimes acted ruthlessly. At any rate, his actual benevolence combined with his self-aggrandizing claims successfully branded his image in history as almost wholly positive.

Herodotus, Xenophon, and Plato highly esteemed Cyrus, despite their commonly negative portrayal of non-Greeks. Contemporary business and military leaders still use Xenophon's *Cyropaedia* for its valuable leadership principles. Both Dante Alighieri and Edmund Spenser allude to Herodotus's account of Cyrus (cf. His*tories*, 1.201-14); Dante refers to his death by Tomyris (*Purgatorio*, Canto 12.55) and Spenser refers to Araxes, the river he crossed just before his death (*Faerie Queene*, Book 4, Canto 11.21). Gioachino Rossini wrote *Ciro in Babilonia* (1812), an operatic composition telling the biblical story of Cyrus overtaking Babylon.

Comparisons have been made between subsequent rulers and Cyrus, particularly ones who acted kindly toward the Jewish people of their respective times. The Jewish community throughout Europe compared Napoleon to Cyrus because the latter allowed the Jewish Sanhedrin to reconvene (1806). Harry Truman referred to himself as Cyrus (1953) for leading the United States in being the first nation to recognize the modern State of Israel (founded 1948). Ottoman Sultan Mehmet II (1432–1481), Emperor Joseph II (1741–1790), and Tsar Alexander II (1818–1881) have also been compared to Cyrus.

Uses of Cyrus in the West have often related to what he did for the Jewish people, reflecting the privileged status the Bible has had as a source of information and symbolism. Today the biblical influence is less direct. He is not seen as just a liberator of the Jews, but more broadly as an early proponent of human rights. The United Nations Headquarters contains a replica of the Cyrus Cylinder (est. 1971) and a replica of the bas-relief recovered at Pasargade was erected in Bicentennial Park, Sydney, Australia (est. 1994); these both look back to Cyrus as a symbol of diversity and tolerance. In popular culture, the Chahaya Group hopes to promote a message of peace and tolerance through a film about Cyrus.

Recommended reading. Yamauchi, Edwin M. *Persia and the Bible*. Baker: 1990.

See also BABYLONIAN CAPTIVITY, THE; DARIUS; EXILE; JEW/JUDAISM; CHRIST; PROMISED LAND [BJL]

D

Dagon. From the Hebrew *dab* (fish) or *dagan* (grain). Dagon was originally worshiped by the Canaanites and became the chief god of the Philistines after they invaded Canaan in the twelfth century BCE. The god of agricultural fertility, Dagon is depicted as a merman, having the face, arms, and torso of a man and the tail of a fish. Though there is mention of his inferiority to the Israelite God in 1 Sam. 5 and of his temple housing Saul's head in 1 Chron. 10, Dagon is most widely known from chaps. 13–16 in the Book of Judges. These chapters trace the story of Samson, the Israelite man whom God imbued with great physical strength, and his undoing by the beautiful Delilah. After Delilah learns that the source of Samson's strength is his hair, she informs the Philistines who promptly shave his head and seize the weakened Samson, gouging out his eyes and imprisoning him in Gaza. Believing that their god had assisted them in the capture of their enemy, the Philistines gathered at Dagon's temple to offer a sacrifice. Brought to the temple and stood between the structure's two load-bearing pillars, Samson prayed, 'Lord God, remember me and strengthen me only this once, O God, so that with this one act of revenge I may pay back the Philistines for my two eyes. . . . Let me die with the Philistines' (Judg. 16.28, 30). God thus reinstated Samson's superhuman strength, enabling Samson to push apart the pillars and topple the temple of Dagon.

Modern cultural references to Dagon appear in a variety of outlets from literary masterpieces to popular music to television shows. In Book One of *Paradise Lost*, for instance, English poet John Milton paraphrases 1 Sam. 5, writing of 'one / Who mourned in earnest, when the captive ark / Maimed his brute image, head and hands lopt off, / In his own temple, on the grunsel-edge, / Where he fell flat and shamed his worshippers: / Dagon his name, sea-monster, upward man / And downward fish' (ll. 457-63). American horror fictionist H.P. Lovecraft wrote a 1917 short story titled 'Dagon', in which a merchant marine officer comes upon a strange white monolith decorated with sculptures of half-men, half-fish just before a giant, scaly creature emerges from the waters below. And in 1968, North Carolina writer Fred Chappell released a novel entitled *Dagon*, which tells the story of a young minister who preaches that Dagon is still worshiped in American culture. He encounters a sinister sect devoted to the pagan deity in the North Carolina mountains.

Perhaps the most comprehensive musical version of the Samson story is the song entitled 'Dagon Undone (The Reckoning)'. Sung by the Christian metal band The Showdown, this song recounts Samson's capture and the subsequent destruction of the temple of Dagon. Famous director Cecil B. DeMille brought Vladimir Jabotinsky's novel *Samson Nazorei* to life on the big screen with the film *Samson and Delilah* (1949). On television, the hugely popular *Buffy the Vampire Slayer* series has a storyline revolving around the Order of Dagon and the Dagon Sphere, and the Stephen Spielberg cartoon *Pinky and the Brain* bends the Samson story to its purposes, turning Dagon into a papier-mâché idol. This pagan god maintains, therefore, a prominent cultural presence even though little is known of him.

Recommended reading. Dahiyat, Eid. 'The Philistine Deity Dagon: The Semitic Origin and Two Possible Derivations'. *Studia anglica posnaniensia: An International Review of English Studies* 20 (1987) 213-16.

See also SAMUEL; PHILISTINES; JUDGES, BOOK OF; SAMSON; DELILAH; CANAAN/CANAANITES   [DN]

Damascus Road. This phrase and similar expressions derive from the NT story of Saul's (later, the Apostle Paul) encounter with the risen Jesus near the city of Damascus.

The Acts of the Apostles describes this event in three places (Acts 9, 22, 26), each new passage providing fresh details while retaining the essential story. Paul (also called Saul) was a zealous Jewish Pharisee on his way from Jerusalem to Damascus to persecute the Jewish Christians there when he was confronted by a blinding light accompanied by a heavenly voice. The speaker identified himself as Jesus, who had been crucified and subsequently resurrected by God, and called on Paul to join the cause of the Christians he had persecuted and to proclaim the Christian message about Jesus to Israel and the Gentile nations. Paul himself in his letters provides the same essential details: in the midst of persecuting Christians as a zealous Pharisee, he experienced a revelation of Jesus near Damascus, a revelation which included a commission to teach about Jesus among the Gentiles (Gal. 1.11-17; cf. Phil. 3.4-11).

Two distinctive elements are especially emphasized in these biblical accounts of Paul's 'Damascus Road' experience. First, this experience was a divine revelation, God making known something otherwise unknown. Acts describes it as a 'heavenly vision'

(Acts 26.19); Paul himself describes it as a 'revelation of Jesus Christ' to him (Gal. 1.12, 16). Second, this experience was a conversion of some sort, though precisely what kind of conversion remains a matter of some dispute among scholars. Clearly it resulted in a radical change in thinking and behavior for Paul, and it certainly brought about a drastic change in Paul's social and even religious situation. However, the biblical accounts do not describe this experience as a change in religion for Paul, or a change from irreligion to religion or from immorality to morality, but more as a call by the same God to serve him in the right way reflecting the changed situation brought about by the resurrection of the crucified Jesus.

Drawing on these two primary elements from the biblical texts, 'Damascus Road' has come to symbolize any sudden and radical change in thinking and behavior resulting from a single, intense experience. Certainly this is the case in religious contexts as the image frequently symbolizes conversion to Christianity from another religion or worldview. The history of Christianity is thus filled with references and allusions to Paul's 'Damascus Road' experience. In literature and art, the story represents an idealized conversion, and the phrase 'Damascus Road' or similar expressions can be found today in everything from church names to song lyrics. But the phrase is not limited to religious contexts in Western culture. For example, someone who ardently opposes a particular political candidate but suddenly becomes a fervent supporter of that candidate after hearing her speak could be said to have had a 'Damascus Road' experience.

Recommended reading. Stendahl, Krister. *Paul among Jews and Gentiles, and Other Essays*. Philadelphia: Fortress Press, 1976. Longenecker, Richard N. (ed.). *The Road from Damascus: The Impact of Paul's Conversion on his Life, Thought, and Ministry*. Grand Rapids, MI: Eerdmans, 1997.

See also CONVERSION; PAUL, THE APOSTLE [MWP]

Daniel. This proper name means, 'God is my judge', or 'Judge of God'. Daniel was the name of one of David's son (1 Chron. 3.1), and the name of one of the four Major Prophets in the HB. While David's son was originally recorded as Chileab the son of Abigail the Carmelite (2 Sam. 3.3), nothing else was said about him. Daniel the prophet however has a book of the Bible named after him that contains some autobiographical content about his experiences among the Jewish exiles.

Daniel was part of a group of young Hebrew nobles trained to serve in the king of Babylon's court (Dan. 1.3). He and his three friends Shadrach, Meschach and Abednego excelled at what they did, and served as magi in the Babylonian court. In Babylon, Daniel was given the name Belteshazzar, meaning 'Bel protect the king'. A wise man and an interpreter of dreams, Daniel's uncanny ability to know and interpret royal dreams and visions endeared him to the Babylonian kings (Dan. 2 and 5). This led to promotion and the offer of gifts.

As a religious vegetarian, he and his three friends refused to defile themselves with the royal food, and opted for water and vegetables (Dan. 1.8-16). Such was his popularity with kings that he was given the oversight of the kingdom by both the Babylonian king Nebuchadnezzar and the Persian king Darius (Dan. 2.48; 6.3). This however, led to jealousy among the other wise men, and they plotted against him. The plot against him lies behind the well-known story of Daniel in the lions' den.

Daniel's colleagues despised him because of the royal favor he enjoyed and they knew the only way to get the king angry was to make Daniel break one of the royal decree. This was only accomplished because of Daniel's refusal to stop praying to God, instead of praying to the king for three days. As a result, Daniel was cast into the king's lions' den, where he was miraculously saved from being devoured by the animals (Dan. 6).

This particular incident is represented in contemporary culture in different ways, most especially as works of art, and in songs. There are different paintings depicting Daniel in the lion's den. Painters like Irish painter and engraver Briton Rivière (1840—1920) depicted Daniel looking out of the window, while surrounded by lions who looked as if they were afraid to go near him. While others like French painter François Verdier (1651–1730) depicted an angel above Daniel, stopping the lions from coming close to him.

A contemporary of Ezekiel, it is possible that this was the same Daniel referred to in Ezek. 14.14, 20 and 28.3. He was a righteous man who found favor with God (Dan. 10.11-12). He was also one of the few in Scripture said to have contact with the angel Gabriel (Dan. 9.21).

See also DANIEL, BOOK OF; APOCALYPSE, APOCALYPTIC; BELSHAZZAR; NEBUCHADNEZZAR [GOA]

Daniel, Book of. Named after the prophet Daniel, the book of Daniel in the HB is considered part of the 'writings' (*Ketubim*). Consisting mostly of historical-narratives and personal visions and prophecies shown to Daniel, the book starts with the story of a young Hebrew boy named Daniel, and ends with prophecies about Israel and the nations. The setting for the narratives in the book is mostly the Babylonian royal court where Daniel and his friends struggle to remain true to their God.

The book has twelve chapters, and the first six are devoted to the historical-narratives. The last six includes three prophecies and lengthy prophetic communications, as well as Daniel's prayer of intercession. Though most of the OT was written in Hebrew, part of the Book of Daniel was written in Aramaic (2.4–7.28). There are also various additions to Daniel included in the (Greek) Septuagint.

The book itself claims Daniel is the author (Dan. 7.1, 28; 8.2; 9.2; 10.1, 2; 12.4, 5) which, if accurate, would locate the time of composition somewhere in the sixth century BCE. Scholars, however, dispute the authorship and the authenticity of the book for various reasons. For instance, extra-biblical sources do not have Belshazzar at any time on the throne of Babylon, and there are no records of Nebuchadnezzar being the father of Belshazzar as the book of Daniel claims (Dan. 5.18). However, there are records of Nabonidus the son of Nebuchadnezzar being away from the palace during the last days of his empire, while his son Belshazzar was left in charge.

A major thrust of the book of Daniel is its emphasis on the fact that Yahweh is still in charge of history and kings. Regardless of location and status, Yahweh still controls nature and humans. This is evident in all of the stories and prophecies recorded in the book of Daniel. There is a definite message of Yahweh's sovereignty over all of times and places. For this reason, it is not surprising that an eschatological message dominates the visions of the book and that it influenced the NT Book of Revelation, which explores similar themes.

A particular understanding of Daniel's visions of the last days are widely used by American evangelical dispensationalists like Tim LaHaye and Jerry B. Jenkins in their bestselling *Left Behind* novels. Some of the characters and names in the Book of Daniel are used in the Wachowski brothers' directed movie *The Matrix* (1999). Morpheus's ship *Nebuchadnezzar* is named after the king of Babylon mentioned in the first chapters of the Book of Daniel. The name of the movie's protagonist Neo Anderson is likely based on Dan. 7.11 and the Aramaic phrase 'one like a son of man'. Anderson is a patronymic for son of Anders/Andrew (man).

Recommended reading. Collins, John J., and Peter W. Flint (eds.). *The Book of Daniel: Composition and Reception*. Leiden: Brill, 2001. Collins, John J. *The Apocalyptic Imagination: An Introduction to Jewish Apocalyptic Literature*. 2nd ed. Grand Rapids, MI: Eerdmans, 1998.

See also APOCALYPSE, APOCALYPTIC; APOCRYPHA, DEUTEROCANONICALS AND INTERTESTAMENTALS; BELSHAZZAR; HANDWRITING ON THE WALL; DANIEL; REVELATION, BOOK OF [GOA]

Darius. The king of Achaemenian Persia, the name Darius is derived from the Persian Darayavahus ('Upholder of Good') and there were three kings with that name. Darius I fits closest to the 'Darius the Mede' of the Bible. However, there are problems as the title 'Darius the Mede' appears in only the Bible, the works of Flavius Josephus, and Jewish Midrash material. Darius captured the city of Babylon in 522 BCE, and did help set up the empire into satrapies, appointing satraps of which Daniel was one (Dan. 6.1). However, the title 'The Mede' goes against this as Darius I was not a Mede (who were a subject people to the Persians at the time). It is possible the term 'Mede' was used imprecisely by Jewish writers. There are, however, some historians who have suggested that there could have been another Mede king, otherwise unrecorded, called Darius who had previously taken the city. It has also been suggested that he was Cyrus as the words in Hebrew are very similar, and a transcription error could have occurred. In Ezra 6.14, there is a reference to 'Cyprus, Darius and King Artaxerxes of Persia' but it could be argued that the context indicates somebody else entirely.

There are occasional references to Darius the Mede in contemporary culture, the most famous being that by Vachel Lindsay in the song 'Daniel': 'Darius the Mede was a king and a wonder, his eye was proud and his voice thunder'. Darius I is immortalized on a forty-foot long relief at Behistun, and in October 1971 for the 1500th anniversary of the Persian Empire, Darius's virtues were extolled by the Shah of Iran and his government. In literature, Darius I appears in Olivia E. Coolidge's novel *Marathon Looks on the Sea* (1967) and in R.F. Tapsell's *Shadow of Wings* (1972). Darius II, the great-grandson of Darius I, although he reigned for 19 years, did not involve himself in Greek affairs, and hence much less is known about him. Darius II's great-grandson, Darius III, was the last Persian emperor who was vanquished by Alexander the Great, an event celebrated in ancient times by, amongst other things, a mosaic at Pompeii (now in the National Archaeological Museum in Naples); and recently in films such as *Alexander the Great* (1956) and Oliver Stone's *Alexander* (2004). Both films draw heavily from the mosaic, and Darius is shown as a bad general and a coward. The defeat is also mentioned in the song 'Alexander the Great' by the heavy metal band Iron Maiden.

See also PERSIA; DANIEL, BOOK OF; CYRUS II (THE GREAT) [JC]

Daughter of my people. The term, *bat-'ammî* (daughter of my people) appears in the Bible fourteen times; it is used once in the poetry of the prophet known as first Isaiah (22.4), numerous instances in the poetry of the prophet Jeremiah, and several times in the poetry of the Book of Lamentations. There are two different understandings of the use of this term: the prophets employ it to refer either to (1) a poetic persona, or to (2) a female person in the community. As such, it refers to a female personification of the people, or it refers to an actual female figure. In the first understanding, it is analogous to 'Daughter of Zion' (or, Daughter Zion) and similar phrases widely recognized as poetically crafted personae representing the people of Jerusalem or Judah. Those phrases have the structure of 'daughter' plus a geographical reference. On the other hand, 'daughter' plus the actual term 'people' is reflected in the use of the phrase 'daughters of your people' by the prophet Ezekiel (13.17); his phrase clearly refers to women prophets active in his context. This pattern supports the second understanding above, and suggests that the singular 'daughter of my people' refers to an unnamed woman prophet in the above books (e.g., Isaiah's wife or woman partner in Isa. 9 who is called a prophet; Jeremiah's reference to an unnamed woman prophet in his context; Lamentations has a central female voice in its poetic composition). This referring to *bat-'ammî* (daughter of my people) by male prophets would reflect historical contexts when a few women prophets were known to exist in the kingdoms of Israel and Judah, and serve as a rhetorical signal pointing to unnamed women prophets hidden in the shadows of history.

Recommended reading. Bowen, Nancy R. 'The Daughters of your People: Female Prophets in Ezekiel 13:17-23'. *Journal of Biblical Literature* 118 (1999) 417-33. Lee, Nancy C. 'Prophetic '*Bat-'Ammî*' Answers God and Jeremiah'. *Lectio difficilior: European Electronic Journal for Feminist Exegesis* 2 (2009), http://www.lectio.unibe.ch/e/infos.htm.

See also DAUGHTER OF ZION; JERUSALEM [NCL]

Daughter of Zion. The phrase daughter of Zion is identical to daughter of Jerusalem since 'Zion' is a symbolic or metaphoric designation for the historical city of Jerusalem (cf. Zech. 9.9). The idiom daughter of Zion appears in the OT, particularly in Isaiah, Jeremiah, Lamentation, Micah, and Zechariah, as a personification of the city of Jerusalem and its inhabitants. This Hebrew idiom, in fact, contains a double metaphor that seemed widespread in ancient Near East culture: a capital city personified as a woman, and its inhabitants collectively as its 'daughter' (cf. 'daughter [of] Sidon' [Isa. 23.12]; 'daughter [of] Babylon' [Jer. 50.42]). Zech. 9.9, for example, addresses, 'Rejoice greatly, O daughter [of] Zion! Shout aloud, O daughter [of] Jerusalem! Lo, your king comes to you; triumphant and victorious is he, humble and riding on a donkey, on a colt, the foal of a donkey' (quoted later in the NT as Messianic prophecy [Matt. 21.5 and John 12.15]). One finds another example in Mic. 4.10: 'Writhe and groan, O daughter [of] Zion, like a woman in labor; for now you shall go forth from the city and camp in the open country; you shall go to Babylon'. As these two cited examples indicate, the idiom is employed in portraying both the glory and the doom of the city and its citizens. The plural form, 'daughters of Zion', occurs in Isa. 3.16-17 and 4.4, denoting the female inhabitants of the city, and in Song 3.11, referring probably to the king's women or the female attendants in the palace (at least in the literary context).

In his early fourth-century defense of Christianity (*Divinae institutiones* [PL 6.542]), Lactantius interprets Song of Solomon (and Jer. 2.13) allegorically, with the effect of designating the Jewish synagogue as the 'daughter of Jerusalem' (synonym to 'daughter of Zion') and the Church as the 'New Jerusalem', thus granting the Church a superior and more ultimate status. On the other hand, the twelfth-century Cistercian St Bernard of Clairvaux views 'daughters of Zion' as worldly and spiritually frail people, in contrast to 'sons', in his sermon on Song 3.11. The idiom, however, is often Christianized. In his twelfth-century sermon, Master Peter Comestor designates the theological students listening to his preaching in Paris as 'daughters of Zion'. Along the same line, yet with a universal perspective, the twelfth-century liturgical poetry of Adam of St Victor identifies the Church with 'Jerusalem, daughter of Zion' (*Dedica-*

tione Ecclesiae). Similarly, when preaching on Song 3.11 at a coronation service, John Flavel (1630–96), an English Puritan, interprets 'Zion' as the Church and 'daughters of Zion' as members of the Church or Christian believers.

Some groups who promoted a new religious movement, within and beyond Christian 'orthodoxy', employed the idiom. For instance, the term 'Daughters of Zion' was used to refer to virtuous Christian women among New England Puritans. On the other hand, a group of early Mormon assassins called themselves 'the Daughters of Zion', which were later named 'the Danites' (i.e., the sons of Dan). Today a number of Christian organizations that consist of only females name themselves '(the) daughters of Zion'. There is also a Jewish example: the 'Daughters of Zion' was a Jewish women's organization founded in America in 1912 with a Zionist background. It was renamed 'Hadassah' in 1914.

See also WOMAN; DAUGHTER OF MY PEOPLE; ZION; JERUSALEM [JOL]

Daughters of Philip. The daughters of Philip appear in Acts 21.8-9, during the account of the Apostle Paul's final journey to Jerusalem: 'The next day we left and came to Caesarea; and we went into the house of Philip the evangelist, one of the seven, and stayed with him. He had four unmarried daughters (*parthenoi;* or virgins) who had the gift of prophecy (*prophēteuousai*)'.

The author of Luke–Acts occasionally emphasizes the contributions of women to the early Christian communities. In Acts 2.17a, Peter invokes the prophecy of Joel: 'In the last days it will be, God declares, that I will pour out my Spirit upon all flesh, and your sons and your daughters shall prophesy'. Though Acts says no more about the daughters of Philip, continuing instead with a description of a male prophet named Agabus who warned Paul of dangers awaiting him in Jerusalem, the prophetic daughters of Philip are mentioned by Papias and Bishop Polycrates of Ephesus, by the Roman Presbyter Gaius, and by the early church historian Eusebius. While women prophets were part of some early Christian communities, and active in the HB, unfortunately their words and the extent of their activities were rarely preserved. Yet the author of Luke–Acts is especially aware of their role. The prophet Anna appears in Luke 2.36 and a woman slave who was a prophet appears in Acts 16.16-18. Also notable in the NT writings are the women prophets described by Paul in 1 Cor. 11. Female prophets also emerge in the later Montanist movement (c. 150 CE). That the biblical canon includes women prophets should not be underestimated, even though the information about them is so minimal. Prophets were recognized as infused with God's Spirit, entrusted with being spokespersons for God, who could guide and critique individuals, and social and religious authorities (mostly male). An interesting development in women's self-determination, perhaps reflected in the story about the daughters of Philip, is the reference to their virginity. There is evidence that some women prophets remained virgins, such as some of the Greek women prophets, oracles of Delphi. Some Christian women chose not to marry and remain virgins as a way of radically freeing themselves from traditional duties expected by the culture, while they followed a fuller life of faith (see references in *Acts of Paul and Thecla*); they were at times also called 'widows', having sacrificed marriage. The daughters of Philip, women prophets, and those women who pursued unorthodox paths for lives of faith, all offer affirmation to today's women. They provide unexpected resources for women seeking opportunity and equity today, in religious or secular spheres, who still struggle against a legacy of gender discrimination. The holiness movement found inspiration from such prophetic women to support women's preaching and ordination in the 1800s.

Recommended reading. Gaventa, Beverly. 'What Ever Happened to Those Prophesying Daughters?' In *A Feminist Companion to the Acts of the Apostles*. Ed. Marianne Blickenstaff and Amy-Jill Levine. Pp. 49-60. New York: Pilgrim Press, 2005. Kraemer, Ross. *Her Share of the Blessings: Women's Religions among Pagans, Jews, and Christians in the Greco-Roman World*. New York: Oxford University Press, 1992. Reimer, Ivoni Richter. *Women in the Acts of the Apostles: A Feminist Liberation Perspective*. Minneapolis: Fortress Press, 1995.

See also ACTS OF THE APOSTLES, THE [NCL]

Daughters of Zelophehad. The episode of the daughters of Zelophehad occurs in the narrative context of the allotment of the land in the wilderness, after the Exodus but before entry into the land (Num. 26.32-33; 27.1-11; 36.1-12; Josh. 17.3-6). Zelophehad and his daughters are minor characters whose story establishes precedents for inheritance by females in a society in which the male is primary and identity is established through kinship groups defined through the male line. Zelophehad died leaving five daughters and no sons. The daughters petition Moses to allocate them the portion of the land that would have gone to their father, so that his memory would be preserved in the association between land and name. The request is granted with divine approval on condition that they marry within their clan. In later interpretation, the story has functioned as a basis for rules of inheritance (particularly in Jewish interpretation) and more recently, served as a model of women asserting themselves without breaching societal boundaries in a context in which they are secondary to males. The story also serves as symbol for the provision of shelter and support to disempowered women, such as victims of domestic violence. A motif of female inheritance of the father's assets appears in modern literature and film (e.g., *Lara Croft*, *The King of Texas*), usually as back-story for a plot about subsequent events. In contrast, the biblical account does not detail the subsequent life of the daughters.

See also HOLY LAND; PROMISED LAND [PT]

David. A straightforward reading of 2 Samuel would lead to the assumption that David ruled Israel c. 1000–960 BCE. According to 1 Sam. 16, he came from a landholding family in Bethlehem, just south of Jerusalem, and rose to power as a warrior and courtier of his predecessor Saul. Though married to Saul's daughter, Michal, he became a rival for the throne, first joining, and then opposing, the Philistines along the Mediterranean coast. David must have had a reputation as a political genius, albeit a ruthless one, because 2 Samuel takes great pains to exonerate him of charges of murder and intrigue (though it does admit his murder of Uriah the Hittite, whose wife Bathsheba David stole).

After his own lifetime, David became a great hero. First Chronicles remembers him as the one who laid the groundwork for the peace and prosperity of Solomon's reign and even for the building of the temple that symbolized such good times. The Chronicler omitted all references to David's sin with Bathsheba, conflict with members of his own family, and other signs of his human frailties. The editors of the book of Psalms prefaced 73 psalms with superscriptions attributing the given psalm 'to David'. However, the Hebrew phrase *l^eDawid* ('to David') does not imply that David wrote these psalms, but merely that they pertain to him or to his royal successors in some way. Later still, the Dead Sea Scrolls contain a short collection of psalms that attributes to David over 4000 hymns (most fictitious), which he composed as a response to prophetic inspiration (11QPs^a). By the time of Jesus, David had become a model king and an inspiration, at least for some Jews, for a coming messiah. Hence, the frequent NT references to Jesus as the 'son of David' (see Matt. 21.9; but contrast Mark 11.10).

In the Middle Ages, artists in various media portrayed many stories of David. His adultery with Bathsheba answered an obvious interest, but the more common portrayal showed him as a composer of music, often with a harp or miniature organ. As the model musician, David was the inspiration for one of the earliest Christian hymnals, Schütz's *Psalmen David* of 1619. (In Calvinist churches, the Psalms were the only permitted songs in church until the end of the seventeenth century, again reflecting the popularity of David.) Statues of him by Donatello and Michaelangelo portrayed him with a flawless male body, perhaps anticipating the modern interest in David as a homoerotic figure (based on a misunderstanding of the biblical stories about him and Jonathan).

In contemporary literature and music, David has become a symbol of the troubled ruler, as in Joseph Heller's *God Knows* and Stefan Heym's *King David Report* (a veiled criticism of East German communism). Arthur Honegger wrote a dramatic opera, *Le roi David* (1921), as did Darius Milhaud (*David*, 1954), while movies starring Gregory Peck (1951) and Richard Gere (1985), among many others, have tried to bring David's life to the screen. In every age, David is a kind of Rorschach test, a symbol of human dreams and fears. Our continued fascination with him testifies to his great, if not altogether commendable, achievements.

Recommended reading. McKenzie, Steven. *King David: A Biography*. Oxford: Oxford University Press, 2000.

See also ABSALOM; BATHSHEBA; SAUL, KING; SOLOMON; SWORD [MWH]

Day of Atonement, the. Anglicized as Yom Kippur, it refers to a yearly ritual for the expiation of sin from the Hebrew community. The foundational text is Lev. 16, where Yahweh offers a series of special instructions to be followed by Moses' brother Aaron, Israel's high priest. Precipitated by the death of Aaron's sons (Lev. 10.1-2; 16.1), the directives are intended to protect the Jewish community from the threat of death (Lev. 16.3, 13) and the contagion of sin (16.16, 30), reinforcing routine purification offerings (Lev. 4). Through a sequence of ritual washing, burnt offerings and sacrifices, Aaron must make atonement for himself and for the community, cleansing Yahweh's inmost sanctuary in the process. Of the animals gathered for the sacrifices, one 'scapegoat' is to be left alive, sent into the wilderness, symbolically expelling all the confessed sins out of the encampment and into regions characterized by chaos and death. The re-ordered community then initiates a Sabbath of disciplined rest and humility.

In the NT, the Yom Kippur tradition remains influential, especially in shaping sacrificial imagery. The author of Hebrews conceptualizes Christ as high priest and mediator, but also paradoxically as the sacrifice itself, entering the Holy Place 'not with the blood of goats and calves, but with his own blood, thus obtaining eternal redemption' (Heb. 9.12). This soteriology forms the basis for the surrounding chapters, underscoring the significance of God's new covenant with his people. Yom Kippur may also inform Paul's motif of the redemptive curse in Gal. 3, while the holiday's austerity is frequently associated with fasting practices in the apostolic and patristic eras.

At stake in this tradition are questions of theodicy; of ostracism and violence; of God's holy presence, welcome but potentially lethal, in human community; and of God's righteousness, held to be incompatible with imperfection and sin. Anticipating Anselm's 'satisfaction' theory, atonement concerns absolving God of injustice as much as it does the eradication of sin and the renewal of covenantal loyalty. These contexts add new urgency to the recitation of the Shema (Deut. 6.4-5).

Yom Kippur was modified in the exilic period, when the first Jerusalem temple had been destroyed and animal sacrifice was impractical for diasporic communities; but the emphasis on confession and rehabilitation continues in modern Jewish observance, reducing the supersessionist temptation to forget the yearly ritual. Setting apart a specific day for atonement prompts reflection on the ways in which people of biblical faiths understand sinfulness, whether as wrongdoing, disloyalty, brokenness, or inherently faulty behavior. Consider the connotations of 'rehab', used as a foreshortened verb and noun in contemporary North American culture: while it can mean the therapeutic restoration of strength and agility, as in sports injuries, it also evokes images of celebrities entering drug-abuse facilities. Often the resulting focus is on the scandal, the sin, rather than the therapy and the hope for true decontamination and rehabilitation. Another secular usage of Yom Kippur evokes judgment, somewhat in the apocalyptic sense, for individual and corporate sin. The eco-prophet hero of Neal Stephenson's novel *Zodiac* (1988) offers a chance for redemption to the scion of a family made rich by illegally dumping toxic waste: 'Yom Kippur, dude. The Day of Atonement is here'.

Recommended reading. Gane, Roy. *Cult and Character: Purification Offerings, Day of Atonement, and Theodicy*. Winona Lake, IN: Eisenbrauns, 2005. Stökl Ben Ezra, Daniel. *The Impact of Yom Kippur on Early Christianity: The Day of Atonement from Second Temple Judaism to the Fifth Century*. WUNT, 163. Tübingen: Mohr Siebeck, 2003.

See also SIN; ATONEMENT; SACRIFICE; REPENTANCE; HOLIDAYS/FEASTS/FESTIVALS, JEWISH; THEODICY [MFL]

Day of the Lord/Judgment/Wrath. Frightening images of 'The Day of the Lord' ('Day of Judgment', 'Day of Wrath') abound throughout the Jewish and Christian Scriptures, as it is often described as a day when the Lord is present in all his holiness. Images of creation shaking, melting and fleeing before his presence are accompanied by the total terror of humanity (Isa. 2.12-22; Nah 1.2-6; Zeph. 1.14–2.3; Joel 2.12-14, 28-32). More than once the description of this day concludes with the question 'Who can stand in his presence?' (cf. Nah 1.6; Rev. 6.17).

This 'day' is portrayed as a response to humanity's rebellion against their Creator. At times, it is directed towards God's people for their covenant infidelity and at other times toward the nations for their wickedness. It is a time when God's capacity for fierce wrath is realized. It is a day when justice is done, God and his people are vindicated, God's rule is established, and the re-creation of Heaven and Earth is imminent.

While both the OT and NT portray this day as a future event that precedes re-creation, they also recognize that the 'The Day of the Lord' is prefigured in many events throughout history. Therefore, it would be a mistake to think of this day in purely futuristic terms. Various prophecies in the OT picture this day as a reality in the immediate future. Isaiah prophesied that this day would be a reality for God's own unfaithful people who were subsequently defeated and exiled in 721 BCE (Isa. 2–3). Nahum similarly prophesied that this day was imminent for Nineveh, which was subsequently destroyed in 612 BCE The most profound prefiguring of 'The Day of the Lord' is found in the crucifixion of Christ. Similarities in Matthew's Gospel between the description of coming judgment (Matt. 24–25) and the passion narrative (26–28) are evidence that Matthew considered the death of Christ as a climactic enactment of 'The Day of the Lord' on behalf of sinful humanity.

'The Day of the Lord' is a pervasive theme in Western culture, although this particular phrase is less common than its ubiquitous alternative 'Judgment Day'. Michelangelo painted a mural on the altar wall of the Sistine chapel in the sixteenth century entitled 'The Last Judgment'. It depicts the second coming of Christ and the judgment of humanity. The movie *Terminator 2: Judgment Day*, starring Arnold Schwarzenegger, is indicative of Western culture's consciousness of this biblical theme. In this movie, the protagonists attempt to avoid the occurrence of 'Judgment Day' which would involve the destruction of humanity in a nuclear war. While the term is used to refer to the end of the world, it is also used to depict individual or localized judgment. A person or group endures a 'judgment day' when they experience a time of testing or a defining moment.

It is interesting to note that western culture often portrays 'Judgment Day' as something to be avoided at all costs and that salvation from it lies within our own ability. This counters the NT picture which portrays 'Judgment Day' not only as imminent, but also sought-after (Matt. 6.9-10; Rev. 22.20) and salvation from it is solely through faith in the One who will execute it (Rev. 7.9-17).

Recommended reading. Allison, Dale C., Jr. *Studies in Matthew: Interpretation Past and Present*. Grand Rapids, MI: Baker Academic, 2005. House, Paul R. 'The Day of the Lord'. In *Central Themes in Biblical Theology*. Ed. Scott J. Hafemann and Paul R. House. Grand Rapids, MI: Baker Academic, 2007.

See also ARMAGEDDON; SECOND COMING [KB]

Deacon/Deaconess. This word derives from the ancient Greek *diakonos*, usually defined as 'servant', 'minister', 'assistant', or 'table-waiter'. In the Hellenistic world, it also came to represent particular cult and temple officials, foreshadowing the technical use of the office within the Christian Church.

As a church office, it originated with the twelve disciples appointing leaders to distribute food (Acts 6.1-6). The responsibilities associated with this office were also liturgical and social, including the care of the poor, widows, and orphans. However, in other biblical passages that use this word and its cognates (Col. 1.7, 23, 25; 4.7; Eph. 6.21; Acts 19.22), the term is applied specifically to preaching, pastoral, and evangelistic work. The only place that gives a technical description of the qualities required of a deacon or deaconess and their household is 1 Tim. 3.8-13.

Today, the role of deacon or deaconess in Christian churches is generally associated with service in all capacities. The role varies throughout different theological and denominational traditions: in some it is an official clerical office, and in others it is filled by the laity. Although predominately considered a male role, there are some denominational traditions that allow women to be ordained as deaconesses.

Although the official role of deaconess gradually disappeared in the later centuries and evolved into the role of celibate religious orders, there is evidence from biblical and other ancient writings that there existed the office of the deaconess. Phoebe was deacon (there was no feminine form of *diakonos* at this time) of the church at Cencreae (Rom. 16.1), and, around 111 CE, Pliny the Younger, governor of Bithynia, reported on a legal case concerning two women called deaconesses in *Epistolae* 10.96.

Today the word 'deacon' is a common surname (e.g., British fashion designer Giles Deacon; British sculptor Richard Deacon; and American electronic musician Dan Deacon). The name Deacon is not as common in given names, however, when actor Reese Witherspoon chose this name for her son (born in 2003) many parents took note of her choice. As a result, the popularity of this name appeared on the US baby-name charts in 2003 and 'peaked' in 2006, still only ranked at #600.

See also PAUL, THE APOSTLE; PHOEBE; POOR, POVERTY; SERVANT; SERVANT OF THE LORD; TWELVE DISCIPLES, THE [RKM]

Dead Sea, the. 'Dead Sea' is a post-biblical name for what the Bible calls the Salt Sea (e.g., Gen. 14.3; Num. 34.12), the Sea of the Arabah (e.g., Deut. 3.17, 4.49), or the East Sea (Joel 2.20). Other extra-canonical names include the Asphalt Lake, the Stinking Sea, and the Sea of Sodom. The Crusaders called it the Devil's Sea, and for Arabs, it is the Sea of Lot.

At 408 meters below sea level, the Dead Sea is the lowest area of the world. It is also one of the world's great wonders where it is virtually impossible for swimmers to drown. The Jordan River's lack of an outlet to the sea and the high level of evaporation have made the Dead Sea a lake of extreme saltiness. Its salinity is over thirty percent while the salinity of the oceans averages only five percent. There are hot springs that feed the Dead Sea, some of which are sulfurous. Petroleum seeps account for the balls of bitumen (pitch) that were gathered from it by the Nabateans and others. The extremely bitter tasting mineral waters were known to the Queen of Sheba, King Solomon, Aristotle, Cleopatra, and to moderns as a medicinal remedy for skin ailments. South of the Dead Sea is the Dead Sea Valley (Wadi al-'Arabah). An extension of the Jordan Valley, it stretches 179 kilometers from the Dead Sea to the port of Aqabah.

In biblical times the Dead Sea was more of an obstacle than anything else so references to it are few. It barrenness prohibited most from entering the area though David sought a place of refuge there, at the spring En-Gedi. He later won a victory over the Edomites there (1 Chron. 18.12), as did King Amaziah (2 Kgs 14.7). Jehoshaphat responded to an army of Moabites and Amorites advancing from the sea for an attack (2 Chron. 20.1-2).

Ezek. 42.1-12 tells of the prophet's vision of a steam of water form the Temple which flows into the Dead Sea and heals its bitter waters. Zechariah prophesied that living waters would flow from Jerusalem to the Dead Sea. This vision might lie behind John's description of a river flowing from the throne of God (Rev. 22.1-2). These prophetic visions contrast with references to the destruction of Sodom and Gomorrah (Gen. 19), which were cities on the Dead Sea plain. Near to a possible site of Sodom are karstic salt pillars called 'Lot's Wife'. Jericho is at the northern end of the lake. On the west is Qumran where the Dead Sea Scrolls were found.

Recommended reading. Kreiger, Barbara. 1997. *The Dead Sea*. Hanover, NH: Brandeis University Press, 1997.

See also DEAD SEA SCROLLS; QUMRAN; LOT'S WIFE; SODOM AND GOMORRAH [AJW]

Dead Sea Scrolls. Popular fascination with the Dead Sea Scrolls began soon after the discovery, in 1947, of seven ancient manuscripts in a cave in the Judean desert, near the Dead Sea. Front-page stories in *The New York Times* and major magazine articles (including a *New Yorker* series by Edmund Wilson that became a bestselling book) celebrated the discoveries. These eventually included eleven scrolls caves, containing fragments of more than 800 manuscripts dating from the second century BCE through the end of the first century CE.

The contents of the scrolls are largely literary and include witnesses to all the canonical books of the HB (except Esther), as well as important ancient Jewish texts such as Enoch, *Jubilees*, and Tobit. Scripture-style texts are common among the scrolls, as are rule texts, prayers, and commentaries of a distinctly sectarian nature. They include almost no documentary material (personal letters, legal documents, etc.), although such material has been found elsewhere in the Judean desert (generally dating to the second-century CE revolt of Bar Kokhba). The messianic expectations and endtimes orientation of the scrolls point to a kind of Judaism that was largely unfamiliar before their discovery.

A key importance of the scrolls lies in the evidence they provide for the historical development of Scripture. In this period, the biblical canon was still in flux. Some books that were authoritative at Qumran did not become part of the biblical canon, while some canonical texts were less important at Qumran. The scrolls also include witnesses to diverse textual forms of Scripture (the Masoretic text, the Septuagint, the Samaritan Pentateuch) which would later become the property of separate religious communities (Jewish, Christian, and Samaritan).

Early views associated the scrolls with the ancient Jewish Essenes and assumed a base for them at Khirbet Qumran, a habitation site located directly opposite Cave 4, where three-quarters of the scrolls were discovered. A large nearby cemetery, with very few female or juvenile skeletons, contributes to the view that Qumran was not home to typical family units, while the presence of some evidence for wealth at the site suggests that the classical descriptions of the Essenes do not fit the picture in every detail.

A wide variety of theories have challenged or modified the classical Essene Hypothesis. Some, including arguments for connections to pious Sadducean priests, have been influential. Others, including many attempts to assign the scrolls to an early Christian community, have had less scholarly impact. Claims that the scrolls represent the library of the Jerusalem Temple, or that the site of Qumran was actually a villa, fortress, or commercial site, remain controversial.

The delayed publication of the fragmentary Cave 4 materials brought renewed attention to the scrolls in the 1980s and 1990s, when many popular publications and videos outlined hidden 'secrets', scandals, and conspiracy theories; chief among these was Baigent and Leigh's *Dead Sea Scrolls Deception*. Robert Eisenman's efforts to associate the scrolls with James the Brother of Jesus have been influential in popular culture, but not among scrolls scholars. In Dan Brown's *Da Vinci Code*, as in other contexts, the scrolls are lumped together with other ancient manuscript discoveries (especially the Nag

Hammadi texts) and treated, incorrectly, as Gnostic Christian scriptures.

Recommended reading. Davies, Philip R., George J. Brooke, and Philip R. Callaway. *The Complete World of the Dead Sea Scrolls.* London: Thames & Hudson, 2002. Schiffman, Lawrence H., and James C. VanderKam (eds.). *Encyclopedia of the Dead Sea Scrolls.* New York: Oxford University Press, 2000. Vermes, Geza. *The Complete Dead Sea Scrolls in English.* New York: Penguin, 1997.

See also ESSENES [MLG]

Deafness. Deafness in the Bible refers to a physical or moral condition of being unable to hear, of dumbness, of silence. The Hebrew *chârash* refers to the latter condition, whereas the word *chêrêsh* means simply *deaf*. Likewise the Greek *kōphos* means silence as well as to be deaf; the word for dumb, *alalos*, is likewise sometimes used to refer to the deaf.

Writers of the OT consider the deaf person as intellectually weak and morally disabled, unable to function as a full citizen in society. In Ps. 38.13, David confesses in anguish to God that sin has made him like a deaf man who does not hear, like a dumb man who does not open his mouth. Isaiah treats deafness as both a moral condition of refusing to hear (6.9) as well as a messianic sign (35.6), in which the coming of the Lord will result in 'the ears of the deaf unstopped'. In Exod. 4.11, Yahweh tells Moses that it is him who causes a person to be 'dumb, or deaf'. In Lev. 19.14, the deaf are due consideration and help—it is a sin and against the law not to help.

Likewise in the NT, deafness or its removal is the will of God. Jesus heals the deaf, dumb, or silent. In Mark 7, Jesus heals a deaf man who is also unable to speak clearly by putting his fingers into the man's ears, spitting and touching the man's tongue. When he says, in Aramaic, *ephphatha*, 'be opened', the man's ears are opened and his tongue loosened. The NT also teaches that a person can be morally and spiritually deaf, refusing or unable to hear the truth. As Jesus puts it with reference to his use of parables (Matt. 13.13), 'hearing they do not hear, nor do they understand'. Depictions of Jesus healing the deaf are popular in later art, evident, for instance, in the 1695 woodcut by the well-known German artist Johann Weigel.

Recommended reading. Rosner, Fred. *Encyclopedia of Medicine in the Bible and the Talmud.* Lanham, MD: Jason Aronson, 2000.

See also BLINDNESS [RL]

Death. Death is the cessation of life. The Bible presents death as a consequence of the sin of Adam and Eve (Gen. 2.17). For the Christian Paul, the first sin introduced both physical and spiritual death, which is to say separation from God (Rom. 5.12-21). The first recorded death is that of Abel, murdered by his brother Cain (Gen. 4.8).

Biblical attitudes about death range from dread to anticipation. In the Hebrew Scriptures, death is ugly because the dead in *Sheol* ('the grave') are separated from loved ones; however; God is in *Sheol* as well as Heaven (Ps. 139.7-8) and can redeem from *Sheol* (1 Sam. 2.6). Paul declared that Death is the Last Enemy (1 Cor. 15.26) and then taunts it, 'Where, O death is your victory? Where, O death is your sting?' (1 Cor. 15.55). The taunt is possible because Christ's death defeated.

Death is of course a recurring subject in religious and philosophical contemplation, among them Dante's *Divine Comedy*, Francis Bacon's essay 'Of Death', Thomas Grey's 'Elegy Written in a Country Church-Yard', and Lord, Alfred Tennyson's *In Memoriam*, to name but a few.

Recommended reading. D'Souza, Dinesh. *Life after Death: The Evidence.* Washington, DC: Regnery Press, 2009. Ratzinger, Joseph Cardinal (Pope Benedict XVI). *Eschatology: Death and Eternal Life.* Washington, DC: Catholic University of America Press, 2007.

See also ADAM; BOOK OF LIFE; ESCHATOLOGY; ETERNAL LIFE; EVE; IMMORTALITY; LIFE; RESURRECTION; SIN; TREE OF KNOWLEDGE, TREE OF LIFE; WAGES OF SIN [AJW]

Deborah. The etymology of the name comes from the Hebrew word for 'bee.' There are two Deborahs in the Bible. The first mentioned is Rebekah's nurse (Gen. 35.8). The second is the better-known Deborah mentioned in Judg. 4–5. This Deborah was not only a prophetess but also the only female judge of pre-monarchic Israel. Her story is told twice: as narrative in chapter 4 and as poetry in the victory song of chapter 5.

Judges 4 describes Deborah as a prophetess, the wife of Lappidoth, and the fourth judge of Israel, who held her headquarters under the 'palm of Deborah' which was located between Ramah and Bethel. She is said to have summoned Barak, by the Lord's command, to lead an Israelite army of ten thousand men against Sisera, the commander of the Canaanite army and his nine hundred iron chariots. Deborah then prophesies that the God of Israel will hand over Sisera and his troops to Barak. However, since

Barak only agrees to go if Deborah accompanies him Deborah prophesies that because of his little faith the Lord would hand Sisera over to a woman and he would receive no honor.

The result of the battle of Kishon in Judg. 4 is the crushing defeat of Sisera's army. As soon as Sisera's troops begin to fall, Sisera flees the battle site in order to find refuge. He ends up finding refuge in the tent of a woman named Jael, the wife of Heber the Kenite, who then seizes the opportunity to take Sisera's life while he is resting. Thus, as Deborah prophesied, the Lord gave victory to the Israelites and the Lord handed Sisera over to a woman.

Judges 5 presents a victory song, which some believe was written by Deborah after the battle victory; it is often called 'The Song of Deborah'. The song summarizes the events of Judg. 4 into poetic form and may well be one of the earliest samples of Hebrew poetry. Judges 5 also gives additional information about Sisera's defeat. It claims a storm flooded Kishon's river and swept away the Canaanite chariotry. Judges 5.7 appropriately speaks of Deborah as 'a mother in Israel', which is consistent with the portrayal of her in chapter 4 as a strong independent woman who is capable of leading Israel.

In rheology, the study of the flow of matter, the 'Deborah number' is a dimensionless number used to characterize the fluidity of a material. The term derives from the biblical Deborah, specifically the KJV translation Judg. 5.5, part of Deborah's victory song: 'The mountains melted before the Lord....'

See also BARAK; CANAAN, CANAANITES; JAEL; JUDGES, BOOK OF; PROPHECY; PROPHETS; REBEKAH; SISERA [RKM]

Decapolis. The NT has three direct references to the Decapolis. Matthew 4.25 says that early in Jesus' ministry great crowds from the Decapolis followed him. Mark 5.1-20 contains the story of Jesus healing the Gadarene Demoniac, in which the exorcised demons enter a swine herd. The ruins of Gadara are on a bluff that overlooks the Sea of Galilee, the Golan Heights and the Yarmuk River Valley at modern day Umm Qeis. The people of Gadara, despite the healing miracle, ask Jesus to leave. The Gaderene Demoniac then spreads the news of his healing in the cities of the Decapolis (5.20). In Mark 7.31, Jesus traveled through the region of the Decapolis where he healed a man who was deaf and dumb.

The Decapolis was a group of ten (Greek, *deka*) city-states (Greek, *polis*) spreading from Damascus in the north to Philadelphia (Rabbath Amon, site of present day Amman, Jordon) in the south. With the exception of Scythopolis (Beth Shan), which was located on the west side of the Sea of Galilee, all of the others were located on the east side of the Jordan River. Ancient authors disagree the identity and number of these cities. Pliny the Elder (*Natural History*, 5.18.74), identifies them as Damascus (Syria), Dion, Gadara, Gerasa (or Galasa), Hippos, (or Hippo in Syria) Canatha (or Kanatha in Syria), Pella, Philadelphia, Raphana and Scythopolis. In the second century CE, Claudius Ptolemy (*Geography*) claimed there were eighteen cities in the group. The Decapolis cities were founded by Greeks beginning shortly after Alexander the Great died in 323 BCE. The region of Coele-Syria (Hollow-Syria) had gone over to Alexander after the defeat of the Persians under King Darius at the Battle of Issus (November 333 BCE) and the capture of Tyre (Arrian, *Anabasis of Alexander*, 2.25.4). Other cities were founded when the Greco-Egyptian Ptolemy dynasty (prior to 198 BCE) controlled the region, and still others during the time of the Seleucid dynasty (198–ca. 160 BCE). The Romans under Pompey controlled the Decapolis from 65 BCE. After taking Sythopolis, Pella and Hippos from the Jews in 63 BCE he made Sythopolis the capital of the Decapolis and the seat of the Sanhedrin as well. The Decapolis cities became part of the Roman province of Syria with municipal freedom.

The Decapolis cities were centers of Hellenistic and later Greco-Roman culture. The cities had forums, market places, amphitheaters, temples, public baths, hippodromes and a stadium. The Jews were hostile to the presence of the morally corrupt Greeks. Their lack of unity made them vulnerable to the attacks of the Hasmonean dynasty in Jerusalem during the Maccabean Era and afterward. Pella and several other cities were captured by Alexander Janneus. The early church flourished in the region during the apostolic age. Pella provided safety for Christian refugees from Judea during the time of the Great Jewish Revolt (67–70 CE). The Decapolis cities continued to have pagan temples into the Byzantine era. Bishops had their seats in many of the cities until the coming of Islam.

Recommended reading. Browning, Iain. *Jerash and the Decapolis*. London: Chatto & Windus, 1982. Kennedy, David. *Gerasa and the Decapolis: A Millennium of Prosperity in Northwest Jordan*. London: Gerald Duckworth & Co., 2007.

See also GADARENE SWINE; MACCABEES; MACCABEES, BOOKS OF [AJW]

Deity. A deity, from the Latin *deus*, is generally a transcendent, immortal, powerful figure who has powers to cause changes to events or conditions on earth. There are great variations in deities among cultures. Some cultures or religious groups accept the existence of a variety of deities (polytheism). Other cultures accept a variety of deities, but only one is supreme or worthy of worship (henotheism), while others believe that there is only one (monotheism), and all others are idols. Deities also vary in their accessibility to humans, their benevolence, and the sacrifice and adoration demanded. The amount of control they exercise over events on earth also varies.

Although the Bible ultimately teaches monotheism, there are reflections of earlier attitudes that are sometimes not resolved. As an example, the early books of the Tanak mention rivalries among deities. The plagues leading to the Exodus from Egypt are a contest between Egyptian deities and Yahweh. Similarly, the stories of Samson (Judg. 16) and the Philistine capture of the ark of the covenant (1 Sam. 5–6) describe contests between Dagon, the deity of the Philistines, and Yahweh, the deity of Israel.

Some of the prophets, among them Isaiah and Jeremiah, affirm that Yahweh is not only Israel's God but also its creator, ruler, and the judge of all the earth. This deity possesses aseity (from the Latin, *a se esse*, existence from himself), and is thus distinguished from the deities of other nations (and the later Greek and Roman deities) in being eternal, infinite and not dependent on any other being or events.

Despite this affirmation, there remains a variety of understandings about the nature of deity in the Bible. The Reformer John Calvin is best known for his theological conclusion that God controls the world absolutely, resulting in the doctrine of predestination. Others find justification for a deity who set the world in motion and left it to operate by natural law. Process theologians conclude that God offers guidance but, in order to be considered ultimately good, is unable to force compliance, thus allowing evil to exist.

Most often, the term 'God' indicates the monotheistic deity of Christianity, Judaish, and Islam. The term 'deity' occasionally appears in technical writings or in comparative religion. 'Deity' appears in the fourth stanza of the Christmas carol 'We Three Kings of Orient Are' by John Hopkins, Jr, 1857, as an offering to a deity. This phrase points to an ongoing Christian debate about the deity of Jesus of Nazareth. This debate led to the development of the doctrine of the Trinity (promulgated by the Council of Nicaea in 325 CE), which seeks to explain how monotheism is compatible with the teaching of Jesus as divine.

See also ARK OF THE COVENANT; ARTEMIS; BAAL; CAESAR; CREATION, CREATOR; DAGON; GOD; IDOL; TRINITY; YAHWEH [TJV]

Delilah. The meaning of the name is uncertain, though 'flirtatious' is one possibility, given the resemblance of the name to the Arabic *dallatum* (flirt or languid), and the Hebrew *dll* (to languish). Delilah is a word play on the Hebrew *layla*, night, which overcomes the sun. In the story in which she figures (Judg. 16.4-22), she is the downfall of the Israelite Samson (*shimshon*, which is related to *shemesh*, sun).

Delilah seduced Samson, accepted money from his enemies to learn the secret of his strength, and then betrayed him. The story raises more questions about Delilah than it answers because other than her name and place of residence (the valley of Sorek), little more is known. The text does not say she loves Samson, though clearly he loves her her (16.4). She accepts a bribe from the Philistines to learn and then reveal the secret of Samson's strength (16.5), which famously is his hair (16.17). She arranges for his hair to be removed, at which point the Philistines gouge out his eyes and place him in prison (16.19-22).

In ancient and medieval literature, Samson is the focus of the story and little is said about Delilah, although the first-century philospher Philo in *De Sampsone* tells of two sons born to Delilah and Samson, one of whom was given some of her silver bribe money. The first-century historian Josephus assumes Delilah to be a harlot. Fifteenth- and sixteenth-satires emphasize Delilah's seduction, something evident in S. Brant's *Ship of Fools* (1494), and J. Wickram's *Weiberlist* (1534). In A. Fabricius's *Samson* (1568), Samson's fatal attraction to Delilah is compared to Catholic attraction to Protestant heresy. J. Lummenaeus's Latin drama, *Sampson* (1628) portrays Delilah as a prostitute. In the Baroque era, jealousy becomes a major motif as in Jean-Antoine Romagnesi's *Samson* (1736), and Voltaire's libretto with music by Rameau (1734). More often, Delilah is neither sensitive nor jealous, but a heroine, as in Milton's *Samson Agonistes* (1671) where Delilah acts out of patriotism, and attempts a reconciliation with Samson. Delilah is heroine also in Handel's oratorio *Samson* (1741).

Eighteenth-century writers return to the love intrigue as in B. Feind's libretto *Der Fall des grossen Richters in Israel, Simson,* (1709). In nineteenth-century Romantic works such as F. Lemaire's libretto *Samson et Dalila* (1877), Delilah is a calculating seductress who rejects Samson once conquered. Camille Saint-Saens's opera *Samson et Dalila* (1877) develops this theme. Late nineteenth-century American writers Eugene Moore and W. Odell depict a repentant Delilah trying to save Samson. In Austrian writer Felix Salten's novel *Samson* (1928), Delilah is a tragic heroine who loves Samson and is faithful to him. Literary theorist M. Bal (1987), reads the story on a psycho-analytical level with Delilah as the mirror that allows Samson to discover himself.

Delilah is often depicted in art as seductress. In much seventeenth-century art, the nude or semi-nude body of Delilah is at center, as in the works of Christian van Coubenbergh, Rembrandt, Adrien van der Werff, Rubens, and Anthony van Dyck. Nineteenth-century Symbolist artist Gustave Moreau's Delilah is the quintessential *femme fatale*. In modern music deceitful Delilah must die, as in Tom Jones's hit song 'Delilah' (1968). Hedy Lamarr stars as a seductive and deceitful Delilah in Cecil B. DeMille's film *Samson and Delilah* (1949) with screen play written partly by Vladimir Jabotinsky, author of a novel, *Samson* (1927).

See also HARLOT; JUDGES, BOOK OF; SAMSON

[EG]

Deliverance. In the Bible, deliverance may be rescue or liberation from something (in Hebrew *yasa, natzal*; in Greek *exaireomai, sozo, lutroomai*) or being given over to something (in Hebrew *magan, masar*; in Greek *anodidomai*). Examples include the deliverance of Noah and his family from the flood, Moses being delivered from the massacre of the innocents, deliverance from the Jewish captivity in Egypt told in the Book of Exodus, and deliverance from impending death in the story of Esther. This deliverance may be from metaphorical bondage, such as physical or spiritual ailments. In the NT, this term is often used to describe salvation from sins. Whether literal or metaphorical, God is consistently pictured as the 'Deliverer'. In the NT, Jesus is not only granted deliverance like Moses while an infant, but becomes a source of deliverance from diseases and demon possession as well as from sin. Eschatological imagery offers a final deliverance from the bondage of death and suffering in this world. This concept of the afterlife as deliverance is central to the NT view of salvation. This deliverance in Christ has the ultimate purpose in the afterlife of returning God's people to Edenic bliss.

In early Christian and medieval literature, deliverance is often associated with the concept of demonic possession and the concept of bondage by sin. In Dante's *Purgatorio* Book XI, penitents must carry stones upon them as the weights of sinful pride to gain deliverance at the top of Mount Purgatory.

Within ancient and modern Jewish culture, Purim and Passover celebrate yearly the deliverance of the Jewish people. Purim remembers God's deliverance of the Jews from genocide through Esther, while Passover remembers God's deliverance from slavery in Egypt. The abolitionist movement similarly used the powerful language of deliverance in the stories of the Exodus and Esther. In the film *Amazing Grace*, John Newton states that William Wilberforce was appointed by God 'for such a time as this', echoing Est. 4.14.

Other modern films such as *The Shawshank Redemption* and *The Planet of the Apes* also echo the Exodus story's deliverance themes. Some modern musicians invert elements of the biblical metaphor of deliverance. For example, the metal band Opeth's album *Deliverance* is coupled with an album called *Damnation*. The themes of the title song 'Deliverance' center around the idea of the paradox of gaining salvation from a sinful act and the pain that such 'deliverance' elicits. Hip-hop artist Bubba Sparxxx's video for his song 'Deliverance' couples a prison escape (in the spirit of *O Brother, Where Art Thou?*) with the idea of salvation.

In Christian circles, deliverance ministries of various sorts are present throughout the world. In these ministries the term 'deliverance' often relates to deliverance from demonic forces, but includes all forms of spiritual warfare and, therefore, all kinds of ailments and struggles from emotional disturbance to the occult to physical sickness to sexual addictions or drug addictions. Central to many of these ministries is the worldview that God and Satan are at war and angelic and demonic forces are real and fighting against one another. Prayer and repentance are usually viewed as key to freedom from demonic attack and the means to 'deliverance', both physical and spiritual. These ministries are often associated with other aspects of charismatic belief including a wide range of spiritual gifts. Other versions of deliverance ministry focus on helping the poor including widows and orphans. Still other versions incorporate trained Christian counselling to promote inner healing.

See also NOAH'S ARK; FLOOD; EXODUS, THE; MASSACRE OF THE INNOCENTS; SATAN; LUCIFER; BELIAL; DEMON; WIDOWS AND ORPHANS; ESTHER, BOOK OF; LOTS, FEAST OF (PURIM); SPIRITUAL GIFTS [BMS]

Demon. A demon (from the Greek *daimon*) is an evil supernatural being who seeks to influence humans negatively. Ideas about demons and evil spirits are quite diverse in the HB. They influence human behavior in destructive ways, such as arousing jealousy (Num. 5.14), stirring up desire for vengeance (Judg. 9.23), creating confusion (1 Sam. 16.14), or encouraging idol worship (Hos. 4.12). There are instances, however, where they are carrying out God's will (1 Kgs 22.23).

First Enoch, a first-century BCE. Jewish pseudepigraphical work, features an influential interpretation of Gen. 6.1-4, which claims the 'sons of God' who had intercourse with human women are in fact fallen angels. The NT writer Jude picks up this tradition (v. 6) and later Patristic writers affirmed that demons were the offspring of this union.

The NT has a more consistent understanding of demons, reflecting Hellenistic and Roman philosophy, and possibly foreign religious elements. They are portrayed as servants of Satan. In the Gospels, Jesus has the authority to cast out demons and cure illnesses (Luke 8.26-39) and successful exorcisms are recorded in the early church (Acts 19.11-16). There was a widespread belief that demonic attack and deception would increase in the last days (1 Tim. 4.1; Rev. 16.13-14; 18.2).

Subsequent Christian tradition affirmed that Satan and demons were angels cast from God's presence because of disobedience (reflecting interpretations of Isa. 14.12-14 and Ezek. 28.12-19). Prominent theologians such as Justin Martyr and Augustine of Hippo claimed that pagan gods were demons. Baptismal rites in the Latin West involved exorcisms prior to baptism. Much speculation occurred during the medieval period, largely concerned with the nature of the sin that led to the fall of Satan and his angels.

Some modern interpreters claim that belief in demons was a pre-modern way of understanding mental and physical illness. American theologian Walter Wink has recently re-interpreted demons as figurative personifications of social and political 'domination systems'. Contemporary 'charismatic' Christian groups often emphasize demonic influence or possession, and the possibility of miraculous cures and deliverance through exorcism. Pentecostal writer Frank Peretti's fictional *This Present Darkness* (1986) represents such an approach, as the human (Christian) protagonists fight against demons that seek to control and manipulate human beings. Demons and exorcisms continue to be important within certain forms of global Christianity, particularly in parts of Africa.

Demons feature in classic literary works such as the Dante Alighieri's *Divine Comedy* (1321) and John Milton's *Paradise Lost* (1667). In Michelangelo's painting *The Last Judgment* (1534–1541), horned demons are shown gruesomely torturing unbelievers in hell. Christian author C.S. Lewis's *The Screwtape Letters* (1942) is written as a correspondence between a senior demon and his nephew.

Interest in the occult increased during the 1960s and 1970s, reflected by the popularity of horror films such as *The Exorcist* (1973), reportedly based on a true story of demon possession. *Jacob's Ladder* (1990) explores the interplay between demons and mental illness. Films such as *Hellboy* (2004) and *Constantine* (2005) are based on comic books and deal with demons in a more fantastical fashion.

Heavy metal music frequently draws inspiration from horror films, occultism, and satanic/demonic imagery. An increasingly popular sub-genre is Christian metal, with bands like Demon Hunter drawing from similar themes, albeit from an evangelical Christian perspective.

Recommended reading. Nugent, Christopher. *Masks of Satan: The Demonic in History*. London: Sheed & Ward, 1983. Pagels, Elaine. *The Origin of Satan*. New York: Random House, 1995.

See also SATAN; ESCHATOLOGY; EVIL [JR]

Deuteronomy, Book of. Deuteronomy is the final instalment of the five-part collection known as the 'Torah' (Judaism) or the 'Pentateuch' (Christianity). The Hebrew title of the book is 'These Are the Words', while the eponymous term 'deuteronomy' in English Bibles is derived from the Greek translation of a passage that commands Israel's king to write a 'second copy' (*to deuteronomiov*) of the law (17.19). The act of duplication inherent in the title 'Deuteronomy' is therefore fundamental to understanding the book, for wherever there is duplication (or 'actualization') there is certain to be modification, adaptation, and appropriation.

In overview, Deuteronomy is comprised largely of a long speech by Moses addressed to his people prior to their march into Canaan. The topics that Moses deems crucial for this pivotal speech event are all directed toward a single issue: How to take and maintain possession of their mythic 'promised land'. The author(s) of Deuteronomy couched these topics and their primary concern within an ancient form of speech known as the Vassal Treaty, an Ancient Near Eastern convention which stipulated the duties and obligations that bound together a group of people to a powerful monarchical overlord. In reduplicating the conventional treaty formula, the author(s) of Deuteronomy placed into the mouth of Moses an agreement that positioned Israel as vassal partner to God as king.

Not only is duplication found at the level of the book's structure, it can also be found in the contents of Moses's speech. For example, Moses's rationale for Sabbath observance is based on Israel's recent escape from Egypt (5.12-15) while God's earlier explanation was rooted in the rhythmic six-on, one-off weekly pattern that was the process of cosmic creation (Exod. 20.8-11). More significant perhaps is Moses's modification of Israel's worship. Where God had originally envisioned multiple locations for divine–human encounters (Exod. 20.22-26), Moses focuses such interactions in the direction of a single location (12.1-28).

The history of reception of the Book of Deuteronomy is also filled with acts of duplication. Many copies of Deuteronomy were found in Cave 4 at Qumran, the site of the famous Dead Sea Scrolls discovery. The NT quotes from or alludes to Deuteronomy some ninety times, with Jesus relying exclusively on the work to refute the devil in the Temptation Scene (Matt. 4). Closer to home, one of the feline characters in T.S. Eliot's *Old Possum's Book of Practical Cats* is named 'Old Deuteronomy'. Andrew Lloyd Weber got into the duplication act when in 1998 he adapted Eliot's book for the musical called *Cats*. Some ten years later, 'Old Deuteronomy' made another appearance in an Australian musical called *Clowns: The Musical*, though by this time 'Old Deuteronomy' no longer purred but punned. Conceivably, one could be found relaxing at 'Deuteronomy 8.3 Café' in Cleveland, Ohio, reading about cat-napping (Eliot) or utopian peace (Deuteronomy) while enroute to a British or Australian musical featuring the long-lived character 'Old Deuteronomy'.

Like Eliot's 'Old Deuteronomy', the biblical Deuteronomy has had many lives. A more sobering duplication however is seen in the pioneering efforts of American settlers who remythologized the 'promised land' motif for their own colonial purposes. They were the New Israel about to enter the 'promised land' of North America; all that stood in their way was the aboriginal population whose unsuspected demise was prefigured in Deuteronomy's extermination directive (Deut. 7 and 20). Duplications modify, adapt, and appropriate, but sometimes they do so for less than positive purposes.

Recommended reading. Francis, R. Douglas, and Chris Kitzen (eds.). *The Praire West as Promised Land.* Calgary: University of Calgary Press, 2007.

See also BOOK OF THE LAW; CANAAN; COVENANT; LAW; MOSES; PROMISED LAND [DAB]

Diaspora. From the Greek *diaspora* (dispersion), this term refers to the spread of both Hebrew peoples and culture beginning with the destruction of the first temple, and to the communities of Jews dispersed throughout the Mediterranean world during Hellenistic and Roman times. Though it carries a different connotation from Exile, the Jewish Diaspora began with the Persian invasion of the kingdom of Judah, and the destruction of the Jerusalem temple in 587/6 BCE, when many Judeans were forcefully removed to Babylon. Though the Persian king Cyrus allowed the captured Judeans to return and rebuild the temple, many instead decided to stay (Est. 2.5-6; Ezra 7.1-8). From then on, a Jewish community existed in Babylon, which would become an important center of rabbinic learning beginning in the third century CE.

Egypt was also home to a great number of Jews in antiquity. As early as the sixth century BCE there existed a Jewish military colony in the city of Elephantine. Eventually Alexandria became an important center for Diaspora Jews, where Greek and Jewish culture could join and intermingle. The most famous Diaspora Jew from Egypt is Philo of Alexandria (c. 20 BCE—50 CE), a prolific writer who wrote philosophical commentaries on the Pentateuch that incorporated Platonic, Pythagorean, and Stoic ideas.

By NT times, there were well-established Diaspora communities, integrated to varying degrees within the Greco-Roman cities, throughout the Roman Empire. The Jewish historian Josephus (37–ca. 100 CE) comments in his history of the Jewish people (*Jewish Antiquities*) that the Jews in Sardis submitted a request to the local governing body for the city to supply a place for them to worship and kosher food in the marketplace, which the city granted (*Ant.* 14.259-61). Jews are referred to in the writings of several Greek and Roman authors, including Juvenal (*Satire* 3) and Horace (*Satires* 1.4). Paul also addresses Jews in several of his letters, including a sizable Jewish community in Rome (Rom. 2.17; 16.7-15).

For Jews who lived outside of Roman Palestine, the temple was still at the heart of their religious life, and they paid an annual temple tax of one half shekel (two denarii in Roman currency). Those who could travelled to Jerusalem for important festivals. Acts 2.9-11 lists the nations from which Jews journeyed for the festival of Pentecost, including Parthia, Media, Mesopotamia, Cappadocia, Pontus, Phrygia, Pamphilia, Egypt, and Rome. Acts also describes Paul visiting Jewish synagogues throughout the Mediterranean during his missionary journeys.

For centuries, Jewish Diaspora communities have made many contributions to Western culture. In the third and second centuries BCE the Jews of Alexandria produced the Septuagint (LXX), a Greek translation of the HB. Integral to the history of Christianity, the LXX is quoted in the NT and was the Bible read by the Apostolic Fathers. Several centuries later, Diaspora Jews formed an important part of the medieval center of learning in Toledo, Spain (eighth century CE). There are numerous references to Jews living in the Diaspora within Western literature, like the infamous character of Shylock in Shakespeare's *The Merchant of Venice*. Even today, many Jews throughout the world think of themselves as living in the Diaspora.

Recommended reading. Barclay, John M.G. *Jews in the Mediterranean Diaspora from Alexander to Trajan (323 BCE—117 CE)*. Edinburgh: T. & T. Clark, 1996. Collins, John J. *Between Athens and Jerusalem: Jewish Identity in the Hellenistic Diaspora*. Grand Rapids, MI: Eedrmans, 2000. Williams, Margaret. *The Jews among the Greeks and Romans: A Diaspora Sourcebook*. Baltimore: Johns Hopkins University Press, 1998.

See also EXILE; ESTHER, BOOK OF; EZRA, BOOK OF; ACTS OF THE APOSTLES, THE; PAUL, THE APOSTLE; SEPTUAGINT [NKB]

Dinah. The name derives from the Hebrew *dîn* (law). Dinah is first mentioned in Gen. 30.21 as the only daughter born to Leah and the patriarch Jacob. Her story, however, takes place in Gen. 34, 'Now Dinah the daughter of Leah, whom she had borne to Jacob, went out to visit the women of the region. When Shechem son of Hamor the Hivite, prince of the region, saw her, he seized her and lay with her by force. And his soul was drawn to Dinah daughter of Jacob; he loved the girl, and spoke tenderly to her' (34.1-3). This is, in essence, Dinah's story.

The continuation of the narrative is based on this episode between Dinah and Shechem, but Dinah herself is not present. Shechem seeks to marry Dinah, and so his father Hamor and Jacob meet. Jacob, however, is silent, letting his sons respond to the situation. Hamor proposes that the Shechemites and the Israelites live together, work together and intermarry. Jacob's sons respond 'deceitfully', according to the text (Gen. 34.13) and say that only if the Shechemites become circumcised can they give their sister in marriage to Shechem. Hamor and Shechem agree, and every male of the Shechemites was circumcised immediately. On the third day after their circumcision, before the men had a chance to fully recover, Jacob's sons took up arms against the Shechemites led by Simeon and Levi, killing and plundering throughout the city. They also took Dinah back home. Jacob, who seems not to have known about the plan, chastises Simeon and Levi, who responded, 'Should our sister be treated like a whore?' (Gen. 32.31)

Dinah is only mentioned once more in Gen. 46.15 in the list of Jacob and Leah's children. Later Jewish Midrash talks of Dinah as the biblical Job's second wife. Early and Medieval Christian interpretation focused on Dinah as somehow causing the rape; that is, something called 'victim's guilt' where only someone who actually deserved to be raped could be. In other Christian interpretation, Dinah also represented the Christian seduced by Satan.

Dinah is discussed often in feminist interpretations of the Bible. Most commonly, her lack of voice in the story of her rape is emphasized; however, there is also a discussion by Lyn Bechtel about the possibility that Dinah chose to be with Shechem, and that he did not, in fact, rape her, but that they had mutual—but illicit—sexual relations. This philological argument is based on the fact that there is no biblical Hebrew word for rape. Instead, the word used in Gen. 34 is *'nah*, which means to humble or to shame. Bechtel argues that the shame is not from rape, but from a crossing of cultural clan lines without regard to the implications for the clan.

Dinah's story is also the focus of the popular historical fiction book by Anita Diamant entitled *The Red Tent*. This book is told from Dinah's point of view, and not only encompasses her childhood, but focuses greatly on her love affair with Shechem. Here, Dinah chose to be with Shechem, but as per the biblical narrative, her brothers disagree and kill the Shechemites. Dinah, instead of returning home with her brothers, fled with Shechem's mother to Egypt and gave birth to Shechem's child.

Recommended reading. Schroeder, Joy A. *Dinah's Lament*. Minneapolis: Fortress Press, 2007. Kugel, James L. *Traditions of the Bible*. Cambridge, MA: Harvard University Press, 1998.

See also GENESIS, BOOK OF; JACOB; JOB'S WIFE [SS]

Dionysius the Areopagite. Along with Damaris, Dionysius the Areopagite was one of the few people who converted to Christianity after the Apostle Paul preached to the members of the Areopagus in Athens (Acts 17.34). The writings of a fifth- or sixth-century Christian Neoplatonist thinker, now known as Pseudo-Dionysius, were mistakenly attributed to Dionysius the Areopagite because the author assumed the name of the biblical character. It is important not to think of the writings of Pseudo-Dionysius as a forgery, as the practice of pseudonymity or *declamatio*, was a common rhetorical device used in the ancient world in order to relate one's writings with an already established intellectual tradition. The writings of Pseudo-Dionysius were an attempt to incorporate Neoplatonist philosophy, particularly the thought of Plotinus and Proclus, into the Christian tradition, and exerted an important influence on Christian thought in both the Greek East and Latin West.

See also AREOPAGUS; PAUL, THE APOSTLE [AS]

Disciple. The Greek term *mathētēs* indicates one who temporarily and socially submits one's life and/or education to a teacher, school of thought, or religious leader, and biblically, a devoted believer and follower of Jesus Christ (cf. Luke 6.13). Discipleship is completely volitional (cf. Luke 9.57; John 6.60-66), and may have had no gender biases (cf. Luke 8.1-3). Jewish authorities considered themselves 'disciples of Moses' (John 9.28), and John the Baptist's followers were called his 'disciples' (Mark 2.18). It was from within the greater corpus of disciples that Jesus choose the Twelve Disciples (cf. Matt. 10.2-4; Mark 3.13-19), and when he commissioned them and bestowed them with authority over principalities, they were subsequently named apostles (Mark 3.14; cf. 6.7, 30). In the early Church, we see the expression 'disciple' transform into 'Christian' (Acts 11.26). Later, the term disciple transformed into 'saint' for those who were martyred or showed exceptional dedication to the Church.

In the Reformation period, Rembrandt was influenced by the model of discipleship evident in Jesus' relationship with his disciples and therefore included himself in the painting, *Supper at Emmaus*. Ernest Hemingway wrote *The Old Man and the Sea* (1952) with the mindset that a lot of his readers would understand the story better if he employed Christian symbolism like discipleship, apostle, and other gospel images. Countee Cullen, part of the 1920s Harlem Renaissance movement used this discipleship image as he choose to highlight a disciple of Jesus, Simon the Cyrene, and portrayed him as a black man suffering civil rights violations. The story about Jesus washing the disciples feet, a great act of humility, inspired Agnes Gonxha Bojaxhiu, better known as Mother Teresa of Calcutta, to take religious vows. Edgar Lee Masters creates a hilarious reinterpretation of the Gospels' depiction of the disciples in his 1993 poem, 'Business Reverses' where he contrasts the Christ's disciples with the disciples of financial gain. He uses Mark 6.30-44 (the feeding of 5000 people) as the backdrop where the disciples of financial gain decide to create a business selling food at inflated amounts to the crowds who follow Jesus, but Jesus knowing this, decides to feed the crowd instead, causing financial ruin.

The word disciple has lost much of its religious connotations in late modernity. The horror film *Disciple* changed the definition of disciple to someone who is studious and a good investigator. Dee Snider, frontman of heavy metal legends Twisted Sister, produced the follow up to the horror film *Strangeland*, called *Strangeland: Disciple*, which depicts disciples as part of a secret society who are required to have body modifications.

Recommended reading. Dunn, J.D.G. *Jesus' Call to Discipleship*. Cambridge: Cambridge University Press, 1992. Longenecker, R.N. (ed.). *Patterns of Discipleship in the New Testament*. Grand Rapids, MI: Eerdmans, 1996.

See also APOSTLE; TWELVE DISCIPLES, THE [CCB]

Divine council, the. One thing that Egypt, Mesopotamia, Canaan, Phoenicia and Israel all have in common is the concept of a divine council, otherwise known as an assembly of gods. This council is comprised of the supernatural ruling elite. Divine council is a modern construct developed to represent a phenomenon that appears in Ancient Near Eastern texts. Simply put, the divine council is the heavenly court, similar to an amalgamation between the modern judicial court and historical royal courts.

Other ancient Near Eastern cultures had a four tier structure in their councils but this structure cannot be found in the HB. It is assumed that this absence was due to the transition from monotheism to polytheism that Israelite religion underwent.

Due to the influence of monotheism, the divine council has not played a major role in the history of interpretation or in popular culture. Instead the various members, such as the *satan* and the messengers of Yahweh, have been the focus of attention. It is far more common to find the Greek pantheon displayed through history and in modern culture. However, traces of this concept can be found in some elements of modern culture.

In contemporary culture, the Divine Council is the name for the Irish band that does the music for the Final Fantasy video games. Also, a revised version of the divine council has appeared in the stand up comedy of Eddie Izzard, the British cross-dresser who often has religion as the focus of his sketches. A divine council is present in the fifth season of the television series *Stargate SG1*. This council even includes Ancient Near Eastern deities such as Baal and uses biblical imagery for its design.

Recommended reading. Handy, Lowell K. *Among the Host of Heaven: The Syro-Palestinian Pantheon as Bureaucracy*. Winona Lake, IN: Eisenbrauns, 1994. Smith, Mark. *The Origins of Biblical Monotheism: Israel's Polytheistic Background and the Ugaritic Texts*. New York: Oxford University Press, 2001.

See also SONS OF GOD; ANGEL; CHERUBIM AND SERAPHIM; YAHWEH; ELOHIM; BAAL   [EW]

Divorce. Divorce is the process of dissolving a marital relationship as well as the state of total separation resulting from marital disunion. While Western democracies practice no fault divorce, civil marriage law prior to the late twentieth century was tied to church law and only permitted divorce when one spouse could be considered to be at fault, usually for reasons of infidelity (e.g., Deut. 24.1-4), although abandonment, cruelty and unbelief were also permitted reasons, a fact highlighted in the opening scenes of the movie *The Alamo* (2004). Thus, biblically and theologically, divorce is a response to a violation of the marital covenant.

Divorce for reason of sexual infidelity recognizes that one spouse has been unfaithful to the covenant commitments of the marriage, despite the apparent faithfulness of the other partner. This theme is frequently portrayed in the media (e.g., television talk shows, movies such as *Dinner With Friends* [2001]).

Theologically, the image of sexual unfaithfulness describes Israel's worship of other gods (e.g., Jer. 3.1-2; Hos. 6.7-10) and God is described as having divorced Israel because of her unfaithfulness (Isa. 50.1; Jer. 3.8). Thus, divorce for reasons of sexual unfaithfulness illustrates the problem of sin and humanity's unfaithfulness to God.

Exod. 21.7-11 describes the rights of a slave woman who has become a man's wife. This text states that the man has a continuing obligation to her, even if he enters into another marriage, and that she is free of her obligations to him (e.g., divorced) if he fails to provide her with food, clothing and marital rights. In other words, the man is considered to have broken covenant with his spouse by virtue of the fact he has abandoned her. In 1 Cor. 7.12-16, the apostle Paul permits divorce when a non-Christian informs his or her Christian spouse that she or he no longer wishes to remain within the marriage. In this situation, the Christian is considered released from his or her obligation to the non-Christian partner because that partner has decided she or he no longer wishes a divorce. A related issue is whether those who are divorced are permitted to remarry. Neither the OT (Deut. 24.1-4) nor the NT (e.g., 1 Cor. 7.27-28) absolutely prohibits the practice of remarriage, although reconciliation is clearly the preferred option (1 Cor. 7.11). Instead, the OT regulates the practice of remarriage by stating that a couple is prohibited from reconciling after one of them remarries (Deut. 24.4). In addition to this, many conservative Christians hold the view that remarriage is only permitted if marital unfaithfulness was the reason for the divorce (Matt. 5.31-32; 19.9). Theologically, the invitation to separated couples to reconcile mirrors God's desire to be reconciled to his wayward people (e.g., Hos. 14.1-9).

John Milton (*Doctrine & Discipline of Divorce*) argues, based on church tradition, that Jesus' reference to the hardness of men's hearts (Matt. 19.8) extends to marital cruelty. For Milton, anger and violence do not serve the goals of marriage, making divorce a valid consequence of spousal abuse. In other words, one spouse's failure to act respectfully towards the other violates the relationship of trust and thus the marital covenant is broken.

Recommended reading. Imstone-Brewer, David. *Divorce and Remarriage in the Bible: The Social and Literary Context*. Grand Rapids, MI: Eerdmans, 2002.

See also COVENANT; IMAGE OF GOD; LOT; MARRIAGE; SLAVE   [KFM]

Docetism. The term derives from the Greek *dokesis*, meaning 'appearance'. Docetism is a doctrine that flourished from the late first century until the third century CE. It states that Jesus' fleshly body was merely an appearance, making him not completely human. Because there has often been an inverse relationship between the extent of Jesus' humanity and his divinity, a strong emphasis on his divinity accompanied this rejection of his human nature. Docetism was often motivated by efforts to distance Jesus from humanity's sinful nature or to ensure his incapability of suffering.

Knowledge of ancient docetic teachings is limited because very few of their own writings have survived. For information, scholars depend largely on the literature of their opponents who had little motivation to describe docetic beliefs accurately. Paul (Rom. 8.3-4), the Gospel of John, Platonic philosophy, and the cultural revulsion at crucifixion all played significant roles in the development of Docetism.

Docetism was among the earliest heresies in Christianity and apparently widespread during the days of the NT, leading one author to write, 'Many deceivers have gone out into the world, those who do not confess that Jesus Christ has come in the flesh; any such person is the deceiver and the antichrist!' (2 John 7; cf. 1 John 4.1-3). This doctrine spread in the second century and was adopted by many Christians, including Marcion, Basilides, and various Gnostic groups, often provoking adverse reactions from orthodox writers. Docetism started becoming sparse by the fourth century and has remained an extremely unpopular idea since that time, aside from its use in isolated sects during the middle ages such as the Catharians. Contemporary Gnostic and new age congregations often renounce Jesus' divinity altogether, thereby ruling out this doctrine that was popular among their precursors.

Docetism has three primary associations in contemporary discourse. First, despite its aforementioned unpopularity among Gnostics and new age groups, various occultists have picked up on the belief—including numerous theosophists and the American Gnostic Church. The compositions of experimental rock group Current 93 fit within this mould, though their most relevant song, 'On Docetic Mountain' (2009), defies straightforward interpretation. This use is self-consciously political, working as an arcane heresy to combat a perceived 'Christian establishment'. Second, Docetism is sometimes employed inadvertently in attempts to separate Jesus from human defects. The astral Christ in Salvador Dalí's paintings *The Sacrament of the Last Supper* (1955), *The Crucifixion* (1954), and *Christ of Saint John of the Cross* (1951) are consistent with this use.

Finally, Docetism is most commonly applied as derisive theological label. It is typically used against theological positions that place an important aspect of Christianity (e.g., the Bible, Jesus, the church) too far from human contingencies. Karl Barth, for example, wrote of biblical infallibility as a form of Docetism. Such charges insinuate that the refusal to root Christian doctrine in *human* history runs in theological parallel to docetic embarrassment over Jesus' humanity.

Recommended reading. Stroumsa, Guy G. 'Christ's Laughter: Docetic Origins Reconsidered'. *Journal of Early Christian Studies* 12 (2004) 267-88. Yamauchi, Edwin. 'The Crucifixion and Docetic Christology'. *Concordia Theological Quarterly* 46 (1982) 1-20.

See also FLESH; GNOSTIC, GNOSTICISM; HERESY; NAG HAMMADI; WORD   [CBZ]

Dove. There are many references to doves in the Bible. In Gen. 8, after the flood, Noah released one at three intervals to find out if the water had subsided enough for the others to leave the Ark. On the second trip, it returned with an olive leaf. Leviticus 12 specifies a pigeon or dove as part of the purification offering after the birth of a child. The Song of Solomon uses it as a term of endearment or comparison to the beloved. Doves appear throughout the Psalms and Prophets as symbols of beauty. Sometimes their call, which resembles a moaning sound, represents distress. The Hebrew word is *yonah*, the name of the prophet who fled God's call to Nineveh; there is much speculation on the significance of this name in relation to the plot.

The Gospel of Luke records that Mary offered doves after the birth of Jesus, generally taken as an indication that the family was poor. All NT Gospels record the appearance of a dove over Jesus at his baptism, and identify it as a manifestation of the Holy Spirit. In Matt. 10.16, Jesus sent the disciples on a mission, charging them to be 'wise as serpents and innocent as doves'. The Gospels also mention doves as being among the items offered for sale during the cleansing of the temple.

Much non-religious as well as religious imagery draws on doves. Coupled with the olive leaf or branch, they are often symbols of peace. Thus in political discourse, 'doves' signifies those preferring peaceful methods compared to 'hawks', who are often aggressive. This most often refers to attitudes toward war, but economists refer to doves as those who prefer low interest rates to encourage consumer spending, whereas 'hawks' prefer higher interest rates in the belief that they reduce inflation. A DC Comics series of 1968–1969 titled *The Hawk and the Dove*, intended to promote the need for balance between the two, produced a variety of caricatures and disputes. Characters based on the two have reappeared in several later series and in other comics.

Many religious organizations also use the dove in their name or logos. The Gospel Music Association (United States) confers 'Dove Awards' for various categories in Christian music. Doves also appear as a symbol of divine approval or guidance in many paintings and other artistic works. Many traditional hymns and newer praise songs also mention the dove as a sign of the Holy Spirit or divine peace.

An early 1930's Nazi poster, with the text 'Es lebe Deutschland!' (Long Live Germany!) seems to proclaim Adolph Hitler as a new messiah. Using the image of Jesus' baptism, it depicts him and brownshirted followers rising from a river, with a stylized bird appearing in a break in the clouds over his head.

See also WINGS LIKE A DOVE; CLEANSING OF THE TEMPLE; FLOOD; HOLY SPIRIT, THE; NOAH'S ARK; SACRIFICE [TJV]

Doxology. Doxology is a liturgical term used to denote an expression of praise or a proclamation about the glory of God. More specifically, the term designates a statement that includes the Greek term *doxa*, glory. These statements are concerned with who God is and his attributes.

The OT Psalms collection is divided into five smaller sections or books, each concluding with a doxology (Pss 41.13; 72.19; 89.52; 106.38). Thus, Ps. 41 closes book one with the phrase: 'Bless the Lord, the God of Israel, from everlasting to everlasting'. In the HB, the Psalter as a whole concludes with Ps. 150, itself a long doxology calling for God to be wholeheartedly praised. Narratives could also be concluded with doxologies, like Apocryphal books *3 and 4 Maccabees* (*3 Macc.* 7.23; *4 Macc.* 18.24).

Early Hebrew prayers tended to separate praise from appeal though after the exile prayers of petition sometimes began with doxological statements. An extended doxology precedes the prayer of King David at the end of 1 Chronicles (1 Chron. 29.10-19). Similarly, Sarah's petition in the Apocryphal book Tobit begins with a doxological statement (Tob 3.11-15), and Abram's prayer pleading for justice against Pharaoh for taking his wife Sari, found in the Dead Sea Scroll the Genesis Apocryphon, begins, 'Blessed are you, O God Most High' (1Qap Gen^{ar} 20.12).

The best known doxology in the NT is found at the conclusion of the Lord's Prayer in the Gospel of Matthew: 'For yours is the kingdom, and the power, and the glory, forever. Amen' (6.13b). However, many scholars believe that this doxology is a later addition to the text and as a result, some modern translations, like the English Standard Version and the American Standard Version, have removed 6.13b from the main text. Additionally, many of the NT epistles conclude with doxological statements (e.g., Phil. 4.20; 1 Pet. 4.11; 2 Pet. 3.18; Jude 24-25).

Doxologies remain an important part of both modern Jewish and Christian liturgies. In the Synogogue, doxologies may be recited after or in response to the *Shema*, the *Kaddish*, or the *Kedusha*. In Christian liturgy, the two most well-known doxologies are the Great Doxology, or *Gloria in Excelsis Deo*, and the Lesser Doxology, or *Gloria Patri*: 'Glory to the Father, and to the Son, and to the Holy Spirit; as it was in the beginning, is now, and ever shall be, world without end. Amen'.

Recommended reading. Brueggemann, Walter. *Israel's Praise: Doxology against Idolatry and Ideology.* Philadelphia: Fortress Press, 1988. Wainwright, Geoffrey. *Doxology: The Praise of God in Worship, Doctrine and Life.* London: Epworth Press, 1980. Werner, Eric. *The Sacred Bridge: The Interdependence of Liturgy and Music in Synagogue and Church during the First Millennium.* London: Dennis Dobson, 1959.

See also PSALM, PSALMIST, BOOK OF PSALMS; EPISTLE [CLH]

Dragon, the. The dragon in the Bible is an enemy of God, present in a number of manifestations generally based around what is known as the 'combat myth'. This tells of the battle for kingship between a fertility god and the dragon, a god of chaos and sterility that threatens continued life. In Middle-Eastern creation myths, the dragon is the dark, chaotic waters that must be subjugated for life to appear. OT texts make poetic use of this imagery to enhance Yahweh's sovereignty over neighboring cosmologies by softening the ferocity of battle and reducing the dragon's power. Yahweh stills the sea, crushing the head of the dragon to create the world and feed his people (Pss. 74, 89; Isa. 51), while in Genesis the dragon is the waters of the deep that are defeated without combat, but by the creative word of God. Pharaoh, the enemy of God's people, is depicted as the dragon in the river that will be flung away (Ezek. 29). In a further shift, the dragon is the awe-inspiring Leviathan, the greatest of all God's creatures, but no challenge to the deity. A sea monster, and perhaps referring to a crocodile, Leviathan has many characteristics found in the medieval and modern dragon, such as smoke, fire, scales, flashing eyes, coiling tail and fearsome teeth.

The image of the red dragon in Rev. 12 gathers together many mythic manifestations of opposition to God and humans. The dragon with seven heads accords with Leviathan of Hebrew and Canaanite tradition, but its attack upon the Woman Clothed with the Sun, hoping to destroy her child when it is born, has mythic precursors in Egyptian and Greek combat myths. This battle for cosmic kingship also draws upon ancient Jewish apocryphal tales of the fall of Lucifer and his angels from heaven and their battle with the angel Michael. Once the dragon is thrown to earth, the focus turns to its attack upon humans as the tempting serpent in Eden, as the devil, and as Satan the accuser of the faithful.

The dragon remains an endless source of fascination in Western culture, its source in the imaginative world allowing for a variety of manifestations. The figure was developed strongly in the early church and Middle Ages as a symbol of evil: the devil, pagan belief, sin and temptation. It is the opponent of many saints (including two women, Martha and Margaret of Antioch) who easily dispatch it without physical battle, but with prayer. Ubiquitous as the enemy of the pious martial champion St George in secular romance and folktale, it is the ultimate spiritual and bestial enemy of the emerging hero. Its gold-hoarding in the Old English *Beowulf* draws upon Norse mythology and the Bible, though the reference here is more oblique. Dwelling always on the margins of civilization, it characterizes the Other and the unknown in story and cartography, but is a dramatic graphic and literary symbol of royal strength for Pendragon and Arthur. The dragon remains a figure of power, but not necessarily of evil, in contemporary fantasy literature, and in children's literature is usually a gentle, misunderstood figure reluctantly playing a role as enemy, as in Martin Baynton's *Jane and the Dragon* (also a TV series).

Recommended reading. Collins, Adela Yarbro. *The Combat Myth in the Book of Revelation*. Missoula, MT: Scholars Press, 1976. Day, John. *God's Conflict with the Dragon and the Sea*. Cambridge: Cambridge University Press, 1985.

See also APOCALYPSE, APOCALYPTIC; CREATION/ CREATOR; WATER; MICHAEL, THE ANGEL [RC]

Dreams. Although many modern theories of dream interpretation focus primarily on the psychological dimensions of the dreamer, in biblical and other ancient literature, dreams are usually identified as one of the expected means by which God, or the gods, communicate with humanity (Num. 12.6; 1 Sam. 28.6, 15).

In the HB, the subject of dreams appears most prominently in the mantic wisdom of the Joseph story (Gen. 37–50) and the early chapters of Daniel (1–7), where dreams reveal information of such value and importance as: the rise and fall of rulers (Gen. 37.5-11; Dan. 4.19-27) and empires (Dan. 2.24-45; 7.15-28); the threat of imminent catastrophe (Gen. 41.25-32) and the means to circumvent its effects (Gen. 41.33-36); and whether or not a person might live (Gen. 40.9-15) or die (Gen. 40.16-19).

In other portions of Scripture, dreams can be seen to offer critical guidance on the navigation of complex personal and social decisions (Matt. 1.20); provide warnings about imminent danger (Matt. 2.2-13, 23); and, with some qualification, be indicative of the outpouring of God's spirit (Joel 2.28; Acts 2.17).

Though highly valued, the imagery of dreams was often obscure and their meanings difficult to discern (Gen. 40.8; Dan. 2.3). Accordingly, gifted interpreters were often called upon to unpack the inherent mysteries of meaning (Dan. 4.18; 7.16). In fact, in many ancient cultures, dream interpretation even became a sort of primitive science that in turn led to the development of a specific class of sages who specialized in dream interpretation (Gen. 41.8; Dan. 2.2).

[TAB]

E

Ears to Hear. In the Bible, hearing is associated with spiritual understanding, seeking knowledge, and the word of God. The symbolic phrase 'ears to hear' is found in the HB exclusively in the context of *not* hearing (Deut. 29.4; Jer. 25.4; Ezek. 12.2). Hearing is obedience to God, and the ancient Israelites are admonished for not having, or not using, their ears to hear.

In the NT, Jesus uses the phrase 'ears to hear' (Matt. 11.15; 13.9, 43; Mark 4.9, 23; 7.15; Luke 8.8; 14.35), as does John the Seer (Rev. 13.9). It can also be found in a number of sayings attributed to Jesus in the apocryphal *Gospel of Thomas* (8, 21, 24, 63, 65, 96), using a similar formulation to the NT.

The phrase is central to the admonition not only to listen to what Jesus is saying, but also to understand. The most common construction is the phrase 'let anyone with ears to hear listen!', which usually follows a parable or a teaching using highly symbolic language. This is an important formula, as it gives the impression that, while Jesus' teachings are open to all people (i.e., Matthew's Sermon on the Mount), not everyone has the aptitude necessary for understanding them.

In modern usage, this phrase has retained much of its initial meaning. However, it now extends beyond listening to and understanding Jesus' teaching to incorporate truth more generally, whether in a religious, political, or literary context. For example, in his famous speech 'Give me Liberty, or give me Death!' (1775), Patrick Henry uses a turn of the phrase in juxtaposition to the fight for liberty and truth: 'Are we disposed to be of the number of those who, having eyes, see not, and, having ears, hear not, the things which so nearly concern their temporal salvation? For my part, whatever anguish of spirit it may cost, I am willing to know the whole truth; to know the worst, and to provide for it'. The phrase 'ears to hear' is widely represented in literature, from Leo Tolstoy's *War and Peace* (1869), to Mark Twain's *The Adventures of Tom Sawyer* (1876), to Bram Stoker's *Dracula* (1897).

See also PARABLE [EJW]

Earth. The Hebrew term *erets* can refer to Earth as distinct from sky, land as distinct from sea, and land as ground, property or country. The same is generally true of the Greek term *gaia*.

There are several accounts of the origins of Earth in the Bible. In Job 38.4-7 God constructs Earth like a building with foundations and a cornerstone. The heavenly beings break into song when the cornerstone is laid. In Ps. 104.5-9 God again sets Earth on its foundations, but then covers her with the waters of the deep before putting them in their place. In Gen. 1, the account begins with a superscription saying God created heaven and Earth. The account then says that 'Earth is without form and life', but lies deep in the waters, like an embryo waiting to be born. On the third day, the waters part, land appears and Earth is born. God names the land 'Earth'. Earth then becomes a partner with God in the creation process, bringing forth all vegetation and all forms of life, except human beings. In Prov. 8.22-31, the feminine figure of Wisdom is present celebrating with God at the beginning before the formation of Earth and the domains of Earth.

The story of Earth from its origins in Genesis to its transformation in Revelation is both extensive and complex. In Gen. 1, humans are given a mandate to dominate Earth (1.26-28) while in Gen. 2 the mission is to serve and preserve (2.15). In the flood narrative, Earth, an innocent party, is to be destroyed along with all life (Gen. 6.13). After the flood, God makes Earth a partner in the covenant never to send another flood (9.13). Domains of Earth are frequently destroyed when God liberates Israel or punishes a nation. Some prophets hear Earth mourning because of human sin or divine punishment (Jer. 12.4, 11; Joel 1.10). The seraphim in Isaiah's vision, however, announce that the 'whole Earth' is filled with God's glory, that is, with God's visible presence (Isa. 6.3).

Some passages speak of a new heaven and a new Earth. In Isaiah this means Earth is transformed into an ideal abode (65.17-25; 66.22-23). In other texts, Jerusalem descends from heaven to transform Earth (Rev. 21.1-4) who is earlier a hero in her struggle with the dragon (Rev. 12.13-17). The groanings of Earth, however, may refer not only to the curses imposed on her, but also to the birth-pangs of a rebirth (Rom. 8.18-25).

The emergence of ecology has added another dimension to how we relate to Earth and how we read the Bible. Reading the text from the perspective of Earth uncovers new insights. The five volumes of *The Earth Bible* illustrate this approach. Ecology has made us aware that Earth is not a series of discrete domains, but a web of interdependent life systems, of which we humans are an integral part. Humans are not separate from Earth, but live in Earth, are made of Earth and are nurtured by Earth. Earth, moreover, is now viewed as a living organism, a concept developed by James Lovelock in *The Gaia Hypothesis*.

Throughout history, Earth has been hailed by artists and poets as mother and mystery. For some writers, like Tolkien, Middle Earth is a magical place. The great adventure writer Jules Verne sought to take a *Journey to the Centre of the Earth* (1864). Great artists like Michelangelo have painted the *Separation of the Earth from the Waters*. Musical works like Hayden's *Creation* or Mahler's *Das Leid von Erde* focus on Earth. Recent songs, like Dilan Lennon's 'Saltwater', reflect the environmental crisis on planet Earth.

See also CREATION, CREATOR [NH]

Earthen vessels. Rooted in the ancient practice of pottery, this biblical reference relates to the role of human beings as vessels that God desires to use for his purposes in the world (Isa. 64.8; Jer18.4, 6). From the Greek word *ostrakinos* (earthen vessels), this term implicitly refers to the frailty of humans since they were created from the dust of the earth. Due to some scriptural references (Rom. 9.21), some have come to understand this biblical reference relating earthen fragility to include humankind's insignificance in the created order. With that in mind, it seems that fragility does not diminish humankind's importance in the larger biblical narrative. More importantly, the biblical language instills grave importance to those who surrender themselves to the handiwork of the potter. Paul, writing to the faithful in Corinth indicates that the treasure of the knowledge of the glory of God is 'in earthen vessels' (2 Cor. 4.7).

Contemporary worship music is filled with expressions connoting humanity's involvement in God's redeeming plan. In 1998, one song by Australian singer-songwriter Darlene Zschech emerged as most relevant. From her album *Touching Heaven Changing Earth*, a song called 'The Potter's Hand' stirred the hearts of congregations for its ability to make the idea of 'earthen vessel' a tangible reality in the life of ecclesial communities.

Recommended reading. Matthews, Victor Harold. *Manners and Customs in the Bible: An Illustrated Guide to Daily Life in Bible Times*. 3rd ed. Peabody, MA: Hendrickson, 2006.

See also VESSEL; PROPHETS; SAINTS [DOMR]

Easter. This important Christian religious festival takes place on the first Sunday after the first full moon, which falls on or after March 21, and coincides with the Jewish festival of Passover. Good Friday and Easter Sunday commemorate the crucifixion of Jesus and his resurrection from the dead. Because of the differences between the Julian and Gregorian calendars, Easter is celebrated later in Orthodox communities.

The English term Easter seems to have come from the Saxon goddess Eostre who was commemorated in spring. In French, the festival is known as Paques, and this is similar in other Romance languages, deriving from the Greek which itself is derived from Passover. Easter in Slavic languages comes from the word for 'Great Day' or 'Great Night'. Traditionally Easter is celebrated by Christians with the symbolic Stations of the Cross, charting the events which led up to the crucifixion of Jesus. Many pilgrims go to Jerusalem for this, but there are also traditional 'stations of the Cross' in Rome which are commemorated by the Popes. In some parts of the world, such as the Philippines, some of the faithful are nailed to crosses themselves as a sign of penitence. Many Christian communities also see it as the best time to baptize children.

Though it appears to have little connection to the religious meaning of Easter, the practice of decorating eggs, initially in bright red, was symbolic of the blood spilled by Christ. The Easter bunny has its roots in non-Christian folklore, reaching back at least to the sixteenth century in festivals commemorating the end of winter and start of spring. Since medieval times, Easter scenes have been shown in Christian carvings and also in illuminations. The former can be seen in churches and cathedrals all around the world, and the latter in museums and libraries which have collections of old manuscripts.

Recommended reading. Clarke, Alison. *Holiday Seasons: Christmas, New Year and Easter in Nineteenth-century New Zealand*. Auckland: Auckland University Press, 2007.

See also CROSS, CRUCIFIXION OF CHRIST; PASSOVER [JC]

Ebenezer. The word Ebenezer occurs in 1 Sam. 4.1; 5.1; and 7.12. It is a combination of the Hebrew words *'eben* and *ha'azer*, which mean 'stone' and 'the help'. In context, the words mean 'the stone of the help'. In the first two instances, the phrase refers to a specific site, but experts disagree as to the exact location. First Samuel 4 and 5 describe a battle at Ebenezer during the time of Eli, the Israelite prophet, where the Philistines defeated the Israelites and captured the Ark of the covenant.

In 1 Sam. 7, Ebenezer refers to a stone monument erected by Samuel. The chapter describes another battle where God delivers Israel from the Philistines. Before this battle, Samuel exhorts Israel that if they remove their foreign gods and serve the LORD alone, they will be delivered from the Philistines. According to 1 Sam. 7.12, after the Israelite victory, 'Samuel took a stone and set it up between Mizpah and Jeshanah, and named it Ebenezer', which is interpreted by the biblical author as, 'Thus far the LORD has helped us'. Therefore, Samuel built the Ebenezer to stand as a physical reminder, or monument, of God's help.

Ebenezer does not appear frequently in art or literature until after the Methodist pastor Robert Robinson, at age 22, incorporated the word into his hymn 'Come Thou Fount of Every Blessing' in 1757. While there are a number of versions of this hymn, the most common version references Ebenezer in the second verse: 'Here I raise my Ebenezer; / Hither by thy help I come; / And, I hope, by Thy good pleasure, / Safely to arrive at home'. Interestingly, the word is misstransliterated, or mispronounced, in the hymn. The original Hebrew vocalization is closer to 'Eben Ha-azer'. The confusion probably stems from the Septuagint transliteration of the word, *abenezer*, which omits the vocalization of the definite article. Thus, the common pronunciation Ebenezer would be translated 'a stone of help' rather than 'the stone of the help', as the Hebrew indicates. The Septuagint vocalization was then carried forward by other English translations such as the KJV.

After the hymn was written, Ebenezer begins to appear with some frequency as both fictional and historical names. The most widely known use is that of the character Ebenezer Scrooge in Charles Dickens's *A Christmas Carol* (1843). Scrooge personifies the theological significance found in 1 Sam. 7.12 of triumph via supernatural intervention after previous defeat.

See also ROCK; SAMUEL; SEPTUAGINT [JMK]

Ecce Homo. *Ecce homo* is a Latin phrase meaning 'behold [*ecce*, in the imperative] the man' (*homo*). The two words appear in the Latin Vulgate at John 19.5 where Pontius Pilate speaks to the Jewish leaders and the crowds assembled for Jesus' trial. By this time Jesus had been scourged (John 19.1), a scene so vividly portrayed in Mel Gibson's *The Passion of the Christ*. Jesus is bleeding, bound and wearing a crown of thorns.

The words *ecce homo* now represents the sufferings of Jesus during his trial, a scene that has inspired artists and thinkers ever since. In the nineteenth century, for instance, John Seeley wrote *Ecce Homo: A Survey of the Life and Work of Jesus Christ* (1865). The book is a liberal portrayal of Jesus as a moral teacher who suffered unjustly. Frederick Nietzsche (1844–1900) wrote an autobiography, translated from German as *Ecce Homo: How Man Becomes What He Is* (1888), completed just weeks before his metal breakdown. Frederick Douglas compared the whippings given to African-American slaves to the trial of Christ in his *Narrative of the Life of an American Slave*. Douglas's 'ecce homo' is similar to applications in the twentieth century which evoke Christ's sufferings to portray forms of human suffering. Artist such as Lovis Corinth (*Ecce Homo*, 1925) and Otto Dix (*Ecce homo with self-likeness behind barbed wire*, 1948) draw an analogy between Jesus' sufferings and war victims. In 1998, the Swedish photographer Elisabeth Ohlson Wallin used the *ecce homo* concept in an exhibition portraying Jesus with homosexuals. In twentieth-century literature, David Gascoyne (1916–2001) published a poem entitled 'Ecce homo' (in *Poems 1937–1942*) that highlights the anguish of Jesus followers and the crowd who saw the savagely beaten man. Gascoyne's subject is the grief occasioned by bombed and battered cities in the aftermath of World War II.

See also CHRIST; SUFFERING SERVANT; TRIAL OF JESUS [AJW]

Ecclesiastes, Book of. Ecclesiastes, or Qoheleth, is found in the third section of the HB, the Writings (*Kethuvim*), and is one of the *Megillot* (the five scrolls, the others being Song of Songs, Ruth, Lamentations, and Esther). This liturgical text is used during the Feast of Booths commemorating the forty years of wilderness wandering—a time for Israel to think about their faith *vis-à-vis* the temporalness of life. The skepticism of Ecclesiastes with all its questioning and doubts seems appropriate for such a festival.

Ecclesiastes challenges the foundations of traditional Israelite wisdom as derived from the Book of Proverbs. It is loaded with irony, setting up a tension between the way things should be and the way they are. For example, Ecclesiastes uses the very tools of the wisdom tradition to question the cherished belief in retributive justice, or, 'you reap what you sow'. The writer observes that in fact good things do not always happen to good people, and bad things do not always happen to bad people. Such skepticism contributes to the pessimistic ethos of the book.

Ecclesiastes's literary structure involves an inclusio beginning at 1.2 and ending at 12.8, meaning the book ends as it begins (*hevel havalim*; 'vanity', 'futile', 'meaningless'). This inclusio indicates that the author remained in an acute faith crisis, contrary to the 'trendy' counter-reading of the book as essentially one of joy. The setting of the book is the royal court, and it addresses, among other things, the delusionary problems facing the politically powerful, and the rich and famous. Ecclesiastes does not represent the 'voice of the common man' because the contents of the book would be irrelevant to the disenfranchised and illiterate masses.

In recent times, the Byrds immortalized Ecclesiastes, bringing it into the mainstream with their song 'Turn! Turn! Turn! (to Everything There is a Season)'. *The Simpsons* cites 9.11 ('the race is not to the swift') and 11.1 ('bread upon the waters') in two different episodes, and *The Brotherhood* uses Eccl. 7.2 ('better to go to the house of mourning than … the house of feasting') as the title for an episode. Cecil B. DeMille has Solomon quoting Ecclesiastes's refrain 'vanity, vanity' in his 1959 movie *Solomon and Sheba* at the point where Solomon's whole life is crumbling around him.

According to Ecclesiastes, 'There is nothing new under the sun' (1.9). The strongest link between this book and contemporary culture may be postmodernism, a term encapsulating philosophical skepticism and epistemological deconstruction. For some, this concept captures a pessimistic ethos that resembles Ecclesiastes's observation that 'Everything is a chasing after the wind and a vexation of spirit'.

Recommended reading. Christianson, Eric S. *Ecclesiastes through the Centuries*. Oxford: Blackwell, 2007. Fox, Michael V. *Qohelet and his Contradictions*. Sheffield: Almond Press, 1989. Leithart, Peter J. *Solomon among the Postmoderns*. Grand Rapids, MI: Brazos Press, 2008.

See also Wisdom [BA]

Edom. Edom was the home of the Edomites, descendants of Jacob's bother Esau (Gen. 36.1). Jacob manipulated Esau out of his birthright, and stole the blessing given to the firstborn in the memorable stories of their contentious relationship (Gen. 25.29-34; 27.1-29). The land of Edom stretched for over 160 kilometers from the Dead Sea to the Gulf of Aqaba. The rock in the area is a reddish sandstone which accounts for name Edom, which means 'red' or 'ruddy'. The term also picks up on Esau's red hair (25.25) and the red food Jacob serves his brother (25.30).

At the time of the desert wanderings the Israelites sought permission to pass through Edom (Num. 20.14-21) though the request was refused. Both Saul and David defeated the Edomites (1 Sam. 14.47; 2 Sam. 8.12-14). During the reign of King Jehoram, the Edomites successfully revolted (c. 850–843 BCE) and they set up an independent kingdom (2 Kgs 22.48-49; 2 Chron. 20.35-37) that remained independent until the middle of Amaziah's reign (c. 800–785; 2 Kgs 14.7; 2 Chron. 25.11-12). At the time of Ahaz (c. 742–725 BCE), the Edomites defeated Judah (2 Chron. 28.17). Edom may have been destroyed by the Babylonians around the time of Jerusalem's destruction in 587/6 BCE.

Recommended reading. Edelman, Diana Vikander (ed.). *You Shall Not Abhor an Edomite for He Is your Brother: Edom and Seir in History and Tradition*. Atlanta, GA: Scholars Press, 1995. MacDonald, B. *Ammon, Moab and Edom: Early States/Nations of Jordan in the Biblical Period (End of the 2nd and during the 1st Millennium B.C.)*. Amman, Jordan: Al Kutba, 1994.

See also Esau [AJW]

Egypt. Egypt is one of the longest lasting civilizations of the ancient world (3050 BCE–30 BCE). It was a place of sanctuary for Abram and Joseph, and later the location of Israel's captivity. Egypt also came to symbolize obstacles to overcome and temptations to resist in later prophetic writings (e.g., Isa. 30.1-5; Hos. 7.11-12; Jer. 42–43).

Egyptian religion includes connections between the physical and spiritual worlds. The pyramids were the mortuary temples of dead Pharaohs. The cult of the dead reveals Egyptian concern with living after death, and interest in knowing all the spells and rituals necessary to achieve this. Another such interaction was through the realm of the gods. Gods were associated with geographical locations (the places of their temples), the physical universe (Re the sun god), or lifecycles (rebirth; Osiris). Some aspects of Egyptian mythology appear contradictory and confusing. For example, Nut the sky goddess was depicted as a naked female overstretching the sky, or as a cow. She was created by the sun god Re but also gave birth to Re each morning. Likewise, Re was referred to as three different gods, depending on the time of the day (Khepri, Re and Atum). Another example is Egypt's various creation stories. The world came out of the word of a god, out of clay, or out of the sneeze of a god, according to different myths. There is some resemblance here with the HB, which includes differing accounts of creation (Gen. 1.1–2.4; Gen. 2.4-25; Ezek. 28.13-19).

Egyptian religion influenced the HB. In the Egyptian creation story from Memphis, Ptah speaks humanity into existence (compare Gen. 1.3) and Khnum forms people out of clay (compare Gen. 2.7). Various parallels occur between the Egyptian tale of two brothers and the story of Joseph (Gen. 39.1-20), and whereas Moses parts the sea (Exod. 14.21), Egyptian literature speaks of a head priest who folds the waters to uncover the sea bottom.

The biblical representation of Egypt continues to influence the popular imagination, as is evident in G.F. Handel's *Israel in Egypt*, which draws on Exod. 1–15, Cecil B. DeMille's film *The Ten Commandments* (1956), and the animated *The Prince of Egypt* (1998). In *The Simpsons* ('The Simpson's Bible Stories', tenth season, 1999), the representation of Egypt is typically biblical. Egyptian religion and culture remains the backdrop for stories still drawing on biblical material, as in *Indian Jones: The Raiders of the Lost Ark* (1981). The series of movies in *The Mummy* (1999) franchise did a little more to engage with Egyptian myth on its own terms, though obviously with fanciful embellishments.

Recommended reading. Shafer, Byron E. (ed.). *Religion in Ancient Egypt: Gods, Myths, and Personal Practice*. Ithaca, NY: Cornell University Press, 1991. Redford, Donald B. *Egypt, Canaan and Israel in Ancient Times*. Princeton: Princeton, 1992.

See also YAHWEH; EXODUS, THE; NILE; PHARAOH
[SWF]

Ehud. Ehud (meaning 'union') son of Gera was a left-hander who assassinated the Moabite king and led Israel to victory. The crude, gory narrative in Judges uses coarse jokes on names and physical defects. Ehud's tribe is Benjamin (meaning 'son of my right hand'), but ironically he is 'bound' or deformed in his right hand (Judg. 3.15). Hebrew culture saw the right hand as favorable (Pss 16.11; 110.1) and the left as sinister—to use a word from the Latin for 'left hand'. In many languages the word 'right' means correct or true, and also skilful. 'Dexterous' is from Greek and 'adroit' from French, whereas 'gauche', with its negative connotations, means left. So Ehud is a flawed hero.

King Eglon ('little calf') of Moab had taken the balmy city of Jericho, 'city of palms', and ruled the area for 18 years. Ehud delivered to him the tribute or tax, probably in the form of farm produce collected from his countrymen, no doubt a demoralizing task.

Ehud made himself a short sword—a major task, especially without full use of one's hands—and took the trouble to give it two cutting edges. He hid the sword under clothing on his right side, expecting to be considered harmless and not be checked. (The modern handshake originates in a traditional check that the right hand did not hold a weapon). Ehud smuggled it into the king's presence. Here the writer tells us Eglon was a very fat man, suggesting a large target or a fattened calf for butchery. However, Ehud did not attack. He left, then turned back claiming to have a secret message for the king.

The Hebrew wordplay gives a number of hints that Ehud had been the victim of sexual harassment by the king. Now the king tells his attendants to leave them alone. Ehud approaches him, saying, 'I have a message from God (or a divine thing) for you'. The king rises from his seat, perhaps in anticipation. However, Ehud's left hand thrusts the hidden sword, burying it hilt-deep in the fat of the king's belly—not the thrust the king was perhaps hoping for. The stab was so deep that 'the dirt came out'. Ehud never retrieved his precious sword, avoiding being sprayed with arterial blood and perhaps worse when he was about to walk past the guards.

When Ehud locked the doors and left, the guards assumed the king was inside 'covering his feet' (the phrase can mean either sexual activity or relieving oneself). While they waited, Ehud escaped to muster an army from Ephraim. In his pre-battle speech, the left-handed, handicapped leader from Benjamin makes a self-deprecating pun about hands: 'Follow after me; for the LORD has given your enemies the Moabites into your hand' (3.24). When Ehud's army cuts off Moab's cross-river escape and inflicts heavy losses on their oppressors, the writer repeats the pun: 'So Moab was subdued that day under the hand of Israel' (3.30).

Ehud fathered three sons (1 Chron. 8.6-7), and later the tribe of Benjamin had 700 left-handers, handicapped in their right hands, who are superb marksmen with the slingshot (Judg. 20.15-16). The name Ehud was not in use until the twentieth century, when Zionism revived many aspects of ancient Jewish culture. Two Israeli Prime Ministers, Ehud Barak and Ehud Olmert, were named for the heroic judge.

Recommended reading. Alter, Robert. *The Art of Biblical Narrative.* New York: Basic Books, 1981. Soggin, J. Alberto. *Judges.* 2nd edn. London: SCM Press, 1987.

See also JUDGES, BOOK OF; MOAB [GK]

Eleazar. Eleazar is one of the sons of Aaron (Exod. 6.23). He was a Levite and high priest, and was responsible for looking after various items in the sanctuary (Lev. 8.1-13; Num. 3.1-4). When Aaron died, Moses anointed Eleazar as his father's successor and after the plague struck the Israelites in the land of the Moabites, Moses ordered Eleazar to conduct a census (Num. 26.1-4). He helped with the distribution of land after the conquest of Judaea, and was buried by his son Phinehas, 'at Gibeah, the town of his son Phinehas, which had been given him in the hill country of Ephraim' (Josh. 24.33). The village of Awarta on the West Bank of the River Jordan is now thought to be the burial place of Eleazar, and each year on the fifth of Shevat (in the Hebrew Calendar, around January–February), a service is held attracting people from Israel and overseas.

The Eastern Orthodox Church recognized Eleazar as a saint, and his Saints' Day is September 2. He is also one of the Holy Forefathers in the Calendar of Saints observed by the Armenian Apostolic Church, his day being July 30. Eleazar is often represented as very tall, with some traditions claiming he was the tallest man in history. In Cecil B. DeMille's *The Ten Commandments* (1956), which had Moses played by Charlton Heston, Paul de Rolf played Eleazar as a boy and Robert Carson as the adult Eleazar.

There are also a number of other people called Eleazar mentioned in the Bible. One of these was a fierce soldier in the army of King David, and another (mentioned in the Books of Maccabees in the Apocrypha) was the brother of Judas who was killed in battle when an elephant fell on him.

See also AARON; LAZARUS; MOSES [JC]

Elder. The word translates the Hebrew *zāqēn* and the Greek *presbyteros*. The word 'priest', semantically closer to the Greek *hiereus* (priest), is etymologically derived from *presbyteros*.

Since pre-monarchical Israelite times, the elders were the heads of families and clans. Collegially, they represented and had authority over the people (Exod. 12.21). They were judges, civic leaders (1 Sam. 11.3), mediators between people, and between people and God (Lev. 4.15). During the monarchic period, the exile, and later in the Second Temple period, the elders played an important role within Jewish society, and their religious and civil authority was recognized in Judea and in the Diaspora. In the Book of Daniel, God is anthropomorphically depicted as an 'ancient of days' (7.9), alluding to his unsurpassed wisdom and to the reverence he inspires. However, the expression was to be appropriated in mystical terms by later apocalyptic literature (Rev. 1.14).

The Romans acknowledged their local power in Jerusalem by granting their assembly (Sanhedrin) a degree of autonomy in dealing with civic matters (Acts 22.5). Elders occasionally refers to the Fathers of the Jewish traditions (Mark 7.3-5), or to Jews holding religious (and political?) power in the city of Capernaum (Luke 7.3).

Greek-speaking Jews and Gentiles also used the word *episcopos* to refer to an elder ('overseer'; cf. LXX Neh. 11.9). This word occurs five times in the NT, and may have initially been used as a synonym of *presbyteros* in primitive Christianity.

Ignatius of Antioch (d. c. 98–117 CE) attested to the development of hierarchical structures within the churches that eventually led to the establishment of Bishops (*episcopos*) and a subordinate Councils of Elders (*presbyterion*). In time, elders focused on sacerdotal (clergy) rather than pastoral functions, meaning the consecration of the Eucharistic body and the performance of rites. The Reformation rehabilitated the pastoral ministry of the Elders, with a single ordination for pastors and lay-elders. In the context of the Counter-Reformation, the Council of Trent (1545–1563) promoted a spiritual/moral reform of the elders-priests, which led to the creation of Seminaries. Today, the elder still holds a position of responsibility in Christian circles as a cleric (e.g., Roman Catholicism, Eastern Orthodoxy, Anglicanism) or as a layperson (e.g., Presbyterianism, Evangelicalism).

Power, knowledge, mediation, and protection are the elders' prerogatives. The Book of Revelation describes twenty-four crowned elders bowing before Christ ('the Lamb') holding in their hands fragrant 'golden vials ... which are the prayers of saints' (5.8; cf. 4.4; 19.4). Noteworthy artistic representations include *Adoration of the Mystic Lamb* (Jan Van Eyck, 1432) and William Blake's *The Four and Twenty Elders Casting their Crowns before the Divine Throne* (c. 1803–1805). Bamberg's *Adoration of the Elders* (c. 1000) highlights the political nature of the Elders by including crown imagery. In contemporary society, the word elder still evokes wisdom and hierarchy, as its adoption into political language (e.g., Electoral district of Elder in South Australia; Global Elders, a group of statesmen and human rights advocates) and fictional language (e.g., Harry Potter's elder wand) shows.

However, power and knowledge are seldom dissociated from abuse and skepticism. Grace Cossington Smith's *I Looked and Behold, a Door Was Opened in Heaven* (1953) has John looking up through the door of heaven only to see the elders on their thrones: despite the mediation of this elite group, God remains unattainable. Artemisia Gentileschi's *Susanna and the Elders* (1610) depicts the biblical story of a beautiful young wife sexually harassed by the elders of her community: the vulnerable Susanna repulses the demands of malicious and conspiratorial men who were supposed to provide guidance, assure protection, and mediate between her and God.

See also ANCIENT OF DAYS [LM]

Election. In the OT, the Hebrew *bachar* and its various inflections indicate choices made by both God and humans (e.g., 2 Sam. 21.6). The word in some form is used almost two hundred times. When God elects (chooses), a relationship is formed between the chosen and the Lord (e.g., Ps. 89.3). Divine choices cover a wide range of relationships. For instance, God chose Israel (Deut. 7.6) and Jerusalem (Deut. 12.5, 11, 14, 18). He also elected or chose individuals, among them Abraham (Gen. 18.19), Moses (Ps. 106.23), and Saul (1 Sam. 10.1). Israel was elected by God, which lies behind references to the Jews as a 'chosen nation' or 'the elect' (cf. Rom. 9). In the NT, the language of choosing and election applies more broadly to the followers of Jesus (e.g., 1 Pet. 1.1-2, 9). Theological discussion about divine election also addresses the related ideas of predestination and divine foreknowledge (cf. Rom. 9.18; 11.2; etc.). These difficult concepts fuel debates to this day about human freedom and responsibility versus divine determination.

Percy Bysshe Shelley rejected the idea of personal election in 'Queen Mab', and the concept is explored further in Chaim Potok's *The Chosen* (1967). Margaret Atwood's dystopian novel *The Handmaid's Tale* (1985) attacked the American theme of the chosen, and Kris Kristofferson's song 'Why Me Lord' ponders the mystery of divine election.

Recommended reading. Berkouwer, G.C. *Divine Election*. Grand Rapids, MI: William B. Eerdmans, 1960.

See also CHOSEN PEOPLE, THE; FREEDOM; GRACE; LOVE, NO RESPECTER OF PERSONS; PREDESTINATION
[AJW]

Eli. Eli was a (high) priest at a local sanctuary in Shiloh and, according to 1 Sam. 4.18, one of the last judges of ancient Israel before the establishment of the kingdom. His name means 'ascent' or 'exalted', possibly a short form for 'Yahweh is exalted'. Eli's story is told in 1 Sam. 1–4. He appears without special introduction in the narrative about Elkanah and his wives Hannah and Peninnah, who make an annual pilgrimage to Shiloh, at that time the site of the ark of the covenant (1 Sam. 1.1-8; 3.3). Eli is portrayed as an ambivalent person. He seems to be of reputable and extended priestly pedigree (1 Sam. 2.27-28), perhaps a descendant of Ithamar, a son of Aaron (1 Kgs 2.27; 1 Chron. 24.3), or of Eleazar (2 Esd. 1.2-3). Yet in his first appearance he misjudges Hannah when reproaching her for being inebriated while she actually prays to receive a son. This scene becomes the overture to the story of her son Samuel, whom Hannah later brings to Eli for apprenticeship in the priesthood. Indeed, the story technique of 1 Sam. 1–4 connects the rise of stature of the young Samuel with the decline of Eli's house. Hophni and Phinehas, the two sons of Eli, are reprobate priests who blaspheme God by disobeying customs of sacrificial rituals (1 Sam. 2.12-17) and misusing female servants at the tent of meeting (2.22). Eli rebukes them because of their inappropriate manners, yet to no avail. Therefore an unnamed prophet pronounces divine judgment upon Eli's house which is corroborated by Samuel (2.27-36; 3.11-18). When ninety-eight years old, blind, and 'heavy', Eli is informed that both of his sons have died in battle and that the ark of the covenant has been lost. The shock causes him to fall down, break his neck, and die (4.12-18). Considering the importance of genealogies and dynasties in ancient Near Eastern cultures, the Eli story conveys that dynasties can fall and leaders can be displaced by subordinate persons.

In the first century CE, the story of Eli and his sons is recounted by Josephus (*Antiquities* 5.338-62). Depictions of Eli include paintings of Hannah presenting her son to a priest by Jan Victors (1645), and this priest advising his young apprentice Samuel by Gerrit Dou (c. 1631).

Recommended reading. Eberhart, Christian A. 'Beobachtungen zum Verbrennungsritus bei Schlachtopfer und Gemeinschafts-Schlachtopfer'. *Biblica* 83 (2002) 88-96. Eynikel, Erik M.M. 'The Relation between the Eli Narratives (1 Sam. 1–4) and the Ark Narrative (1 Sam. 1–6; 2 Sam. 6:1-19)'. In *Past, Present, Future: The Deuteronomistic History and the Prophets*. Ed. Johannes C. de

Moor, Harry F. van Rooy. Oudtestamentische Studiën, 44. Pp. 88-106. Leiden: Brill, 2000.

See also HANNAH; PRIEST; SACRIFICE; SAMUEL; SHILOH [CAE]

Elihu. While there are several characters in the Bible named Elihu (1 Sam. 1.1; 1 Chron. 12.21; 1 Chron. 26.7; 1 Chron. 27.18), it is usually Job's youthful fourth opponent (Job 32.2–37.24) who generates most interest. Since he is unmentioned alongside Job's three friends in the prologue (2.11) and epilogue (42.7), some scholars speculate that Elihu's speeches are later additions to the text. It is also interesting to observe that he is not condemned by God in the epilogue along with the three friends.

In the Hellenistic work *The Testament of Job* (dated between 100 BCE and 100 CE), Elihu is described as an unmistakably negative figure, as 'not a human but a beast'. In sharp contrast, among medieval Jewish commentators (for whom *The Testament of Job* had little authority), such as twelfth-century thinkers Nahmanides and Maimonides, Elihu's speeches are deemed more central to the message of the book. Ascribing to Elihu's contention that Job speaks 'without knowledge' (34.35) and 'adds rebellion to his sin' (34.37) allows the possibility, especially attractive for theologically conservative readers, of criticizing the protagonist's defiance without needing to express sympathy with Job's three explicitly maligned friends.

William Blake's *The Wrath of Elihu* (1825), part of his series of illustrations on the biblical book, presents Elihu in a more positive light than Job's other interlocutors. Elihu appears in the pose of an inspired preacher, speaking under a star-filled sky, which contrasts with the murky and oppressive hue in illustrations of the other friends. In the Elihu illustration, Job appears more receptive than during the earlier dialogues with the three others.

A more recent literary appropriation of themes related to Elihu's ambiguous and unannounced appearance in Job appears in the writings of Holocaust survivor Elie Wiesel. In his 1979 play *The Trial of God*, which includes various allusions to Job, a mysterious stranger named Sam emerges during a trial of God's culpability for human suffering. Despite a majority of the characters being deeply impressed with Sam's Elihu-like defense of God, he is revealed in the final scene to be a misleading and satanic figure.

Recommended reading. Newsom, Carol A. *The Book of Job: A Contest of Moral Imaginations*. Oxford: Oxford University Press, 2003.

See also JOB, BOOK OF; JOB'S FRIENDS [DCT]

Elijah. Elijah is a prophet in Israel whose name in Hebrew means 'My God is Yahweh'. His ministry started during the reign of Ahab and was a reaction to the king's and his wife's idolatry. He enters the narrative without any introduction but with a message of a drought, which was aimed against Baalism, for Baal was a storm God (1 Kgs 17.1–19.21). After that pronouncement, the prophet hid himself by the wadi Cherith, where he was fed by ravens. Then, he moved to Zarephath where he supported a widow by providing a perpetual source of flour and oil until the rain came back upon the land. He also resurrected the widow's son who died during the prophet's stay in the widow's house. Elijah, then, went back to Israel where he confronted 450 prophets of Baal on Mount Carmel. During this confrontation, Yahweh, on Elijah's request, sent fire from heaven proving his supremacy over Baal and his prophets (1 Kgs 18.20-40). After this victory Jezebel, Ahab's wife, threated to kill Elijah, forcing him to flee (1 Kgs 19.1-10). In his despair, he experienced a theophany and was commissioned to anoint two kings and then his successor, Elisha. After the death of Ahab, Elijah predicted the death of Ahaziah, the king of Israel, and called fire from heaven killing two groups of fifty soldiers sent to seize him. At the end of his earthly ministry he split the Jordan, crossed it, and was taken to heaven in a chariot of fire (2 Kgs 2.11-12)

Elijah, in the Books of Kings, is presented as a second Moses (cf. his appearance with Moses on the mount of transfiguration [Matt. 17.3; Mark 9.4; Luke 9.30]). Although the prophet's image in the Books of Kings is not totally positive, he becomes an awaited hero in the NT. This is partially due to Mal. 4.5, which makes Elijah the forerunner of 'the great and terrible day of the Lord', and partially due to the Jewish tendency in the intertestamental period to idealize their national heroes. The latter tendency is reflected, for instance, in Sir. 48.1-14, especially 48.4: 'How glorious you were, Elijah, in your wondrous deeds! Whose glory is equal to yours?' The Synoptic Gospels apply the prophecy of Mal. 4.5 to John the Baptist (Matt. 11.14; 17.10-13; Mark 9.11-13; Luke 1.13-17). Jas 5.17, the last reference to the prophet in the NT, uses Elijah as an example of a fervent prayer.

Elijah is a symbol of zeal for morality, intransigence, and the desire to escape death and go directly to heaven. Hints of these ideas appear in Wallis Willis's song 'Swing Low, Sweet Chariot', Mendelssohn's oratorio *Elijah*, Chi Coltrane's 'Go like Elijah', or Rembrandt's *God's Judgment on Mount*

Carmel. Elijah's story also exemplifies God's care for his servants, which is nicely presented by Rubens in his painting *The Prophet Elijah Receiving Bread and Water from an Angel* or in Escalante's *The Angels Awakens the Prophet Elijah*. Among the literary works that allude to Elijah are Dickens's *The Life and Adventures of Martin Chuzzlewit*, Melville's *Moby-Dick*, and Coelho's *The Fifth Mountain*.

Recommended reading. Öhler, Markus. 'The Expectation of Elijah and the Presence of the Kingdom of God'. *Journal of Biblical Literature* 118 (1999) 461-76.

See also ELISHA; AHAB; JEZEBEL; MOUNT CARMEL

[RJM]

Elisha. Elisha son of Shaphat from Abel-meholah was an Israelite prophet and successor to Elijah. Elisha's Hebrew name means 'God is salvation' or 'God helped'. He was called to be a prophet by Elijah after the latter's return from Mount Horeb (1 Kgs 19.19-21). His ministry, at least as it was recorded in the Bible, was limited to the land of Israel and took place during the reign of the ninth-century Israelite kings Jehoram, Jehu, Jehoahaz, and Jehoash (2 Kgs 2–13). He inherited two parts or a double portion of Elijah's spirit (the exact meaning of the phrase is debated).

After Elijah's ascension to heaven, Elisha split the Jordan repeating Elijah's miracle. In his ministry he purified the water in Jericho, purified a stew for the sons of prophets, multiplied oil, multiplied bread, and promised the birth of the Shunammite woman's son whom he later raised from the death. He healed Naaman, a foreigner, but brought a skin disease (traditionally associated with leprosy) upon his servant Gehazi for the latter's greed. He also blinded an Aramean unit sent to capture him, and cursed 42 young lads from Bethel for mocking him thus causing their deaths. Elisha made an axe-head float, prophesied the end of the siege of Samaria, as well as Israelite victories over Aram. Even after his death his bones made a dead man live. This diversity of Elisha's miracles makes it difficult to find any unifying theme or a main purpose lying behind their appearance in the narratives of Kings. It can be said, however, that some of the miracles performed by Elisha were a kind of repetition of Elijah's miracles. Besides being a miracle worker, Elisha is also known for being a patron of the group called 'sons of the prophets', a name used ten times in 1 Kgs 20.35—2 Kgs 9.1 and nowhere else in the HB. Elisha was also the one starting Jehu's revolt which ended the reign of the Omride dynasty in Israel.

In the NT, Elisha is directly referred to only once—in recollection of the cleansing of Naaman (Luke 4.27). However, it seems that the description of the ministry of Jesus was fashioned after Elisha's prophetic ministry for there are many parallels between the two.

Allusions to Elisha in music, literature, and art are quite frequent mainly due to the number of miracles he performed. Among such works are Thomas Hull's oratorio *Elisha*, Miquel de Cervantes's *Don Quixote de la Mancha*, Matthaeus Merian's *Icones Biblicae*, and Charles Lamb's *Essays of Elia*. A motif that deserves a separate treatment is the ripping of forty-two children by two bears. This gruesome scene became an inspiration for such authors and painters as M. Cervantes, W. Shakespeare, W. Bundel, La Hyre, J. Ruskin, F. Dostoevsky, F. Kafka, T. Mann, and J. Kosinsky.

Recommended reading. Moore, Rick D. *God Saves: Lessons from the Elisha Stories*. JSOTSup, 95. Sheffield: Sheffield Academic Press, 1990. Shemesh, Yael. 'The Elijah Stories as Saint's Legends'. *Journal of Hebrew Scriptures* 8 (2008) 1-41. Ziolkowski, Eric. *Evil Children in Religion, Literature, and Art*. Cross-Currents in Religion and Culture. New York: Palgrave, 2001.

See also ELIJAH; NAAMAN; KINGS, BOOKS OF

[RJM]

Elizabeth. Saint and mother of John the Baptist, Elizabeth appears only in the Gospel of Luke. A descendant of Aaron, the priest (Luke 1.5), Elizabeth was married to the priest Zechariah and Luke calls them 'righteous before God'. The aged couple had no children due to the Elizabeth's barrenness (Luke 1.7, 24-26), thereby eliciting a comparison to Abraham and Sarah (Gen. 16). Elizabeth's story is intertwined with her relationships to others, for instance, to her husband Zechariah; to her son John the Baptist; and to her relative Mary the mother of Jesus. Luke maintains a familial relationship between Elizabeth and Mary (Luke 1.36), although the word *suggenis* denotes an inexact connection. The vagueness of the relationship was reflected in the Vulgate's use of *cognata tua*, but an early Christian tradition that the women were cousins was perpetuated by the use of 'thy cousin' in the King James Bible of 1611. Subsequent English translations have reasserted the vagueness of the kinship.

After the angelic annunciation to the aged Zechariah, Elizabeth miraculously conceived six months prior to the Annunciation of Mary (Luke 1.24-26, 36). Elizabeth demonstrated the power of the Holy

Spirit upon her by proclaiming Mary to be the 'mother of my Lord' (Luke 1.43-44). Furthermore, her report of John leaping in her womb at the salutation of Mary evinced the pre-natal grace given to John.

The parallelism between Elizabeth and John the Baptist as precursors of the Messiah appears in Elizabeth's blessing of Mary and the unborn Christ, and in John's later declaration of the coming Messiah (Luke 3.15-17). While John functions as the forerunner of Jesus the Christ, the conception by the barren Elizabeth has been understood as a congruent preceding miracle to the virginal conception of Mary. Leo the Great asserted that Mary's faith was reassured by Elizabeth's surprising fertility and Thomas Aquinas argued in his *Summa Theologiae* that the angel's declaration of Elizabeth's pregnancy to the Virgin Mary functioned as a figurative example to encourage Mary and the readers of Luke to believe in the possibility of her virginal conception.

Elizabeth was a paragon of feminine faith and she is the only woman declared 'righteous' in the NT. Elizabeth and Anna the prophetess (who make their only biblical appearances in the early chapters of Luke) and Mary serve as models of submission to the divine will in the first chapters of Luke.

Elizabeth appeared in the non-canonical *Protevangelium of James*, which used the Lukan account as a source. This text introduced the legend of the escape of Elizabeth and John during the Murder of the Innocents (cf. Matt. 2.16-18), and the martyrdom of Zechariah at the temple. The Proto-Gospel details how the absconding Elizabeth and her infant son were miraculously hid in a mountain. This legend became so integrated into Christian piety that a church celebrating the miraculous preservation of Elizabeth and John was built at Ain Karim in Jerusalem where Elizabeth was believed to reside, and a later church was built to commemorate the Visitation of Mary.

Frequently depicted as an elderly matron, Elizabeth usually appears with her child or with Mary and the Holy Family. Fine Renaissance representations include *Bestowal of the Name of John the Baptist* (fifteenth century) by Fra Angelico, *The Virgin and Child with Saint Elizabeth and John the Baptist* (c. 1545) by Francesco D'Ubertino Verdi, and *Holy Family with St Elizabeth and St John the Baptist* (c. 1651) by Nicolas Poussin. Elizabeth is celebrated as a saint in the Roman Catholic Church on November 5.

Recommended reading. Getty-Sullivan, Mary Ann. *Women in the New Testament*. Collegeville, MN: Liturgical Press, 2001.

See also JOHN, THE BAPTIST [BVH]

Elohim. *Elohim* is one of the names used to refer to the supreme God of the HB. It is actually the generic noun that means 'god(s)' and is grammatically plural; however, when it operates as a name for the chief God it is usually translated as singular because it is paired with singular verbs. Various theories have been put forward as to why the plural form is used, such as a plural of majesty, but there is no consensus among scholars.

The potential for plurality located in the word has led to a long history of interpretation by various groups. In the Mormon Church, *elohim* is generally used to distinguish the Godhead from God the father. It is also believed to carry the concept of the divine council rather than referring to one deity individually. Rudolph Stiener developed a philosophy/anthroposophy, which believes there is a knowable spiritual world and the *elohim* make up the sixth realm of the angelic hierarchy. Yahweh is a member of the *elohim* and the Trinity that emanates from him rules this level. Raëlism (a religion centered on belief in extraterrestrials) also focuses on the pluralness of the word and translates it to mean 'those who came from the sky'. This allows them to use the term to justify their belief in extraterrestrial life which has visited the earth in order to promote knowledge. These traditions are similar to the Summit Lighthouse movement that relates the *elohim* to the ultimate connection between male and female. These beings are associated with light and creation.

The name still appears in popular culture. For instance, it is the name of a character in the videogame *Homeworld 2*. The band Morbid Angel has a song called 'A Blade of Elohim'. It is also a race of beings in Stephen Donaldson's *Chronicles of Thomas Covenant*.

Recommended reading. Day, John. *Yahweh and the Gods and Goddesses of Canaan*. Sheffield: Sheffield Academic Press, 2000. Lang, Bernhard. *The Hebrew God: Portrait of an Ancient Deity*. New Haven/London: Yale University, 2002.

See also YAHWEH; SONS OF GOD; DIVINE COUNCIL, THE; ANGEL [EW]

***Eloi, Eloi, lama sabachthani?*.** The phrase *Eloi Eloi, lama sabachthani* is the opening of Ps. 22, which is translated as 'My God, my God, why have you abandoned me'. This is a psalm of individual lament that follows the standard structure of lament psalms: invocation, complaint, motive(s) for God to hear, request for help, answer, praise, and thanksgiving. This phrase is the invocation but it probably also served as the name for the Psalm, as the title Ps. 22 was not created until the Middle Ages. Like all psalms of lament, this one ends with praise and thanksgiving as the certainty of God's rescue comes with the implied answer.

All four canonical Gospels make reference to Ps. 22 in their passion narratives. Mark places the words *Eloi Eloi, lama sabachthani* in the mouth of Jesus from the cross before he died (15.34; cf. Matt. 27.46). It is interesting the Luke omits this proclamation despite it being in his source. One interpretation believes that this exclamation was uttered in a moment of pure humanity and despair. However, based on the insights of form criticism, it is likely a statement of hope. In effect, Jesus is saying things are bad at this moment, but that God's deliverance is certain because Ps. 22 teaches this. In the Roman Catholic tradition, Ps. 22 is the liturgical psalm for Palm Sunday with the opening phrase serving as the refrain. The phrase itself has almost become a catchphrase for those who are living in crisis.

Recommended reading. Craigie, Peter C. *Psalms 1–50*. Word Biblical Commentary. Waco, TX: Word Books, 1983. Patterson, Richard. 'Psalm 22: From Trial to Triumph'. *Journal of the Evangelical Theological Society* 47 (2004) 213-33.

See also PSALM/PSALMIST/PSALMS, BOOK OF; SEVEN LAST WORDS OF CHRIST; JESUS OF NAZARETH [EW]

Emmanuel. Emmanuel (or Immanuel) is a Hebrew word meaning 'God [is] with us'. The title recalls the covenant between Israel and her God (Exod. 19.5; Jer. 31.33). The most familiar passage using the term is Isa. 7.14 ('the young woman is with child and shall bear a son, and shall name him Immanuel'), which Matthew cites at 1.23 with reference to Jesus ('the virgin shall conceive and bear a son, and they shall name him Emmanuel,' which means, 'God is with us').

Matthew adapts Isa. 7.14 to express the idea of 'fulfillment'. Several features of the Isaiah passage made it suitable for Matthew's purposes: (1) the ambiguity surrounding the sign given by the prophet to Ahaz; (2) Isaiah's oracle was addressed to 'the House of David', and Matthew stresses Jesus' Davidic descent; (3) the Hebrew text uses the term *almah* ('young woman') but the Greek translates this as *parthenos* ('virgin'), which is appropriate with his conviction of the virginal conception of Jesus as Son of God; (4) the symbolic name 'Emmanuel' emphasizes Jesus' abiding presence in the community, which becomes a centerpiece of Matthew's Christology.

Emmanuel is not simply another name for Jesus but rather the term highlights God's abiding presence among his people. This is a guiding concern for Matthew's Jesus who promises that 'where two or three are gathered in my name, I am there among them' (18.20) and, in a clear echo of the Emmanuel language of 1.23, 'I am with you always, to the end of the age' (28.20).

The Emmanuel title figures in Christmas messages and inspirational music, such the Mississippi Mass Choir's rendition of 'Emmanuel' by Doug Williams and Melvin Williams, 1999, and Mercy Me's performance of 'Emmanuel' on the album *All That Is within Me* (2007).

Recommended reading. Senior, Donald P. *Matthew*. ANTC. Nashville, TN: Abingdon Press, 1998.

See also INCARNATION; INFANCY NARRATIVES; ISAIAH, BOOK OF; MATTHEW, GOSPEL OF [DR]

Emmaus Road. Emmaus (in Greek, *Emmaous*, in Hebrew *Hammat*, meaning warm spring) appears only once in the Second Testament, in Luke 24.13, as the village of destination of the two disciples going away from Jerusalem after Jesus' death on the day of resurrection. Emmaus is said to be sixty stadia from Jerusalem and this is often translated as about 11 or 12 kilometers. The location of the ancient village is not clear and the favored site of Emmaus Nicopolis is 160 stadia from Jerusalem. What is clear from the Lukan Gospel is that these two disciples, one whom is named Cleopas, are going away from Jerusalem. Emmaus was also one of the cities where, according to 1 Maccabees (see 3.40, 57; 4.3; 9.50) the armies regrouped after defeat in Jerusalem.

As the disciples walked and discussed all the 'things that had happened [referring to the death and resurrection of Jesus]… Jesus himself came near and went with them, but their eyes were kept from recognizing him' (Luke 24.14-16). They refer to the people's reception of Jesus during his ministry ('a prophet mighty in deed and word before God and all people' [24.19]) and they tell their version of the death and resurrection. Jesus eventually admonishes them and instructs them in the full story of his death and resurrection. It is not until 24.32 that these disciples finally recognize Jesus.

The story of disciples walking while Jesus gives further instructions for the journey ahead is familiar motif in the church. The setting of the story is the first day of the week, resurrection day, which in the Christian tradition is Sunday, when the community gathers to renew their story in Jesus, to recognize him in the breaking of bread, and be strengthened and encouraged to continue on the way (cf. Luke 24.30-35).

Recommended reading. Tannehill, Robert C. *The Narrative Unity of Luke–Acts*. Vol. 1. Philadelphia: Fortress Press, 1986. Trainor, Michael. *According to Luke: Insights for Contemporary Pastoral Practice*. North Blackburn, Victoria: CollinsDove, 1992.

See also DISCIPLE; GOD; LUKE, GOSPEL OF; RESURRECTION [RAHC]

Emperor. This is the common English title for the conventionally male leader of an empire; in the Bible, it usually applies to the head of the Roman Empire. Previous empires of the Ancient Near East played major roles in Israel's formation and the OT's account of it, most significantly in the Exodus, and in the Assyrian and Babylonian Exiles (722 and 586–539 BCE), but in these earlier cases the rulers were called kings, or pharaohs in the case of dynastic Egypt. The NT refers to the head of the Roman state as *Kaisar*, or Caesar, a prestigious name passed down in quasi-hereditary fashion from the dictator Julius Caesar to his successors, beginning with Octavian (Augustus Caesar, reigning 27 BCE –14 CE). Biblical authors seldom name the emperor explicitly, and he never appears in person, but the military, commercial, and ideological power wielded by this 'offstage' character has a far-reaching impact on the texts themselves.

Matt. 22.15-22, Jesus' well-known rejoinder to a trick question about Roman taxes, has made 'Caesar' into a cipher in traditional interpretation, essentially synonymous with secular political power, though Jesus' actual response points to God's comprehensive sovereignty. Luke is also attentive to the emperor's position, placing Jesus' birth amid census activities ordered by Augustus (Luke 2.1) and orienting the later chapters of Acts as a journey toward Ceasar's tribunal court. The Pauline epistles shrewdly apply titles and evocative language to Jesus which were normally reserved for the emperor, as in the lord who deserves universal submission and receives the name 'that is above every name' in Phil. 2.9-11, or the patronal ascription of 'savior' to the death-destroying, life-bringing Christ in 2 Tim. 1.10. Other influential examples surface in the Book of Revelation, where the civic obligation to worship Caesar shapes the form of Christian resistance and liturgical praise.

There are echoes of the ancient Caesars in contemporary culture. Emperor penguins, Caesar salads and haircuts, and the 'Caesarian section', the medical procedure reportedly used at Caesar's birth and increasingly frequent in its modern form, are readily apparent derivatives; so too are *czar* and *kaiser*, political titles of clear imperial mimicry. Individual emperors from the NT era reappear in Shakespeare, in Robert Graves's *I, Claudius*, and many other art forms. Nero's name (Emperor, 54–68 CE; likely the 'Caesar' Paul appealed to in Acts 25.10-12, and suspected for setting a catastrophic fire in Rome) is especially prominent, from Rex Stout's Nero Wolfe, to the Romulans of *Star Trek*, to a cleverly named software application for 'burning' digital media. Less obvious is the continuing deployment of the power of famous names, paralleling the Roman practice. American politicos regularly invoke the name of Abraham Lincoln. Hailed as a skilled orator, unifying his country and emancipating slaves, Lincoln becomes a sanctioning device, a rhetorical tool for furthering 'patriotic' causes. Caesar's name has thus become a model for the adoption of other great names.

Recommended reading. Howard-Brook, Wes, and Anthony Gwyther. *Unveiling Empire: Reading Revelation Then and Now*. Maryknoll, NY: Orbis, 1999. Kim, Seyoon. *Christ and Caesar: The Gospel and the Roman Empire in the Writings of Paul and Luke*. Grand Rapids, MI: Eerdmans, 2008. Suetonius. *The Twelve Caesars*. Trans. Robert Graves. Revised by Michael Grant, with Sabine MacCormack. New York: Penguin, 1980.

See also ROME; ROMAN EMPIRE; KINGSHIP [MFL]

Enoch. In the Bible, there are several Enochs. One was the son of Cain, mentioned in Genesis, who has a city named after him (Gen. 4.17). The most famous Enoch, however, is the son of Jared, who, when he was sixty-five, became the father of Methuselah and lived for 365 years (Gen. 5.25). He possibly took his name from Enosh, his great-grandfather, who was a grandson of Adam. Enoch, the son of Jared, was also the great-grandfather of Noah. This Enoch, Genesis tells us, 'walked with God; then he was no more, because God took him' (5.24). This curious incident stimulated various reflections on this character and lies behind pseudepigraphal writings in the pre-Christian centuries. The influence of the Jewish pseudepigraphal books 1–2 Enoch are evident in the NT epistle Jude 14-15. There are also references to him in the Dead Sea Scrolls.

See also METHUSELAH [JC]

Ephesians, Epistle to the. Ephesians presents itself as a letter from Paul the Apostle to 'the saints in Ephesus'. The manuscript evidence, however, along with the general content of the letter, suggests that it was a circular document not meant specifically for the church in Ephesus, but for a number of congregations. It does not address specific issues as do other Pauline letters, and has a more sermonic tone. It is characterized by long sentences and by wording that speaks of fullness of salvation already in the present and of believers being already raised and seated with Christ in heaven (e.g., 2.4-8). Ephesians emphasizes the union of Jews and Gentiles in Christ (2.11-22). Due to its language and style, most scholars think that Ephesians was not written by Paul. It has many literary affinities with Colossians.

Ephesians falls naturally into two long sections. The first three chapters (1.3–3.21) describe the saving action of God in Jesus Christ for the sake of humans. From before creation (1.4) God planned to save humans who are dead in sin (2.1-3) and bring them together in a holy and unified body. The last three chapters (4.1–6.20) form an extended moral exhortation. Christians are to behave in ways appropriate to the calling they have in Christ (4.1-3). They should aim toward maturity and love (4.12-16). They should live orderly lives in community and domestic environments. They should be conscious of the forces of evil and 'put on the armor of God' in order to withstand them (6.10-18).

Ephesians has been very influential in Western Christian culture. Perhaps among its most familiar words are 'For by grace you have been saved through faith' (2.8) and 'do not let the sun go down on your anger' (4.26). But also well known are the exhortations to 'be filled with the Spirit' (5.18) and 'Put on the armor of God' with the descriptions of various pieces of military equipment (6.10-20). Its description of God choosing people before the foundation of the world and predestining them as adopted children (1.4-5) has figured strongly in the theological debates about predestination versus free will. The wording of Eph. 4.9 has been thought by many to support the notion of a *descensus ad inferos* or descent to hell of Jesus between his death and resurrection.

Ephesians is classified as a 'prison epistle' on the belief that Paul was imprisoned in Rome when it was written. Rembrandt's famous *St Paul in Prison* reflects this view. The traditional roles for men (husbands), women (wives) and children seen in the domestic code (3.18–4.1) seems to be reinforced by such things as the song 'Tradition' in the musical and film *Fiddler on the Roof* (1971). Popular images and thinking about ancient (and more recent) slavery are aroused by the discussion of the roles of slaves and masters in Eph. 5.22–6.9, drawing the mind to recall such films as *Spartacus* (1960) and the institution of African slavery in the sixteenth to nineteenth centuries.

Recommended reading. Jeal, Roy R. 'Rhetorical Argumentation in the Letter to the Ephesians'. In *Rhetorical Argumentation in Biblical Texts*. Ed. A. Eriksson, T.H. Olbricht and W. Überlacker. Pp. 310-24. Harrisburg, PA: Trinity Press International, 2002. Perkins, Pheme. *Ephesians*. Abingdon New Testament Commentaries. Nashville, TN: Abingdon Press, 1997.

See also PAUL, THE APOSTLE; COLOSSIANS, EPISTLE TO THE [RRJ]

Ephod. In the HB, the term ephod designates three different objects: a special garment made of expensive thread and gold worn by the high priest for work in the temple, a linen garment, and an idol/tool employed to discern the will of and facilitate communication with the divine. In Exod. 28, the term ephod refers to an outer garment made for the high priest of gold, blue, purple, and scarlet thread and fine linen woven together. To this garment a breastplate displaying twelve precious stones engraved with the names of the twelve tribes of Israel was attached. Inside the breastplate were the Urim and Thummim, sacred lots used for discerning the will of Yahweh. The exact shape and length of the garment is debated.

Judges relates two stories about objects called an ephod. In chapter 8 Gideon, a leader over Israel, forms gold gained from plundering his enemy into an 'ephod'. Whether this 'ephod' was a garment made of gold or some sort of solid object is uncertain, however the text does say that the Israelites worshiped the object (8.27), an action condemned in the very next phrase of the verse. Later, in Judg. 17–18, a man named Micah makes an 'ephod' out of silver. He installs this object along with other idols and his household gods into a shrine on his property, hiring a priest to tend to them. The significance of these objects becomes clear when men from the Israelite tribe of Dan steal them and his priest. Micah musters a force to pursue the thieves exclaiming to the Danites, 'You took the gods that I made and the priest and went away. What else do I have?' (Judg. 18.24).

In 1 Samuel, the term ephod firstly designates a garment, usually made of linen worn by those ministering at sacred locations (1 Sam. 2.18, 28; 14.3; 22.18). When bringing the ark of the covenant to Jerusalem, David, the second king of Israel, clothes himself in a linen ephod while performing ritual dance. Finally in 1 Sam. 23.9 and 30.7 the ephod refers to a special object kept by priests for obtaining oracles from Yahweh.

Interestingly, Deut. 21.11 forbids the mixing of material when constructing a garment. A later rabbinic tradition discusses the seeming contradiction between the directions given for the creation of the high priests ephod in Exod. 28 and the prohibition against mixing wool and linen in Deut. 21.11. The Talmud states that as long as the mixed garment was worn only while the priest performed his duties in the temple, no law was broken (*Kilayim* 9.1).

Recommended reading. Rowley, H.H. *Worship in Ancient Israel: Its Forms and Meaning*. London: SPCK, 1967.

See also Urim and Thummim; Idols, Idolatry; Gideon; David [CLH]

Epistle. The term epistle has a rich heritage in biblical scholarship. No wonder—over two thirds of the NT is composed of epistles. The term is actually not as current in biblical scholarship as it used to be; nevertheless, this description remains quite popular in Western church culture, not least because most of the standard Bible translations still use the term: 'The Epistle to the Romans', 'The Epistle to the Galatians', and so on, are the types of headings found at the top of the NT letters in most cases.

The reason that the term epistle has fallen on hard times among biblical scholars has a lot to do with NT scholar Adolf Deismann, who did a significant amount of work on the papyri letters when they were first being discovered in Egypt around the turn of the nineteenth century. Deismann made the unfortunate error of distinguishing rigidly between epistles on the one hand, which he described as pieces of literary art (for example, a piece of poetry in letter form), and letters on the other, which he said were intended more for the common purposes of every day life (for example, a letter home to one's family). Paul, he said, wrote letters, not epistles. His error here had to do with the fact that he failed to recognize the wide range of letters in the ancient world. Today, scholars believe that Paul's writings are neither epistles nor letters, to use Deissmann's terminology, but instead fall somewhere in between. This is why interpreters tend to prefer to get rid of the term epistle altogether and speak of more and less literary letters. The NT letter of 1 John, for example, is quite non-literary whereas some of Paul's writings tend to have a number of literary features.

Letters in the ancient world usually follow a predictable structure: Greeting; Thanksgiving; Body; Closing. Paul's letters to the churches all conform to this structure with the exception of Galatians, which is missing a thanksgiving—partly due to the fact, it seems, that Paul was not too thankful for the way that the Galatians had been behaving.

It is interesting that in biblical culture, the letter functions as a central means of communication for people at all levels of society—we even have letters written by slaves in the ancient world. But in contemporary Western culture the letter has become almost obsolete, being reserved mostly for formal documents and contracts. What has taken its place? Email, of course, and more recently text messaging, Twitter, Facebook and other social networking tools. Paul was a man of his culture and used the means of communication current in his day so one cannot help but wonder whether, if the Bible had been recorded in today's culture, it would have consisted of a number of Paul's emails to the churches that he had planted.

Recommended reading. Klauck, Hans-Josef. *Ancient Letters and the New Testament: A Guide to Context and Exegesis*. Waco, TX: Baylor University Press, 2006.

See also Paul, the Apostle; New Testament [AWP]

Esau. Esau (which means 'hairy') is the eldest son of Isaac and Rebekah, the grandson of Abraham, and the twin brother of Jacob (Gen. 25.19-28). Esau was a hunter and is best remembered for selling his birthright to Jacob (Gen. 25.29-34), and for being swindled out of his father's blessing. To do this, Jacob impersonated Esau, wearing his clothes and covering himself in skins so that he would resemble and smell like his twin (Gen. 27.1-40). This was enough to fool his semi-blind father who bestowed the blessing due the firstborn son (Esau) on Jacob. The two brothers became violently estranged, but were reunited for the burial of their father. Esau later became the ancestor of the Edomites. Edom means 'red', and there are various references to 'red' in the story of his life. For instance, Esau sold his birthright for the pleasure of eating some 'red stuff' (Gen. 25.29-34), and Edom is an area with many red rocks. Some traditions claim the Edomites are the ancestors of the Romans. When the Romans occupied the Holy Land, it was considered fulfillment of a prophecy that the descendants of Esau would have revenge on those of Jacob.

Because of the importance in the story of Esau and Jacob, Esau has been the subject of many paintings. The American-born painter Benjamin West (1738–1820) painted the birth of Esau and Jacob, showing the two babes being held by midwives and family members while Isaac comforts his wife who lies on silken sheets on a bed. The drawing by George Frederick Watts (1817–1904) shows Esau, with strong legs and arms and wearing a quiver full of arrows, embracing Jacob who has his body covered and is clearly the weaker, physically, of the two. The story also appears in a number of novels. For example, Irving Fineman wrote *Jacob: an Autobiographical Novel* (1941), and Jean Cabries wrote *Jacob* (1958). Both portray Esau very much like his biblical counterpart, as does the famous German writer Thomas Mann (1875–1955) in his *Tales of Jacob* (1948; the US title is *Joseph and his Brothers*).

See also ABRAHAM; ISAAC; JACOB [JC]

Eschatology. The term combines the Greek *eschatos* meaning 'last' and *logos*, with the sense, 'the study of'. In a Christian context, eschatology is the theology and philosophy of the final events of: (a) a human life (death and personal judgment that determines the destination of the soul, either to heaven or hell; and in Catholic theology, purgatory); (b) history (the end of the age as outlined in the Book of Revelation, whether understood literally or metaphorically, including, in some traditions, such concepts as the coming of an antichrist, Christ's return, the resurrection of the dead, the rapture, the tribulation, and the millennium); (c) the ultimate destiny of creation (the last judgment, the banishment of Satan and his followers to the lake of fire, and the creation of the new heaven and new earth). Christian eschatology is rooted in Jewish apocalyptic writings, particularly the Book of Daniel.

Though many of the early church fathers (e.g., Ignatius of Antioch, Justin Martyr) wrote about Christ's second coming, eschatology is often characterized as an interest of radical or fringe Christian thinkers or groups, such as Jack Van Impe, Hal Lindsay, the Millerites, the Campbellites, and the Jehovah's Witnesses, to name a few. As eschatology is based on highly symbolic, allegorical apocalyptic texts, scholars and laypeople have argued a variety of interpretations and timelines of these events.

Eschatology has been a particularly common subject in popular culture since World War II and the beginning of the nuclear age. These narratives tend to explore destructive, dystopian fantasies of humanity's powerlessness against natural disasters, computers, aliens, and the like—consider, to name but a few films, *End of Days* (1999), *2012* (2009), *Terminator* (1984), *Legion* (2010). Post-apocalyptic novels and films like *Mad Max* (1979), Cormac McCarthy's *The Road* (novel, 2006; film, 2010), and *The Book of Eli* (2010), for instance, are set in savage wastelands following some usually unspecified diaster. Jewish and Christian eschatology, however, portray the 'last things' as the fulfillment of God's perfect creation and the expectation of greater things. Fundamentalist Christian writers like Tim La Haye, Jerry B. Jenkins and Robert Van Kampen have popularized end times fiction, typically following the events of the biblical sources closely (as interpreted through a particular theological lens) but, like their secular counterparts, foregrounding the horror of these events.

See also APOCALYPSE, APOCALYPTIC; TRIBULATION, THE; LAKE OF FIRE; MILLENNIUM [MWB]

Esdras, Books of. 'Esdras' is the Greek transliteration, then Latin, of the Hebrew/Aramaic personal name Ezra (meaning 'help'), a figure appearing in Ezra and Nehemiah. These texts continue the story of life in Judah beyond the account given in 1–2 Chronicles, which ends with the fall of the Babylonian empire, and Judah's incorporation into the successor kingdom, Persia.

Though the first book bears Ezra's name in its English title, he himself does not make an appearance until chapter 7. A Hebrew scribe commissioned by the Persian ruler Artaxerxes, Ezra is to deliver resources to Jerusalem in order to help rebuild the temple to Yahweh there. (The Babylonians had destroyed its temple a century earlier). After quoting Artaxerxes's authorizing letters, the narrative switches to first person singular ('I') through to the end of chapter 9, apparently quoting Ezra's 'diary' of the journey back to the Judean capital. The book's last chapter (10) recounts measures for re-establishing ethnic purity among the Judean ruling class, and the expulsion of 'foreign' wives and children.

Ezra also appears late in the narrative of the second book, Nehemiah 8, where alongside the Hebrew governor appointed by the Persians, he re-introduces the Judean people to their own original law-code, the Torah. Ezra provides his people with a running translation of its original Hebrew into the now prevailing language of commerce and government, Aramaic.

The two canonical books in which Ezra appears are complex works literarily—a mix of narrative, genealogy, correspondence, and diary. Greek translators of this part of the HB prefaced it with a clearer summary of its action, drawing on the latter chapters of 2 Chronicles, the whole of Ezra, sections of Nehemiah, as well as other narrative material—a work they titled 1 Esdras. Aramaic Ezra and Nehemiah were then translated as the single, subsequent, work, 2 Esdras.

These two texts attributed to Ezra/Esdras in the (Greek) Jewish Bible seem to have sparked a greater interest in the role this scribe played in the recovery of his people's ethnic identity. In the later Second Temple period Ezra joined a host of historic Hebrew figures who had had visions of their people's future, and late in the first century CE an apocalypse appeared under his name (compounded with the nickname 'Salathiel' = 'Ask God'). Though portrayed as the scribe mourning the first temple destroyed by the Babylonians in 586 BCE, in this text he instead represents all those mourning the loss of the second temple to the Romans, in 70 CE. In this apocalypse, his phenomenal memory allows him to re-dictate the whole of Torah, along with other texts, canonical and apocryphal, so that none of the literature sacred to Judaism is lost.

This apocalypse of Ezra has received a variety of titles in its various translations—4 Esdras in the Latin Vulgate, 3 Esdras in the Russian Bible, and 2 Esdras in the English tradition since the Geneva Bible of 1560 (which restored the original Hebrew/Aramaic titles to the books of Ezra and Nehemiah.

The figure of Ezra continued to inspire literature composed in his name after 100 CE. Over the next few centuries, there appeared another apocalypse, a vision, a revelation, and a text called *Questions of Ezra*. Ezra as the visionary who helped his people recover their own identity has continued to have an influence, particularly in Western Christianity. Columbus, Milton, Ruskin, and Kipling, for example, all read the Apocalypse that circulated under his name as prophetic of both the mysterious nature of the world, and of its still unfolding history.

See also EZRA, BOOK OF   [BR]

Essenes. The piety, communalism, and self-discipline of these Jewish sectarians attracted the attention of ancient writers. Modern scholars view the Essenes as a witness to pre-Christian Jewish asceticism and connect them to the sectarian community of the Dead Sea Scrolls. Popular culture associates Essenes with esoteric wisdom and prophecy.

Our most extensive descriptions of the Essenes come from the philosophical treatises of Philo of Alexandria, Jewish histories written by Josephus, and the travel writings of Pliny the Elder, all dating from the first century CE. Neither the NT nor the rabbinic literature mentions Essenes.

The etymology of the word Essene is unclear. Philo associates it with the Greek term for holiness or piety. Other possibilities include connections to healing or to the observance ('doing') of Torah. Pliny's description is brief but has been influential: he asserts in his *Natural History* that the Essenes are a unique and admirable people, who live together, west of the Dead Sea and above En Gedi. They live entirely without women or money, and they experience a regular influx of new members from outside.

Philo and Josephus paint a rather different picture, nor do they always agree with one another. Both number the Essenes at about 4,000 and state that they live all over Palestine, rather than in any one place (Philo adds that they avoid cities, because of their potential for moral taint). They hold all property in common, provide care for their aged and infirm, and submit to the authority of an elected group leader. They reject luxury, eat sparingly, and have no possessions beyond a single set of clothing (Josephus also mentions a hand-axe, used in digging and covering over latrine facilities).

Josephus extensively describes the group's initiation process, which takes three years to complete, and their daily activities, which include pre-dawn prayers, long hours of work, and collective meals preceded by ritual baths. Their work includes farming and artisanry; they also take an interest in the study of ancient texts. Both authors assert that Essenes do not marry, although Josephus describes a second type of Essenes, who marry for purposes of procreation.

Much has been made of the esoteric and philosophical aspects of Essenism. Josephus notes that they believe in the immortality of the soul and the power of fate over free will. He describes Essenes who prophesied the future or interpreted dreams, and he mentions an Essene interest in healing and the power of stones and plants.

Parallels between the ancient descriptions of the Essenes and the evidence of the Dead Sea Scrolls are striking, reflecting both general similarities and points of precise equivalence. The classical Essene Hypothesis understood the Dead Sea Scrolls community as coterminous with 'the Essenes' and located them at Qumran, where the scrolls were discovered. More recent theories acknowledge a more complex picture, but some connection between the scrolls and the Essenes is still asserted by the majority of scrolls scholars.

Modern readers have sometimes sought to place John the Baptist or (less plausibly) Jesus in an Essene context. An imagined Essene community provides a backdrop for H. Rider Haggard's *Pearl Maiden: A Tale of the Fall of Jerusalem* (1903). More recently, the Internet has provided a home for a wide variety of neo-Essene churches and fellowships, often with 'Nazorean' or esoteric Christian aspects.

Recommended reading. Beall, Todd S. *Josephus' Description of the Essenes Illustrated by the Dead Sea Scrolls*. Cambridge: Cambridge University Press, 1988. Vermes, Geza, and Martin D. Goodman (eds.). *The Essenes according to the Classical Sources*. Sheffield: JSOT Press, 1989.

See also DEAD SEA SCROLLS; PHARISEES; SADDUCEES [MLG]

Esther, Additions to. The Greek version of the book of Esther contains six extended passages that are not found in the HB. These additions do not appear in many protestant versions of the Bible and are considered 'apocryphal' by Protestants and Jews. Roman Catholics deem these additions to be 'deuterocanonical' and include them in Catholic Bible translations, usually restoring the Septuagint (the Ancient Greek version of the Old Testament) order, which intersperses the additions among the original text and indicates the additions with footnotes that tell the reader that the additions did not appear in the Hebrew text. Jerome, in composing the Latin *Vulgate* version of the Bible, placed them at the end of his translation as chapters 10.4–16.24.

While the exact date and origin of the additions is unknown, some scholars suggest that they emerged in the second century BCE, although others place them later. Regardless of their origin and reason for being written their impact on the shape of the story is significant. They add detail to the main characters, drama to the events of the story, and most noticeably, they introduce God explicitly into the narrative. Whereas the character or name of God does not appear at all in the Hebrew version, God's name shows up over fifty times in the additions, making Esther a far more religious tale than it is without the additions.

Over the years, the additions have received a certain amount of debate in terms of their canonical worthiness. Particularly during the Protestant Reformation when Martin Luther, who did not have much appreciation for the original Hebrew version of Esther itself, strongly denied their canonical value as did other Reformers. It may be because of the late nature of the additions coupled with its lack of overt religious tone that the book of Esther has long (until recently) been overlooked in Western biblical scholarship. References to the book in any of its forms are rare among the church fathers and a Christian commentary was not written on it until the ninth century.

While this may have been the case in the world of biblical studies, in the world of popular culture the story of Esther has been an inspiration to many and has been retold in a variety of media. Like the author(s) of the additions to Esther, these interpretations of the Esther story have added new plot twists and color to the characters. Examples of these interpretations include the 1960 film *Esther and the King* (1960), an episode of the TV miniseries *The Greatest Hero's of the Bible* (1978), the animated Veggie Tales movie, *Esther: The Girl who became Queen* (2001), the novel *The Gilded Chamber* (2004), the movie *One Night with the King* (2006), and the British rock opera *Luv Esther* (2008).

Recommended reading. Fox, Michael V. *The Redaction of the Book of Esther*. Atlanta: Scholars Press, 1991. Orlinsky, Harry M. (ed.). *Studies in the Book of Esther*. New York: Ktav, 1982.

See also ESTHER, BOOK OF; MORDECAI; SEPTUAGINT [LB]

Esther, Book of. For many reasons, not the least of which is its neglect of any direct reference to God, the book of Esther is one of the most unusual books in the Bible. Martin Luther disliked the book so much he indicated that it carried no value for Christian readers (Table Talk XXIV). While clearly set in the Persian period, when King Ahasuerus (Xerxes I) was ruler (486–465 BCE), scholars agree that a precise date for the book, also known as the Megilla, is hard to determine although it is generally assumed that the final Hebrew form of Esther is of late Persian or early Hellenistic origin. From a purely literary perspective it seems obvious that Esther is written to demonstrate the potential for Jewish life for those trapped in an exilic existence.

Esther was, or came to be understood as, a story which informed the Diasporic experience of Israel. Its content depicts the lived experience of a subjugated people, and creates the potential for them to see their lives through the lens of an orphan girl who becomes a queen and courageously acts to rescue her people. Over time the book was included in the HB, not because it talked about God, but because it helped the nation understand its own story.

While its place in the canon has been tenuous, as an engaging story it has generated great enthusiasm and inspired a diverse vista of cultural expression. As a part of religious culture the book of Esther is the foundation for the annual Jewish festival of Purim, a time of high celebration for Jewish people.

Socially, the heroic quality of Esther's character has inspired many movements such as the rabbis of medieval Europe who often saw the Book of Esther as a how-to book for Jewish survival among the elite classes in Diaspora communities. In 1873 Harriet Beecher Stowe commented on the Book of Esther in relation to slavery in the United States and 'Hadassah', a movement that supports health care, education and youth initiatives in Israel and America takes Esther as its model and her Jewish name as the name of the organization.

In literature, art, stage, film and television the story of Esther has received numerous treatments like the renaissance poem about Queen Esther by Joao Pinto Delgado (c. 1585–1653), and the play *Esther: A Tragedy* (1689), upon which Handel based his oratorio *Esther* (1718). Esther was the subject of paintings by English artist John Millais (1829–1896), and the 1960 film *Esther and the King* (1960). More recently Esther's story has been depicted in such diverse media as an episode of the TV miniseries *The Greatest Hero's of the Bible* (1978), the animated Veggie Tales movie, *Esther: The Girl who became Queen* (2001), the novel *The Gilded Chamber* (2004), the movie *One Night with the King* (2006), and the British rock opera *Luv Esther* (2008).

In a larger way the story of Esther embodies a particular archetype in storytelling. She is the heroine with humble beginnings who is lead to a place of influence by using her beauty, brains and determination to overcome a more powerful (usually male) opponent for the good of others.

Recommended reading. Greenspoon, Leonard J., and Sidnie White Crawford. *The Book of Esther in Modern Research*. London: T. & T. Clark International, 2003. Fox, Michael V. *Character and Ideology in the Book of Esther.* Columbia, SC: University of South Carolina Press, 1991.

See also MORDECAI; ESTHER, ADDITIONS TO   [LB]

Eternal life. The compound term appears in the OT at Isa. 45.17; 57.15, and Eccl. 3.11. However, the ideas it expresses are found in earlier Israelite and Near Eastern texts (e.g., *The Epic of Gilgamesh*, Egyptian papyri), as well as Nordic (Valhalla) and Greek traditions (Elysium). The term is found throughout the NT. Belief in eternal life requires consideration of the social and religious context that gave rise to it.

The Bible makes assumptions that shape its own narrative. One central belief is the creation accounts of Genesis where the polarities of life and death are presented. Death is anti-creation and is viewed as symptomatic of the destruction of the moral order inherent in creation. Human culpability is identified as a principle reason for death's universal existence in tension with the narrative's depiction of humankind made in God's image. This tension is assumed in, for example, Eccl. 3.11 where eternity as a human desire is derived from God though bounded by death. Humans grasp something of it because they are made in the image of God despite Ecclesiastes stress on the circularity of life's rhythms.

The biblical writers use a variety of synonyms for eternal life. The life (*zoe*) in view is mainly qualitative and is not defined by questions of duration. It is life unbounded by death and can therefore only be given by God whose sovereignty is over both. It is God's character that makes eternal life the centre of human desire. Late OT writings such as Daniel and other apocalyptic works, including intertestamental texts such as 1–2 Maccabees, develop the implications of the doctrine of creation for the fate of individuals beyond death. These are stimulated by theological and ethical reflection on the consequences of sin, (unjust) suffering, and the fate of the individual. NT writers are consistent in their emphasis on eternal life because of their central conviction that God raised Jesus of Nazareth from physical death (e.g., 1 Cor. 15.3-7, 20, 26, 53). The concept of eternal life was present in both Jewish and Gentile contexts though in different ways. The problem was how to obtain this life and for whom it might be given (e.g., Luke 10.25). The NT conclusion concerning eternal life was, apart from divine grace, unattainable by personal moral exertion or interior discipline. St Paul avers that while 'the wages of sin is death ...

the free gift of God is eternal life in Christ Jesus our Lord' (Rom. 6.23). The distinction made by Paul is the source of eternal life, which he associates with the resurrection of Jesus, not obedience to the Torah.

Eternal life is frequently identified with existence that survives death. It is often viewed as a natural though transcendent extension of biological life unrelated to specific religious commitments. Such spirituality is common in the West and may be a reaction to widespread rejection of religious authority. The universal questions of life's meaning in the face of mortality are characteristic of all human societies reflected in contemporary art, film and literature. The movie *Avatar* (2010) explores these themes (among many others). Christian popular art often conflates the hope of eternal life and paradise in the presence of Christ (cf. Luke 23.42-43) to produce utopian emotional effects. By contrast, the late medieval allegory of Dante's *The Divine Comedy* (c. 1308–21) produced art which depicted not only paradise but also hell and purgatory.

[JKS]

Eternity. The term derives from the Latin *aeternus* and is itself related to the Greek *aionios*. Contemporary speech uses hyperbolic phrases like 'I'll love you forever' or 'I've been waiting for an eternity' but the words are rarely used in their literal sense. Similarly, the biblical words usually translated 'eternal' or 'everlasting' encompass both the timeless and the temporal, although thanks in large part to the influence of the Greek philosophers Plato and Aristotle (especially in the latter's *Physics* and *Metaphysics*), we tend to read into texts the literally infinite when the finite may be more appropriate to the biblical context, especially in the OT.

The Hebrew word *'olam* has at least three distinct usages. It refers to God, as in the phrase 'from everlasting to everlasting' (Ps. 41.13; 90.2). In Gen. 21.33, God is named *'El 'Olam*, 'The everlasting God'. This use seems closest to our modern concept of 'eternal'. A second use indicates the distant—but not infinite—past. For instance, we read about 'days of old' in Isa. 63.9, 11; 'ancient doors' in Ps. 24.9; and 'eternal mountains ... everlasting hills' in Gen. 49.16. A third use indicates the indefinite—but again, finite—future, as in, 'he shall be your slave forever' (Deut. 15.17); and 'May my lord King David live forever' (1 Kgs 1.31). Here the meaning is something like 'as long as he may live'.

In the NT, the Greek word *aionios* has roughly the same three categories as the Hebrew *'olam*, but each of them generally has the more familiar sense of literal eternity, reflecting presumably Greek philosophical influence: 'eternal God' (Rom. 16.26); 'the eternal Spirit' (Heb. 9.4); 'for long ages past' (Rom. 16.25); 'before the ages began' (2 Tim. 1.9; Tit. 1.2); 'eternal dominion' (1 Tim. 6.16); 'eternal punishment ... eternal life' (Matt. 25.46). Paul in 2 Cor. 4.18, contrasts 'eternal' with 'temporary'.

The idea of eternal punishment is the basic premise of the medieval Italian poet Dante's *Inferno*, in which the souls of the wicked are punished in various creative ways, often based on crimes committed during their lifetimes. Dante uses the Italian adjective *etterno* some 83 times in the whole of his *Divine Comedy*, 42 of them in the *Paradiso*, and 5 of those in the very last canto (more than in any other canto of the whole work), helping to point climactically towards blessed eternity with God in heaven.

John Milton uses the word 'eternal' over forty times in his *Paradise Lost*, almost exclusively of God or of eternal rewards and punishments, as in the phrases, 'I may assert eternal Providence' (1.25), and 'immortal, infinite / Eternal King' (3.373-74). John Keats's 'Ode on a Grecian Urn' contains the words, 'Thou, silent form! dost tease us out of thought / As doth eternity: Cold Pastoral!' (ll. 44-45). The science fiction writer Arthur C. Clarke introduced the concept of 'eternity circuits' in his 1953 book *The City and the Stars* as a way of imagining how futuristic machinery might last forever without breaking down or wearing out. The John F. Kennedy Eternal Flame is a presidential memorial at the gravesite of US President John F. Kennedy, in Arlington National Cemetery, dedicated on March 15, 1967.

See also HEAVEN; HELL [GDB]

Eucharist. The Eucharist (e.g., Mark 14.23) is one of the names for the 'Lord's Supper' or 'Holy Communion' or 'The Breaking of Bread' (see also 1 Cor. 10.16; 11.20; Acts 2.42, 46). Roman Catholicism calls this ritual 'Mass'. The word 'Mass' comes from the Latin words at the end of the service when the people were dismissed (*massa est*). The name Eucharist comes from the Greek word *eucharistia*, which means, 'the giving of thanks'. Thanks and thanksgivings are words used many times in the Bible. In the OT, to bless (*barak*) is a synonym for *yadah*, to thank or praise someone. In the NT, giving thanks to God is an appropriate expression of gratitude.

In church tradition, the Eucharist refers to the memorial meal instituted by Christ himself shortly before his death. The meal involves remembrance (*anamnesis*) of, and thanksgiving for his sacrificial death. Jesus instructed his disciples to eat bread and drink wine 'in remembrance of me' (1 Cor. 11.24-25).

Saint Ignatius of Antioch described the Eucharistic bread as 'medicine of immortality' in his *Letter to the Ephesians* (20.2). Directly and indirectly the Eucharist has been widely celebrated, expounded, alluded to, and abused in Western literature. Many hymns have been written for use in the Eucharistic meal both before, during and at the end. Examples include Philip Doddridge's 'My God, and Is Thy Table Spread', Horatio Bonar's 'The Supper of Thanksgiving', and Charles Wesley's 'The Eucharistic Mystery'. William Cowper's 'There is a Fountain Filled with Blood' captures well some of the drama and mystery of the Eucharistic celebration.

Recommended reading. Barron, Robert E. *Eucharist.* Maryknoll, NY: Orbis Books, 2008. Wainwright, Geoffrey. *Eucharist and Eschatology.* New York: Oxford University Press, 1981.

See also BREAD; BREAD OF LIFE; COMMUNION; CUP; LORD'S SUPPER; SACRAMENTS; UPPER ROOM; WINE

[AJW]

Eunuch. The term originates from the Greek words *eunen* (bed) and *echein* (keeper, guard), and is translated loosely as 'bed-guard'. The word translated eunuch in the HB is *saris* meaning (court) official, and has its origin in the Akkadian word *saresi, sarri*, meaning 'the one of the (king's) head'. Often interpreted as a male official who has been castrated in order to work in the king's quarter, this is not always true. In certain Ancient Near Eastern and Mid-Eastern cultures, the eunuch was not always a castrated male. The reason for this widespread belief of eunuchs being castrated males emanated from the fact that eunuchs were mostly chamberlains who had access to the king's harem (2 Kgs 9.32; Est. 2.3). To avoid the possibility that a servant would have sexual relations with the king's wives or concubines, some ancient monarchs castrated their eunuchs.

The use of eunuchs in wealthy households, and not necessarily the king's court, was also a common practice. A eunuch's job description varied from being in charge of the king's harem to taking care of the operation of a house. The Greeks and Romans in antiquity used eunuchs in their households, as well as the ancient Egyptians. In some places in Africa where monarchical systems still operate, the use of eunuchs is still very much present. Joseph's master Potiphar was a *saris* in Pharaoh's palace (Gen. 29.1). Joesph's role in Potiphar's house was also similar to that of a eunuch (Gen. 39.4), though the Bible did not use this word to describe him. Nehemiah, who led the exiles that returned to rebuild the walls of Jerusalem, may have been a eunuch (Neh. 2.1).

Such was the influence and power wielded by some eunuchs that they usually had the king's ears (Jer. 38.7-12). In wealthy households, some were even entrusted with finances. Eunuchs were some of the most educated people in the Greco-Roman world. While some were freedmen, a number of eunuchs were slaves attached permanently to the household of their masters.

In different biblical accounts, being a eunuch is used interchangeably or as a euphemism for being impotent (Isa. 56.3-4), and other times for celibacy (Matt. 19.12). Though there are two Ethiopian eunuchs mentioned in the Bible, Ebed-melech (Jer. 38.7) and the one Philip had an encounter with (Acts 8.27), the latter is better known.

The most significant explanation on eunuchs in the NT is Jesus' comment in Matt. 19.12. In response to his disciples' protest, Jesus responded by using the word eunuch to describe someone who either willingly abstains from sex, or is unable to have sexual intercourse. In his words, 'For there are eunuchs who have been so from birth, and there are eunuchs who have been made eunuchs by others, and there are eunuchs who have made themselves eunuchs for the sake of the kingdom of heaven'.

See also SEX, SEXUALITY

[GOA]

Euphrates. A major river in Mesopotamia, there are 36 references to the Euphrates in the Bible, all but two of them in the OT. It is described first in Gen. 2.14, as the third great river of the Middle East, and rapidly became one of the major transport routes through Sumer, with ditches and canals being used to provide irrigation and drinking water for the people nearby. As such, it became crucial in the 'Cradle of Civilization'. It was also a natural boundary, with the Lord making a covenant with Abraham in Gen. 15.18, whereby the Euphrates represented the eastern boundary of the land promised to the Jews. Memory the Euphrates as an ancient boundary marker continued long after the Israelites returned from Egypt (Deut. 1.7; 11.24; Josh. 1.4).

During the 1920s and 1930s, archaeological work along the Euphrates led to Leonard Woolley and Max Mallowan (the husband of the crime writer Agatha Christie) uncovering the site of Ur of the

Chaldees, which led to a much greater understanding of life in, and the wealth of Ancient Sumer. The famous city of Babylon was built on the banks of the Euphrates, and water from the river was vital in the watering of the famous 'Hanging Gardens'. In 1831, a British army officer, Francis Rawdon Chesney, travelled down the Euphrates in search of a new route to India, and the intrepid British explorer Freya Start was later to title one volume of her autobiography as *Beyond Euphrates* (1951).

With the creation of modern Iraq after World War I, the country came to be known as the 'Land of the Two Rivers'—the other being the Tigris. The irrigation water from the Euphrates became a large part of the various National Development Plans of the country celebrated on a postage stamp issued in 1970, as was the dam across the Euphrates. Many of the places along the Euphrates became famous in the 2003 US invasion of Iraq, and the subsequent occupation: Falluja, Karbala, and Nasiriyah.

The Euphrates appears in various literary works, such as Deborah Alcock's *By Far Euphrates* (1897), Carol Edgarian's *Rise the Euphrates* (1990), and Aryeh Lev Stollman's *The Far Euphrates* (1997). The phrase 'by the waters of Babylon' (from Ps. 137.1) refers to the Euphrates. It appears in the post-apocalyptic short story by Stephen Vincent Benét, first published in 1937, and in the song with music by Nikolai Rimsky-Korsakov. It was also used by Steve Misarski, a military chaplain with the US forces, who wrote a hymn while sitting beside the Euphrates. It also appears in songs by Martin Oxenham and Clifford Boyd. The Pixies has a song called 'River Euphrates'.

See also MESOPOTAMIA [JC]

Eutychus. According to the story told in Acts 20.7-12, Eutychus, a young man whose name means 'Good Fortune' or 'Lucky', was sitting in a third storey window while listening to Paul proclaim the word in the city of Troas. While Paul extended his speaking far into the night, Eutychus was overcome with sleep, fell from the window, and was found dead. Paul went downstairs and embraced the boy who was subsequently taken away alive, to the great comfort of many. The overall story is straightforward enough, though there are a number of critical questions about the details given in it, and about its place in the narrative flow of Acts. It draws on stories of dead young persons being raised to life by Elijah, Elisha and Jesus (1 Kgs 17.17-24; 2 Kgs 4.32-37; Mark 5.35-43). Paul is portrayed as both teacher and miracle worker who cares enough about believers to engage them in dialogue about the word long into the night, and to raise the sleepy and implicitly careless Eutychus back to life in the community. After embracing Eutychus and declaring that life was in him, Paul returns casually upstairs to eat (perhaps including the Lord's Supper) and continues conversation with those assembled until dawn. Eutychus was indeed 'lucky' that Paul was there to declare that life was still in him and raise him up.

The story of Eutychus has been a popular feature in sermons. The most famous is 'Upon Sleeping in Church' by Jonathan Swift, Dean of St Patrick's Cathedral in Dublin, satirist, and author of *Gulliver's Travels*. Swift castigated persons who fall asleep during sermons ('Opium is not so stupefying to many persons as an afternoon sermon') as well as preachers who are unable to keep the attention of their audiences ('…preachers now in the world, however they may exceed St Paul in the art of setting men to sleep, do extremely fall short of him in the working of miracles, therefore men are become so cautious as to choose more safe and convenient stations and postures for taking their repose without hazard of their persons…'.).

References to Eutychus appear in literature, for example in Charlotte Brontë's *Jane Eyre* (1847). The raising of Eutychus has been the subject of many paintings and other artistic works including *Paul Raiseth Eutychus to Life* by Gerard Hoet (1648–1733).

Recommended reading. MacDonald, Dennis R. 'Luke's Eutychus and Homer's Elpenor: Acts 20:7-12 and Odyssey 10–12'. *Journal of Higher Criticism* 1 (Fall 1994) 4-24. Swift, Jonathan. 'Upon Sleeping in Church'. In *The Prose Works of Jonathan Swift*. Vol. 9. Pp. 210-18. Ed. Herbert Davis. Oxford: Basil Blackwell, 1948.

See also PAUL, THE APOSTLE; ACTS OF THE APOSTLES, THE [RRJ]

Eve. The first woman to appear in the biblical text is Eve. She is created from Adam's side in order to provide companionship. Eve engages in the first theological conversation with the serpent, trying to determine what God meant by his command against eating the fruit of the tree of knowledge, and what the consequences of violation would be. As a result of this conversation, she and Adam ate the fruit, traditionally understood to mean sin's entrance to the world. The woman's punishment for this disobedience is described: 'I will greatly increase your pangs in childbearing; in pain you shall bring forth children, yet your desire shall be for your husband, and he shall rule over you' (Gen. 3.16). In addition, the humans expelled from the Garden of Eden.

Eve is known as the mother of all living. Genesis narrates the birth of three of her sons (Cain, Abel, and Seth) though there were others (Gen. 5.4). These additional children are discussed further in the *Book of Jubilees*, *Genesis Rabba*, and *The Book of Adam and Eve*, but none of them agree on the number of these children or their names. *The Apocalypse of Moses* presents many details of Eve's life outside the Garden of Eden.

The NT refers to Eve in 2 Cor. 11.13 and 1 Tim. 2.13, passages used to support the notion of women's subordination: the former because it blames Eve (and with her all women) for the sin in the garden; the second because it claims Eve is inferior due to the order of creation.

This perceived role of Eve has been used in many ways through history. Gregory of Tours argued that women should not be included in the term 'man' at the Council of Macon (585 CE) because the actions of Eve caused man to fall. This led to the inspiration for Valentius Acidalius's sixteenth-century work entitled *Women do not have a soul and do not belong to the human race, as is shown by many passages of Holy Scripture*. It was also used as an argument against witches in the fifteenth-century *Malleus Maleficarum*, a document developed in order to purge the world of 'witches'.

Eve is the second wife of Adam in the Midrash and the medieval Alphabet of Ben Sira. Adam's first wife Lilith abandons Adam and procreates with demonic beings in order to produce more demonic beings. However, the Midrash Rabbah states that the original human being was a hermaphrodite and that the creation of Eve was really a splitting of one human being into two distinct sexes. This interpretation has been picked up by modern interpreter Phyllis Trible in her attempt to rescue Gen. 2–3 from a history of misinterpretation. Most art focuses on Eve as temptress, and in association with the serpent. Perhaps the most famous depiction of the creation of Eve was painted by Michelangelo on the ceiling of the Sistine Chapel in Vatican City.

Recommended reading. Edwards, Katie. *Admen and Eve: The Bible in Contemporary Advertising*. Sheffield: Sheffield Phoenix Press, 2012. Trible, Phyllis. *God and the Rhetoric of Sexuality*. Philadelphia: Fortress Press, 1978.

See also ADAM; CAIN AND ABEL; CREATION; FINGER OF GOD; GARDEN OF EDEN; GENESIS, BOOK OF; GOD; TREE OF KNOWLEDGE, TREE OF LIFE   [EW]

Evil. Except for several rare uses of other terms to convey iniquity (Prov. 12.22, *aven*), worthlessness (Ps. 41.8, *beliyyaal*), or an evil report (Gen. 37.2 *dibbah*), the OT uses the Hebrew word *ra* in all of its inflections to name and describe evil as something that 'spoils'. The NT uses almost exclusively the Greek words *kakos* and *poneros* to name evil or evil practices. The biblical words for evil are different from words for sin. In Hebrew, sin is *hata*, in Greek *harmatia*. Evil is a comprehensive word for something that disturbs the divinely ordained good order of the creation. It also is a force that opposes God's work of salvation in the world (Rom. 7.8-19). It originates with the fall of Adam and Eve (Gen. 3). The devil was the author of the fall (Matt. 13.19; Luke 8.12). According to the NT, there will be an end to evil (Rev. 20.10; Rev. 21.9-11).

Theologians have long debated the problem of presented by the existence of evil. Why does it exist, when everything God made is 'very good' (Gen. 1.31)? Ancients like Qoheleth (Eccl. 6.1-2) was puzzled by this, as was Gottfried Wilhelm Leibniz (1646–1716) who wrote, *Theodicy*, and countless others.

Recommended reading. Adams, Marilyn McCord, and Robert Merrihew Adams (eds.). *The Problem of Evil*. New York: Oxford University Press, 1990. Hart, William. *Evil: A Primer*. New York: MJF Books, 2007. Ricoeur, Paul. *Evil: A Challenge to Philosophy and Theology*. New York: Continuum International Publishing Group, 2007.

See also APOCALYPSE, APOCALYPTIC; DEVIL; LUCIFER; SATAN; FALL, THE; HELL; PROFANE; RIGHTEOUSNESS; SERPENT, SNAKE; SIN; TEMPTATION; WAGES OF SIN   [AJW]

Exile. The exile was a formative experience for Israel in its identity as a people. The Assyrians conquered the northern kingdom of Israel in 722 B.C.E when they were the unrivalled national power of the Ancient Near East, however by 605 BCE the Assyrian empire was waning and the Babylonian empire was ready to fill the power vacuum that was created. The Babylonians under Nebuchadnezzar overtook the southern kingdom of Judah in three stages (591, 587 and 581 B.C.E). The militaristic subjugation of both kingdoms threw the people into a new reality, which for some meant forced relocation to the land of their conquerors. Ultimately it meant a loss of land, temple, and king; the three main physical signs of God's covenant with Israel as his people. The Babylonians were later conquered by the Persian Empire in 540 BCE. Under Persian rule many were allowed to return to their land, however the experience of living as a conquered people did not end with a return to the land.

A significant section of biblical literature offers a perspective on these events, including 2 Chron. 36.15-23, which presents the most concise historical overview. This is augmented by prophetic books like Jeremiah and Ezekiel which feature prophecies and historical perspectives on life before and during the time of Judean captivity. The book of Lamentations offers an experiential perspective on the events of exile and Isa. 40–66 is devoted to casting a hopeful vision of the possibility of restoration from exile.

As has been pointed out in a range of literature, exile is not an uncommon experience for both historical and contemporary people. Further, exile can also encompass other aspects of 'living away from home' that may be the result of some kind of displacement other than physical dislocation. Exile, in a broad sense, is a major historical and personal phenomenon that acts as a focal point for reflection on individual and cultural identity. Artists and commentators capture the interiority of exile and remind us that in certain ways we are all, at times, in exile. In this way the biblical story of exile resonates with universal human experience.

The motif of exile has been appropriated culturally throughout the centuries. Bartlett Giamanti has noted that it is a theme that runs throughout Renaissance literature. James Joyce uses exile as a metaphor in his *Exiles: A Play in 3 Acts* (1918), which depicts an Irish writer who has spent much time abroad and feels estranged from Irish society upon his return to Dublin. Camus emphasizes the theme of separation through a collection of short stories entitled *Exile and the Kingdom*. The motif of exile is at the heart of the musical *Fiddler on the Roof*, which depicts the ongoing exile of Jews in Tsarist Russia. A Jewish father struggles to maintain his cultural and religious traditions while outside influences encroach on his family. Even the Rolling Stones employed the motif when, in 1971 they were forced to abandon their homeland of England because of the amount of taxes the government expected them to pay. Facing the possibility of their assets being seized they settled in France and recorded the album *Exile on Main Street*.

While the experience of exile is not historically exclusive to biblical literature, the biblical experience reflects and informs an experience that is universally human.

Recommended reading. Tabori, Paul. *The Anatomy of Exile: A Semantic and Historical Study*. London: Harrap & Co., 1972. Brueggemann, Walter. *Cadences of Home: Preaching to Exiles*. Louisville, KY: Westminster John Knox, 1997.

See also DIASPORA; PERSIA; BABYLON [LB]

Exodus, the. Israel's departure from Egypt (Exod. 2–14) and settlement in its own land is one of the key events of the biblical narrative. But what actually happened? Since the biblical texts were written long after the events they record, and vary among themselves, and since the Egyptian texts say nothing about such an event, what do we know for sure? Many scholars would answer 'nothing', arguing that much of the biblical story is simply legendary. However, at least the basic idea of a group of Semitic-speaking people leaving Egypt and settling in Palestine makes sense of the historical evidence we do have.

What is this evidence? First, in the late 1200s BCE, Pharaoh Merneptah left an inscription in which he listed cities and tribes he had conquered in Palestine. One group, located in the hill country and designated an ethnic unit rather than a city-state, was Israel. In one of the most premature obituaries ever written, Merneptah claimed, 'Israel is no more'. Second, the emergence of a culture based in villages (not walled cities) in the hill country of Palestine during the thirteenth century BCE, for which archaeology supplies ample evidence, fits well with the biblical Book of Judges. The absence of pig bones in these settlements would dovetail well with the biblical portrayal of Israelite beliefs, as well. Third, such names as 'Moses' and 'Phinehas' are definitely Egyptian, and compounds of *Mose* ('son of X') were common during the New Kingdom (think Ra-mose, Tut-mose, etc.). Fourth, the hymn commemorating the crossing of the Reed (not 'Red') Sea in Exod. 15.1-18 is very ancient Hebrew, probably from the second millennium BCE. The very antiquity of the hymn shows that, whatever happened to Moses and his colleagues, Israelites remembered the event as an act of divine deliverance against impossible odds.

It may be that the biblical stories as we have them have undergone many stages of oral telling and retelling, and then revisions in written form. Arguably, the stories remember even earlier events, such as the Egypt expulsion of Asiatic invaders (the Hyksos) in the fifteenth century BCE. More importantly, later theological reflections and narratival embellishments on the great events of the flight from Egypt worked their way into the basic storyline.

However, the core elements appear to come from the time of the events they describe.

Modern adventurers and amateur archaeologists often look for evidence 'proving' the exodus. Such endeavors, though understandable, often bend the facts to suit preconceived (sometimes, theologically motivated) ideas. Moreover, they miss the point: ancient people, like us, report events along with their interpretations of them. Interpretation could take the form of metaphor and mythological language, just as it does, in different ways, for us. Confusing fact and interpretation solves nothing and may rob us of the power of the story as a whole. The exodus story, whatever its facticity in detail, reveals important truths about human freedom before God. As such, it deserves to be celebrated, remembered, and lived out today.

Recommended reading. Hoffmeier, James K. *Israel in Egypt: The Evidence for the Authenticity of the Exodus Tradition*. Oxford: Oxford University Press, 1996. King, Philip J., and Lawrence Stager. *Life in Biblical Israel*. Louisville, KY: Westminster John Knox, 2001.

See also EXODUS, BOOK OF; MOSES; PHARAOH
[MWH]

Exodus, Book of. The Book of Exodus gets its name from the Greek word for 'the way out' (*ex* 'out' + *hodos* 'road, way'; the Hebrew title is *Shemot*, or 'names', from the book's first line). It combines the story of Israel's departure from Egypt and slavery with an elaborate description of the building of the tabernacle, a portable tent-shrine. At the beginning of the book, Israel does not know the name of its God but by the end, Yahweh's presence is so overwhelming as to make entering the tabernacle temporarily impossible. The revelation of Yahweh's identity, and thus Israel's identity is the major theological theme of the book.

Exodus combines sources that appear elsewhere in the Pentateuch, including narrative material (Exod. 1–19, 24, 32–34), law codes (Exod. 20–23), and hymns (Exod. 15.1-21). In its current form, Exodus plays a role in a larger work, the Pentateuch, which describes Israel's story from the beginning of the human race to the verge of settlement in the promised land. Although the book contains authentic information about the time of Moses—his very name ('Mose'—'son of X') is Egyptian from the time of the New Kingdom, and the names of Pharaoh's cities are correct—the book as we have it is the product of a much later time period, and it probably grew in several stages.

The story of Exodus begins in a time of terrible oppression and intermittent resistance (the story of the midwives). Much of this material seems to resemble folklore in other parts of the world, as appears in such elements as the test of the hero by the one calling him to act (Exod. 3–4), the branding of the hero (4.24-26), the villain's pursuit of the hero (Exod. 14.2-10), and the hero's return home (14.15–15.21). However, Exodus has reworked this material into a highly sophisticated story.

The story of freedom serves as a prelude to the giving of the Law at Mount Sinai, the central event of Jewish history. The Ten Commandments (Exod. 20.1-17) and the Covenant Code (Exod. 21.22–23.33) give basic laws, though in different formats. The Ten Commandments are apodictic law ('thou shalt [not]'), admitting of no variation, while the Covenant Code uses the more common ancient Near Eastern casuistic ('if ... then') form, acknowledging the complexity of many social situations. The two descriptions of the tabernacle (Exod. 25–31, 35–40) describe a site holy enough for Israel's deliverer God. The tabernacle descriptions also frame the story of the golden calf, creating a dramatic contrast between appropriate and inappropriate ways of worshiping Yahweh.

It would be hard to overestimate the importance of the Book of Exodus in Jewish and Christian tradition. The stories of Moses have inspired many painters in the West (Rembrandt, Michaelangelo) and authors as unexpected as Sigmund Freud (*Moses and Monotheism*, 1937). Cecil B. DeMille made not only his famous 1956 film *The Ten Commandments*, starring Charlton Heston and Yul Brenner but also a pioneering silent film version (partly in early Technicolor) in 1923. The earlier version pioneered dramatic special effects, and it wove the ancient story into a contemporary tale of greed and profiteering in order to illustrate the folly of violating the Ten Commandments. A recent release of both films is available on DVD. An animated film of the story, highly dependent on the 1956 version but cast in a postmodern vein, is *The Prince of Egypt* (1998).

Recommended reading. Berrigan, Daniel. *Exodus: Let My People Go*. Eugene, OR: Cascade Books, 2008. Propp, William H.C. *Exodus 1–18*. New York: Doubleday, 1998.

See also COVENANT; EXODUS, THE; MOSES; LAW; PENTATEUCH; TEN COMMANDMENTS   [MWH]

Eye. Ancient people sought to understand how the various parts of the body worked, and sometimes they did quite well given their pre-scientific knowledge. But the eyes were the most mystifying part of the body, and theories abounded on how they worked. Some believed they projected beams of light that attached themselves to things that the eye could then see; others thought vision was based on color, like-colored images detaching themselves from their objects and reaching the eye; still others argued that vision occurred when light from an object and light from the eye met each other. Aristotle argued it was light emanating from an illuminated object reaching the eye that caused the sensation of seeing, which comes closest to the modern understanding.

The eye also had a moral component as well: the eyes were windows to the soul, which means they expressed and betrayed emotion: delight (Ezek. 24.16); sympathy (Deut. 7.16); and generosity (Matt. 6.22); but also hatred (Job 16.9); lack of sympathy (Matt. 13.5), and stinginess (Matt. 7.22). The eye was a miniature version of the whole person, which explains the Hebrew word for 'pupil' (*ishon* = 'little man').

The moral aspect of the eye also had to do with the eye's natural tendency towards covetousness. Hellenistic Jewish folklore tells that when Alexander the Great asked to enter the gates of paradise, he was given an eye instead. His wise men placed the eye on a scale and it outweighed Alexander's entire kingdom! The moral of the story is that the eye is never satisfied, it always yearns for more. The natural covetousness of the eye is likely what leads to belief in the evil eye—a look based in envy that harms everything it touches.

Belief in the evil eye is probably the most widespread superstition in the world. Residuals of these superstitions persist even in contemporary culture, such as brides wearing veils to protect from the evil eye, since she would be an obvious target for envy; and averting one's eyes when rice is thrown, thereby casting aside the evil eye. Baby boys are dressed in blue because the color blue wards off the evil eye and baby boys will be natural targets of envy. Gesturing with the middle finger was originally a Roman way of expressing contempt for the evil eye, since the upstanding middle finger resembles an erect penis, which because of its power can repel the evil eye. Finally, notice that the Great Seal of the United States, with an eye in a pyramid, seen on the back of an American one dollar bill, is related to the power of the eye.

Biblical references to the evil eye abound, but English translations are rarely faithful to the original: Prov. 23.6 warns against taking food from someone with the 'evil eye' (NRSV calls the person 'stingy'); Matt. 6.23 warns that when your eye is 'evil' (NRSV offers 'unhealthy'), your body is filled with darkness. Galatians 3.1 (NRSV) has Paul ask the Galatians 'Who has bewitched you?' The Greek word behind 'bewitched' is *baskainō*, which the Greeks used for the evil eye. The Greek *bask*- changes to the Latin *fasc*-, which becomes the English word 'fascinate'. Thus, to be fascinated by something is to be influenced by the evil eye.

Recommended reading. Dundes, Alan (ed.). *The Evil Eye: A Case Book.* Madison, WI: University of Wisconsin Press, 1992. Elworthy, Frederick. *The Evil Eye: The Origins and Practices of Superstition.* New York: Collier Books, 1958.

See also BLINDNESS; EYE FOR AN EYE, TOOTH FOR A TOOTH; TWINKLING OF AN EYE [ZAC]

Eye for an eye, tooth for tooth. Also referred to as the *lex talionis* (Latin for law of retaliation in kind), the phrase refers to Exod. 21.22-25 (also see Lev. 24.20; Deut. 19.16-21). The *lex talionis* is not limited to the 'eye for an eye' expression, but the laws including and surrounding it that deal with injury and compensation. A famous Mesopotamian law code helps one's understanding of the 'eye for an eye' biblical law. Like Moses on Sinai, Hammurabi (Babylonian king 1792–1750 BCE) receives the law code of 282 articles (now called the Code of Hammurabi) from the sun god Shamash; divine origin being a common motif for legitimating the law in the Ancient Near East. Also the context of Exod. 21.22-25 matches the context of Hammurabi's law code (articles 196–214).

In the Code of Hammurabi (1792–1750 BCE) retribution for crime is based on social class. Thus if an *awilum* (a citizen) knocks out the tooth of another *awilum*, his tooth will be knocked out. But if the same is done by an *awilum* to a *muskenim* (a commoner), the *awilum* only needs to pay one mina of silver. Some have suggested the biblical law (Exod. 21.22-25) is a hyperbolic response against such class distinctions.

Interpretive problems with 'eye for and eye' were encountered early on. The NT cites Exod. 21.24 in Matt. 5.38. It suggests a reversal on the 'eye for an eye' statement; the result is Jesus' famous 'turn the other cheek' saying, set after the ten beatitudes (just as the *lex talionis* is set after the Ten Commandments in Exodus). Later the Qur'an upholds the law, applying it to unbelievers, but encourages payment instead (5.45). In Emily Brönte's *Wuthering Heights*, Isabella says she will forgive only if she has the power to enact the *lex talionis*. While in A.L. Tennyson's *Beckett*, King Henry tries to enact *lex talionis* when the clergy will not.

In contemporary contexts, the 'eye for an eye' text has been utilized in a variety of ways and such usages are good examples of limitations of literalistic readings void of historical context. Due to the connection of the *lex talionis* with causing miscarriage, (Exod. 21.22), some have connected the *lex talionis* with current abortion debates. Fundamentalist interpretations argue that since the *lex talionis* follows the death of a fetus, for them, this is a clear indication that God commands death for death. However, this interpretation does not deal with the fact that the law says the woman must be paid if the fetus is killed.

The theme of this biblical passage has been a favorite in literature and movies where justice fails and the main character has to carry out their own justice in movies like *Eye for an Eye* (1996) and *Double Jeopardy* (1999). The Credence Clearwater Revival song 'Bad Moon Rising' alludes to the *lex talionis* in 'one eye is taken for an eye'. Bruce Springsteen's song 'Empty Sky' uses this phrase. Likewise, rap star G-Unit uses the text in a song called 'Eye for an Eye' as a defense for street justice. More famously, Mahatma Gandhi (1869–1948) used the phrase 'An eye for an eye, and soon the whole world is blind'. Interestingly, contemporary usage maintains a literalistic reading and avoids historically nuanced possibilities despite advances in comparative studies of the biblical law with law codes of the Ancient Near East.

See also LAW [SWF]

Ezekiel, Book of. The biblical book of Ezekiel is part of the second division of the HB, the prophets (Nevi'im), in the Jewish order of the HB. The Christian arrangement of the OT includes the book of Ezekiel as one of the three Major Prophets, alongside Isaiah and Jeremiah. Ezekiel received his prophetic call while exiled in Babylon in 593 BCE as part of the first wave of exiles who were deported from Jerusalem in 597 BCE. The first part of the book (Ezek. 1–24) is composed of oracles of doom leading up to the fall of Jerusalem in 587 BCE. Chapters 25–32 outline oracles of judgment against the nations that threatened Israel following the destruction of Jerusalem. In the second half of the book the tone becomes more hopeful (Ezek. 33–39) and God's restoration of Israel is portrayed in powerful visions like that of the valley of dry bones (Ezek. 37.1-14). Finally, in chapters 40–48, the prophet Ezekiel expands his message of hope through his visions of a restored temple, priesthood, and tribal boundaries. The climax of this section is Ezekiel's vision of the return of God's glory to the temple (Ezek. 43.1-5).

During the Second Temple Period, the visions of Ezekiel were an important source of inspiration. In particular, Ezekiel's vision of the throne room of God (Ezek. 1) became a blueprint for later works like *1 Enoch* and the Book of Revelation (Rev. 21). Later rabbinic interpretations of Ezekiel focused on the description of the *merkabâ* (heavenly throne-chariot) that are also found in Ezek. 1.

Ezekiel's visions of the four living creatures with the four faces (human, lion, ox and eagle) and their wheels (Ezek. 1.5-21; 10.9-14) have captured the imagination of artists. In his painting, *Ezekiel's Vision of the Eyed Wheels*, William Blake (1757–1827) attempted to capture this fantastic vision of Ezekiel. The popular television show, *The X-Files*, also picked up on the imagery of the four living creatures in their episode 'All Souls' in which an angel is depicted with the four faces of a human, a lion, an eagle and a bull. One of the most far-fetched interpretations of the Book of Ezekiel was made by Josef F. Blumrich in his 1974 book entitled *The Spaceships of Ezekiel*. In this book, Blumrich puts forth the view that the wheels of Ezekiel 1 represent UFOs.

Apocalyptic elements in the book of Ezekiel (as well as Daniel) have been singled out by some Christian groups as a way to interpret the Book of Revelation. Typical of this type of interpretation is Hal Lindsey's *The Late Great Planet Earth* (1970) which interprets Ezek. 38–39 as a prophecy predicting the rise of a Russian-led invasion of the Middle East prior to the great battle of Armageddon. This interpretation is largely rejected by scholars but was recently popularized in Tim LaHaye and Jerry B. Jenkins's *Left Behind* series.

Recommended reading. Block, Daniel I. *The Book of Ezekiel: Chapters 1–24*. The New International Commentary on the Old Testament. Grand Rapids, MI: Eerdmans, 1997. Idem. *The Book of Ezekiel: Chapters 25–48*. The New International Commentary on the Old Testament. Grand Rapids, MI: Eerdmans, 1997. Odell, Margaret S. *Ezekiel*. Smyth & Helwys Bible Commentary. Macon: Smyth & Helwys, 2005.

See also BABYLONIAN CAPTIVITY, THE; EZEKIEL; APOCALYPSE, APOCALYPTIC; PROPHECY [HM]

Ezekiel, Prophet. The prophet Ezekiel received his prophetic call in 593 BCE while living among the exiles by the river Chebar (Ezek. 1.1-3). He is described as the son of the priest Buzi and was most likely a priest or at least closely connected with a priestly group. Ezekiel was taken away into captivity in 597 BCE in one of the first deportations before the final destruction of Jerusalem in 587 BCE.

The visions and oracles of Ezekiel are considered some of the strangest in the entire HB. He is well known for living out his prophecies in symbolic actions that are truly bizarre. These include lying on his left side for three-hundred and ninety days and then on his right for forty days while cooking his food over excrement (Ezek. 4.4-8), digging a hole in a wall with his baggage on his back (Ezek. 12.1-7), and refusal to mourn his wife's death in obedience to the Lord's instructions (Ezek. 24.15-18). Ezekiel performs these puzzling actions in the sight of his fellow exiles to demonstrate the judgment of God in the coming destruction of Jerusalem. Ezekiel is also famous for his use of extended metaphors to capture and retell the history of Israel (Ezek. 16, 17, 23). In recent years, chapters 16 and 23 have come under scrutiny by feminist scholars for Ezekiel's graphic and shocking portrayal of Israel as an adulterous wife.

Unlike other prophetic books, the Book of Ezekiel contains very little personal information about the prophet. However, references to the prophet's strange actions and occasional inability to speak (Ezek. 3.15) have led to speculation about the state of his mental health. In 1946, Edwin C. Broome argued that the prophet Ezekiel suffered from paranoid schizophrenia. He pointed to various 'symptoms' that he found in the text of Ezekiel such as paranoia, hearing voices and delusions of grandeur. Although the majority of scholars rejected Broome's theory, David Halperin has recently revisited this psychoanalytic method of interpretation. Halperin's own assessment of Ezekiel is that the prophet suffered sexual abuse as a child, which is dramatized in the prophet's negative portrayal of women (Ezek. 16, 23). Neither of these interpretations have gained a wide following but they demonstrate the fascination that the strange prophecies of Ezekiel hold for people throughout history.

Recommended reading. Broome, Edwin C. 'Ezekiel's Abnormal Personality'. *Journal of Biblical Literature* 65 (1946) 277-92. Halperin, David J. *Seeking Ezekiel: Text and Psychology.* University Park, PA: Pennsylvania State University Press, 1993. Odell, Margaret S. *Ezekiel.* Smyth & Helwys Bible Commentary. Macon: Smyth & Helwys, 2005.

See also BABYLONIAN CAPTIVITY, THE; HARLOT; PROPHETS; EZEKIEL, BOOK OF [HM]

Ezra, Book of. The Book of Ezra is roughly divided into two primary sections. The first section begins where the book of 2 Chronicles ends, the defeat of the Neo-Babylonian Empire by Cyrus II's newly established Persian Empire. Once the Babylonians were defeated, both 2 Chronicles and Ezra record that King Cyrus made a decree allowing all of the Israelites who had been exiled from their homeland during the Babylonian captivity, initiated by king Nebuchadnezzar II, to return to Judah and rebuild the temple (2 Chron. 36.22-23; Ezra 1.1-4). Chapters 2 to 7 largely recount the first wave of returning Israelites to Judah, which began in 538 BCE (Ezra 2), and the restoration of Israel's cultic establishment, namely the rebuilding of the altar and the temple (Ezra 3–7). The second section of the Book of Ezra begins in chapter 7, and centers on a second wave of returning Israelites, which included the scribe, Ezra, who provided moral and political leadership to the fledgling Israelites, and administered the reestablishment of Israel's cultic structure (Ezra 7–10).

Until the third century CE within Christianity, and the fifteenth century CE within Judaism, the books of Ezra and Nehemiah formed a single and cohesive work. Both in the Hebrew manuscripts and in the Septuagint (the Greek translation of the HB initiated in the third century BCE), the two books formed a whole. The Latin Vulgate, however, separates the books into 1 and 2 Esdras (the Greek word for Ezra). While the two books definitely contain distinguishing characteristics, they should be read with attentiveness toward their original narrative unity. Jewish scholars and the rabbinic tradition have traditionally viewed the character of Ezra as a hero who reestablished moral, political, and religious order within the nation of Israel. Until recently, however, Christian scholars have historically interpreted Ezra either typologically, paying little attention to the historical and theological content of the book, or negatively, portraying Ezra as the individual primarily responsible for reestablishing what some understood to be an inferior form of Judaism.

The central theological motif of the Book of Ezra is that regardless of any temporary set-back experienced by the nation of Israel, in this case the disorientation and humiliation suffered as a result of the Babylonian exile, God is faithful to work providentially through the processes of human history and politics to safeguard his people and their future as a nation. The Israelites' return from Babylon closely intimates the Israelites' exodus out of Egypt, and the rebuilding of the temple provides an important sense of continuity with the memory of pre-exilic Israel, and the promises made by God to the nation of Israel throughout previous generations.

Recommended reading. Conti, Marco (ed.). *1–2 Kings, 1–2 Chronicles, Ezra, Nehemiah, Esther. Ancient Christian Commentary on Scripture.* V. Downers Grove, IL: InterVarsity Press, 2008. Levering, Matthew. *Ezra and Nehemiah.* Grand Rapids, MI: Brazos Press, 2007.

See also BABYLONIAN CAPTIVITY, THE; HAGGAI, BOOK OF; NEHEMIAH, BOOK OF; TEMPLE; ZECHARIAH, BOOK OF [AS]

F

Faith. From the Hebrew *munah* (which can also be rendered 'faithfulness') and Greek *pistis* (noun) and *pisteuō* (verb), faith is an important biblical theme that defines the appropriate relationship of human beings to God, namely, one of unreserved confidence in, and complete reliance on the Creator. According to Hab. 2.4, 'the person of integrity will live by his faithfulness'. Paul cites this passage in Rom. 1.17, 'The righteous by faith will live'. It follows that biblical faith is not primarily a set of theological propositions or a mental exercise but rather a practical way of living. In Rom. 4, for instance, Paul links Abraham's obedience to faith.

In a more popular religious vein, faith has come to be synonymous with religious sects or communities, as in the phrases the 'Roman Catholic faith' or the 'Muslim faith'. For many, to have faith is simply to subscribe to the tenets of a particular system.

During the twentieth century (and still popular in many quarters) the 'Word of Faith' movement arose alongside of the charismatic renewal. It purports that a Christian can and should live in perpetual health and material abundance by the simple exercise of one's faith. Popularized by E.W. Kenyon and Kenneth Hagin, the philosophy of the Word of Faith movement may be summed up as, 'if you have enough faith, it will happen', whether your desire is for healing, money, or success.

A more secular rendition of the faith movement prevails in Oprah Winfrey's endorsement of 'the Secret', which is a desacralized version of Norman Vincent Peale's 'power of positive thinking'. If you know how to focus your attention and will on what you want, you will achieve it. A somewhat politicized version may be found in President Obama's 'Yes, you can!' election campaign.

See also HOPE; ABRAHAM [DLS]

Fall, the. The term refers to the story of Adam and Eve in the Garden of Eden and their disobedience to God's instructions (Gen. 3). God instructed them not to eat from the tree of the knowledge of good and evil but they both ate the forbidden fruit, giving way to the serpent's seductive speech (Gen. 3.1-7). Adam and Eve were expelled from the Garden of Eden and forced to earn their living with low yielding labors (Gen. 3.16-24). Other biblical writers build on this foundational narrative. The Apostle Paul, for one, parallels Adam and Christ, teaching that through the First Adam came sin and through the Second Adam (Christ) came salvation (Rom. 5.12-19; 1 Cor. 15.22). The Fall has also been a regular theme in English literature, most notably in John Milton's *Paradise Lost* (1667) and John Dryden's 'The State of Innocence and Fall of Man' (1712).

Recommended reading. Maine, David. *Fallen*. New York: St Martin's Press, 2006. Murdoch, Brian. *Adam's Grace: Fall and Redemption in Medieval Literature*. Rochester, NY: Boydell & Brewer, 2000.

See also ADAM; EVE; DEATH; GARDEN OF EDEN; ORIGINAL SIN; SERPENT/SNAKE [AJW]

Fall of Jericho, the. Jericho is the world's lowest town (258m below sea level) and one the oldest, as nomads at the dawn of history sought its balmy climate. Its name (Hebrew *Yericho*) likely came from the Canaanite moon-god Yarich. Jericho, modern Tel es-Sultan on the West Bank, is located by a large freshwater spring in the southern Jordan River valley, approximately 18 kilometers from the mouth of the Dead Sea, and located on the main East–West road.

Jericho had been built, invaded, and rebuilt long before the Israelites under Moses arrived. It was prosperous during the time of Abraham, judging by lavish pottery and ornaments found in tombs. Early biblical references describe the twelve tribes coming to the Jordan River opposite Jericho, and then camping in the 'plains of Jericho' (Josh. 4.13; 5.10). Jericho was then ruled by a Canaanite king and is called the 'city of palm trees' (Deut. 34.3) because of its fertility. In the well-known story, Joshua's spies were protected by the local prostitute Rahab, who in return was protected when Jericho's walls fell down and its population killed (Josh. 2.1-24; 6.17-25).

Various archaeological excavations since 1867 have examined Jericho. J. Garstang, digging from 1930 to 1936, believed he had discovered the major defensive wall, collapsed and heavily burned, and dated its fall to c. 1400 BCE. Dame Kathleen Kenyon, digging 1952–1958, claimed Garstang had the wrong wall, yet she identified a burnt layer suggesting violent destruction which she dated to 1560 BCE. Kenyon said this could have been Israelite invasion, though she found the date a little early. After this there are scant signs of life until the city is poorly re-settled centuries later, probably without a wall. More recently, J.J. Bimson re-dated the destruction to c. 1400 BCE and connected it with Israelite invasion. Yet J.M. Miller, Israel Finkelstein and others believe archaeological findings contradict the biblical record. The debate continues.

Moabites occupied Jericho for 18 years (Judg. 3.13). It is mentioned once during King David's reign (1 Sam. 10.5), but was probably just a small village. Various stories about the Elijah and Elisha period are set here (2 Kgs 2.1-22).

Joshua had cursed anyone who would rebuild Jericho (Josh. 6.26), and centuries later (c. 870 BCE), Hiel of Bethel tried to rebuild it, but at the cost of two sons' lives—presumably through child sacrifice in the religion of Baal (1 Kgs 16.34). Kenyon found one tomb associated with this rebuilding. Later King Zedekiah of Judah, in attempting to escape the armies of Babylon, would reach the plains of Jericho only to see his sons killed in front of him, then be blinded and taken to Babylon (2 Kgs 25.2-7; Jer. 39.1-7; 52.4-11). After the return from Exile, 345 people from Jericho helped rebuild the wall of Jerusalem (Ezra 2.34; Neh. 3.2; 7.36). The NT records Jesus healing blind men on the road outside Jericho (Matt. 20.29; Mark 10.46; Luke 18.35). Jesus sets the Good Samaritan story on the narrow Jerusalem–Jericho road (Luke 10.30-37). The wealthy Zaccheus lives in fashionable Jericho (Luke 19.1).

'Joshua Fit De Battle at Jericho' is a traditional spiritual recorded by Mahalia Jackson, Elvis Presley, and others. Jericho is also the name of a television drama series set in a post-nuclear United States, and an album by The Band. Operation Jericho was a World War II Allied bombing raid on the walls of Amiens Prison in Nazi-occupied France, aiming to liberate Resistance members.

Recommended reading. Murphy-O'Connor, Jerome. *The Holy Land: An Oxford Archaeological Guide from Earliest Times to 1700*. 4th edn. Oxford: Oxford University Press, 1998

See also RAHAB; JOSHUA; JOSHUA, BOOK OF; JERICHO [GK]

Fall of Jerusalem, the. Jerusalem was captured by the Romans in 70 CE under the command of Titus, son of then Emperor Vespasian. Titus himself became emperor nine years later. This was a major event in ancient Jewish history, one that followed years of Roman presence in the city, and a crisis resulting in the scattering of the Jewish people (diaspora). The fall of Jerusalem in 70 CE was not the first time pagans destroyed the city. It was captured by the Babylonians in 586 BCE, which resulted in the Babylonian Exile. In 538 BCE, the Jews returned to the city, then under Persian rule, and from that time to 70 CE Jerusalem was a great center of learning in the region, and the site of the 'Second' Temple built by Herod the Great. Its fall was anticipated in a number of prophetic writings (e.g., Isa. 10.3, which refers to the 'day of punishment in the calamity that will come from afar', and Zech. 14.2, which announces 'the city shall be taken'). Jesus also announces the fall of the city in Mathew, Mark and Luke, in the so-called Olivet Discourse (Matt. 24; Mark 13; Luke 21).

After the capture of the city, the Arch of Titus was built at the entrance of the Roman Forum to commemorate the victory. It depicts the campaign and its detail supplies information about the Roman army and its fighting techniques. The image of Roman soldiers carrying the menorah is suggestive, leading some historians to speculate the army carried holy relics to Rome, and that the later Visigoths (who sacked Rome in 410 CE) then took them to southern France and the French village of Rennes-le-Château. This highly speculative theory figures in *The Holy Blood and the Holy Grail* (1982) by Michael Baigent, Richard Leigh and Henry Lincoln, and Dan Brown's popular novel *The Da Vinci Code* (2003).

The earliest account of the fall of Jerusalem is that of Flavius Josephus, written in the first century. The sacking of Jerusalem also forms the backdrop for various works of fiction, including G.J. Whyte-Melville's novel *The Gladiators: A Tale of Rome and Judaea* (1863), and H. Rider Haggard's *Pearl Maiden* (1902). Mention should also be made of J.B. Webb's *Naomi: The Last Days of Jerusalem* (1840), a boy's adventure story about the fall of the city. Howard Fast's *Agrippa's Daughter* (1964) follows the life of a daughter of Herod the Great and her husband during the destruction of the holy city.

See also JERUSALEM; OLIVET DISCOURSE [JC]

Fallen Angels. Fallen angels are angels who, both through willful rebellion against God or by falling into temptation, have been deprived of their position in the celestial hierarchy, and sentenced to an existence of punishment. While the HB contains several passages that were later used to construct the myth of fallen angels (Gen. 3, 6; Ps. 82; Isa. 14), the idea of fallen angels is not explicitly found in the HB. A coherent concept of fallen angels first emerges within Judaism in the pseudepigraphal writings, most notably, *1 Enoch* and *Jubilees*, in which it is explained that a group of 200 angels were so overcome by lust that they descended from their place in heaven in order to marry and have children with earthly women. The authors of these books developed the idea of fallen angels as a way to explain the existence of evil in the world without attributing it to God who they believed was incapable of creating evil.

The NT authors advanced a much more developed concept of fallen angels than that found in the HB. The idea of fallen angels, and particularly of Satan, as instruments or testers of God, was largely abandoned by the NT writers in favor of the idea of fallen angels as the diametrically opposed enemy of God. Many early Christian writers, such as Justin Martyr, Tatian, Athenagoras of Athens, Irenaeus, Tertullian, Lactantius, the Pseudo-Clementine writings, and Ambrose, largely accepted the Jewish pseudepigraphal account of the origin of fallen angels as the result of their lust for human women. Christian thinkers writing in the third through the fifth centuries, however, such as Sextus Julius Africanus, Origen, Jerome, and Augustine, began to express serious doubt concerning the traditional myth of fallen angels derived from Gen. 6 and *1 Enoch*. Origen, who understood there to be three levels of meaning in Scripture, the literal, moral, and figurative, thought that the story of the fallen angels should not be read as a literal description of the fall of spiritual beings from heaven to earth but rather as an allegory of the descent of the soul into the human body. Augustine further argued in the *City of God* that Gen. 6 did not speak of the union of humans and angels but rather of the intermarriage of the clans of Seth and Cain. With these substantial revisions made by Origen and Augustine, the existence of evil and fallen angels came to be understood as a result of Satan's rebellion against God rather than the carnal lust of heavenly beings.

The lore surrounding fallen angels has undergone numerous resurgences and development throughout history, evidenced by the ninth-century Jewish Midrashim, Pirke de-Rabbi Eliezer, and John Milton's, *Paradise Lost* (1667). Although Milton's epic poem did not play as great a role in perpetuating the myth of fallen angels among common Anglo-Americans as did John Bunyan's *The Pilgrim's Progress* (1678), it would be difficult to overestimate its influence among subsequent authors and more educated readers. A contemporary resurgence of interest in fallen angels has also taken place within twentieth-century evangelical Christianity, largely influenced by such popular books as *The Screwtape Letters* (1945) by C.S. Lewis and *This Present Darkness* (1986) by Frank E. Peretti.

Recommended reading. Bamberger, Bernard J. *Fallen Angels: Soldiers of Satan's Realm*. Philadelphia: Jewish Publication Society of America, 2006. Reed, Annette Yoshiko. *Fallen Angels and the History of Judaism and Christianity: The Reception of Enochic Literature*. Cambridge: Cambridge University Press, 2005.

See also ANGEL; EVIL; SATAN; LUCIFER [AS]

False Prophet. Although there are many references to false prophets in the Bible (Deut. 18.20; Jer. 29.26; Acts 13.6) there is one character who is designated as the False Prophet. The False Prophet emits one of three unclean, demonic spirits from its mouth to perform signs and gather the armies for battle against God Almighty at Armageddon (16.13-14). The implications for prophetic or verbal deception are clear. This personage appears in John's portrayal of the allies called upon by the Devil to help amaze and deceive the nations into worshiping the Beast (13.1, 11). When the judgment on the False Prophet is rendered on the False Prophet in judgment scenes (Rev. 19.20; 20.10), we receive the fullest information about its activity and role in the conflict.

It is important for the message and visions of Revelation to recognize the work of deception that this prophet along with the Beast carries out. Although not much is said about the identity of this character, its work of deception and its collusion with the first beast is crucial for the unfolding drama of the book. Even those who bear the mark of the Beast have been deceived (Rev. 19.20). Revelation's theology presents a conflict between those who bear the true word of God and those who try to inspire God's people to worship and serve other gods and shift their allegiances. This conflict between false and true prophecy appears in the churches (Rev. 2.14, 20) and on the world stage (11.1-12).

False prophets are certainly present in Israel's history. Israel was warned there would be false messengers and prophesiers (Deut. 13.1-18), and the prophets of God have had to deal with them as they led the people to serve and worship other gods (1 Kgs 22.1-28; Jer. 5.30-31; etc.). A classic scene of prophetic conflict is found in Elijah's confrontation with the prophets of Baal on Mount Carmel (1 Kgs 18.90). In the NT, Paul the apostle had to deal with a false messenger in his ministry (Acts 13.6-12) and Jesus gave warnings about following false prophets and prophecies (Matt. 7.15; 24.11, 24).

In literature and film, the false prophet motif appears often closely tied to the work and role of the Beast in Revelation. The activity of the False

Prophet or the Beast is a prelude to a disaster of some kind such as in the film *The Omen* (1976/2006). A concern about true and false prophets is also evident in the Qur'an (Sura 21) and throughout Muslim history and culture. This role is also seen wonderfully portrayed in the film version of J.R.R. Tolkien's *The Two Towers* by the character of Grima Wormtongue and his devastating counseling of King Theoden of Rohan.

See also BEAST; ANTICHRIST [DMAC]

Family. In Western societies, family is a kinship grouping idealized as a man and woman and their biological offspring. This definition is, however, frequently extended to include a variety of other configurations.

Two pairs of words are used in the Scriptures to denote family. The first pair of words, *mishpāḥâ* (Hebrew) and *patria* (Greek), focus on a person's lineage or kinship. These words denote a level of relationship that is between a person's immediate household and his or her tribe (i.e., the extended family). While *mishpāḥâ* and *patria* primarily emphasize the relatedness of kinship, the Scriptures also stress the responsibilities of kinship, particularly in passages that speak of caring for one's parents, widows, and orphans (e.g., Deut. 24.19-21; Mark 7.10-12). Thus, the first role of family outlined in scripture is to provide for the physical and emotional needs of the kinship group. This is reflected in songs like 'I Will Take Care of You', which emphasizes family commitment, and, iconic figures like Homer and Marge Simpson who manage to provide for themselves and their family despite their obvious failings.

The second set of Biblical words associated with the idea of family, *bayît* (Hebrew) and *oikos* (Greek), refer to the community of individuals who live within a household and corresponds most closely with the contemporary sense that one's family is comprised of those with whom he or she lives. In biblical times, households such as Jacob's, which included three generations of the family (Gen. 45.8-11), and Abraham's, which included his servants, herdsmen, their spouses and offspring (Gen. 14.14), included multiple parent–child constellations.

If the first role of the family is to provide for the physical needs of the family, its second role is to contribute to the spiritual health of its members. Thus, one of the critical biblical roles of the household is the transmission of faith values from one generation to the next. This is seen both in the examples of biblical families (e.g., 2 Tim. 1.5) as well as the instructions to teach each generation about God's mighty acts (Exod. 12.24-27; Deut. 6.4-9; 11.18-21; Josh. 4.4-7). It is also captured in films such as *Fiddler on the Roof*, which portrays a Jewish household observing and transmitting the teachings of the Law. In the Christian era, Chrysostom advised parents in *Homily IX* of his *Homilies on Timothy* to attend to the spiritual formation of their children. Similarly, the Puritans and their successors counselled Christian parents to read Scripture and pray as families.

A significant NT development is the role of the household in the transmission of the Gospel (e.g., Acts 16.15) as well as the role of households in providing places to worship for communities of believers (e.g., Acts 12.12). Thus, the household became a foundational unit of the community of faith and a metaphor for the church. The contribution of important households to the work of the church is seen in the Duke of Saxony's protection of Martin Luther during the Protestant Reformation and the support provided by wealthy families for both the early Methodist movement and the movement to abolish slavery. Today in many parts of the world, especially in what are known as limited access countries, households continue to serve as places where communities of Christian believers gather for worship and to study the Scriptures.

Recommended reading. Anderson, Ray, and Dennis B. Guernsey. *On Being Family: A Social Theology of the Family*. Grand Rapids, MI: Eerdmans, 1985. Clapp, Rodney. *Families at the Crossroads*. Downers Grove, IL: InterVarsity, 1993.

See also CHILD; COVENANT; FIRSTBORN; IMAGE OF GOD [KFM]

Fasting. From *tsum* (Hebrew), and *nesteia* (Greek) both meaning to abstain from food, fasting is the practice of self-denial. A common practice among Jewish and Christian communities in both the HB and NT, it was mostly a religious practice associated with mourning, intercessions, repentance, and penance. It was principally an act of self-discipline, sometimes in contrition or humility (1 Kgs 21.27-29; Ezra 8.21), practiced by individuals as well as corporate entities like Israel. Most often practiced in times of crisis, either to appease or invite a favorable decision from God (see 2 Sam. 12.16; Est. 4.16; Jonah 3.6-10), fasting also occurred in response to catastrophes.

Fasting in the Bible was primarily a way to seek God and/or influence spiritual encounters. Moses was on the mountain for forty days and nights presumably fasting while meeting with God (Exod. 24.18). Elijah also fasted for forty days and nights while preparing to meet with God on the mountain (1 Kgs 19.8), and Jesus fasted for forty days and nights after he was baptized (Matt. 4.2). This particular practice of fasting for forty days is replicated in the Catholic tradition of Lent, in preparation for the Holy Week, which culminates in the celebration of the death and resurrection of Jesus Christ during Easter. Fasting was part of the worship life of the earliest Christians (see e.g., Acts 13.3; 14.23; 2 Cor. 6.5). Although practiced in other religions as well, fasting is a prominent feature in both Judaism and Islam. In Judaism, the holiest day in the Jewish calendar is Yom Kippur, the Day of Atonement. This day is preceded with fasting. An act of spiritual discipline, fasting is the fourth pillar of Islam As-Sawm and observed primarily in the month of Ramadan.

There are non-relgious fasts as well. Hunger strikes are dramatic statements for political activists, an idea popularized by Mahatma Gandhi during his non-violent struggle against British colonialism. American actress and UNICEF Goodwill Ambassador Mia Farrow called attention to the crisis in Darfur with her twenty-one day fast. Some members of the Irish Republicans protested the British government's treatment of Ireland using this method as well. Several of the prisoners died during their Irish Hunger Strike in 1981. Common to all these hunger strikes is the theme of oppression and creating awareness for injustice (cf. Isa. 58). On a less serious note, Homer Simpson demonstrated the power of this form of non-violent protest in an episode of *The Simpsons* ('Hungry, Hungry, Homer'). Some non-profit and/or religious organizations like the World Vision and the Salvation Army have annual events that utilize fasts to bring awareness to different social problems. The 30-hour famine started in 1992 by World Vision, for one, is a program sensitizing young people to the need for social responsibility as well as a fundraiser.

Recommended reading. Diamond, Eliezer. *Holy Men and Hunger Artists: Fasting and Asceticism in Rabbinic Culture*. Oxford: Oxford University Press, 2003. Shaw, Teresa M. *The Burden of the Flesh: Fasting and Sexuality in Early Christianity*. Minneapolis: Fortress Press, 1998.

See also MOURNING; REPENTANCE; PROPHETS [GOA]

Fat of the Land. This phrase is spoken by Egypt's Pharaoh to Joseph, son of Israel (Jacob). Pharaoh commands Joseph to tell his family that they may come from Canaan so that they may receive 'the best of the land' and they may 'enjoy the fat of the land' (Gen. 45.18). This command would save Joseph's brothers from the famine in Canaan (Gen. 42.5). The only place in the Bible with the exact Hebrew phrase 'fat of the land' is found here. The meaning of 'fat' as the 'choicest' or 'richest' part of the land is echoed with other phrases in the OT (Num. 13.20; Neh. 9.35; Ezek. 45.15). The use of 'fat' in these three verses is only found in the King James Version and is actually three different Hebrew roots.

The English phrase 'living off the fat of the land' is derived from this phrase and means 'living well', 'being wealthy', or, more literally, 'being fed and sustained by abundant crops'. More recently it is used as a collective term to connote the best of something. *The Fat of the Land* is the title of the third studio album of the English electronic music group The Prodigy. *Fat of the Land: Adventures of a 21st Century Forager* (2009) is a creatively told nonfiction story and recipe book combination by Langdon Cook.

See also GENESIS, BOOK OF; JOSEPH, SON OF JACOB; EGYPT; PHARAOH; KING JAMES VERSION (KJV) [ACW]

Father. The Hebrew *avi* and Greek *pater* occur over one thousand times in the HB and NT. In the HB, 'father' is most frequently used to refer to a child's biological parent. When used in the plural, it usually means 'ancestors' (e.g., Gen. 47.30-31; Exod. 4.5; 20.5; Num. 20.15; Deut. 1.11). In keeping with this usage, God is sometimes called 'the God of your fathers' (e.g., Exod. 3.13; Deut. 4.1; 6.3; 12.1; 2 Chron. 13.12; Ezra 8.28), referring broadly to all the generations of Israelites. The term can also refer specifically to 'Abraham, Isaac, and Jacob', from whom the twelve tribes of Israel were believed to be directly descended (e.g., Exod. 3.16; Deut. 1.28; 6.10; 1 Chron. 29.18). Abraham alone, too, could be designated 'father' (e.g., Gen. 17.4; Isa. 51.2). There are, moreover, several passages in which God is referred to as 'Father' (e.g., Deut. 32.6; 2 Sam. 7.12-14; Ps. 68.5-7; 89.27-29).

In the NT, 'father' can similarly refer to a biological parent, especially in the genealogical list in the Gospel of Matthew (1.1-17). There are only two instances in which the term 'fathers' designates Abraham, Isaac, and Jacob (Acts 3.13; 7.32). Far more common is the use of the term 'father' to refer to Abraham alone. To claim Abraham as one's father is to claim faithfulness to God and inclusion in God's covenant (cf. Matt. 3.9; Luke 3.8; John

8.39; Rom. 4). The most prominent use of the term, however, is the designation of God as 'Father'. In the Gospels, Jesus frequently calls God 'Father', perhaps most famously in the Lord's Prayer (Matt. 6.9-15; Luke 11.2-4). Jesus considers God to be his father in a unique way (cf. John 5–6, 10, 12), designating a shared will and purpose, but he also encourages his followers to call God 'Father'. In his epistles, the Apostle Paul uses the term 'God our Father' as a proper title alongside 'Lord Jesus Christ' (cf. Rom. 1.7; 1 Cor. 1.3; 2 Cor. 1.2; Gal. 1.3; Phil. 1.2; 2 Thess. 1.1). Paul also develops the notion that Gentiles are adopted as children of God through their faith in Jesus Christ (cf. Rom. 8).

The confession of God as 'Father' became a central tenet of Christian Trinitarian theology. In the fourth century, there was a fierce debate, which came be known as the 'Arian controversy'—named after Arius, a presbyter in Alexandria—about the relationship between God the Father and Jesus Christ the Son: did they share the same divine substance? The debate hinged on the issue of whether Christ was eternal, like the Father, or was a being created in time. A key point in the affirmation that the Son was eternal was the argument put forth by Athanasius (c. 296–373) that if God is called 'Father', he must eternally have been Father, meaning Christ must eternally have existed as Son. In late medieval and Renaissance painting, God the Father came to be portrayed in strikingly anthropomorphic terms, as a white-bearded old man (e.g., Michelangelo, *Creation of the Sun and Moon* [1501]). Contemporary feminist theologians, such as Daphne Hampson (cf. *After Christianity* [1996]), have critiqued Christianity as patriarchal and oppressive towards women, owing in large part to its overt depictions of God as male.

See also ADOPTION; TRINITY [KAS]

Fear of God. This term is synonymous with 'the fear of the Lord'. It is taken to mean the experience of fear when contemplating the power and impartiality of God when personal or collective behavior is judged by God (2 Chron. 19.7). This gives rise to the belief that human actions are 'seen' by God. As such no relationship with God is possible that assumes divine indifference since God judges human decisions with dispassionate (though not arbitrary) clarity (Isa. 11.3). Behind this lies the idea that thoughts and motives are transparent to God. Many religious traditions hold that humans possess an inherent perception of the quality and accountability of their actions—conscience—and the Bible is no exception. Thus, humans are accountable to God.

Although some biblical texts use the term this way, more is involved; the actions of God rightly precipitate fear in the sense of awe since fear is a primal emotion (e.g., Gen. 28.10-17; Luke 18.4; Rom. 3.18). However, the term is a compound expression that normally speaks objectively to a person's actions in keeping covenant with God (Gen. 22.12). Abraham keeps faith with God and trusts him despite the difficulty of doing so. The same is true of Moses. To keep the covenant is to 'fear God' which means obedience to the standards of the Torah.

This key religious precept of ancient Israel naturally spilled over from the HB to the NT (e.g., 2 Cor. 5.11). The term is found throughout Wisdom literature (e.g., Job 28.28; Prov. 14.27) where it clearly connects obedience to the covenant (in both its moral and cultic aspects) with the promised outcomes of blessing (or curse in the case of covenant violations, as in Deut. 27.26; 29.22-29; 30.15-20). These verses from Deuteronomy explain the reward of prolonged life to a person who 'fears God' (cf. Prov. 10.27). This concept lies behind the persistent efforts of Israel's prophets to reform the life of Israel during times of individual or national apostasy. The prophets understood the remedy to be the return to a piety focused on the fear of God from which right actions would then proceed.

The term found frequent use among Puritans with considerable emphasis on the physical experience of fear. More radical Puritans equated fear as a negative emotion, with loss of faith and the assurance of salvation. John Bunyan (1628–1688) wrote *The Fear of God* which explores the inner condition of the soul in relation to God. The perceived darkness of the term is picked up by contemporary heavy metal bands such as Fear of God that incorporates powerful themes of divine wrath, hence the play on 'fear'.

Some modern agnostics (and gnostics) hold that the worship of God is motivated mainly by fear of divine judgment. They take a contrary view to the Bible: 'The fear of God is not the beginning of wisdom. The fear of God is the death of wisdom', according to Clarence Darrow, in his *Why I Am An Agnostic*. Darrow is famous for his part in the 1925 *Scopes Trial*. In the seventeenth century, Thomas Fuller (1608–1661) claimed, 'Those that worship God merely for Fear, Would worship the Devil too, if he appear[ed]'.

Contemporary understanding of this important biblical expression has focused on its more subjective psychological and therapeutic aspects. The 2007 movie by Ozer Kiziltan, *A Man's Fear of God*, adopts biblical language to connect behavior and accountability.

See also COVENANT; DAY OF THE LORD/JUDGMENT/ WRATH [JKS]

Feasts. The earliest reference to a feast occurs in Genesis. Abraham serves a meal to three guests, one of whom states that his long-barren wife Sarah will give birth to a son that year (Gen. 18.1-15). Abraham then 'made a great feast on the day that Isaac was weaned' (Gen. 21.8). The Passover feast is described in Exod. 12.1-42; it includes discussion of the origin of the unleavened bread. As Moses and Israelites eat standing at Passover, it may be considered a less traditional 'feast' than others, but Passover is one of the most important festivals of the OT. The rather elaborate Feast of Belshazzar is depicted in Dan. 5. Belshazzar hosts a grand celebration, bringing in vessels from the temple after much wine. Writing appears on the wall and Daniel is brought in to interpret it, telling the king that his reign is at an end.

Many significant feasts are recorded in the Gospels. The beheading of St John the Baptist occurs at the Feast of Herod (Mark 6.17-29). Herod's wife, Herodias, wanted to kill John, and after her daughter pleased Herod with her dancing at his birthday celebration, he tells her that he will give her anything she wishes. After consulting her mother she rushed back to the king and requested 'the head of John the Baptist on a platter' (Mark 6.25). Many other feasts occur during the life of Christ, including the marriage feast at Cana, where Christ turns water into wine (John 2.9-10). Christ dines at Bethany with Simon the leper, and a woman pours a jar of oil over his head, which Christ interprets as an anointing preparing him for burial (Mark 14.3-9).

The final Passover meal taken between Christ and his disciples is generally referred to as the Last Supper, or the Lord's Supper, and is described in all four Gospels (Matt. 26.17-29; Mark 14.12-25; Luke 22.7-38; John 13.1-30). Its significance lies in the fact that it is Christ's final earthly meal, where he tells his disciples to eat the bread and drink the wine in memory of his body and blood. He also tells them that one will betray him, which occurs just after the meal ends. This event has been artistically represented hundreds of times, most notably by Leonardo da Vinci (Santa Maria delle Grazie, Milan, 1495–1498). Both Leonardo's fresco and the ideas and characters of the Last Supper play a major role in Dan Brown's 2003 novel *The DaVinci Code*. After his resurrection, Christ appears to two of disciples on the road to Emmaus and dines with them (Luke 24.13-53). As he breaks bread they recognize him at last, reminding readers of the Last Supper and the statements Christ made at that meal.

Recommended reading. Hicks, John Mark. *Come to the Table: Revisioning the Lord's Supper*. Abilene, TX: Leafwood, 2002. Juengst, Sara Covin. *Breaking Bread: The Spiritual Significance of Food*. Louisville, KY: Westminster John Knox, 1992.

See also COMMUNION; EMMAUS ROAD; FASTING; FESTIVALS; FOOD, SYMBOLISM OF; HANUKKAH; LORD'S SUPPER; MARRIAGE FEAST, PARABLE; PASSOVER; UNLEAVENED BREAD, FEAST OF; WEDDING AT CANA [ACF]

Feeding of the five (four) thousand. The miracle story of Jesus feeding 5000 people with a small amount of food is one of the few stories found in all four Gospels (Matt. 14.13-21; Mark 6.30-44; Luke 9.10-17; John 6.1-15). Jesus withdraws to a 'deserted place', but many people follow him. At the end of the day, his disciples want to send the people to get some food but Jesus says, 'You give them something to eat'. When the disciples say they do not have enough money, Jesus asks them what they have: 'Five loaves and two fishes'. Jesus takes this food and gives it to the disciples who distribute it to 5000 men (Matthew adds 'besides women and children') and they are 'satisfied'. The disciples collect twelve baskets of leftover bread and fish. Although the Synoptic Gospels agree for the most part, John claims that (1) it was Passover; (2) Jesus 'tests' Philip; (3) a boy provides the bread and fish; (4) Jesus himself feeds the people; and (5) when the people see this 'sign', they say Jesus is a prophet and want to make him king. Both Matt. 15.32-39 and Mark 8.1-10 recount an additional story with these differences: Jesus multiples seven loaves and a few fish to satisfy 4000 men (plus women and children), and the disciples collect seven baskets of leftovers. Jesus later rebukes the disciples for forgetting about these miracles (Matt. 16.5-12; Mark 8.14-21).

The story mocks Satan's request to 'turn these stones into loaves' (Matt. 4.3; Luke 4.3), and supports the Lord's Prayer ('Give us this day our daily bread' [Matt. 6.11; Luke 11.3]). The miraculous bread is linked to the 'manna from heaven' which God fed to the Israelites in the wilderness (Exod. 16.1-15; cf. John 6.22-59) and to Elijah's multiplication of oil and meal (1 Kgs 17.14). Early Christian art frequently represents this story. In the catacombs, symbols of loaves and fishes were painted near buried Christians; the mid-fourth-century catacomb of Domitilla shows Jesus blessing the loaves. The 'Trinity' sarcophagus (c. 315, Rome) shows Jesus standing between two disciples with his hands on the loaves and fishes; this picture is flanked by the marriage of Cana on one side and the raising of Lazarus on the other (perhaps suggesting that the wine and bread of the Eucharist result in eternal life). A common image is of Jesus blessing the fish and touching the bread in a basket with his staff, found on the fifth-century doors of St Sabina in Rome, the early-sixth-century mosaic in the Sant'Apollinaire Nuovo, Ravenna, and in the Codex Aureus of Echternach (1020-1030). By the twelfth-thirteenth century, the image appears less frequently, mainly in French medieval churches, mosaics in Siciliy, and Serbian frescoes. The image appears in a large painting by Tintoretto found at the Scuola Grande di San Rocco in Venice (1579-1581) and in a series by the Master of Alkmaar (1504 Amsterdam). In the Church of the Multiplication of the Loaves and Fishes, Tabgha, Israel, a mosaic of two fishes flanking a basket of bread marks the stone upon which Jesus supposedly laid the miracle meal.

The story speaks to 'making do' with what is available, of trusting God to provide when resources are scarce. Many associate the story with an old fairy tale that describes a hungry stranger who stirs a pot with just water and a stone in an attempt to entice misery villagers to contribute real food, making 'stone soup'.

See also LOAVES AND FISHES; BREAD [JSW]

Feet of clay. This phrase comes from an incident related in the second chapter of Daniel. According to the story line, when the Babylonian exile began, Nebuchadnezzar chose Daniel, along with several others, for training to become royal attendants. Later (the chronology of the account is difficult to follow), the king had a frightening dream. Although he refused to relate the contents, the king demanded an interpretation from his advisors. After prayer, and while giving God the credit for the revelation, Daniel told the king the contents of a dream and its interpretation. The dream centers on a large figure with a gold head, silver chest and arms, a brass middle and thighs, iron legs, and 'feet partly of iron and partly of clay' (2.33). This mixture caused the kingdom represented by the statue to be unstable, so that it broke apart and was scattered.

The dream incident is the first in a section of the book that is written in Aramaic (from 2.4b to the end of chapter 7), not the Hebrew that is typical of most of the Tanak. This Aramaic section contains six stories that focus on the faithful witness of Jewish exiles at the Babylonian court.

To some, this and the following stories are predictions (sometimes claimed to be predictions of events of our own day). To others, they symbolically recount the decline of Babylon. These commentators argue that the stories were collected during the reign of Antiochus IV Epiphanes (175-163 BCE) as examples of faithfulness during a time of persecution. Recent scholarship suggests that the image of iron mixed with clay was popular in the Hellenistic period, referring to idolatry and royal intermarriage. This and similar metaphors in Wisdom and Sirach lend support to later composition. Others question whether the stories are historical accounts or legendary examples. In this line of thought, the story parallels that of Joseph and Pharaoh, and is viewed as recasting the older stories of trouble and triumph to give hope to the exiles.

Underlying all interpretations is a message of faithful living and resistance to oppression. In modern culture, this message is less frequent than that of someone who is admired but ineffective, or any person or institution which appears strong but whose foundation is weak. This image appears in Lord Byron's 'Ode to Napoleon Bonaparte' (1814), and has been used several times since then as the title of books, articles, and groups. Examples range from Ellen Martin, *The Feet of Clay: A Novel*, published in 1882, to Terry Pratchett, *Feet of Clay* (1996), a fantasy mystery novel. Anthony Storr used the title for a 1977 book that analyzed charismatic personalities such as Jim Jones and David Koresh.

See also ANTIOCHUS IV EPIPHANES; BABYLONIAN CAPTIVITY; DANIEL; DANIEL, BOOK OF; EXILE; JOSEPH, SON OF JACOB; MOSES; NEBUCHADNEZZAR [TJV]

Festivals. As with modern day observances, festivals for biblical Israel were a time for the worshiping community to gather together, refrain from work, thank God for his material blessings, and remember his salvific acts in history.

Deut. 16.1-17 (cf. Exod. 23.14-16; Num. 28.16-31; 29.12-38) calls for the observance of three annual festivals: Passover (16.1-8), Weeks (16.9-12), and Tabernacles (16.13-17). The feast of Passover, or Unleavened Bread, commemorates Israel's deliverance and hasty departure from Egypt (Exod. 12).

The feast lasted seven days, and during this week the Israelites sacrificed the Passover animal, ate unleavened bread, and had to remove all yeast from their possession (Deut. 16.3-4). The Feast of Weeks, also known as Pentecost in the NT because it took place fifty days after Passover, was a harvest festival thanking God for his agricultural blessings. The feast was also called the 'day of firstfruits' (Num. 28.26) and the 'feast of harvest' (Exod. 23.16) and involved an assembly and sacrifices to God (Lev. 23.15-21). The third annual festival, the Feast of Tabernacles, also known as the 'feast of booths' and the 'feast of ingathering' (Exod. 23.16, 34.22), commemorates Israel's wilderness wanderings following the exodus (Lev. 23.42-43). This was a week long harvest festival during which time the Israelites lived in shelters made of branches and presented thank-offerings to God.

The weekly observance of the Sabbath (Lev. 23.3), which comes from the Hebrew meaning 'to cease', was another important festival that mirrored God's rest following the six days of creation (Exod. 20.8-11; Gen. 2.2-3). Besides these four key festivals, the HB also commands the observation of the Feast of Trumpets (Num. 29.1-6), also known as Rosh Hashanah, and the Day of Atonement (Lev. 23.26-32), also called Yom Kippur. Additionally, Est. 9 describes the historical setting for the joyful feast of Purim, when the Jews were delivered from the murderous plot of Haman.

Festival observances are the setting for some important NT events. In the Gospel of Luke, a twelve-year old Jesus questioned leaders at the temple following the Passover, and the Passover and Feast of Unleavened Bread also form the background to the events surrounding Jesus' Last Supper (Luke 22.1, 7). In Acts, the arrival of the Holy Spirit at Pentecost resulted in Peter's sermon and the birth of the Church (Acts 2). For this reason Pentecost remains an important day on the Christian calendar, especially among the Eastern Orthodox Churches. In the Gospel of John, Jesus is accused of blasphemy during the Feast of Dedication, also known as Hanukkah, which is a feast first mentioned in the inter-testamental book of Macabees (1 Macc. 4.56-59).

The musical *Fiddler on the Roof*, which begins with the preparation for a Sabbath meal and is centrally concerned with the importance of Jewish traditions, is one of the longest running musicals in Broadway history. The celebration of Purim is examined in Christopher Guest's *For Your Consideration*, and the story of the Passover has been recounted in films from Charlton Heston's *The Ten Commandments* to the animated movies *A Rugrats Passover* and *The Prince of Egypt*. Adam Sandler's 'The Chanukah Song' and the movie *Eight Crazy Nights* are comedic takes on the Festival of Lights.

Recommended reading. Craigie, Peter C. *The Book of Deuteronomy*. New International Commentary on the Old Testament. Grand Rapids, MI: Eerdmans, 1976. Gane, Roy. *Leviticus, Numbers*. The NIV Application Commentary. Grand Rapids, MI: Zondervan, 2004.

See also FEASTS; PASSOVER; DAY OF ATONEMENT, THE; FEAST OF LOTS (PURIM); BOOTHS, FEAST OF (SUCCOT) [JL]

Field of Blood. The term refers to a public burial place for poor and unknown people. The terms 'field of blood' and 'potter's field' derive from the story in Matt. 27.3-10 in which a plot of land owned by a potter outside the walls of the city of Jerusalem is purchased 'as a burial place for foreigners' with the 30 pieces of silver that Judas Iscariot received for betraying Jesus. A repentant Judas returned the money to the chief priests, but they realized that they could not put it into the treasury since it was 'blood money'. The traditional site for this first potter's field is the valley Hinnom, a source of potter's clay.

In 1794, a potter's field was established near what is now Madison Square Park in New York City. Three years later it was moved to Washington Square Park. By the mid-1820s, the city had grown to surround Washington Park and burials were prohibited there. New corpses were buried in what is now Bryant Park. New York City's current potter's field on Hart Island was opened in 1869. With more than 800,000 burials it is the largest cemetery in the United States. During each weekday, prisoners from nearby Riker's Island are bused to Hart Island to unload unpainted plywood coffins and stack them eight or 10 deep in trenches. The mass graves are then filled by earthmoving equipment until the ground is leveled, and the backhoes move on to dig the next trench.

Other cities also have potter's fields. In 1825, a potter's field was started on four acres of land at the corner of Yonge and Bloor Streets in Toronto. The cemetery was closed in 1855 because city officials decided it was located at the wrong place. Most of the 900 caskets were removed to the Toronto Necropolis, although an occasional casket is uncovered during construction activities in the Yorkville district.

'Potter's field' has found a place in popular culture. Patricia Cornwell wrote the mystery novel *From Potter's Field*. *The Potter's Field* is the title of one of the *Brother Cadfael* detective novels written by Ellis Peters; the book was turned into an episode for the television series. The heavy metal band Anthrax recorded the song 'Potter's Field' on its 1993 album *White Noise*. Potter's Field is a housing development owned by the greedy banker Potter in Frank Capra's 1946 movie *It's a Wonderful Life*. In Victor Hugo's *Les Miserables*, Jean Valjean is buried in Potter's Field.

See also CHIEF PRIESTS; JUDAS ISCARIOT [JDR]

Fight the good fight. This phrase, from the Greek *ton kalon agōna ēgōnismai* (I have fought the good fight), appears in 2 Tim. 4.7: 'I have fought the good fight, I have finished the race, I have kept the faith' (see also 1 Tim. 6.12). The second letter to Timothy is attributed to Paul who was in prison at the time of writing. Knowing that he was at the end of his life, he transmitted various instructions to the young Timothy. Taken from the vocabulary of sports (strife and race), this metaphor (2 Tim. 4.6-8) reminds Timothy that life for the believer is a struggle between good and evil. Wrestling and racing were popular sporting activities in the Hellenistic world. Preachers and philosophers commonly referred to them to describe the fight against an enemy, either physical or metaphorical.

The sentence 'I have fought the good fight' carries at least two important ideas. First, it is a statement of an intelligent choice, since the author has chosen to fight on God's side, the final victor. Second, Paul implies that he has fought well, respecting ethical rules and keeping a clear conscience until the very end of his life. In other words, the athlete decided to fight for the winning team, and at the same time, to fight fairly until the end of the contest.

In the history of literature the theme of fair play in the conflict against evil permeates many works. In recent times, this concept has inspired literary productions such as the epic novels by J.R.R. Tolkien, *The Lord of the Rings* (1937-1949), and the film trilogy of the same name (2001-2003). Similar in this respect are the *Star Wars* (1977-2005) movies and Michael Ende's novel *The Never-ending Story* (1979), which was later adapted to film (1984). Working on the same basic plot, the biographical film *Gandhi* (1982) describes Mahatma Gandhi's non-violent resistance movement for the liberation of India.

See also PASTORAL EPISTLES [DAVS]

Filthy lucre. Used five times in the KJV (1 Tim. 3.3, 8; Tit. 1.7, 11; 1 Pet. 5.2) and four times in the American Standard Version (which translates 1 Tim. 3.3 differently), the words filthy and lucre (from the Latin *lucrum* meaning monetary gain or profit) could literally be translated dirty money/wealth/gain.

The moral concern implied by this biblical expression is nicely illustrated in John Bunyan's *Pilgrim's Progress*. In the seventh stage of the book, Pilgrim comes to a hill called 'Lucre', which is close to the silver mine that lured Demas (see 2 Tim. 4.10a) from the journey. Also mentioned in association with the hill is the pillar of salt (Gen. 19.26) in view of Sodom. Pilgrim learns that regardless of knowledge or maturity, anyone can be blinded by the allure of lucre.

While the Bible does not expressly condemn the search for wealth, it does warn against undue love for it. According to the 1 Tim. 6.10, 'the love of money is a root of all kinds of evil'. Most often misquoted, as 'money is the root of all evil', this verse does not speak against acquiring wealth, but strongly suggests that the love of it will lead to pain, and away from faith.

See also KING JAMES VERSION (KJV); MONEY; WEALTH [GOA]

Finger of God. The psalmist's words 'When I look at your heavens, the work of your fingers' (Ps. 8.3), has inspired poetic and artistic retellings of the creation story. Geoffrey Chaucer's poem on the creation of Adam in 'The Monk's Tale' (*The Canterbury Tales*, 1387-1400) develops the epic image of Yahweh using his hands to mold man (Gen. 2.7-8): 'Lo Adam, in the field of Damascene with Goddë's owen finger wrought was he, and not begotten of mannë's sperm unclean'. Michelangelo's *The Creation of Man* (1510) portrays God floating through the heavens and extending his life-giving forefinger to touch the lifeless finger of the newly created Adam. Michelangelo's representation is influenced by Lorenzo Maitani, whose façade relief (1320) portrays God giving life to Adam's body with outstretched right arm and forefinger. God also gives Eve the spirit of life by placing his fingers on her forehead in Paolo Veronese's *The Creation of Eve* (1570). With direct reference to Michelangelo, Domenichino's *The Reproach of Adam and Eve* (1623-1625) depicts the Creator floating within a wide cloak and raising his forefinger to accuse

Adam of having eaten the prohibited fruit of the tree of knowledge (Gen. 2.9-12).

God's finger represents his power to perform miracles. In fulfillment of God's command to Moses, Aaron strikes the earth's dust with his rod to bring forth gnats throughout Egypt, and Pharaoh's magicians react to the scourge: 'This is the finger of God' (Exod. 8.16-19). Jesus declares that it is by the finger or Spirit of God that he expels demons (Matt. 12.28; Luke 11.20). In Herman Melville's *Moby-Dick* (1851, chap. 119) 'God's burning finger' or destructive power has been laid on many a ship in stormy seas, and his message of doom, '*Mene, Mene, Tekel Upharsin* has been woven into the shrouds and the cordage' (cf. Dan. 5.24-28). William Blake composed the lengthy poem *Jerusalem* (1804), whose furnaces are heated by Los, the mythological blacksmith, who sees the finger of God touch the seventh furnace (12.5-14; 46.17-22; 48.45), a vision in which the universe is regenerated by metal and fire before the New Jerusalem emerges as the symbol of liberty and civilization.

The biblical God is also a legislator who inscribes the Decalogue on two stone tablets with his finger (Exod. 31.18; Deut. 9.10). The early twelfth-century Persian poet Omar Khayyám declares in *Rubaiyat* that God does not edit or revoke what he has written: 'The Moving Finger writes, and having writ, moves on; nor all Thy Piety nor Wit, shall lure it back to cancel a line, nor all Thy Tears wash out a word of it'. In the Prologue to *Gates of Paradise* (1793, 1810), William Blake interprets God as regretting his authorship of the Law: 'Jehovah's Finger Wrote the Law; then Wept; . . . in the midst of Sinai's heat, buried it beneath his Mercy-seat!' In Blake's *The Everlasting Gospel* (1810), Jesus calls a halt to God's writing—'Cease finger of God to write'—and writes this counter message: 'Upon his heart with iron pen he wrote, "Ye must be born again."'

Recommended reading. Frye, Northrop. *Fearful Symmetry: A Study of William Blake*. Princeton: Princeton University Press, 1947. Hartt, Frederick. *Michelangelo Buonarroti*. New York: Harry N. Adams, 2004. Thompson, Edward P. *Witness against the Beast: William Blake and the Moral Law*. Cambridge: Cambridge University Press, 1993. Zuffi, Stefano (ed.). *Old Testament Figures in Art*. Trans. Thomas M. Hartmann. Los Angeles: Getty Museum, 2003.

See also ADAM; BELSHAZZAR; BOOK OF THE LAW; CREATION, CREATOR; TEN COMMANDMENTS; EVE; GOD; HANDWRITING ON THE WALL; JESUS OF NAZARETH

[JRW]

Fire. In ancient cultures, fire was sparked by rubbing wooden sticks or striking flint stones (2 Macc. 10.3). Fire was kept in brick ovens for domestic use such as the preparation of food (Lev. 2.4; 7.9) and heating, and for industrial use and crafts like metal refinement. Due to its destructive power, fire was used in warfare as well and could be employed as a general metaphor for oppression. During the Babylonian exile, Judah hoped that God would protect them from 'fire' (Isa. 43.2; cf. Ps. 66.12). In the religious language of the HB, fire appeared as representing the divine: its immaterial quality and light symbolized God's otherness and aloofness. Thus theophanies were usually accompanied by fire (burning bush, Exod. 3.2-3; pillar of fire, Exod. 13.21-22). When proclaiming the covenant and giving the commandments at Mount Horeb, God is described as speaking 'out of the fire' (Deut. 4.12). According to Ps. 18.8 (= 2 Sam. 22.9), God's mouth emits devouring fire, and the prophet Jeremiah compares the power of God's word to fire (Jer. 23.29). Fire also appeared as an expression of divine wrath, punishment, or jealousy. It consumed those who followed Korah's rebellion against Moses (Num. 16.35) and will cleanse Israel on the Day of the Lord (Isa. 66.15-16.; Zech. 13.9). Fire as a theopanistic manifestation is paralleled by clouds and smoke (Exod. 19.18; Isa. 6.4).

Because it symbolized the divine, fire was the central feature of altars. At the tabernacle sanctuary God sparked the fire on the altar of burnt offering in order to 'consume' the sacrifices brought by the Israelites (Lev. 9.24). Thus God not only accepted but also initiated the sacrificial cult as the HB depicts it. Divine fire also 'consumed' the burnt offering prepared by Elijah in his contest with the Baal's prophets on Mount Carmel (1 Kgs 18.23-40). Priests at Israel's sanctuary were preoccupied with maintaining the altar fire. It was not to be extinguished (Lev. 6.12 ET) and fire of different origins was prohibited (Lev. 10.1-2). Later sources even relate that the altar fire, hidden in a fountain, survived the destruction of the Solomonic temple and the Babylonian exile (2 Macc. 1.19-2.1).

Early Christianity adopted much of this religious symbolism when depicting the presence of God's Spirit at Pentecost as tongues of fire (Acts 2.3-4). During the transfiguration Jesus' clothes shined and glistened (Mark 9.3), hinting at his divine nature, and in John's vision Christ appeared with 'eyes of fire' (Rev. 1.14; 2.18). The description of hell as a place of eternal fire (Mark 9.43; Rev. 19.20) continued HB concepts of divine punishment while dissociating them from God due to the dualistic apocalyptic worldview.

Because of its domestic and industrial importance and its central place in religious symbolism, fire has remained a key symbol in Western culture. An example is the Olympic flame, chief symbol of the Olympic Games, which commemorates that Prometheus stole fire from Zeus, the highest god of the Greek pantheon. The Olympic torch thus symbolizes divine presence, protection, and peace. Borrowing from the tradition of altar fire at the Judean sanctuary, Roman Catholic churches normally feature red candles close to their altars to signify God's presence. At the beginning of winter, Christmas lights infuse the hope that life will prevail despite shorter days once perceived as dangerous. During times of the church inquisition, religious tribunals sentenced opponents to be burnt at the stake in efforts to suggest that divine judgment was executed.

Recommended reading. Eberhart, Christian. 'A Neglected Feature of Sacrifice in the Hebrew Bible'. *Harvard Theological Review* 97 (2004) 485-93.

See also ALTAR; BURNING BUSH; PENTECOST [CAE]

Fire and brimstone. Brimstone is also called sulphur, and is an odorous mineral discharged during volcanic eruptions. The phrase 'fire and brimstone' comes from the KJV and describes the way God judges the wicked. For example, in Gen. 19 God rains fire and brimstone on the cities of Sodom and Gomorrah, bringing both cities to ashes (Gen. 19.24). Psalm 11.5 states that God will similarly judge all of the wicked, while the righteous will have God as their 'portion'. Luke 17.28 records Jesus likening the judgment exacted on Sodom and Gomorrah (above) with what will happen in the day that he is revealed. Revelation has more references to 'fire and brimstone' than any other book of the Bible. Here God and 'the Lamb' (the primary title for Jesus in this book) are recorded as using fire and brimstone to punish Satan and his unbelieving followers (Rev. 14.10; 20.10; 21.8).

'Fire and brimstone' is often used as a pejorative term to caricature a religious message or ministry that seems unduly focused on God's judgment. However, historic Christianity has always strongly believed that the judgment of God will fall on those who do not worship Jesus. To be sure, the NT records Jesus himself teaching that the 'fire and brimstone from heaven' is an imminent consequence for not following him (Luke 17.29).

The 'fire and brimstone' theme has achieved a mild popularity in video games and other forms of entertainment. Fire and Brimstone is a spell in the video game *World of Warcraft* that increases the destructive power of certain weapons a player uses. Matthew Damon and Ben Affleck play angels in the 1999 satire *Dogma*, where Damon's character, Loki, says, 'I'm talking about Divine Justice here. I'm talking about raining fire and brimstone, punishing the wicked'. Author Laurinda Brown has a book called *Fire & Brimstone: A Novel*, which discusses the interface between lesbianism and religion. Rock band Black Lungs has a song entitled 'Fire and Brimstone', where the songwriter laments, 'Will you let me go to hell however I choose?' During the 2008 Olympics, prior to the passing of the Olympic torch, one journalist called the China–Tibet conflict 'Olympic Fire and Brimstone'. Such uses of the expression in popular culture illustrate how the phrase remains a trendy way to refer to judgment or disaster with or without the religious overtones.

Recommended reading. Vincent, Thomas. *Fire and Brimstone from Heaven, from Earth, in Hell*. Morgan, PA: Soli Deo Gloria, 1999. Almond, Philip C. *Heaven and Hell in Enlightenment England*. Cambridge: Cambridge University Press, 2009. Casey, John. *After Lives: A Guide to Heaven, Hell, and Purgatory*. Oxford: Oxford University Press, 2010.

See also HELL; DAY OF THE LORD/JUDGMENT/WRATH; HARROWING OF HELL [MB]

Firstborn. In the biblical texts the term firstborn usually refers to the first son (Gen. 10.15; Luke 2.7). In the OT, the birth of the firstborn son is symbolic of the father's strength or virility (Deut. 21.17), and this child receives a special blessing from the father (Gen. 27), a double inheritance (Deut. 21.17), and in turn becomes the family head following the father's death. This practice, known as primogeniture, is conspicuously evident throughout European culture, as in the laws of succession for royalty and British laws of inheritance that favored the firstborn son until well into the twentieth century. As a consequence, less favored children were sometimes forced into religious life, a fact decried by Wyclif (*Weddid Men and Wifis and of Here Children Also*). Two subplots in the movie *Kingdom of Heaven* (the priest's relationship to Balian, Godfrey's relationship to the village lord) also serve to illustrate the effect of primogeniture in medieval life as both the priest and Godfrey wish to benefit from an inheritance.

In the Passover event, God lays claim on every firstborn male in Egypt, killing the firstborn of the Egyptians (see e.g., Alma-Tadema's painting *Death of the Firstborn*), and sparing Israel's firstborn because these children were redeemed by blood of the Passover lamb (Exod. 12.12-13, 29; cf. Exod. 4.22). Following the Passover, all Israel's firstborn males, human and animal, were understood to be devoted to God. Thus firstborn children were to be redeemed (Exod. 13.13; 34.20; Num. 18.15) and the Levites took their place in God's service (Num. 8.14-19). In the case of animals, the firstborn of clean animals (calves, lambs, and kids) were to be given as an offering to the Lord (Num. 18.17). As for the firstborn of unclean animals, everything except donkeys was to be redeemed with money (Num. 18.15). In the case of donkeys, the owner was either to offer a sheep (Exod. 13.13; 34.20) or break its neck (Exod. 13.13).

In the NT, figurative uses of the term firstborn (Greek *prototokos*) dominate. Metaphorically it describes Christ's authority over both creation (Col. 1.15) and the church (Rom. 8.29; Heb. 1.6). In addition to this, by his resurrection from the dead Christ is the *prototokos* (Col. 1.18, Rev. 1.5) in that his resurrection both speaks to the transforming power of Christ's act of redemption and anticipates the resurrection in the last days, truths conveyed by C.S. Lewis in the *Lion, Witch and the Wardrobe*.

Because of God's mighty acts of salvation, both Israel (Exod. 4.22-23) and the church (Heb. 12.23) are described as his firstborn. In the OT, this title signifies Israel's covenant relationship with God as well as its role as God's saving light to Gentile peoples. This theme is carried over to the NT where the new covenant mediated by Jesus Christ has created a new people of God who, like their predecessors, are to bear witness to the nations of God's mighty acts.

See also CHILD; FAMILY; BIRTH [KFM]

Fish, Fisher, Fishing. Fish referred to in biblical texts are either salt-water fish found in the Mediterranean Sea and the Gulf of Aqaba, or fresh-water fish living in the Nile (Exod. 7.18; Num. 11.5), in the Sea of Galilee, or in the Jordan River. Fish cannot survive in the Dead Sea due to its high concentration of salt. The Israelites were not a seafaring nation. They relied on fish trade, a possible reminder of which is the 'Fish Gate' in the north wall of Jerusalem (2 Chron. 33.14; Neh. 3.3; Zeph. 1.10). Due to the Israelites' lack of familiarity with seafood, the HB features no references to any particular fish species. Thus, the 'great fish' which swallowed and eventually spit out the prophet Jonah is never further specified (Jonah 1.17–2.10). In addition, the Levitical laws on clean and unclean foods allow only fish with fins and scales for human consumption, but never mention any species (Lev. 11.9-12; see also Deut. 14.9-10).

In the NT, fish are known as a basic staple (Mark 6.38; 8.7; Luke 11.11). Some of the disciples of Jesus were fishermen who had worked on the shores of the Sea of Galilee. In this lake, at least twenty-four species of fish are found today, including the Siluridae (a type of catfish), the Cichlidae, and the Cypinidae. In NT times, fishermen would have used dragnets (John 21.1-9). Because of their vocation of proclaiming the gospel, Jesus calls his first disciples 'fishers of humans' (Mark 1.17).

Early on in Christian church history, the fish became the symbol of a (secret) christological confession. *Ichthys*, the Greek word for 'fish', was read as an acronym for 'Jesus (is) Christ, God's Son, (and is) savior'. Preceding the cross as a central symbol of the Christian faith, the fish can be found scratched into the walls of early Roman catacombs. Still today, the fish symbol is used as a discrete interdenominational self-identification of Christians throughout the Western world.

See also ANIMALS, SYMBOLISM OF; CHRIST; GALILEE, SEA OF; JORDAN [CAE]

Flaming Sword. When Adam and Eve were banished from the Garden of Eden and passed through the Gates of Paradise, God placed there a cherubim and a 'sword flaming' (Gen. 3.25). This image has remained an important part of biblical iconography. According to Eastern Orthodox tradition, when Jesus was born the flaming sword was removed from the Gates of Paradise which allows people to re-enter Eden. It is portrayed in a painting by Ferdinand Victor Eugène Delacroix (1798–1863).

The idea of a flaming sword represents destructive power. In Norse mythology, Surtr, the leader of the Giants of Muspelheim used a flaming sword so it would shine in darkness. Flaming swords also appear in many fantasy books and is one of the magical swords that can be used by players of the game *Dungeons and Dragons*. There is a priest wielding a flaming sword in *A Song of Ice and Fire*, a series of fantasy novels by George R.R. Martin published from 1991 until 1996. The British New Wave group Care also performed a song entitled 'Flaming Sword', and novelist Thomas Dixon wrote *The*

Flaming Sword (1939) about black–white relations in the United States.

See also GARDEN OF EDEN [JC]

Fleece, setting out. In Judg. 6.36-40, Gideon tests the Lord two times to make sure that he is meant to deliver the Israelites from the oppression of the Midianites. In his first test, Gideon sets out a wool fleece overnight and asks God to make the fleece wet with dew but leave the ground around it dry. In the second test, he reverses the request, asking God to make the ground wet with dew but leave the fleece dry. Both nights God does exactly as Gideon asks, giving Gideon the confidence to lead the Israelite army to victory in chapters 7 and 8.

The theme of testing runs throughout the Bible. While testing God is usually condemned (Exod. 7.2; Num. 14.22; Deut. 6.16; Isa. 7.12; Matt. 4.7; 22.18; Acts 5.9), there are exceptions. In Malachi, the Lord instructs his people to test him by tithing to see if he will not bless them (3.10), yet a few verses later, testing God is frowned upon (3.15). In the NT, testing God or Jesus is usually denounced, but the author of 1 John instructs his audience to 'test the spirits' to see if they are from God (4.1). An example of a human testing God in the NT is the disciple Thomas, who refuses to believe that Jesus has risen from the dead until he puts his hands in Jesus' wounds, a request which is honored a week later (John 20.24-29). For Augustine, the fleece symbolized Israel, to which Christ came like the dew (*Ennar. in Ps.* 72.9). Because Christ came to a 'chosen mother', the fleece also came to symbolize the miraculous conception of Mary, a theme echoed in medieval lyric poetry. In James Joyce's *Ulysses*, this connection is reversed, the wet fleece instead standing for sexual experience: 'thy fleece is drenched'.

Recommended reading. Beck, John A. 'Gideon, Dew, and the Narrative-Geographical Shaping of Judges 6:33-40'. *Bibliotheca sacra* 165 (2008) 28-38.

See also GIDEON [MH]

Flesh. The term derives from the Hebrew *basar* (flesh, body) and is different from skin and meat, and from *she'er* (flesh, meat), which denotes food in most uses. The OT view of flesh is as something vital, important, and in connection with God (Gen. 9.16; Lev. 17.11; Ezek. 11.19; 36.36). Flesh is also tied with food, life, and covenant, and served as a means of atonement for sin (cf. Exod. 29.14; Deut. 12). The word *sarx* (flesh, the material that covers bones) in the NT refers to humankind or the entire person. The Apostle Paul uses *sarx* to describe flesh in spiritual terms, made prominent with the use of *kata sarx* 'according to the flesh' (cf. Rom. 8.4, 5, 12, 13).

Religious and philosophical understandings of flesh have facilitated discussions ranging from Luther's work on transubstantiation, a term referring to the transformation of the wine and bread into the blood and flesh of Christ, to the objective studies of modern science arising from Kantian philosophy, which gives way to discussions on mind–body dualism.

See also ADAM; EVE; FOOD, SYMBOLISM OF; SIN; HOLY SPIRIT; RITUAL PURITY, IMPURITY; RESURRECTION [PEN]

Flood. Although not the oldest of the world's flood stories, the HB flood narrative (Gen. 6–9) has captivated audiences for well over 2500 years. According to the biblical account, the flood occurs primarily as a divine response to the problem of human corruption. The world had become exceedingly violent and the human heart relentlessly wicked (6.5, 11-13). This corruption is further underscored by the episode of the intermarriage of the 'sons of God' with the 'daughters of men' (6.1-4), an event which suggests the violation of the divinely ordained boundaries of God's creation. The only exception to humanity's impoverished state appears in the righteousness of Noah, who is accordingly spared the ravages of the flood, along with his family and breeding pairs of all non-aquatic creatures by means a handcrafted vessel of cypress wood and pitch.

For this reason, the flood is presented as an act of 'uncreation' that returns the earth to the original primordial state out of which it was created. This is suggested by (a) the portrayal of the flood waters as descending from the floodgates of heaven above and arising from the great abyss below (7.11); (b) the disappearance of all land beneath the chaotic waters (7.19-20); and (c) the blotting out of all land-dwelling and aerial creatures (7.21-23)—details that each describe the undoing of God's intentional acts of creation in Gen. 1. In this respect, the subsequent closing up of the flood gates of heaven and the great abyss (8.2 cf. 1.6-7), the recession of the flood waters and the emergence of dry land (8.3-5; cf. 1.9), and the release of Noah, his family, and the other living creatures into the world (8.15-19; cf. 1.20-27) are to be regarded as a reciprocal act of recreation—a point underscored by the repetition of the command of God to 'be fruitful and multiply, and fill the earth' (9.1; cf. 1.28).

The unfortunate irony of the biblical flood is its failure to accomplish its intended purpose of eliminating human corruption. God himself acknowledges this in his post-flood reflections on the persistence of evil in the human heart (8.21)—a detail illustrated ever so tragically by the subsequent incidents of drunkenness, dishonor, and cursing (9.18-27). Even so, the value of the flood as a symbol of divine judgment, destruction, and recreation was not lost on the Second Temple and early Christian apocalyptic writers who frequently employed the flood narrative typologically in their anticipations of a great fiery conflagration that would bring the current world age to an end (e.g., 2 Pet. 3.1-13).

Beyond its obvious apocalyptic appeal, the flood narrative also came to be used in a variety of other creative ways. For example, the writer of *Jubilees*, who expanded the flood narrative's latent priestly details of covenant, purity, and sacrifice, went to great lengths to tweak the chronological details of the flood narrative in order to give legitimacy to the use of the 364-day calendar (*Jub.* 6.1–7.39).

Other creative embellishments and usages of the flood narrative include the identification of Noah with the Greek flood hero Deucalion (*Apoc. Adam* 5.5; Philo, *Praem.* 23; Justin Martyr, *Apol.* 2.7.2; Epiphanius, *Haer.* 26.1.6); the presentation of Noah as a preacher of repentance (*Sib. Or.* 1.147-98; 2 Pet. 2.5; *Apoc. Paul* 50); its reconfiguration for liturgical and didactic usage within the Qumran community (4Q508 [Festival Prayers]; 4Q370 [Admonition Based on the Flood]); and 1 Peter's remarkable correlation between the flood and baptism (3.20).

Recommended reading. Garcia Martinez, Florentino, and Gerard P. Luttikhuizen (eds.). *Interpretations of the Flood.* Leiden: Brill, 1998.

See also GENESIS, BOOK OF; NOAH'S ARK   [TAB]

Food, symbolism of. Symbolic references to food abound in the Bible as a few examples illustrate. Food is notably encountered in Gen. 3.6, when Adam and Eve eat the forbidden fruit, often interpreted as an apple, from the Tree of Knowledge. Other significant fruits are the pomegranate, fig, and grape. References to grapes, and wine made from them appear in dozens of references, as they are symbolically connected to the blood of Christ and the institution of the Eucharist.

There are numerous discussions of the separation of meat and milk in the OT, the basis for eating kosher (Lev. 11.1-22; Deut. 9.1; Exod. 23.19). The unleavened bread of Passover is discussed in Exod. 12.15-20. Deuteronomy 8.8 gives an image of the promised land, with wheat, barley, vines and figs. Bread from heaven rained down and they 'called it manna; it was like coriander seed, white, and the taste of it was like wafers made with honey' (Exod. 16.31).

Wheat was such a staple that it becomes metaphor for existence. Christ says, 'I am the bread of life' (John 6.35). John the Baptist points to Christ as the judge who will separate wheat from chaff (Matt. 3.12). Among Christ's parables are those of sowers of wheat (Matt. 13.1-9), weeds amidst wheat (Matt. 13.24-30), and flour and yeast (Matt. 13.33). Bread is the object of numerous miracles described throughout the Gospels. These include the institution of the bread and wine of the Eucharist (Matt. 26.26-29), and the multiplication of the loaves and fishes (Matt. 14.13-21; 15.32-39; John 6.1-14). Two significant passages pertaining to grains and seeds are found in the OT: 'God said, 'See, I have given you every plant yielding seed that is upon the face of all the earth, and every tree with seed in its fruit; you shall have them for food' (Gen. 1.29); 'And you, take wheat and barley, beans and lentils, millet and spelt; put them into one vessel, and make bread for yourself' (Ezek. 4.9).

Fish figure symbolically in the NT. Christ says to his disciples, 'Follow me and I will make you fish for people' (Mark 1.17). The story of Peter and the tribute money involves Peter finding a coin in a fish's mouth to pay the tax collector (Matt. 17.27). The feeding of the five thousand (the multiplication of the loaves and fishes) is one of Christ's great miracles (John 6.1-14). Christ's third appearance to his disciples after his resurrection occurred while they were fishing; he appeared on shore with a fire and they brought in fish for a feast (John 21.1-14). A fish later became an early Christian symbol for Christ. The acronym for Jesus Christ, Son of God, Savior, in Greek spells ICHTHYS, meaning fish. The Roman catacombs were decorated with paintings and sculptures of fish, to represent Christ in the days when the religion was still illegal. The 'Jesus fish' motif is still used by Christians on bumper stickers and t-shirts.

Recommended reading. Vamosh, Miriam Feinberg. *Food at the Time of the Bible. From Adam's Apple to the Last Supper.* Herzliya: Palphot, 2007. Juengst, Sara Covin. *Breaking Bread: The Spiritual Significance of Food.* Louisville, KY: Westminster John Knox, 1992.

See also APPLE; BREAD; BREAD OF LIFE; FEASTS; FASTING; FISH; FEEDING OF THE FIVE THOUSAND; FORBIDDEN FRUIT; HARVEST; LAND OF MILK AND HONEY; LOAVES AND FISHES; MANNA; PLANTS, SYMBOLISM OF; POMEGRANATE; WINE [ACF]

Fool, Foolishness, Folly. The unabridged *OED* defines fool as 'One deficient in judgment or sense, one who behaves or acts stupidly, a silly person, a simpleton ... [Moreover t]he word has in mod[ern] Eng[lish] a much stronger sense than it had at an earlier period; it now has an implication of insulting contempt which does not in the same degree belong to any of its synonyms, or to the derivative foolish'. Hence common parlance knows such aphorisms as 'no fool like an old fool', 'a fool has himself for a lawyer', or 'a fool and his gold are soon parted' (cf. William Shenstone [1714–1773], *Essays on Men and Manners*: 'a fool and his words are soon parted'). Alexander Pope in his *Essay on Criticism* (1711) coined another well-known proverb: 'Fools rush in where angels fear to tread'.

Applications of the word fool in the English Bible do not indicate mental incompetence on the part of its intended referent, but rather a wilful rejection of God and his counsel. A number of Hebrew words in the OT underlie use of the term fool in English translation. Its cognates foolishness and folly carry such nuances as 'arrogance', 'overconfidence', 'senselessness', 'thickheadedness', or less frequently 'evil'/'wrong-doing'. The psalmist deems atheism a form of 'senselessness' (Heb. *nabal*, 14.1; 53.1). Interestingly, Jesus' proscription against the denunciation of one's brother as a fool (Gk *ho mōros*, Matt. 5.22) reflects a similar connotation of the Greek *mōros* (but cf. the LXX in Ps. 14.1; 53.1, *aphrōn*).

The adjective *mōros* with its substantive/verbal cognates is the most common designation of foolishness among the NT writers. The NT carries the same range of nuances as those mentioned in connection with the OT corpus. Thus, the Lukan parable of the rich fool (12.16-21) teaches that reliance on material wealth as the ultimate source of security proves one to be a fool (v. 21).

The classic juxtaposition of folly and wisdom in the Bible is most obvious in the Book of Proverbs. Its personification of wisdom as the desirable woman serves to extol virtue and prudence, while the presentation of folly as the beguiling harlot denigrates idolatry and wastefulness. Dame Wisdom's role in later literature reflects the influence of Proverbs. Geoffrey Chaucer's *Tale of Melibee* illustrates the point.

Paul contrasts worldly and divine wisdom (1 Cor. 1.8–4.21). One earns acceptance in the eyes of others but God's disfavor. However, divine wisdom evokes scorn from the world but God's approval. Better to be a 'fool for Christ', Paul concludes. Secular literature also knows the 'wise fool'. The court jester in William Shakespeare's tragedy *King Lear* continues to provide the king with wise counsel, while other characters utter lies and treachery. The 'fool for Christ' has also infiltrated modern literature, as in Harold Fickett's comic novel *The Holy Fool* (1983), which relates the story of a Los Angeles clergyman who decides to place moral integrity ahead of the security of his position.

See also PROVERBS, BOOK OF; RICH FOOL, PARABLE OF THE; WISDOM; WISDOM OF SOLOMON [NRP]

Foot washing. The action of foot washing depicts the proper relation of a servant to a master. It is found in various places in the Bible and is viewed as culturally normative for hospitality. Its omission constitutes a breach of protocol especially when considered deliberate as in Luke 7.36-50 where Simon, though outwardly according Jesus the status of teacher, inwardly considers him inferior. Simon communicates this attitude unmistakably by a pointed failure of etiquette. For Jesus to note such an omission in his host (Luke 7.44) is also a breach thus contributing to the tensions in the narrative. Judges 19.21 associates foot washing with hospitality to a stranger. During the courtship of David and Abigail, Abigail declares her great humility as 'a servant to wash the feet of the servants of my lord' (1 Sam. 25.41). In the story of David and Uriah, David invites Uriah to go to his home to wash his feet. This is probably a euphemism for sexual intercourse since 'feet' (Heb. *regelim*) is also sometimes used to describe the genitals. When Abraham's servant visits Laban (Gen. 24.32), water is provided for foot washing though not by another servant.

There is no doubt that foot washing in the Bible is regularly connected with hospitality and the task always given to servants. The Bible assumes this cultural pattern. Servanthood is also a characteristic of church leadership (1 Tim. 5.10). The basis for the formal links between foot washing and ministry reside in the known teachings and actions of Jesus of Nazareth (cf. Phil. 2.5-7). Jesus' own teaching on servanthood was understood to reflect his own life and thus essential for the pattern of Christian discipleship. This is clear in the Johannine account of the Upper Room (John 13.3-15) where Jesus washes his disciples' feet. It is a radical cultural reversal consistent with Jesus' frequent adoption and subversion of plausible audience expectations. Thus, the reader is expected to respond with surprise at the new concept of servanthood and humility applied by Jesus to himself. The text of John 13 recalls Peter's initial refusal to submit to Jesus' insistence that he wash the disciples' feet. Peter's vigorous rejection (though he eventually relents) gives a measure of the dissonance such an enacted parable produced in the minds of the disciples.

Of special interest is the exceedingly intimate gesture of women wiping Jesus' feet with their hair recorded in John 11.2; 12.3; Luke 7.37-38, 44-46. This raises the question of dissonance to new levels inasmuch as 'feet' has sexual connotations. Such intimacy is heightened in these texts by the women's use of their hair normative only in the context of married relations. That a man would even speak to a woman who was not a relative or husband seems implied by John 4.27.

Foot washing is a popular subject in art and iconography. In some instances, the emphasis lies with Jesus' reasoning with Peter (as in the work of Giotto di Bondone, 1267–1337). The contemporary artist Leszek Forczek brings a luminous and transcendent quality to the physicality of foot washing. For Canadian poet Rachel Vigiers, the foot washing associated with Mary Magdalene becomes emblematic of any act of surprising service (in her poem 'Shoes'). Some Christian traditions celebrate Maundy Thursday with a footwashing service modelled on Jesus' actions as described in John 13.

See also SLAVE; DISCIPLE [JKS]

Forbidden fruit. God warned Adam and Eve not to eat from the tree of the knowledge of good and evil in the center of the Garden of Eden (Gen. 2.16-17) but they eventually ate this forbidden fruit. The term usually refers to this act of disobedience and fall from grace (Gen. 3), becoming a metaphor for anything that seems desirable but is potentially disastrous. In the first couple's case, the fruit seemed to them beautiful in appearance, delicious in taste, and capable of making them wise, but the result of their eating it was guilt, shame, and alienation from God and each other.

Many have wondered what the forbidden fruit in the garden was. In the East, it was thought to be an olive or fig; in the West, usually an apple. The Bible does not enlighten us. Early Christian teaching interpreted the forbidden fruit metaphor as sexual activity. Many of the early church fathers, like Tertullian, Jerome, and Augustine, fought their own sexual demons and considered sexual activity as the temptation of the Devil. In spite of God's having commanded Adam and Eve to be fruitful and multiply—and despite basic biblical teaching of the goodness of sex in its proper context of marriage—there remain Christians with lingering suspicions that sexual attraction and activity are the forbidden fruit.

In the sexual context, some have seen forbidden fruit as a metaphor for miscegenation, or relationships between two people of different races. Such is the theme of the 2006 motion picture, *Forbidden Fruits*, written and directed by Marc Cayce, which details a romance between an African American Christian girl and an Arabic Muslim man, together with the racial and cultural tensions engendered.

Recommended reading. Pagels, Elaine. *Adam, Eve, and the Serpent*. Toronto: Random House, 1988.

See also GENESIS, BOOK OF; FALL, THE; ADAM; EVE [DLS]

Forgiveness. Forgiveness is the cessation of anger or resentment toward someone for an offense, flaw, or mistake. There are two categories of forgiveness in the Bible: human forgiveness, which involves the restoration of right relationship between two people in the wake of some offense, and divine forgiveness, which is an act of God that removes sin and its consequences from human beings.

A prominent example of human forgiveness in the HB is Joseph's forgiveness of his brothers (Gen. 50.15-21), even though they sold him into slavery and lied about his death (Gen. 37). One can also intercede and ask God to forgive others, as when Moses cries to God, 'Forgive the iniquity of this people according to the greatness of your steadfast love' (Num. 14.19). The sacrificial system describes the process by which people make 'sin-offerings' for purification: 'The priest shall make atonement on your behalf ... and you shall be forgiven' (cf. Lev. 5.16).

In the NT Gospel of Matthew, Jesus instructs his followers to forgive one another seventy-seven times (18.22), meaning without limit, because God will not forgive those who do not forgive others (6.12, 14-15; 18.35). In Luke, Jesus teaches that forgiveness depends on repentance (17.3-4), and in some manuscripts Jesus intercedes for those who crucify him (23.34a). Regarding divine forgiveness, Jesus' death is understood as an atoning sacrifice for all time, delivering humanity from the burden of sin (e.g., Rom. 3.24-25; Heb. 10.10; 1 John 2.2). The Synoptic Gospels cite blasphemy against the Holy Spirit as an 'unforgivable sin' (Matt. 12.31; Mark 3.29; Luke 12.10). Some NT texts discuss forgiveness without mentioning the term, as in the parable of the prodigal son (Luke 15.11-32) and the story of the woman caught in adultery (John 7.53–8.11). The Greek word most commonly translated 'forgive' in the NT is *aphiēmi*. It appears 146 times in the NT, but only 38 of those are translated 'forgive'. Elsewhere it is rendered 'leave', 'let', or 'allow'.

The topic of forgiveness is prominent in the world of self-help and popular psychology, especially the notion of self-forgiveness. Public apologies and appeals for forgiveness have become commonplace, delivered by such figures as Pope Benedict XVI (2010), Bill Clinton (1998), John Edwards (2010), as well as sports celebrities Michael Vick (2007) and Tiger Woods (2009). In 2000, German president Johannes Rau addressed the Israeli parliament and asked for forgiveness for the Holocaust on behalf of the German people. After the shooting of five young Amish girls in Nickel Mines, Pennsylvania in 2006, the Amish community enacted their religious commitment to forgiveness by reaching out in support of the family of the shooter. This emphasis on forgiveness and reconciliation was widely celebrated in the national media. In post-apartheid South Africa, Archbishop Desmond Tutu presided over the Truth and Reconciliation Commission that recorded testimony of victims and conducted amnesty hearings for perpetrators. The title of his memoir of this period, *No Future Without Forgiveness* (1999), contributes to the veneration of forgiveness in contemporary culture.

Motifs of forgiveness figure prevalently in many of William Shakespeare's dramas, most notably *Hamlet* and *King Lear*. **See also** novels such as Alexander Dumas, *The Count of Monte Cristo* (1844); Nathaniel Hawthorne, *The Scarlet Letter* (1850); Harper Lee, *To Kill a Mockingbird* (1960); Ian McEwan, *Atonement* (2001); and Alice Sebold, *The Lovely Bones* (2002). Films that take up issues of forgiveness include *Unforgiven* (1992), *Schindler's List* (1993), *Dead Man Walking* (1995), *In the Bedroom* (2001), and *Mystic River* (2003).

See also SIN AGAINST THE HOLY SPIRIT; ATONEMENT; REPENTANCE; SEVENTY TIMES SEVEN [MM]

Former Prophets. The term Former Prophets refers either to the acting prophets named in Joshua, Judges, 1–2 Samuel, and 1–2 Kings, or, more often, the books of Joshua through 2 Kings themselves. Some of the acting prophets in Joshua through 2 Kings are obscure, as is the case with the prophet Micaiah who prophesied against King Ahab (1 Kgs 22.1-40) and then disappears from the text. Others, particularly Elijah and Elisha (sporadically throughout 1 Kgs 17–2 Kgs 13), figure more prominently in the narratives. Elijah, among other things, opposed the prophets of Baal that had been instituted by King Ahab and his wife Jezebel. Elisha succeeds Elijah when the latter is carried alive into heaven by chariots over the Jordan River. The acting prophets also denounce the abuses of power by the kings of their day. In the case of King David's adultery and murder in connection with Bathsheba, the prophet Nathan delivers the rebuke of God (2 Sam. 12.1-15). Elijah denounces King Ahab when he takes possession of a vineyard through the judicial murder arranged by Queen Jezebel (1 Kgs 21.1-29).

Discussions on the formation of the Former Prophets involve issues related to the Pentateuch, that is, to the first five books of the Bible (Genesis to Deuteronomy). Scholars who have followed the JEPD Theory of the origins of the Pentateuch believe that the books were formed from earlier materials in ancient Israel by writers who either referred to God as Yahweh (J), Elohim (E), were priests (P), or were associated with an unknown author designated the Deuteronomistic Historian. Other scholars believe they were once part of a large Deuteronomistic History. They also mention a number of books that have been lost such as the Book of the Wars of Yahweh, the Book of Jasher, the Book of the Acts of Solomon, the Book of the Chronicles of the Kings of Israel, and the Book of the Chronicles of the Kings of Judah.

Recommended reading. Christensen, Duane L. *Former Prophets*. North Richland Hills: D. & F. Scott Publishing, 2002.

See also ELIJAH; ELISHA; JOSHUA, BOOK OF; JUDGES, BOOK OF; KINGS, BOOKS OF; SAMUEL, BOOKS OF; LATTER PROPHETS; NATHAN; OLD TESTAMENT; PROPHECY; PROPHETS [AJW]

Four horsemen of the Apocalypse, the. The four horsemen of the apocalypse appear in Rev. 6. They each ride a different colored horse (white, red, black, pale green) and represent four trials released upon the earth by the Lamb, Jesus Christ (5.2, 7): conquest, slaughter, inflation or famine, and death. He opens the seals of the scroll that they lock (6.1-8). The scroll appears first in the hand of the One on the throne (5.1). Most interpreters of the four riders do not see Christ as the first rider on the white horse here (even though Christ rides a white horse later, in 19.11-13). The scene is reminiscent of the use of the three colored horses in the events depicted in Zech. 1 and 6 when judgment on Israel takes place. The role of the Lamb (Jesus Christ) in these scenes from Revelation, however, is an issue in the interpretation of this book since Christ represents the grace of God in the whole drama and not the destruction apparently released by the horsemen.

The image of the four horsemen has been a favorite way of representing natural and human disasters in film, literature, and art. They can symbolize the impact of terrible episodes in human history in any age such as the traditional events of death, famine, pestilence, and war. Their name and symbolic value can even serve an antiwar theme. The silent film *The Four Horsemen* in 1921 with Rudolph Valentino does just this and so does its 1969 remake set in Nazi Germany. The four horsemen are dramatically represented by the woodcuts of Albrecht Dürer produced between 1495 and 1498. His portrayals reflect tragic images of his own age just as Vasko Taskovski's oil painting, *The Riders of the Apocalypse*, reflect disturbing twentieth-century scenes.

Some incarnations of the four horsemen image in contemporary culture have no real connection to the biblical Apocalypse. The symbol of the horsemen was used to describe the four running backs of Notre Dame's Fighting Irish football team in 1924 and, in turn, they had a United States Postal Service stamp issued in 1998 depicting each of them sitting on four horses. Individually, the horsemen and their symbolic impact can be seen in various ways in art and literature from Jan Vermeer's seventeenth-century painting, *A Lady Weighing Pearls*, to Agatha Christie's novel, *The Pale Horse*.

Recommended reading. Witherington, III, Ben. *Revelation*. The New Cambridge Bible Commentary. Cambridge University Press: Cambridge, 2003.

See also REVELATION, BOOK OF; APOCALYPSE, APOCALYPTIC; JOHN OF PATMOS [DMAC]

Freedom. The concept of freedom is a highly significant motif in the Bible. It most often refers to the literal release from a physical condition (e.g., slavery) or to the metaphorical release from the bondage of a spiritual condition (e.g., sin). The creation story in Gen. 1 begins with a picture of God giving to each living creature the freedom to thrive on earth and to humans, the authority and freedom to rule over the other creatures (Gen. 1.26-31). However, Adam and Eve's disobedience of God's decree in Gen. 2.16-17 led to the loss of freedom, and the entrance of sin and death upon all humanity. In the Book of Exodus, the Israelites experienced bitter slavery under the harsh rule of the Pharaoh of Egypt, at which point God brought liberation through Moses.

Following their freedom from Egyptian rule, the Israelites entered the promised land (Palestine) in the Book of Joshua. Israelite history then is riddled with either bondage to enemy nations or freedom through leaders called 'judges' (Judg. 2–16). As the Israelite monarchy began to deteriorate after the time of Saul and David, the Israelite kingdoms were eventually overrun by the Assyrian and the Babylonian empires (Israel and Judah fell in 722 and 586 BCE respectively). This motif of freedom then became a powerful force in the Jewish national psyche, with a longing to re-establish the nation of Israel in the promised land. In addition, in the NT, this 'exodus' motif is then metaphorically and spiritually applied to a desire for freedom from the tyranny of sin and Satan (cf. Luke 4.18; John 8.34; Gal. 5.13; 1 Pet. 2.16).

Not surprisingly, this motif resonates in contemporary struggles for independence and freedom from oppression, evident in such events as the American struggle for independence, the abolitionist movement, the Mormons' westward trek to flee oppression, and the American civil rights movement. During the American Revolution, the colonists viewed America as 'God's new Israel' and caricatured King George III as a 'British Pharaoh'. In addition, both the abolitionist movement in America and the Mormons' search for religious freedom was framed in exodus language. In the 1960s, Oscar Peterson composed 'Hymn to Freedom' in honor of the African-American civil rights movement.

This biblical theme of subjugation and repression with a powerful desire for liberation became a popular theme in the film industry. In *The Ten Commandments* (1956), Charlton Heston plays Moses, in a popular film adaptation of the Exodus story. In 1998, DreamWorks released a very popular animated film, *The Prince of Egypt* also based on the story of the Exodus. On a more general and popular level, the word freedom in the context of film brings *Braveheart* to mind. In this movie, the freedom motif is heard from the lips of William Wallace (played by Mel Gibson). Instead of declaring King Edward I as the king over Scotland, the leader of the Scottish resistance cries just before his beheading, 'Freedom!' which provided the inspiration for Robert the Bruce's eventual victory in the struggle for Scottish independence.

Recommended reading. Roncace, Mark, and Patrick Gray (eds.). *Teaching the Bible through Popular Culture and the Arts*. Atlanta: SBL Publishing, 2007. Schippe, Cullen, and Chuck Stetson. *The Bible and its Influence*. New York: BLP, 2006.

See also DELIVERANCE; EGYPT; EXILE; EXODUS, BOOK OF; SIN; SLAVE [MKWS]

Fruit of the Spirit. The fruit of the Spirit are listed in Gal. 5.22, where Paul identifies nine characteristics indicating spiritual maturity or the work produced by the Holy Spirit in the lives of Christians: love, joy, peace, patience, kindness, goodness, faith or faithfulness, gentleness, and self-control (see NASB). These qualities contrast with others Paul describes as 'the works of the flesh': immorality, impurity, sensuality, idolatry, sorcery, enmities, strife, jealousy, anger, disputes, dissension, factions, envy, drunkenness, carousing, and similar things (Gal. 5.19-21 NASB).

The fruit of the Spirit are not a set of rules or standards. As Paul says, there is no law against such qualities of the Spirit-led life. More than that, those who belong to Christ have crucified the fleshly elements, and now walk in the Spirit, in which it is now possible to produce spiritual fruit. Paul is consistent in Galatians with how he treats these virtues elsewhere in his letters. The list begins with love, one of the cardinal Christian virtues. In 1 Cor. 13.13, Paul states that faith (or faithfulness?), hope, and love remain, and the greatest of these is love. Joy is one of the qualities of a follower of Christ, not based on circumstances but based on their position in Christ, as Paul states in Phil. 1.25. Similarly, peace is the state that results from the absence of strife with God, as stated in Rom. 5.1. Joy and peace, in Paul's mind, belong together, as in Rom. 15.13. Patience is a quality based on God's own long-suffering with humans resulting in the ability to endure the failings of others. This is expressed well in 2 Cor. 6.6, where Paul has a list of virtues similar to the fruit of the spirit in Gal. 5. Kindness is linked here and in 2 Cor. 6.6 with patience, also a quality of God to be manifested in the life of the Christian. Goodness indicates the characteristic of doing good acts for others, and is one of three characteristics, along with righteousness and truth, in a small list of 'fruit' of light in Eph. 5.9. Faith or faithfulness, as mentioned above, is elsewhere linked with the characteristics of the Christian life, and may indicate the act of leading a believing life or the result of believing. Gentleness indicates control of the emotions that Paul attributes to Christ and that he desires in those who follow Christ, as he says in 2 Cor. 10.1. Finally, self-control addresses physical passions, which should be under control (see 1 Cor. 7.9; 9.25, using the verb form of this noun). The fruit of the spirit represent the idealized virtues to be sought in the mature Christian life.

See also GALATIANS, EPISTLE TO THE [SEP]

G

Gabriel, the angel. From the Hebrew *Gavriel*, this name means 'man of God' or 'hero of God'. Gabriel is one of God's seven arch, meaning chief or primary, angels. He appears in the Bible four times, speaking with individuals of great faith and providing an understanding of God's plan for man's salvation and the end of time. Jewish tradition indicates that Gabriel is the angel of judgment, and in Islamic belief, Gabriel dictates the Qur'an to Mohammed. Gabriel's identity as God's messenger continues to the present day with some exceptions.

In the OT, Gabriel appears twice to the prophet Daniel to explain Daniel's visions. In 8.16-26, Daniel has seen a ram with two horns being defeated by a male goat. Gabriel appears in human form and explains that a Greek leader, the goat, will overcome the empires of the Persians and the Medes, signified by the two horns on the ram. Scholars often argue the image refers to Alexander the Great. In Dan. 9.21-27, Daniel sees Gabriel flying down to talk with him and foretelling the destruction of Jerusalem and the temple.

In the NT, Gabriel appears to the priest Zechariah while he is burning incense at the altar to announce the birth of Zechariah and Elizabeth's son, John the Baptist. When Zechariah doubts the message, Gabriel takes away Zechariah's power of speech until the baby is born (Luke 1.5-23). Gabriel's fourth and best-known appearance is to Mary: 'The angel came to her and said, 'Peace be with you! The Lord is with you and has greatly blessed you!' (Luke 1.28). He tells Mary she will give birth to the savior Jesus.

The character Gabe in August Wilson's 1987 Pulitzer Prize winning play *Fences* parallels the biblical Gabriel. Gabe carries a trumpet, even after the neighbors take away its mouthpiece, and due to a war-time head injury, Gabe does not concern himself with earthly matters such as earning a paycheque or paying rent. After his brother Troy's death, Gabe blows on his trumpet three times and Wilson's stage directions suggest that the doors of heaven are opening to allow Troy, an imperfect man, to enter.

The 2005 movie *Constantine* presents Gabriel as an androgynous messenger (played by Tilda Swinton) who must make Constantine, a human detective who can see angels and demons, accept that his occupational demon killing will not save him from his own death and the punishment for an attempted suicide when he was younger.

Other depictions of Gabriel explore conflict arising from implicit differences between humans and angels. In the 1995 film *The Prophecy*, humans have replaced angels in the celestial hierarchy and Gabriel attempts to gather a soul he believes will re-establish angelic superiority. When the soul is housed in a young girl, Gabriel is defeated. In the 2007 movie *Gabriel*, angels are battling demons for control of purgatory. Gabriel is the youngest and strongest angel to fight, but he is burdened by human emotions and does not know how to deal with them. His inner emotional struggle is a greater conflict for him than the battle with the demons.

See also ANGEL; MICHAEL, THE ANGEL; RAPHAEL, THE ANGEL [KAM]

Gadarene swine. The story of the Gadarene swine appears in all three Synoptic Gospels (Matt. 8.28-32; Mark 5.1-20; Luke 8.26-32). The incident occurs in the region known as Gadara near a town called Gerasa/Gergasa, hence the alternative story-names Gadarene swine and Gerasene/Gergasene swine. In this passage, Jesus is confronted by a demoniac, and after exorcizing the evil spirits who call themselves Legion, he sends the spirits, at their request, into a nearby herd of pigs who then rush over and cliff and are destroyed.

Jerome and the early church fathers understand this passage to indicate Jesus' authority over evil spirits, a sign of his role as the Christ, the Messiah. Chrysostom and others also suggest that the demon's desire to enter into the herd of swine is a moral allegory indicating Satan's desire to enter into humanity through it base, bestial nature in order to destroy it from within. Tertullian further suggests that Jesus permits the evil spirits' desires to control this bestial nature because it may motivate the individual to resist sinful living and return to the Father (cf. Jesus' story about the prodigal son).

The story of the Gadarene swine enters into Western culture through works such as John Milton's *Paradise Regained*, which refers to the fallen angels fleeing from Christ and wanting 'to hide … in a herd of swine, lest he command them down into the deep, bound'. Edmund Spenser's *Faerie Queen* blends the imagery of the Gadarene swine with the Homeric tale of Odysseus and his confrontation with Circe, who changes his crew into swine. Spenser, writing on the virtue of temperance calls on the legend of

Circe as a reminder that in greed and gluttony we may 'see the mind of beastly man'.

Fyodor Dostoevsky prefaces his novel *The Possessed* with Luke's account of the Gadarene swine. The story critiques the rise of democratic liberalism and the response of the conservative establishment in nineteenth-century Russia, and proposes that ideas themselves can be demonic, that ideologies have the power to possess the minds of humanity and lead it away from God. In formal logic, the story of the Gadarene swine forms the basis for a logical fallacy called the 'Gadarene Swine Fallacy', which assumes that because a group is in the right formation it is necessarily on the right course, or conversely that because an individual is not in right formation with the group, then the individual is necessarily off-course. The film *Gadarene Swine* (2009) from director Brian Smolensky uses the imagery of the Gospel story to weave together three separate tales illustrating the destructive power of our personal demons.

See also DEMON; LEGION; SIN [RLM]

Galatians, Epistle to the. The ninth book of the NT, the Epistle to the Galatians, deals with a defense of Paul's apostleship and the relationship of faith and works. It was written by Paul the Apostle to rebuke and correct the churches of the ancient Roman province of Galatia (present-day central Turkey). Dating of Galatians is complicated by uncertainty about the intended audience. If Paul addressed northern cities, then a date of c. 54–55 CE is likely. If Paul wrote to Christian churches in the south, then an earlier date around 49 CE best fits the available data (making it Paul's earliest epistle).

In Galatians, Paul addresses questions about the relationship of faith to the Mosaic law. Some were convinced circumcision was necessary for Christians to find favor with God, and they challenged Paul's claim of authority to speak to this and other issues. The Epistle to the Galatians begins with a defense of his apostleship (chs. 1–2) before demonstrating that faith in the promised Messiah (Jesus) has always been central for the people of God (chs. 3–4; cf. Rom. 4.1-25). Paul concludes with instructions on how to live a godly life free of legalistic pursuits (chs. 5–6). The thrust of Paul's main argument appears in 3.3: 'Are you so foolish? Having started with the Spirit, are you now ending with the flesh?' The Galatian churches had been committing this error by demanding mandatory circumcision as part of the cultic initiation rite to become a Christian. Paul argues that the Galatian church is seeking to follow the OT Mosaic law, which promises earthly land, instead of Jesus Christ who fulfilled the demands of the Mosaic law, which promises eternal blessings.

Galatians has been widely influential on the arts. Peter Paul Rubens's painting *Hagar Leaves the House of Abraham* draws on Paul's allegorical account of Sarah and Hagar in Gal. 4.21-31. Rembrandt created a series of paintings of what Paul might have looked like during the writing of such letters as Galatians in his painting series *St Paul in Prison*. In the modern era, Felix Mendelssohn found inspiration in a misreading of Galatians that showed Paul to be anti-Semitic, resulting in his *Paulus*, Op. 36. The defense of Paul's apostleship is a theme the 1980s Alternative Rock band Momus explores in their song 'Lucky like St Sebastian'. In motion pictures, the phrase 'Christ crucified' (Gal. 2.13) gave Stanley Kubrick a mental image for his 130-mile stretch of crucifixions in the four-time Academy Award winning 1960 movie *Spartacus*.

Galatians has been used as a platform in the last few centuries to educate people on unity and diversification. Paul's great statement about freedom in 3.28 ('There is no longer Jew or Greek ... slave or free ... male or female') has been transformed into modern tolerance and social justice movements. In the mid 1800s, England's William Booth (The Salvation Army) and George Williams (YMCA) were specifically inspired by this verse to start programs that reached out to those in need. These social programs now service millions of people worldwide. During this same period, England's William Wilberforce and America's Abraham Lincoln were inspired by this verse in their respective efforts to abolish slavery, even quoting this verse in speeches. In the later civil rights movement, this statement gave hope and fervor to activists, such as Modjeska Simkins and Martin Luther King, Jr.

Recommended reading. Wright, N.T. *Justification: God's Plan and Paul's Vision*. Downers Grove, IL: IVP Academic, 2009.

See also APOSTLE; PAUL, THE APOSTLE; CIRCUMCISION; JUSTIFICATION; LAW; ROMANS, EPISTLE TO THE [CCB]

Galilee. The name is from the Hebrew term for 'wheel'. With the definite article, it refers to the region of the Levant that is bounded by the Lebanon Mountains and Lake Huleh (north), the Esdraelon Plain (south), the Sea of Galilee and the Jordan River (east), and by the Phoenician cities of the

Coastal Plain (west). OT references to this area include 2 Kgs 15.29, which describes the invasion of the northern kingdom of Israel by the Assyrian king Tiglath-Pileser, and Isa. 8.23, which refers to 'Galilee of the Nations' (*Glyl hagoyim*), an appellation likely derived from the surrounding Canaanite population. In the NT, the Isaiah passage is referred to at Matt. 4.15. The Galilee is mentioned in the Gospel narratives of Jesus' birth (Matt. 2.22; Mark 1.9; Luke 1.26) and his mission (e.g., Matt. 4.12; Mark 1.28; Luke 4.14; John 1.43).

Galilean sub-regions in the first millennium BCE are listed at Josh. 15.10-48, which describes the locations of the tribes Asher, Dan, Issachar, Napthali, and Zebulun. By the first century CE, the Galilee consisted of three sub-regions, each with unique geographic characteristics. 'Upper Galilee' has elevated mountainous terrain and the sites of Dan and Gischala. Further to the south, 'Lower Galilee' possessed fertile valleys, which separate lower altitude east–west mountain ranges. Important sites include the city of Sepphoris, and Nazareth, the town associated with Jesus' birth. The region surrounding the 'Sea of Galilee' was not only agriculturally fertile, but also symbiotically linked with the lake's fishing activity (Luke 5.1). Important towns included Capernaum, Magdala, and Tiberias. Products of the Galilee included barley, grapes, and olives (Josephus. *Jewish War* 3.35-44).

In 363 CE, the Roman Emperor Julian penned a treatise (now lost) entitled *Against the Galileans*, which outlined his plans to restore traditional Greco-Roman mores; it referred to Jesus as 'that new-fangled Galilean God'. Julian's work resonated with the Norwegian playwright Henrik Ibsen, who published *The Emperor and the Galilean* (1873). The plot revolved around the Emperor's defection from Christianity and paints his rule with a negative brush. English poet Algernon Swinburne wrote the *Hymn to Proserpine* (1866) as a lament over the demise of Greco-Roman religion. Well known is the opening line: 'Thou hast conquered, O Galilean'.

Recently, the Galilee has been employed in children's literature. Marjorie Holmes's *Two from Galilee* (1982) turns the story of Mary and Joseph into a modern day love story, with Christ's conception serving as the focal point. Annie Johnston's *Joel: A Boy of Galilee* (1992) presents Christ's infancy to a young audience and focuses on Jesus as the Messiah. In adult fiction, Clive Barker's *Galilee* (1998) relates the intrigue that surrounds the lives of two rival elite American families, the Gearys and the Barbarossas. Galilee is the name of the protagonist, a Barbarossa, who enters into a forbidden liaison with his rival's fiancée, Rachel.

In modern cinema, director Michel Khleiffi's *Wedding in Galilee* (1987) takes up the story of a young Palestinian couple whose nuptials must involve an Israeli official. Finally, restaurants like the 'Taste of Galilee' (Dallas, Texas) and 'Galilee Catering' (Toronto, Ontario) reflect the North American penchant for Mediterranean cuisine.

Recommended reading. Freyne, Sean. *Galilee from Alexander the Great to Hadrian, 323 BCE—135 CE: A Study of Second Temple Judaism.* Wilmington, DE: M. Glazier, 1980. Meyers, Eric M. (ed.). *Galilee through the Centuries: Confluence of Cultures.* Winona Lake, IN: Eisenbrauns, 1999. Reed, Jonathan L. *Archaeology and the Galilean Jesus: A Re-Examination of the Evidence.* Harrisburg, PA: Trinity International, 2000.

See also GALILEE, SEA OF; JESUS OF NAZARETH; INFANCY NARRATIVES [MiWH]

Galilee, Sea of. This lake is referred to in the OT as the Sea of Chinnereth (Num. 34.11; Deut. 3.17; Josh. 13.27; 'Chinneroth' in Josh. 11.2; 12.3). It is located in northern Israel and was referred to by NT times as the Galilee. The lake is approximately 21 kilometers long by 13 kilometers wide. Fed and drained by the Jordan River, the lake is part of a geographical phenomenon known as the Jordan Rift.

The lake and its environs figure prominently in the Gospels Matthew, Mark, Luke, and John as much of Jesus' ministry occurred in the region. For instance, on the banks of the Galilee at Kursi, Jesus exorcised demons and sent them into a herd of swine (Matt. 8.28-32). Some of his disciples were fishermen who made their living from the Galilee (Matt. 4.13-22). It was here that Jesus calmed a violent storm with a word (Matt. 8.24-26) and walked on water (Matt. 14.25-29).

Many artists through the centuries have depicted the events of Jesus' life in and around the Galilee. One of the favorites of painters is the call of the Galilean fishermen by Jesus. Others have covered the post-resurrection scene, with Jesus preparing a meal for the disciples on the lake's shore. Well-known works include Borrassa's fifteenth-century *St Peter Is Walking on the Water*, Tintoretto's sixteenth-century *Christ at the Sea of Galilee*, and probably the most elegant and readily recognizable is Rembrandt's seventeenth-century *Christ in the Storm on the Lake of Galilee*. Donatello's Mary Magdalene sculpture is a depiction of an exorcism by Jesus

(Mary's hometown, Migdal, was on the western shore of the lake, according to Luke 8.2).

Many songs depict scenes or use language from the biblical events linked to the Galilee. Country music legend Randy Travis used the walking on water event in the hit 'He Walked on Water' (referring to a great-grandfather, not Jesus). In an altogether different genre, Nicole Mullen recorded 'When I Call on Jesus' (2001) which employs the line, 'Oh, I have never walked on water, / And I have never calmed a storm'. Additionally, Dean Himes in a cross-genre composition recorded 'The Man from Galilee' in 2004. Fr. Frank Andersen's 'Galilee Song' has been a hit with many artists globally.

Western culture owes much more to the events surrounding the Sea of Galilee. The literary world would recognize Clive Barker who has added the title *Galilee*. The sea has influenced many filmmakers including Michel Khleifi's *Wedding in Galilee* (1987); Spielberg's Jewish Film Archive's *To the Galilee* (1937); and Alfred Newman's *Man of Galilee* film music collection. The mosaic of the loaves and fishes (another miracle by Jesus on the seashore) appears in the floor of The Church of the Multiplication at Tabgha and has lent itself to other works of art and humanitarian ministries using the name 'loaves and fishes'. Finally, one ministry targeting surfers is titled walkingonwater.org. Today, the lake is a source of drinking water, commercial fishing, and tourism for the State of Israel.

See also BETHSAIDA; GALILEE; JESUS OF NAZARETH, JORDAN RIVER [MBW]

Gamaliel. Six leading figures (or patriarchs) in Jewish history bear the name Gamaliel, which means 'reward of God'. The earliest biblical reference to a Gamaliel occurs in the Book of Numbers where he is described as 'the son of Pedahzur' and the leader of the tribe of Manasseh (Num. 2.20; cf. 1.10; 7.54; 10.23). Gamaliel II, who was born c. 50 CE is generally recognised for two things. Following the destruction of the Temple in 70, he was instrumental in bringing about unity within Judaism, especially between the rivalling Pharisaic schools of Hillel and Shammai. Gamaliel II is also said to have inserted a statement into the *Eighteen Benedictions* that served as an indictment against Christianity (cf. *Ber.* 28b; *Meg.* 17b), although this is debated. The final historical figure is Gamaliel VI, who by an imperial decree in 415 CE was denied his prestige and office as a patriarch because of assumed religious obstinacy. He died shortly thereafter, most likely before 426 CE, which was when another imperial decree required all patriarchal taxes to be given to the Empire.

The best known biblical figure is Gamaliel I (died c. 50 CE), also known as 'the Elder'. In Acts 5.34, Gamaliel I is described as 'a Pharisee' and 'a teacher of the Law', which finds conceptual support in the Jewish text *Abot.* 1.5. In this latter text, Gamaliel I is also called Rabban, usually translated as 'our Master', which was a title exclusively reserved for religious leaders of the highest order. (Only seven in Jewish history received this title). This reverence harmonises with the tradition that Gamaliel I was the first leader of the Great Sanhedrin in Jerusalem and that he served as such in an unparalleled fashion. Acts 5.34 suggests as much when it describes Gamaliel I as one 'respected by all the people'. Usually considered to be on the more liberal side of Pharisaic Judaism, stemming from the school of Hillel, Gamaliel I was influential in making several legal reforms in the Jewish world. For example, he placed stronger restrictions on certain divorce procedures (see *Git.* 4.2), relaxed the conditions for a woman's ability to remarry (see *Yebam.* 16.7), and extended the allowed distance one was permitted to travel on the Sabbath (see *Roš. Hoš.* 2.5).

Gamaliel I was also known for his high regard for moral purity and religious piety, both of which he saw as arising from a loyal devotion to the Torah; he also stressed the need for living out both in every day life. One later Jewish text notes that when Gamaliel died, reverent respect for 'the Torah ceased, and purity and piety became extinct' (*Sotah* 15.18). Pertinent to NT and Pauline studies are the references in Acts 5.33-39, where Gamaliel I is said to call for patient restraint in response to the activity of the apostles. According to Acts 22.3, Paul studied under the direct supervision of Gamaliel I. However, some scholars debate the legitimacy of both of these descriptions. Despite the claims found in *Ps-Clem.*, where Gamaliel I is said to be 'secretly our brother in the faith' (1.65), it is certain that he remained loyal to Judaism and did not become a follower of Jesus.

See also ACTS OF THE APOSTLES, THE; RABBI [CSS]

Garden of Eden. The story of humanity's blessed infancy and the subsequent estrangement from God is recounted in Gen. 2.4b–3.24. Genesis may contain fading memories of pre-agrarian foraging or alternately, of the world's first cities in Sumer, and perhaps even a veiled polemic against the imperial gardens of Babylon contemporary with the composition and editing of parts of the Pentateuch. Genesis 2.10-

14 gives what appears to be a geographical setting to the story, by naming two 'lands' and four rivers, only two of which—the Tigris and the Euphrates—can be identified with any certainty.

However specific or historical Eden may once have been, the story of the original, protected garden of bliss and delight into which humanity was placed became a powerful cultural and religious symbol. It operates as a term-of-reference in works as diverse as John Steinbeck's *East of Eden* (cf. Gen. 4.16), Gauguin's paintings of Tahitian women (and perhaps the whole of eighteenth-century Europe's preoccupation with 'the noble savage'), John Berendt's book (1994) and film (1997) *Midnight in the Garden of Good and Evil*, Hieronymous Bosch's *The Garden of Earthly Delights* (c. 1504), heavy metal band *Today is the Day*'s October 2007 release *Axis of Eden,* and, perhaps most monumentally in the English-speaking world, Milton's *Paradise Lost.*

In contemporary culture, the image of the garden lies behind such films as *The Milagro Beanfield War* or the spoiling of paradise themes of *King Kong* or *Jurassic Park*. In its most general sense, the longing of humanity to return to a time of innocence and bliss is amply recorded in the pastoral and primitivist movements in art, as well as in the writings of poets such as Wordsworth and William Blake (cf. *Jerusalem*).

Despite the clearly metaphorical nature of the Genesis passages ('Adam' for instance, is used both as a proper name and yet means 'the man' in the text), modern-day Eden hunters use ever-more-sophisticated tools of technology including satellite photography to search for a presumed original location of the Garden of Eden. Settings have been suggested virtually everywhere on the planet, ranging from Jackson Country Missouri, through the Anatolian highlands, to the equally meta-historical Atlantis.

Associated symbols include: the tree of life, the tree of the knowledge of good and evil, the river of life, paradise, the fig leaf, the serpent, the cool of the evening, the apple (identified only as a fruit in Genesis), and the expulsion. Within religious tradition, especially under the influence of Ezekiel, the Garden of Eden was contrasted with the wilderness (= time of testing) and became an apocalyptic cipher for the restoration and glorification of Israel and Mount Zion/the temple. In the NT, this image was broadened explicitly to include all humanity, and Rev. 21, while describing the heavenly 'city', specifically opens paradise's doors (banishing 'the angel') and rescinds the curses of Genesis. The Bible contains four primary garden images, in turn the Garden in Eden, Mount Zion as garden, the Garden of Gethsemane, where betrayal is replayed, and finally, the eschatological Garden of Paradise.

The terms Eden and 'garden of Eden' are often used to describe, and have become synonymous with, lush and cloistered spaces ranging from monastery gardens, to the national parks of Canada and the United States, to monumental public spaces such as Versailles and Frederick Law Olmsted's Central Park in New York City. Although technically not gardens, the evolution of fantasy theme-parks such as Disneyland and Disneyworld as places that children with terminal illnesses wish to see before they die, and where adults themselves are returned to a state of childhood naiveté and wonder, rely on the cultural currency of Eden.

The Garden of Eden symbolizes the innocent and beautiful finding pleasure in an unspoiled paradise. The irony within popular notions of paradise is that so many self-styled contemporary 'Edens' begin, rather than end, with the eviction of the original inhabitants.

See also GENESIS, BOOK OF; ADAM; EVE; SERPENT

[MRA]

Garden of Gethsemane. The Garden of Gethsemane has an important place in the life of Jesus of Nazareth. This garden, orchard or estate was located just outside the city of Jerusalem. It is believed to derive from the name 'oil press' suggesting that it might have been an olive orchard at the foot of the Mount of Olives, and it was there that Jesus Christ sought solace and where he was arrested prior to his trial and execution. It is in the garden that Judas kissed Jesus, and where Jesus was seized by guards of the high priest Caiaphas (Matt. 26.36-56; Mark 14.32-51; Luke 22.39-53).

As a result of its importance, the Garden of Gethsamane was visited by many early Christian pilgrims. The anonymous 'Pilgrim of Bordeaux' who went to the Holy Land in the 330s, managed to get to the Garden, as did Eusebius of Caesarea who noted that there were worshippers praying there regularly. The Church of the Agony, also known as the Church of All Nations, was built in the gardens probably in the fourth century, but it was damaged by the Sassanian Persians in 614, and what was left was destroyed in an earthquake in the 740s. A Crusader Church was later built on the site, but it was badly damaged in 1219, and abandoned in 1345. The area was surveyed by Sir Charles Warren from the British Royal Engineers in the late 1860s—he later became famous for his work as Commissioner of the Metropolitan Police in London where he led the investigations into the murders attributed to Jack the Ripper.

Tsar Alexander III (reigned 1881–1894), built the Church of St Mary Magdalene near the Garden of Gethsemane, and it remains one of the landmarks of the area. Part of the church was built on the grounds of the gardens. In 1924, the Church of All Nations was built by contributions from wealthy people from twelve countries. When the British writer H.V. Morton visited the garden in 1933 he found a peaceful place with the garden being tended to by Franciscan friars, the sound of the rake on the leaves occasionally reminding him of the whiplash of the scourging before the crucifixion. The garden remains open to the public from 8:30 until 11:30 am, and 2:30 to 4:00 pm each day.

There are many images of the Garden of Gethsemane. The Italian painter Andrea Mantegna (c. 1431–1506) in his *Agony in the Garden* (ca.1460) showing it as a rocky place with little in the way of olive trees. The garden is shown with a few more trees in *Gethsemane* by Pedro Berruguete (d. 1504). The stone carvings on the walls of Ulm Munster show the Garden of Gethsemane. The German painter Heinrich Hoffman's (1824–1911) *Christ in Gethsemane*, located in the Riverside Church in New York City, goes back to the Renaissance theme of a stony 'garden' devoid of trees.

Recommended reading. Armstrong, Karen. *A History of Jerusalem: One City, Three Faiths*. London: HarperCollins, 1996. Gray, John. *A History of Jerusalem*. London: Hale, 1969.

See also JESUS OF NAZARETH; MOUNT OF OLIVES
[JC]

Gehenna. The word is the Latin form of the Greek *geenna*, which is a transliteration of the Hebrew *Gey Hinnom* (the Hinnom Valley). The valley demarcated the territories of Judah and Benjamin (Josh. 15.8; 18.16) and later was said to lie outside the walls of Jerusalem (e.g., Jer. 19.2), most likely to the south. There is no ancient evidence to support the widely circulated view that the Hinnom Valley served as Jerusalem's garbage dump in the first century CE.

The prophet Jeremiah condemned the people of Judah for burning their sons and daughters for the gods Baal and Molech at the high place of Topheth in the Hinnom Valley (Jer. 7.31-32; 19.1-6; 32.35). Probably because of that association with abomination, fire, and death, Gehenna became a representative term within early Judaism, Christianity, and Islam for the place of fiery judgment in the afterlife. For example, 4 Ezra says that on the Day of Judgment, 'The pit of torment shall appear, and opposite it shall be the place of rest; and the furnace of hell (Latin *gehenna*) shall be disclosed, and opposite it the paradise of delight' (7.36).

In the NT, the Letter of James says, 'the tongue is a fire' that is 'set on fire by hell (Greek *geenna*)' (3.6). All other NT references to Gehenna occur in the Synoptic Gospels as judgment sayings by Jesus, among them: 'If your right eye causes you to sin, tear it out and throw it away; it is better for you to lose one of your members than for your whole body to be thrown into hell (Greek *geenna*)' (Matt. 5.29). In some instances Gehenna is juxtaposed with 'fire' (Matt. 18.9) and 'unquenchable fire' (Mark 9.43), and it is also called the place where God 'can destroy both body and soul' (Matt. 10.28). In early Judaism, the Mishnah tractate *Eduyyot* records Rabbi Akiba's view that judgment of the wicked in *Gey Hinnom* lasts twelve months, to which Rabbi Yohanan ben Nuri replies that judgment lasts only from Passover to Pentecost (*m. 'Ed.* 2.10). In Islam, the Arabic cognate *jahannam* occurs over 75 times in the Qur'an, usually denoting the eternal abode of unbelievers (e.g., 3.10).

There is one reference to Gehenna in John Milton's *Paradise Lost*: 'The pleasant valley of Hinnom, Tophet thence / And black Gehenna called, the type of hell' (1.404-405). At the end of Part I of 'William the Conqueror' (1899), Rudyard Kipling refers to famine-ridden southern India as 'the baked Gehenna of the South'. Madison Jones's allegorical coming of age romance is entitled *Passage Through Gehenna* (1978). In late 1989 'The Gehenna Stone Affair' was a story arc involving Baal and vampires in issues 11-16 of Marvel Comics' *Wolverine* series.

See also DAY OF JUDGMENT/OF THE LORD/OF WRATH; ESCHATOLOGY; HADES; HELL; MOLOCH, MOLECH; WRATH
[JWB]

Genealogy. Genealogies comprise the least understood and most flagrantly abused genre in the Bible. The function of genealogies in oral and other kinship based societies is never strictly about who begat who, unlike modern Western usages of genealogies. Rather, genealogies function to explain contemporary social and political structures, justifying the current social structures as authoritatively rooted in the past.

Establishment of order within kinship matters, as most people in these societies interact almost exclusively with kin members in their villages. Social hierarchies are created; marriage partners are defined by kinship, as one must satisfy that an individual is close enough in kin to marry, yet not close enough to meet a given society's definition of incest; trade relationships are defined; and military obligations are established, to name but a few functions.

One finds differing genealogies in the Bible, as any given genealogy can serve multiple purposes. For example, the genealogies of Jesus found in Matt. 1 and Luke 3 are markedly different, Matthew listing 14 generations from Abraham to David, and Luke listing 17. Neither are right or wrong. They are filling the specific needs of the author. Matthew, for instance, introduces the genealogy by calling Jesus the 'son of David, the son of Abraham' (1.1). This is clearly a shorthand, succinctly declaring his royal and pure Jewish (and for that matter, human) ancestry.

The genealogies of the tribes found in Gen. 49 and 1 Chron. 7 differ, as the circumstances of different kin groups change throughout the centuries. Thus, different ancestors are emphasized in the genealogies. Not every member of the descent groups are listed, but only the ones that are direct ancestors of the people in question in these differing historical circumstances.

Genealogies are also a way of understanding political and ethnic relationships. The ancient Israelites held that their geographic neighbors were related to them, although distinct from them thanks to diverging ancestors. For example, Moab and Ammon were also descendents from Terah, Abraham's father. However, their inferiority is sealed by their descent from Lot and his daughters. The table of nations genealogy found in Gen. 10 is an expression of political relationships, rather than biological ones. Cushites, Egyptians, Assyrians, Babylonians, Hittites, and Canaanites are all lumped together as descendents of Ham (although Asshur appears as a descendent of both Ham and Shem). These peoples have nothing biologically, ethnically, or linguistically in common. What they do share is that they have been politically overshadowed by Israel (according to the author of the table).

The genealogies of David and Jesus are remarkable, in that they share as ancestors a prostitute (Rahab) and a foreign widow (Ruth). Both males ultimately receive their authority from God, despite these comparative ancestral shortcomings. This stands in contrast to the genealogical purge under Ezra and Nehemiah in the wake of the Assyrian resettlement of what had been the northern kingdom of Israel, and the Babylonian Exile and return, in which Jewishness could only be granted in the cases of undisputed Jewish ancestry in both lines (Ezra 10.6-44; Neh. 13.3, 23-31).

Given that genealogies do not exist in societies to list systematically every descendent or even every generation, efforts such as those of Bishop Ussher to use genealogies as dating tools are attempting to make the genealogies do something they were never intended to do. Thus, the earth could not possibly have been created in 4004 BCE on an August morning.

Recommended reading. Johnson, M.D. *The Purpose of the Biblical Genealogies*. 2nd edn. Cambridge: Cambridge University Press, 1988. Wilson, R.R. *Genealogy and History in the Biblical World*. New Haven: Yale University Press, 1977.

See also EZRA, BOOK OF; NEHEMIAH, BOOK OF; MATTHEW, GOSPEL OF; LUKE, GOSPEL OF [MAP]

Generation. The term 'generation' in the HB and NT can refer to several things, including: (1) a grouping of people born approximately the same time (e.g., Gen. 50.23; Matt. 24.34; Acts 13.36); (2) a length of time between two individuals (Matt. 1.17); (3) a passage of time during which knowledge of the Lord and his deeds is passed along (Judg. 2.10; Ps. 71.18; 78.4, 6; 102.18; 145.4); and a way of indicating God's patient endurance over time (Dan. 4.34; Lam. 5.19; Ps. 33.11; 79.13; 89.1; 90.1; 135.13; 145.13).

How many years are to be assumed for one generation, that is, from the birth of the father to the birth of the son? Some scholars count 30 years per generation, others 27.5 or 25, but most scholars calculate 20 years per generation. In the nineteenth century, A. Kamphausen claimed that the average duration of one generation is 23 years. He based this on the accounts of the reigns of Israelite kings as they are related in the Book of Kings. Indeed, the information about the duration of the Babylonian exile as expressed in Jeremiah supports a time of approximately 23–24 years per generation. Jeremiah 27.6-7 states, 'Now I have given all these lands into the hand of Nebuchadnezzar, the king of Babylon .... All the nations shall serve him and his son and his grandson, until the time of his own land comes'. According to this text, Jeremiah counts three generations for the time of the Babylonian exile. Elsewhere, he gives the absolute number of 70 years for the same period: 'and these nations shall serve the king of Babylon 70 years. Then after 70 years are completed, I will punish the king of Babylon and that nation, the Chaldeans, for their iniquity, says the Lord' (Jer. 25.11-12; cf. 29.10). Jeremiah's words, however, cannot be viewed, historically, as absolutely correct, for Nebuchadnezzar II was followed by his son, Awil-Marduk. A revolt broke out after him, and Nergal-šar-uṣur, Labaši-Marduk and Nabonidus reigned successively. Only at some point in the reign of Nabonidus, Babylon was ruled by the Persian emperor Cyrus II (539 BCE). In addition, the number seventy might better be understood typologically, such as, for example, 'seventy years' (Zech. 1.12; 7.5), 'seventy days' (Gen. 50.3), 'seventy descendants' (Exod. 1.5; Deut. 10.22), 'seventy sons' (Judg. 8.30; 9.2.5), rather than literally. Indeed, it is barely fifty years from the destruction of the Kingdom of Judah (587/6 BCE) to the beginning of the return from the Babylonian exile (538 BCE). Similarly, 'seventy years' was the time that the city of Babylon should stay in its ruin (since its destruction by Sennacherib), as it was written down by Marduk in the Book of Fate. However, 'the merciful Marduk—his anger lasted but a moment—turned it [the book] upside down ordered its (the city's) restoration in the eleventh year'. Nevertheless, this does not impair the literary parallel, nor is the common biblical understanding of the duration of one generation affected by it.

The concept of generation remains familiar in the modern world, obviously in the context of families but also in societies more broadly (e.g., Baby Boom Generation, Generations X, Y, Z) and cultural phenomena (e.g., The Beat Generation).

Recommended reading. Kalimi, I. *An Ancient Israelite Historian*. Studia Semitica Neerlandica 46. Assen: Van Gorcum, 2005.

See also GENEALOGY [IK]

Genesis, Book of. Genesis is the first book to appear in the canons of Jewish and Christian Scripture and opens the Pentateuch and Torah. Genesis is the Greek word meaning 'origin'. The Hebrew name for this book is *bereshit* meaning 'in a beginning', and is taken from the first word in the narrative. It is written mostly in narrative form and consists of two distinction sections. The first section is the prologue which deals with the creation and flood myths and focuses on the entire human race. Some of the most popular biblical stories are found in this section, such as the seven days of creation, Adam and Eve, Cain and Abel, the flood, and the Tower of Babel.

In chapter 12, the founding family narratives begin and the focus narrows to one family that will eventually grow into the nation of Israel. The founding family narratives exist in three cycles: the Abraham–Sarah cycle, the Rebekah–Isaac cycle, and the Jacob–Leah–Rachel cycle. These stories trace God's threefold promise of land, seed, and blessing through the earliest stages of Israel's history.

The narratives of the prologue have had a long cultural history. The first creation narrative provided a staging ground for the battle between science and religion. Creationists take the description of the seven days of creation literally and then based on the timeline provided in the rest of the book come to a young earth theory. The debate between this group and evolutionists, who believe in an extended process of origin and an old earth, came to a head with the Scopes Monkey trial in 1925. This is not the only area in which the creation myths have played a role in western culture. Often they have been used as examples of supposed natural order. Gender and sexual relations have been modeled on interpretations of the second creation narrative. This book, and particularly the prologue, has been used in the debates surrounding gay-marriage and the roles of women, particularly in Papal encyclicals, such as the 2004 *Letter to the Bishops on the Collaboration of Men and Women in the Church and in the World*.

In the art world many of the narratives of Genesis have been imagined by artists throughout the ages. The most famous depictions are those painted by Michelangelo on the ceiling of the Sistine Chapel. His *Creation of Adam*, panel four of the Genesis series, is perhaps the most famous with a popular culture legacy of its own, including the inspiration of ET's most famous gesture. Genesis also provided much inspiration for Rembrandt.

The stories of Genesis have also been used throughout literary history. Perhaps the most famous example is John Milton's *Paradise Lost*, an epic blank verse poem that traces the biblical stories of origin. Certain stories have also provided inspiration to J.R.R. Tolkien's *Two Towers* and Ernest Hemingway's *The Sun also Rises*.

Reggae artist Bob Marley used Genesis as the basis for several of his songs, including 'We and

Dem' and 'Adam and Eve'. Bob Dylan borrowed ideas from Genesis for 'Man Gave Names to All the Animals' and 'Highway 61 Revisited'. Other artists that based material on Genesis include Ice Cube ('When I Get to Heaven'), Garth Brooks ('Against the Grain'), Leonard Cohen ('Story of Isaac'), the Grateful Dead ('My Brother Esau'), and Dolly Parton ('Coat of Many Colors').

Recommended reading. Alter, Robert. *Genesis: Translation and Commentary*. New York: W.W. Norton, 1996. Phipps, William E. *Genesis and Gender: Biblical Myths of Sexuality and their Cultural Impact*. New York: Praeger, 1989.

See also CREATION; GARDEN OF EDEN; FLOOD; NOAH; TOWER OF BABEL; ABRAHAM; SARAH; REBEKAH; ISAAC; JACOB; LEAH; RACHEL; JOSEPH [EW]

Gentiles. The term is a common translation for the Hebrew *gôyîm* and *'ammîm*, and the Greek *ethnē*. In English translations interpretive decisions have to be made as whether or not to translate these words as 'people(s)', 'nations', or 'Gentiles'. Whenever these words are used in contexts that seem to be speaking about those who are not Israelite or Jewish ethnically, they are usually translated as 'Gentiles'. This term can be used to simply refer to non-Israelites or non-Jews but it can also have more specialized connotations as well. It can refer to God or Israel's enemies, as in Num. 24.8 and Deut. 7.1, who are often portrayed very negatively, as in Ps. 9.6. At other times in the HB, this term is placed in eschatological contexts—the nations are seen as an inheritance of Israel (Ps. 2.8) and at the end the nations will pour into Jerusalem to worship God (Jer. 3.17; Mic. 4.2). The Israelites are called to be 'a light to the nations' (Isa. 42.6). In the NT, 'Gentiles' has a similar range of meanings. One specialized usage is that Paul believes that he is called by God to bring the gospel to the Gentiles (Gal. 1.16; Rom. 15.16), which he sees as a fulfillment of God's plan (Rom. 15.8-12). This mission caused a major conflict in the early church, which revolved around the circumcision of Gentiles who had faith in Jesus (Acts 15; Gal. 2). Paul's understanding of the situation (that Gentiles should be included as they are) won the day, though tension would remain between Jewish and Gentile Christians for generations to come.

For the most part these same levels of meaning continued through the first generations of Christians, though at times they seem to have believed themselves to be a third category of people, distinct from Jews and Gentiles or pagans. Over time, people who were ethnically Jewish made up a smaller and smaller percentage of Christians until the Church was largely Gentile ethnically, as it is still true today, though there have always been enclaves of Jewish Christians. Some religious groups, such as the Latter-Day Saints (Mormons), have begun to use 'Gentiles' to refer to people outside of their faith and some Jehovah's Witnesses talk about an epoch in history, called 'Gentile time', in which God's favor left the Jewish people and rested only on Gentiles.

Often times the differences between Jews and Gentiles, such as circumcision, holidays, language, history, and diet, are highlighted in comedies and dramas on TV, in movies, on the stage, and in songs. One example is on the television show *Curb Your Enthusiasm* where the character Larry David, who believes himself to be Jewish, discovers that his birthparents were both Christians. He responds by saying, 'Oh, my God. *I'm* gentile'. Another example is from comedian/musician Weird Al Yancovich's song 'The Night Santa Went Crazy' from the album *Bad Hair Day*. The song opens as follows: 'Down in the workshop all the elves were makin' toys / For the good gentile girls and the good gentile boys'.

See also CIRCUMCISION; ESCHATOLOGY; JEW, JUDAISM [JMB]

Gentle as a nurse. This description is found in 1 Thess. 2.7 (cf. 1 Cor. 3.2). From the Hebrew *'ōmeneth*, *yānaq*, or *mēneqeth* and Greek, *trophos*, 'nurse' denotes a woman nursing her own (Gen. 21.7) or another's child (Ruth 4.16; 2 Sam. 4.4) and symbolizes the messianic era in Jerusalem (Isa. 66.11-13). In 1 Thessalonians, likely the oldest document in the NT, Paul describes his apostleship employing metaphors and kinship language. In addition to 'brothers and sisters' (2.1, 9, 14, 17a), 'father' (2.11), and 'orphan' (2.17b), in 1 Thess. 2.7 Paul taps on the socio-cultural richness of being a 'gentle nurse tenderly caring for her own children'.

Paul's use of this metaphor is doubly striking. First, as a man, he uses a feminine metaphor to describe his ministry to the Thessalonians. By doing so, Paul parallels Moses's self-identification in Num. 11.12. However, Paul uses the metaphor positively whereas Moses employs it negatively as he complains against the Israelites. Second, from the socio-cultural context of Thessalonica and of early Greek literature, a nurse evokes images of one who nurtures, who cares for infants or young children, an attendant to a young woman, and one who remains in the affection of young men even when they have grown up. Paul, in 1 Thess. 2.7, evokes these images as he explicitly claims to be the Thessalonian Christians' nurse and implies being their mother. In defending his own work among them against other preachers, Paul underscores the way he worked with them: being a *gentle* nurse *tenderly* caring for his *own children*. Paul wants to keep the community from following the other preachers and reminds them how they belong to the apostle who has given himself to them (v. 8). We find an example of Pauline maternal imagery in 1 Thess. 2.7 that refers to the ongoing nature of his relationship with his communities. This is reflected in a prayer by Anselm of Canterbury (1033–1109 CE) who calls Paul 'Sweet nurse, sweet mother'.

The image of Paul in 1 Thess. 2.7 is not widely popular in artistic images. However, the nursing or breastfeeding figure behind it is a significant motif. A number of pre-Reformation *Virgo Lactans* paintings show Mary breastfeeding Jesus (for example, Leonardo da Vinci, c. 1490). The decline during the Reformation was due to controversies about the 'carnality' of the images. In 2008, the Vatican encouraged the retrieval of these images to underscore the Mystery of the Incarnation.

Non-biblical images of nursing women are found in artworks like Jacopo Tintoretto's *Origin of the Milky Way* (c. 1575), Morisot's *The Wet Nurse* (c. 1880), and Renoir's *Aline allaitant son fils* (c. 1888), to name but a few. In literature, the nurse features in Shakespeare's 1590's classic *Romeo and Juliet*, William Blake's 'Nurse's Song', and Erica Eisdorfer' *The Wet Nurse's Tale* (2009).

Recommended reading. Collins, Raymond F. *The Power of Images in Paul*. Collegeville, MN: Liturgical Press, 2008. Gaventa, Beverly Roberts. *Our Mother Saint Paul*. Louisville, KY: Westminster John Knox, 2007.

See also PAUL, THE APOSTLE; THESSALONIANS, EPISTLE TO THE [MALOUSI]

Gershom. Gershom was the name of the first-born son of Moses and Zipporah (Exod. 2.22). Moses took Zipporah and Gershom with him when he returned to Egypt, sending them to live with Jethro, Zipporah's father.

See also MOSES; ZIPPORAH [JC]

Get thee behind me, Satan!. 'Get thee behind me, Satan' is the popularly retained KJV translation of the words of Jesus to the disciple Peter (Matt. 16.23; Mark 8.33). In the Gospel narratives, these words are precipitated by Peter's rebuking of Jesus for telling the disciples that the Son of Man must suffer and die (Matt. 16.21-22; Mark 8.31-32). In the Gospel of Mark, Jesus responds, 'Get behind me, Satan! For you are setting your mind not on divine things but on human things'. Matthew's version sheds extra light on the story. After the initial reference to Satan, Jesus also says, 'you are a stumbling block to me', intimating that Peter's rejection of Jesus' prediction of suffering was something of a fourth temptation (cf. Matt. 4.1-11). Jesus was tempted by Satan's efforts to thwart his ministry but ultimately rebuked the devil and withstood the temptation. In the Gospels, these harsh words of Jesus also reveal a certain level of ignorance on the part of the disciples concerning the true nature of Jesus' messiahship. Whereas Peter's expectation of Jesus' vocation seems to have had strong political connotations, Jesus understood himself to be Israel's messiah who was destined to suffer and die for her sake, and he therefore rejects Peter's admonishment since he was focusing only on 'human things'.

Jesus' expression has become a shorthand means of rebuking one for their evil intentions. Such uses can be found in works of literature including Sir Walter Scott's *Ivanhoe* (1819) and James Joyce's *Dubliners* (1914). John Milton's *Paradise Regained* (1671) contains a more direct allusion to the phrase: 'Get thee behind me: plain thou now appear'st / That Evil one, Satan for ever damn'd'. The phrase has been popularly adopted and appropriated in music as well. For instance, the American lyricist Irving Berlin penned the song, 'Get Thee Behind me Satan' for the 1936 film, *Follow the Fleet*. More recently, the American alternative rock band The White Stripes entitled their 2005 album, *Get Behind Me Satan*. In an anagrammatic play on Jesus' rebuke, American indie-rock artist Sufjan Stevens entitled a track in his five-volume Christmas album, *Songs for Christmas* (2006), 'Get behind me Santa', a song which mocks the commercial nature of the Christmas season in Western culture. From Milton to Joyce to The White Stripes, the words of Jesus' harsh rebuking of Peter have remained familiar. And though the archaic KJV of the Bible is perhaps the most memorable rendering of Jesus' words, allusions to this phrase show a certain level of pliability in their appropriation of it.

Recommended reading. Stoutenburg, Dennis C. "Out of my Sight!', 'Get Behind Me!', or 'Follow After

Me!': There Is No Choice in God's Kingdom'. *Journal of the Evangelical Theological Society* 36 (1993) 173-78.

See also SATAN; PETER, THE APOSTLE; TEMPTATIONS OF JESUS [DRB]

Giants (Nephilim). The Bible claims that races of giants originally inhabited the lands of Israel's immediate enemies: '*Anaqim* in Canaan, *Repha'im* in Bashan, *Zamzummim* in Ammon, *'Emim* in Moab, *Horim* in Edom, and '*Avvim* in Philistia. The term *repha'im* (perhaps meaning 'healers', 'saviors' or 'great ones') is also used generically to denote all of these ancient giants (Deut. 2.11, 20; cf. 2 Sam. 21.16-22), or alternatively, to denote the dead, in particular, deceased warrior-kings (Isa. 14.9). In addition, the term *gibborim* is sometimes employed to refer to giants (Gen. 6.4; cf. 1 Sam. 17.51), although *gibborim* can merely mean 'men' or 'heroes' (2 Sam. 23.8).

Gen. 6.4 recounts the story of sexual intercourse between 'sons of god' ('angels', 'divine beings' or 'potentates') and 'daughters of men' (human women), which produces hybrid offspring called *Nephilim* (perhaps meaning 'fallen ones'). Although these *Nephilim* seem to be destroyed by the flood, *Nephilim* feature in one later narrative, where their gigantic size makes the Israelites appear like grasshoppers (Num. 13.33). The KJV, following the Septuagint, thus translates *Nephilim* as 'giants' in an oft-quoted translation of Gen. 6.4: 'There were giants in the earth in those days'. The stories about these giants are developed in greater detail in early Jewish works such as *1 Enoch* and the *Book of Giants*.

Based on biblical and classical stories about giants, 'gigantologists' since antiquity have attempted to adduce the reality of giants from large skeletal remains (usually of mastodons and whales) and ancient monolithic architecture. In *Genealogy of the Gods* (1472), Boccaccio tells of a 300-foot-high skeleton of a giant man, discovered in Trapani, Sicily. Most of the cathedrals of Europe once displayed skeletons purportedly belonging to biblical giants. The widespread belief in giants was slow to recede. Although Cervantes portrays Don Quixote's belief in giants as comical in 1605, as late as 1878 the *Encyclopedia Britannica's* 'Giants' entry carefully weighs arguments for and against their historicity—only cautiously concluding their non-existence. Contemporary creationists continue to interpret fossilized remains as those of giants, such as the dinosaur footprints at Paluxy Creek, Texas. Theosophy and many UFO religions also interpret the *Nephilim* as ancient historical beings.

Giants typically represent the uncultured, barbaric, and irreligious enemy of Israel or Christendom. Augustine, quoting Bar. 3.26-28, claims giants perished because they lacked knowledge and wisdom (*City of God* 15.23). In John Milton's *Samson Agonistes* (1671), the giant Harapha (meaning 'the giant' in 2 Sam. 21.18) is a haughty Canaanite, a 'vain boaster', who is contemptuous of Samson's God. In *Beowulf*, the cannibalistic giant Grendel is referred to as 'Cain's kin'. The connection of giants with Cain stems from Augustine's tendentious yet influential interpretation of the 'sons of God' in Gen. 6.4 as 'the sons of Seth' who marry Cain's descendants (*City of God* 15.23-24). In Dante's *Inferno* (c. 1310), the giants appear as towers around the pit of lower hell, and the giant Nimrod is the exemplar of defeated pride. Based on the biblical notion that giants had to be destroyed before human settlement, many medieval towns paraded effigies of 'town giants' they claimed their ancestors had conquered. The town giants frequently received biblical names such as Gogmagog (London) or Goliath (Ath, Nieuport, and Troyes).

Recommended reading. Auffarth, Christoph, and Loren T. Stuckenbruck (eds.). *The Fall of the Angels*. Leiden and Boston: Brill, 2004. Rouillard, H. 'Rephaim'. In *Dictionary of Deities and Demons in the Bible*. Ed. Karel van der Toorn, *et al.* Pp. 692-700. 2nd edn. Leiden: Brill, 1999. Stephens, Walter. *Giants in Those Days*. Lincoln and London: University of Nebraska Press, 1989.

See also GOLIATH; OG OF BASHAN [DG]

Gibeonites. The Gibeonites are a group of people that interacted with the Israelites as they moved out of Egypt. The story of their deception of the Israelites is found in Josh. 9–10. In this passage, they are cursed to be always cutters of wood and drawers of water for the Israelites. As the result of the treaty between Gibeon and Israel, the Gibeonites integrated with the tribe of Benjamin. The Gibeonites reappear in 2 Sam. 21 as a people abused by Saul and later, as aiding in the rebuilding of Jerusalem and the temple (Neh. 3.7; 7.25). Gibeonites are also mentioned in genealogies in 1 Chron. 8–9.

The Gibeonites were part of a group of people known as Hivites, who lived in the land of Canaan. They inhabited the cities of Gibeon, Chephirah, Beeroth and Kiriath-jearim. Gibeon, Chephirah, and Beeroth were located within the inheritance of the tribe of Benjamin. Kiriath-jearim was listed within the inheritance of both Benjamin and Judah as it was on their border, and Gibeon itself is often identified with El-Jib, which is about 10 kilometres north of Jerusalem.

Recommended reading. Blenkinsopp, Joseph. *Gibeon and Israel: The Role of Gibeon and the Gibeonites in the Political and Religious History of Early Israel*. Society for Old Testament Monograph Series, 2. London: Cambridge University Press, 1972.

See also EXODUS, THE; SAUL, KING [J-AS]

Gideon. Gideon (Hebrew *gid'on*), or Jerubbaal (Hebrew *yerubba'al* cf. Judg. 9; 1 Sam. 12.11) was an Israelite military leader in the period of the Judges (see Judg. 6–8) who freed the Israelites from Midianite oppression. Despite receiving repeated assurances of his success, Gideon struggled to follow God's calling, testing God by laying out a wool fleece and asking that it be wet while the ground around it remain dry, and then requesting the reverse the following night (Judg. 6.36-40).

In preparation for the battle against the Midianites, Gideon was told to scale back the 32,000 men he had mustered to a mere three hundred, thereby placing the focus of the eventual victory on the LORD, the divine warrior who would fight on Israel's behalf. Gideon then overheard enemy soldiers relate a dream, a common ancient Near Eastern omen indicating future divine action, describing their impending destruction at Gideon's hand (Judg. 7.13-15). This gave Gideon the assurance he needed to lead a nocturnal attack that utilized trumpet blasts, the smashing of pots, and the lighting of torches to throw the Midianite camp into confusion.

After the victory, Israel offered Gideon the position of king (Judg. 8.22-23) but he refused, saying God was their king. In subsequent narrative (Judg. 8.24-32), however, he acts much like a king. He sets up an ephod (a type of priestly garment, possibly covering a statue-like idol) as part of an idolatrous worship installation (1 Kgs 12.26-32), marries multiple wives and a concubine (cf. 1 Kgs 11.3), and fathers seventy sons including Abimelech (which means 'my father is king'; cf. Judg. 9). Gideon's actions lead Israel astray (8.27) and further the 'canaanization' of Israel in the period of the Judges.

The story of Gideon is among the most widely interpreted texts in the Book of Judges and evokes mixed responses. The NT book of Hebrews (11.32) lists Gideon among the models of faith. Milton's *Paradise Regained* (1671) also praises Gideon as an example of virtue, valor, and wisdom, and in Bunyan's allegory *Pilgrim's Progress* (1678), when Christian reaches The House Beautiful, he sees Gideon's pots, trumpets, and torches—tools used to accomplish wonderful things.

Early Jewish interpreters such as Rashi (1040–1105) saw Gideon as well intentioned, but leading Israel astray through his idolatrous ephod, and the Reformer John Calvin (1509–1564) saw Gideon's repeated doubts as a warning that every saint has flaws. This mixed evaluation of Gideon has continued into the modern era.

The Broadway play *Gideon* (1961) by Paddy Chayefsky is a whimsical portrait of a man who hesitates to trust God despite witnessing several miracles. By contrast, the 2006 Veggie Tales children's video *Gideon: Tuba Warrior* omits the largely negative portrait of Gideon in Judg. 8, depicting Gideon as a hero of hesitant faith. Some evangelical Christians see the story of Gideon's fleece as a model for determining the will of God, illustrating God's willingness to provide tangible signs. The Gideons International is an association of Christian businesspersons whose mandate is to introduce people to God through the distribution of Bibles in places like hotel rooms and schools, taking their inspiration from Gideon's humility and obedience.

Recommended reading. Bluedorn, Wolfgang. *Yahweh versus Baalism: A Theological Reading of the Gideon–Abimelech Narrative*. JSOTSup, 329. Sheffield: Sheffield Academic Press, 2001. Block, Daniel I. 'Will the Real Gideon Please Stand Up? Narrative Style and Intention in Judges 6–9'. *Journal of the Evangelical Theological Society* 40 (1997) 353-66.

See also JUDGES, BOOK OF; MIDIAN; EPHOD; FLEECE, SETTING OUT [GO]

Gird up your loins. The English idiom 'Gird up your loins' translates several Hebrew phrases that convey readiness for action, both metaphorical and tangible. Perhaps the best known is a Hebrew imperative translated literally, 'gird up your loins like a man', which appears in Job 38.3 and 40.7. In the story, the righteous man Job has endured much suffering and loss and repeatedly seeks an explanation for his misfortune. Near the work's conclusion, God responds to Job from the midst of a tempest saying, 'Who is this that darkens council with words lacking knowledge. Gird your loins like a man; I will question you, and you will answer me.'

The physical action behind the phrase 'girding one's loins' involves wrapping up one's traditionally long garment into a belt to be ready for running, battle, and so on. In 1 Kgs 18.46, the prophet Elijah 'girded up his loins' to run ahead of King Ahab's chariot all the way to the ancient town Jezreel. In 2 Kgs 4.29, the prophet Elisha commands his servant Gehazi to 'gird up [his] loins', take the prophet's staff, and go directly to the house of a woman who had lost her child to raise the child from the dead.

Similar to Job, the Epicurean poet Titus Lucretius Carus (d. c. 50 BCE) challenges those reading his treatise to weigh his arguments, and if Lucretius is correct, admit their own defeat, but if they consider him incorrect, to gird up your loins to fight (*On the Nature of Things*, Book II). In the NT, the expression is metaphorical, though the challenge is not only for readiness but also fortitude (Luke 12.35; 1 Pet. 1.13).

Later authors echo the senses of fortitude, readiness, and challenge. In *Civil Disobedience*, nineteenth-century poet and author Henry David Thoreau writes near the end of the essay, 'They who know of no purer sources of truth, who have traced up its stream no higher, stand, and wisely stand, by the Bible and the Constitution, and drink at it there with reverence and humility; but they who behold where it comes trickling into this lake or that pool, gird up their loins once more, and continue their pilgrimage toward its fountain-head.' English author Samuel Butler utilized the idiom in his posthumously published novel *The Way of All Flesh*. In chapter 49, the Evangelical preacher Mr. Hawke exhorts a gathering of young men at Cambridge, 'Oh! my young friends, turn, turn, turn, now while it is called to-day … stay not even to gird up your loins; look not behind you for a second, but fly into the bosom of that Christ who is to be found of all who seek him.' Finally, Robert W. Service, sometimes called the 'Bard of the Yukon', relates in verse how the old miner Jock MacPherson was sought to play the bagpipes at a local ball. Before taking the floor, he is pressed by the treasurer to "Drink down your *doch and doris*, Jock', cried Treasurer MacCall; 'The time is ripe to up and pipe; they wait you in the hall. Gird up your loins and grit your teeth … Play on and on for all you're worth; you'll shame us if you stop. Remember you're of Scottish birth—keep piping till you drop" ('The Ballad of How MacPherson held the Floor').

See also JOB, BOOK OF [CLH]

Glass, mirror. The ancient Egyptians used polished copper for mirrors that exhibited a high lustre but offered only poor quality reflection. Over time, the metal rusted as well. Some scholars suggest that Hebrew women took mirrors from Egypt while escaping into Canaan. Later, during NT times, the Romans began to make mirrors from glass, but their reflection was cloudy. Hence, mirrors from ancient times, though useful, yielded distorted images.

This topic is of interest to readers of the Bible because of various symbolic and metaphoric uses of glass and mirrors. For instance, when Job endures catastrophic misfortune and bemoans his state, Elihu reminds him that God is all-powerful and asks Job a rhetorical question: 'Can you, like him, spread out the skies, hard as a molten mirror?' (Job 37.18). The question compels Job to realize his dependence on God. In the NT, Paul the apostle anticipates the wonders of the coming kingdom, describing it in these terms: 'now we see in a mirror, dimly, but then we will see face to face. Now I know only in part; then I will know fully, even as I have been fully known' (1 Cor. 13.12). He explains to the recipients of this letter that following God requires a maturation process. The cloudy mirror, through which Paul looks for truth, reflects an incomplete or dim revelation of something he will see clearly in God's presence. James writes of one who hypothetically looks into a mirror, discerns his poor condition, and chooses to walk away without making necessary changes to his life (Jas 1.23).

This kind of symbolic use of mirrors and glass is familiar in Western cultures. In Greek mythology, Medusa sees her harsh reflection in Perseus's mirror-like shield and, unable to bear it, dies. The Greek Narcissus, condemned to regard his beautiful reflection in a pool for being cruel to others, does not realize he needs to change. Much later in Alfred, Lord Tennyson's poem 'Lady of Shallot', the protagonist, cursed to remain in a tower and see the world through a mirror's dissatisfying reflection, dies because she chooses to leave. In a popular Disney version of *Snow White*, the evil queen uses a mirror to divine truth, but she rejects it and later dies in the story. In Michael Jackson's song 'Man in the Mirror', the singer asks the one staring back at him to 'change his ways'.

See also EYE [GM]

Glory. Central for biblical passages and themes, glory describes magnificence and beauty both in people (1 Chron. 29.28) and things (Ezek. 31.18) as well as worthiness of respect or reverence (Mal. 1.6). Whatever is glorious has honor and significance. In the Bible, glory often characterizes God's presence. He is the creator who fills the earth with his glory (Isa. 6.3; 40.1-8). Although humanity distorted its creaturely glory through sin, God is the redeemer that made his glory known through mercy (Rom. 9.22-23). After Israel broke their covenant with God at Mount Sinai, Moses begged for God's presence to stay with them. When God agreed, Moses asked for reassurance, requesting to see his glory and in response, God's glory passed in front of him with such magnificence that its brilliance had to be veiled from Moses (Exod. 33.12–34.8). Despite Israel's continued attraction to idols, the prophets anticipated a day when the earth will be filled with the knowledge of the glory of the LORD, as the waters cover the sea (Hab. 2.14). Then Israel would declare his glory among the nations (Isa. 66.19) and the nations would tremble at his glory (Isa. 40.5; 59.19).

According to NT authors, Jesus reveals God's glory on earth (John 1.14-18; Heb. 1.3). After his life, death, and resurrection, he is 'crowned with glory and honor' (Heb. 2.9; Rev. 5.12-13), and he is proclaimed in 'the gospel of the glory of Christ' (2 Cor. 4.4). Through his sacrifice, Christ brings 'many children to glory' (Heb. 2.10). Although hindered in this life through suffering and difficulty, believers begin the transformation into the glory of the Son. When Christ returns in his glory (Luke 9.26), believers will finally 'appear with him in glory' (Col. 3.4; Rom. 8.18). Forever in the New Jerusalem, the nations will walk in the light of God's glory (Rev. 21.22-27).

Among contemporary uses, the term glory often associates with military honors, as in the American Civil War era 'Battle Hymn of the Republic' (1861). Inspired by the Battle of Balaclava during the Crimean War, Alfred, Lord Tennyson wrote an influential narrative poem, 'The Charge of the Light Brigade': 'When can their glory fade? / O the wild charge they made! / All the world wonder'd. / Honour the charge they made! / Honour the Light Brigade, / Noble six hundred!' (1854).

See also WORSHIP; GOD; HOLY, HOLINESS [SP]

Gnostic, Gnosticism. The gnostic tradition is a belief system that maintains divine souls are trapped by an imperfect God in a material world. In the second and third centuries CE it became popular in the Eastern Mediterranean where it became associated with the concept of dualism. This went against Christian teaching and literature deemed gnostic was often destroyed. Some who held such beliefs remained into later periods, including the Bogomils and later the Cathars, who were ruthlessly suppressed, the latter in the Albigensian Crusade.

In the nineteenth and twentieth centuries, philosophers highlighted the gnostic traditions which have increased in popularity. There are many books which feature the Cathars, the most famous being Zoe Oldenburg's account of the destruction of the Cathars in *Massacre at Montségur: A History of the Albigensian Crusade* (1961), and Stephen O'Shea's *The Perfect Heresy: The Life and Death of the Cathars* (2000). They also feature in the story of *The Holy Blood and the Holy Grail*, by Michael Baigent, Richard Leigh and Henry Lincoln, published in London in 1982. This work was a major source for the information for Dan Brown's *The Da Vinci Code* (2003). Most of the novels exploring these subjects, such as Sophy Burnham's *The Treasure of Montségur* (2002), portray the Cathars as the people greatly wronged in the Albigensian Crusade, as fundamentally good people who are persecuted by the French who were anxious to seize the Cathars' wealth. However a different view appears of dualists, in this case the Bogomils whose ideas originated in the region around what is now Albania. One of them appears in Edward Marston's novel *The Serpents of Harbledown* (1996) about a Bogomil who is involved in murders in the eastern English city of Canterbury.

Certainly the scholarship exploring gnosticism is not new but the discovery of ancient gnostic books at Nag Hammadi in Egypt in 1945, dating back to as early as the second century, has renewed academic interest in the subject. These writings are particularly valuable for understanding better the NT and early Christian history.

Recommended reading. Layton, Bentley. *The Gnostic Scriptures*. London: SCM Press, 1987. Newman, Sharan. *The Real Story behind the Da Vinci Code*. London: Penguin Books, 2004. Pagels, Elaine. *The Gnostic Gospels*. New York: Random House, 1979. Rudolph, Kurt. *Gnosis: The Nature and Structure of Gnosticism*. London: Harper & Row, 1987.

See also NAG HAMMADI [JC]

God. God talk was controversial in ancient Israel where the interaction of writers led to a literary tradition and the growth of culture in the Mediterranean. The debate was over God as human or transcendent. In the earliest epic Yahweh forms man by hand and walks in the garden (Gen. 2.7-8; 3.8). In the updated version, God is outside the cosmos and creates by the word (Gen. 1). The epic narrative depicts Yahweh descending on Mount Sinai 'before the eyes of all the people' (Exod. 19.11, 20), but in priestly writing the people see only the appearance of Yahweh's glory (Exod. 24.16-17). Another author insists that the people never saw God but only heard his voice (Exod. 19.21-24; 20.18-22). Hosea portrayed God as a 'man' (Hos. 2.2, 16 ET), but his editor says, Yahweh is 'God and not man', 'the Holy One' (Hos. 11.9). For many God resided in the Jerusalem temple (2 Kgs 18.16-22; Ps. 24), for others in the distant heavens (Deut. 4.39; 1 Kgs 8).

In Michelangelo's first scene of the figure of God, he stands on earth and gestures to Eve who emerges out of Adam's side (1509–1510). Floating within a crimson cloak, a muscular silver-haired God puts one arm around Eve and stretches out the other to touch Adam's finger, to infuse him with life (1510). Three scenes of creation represent God's infinite mobility (1511). From Michelangelo onwards God is recognizable by his flowing beard and aged appearance.

'A man wrestled with Jacob until daybreak' (Gen. 32.24), after which the assailant addresses Jacob, 'Your name shall be Israel for you have struggled with God and prevailed' (Gen. 32.28). Tales of heroes wrestling with some god in human form were well known (e.g., Heracles and Zeus). In the revised tale, Jacob meets angels, and his adversary is Esau (Gen. 32.1-2, 6-21). According to Hosea, Jacob struggles with God but prevails over the angel (Hos. 12.4-5). What artists usually depict is Jacob's combat with the angel (Gustave Doré 1855; Eugène Delacroix 1861; Paul Gaugin 1888).

Three men on a journey visit Abraham. One of the men is God himself (Gen. 18.2-15). Western art usually portrays the male visitors as angels, as in the revised version of the tale (Gen. 19.1). Rembrandt's 1656 etching, however, presents God as a gregarious sage seated on a carpet between a winged warrior and monk, with wine cup raised. In Rembrandt's 1650's drawing, Abraham kneels before God, a young tall man standing between two angels. Jesus is God in human form and travels with two disciples on the road to Emmaus in Luke's version of the Genesis tale (Luke 24). In an unnamed American painting (1720–1740), Jesus walks with two men along a country road in upstate New York.

God is dramatized as a character in Mediaeval English *Corpus Christi* cycles of plays performed in such cities as York, Chester, Coventry, circa 1360–1560. The actors playing God in episodes such as *The Building of the Ark* (Gen. 6–7) or *Moses and Pharaoh* (Exod. 3–14) often wore a gilded mask or visor to distance God from the audience. Modern literary representations include Timothy Findley's novel on the biblical flood, *Not Wanted on the Voyage* 1984: 'God descends from his carriage, lowered by angels. We gaze at a fragile and foolish human who makes equals of us all just by putting in a personal appearance.'

Recommended reading. Beagle, Richard, and Pamela King (eds.). *The York Mystery Plays*. Oxford: Oxford University Press, 1995. Gamba, Claudio (ed.). *Michelangelo*. New York: Rizzoli, 2005.

See also ABRAHAM; ADAM; ANGEL; DEITY; EVE; FINGER OF GOD; HOSEA, BOOK OF; IMAGE OF GOD; JACOB; YAHWEH [JRW]

Gog and Magog. In post-NT cultural representations, Gog and Magog usually refer to two fairly unspecific apocalyptic tribes sent by Satan at the time of the Last Judgement but overcome by Christ. This, however, only takes account of the NT reference found in Rev. 20.8. In the OT, Magog appears in the table of nations (Gen. 10.2) among the sons of Japhet. Gog descends from Reuben (and hence Jacob) according to 1 Chron. 5.3-4, and both names appear together in Ezek. 38.2-3, where Gog is the prince of Magog. Moreover, the Qur'an mentions some Dhū l-Qarnain ('he who has two horns') who fought against Ya'dschudsch und Ma'dschudsch (Sura 18.83-98), which are usually identified with Gog and Magog. The etymologies of all these named references remain uncertain.

Throughout the centuries, Judaic, Christian, and Muslim exegetes have tried to identify these tribes with existing groups (such as the Mongols, Goths, Russians, or Khazars) or other mythical people, and artists have depicted them as fearsome folks. Speculations about their real existence was deeply rooted in both the Christian and Islamic imagination throughout the Middle Ages. The *Anglo-Saxon World Map* of c. 1000, for instance, locates the kingdom of Gog and Magog near the Polar Circle, north of Aserbaidschan and the Caspian Sea, the famous *Ebsdorf World Map* (long time attributed to Gervasius of Tilbury, now dated c. 1300) even depicts the people of Gog and Magog as giant, monstrous cannibals.

Indeed, a whole branch of Christian popular tradition has made Gog and Magog two giants, who at times even lost their apocalyptic connotation. English sagas, for instance, tell of the two giants Gog and Magog, who were brought into London right after its founding to guard the king's newly edified palace. At least from the times of Henry V (1387–1422) through to the Great Fire of 1708, two giant figures of them stood in front of London Guildhall. Two smaller ones can still be seen there today. This popular tradition of identifying Gog and Magog as men rather than nations or people—while still apocalyptic and fearsome—has also inspired many modern representations, such as Nikolai Gogol's 1842 novel *Dead Souls* where Sobakewitsch compares a govenor and his delegate with Gog and Magog 'who will cut your throat for one single copeck', or the two non-humanoid laboratoy robots in Herbert L. Strock's 1954 science fiction movie *Gog*.

Other such representations comprise the species of 'Magog' in the science fiction series *Andromeda*, who reproduce themselves only for the purpose of killing (and are sometimes also cannibalistic), and know neither music nor literature nor arts. There are also the two demons Gog and Magog in Wolfgang Holbein's 2003 novel *Magog*. This demonic aspect is accentuated in some computer games, such as *Heroes of Might and Magic* (1990). Gog and Magog are popular figures in comic books as well, such as *Cosmonaut Keep* (2000), *X-Men* (1991), and other Marvel creations where they are demons sent by the Egyptian god Seth to punish the Israelites.

In Genesis's twenty-three minute song 'Supper's Ready' (on the album *Foxtrott*, 1972), Peter Gabriel sings 'With the Guards of Magog swarming around / The pied piper takes his children underground...' This is in the fifth section of this orchestral song, entitled 'Apocalypse in 9/8'. Gabriel would wear a special Magog-outfit and hair-cut when performing it, which can be seen on the cover of the *Genesis Live* album (1973). Several traditions and even conflicting elements are combined here that give a good idea of the fragmented traces Gog and Magog have left in popular imagery.

See also EZEKIEL, BOOK OF; QUR'AN, THE BIBLE IN THE [CC]

Gold. This precious metal, used since ancient times to make coins an ornaments, is mentioned 106 times in the Bible, all but nine of them in the OT. Gold was not mined in Palestine but imported in significant amounts from other places. King Solomon certainly desired gold and used it in coinage. From information in the Bible and elsewhere, it is believed that 1 shekel was measured by 2/5 ounce (11.4g), 50 shekels being the same as 1 mina, representing 20 ounces or 571g of gold; and 60 minas being the same as one talent which represented 75 pounds (or 34 kg). The gradual introduction of coinage into transactions throughout the region helped make trade much easier.

However gold in the Bible, although associated with wealth, is not always in the form of coins. It is used to lavishly adorn the tabernacle (Exod. 25.1-3; etc.) and also, obviously, to construct the idolatrous golden calf (Exod. 32.1-6) shortly after the Israelites left Egypt. David built up a large cache of gold and Solomon used that gold to help build the temple (e.g., 1 Kgs 6.28, 30, 32, 35).

The origin of the gold used in Palestine is much debated. Some was certainly brought in from the legendary port of Ophir, and some in coins for trade. It probably came from Arabia or the Red Sea, and the Egyptians had found deposits in ancient times. Curiously, in Ancient Egypt there was a lack of silver, and considerable quantities of gold, making the exchange rate of the two there favorable to people who had access to silver. This was obviously not the case in Palestine for much of this period as many of the references to gold are to gold *and* silver.

By the time of the NT, most of the gold in Palestine was in the form of Greek and Roman coins. The Magi brought with them 'gold, frankincense, and myrrh' (Matt. 2.11) for the baby Jesus. Revelation refers to streets of gold, which remains a familiar expression in contemporary speech (Rev. 21.21).

Recommended reading. Sutherland, C.H.V. *Gold: Its Beauty, Power and Allure*. London: Thames & Hudson, 1969.

See also GOLDEN CALF; OPHIR; SOLOMON [JC]

Golden calf. Exodus 32.1-35 reports that during the Israelites' migration from Egypt to the promised land, the exiled people demanded that their priest Aaron erect a cult statue, called the 'golden calf' because of its shape (a bovine) and material (made from gold jewelry collected from the worshippers). At that time, Moses was on Mount Sinai, where he received the tablets of the law from God, who also informed him of the Hebrews' disobedience to the commandment forbidding sacred images (Exod. 20.4-6). As their sin broke the covenant with God, the Israelites had to suffer a consequence: embodying divine wrath, Moses shattered the Decalogue, destroyed the sculpture, and ordered the execution of 3,000 men.

Most commentaries on the episode focus on the theme of idolatry and its condemnation. In his *Life of Moses*, Gregory of Nyssa considers the golden calf as a prophecy of the events that occurred during his time: the forbidding of pagan cults by the Christian emperor Theodosius I, marking the end of idolatry. In the opera by Arnold Schoenberg *Moses and Aaron* (1932), there is a theological debate. Some oppose Moses who is convinced that God is inexpressible, and Aaron chooses to give the people a language to understand the divinity; the golden calf is a visible image of an otherwise abstract God. Other interpretations of the golden calf as idolatry include the TV cartoon *The Simpsons* (season 2, episode 13) with the character Azran, a carver, producing figurines of calves at the foot of Sinai in 1220 BCE.

The symbolism of the biblical episode progressively extended to other sins. Lust emerges in the representations of the feast and dances welcoming Moses on his return, like the motive of the *Adoration of the Golden Calf* in European painting (see the version by Nicolas Poussin, London, 1634) and the orgiastic scenes of sex, rape and murder in Schoenberg's opera and in *The Ten Commandments* by Cecil B. DeMille (1956). Greed is present in *Faust,* an opera by Charles Gounod (1859), in the hymn devoted to the Golden calf sung by the diabolic Mephistopheles and in the popular expression 'to worship the Golden calf'.

God and Moses's wrath and its corollary, punishments, are the central point of other interpretations. Analyzing Moses's temper in *Moses and Monotheism* (1939), Sigmund Freud describes a personality dominated by anger. This is represented in art in *Moses Breaking the Tablets of the Law* by Rembrandt (1659). Michelangelo's *Moses* (1515) shows the prophet overcoming his anger after the vision of the golden calf, a psychic achievement far beyond anything in the biblical text. In Kevin Smith's film *Dogma* (1999), two fallen angels, willing to regain God's favor, reach the headquarters of a company whose mascot is an anthropomorphic cow named *Mooby the Golden Calf,* and kill the board of directors as a punishment for idolatry. And in 'If I'm lyin' I'm dyin'' (2000) of the animated series *Family Guy,* Peter suffers the plagues of Egypt in his own way after accepting the idolization directed to him as a faith healer when people adore his golden portrait.

Recommended reading. Schippe, Cullen. 'The Golden Calf'. In *The Bible and its Influence.* Ed. Cullen Schippe and Chuck Stetson. Pp. 75-79. New York and Fairfax: BLP Publishing, 2006.

See also GOLD; TEN COMMANDMENTS; MOSES; AARON [CD]

Golden rule. The golden rule is an oft-repeated axiom: 'In everything do to others as you would have them do to you.' The form of the expression varies context to context, but the expression calls for positive actions between individuals, informal groups, and even formal organizations. In short, it is a guideline for ethical behavior. We find versions of the golden rule throughout the Bible as well as other ancient sources. It appears in the OT in a passage on ritual and moral holiness (Lev. 19.18), and in the NT, Jesus speaks the words as part of the Sermon on the Mount (Matt. 7.12; cf. Luke 6.31). We find a similar sentiment in Luke 10.25-28, in the popular Parable of the Good Samaritan. It appears in deuterocanonical literature in Tob 4.15. Other variations on the golden rule appear in the Talmud (*Shabbat* 31a) and the Qur'an (83.1-6). In fact, variations of this simple phrase appear in the philosophies, the writings, or both, of many of the world's religions, including Buddhism, Christianity, Confucianism, Daoism, Hinduism, Islam, Jainism, Judaism, Zoroastrianism, and others. The ideal represented in this expression remains appealing in contemporary society, even serving as a nickname for the State of Arizona.

Recommended reading. Neusner, Jacob, and Bruce Chilton (eds.). *The Golden Rule: The Ethics of Reciprocity in World Religions.* London and New York: Continuum, 2008. Wattles, Jeffrey. *The Golden Rule.* New York: Oxford University Press, 1996.

See also GOOD SAMARITAN; GOODNESS; HOLY/HOLINESS; QUR'AN, THE BIBLE IN THE; SERMON ON THE MOUNT [RF-C]

Golgotha. Golgotha is the biblical name for the place where Jesus was crucified. It was probably a small hill just outside the walls of ancient Jerusalem. According to Christian tradition, it was within the area now occupied by the Church of the Holy Sepulchre but most biblical scholars doubt this is the correct location. The name 'Golgotha' is derived from the Aramaic word *gulgulta*. In the KJV and NKJV, Matt. 27.33 and Mark 15.22 give its meaning as 'place of the skull'. When Saint Jerome translated these verses into Latin, he used the Latin word for skull, *calvaria*, which was later converted into the English word Calvary. The Gospels do not say why Golgotha was called the 'place of the skull'. One suggestion is that the site was on a hill or near a rock that resembled the shape of a human skull. Another suggestion, first made by the third-century scholar Origen, is that the name referred to the burial place of Adam's skull, traditionally believed to have been buried at Jerusalem. The NT does not provide clear geographic information about the location of Golgotha but there are three clues providing some indication of its whereabouts. According to John 19.41-42, Jesus' body was carried only a short distance before it was placed in the tomb. This infers that the site was probably near a cemetery. The writer of Heb. 13.12 posits that the site was 'outside the city gate', but unfortunately does not indicate which gate. Matthew indicates that the location was near a heavily traveled road (27.39). Additionally, executions had to take place outside the city, pursuant to Jewish religious tradition, a requirement which the Romans generally honored. Finally, the Romans often crucified people on elevated locations adjacent to major roads, to serve as a warning of the fate of those who contested their authority. Golgotha served both aims well.

In literature, the term 'Golgotha' was used by writer Grigoris Balakian in his book *Armenian Golgotha*. The book provides a striking account of the Ottoman Empire's systematic attempt to eliminate the Armenian people from Turkey, chronicling the immeasurable suffering endured by the Armenian people. In 2007, Ian Wilson published *Murder at Golgotha: A Scientific Investigation into the Last Days of Jesus' Life, his Death, and his Resurrection*, which approaches Jesus' crucifixion from the perspective of a crime scene investigator.

In contemporary film, Golgotha is a 1935 French film about the death of Jesus Christ, directed by Julien Duvivier and featuring actors Harry Baur as Herod, Jean Gabin as Pontius Pilate and Robert le Vigan as Jesus Christ. It opened in the US in 1937. Le Vigan's performance marks the first direct portrayal of Christ in a sound film. This film is significant in that Jesus is seen speaking and in closeup, not merely from a distance as in films such Ben-Hur or The Robe. The National Board of Review named the film the sixth best foreign film of 1937. This film laid the groundwork for others such as Behold the Man (1965) and Mel Gibson's 2004 film The Passion of the Christ. In both films, the crucifixion scene at Golgotha is prominent. In popular music, the band Horror featured the song 'Golgotha' on their album With Blood Comes Cleaning (2006). More generally, the hill known as Golgotha symbolizes a place of suffering and sorrow but it is also seen as a place of victory and redemption for Christians.

See also CALVARY; CROSS, CRUCIFIXION OF CHRIST

[SNW]

Goliath. One of the most famous of all Bible stories is the duel between the Philistine giant Goliath of Gath (Hebrew *Golyath*), and the inexperienced and youthful Israelite David (1 Sam. 17). The story begins with a standoff between the Israelite and Philistine armies, during which Goliath repeatedly challenges the Israelites to a one-on-one duel. David persuades King Saul he is able to fight Goliath and goes out to meet the giant armed with only a staff, slingshot, and five stones. David brings Goliath to the ground with a single stone to the forehead, before decapitating him with the giant's own sword. As a result, the Philistine army flees and Israel is victorious. Goliath's height is given as a gigantic 'six cubits and a span' (9.75 feet) in the MT, yet only 'four cubits and a span' (6.75 feet) in some Septuagint manuscripts and Dead Sea scroll 4QSam^a.

An alternative account (2 Sam. 21.19) attributes Goliath's defeat to Elhanan instead of David. It is alluded to in Charles Reznikoff's poem, 'I do not believe that David killed Goliath' (1941), and in *The Simpsons* (season 10, episode 18), when Bart (playing David) has to kill both 'Goliath I' and 'Goliath II'.

The term 'Goliath' has come to signify the abnormally large, for example, the world's largest spider (Goliath birdeater), largest frog (Goliath frog), and heaviest beetle (Goliath beetle). It often also infers tyrannical size, as it does for the Goliath Corporation, a megalithic company in the *Thursday Next* novels (2001–) by Jasper Fforde.

In early Christian interpretation, David's defeat of Goliath is viewed as a prototype of Christ's defeat of Satan. In modern usage, a 'David and Goliath struggle' is proverbial for a seemingly unequal contest between an overpowering opponent and a small but courageous contender. Ann Fairbairn, in *Five Smooth Stones* (1966), portrays the American Civil Rights Movement as a struggle against the Goliath of racism, fought by a protagonist named David. The David and Goliath metaphor has frequently been employed to provoke sympathy for a heroic Israeli underdog against a surrounding Arab coalition—despite Israel's overwhelming military superiority since 1948. The truth of the metaphor itself is brought into question by Robert Graves, who questions whether an individual soldier can realistically maintain hope amidst the overwhelming horror of WWI. Therefore, Goliath kills David in his 'Goliath and David' (1916). Emily Dickinson likewise despairs she is too small to face her 'Goliath' in 'I Took My Power in My Hand'.

David's military victory is celebrated in Donatello's bronze *David* (c. 1430s) and Phillis Wheatley's poem 'Goliath of Gath' (c. 1773). In the 1980s television series *Knight Rider*, the heroic car K.I.T.T. destroys his nemesis Goliath, an armored truck, by 'decapitating' truck from trailer with a laser beam. Caravaggio challenges such militant triumphalism by using his own head to model Goliath's severed head, while modeling the beautiful young David on his boy lover Cecco.

David's 'perfect Symmetry' is contrasted with Goliath's monstrous form in Michael Drayton's 'David and Goliath' (1630). Similarly, Michelangelo's fresco in the Sistine Chapel (1508–1512) depicts Goliath as a beast, crawling on all fours, with David standing heroically above. The medieval Goliards took advantage of the common association of giants with the uncultured and immoral, by claiming their patron was Bishop Goliath (Latin *Golias*), under whose fictitious name they wrote songs of gluttony, drunkenness, fornication, and vagrancy—including *Gaudeamus Igitur*.

Recommended reading. Isser, Stanley Jerome. *Sword of Goliath*. Atlanta: Society of Biblical Literature, 2003. Tov, Emmanuel. 'The David and Goliath Saga'. *Bible Review* 34 (1986) 35-41.

See also DAVID; GIANTS; PHILISTINES; SWORD

[DG]

Gomer. This Hebrew name means perfection or completion. The best-known biblical character of this name is Gomer, daughter of Diblaim and wife of the prophet Hosea. Gomer gives birth to three children: Jezreel, whose father is Hosea (Hos. 1.3-4); Lo-ruhamah (not loved) and Lo-ammi (not my people), who may have been conceived through illicit relationships with other men (Hos. 1.6; 1.8-9). Gomer's marriage to Hosea symbolizes God's relationship with Israel (Hos. 1–3) who, like a prostitute, often wanders away and gives her love and loyalty to other gods. The prophet's marriage to the unfaithful woman sets the stage for the following chapters of the book in which the author reveals a pattern of divine judgment followed always by divine restoration; God judges Israel but never forsakes her entirely. Rather, it is only through her relationship with God that Israel will eventually reach perfection, as the name 'Gomer' implies.

The use of this marital/sexual metaphor has given rise to several questions about Gomer and her story. Was the 'marriage' an actual historical event or just an allegory? Did the breach between Hosea and Gomer consist of a legal divorce or merely an informal separation? Was Gomer a promiscuous wife or actually an independent prostitute whom Hosea pursued and took for his own? And if one assumes Gomer was actually the prophet's wife, was she promiscuous before their marriage, as well as during?

Analysis of the relationship between Hosea and Gomer has led to scholarly disagreements regarding the dating of the text. Traditionally, the book is thought to have been written just after the fall of the northern kingdom of Israel to the Assyrians in 722 BCE. More recently, it has been suggested that it was written during the Persian period. Hermeneutical issues have also arisen, especially regarding the value and limitations of the use of a metaphor that may be interpreted as excusing violence against women. The text has also been used in our modern day as the basis for a marital counseling model that suggests that divorce is not the preferred solution to marital crisis involving infidelity.

Another biblical character named Gomer is the grandson of Noah by his son Japheth (Gen. 10.2 and 1 Chron. 1.5). Ezekiel also prophesies that the descendants of Gomer will be defeated as part of God's judgment against Gog and its allies (Ezek. 38.1-6).

Recommended reading. Hornsby, Teresa J. '"Israel Has Become a Worthless Thing": Re-reading Gomer in Hosea 1–3'. *Journal for the Study of the Old Testament* 82 (1999) 115-28. Weems, Renita J. 'Gomer: Victim of Violence or Victim of Metaphor?' *Semeia* 47 (1989) 87-104.

See also HOSEA, BOOK OF

[EAG]

Good Samaritan, the. One story dominates Western justifications of welfare, social justice, community care, and international aid—the parable of the so-called Good Samaritan. The parable has a single appearance in the NT (Luke 10.29-35) at the beginning of Jesus' long journey to Jerusalem (Luke 9.51–19.57). The setting of the parable is one of conflict (Luke 10.25-37) that uses wording familiar in other contests (Matt. 22.35-40; Mark 12.28-31; Luke 18.18-20). The story itself focuses on a badly injured victim who is ignored by two exemplars of religious scruples within ancient Judaism but who is tended and rescued by a Samaritan merchant. Modern scholarship and popular literature have adopted a meaning that counsels the privileged to care for the less fortunate.

This reading of the parable dominates literary improvisation, especially in nineteenth-century novels (for example, William Thackeray's *The Adventures of Philip on his Way Through the World* [1861–1862] and Samuel Butler's *The Way of All Flesh* [written 1873–1884]). It continues to remain a motif in cinematography (e.g., Carlo Lizzani's *L'indifferenza* [1969], and Michael Bay's *The Island* [2005]). The term good Samaritan provides the identification for a Catholic religious order, numerous welfare groups, even medals of honor and legislation summarized as Good Samaritan laws.

The parable began to receive the title 'the good Samaritan' in the sixteenth century under humanist literary and artistic influence. The earliest manuscript headings for this section of Luke's Gospel title it the parable of 'the man who fell among thieves', a heading that survived through to the printing of Erasmus's editions of the NT. This categorization did not see the story as an exhortation about charitable behavior but as a theological story about salvation, with Jesus in the starring role of the Samaritan savior and the victim as the man Adam, fallen into sin. By a striking correlation of the parable with a literal reading of John 8.48-49, Jesus' failure to deny that he was a Samaritan, whilst he did deny being demon-possessed, was taken as proof. Accordingly, not only was Jesus distanced from Jewish connections in the parable (characterized in the priest and Levite who passed by the wounded traveler) but he became the exemplary savior who brought a sinner into the embrace of the church (allegorized from the reference to the inn, St Peter playing the role of the inn-keeper, and the two coins taken as the sacraments of baptism and Eucharist, or as the OT and NT). This interpretation featured prominently in early manuscript illumination (such as in the gospel book, Codex Rossanensis) and in medieval allegories, such as William Langland's *The Vision of Piers Plowman*.

Criticism that is more recent notes that the anchor to the whole story is the wounded man. The question in Luke's narrative directed to the lawyer ('Which ... was a neighbor to the man?') echoes the lawyer's question ('And who is my neighbor?') which places the professional not into the role of the Samaritan but into that of the wounded man. Such a reading notes that the epithet 'good' is nowhere used in the story. The exaltation of the wounded man to the center of the story is the key to Vincent van Gogh's striking painting of the parable, the masterpiece contesting its own title of *The Good Samaritan* (1890).

Recommended reading. Cadwallader, A. 'Where to Now, Good Samaritan?' *St Mark's Review* 196 (2004) 7-15. Oakman, D. 'Was Jesus a Peasant?: Implications for Reading the Samaritan Story (Luke 10:30-35)'. *Biblical Theology Bulletin* 22 (1992) 117-25.

See also PARABLE; LUKE, GOSPEL OF; SAMARITANS

[AHC]

Good shepherd, the. In John's Gospel, Jesus describes himself as 'the good shepherd' (10.11), and the author of Hebrews describes Jesus as 'great shepherd' (Heb. 13.20), but the phrase has its origin in the HB's depiction of God as shepherd. The shepherd metaphor in the HB and NT usually presents persons in authority (kings, leaders, or God) as caretakers of the people, who are represented as sheep. Examples include Ps. 23; 119.176; Isa. 53.6; Jer. 50.6; Ezek. 34.11-23; Matt. 10.6; 15.24; John 10; Luke 15.1-8. At times, shepherds may be positive or negative figures, but when God is described as shepherd, the association is a naturally positive one. Thus, Jesus' use of this language in John 10 may point to God and/or involve a comparison between the current evil shepherds (i.e., the Jewish leaders) and Jesus as the good shepherd (i.e., the good leader). Some suggest John 10 alludes to Ps. 23. The good shepherd also links to symbols of Jesus as the Lamb of God, the lamb to the slaughter, and other pastoral metaphors. This association is further encouraged by Jesus' discussion of shepherding in several parables.

Early Christian and medieval art were particularly inspired by the symbol of the good shepherd. Some of the earliest depictions of the sheep/shepherd metaphor in art are present in the figure of the good shepherd in early Christian catacombs. The use of this image in the third century CE rose to its full development and is present in the catacombs of St Calixtus, St Nereus and Achilleus, St Domitilla, St Lucina, St Praetextatus, St Priscilla, and St Agnese, among others. Small statues of the good shepherd carrying a lamb have also been found dating to the third and fourth centuries as well as depictions of the good shepherd on Christian sarcophagi.

The good shepherd has also been a title transferred from Jesus to the Pope at various times in the history of the Roman Catholic Church. This comparison sees the Pope's authority as shepherd over the Church, his sheep, as derived from Jesus as the ultimate Good Shepherd.

In modern usage, literary and artistic references to the good shepherd include Spenser's *Shepheardes*

Calendar, Milton's *Lysidas*, Bunyan's *Pilgrim's Progress*, Handel's 'He shall feed his flock' in the *Messiah*, Murillo's 'The Good Shepherd', and 'The Christ Child as the Good Shepherd'. The movie, *The Good Shepherd* (2006), uses the metaphor to depict a man who sacrifices aspects of his life for the sake of his work in the CIA, protecting the 'sheep' of America.

Recommended reading. Nielsen, Kirsten. 'Old Testament Imagery in John'. In *New Readings in John*. Ed. Johannes Nissen and Sigfred Pedersen. Pp. 66-82. Sheffield: Sheffield Academic Press, 1999. Ham, Clay Alan. *The Coming King and the Rejected Shepherd: Matthew's Reading of Zechariah's Messianic Hope*. New Testament Monographs, 4. Sheffield: Sheffield Phoenix Press, 2005. Gan, Jonathan. *The Metaphor of Shepherd in the Hebrew Bible: A Historical-Literary Reading*. Lanham, MD: Rowman & Littlefield, 2007.

See also SHEEP; JOHN, GOSPEL OF; LOST SHEEP, PARABLE OF THE; SHEEP AND THE GOATS, PARABLE OF THE; ANIMALS, SYMBOLISM OF; LAMB, SACRIFICIAL

[BMS]

Good thief, the. The Gospels record that Jesus was crucified with two other men (John 19.18), called *lestai* (robbers, bandits) in Matt. 27.38, 44 and Mark 15.27, and *kakourgoi* (criminals, evil-doers) in Luke 23.33, 39. 'The Good Thief' is the name commonly given to the unnamed malefactor, crucified alongside Jesus, who repented of his sins and asked Jesus to remember him in his kingdom (Luke 23.32, 39-43).The text tells us that Jesus responded to the converted thief saying that he will be with him in Paradise.

In Christian tradition, from the fourth century on, the so-called good thief received the name of Dimas (sometimes spelled *Dysmas*, or even *Dumas*). The apocryphal Arabic Infancy Gospel calls him Titus, and the Russian tradition Rakh. Although the good thief was never formally canonized by Christianity, he was generally regarded as a saint on the basis of the promise made to him by Jesus that he will be in heaven. In the Roman Catholic and Eastern Orthodox Churches, Saint Dismas is especially venerated by condemned prisoners, repentant criminals and even undertakers as their patron. His feast is celebrated on March 25. The town of San Dimas, California, is named after him. Many prison chapels are dedicated to Saint Dismas, since he represents the perfect example of a repentant malefactor saved *in extremis*. His story is an outstanding paradigm of God's grace and his willingness to forgive even at the last moment of life. This moving story inspired the famous painting by Titian, *Christ and the Good Thief* (Tiziano Vecellio, 1566).

The theme of the conversion *in extremis* of a criminal was very influential in the way Fyodor Dostoyevsky (1821–1881) described the repentance and redemption of Raskolnikov in *Crime and Punishment* (1866). One of the most moving hymns of the Eastern Orthodox Church is based on the story of the good thief. It is entitled *The Good Wise Thief* (in Slavonic *Razboinika blagorazumnago*), and often sung in the Matins service on Good Friday in Russian Orthodox churches. The good thief story has appealed to many artists throughout history, and continues to do so today. Thus, Dimas plays an important role in Cecil B. DeMille's movie *The King of Kings* (1927). More recently, the title *The Good Thief* was given to a film directed by Neil Jordan (2002), to an album by John Brannen (2004), and to a novel written by Hannah Tinti (2008).With the title *Thief of Heaven*, Glenn Hefley published (2009) a novel based on the life of Dismas.

Recommended reading. Smith, Robert Harry. 'Paradise Today: Luke's Passion Narrative'. *Currents in Theology and Mission* 3 (1976) 323-36.

See also CROSS, CRUCIFIXION OF CHRIST; CONVERSION

[RB]

Goodness. The words goodness and good are generally expressed in the Bible by the Hebrew term *tôb* and the Greek terms *agathos* and *kalos*. The concept of goodness is sometimes given an aesthetic meaning (e.g., Gen. 6.2; Est. 1.11), but it is mainly used in a moral sense. In the Bible goodness is most often associated with God, expressing his essential quality in relationship with his creation, namely benevolent kindness and love: 'O taste and see that the LORD is good' (Ps. 34.8; cf. 1 John 3.7-8). When Moses asked to see God, He answered 'I will make all my goodness pass before you' (Exod. 33.19-20). When the glory of God passed before Moses, he defined the Lord as 'a God merciful and gracious, slow to anger, and abounding in steadfast love and faithfulness, keeping steadfast love for the thousandth generation, forgiving iniquity and transgression and sin' (Exod. 34.6-7). God reveals himself in goodness and manifests his goodness by doing good (Ps. 119.68). Thus, after the creation, 'God saw everything that he had made, and indeed, it was very good' (Gen. 1.31).

The Bible states that goodness belongs to the very nature of God, and that human beings were also created good, in God's image. After the fall, however, they are never considered 'good' in themselves, and are therefore only capable of goodness through the action of God. Sin has defiled human nature to the point that Paul declares there is no one who does good (Rom. 3.12). In spite of this situation, human beings can be morally restored through redemption. By the grace of God, men such as Hezekiah (2 Chron. 32.32), Joseph of Arimathea (Luke 23.50), and Barnabas (Acts 11.24) are described as capable of doing good. Goodness is one of the fruits of the Spirit, manifested in those who live in communion with God (Gal. 5.22-24).

The Bible never presents the concept of goodness in the abstract, and therefore includes the concept of right behavior. Goodness is often expressed through the words translated as upright, right, or righteousness. These qualities do not describe people without faults, but those who struggle to avoid evil, who choose to act in a good way, and who strive for goodness in their everyday lives. The search for 'goodness' in the Bible is related to the resolution of the cosmic conflict between good and evil. A prime responsibility for believers includes ethical discernment: to discern good from evil (2 Sam. 14.17; Heb. 5.14), and to strive for goodness instead of evil (Ps. 34.14; 37.27; Amos 5.14; Rom. 12.9). Siding with goodness against the evil forces in this world is an essential part of the mission of God's people (Eccl. 12.14; 2 Cor. 5.10).

The self-evident superiority of goodness over any other behavior is also a main theme in literature. The concept of goodness has inspired novels such as *The Green Mile* (1996) by Stephen King (see also the film on the same subject, 1999), and the best-selling novel by Morris West, *The Shoes of a Fisherman* (1963), and a film on the same subject (1968).

See also CREATION, CREATOR; EVIL; GOD; WISDOM

[DAVS]

Gospel. Gospel is a term that is used to encapsulate the entire Christian message, but is usually confined to the message of 'good news' (its literal translation) that each of the Gospels conveys. The earliest use of the term 'good news' or Gospel is probably found in Mark 1.1: 'the beginning of the good news of Jesus Christ'.

Scholarship has long been intrigued by the question of the type of literature of the Gospels. There have been five major, recurring proposals. (1) With the development of form criticism in the early years of the twentieth century, many scholars believed that the Gospels were unique, a type of literature that was neither literary nor simply commonplace. Form criticism attempted to show that the Gospels were simply compilations of individual smaller literary units, without an authorial unifying voice or literary character. (2) The comparative study of the Gospels has resulted in analogies being drawn with other ancient tales of 'divine men'. These aretalogies, such as the life of Apollonius of Tayana, depict their heroes as semi-divine figures performing supernatural acts, supposedly in the same vein as the acts and wonders performed by Jesus. (3) The study of genre in many ways goes back to Aristotle, and with it the presumption that the Gospels may have been written as forms of Greek tragedy. Such studies often analyze common plot patterns, including rising, climactic, and falling action, especially in Mark's Gospel, with its turning point being Peter's confession in chapter 8. (4) Whereas many proposals have looked to Greco-Roman literature, some proposals believe that the Gospels reflect Jewish forms of writing. These might include midrashic or lectionary forms of literature that interpret events in terms of Jewish hermeneutical techniques. They might also involve depictions of Jesus in the same light as heroes of the OT, such as Moses. (5) Before form criticism proposed that the Gospels were assembled from individual story-units, many scholars proposed that the Gospels were forms of Hellenistic biographies.

One of the major issues in determining literary genres is the tension between prescriptive and descriptive categories. Rather than simply prescribing a literary genre, or attempting simply to describe a given work without reference to similar categories, it is probably best to realize that genre is a flexible and developing category as each new work transforms the genre. The same is true of the Gospels. There are many characteristics that the Gospels share with ancient Greco-Roman biography. However, they also depict a figure in ways that also alter and shape the genre itself, such as including characteristics of his Jewishness, his coming from the common people, and his distinctive sense of divine calling.

Recommended reading. Burridge, R. *What Are the Gospels? A Comparison with Greco-Roman Biography*. 2nd edn. Grand Rapids, MI: Eerdmans, 2004.

See also SYNOPTIC GOSPELS; MATTHEW, GOSPEL OF; MARK, GOSPEL OF; LUKE, GOSPEL OF; JOHN, GOSPEL OF; Q DOCUMENT

[SEP]

Grace. Grace is generally the disposition to show kindness, favor, and loyalty to another. In the HB grace (*hen*; *hesed*) is bestowed by humans (Gen. 21.23; 40.14; Josh. 2.12-14), but more often represents God's covenant loyalty which he dispenses to individuals (Gen. 39.21) and Israel (1 Kgs 8.23; Neh. 1.5; 9.32). God initiates grace but he demands loyalty and obedience from his people (Exod. 20.5-6; Deut. 7.6-12). In return for faithful Torah-observance, God promised to show grace to Israel through covenant blessings (Lev. 26.3-13; Deut. 28.1-14). For unfaithfulness and disobedience God promised exile and curses (Lev. 26.14-39; Deut. 28.15-68), although God's people need only to confess their sins and return to Torah-observance to recover God's grace (Lev. 26.40-45; Deut. 30.1-10).

Grace (*charis*) in the NT is embedded in the reciprocity system of the Greco-Roman world. In this context, when an individual was presented with a gift, the beneficiary was socially obligated to return the favor in an equal or greater manner. The term grace, then, can refer to (i) the willingness and initiative of the giver to bestow gifts to a person or group, (ii) the content of the gift itself, and (iii) the beneficiary's gift, gratitude, and/or loyalty offered in return.

Grace serves many functions in the NT. In conformity with standard letter writing practices, 'grace' in many NT documents is a greeting (Rom. 1.7; Rev. 1.4) and farewell (Gal. 6.18; Heb. 13.25). Grace is observed in the exchange of favors between individuals (Acts 24.27; Eph. 4.29). Paul's discussion of the collection in Corinth (2 Cor. 8–9) is perhaps the clearest example of grace language within the ancient reciprocity system. Interestingly, Paul refers to the gift of Christ to signal how the Corinthians were obligated to express gratitude to God and support the Jerusalem church financially (2 Cor. 9.10-15).

The NT authors often use grace to convey God's generous and uncoerced initiative in redeeming sinful humanity from condemnation (Rom. 5.20–6.1; Tit. 3.4-7). The Pauline doctrine of salvation by grace through faith opposes the possibility of entrance into God's people through the observance of works of the Law (Rom. 3.27-28; Gal. 2.16; Eph. 2.8-9). Grace is equated with the death of Jesus (Rom. 5.15) and is the appropriate response to God for salvation (Rom. 6.17; 7.25). Paul also credits the grace of God for his commission into apostolic ministry (Rom. 1.5; 12.3; 1 Cor. 3.10).

In Western culture, grace has all but fallen out of popular usage. Grace continues to carry significant theological weight in Christian discourse and spirituality, as evident in the Reformation cry '*sola gratia*' ('grace alone') and John Newton's famous hymn '*Amazing Grace*' (1772). Grace is a feminine forename, as represented in the television sitcom *Will & Grace*. Grace also refers to a short prayer spoken before a meal, which is depicted in Jean-Baptiste-Siméon Chardin's eighteenth-century painting *Le bénédicité* ('Grace'). The concept of grace as an uncoerced gift is analogous to the modern concept of charity, although modern charity lacks reciprocity. Still, the etiquette of mutuality in gift exchange persists as confirmed in the all too familiar Christmas confession, 'But I didn't get anything for you!' A modified version of the ancient concept of grace is perhaps best displayed in the film *Pay It Forward* (2000).

See also COVENANT; FORGIVENESS; SALVATION

[JKG]

Great commandment, the. The great commandment is found first in Lev. 19.18: 'You shall love your neighbor as yourself: I am the Lord.' This is a positive formulation of the so-called golden rule, which requires a person to treat others the way that same person would like to be treated. The principle is given in its negative formulation by Rabbi Hillel, in *b. Šabb.* 31a: 'What is hateful to you, do not do to your neighbor.' The Apostle Paul writes something similar in Gal. 5.14: 'You shall love your neighbor as yourself.' In Luke 10.25-37, Jesus tells the parable of the Prodigal Son in part to address the social implications of this principle with regard to the identity of the neighbor. In Matt. 22.37, Jesus also elevates another principle—loving God with the entirety of one's being. He does this by quoting Deut. 8.5, part of the *Shema*, which was central to the religious life of an Israelite: 'You shall love the Lord your God with all your heart, and with all your soul, and with all your mind.' Jesus then takes the view that this dual formulation is the greatest commandment, thus engaging in an ongoing debate within early Judaism (cf. *Gen. Rab.* 24.7; *Mek.* 6). So, for Jesus, the great commandment is actually two principles held together: (1) loving God; (2) loving your neighbor (Mark 12.31). The great commandment is often conflated with the golden rule, but as seen above, Jesus extends the focus on communal reciprocity to an equal concern for full devotion to God. In Mark 12.29, Jesus' teaching on this topic has a monotheistic focus, 'Hear, O Israel: the Lord our God, the Lord is one.' This is similar to Sir. 18.2: 'The Lord alone is just.' Sirach goes on to write in 31.15a, 'Judge your neighbor's feelings by your own.' The monotheistic focus of both Jesus and Sirach provide a contrasting ideological foundation when compared to Seneca, whose universalistic ethic relates more to the good ordering of society (*Ep.* 47.11; *De ira* 3.12.3; but see *Ben.* 1.1.9-13, 4.25.2). For Jesus, loving God and loving one's neighbor together form the great commandment.

Wolfgang Amadeus Mozart composed an oratorio in 1767 entitled, 'The Obligation of the First and Foremost Commandment'. It addresses issues of justice, mercy, and worldliness in the life of an uncommitted Christian, who later becomes zealous. In 1939, Irving Pichel directed a movie entitled, *The Great Commandment*, which looks at the complex way the principle of loving one's neighbor is lived out in the context of the Roman Empire. In 1988, the German new wave band Camouflage reached the Billboard charts with its single 'The Great Commandment'. This song laments what happens to those who try to live out this principle and the way in which hegemonic political structures oppress those under their control and ignore this basic principle for a society. In 1998, Eleanor Humes Haney provided a feminist reading of Jesus' principle in *The Great Commandment: A Theology of Resistance and Transformation*. She brings to the fore the radical nature of Jesus' teaching on collective justice. The overall focus of the great commandment is loving and knowing God and then reaching out in that love to others.

Recommended reading. Haney, Eleanor Humes. *The Great Commandment: A Theology of Resistance and Transformation*. Cleveland, OH: Pilgrim Press, 1998. Lee, Matthew T., and Margaret M. Poloma. *A Sociological Study of the Great Commandment in Pentecostalism: The Practice of Godly Love as Benevolent Service*. Lewiston, NY: Edwin Mellen Press, 2009.

See also GOLDEN RULE; SHEMA [JBT]

Great commission, the. This refers to the concluding episode of Matthew's Gospel, an episode in which the resurrected Jesus dispatches or 'commissions' his disciples to continue his preaching about the good news of the coming kingdom of heaven (Matt. 28.18-20). Consisting of Jesus' statements of his rule (v. 18), of the need 'to baptize and to instruct' (v. 19), and of his continuing presence 'until the end of the age' (v. 20), the commission episode argues, with the larger passion–resurrection narrative to which it belongs, for the ultimate triumph and legitimacy of Jesus' mission.

The historicity of the commission episode falls outside scholarly analysis since it narrates alleged actions and words of the risen Jesus. Might Jesus nevertheless have spoken something like this commission? For several reasons, the answer is essentially negative. For one, the commission's emphases on Jesus' 'authority' and on the global scope of the mission point not so much to the historical Jesus as to the thinking of Christians in the late first century CE, while redactional themes of Matthew (for instance, the reference to Jesus being 'with you' in v. 20 [cf. Matt. 1.23-24]) betray the evangelist's hand. Moreover, Matthew's commission episode appears in neither of his written sources (the Gospel of Mark and sayings gospel Q), although independent commission traditions appear in Luke 24.47-49 and John 20.21.

The episode's rhetorical or persuasive function, as part of the passion–resurrection narrative, reflects the function of conclusions in the larger genre that the canonical Gospels best approximate, the ancient biography (or *bios*). Such conclusions characteristically emphasize the protagonist's stature and legacy.

In the Christian culture of the West, the great commission has had an impact out of proportion to its verisimilitude. And perhaps its most powerful impact has been in justifying Christian evangelism. Although not understood in an evangelistic sense before roughly 1500 CE, it took on this sense among various Christian missionaries after this point, particularly after 1800, and remains influential today in conservative Christian communities. At times, however, the text has proven a double-edged sword, for the oppression that often accompanied missions led the Spanish priest Bartolomé de las Casas (1484–1566) to employ this text to help argue against the prosecution of non-Christian natives. Quite apart from its evangelistic role, the text has also played a strong role in the development of the influential Anabaptist or adult-baptism tradition (c. 1520), and has doubtless contributed to popular views about baptism and Christian pedagogy. Influences such as these help to account for visual depictions of the commission in the early modern period, for instance in woodcuts by Johann Christoph Weigel (1695), and by the anonymous artist of the *Evangelicae Historiae Imagines* (1593). In the modern period too, the commission remains a subject of interest in

Christian media. For instance, one American Christian band calls itself The Great Commission. In mainstream culture, the great commission has a less evident impact, although it is the title of Rockmond Dunbar's 2003 film portraying the nexus of Christian mission and prostitution.

Recommended reading. Luz, Ulrich. *Matthew 21–28: A Commentary*. Trans. James E. Crouch. Hermeneia. Minneapolis: Fortress Press, 2005. Sugirtharajah, R.S. *The Bible and the Third World: Precolonial, Colonial and Postcolonial Encounters*. Cambridge: Cambridge University Press, 2001. [AD]

Great physician, the. The great physician is a title often given to Jesus of Nazareth in recognition of his healing ministry. It is not a phrase from the Bible. However, in the early stages of his ministry, Jesus mentioned physicians and compared himself to them: 'Those who are well have no need of a physician, but those who are sick; I have come to call not the righteous but sinners' (Mark 2.17; compare similar statements in Matt. 9.12 and Luke 5.31). In Luke 4.23, Jesus quoted a popular saying about physicians as an introduction to a statement about the inclusiveness of God's love, which incited the crowd into an attempt to throw him off a cliff.

The healing and miracle stories of the Gospels often mix physical cures with forgiveness of sin. As a result, many readers have concluded that physical illness or disabilities are the result of sin, often leading to social stigma within religious cultures. In response, commentators have distinguished cures from forgiveness or taken wider views of healing. For example, this approach notes that physical cures are not always linked to forgiveness, and that Jesus often warned of the consequences of sin to people without disabilities. A social response has emerged from the field of disability studies, which considers disabling conditions primarily through their social effect, rather than as being purely medical conditions. This approach has focused on the subject's role in an interdependent community. To these commentators, healing is restoration, and the long-term healing results come to those who have suffered themselves and share the liberating story. This leads to wider acceptance of all conditions and acknowledgement of a need for diversity to complete the 'image of God' behind humanity's creation.

In 1859, William Hunter wrote the hymn 'The Great Physician'. It portrays 'the sympathizing Jesus' who brings hope and forgiveness of sins. This hymn portrays Jesus as calling for a decision to accept him as Savior. As it progresses, however, it is a hymn of personal dedication rather than any theological statement about healing.

The phrase great physician appears often in devotional and self-help literature. Self-help topics include the idea of restoration of Edenic balance, promotion of particular health techniques claimed to have a biblical foundation (such as vegan or vegetarian diets), as well as a Buddhist-like mindfulness. The best-known movement based on such ideas is probably the Church of Christ, Scientist. Mary Baker Eddy founded it in 1879 after she read various healing stories in the Gospels. Instead of medical techniques, Christian Science uses practitioners who assist the patient in gaining spiritual wholeness and rejecting illness through devotional exercises. Other Christian groups also reject medical techniques in favor of prayer. More mainline denominations accept the role of physicians, while recently emphasizing spiritual care as a complementary part of healing. Islamic traditions also include a great physician and enjoin followers to use the many tools (including medical science) which God has provided to humanity.

See also GARDEN OF EDEN; IMAGE OF GOD; MIRACLES; THORN IN THE FLESH [TJV]

Greek language. The Greek language dominated in the Roman Empire of the first century CE, and *Koine* (common) Greek is the language of the NT. At one time it was believed that the Jews in Palestine were less affected by Greek language and culture than Jews living abroad in more Hellenized (Greek influenced) cities but recent scholars have shown that Greek culture dominated even in Jewish centers such as Jerusalem. All Judaism around the turn of the era was in some measure impacted by Hellenism so it is no surprise that several Jewish and early Christian writings are Greek, and that the NT authors, as a rule, relied on the Greek translation of the Jewish Scriptures (the Septuagint). This does not mean all Jews spoke Greek. It is likely that Jesus spoke Aramaic, which means the Gospel records of his words are translations.

See also NEW TESTAMENT; SEPTUAGINT; LANGUAGES OF THE BIBLE [AWP]

Green pastures. The phrase 'green pastures' comes from a psalm of David: 'He makes me lie down in green pastures' (Ps. 23.2). It serves to represent an area of natural abundance and appears often in titles of books. The most famous of these is the play *The Green Pastures*, written by Marc Connelly in 1930. A folk version of the OT, it dramatizes the story by portraying it through the lives of African Americans living in the southern United States. There is also the 1936 film *The Green Pastures*, adapted by Marc Connelly from the story *Ol' Man Adam an' his Chillun* (1928) by Roark Bradford (1896–1948). Revived in 1951, it attracted criticism on account of its stereotyping of African Americans. Una Lucy Silberrad (1919), Aphra White (1924), Rev. C.E. Yates (1954), George A Birtill (1968), and Clarke Hockley (1990) have also used the term green pastures as the titles of books.

See also PSALM/PSALMIST/PSALMS, BOOK OF [JC]

H

Habbakuk, Book of. The Book of Habakkuk is the eighth book of the twelve Minor Prophets in the HB, penned sometime between 610 and 605 BCE. It illustrates God's willingness to judge, protect, sustain, and deliver his people. The book also illustrates humanity's capacity to question God's actions during times of suffering. God responds to the prophet's line of inquiry and ultimately, Habakkuk's faith is restored. The prophetic book contains three short chapters, but they present a striking contrast. In the first two, Habakkuk protests, complains, and questions God. However, the final chapter is a psalm of praise.

Habakkuk starts his book with a cry of woe. Injustice is rampant, the righteous are surrounded by the wicked, the law is powerless, and God does not appear to be concerned about the plight of his people (1.1-4). The prophet wonders why God is allowing these things to happen and God's response brings little comfort. He explains that inevitably, the armies of Babylon will move throughout the ancient world on a campaign of death and destruction. By the time Habakkuk received this vision, the Babylonians had already defeated Assyria and Egypt. The implication is that Habakkuk's nation, Judah, will be the next to fall.

The prophet is stunned at the news and reminds God of his justice and holiness (1.12-13). How could God use the wicked Babylonians to destroy his chosen people? Surely, he reasons, God realizes that the sins of Judah were miniscule compared to the atrocities of the pagan Babylonians (1.13). The question posed to God in this verse indicates Habakkuk's tremendous faith. God assures Habakkuk that the Babylonians will prevail not because they are righteous but because they are his temporary instrument of judgment (2.4). He then pronounces five burdens of woe against the Babylonians (2.6, 9, 12, 15, 19). Utimately God will vindicate his righteous character (2.14). After this assurance, Habakkuk offers his psalm of praise to God. The second half of Hab. 2.4 is frequently quoted by early Christian writers. In the NT, the Paul quotes this verse twice in his letters, first in Rom. 1.17 and again in Gal. 3.11 (cf. Heb. 10.37-38).

The Book of Habakkuk seldom appears in popular culture though it is a favorite book for televangelists like Richard Roberts, John Hagee and Creflo Dollar who frequently utilize its language in sermons about the need for faith in the midst of suffering.

Recommended reading. Brueggemann, Walter. *Theology of the Old Testament*. Minneapolis: Fortress Press, 1997.

See also PROPHETS [SNW]

Hades (Gk 'invisible'; Lat. *Pluto* or *Dis*, 'the wealthy one') is the name of the Greek god of the underworld and, by extension, of his realm. Originally, the 'house of Hades' was perceived as a dark and indistinct place where the deceased dwell in near-oblivion, regardless of their actions in life. However, already in the eleventh book of Homer's *Odyssey* the idea existed that some individuals are singled out for severe punishment, while a select few never go to Hades but to Elysium, a place of eternal bliss at the far end of the world. Towards the Hellenistic and Roman era, ethical notions of punishment and reward had led to more sophisticated ideas on the afterlife, due in no small part to the influence of Platonist, Orphic and Stoic philosophy. The classical image of Hades, with its tripartite division into the Elysian Fields, the Plains of Asphodel and Tartarus, can be found in the sixth book of Virgil's *Aeneid*.

A similar evolution from the indiscriminate abode of the dead to a place of punishment or reward, in anticipation of resurrection and final judgment, characterizes *Sheol*, the Jewish concept of the afterlife. In Greek, Jews naturally referred to this place as Hades, without concern for any implied polytheism. Both in the Septuagint and in the NT, Hades commonly refers to the abode of the dead (Acts 2.27) or to death itself (Wis. 1.12-16). Apparent personification of Hades is rare, but does occur (Rev. 6.8). In any case, Hades in the Bible rarely refers to what we would call hell, contrary to what, for instance, the KJV implies.

Typical of the later Christian tradition is an ambiguous mixture of biblical and pagan concepts of the hereafter. In time, this resulted in the distinction of heaven, purgatory, and hell, echoing the threefold layout of the Greco-Roman afterlife. As heaven and purgatory were physically separated from it, Hades became virtually synonymous with hell. Medieval imagery of a king and queen presiding over hell probably goes back to Hades and his spouse, Persephone (compare their depictions as rulers of the underworld in the Etruscan *Tomba dell'Orco* at Cerveteri, Italy). An interesting Byzantine ivory (tenth century) depicts a bearded man, identified as Hades, impaled on the Cross of Christ. This is one of the very few depictions of the god in an explicitly Christian context. From the Renaissance onwards, depictions of Hades are largely limited to the abduction of Persephone (sculpted by Bernini 1622; painted by Rembrandt 1632).

There are no significant portrayals of the god Hades in literature. Evocations of his realm are more common, though. The archetypal representation of medieval views on Hades/hell, incorporating numerous Christian and classical elements, is offered by Dante Alighieri in his *Inferno* (1309). Other noteworthy descriptions of Hades include Milton's *Paradise Lost* (1667) and the sixth chapter of Joyce's *Ulysses* (1922). Outside literature the god is part of the supporting cast of Monteverdi's opera *Orfeo* (1607) and, more recently, the Walt Disney motion picture *Hercules* (1997).

See also DEATH; GEHENNA; HELL; SHEOL [DDEC]

Hagar. Hagar was Sarah's maidservant (Gen. 16.1). When Sarah realized she could not conceive, she said to Abraham, 'go in to my slave-girl; it may be that I shall obtain children by her' (16.2). Hagar eventually gave birth to a son named Ishmael, but Sarah also gave birth to a son, Isaac, unexpectedly. Before Isaac was born, Sarah treated Hagar harshly and so she ran away. Despite Sarah's cruelty, God instructed Hagar to return to her master Sarah and submit. He also promised to make Ishmael a great nation because legacy was highly desirable in the Ancient Near East. After Hagar returned, there was tension between the two boys so Sarah demanded that Abraham reject Hagar and her son and banish them from the household. Once again, Hagar found herself in the wilderness and once again, God communicated with her and promised to make Ishmael flourish (Gen. 21.1-21). In the NT, Hagar is referred to in Gal. 4. She appears in an allegory about the God's covenant with Israel.

In rabbinic tradition, Hagar is identified as the daughter of Pharaoh who gave her to Sarah when Sarah was part of his harem. This idea is also present in the Islamic traditions though the reason for the gifting of Hagar varies. Because Hagar is the mother of the Patriarch Ishmael, the Islamic text portrays her in a positive light and views her expulsion from the home of Abraham as a means of testing and relocation. There are two Muslim pilgrimages that commemorate Hagar's experience in the desert, Hajj and Umra.

Hagar has come to serve as an example for women who have experienced oppression, especially among those who engage in womanist criticism of the biblical text. Black scholars relate to Hagar due to the themes of racism, slavery, and subjugation involved in her story.

Hagar also plays an important role in Middle East politics. Many Palestinians used Hagar as an exemplar of their situation after the Israeli War of Independence. When people name babies Hagar, it is often a political statement of sympathy with Palestinian reconciliation. Hagar was the subject of debate in the Knesset regarding proper school curriculum. Recently the creation of the journal *Hagar: Studies in Culture, Polity and Identities* has solidified the connection between Hagar and Israeli–Palestinian relations.

Authors such as William Shakespeare, Daniel Defoe, and Samuel Taylor Coleridge have used Hagar as mean of expressing rejection. More positive images appear in Pearl River's *Hagar*, *Hagar in the Wilderness* by Nathaniel Parker Willis, and Augusta Moore's *Hagar's Farewell*. Hagar or allusions to her can also be found in Salman Rushdie's *The Satanic Verses*, Toni Morrison's *Song of Solomon*, and *The Stone Angel* by Margaret Laurence. Scenes from the life of Hagar have been depicted by artists such as Lucas van Leyden, Rembrandt, Pieter Lastman, Gustave Doré, Sir Robert Strange, and Marc Chagall. A large collection of Hagar art can be found at the Fine Arts Museums of San Francisco.

Recommended reading. Weems, Renita. *Just a Sister Away: Understanding the Timeless Connection between Women of Today and Women in the Bible*. Farmington Hills, MI: Walk Worthy Press, 2005.

See also ABRAHAM; GENESIS, BOOK OF; ISHMAEL; ISAAC; SARAH [EW]

Haggadah. The term derives from the Hebrew *naggid*, meaning 'to tell or proclaim'. It often appears as *aggada*. Most commonly the term *aggada* refers to the narrative portions of Jewish commentaries on the Bible known as *midrash*, the narrative portions of other early Jewish literature such as the Babylonian or Jerusalem Talmuds, or to the narrative expansions of the Aramaic Targums (early Jewish translations of the Bible). *Aggadah* can narrate exegetically derived stories concerning biblical characters, filling in the gaps of the biblical narrative. It can also convey stories of early Jewish rabbis to illustrate either an exegetical point in the context of *midrash*, or a legal (*halakhic*) perspective in the context of legal *midrash* or the Talmuds. Often *aggadic* narratives employ fantastic elements including the working of miracles, exaggerated characterizations, or folktale motifs. Recent research into *aggadic* literature has often emphasized aspects of early Jewish culture such as gender, sexuality, and the relationship between early Judaism, early Christianity, and Greco-Roman culture. Some argue *aggadic midrash* manifests folklore motifs and evidence of cross-cultural interaction, both between high and low Jewish culture, as well as between Jews and other Middle Eastern peoples. In the 1980s and 90s, it was popular to analyse *aggada* using the methods of poststructuralist literary criticism due to the high levels of indeterminancy and polysemy manifest in this literature. Such analysis has fallen out of fashion, however, for both theoretical and historical reasons; many scholars felt it was inappropriate to read twentieth-century concepts into literature originating from the early centuries of the Common Era. Yet in contemporary Judaism, the practice of creating *aggadic* narratives after the fashion of *midrash* has been revitalized, especially as a means for recovering the lost or hidden voices in the Bible. For many Jewish feminists this is a legitimate way to uncover the voices of women obscured by the masculine narrators of the Bible and male dominated post-biblical literature.

The term Haggadah, this time spelled with an 'H', can refer more specifically to the scrolls, codices, and modern books containing the Passover service or *seder*. These *Haggadot* (plural of *haggadah*) consist of multiple parts, including prayers, readings from the Bible and from rabbinic literature, as well as directions concerning how to perform the Passover rituals. Many portions of the Passover *Haggodot* are sung, in keeping with the synagogue custom of chanting psalms and prayers. It is common to find illuminated *Haggadot* dating from the Middle Ages. Similarly, in modern times, various *Haggadot* have been produced by a variety of Jewish publishers for specific branches of Judaism (Orthodox, Conservative, Reform, Reconstructionist, etc.). Sometimes individual synagogues will write their own *Haggadot* based on the preferences of the particular communities and their rabbis. Feminist, humanist, and universalist *Haggadot*, as well as *Haggadot* written specifically for children are also growing in popularity.

See also PARDES [SL]

Haggai, Book of. Haggai was one three prophets sent to the people who returned from exile to the Holy Land. About Haggai almost nothing is known. Some argue that 2.3 implies he saw Solomon's temple and was quite elderly at the time of his prophetic ministry. Some ancient traditions say he was of priestly lineage.

The Book of Haggai is the tenth in the Book of the Twelve (the Minor Prophets) and it is the first of the Latter Prophets addressing the exiles who returned to Jerusalem. His prophecy was linked Zechariah (Ezra 5.1) and the written form of this message was was dated in relation to the gentile Persian king, Darius I, Hystaspes (521–485 BCE). Haggai received his call in the second year of the reign of Darius in the sixth month and on the first day of the month (August–September 520 BCE) according to the Babylonian lunar calendar. He also received three additional oracles through November–December in a ministry lasting only four months.

Haggai received 'the word of the Lord' and delivered his message to Zerubbabel son of Shealtiel, the governor of Judea, and to Jehozadak the high priest. It was an oracle delivered to them as the civil and temporal leaders of the renewed community of faith in Jerusalem. It also concerned the people because it was specifically addressing their claim that the time for rebuilding the temple had not come. This inattention to rebuilding was one of Haggai's concerns. The people were putting themselves—their homes and businesses—ahead of the service of God. He also declares there will be political upheavals that will 'shake the heaven and the earth' (2.21-22). Given all of the preaching of the pre-exilic prophets against the worship at the temple, this message in support of rebuilding the temple is remarkable. Dedication services for new church buildings often use Hag. 2.1-9, and lectionaries include a few reading from Haggai in evening prayer services.

Recommended reading. Newsome, James D. *The Hebrew Prophets*. Atlanta: John Knox Press, 1984.

See also DARIUS; FORMER PROPHETS; HIGH PRIEST; LATTER PROPHETS; PERSIA; PROPHECY; PROPHETS; TEMPLE, ISRAEL'S; ZERUBBABEL [AJW]

Hallelujah. The term derives from the Hebrew *hallel* (to praise) and *yah* (the Lord, Yaweh). It appears twenty four times in the HB, primarily in the Psalms as an instruction for the congregation to join in praise, notably in the Hallel prayer (Pss 113–118), which is recited at times of joy. It appears four times in the NT (all in the Book of Revelation). Hallelujah is also used as an expression in Christian liturgy and prayer not as an injunction, as in Jewish liturgy, but as a proclamation of joy or thanksgiving. Some traditions omit use of the word from the liturgy during Lent, a season of prayer and self-denial, and reintroduce it at Easter. In many free-church traditions, hallelujah is used as a joyful, spontaneous exclamation of praise.

In modern usage, hallelujah does not always hold the religious connotation of the word; instead, the word is often an expression of general happiness. The so-called 'Hallelujah Chorus' from George Frideric Handel's *Messiah*, and Leonard Cohen's oft-covered song 'Hallelujah' illustrate familiar uses of the term. Handel's upbeat, ecstatic piece concludes the section entitled 'The Passion', which outlines Christ's death, resurrection, and triumph over the powers of evil. Cohen's 'Hallelujah' contrasts OT imagery (mostly through references to David, traditional author of many Psalms) and a contemporary romantic relationship. Hallelujah, in Cohen's song, becomes an intentional, self-conscious expression of joyfulness in the face of despair, heartache and loss.

See also PSALM/PSALMIST/PSALMS, BOOK OF; WORSHIP [MWB]

Ham. Ham is identified as the second son of Noah who was saved with his family from the flood (Gen. 5.32; 6.10; 9.18). God establishes his covenant with Noah, his sons and their descendants that waters will never again destroy the earth (9.1, 9-17, 28-29). God's covenant with humankind includes the African nations around the Red Sea that originated from Ham, including Egypt and its province of Canaan (10.1, 6-7, 20; 1 Chron. 1.8-16). Another writer tells an unflattering tale about Ham (9.18-27). Ham saw Noah naked and drunk in his tent, but his brothers Shem and Japheth averted their eyes. The expression 'saw nakedness' suggests carrying out a sexual act (see Lev. 20.17; Ezek. 16.37; cf. also the story of Lot's incestuous union with his daughters in Gen. 19.30-38). When Noah wakes up and realizes what Ham did to him, he curses his youngest son: 'Cursed be Canaan; lowest slaves shall he be to his brothers' (Gen. 9.25). Presumably, the story provides justification for the later conquest and enslavement of the Canaanites.

Postbiblical Jewish sources relate that Ham disobeyed Noah's prohibition against sexual intercourse on the Ark during the world's destruction. As punishment God turned Ham's skin black (e.g., *Sanhedrin Tractate* 108b). In another tradition, Ham's crime was sodomy (*Sanhedrin* 70a). Some legends say that Ham unmanned Noah (e.g., *Pesahim* 113b), which is based on the Greek myth of Cronus's castration by his youngest son Zeus. Other interpreters acquit Ham (e.g., *Tanhuma Noah* 9). From the fourth century into the fifteenth, Christian theologians found the origins of servitude in Ham's sinfulness (Augustine, Chrysostom, Augustodunensis). German jurist Eike von Repgau (*Sachsenspiegel*, 1200) and English scholar John Wyclif (tract, 1378) refuted the servile status of Ham and the notion of lower servile classes. Mediaeval legend also connected Ham's laughter at Noah (Josephus, *Antiquities* 1.6.3) with the laughter of the Persian poet-prophet Zoroaster (Pliny, *Naturalis historiae* 7.16). In *Commentaria* (1498) Dominican scholar Annius of Viterbo popularized Ham's family as gods and kings who founded Italy, Spain and Britain, as evidenced by a 1560 woodcut portraying Ham as a Roman king and ancestor of Elizabeth I.

The curse of Ham entered Western cultural history as the single greatest justification for the African slave trade of the eighteen and nineteenth centuries. Bishop Thomas Newton (*Dissertations on the Prophecies*, 1754) declared that Noah's curse on Ham is 'shown to be fulfilled from the earliest times to the present'. Baptist minister Thornton Stringfellow (*Slavery . . . in the Light of Bible Teachings*, 1861) described Ham as 'a slave of shameless animal propensities', representing nations and individuals who 'should be subjected to the control of superiors' for the good of the world. Slavery was 'God's plan' and the way to control and elevate 'the inferior and degraded man'. This popular belief that Ham was cursed by God persisted well into the twentieth century, the ideological endorsement of racial segregation and resistance to the United States Civil Rights Act (1964).

Recommended reading. Alter, Robert. *Genesis: Translation and Commentary*. New York: Norton, 1997. Goldenberg, David M. *The Curse of Ham: Race and Slavery in Early Judaism, Christianity, and Islam*. Princeton: Princeton University Press, 2003. Graves, Robert, and Raphael Patai. *Hebrew Myths: The Book of Genesis*. London: Arena, 1989. Whitford, David, M. *The Curse of Ham in the Early Modern Era: The Bible and the Justifications for Slavery*. Burlington, VT: Ashgate, 2009.

See also CANAAN; JAPHETH; NOAH'S ARK; SHEM [JRW]

Haman. Haman, the son of Hammedatha the Agagite, first appears in Est. 3.1 as the chief advisor to King Ahasuerus. Following his promotion by King Ahasuerus and interaction with Mordecai, Esther chronicles Haman's vehemence towards Jews, his desire to obliterate them, the unraveling of his plans, and his subsequent demise. Though appearing in only six chapters of the Bible, Haman remains perhaps the most vilified character in all of Jewish history.

Each year, on the holiday of Purim, through the public reading of Esther, varying practices of nullifying Haman's name are performed. Listeners, upon hearing Haman's name, shake a *gragger* or other form of noisemaker, stomp their feet, clap their hands, and yell in order to drown out Haman's name. This practice of obliterating Haman's name reflects both his wicked actions as the chief advisor as well as his genealogical lineage. As a direct descendant of Agag, king of Amalek (1 Sam. 15.8), Haman is subject to all acts reserved for Amalekites as mentioned in Deut. 25.17-19. Specifically, the Bible commands the recalling of Amalek's actions to the Israelites in the wilderness, as well as the need to 'blot out' Amalek's remembrance from under heaven.

Within rabbinic literature, Haman's identifications and associations extend beyond chief advisor. The Midrash and Babylonian Talmud describe Haman as a barber, astrologer, and former servant of Mordecai. Additionally, Haman is likened to both a wolf and serpent. This pairing of Haman and serpents is treated by Renaissance painter Michaelangelo Buonarrati (1475–1564) within two of his four pendentives in the Sistine Chapel. In *The Brazen Serpent* (1511), Michelangelo visualizes the biblical account of the Israelites' grumblings against God, as mentioned in Deut. 21.4-9; and, in *The Punishment of Haman* (1511), Michelangelo refigures Haman's expiration. As opposed to the literal reading of Haman's execution through hanging, Michelangelo visibly elaborates Haman's end through a pronounced foreshortening of his supposed crucifixion. This substitution of hanging for crucifixion enables Michelangelo to claim Haman as a precursor to Jesus.

Haman reappears in several other Renaissance paintings including Filippino Lippi's *Three Scenes from the Story of Esther* (1475); here, Haman appears before Esther begging for forgiveness. Within Frans II Fracken's *The Feast of Esther* (1630), Haman is again crucified, though this time in the far corner of the painting. Within Jan Victor's *The Banquet of Esther and Ahasuerus* (1640s) and *Esther and Haman before Ahasuerus* (1638–1640), Haman is seated at a table along with Esther and Ahaseurus.

Within Rembrandt Harmenszoon van Rijn's works, Haman appears in *Haman Begging Esther for Mercy* (1655), and *Ahasuerus, Haman, and Esther* (1660), and possibly *Haman in Disgrace* (1660).

Haman's resurgence in Renaissance art coincides with a renewed interest in the HB, and rabbinic literature among Christian Hebraists and contemporary authors. Between 1536 and 1537, Friar John Pickering of Bridlington wrote a poem comparing Haman with Thomas Cromwell, the first Earl of Essex. Later, in 1543, Thomas Kirchmayer published a play about Haman titled *Hamanus: Tragoedia nova sumpta e Bibliis*. Following Joseph Swetnam's misogynistic invective, *The Arraignment of Lewd, Idle, Froward, and Unconstant Women* (1615), Esther Sowernam utilized the Haman imagery in a rebutting pamphlet titled *Ester Hath Hang'd Haman* (1617).

Through the Renaissance, Haman's lore was redistributed via differing means. In both word and image, Haman was reconstituted for contemporary purposes. Nonetheless, it is through Esther and its perennial reading that we are reminded most of this character's machinations.

Recommended reading. Anastaplo, George. *The Bible: Respectful Readings*. Lanham, MD: Lexington Books, 2008. Graham-Dixon, Andrew. *Michelangelo and the Sistine Chapel*. New York: Skyhorse Publications, 2009.

See also ESTHER, ADDITIONS TO; ESTHER, BOOK OF; LOTS, FEAST OF (PURIM); MORDECAI [ADAMR]

Hand. The English term hand translates Hebrew *yad* (*yāmîn*, right hand) and Greek *cheir* (*dexios*, right hand). In the HB and the NT, the word hand is used in three distinct senses: (1) as a physical part of the human body; (2) in a broader symbolic sense, the hand denotes human or divine power, agency, or ownership; (3) various idiomatic phrases employ the word hand, e.g., the banks of a river are sometimes called the hands of the river (e.g., Num. 13.29), and in Ezek. 21.9, a signpost is called a hand.

The most common use of the word hand in the Bible involves the agency of a human or group, as in Ps. 71.4: 'Rescue me, O my God, from the hand of the wicked, from the grasp of the unjust and cruel' (see also Acts 4.27-28). In reference to Israel's God, the hand can designate an instrument of either blessing and empowerment (1 Esd. 8.61) or affliction (1 Sam. 5.11). Laying hands on an individual is a mark of dedication for a task or a conferral of some status (whether for blessing or for cursing), as in Gen. 48.13; Exod. 29.10; Lev. 16.21-22. The hands' status as either 'clean' or stained with blood is an image of innocence or guilt, respectively (Gen. 4.11; Job 17.9; Jas 4.8; cf. Matt. 5.30; Mark 9.43).

The symbolism of the right hand (blessing, chosenness) and the left hand (curse, rejection) plays an important role in several biblical passages (e.g., Gen. 48.13-18), and the NT repeatedly describes Jesus as exalted to, or sitting at, 'the right hand of God' (Mark 16.19; Acts 2.33; 7.55, 56; Rom. 8.34; Col. 3.1; Heb. 10.12; 1 Pet. 3.22). In Mark 10.37-40, Jesus' disciples request to be seated in the place of honor at Jesus' right hand in the coming kingdom. In other places (specifically Judg. 3.15; 20.16), being left-handed is viewed as a code for crafty behavior or for some unusual talent, a meaning reflected in the Latin etymologies for the modern English words sinister (*sinistra* = left handed) and dexterous (*dextra* = right handed).

The sense of hand in terms of human agency is a natural biological idiom that was commonly used in ancient contexts and continues to be widely used throughout the world today. Witnesses in contemporary legal settings still raise their right hand before testifying, and Adam Smith's seminal description of capitalism in *The Wealth of Nations* (1776) famously referred to an 'invisible hand', namely, the role of the capitalist market in its own self-regulation. The phrase 'hand of God' (e.g., 2 Chron. 30.12; Job 2.10; 19.21; Eccl. 9.1; Wis. 3.1; 1 Pet. 5.6; etc.) has acquired significance in modern popular culture as a description of an unexplained or seemingly mysterious event (similar to the legal term 'act of God' in reference to a natural disaster). In the sports world, the 1986 FIFA World Cup quarter-final soccer match between Argentina and England featured the so-called 'hand of God goal', scored by Diego Maradona on an unnoticed handball. A last second field goal in a 2006 American football game between the Washington Redskins and Dallas Cowboys seemed, to Redskins fans, to miraculously move from right to left and give the Redskins the victory, causing many fans to dub the game 'the hand of God game'. In 2009, NASA's Chandra X-ray observatory captured an image in deep space of a hand-like shape, which was quickly labeled the 'hand of God' by viewers and news media outlets.

See also Body; Finger of God [BRD]

Handmaiden. This term is used in various ways in the Bible. It refers to a female servant or slave. One example is Hagar, 'an Egyptian slave-girl' (Gen. 16.1; see 16.1-16; 21.8-34). In many cases, the handmaiden is the personal servant of a wealthy woman. The handmaiden may be called upon to act as a surrogate mother for her mistress, as in the story of Hagar and Sarah; any children she had would belong to the mistress. Sometimes, a handmaiden (or simply, maid or maiden, in some English translations) refers to a young girl or woman and is not associated with her social status. Often, this reference is made to a young girl who is also a virgin. Finally, the term handmaiden is used as a term of humility and respect by many women to describe themselves when they are addressing an elder or king, or praying to God. Although the term is now outdated, there is a loose echo of the idea in the modern idea of a bridesmaid.

See also Slave [MHH]

Handwriting on the wall. Rembrandt's painting *Belshazzar's Feast: The Writing on the Wall* (1635) faithfully represents the biblical legend of Belshazzar king of Babylon who desecrates the temple's gold and silver vessels at an all-night drinking party (Dan. 5). The banquet is interrupted by a mysterious hand writing the Hebrew words *mene, mene, tekel, uparsin* on a wall. The prophet Daniel interprets the message 'numbered, weighed and divided' as foretelling the fall of Babylon and Belshazzar. Rembrandt represents the Hebrew script, in contrast to most artists who omit the ominous writing (e.g., Mattia Preti 1658; John Martin, 1821). Rembrandt's Hebrew words read vertically downwards, beginning at the top right, with the hand resting on the final character at bottom left. His script closely resembles the inscription of his friend Rabbi Menasseh ben Israel who, in his essay *De termino vitae (Of the Term of Life,* 1639), follows ancient rabbinical interpretation in suggesting that God made his handwriting incomprehensible to Belshazzar but decipherable to Daniel.

Georg Friedrich Händel's oratorio *Belshazzar* (1744), with librettist Charles Jennens, includes the Hebrew words and their meaning but embellishes the biblical plot. 'Behold! See there!' is tenor Belshazzar's familiar reaction to the handwriting, but Handel includes a response from the Chorus of Babylonians: 'O dire portentous sight! But see, 'tis gone, and leaves behind it types unknown; perhaps some stern decree of fate, big with the ruin of our state!' (Act two, scene 2). Another significant change occurs when soprano Nitocris the Queen Mother (Herodotus, *Histories* 1.185-88) narrates that Belshazzar repented and God reversed the handwritten message of doom. What follows the resumption of

Belshazzar's 'impious feasts' is a Martial Symphony in which the Babylonian king and his attendants are killed in battle (Act two, scene 1; cf. Dan. 5.30). Belshazzar's kingdom is seized by Darius the Persian king (5.31), but Handel's Daniel instructs Cyrus of Persia to read the lines on the wall, 'the great prediction', which he has already in part accomplished (scene 3).

In his poem 'To Belshazaar' (1814), Lord Byron (George Noel Gordon) opposes autocratic government by way of Daniel's defiant address to Belshazzar, against the 'weakest and worst' of men who are 'crowned and anointed'. But the truly wise or perceptive person is not deluded, thus Daniel sees and understands the meaning of 'the graven words': 'Is it not written, thou must die?' In Byron's *Vision of Belshazzar* (1815), Babel's aged statesmen 'were not sage', but youthful Daniel 'saw that writing's truth'.

German poet Heinrich Heine denounces tyrannical rule in *Belsazar* (1822), a Gothic ballad, which characterizes the king as an absolute monarch. Heine omits the figure of Daniel and transforms the biblical story of 'the flaming script' into a prophecy of doom for German despotism. The revolutionary call for political change is indicated by 'the letters of fire', by the king's claim of sovereignty over God himself, and by the report that the knights murdered their monarch during the drunken feast.

In William Walton's oratorio *Belshazzar's Feast* (1931) and Osbert Sitwell's libretto (1930), the writing on the wall is eerily depicted, without reference to Daniel. By combining biblical texts (Isa. 13; 39; Pss 81, 137; Dan. 5; Rev. 18) with grandiose and rousing orchestration, the oratorio emphasizes the fall of Babylon, the symbol of civilization but also a city of evil and decadence.

Recommended reading. Porteous, Norman W. *Daniel: A Commentary*. Philadelphia: Westminster Press, 1965. Kitson, Michael. *Rembrandt*. Rev. 3rd edn. London: Phaidon Press, 1992. Westermann, Mariët. *Rembrandt*. London: Phaidon Press, 2000.

See also BELSHAZZAR; DANIEL; DANIEL, BOOK OF; GOD [JRW]

Hannah. The books of Samuel describe the introduction and establishment of kingship in Israel. At the start is a transition phase where Samuel serves as prophet, priest and national leader. The book opens with the story of his birth, and at the center of that story is a woman named Hannah (1 Sam. 1.1–2.21). The Hebrew name Hanna means 'favored'.

Hannah is the first of two wives married to Elkanah. The second wife, Peninnah, has given Elkanah numerous children, but Hannah is barren. In ancient culture, barrenness is viewed as a social stigma. Peninnah intensives Hannah's painful situation by provoking her to anger until eventually, Hannah becomes despondent and will not eat. Every year, the family goes to worship and make a sacrifice to the LORD. Elkanah has a special love for Hannah and gives her a double portion of meat for the sacrifice. Yet, he shows that he doesn't truly understand the situation, remarking that surely he is better to her than ten sons. Hannah, in her state of desperation, goes to the temple and pours out her heart before God. She vows that if God would give her a son, she would dedicate him to the LORD and he would serve the LORD at the temple.

The priest observes Hannah quietly, but fervently, praying and accuses her of being drunk. When she explains that she is not drunk, but praying in great anguish, the priest responds that surely her prayer will be answered. Indeed, Hannah conceives and eventually gives birth to a boy. As promised, she dedicates him to the LORD and when he is old enough, the boy goes to serve the LORD at the temple.

This story takes place during a time of spiritual darkness in Israel. The priest's sons are wicked and unfit to minister to the nation. Hannah's son, Samuel, is raised up by God to be a great leader and a powerful character in Israel's history. Samuel's notable life is a legacy to the faithfulness and prayerful request of his mother, Hannah. The story of Hannah is also important for the role of women in Scripture. Her character reflects the struggles and dynamics of other women in the Bible, especially the motif of the barren wife and the rivalry between barren and fruitful wives. It is an important example that women can boldly approach God through prayer and can make vows and sacrifices, and that God hears and answers the prayers of women and cares about their hardships. A lengthy section in 1 Sam. 2 is given to a prayer of praise that is attributed to Hannah. This is a significant contribution to the voice of women in the OT.

Recommended reading. Cook, Joan E. *Hannah's Desire, God's Design: Early Interpretations of the Story of Hannah*. Sheffield: Sheffield Academic Press, 1999.

See also SAMUEL; SAMUEL, BOOKS OF [MHH]

Hanukkah. The Jewish festival Hanukkah (also known as the Feast of Dedication) commemorates the repair, rebuilding and reinstitution of worship in the Jerusalem temple in 165/4 BCE. Hanukkah is unique among the festivals of the Jewish calendar as it originates from an event not recorded in the HB itself but from the books 1 and 2 Maccabees (included in the Septuagint, and among the Apocrypha in Catholic and Orthodox Bibles). In the Maccabean saga, the antagonistic Syrian ruler Antiochus IV Epiphanes desecrated the Jerusalem temple and instigated pagan worship on its altar (1 Macc. 1.40-64; 2 Macc. 6.1-9). Such profanation spurred Judas Maccabeus to lead a guerilla revolt against their oppressors. This movement experienced a degree of success culminating in the rededication of the temple (1 Macc. 4.36-61; 2 Macc. 10.1-8). The inaugural event of rededication is recorded as taking place on the twenty-fifth day of Kislev (the lunisolar month coinciding with November–December) and lasting for a period of eight days (1 Macc. 4.59). During this time, incense and sacrifices were offered anew on the rebuilt altar and lamps were lit within the precincts of the temple in celebration (1 Macc. 1.59-60; 2 Macc. 10.3).

Within later Jewish tradition, Hanukkah was considered a relatively minor event in the religious calendar until the emergence of the Jewish enlightenment movement (*Haskalah*) in the nineteenth century CE. After that time, particularly in post-World War II America and Europe, the celebration of Hanukkah had a significant impact both internally on Jewish tradition as well as externally in regards to secular perception of Jewish life and practice. While many of the practices involved in celebrating Hanukkah find their roots in the Maccabean tradition, such as celebrating for eight consecutive days beginning on the twenty-fifth day of Kislev, other celebratory elements appear to have evolved over time. For instance, while the lighting of individual candles in the candelabrum (also known as a menorah) and recitation of prescribed blessings is reflective of lighting the lamps in the temple, this practice evidences the growth of the tradition. Hanukkah is a predominantly home oriented festival as only two minor additions associated with the celebration are evident in the Jewish liturgy.

More recently, Hanukkah has become something of a commercial parallel to Christmas. Consumers are able to purchase seasonal items such as Hanukkah cards and decorations, and in some circles, the exchange of gifts has become common practice. Evidence of this trend in popular culture is Adam Sandler's 'The Hanukkah Song' (1996) which was later expanded into the animated seasonal film '8 Crazy Nights' (2002). Beyond this, a niche market has developed for Jewish-Christian interfaith families to celebrate the fusion holiday of 'Chrismukkah'. Online retailers such as chrismukkah.com make celebrating the hybrid holiday an easy and unique experience. In popular culture, Chrismukkah was celebrated in the Cohen household on the television series The O.C. (2005).

Recommended reading. Robinson, George. *Essential Judaism: A Complete Guide to Beliefs, Customs and Rituals*. New York: Pocket Books, 2000. VanderKam, James C. 'Hanukkah: Its Timing and Significance according to 1 and 2 Maccabees'. *Journal for the Study of the Pseudepigrapha* 1 (1987) 23-40.

See also FESTIVALS; JUDAS MACCABEUS; MACABEES, THE; MACCABEES, BOOKS OF [ABP]

Haran. Haran is both a personal and a place name. According to Gen. 11.26-31, Haran is the third son of Terah and the youngest brother of Abram (Abraham). Genesis 11.28 says Haran predeceased Terah and was buried in Ur of the Chaldeans, which was his birthplace.

Lot, Abram, Sarai, and Terah left Ur, migrating up the Euphrates valley to Haran where they settled (cf. Acts 7.2, 4). Haran is located in modern Turkey about 40 kilometers north of the Syrian border on a tributary of the Euphrates called Balikh. After a season Terah died at Haran at the age of two hundred and five years. It was at Haran ('crossroads' in Hebrew) that the descendants of Nahor established themselves, thus causing it to be called the city of Nahor. It is located in a farming district called Padan-aram between Khabour and the Euphrates. Ezekiel 27.23-24 refers to it as a trading center for choice garments, embroidered and dyed blue.

When Abraham was old he sent his servant to the city of Nahor to find a wife for Isaac. When he arrived, he met Rebekah whom he discovered to be the daughter of Bethuel, son of Milcah. Her brother was Laban (Gen. 24.10). Years later Jacob left Beer-sheba to go to Haran (Gen. 28.10). When he arrived in the Paddan-aram district, he went to a well near Haran (Gen. 29.4-5) where he met Rachel and her father Laban, son of Nahor.

The Assyrians captured the city, and it is identified as a token of their power in a letter sent by King Sennaherib of Assyria (2 Kgs 19.12). After the fall of Nineveh to the Babylonians and Medes in 612 BCE, Ashur-uballit II (612–609) retreated to Haran. The Babylonian took it in 610. Nabonidus (556–539) the last king of Babylon was from Haran.

There are a few minor biblical characters with the name Haran. Caleb was one of the twelve spies. He later had a concubine named Ephah by whom he had a son named Haran as well as other sons (1 Chron. 2.46). Levi had three sons, one of whom was Gershom. In King David's time a Gershonite Levite from the family of Shimel was named Haran (1 Chron. 23.7-9).

See also ABRAHAM; ASSYRIA; BABYLON; CHALDEANS; EUPHRATES; GERSHOM; UR [AJW]

Harlot. A harlot is a prostitute (Hebrew *zonah*) who offers sex for payment (Deut. 23.17-18; Josh. 2.1; 6.17; Judg. 11.1; 16.1-3; Hos. 3.1-3). Not all stories referring to harlots are concerned to condemn their profession. One story presents a prostitute in a positive light in her legal dispute over a baby; Solomon judges in her favor (1 Kgs 3.16-28). Bertolt Brecht's play *The Caucasian Chalk Circle* (1944–1945) reverses the tale when a judge establishes the true mother as the non-biological one. Usually a biblical female is called a harlot, not for sexual irregularity, but for engaging in foreign alliances and worship (Hos. 1.2; 2.2-13; Jer. 2.20, 3.1, 6, 8; Ezek. 16). The way a woman dresses and behaves is how she identifies her social standing. Tamar puts on a harlot veil to cover her face and sits on a public road so that she can be immediately identified as a prostitute (Gen. 38.14-30). Jerusalem and Babylon (Rome) appear as harlots dressed in scarlet and gold jewels (Jer. 4.29; Rev. 17.1–19.5).

Biblical imagery of the good and bad harlot, either prostitute or the disgraced woman, structures the epic drama of *Gone with the Wind*, a 1939 film adapted from Margaret Mitchell's 1936 novel on the American Civil War. Just as Rahab protected the Israelite spies by housing them at her brothel (Josh. 2; 6; Heb. 11.31), so Belle, madam of Atlanta's Red Horse Saloon, saves the lives of men walking into a Yankee trap by providing sanctuary in her bordello. Her archetypal counterpart is the beautiful Scarlett O'Hara, a strong, shrewd and scheming Delilah figure who exhibits prostitute-like behavior. For compensation of 1100 silver pieces from every Philistine lord, Delilah seduces Samson to make him reveal the secret of his strength (Judg. 16.4-6). So Peter Paul Rubens (1609) represents Delilah as a red-headed prostitute wearing a red dress, in company with an elderly madam. Scarlett tries to sell sex to Rhett Butler until he tells her, 'You're not worth $300'. After tricking a prosperous merchant into marriage, Scarlett's beloved Ashley says, 'You've sold yourself'. Belle acknowledges she stands outside respectable society, but Scarlett thinks she belongs. Because she sacrifices all moral principles for self-interest, Butler makes her put on a red dress and plenty of rouge to be seen as she really is, a harlot out of place within her social context.

Jezebel, daughter of a Sidonian king, is treated as a harlot because she introduced Canaanite Baal worship into Northern Israel (1 Kgs 16.31; 18.19, 2 Kgs 9.22). In the 1993 oratorio *Jezebel* composed by Derek Holman, librettist Robertson Davies calls the heroine a harlot because she seized Naboth's vineyard in exchange for Ahab casting off his desert god to worship Baal, her city god bringing wealth through his Stock Market, 'The Market of Phantoms' (cf. 1 Kgs 21). The biblical Jezebel, eyes painted and head adorned, does not present herself as a harlot (cf. *Jezebel* 1938 film) but as the Israelite queen-mother, Asherah-devotee, meeting her death (2 Kgs 9.30). By contrast, Davies' painted Jezebel, clad in purple gown with gold necklace, calls herself 'a great Queen' and 'Queen of Market riches'.

Recommended reading. Ackerman, Susan. *Warrior, Dancer, Seductress Queen: Women in Judges and Biblical Israel*. Anchor Bible Reference Library. New York: Doubleday, 1998. Levitt Kohn, Risa. 'In and out of Place: Physical Space and Social Location in the Bible'. In *From Babel to Babylon: Essays on Biblical History and Literature in Honour of Brian Peckham*. Ed. Joyce Rilett Wood, John E. Harvey, and Mark Leuchter. LHBOTS 455. Pp. 253-62. New York: T. & T. Clark, 2006.

See also ASHERAH; BAAL; CANAAN, CANAANITES; DELILAH; JEZEBEL; RAHAB; SOLOMON; TAMAR [JRW]

Harp and lyre. Both the harp (*kinnor*) and lyre (*nevel*) are chordophones, instruments whose strings are stretched across the surface. When struck, the strings vibrate to produce sound, amplified by a sound box. The modern harp has a roughly triangular frame, with a pillar supporting its 47 strings, and pedals which allow key changes. Scandinavia, England, and Ireland claim the harp originated in their country; it actually became the national instrument and emblem of Ireland.

The ancient lyre was the chief instrument of the temple orchestra. Based on the biblical text, King David excelled at playing the lyre. According to first-century CE Jewish historian Josephus (*Antiquities* 8.3.8), the lyre had ten strings plucked with a plectrum (a thin flat piece made of tortoise shell).

The lyre was box-shaped, with two arms and a yoke, roughly 48–58 centimetres high. The word 'lyric' derives from lyre. The lyre became one of the earliest bowed instruments in Europe.

In the HB, *kinnor* and *nevel* occur together in the same verse 24 times. The lyre is mentioned alone in 17 places, the harp in 11. In the NT, only the harp is mentioned, four times. The two instruments are usually interchangeable (Ps. 57.8; 81.2; 108.2.); the function of both is to make melody, usually for God (Ps. 43.4; 98.5; 137.2; 44.9; 147.7; 149.3; 150.3). Harp and lyre are used as parallelisms in several psalms (Ps. 33.2; 71.22; Ps. 92.3).

The earliest biblical mention of a plucked instrument is in Gen. 4.21; Jubal is named as the ancestor of all who play the lyre. Connections between playing the lyre and prophesying are found in 1 Sam. 10.5, where a group of prophets playing the lyre and other instruments falls into a frenzy; and in lists of those who prophesy 'with lyres and harps' (1 Chron. 25.1, 3).

The most common association of lyre is with David, playing for Saul (1 Sam. 16.16, 23; 18.10). David plays for Saul to ease his depression in probably the earliest known reference to music therapy. The traditional figure of David as the divine singer and lyre-player persisted throughout the Middle Ages, when harp music was considered spiritual. Yet at the same time, minstrels and troubadours, who accompanied themselves on a small harp, created the earliest form of secular music.

The harp and lyre are most frequently found in connection with celebration and singing for temple rites (2 Sam. 6.5; 1 Chron. 13.8; 15.28; Neh. 12.27). The connection between Levites, singers, and these instruments is found in several places (1 Kgs 10.12; 1 Chron. 15.16, 20, 21; 16.5; 25.6; 2 Chron. 9.11; 5.12; 29.25). Music making was so basic to life that when a group of victorious soldiers returned to Jerusalem, the text specifies that they had their harps and lyres (2 Chron. 20.28).

Harps and lyres occasionally appear as symbols of decadence (Amos 5.23; 6.5), equated with pomp (Isa. 14.11), feasting without praising God (Isa. 5.12), and prostitutes (Isa. 23.16). The silencing of these instruments represents defeat and punishment (Ps. 137.2; Isa. 24.8; 30.32; Ezek. 26.13). Figurative uses of harp or lyre are seen in Job 30.31 and Isa. 16.11. Such abundant references imply that the use and sound of harp and lyre were well known to the contemporary readers of these texts.

NT writers refer to harps in 1 Cor. 14.7, where the inanimate sound of instruments is compared to speaking in tongues, and in Rev. 14.2; 15.2; 18.22, where the harp is a heavenly sound.

See also Music [HL]

Harrowing of Hell. The harrowing of hell, alternatively referred to as the Descent of Christ to Hell or the *descensus ad inferos* is, contrary to Christian and Western cultural myth, not mentioned in the Bible. In his descent to hell Christ is said to have taken the devil and death as captives and freed people suffering there in torment. It emerges very early in the development of Christian thought, seen in Irenaeus (*Adversus haereses* 4.27.2) and Tertullian (*De anima* 55.2) and, by the late fourth century, it appears in the Apostles' Creed ('I believe...in Jesus Christ... who...suffered under Pontius Pilate, was crucified, dead and buried, and descended to hell').

From very early Christian times, two NT passages—Eph. 4.8-10; 1 Pet. 3.18-20—have been held to describe the harrowing of hell. In Eph. 4.9 the words 'He had also descended into the lower parts of the earth' were imagined to speak of Christ going to Hades, the underworld or place of the dead. In 1 Pet. 3.18-20, Christ is visualized as being 'put to death in the flesh, but made alive in the spirit, in which also he went and made a proclamation to the spirits in prison, who in former times did not obey, when God waited patiently in the days of Noah'. This language was similarly understood to describe Christ preaching the gospel to persons who had died long ago and were in hell, perhaps those mentioned in Gen. 7.21-24 who were killed by the Noachian flood. Other passages such as Matt. 12.40; Acts 2.24, 27, 31; and 1 Pet. 4.6 have been adduced to support the descent. Modern biblical scholarship has rejected these views. None of these texts say anything explicitly about a supposed harrowing of hell and there is no interpretive reason to support the view that they allude to the descent. They likely refer to the work of Christ during his ministry.

The idea of the descent has persisted in Western culture. It has been a feature of many ancient and medieval writings including St John Chrysostom's *Paschal Homily*, the late fourth century *Gospel of Nicodemus* (chapters 17–27), and Dante's *Inferno*. There are many artistic depictions of the harrowing of hell. Among these are *Christ leads the patriarchs from Hell to Paradise* (Bartolomeo Bertejo, c. 1480), and *Harrowing of Hell or Christ in Limbo* (Albrecht Durer, 1510). Reformers Martin Luther and John Calvin preached about the descent and the work of Christ in conquering the devil, death and hell. It is a teaching of the *Catechism of the Catholic Church*. Despite relatively widespread recognition and acceptance, clear biblical support for a doctrine of the harrowing of hell is lacking.

Recommended reading. Bernstein, Alan E. *The Formation of Hell: Death and Retribution in the Ancient and Early Christian Worlds*. Ithaca, NY: Cornell University Press, 1993. Harris, W. Hall. *The Descent of Christ: Ephesians 4:7-11 and Traditional Hebrew Imagery*. Leiden: Brill, 1996.

See also HELL [RRJ]

Harvest. This term translates the Hebrew *qasir* and Koine Greek *therismos*. In the OT, harvests were cause for celebration, thanksgiving, and reflection. Within Israelite culture the three major harvest seasons of barley, wheat and fruit were linked to three principle feasts: Passover/Unleavened Bread (April), Pentecost (June) and Ingathering (October). See, for example, Exod. 23.14-17; 34.21-28; Lev. 23.4-8, 15-22, 33-36. Harvests were also strictly regulated. Harvesting the corners of a field and gathering fallen grapes were forbidden. These were to be left 'for the poor and the foreigner' (Lev. 19.9; 23.22; Deut. 24.19). The first fruits from the harvest were also to be given to Yahweh as an offering (Lev. 23.9-14). Also, every seventh year the Israelites were to give the land 'a Sabbath of complete rest' (Lev. 25.1-7).

Throughout the OT, harvest was used both literally and figuratively. The loss of a harvest was often used to symbolize devastation, suffering, or calamity (e.g., Job 5.5; Isa. 17.11; Jer. 50.16). Harvest was also used to represent God's judgment as manifested through the destruction of a nation (e.g., Jer. 51.33; Hos. 6.11). In contrast, the idioms 'joy in harvest' and 'harvest of the Nile' signified great joy and abundance (Isa. 9.3; 23.3)

In the NT Gospels, Jesus often used the harvest to teach his followers about certain spiritual needs and realities. On one occasion, Jesus told a parable about the wheat and the tares. In his explanation of the parable, Jesus noted, 'The harvest is the end of the age' (Matt. 13.24-30, 36-43). At another time, after he was overtaken by compassion for the crowds that sought him, Jesus noted, 'The harvest is plentiful, but the workers are few'. He then asked his disciples to 'ask the Lord of the harvest to send out workers into his harvest' (Matt. 9.37-38). Furthermore, in Rev. 14.14-20 John refers to a great harvest of the earth.

In the Western world, throughout the middle ages and the early modern period, the harvest season was a time of communal co-operation and celebration. The harvest was also captured by Western artists, like the nineteenth century French realist, Jean-François Millet in his works entitled *Harvesters* (1849), *The Sower* (1850), *Harvesters Resting (Ruth and Boaz)* (1853), and *The Gleaners* (1857). In the year 2000, French filmmaker Agnes Varda produced a film entitled *Les Glaneurs et la Glaneuse* (*The Gleaners and I*) in which she examined the tradition and practice of gleaning in France.

The triumph of urbanization in Western culture has somewhat diminished the social significance and relevance of the harvest. Many urban-dwellers have little knowledge of agriculture or the modern harvest. Still, the thanksgiving holiday, a very modern form of an autumn harvest festival, is celebrated in many countries to this day.

Recommended reading. King, Philip J., and Lawrence E. Stager. *Life in Biblical Israel*, 2001. Snell, Daniel C. *Life in the Ancient Near East*, 1997. White, K.D. *Roman Farming*, 1970.

See also PLANTS, SYMBOLISM OF; SOUR GRAPES; VINE/VINEYARD; WINE [PRW]

Head. Head translates the Hebrew *rōsh* and the Greek *kephalē*. The foundational sense of head is anatomical but figuratively, the term can represent a whole person or, in apocalyptic symbolism, power over an entire kingdom (e.g., Dan. 2.37-38; cf. Rev. 13.1). In Hebrew, head metaphorically designates beginning (e.g., Judg. 7.19), top (e.g., 1 Sam. 26.13), or leader of a group (e.g., Job 12.24), and whilst the Greek usage overlaps the second of these senses, there is some dispute regarding its application to persons (e.g., 1 Cor. 11.3). On this question, scholarly opinion is divided between the meaning 'authority over' and the alternatives 'origin' or 'pre-eminence'.

In the HB, the head is an important location for the performance of various ritual acts. Hands are laid upon the head during blessings (Gen. 48.14); atonement rituals (the animal's head, Lev. 1.4; 16.21); acts of judgment (Lev. 24.13); and, during consecration, the head of the priest or king is anointed with oil (Lev. 8.12; 1 Sam. 10.1). Accordingly, the NT accounts of the anointing of Jesus' head at Bethany (cf. Matt. 26.6-13; Mark 14.3-9) are rich in allusions to the ritual life of ancient Israel.

Ephesians and Colossians designate Christ as head of the Church (Col. 1.18; Eph. 1.22), with the latter described as the 'body' (*sōma*). This combined head–body metaphor is likely to be more than a simple extension of Paul's 'body of Christ' language (cf. 1 Cor. 12.12-27), since it also applies to Christian marriage (Eph. 5.23-32). The assertion that 'the husband is head of his wife' (1 Cor. 11.3; Eph. 5.23) has become particularly controversial since the emergence of feminist interpretation. This controversy is partly responsible for the disagreement over the application of the *kephalē* metaphor to persons, and the emergence of male 'headship' movements, particularly in American evangelicalism.

The head of Christ wearing the crown of thorns has been a longstanding object of Christian devotion, perhaps because attention to Christ's face evokes a more personal response to his suffering. Notable artworks include Bosch's *Christ Crowned with Thorns* (c. 1495–1500), and van Honthorst's (c. 1620) beautiful, but darker, painting of the same name. In terms of film, the iconic shots of Christ's crowned head in Franco Zeffirelli's *Jesus of Nazareth* (1977) and Mel Gibson's *The Passion of the Christ* (2004) appeal to different strands of this ongoing tradition of representation. By contrast, Dalí's attention to Christ's head in his crucifixion scene *Christ of Saint John of the Cross* (1951) is singular, in that not only are there neither nails nor crown of thorns, but the scene is observed from directly above Christ's head.

Lastly, it is ironic that another culturally significant biblical 'head' story concerns the removal of John the Baptist's head (cf. Mark 6.14-29). This story informs numerous paintings, including Caravaggio's melancholy *Salome with the Head of John The Baptist* (c. 1607). Although published as a short story by Flaubert (1877) and as an opera by Massenets (1881), the most famous version of the tale is the macabre and erotic single-act play by Oscar Wilde (*Salomé*, 1891, 1894), and the Richard Strauss opera (*Salome*, Op.54, 1905) based upon it.

Recommended reading. Fitzmyer, J.A. '*Kephalē* in I Corinthians 11:3'. *Interpretation* 47 (1993) 32-59. Thiselton, A.C. 'Κεφαλή'. In *The First Epistle to the Corinthians*. Edited by I.H. Marshall and D.A. Hagner. Pp. 812-22. Grand Rapids, MI: Eerdmans, 2000.

See also BODY; BODY OF CHRIST; CHRIST; CROWN OF THORNS; SALOME; HERODIAS [MJL]

Heart. The heart (Heb. *lēb*, *lēbāb*, Gk *kardia*), is the most frequently occurring anthropological term in the Bible but only rarely does it refer to the physical organ. Metaphorically, it indicates the innermost part of the human being. As such, the biblical heart was the location of thinking, understanding, feeling, and volition, and it encompassed a human's character and intellect. Since the biblical heart includes faculties of reasoning, emotion and will, biblical translations, in some cases, translate either *lēb(āb)* or *kardia* as 'mind' instead of 'heart'.

The heart is both receptive and active. A person 'hears' the words spoken by another with her or his heart (Acts 16.14), and thinks (Luke 2.19) and understands with the heart (Deut. 29.4). A range of feelings are experienced in the heart including joy (Sir. 30.16), anguish (Isa. 65.14), fear (Ps. 27.3), love (1 Pet. 1.22), and hope (Jdt. 6.9). Planning and volition come from the heart (1 Kgs 8.17). A heart is firm in courage and resolve (Ezek. 22.14) and idiomatically one 'fortifies oneself' by 'feeding one's heart' (Judg. 19.5).

Since the relationship between God and humanity marks the principal biblical relationship, it is not surprising that the workings of the human heart are contextualized within it. Thus, the general objective of 'listening' with the heart is to understand God's teaching and will (Acts 28.27). In addition, most examples of 'obstinacy' denote resistance to or rejection of God's will and may be evoked by images of a 'hard heart' (Eph. 4.18) or 'heart of stone' (Ezek. 36.26). Morality is expressed within this divine–human construct and therefore 'crooked hearts' are an abomination to God (Prov. 11.20) while Simon the Magician's attempt to purchase the power of the Holy Spirit signals that his 'heart is not right before God' (Acts 8.21). Turning to God with all one's heart and soul implies obeying (literally, listening to God's voice) and observing God's commandments (Deut. 30.10). God knows and examines the human heart (Acts 15.8; Rom. 8.27).

When acting in judgment, God is described as 'he who weighs the heart' (Prov. 24.12; 21.2). The ancient Egyptians, who also understood the heart to be the integrative center of the human, described a judgment process, involving the weighing of the heart in funerary literature called *The Book of the Dead*. In it, the heart of the deceased was to be placed on a scale and weighed against a feather of truth. Inscriptions on heart scarab amulets, which were wrapped along with a deceased's body, beseeched the heart to not testify against its owner at the judgment.

The ancient Mediterranean understanding of personality was deeply intertwined with the community to which a person belonged. As a result, many biblical texts involve the heart of 'a people', frequently the people of Israel (Deut. 10.12) or the community of the early Jesus-movement (Acts 4.32). The current Western understanding of heart, in contrast, reflects an individualistic perspective on personality and usually refers to the heart of an individual. Moreover, the divine–human framework governing the heart's functioning has been replaced by a human–human one in which, for example, phrases such as the title of the Rolling Stones' song 'Heart of Stone' convey a lack of interpersonal emotion. Furthermore, while the biblical heart was an integrative center, the post-Enlightenment separation of reason and emotion has narrowed the current popular understanding of heart to the emotional realm. At the same time, the recent growth in literature on what is termed 'emotional intelligence' signals a trend toward a re-emerging integrative 'biblical heart' understanding of cognition.

Recommended reading. Schroer, Silvia, and Thomas Staubli. *Body Symbolism in the Bible*. Trans. Linda M. Maloney. Collegeville, MN: Liturgical Press, 2001.

See also SOUL [AG-M]

Heaven. Biblically speaking, the term heaven is capable of more than one meaning. On the one hand, the term is often applied to that portion of the created order that exists above the earth, in other words, the visible realm of the sun, moon and stars (see Gen. 1.1, 6-8; Ps. 33.6). In modern usage, this concept of heaven is roughly equivalent to our employment of the term 'sky'.

On the other hand, there is a rich stream of biblical tradition which uses heaven in a more theological sense, to refer to the abode of God and his angels, a realm that is normally invisible to human perception (1 Kgs 8.27; 1 Tim. 6.16). The degree to which God is the defining resident of heaven is made clear by the way the terminology of heaven can be used as a substitute for God in certain expressions. Thus, Dan. 4.26 speaks of the sovereignty of heaven, by which is meant the sovereignty of God, whilst the Gospel of Matthew often substitutes the phrase kingdom of heaven for kingdom of God (Matt. 3.2; 4.17; etc.).

The enduring legacy of the imagery and language of heaven upon Western culture primarily lays in its application to the field of eschatology, in particular the personal experience of an afterlife. The logic works as follows: Because heaven is God's dwelling place, and ultimate salvation involves the full and unmediated experience of God's personal presence, then post-mortem experience comes to be defined in terms of 'going to heaven'. In many respects, the use of such expressions is unhelpful, for it tends to marginalize the actual ways the Bible does speak about the eternal state, which is usually in 'earthly' terms of a new creation (see Isa. 65.17-25; Rom. 8.19-23; Rev. 21–22). Nevertheless, the biblical language and imagery of heaven, understood within an eschatological frame, has left an indelible stamp on Western art and literature.

Prominent visions of heaven in literature include Dante's *Paradiso* (part of his *Divine Comedy*), the heavenly city of Bunyan's *Pilgrim's Progress*, and the two epic poems by Milton, *Paradise Lost* and *Paradise Regained*. Indeed, the influence of Milton's grand Edenic vision was so great that the gardens of the English gentry were occasionally modelled on Milton's conception of paradise.

In the realm of music, perhaps one of the most prominent applications of heavenly language by a musical tradition is the African-American spiritual, where in songs like 'All God's Children Got Wings' heavenly language became a repository of hopes to be freed from oppression.

Yet with the rise of the Enlightenment, the notion of heaven has increasingly come under attack within Western culture. The arguments of such thinkers as Feuerbach, Marx and Freud, all of whom variously argued for the illusory nature of religious thinking (including thinking about heaven), has generated an ongoing discourse that questions the value of heaven as a concept. No better example of this can be given than John Lennon's song 'Imagine', in which the absence of heaven, together with the absence of all organised religion, is part of the means by which the world will be brought to true harmony.

Recommended reading. McDannell, Colleen, and Bernhard Lang. *Heaven: A History*. New Haven: Yale University Press, 1988. McGrath, Alister E. *A Brief History of Heaven*. Oxford: Blackwell, 2003. Wright, N.T. *Surprised by Hope: Rethinking Heaven, the Resurrection, and the Mission of the Church*. New York: HarperCollins, 2008.

See also NEW HEAVEN, NEW EARTH [MBS]

Hebrews, Epistle to the. Hebrews is the nineteenth book of the NT. Although its formal title in the KJV is 'The Epistle of St Paul the Apostle to the Hebrews', modern scholars dispute each point of this designation: it is not an epistle, it was not written by Paul, and it was not addressed to 'the Hebrews'.

Hebrews is a sermon, a product of rhetorical art designed primarily to be heard rather than read. The author refers to the book as a 'word of exhortation' (13.22), a phrase used to describe a synagogue address in Acts 13.15. Commentators have identified examples of Hellenistic rhetorical techniques throughout Hebrews.

The list of proposed authors of Hebrews includes Paul, Apollos, Barnabas, Priscilla, Epaphras, the Virgin Mary, and seemingly everyone else in the NT. That scholars can suggest so many candidates is itself evidence that more information is needed. The search for the name of the author of Hebrews has largely been abandoned.

Based on the book's extensive use of the OT, it is often assumed that Hebrews was written to Jewish believers. Even so, the OT was the Bible of the entire Christian community—both Jew and non-Jew. Therefore, the book's recipients need not have been exclusively or even predominantly Jewish.

The author continually returns to the theme that Jesus is 'better' than anything the old covenant can offer. In successive chapters, he argues that Jesus (1) is better than angels (1.1–2.18); (2) is better than Moses (3.1–4.13); (3) is better than Aaron (4.14–6.20); (4) belongs to a better priesthood (7.1-28); (5) inaugurates a better cultic order (8.1–10.18); and (6) makes possible a better spiritual experience (10.19–13.25).

The author elaborates upon this theme through a lengthy exposition of OT texts linking Jesus with the main elements of ancient Israel's religious and sacrificial system. By his own admission, the author's 'main point' is Jesus' high priestly status (8.1). He further elaborates on the setting and content of Jesus' ritual activity: the sanctuary and its sacrifices (see 9.1).

The primal (some have said 'primitive') nature of the argument of Hebrews has long been noted. The author defines humanity's problem and its solution in language the average preliterate hunter–gatherer could grasp: transgression produces a state of spiritual defilement; ritual cleansing is necessary for purgation. The author reveals a preoccupation with sin, conceived as an almost physical defilement, and sacrificial blood as the definitive cleansing agent

Although the idea of blood sacrifice is repulsive to most Westerners, the idea of sin as a form of defilement remains a fixture in Western culture. English speakers are familiar with expressions like 'dirty movies' or 'filthy language' that connect feelings of moral guilt with feelings of physical dirtiness. When Shakespeare described Lady Macbeth compulsively making washing motions with her hands after conspiring to kill King Duncan, he was tapping into feelings of impurity with which most people can identify.

Ancient cultures proposed a great number of cleansing agents to remove moral defilement through ritual means: water, salt, smoke, oil, etc. The preeminent cleanser of sin, however, was blood, and that is the mental picture the author of Hebrews provides for his audience. The blood of Jesus surpasses the cleansing power of any other, so that believers may enter the presence of God undefiled, not by the blood of bulls and goats (9.12), but by the blood of Christ.

Recommended reading. Lane, William L. *Hebrews*. 2 vols. Word Biblical Commentary. Dallas: Word, 1991.

See also ATONEMENT; BLOOD; HIGH PRIEST [DJP]

Hebrew language. The Hebrew of the Jewish Bible represents a sixth century BCE redaction of earlier stages of the language. This stage, called classical Hebrew, became the basis for modern Hebrew as developed by Eliezer Ben Yehudah in the late nineteenth century; it is derived from the tri-consonantal form evidenced in biblical Hebrew. Jewish tradition explains that the name for the language, *Ivrit* in Hebrew, can be traced to the name of one of Abraham's ancestors, Eber or *Ever* (Gen. 20.10). Those who adhered to the faith exercised by Abraham were designated *Ivri*. A cognate of this term was applied to the language that they spoke, producing the term *Ivrit* or Hebrew. Material evidence of *Ivrit* is until now limited to a few fragmentary remains dating no earlier than three millennia ago, alongside greater evidence of its contemporary counterparts that included Egyptian hieroglyphs, Phoenician, and Proto-Sinaitic. Common reconstruction of the Hebrew language advances five stages beginning with early archaic Hebrew, from the monarchic period through the Babylonian captivity. This stage was written in a Canaanite script and is known as Paleo-Hebrew or Old Hebrew. Classical (biblical) Hebrew overlaps the last two centuries of this stage. The next stage, written in Imperial Aramaic script, is evidenced during the Persian period and is called Late Biblical Hebrew. It finds expression in texts such as Ezra and Nehemiah. Qumran Hebrew, also known as Dead Sea Scrolls Hebrew, was written in the familiar square letters that modern Hebrew has adopted. Qumran Hebrew extended from the Hellenistic through the Roman period up to the first century CE. Mishnaic Hebrew, also called Early Rabbinic Hebrew, completes the evolution of the Hebrew language, dating from the first through the fourth centuries CE. Its sources include Mishnah and Tosefta in the Talmud, the Bar Kokhba letters, and the Copper Scroll from the Qumran cache that alleges to be a codified map of where the Second Temple furnishings were hidden during the Roman siege of 68–70 CE.

According to Flusser, there is every reason to trace the use of Hebrew from biblical times through to the rabbinic era, including the intermediate NT period, in the following manner: the language of the HB was relatively constant with only a few Aramaic pericopes in late writings; discovery of a Hebrew Ben Sira (Ecclesiasticus) provides a subsequent chronological link; the Dead Sea Scrolls testify to a predominantly Hebrew corpus in a time just prior to the NT writings; the Bar Kokhba Letters, also written in Hebrew, provide a terminal bookend for the NT with the rabbinic literature closely following thereafter. He further demonstrates linguistic logic to support a Hebrew-based Gospel collection in the original form: the Synoptics, so narrowly interconnected due to shared influences and mutual oral sources, provide an early stage for sayings developed in later Talmudic and Midrashic literature; sayings of Jesus that can be rendered into either Hebrew or Aramaic originals can be reduced to the former language in every instance but only into the latter in a very few instances; the occasional Aramaic terms employed by Jesus serve to reveal common expressions and familiar adaptations of the day rather than that of a spoken language for an entire religious community; the second stage of Christianity's development, that established by the Apostle Paul and others, separated itself from the principal stage in both language and theology by focusing on largely Greek-speaking audiences with the message of a resurrected Christ.

Recommended reading. Flusser, David. *Jewish Sources in Early Christianity*. Trans. John Glucker. Tel Aviv: MOD Books, 1989.

See also ARAMAIC LANGUAGE; GREEK LANGUAGE; LANGUAGES OF THE BIBLE [DM]

Hell. The English word hell has its origins in the Anglo-Saxon root *hel* or *hol*, meaning 'to conceal' or 'to hide' and is used to translate four biblical terms. The Hebrew *sheol*, which can be translated as 'hell', 'the grave' and 'the pit'; Greek *hades*, which parallels *sheol*, both of which generally refer to the world of the dead or under world; the Greek verb *tartarus*, which appears only once in the NT in 2 Pet. 2.4 and means to 'put in hell' or 'cast into hell'. According to this verse, God did 'not spare the angels when they sinned, but cast them into hell and committed them to chains of deepest darkness to be kept until the judgment'. Finally, the Greek *gehenna* is derived from the Hebrew *gê ben hinnōm*, which means the 'Valley of the Sons of Himmom', a ravine south of Jerusalem. The majority of the biblical teaching on hell comes from Jesus, most notably in Matt. 25.31-46 and Mark 9.43.

Throughout the history of the Church, there have been three main views on hell: the literal view, the metaphorical view and the conditional view. The literal view understands hell to be a place of eternal conscious torment and/or torture (the difference between torment and torture being that the former is done by a person to themselves and the latter is done by another against the will). This view holds the language in the Bible about hell as literal, straightforward truth. Thus, when the Bible speaks of hell as a 'lake of fire' (Rev. 20.14) and 'where there will be weeping and gnashing of teeth' (Matt. 13.42), it means just that. On the other hand, the metaphorical view takes the biblical language about hell to be symbolic. In this view, hell is a real place where people go after death, but the biblical language about hell, such as that cited above, is to be understood as metaphors pointing toward a real state of existence that is unable to be described in its fullness. The conditional view holds that hell is not eternal, that punishment is temporal and will end. Under this view, hell is a place where people go after death for temporary punishments and then eventual annihilation, being snuffed out of existence forever.

The *Divine Comedy*, by Dante Alighieri (c. 1265–1321) is, perhaps, the most notable example of a literary depiction of hell outside of the biblical texts. This poem is composed of well over 14,000 lines divided into three sections: *Inferno* (Hell), *Purgatorio* (Purgatory), and *Paradiso* (Paradise). The poem is written in the first person and tells of Dante's journey through the three levels of the dead. In the *Inferno*, Dante experiences hell as a literal place of fire. This fits with the fact that the literal view of hell was the dominant one at the time this poem was written (somewhere between 1308 and 1321).

Recommended reading. Alighieri, Dante. *The Divine Comedy*. New York: Penguin Group, 2003 [original: 1308–1321]. Crockett, William. *Four Views on Hell*. Grand Rapids, MI: Zondervan Publishing, 1996.

See also HADES; DAY OF THE LORD/JUDGMENT/WRATH; HARROWING OF HELL [JFW]

Hem of his garment. The account of the woman suffering from a hemorrhage who touches the hem of Jesus' garment and is healed is found in all three of the Synoptic Gospels (Matt. 9.20-22; Mark 5.25-34; Luke 8.43-48). The woman is in a crowd of people in Capernaum surrounding Jesus as he walks through the streets in the aftermath of the healing of the Gerasene demoniac. Jesus has just heard that the synagogue official Jairus's daughter is on the point of death (or dead) and is hurrying to his house. The woman, the Gospels tell us, has been suffering from the bleeding for twelve years. Mark adds that she has spent all of her money for cures to no avail. She has such faith that she convinces herself that merely by touching the hem of Jesus' garment she will be healed. Upon touching the garment, the bleeding ceases, and she feels that she has been cured. All the while, she wishes to remain anonymous. In Matthew's account, she is not healed until Jesus turns to see her and proclaims her to be healed. In Mark and Luke, however, Jesus feels power (Greek *dynamin*) has gone from him to someone else, but he does not know to whom. The word *dynamin* also means virtue. Therefore, when people touch Jesus power/virtue goes from him into them and they are healed. This is not just a spiritual occurrence, as the Gospels state clearly that a moral and physical connection or process has occurred.

After this empathetic connection of two people, the woman is healed, and Jesus asks who has touched him; the woman comes forward, afraid that she has committed an error. However, Jesus tells her that her faith as cured her, and to go in peace.

In the Gospel accounts, Jesus heals by touch or by word, requiring usually faith in the recipient. The account of the hemorrhaging woman is the only account in the Gospels of a person healed merely by touching the hem of his garment. Depictions of the event occur throughout Western culture, ranging from a beautiful painting on a wall in the catacombs in Rome to the song by Sam Cooke, 'Hem of his Garment'.

See also JAIRUS AND HIS DAUGHTER; PHYSICIAN [RL]

Heresy. Heresy comes from the Greek word *hairesis*, which means a 'choice' in the sense of an opinion or way of thinking. The classical Greeks used the term to refer to a philosophical school that someone chooses to identify with. Similarly in the NT, *hairesis* can mean a self-willed decision to align with a particular party or sect, such as the Pharisees (Acts 15.5; 26.5), Sadducees (Acts 5.17) or Christians (Acts 24.5). A second meaning arises from the dissensions resulting from heresies, as a variety of interests are brought into conflict (e.g., Gal. 5.20). A third meaning is a doctrinal departure from divinely revealed truth (e.g., Tit. 3.10; 2 Pet. 2.1, Jude 4). The apostles give numerous warnings against departing from the truth (Acts 20.29; Phil. 3.2). Paul called parties within the church heresies (1 Cor. 11.19). In 2 Pet. 2.1, the term heresy refers to the opinions those who deny Jesus Christ as the Redeemer.

The early church fathers fought vigorously against several belief systems identified as heresies. Among the major targets were Marcionism, Arianism, Pelagianism, Monarchianism, Nestorianism, Monophysitism, Manicheanism, Donatism, Docetism, and a variety of Gnostic doctrines.

Recommended reading. Kenyon, J. Douglas (ed.). *Forbidden Religion: Suppressed Heresies of the West.* Rochester, VT: Inner Traditions, 2006. Evans, Grubbs R. *A Brief History of Heresy.* New York: John Wiley & Sons, 2003.

See also ATONEMENT; CHRIST; FALSE PROPHET; GRACE; JUSTIFICATION; SANCTIFICATION; SIN [AJW]

Hermeneutics. After mentioning the pool of Siloam, the author of the Fourth Gospel includes a short aside about the name, explaining it 'means Sent' (John 9.7). The author of Hebrews explains that Melchizedek 'means' king of righteousness, and that he was the king of Salem, which 'means' king of peace (Heb. 7.2). Luke records a story of Jesus walking along the Emmaus road with two disciples: 'beginning with Moses and all the prophets, he interpreted to them the things about himself in all the scriptures' (Luke 24.27). Each verse uses the Greek word *hermeneuō*, usually translated as explain, interpret, or translate.

When scholars discuss hermeneutics, more specifically biblical hermeneutics, they have in mind the strategies and theories of interpretation that shape the reading of a text, as well as the presuppositions they bring to that work. This might include a theological frame of reference (e.g., the Bible is inspired by God), or an explicit resistance to such notions and insistence that we study the Bible as we would any other ancient text (enlightenment rationalism). Theories of interpretation might also involve guiding concerns like attention to social and political inequities (e.g., postcolonial theory or feminist interpretations), or guiding ideological perspectives (e.g., Marxist criticism). As an academic subject area, hermeneutics usually refers to the history of biblical interpretation as well as principles representing particular reading strategies.

Recommended reading. Kaiser, Walter C., Jr, and Moisés Silva. *Introduction to Biblical Hermeneutics: The*

Search for Meaning. Rev. and expanded edn. Grand Rapids, MI: Zondervan, 2007.
See also PARDES [MJG]

Herodias. Feminine form of Herod, from the Greek *heros* (hero, heroic), the name can also refer to the revered, deified dead (Mark 6.17-28; Matt. 14.1-11; Luke 3.19-20).

In the Synoptic Gospels, John the Baptist criticizes Herod Antipas for marrying Herodias, who was his brother Herod Philip's wife. Herod, in return, imprisons John. In Mark, Herodias wants John killed, but is thwarted by Herod who fears him as a holy man. In Matthew, it is Herod who wishes to kill John, but he fears the crowd which sees John as a prophet. Herodias's role is minimized. In both Mark and Matthew, the daughter of Herodias pleases Herod by dancing at a celebratory banquet, and at the prompting of her mother, requests the head of John on a plate.

The historian Josephus contradicts the Gospels. He relates that the royal couple had intentionally transgressed ancestral traditions by marrying, and blames both Herod and Herodias for their irregular marriage. John is never said to have criticized the marriage, and Herod is shown to be solely responsible for John's death. Herodias's complicity in John's death is thus historically suspect.

The historical Herodias, granddaughter of King Herod the Great, and daughter of Aristobulus and Bernice, lived amid constant intrigue and murder. Her grandfather executed his son, and her father, Aristobulus. He then engaged her to Herod II Boethus/Herod Philip I, her half-uncle. Herodias later divorced him and married his younger half-brother, Herod Antipas, to whom she remained faithful, even in his later time of exile.

In ancient Syrian legends, Herodias's name is Polia, and she has John tortured because he has publicly insulted her. Herodias, in sixteenth–eighteenth-century German dramas is sometimes depicted as an evil spirit and as the main driving force in John's death, while Italian dramas celebrate Herodias's genuine love for Herod. In Heinrich Heine's nineteenth-century epic, *Atta Troll*, Herodias appears in a procession of ghosts carrying the head of John, whom she had passionately loved. Late nineteenth-century literary and musical works explore the erotic potential of the story. In Flaubert's short story, *Hérodias* (1877), Salome dancing is likened to Herodias in her youth. In Massenet's opera *Érodiada,* (1881), Herodias uses her innocent daughter to obtain John's death. Herod does not know that Salome is his wife's daughter. Salome wants to kill Herodias, but on learning that she is her mother, she instead stabs herself. In Oscar Wilde's play *Salome* (1893), Herodias is disillusioned, cynical and ignored by Herod and Salome, and has no influence on the action. Richard Strauss's opera *Salome* (1905) follows Wilde, and Herodias is usually played as half-drunk.

Medieval paintings usually place Herodias at the table with Herod while Salome dances but it was not customary for women and men to eat together in the Middle East. Herodias in Aubrey Beardsley's drawings for Wilde's *Salome* (1894) is the decadent evil, emasculating woman. In Moreau's paintings of Salome, Herodias is often in the background.

Recommended reading. Kokkinos, Nikkos. *The Herodian Dynasty: Origins, Role in Society and Eclipse*. JSPSup, 30. Sheffield: Sheffield Academic Press, 1998.
See also SALOME; HEAD [EG]

Herods, the. There were a number of rulers called Herod in the NT, the main one, and the first mentioned in the Bible is Herod the Great, son of Antipater, Procurator of Judaea from 47 to 43 BCE. Herod assumed the title of king, and he ruled from 37 until his death in 4 BCE. During this time, he was involved in major building projects in Jerusalem, including the construction of the Second Temple. This Herod was the ruler who, on hearing of the arrival of the wise men seeking the newborn Jewish king, wanted to find out about the child himself (Matt. 2.1-12). Herod then ordered the killing of all children under two years old in the area (the 'Massacre of the Innocents') to ensure that he has killed this rival king. Another Herod mentioned often in the Gospels is Herod Antipas, the Tetrarch of Galilee from the death of his father in 4 BCE until his banishment in 39 BCE. He is responsible for the beheading of John the Baptist, and for turning away Jesus just before the crucifixion. Curiously, these two Herods—one at his birth and one just before his death—help with the dating of the life of Jesus, and show that the calculation of the Christian calendar was in error. Jesus had already been born, and taken by his parents to Egypt before the death of Herod the Great in 4 BCE.

Herod the Great appears in many novels including Richard Sullivan's *The Three Kings* (1956), H. Ellsworth Nightingale's *Herod* (1967), Par Lagerkvist's *Herod and Marianne* (1968), and Leslie Hunt's *At the Point of the Sword* (1984), as well as in Dorothy Sayers's radio play *The Man Born to be King* (1942). In film, Herod the Great was played by Joseph Schildkraut in *Cleopatra* (1934), by Gregoire Estaire in *King of Kings* (1961), by Claude Rains in *The Greatest Story Ever Told* (1965), by Peter Ustinov in *Jesus of Nazareth* (1977), by Leo McKern in *The Nativity* (1978), and Ciara'an Hinds in *The Nativity Story* (2006). Herod Antipas appears in Emery Bekessy's *Barabbas* (1946), as well as in Andrew Lloyd Webber's *Jesus Christ, Superstar* (1970), played by Josh Mostel in the 1973 film version. Luca de Dominicis played this character in Mel Gibson's *The Passion of Christ* (2004). The term 'Herod' (referring to Herod the Great as a killer of small children), and as a vicious murderer, appears regularly in fiction. In William Shakespeare's *Hamlet* (Act 3, Scene 2), Hamlet makes a condemnation in which he tells various players 'it out-herods Herod'.

See also MASSACRE OF THE INNOCENTS [JC]

Hewers of Wood. This phrase originates with the story of Israel's conquest of the promised land. After entering the land and conquering Jericho and Ai, the kings of the North banded together to engage the invading armies of Israel. The people of Gibeon, however, did not join with them (Josh. 9). Instead they decided on a ruse to trick Israel into forming a treaty with them. They sent representatives who were dressed in worn out clothes and carrying moldy bread to Joshua and the elders. The representatives claimed to come from afar and left with fresh bread and new clothing. The people of Israel had been forbidden to form any treaty with the Canaanite residents of the land. But Joshua and the elders did not consult with God regarding these people and, because they believed that they were not residents of Canaan, they made a treaty with them. Three days later, when the deception was discovered, and Israel learned that they had come from a Canaanite city nearby, they were angry and wanted to void the treaty. Joshua insisted that it had to be respected but agreed that there needed to be consequences. So the Gibeonites were designated to be servants to the community and to the sanctuary as 'hewers of wood and drawers of water' or 'woodcutters and water carriers' (Josh. 9.27).

The term thus came to describe those who were reduced to servant status, doing menial labor in the community. The phrase would be used with this sense in English literature. Chaucer uses it to refer to the disguise that Arcite adopts in order to be near his beloved Emelye. In Tennyson's poem 'Idylls', Gareth clothes himself in the garments of a laborer who will 'hew wood and draw water'. Allusion is made to this phrase in Shakespeare's *The Tempest*, where Caliban is made to fetch wood. The phrase also appears in Canadian economic language where it is used to refer to those who engaged in Canada's first resource industries of logging and fishing.

See also PROMISED LAND; GIBEONITES; SLAVE

[BW]

Hezekiah. Hezekiah is the thirteenth king of post-schism Judah who is known primarily for his piety and his extensive religious reforms. The biblical data regarding Hezekiah is drawn primarily from 2 Kgs 18–20, 2 Chron. 29–32, and Isa. 36–39, although this information is also confirmed, clarified, or counterbalanced by data derived from Assyrian annals, Israelite epigraphy, and archaeological findings.

Hezekiah succeeded his father Ahaz at the age of twenty-five, and ruled Judah for twenty-nine years between 715–687 BCE—although given the inconsistencies within the data, the inauguration of his reign could be placed as early as 727 BCE. Some have suggested a possible correlation between Hezekiah king of Judah and the great-great-grandfather of the prophet Zephaniah (1.1), indicating that the prophet was of royal blood, but the data required to validate this is wanting.

He is regarded favorably by the writer of 2 Kings as one who did 'what was right in the sight of Yahweh just as his ancestor David had done' (18.3), as one who was unique among the kings of Judah in his trust in the God of Israel (18.5), and as one who was steadfast in his allegiance to Yahweh and his commandments (18.6). This exemplary commitment to Yahweh prompted a series of religious reforms that included the removal of idolatrous places of worship (18.4), the restoration of the temple (2 Chron. 29.3-19), and the renewal of temple worship (29.20-36). He is also credited with renewing the tradition of the Passover pilgrimage, inviting the remnants of the northern tribes to participate in the festival for the first time since the division of the kingdom (30.1-27). Tragically, his son Manasseh would undo all of these reforms shortly after his death (2 Kgs 21.1-18).

On a political level, Hezekiah is most famous for his rebellion against Sennacherib, and for withstanding the siege of Jerusalem by the Assyrian king in 701 BCE—a victory of sorts made possible in large part by his construction of a 533 meter tunnel that diverted fresh water from the Gihon spring (located outside the city) into Jerusalem

(2 Kgs 20.20; 2 Chron. 32.4). The biblical writers go beyond other accounts of the seige by attributing victory to a mighty angel who slew the Assyrian camp (2 Kgs 19.35-37; 2 Chron. 32.20-23), a detail depicted wonderfully in Johann Christoph Weigel's engraving, *Angel of Death* (1695), Gustave Doré's *Destruction of the Army of Sennacherib* (1865), and James Tissot's watercolor, *The Slaying of the Assyrians* (1896–1900).

Outside of biblical literature, Hezekiah reappears in the pseudepigraphical work, the *Ascension of Isaiah*, where he functions passively as a sympathetic ear for the recounting of Isaiah's visions and prophecies. A Christian portion of this text, the *Testament of Hezekiah* (3.13–4.22), bears his name, although this is misleading, since this too is actually an account of a vision seen by Isaiah.

Recommended reading. Rowley, H.H. 'Hezekiah's Reform and Rebellion'. *Bulletin of the John Rylands University Library of Manchester* 44 (1961) 395-431. Vaughn, A.G. *Theology, History, and Archaeology in the Chronicler's Account of Hezekiah*. Atlanta: Scholars Press, 1999.

See also KINGS, BOOKS OF; JUDAH, KINGDOM OF [TAB]

Hittites. The Hittites were an ancient people in Anatolia (Asia Minor) in modern-day Turkey, and they inhabited the region from the eighteenth century until the twelfth century BCE, with the peak of their civilization in the fourteenth century. In the Bible, they are mentioned eleven times in Genesis, eight times in Exodus, once in Numbers, twice of Deuteronomy, five times in Joshua, twice in Judges, three times each in Kings and Chronicles, and once each in Ezra and Nehemiah. They are counted among the Canaanites, and there is some debate as to whether the Hittites of Asia Minor are actually the same as those mentioned in the Bible. Some of the Hittites in the Bible served as officers in the army of King David.

In fiction, Mika Waltari's *Sinuhe, the Egyptian* (1945, translated into English in 1949), has Sinuhe learning of the power of iron in battle from the Hittites. After treating their king, the only payment he wanted was one of their iron swords, which he brought back to Egypt where he demonstrated its superiority over bronze weapons to Horemheb. This famous scene appears in the film *The Egyptian* (1954). The Hittites retain their reputation for fighting and scheming in the novels of Christian Jacq, as in *Ramses: The Temple of a Million Years* (1998) where the Hittites are planning to take over Egypt by stealth. In *Ramses: The Battle of Kadesh* (1999), set around the great victory by Ramses over the Hittites, the Egyptian government is ever in danger of being undermined by Hittite spies. In *Ramses: Under the Western Acacia* (1998), the Hittite king schemes to get Ramses to marry his daughter.

Recommended reading. Bryce, Trevor. *Life and Society in the Hittite World*. New York: Oxford University Press, 2002.

See also EGYPT [JC]

Holy, Holiness. From the Hebrew *qadesh* and Greek *hagios*, the concept of 'holiness' permeates the entire Bible and is considered a definitive attribute of God. To label God as 'holy' is to refer to him as 'wholly other', and distinct from any human category (see 1 Sam. 2.2). A number of other concepts are often associated with God's holiness such as his power (Ps. 78.41), righteousness (Hos. 11.9), glory (1 Chron. 16.29), and transcendence (Ps. 47.8). But, the notion of holiness is bound up in the covenant which brings the God of Israel into a relationship with Israel where he promises he will be near to his people and walk with them (see Exod. 6.7).

The covenantal relationship between Israel and the Lord contained stipulations and commands for obedience. An important articulation of the nature of this obedience is found in Lev. 19.2: 'You shall be holy, for I the Lord your God am holy'. For the Israelites to be holy, there needed to be complete dedication to the Lord and a distinct separation from the evil ways of their pagan neighbors and enemies, and their former lives. As Israel stands in covenantal union with the Lord, they can be referred to as his 'holy people' (Isa. 63.18). Of course 'holiness' was a key conceptual category of cult whereby those objects and people that worked in the temple (and thus near the presence of God) had to be 'consecrated' to him. This entailed ceremonial cleansing and moral purity (for, e.g., priests and Levites) as they served God. Strict protocols of purity were enforced, then, to protect the Israelites from breaching God's holy standards and incurring the consequences of improper exposure to his dangerous perfection (see Num. 3.4).

According to the NT, the holy presence of God finds a new locus in the person of Jesus Christ, the Son of God, who became incarnate and brought God's holiness to humanity in a new and special way (see John 1.14; 6.69). Christ also promised to send the Holy Spirit who would enable Christian believers to live and behave as 'holy ones' (2 Thess. 2.13).

In modern culture, the language of holiness remains preeminently a religious term, and can sometimes be used in a pejorative sense as in the phrase 'holier than thou'. When this phrase is used in reference to someone, it often carries the idea that the referent feels that he or she is morally superior. This association may derive in part from Matthew's rephrasing of Leviticus so that 'You shall be holy as I am holy' (Lev. 19.2) becomes 'Be perfect, therefore, as your heavenly father is perfect' (Matt. 5.48).

The synonym 'sanctity' does appear in modern ethical discussions of issues such as euthanasia and abortion where conservatives appeal to the idea of the 'sanctity of human life'—the notion that all human life has inherent value and inviolability. Thus, on January 13, 1984, President Ronald Reagan instituted a 'National Sanctity of Human Life Day'. Though this language does not necessarily presume a belief in God for its advocates, the earliest roots of the expression trace back to Christians who argued against abortion on the basis of the holiness of life as a creation of God.

Recommended reading. Barton, S.C. (ed.). *Holiness: Past and Present*. London: T. & T. Clark, 2002. Otto, R. *The Idea of the Holy*. Trans. J.W. Harvey. New York: Oxford University Press, 1958.

See also HOLY OF HOLIES; SAINTS; SANCTIFICATION; PURIFICATION [NKG]

Holy of Holies, the. Holy of holies is a translation of *qodhesh haqqodhashim*; this phrase is also rendered as 'most holy place', 'sanctum sanctorum', 'adytum' or 'shrine'. Similarly, the word *děbîr*, which is usually translated 'oracle', can refer to the 'back room' of the temple[s], which is the same as the holy of holies or 'inner sanctuary' (cf. 1 Kgs 6.16; 8.6, 8). The holy of holies was located behind a veil (Exod. 26.31-35; 2 Chron. 3.14) within the *qodhesh* ('holy place') and was the site of the golden altar of incense and the ark of the covenant (1 Kgs 6.19; 8.6; 2 Chron. 5.7). Israelite and early Jewish belief held that the presence of the God of Israel resided here. Once a year, on the Day of Atonement the high priest alone was allowed to enter the sanctum to make atonement for all of Israel (cf. Lev. 16).

According to 1 Kgs 6.20, this area was twenty cubits in length, breadth and height, overlaid with gold (cf. 2 Chron. 3.8; Ezek. 41.4). It is believed to have been raised ten cubits above the *qodhesh* (cf. 1 Kgs 6.2). The doors of the adytum were decorated with carvings of palm trees, flowers, and cherubim and overlaid with gold (1 Kgs 6.32; Ezek. 41.18). Two olivewood cherubim, overlaid with gold, stood ten cubits high with wings spread in a span of ten cubits so that, side by side, they touched both the walls and each other while standing over the ark of the covenant (1 Kgs 6.23-28; 2 Chron. 3.10-13). Ezekiel makes reference to a holy district of 25,000 x 10,000 cubits that would serve as the most holy place (Ezek. 45.3).

The Eastern Orthodox Church has continued the use of such a sanctum by placing their 'Holy Table' in a restricted area behind the iconostasis called the 'Holy Place'. The room is located in Orthodox temples behind the Holy Doors and a veil embroidered with cherubim. The Ethiopian Orthodox Church has a similar room, called *Qidduse Qiddusan*, which only clergy may enter. In the Salt Lake Temple of The Church of Jesus Christ of Latter-Day Saints there resides a 'holy of holies' where the church's president, taking on the role of Presiding High Priest for the church, enters to speak with God concerning important decisions.

'Holy of holies' as a term is sometimes applied secularly to any place that is specially venerated. It may also be used humorously or sarcastically for places that are unimpressive or not venerated. The term has also taken on a sexual connotation, especially after the 1994 film *Pulp Fiction* used it to refer to the vagina. In Dan Brown's *The Da Vinci Code*, Brown describes the holy of holies as a massive, underground chamber. In the visual arts, various interpretations of the holy of holies have been painted by Zely Smekhov. The Christian rock band Kutlass sings about the holy of holies in their song 'Take Me In'.

Recommended reading. Kaufman, Asher S. *Temple Mount*. Temple of Jerusalem. Jerusalem: Har Year'eh Press, 2004.

See also TEMPLE, ISRAEL'S; JERUSALEM; KINGS, BOOK OF; EZEKIEL, BOOK OF; CHRONICLES, BOOKS OF; HIGH PRIEST; ARK OF THE COVENANT; DAY OF ATONEMENT, THE [ACW]

Holy Land, the. The identification of the land of Israel as the Holy Land is common to several streams of Jewish and Christian thinking. The term holy means 'set apart', and marking the land of Israel as holy means to distinguish it as being in some way closer to God than other lands. The Bible does not always make clear just how the land is holy, but the simple notion that it is God's own possession crops up in some connections. For example, the OT law of giving ten percent of the produce of the land (known as 'tithing') applies only to those crops grown within the boundaries of the holy land. Crops grown outside the land were exempt from this requirement because the idea behind it is that of a payment for tenancy of God's land.

In the late Middle Ages, accounts of travel to the land of Palestine (e.g., *Mandeville's Travels* [1357?], attributed to a Sir John Mandeville, but no longer believed to be a firsthand report) endeared the idea of a Holy Land to people throughout Europe. Travel accounts of the Holy Land had actually begun to appear a thousand years earlier (e.g., Egeria's late fourth-century account), and continued to appear into the first part of the twentieth century.

When most modern Christians refer to the modern state of Israel as the Holy Land, they mean nothing more than to call attention to the fact that most of what is related in Scripture happened there. For many present-day pilgrims to modern Israel, it is the fact that Jesus travelled throughout the land, and that many of the locales of his ministry are recorded in the Gospels, that makes the land 'holy'. This last sense lies behind a good deal of modern religious poetry. For instance, Lucy Maud Montgomery wrote of Jesus 'making holy the land' ('If Mary Had Known'). In a quite different way, John Greenleaf Whittier applied the related concept of 'holy ground' (see Exod. 3.5) in a new way in 'The Miracle of Autumn', and in 'Laus Deo' (the latter celebrating the abolition of slavery in America).

Recommended reading. Brueggemann, Walter. *The Land: Place as Gift, Promise and Challenge in Biblical Faith.* Overtures to Biblical Theology. Minneapolis: Fortress Press, 1995. Kugel, James. 'The Holiness of Israel and the Land in Second Temple Times'. In Michael V. Fox, *et al.* (eds.). *Texts, Temples, and Traditions: A Tribute to Menahem Haran.* Pp. 21-32. Winona Lake, IN: Eisenbrauns, 1996. Wilken, Robert L. *The Land Called Holy: Palestine in Christian History and Thought.* New Haven: Yale University Press, 1994.

See also LAND OF MILK AND HONEY; PROMISED LAND; ISRAEL [JCP]

Holy Spirit, the. The title Holy Spirit (Hebrew *ruah haqodesh*) occurs three times in the HB (Ps. 51.11; Isa. 63.10, 11). In each instance the title appears in a moral context and it represents God's presence with his people. The title occurs seven times in the Greek Septuagint (Ps. 51.11; Isa. 63.10, 11; Wis. 9.17; Dan. 5.12; 6.3; Sus. 1.45). 'Spirit' refers to God's spirit at least 90 times in the HB and 100 times in the Septuagint.

In the NT, 'Holy Spirit' bears new theological significance. The Holy Spirit, as the Spirit of God, is portrayed as a personal agent who works to grace the church with the knowledge, power, and presence of God. The Synoptic Gospels and the Acts of the Apostles include the Holy Spirit in most of the significant aspects of Jesus' life and ministry, indicating that the Spirit empowers Jesus, and that readers are to understand Jesus' vocation as the joint-work of the Son and Spirit of God. The Acts of the Apostles also presents the apostolic ministry as the continuation of Jesus' own mission. After receiving the Holy Spirit on the day of Pentecost, the apostles continue to proclaim the gospel through the empowering presence of the Spirit.

In the Gospel according to John, the Holy Spirit helps Jesus' audience to perceive the latter's divine identity. The Spirit is also given the title 'Paraclete' (Greek *paraklētos*) or 'Advocate'. As Paraclete, the Spirit comforts, teaches, and communicates the post-resurrection presence of Jesus to Christians. In the Acts of the Apostles, the Spirit continues Jesus' ministry by equipping the apostles and early church with power to proclaim the gospel of Christ throughout the Roman Empire. In the Pauline Epistles the Spirit is said to contribute to the conversion and maturation of Christians. According to Paul, the Holy Spirit gives spiritual gifts, enables faith and holiness, and communicates the knowledge, love, and presence of God. The Holy Spirit is also credited with inspiring the OT (Heb. 3.7; 1 Pet. 1.10-11; 2 Pet. 1.21). Additionally, NT authors often interpret references to 'spirit' in the OT as inspired allusions to the Holy Spirit, whom they and other early Christians believed was known through the life and worship of the church. These experiences, coupled with the centrality of the Spirit in the Scriptures and early Christian tradition, led to the later affirmation of the Spirit as the third member of the Trinity.

The Holy Spirit is commonly featured in Western art and music. Artists including Duccio di Buoninsegna, Giotto di Bondone, El Greco, and Anthony van Dyck have depicted the descent of the Spirit upon the disciples at Pentecost. Johann Sebastian Bach composed multiple Pentecost cantatas, including BWV 34, 59, 74, 172. The Spirit has been referred to in Leonard Cohen's 'Hallelujah', Iron Maiden's 'The Pilgrim Press', and U2's 'Mysterious

Ways'. Episode 7ABX09 of the X-Files features a fictional cult dedicated to the Holy Spirit.

Recommended reading. Brown, Raymond E. *The Gospel according to John.* 2 vols. Anchor Bible, 29–29a. New York: Doubleday, 1966.

See also PENTECOST; SIN AGAINST THE HOLY SPIRIT; TEMPLE OF THE HOLY SPIRIT, TRINITY [KDH]

Hope. The term translates *qawa* (Hebrew) and *elpis* (Greek). Both words mean awaiting or looking in eager expectation for something. The OT refers to trust in the God of Israel (Ps. 71.5) in spite of oppression and difficult situations encountered. Sometimes hope looks forward (Jer. 29.11), at other times it involves continuous trust in God's ultimate protection in the present (Ps. 130.7; 131.3). God is called the 'hope of Israel' (Jer. 14.8; 17.13) and the words of God are a constant source of hope (Ps. 119.43, 49, 74, 81, 116). In the NT, Christians hope for existence after this present world (1 Thess. 4.13). As is the case with writers in the OT (see e.g., Prov. 10.28), hope in the NT was the exclusive right of those who believed in God (1 Tim. 4.10). Jesus' disciples linked hope to the restoration of the kingdom (Acts 1.3-8) and Paul combined it with faith and love (1 Cor. 13.13). It figures in the definition of faith provided by the writer of Hebrews (11.1).

In contemporary society, the use of hope ranges from the mundane to the esoteric. During natural disasters, acts of terrorism, economic crises, and the like, there is a grounding fact that the future holds something better. Sometimes used as a political rhetoric, hope is used rather effectively at times to reassure the electorate of a better future, and to garner votes. A classic example is the use of hope as a vehicle for change in the 2009 US Presidential election, where a first term senator from Illinois, Barack Obama, persuaded Americans from all walks of life with the slogan 'Yes we can'.

African-American slaves held on to the Christian promise of hope for a better world beyond this one, where there would be no more sorrow or pain. It is not surprising, then, that it was a theme in Martin Luther King, Jr's 'Dream' speech. There is a certain audacity to hope that stuns even the direst of circumstances. This is what Obama called 'a relentless optimism in the face of hardship'. Despite all the evidence to the contrary, humans believe in a better future and the search for that utopian world.

Recommended reading. Obama, Barack. *The Audacity of Hope: Thoughts on Reclaiming the American Dream.* New York: Crown Publishers, 2006. Tutu, Desmond. *God Has a Dream: A Vision of Hope for our Time.* London: Rider, 2004.

See also DREAMS; FAITH; LOVE; KEY OF DAVID [GOA]

Hophni and Phinehas. The story of Hophni and Phinehas can be found in 1 Sam. 2.4. They were priests, the sons of a priest, Eli, who ministered in Shiloh. Hophni is a name derived from an Egyptian word meaning 'tadpole'. Phinehas is derived from the Egyptian word that means 'southerner'. The Egyptian etymology behind their names illustrates the influences of Egypt upon Israelite culture which were cautioned against in the Torah. Known as scoundrels, the brothers had no respect for their roles as priests, or the laws and customs of their people (1 Sam. 2.12-17). They brought the wrath of God upon their family and it was prophesied that none of their descendants would live to see old age (1 Sam. 2.31). It was not long before this prophesy was fulfilled, and Hophni and Phinehas were both killed (1 Sam. 4.11). The narrative concerning Hophni and Phinehas is interrupted a number of times with events that involve the prophet Samuel. In this manner, Hopnhi and Phinehas become literary foils for Samuel. There are a number of paintings that portray the events of 1 Sam. 2 and 4. Two that portray Hophni and Phinehas specifically are *Death of Eli; Hophni and Phinehas, sons of Heli, eating the meat reserved for sacrifices* (unknown artist, fourteenth century) and *The Philistines capture the ark, and the slaying of Hophni and Phinehas* (unknown French Master, 1250–1300).

See also SAMUEL; SAMUEL, BOOKS OF; ELI [J-AS]

Horeb. This mountain is mentioned in the Book of Deuteronomy as the place where the Ten Commandments were given by God to Moses. It is mentioned also in 1 Kgs 8.9 and 2 Chron. 5.10, which refer to the ark of the covenant containing the tablets delivered to Moses at Horeb. Elsewhere there are references to the Ten Commandments being given to Moses on Mount Sinai. There have been many disputes over whether or not the two are actually the same place, with the British writer H.V. Morton citing this to be probable, and many years earlier, the German theologian George H.A. Ewald (1803–1875) suggesting that Horeb could have been an earlier name for Sinai. Others associate Horeb with Djebel Mousa. Elijah visits Horeb in 1 Kgs 19.8 in a context which suggests that it was a familiar place, perhaps for pilgrimage.

The term Horeb is believed to mean 'glowing' or 'heat' and it is first mentioned in Exod. 3.1, which refers to the story of Moses and the burning bush leading some scholars to associate the two. As Sinai is believed to derive from the Semitic lunar deity Sin, Mount Horeb and Mount Sinai possibly referred to the mountains of the sun and the moon, this could possibly mean that the two were different sides of the same mountain, or that they are quite different places. Alternatively, some scholars suggest that Mount Horeb could have been a lower peak, and Mount Sinai a higher one, or that Horeb was the name of the mountain range, and Sinai a specific mountain. Novels on Moses tend to use Sinai as the place where the Ten Commandments were given by God to Moses.

Recommended reading. Galey, John. *Sinai and the Monastery of St Catherine*. Stuttgart: Massada, 1980.

See also MOSES; SINAI; TEN COMMANDMENTS   [JC]

Horns of the Altar. Most altars mentioned in the HB would have had horns protruding from each corner. While their purpose is uncertain (unless it was to facilitate the binding of the animal to the altar), they came to be a symbol for protection. An individual who unintentionally killed another could seek sanctuary by fleeing to the altar and grasping its horns. Adonijah sought protection from Solomon by grasping the altar's horns (1 Kgs 1.50-53). In response, Solomon spared his life. In 1 Kgs 2.28-35, Joab also sought refuge by grasping the horns. On this occasion, Joab was struck down for his treachery. The horns were also a symbol for power. As punishment for Israel's transgressions, the horns of the altars are to be cut off, symbolizing the destruction of their religious authority and their loss of power (Amos 3.14).

The horns of the altar were significant in atonement rites. Sacrificial blood was spread on the horns (Exod. 29.12; 30.10) for certain occasions. As Ezekiel received a vision for a new temple, he was also directed to smear blood on the horns for purification purposes (Ezek. 43.20). In Rev. 9.13, the horns of the altar signify God's presence as he gives directions to the sixth angel.

Writer Thomas de Quincey used the imagery of the horns of the altar in 'Dream Fugue', found in *The English Mail Coach*. Sir Walter Scott compares vows to the cords holding sacrifices to the horns of the altar, in that vows bind the issuer to God (*Ivanhoe*). The abolitionist, John Greenleaf Whittier, compares slavery to hell, and compares the slaves' search for sanctuary to those grasping the horns of the altar for refuge: 'We gather, at your summons, above our fathers' graves, / From Freedom's holy altar-horns to tear your wretched slaves!'

See also ALTAR; JOAB; SACRIFICE   [DP]

Hosanna. The term hosanna is a liturgical one in Judaism and Christianity meaning 'save now', or 'please save'. It comes from Ps. 118, and is used in the NT to refer to the triumphal procession of Jesus Christ into Jerusalem with people crying, 'Hosanna to the Son of David! ... Hosanna in the highest heaven!' (Matt. 21.9). The term also appears in Mark 11.9 and John 12.13. As a result of this, the term Hosanna is used in many hymns as a Christian cry of adoration to hail the coming of the Messiah.

Many of the hymns which use the term 'Hosanna' have a call-and-response style, by which a body of people respond to a question with 'Hosanna', or have 'Hosanna' in a chorus (e.g., the Moravian anthem 'Hosanna Anthem', written by Bishop Christian Gregor). In 1956, the singer Harry Belafonte recorded a song called 'Hosanna', and the term appears in the rock opera *Jesus Christ Superstar* (1971) by Tim Rice and Andrew Lloyd Webber. It is also used by the British rock band Kula Shaker in *Peasants, Pigs and Astronauts* (1999), and by the New Zealand singer Brooke Fraser in *All of the Above* (2007).

See also PRAYER   [JC]

Hosea, Book of. The Book of Hosea is the longest of the so-called minor prophetic writings. It is ascribed to Hosea the son of Beeri whose prophesies spanned about thirty years during the reigns of the Judean kings Uzziah, Jotham, Ahaz, and Hezekiah, and also during the days of King Jeroboam of Israel. The reigns of these kings were roughly 750–725 BCE.

The prophetic ministry of Hosea occurred in prosperous times; however, all worsened when the political situation changed from one in which the threatening political power was the Syrians in Damascus to the Assyrian Empire. Instead of appealing to God for help Northern Kingdom of Israel put its trust in alliance, politics, and military power. This failure to trust in God is for Hosea a failure of love that is the theme of his prophetic message. The most memorable part of Hosea's story is that God instructed him to marry a prostitute (Hos. 1.2-3), an act illustrating how 'the land commits great whoredom by forsaking the LORD'. Hosea's dedicated pursuit of this woman parallels God's love for idolatrous (unfaithful) Israel. Many commentators, including John Calvin, the Reformed pastor of Geneva, and the medieval physician-philosopher Rabbi Moses Maimonides (*Guide to the Perplexed*) have seen the marriage of Hosea and Gomer as a fiction. The idea that God would literally command such a thing seemed unusual.

Hosea's images, themes, names, and allusions have been used to present a variety of issues from love to injustice in sermons, speeches, and poems. Its influence is evident in such diverse works as the play *A Looking Glass for London and England* by Thomas Lodge and Robert Greene (c. 1590s) and Thomas Hardy's novel *Tess of the d'Urbervilles* (1891).

See also ADULTERY; FORMER PROPHETS; LATTER PROPHETS; LOVE; MARRIAGE; PROPHECY; PROPHETS

[AJW]

House. In the Greek NT, *oikos* occurs 114 times in the NT and designates either the people who reside in the dwelling as family or household or the dwelling itself. While most commonly used in relation to domestic housing, *oikos* can also be used for public buildings such as temples or treasuries. In the Septuagint (the Greek version of the HB), *oikos* appears 1545 times and is mostly used in relation to a house or household but is also used for the Jerusalem temple as 'house of God', 'house of the Lord' or just 'house'. *Oikia* is less common, appearing 94 times in the NT. It usually denotes a dwelling though it can also indicate the household or family that resides in it. This included wives and could also extend to guests, friends, slaves and craftspersons. Paul uses *oikia* to describe 'those in the House of Caesar' (Phil. 4.22) meaning not the Imperial family but those connected with it. *Oikos* could stretch to tribe or clan. In 1 Corinthians, Paul uses both terms in his discussion of the Lord's Supper: in 11.22 he asks whether they have houses (*oikia*) for the purpose of eating and drinking and in 11.34 he says that anyone who is hungry should eat at home (*oikos*)

In the first centuries CE, *oikos/oikia* is the basic unit of society. It designates social identity, is the base economic unit, defines the mores of cultural interaction and ethics, and is the emotional and psychological place of belonging. The Pauline communities harnessed *oikos/oikia* as a symbol of community for the assembly/church (*ekklēsia*) of God. In this way, the bases of social identity moved from kin and lineage to the family of God. According to first-century Platonism, an earthly house is a metaphor for the human body. Paul effectively used this metaphor to describe the assembly/church (*ekklēsia*) of God. This may also have begun to make the distinction of the 'church of God' that was the Christian community from the 'house of God' that was temple.

Recommended reading. Gehring, Roger W. *House Church and Mission: The Importance of Household Structures in Early Christianity*. Peabody, MA: Hendrickson Publishers, 2004. Trainor, Michael F. *The Quest for Home: The Household in Mark's Community*. Collegeville, MN: Liturgical Press, 2001. White, L. Michael. *The Social Origins of Christian Architecture: Building God's House in the Roman World: Architectural Adaptation among Pagans, Jews and Christians*. 2 vols. Harvard Theological Studies, 42. Valley Forge, PA: Trinity Press International, 1990.

See also CHURCH; FAMILY [RAHC]

How are the mighty fallen! These powerful words occur in David's lament over the death of Saul and Jonathan as recorded in 2 Sam. 1.18-27. In fact, these words occur not once, but three times over the course of the lament (in vv. 19, 25, and 27), and as such serve as the refrain of the lament. The lament itself is a very moving and elegant piece of Hebrew poetry. David begins his lament with our refrain and then quickly moves from a focus on Israel's enemies and the battlefield itself in vv. 19-21 to a focus on Saul and Jonathan as heroes to be mourned in the rest of the lament. In words that would seem to fit well the image of the heroic last stand, our heroes are portrayed as fighting to the last and exhibiting the characteristics of eagles and lions, with their death mourned as a tragedy (vv. 22-27).

It is generally agreed that David wrote this lament, as its content seems to agree with what we know of his relationships with both Saul and Jonathan from 1 Samuel. This can be seen in David's mourning of Saul as one who brought prosperity to Israel (v. 24), without dwelling on their personal relationship. In contrast, Jonathan is mourned in the most intimate of terms, as David says, 'your love to me was wonderful, passing the love of women' (v. 26). It is also striking that God is not mentioned in this lament, it is focused entirely on Saul and Jonathan. In v. 18, we learn that David instructed the men of Judah to learn this lament. This may well have been motivated by a political as well as a personal desire, as David may have wanted to show that his tribe did not rejoice in the death of his oppressor and rival, Saul, but mourned him as the king of Israel.

Our refrain also resounds well with a major theme of Anglo-Saxon and medieval literature, the thematic *Ubi sunt,* which means literally 'where are'. This phrase came to serve as an important source of reflection on the temporary nature of all human glory. In some cases, such as Dunbar's 'Of Manis Mortalitie' both classical and biblical heroes are listed among the mighty fallen. Within this tradition, our refrain would be at home, understood not only as a lament but also as a question: 'How have the mighty fallen?'

In popular culture, the phrase 'How the mighty have fallen!' has come to be used primarily with reference not to death or mortality but rather to the loss of power or prestige, such as in the case of a failure in business or sports or in politics. For example, Sherry Bebitch Jeffe said the following of Governor Arnold Schwarzenegger in 2005: 'Their polling must be telling them that he's a drag on his own initiative. How have the mighty fallen'. In another vein, the Christian alternative rock band The Choir titled their 2005 release *O How the Mighty Have Fallen,* while John Christian Orndorff published a novel *How the Mighty Have Fallen* in 2006.

Recommended reading. Barrick, W. Boyd. 'Saul's Demise, David's Lament, and Custer's Last Stand'. *Journal for the Study of the Old Testament* 73 (1997) 25-41. Shea, William H. 'Chiasmus and the Structure of David's Lament'. *Journal of Biblical Literature* 105 (1986) 13-25.

See also DAVID; JONATHAN; SAUL, KING   [MP]

Huldah. This name derives from the Hebrew word for 'weasel'. Huldah is one of the five women described as 'prophetess' in the HB (Exod. 15.20; Judg. 4.4; Isa. 8.3; Neh. 6.14), and is the lone prophetess mentioned in the Books of Kings. She is the 'wife of Shallum son of Tikvah (Tokhath), son of Harhas (Hasrah), keeper of the wardrobe. She resided in Jerusalem in the Second (new) Quarter, where they consulted her' (2 Kgs 22.13-20; 2 Chron. 34.22-28). Through his emissaries, Josiah asked her to 'inquire of the Lord' about the Book of the Law that Hilkiah discovered during the restoration of the Temple.

Rabbinic interpretation explains that Josiah consulted Huldah instead of Jeremiah because women are deemed to be more compassionate and, therefore, would intercede for God on his behalf. Moreover, they were both believed to be descendants of Rahab. It is said that while Jeremiah admonished and preached repentance to the men, Huldah did the same to the women. Some rabbis think that she taught publicly in the school and that the Huldah Gates in the Second Temple formerly led to the gate of her schoolhouse. These two sets of gates at the southern wall of the Temple Mount are now blocked.

The biblical story of Huldah and her oracle present her as someone whom Josiah and his officials regard as a legitimate prophet. They know where to find her and she did not have any reservations in receiving them and reciting the oracle of the Lord for the king and the nation. The use of the phrase 'Thus says the Lord' and 'indeed' (2 Kgs 22.16) lend divine perspective on the matters and recognize that the words on the new found books are the Lord's. The first part of the oracle announces the upcoming disaster and the reason behind it (i.e., apostasy as betrayal of the Lord). The second part addresses the king directly and acknowledges his piety and sincerity. Josiah's show of repentance assured him of not seeing the adversity in his lifetime and having a 'peaceful death'. Huldah's confirmation endorsed Josiah's subsequent reform.

Modern scholars debate on the role of Huldah as a prophetess and the nature and effect of her oracles. Some say she is a court prophet since she was consulted by Josiah on matters of state. Others argue that she is a cult prophet as the vocabulary of the second part of her oracle ('you will be gathered to your fathers', usually found in Priestly sections) suggests. Still others propose that she may have been a prophet of Asherah, the consort of Yahweh in earlier belief. As the worship of Asherah was associated with women (2 Kgs 23.7), a critical reading of Huldah's story characterizes her as being set up by the high ranking policy makers to justify the removal of the Asherah, which was against her own particular cultural heritage. Read from gender and postcolonial lenses, the implications of pitting women against their own people and native culture are numerous. A contemporary example of this is the predicament that the Maori members of parliament, including three women members, found themselves in the current seabed and foreshore debate in New Zealand.

Recommended reading. Cohn, Robert L. *2 Kings.* Berit Olam. Collegeville, MN: Liturgical Press, 2000. McKinlay, Judith E. 'Gazing at Huldah'. *The Bible and Critical Theory* 1.3 (2005) 15.1–15.11.

See also JOSIAH; DEUTERONOMY, BOOK OF; KINGS, BOOKS OF; ASHERAH (ASHTORETH)   [MARICELSI]

Human. In colloquial usage an acknowledgement of one's humanity is frequently an admission of a person's limitations, as in the expression, 'I'm only human'. While an admission of one's humanity may be seen as an attempt to excuse poor judgment or unacceptable behavior, it may also be a plea for compassion. Thus, Alexander Pope invites the critic not to lose sight of the person one is criticizing and to practice compassion, remembering that 'To err is human, to forgive divine' (Alexander Pope, *An Essay on Criticism*, 3.325).

Various contemporary literary and cinematic genres reflect on what it means to be human and, in particular, highlight the tensions between human potential and the limitations of the human condition. Detective and crime stories, for example, invite us to reflect on human depravity, the problem of evil, and the role of the conscience. Within these stories the offenders who seem most human to us are those who wrestle with their consciences (cf., Rom. 2.14-15) while the worst type of offender, those who seem least human, are so depraved that they have no conscience (cf. Rom. 1.28-32). Science fiction writers not only explore questions related to the moral character of our humanity, they also explore questions relating to the role of humans within the cosmos. Indeed, as they look to the vastness of the created order, these writers seem to be asking 'in light of all this, and all that we do not yet know, of what significance is it to be human?'—a question which seems to echo the words of Ps. 8.3-5. This question is voiced in stark reality in an episode of *Star Trek: The Next Generation* where Data observes that while Q viewed life as a human to be a hardship, it was the life Data himself aspired to live ('Déjà Q', Season 3, episode 13).

The Scriptures portray the tension between human potential and the limitations of the human condition differently, employing the words *ādām* (MT) and *anthropos* (LXX and NT) to refer generically to all of humanity. The HB creation accounts affirm that to be human is a level of existence, which is differentiated from all other forms of existence, inanimate, creaturely or divine (Gen. 1.26-31; 2.4-9, 18-25). Thus humans are portrayed as biopsychosocial-spiritual beings who, in their original state, were created in a state of moral perfection which was lost when Adam and Eve ate the fruit of the tree of the knowledge of good and evil. What makes humans distinct from other created beings is not that we are biological beings who are part of the biosphere; or, that we are sentient beings with cognition, rationality, emotions, and a will; or, that we are social creatures; or, even that we are spiritually oriented creatures. Rather, humans are distinct because we exist simultaneously in all four domains. Thus Christians emphasize that humans were created and exist to be in relationship with God and are the objects of his redeeming love, have been given the specific mandate of being stewards of the earth, and, though marred by sin, have the capacity to know the difference between good and evil.

Recommended reading. Anderson, Ray S. *On Being Human: Essays in Theological Anthropology.* Grand Rapids, MI: Eerdmans, 1982.

See also IMAGO DEI; MAN; WOMAN; SIN [KFM]

Humble, Humility. In antiquity, humility was not the prized virtue that it is now. The Greek adjective for humble (*tapeinos*) and its verb (*tapeinoo*) had a derogatory sense, referring to servile, grovelling or demeaning behavior. This vice was overcome by the great man performing glorious deeds or by the philosopher avoiding the extremes of pride and servile behavior. In the case of the noble families of republican Rome, the leading men competed against each other for glory, hoping to surpass the fame of their consular ancestors. The epitaphs of deceased family members listed their military achievements, civic magistracies, and priesthoods. At funerals not only were eulogies of the deceased delivered but also eulogies of other famous ancestors (see e.g., Cicero, *Brut.* 16.61-62). The living descendants at funeral processions held wax masks of their ancestors, including the deceased. This enhanced a renowned family's reputation, and spotlighted ancestors worthy of imitation (Polybius 6.53.1-6.54.4; Valerius Maximus 5.8.3).

This boasting in great men intensified in the mid-first century BCE. Famous generals erected public monuments on a grand scale, with the Theatre of Pompey and the Forum of Caesar being conspicuous examples. In the Forum of Augustus the emperor portrayed himself as the fulfillment of Roman history, erecting statues of Julian family members descended from Aeneas and statues of illustrious Republican heroes descended from Romulus. Augustus, the apex of Roman history and founder of the new Rome, had arrived. The imperial propaganda proclaimed that his rule was eternal and godlike. The glory for which Republican nobles had competed was now concentrated in Augustus and his family.

The boasting culture of the Latin West was no different in the Greek East. Greek cities erected inscriptions registering their gratitude for the benefits of their benefactors, granting them honors, and eulogising them in the language of virtue (their 'zeal', 'piety', 'good will'). The celebrity of modern sport stars like David Beckham, Magic Johnson and Tiger Woods had its parallels in antiquity. The achievements of Greek athletes in the games were recorded on public inscriptions and celebrated in poetry for posterity.

In contrast to Greco-Roman culture, Second Temple Judaism prized humility towards God and his people. Humility originates with Israel's consciousness of her delivery from slavery in Egypt by divine grace (Deut. 7.7-8). Yahweh humbles the proud (Exod. 10.3; Deut. 8.2-3, 16) and exalts the humble (1 Sam. 2.7 [cf. 1.11, 16]; 2 Sam. 22.28). The humble poor are objects of God's concern (Exod. 23.6, 11; Deut. 15.4, 7, 11; 24.14). The Dead Sea Scrolls portray their community of the spiritually poor as walking humbly before God (1QS 2.24; 3.8; 4.3; 5.3, 25). In the wisdom and inter-testamentary literature, too, God saves the humble (Job 5.11) and favors them because of their humility (Prov. 3.34; 2 Esd. 8.47-54; Sir. 3.17-18; *T. Gad* 5.3).

In the NT, the humble poor announce the arrival of God's Messiah (Luke 1.48, 52). While humility informs Jesus' teaching and example (Luke 18.1-5; Mark 10.35-45; Matt. 5.5; Matt. 11.29), it is supremely displayed in Christ's incarnation and crucifixion (Phil. 2.7, 8c). Humility becomes the transforming paradigm for social relations (Rom. 12.16; Col. 3.16; Jas 1.9; 4.6, 10) and ministry (2 Cor. 11.7; 12.21 Acts 20.19). The demise of the great man in antiquity occurred imperceptibly but relentlessly through the triumph of humility as a virtue in the Western intellectual tradition.

Recommended reading. Wengst, K. *Humility: Solidarity of the Humiliated*. Philadelphia: Fortress Press, 1988. Harrison, J.R. *Paul and the Imperial Authorities at Thessalonica and Rome*. Tübingen: Mohr Siebeck, 2011.

See also WISDOM; REPENTANCE; MEEK SHALL INHERIT THE EARTH, THE [JRHA]

Hunger. The Hebrew *rā'āb* and the Greek *peinaō* can both denote simple hunger and starvation. The concept also appears metaphorically in several biblical contexts (Ps. 34.10 and Matt. 5.6).

Physical hunger is prominent in Exod. 16. Longing for the food in Egypt, the people complained to Moses of hunger and the Lord fed them with manna. The significance of this story is recalled elsewhere in the Bible (Deut. 8.3; Ps. 78.24; John 6.31). Experiences of hunger are signs of God's absence or punishment because of breaking the covenant or not obeying God (Deut. 28.47-48; Isa. 5.13; Lam. 4.9). God's favor is manifested when hungry people are filled (Jer. 50.19; Ps. 107.4-5; 146.7). In the NT, Jesus is described as hungry and tempted by the devil in the desert (Matt. 4.2). In Jesus' parables, he describes hungry characters like Lazarus (Luke 16.21) and the prodigal son (Luke 15.17). Paul enumerates hunger as one his apostolic trials (2 Cor. 11.27; Phil. 4.12). He comments on the Corinthians worship life because the have-nots in the community go hungry (1 Cor. 11.21).

Freedom from hunger is one of the important symbols of God's providence and a vision of the messianic age (Isa. 49.10; Ezek. 34.29; Luke 1.53; 6.21). In the NT, it is illustrated in Jesus' miraculous feeding of a multitude (Matt. 15.32-38; Mark 8.1-10; Luke 9.12-17). To feed the hungry is a work of righteousness, whether among one's kindred (Isa. 58.7; Tob 1.17; 4.16; Acts 6.1) or as an expression of hospitality to strangers and even enemies (Prov. 25.21; Rom. 12.20). It is also a measure of righteousness. Unwillingness to help the hungry deserves condemnation (Matt. 25.35, 37, 42, 44).

Hunger signals the bodily need for food in order to survive. Freedom from hunger remains a global aspiration. On December 10, 1948 the General Assembly of the United Nations adopted and proclaimed the Universal Declaration of Human Rights including the right to food (Article 25). The concern for defeating global food hunger is the main thrust of the UN Food and Agriculture Organization. Contemporary musical works support efforts to end hunger. Concern for the hungry in Africa inspired the song 'We are the World' by American artists in 1985. It has become the biggest-selling single of all time.

In another note, hunger strikes are a form of nonviolent protest, most famously illustrated in Mahatma Gandhi. The suffragists in England achieved the Franchise Act of 1918 with a hunger strike. In 1981, Bobby Sands died during a hunger strike protesting the Special Category Status as a republican prisoner in HM Maze prison near Belfast, Northern Ireland. The story is told in the multi-award winning movie *Hunger*.

See also BEATITUDES, THE; LAZARUS AND THE RICH MAN, PARABLE OF; FEEDING OF THE FIVE THOUSAND (FOUR THOUSAND); FOOD, SYMBOLISM OF [MALOUSI]

Hur. The name Hur is used infrequently in the biblical text (16 times), but may refer to several different characters. One of these characters the HB mentions only twice, Hur the Moabite king who was killed by the Israelites (Num. 31.8; Josh. 13.21). The most prominent figure with this name in the HB is Hur, of the tribe of Judah, son of Caleb (according to 1 Chron. 2.19), and presumed grandfather of Bezalel, the chief architect of the tabernacle (Exod. 31.2; 35.20; 38.22). This Hur appears as an aid to Moses in Exod. 17 during the Battle of Rephidim, where he and Aaron hold Moses's arms in the air, allowing the Israelites to defeat the Amalekites.

Modern scholarship has noted that very little explicit connection exists between the various occurrences of the name Hur in the biblical text. However, some theories exist which serve to connect many of them. If Josephus is correct (*Ant* 3.54, 105), Hur is the husband of Miriam, Moses's sister, and might have had a significant degree of tribal prominence. Accordingly, modern scholars have linked references to other persons named Hur (1 Kgs 4.8; Neh. 3.9) to a clan descended from the Hur of Exodus.

Modern cultural references to the biblical Hur are few but notable. Lew Wallace's 1880 book *Ben-Hur: A Tale of the Christ*, stars the character Judah Ben-Hur, who, it may by presumed, belongs to the lineage or clan of the Hur of Exodus. In 1871, artist John Everett Millais painted *Victory O Lord!*, which depicts Aaron and Hur hold up Moses's arms during the battle of Rephidim recounted in Exod. 17. In the 1956 movie *The Ten Commandments*, starring Charlton Heston and directed by Cecil B. DeMille, Hur ben Celeb is played by Lawrence Dobkin. In the 1959 film *Ben-Hur*, based on the Wallace novel, Charlton Heston played Judah Ben-Hur.

See also MOSES; EXODUS, BOOK OF [NDL]

Hypocrite. Originating from the Greek *hypocritēs*, a stage actor, the term means one who pretends to be what he or she is not. The resulting verb is *hypokrinō*, to answer or pretend, and a related noun, *hypokrisis*, means hypocrisy or pretence. Jesus accused the Pharisees (religious leaders) of his day of honoring God with their words but not their lives; he applied Isa. 29.13 to them: 'Isaiah prophesied rightly about you hypocrites, as it is written, "This people honors me with their lips, but their heart is far from me; in vain do they worship me, teaching human precepts as doctrines"' (Mark 7.6-7). Hypocrisy is not so much a deliberate act of pretending to be what one is not as it is an innate and stubborn blindness to what one genuinely is like. Jesus applied this epithet to all who fail to practice what they preach.

Throughout the centuries, especially in Christianized countries, hypocrisy has been held to be a major sin that blots out all possible virtues a person possesses. In recent years, however, a new view has arisen that sees hypocrisy as a misleading vice that is used to obfuscate truth and lead people away from doing what may be rightly advocated by the hypocrite. Charges of hypocrisy draw attention away from focusing on the true foundations of an argument. For example, Ted Haggard, head of the National Association of Evangelicals (USA) and advocate of righteous living, was caught using male prostitutes. His hypocrisy in failing to practice what he preached does not invalidate the concept of biblical morality. When parents tell their children that using drugs is harmful, and then the children find out that their parents used marijuana when they were young, that the children may think of their parents as hypocrites does not lessen the fact that using such drugs is harmful.

That hypocrisy is still considered a Christian vice may be seen in the modern death metal band, Hypocrisy, established by Peter Tägtgren in Sweden in 1990. Early lyrics were antichristian and pro-Satanic; now they focus on the paranormal and extraterrestrial. Their 2009 album featured such titles as 'Valley of the Damned', 'Taste the Extreme Divinity', 'The Sky Is Falling Down', and 'No Tomorrow', typical death metal themes.

See also WORSHIP; GOODNESS [DLS]

I

I Am. Exodus 3 records the first time that God enigmatically declares, 'I Am'. It forms part of a threefold statement where God reveals himself as: 'I am who I am'; 'I am'; and 'The LORD'. All three self-designations are closely related. The last title, 'The LORD' is an unfortunate English translation of the Hebrew word *yhwh* which is commonly transliterated as Yahweh. It is important to realize that 'Yahweh' is a shortened form of the first declaration 'I am who I am'.

There have been many attempts throughout history to explain the meaning of this name. Some have suggested that it represents a refusal of God to reveal himself to Moses and humanity. While this conclusion is overstated, the name does not reveal much in and of itself. God's self-designation as 'I am' is clearly related to the idea that God exists, he is present, he is real. However, to limit the meaning of this name to its semantic domain is to miss the more important reasons for this declaration. The key to understanding its meaning is the narrative context in which it first occurs.

In Exod. 3, God asks Moses to return to Egypt and lead his people out of slavery. Moses attempts to persuade God that he is not the man for the job, firstly by asking who he is that God should choose him, and secondly, by asking who God is that he should send Moses. It is here that God responds with the threefold self-designation.

Moses did not need to ask God his name, as God had already introduced himself as the 'the God of your father, the God of Abraham, the God of Isaac, and the God of Jacob'. Moses's real question was not who God was but whether God was willing and able to save his people. They had been crying out for hundreds of years and he had not saved them yet. In the immediate chapters surrounding this text, God is portrayed repeatedly as one who sees their situation, hears their cries, remembers his covenant, and knows their pain (Exod. 2.23-24; 3.7-10; 6.2-8). When God responds in this dialogue 'I am', he is reassuring Moses and the community that he is the covenant God who keeps his covenant promises. The names 'I am', 'I am who I am', and 'Yahweh' are a statement that God is real, he is present, he cares about his people, he can be trusted to keep his promises, and he has a track record to prove it.

The self-designation 'I am' is found on the lips of Jesus in John's Gospel. While many of these statements include a predicate noun (e.g., the good shepherd, the bread of life, etc.), a few statements have no predicate and clearly allude to the dialogue in Exod. 3 (John 18.1-11).

In terms of popular usage, the statement 'I am' is rarely used. The longer version 'I am who I am' is found in a number of songs and writings as a petition to accept the author 'as they are' (e.g., 'I Am who I Am' in the play *The Teddy Pendergrass Story*, and Popeye's famous expression, 'I yam what I yam'). In this way, they may mirror God's desire to be understood and trusted on the basis of how he has revealed himself.

See also GOD; YAHWEH [KB]

I know that my redeemer lives. The meaning of the phrase 'I know that my redeemer lives' from Job 19.25 varies significantly between its function in the Book of Job and its subsequent history of interpretation. In ancient Israelite culture, a redeemer refers to a close relative who either acquires some sort of lost property in behalf of another (Lev. 25.25; Num. 5.8; Ruth 4.4-6; Jer. 32.6-7) or avenges a murdered kinsman (Deut. 19.6-12; Josh. 20.1-9; 2 Sam. 14.11). In the context of the Book of Job, 'redeemer' likely refers to the latter and relates in some ways to Job's stated desire for an (heavenly?) adjudicator between himself and God earlier in the book (cf. 16.18-21; 19.23-26; 33.23-24). The idea being that, when God's unwarranted punishment of Job leads to Job's death, someone or something will call God to account for the unjust shedding of Job's blood.

Of course, there is much debate on whom or what this someone is. Some say an intercessory angel such as *ha-Satan* in Job 1–2, others believe it refers to Job's cry and interpret this phrase as intimating the survival of Job's testimony after his death, and still others interpret Job's redeemer to be God (for God as redeemer cf. Prov. 23.11; Jer. 50.34; Ps. 119.154; Lam. 3.58). In spite of disagreement on the identity of the redeemer, almost all modern commentators agree that this passage does not refer to bodily resurrection.

This is not the case in the history of interpretation in which interpreters have almost unanimously treated this verse as a witness to bodily resurrection (though the great early Christian preacher John Chrysostom [347–407 CE] is an exception), and for Christian interpreters it represents in particular the bodily resurrection of Christ. For example, in the appropriation of this phrase in music, whether one refers to Handel's aria 'I Know That My Redeemer Liveth' from the *Messiah* or hymns with this verse as their title (see Charles Wesley's, Samuel Medley's, and Fred Fillmore's hymns, 'I Know That My Redeemer Lives' and Jessie Pounds's hymn, 'I Know That My Redeemer Liveth'), all connect the redeemer to Christ and the act of living to the resurrection. This same connection between Job and Christ occurs in Christian art. The image of Christ in distress in the Middle Ages and the iconography of the suffering of Job in early Christian art bare a striking resemblance to the extent that the latter may be the prototype for the former. Regardless, Job served as a Christ-figure in early Christian thought, and Job 19.25 is one of the main passages behind this typology. Finally, there are several statues that depict Christ as a redeemer, the most famous of which are Michelangelo's *Cristo della Minerva* (1521) and *Christ the Redeemer* in Rio de Janeiro, Brazil (1931). Hence, humanity's fascination with bodily resurrection, in particular the resurrection of Christ, has almost entirely engulfed the original meaning of this passage.

See also JOB, BOOK OF; REDEEMER; RESURRECTION [DAS]

I stand at the door and knock. 'Behold, I stand at the door and knock; if anyone hears my voice and opens the door, I will come in to him and eat with him, and he with me' (Rev. 3.20). In order to interpret this verse correctly we must consider it in its context. In today's preaching, this verse is often used as an invitation to outsiders to become Christians but in fact it was originally addressed to those who already were Christians. It comes at the end of a message from the risen Jesus to the church in the city of Laodicea in Asia Minor (3.14-22). The Laodicean Christians are like the water that the city had to bring in from aqueducts: neither cold nor hot. Cold water and hot water each have their uses, but lukewarm water is useless.

The reason that the Laodicean Christians are useless is that their prosperity has made them spiritually complacent (Laodicea was a wealthy city, known for banking and the production of medicine and fine black wool; contrast the refined gold, white garments, and eye salve that Jesus offers at 3.18). They are unaware that they have lost the closeness of their relationship with Jesus. The risen Jesus calls on them to renew the intimacy of this relationship (in ancient Mediterranean cultures, sharing food with someone was a sign of intimate fellowship). It is noteworthy that Jesus says that he is knocking at the door, for in the ancient Mediterranean a friend usually called at one's door (cf. Luke 11.5). This is another sign of disruption in the relationship between the Laodicean church and its Lord.

This verse inspired William Holman Hunt's famous painting *The Light of the World* (1851–53; Keble College, Oxford). Hunt's painting in turn inspired many artists and poets of the late nineteenth century, including W. Rainey's woodcut *Christ before thy Door is Waiting* (c. 1883). Hymns inspired by this verse include Joseph Grigg, 'Behold a Stranger's at the door' (1775) and 'O Jesus, Thou art standing' by William Walsham How (1823–97). It is noteworthy that the latter is addressed to the church.

See also REVELATION, BOOK OF [ED]

Ichabod. Ichabod was a wartime baby born into the high priest's family but orphaned on the day of his birth. In the narrative of 1 Samuel, Eli the high priest had tolerated corruption in his sons, the priests Hophni and Phinehas, who slept with female attendants and took for themselves an unlawfully large share of the meat offerings given by worshippers. An anonymous prophet delivered God's rebuke to Eli, punning on two meanings of the Hebrew word *kabad*, meaning 'to be heavy' and 'to be honored': 'Why do you... honor [or make heavy] your sons more than me by fattening yourselves on the choicest parts of every offering of my people...? [God says]: "those who honor me I will honor, and those who despise me shall be treated with contempt"' (1 Sam. 2.29-30). He predicted Eli's actions would result in destruction for his family.

Later the Philistines defeated Israel's army, killed Hophni and Phinehas and took the ark of the covenant, a golden box from the most holy place of the temple. The ark was an important symbol of God's presence because his glory was thought to be enthroned between its carved cherubim or angels, though the ark could be misused something like a magic charm (Exod. 25.10-22; 37.1-9; 1 Sam. 4.3-4). The news of the ark shocked Eli and he fell backwards off his chair and broke his neck because 'he was an old man and heavy (*kabod*)', the word ironically linking his death to his sin and the prophet's judgment.

Phinehas's wife was about to give birth, and the news traumatized her. She delivered and was congratulated but was dying in despair. She named her son Ichabod (*kabod* meaning 'glory' and *i* meaning 'no' or 'where is?'), and she said, 'The glory has departed from Israel, for the ark of God has been captured' (1 Sam. 4.22). Nothing is recorded about Ichabod's life or his descendants, but he is a tragic symbol of failure in a once-great family.

In Washington Irving's story *The Legend of Sleepy Hollow*, schoolteacher Ichabod Crane is rejected by a local girl and leaves town, meeting the ghostly Headless Horseman who fells him by throwing his own head. There are several film adaptations, including *Sleepy Hollow* with Johnny Depp as Ichabod. In the TV sitcom *Frasier*, Niles Crane makes a prep school booking for his son Ichabod, who is not yet conceived.

'Ichabod' is a John Greenleaf Whittier poem, which laments Daniel Webster's loss of honor by supporting slavery. The phrase 'Ichabod, Ichabod / The glory is departed' appears in Robert Browning's 1842 poem 'Waring', about a friend who moved overseas.

Country-rock band Th' Legendary Shack Shakers sing 'Ichabod', a song about a man who dies but cheats hell and heaven and comes back to see his lover. It uses biblical imagery satirically. A bear named Ichabod appears in *Dr Seuss's ABC* in the line: 'Ichabod is itchy, and so am I.'

Recommended reading. Alter, Robert. *The David Story*. New York and London: W.W. Norton & Co., 1999. Arnold, Bill T. *1 and 2 Samuel*. The NIV Application Commentary. Grand Rapids, MI: Zondervan, 2003.

See also ELI; HOPHNI AND PHINEHAS; ARK OF THE COVENANT [GK]

Idols, idolatry. Idolatry represents the most constant threat to the relationship between God and his people in biblical narrative. Avoidance of idolatry is basic to the ethics that mold Israel's identity: the second commandment, proscribing idol manufacture and worship, is founded on the first, prohibiting the worship of any other gods before Yahweh. The Decalogue consistently refers to God as 'your' God, a 'jealous' God, underscoring God's deep commitment to his people and his uncompromising view of potential rivals; it is no accident that the golden calf (Exod. 32), one of the most famous biblical incidents of idolatry, appears so soon after the Ten Commandments are given. Israel's prophets similarly repudiate idolatrous practice, variously mocking idols as powerless, manufactured from the same substances used for cooking fuel (Isa. 40.18-20; 44.9-21); presenting them as valueless, lifeless objects, whose worship is closely tied to the breakdown of social justice (Hab. 2); and condemning idolatry as an adulterous, covenant-breaking pattern leading to exile, from which God will redeem Israel when he sees true repentance (Hosea).

The NT polemic against idols takes on political and commercial dimensions. Paul reminds his readers that while meat purchased in Corinth's marketplaces had been sacrificed to idols (i.e., in pagan temples), these 'many gods and many lords' are powerless to threaten or save, particularly in comparison with Israel's 'one God' and 'one Lord, Jesus Christ' (1 Cor. 8–10). Paul later heightens this rhetorical contrast in references to the 'living God' (2 Cor. 3.3; 6.16), an antithesis to idols anticipated in the Septuagint, where the same epithet is placed in the mouth of faithful Daniel and repentant Darius (Dan. 5.23; 6.27-28 LXX). Other Pauline epistles connect idolatry to greed (Eph. 5.5; Col. 3.5), recalling Jesus' warning about conflicting devotions to God and acquisitions (Matt. 6.24).

Questions about devotion and service remain crucial to contemporary issues of idolatry. Distilling many earlier biblical voices, Rom. 1 emphasizes the dehumanizing effects of service and obedience when hearts are given fully to any image other than God. 'A "graven image"', Robert Heinlein comments wryly in *To Sail Beyond the Sunset* (1988), 'is any idol that could rival the official god; it has nothing to do with sculpture or etchings'. Idolatry remains pernicious and pervasive because anything can become an idol, ultimately captivating the heart and the imagination, even if the object itself makes no explicitly theological claims. Sport, sex, war, the marketplace, nationalism, and fame are rife with potential examples, especially in societies that lavish so much attention on 'celebrity' status and so many resources on meeting every conceivable human desire, often at others' expense.

Recommended reading. Meadors, Edward P. *Idolatry and the Hardening of the Heart: A Study in Biblical Theology*. New York: T. & T. Clark, 2006. Rosner, Brian S. *Greed as Idolatry: The Origin and Meaning of a Pauline Metaphor*. Grand Rapids, MI: Eerdmans, 2007.

See also TEN COMMANDMENTS; WORSHIP; COVENANT; DAY OF THE LORD/JUDGMENT/WRATH [MFL]

Image of God. When God deliberates on making humans in the creation account (Gen. 1.26-27), it is 'in our image and according to our likeness', and when he creates them it is 'in his image'. In the OT, the phrase only appears in Genesis where 'image' underscores the solidarity of humanity (5.3) and human life's unique and intrinsic value (9.6). When translated into Greek the phrase became 'according to our image and likeness' and was freighted with vocabulary redolent of Greek philosophy, allowing a later fusion of biblical ideas with philosophical concepts to support far-reaching anthropological and soteriological claims.

The NT rarely makes use of 'the image' but when it does so, the phrase appears at notable and important passages. Paul's soteriological concept of Christ as the 'second Adam' relies on humanity's solidarity (Rom. 5.12-21; 1 Cor. 15.21-22, 44-47). Paul adopts the idea that humanity is not itself the image of God but is instead created 'in accordance' with the image. The image itself he refers to Jesus, the Son of God (Col. 1.14; 2 Cor. 4.4). Nevertheless, in Pauline theology, humanity's affinity with the image of God allows for increasing conformity to Christ, and so the image remains anthropologically constitutive both structurally and as the goal of Christian life (Eph. 4.13). Paul's usage would prove most incisive for Christian thought.

Patristic authors relied on Paul's understanding to focus salvation along anthropological lines: humanity, created in accordance with the image of God, was free and rational, ruling itself and the natural world. Adam's sin was to deny these elements and give up proper rule of himself by following irrational desires, which allowed all things to enter a trajectory of corruption and death. Christ reconstituted the image in himself, effectively re-creating humanity and enabling it to again relate properly to God.

By the late fourth century CE, as the Scriptures were translated into Latin, the 'according to' lost its force as did 'likeness'. Humanity, rather than the Son, became the 'image of God' and, since Trinitarian theology was by then firmly entrenched, anthropology received a Trinitarian structure in authors like Augustine and Boethius. In the Greek-speaking East, emphasis came to rest on 'likeness' as a process of perfection. 'Likeness to God' therefore defined the goal of the Christian life. These affirmed the Son as 'image of God' and as fully God, allowing 'image' to shake off its Platonic and Jewish stigma of imperfection or separation from its object. This distinction eventually found its way into Eastern Christian liturgy through the veneration of icons (images of Christ, Mary, Saints, or scriptural events). The East developed a thorough doctrine of icons based on the belief that the honor given to the image passes to that which the image represents, and so the veneration of images of Christ passes to Christ himself.

The currency of 'image' generally lessened following the Reformation. Nevertheless, following Augustine, the 'image of God' provided a driving argument whenever theological positions were adduced on either side of debates surrounding bioethics, euthanasia, or contraception. The 'image of God' has become a tool for theologians looking to safeguard the sanctity of life, and its re-appropriation in terms of stewardship over the world may have implications for the future of theology and ecology.

Recommended reading. Hughes, Philip Edgcumbe. *The True Image: The Origin and Destiny of Man in Christ*. Grand Rapids, MI: Eerdmans, 1989. Lossky, Vladimir. *The Image and Likeness of God*. New York: St Vladimir's Seminary, 1974.

See also CREATION, CREATOR; GENESIS, BOOK OF; GOD; SECOND ADAM [JLZ]

Immaculate Conception. Defined by Pope Pius IX in his constitution *Ineffabilis Deus* on December 8, 1854, the doctrine of Immaculate Conception teaches the Virgin Mary was without any 'stain' of original sin because of the salvific merits of Jesus Christ. Mary's salvation was achieved through the life, death, and resurrection of her son, Jesus Christ and not by her own merits. The Immaculate Conception is one of the four dogmas in Roman Catholic Mariology. According to this dogma, Mary was preserved by God and filled with divine grace, without need of sanctifying grace, connoting that she lived a life without sin.

Originally, the feast of the Immaculate Conception, celebrated on December 8, was established as a universal feast in 1476 by Pope Sixtus IV. Pope Sixtus IV did not define the doctrine of the Immaculate Conception as dogma, which allowed Roman Catholics the freedom to hold this belief or not. It was in the papal bull, *Ineffabilis Deus*, by Pope Pius IX, that the doctrine was defined as a dogma. Catholic theology still maintains that since Jesus Christ became Incarnate through the Virgin Mary, it is appropriate that Mary would be completely free of sin.

This dogma finds support in Gen. 3.15, which states, 'I will put enmity between you and the woman, and between your offspring and hers; he will strike your head, and you will strike his heel.' For Catholicism, this is a prophecy of a 'woman' who would always be at enmity with the serpent; that is, a woman who is never under the bondage of sin or the power of the serpent. Scriptural support is also found in Luke 1.28, when the angel Gabriel says to Mary, 'Greetings, favored one! The Lord is with you.' Some of the early church fathers, including Justin Martyr, Tertullian, Irenaeus, and Jerome, also support the notion of Mary's sinless nature.

Views on Mary's relation to sin vary in Eastern and Oriental Orthodoxy, Anglo-Catholicism, Old Catholicism, and Lutheranism. The sinless nature of Mary is also attested in Islam. Most Protestants reject the doctrine based on biblical exegesis: Jesus is the only one who is portrayed in the Bible as sinless. There are implications regarding Mary's salvation (what exactly was she saved from?) and Christ's Incarnation and sharing of sinful humanity (if he does not share, then can he actually redeem?).

In today's vernacular, the term Immaculate Conception is most commonly applied to names of Catholic schools and parishes. The independent comedic film *The Immaculate Conception of Little Dizzle*, directed by David Russo and released in 2009, spoofs the doctrine. However, the film indicates the misunderstanding of the Immaculate Conception present in mass media. Virginal conception and the Virgin Birth are not the same as the Immaculate Conception of Mary though the doctrines are oftentimes confused with one another.

Recommended reading. Perry, Tim. *Mary for Evangelicals: Toward an Understanding of the Mother of our Lord.* Downers Grove, IL: InterVarsity Press Academic, 2006.

See also FEASTS; GABRIEL, THE ANGEL; MARY, CHILDHOOD OF; MARY, MOTHER OF JESUS; PROPHECY; ROME; VIRGIN, VIRGIN BIRTH [RKM]

Immorality. The unabridged *OED* defines immorality this way: 'Immoral quality, character, or conduct; violation of moral law; wickedness, viciousness', and with the indefinite pronoun or in the plural '[a]n instance or species of [immorality]; an immoral act or practice; a vice'. Likewise the modifier immoral serves to define persons, things or actions as 'not consistent with, or not conforming to, moral law or requirement; opposed to or violating morality; morally evil or impure; unprincipled, vicious, dissolute'.

The words 'immoral' and 'immorality' are now used predominantly of sexual impurity; hence the use of the modifier 'sexual(ly)' with them is practically redundant. Nonetheless, the concept of morality does not limit itself to sexual conduct. Thus the prophet could deem exploitation of widows and orphans (e.g., Isa. 10.1-2), for example, as an immorality insofar as it constituted a violation of the Mosaic Law (Exod. 22.22). The terms of God's covenant with the Israelites demanded not only unflagging loyalty to her sovereign but also just relations among the people. Indeed the latter was to mirror the former. The purpose of the Law was to guarantee the greatest good for the greatest number and an equitable treatment of its weakest members.

The Greek verb *porneuō* and its cognate forms underlies the NRSV rendition 'immoral' and 'immorality' (e.g., 1 Cor. 5.1-12) and serves to denote a variety of proscribed sexual behaviors like fornication, adultery and sodomy (1 Cor. 6.9; cf. Mark 7.21-22). Notably Paul also includes 'sins' like drunkenness and robbery.

The Greek verb *porneuō* and its cognate forms denote various forms of sexual immorality in the Septuagint. This pre-Christian translation employs such terminology as its rendition of a variety of Hebrew roots. The writers of the OT do not condemn fornication or prostitution *per se*; the latter does not always entail a violation of the marriage bond. However, the monarchical period witnessed widespread influence of Canaanite practices including temple prostitution. This association (cf. Lev. 21.7, 9) engendered opposition to fornication which, along with adultery, came to symbolize idolatry. The NT uses the same metaphor (e.g., Rev. 17). Ultimately, the opposition to sexual relations between unmarried individuals underwent a hardening into legal prescription within early-church communities.

The purpose of moral codes is to establish accepted norms within a society with a view to the general well-being of that society. Indeed law and custom afford individual security in regard to society's expectations and understandably many people experience considerable anxiety in the face of changing values. This was true of the so-called 'new morality' of the 1960's and has remained true of the developments since that time. Here a generalizing paraphrase of the Markan Jesus serves to place the matter in Christian perspective: the Law was made for humanity, not humanity for the Law (2.27).

See also ADULTERY; CANAAN, CANAANITES; IDOLS, IDOLATRY; SEX, SEXUALITY [NRP]

Immortality. This word translates the Greek *athanatos* (immortality), in addition to *aphtharsia* (incorruptibility, imperishability). With the problem of death noted from the first book of the Bible (Gen. 2.17), the restoration of life serves as a central aspect of biblical soteriology. While some argue that the concept of immortality is implicit in the HB with such concepts as Sheol, the explicit use of the terminology in biblical literature does not arise until the intertestamental period (e.g., Wisdom of Solomon; *4 Maccabees*; and *1 Enoch*). In particular, these writings describe immortality as a hope for the faithful after death. Wisdom speaks of being honored and remembered among the community after death as immortality (Wis. 4.1; 8.13) but also of an ontological experience of immortality after death (Wis. 2.21-24; 15.3). Along with its anthropological use, immortality also is an important description of the divine. For instance, for the Greeks immortality is what distinguished humans from gods (e.g., Plato, *Timaeus* 41d).

In the NT, immortality language is used to describe both the divine state of being (Rom. 1.23; 1 Tim. 1.17; 6.16) and the hope of the resurrected state for believers (Rom. 2.7; 1 Cor. 9.25; 15.42-54; 2 Tim. 1.10; 1 Pet. 1.4), particularly because of Christ's defeat of death. While often popularly associated with the soul, NT writers usually associate immortality with the person as a whole or the body, in particular. Paul associates glory (*doxa*) and immortality/incorruption (Rom. 1.23; 8.21; 9.22-23 and 1 Cor. 15.40-44). Greek patristic theologians focus upon the experience of immortality as central for soteriology. In addition, they describe the process of believers becoming immortal as deification (*theopoiēsis, theōsis*), or becoming 'gods' (*theoi*), since they are participating in divine attributes, based on their exegesis of Ps. 82.6 (81.6 LXX) and other passages.

The search for immortality has captured the interest of many who want to escape the limitations of death. For instance, the legend of the Fountain of Youth prompted Ponce de León and others to scour the area of present day Florida in search of it. In a modern quest for immortality, cryogenics and transhumanism are promoted as means to cheat death. In the film *Indiana Jones and the Last Crusade*, immortality was promised for all who drank from the Holy Grail. While often seen as positive, some see immortality as negative or ambiguous. For instance, Def Leopard's song 'Immortal' presents a mixed picture about immortality. The search for immortality is disparaged in the *Harry Potter* series, especially Voldemort's attempts at attaining immortality through horcruxes. In addition, J.R.R. Tolkien presents the immortality of the elves as both a gift and a curse in *The Silmarillion*.

In art, the peacock and its feathers became a symbol of immortality due to an ancient legend that its flesh did not decay, thus providing an image of the resurrection. This association was noted from the early church and appeared regularly in art from that time onwards. An example of a painting with a prominent peacock is Fra Filippo Lippi's *The Adoration of the Magi* (c. 1440–1460).

See also LIFE; ETERNAL LIFE [BCB]

Incarnation. Derived from the Latin *carnis* (flesh), incarnation has its closest English equivalent in the word enfleshment. The concept is of central importance in the Christian tradition and refers to the theological belief that God became human (incarnate, enfleshed) in the person of Jesus of Nazareth.

Belief in the incarnation is associated in the NT most particularly with the Gospel of John: 'the Word became flesh and lived among us' (John 1.14). The Word of God, through whom the world was made (John 1.3; Gen. 1.1–2.3a), is to be understood in personal and relational terms, while intimately linked to the being and activity of God. John identifies the Word with the Son, eternally present to the Father yet also incarnate in Jesus Christ: in his life, ministry, death and resurrection.

Although incarnation is associated with John's Gospel, ideas of a parallel nature are found elsewhere in the NT: in the Gospel of Matthew, for example, in the title Emmanuel used of Jesus ('God with us' [Matt. 1.23]); in the Philippians' hymn where Christ is described as possessing divine form yet emptying himself in the incarnation and cross (Phil. 2.6-11); in the Colossians' hymn where Jesus is portrayed as 'the image of the invisible God' who is 'before all things' (Col. 1.15-19); and in the opening verses of Hebrews which speak of God creating the worlds through the Son who is 'the reflection of God's glory and the exact imprint of God's very being' (Heb. 1.2-3).

For several generations in the early Church, theologians struggled to maintain their commitment to monotheism (belief in one God) with the conviction that, in Jesus, God had become incarnate. These struggles led to the development of formal, Trinitarian theology, expressed in several councils and creeds. In particular, the definition of Chalcedon in 451 CE asserted belief in Jesus Christ as both divine and human, begotten of God yet born of Mary, his two natures divided yet unconfused, united yet different, separate yet harmonious. This kind of paradoxical theology became the basis of orthodox Christian theology across the various Christian denominations that were later to emerge.

The retrieval of a more strongly Trinitarian focus in contemporary theology has given considerable space to the doctrine of incarnation. Yet it has also had its detractors. There are those, for example, who interpret the incarnation as a myth that does not seek to describe a literal, historical event but rather a general maxim of symbolic import. Some forms of feminism have been troubled by the maleness of God incarnate in Jesus and see it as either unacceptable for contemporary women or as metaphorical for a truth about all people, and not confined to Jesus. Mainstream Christian theology in the West, however, continues to confirm the centrality of the incarnation alongside the uniqueness of Jesus, including a number of feminist theologians. For Christians from the Orthodox East, where the incarnation has never been other than central, the doctrine is both specific and general. It expresses the unique personhood of Jesus Christ, divine and human, yet points also to the ultimate identity of all Christians: to share in the divine nature by grace (*divinization, theosis*). This view is encapsulated in the Patristic maxim which summarises the orthodox understanding of incarnation: 'God became what we are so that we might become what God is'.

Recommended reading. Studer, Basil, *Trinity and Incarnation: The Faith of the Early Church*. Edinburgh: T. & T. Clark, 1993. Lee, Dorothy, *Flesh and Glory: Symbol, Gender and Theology in the Gospel of John*. New York: Crossroad, 2001.

See also EMMANUEL; CHRIST; JOHN, GOSPEL OF; MARY, MOTHER OF JESUS; TRINITY [DL]

Infancy narratives. The term infancy narratives refer to the first two chapters of both Matthew and Luke that relate various episodes concerning Jesus' birth and infancy. Scholars generally agree that the Matthean and Lukan stories are independent of each other. There are similarities between them which indicate pre-Gospel traditions used by each writer in his own way. The infancy narratives are not historical narratives in the historiographical sense of the word, meaning a simple list of historical facts, presented in chronological sequence. Neither are they myths, lacking connection to historical events. The evangelists' presentation of these stories is primarily theological in nature and it makes sense as part of their respective Gospels. Both writers present Jesus in relation to Israel's story and as part of God's plan for his people as told in the Scriptures.

Matthew's account identifies Jesus as the Messiah, the Son of David and Abraham, Emmanuel, 'God with us', and the New Moses. Matthew indicates that Jesus is Son of God by pointing out Jesus' conception—through the Holy Spirit without a human father (1.18-25). Quoting Isa. 7.14, Matthew articulates Jesus' identity and his divine origin. The focus on the magi in Matt. 2 expands another side of Matthew's theology, namely that Jesus came also to save the gentiles.

The Lukan infancy narrative serves as overture to the rest of the Gospel, revealing major themes developed throughout his portrayal of Jesus. OT characters representing Israel (Zechariah, Elizabeth, the shepherds, Simeon, Anna) come to meet Mary and Jesus. The core message in the whole infancy narrative is 2.11: 'For to you is born this day in the city of David a Savior, who is Christ the Lord' (cf. Isa. 9.6). Luke's narratives are interspersed with canticles that feature prominently in Christian liturgies: *Benedictus, Magnificat, Nunc Dimitis, Gloria*. Early Christian writers expanded on the brief canonical references to Jesus' birth and childhood, in such writings as the *Infancy Gospel of Thomas* and the *Infancy Gospel of James*. Infancy stories, especially the nativity scene, are evocative themes for artists, storytellers, and poets. Christian hymnody often incorporates elements of the birth narratives into the stories told, as in Joseph Mohr's 'Silent Night' (1816) and John Henry Hopkins's 'We Three Kings' (1857).

See also CHRISTMAS; EMMANUEL; INCARNATION; MARY, MOTHER OF JESUS; MAGI [DR]

Inspiration. Inspiration refers to the influence of a spirit, or to the quality of that influence, on a particular task. In connection with the Bible, the most obvious instance of inspiration proper lies in the interaction between spirit and messenger that provided the prophets with their message. For most that have learned to read the Bible by way of the Church's traditional approaches, the concept of 'inspiration' has an important second application in the idea of the inspiration of the biblical text itself. According to this idea, the wording of the text of Scripture is ultimately tied (whether strictly or loosely) to the inspired state of its writers. For many who accept the idea of the inspiration of Scripture, these two notions are related to each other, in that the text is inspired in a way similar to the prophets of old. That a writing within the Bible should be inspired in the same way as spoken prophecy is easily enough understood in the case of the writing prophets (i.e., that section of Scripture commonly called 'the Prophets'), because the writing is largely a transcript of the prophecy itself, but it is less clear in the case of wisdom writings, historical narratives (including the Gospels), NT epistles, and so on. Because of the difficulty of explaining the mechanics of the latter, claims of these writings' inspiration usually avoid any sort of detailed explanation of how it actually works out.

The primary supporting passage for the Christian understanding of the inspiration of Scripture is 2 Tim. 3.16: 'All scripture is inspired by God and is useful for teaching, for reproof, for correction, and for training in righteousness'. The word translated 'inspired' literally means 'God-breathed'. Theologians throughout Church history have occupied themselves with this aspect of the doctrine of Scripture, but it was not until the second generation of the Reformation, with the influential writings of John Calvin, that the doctrine of inspiration took on any measure of importance. Since then it has represented an area of contention between the opposing traditions within the Church, with one side confidently reading the ideas of infallibility into the wording of 2 Timothy, and the other side holding that such a reading is unwarranted. There are also some notable variations on the doctrine of Scripture's inspiration. One scheme attributes a mechanism of inspired scriptural *interpretation* to the Church, a notion better known as the indefectibility of the Church.

The basic idea of inspiration is widespread in poetry, but there it is especially due to the idea of poetic inspiration as caused by the muses of Greco-Roman antiquity, going back much farther than the NT. At times, however, scriptural-sounding ideas are mixed in. A pagan notion of inspiration underlies Ralph Waldo Emerson's 'O what are heroes prophets men', and a more neutral notion can be found in Paul Laurence Dunbar's 'Inspiration', Emerson's 'Ah! Not to me these dreams belong', and Henry David Thoreau's 'Inspiration'. But a more biblically related concept of inspiration underlies Robert W. Service's 'Inspiration'.

Recommended reading. Abraham, William J. *The Divine Inspiration of Holy Scripture*. New York: Oxford University Press, 1981. Aune, David E. *Prophecy in Early Christianity and the Ancient Mediterranean World*. Grand Rapids, MI: Eerdmans, 1983.

See also PROPHETS; WORD [JCP]

Isaac. The son of Abraham and Sarah in the HB, Isaac was born when his father was 100 years old (Gen. 21.1-7). He was also the father of Jacob and Esau, and was the biblical patriarch who lived the longest. He is mentioned about seventy times in the Book of Genesis and is the child in the famous story called the Aqedah, when Abraham shows willingness to sacrifice his son to God (22.1-19).

Over the years, there have been many paintings depicting episodes in Isaac's life, though the Aqedah is particularly well represented. One of the early representations of this story is on the sarcophagus of the Roman Consul Junius Bassus (c. 359 CE), which shows a bearded Abraham about to kill his young son when an angel intercedes. Caravaggio (1571–1610) in a 1603 painting (now at the Uffizi Gallery in Florence), shows Abraham pushing his son by his neck onto the altar and holding the knife, with an angel interrupting him to point out the goat in the background. In the painting by Rembrandt (1606–1669), Abraham in dark clothes is about to cut the throat of a largely naked Isaac who has his arms bound behind his back, but the angel has grabbed his right hand and the knife has fallen from it. The sculptor Donatello (ca.1386–1466) made a bronze image of Abraham looking to heaven as he moved the knife towards his son's throat. Another popular story about Isaac often represented in art involves Jacob deceiving his father, pretending to be Isaac's other son Esau, in order to gain the blessing intended for the eldest child (Gen. 27.1-29).

Issac is also mentioned in the many novels about his son Jacob, including Irving Fineman's *Jacob: an Autobiographical Novel* (1941); Thomas Mann's *Tales of Jacob*, a part of *Joseph and his Brothers* (1948); Jean Cabries's *Jacob* (1958); Robert Hoyer's *Jabbok: A Novel* (1958); Jean A. Rees's *Jacob I Have Loved* (1963); and Frederick Buechner's *The Son of Laughter* (1993). He was played by Alberto Lucantoni in film *The Bible: In the Beginning* (1966).

See also ABRAHAM; ESAU; JACOB; SARAH; AQEDAH [JC]

Isaiah. The name derives from the Hebrew *yesha'yahu*, meaning salvation of Yahweh. A major prophet whose ministry began c. 740 BCE in 'the year that King Uzziah died' (Isa. 6.1; cf. Isa. 1.1) and ended closely after the Assyrian King Sennacherib's attempt to conquer Jerusalem in 701 BCE (2 Kgs 19.16-19). Isaiah spoke Yahweh's words of the tragic impending doom of Jerusalem, Judah, and several foreign nations, while paradoxically offering hope for future restoration (cf. Isa. 1–39; 2 Kgs 19–20; 2 Chron. 26; 32).

Many Christians believe Isaiah's prophecies foretold future events (e.g., the return from the exile, the virgin birth, the coming of the Messiah). Isaiah is quoted (by name) by Jesus (Matt. 15.7; cf. Mark 7.6; John 12.39-43), John the Baptist (John 1.23), and the apostles (e.g., Rom. 9.27-29; 10.16-21; Acts 28.24-28). Both Jesus and John the Baptist take up an Isaiah-like prophetic calling, critiquing their society and offering the reconciliatory hope of God.

Isaiah's prophetic call and commission has profoundly influenced Western literature. Poet John Milton in 1629, while crediting the 'infinite God' as his poetic muse, relates his life to Isaiah's calling. He alludes to Isaiah's vision of the seraphim and Yahweh of Hosts ('On the Morning of Christ's Nativity', 4.27-28; cf. Isa. 6.7). William Blake, in 'A Memorable Fancy' (c. 1789–1790), dialogues with Ezekiel and Isaiah over dinner. In the poem, Isaiah says, 'I saw no God, nor heard any, in a finite organical perception; but my senses discover'd the infinite in every thing' (*The Marriage of Heaven and Hell*, plate 12.6-8). Blake expands Milton's practical understanding of Isaiah's divine inspiration by interpreting all matter through mystic (non-scientific) lenses. The abrasive parts of Isaiah's message are embraced by Blake (plate 12.8-11). Isaiah's three-year choice to be naked and barefoot is even explicitly mentioned, and paralleled with Greek cynical philosophy (plate 13.17-19; cf. Isa. 20.3).

In the Sistine Chapel (1509), Michelangelo portrays a clean-shaven European Isaiah, deep in thought, dressed like a Roman philosopher (cf. Blake). He holds a book and is accompanied by two cherubim. Raphael's fresco is much more Jewish—the prophet has a beard and holds a Hebrew scroll (1511–1512). Gustave Doré (1832–1883) engraved a prayerful, Jewish Isaiah. The mid-twentieth-century American artist Guy Rowe presents a preaching Isaiah, with an American symbol of freedom as a backdrop—the bald eagle. Rowe uses Isaiah's words, 'they shall mount up on wings like eagles' (Isa. 40.31), as a point of contact with his own culture. Each artist represents the idealism of their period, while showing an aspect of Isaiah's dichotomous life and message.

Isaiah embodies the concept of a life calling, often referred to simply as *the* prophet *par excallance*. In Western literature and art, Isaiah is a point of interest, contention, and theological empowerment

Recommended reading. Childs, Brevard S. *The Struggle to Understand Isaiah as Christian Scripture.* Grand Rapids: Eerdmans, 2004. McKinion, Steven A., and Thomas C. Oden (eds.). *Isaiah 1–39.* Ancient Christian Commentary on Scripture. Downers Grove, IL: InterVarsity Press, 2004. Seitz, Christopher R. *Isaiah 1–39.* Interpretation. Louisville, KY: Westminster John Knox Press, 1993.

See also ISAIAH, BOOK OF; EMMANUEL; PROPHETS

[JDB]

Isaiah, Book of. The biblical book of Isaiah is the first book included in the second division of the HB, the prophets (*Nevi'im*). It is also the first book in the fourth division of the Christian Bible (the prophets). In chapters 1–39, a narrator recounts the life of Isaiah, dispersing first-person divine oracles (written in Hebrew poetry) throughout this section. At the end of chapter 39, the narrator ceases to speak. From this point forward, the words are only those of an unnamed prophet, who brings a comforting message—Yahweh will redeem his people by means of his servant(s). Chapters 56–66 offer an eschatological (future) hope for all nations—those who follow Yahweh will be saved when he restores his creation (e.g., Isa. 65.17-25; 66.18-21). However, those who are not obedient to Yahweh will suffer and/or die (e.g., Isa. 66.24).

Isaiah is one of the most quoted books in the NT. Perhaps the most famous scene involves Jesus reading from 'the scroll of the prophet Isaiah' (Luke 4.16-21). Following his reading, he says, 'Today this scripture has been fulfilled in your hearing', signalling that he is the culmination of the prophecy. Throughout the earliest Christian writings, there are allusions to Isaiah's characters: Immanuel, the Man of Sorrows, and the Servant of the Lord.

Isaiah was popular among the Essenes who lived at Qumran (c. second century BCE—first century CE). There are 19 copies of Isaiah discovered among the Dead Sea Scrolls and five commentaries (*pesharim*) on Isaiah. In the *pesharim*, various figures of the period are identified with characters in Isaiah. A group of the Essene sect is even depicted in one *pesher* as 'the sapphires' that are the foundation of God's restored people (4QpIsa^d 1.1-3; cf. Isa. 54.11-12). Isaiah's impact is typified by the Great Isaiah Scroll, which has become a symbol of public pride for Israelis and an icon of intrigue throughout the world.

Shakespeare capitalized on the popularity of the Geneva Bible version of Isaiah in his era when writing *Henry V* (c. 1599). He used allusions and glosses affiliated with Isaiah's character archetypes to describe the king, the French nobles, and the London rascals. Likewise, J.R.R. Tolkien used Isaiah's archetypes in *The Silmarillion* (c. 1914–1950). Tolkien depicts Melkor with imagery affiliated with the spirit 'Day Star, son of Dawn', commonly known as Lucifer (Isa. 14.12). Melkor too falls from splendor to lowliness (*The Silmarillion* 34-35; cf. Isa. 14.11-12).

Handel's famous oratorio *Messiah* (c. 1741) opens with a direct citation from Isa. 40.1: 'Comfort ye, comfort ye, my people, saith your God' (Part 1.2-4). Handel recognized the NT writers' intentional connection of Isaiah's prophecies with Jesus' life. The composer even makes some christological claims about the book of Isaiah himself. Isaiah 40 was also William Blake's inspiration for *All Religions are One* (c. 1788). Blake identifies with the prophetic oracles of Isaiah by opening his poem with the words, 'The Voice of one crying the Wilderness' (Isa. 40.3; cf. John 1.23). The drama and intrigue of the Book of Isaiah has been an archetypal and poetical source for many influential Western figures. No doubt, it will continue to be a foundation of fruitful thought.

Recommended reading. Childs, Brevard S. *Isaiah*. Old Testament Library. Louisville, KY: Westminster John Knox Press, 2000. McKinion, Steven A., and Thomas C. Oden (eds.). *Isaiah 40–66*. Ancient Christian Commentary on Scripture. Downers Grove, IL: InterVarsity Press, 2007. Motyer, J. Alec. *The Prophecy of Isaiah: An Introduction and Commentary*. Downers Grove, IL: InterVarsity Press, 1993.

See also ISAIAH; SUFFERING SERVANT; MAN OF SORROWS [JDB]

Ishbaal. Ishbaal is one of the sons of King Saul. He was installed as king over Israel by Abner, commander of Saul's army, after the death of his father and his three brothers at the battle of Mount Gilboa (2 Sam. 2.8-9; cf. 1 Sam. 31.1-6). This installation contrasted with the southern enthronement of David in Hebron (2 Sam. 2.1-4). Ishbaal was 40 years old when he began his rule as a powerless king. He was Abner's creation and he feared him so much that he dared not stand up to him even though he could not tolerate Abner's relationship with Rizpah, concubine of Saul (2 Sam. 3.6-11). After reigning for two years, Ishbaal was assassinated by two of his own captains in the palace (2 Sam. 4.5-8, cf. 2.10). From then on, David became king over the whole of Israel.

The name Ishbaal only appears in 2 Sam. 2–4, where the rise and fall of his kingship is recounted. When the same name recurs in the genealogy of Saul in 1 Chronicles, it is changed to Eshbaal (1 Chron. 8.33; 9.39). The NRSV uses the word 'Ishbaal' as the rendering of its Hebrew counterpart 'Ishbosheth', a transliteration adopted in most English versions. Ishbosheth in 2 Samuel means 'man of shame' while Eshbaal in 1 Chronicles denotes 'man of Baal'. Most scholars believe that the original name should be Eshbaal rather than Ishbosheth. (Note the similar alteration from Merib-baal in 1 Chron. 8.34; 9.40 to Mephi-bosheth in 2 Sam. 4.4).

The word Baal, which means 'lord' or 'master', was originally a title of dignity. It appears to have been an accepted epithet for Yahweh until the early monarchic period, but after that time, this name came to be increasingly associated with the Canaanite storm god Baal. Baal-worship flourished especially under the rule of King Ahab whose wife Jezebel had brought the idol Baal from Sidon with her when she married him (1 Kgs 16.31). Because of this, the Hebrew editors substituted '-bosheth' (shame) for '-baal' (Baal) in order to avoid any association with Baal-worship. This alteration to satisfy religious sensibilities was particularly essential when biblical texts were frequently read in public worship.

Recommended reading. Brueggemann, Walter. *First and Second Samuel*. Interpretation: A Bible Commentary for Teaching and Preaching. Louisville, KY: John Knox Press, 1990.

See also SAUL, KING; DAVID; BAAL; AHAB; JEZEBEL [ASYL]

Ishmael. Ishmael (Hebrew, 'God will hear') was the elder son of Abraham by his wife Sarah's Egyptian handmaiden. In the customs of the time Sarah, being barren, could give her handmaiden to her husband. He could accept her as a concubine and have children by her which would legally belong to Sarah.

Ishmael was born when Abraham was eighty-six years old (Gen. 16.15-16) at Mamre. Isaac his half-brother was born naturally to Sarah fourteen years later (Gen. 21.5). When Ishmael was thirteen year old he was circumcised, along with Abraham and all of the other males in the camp because of God's covenant with Abraham (Gen. 17.25). However, the covenant was to be with Abraham's son Isaac and not with Ishmael. Abraham's plea (exposing great affection for Ishmael) that the covenant would be with Ishmael was rejected, but God promised to bless Ishmael, to make of him the fruitful father of many descendants and the father of twelve princes (Gen. 17.20).

When Isaac was weaned there was a great festival in the camp of Abraham. When Sarah saw Ishmael playing with little Isaac in a manner she disapproved, she demanded that Abraham send both Ishmael and Hagar away. Abraham did so very reluctantly following a divine admonition that it would all work out. Hagar and Ishmael are sent out with bread and water. Hagar and Ishmael wandered in the wilderness of Beer-sheba until their water was gone. Putting him under a bush she moved off a bowshot's distance and wept. Her voice was heard by God. The angel of the Lord repeated the promise of blessing and showed her a well of water saving their lives. Ishmael grew up in the desert wilderness of Paran with the blessing of God active in his life. He became a skilled archer and hunter with an Egyptian wife (Gen. 21.8-21).

Abraham died at the age of one hundred and seventy-five years. His sons, Isaac and Ishmael, buried him in the cave of Machpelah in the field of Ephron son of Zohar the Hittite, east of Mamre, where Sarah was also buried (Gen. 25.9). Ishmael's sons in order of their birth were: Nebaioth, Kedar, Adbeel, Mibsam, Mishma, Dumah, Massa, Hadad, Tema, Jetur, Naphish, and Kedemah (Gen. 25.13-15). The villages and camps bore the same names spreading out from Havilah to Shur.

The biblical references to Ishmael can be found at Gen. 16.11, 15-16; 17.18, 20, 25-26; 25.9, 12-13, 16-17; 28.9; 36.3; and at 1 Chron. 1.28-31. Several individuals in the OT are named Ishmael. Esau married Ishmael's daughter, Mahalath. Both Mahalath (Gen. 28.9) and Basemath (Gen. 36.3) were sisters of Nebaioth. Ishmael died at age one hundred thirty-seven. His descendants were the Ishmaelites (the eventual enemies of the Israelites, Ps. 83.6) and ultimately the Arabs.

In Gal. 4.22-31, Paul used Sarah and Hagar (Isaac and Ishmael) as allegoric symbols of the conflict between the covenants of Sinai and Jerusalem. Carnality and spirituality are thereby represented which was the theme followed by a number of the church fathers, by Luther, Calvin and others. Literature since the 1600s has followed similar themes. Ishmael appears as good (e.g., William Blake's painting *A Vision of the Last Judgment*, 1808 [known only by description]) and as a symbol of evil (e.g., Samuel Taylor Coleridge's play *Zapolya*, 1817).

Recommended reading. Bakhos, Carol. *Ishmael on the Border: Rabbinic Portrayals of the First Arab*. Albany, NY: State University of New York Press, 2006. Maalouf, Tony. *Arabs in the Shadow of Israel: The Unfolding of God's Prophetic Plan for Ishmael's Line*. Grand Rapids, MI: Kregel Publications, 2003.

See also ABRAHAM; ESAU; HAGAR; HANDMAID; ISAAC; SARAH [AJW]

Israel. This name signifies the people of God in the HB. It arose from the story of Jacob wrestling with the angel in Gen. 32.28. In the struggle Jacob is renamed Israel and the meaning given for the name is one who wrestles with God. The meaning could also be applied to the history of the people Israel through the ages. The name Israel can also mean the land where Jacob's descendants settled in ancient Palestine. Jacob had twelve sons and each son or tribe received a portion of the land of Canaan in which the people settled after the Exodus and desert wanderings.

There is a distinction made between the northern ten tribes called collectively Israel, and the two southern tribes of Judah and Benjamin. The split between the ten and the two tribes took place after the death of Solomon when his grip upon the federation of the twelve tribes broke apart. From this point on, the northern tribes were called Israel and the souther tribes Judah. (Occasionally the south, Judah, was called Israel, as in Isa. 1.3-4; Ezek. 2.30.) Israel in the north fell first, in 722 BCE. The south was defeated in 586 BCE After these events and as the Jews slowly returned to their country, Israel referred to the nation as a whole and the distinction among the tribes became more and more an exception.

In the NT, Israel often signifies the whole nation of the Jewish people (Matt. 10.6; Luke 1.16). The term indicates the Jews outside the church in Paul's discussion of the Jews in Rom. 9–11. In the course of that reflection he says, 'not all Israelites truly belong to Israel' (Rom. 9.6). Paul also speaks about the Israel of God by which he means both the Gentile and Jewish followers of Jesus (Gal. 6.16; see also Jas 1.1). For most of the Church's history, interpreters of Scripture assumed that the true or real Israel of God was the Church and eventually the Jews who did not believe in Christ would be converted. Paul's argument is more sophisticated than this but he has contributed to the Church's assumption that it has become the people of God and replaced Israel or the Jewish people in that role. Since the Holocaust, however, Christians have been rethinking this assumption very deeply. Israel is still treated as a harbinger of the end times in much fundamentalist theology because of the expectation that the Jews will be converted to Christ at or near the end time as expressed, for instance, in *The Beginning of the End* by Tim LaHaye.

There is a distinction to be made today between Israel as a nation in the Middle East and Judaism the living faith as practiced by Jewish believers. Israel as a nation encompasses both secular and religious Jews and the various expressions of Judaism. The film *Exodus* portrays the story of the establishment of the modern state of Israel, as the *Ten Commandments* explores the beginning of the nation as a people.

See also GOD; JACOB WRESTLING AN ANGEL; TWELVE TRIBES OF ISRAEL [DMAC]

J

Jacob. Born grasping the heel of his elder twin Esau (Gen. 25.26), this second son was thereafter named Jacob, a derivation from the Hebrew word *'āqab* ('grasped by the heel'; 'cheat'). The entire story of Jacob and his immediate family is found in Gen. 26–50. He is considered the great patriarch, the father of Israel, who is eventually named 'Israel' by God in Gen. 32.28 and 35.10.

Fulfilling God's prophecy to Rebekah (Gen. 25.23), wife of Isaac, who was the son of Abraham, Jacob's cunning demeanor is evident from birth: Jacob's destiny to overtake his brother begins with the grasping of his twin brother's heel. Soon after, Jacob tricks Esau into giving him the birthright of the eldest son in exchange for red stew (Gen. 25.30) and then beguiles his father Isaac, whose sight has become poor, into giving him the blessing specially put aside for the firstborn. Through deceit and trickery, Jacob supplants his elder brother and takes the important and powerful position of firstborn in the family.

Afraid of his brother's wrath towards him, Jacob flees to Laban, his mother's brother, in hopes that his brother's vengeance will eventually die out. Jacob is then promised Laban's second daughter, Rachel, but gets tricked into marrying Leah, the eldest daughter. Jacob continues to exercise his clever wit and cunningness and ends up acquiring both daughters as wives and the majority of Laban's flock through crossbreeding strategies (Gen. 30.25-43). Once Laban realizes that he has been tricked, Laban pursues Jacob, but by that time, Jacob has already fled. Thereafter, Jacob eventually reconciles with both Laban and Esau (Gen. 31–33).

By his two wives, Leah and Rachel, and their maidservants, Bilhah and Zilpah, Jacob brings forth twelve sons and several daughters (Gen. 37.35). The twelve sons of Jacob become the twelve tribes of Israel: Reuben, Simeon, Levi, Judah, Dan, Naphtali, Gad, Asher, Issachar, Zebulun, Joseph, and Benjamin. The only daughter of Jacob who is named is Dinah.

The two more widely popularized stories of Jacob are usually entitled, 'Jacob's Ladder' and 'Jacob Wrestles with God'. Regarding the former, while on his way to Haran, fleeing from his brother Esau, Jacob stops for a night to sleep. While he sleeps, he has a dream of stairs reaching to heaven with angels of God ascending and descending. Above the staircase stands the Lord, who reaffirms the covenant he has made with Jacob's grandfather and father, Abraham and Isaac, respectively. In the story commonly entitled, 'Jacob Wrestles with God', the night before Jacob meets with Esau to reconcile past differences, Jacob wrestles all night with a man who infers that he is God. Unable to overcome Jacob, the man touches his hip socket and wrenches it out of place. Jacob persists and will not let the man go unless the man, who is God, blesses Jacob.

The amount of space given to the story of Jacob and his family speaks to its religious significance for ancient Judaism but the story continues to resonate in post-biblical art and literature. One interesting example is Anita Diamant's novel *The Red Tent* (1997), a retelling of the story of Dinah, Jacob's daughter.

See also DINAH; ESAU; FIRSTBORN; GOD; ISAAC; JACOB WRESTLING AN ANGEL; JACOB'S LADDER; LABAN; LEAH; RACHEL; REBEKAH; TWELVE TRIBES OF ISRAEL, THE

[RKM]

Jacob wrestling an angel. Recounted in Gen. 32.22-32, the story of Jacob's dusk-to-dawn struggle with a mysterious being at Peniel is perhaps the most significant event in the patriarch's colorful career, and a notable moment in the formative stages of biblical Israel. Reluctant to reveal his name, the identity of Jacob's opponent remains mysterious. Often referred to as an 'angel' (Hos. 12.4), the being is described by the narrator simply as a 'man' (Gen. 32.24). Jacob, however, is convinced that he has seen God face-to-face (32.30), a detail that was not lost among the early Christian apologists who often regarded the being as an appearance of the pre-incarnate Christ, and thus an invaluable resource in Trinitarian arguments (e.g., Novatian, *De trinitate* 19).

The issue behind the struggle, made clear by Jacob's insistence that the being bless him, is the renewal of the promise given to Abram and his descendants in Gen. 12.1-3, the urgency for which was heightened by Jacob's anticipation of an imminent violent encounter with his older brother Esau (32.3-21) from whom he had previously stolen the birthright (27.1-40). The struggle with the being ensued throughout the night, during which time Jacob sustained a serious wound to the hip that, according to the narrator, would later form the basis of the dietary prohibition against eating 'the thigh muscle that is on the hip socket' (32.32). Eventually the being relinquished the struggle at dawn, and at Jacob's request, the being blessed the Patriarch and gave him the name Israel, since he had 'struggled with God and with humans and [had] prevailed' (32.28). Significantly, this name would also be applied to Jacob's twelve sons, and eventually to the nation that would derive from them.

The story is one of great triumph and has accordingly captured the imagination of many notable artists throughout history including Rembrandt, Gustave Doré, and Paul Gauguin. In recent years, in addition to receiving mention in Margaret Laurence's *The Stone Angel* and Tony Kushner's *Angels in America*, the struggle between Jacob and the angel also continues on in U2's classic protest tune, 'Bullet the Blue Sky'.

See also GOD; ISRAEL; JACOB; JACOB'S LADDER [TAB]

Jacob's ladder. This biblical image, appearing in Gen. 28.11-19, refers to a dream by Jacob about a ladder connecting earth to heaven on which various angels are ascending and descending. Standing above the ladder is the 'Lord' (Gen. 28.12-13), who proclaims a renewal of the covenant with Jacob, thereby ensuring divine blessings on Jacob's descendants. The awe-inspiring nature of the dream compels Jacob to awake and exclaim that the very place at which he was sleeping is holy. He renames it 'Bethel' meaning House of God.

The story provides allegorical content for much theological and literary reflection. Jewish midrash discerns various levels of meaning in the image. One interpretation sees the ladder as representing a type of *axis mundi* (world axis) connecting earth with heaven and foreshadowing Solomon's temple. To others it represents divine transcendence and immanence, and to others still, the ladder denotes the various exiles of the Jewish people until the arrival of the Messiah. Of particular note is Philo, whose *De somniis* provides extensive allegorical commentary on the image including the view that the ascending and descending angels symbolize the movement of souls to and from bodies.

With the advent of Christianity, the image of Jacob's ladder was primarily reinterpreted to signify Christ as the conduit, ladder and way connecting heaven and earth, which is alluded to in a verse in the Gospel of John, 'you will see heaven opened, and the angels of God ascending and descending upon the Son of Man' (1.51).

Among Christian writers, the ladder symbolized different things and held a wide range of meanings including the incarnation (St Augustine), human fellowship with angels (St Ambrose), the two Testaments (Zeno of Verona), and mystical progress of the soul toward God (St Bonaventure). In St John Climacus's work, *Ladder of Divine Ascent,* the ladder was an analogy for progression on the path of Christian asceticism. Within Eastern Orthodoxy, the movement of angels up and down the ladder is understood as a two-way interaction with God; God descends to humanity and humanity aspires upward toward God.

During the Middle Ages, the motif of Jacob's ladder was often used an analogy for spiritual growth, as noted in 'steps' of self-discipline found in St Benedict's Rule, for example. Correspondingly, Pope Gregory's *Regulae pastoralis* used 'rungs' as virtues, and Rabanus Maurus spoke of the ladder as symbolic of works of charity.

Politically, the story of Jacob's ladder had an impact on European aristocracy for the coronations of Scottish kings occurred on the Stone of Scone, which was alleged to be the rock upon which Jacob slept while dreaming.

In English literature, various writers employed the ladder as motif in their prose including Walter Hilton's, *The Ladder of Perfection*, John Milton's *Paradise Lost* (3.510-15), and Thomas Gray's *The Characters of Christ-Cross Row*. Additional ladder symbolism appears the writings of William Wordsworth, Robert Browning, Henry Wadsworth Longfellow, and George Bernard Shaw.

Western music also became a repository of ladder lore. For the Reformation writers, the story was an inspiration for many religious hymns. Musical echoes of the motif continue to be heard in the modern folk song, 'We are Climbing Jacob's Ladder', in Arnold Schoenberg's German Opera, *Die Jakobsleiter*, and in Led Zeppelin's famous 'Stairway to Heaven'. Several recent bands also refer to Jacob's ladder in song titles, including Chumbawamba, Bruce Hornsby, Huey Lewis and the News, Patrick Wolf, Rush, and The Monochrome Set. In the movie industry, *Jacob's Ladder* was the title of a psychological horror film (1990), and a *South Park* episode was titled 'A Ladder to Heaven' (2002).

See also JACOB; JACOB WRESTLING AN ANGEL; SON OF MAN [SDD]

Jael. Jael (*yael*, meaning mountain goat) was a nomadic Kenite tribeswoman who killed Sisera, Israel's oppressor, with a tent peg. Sisera, feared general of the Canaanite king Jabin of Hazor, had superior weapons technology: 900 iron chariots. When his chariots were defeated by a flash flood and his army suffered heavy losses and retreated

West, Sisera ran North towards Hazor. En route he encountered a small Kenite camp. The Kenite people, originating in the northern Sinai and descended from Moses's father-in-law Jethro (Judg. 1.16), were generally friendly towards Israel. Being skilled metalworkers, they were likely recruited by Jabin to help with his army (Judg. 4.17).

Jael came out of her tent to offer hospitality to the fleeing Sisera. She gave him a place to rest before completing his escape. He asked for the standard desert kindness of water and she offered even more: milk. He asked her to stand sentry and, if asked, to say no man was in her tent. Yet while he slept she came quietly and hammered a tent-peg through his temple right into the ground.

Her motives are not revealed. Perhaps she figured Sisera would cover his tracks by killing her household. Perhaps she was sympathetic to Israel and even to their God. Or perhaps she was pragmatically joining the new winning side. When Barak came looking for Sisera, she showed him the corpse in her tent and earned heroine status, being commemorated in the narrative and in Deborah's song (Judg. 4–5), which delightedly repeats the kill moment when she 'shattered and pierced his temple' and he fell endlessly at her feet (4.24-27). This barbaric delight in violence, though hardly an example of peacemaking ethics, may be understandable in people violently oppressed, and may be theologized as God finally righting wrongs.

Scholars have debated the ethics of her action as a breach of trust, fracturing hospitality. Jael is associated with the motherly imagery of milk and a blanket and protection in sleep. Yet she contrasts with the description of Sisera's own mother worrying about her little boy, then comforting herself that he is out there raping—'a girl (literally 'womb') or two for every man'—and bringing home stolen, second-hand clothes for her to wear (Judg. 5.28-30). If Jael is a dangerous mother, she at least looks better by contrast.

The Song of Deborah uses Sisera's destruction as a microcosm of God's ultimate destruction of all evil (Judg. 5.31). Jael is an early *femme fatale*, a popular archetype in literature and film, particularly Film Noir.

Recommended reading. Block, Daniel I. *Judges, Ruth*. Nashville, TN: Broadman & Holman, 2002. Herzog, Chaim, and Mordechai Gichon. *Battles of the Bible*. London: Greenhill Books, 2002. Schneider, Tammi J. *Judges*. Collegeville, MN: Liturgical Press, 2000.

See also DEBORAH; HAZOR; KENITE [GK]

Jairus and his daughter. All three Synoptic Gospels—Matthew, Mark, and Luke—tell the story of Jesus raising Jairus's daughter from the dead (Matt. 9.18-26; Mark 5.21-43; Luke 8.40-56). Jairus, whose name means 'enlightener', was a local synagogue official in Capernaum in the region of the Sea of Galilee. Jesus having recently healed the Gerasene demoniac, was drawing quite a crowd of people about him, especially those who needed healing. Jairus approaches Jesus and asks that he come to his daughter, who is dying, according to Mark and Luke. Matthew says she was already dead. Jairus has faith that Jesus can either heal her from the brink of death (Mark and Luke) or bring her back from the dead (Matthew). Along the way to Jairus's house, a woman suffering from a hemorrhage touches the hem of Jesus' garment and is healed. Soon after, according to Mark and Luke, a man arrives from Jairus's house to inform them that the little girl, age 12, is dead. However, Jesus replies that Jairus must continue to have faith. He proceeds to Jairus's house and upon arriving mourners are crying out and playing music for the dead. Jesus causes laughter and derision among them when he proclaims that the little girl is not dead, rather asleep. He enters the house accompanied by Jairus and his wife, and his disciples Peter, James, and John. There he takes the girl's hand and, according to Mark, says in Aramaic, *'Tal'itha cu'mi'*, which the Gospel writer translates as 'Little girl, I say to you, arise'. The girl immediately revives and Jesus tells them to feed her.

The raising of Jairus's daughter is one of several accounts in the NT in which Jesus shows his power over death. Artistic depictions of the story of Jairus and his daughter include the Paolo Veronese painting *Raising of the Daughter of Jairus* (1546), and in music, *The Daughter of Jairus* (1878) by the English composer Sir John Stainer.

See also HEM OF HIS GARMENT; MIRACLES [RL]

James, the Apostle. James is the English rendering of the Greek form of the name Jacob, meaning possibly 'one who catches the heel' or 'supplanter' (see Gen. 25.26). He was one of Jesus' twelve apostles. The apostles were Jesus' ambassadors, sent to do particular tasks (e.g., Mark 6.7-13) and witnesses of his words and deeds (e.g., Matt. 1.29; 9.2; 17.1; 14.33; 26.37; Luke 8.8:51; 9.28). James and John were the sons of Zebedee, and apparently, they were well off because they employed other people (Mark1.20). Jesus called James and his brother at the Sea of Galilee/Genessaret (Luke 5.1), at which time they left everything, including their father. It seems James was close to his brother because they are always presented together (Mark 1.20; Matt. 20.20; Luke 9.54). They were choleric in character (see Luke 9.54), which explains Jesus' use of the nickname Boanerges for them; the words means 'sons of thunder (Mark 3.17). According to Mark, they asked Jesus for a favor, namely that they might 'sit, one at your right and one at your left, in your glory (17.35). As Matthew tells the story, it is their mother asked Jesus this favor on their behalf (Matt. 20.20). Jesus prophesied that the brothers would die as martyrs, and indeed, James died at the hands of Herod Agrippa I in 42 C.E (Acts 12.1-2). We do not know the fate of his brother from the Bible though later tradition claims he was executed because of his faith. Because there are many people with the name James in the NT, this James is often confused with the brother of the Lord and others with the same name. For convenience, he is often called James the Major/Elder/Greater, as opposed to the Just/Presbyter/Righteous (i.e., Jesus' brother).

He is a legendary figure and today he is believed by the Roman Catholics to be the patron of Santiago de Compostela in Spain. Catholic pilgrims visit what is believed to be his tomb annually. Rembrandt painted this character (see his *Saint James the Elder*).

See also APOSTLE; DISCIPLE; BOANERGES; JOHN THE APOSTLE [ET]

James, Epistle of. By all appearances, this letter did not circulate widely in earliest Christianity. It is not included in the second-century Muratorian Canon, one of the earliest canon lists. Origen was the first of the early church fathers to quote this text in Greek. Hilary of Poitiers (*On the Trinity*) was the first to quote James in Latin (c. 357). Jerome included James in the Vulgate though he was still uncertain about the identity of its author.

There are five men named James in the NT: James son of Zebedee; James the son of Alphaeus; James the Less; James the father of the Judas (not Iscariot); and James the brother of Jesus. Since James the son of Zebedee was martyred early, the most likely candidate for authorship is James the half-brother of Jesus who presided over the early Jerusalem church (Acts 15.13-21), though this is far from certain. It is possible an otherwise unknown James penned the letter. The time of composition is equally uncertain. James is one of the 'general' or 'catholic' letters of the NT. It is addressed somewhat vaguely to 'the twelve tribes in the Dispersion' (1.1) which, judging by the contents of the letter (e.g., 2.1) is a Christian readership.

It is really more like a hard-hitting sermon than a letter that seeks to encourage the readers' waning faith. James tells them to meet persecution with patience and joy, teaches that wisdom is a gift from God, that God is not the author of evil, and that that they should be slow to anger. James teaches that good works are an evidence of faith. The ethical content of the book resembles the OT and the Sermon on the Mount in certain respects.

Some find tension between James's letter and Paul's writings, suggesting the former stresses the need for good works over faith, the latter faith over works. This was a concern for Martin Luther in the Reformation period. He considered James 'an epistle of straw' yet still kept it in his German translation and quoted it often. This perceived contradiction tends to be overstated, however, as Paul assumes faith leads to good works, and James presupposes faith when he urges particular behaviors. James also preaches against the evils wrought by the human tongue. He opposes wars, pride, and vain confidence in worldly things. He denounces the rich who exploit the poor. James's eschatology includes references to the kingdom of God, judgment, and the second coming.

Christopher Smart (1722–1771) used Jas 1.26-27 as the basis for his poem 'Jubilante Agno'. A number of hymns have been based on James, including 'From Thee All Skill and Science Flow' (1871), and 'O Grant Us Light' (1885). Jas 4.8 was the inspiration for, 'Nearer, My God to Thee' by Sarah Flower Adams (1805–1848). This hymn was performed at memorable tragic scenes such as the Johnstown City Flood (May 21, 1889) and the deathbed of President William McKinley. The band apparently performed the song during the sinking of the Titanic (April 10, 1912).

Recommended reading. McKnight, Scot. *The Letter of James*. Grand Rapids, MI: William B. Eerdmans, 2010. Johnson, Luke Timothy. *The Letter of James*. New Haven, CT: Yale University Press, 2007.

See also JAMES, THE BROTHER OF JESUS; FAITH; CATHOLIC EPISTLES [AJW]

James, the brother of Jesus. James is derived from the Greek *Iakōbos* which comes from the Hebrew name Jacob (*ya'aqov*). James is a complicated figure in the NT. In the Gospels, he has a minimal role. James is not explicitly listed among the twelve disciples and there are many passages that diminish the role of the immediate family of Jesus and their belief in him. However, in Acts James plays a prominent role in the Christian community in Jerusalem, especially during the so-called Jerusalem conference in Acts 15. In Paul's letters, James is described as both a leader and a pillar. Additionally, in Gal. 2.12, Paul states that Peter ate with Gentiles in Antioch until representatives of James came to the community. Most church fathers also attribute the Epistle of James to him.

The status of James in the NT becomes even more complex because James, the brother of Jesus, has often been connected to both James the Lesser and James, the son of Alphaeus. The latter was a disciple of Jesus and thus many have concluded that James, the brother of Jesus, was in fact one of the twelve disciples. This was Jerome's position and his conclusions remain influential, especially for those within the Roman Catholic Church.

In later, extra-biblical documents, James is an important and respected figure. In Nag Hammadi texts such as the *Apocryphon of James*, the *First* and *Second Apocalypse of James*, and the *Gospel of Thomas*, James is designated as either the leader of the Christian community or a bearer of secret knowledge. James is also a respected and influential figure in other texts including the *Pseudo-Clementines*, the *Protevangelium of James*, and the *Gospel of the Hebrews*.

Many church fathers concluded that James had an important position in the early Church. Epiphanius referred to James as the Just, the *Oblias* (rampart or bulwark), and the first bishop of the Christian community. Eusebius also cites many sources in his *Ecclesiastical History* such as Hegesippus who stated that James was called the Just, was the leader of the church and was the only one allowed to enter the holy of holies, where he prayed for the people so often that his knees grew hard like those of a camel.

Since James, the brother of Jesus, is often associated with the apostle James, there have been many paintings that either include or feature the apostle such as Leonardo da Vinci's *Last Supper* (1495–1498) and El Greco's portrait of James (1610–1614). James the Lesser is also featured in many movies about the life of Jesus including *The Greatest Story Every Told* (1965). Additionally, St James Palace in London housed the royal family of England from the sixteenth to the nineteenth century.

James has been the focus of many scholarly works and news items in the last decade. In 2002, an antiquities dealer revealed an ossuary, or bone box, inscribed with the words James, the brother of Jesus. However, most scholars have questioned its authenticity. Recently some scholars have attempted to link this ossuary to others found in the Talpiot Tomb, located near Jerusalem, which contains ossuaries bearing the names of other family members of Jesus of Nazareth. In 2007, James Cameron produced a documentary that featured this tomb and attempted to connect it to the family of Jesus.

Recommended reading. Chilton, Bruce, and Jacob Neusner (eds.). *The Brother of Jesus: James the Just and his Mission.* Louisville, KY: Westminster John Knox Press, 2001. Painter, John. *Just James: The Brother of Jesus in History and Tradition.* Columbia, SC: University of South Carolina Press, 2004.

See also JAMES THE APOSTLE; JAMES, EPISTLE OF

[KS]

Japheth. In the HB, Japheth is one of the sons of Noah, with the KJV of the Bible recording that he was older than his brother Shem, but the Revised Standard Version listing Shem as the older brother. According to Gen. 10.2-5, Noah's three sons, Japheth, Ham, and Shem, were all born after the flood, and indeed, after Noah passed his 500th birthday. They went their separate ways with the 'descendants of Japheth' being the 'coastland peoples' (Gen. 10.5). Some considered Japheth the ancestor of the Greeks, and hence the ancestor of most European people. This view was reinforced by the first-century CE historian Josephus who, in *The Antiquities of the Jews*, notes that Japheth had seven sons, and their descendants lived between Cadiz (in modern-day Spain) and the Don River (in modern-day Russia). As a result the view in medieval and early modern Europe was that all Europeans had Japheth as their common biblical ancestor. The English playwright William Shakespeare makes light of this in his play *2 Henry IV*, when Prince Hal (later Henry V) talks of people who claim to be related to royal families: 'they will be kin to us, or they fetch it from Japhet'. As a result the term 'Japhetic' was used by William Jones (1746–1794) and other linguists to describe the Indo-European language group.

The stories set around the life of Noah obviously include Japheth, and he is a major character in Madelein L'Engle's fictional story *Many Waters* (1986) where as a youth he marries, at the behest of his father, Oholibamah, a lady with black hair but fair skin. He comes over as a kindly man who tries to patch up problems with his feuding family members. Rudyard Kipling in *A Truthful Song* also mentions Japheth. He was played by Eric Leutzinger in *The Bible: In the Beginning* (1966).

Recommended reading. Bailey, Lloyd R. *Noah, the Person and the Story*. Columbia, SC: University of South Carolina Press, 1989.

See also NOAH; HAM; SHEM [JC]

Jebusites. The Jebusites appear a number of times in the Bible, including Gen. 10.15-16, and 1 Chron. 1.14 where they clearly lived in the land of Canaan prior to their conquest at the hands of King David. In Genesis, the Jebusites are noted third in the list of Canaanite tribes, after the Hittites and before the Amorites, with the result that some authorities argue they might have been related to either group. It seems that they might have assimilated with the Israelites.

Some traditions link the Jebusites with the city of Jebus, which some believe is a pre-Israelite name for Jerusalem but there is no real evidence for this. There is also a theory that Zadok may have been a Jebusite. The English poet and essayist Coventry Patmore (1823–1896) mentions the Jebusites in his poem 'To the Body': 'The Jebusite, / That, maugre all God's promises could do, / The chosen People never conquer'd quite'. Because of the disputes over the ownership of Jerusalem, the tradition that it might have been a significant settlement and occupied by the Jebusites before King David has led to some Palestinian writers seeking to associate the Palestinian people with the Jebusites.

See also DAVID; JERUSALEM; CANAAN, CANAANITES [JC]

Jehoiachin. The name derives from the Hebrew *yoyakin* meaning 'Yahweh establishes' or 'let Yahweh establish'. Jehoiachin's given name was Jeconiah (1 Chron. 3.16-17). He is the son of King Jehoiakim of Judah (2 Kgs 24.6) and Nehushta (2 Kgs 4.8). At the age of eighteen (2 Kgs 24.8) he succeeded his father on the throne. His reign as king of Judah spanned a period of three months (597 BCE). The biblical text summarizes Jehoiachin's time on throne with this description; 'He did what was evil in the sight of the LORD, just as his father had done' (2 Kgs 2.9). It was at this juncture that the Babylonian king Nebuchadnezzar besieged the city of Jerusalem, forcing Jehoiachin's surrender, resulting in the plunder of the temple and the appointment of Jehoiachin's uncle Zedekiah as king of Judah.

While the biblical text fails to provide a record of Jehoiachin's time in captivity, the Deuteronomistic History closes with a passage that recounts the story of Jehoiachin's release in late 561 or early 560 BCE (2 Kgs 25.27-30). According to the biblical account, the newly released Jehoiachin enjoyed a place of honor above the other kings who were in exile. Jeremiah provides us with information that suggests that he was afforded an allowance 'by the king of Babylon, as long as he lived, up to the day of his death' (Jer. 52.34).

Outside of the OT, references and allusions to Jehoiachin are few and muddled. The gospel writer Matthew includes the young king as part of the genealogy of Jesus, describing him as the son of Josiah (Matt. 1.11). The earliest extant postexilic Hebrew chronicle *Seder Olam Rabbah* notes of King Jehoiakim, with reference to his sons, 'That a dog brings forth no good progeny'. Writing in the first century CE, the Jewish historian Josephus suggests that it was only after he forced Nebuchadnezzar into taking an oath that neither his family nor the city of Jerusalem would be harmed that Jehoiachin reluctantly surrendered and gave up the city.

In contemporary culture, the biblical story of Jehoiachin has become a major point of contention for some Christians with respect to both Dan Brown's book *The Da Vinci Code* (2003) as well as the film of the same title (2006). Some Christians have asserted that Matthew's Gospel presents us with the legal lineage of Jesus, whereas Dan Brown presents his readers with a natural genealogy that disregards the curse that was placed upon Jehoiachin thereby denying the validity and inerrancy of both the OT and NT texts.

Other allusions in popular culture to Jehoiachin and his legacy have approached the story in allegorical fashion, treating it as a story that has the potential to reveal a hidden moral. The 1993 movie *Dave* starring Kevin Kline and Sigourney Weaver, for example, provides its viewers with a humorous tale about a presidential look alike that ends up running the day-to-day affairs of the country after the real President becomes incapacitated. The result is a funny but serious lesson about the dangers of irresponsible leadership based upon illusions of one's abilities.

Recommended reading. Murray, Donald F. 'Of All the Years the Hopes—or Fears? Jehoiachin in Babylon (2 Kings 25:27-30)'. *Journal of Biblical Literature* 120 (2001) 245-65.

See also JEHOIAKIM; NEBUCHADNEZZAR; TEMPLE, ISRAEL'S; BABYLONIAN CAPTIVITY, THE; KINGS, BOOKS OF; CHRONICLES, BOOKS OF [JNR]

Jehoiakim. Jehoiakim, the second son of Josiah, was the eighteenth and next to last king (609–598 BCE) of Judah. His birth name was Eliakim and his mother was Zebidah, daughter or Pedaiah of Rumah. He was twenty-five when he became king having been previously passed over by the people in favor of his younger brother whose throne name was Jehoahaz. The name Jehoiakim in Hebrew means 'Yahweh raises up'. It was given to him by Pharaoh Necho II as a sign of vassalage. Jehoahaz (birthname Shallum; Jer. 22.11), the son Hamutal daughter of Jeremiah of Libnah, came to the throne of Judah in 609 BCE at the age of twenty-three upon the death of his father, good king Josiah who was killed at the Battle of Meggido as a Babylonian ally. The Egyptians and their Assyrian allies were in turn defeated at the Battle of Harran.

Despite the defeat, Egyptian power was still sufficient for Jehoahaz to be deposed by Pharaoh Necho II after he had ruled just three months. Imprisoned at Riblah in the land of Hamath, he was taken into Egyptian captivity (2 Kgs 23.31-34). Jehoiakim was installed as an Egyptian puppet. He collected heavy taxes to pay the Egyptians one talent of gold and one hundred talents of silver (2 Chron. 36.3).

The foreign policy of the Kingdom of Judah under Jehoiakim was pro-Egyptian much to the consternation of the prophets Jeremiah (Jer. 22.13-19) and Uriah son of Shermiah from Kiriath-jearim (Jer. 26). Both prophesied against the kingdom while calling for repentance. Jeremiah also denounced Jehoiakim as irreligious, greedy, and cruel. Uriah fled to Egypt, but was (2 Chron. 36.3) returned and was vindictively put to death. Jeremiah was protected by sympathetic court officials.

Jeremiah dictated a scroll of prophecies to Baruch his scribe who took the scroll to Jehoiakim to read. The prophecies called for repentant obedience to the law of God. Jehoiakim was warming himself against the winter cold with a flaming brazier. He read and then impiously burned strips of the scroll as it was read.

In 605 Nebuchadnezzar defeated the Egyptians at the Battle of Carchemish. He captured Jerusalem, took Jehoiakim prisoner, and took some temple treasures. He released Jehoiakim, but three years later the Babylonians were defeated by an Egyptian army. Following bad advice from the Egyptian party in his court he rebelled against the Babylonians. The kingdom was then plagued by bands of Chaldeans, Arameans (Syrians), Moabites, and Ammonites led by Babylonians (2 Kgs 24.1-7).

Jehoiakim died in 598 with Jerusalem under siege. The Bible does not tell the details of his death, whether it was natural or violent. According to Jeremiah's prophecy (Jer. 22.18-19) he would be buried unlamented, dragged to a dump like a dead donkey. Josephus said his body was thrown over the city wall at the instigation of Nebuchadnezzar (*Antiquities* 10.97). He was succeeded by his eighteen year old son Jehoiachin (2 Chron. 36.9), who reigned three months before being taken into exile in Babylon. He is listed in Matthew's genealogy of Jesus, which means that Jehoiakim is an unsung ancestor of Jesus. The biblical assessment of Jehoiakim is: he 'did evil in the sight of the Lord as his ancestors had done' (2 Kgs 23.36-37; 2 Chron. 36.5).

Recommended reading. Grabbe, Lester L. *Good Kings and Bad Kings: The Kingdom of Judah in the Seventh Century* BCE. London: Continuum International, 2007. Wiseman, Donald J. *1 and 2 Kings: An Introduction and Commentary.* Downers Grove, IL: IVP Academic, 2008.

See also BABYLON; BABYLONIAN CAPTIVITY; CHRONICLES, BOOKS OF; JEREMIAH; JOSIAH; JUDAH, KINGDOM OF; KINGS, BOOKS OF; MEGGIDO; NEBUCHADNEZZAR; JEHOIACHIN [AJW]

Jehoshaphat. Jehoshaphat is the fourth king of Judah (870–846 BCE). He is the son of King Asa and his wife Azubah. The accounts of his reign are found in 1 Kgs 22.1-50; 2 Kgs 3.1-27; and 2 Chron. 17—20. Jehoshaphat formed an alliance with the northern kingdom by the marriage of his son Jehoram to King Ahab's daughter Athaliah. Ahab later called on Jehoshaphat to assist Israel in a military strike against the King of Aram. Jehoshaphat agreed to come and entered the battle in full regal attire, while Ahab, in an attempt to spare his own life, battled in disguise. Jehoshaphat survived the battle but King Ahab was killed. Jehoshaphat later formed an alliance with Ahab's successor, Ahaziah. They constructed a fleet of ships but the prophet Eliezer condemned this alliance and the ships were wrecked (2 Chron. 20.37). Although Jehoshaphat was reprimanded for his connections with the northern kingdom, he received commendation for his judicial reforms. He appointed priests and Levites to act as judges for the people (2 Chron. 19.8) and was remembered for 'doing what was right in the sight of the Lord' (2 Chron. 20.32).

There were three other individuals named Jehoshaphat: the recorder who served under David and Solomon (2 Sam. 8.16; 1 Kgs 4.3); the official over the district of Issachar during the reign of Solomon (1 Kgs 4.17); and the father of King Jehu (2 Kgs 9.2).

Michelangelo portrays King Jehoshaphat in the Sistene Chapel, where he is included in the frescos of Jesus' ancestors. Jean Fouquet represented Jehoshaphat's triumphant return to Jerusalem in his painting, *Triomphe de Josaphat*, and Frans Boels painted Jehoshaphat's plunder in *Jehoshapat, King of Judah, Plunders the Ammonites and Moabites*. The king's name may also lie behind the exclamation 'Jumping Jehosaphat', in which the king's name is used as a euphemism for Jesus or Jehovah. The phrase is first recorded in Thomas Mayne Reid's 1866 novel *The Headless Horseman*.

See also AHAB; CHRONICLES, BOOKS OF; JUDAH, KINGDOM OF; KINGS, BOOKS OF [DP]

Jephthah's Daughter. A character without a name, Jephthah's daughter is discussed in Judg. 11.34-40. Jephthah was a judge of Israel at the time, and a fierce warrior. Before a battle with the Ammonites, Jephthah vowed that if God would make him victorious, 'whoever comes out of the doors of my house to meet me, when I return victorious from the Ammonites, shall be the Lord's to be offered up by me as a burnt offering' (Judg. 11.30-31). Jephthah's campaign was successful, and upon returning home, his daughter came out of his house first, celebrating his victory. Jephthah was distraught but kept his promise. Jephthah's daughter agreed that he must follow through with his promise, but requested she be granted 'two months, so that I may go and wander on the mountains, and bewail my virginity, my companions and I' (Judg. 11.37). Her request was granted, and at the end of the two months, she returns to her father 'who did with her according to the vow he had made' (Judg. 11.39).

Jewish interpreters of the rabbinic period usually condemned Jephthah's rash vow and denounced the human sacrifice aspect of the story. Some medieval Jewish interpreters suggested that Jephthah did not actually sacrifice his daughter but instead kept her secluded and dedicated to God. Patristic writers read the story allegorically, with Jephthah's daughter often representing the Church, due to her perpetual virginity, or Jesus himself, as a child sacrificed for God.

Due to the tragic nature of the story, Jephthah's daughter is well represented in Western culture, including more than 100 musical interpretations and numerous paintings, etchings and sculptures; the list of musicians and artists is impressive, including pieces by Giacomo Carissimi, William Blake, Edgar Degas, Gustave Doré, Florentine Lorenzo Ghiberti, and Naum Aronson.

In *Hamlet*, Shakespeare surreptitiously refers to the incident with Jephthah's daughter. The scene unfolds in Act 2, scene 2 where Hamlet is mocking Lord Polonius, calling him Jephthah—that is, as one who loves his daughter 'passing well' and yet, will sacrifice her for his own benefit. Chaucer also refers to the story of Jephthah's daughter in *Canterbury Tales* ('The Physician's Tale', 6.238-44). Scotsman George Buchanan wrote a drama entitled *Jephthes* which covers the story of Jephthah and his daughter. In fact, between the sixteenth and eighteenth centuries more than fifty dramas were recorded on the theme of Jephthah and his daughter.

Poetry on the topic is also not lacking: Byron, James Campbell, Hartley Coleridge and Tennyson all lay claim to the story in some fashion, as do American poets N.P. Willis and Mark Van Doren and British lyricist Karen Gershon. Modern Yiddish writers such as I.I. Schwartz and Yehoash write about the theme of Jephthah's daughter, as does Lion Feuchtwanger in his last novel published in 1957. Here, Feuchtwanger offers voice through the story of Jephthah and his daughter to his own experiences during World War II. Author Naomi Ragen uses the story of Jephthah's daughter as model for her book, *Jepthe's Daughter*, which fictionally addresses domestic abuse in the ultra-Orthodox world in Jerusalem. Modern feminists also have much to say, including a comparison between the almost-sacrifice of Isaac (see Gen. 22) the male child and the actual sacrifice of Jephthah's daughter, the female, noting how God steps in save the male child but not the female.

Recommended reading. Bellis, Alice Ogden. *Helpmates, Harlots, and Heroes: Women's Stories in the Hebrew Bible*. Louisville, KY: Westminster/John Knox Press, 1994. Kugel, James. *Traditions of the Bible*. Cambridge, MA: Harvard University Press, 1998.

See also JUDGES, BOOK OF [SS]

Jeremiah. The Hebrew prophet Jeremiah was active in the late seventh and early sixth centuries BCE, a period of dramatic political upheaval culminating with the fall of Jerusalem in 586. His unpopular announcement of Judah's inevitable demise brought him into conflict with the political establishment which rejected his prophetic pronouncements (e.g., 36.17-32) and frequently imprisoned him (20.1-2;

32.2-3; 36.26; 37.11-21; 38.6-13, 28; cf. 43.4-7; 42.19).

Though Jeremiah appears a strong, courageous figure carrying out God's work without care for his own safety, this 'weeping prophet' candidly reports an emotional frailty that sets him apart from other biblical characters. He is timid (1.6), especially when threatened (11.18–12.4). We even catch glimpses of extreme internal anguish (4.19; 9.1; 10.19-20; 23.9): 'O that my head were a spring of water, and my eyes a fountain of tears, so that I might weep day and night for the slain of my poor people!' (9.1). But despite his sorrows, and despite doubts about his ability to complete his work (1.6), Jeremiah never loses sight of his divinely appointed role (1.4-5, 17-19). Perhaps this mix of determination and emotional turmoil explains in part why, centuries later, some confused Jesus with Jeremiah (Matt. 16.14).

The influence of the poetic and emotionally charged writings attributed to Jeremiah, along with his distinctive personality, extends well beyond the HB itself. The term 'jeremiad', for instance, indicates a pattern of diatribe and harangue characteristic of the prophet. Jeremiah attributes Israel's calamities to disregard of the covenant: 'Cursed be anyone who does not heed the words of this covenant' (11.3); 'Therefore ... I am going to bring disaster upon them' (11.11). Similarly, a jeremiad in contemporary speech condemns moral failure and calls for change. This is not condemnation without hope, however. Jeremiah promised a reversal of fortunes for a repentant Israel (e.g., 30.3; 31.1-40). The jeremiad is widely used as a narrative framework in the arts, associated with writers as diverse as American Puritan preacher Increase Mather (*The Day of Trouble Is Near*, 1674) and Scottish social commentator Thomas Carlyle who condemned social and economic injustices during the Victorian period. More recently, the Quebec-based band Arcade Fire chastises contemporary institutional Christianity for its abusive nature in songs well described as jeremiads (*Neon Bible*, 2006).

Beyond the ubiquitous jeremiad, evocations of the prophet include classical music (e.g., Leonard Bernstein's *Symphony No. 1, Jeremiah*, 1942), painting (e.g., Michelangelo's *The Prophet Jeremiah*, 1512), and rock and roll (e.g., U2's *All That You Can't Leave Behind*, 2000). The latter alludes to Jeremiah's writings and his personal struggles as a prophet denouncing abusive political powers. The band uses Jeremiah's story to relate the story of a modern-day political prophet, the Burmese activist and Nobel Peace Prize laureate Aung San Suu Kyi. U2 dedicates the song 'Walk On' to her, and the liner notes urge fans to 'Remember Aung San Suu Kyi, under virtual house arrest in Burma since 1989'.

Recommended reading. Brueggemann, Walter. *The Theology of the Book of Jeremiah*. Old Testament Theology. New York: Cambridge University Press, 2007.

See also JEREMIAH, BOOK OF; JEREMIAH, EPISTLE OF [MJG]

Jeremiah, Book of. The Book of Jeremiah is a composite text. It includes the dramatic poetry Jeremiah composed, with its imaginative vision of an unnamed invader from the north who will occupy Judah and destroy Jerusalem (e.g.,4.5–10.25 *passim*). The poetry is reflective of a dialogue in which distinct voices interact, dispute, interrupt and disappear. Stages of editorial activity updated and transformed the original work. The consequence was a shift in focus to the biography of Jeremiah, to the prophet and his times. His life and work are linked with the reigns of Josiah, Jehoiakim, and Zedekiah from 627–587 BCE (1.1-3); the book's contents cover events before, during and after the fall of Jerusalem and contain laments in response to the disaster Jeremiah proclaims (e.g., Jer. 11.18-23; 12.1-6; 15.10-12).

During World War I Stefan Zweig composed a brilliant play *Jeremias* (English translation, 1922) based on the book's prose narratives and historical figures in chaps. 19–29, 32–46, 50–52. The action takes place in Jerusalem during the Babylonian invasion of the city. Inspired by the figure of Jeremiah, Zweig's drama is a passionate protest against war. Jeremiah counsels peace, but the political establishment—its king, prophets and priests—want war. Zweig uses historical allegory to express the thoughts of thousands of his generation who were opposed to war, in a time when even the desire for peace was considered cowardly and criminal. Because Zweig's drama retells a biblical story, it seemed remote from the conflicts of Europe and thus passed German censorship to be first performed in Zurich in 1917, his tragedy bearing witness to the prevailing conditions and attitudes of wartime.

Holocaust survivor and writer Elie Wiesel understands Jeremiah's war imagery of quaking mountains and reversion of earth to chaos (Jer. 4.23-28) in light of the 1941 Nazi massacre of 80,000 Jews and their burial at Babi-Yar, a ravine outside Kiev: 'The ground was shaking for weeks on end. The mountains of corpses made the earth quake'. As for Jeremiah's vision of no birds in the sky, Wiesel recalls that birds fled the skies above the crematorium death-camps of Auschwitz and Birkenau.

Leonard Bernstein composed his 1942 *Symphony No. 1, Jeremiah*, as he was wrestling with a crisis of faith, not so much in God but in human beings. The score has three movements: 'prophecy' represents Jeremiah's warnings to the people, 'profanation' narrates the destruction caused by idolatrous priests (e.g., Jer. 2.8, 26-28), and 'lamentation' commemorates Babylon's destruction of Jerusalem. Since Jeremiah composed laments (2 Chron. 35.25), he has traditionally been identified as the poet who mourns beloved Jerusalem in the Book of Lamentations. Bernstein scored verses from the biblical book Lamentations for the final movement of his *Jeremiah* (Lam. 1.1-3, 8; 4.14-15; 5.20-21) in keeping with many earlier settings of Lamentations for solo and choral performance (e.g., Thomas Tallis; William Byrd; Robert White). Jeremiah and the poet of Lamentations personify ruined Jerusalem as an abandoned woman, overwhelmed with grief (e.g., Jer. 4.30-31; 30.12-17; Lam. 1.1-4, 17). In Bernstein's setting of the Hebrew verses from Lamentations, a mezzo-soprano sings the dirge over the fallen city. By contrast, Jeremiah's own choral verses on the coming defeat of Jerusalem wait for a performance setting. Yet the book's subject of war reaches across the centuries and speaks to people living in very different times and places.

Recommended reading. Brueggemann, Walter. *A Commentary on Jeremiah: Exile and Homecoming.* Grand Rapids, MI: Eerdmans, 1998. Wiesel, Elie. 'Jeremiah'. In his *Five Biblical Portraits*. Pp. 97-127, Notre Dame, IN: University of Notre Dame Press, 1981.

See also JEREMIAH; LAMENTATIONS, BOOK OF [JRW]

Jeremiah, Epistle of. The Epistle of Jeremiah is a Jewish writing composed some time between the end of the Babylonian exile and NT times. The oldest extant copies are in Greek (the Septuagint), including a papyrus fragment found in the Dead Sea Scrolls, though it may have been written originally in Hebrew or Aramaic. This letter is a pseudepigraphical work, written in a biblical style by an unknown author but attributed to the prophet Jeremiah. The epistle was inspired by the letter in the Book of Jeremiah (29.1-23) addressed to Babylonian exiles, and it seeks to warn readers of the dangers of idolatry. The Epistle of Jeremiah is included in the Apocrypha. It is not considered canonical by Jews and most Protestants though Roman Catholics accept it as deuterocanonical Scripture and the Eastern Orthodox as *anagignoskomena* ('things that are read'). It appears in Syriac and Vulgate versions as chapter 6 of the Book of Baruch. However, Baruch and the Epistle of Jeremiah are separated in the Septuagint by Lamentations.

There are only seventy-three verses in this epistle and they assert the impotency of idols. The anonymous author of the Epistle of Jeremiah tells his readers not to be like the 'foreigners' who worship idols. He uses sarcasm to ridicule idols and the gods or goddesses they represent. He says that artisans made them out of natural materials that can tarnish. These idols are spiritually impotent, they cannot speak, and they cannot defend themselves against robbers or those who may pillage temples. They cannot even see even if lamps are lit in their temples. The writer adds that the priests who serve these idols are corrupt.

See also JEREMIAH; JEREMIAH, BOOK OF [AJW]

Jeroboam. The name Jeroboam means 'may the people be great' or 'may Baal prove himself to be great'. Jeroboam was the first king of the northern kingdom of Israel (c. 922–919 BCE) and he reigned twenty-two years (1 Kgs 11.26–14.20; 2 Chron. 10.1-19; 11.1-4). He began his career as a high-ranking official in King Solomon's court, in charge of tribal territories in the North. Problems arose because of heavy taxation and Solomon's despised policy of forced labor, the temporary conscription of workers needed to support ambitious building projects. Jeroboam came into conflict with Solomon and fled to Egypt. En route, the prophet Ahijah informed Jeroboam that because of Solomon's idolatry, Yahweh would divide his nation and give Jeroboam the northern tribal territories. If he remained faithful and obedient, his nation would prosper.

During Rehoboam's reign, the nation divided into Israel (ten northern tribes) and Judah (two southern tribes) and the northern nation crowned Jeroboam as king. Jeroboam feared his nation's ties to Judah because the temple in Jerusalem was still the religious center for worshippers of Yahweh. To address this problem, he established two rival temples in Israel, placed a golden calf in each and appointed priests who were not Levites. Jeroboam also instituted a rival religious calendar. These forbidden practices confused the common people and led them away from pure worship of the true God, Yahweh. Jewish and Christian history remembers him for this act, which is depicted in the paintings *Jeroboam's*

Sacrifice at Bethel by Gerbrand van den Eeckhout, a seventeenth-century Dutch painter, and *Jeroboam Sacrificing to the Golden Calf,* by Jean-Honoré Fragonard, an eighteenth-century French painter. Jeroboam and his golden calves are discussed in Mark Twain's time-travelling adventure, *The Innocents Abroad* (1869).

The prophet Ahijah, who earlier offered Jeroboam Yahweh's blessing if he followed obediently in his ways, declared the corresponding curse upon Jeroboam. The Israelites would ultimately be uprooted from their land and scattered to the land of the Assyrians. Jeroboam was the first of a long line of kings of Israel who practiced idolatry instead of faithful worship of Yahweh, which continued in varying degrees until the nation's destruction at the hands of the Assyrians in 722–721 BCE.

See also REHOBOAM; JUDAH, KINGDOM OF [KK]

Jerusalem. First mentioned in Egyptian curse tablets of the nineteenth and eighteenth centuries BCE, *Urushalimum* (derivation uncertain) was originally a Canaanite city, later conquered by King David in the tenth century BCE. His city covered about twelve acres, but his son Solomon expanded it by building a temple to its immediate north. The city later expanded to include Mount Zion and the Kidron Valley. It was destroyed by the Babylonians in 586 BCE, rebuilt by Jews at the end of the sixth century, destroyed again by the Romans in 70 CE, and then rebuilt by Hadrian as Aelia Capitolina in the 130s. It was governed, in turn, by the Romans, the Byzantines, Arabs, European crusaders, Mamelukes, Turks, and the British Empire. At last, Jerusalem became part of the autonomous state of Israel. Jerusalem is one of the world's oldest continuously inhabited cities. A day's walk around the old city reveals remains of all these periods.

The city is holy to Judaism, Christianity, and Islam. The most famous site is a building that no longer exists, the temple of Solomon, rebuilt by Herod. However, the massive retaining walls of Herod's platform remain intact, and Jews still pray at the base of them at a site called the 'Western Wall' (before 1967, often called the 'Wailing Wall'). Numerous Christian churches grace the old city and its suburbs, with the most famous being the Church of the Holy Sepulchre begun by Constantine in the fourth century CE and remodeled many times since. The current façade of the building dates to the crusader period. The basic shape of the old city, however, comes from the Islamic constructions in it.

Atop the Temple Mount lies the Dome of the Rock, first built by Abd al-Malik in the late seventh century, following the octagonal floorplans of contemporary Byzantine churches. The Dome of the Rock sits atop the site of Herod's temple. South of it lies the mosque of al-Aqsa. The city's walls were erected by the Turkish emperor Suleiman the Magnificent in the sixteenth century, though he followed the lines of walls dating back to Roman times. The worshipers of all three religions continue to make pilgrimage to the city, which is the holiest site in Judaism, and arguably Christianity, and the third holiest site in Islam.

Beginning in the biblical period, Jerusalem became more than a city. It became a symbol. Thus, for example, Ps. 84.3 praises the city: 'Even the sparrow finds a home, and the swallow a nest for herself … at your altars, O Lord of hosts'. Ps. 48.2 describes it as God's 'holy mountain, beautiful in elevation… the joy of al the earth, Mount Zion in the far north'. The reference to the 'far north' is mythological language, drawn ultimately from Canaanite religious language, and referring to Zion's status as the metaphorical home of God, an earthly copy of the heavenly temple. This powerful symbolism later shapes Jewish and Christian visions of the heavenly city, as in the Book of Revelation and numerous hymns such as 'O Zion Haste', 'Jerusalem the Golden', or 'We're Marching to Zion'.

Jerusalem is such a powerful symbol of freedom and spirituality that Moses Mendelssohn, the great Jewish philosopher and grandfather of the composer Felix Mendelssohn-Bartholdy, entitled his very influential volume pleading for human freedom *Jerusalem* (1783). With the Zionist movement of the early twentieth century and the creation of the state of Israel in 1948–1949, Jerusalem became a prominent feature in literature and music. Novelists such as Elie Wiesel and Amos Oz describe the longing for Jerusalem and the peace it symbolizes, often in conflict with the endemic warfare there. The contrast between symbol and reality continues to be a significant issue for Jews and Palestinians (both Muslims and Christians), who contest the ownership of the city.

Recommended reading. Rosovsky, Nitza. *City of the Great King: Jerusalem from David to the Present*. Cambridge, MA: Harvard University Press, 1996. Shanks, Hershel. *Jerusalem's Temple Mount: From Solomon to the Golden Dome*. New York: Continuum, 2007.

See also DAVID; JEBUSITES; SOLOMON; TEMPLE, ISRAEL'S [MWH]

Jesse. In the OT, Jesse was the father of David (1 Sam. 16.1-13). He is particularly famous as the ancestor of Jesus (Matt. 1.5-6). As such he appears on illuminated manuscripts, on stained glass windows, and in carvings illustrating the 'Tree of Jesse', indicating Jesus' family line. The image of him in the stained glass window at All Saints Church, Hove, in East Sussex, in the south of England, portrays him in colored robes not that different from the other OT figures shown. Because of his great age, he is bearded and hugging the tree as he rests his head on his hands.

Recommended reading. Ash, Paul S. *David, Solomon and Egypt: A Reassessment*. Sheffield: Sheffield Academic Press, 1999. Massie, Allan. *King David*. London: Sceptre, 1995.

See also DAVID; TREE OF JESSE [JC]

Jesus, Childhood of. Of the four canonical Gospels, two (Mark and John) say nothing about Jesus before he appears in the Galilee as an adult, poised to begin his preaching mission. Matthew relates that Jesus spent time in Egypt as a child. It is quite likely that Matthew invented this story in order to have Jesus 'fulfill' the prophecy of Hos. 11.1. Regardless, this detail tells us little about Jesus' childhood since Matthew says nothing about where they stayed or how long they were there. Matthew says only that Jesus and family did not return to Judea until after Herod the Great had died (4 BCE). Luke, on the other hand, skips from Jesus at 40 days old (Luke 2.22) to Jesus at twelve years old, at which time he is at the temple debating ably with the teachers there. Next we see Jesus when he is 'about thirty years old' (Luke 3.1). This reflects the full interest of the biblical account of Jesus' childhood.

Later writers were much more interested in this subject. The most famous of these is the *Infancy Gospel of Thomas (IGT)*, which speculates on what it might have been like to be 'the son of God' as a child. The *IGT* is a pseudepigraphal text, which means it was written in someone else's name, in this case 'Thomas the Israelite'. Usually the pseudepigrapher writes in the name of someone famous, and so it is possible, though uncertain, that the author is claiming to be one of the disciples (Matt. 10.3; Mark 3.18; Luke 6.15; and Acts 1.13 all list a Thomas as a disciple).

The *IGT* purports to tell the life of Jesus from five years to twelve years old—the gap left by the Gospel writers. Here Jesus is a petulant bully with a bad attitude *and* divine powers! One of the more famous stories from the *IGT* is the one in which Jesus makes clay birds by a stream on the Sabbath; when he is criticized for it, he makes them fly away (*IGT* 2). In several other stories, Jesus kills other children who anger him (say for bumping into him in the market, as in *IGT* 4), causing the town to plea with his parents to control the boy. When Joseph admonishes the boy, he threatens his father ominously. About half way through the gospel, however, Jesus begins to use his powers for good, healing people, and even bringing a man back to life (*IGT* 18). The text ends by creatively retelling Luke's story of Jesus left behind in Jerusalem at twelve years old.

The British Museum houses the Tring Tiles, a series of tiles from fourteenth-century England that show a young Jesus at school trying to learn, being chastised by his teacher, and coming into conflict with his classmates. Modern country-folk singer John Prine sings a song called 'Jesus, the Missing Years' (1991) in which Jesus travels around the Mediterranean as a vagrant, and settles in cosmopolitan Rome before inventing Santa Claus and discovering the Beatles. There have been a few attempts in literature to tell the childhood of Jesus, most notably D.T. Bunker, *The Boy Jesus* (1943) and Anne Rice, *Christ the King: Out of Egypt* (2005).

Recommended reading. Barnstone, Willis (ed.). 'The Infancy Gospel of Thomas'. In *The Other Bible*. Ed. Willis Barnstone. Pp. 399-403. New York: HarperSanFrancisco, 1984. Bunker, D.T. *The Boy Jesus*. Notre Dame, IN: Ave Maria Press, 1943. Rice, Anne. *Christ the King: Out of Egypt*. New York: Knopf, 2005.

See also INFANCY NARRATIVES [ZAC]

Jesus, titles of. Jesus has many titles but the best known, of course, is Christ or Messiah. In the OT, David is considered a type of messiah and the title 'son of David' became synonymous with Messiah or Christ (2 Sam. 7.1-17; cf. Matt. 1.1). The Messiah is called prophet (Deut. 18.15-18), priest (Ps. 110.4), branch (Zech. 6.12-13), king (Zech. 9.9; cf. Mic. 5.2), 'Holy One' (2 Kgs 19.22; Ps. 16.10; Isa. 1.4; 49.7; Dan. 4.13), and 'Wonderful Counselor, Mighty God, Everlasting Father, Prince of Peace' (Isa. 9.6).

The NT draws on OT notions about the Messiah (cf. John 6.14) as seen from the titles 'Christ' (Rom. 5.6), 'Root of David' (Rev. 5.5), 'Son of God' (Luke 1.35), 'Son of Man' (Matt. 8.31), 'Holy One' (John 6.69), 'Last Adam' (1 Cor. 15.22), and 'King of kings and Lord of lords' (1 Tim. 6.15; cf. Deut. 10.17; Dan. 2.47). Other titles include 'the/our Lord

Jesus Christ' (Acts 11.17), 'Jesus Christ' (1 Pet. 1.1), 'Christ Jesus' (Rom. 2.16), 'Christ Jesus our Lord' (Rom. 6.23), 'Jesus Christ the/our Lord' (1 Cor. 1.9), 'His Son Jesus Christ' (1 John 1.3), 'the Lord of glory' (Jas 2.1), 'Lord' (Luke 2.11), 'the Way, the Truth, and the Life' (John 14.6), 'Savior' (Eph. 5.23), 'Advocate' (1 John 2.1), 'Almighty' (Rev. 1.8), 'Word' (John 1.1), 'Word of God' (Rev. 19.13), 'Wisdom of God' (1 Cor. 1.24), 'Master and Lord' (Jude 4), 'Lord and Savior' (2 Pet. 3.18), 'God and Savior' (2 Pet. 1.1), 'Jesus Christ the righteous' (1 John 2.1), 'Chief Cornerstone' (Eph. 2.20), 'Chief Shepherd' (1 Pet. 5.4), 'Alpha and the Omega' (Rev. 1.8), 'First and Last' (Rev. 1.17), 'Great High Priest' (Heb. 4.14), 'King Eternal' (1 Tim. 1.17), 'King of Israel' (John 1.49), 'King of the Jews' (Matt. 27.11), 'Lamb of God' (John 1.29), and 'Morning Star' (Rev. 22.16).

Modern understandings of Jesus' identity vary. The question of whether or not the title savior would have changed depending upon the circumstances of Jesus' death, is the premise of rap artist KRS-One's 1995 song, 'The Truth'. Dishwalla, an alternative rock band, played with Christ's gender in their song 'Counting Blue Cars', saying, 'I'd really like to meet her'. The 1973 play and film *Jesus Christ Superstar* asks Jesus the question, 'Do you think you're what they say you are?'

Modernity has consistently rejected the Bible's claims about Jesus' identity. The 1916 silent film *Intolerance* introduces Jesus with the non-biblical title, 'the greatest enemy of intolerance'. Martin Scorsese's interpretation of the Passion story in the 1988 film *The Last Temptation of Christ* rearranges the titles of Christ and presents Jesus as weak, whiny, lustful, and psychopathic.

Some have favored certain titles above others as seen in the 1927 film, *The King of Kings* that depicts Christ as victorious. However, the director Cecil B. DeMille withdrew the line, 'My God, why have you forsaken me?', not allowing the audience to see the humanity of the 'Son of Man'. Mel Gibson reverses DeMille's emphasis, making Jesus quite human and at times neglecting the divinity of the 'Son of God', in his film *The Passion of the Christ* (2004).

Recommended reading. Bateman, Herbert W. 'Defining the Titles 'Christ' and 'Son of God' in Mark's Narrative Presentation of Jesus'. *Journal of the Evangelical Theological Society* 50 (2007) 537-59.

See also CHRIST; JESUS OF NAZARETH; KING OF KINGS; LORD; PRIEST; SECOND ADAM; SON OF DAVID; SON OF GOD; SON OF MAN [CCB]

Jesus of Nazareth. Minimally, Jesus of Nazareth was a Palestinian Jew executed in Jerusalem by the Romans at Passover around 29 CE. Some of his disciples and family believed that they had encountered him alive after his execution and, infused with his spirit, expanded his movement in Jerusalem and abroad among Jews and non-Jews. The Common Era of the Western calendar is based on a sixth-century estimate of his birth-date (which was more probably a few years BCE).

Three broad images of Jesus dominate both Christian and wider cultural receptions: the crucified Jesus, the teacher-prophet Jesus, and the baby Jesus. All representations of Jesus are informed more or less by Christian biblical references to him as Messiah, Lord, and Savior. Later references to Jesus in the Talmuds and especially in the Qur'an have affected popular imagination in their respective spheres of influence (for example, through the 2008 Iranian film *The Messiah*).

Christian biblical and credal accounts of Jesus emphasize the central significance of his execution. Especially in Western (Latin) Christianity, the crucifix and the empty cross of the risen Lord have become the central symbolic representation of Jesus. Paul speaks of Jesus almost exclusively as the crucified and risen Lord; the canonical Gospels relate Jesus' death to traditions of Jesus as a speaker, leader, and miracle-worker. In late modern popular culture, representations as different as the Andrew Lloyd Weber and Tim Rice musical *Jesus Christ Superstar* (1971) and Mel Gibson's *The Passion of the Christ* (film 2004) share a predominant emphasis on the cross as the decisive event for understanding Jesus.

Other representations build on accounts of Jesus' prior activities in Galilee. The Galilean Jesus is portrayed as idealistic and charismatic, healing the sick, loving the marginal, offending the powerful and insincere, and calling disciples from among the ordinary and sinful: 'The man from Galilee' (Gene Maclellan, 1970) is able to assist sinners and inspire disciples without much reference to the cross. A 1999 Easter advertising campaign in Britain imaged Jesus as a thorn-crowned Che Guevara, to suggest revolutionary content behind sacrificial death. William Holman Hunt's famous nineteenth-century painting *The Light of the World* (in several versions) pictures Christ as teacher, illuminator, and friend. The tension between Galilean prophet and Jerusalem sacrificial apocalypse also informs such divergent cinematic representations as *Godspell* (musical, 1971; film, 1973) and *Life of Brian* (1979).

Martin Scorsese's 1988 film adaptation of the novel *The Last Temptation of Christ* (1951) by Greek writer Nikos Kanzantzakis experimented even more daringly with the idea of a Jesus without the cross. The 1989 Denys Arcand film *Jésus de Montréal* portrays Jesus as a dramatic presence in a post-Catholic Quebec (echoing, perhaps unintentionally, the plot of another Kanzantzakis novel, *The Greek Passion* or *Christ Recrucified* [1948]). A more recognizable Jesus is Pier Paolo Pasolini's 1964 *Il Vangelo Secondo Matteo*, which sets Jesus' teaching ministry and death in a stark South Italian peasant milieu reminiscent of Caravaggio's renaissance use of ordinary people to model biblical saints and sinners.

A third image of Jesus, deeply embedded in popular culture is that of 'the Christmas story' and 'the manger scene'. Especially under the influence of medieval Franciscan theology and devotion to the humanity of the incarnate God and perhaps the transcendent potential of humanity, and mixing elements from Matthew and Luke and diverse European folk cultures, Christmas has resisted repeated attempts at suppression and may even survive Santa Claus.

Recommended reading. Sanders, E.P. *The Historical Figure of Jesus*. London: Penguin, 1993. Reinhartz, Adele. *Jesus of Hollywood*. Oxford: Oxford University Press, 2007.

See also MATTHEW, GOSPEL OF; MARK, GOSPEL OF; LUKE, GOSPEL OF; JOHN, GOSPEL OF [IHH]

Jethro. Jethro was Moses's father-in-law. He was a Kenite shepherd and a priest of Midian, the land that stretched from the Dead Sea to the Sinai Peninsula (Exod. 18). When Moses fled Egypt after killing an abusive Egyptian overseer, he went into hiding, and found work as a shepherd working for Jethro. It was through this that he met Jethro's daughters and fell in love with Zipporah, whom he later married (Exod. 2.21). He found Jethro an inspirational father-in-law, and as a result it was Jethro who suggested to Moses that he minister to the Jewish community. People from the Druze community view him as a prophet in his own right. Traditionally, Jethro's tomb is located near the city of Mahis in Jordan.

See also MIDIAN; MOSES; ZIPPORAH [JC]

Jews, Judaism. From ancient Hebrew *cultus* and subsequent Israelite religious expression, Judaism emerged as a religion based on the Oral and Written Torah under the supervision of the Rabbis around the time of the writing of the Mishnah (c. 200 CE). In this sense, Christianity is older than its 'parent' religion. Contemporaneous with nascent Christianity, a variety of 'Judaisms' competed for religious predominance in the late Second Temple period, all with unique sectarian community expressions (for example, the Sadducees, the Pharisees, the Zealots, and the Essenes). From earliest times, the Roman authors perceived Judaism as a monotheistic and rigorous superstition (so Tacitus, *Annals* 5.13: *Gens superstitioni obnoxia, religionibus adversa*, 'A race prone to superstition, opposed to religion'). Christian writers followed suit: 'It is out of place to preach Jesus Christ and to practice Judaism. For Christianity did not believe in Judaism, but Judaism believed in Christianity; it was in the latter that the men of every language believed and were gathered together in God' (Ignatius of Antioch, *Letter to the Magnesians*, second century). Judaism, however, cannot be understood through hermeneutical lenses of either of its monotheistic counterparts, Christianity or Islam. Judaism needs to be defined by those within its own circle. Russian poet Marina Tsvetaeva (1892–1941) understood the tragic history of Jews and Judaism in a self-identifying epithet, 'In this most Christian of worlds all poets are Jews' ('Poem of the End' [1924]).

See also ABRAHAM; MOSES; TWELVE TRIBES OF ISRAEL, THE [DM]

Jezebel. Jezebel was queen of the northern kingdom of Israel, daughter of Ethbaal of Tyre, and wife of King Ahab in the mid-ninth century BCE. Her story is told in 1 Kgs 16.31—2 Kgs 9.37. As a promoter of the cult of the Phoenician gods Baal and Asherah (1 Kgs 18.19), she incurred the wrath of the prophets Elijah and Elisha. Elijah fled from her in fear after his triumph over the prophets of Baal (1 Kgs 19.1-3); her plot to appropriate Naboth's vineyard (1 Kgs 21) illustrates her power and ruthlessness. The unjust stoning of Naboth at Jezreel provoked Elijah to prophesy that the dogs would lick up her blood there (1 Kgs 21.23), a fate that would also befall Ahab (1 Kgs 21.21; cf. Hos. 1.4). The prophecy was fulfilled in Elisha's time during a coup against Jezebel's son, Joram, when a eunuch pushed her out of the palace window as she defiantly waited with 'painted eyes and adorned head' for the usurper Jehu (2 Kgs 9.30). Her daughter Athalia was the only reigning queen of Judah, c. 841–835 BCE (2 Kgs 18.8). Jezebel is reputed to have been the grandaunt of Dido, the founder of Carthage. In the NT, the Apocalyptist nicknames a female prophet of Thyatira whose teachings he opposes 'Jezebel', accusing her and her followers of 'fornication' and eating food sacrificed to idols (Rev. 2.18-23a).

The *OED* defines a 'Jezebel' as 'a depraved woman; a woman who puts garish color on her face'. In Western culture, she has become identified with prostitution (a 'painted Jezebel', also a species of butterfly), although she is not accused of sexual immorality in the biblical story (but cf. 1 Kgs. 9.22; Rev. 2.21-22). Portrayals of her in Western art dwell mostly on her supposed vanity and sensuality and her gruesome death. In the antebellum South, the term 'jezebel' stereotyped slave women as sexually seductive. The 1938 film *Jezebel* stars Bette Davis as a spoiled southern belle who schemes to win her ex-fiancé from his new wife. *Jezebel*, a magazine of 'Atlanta Luxury Living' trades on this image. Jezebel is also a frequent motif in pornography. The character of Ellen Cherry in Tom Robbins's *Skinny Legs and All* (1990) mirrors and parodies the biblical figure. In popular evangelical discourse, the 'Jezebel spirit' is a demonic force besetting the modern world.

Elizabeth Cady Stanton's *Woman's Bible* (1895) archly remarked that Jezebel was 'a brave, fearless, generous woman, so wholly devoted to her husband that even wrong seemed justifiable to her, if she could make him happy. (In that she seems to have entirely fulfilled the Southern Methodist's ideal of the pattern wife entirely fulfilled by her husband'). Contemporary feminist scholarship has challenged the excessively negative reputation of Jezebel in Western culture, pointing out that her devotion to the gods of her people is hardly reprehensible, and her devious politicking is typical of ancient near eastern rulers, including such biblical heroes as David and Solomon.

Recommended reading. Beach, Eleanor Ferris. *The Jezebel Letters: Religion and Politics in Ninth-Century Israel*. Minneapolis: Fortress Press, 2005. Dutcher-Walls, Patricia. *Jezebel: Portraits of a Queen*. Collegeville, MN: Liturgical Press, 2004. Gaines, Janet Howe. *Music in the Old Bones: Jezebel through the Ages*. Carbondale/Edwardsville: Southern Illinois University Press, 1999.

See also AHAB; ELIJAH; ELISHA; HARLOT

[MALB]

Jezreel. From the Hebrew *yizrĕ'e'l*, 'God sows', Jezreel is an OT city located on the eastern edge of a strategic fertile plain that shares the same name (Jezreel Valley). The city was within the inheritance of the tribe of Issachar (Josh. 19.18), and the Valley was the location of a major trading route between Egypt and Damascus (the Via Maris), and as a result, was the site of many important conflicts. From biblical texts, the Jezreel Valley is first mentioned by name in Josh. 17.16, where the tribe of Joseph complains that the people of the Valley have iron chariots, then again in Judg. 6.33, when Gideon's enemies, the Midianites and Amalekites, cross the Jordan River and set up camp. In 1 Sam. 29.1, King Saul gathered Israel's forces at the spring of Jezreel before engaging the Philistines at Gilboah. The city of Megiddo, which is also within the confines of the Valley, has been the setting of many battles throughout history and is the basis for the term 'Armageddon' found in Rev. 16.16.

The city of Jezreel is most closely associated with the reign of King Ahab who used it as a royal residence and possible winter capital (1 Kgs 21.2). Following the events on Mount Carmel, the prophet Elijah, who was on foot, outran Ahab and his chariot to the city (1 Kgs 18.46). It was also in Jezreel where Ahab, in conjunction with his wife Jezebel, arranged for the murder of Naboth the Jezreelite in order to seize his vineyard (1 Kgs 21.1-16). The prophet Elijah cursed Ahab and Jezebel because of this (1 Kgs 21.17-28), and following Ahab's death, Jehu fulfilled the words of the curse by killing Ahab's son Joram outside of Jezreel (2 Kgs 9.24), and having Jezebel thrown from the city's palace window (2 Kgs 9.30-37). Jehu, who had been a commander of the army under Joram, also had Ahab's seventy sons killed and placed their heads in two piles outside the city gate (2 Kgs 10.8), thus eradicating the Ormride dynasty (2 Kgs 10.11, 17).

The slaughter linked to Jehu's rise to power is later referred to by the prophet Hosea, who named his son Jezreel as a sign to the people of the coming judgment against the dynasty of Jehu, and the kingdom of Israel as a whole (Hos. 1.4-5). While the meaning of the passage is debated, it is apparent that the name Jezreel had become associated with violence and bloodshed. Hosea later reverses this destructive image by using Jezreel, and the meaning 'God sows', to emphasize a coming restoration initiated by God (Hos. 1.11; 2.22).

Archaeological evidence attests to the possibility of Jezreel functioning as an Iron Age Israelite military base, complete with a large royal enclosure, a six-chambered gate, a wall supported by earthen ramparts, and a moat. Besides the modern use of the term Armageddon, a derivative of a city found in the Jezreel Valley, the name Jezreel itself has not been significantly popular. In the 1870s, a British army officer named James White changed his name to James Jershom Jezreel and founded a Christian sect called the Jezreelites. The sect's most famous contribution was Jezreel's Tower, or Jezreel's Folly, in Gillingham, Kent. Construction on the massive tower began in 1886, but work was never completed, and the tower remained unfinished until its destruction in 1961.

Recommended reading. Ussishkin, David. 'Tel Jezreel'. In *The Oxford Encyclopedia of Archaeology in the Near East.* Ed. Eric M. Meyers. III. Pp. 246-47. Oxford: Oxford University Press, 1997. Na'aman, Nadav. 'Naboth's Vineyard and the Foundation of Jezreel'. *Journal for the Study of the Old Testament* 33.2 (2008) 197-218.

See also MEGIDDO; AHAB [JL]

Joab. The nephew of King David, Joab was the son of Zeruiah appointed as the commander of David's army. He got that position after leading the Israelites in the attack on the fortress of Mount Zion (1 Chron. 27.34), and then leading the soldiers in the invasion of Syria. Joab was loyal to David and involved in many of the machinations in David's court. Joab figures in various films centerd on the life of King David. Harry Shields plays the part 1917's *The Chosen Prince* and Earl Crain in *The Queen of Sheba* four years later. In *David and Bathsheba* (1951) it was Dennis Hoey, and in 1085's *King David*, Tim Woodward.

See also DAVID [JC]

Joanna. Joanna (Greek *Ioanna,* the feminine form of *Ioannes,* itself a transliteration of the Hebrew masculine name *Yohanan,* 'God is gracious') is one of Jesus' female followers in the Gospel of Luke. She is first mentioned in Luke 8.1-3, where she is grouped with Mary Magdalene and Susanna. The trio is said to have been 'cured of evil spirits and infirmities' (8.2) and to have subsequently 'provided for [Jesus and the disciples] out of their resources' (8.3). Joanna appears again in Luke 24.10, where she is noted to be among the women who discover Jesus' empty tomb and report this finding to his other disciples. Again, as in Luke 8, though there are a number of women present, Joanna is one of the few mentioned by name. Her status is increased somewhat by the mention in 8.3 that she is 'the wife of Herod's steward Chuza', demonstrating her relationship to the royal court. Some scholars have argued that Joanna is to be identified with the apostle called 'Junia' found in Rom. 16.7.

In the Catholic Church, Joanna is memorialized as St Joanna, and her feast day is celebrated May 24. In the Eastern Orthodox Church, Joanna is recognized the third Sunday of Pascha (two Sundays after Easter) on the 'Day of the Myrrh-Bearers', a reference to her bringing embalming agents to Jesus' tomb. She is also credited within the Eastern tradition with being the one to give the decapitated head of John the Baptist a proper burial. In contemporary culture, Joanna is the narrator of Mary Rourke's 2006 novel *Two Women of Galilee,* in which she is healed by Jesus of a lung condition and is later suspected of attempting to poison her husband. She also plays a role as Jesus's second female disciple in Margaret George's 2002 novel *Mary, Called Magdalene.*

Recommended reading. Bauckham, Richard. *Gospel Women: Studies of the Named Women in the Gospels.* Grand Rapids, MI: Eerdmans, 2002. Boer, Esther A. de. 'The Lukan Mary Magdalene and Other Women Following Jesus'. In *A Feminist Companion to Luke.* Ed. Amy-Jill Levine and Marianne Blickenstaff. Pp. 140-60. Cleveland, OH: Pilgrim Press, 2001. Witherington III, Ben. 'On the Road with Mary Magdalene, Joanna, Susanna and Other Disciples—Luke 8:1-3'. In *A Feminist Companion to Luke.* Ed. Amy-Jill Levine and Marianne Blickenstaff. Pp. 1333-39. Cleveland, OH: Pilgrim Press, 2001.

See also JUNIA [KJV]

Joash. Joash is the name given to several men in the OT, including a king of Judah, and a king of Israel. Other men with the name Joash include Gideon's father (Judg. 6.11) and a son of King Ahab of Israel (1 Kgs 22.26).

King Joash of Judah (c. 837–800 BCE) was acclaimed the eighth king of Judah at the age of seven. When he was an infant, his grandmother Athaliah sought to annihilate the royal line of Judah, and only the intervention of his aunt saved the infant. For the next several years, Joash was sequestered in the temple and raised by his aunt and her husband, Jehoiada, the high priest. After a highly organized revolt, Joash was introduced to the population as the rightful king, and Athaliah was executed. As he reigned, Joash rebuilt the temple but let pagan practices intrude. The prophet Zechariah, Jehoiada's son, intervened but the king had him executed. Joash was later assassinated by his servants. One rabbinic tradition maintained that Joash was recognized to be the rightful king because at his coronation, the crown fit perfectly upon his head. Another rabbinic tradition maintained that his assassination was retribution for a self-proclamation of divinity.

King Joash of Israel (c. 801–786 BCE) was the twelfth northern king. This Joash followed in the tradition of other Israelite kings, and 'also did what was evil in the sight of the LORD' (2 Kgs 13.11). Joash consulted the prophet Elisha to achieve victory over the Arameans. However, Joash did carry out the prophet's full intentions, and Elisha died shortly thereafter. Joash also fought against Judah, and was able to sack Jerusalem, breaking down a portion of that city's walls and carrying out valuable items from both the temple and the king's palace.

King Joash of Judah came to recent attention when an artefact surfaced in Israel in 2003. It bore an inscription describing repairs to the temple made by the Judean king. The artefact reignited the conflict surrounding the Temple Mount in Jerusalem, with some calling for the mosque on the Temple Mount to be demolished and a new temple constructed. The Israeli Antiquities Authority has deemed this inscription a forgery.

See also CHRONICLES, BOOKS OF; JUDAH, KINGDOM OF; KINGS, BOOKS OF [DP]

Job, Book of. The biblical book of Job is included in the third division of the HB, the writings (*Ketubim*), and concerns the (mis)fortunes of a wealthy, righteous man in the fictional land of Uz. In the divine court, the Satan, here portrayed similarly to a prosecuting attorney and not as the incarnation of evil familiar from Christian mythology, suggests to God that Job's fidelity and righteousness would disappear if he lost his health, wealth and family. God then gives the Satan permission to take away all these things from Job. The bulk of the work is written in Hebrew poetry and here Job questions his fate and the common religious teaching of his day, which insists that the quality of one's life is a result of one's actions. Against this common wisdom, Job insists that he is righteous and his suffering undeserved. A folktale frame encloses the poetic sections and it is from these sections of the book that the proverbial Job, who patiently and calmly accepts his suffering and has his fortunes eventually restored, arises. The poetic body stands in tension with the happy conclusion and complacent character of Job in the folktale framework.

Possibly as an attempt to avoid dealing with the bleak vision of the poetic sections, early interpretation of the book focused on the Job of the folktale rather than on the Job of the poetic sections. The sole reference to Job in the NT refers to 'the patience of Job' (Jas 5.11) but makes no mention of Job's agonized laments. The Hellenistic novel *The Testament of Job*, composed somewhere between 100 BCE and 100 CE, also focuses on Job's patience and excludes the heavy theological questions raised in the poetic sections. Some modern interpretations have continued this trend. In the gospel song 'I Got Confidence', popularized by Elvis Presley, it is noted that, 'Job was sick oh so long / Til the flesh fell from his bones / His wife, his cattle, his children / Everything that he had was gone / But Job he didn't despair / He knew that God still cared / Sleepless days and sleepless nights / Job said "Honey, that's all right!"'

Other twentieth-century interpretations of Job have been more faithful to actual content of the book. The popular cartoon *South Park* also contains a re-telling of Job, which is surprisingly faithful to the biblical text. Archibald MacLeish's verse play *J.B.*, which won both the Pulitzer Prize and a Tony award, is a modern telling of Job concerning the fortunes of a twentieth-century millionaire. In Canadian literature, Job has been the subject of a cycle of poems by Elizabeth Brewster (*Footnotes on the Book of Job*, 1995) and a novel by Gail Anderson Dargatz (*The Rhinestone Button*, 2002). The former concerns the poet's reading of Job during a Canadian winter and engages with questions of divine justice and the problem of suffering. The latter is a comic novel about an Albertan farmer named Job who, like the biblical Job, feels estranged from the religious world around him, in this case evangelical, charismatic Christianity. During and after the holocaust, Job became a symbol for the Jewish people. A statue of Job can be found at Yad Va-Shem, the Holocaust museum in Jerusalem.

See also JOB'S WIFE; JOB'S FRIENDS; JOB'S DAUGHTERS [JZ]

Job's daughters. Job 42.14-15 describe the daughters of Job, born after his trials, as incomparably beautiful. They had unusual names: Jemimah (Hebrew *yemimah*) means 'dove'; Keziah means 'cassia' or 'saffron'; and Keren-happuch means 'mascara palette' or 'horn of antimony', referring to women's cosmetics. Moreover, unlike most women in the ancient world, they received a share of their father's estate equal to those of their brothers (but see Num. 27 and 36).

Later Jews and Christians were fascinated by these women. In the first-century BCE text *The Testament of Job*, the girls receive from their father, in lieu of money, three magic cords or girdles. These girdles have the power of healing their wearers. The English Romantic poet and engraver William Blake (1757–1827) produced two sets of engravings on

Job (*Illustrations of the Book of Job*, 1818–1825), which began and ended with scenes of domestic bliss, including Job's two sets of daughters (the first of whom died). Plate 20 shows Job telling the story of his trial to awestruck and caring women of considerable beauty, with the caption, 'If I ascend unto Heaven thou art there.... If I make my bed in Hell behold thou art there', obviously implying that the birth of the daughters was a token of divine mercy. Though the daughters do not figure prominently in either Job or the vast literature based on it, they do provide a charming sidebar to the book's serious questioning of divine justice in the world's governance.

Recommended reading. Machinist, Peter. 'Job's Daughters and their Inheritance in the Testament of Job and its Biblical Congeners'. *The Echoes of Many Texts.* Ed. William G. Dever and J. Edward Wright. Pp. 67-80. Atlanta: Scholars Press, 1997. Terrien, Samuel. *The Iconography of Job through the Centuries.* University Park, PA: Pennsylvania State University Press, 1996.

See also JOB, BOOK OF; JOB'S WIFE; WISDOM
[MWH]

Job's friends. The story of Job chronicles the torment of a blameless and upright man (1.1) at the hands of Satan (1.6–2.8) and his subsequent restoration to wealth and prosperity by God following his period of suffering (42.10-17). The bulk of the work's 42 chapters, however, add little to the narrative, but form a treatise on sin and righteousness, suffering and blame, and the role of God in human activity. The bulk of these themes appear in the conversation between Job and his friends Eliphaz the Temanite, Bildad the Shuhite, and Zophar the Naamathite (2.11).

Job's friends first appear in a genuine act of friendship as they 'heard of all these troubles that had come upon him ....They met together to go and console and comfort him' (2.11). There they remained in silence sitting upon the ground with Job for seven days and seven nights. Job ultimately began the dialogue when he 'opened his mouth and cursed the day of his birth' (3.1). Following Job's initial lamentation, three cycles of speech ensue: chapters 4–14; chapters 15–21; chapters 22–27. The cycles are standardized so that the speech order of Eliphaz, Bildad, and Zophar is maintained with Job's response to each friend lying between speakers.

The form of the speeches is one of disputation whereby Job's three friends argue that an individual's fortunes and misfortunes are determined according to their righteousness or unrighteousness before God. Job, on the other hand, is left bewildered and angry since his own experience of suffering does not match the pattern advocated by his friends. He is innocent (e.g., 12.4). Ironically, the reader also knows that Job's righteousness is not at issue, and ultimately God both confirms Job and rebukes his friends: 'My wrath is kindled against you [Eliphaz] and against your two friends; for you have not spoken of me what is right, as my servant Job has'. How exactly the friends have not spoken, 'what is right' is not fully clarified. Job's descriptions of his friends have given rise to later uses of the expression or concept of Job's friends or Job's comforters. Job suggests that his friends scorn him (16.20), have failed him (19.14), abhor him (19.19), and in 19.21 Job begs his friends to have mercy upon him. Speaking of his friends, Job declares, 'miserable comforters are you all'.

Artists such as Jean Fouquet in his *Job sur le fumier*, or William Blake in *Job's Comforters* and especially in *Job Rebuked by his Friends*, depict vividly the gap between Job and his friends both in situation and perspective. Writer Adam Lindsay Gordon, in 'Ars Longa', suggests that all have met 'Job's comforters' whom he describes as those who 'could not help themselves, and yet; To judge us they were ready'. Herman Melville makes the comparison even more vivid: 'Friends? I should like to know who you call foes?' A more positive portrayal of Job's friends occurs in Charles Heavysege's poem 'Jephthah's Daughter' where they are depicted as comforting Job by empathetically sitting in silence with him. Usually, however, to be 'Job's Friend, Job's Comforter' is to increase sorrow through accusation.

Recommended reading. Newsom, Carol. 'Job and his Friends: A Conflict of Moral Imaginations'. *Interpretation* 3 (1999) 239-53.

See also JOB, BOOK OF; WISDOM LITERATURE
[SHW]

Job's wife. Job's unnamed wife plays a minor role in the book telling his story, with only three references to her. Job mentions her indirectly in Job 19.17 and 31.10. He states that his breath has become repulsive to his wife, and that if he has committed adultery, then she would work for and sleep with other men. The only direct reference to Job's wife appears in Job 2.9, in which she responds to her husband's reaction against the calamities that have befallen him. She says, 'Do you still persist in your integrity? Curse God, and die'. Despite the brevity of this speech, different translations are possible. In the Hebrew text, no interrogative particle appears in the first sentence. Therefore, Job's wife could have meant 'You still persist in your integrity', an affirmation that resembles what the Lord has done earlier (2.3). For the second sentence, the verb conventionally rendered 'curse' in most English translations is literally 'bless' in Hebrew. Such a translation assumes that the author uses the verb euphemistically here. The literal translation, however, is also defensible, and this may give a more positive portrayal of Job's wife in the story. Due to the ambiguity of her speech, interpretations of this woman differ radically throughout history. She is an unwitting instrument of the devil on one end of the spectrum, and a pious and compassionate woman of wisdom on the other.

In *The Testament of Job*, a pseudepigraphical work dated between 100 BCE and 100 CE, Job's wife is named as Sitidos, and she is so devoted to her husband that she is even willing to sell her hair in order to buy some bread for him. In *La Patience de Job*, a Middle French play, Job's wife is the character who regrets her birth, yearns for death and complains of her losses, while Job urges her to be patient. At approximately the same time, *Le livre du chevalier de La Tour Landry* presents her as a caring wife who sustains Job with food and suggests her husband to seek death in order to relieve his pain. In his *Jabach Altarpiece* (1503–1504), the German artist Albrecht Dürer illustrated Job's wife standing beside her suffering husband and pouring water over his head. The English poet and painter William Blake created a series of illustrations on the Book of Job (1825) in which Job's wife shares her husband's suffering as well as his glorious restoration. *Job's Wife* (1992) is also the name of a play written by the Canadian playwright Yvette Nolan. The story describes a middle class Catholic white woman pregnant with the child of a Native man who prays to her god who turns out to be Native.

Recommended reading. Gitay, Zefira. 'The Portrayal of Job's Wife and her Representation in the Visual Arts'. In *Fortunate the Eyes That See: Essays in Honor of David Noel Freedman in Celebration of his Seventieth Birthday*. Ed. Astrid B. Beck, *et al.* pp. 516-26. Grand Rapids, MI: Eerdmans, 1995. Seow, C.L. 'Job's Wife, with Due Respect'. In *Das Buch Hiob und seine Interpretationen*. Ed. Thomas Krüger, *et al.* Pp. 351-73. Zurich: Theologisches Verlag Zürich, 2007.

See also JOB, BOOK OF; JOB'S FRIENDS; JOB'S DAUGHTERS [EH]

Joel, Book of. The name Joel means 'the Lord is God'. He is identified as the son of Pethuel but no other information is provided. He may have lived in Jerusalem because he speaks of the city and Judah with apparent knowledge. The time of writing is also uncertain, with opinions ranging from the ninth century to as late as the second century BCE. Those who argue for an early date point to its position between Hosea and Amos in the HB. An early date could place it in or near the reign of King Joash (c. 835–825 BCE), described in 2 Kgs 12.1-21 as the time of the regency of the priest Jehoiada. An early date would explain its attack on Baal worship. A middle date between (630–500 BCE) appeals to some because of the book's close similarities with other minor prophetic works. Others consider Joel a postexilic writing (c. 400–188 BCE). The book is a call to repentance because a locust plague signals that the Day of the Lord is near. A natural event is thus interpreted theologically as a sign that God's wrath is at hand. For Joel, the Day of the Lord is also a day of salvation, just as light follows darkness. The eschatological language and the apocalyptic imagery in the latter part of Joel were cited in Peter's Pentecost Sermon (Acts 2.16) as a fulfillment of God's promise to pour out his Spirit 'upon all flesh' so that 'your sons and daughters shall prophesy'.

The image of the plague of locusts reappears in A.E. Holdworth's *The Years That the Locust Hath Eaten* (1897). J.B. Priestly uses the locust image to refer to the years lost to British veterans of World War I (*The English Journey*, 1934). Thomas Wolfe used it in *The Web of the Rock* (1939).

See also DAY, OF JUDGMENT/OF THE LORD/OF WRATH; FORMER PROPHETS; LATTER PROPHETS; OLD MEN SHALL DREAM DREAMS; PENTECOST; PROPHECY; PROPHETS [AJW]

Johannine literature. This is a collection of four (for some, five) books in the NT: the Gospel of John and the short letters, 1, 2, and 3 John. Some include the Book of Revelation. The Johannine Gospel and letters resemble one another in language, themes, and theology. Some scholars think they are the works of John the Apostle but others hold the view they are products of a community, namely the followers of the beloved disciple, an unnamed character appearing in the Gospel of John (19.26 etc.).

Recommended reading. Brown, Raymond E. *The Community of the Beloved Disciple: The Life, Loves, and Hates of an Individual Church in New Testament Times*. New York: Paulist Press, 1979.

See also JOHN, GOSPEL OF; JOHN, EPISTLES OF; CATHOLIC EPISTLES; BELOVED DISCIPLE [ET]

John, the Baptist. The forerunner of the Messiah, John appears in all four Gospels. Gabriel's declaration to Zechariah regarding John's birth (Luke 1.5-25) introduces biblical themes associated with John: he was identified with the prophetic tradition; he called for repentance and a right relationship with God; and he prepared the people for the Messiah's coming. The Gospels characterize John's ministry as the fulfillment of Isa. 40.3-5, in which John was 'the voice of one crying out in the wilderness: Prepare the way of the Lord, make his paths straight' (Mark 1.3; Matt. 3.3; John 1.23).

A prophet like Elijah (2 Kgs 1.8; cf. Luke 1.17), John lived an ascetic lifestyle marked by camel-hair attire and a diet of locusts and wild honey. John's message, 'Repent, for the kingdom of heaven has come near' and 'the axe is laying at the root of the trees' (Matt. 3.2, 10) called for the rebirth of Israel through repentance and metaphoric baptism in the Jordan River. He warned of fiery judgment for the unrepentant. John's preaching proved popular and he had numerous disciples (Mark 1.5; Matt. 3.5; Acts 13.24-25). Despite significant differences, similarities have been noted between John and the Qumran community including emphases on eschatology, repentance, ritualistic washing, and the theological centrality of Isaiah.

John's role as forerunner was defined prior to his birth in the promises surrounding his conception and in his rejoicing within Elizabeth's womb at Mary's salutation (Luke 1). The apogee of John's ministry was his public recognition of Jesus as the Messiah and his baptism of Jesus in the Jordan, marking the commencement of Jesus' ministry (Matt. 3.13-17; John 1.29-36). John's baptism was then surpassed by the Messiah's baptism by the Holy Spirit and fire (Luke 1.16). John receded into the background until his arrest and decollation (beheading). Josephus (*Ant.* 18.5.2) and the Gospels assert the execution was for John's criticism of Herod Antipas. The Gospels focus on John's criticism of Herod's marriage to Herodias (his brother's wife). This part of the story, involving an antagonistic relationship between prophet and ruler, is analogous to the story about Elijah who criticized Ahab and Jezebel (Mark 6.14-29).

The Baptist was venerated in traditional piety as saint, martyr, and possible relative of Jesus (Luke 1.36). Churches and monasteries were founded on the Jordan River by the fifth century to commemorate John and the baptism of Jesus. Traditional resting-places for his relics (particularly his head) were places of pilgrimage. Western Christianity celebrated John's martyr-like death (August 29), and the celebration of his birth (June 24) was one of the most important liturgical feasts. The Feast of the Nativity of John the Baptist fell upon the summer solstice and was one of the syncretistic holidays associated with pre-Christian calendars.

John was frequently invoked in oaths: Richard II (depicted with the Baptist, Virgin, and Child on the Wilton Diptych) preferred swearing by the Baptist. Originally depicted only in relation to Jesus' baptism, John later appeared in art inspired by his ministry or the scintillating tale of Salome's dancing and John's decollation. Medieval representations of John's martyrdom bedecked churches like the Parish Church of Chalfont St Giles (Buckinghamshire). John was a popular subject for art from the Renaissance forward, appearing in *St John in the Wilderness* (c. 1450) by Giovanni di Paolo, *Herod's Banquet* (c. 1480) by Antonio di Salvi, and *Salome with the Head of Saint John the Baptist* (c. 1530) by Lucas Cranach the Elder. Modern depictions of John have appeared in film and stage adaptations of *Salome*.

Recommended reading. Taylor, Joan E. *The Immerser: John the Baptist within Second Temple Judaism.* Grand Rapids, MI: Eerdmans, 1997.

See also BAPTISM; ELIZABETH; HERODS, THE; SALOME; HERODIAS [BVH]

John, Epistles of. The three short works titled 1–3 John are sometimes categorized among the so-called catholic or general epistles of the NT because they are not addressed to a named church or person, which is the case with Paul's letters. The author is unknown though similarities with the Gospel of John exist, which accounts for the names given to these writings. Similarities include use of the term Paraclete to identify the Holy Spirit and Jesus Christ as 'comforter' 'counselor' and 'advocate' (John 14.15; 14.26; 15.26; 16.7; cf. 1 John 2.1). Both John's Gospel and the Johannine epistles emphasize love as a characteristic of God and the Christian life. Some scholars believe the letters are products of the Johannine community, followers of the 'beloved disciple' mentioned in the Gospel of John.

First John is not actually a letter because it lacks key elements of epistolary writing including an opening greeting and valediction. Written with personal affection, it is a doctrinal tract on the true nature of Jesus Christ and appears to counter elements of nascent Gnostic teachings that included a matter–spirit dualism. Whereas as some downplayed Christ's physical nature, 1 John (and the Gospels) emphasize his humanness (e.g., John 1.1-7; 1 John 1.1-4). The writer of 1 John warns against 'antichrists' (4.1-6) who deny certain teachings about Jesus. This emphasis on orthodoxy and orthopraxy continues in the much shorter 2 and 3 John. The second letter warns of 'deceivers' who have gone out into the world who deny that Jesus Christ has come in the flesh (2 John 7). In 3 John, the emphasis shifts to issues of authority in the church, a problem centered on on one Diotrephes, 'who likes to put himself first' (v. 9). Both 2 and 3 John reflect the struggle for orthodoxy in the early church.

Poems have been written on verses in 1 John, among them, 'The World' by Henry Vaughn (cf. 1 John 2.15-17), 'What We, When Face to Face' by Arthur Hugh Clough (cf. 1 John 3.1-2), and 'The Praise of Godly Love out of 1 John 4' by John Hall (cf. 1 John 4.4-21). The hymns 'Holy Spirit, Truth Divine', 'Christ is the World's True Light', 'God is Love: Let Heaven Adore Him', 'Love Divine, All Loves Excelling', and 'Near to the Heart of God' are based on verses in 1 John.

Recommended reading. Smith, D. Moody. *First, Second, and Third John.* Louisville, KY: Westminster John Knox, 1990.

See also JOHN, THE APOSTLE; CATHOLIC EPISTLES; JOHANNINE LITERATURE; GNOSTIC, GNOSTICISM   [AJW]

John, the Apostle. John the Apostle is mentioned over thirty times in the NT. John was one of Jesus' disciples, and a member of the inner circle of his closest followers. Along with James his brother (both sons of Zebedee) and Peter, John was a disciple to whom Jesus chose to reveal himself in special ways on a few occasions. John is one of the first disciples called, along with his brother (Matt. 4.21; 10.2; Mark 1.19; 3.17; Luke 5.10; 6.14) and is present for the healing of Peter's mother-in-law (Mark 1.29). He is also one of the three disciples that accompany Jesus to heal Jairus's daughter (Mark 5.37; Luke 8.51) and witness the transfiguration (Matt. 17.1; Mark 9.2; Luke 9.28). John enquires of Jesus regarding those casting out demons in his name (Mark 9.38; Luke 9.49, 54) and with James asks Jesus for a special favor, something angering the other disciples (Mark 10.35, 41). John is one of the disciples who question Jesus about future events (Mark 13.3), is sent with Peter to prepare for the Passover (Luke 22.8), and with James and Peter goes to the garden when Jesus prays (Mark 14.33). In the Book of Acts, John's role diminishes. The only major role he plays is when he enters with Peter into the temple area when Peter heals the lame man (Acts 3.1, 3, 4, 11). Paul refers to John, along with James (Jesus' brother) and Peter (Cephas), as the pillars of the church (Gal. 2.9). Traditionally, John the apostle is also identified as the John mentioned in Revelation as its author (Rev. 1.1, 4, 9; 22.8) but a number of scholars, even those who hold to John's authorship of other books, believe that the John of Revelation is not John the apostle. John the apostle is also traditionally said to be the author of the Gospel of John and three epistles (1–3 John). Discussion of Johannine authorship of the Fourth Gospel often refers to an ambiguous statement by Papias quoted from Eusebius (*Hist. Eccl.* 3.39.4) regarding the Elders and an Elder John. Some think that the Elder John referred to is a second generation Christian, while others think that the Elder John, who appears to be listed with the other Elders who are also called disciples, is the same person as John the apostle. Tradition states that John the apostle died in Ephesus near the end of the first century, after having composed the Gospel and the other works attributed to him.

See also JOHN, GOSPEL OF; JOHN, EPISTLES OF   [SEP]

John, Gospel of. The Fourth Gospel of the NT is traditionally ascribed to John the son of Zebedee (Jesus' disciple) and written around 90 CE. Like the other canonical Gospels, it recounts Jesus' life, but with significant differences. It includes no parables or exorcisms, and provides an alternative order of some events (e.g., the temple cleansing is earlier; Jesus dies on the day before Passover; Jesus does not serve the Last Supper but washes the disciples' feet). It recounts unique miracles, called 'signs' (see 20.31), such as turning water into wine (2.1-11) and raising Lazarus from the dead (11.1-44), and incorporates different characters, such as the Samaritan woman, Nicodemus, the beloved disciple, and 'Doubting Thomas'. Jesus speaks in long discourses instead of short pithy sayings. Most distinct is John's equation of Jesus with God. For example, Jesus pre-exists and participates in creation (1.1-18) and has supernatural knowledge (1.48; 2.24-25; 4.29; 6.15; 13.21; etc.). Jesus states that he and the 'father' (God) are 'one' (e.g., 17.11, 22), and uses the divine name 'I am' (4.26; 6.20, 35, 41, 48, 51; 8.12, 24, 28, 58, etc.). Jesus also has unique titles such as the 'word' (1.1), the 'lamb of God' (1.29), and 'the good shepherd' (10.11). Because of the abundant metaphorical language, interpreters named this the 'spiritual gospel' and dismissed it as a historical source for Jesus (a recently challenged assumption). It was a favorite gospel of early Gnostics.

Protestant Reformers drew on the idea of 'Jesus as the word' to promote biblically based faith, and American evangelicals often speak of the 'word of God' ambiguously, conflating the person of Jesus, his words, and the words of the Bible. John contributes extensively to the language of 'God the Father' and the popular evangelical phrase denoting conversion, being 'born again' (3.3).

Because it establishes many dualisms such as light/dark, seeing/blind, believers/unbelievers, heaven/world, above/below, God/Satan, and life/death, John inspires dualistic theology, favoring the spiritual (cf. Plato's *Republic*). In particular, Jesus' claim, 'I am the way, and the truth, and the life. No one comes to the father except through me', fuels Christian exclusivity (e.g., *Augsburg Confession* 20.10) as well as the missionary impulse (St Francis Xavier, sixteenth century). Its pejorative treatment of the Jews (*Ioudaioi*, 8.37-47) is frequently cited as a source for anti-Semitism (e.g., James Tissot's nineteenth-century painting rendering the chief priests consulting together; one has devilishly pointed ears and cap).

The essence of the Gospel is captured in the most frequently cited biblical verse, John 3.16 ('For God so loved the world that he gave his only Son, so that everyone who believes in him may not perish but may have eternal life'). This verse—or just '3.16'—appears on billboards, in stadiums, in episodes of *The Simpsons* and *South Park*, on the bottom of coffee cups and shopping bags, and book titles, and serves as the 'gospel in a nutshell' for many.

There are multiple films, some specifically based on John: *The Visual Bible: The Gospel of John* (2004), and Bruce Marchiano's *Gospel according to John*. Others allude to John's presentation of Jesus, including *The Matrix*. The symbol of John the evangelist is the eagle.

Recommended reading. Anderson, Paul N., Felix Just, and Tom Thatcher (eds.). *John, Jesus, and History.* I. *Critical Appraisals of Critical Views.* Atlanta: Society of Biblical Literature, 2007.

See also JOHANNINE LITERATURE; JOHN, THE APOSTLE; GOSPEL [JSW]

John of Patmos. This title refers to the author of the Book of Revelation. It is derived from biographical material found in the book, where the author refers to himself as John (1.1) and states that he was on the Greek Island of Patmos (1.9), where he received his visions and wrote it down. Scholars debate whether this is John the apostle, John Mark, John the Elder, an otherwise unknown disciple named John, or someone using a pseudonym, which was common in apocalyptic literature. The author does not introduce himself as an apostle, or as the beloved disciple who is associated with the Fourth Gospel, or as the Elder who wrote the epistles. The author simply describes himself as John. This simple designation follows in the tradition of the Hebrew prophets (Isa. 1.1; Joel 1.1; Amos 1.1), and further establishes John's claims to be a prophet (e.g., 1.1-3, 10-19; 4.1-2; 22.19). He claims the visions recorded were seen by him while on the island.

Patmos lies off the SW coast of Asia Minor, it is one of the Sporades in the Greek Archipelago, and is now called Patino. It is a barren, rocky island about 18 kilometers long and 10 wide. The Romans often punished people by exiling them to an island and this may be the case with John. He states that he was on the island for spreading the word about Jesus (1.9).

John's influence rests not in his personal character, but in his written work. The imagery of Revelation is imbedded in much of Western culture. This is witnessed by its influence in all areas of society including theology, literature and art. John's highly symbolic vision provided rich imagery for Christian monumental art after Christianity became the established state religion, such as the 'Adoration of the Lamb' a triumphal arch mosaic by Santi Cosma e Damiano. During the Middle Ages exegetes would often read their situations into the imagery of the text and thus any opposition to the church was seen as Satanic and from the antichrist. During the Reformation, the Pope was often characterized as the antichrist of Revelation. John's Revelation also found its way into literature. The visions focus on Divine justice inspired Dante (Durante degli Alighieri) to write the *Divine Comedy*, which describes his journey through hell, purgatory and paradise.

Contemporary culture uses the Greek title given to John's work (Apocalypse) to refer to catastrophic events and pessimistic ideas resonating with the wildly devastating images recorded in the Apocalypse. For instance, Mel Gibson's *Apocalypto* takes viewers into the disturbing violence that permeated the fall of Mayan civilization. The Crash Test Dummies' album *Songs of the Unforgiven* (2004) uses biblical imagery from John's Revelation to reflect upon the events of 9/11. In the 1930s, Blind Willie Johnson recorded 'John the Revelator', a traditional gospel/blues call and response song, that has taken its place in the American music tradition, being covered by modern bands such as The White Stripes and the Dave Matthews Band.

Recommended reading. Barr, David L. *Reading the Book of Revelation: A Resource for Students*. Atlanta: Society of Biblical Literature, 2003.

See also APOCALYPSE, APOCALYPTIC; MILLENNIUM; REVELATION, BOOK OF [AC]

Jonah, Book of. Jonah appears among the Minor Prophets but a variety of unique features distinguish the book from its canonical neighbors. For example, while prophetic books typically contain collections of poetic oracles, Jonah includes none. Instead, an extended narrative and a single psalm (2.2-9) comprise the book's entire contents. In addition, Jonah's humorous and mythical qualities may suggest a genre more akin to parable or folk tale than prophecy.

Similarly, while 1 Kgs 14.25 suggests that the book's eponymous main character is indeed a prophet, Jonah's unusual behavior distinguishes him from his prophetic colleagues. When the LORD commands Jonah to preach repentance to Nineveh, Jonah resists, boarding a ship headed in the opposite direction. Later, when Jonah's Ninevite audience repents *en masse* and God decides against overthrowing the city, Jonah, far from rejoicing, sulks angrily. The book's structure further highlights this strikingly 'unprophetic' behavior; literary analysis of the book reveals a tight parallelism between chapters 1–§2 and chapters 3–§4. In both sections, Jonah 'arises' in response to God's call (first in disobedience, then in obedience) and the piety of pagan outsiders (the sailors and the Assyrians) leads to Jonah's response (first prayer, than anger).

Some interpretations of Jonah attempt to make sense of this unusual characterization. The pagans' exemplary, effective repentance may have been intended to challenge an overly exclusive view of God's mercy. Accordingly, many scholars date Jonah to the postexilic period, when (it is argued) the Jewish community grew increasingly resistant to outsiders. Early Christian interpretations, meanwhile, highlighted the so-called 'sign of Jonah', drawing a parallel between Jonah's time in the fish and the three-day interval between Christ's crucifixion and resurrection (cf. Matt. 12.39-40). Images from Jonah thus served as symbols of resurrection in early Christian paintings in catacombs.

Several well-known authors have drawn upon Jonah's story. Herman Melville's *Moby-Dick* references the tale frequently; the shared motif of a great whale (Heb. . 'great fish') invites comparisons. Robert Frost's *A Masque of Mercy*, meanwhile, imagines a modern conversation about God's character between a contemporized Jonah and Paul.

Since the advent of historical-critical scholarship, debates on biblical authority and reliability have also centered on Jonah. The book's many hyperbolic and fanciful details present challenges to those determined to defend it as accurate historiography. Still, some have gone to lengths to demonstrate that Jonah could have survived three nights inside the giant fish. The book's genre (likely folk tale or parable) renders such historical questions moot. Still, Jonah remains a battleground for those who insist on the entire Bible's literal historicity.

See also ASSYRIA; LATTER PROPHETS; NINEVEH; PROPHECY [MATTH]

Jonathan. There are fourteen individuals named Jonathan in the Bible, all of them are in the OT. They include a Levite, the son of Gershon (Judg. 18.30); the son of the High Priest Abiathar (2 Sam. 15.27, 36); a son of Shima, David's brother (2 Sam. 21.21); one of David's valiant men (2 Sam. 23.32); a son of Jada (1 Chron. 2.32-33); one of David's uncles (1 Chron. 27.32); the son of Ebed who returned with Ezra (Ezra 8.6); the son of Asahel who was employed in the matter of the strange wives (Ezra 10.15); a descendant of Jeshua the priest (Neh. 12.11); a priest descended from Melicu (Neh. 12.14); a priest descended from Shemaiah in the days of Joiakim (Neh. 12.35); a scribe in whose house Jeremiah was imprisoned (Jer. 37.15, 20); and a son of Kareah who went to Gedaliah the governor (Jer. 40.8).

The most important individual named Jonathan was the son of King Saul. He was a Benjamite, the first born of King Saul, and the bother of Michal who loved David and became his wife. Jonathan was a valiant warrior who defeated the Philistine garrison at Geba (1 Sam. 13.3) and also initiated the Battle of Michmash Pass (1 Sam. 14).

Jonathan was David's close friend and the two made a covenant with one another (1 Sam. 18). When King Saul sought to kill David because he was afraid David would usurp the throne, Jonathan protected him as a secret negotiator and then as an informant. He defied Saul and his filial duties to help his friend escape. At the Battle of Mount Gilboa, Jonathan, King Saul, and some of Saul's other sons were killed by the Philistines (1 Sam. 31). David lamented Jonathan's death in a powerfully moving poem (2 Sam. 1.17-27). After David became king, he brought the lame son of Jonathan, Mephibosheth, into his own household out of devotion to Jonathan (2 Sam. 9.1-11).

The seventeenth-century poet Francis Quarles represented David's eulogy for Jonathan in 'David's Epitaph on Jonathan'. In 1917, Major Vivian Gilbert, commanding a unit of British General Edmund Allenby's army was facing Ottoman forces at the same Michmash location where Jonathan and his armor bearer had fought. As the story goes, he remembered the story of Jonathan from Samuel and used it to find the same path used by Jonathan and his armor bearer. The British moved through the pass to out maneuver the Ottomans and gain an important victory. The account of the covenant between Jonathan and David, which includes the description of their relationship as 'surpassing the love of women' (2 Sam. 1.26), has been interpreted by Jewish interpreters and the Church as a platonic, selfless love. Others see this relationship as homoerotic, an approach to this passage that reaches back at least to the Renaissance sculptures of Donatello and Michelangelo.

Recommended reading. Gagnon, Robert A.J. *The Bible and Homosexual Practice: Texts and Hermeneutics.* Nashville, TN: Abingdon Press, 2001.

See also DAVID; SAUL [AJW]

Jordan River. The word Jordan means 'that which goes down'. The Jordan River begins at the heights of Mount Hermon (2814 meters). The distance from Mount Hermon to the confluence of the Jordan with the Dead Sea is virtually a north to south run of about 190 kilometres. However, the meandering of the River, especially after it leaves the Sea of Galilee gives it a surface distance of 360 kilometres. From Mount Hermon the Jordan River first descends to the basin of Lake Huleh, a dramatic drop in elevation of 275 meters in a distance of about 16.1 kilometres. From Lake Huleh the Jordan River descends nearly 305 meters through steep, rocky gorges. Just before entering the Sea of Galilee the descent slows and waters a plain near the village of Bet Zayda (Bethsaida). When the Jordan River leaves the Sea of Galilee it flows for about 39 kilometres through a fertile region that supported a variety of agriculture in ancient times as it does today. It is joined by the Yarmouk River flowing from the Transjordan plateau soon after it leaves the Sea of Galilee. South of the ancient city of Pella (Arabic, Tabaqat Fahl), one of the cities of the Decapolis, the Jordan flows through the Ghor Plain, an ancient sea bed composed of chalky limestone marls.

The descent to the Dead Sea is accompanied by an increase in temperature. The whole rift valley floor is called the Ghor (Plains of Moab). Its narrow flood plain (Zor) contains thickets of thorn scrub and tamarish along its banks ('jungle of the Jordan').

The Jordan River Valley figures frequently in the landscape of the Bible in passages such as the separation of Abraham and Lot, the Israelites crossing the Jordan on dry land to fight the Battle of Jericho, and the baptism of Jesus.

In Deut. 9.1 and 11.31 the Israelites were commanded to 'pass over Jordan' into the promised land carrying the ark of the covenant. To 'pass over Jordan' is an expression used among Christians for dying. It has been used in baptismal liturgy as a 'passing' from the wilderness of sin to the sinless promised land where woes are absolved as George Herbert wrote in 'Jordan I' and 'Jordan II' (1633). For African-American slaves, the phrase 'on Jordan's banks' symbolized crossing to freedom. The translation of the prophet Elijah to heaven in a whirlwind, which is usually interpreted as a fiery chariot, is widely know from spirituals such as 'Chariots a Comin'' or 'Swing Low, Sweet Chariot'. Emily Dickinson wrote the poem 'Elijah's Wagon Knew No Thrill' about it. Another event along the Jordan was the washing of the Syrian captain Naaman (2 Kgs 2.6-12) to be cleansed of his leprosy. Rudyard Kipling put the story to verse in 'Naaman's Song'. Namaan's washing has been used as a symbol of penitent self-abasement.

Recommended reading. Glueck, Nelson. *The River Jordan: An Illustrated Account of Earth's Most Storied River.* Philadelphia: Westminster Press, 1946.

See also BAPTISM; ELIJAH; ELISHA; FALL OF JERICHO, THE; JOHN THE BAPTIST; NAMAAN [AJW]

Joseph, husband of Mary. Joseph was the husband of Mary the mother of Jesus but not, according to the NT, Jesus' father. Matthew claims, 'the child conceived to [Mary] is from the Holy Spirit' (1.20). Joseph was a descendant of King David and it is through this line that Matthew traces Jesus' ancestry

(1.1-17). Presumably Joseph was from Bethlehem since he took his pregnant wife there for the census (Luke 2.2-5). The Gospels record that the family lived in Nazareth and that Joseph the son of Jacob was a carpenter or tradesman (Matt. 13.55). Little is known about Jesus' childhood except for his visit to Jerusalem when he was twelve (Luke 2.41-51). Jesus' words from the cross entrusting his mother Mary to the care of the beloved disciple likely indicate Joseph was dead by this time (John 19.26-27).

Artistic accounts of Joseph often present him as a kind man who was older than Mary. He appears in many fictional accounts of the life of Jesus, such as the novel by Marjorie Holmes, *Two from Galilee: A Love Story* (1972). In film, Monsieur Moreau played him in *Behold the Man* (1921), Laurence Payne in *Ben-Hur* (1959), Gerard Tichy in *King of Kings* (1961), Robert Loggia in *The Greatest Story Ever Told* (1955), Yorgo Voyagis in *Jesus of Nazareth* (1977), Joseph Shiloach in *Jesus* (1979), David Threlfall in *Mary, Mother of Jesus* (1999), Dallyn Vail Bayles in *The First Christmas* (2005), and Oscar Isaac in *The Nativity Story* (2006).

See also JESUS OF NAZARETH; MARY, MOTHER OF JESUS; INFANCY NARRATIVES [JC]

Joseph, son of Jacob. The biblical narrative centering on Joseph, son of Jacob, at one level appears fixed on presenting the patriarchal family unit as the site of a family romance gone wrong. The story highlights Joseph as the favorite son of Jacob who is consequently hated by his ten older brothers (Gen. 37.2-4); as Genesis draws to a close, these same brothers, though reconciled to Joseph, still fear Joseph will avenge himself for their earlier act of kidnapping and selling Joseph into slavery (Gen. 50.15-21). But the sense of the narrative cannot be reduced to familial relations alone. The importance of the Joseph character is reflected in Joseph's main activity throughout this narrative: his propensity to dream, and the effect that these dreams have on the players in the biblical scene.

Joseph's dreams are presented as particularly destabilizing. The first set of dreams seems to need no specific interpretation, since it is obvious to all those who hear these dreams that Joseph is keen to announce his superiority and future control over the brothers who, at this juncture, are united in disdaining him. But Joseph's dreams soon take on a larger significance. Importantly, Joseph does not grow into his public character until he stops proclaiming his own sense of himself and starts, instead, to listen to the narratives that other people recount. As in the case of his interpretation of dreams for his fellow prisoners in Egypt, Joseph is able to re-contextualize Pharaoh's dream from a disturbing personal experience to a message of national import. This time, however, Joseph uses his interpretative opportunity to recommend a major transformation of Egyptian power structures, with the introduction of economic centralization and agricultural management to defuse the horror of the oncoming famine. In effect, Joseph is the Bible's first economic planner, and his advice, while allowing the people of Egypt and the surrounding environs to survive, also is responsible for the establishment of what today is identified as centralized planning (this approach has been variously identified historically as 'hydraulic despotism' [Adam Smith] and 'oriental despotism' [Karl Marx], and has been incarnated in regimes ranging from fascist to communist). On a more transcendent note, by placing Joseph's political advice within the context of dream interpretation, the Bible encourages its readers to view politics, with all of its attendant power concerns, as a function of the interpretation of dreams and (anticipating, and perhaps even recalibrating, Freud) the personal conceptualization of better worlds to come.

When Joseph meets his brothers after many years of absence, he recognizes them but they do not recognize him. Given the asymmetrical nature of their respective levels of knowledge, it is natural to conclude that Joseph wishes to close the epistemic circle by proving to his brothers that his dreams of power and grandeur had indeed been fulfilled. Instead, Joseph utilizes his interpretative skills to rethink the past as a conduit to a future, peaceful national existence for the previously quarrelsome band of brothers, invoking the Divinity as having prepared the way to reestablish the torn family as the basis for a new national identity. The Israelites accede to full national identity within the borders of the ancient Egyptian Empire. On a more acerbic note, biblical texts describing later historical periods reveals that the division between the brothers (as incarnated in the Joseph–Judah encounter in Genesis) is revisited in the future partition of the Solomonic kingdom into its Judah and Joseph components (see e.g., 1 Kgs 11–12).

See also JACOB; TWELVE TRIBES OF ISRAEL
[MIRAM]

Joseph of Arimathea. Although mentioned in all four Gospels, little is actually stated about Joseph of Arimathea except that he was a 'rich man from Arimathea, named Joseph, who was also a disciple of Jesus' (Matt. 27.57; cf. Mark 15.43; Luke 23.50; John 19.38). Joseph was the man who asked Pontius Pilate for the body of Jesus to bury in his (Joseph's) 'rock-hewn tomb' (Luke 23.53). Mark also states that Joseph was the man who bought the cloth, and wrapped the body of Jesus in what became known as the 'Holy Shroud'.

There is some doubt as to the exact location of Arimathea, with some believing it to be Ramath-aim-Zophim, the birthplace of Samuel, although this is not certain. Because of his important place in the story of the burial of Jesus, much has been inferred about Joseph. The 'Council' mentioned in Mark 15.43 and Luke 23.50 might have been the Sanhedrin, and he being a disciple of Jesus has lent credence to the view that Jesus had attracted support from a number of powerful Jews. There are also scholars and other writers who have supposed that he was a relative of Jesus. Their argument is essentially that people were buried in family vaults, and that it would have been normal for a senior member of Jesus' family (usually the oldest male member) to ask for his body for burial in this manner. Assuming Joseph of Arimathea was older than Jesus, and since Jesus had no older brothers, this has led some writers to conclude he was Jesus' uncle. Others suggest he could have been the brother of Mary, Jesus' mother.

Joseph of Arimathea appears in a number of early Christian writings, and although many accept that these may not be given much credence, they are central to the emergence of Joseph as a major figure in the propagation of Christianity. Indeed some fictional accounts claim that Joseph was a trader who was involved in trading for tin from Cornwall, and suppose that he might have taken the young Jesus to England long before the start of his ministry.

However the more persistent tradition—and it remains only that—is that Joseph left the Holy Land after the crucifixion of Jesus, and went to southern France, then to the Pyrenees, and to Andorra, and from there to England where he started British Christianity in about 63 CE, before it had become a major religion in Rome. Some of this tradition, entwined with folklore and recent historical fiction, has it that Joseph took with him the 'Holy Grail' which was then concealed near Glastonbury in England where it later was to play a part in the story of King Arthur. The earliest known version of this story was by Robert of Boron in the late twelfth and early thirteenth centuries. He was living in eastern France at that time. Queen Elizabeth I, in 1559, cited the missionary work of Joseph when she told Roman Catholic bishops that the Church of England predated the Roman Catholic Church in England. He is also a central figure in Bertram Brooker's novel *The Robber* (1949).

Regardless of the merit of these later writings, and additions to the stories, Joseph of Arimathea is regarded as a Saint in the Roman Catholic, Lutheran, Eastern Orthodox, and some Anglican churches.

See also PASSION NARRATIVE; CROSS, CRUCIFIXION OF CHRIST [JC]

Joshua. One of the most famous figures in the OT, Joshua became the leader of the Israelites after the death of Moses whom he served. Born in Egypt, he was a loyal follower of Moses and accompanied Moses part way up Mount Sinai when he went to receive the Ten Commandments. He was then one of the twelve spies who was sent by Moses into Canaan to explore the land (Num. 13.1-16), and was one of the two who gave a good report of the land. Moses then appointed Joshua to succeed him and Joshua then led the Israelites into Canaan. Joshua is best remembered for his role in the Battle of Jericho, and he subsequently gave the land to the twelve tribes. He was aged 110 when he died in about 1400–1380 BCE As there is no evidence of Joshua from contemporary non-biblical records, a few historians believe that he did not exist, or at least not as a single person.

Muslims also revere Joshua, and he is mentioned in many Islamic theological works. By some traditions, his tomb is in a place known as Yusa Tepesi ('Joshua's Hill') on the Asian side of the Bosporus, opposite the old city of Constantinople (now Istanbul). The Italian writer Dante mentions Joshua in *The Divine Comedy*, and this was probably an influence on the composer Georg Frederic Handel who composed an oratorio called *Joshua* in 1747. Another composer, Franz Waxman, also composed an oratorio called *Joshua*, which was completed in 1959.

There are several novels that feature Joshua, among them Ella M. Noller's *Ahira, Prince of Naphtali: The Story of the Journey into Canaan* (1947); Konrad Bercovici's *The Exodus* (1947); Shalom Asch's *Moses* (1951); Frank G. Slaughter's *The Scarlet Cord: A Novel of the Woman of Jericho* (1956); and Noel Bertram's *The Hittite* (1961). Moreover, in films about the life of Moses, Joshua naturally plays a key role, as is the case with *The Green Pastures* (1936) and *The Ten Commandments* (1956).

Recommended reading. McShane, Albert. *Joshua: Possessing the Land*. Kilmarnock, E. Ayrshire: John Ritchie, 1994. Slaughter, Frank. *The Scarlet Cord: A Novel of the Woman of Jericho*. Garden City, NY: Doubleday, 1956.

See also JOSHUA, BOOK OF; MOSES; FALL OF JERICHO, THE [JC]

Joshua, Book of. The Book of Joshua combines two different histories of Israel's settlement in Palestine. The earliest version is a dramatic narrative of a swift and successful conquest under the leadership of Joshua resulting in complete possession of the land (11.23). It recounts the capture of Jericho, the battle of Ai, the peace-treaty with Gibeon, and the victory over northern and southern kings (Josh. 6, 8–11 *passim*). The conquest narrative was revised by an exilic historian who characterizes Israel's occupation as a gradual and partial dispossession of other peoples, with the shift in leadership from Joshua to individual tribes (11.18; 13.1-6; 15.13-19; 16.5-10; 17.14-18; 23.1-13).

The exilic layer of Joshua includes the repugnant idea of the conquest as holy war (*herem*), the total extermination of the inhabitants of Canaanite cities, commanded by God and in accordance with the legislation on war in Deut. 7 and 20. Reports in Joshua of genocide at Jericho, Lachish, Hebron and Hazor are not factual accounts but serve as propaganda for returning exiles to reclaim the land of Palestine (Josh. 6.17-19, 21; 10.1, 31-40; 11.10-15). Nevertheless, Joshua's ideology of subjugation and slaughter of the peoples of the land is morally offensive—not least in light of the atrocities in Nazi Europe, former Yugoslavia and Rwanda—and runs counter to Deuteronomy's overriding principle of justice and humanitarian concerns as old as civilization itself (Deut. 4.8, 16.20; 25.17-18; 32.4). The moral foundation of Western society is rooted in ancient Israelite law that protects the rights of the sojourner *(ger)*, the minorities who live among us (Deut. 10.17-19; 24.14-22).

The rhetoric in Joshua against the rights of Canaanites to the land is pertinent to the experience of indigenous Native Americans, Black South Africans, and Australian Aborigines. It is specifically applicable to the Israeli–Palestinian conflict. Otto Preminger's 1960 film *Exodus*, screen play by Dalton Trumbo, based on the novel by Leon Uris (1958), looks ahead to future generations who expect an appreciation of both sides of the story. Ari the Jew and Taha the Arab have grown up as brothers sharing the same land, so Taha welcomes young European Jews to Palestine in 1948: 'In this valley of Jezreel we dwell together as friends. It is natural that we should live in peace, since even our words for it are almost exactly the same. We say *salaam* and you *shalom*. Let us seal our friendship forever with that most beautiful of Hebrew toasts: *L'chaim*, to life'. Even an Israeli militant acknowledges: 'One can argue the justice of Arab claims on Palestine, just as one can argue the justice of Jewish claims'. The film's final scene of a Jew and an Arab being buried alongside each other concludes with Ari's address: 'I swear on the bodies of these two people that the day will come when Arab and Jew will share in a peaceful life in this land that they have shared in death.'

Recommended reading. Barr, James. *Biblical Faith and Natural Theology*. Oxford: Clarendon Press, 1993. Collins, John Joseph. *The Bible after Babel: Historical Criticism in a Postmodern Age*. Grand Rapids, MI: Eerdmans, 2005. Habel, Norman C. *The Land Is Mine: Six Biblical Land Ideologies*. Minneapolis: Fortress Press, 1995. Peckham, Brian. *The Composition of the Deuteronomistic History*. Atlanta: Scholars Press, 1985.

See also BOOK OF THE LAW; CANAAN, CANAANITES; COVENANT; DEUTERONOMY, BOOK OF; JEZREEL; JOSHUA; JUDGES, BOOK OF; PROMISED LAND [JRW]

Josiah. From the Hebrew name *yoshiyahu* (possibly meaning 'Yahweh will give' or 'Yahweh brings forth'), Josiah reigned over the Southern Kingdom of Judah c. 640–609 BCE. The grandson of the apostate Davidic king, Manasseh, Josiah was remembered for faithfully instituting reforms aimed at ridding the land of the foreign influences established during the reigns of his ancestors. According to 2 Kgs 23.25, 'there was no king like him, who turned to the LORD with all his heart [...]'. Because of his faithfulness, the prophet Huldah assured Josiah that he would not witness the destruction of Jerusalem in his lifetime (2 Kgs 22.14-20).

Josiah was installed as king when he was only eight years old, after the assassination of his father, Amon (cf. 2 Kgs 21.19-22.1; 2 Chron. 34.1). The biblical record is silent regarding the early years of Josiah's reign, but 2 Chron. 34.3 notes that in his eighth year on the throne, Josiah 'began to seek the God of his ancestor David', and that in the twelfth year of his reign, 'he began to purge Judah and Jerusalem' of the influence of foreign religion.

Both 2 Kings and 2 Chronicles highlight the importance of the discovery in the temple of 'the book of the Law' in the eighteenth year of Josiah's reign. Likely an early form of Deuteronomy, the discovery prompted Josiah to implement (2 Kings)—or perhaps, to intensify (2 Chronicles)—wider-ranging reforms. These included the removal of objects of foreign religion from the temple, a covenant renewal ceremony, the destruction of unauthorized sanctuaries in Judah and even the former Northern Kingdom of Israel (cf. 2 Kgs 22.3–23.20 and 2 Chron. 34.1-33), and a monumental Passover celebration (cf. 2 Kgs 23.21-23 and 2 Chron. 35.1-19).

In Josiah's day, the international political scene was volatile. At Megiddo, Josiah opposed an Egyptian advance, and he died in battle. While 2 Kings does not offer theological comment (2 Kgs 23.29-30), 2 Chronicles presents Josiah's death as being due to his failure to heed God's instructions (2 Chron. 35.20-25).

Throughout history, Josiah-like leaders have championed various types of reforms. Martin Luther, John Calvin and other leaders of the Protestant Reformation sought to address perceived heresy and apostasy in the Church. Some sixteenth-century Calvinists encouraged magistrates to model their careers after Josiah. Modern-day politicians promise 'accountability' and 'transparency', pledging to end corruption. A similar theme is also common in major motion pictures, especially of the 'Western' and 'Super Hero' genres, for example *Tombstone* (1993) and *Batman Begins* (2005), where the main protagonists seek to rid their towns of injustice.

Josiah has been the subject of many works of art, especially in the wake of the Protestant Reformation: an engraving by Matthäeus the Elder (c. 1625–30) remembers Josiah's discovery of 'the book of the law'; a woodcut by Johann Christoph Weigel (c. 1695) depicts Josiah's reforms; and perhaps most significant is Michelangelo's fresco (c. 1511–12), which pictures Josiah holding one of his infant sons.

Contemporary culture has had its specific references to Josiah. African reggae artist Majek Fashek, penned the song, 'Josiah is the King of Kings' (2005), in which he laments the perils of twenty-first-century idolatry. 'King Josiah' is also the stage name for two independent Christian hip-hop artists.

Recommended reading. Sweeny, Marvin A. *King Josiah of Judah: The Lost Messiah of Israel*. New York: Oxford University Press, 2001.

See also CHRONICLES, BOOKS OF; HULDAH; ISRAEL; JUDAH, KINGDOM OF; KINGS, BOOKS OF [MLW]

Jot or tittle. The unabridged *OED* provides the following definition of the word jot: 'The least letter or written part of any writing; hence, generally, the very least or a very little part, point or amount; a whit'. The term derives from the Greek noun *iōta*, the name of the ninth and smallest letter of the Greek alphabet (cf. the Hebrew noun *yôd*, the name of the tenth and smallest letter of the Hebrew alphabet).

The unabridged *OED* provides the following definition of the word tittle: 'A small stroke or point in writing or printing', hence, 'the smallest point of that which was written or prescribed'. The Hebrew word for thorn lies behind this term; it later came to signify the smallest point of that which was written or prescribed and was represented in the NT by the Greek noun for horn or projecting point. The KJV use of tittle denotes the little lines or projections by which Hebrew letters, similar in other respects, differ from each other.

The two words often occur together in the somewhat redundant idiom 'jot or tittle'. This figure introduced itself into English parlance via William Tyndale's 1525 translation (and is preserved in the 1611 KJV): 'For truly I tell you, until heaven and earth pass away not one letter [KJV: jot], not one stroke of a letter [KJV: tittle], will pass from the law, until all is accomplished (Matt. 5.18; cf. Luke 16.17).

The idiom has found its way into a number of literary classics. One example is John Bunyan's allegory of a Christian's journey, *The Pilgrim's Progress* (1678). At one point, Faithful gives Hope 'a Book of Jesus' wherein 'every jot and tittle thereof stood firmer than Heaven and Earth'. Yet another instance is Edmund Gosse's autobiography *Father and Son* (1907). In the 'Epilogue', Gosse says of the father that in his increasing disappointment with his son, 'he abated no jot or tittle of his demands upon human frailty'. On occasion, one might still hear such things as: 'There's not a jot or tittle of truth in the story'.

See also LAW; SERMON ON THE MOUNT [NRP]

Joy. The Bible has over a dozen words for joy plus another dozen for different modes of joyous experience. Hebrew words for joy include *gil*, rejoicing (Ps. 43.2; Isa. 16.10). Isaiah says to rejoice with joy (35.2; *gilah*). Nehemiah 8.10 declares, 'the joy of the Lord is your strength', using the term *chedvah*. The Psalms urge the people to give loud cries, to proclaim and sing with joy (*rinnah*; Ps. 30.5; 42.4). Joyous gladness (*simchah*), expressed in excited singing and dancing, is the kind of joy that greeted King Saul returning from war (1 Sam. 18.6). Qoheleth (Eccl. 2.26) says that God gives wisdom, knowledge, and joy (*simchah*) to the one who pleases him. He also confesses his own pursuit of pleasure as joy (Eccl. 2.10). Isaiah refers to the loss of joy because of divine punishment (Isa. 24.11). However, a future restoration will be a time to sing for joy (Isa. 24.11). In the Lord's comfort for Zion there will be joy, gladness and thanksgiving with the voice of song (Isa. 51.5). The work of the Lord in salvation will produce great joy (Isa. 55.12). Isaiah 61 proclaims that the redeemed will know everlasting joy (Isa. 61.7). Esther (8.16) and various Psalms (e.g., 51.8, 12) refer to joy (*sason*) in the presence of the Lord. Jeremiah says that the word of the Lord was joy unto him (Jer. 15.26). God promises that when the time comes, the exiles shall have their mourning turned into joy (Jer. 31.13). There is shouting for joy (*teruah*) in Job 33.26 and Ps. 27.6.

In the NT, the Greek words *agalliasis*, *euphrosune*, and *chara* mean joy, with most references to joy being some form of *chara*. Spiritual joy is a 'fruit of the Spirit' (Gal. 5.22). This joy in the faith has as its objects God, the gospel, or the future state of the blessed. It is permanent (John 16.22) and beyond words (1 Pet. 1.8).

Recommended reading. Lewis, C.S. *Surprised by Joy: The Shape of my Early Life*. Boston: Houghton Mifflin Harcourt, 1966.

See also BRIDE; BRIDEGROOM; FESTIVALS; HARP; MUSIC [AJW]

Jubilee, Year of. The Year of Jubilee was to be an important period in the Israelite calendar, as it was created to prevent the rise of a class-oriented system. The Year of Jubilee concerns the management and ownership of the land, as well as the place of slaves within Israelite society. Following seven cycles of sabbatical years, each person was to be released from debt and slavery and have their property returned to them. The Jubilee Year was significant as it ensured justice for both the land and the people by returning the land to its rightful heirs. Thus, the people were reminded that the land is owned by God, as the land was not to be perpetually changing owners. The regulations for the Jubilee Year are found in the holiness code in Lev. 25 and 27. The term Jubilee comes from the Hebrew, *yobel*, which is derived from the Hebrew term for ram, *yobhel*. The Year of Jubilee was announced by the sounding of a ram's horn.

There is debate over the actual dating of the Jubilee Year, whether it was intended to happen in the last year of the seven sabbatical cycles (the forty-ninth year), or in the year following the cycles (the fiftieth year). There is also speculation concerning the utopian ideals of the Jubilee. There is no evidence that the Jubilee Year was ever practiced in Israel; certainly there was no regularity in its implementation. Other than a brief mention in Num. 36, the Year of Jubilee is not directly mentioned again in the Bible. However, the year of the Lord's favor in Isa. 61.2 is seen by many as a reference to the Year of Jubilee. Thus, Jesus' use of that passage in Luke 4 indicates that his Messianic kingdom will be characterized by Jubilee principles.

The Jubilee legislation has become a significant symbol for oppressed peoples. Many faith-based groups sought to enact a Jubilee at the turn of the millennium. They desired the forgiveness of debts for many poorer nations as the impoverishment of the third world has resulted in great injustices. These groups desired to bring justice to those who are oppressed. This movement continues in the form of an organization titled the Jubilee USA Network. In addition to being a rallying cry for oppressed nations, jubilee is also used as a celebratory term denoting wedding anniversaries. A fiftieth wedding anniversary is called a golden jubilee.

The term has been given to a number of locations, including the Jubilee Tower in Darwen commemorating Queen Victoria's jubilee anniversary. The two Jubilee auditoriums in Alberta were built to celebrate that province's fiftieth anniversary. Jubilee has been widely used in modern culture, including a Marvel Comics character and the 2002 album title of the British punk band, Sex Pistols. Margaret Walker's 1966 novel also uses Jubilee as its title. This novel concerns a biracial slave in the American civil war era.

Recommended reading. Lowery, Richard H. *Sabbath and Jubilee*. St Louis: Chalice Press, 2000. Milgrom, Jacob. *Leviticus: A Continental Commentary*. Minneapolis: Augsburg Fortress Press, 2004.

See also JUSTICE; LEVITICUS, BOOK OF; SABBATH [DP]

Judah, Kingdom of. After the reign of David's son Solomon (c. 961–922 BCE), the United Kingdom of Israel was divided into the Northern Kingdom of Israel and the Southern Kingdom of Judah. The geographically smaller Southern Kingdom consisted of the tribal territories of Judah (the Kingdom's namesake) and Benjamin, including the capital city of Jerusalem.

In dramatic fashion, the prophet Ahijah informed Jeroboam, son of Nebat, that God was going to tear a significant portion of the kingdom away from the house of David because of covenant violations committed by Solomon (1 Kgs 11.1-40). During the reign of Solomon's son Rehoboam, Ahijah's prediction was realized when the ten northern tribes, led by Jeroboam, withdrew and declared their independence (2 Kgs 12.1-19). While numerous individuals and dynasties sat on the throne of Israel, the kings of Judah were solely the descendants of David (cf. 2 Sam. 7.1-17).

If the books of 2 Kings and 2 Chronicles remember the northern confederacy as being 'in rebellion against the house of David' (cf. 2 Kgs 12.19 and 2 Chron. 10.19) because of idolatrous practices, unfaithful leaders, and its failure to recognize the Davidic king as the true monarch, Judah was viewed more favorably due in large part to the occasional God-fearing king. Hezekiah (c. 715–687 BCE) and especially Josiah (c. 640–609 BCE) were considered the most faithful of Judah's rulers. Such kings, however, were the exception, not the rule.

The reign of Josiah's grandfather, the apostate king Manasseh (c. 687–642 BCE), was the religious low point for Judah, but also the point of no return (cf. 2 Kgs 21.10-15, 23.26-27, and 2 Chron. 33.1-25). Even the righteous reign of Josiah and his reforms were not enough to avert divine judgment. As the Assyrians conquered Israel in 722/1 BCE, the Babylonians conquered Jerusalem in 586 BCE. Nebuchadnezzar's forces destroyed the temple, taking many citizens of Judah into exile in Babylon, thus ending what was by this time even the limited independence of Judah (cf. 2 Kgs 25.1-21 and 2 Chron. 36.15-21).

In 539 BCE, the Persian king Cyrus the Great conquered Babylon and authorized the return of the exiles to Judah (Ezra 1.1-11). While the returnees and the remnant of Judah eventually began to reconstruct the temple and the walls of Jerusalem under the guidance of Ezra, Nehemiah, Zerubbabel, and Joshua, Judah never again established a monarchy as it had before the Babylonian exile. Other than a brief period in the wake of the Maccabean uprising in the late second and early first century BCE, the former Kingdom of Judah would remain under the thumb of various international superpowers until the Jewish revolt of 70 CE, when Jerusalem was sacked and the rebuilt temple was destroyed by the Romans.

In addition to works by unknown Protestant Reformation-era artists, Ahijah's prophetic announcement to Jeroboam that the United Kingdom would be torn in two has been the subject of a painting by Domenico Veneziano (c. 1570–75), a copper engraving by Casper Luiken (c. 1672–1708), and an engraving by Bernard Picart (c. 1728).

See also CHRONICLES, BOOKS OF; HEZEKIAH; ISRAEL; JEROBOAM; JOSIAH; JUDAH, KINGDOM OF; KINGS, BOOKS OF; MANASSEH; NEHEMIAH; REHOBOAM; ZERUBBABEL

[MLW]

Judah, Son of Jacob. The Hebrew name *Yehuda* means 'thanksgiving' and 'praise'. As the fourth son of Jacob and the progenitor of David and Jesus, Judah's role in both Jewish and Christian history was profound (see Matt. 1.1-17). Lineage was an important matter in the Ancient Near Eastern and Greco-Roman worlds. Judah married the daughter of a Canaanite named Shua. Judah had three sons, Er, Onan and Shelah. Er and Onan were killed by Yahweh for their disobedience. Only Shelah produced many children and grandchildren. After the death of his wife, Judah had an illicit relationship with his daughter in law, Tamar, which produced two more sons, Perez and Zerah (see Gen. 38.1-30). The tribe of Judah became the largest of the twelve tribes of Israel with its center at Hebron, and during the divided monarchy the southern kingdom was known as 'Judah'.

In the Joseph narratives, Judah emerges as the spokesman for his brothers. Such a role signified the respect accorded him and his own powers of persuasion. Judah, like his brother Rueben, successfully convinced his brothers not to kill their dreaming, favored brother Joseph and instead sell him to the Ishmaelites for twenty pieces of silver (Gen. 37.25-28). Judah communicated to his father Jacob that Joseph demanded Benjamin come to Egypt when they came again to buy food. And it was Judah who pledged security to Joseph for Benjamin's safety (Gen. 43.1-10). Furthermore, after the discovery of Joseph's silver cup in Benjamin's sack of grain, Judah interceded on his youngest brother's behalf and offered to take his place as a slave to Joseph (Gen. 44.18-34).

Before his death, Jacob pronounced a blessing on his son Judah (Gen. 49.8-12). In that blessing Judah was called a 'young lion' and a great national and spiritual symbol, the Lion of Judah, was born. In Western Christian tradition, the Lion of Judah is often assumed to represent strength and preeminence. This assumption is based in part on Rev. 5.5 where the Lion of Judah opens the book which loosens the seven seals. In his *Chronicles of Narnia*, C.S. Lewis uses a lion named Aslan as an allegorical messianic figure that represents Jesus who was a descendant of Judah.

Many of the key events in Judah's life also became subjects for Western artists. For example, in 1700 the story of Tamar offering herself to Judah was painted by Aert de Gelder, a student of Rembrandt. In 1840, the French orientalist painter Emile Vernet produced his version of the same event in a painting entitled *Judah and Tamar*. Modern artists, such as Marc Chagall and April Aharon, have also captured this pivotal event in their works. Other events in Judah's life, like the sale of his brother Joseph into slavery and Joseph's revelation of himself to Judah and his other brothers, were illustrated in the nineteenth century by the French artist Gustave Doré.

Recommended reading. Alexander, T. Desmond. 'From Adam to Judah: The Significance of the Family Tree in Genesis'. *Evangelical Quarterly* 61 (1989) 5-19. Arnold, Bill T. *Genesis,* 2009. Dever, William G. *Who Were the Early Israelites and Where Did They Come from?* 2003.

See also TWELVE TRIBES OF ISRAEL; JACOB   [PRW]

Judas Iscariot. Judah from the city of Keriyot—known to us as Judas Iscariot—is a character in the NT Gospels who, for 30 pieces of silver, betrayed Jesus with a kiss. The NT narratives, however, cannot agree on many of the details about why Judas did this. In Mark, there is no logical explanation for Judas's actions, and it is definitely not greed (Mark 14.10-11). In Matthew, Judas is motivated by greed to handover Jesus (Matt. 26.14-15). In Luke, the motivation is not greed but Satan (Luke 22.3), thus rendering Judas powerless in the whole affair (and, some argue, blameless). In the Gospel of John, Judas betrays Jesus because he is told to (13.27).

The canonical writers also disagree on the death of Judas. Matthew claims that Judas hangs himself in guilt (hence the origin of the 'Judas tree'). The writer of Acts, on the other hand, claims that Judas buys a field into which he throws himself and explodes (Acts 1.18-19). Papias claims Judas became grotesquely obese and filled with worms and pus, and that he died alone because of his stench (*Expositions of the Sayings of the Lord* 4.4). It is worth pointing out that the Greek word used to describe Judas's action, *paradidōmi*, is more literally translated 'to hand over'.

The *Gospel of Judas* is an object of current scholarly debate. According to the National Geographic team that released the document, Judas is a wise hero who alone among the disciples has the courage to free Jesus from his bodily prison. According to others, the text reveals that Judas is as demonized as ever. Dante pictures Judas in the deepest (ninth) level of Hell; the only other people there are Brutus and Cassius who assassinated Julius Caesar! All three are being chewed on by Satan (*Inferno* 34.61-67). Judas and his treachery feature in works as diverse as Chaucer's 'The Friar's Tale' and Emily Brontë's *Wuthering Heights*.

Modern writers of fiction, from Jewish to evangelical Christian authors, have been much more generous with Judas. Typically, Judas is a Zealot, and unlike the other disciples an independent thinker, who abandons Jesus when he realizes the promised kingdom does not involve rebelling against the Romans (Nino Ricci 2002, Anthony Burgess 1979, Nikos Kazantzakis 1960). Other authors depict Judas as simple-minded, unwittingly tricked into his actions (Walter Wangerin 2005, José Saramago 1994). Like some of these authors, Bob Dylan wonders whether Judas 'had God on his side' ('With God on our Side' from the album *The Times They Are A-Changin'*, 1964).

In popular usage, the name Judas is synonymous with betrayal and treachery. A 'Judas goat' lures sheep and cows to their slaughter; a 'Judas kiss' is the appearance of affection with the intent to betray; 'Judas-colored' is red, based on the mediaeval belief that Judas had red hair; a 'Judas trap' is a small door in a window from which one can look without being seen.

Recommended readings. DeConick, April D. *The Thirteenth Apostle: What the Gospel of Judas Really Says*. London: Continuum, 2007. Ehrman, Bart D. *The Lost Gospel of Judas Iscariot: A New Look at Betrayer and Betrayed*. New York: Oxford University Press, 2006. Klassen, William. *Judas: Friend or Betrayer of Jesus?* Minneapolis: Fortress Press, 1996.

See also CHIEF PRIESTS; GNOSTIC, GNOSTICISM; LORD'S SUPPER; FIELD OF BLOOD; TWELVE DISCIPLES, THE; ZEALOTS   [ZAC]

Judas Maccabeus. The third of five sons of Mattathias the Hasmonean, Judas (Maccabeus) is best known for his military leadership against Seleucid rule which eventually led to the re-dedication of the Jerusalem temple and the installation of the Hasmonean dynasty (160–37 BCE). Although Judas and his family were known as the Hasmoneans, Judas himself was often referred to as 'the hammer', or simply 'Judas Maccabeus' (e.g., 1 Macc. 2.66; 5.24; cf. 2.4). Accounts of his military campaigns can be found in the books of 1 Maccabees and 2 Maccabees as well as in the writings of Josephus.

After taking over a group of Jewish revolutionaries following the death of his father (1 Macc. 2.65-68; 3.1-2), Judas began his military career by defeating Apollonius and Seron, leaders of the Syrian government (1 Macc. 3.10-26; cf. Josephus *Ant.* 12.7.1). Judas's initial success continued as he then turned back the Syrian government's retaliation by defeating first the general Gorgias at Emmaus (1 Macc. 4.1-25) and then Lysias, the ruler of the western part of the Seleucid empire (1 Macc. 4.26-35). Following these victories, Judas then expelled his enemies from Jerusalem, regaining much of the city and famously purifying and re-dedicating the temple, the event which has since been commemorated by the Jewish festival of Hanukkah. From there Judas and his brothers rescued Jews in the areas of Galilee, Transjordan, and Gilead (1 Macc. 5.1-68), and then returned to attempt to recapture the citadel of Acra, which had remained in the hands of the Seleucids. However, Lysias led the Syrians to their first victory over Judas and his army at the Battle of Beth Zechariah (162 BCE), though Lysias was forced to return to Syria due to internal conflict and a peaceful agreement was made. Conflict with the Seleucids soon returned, and Judas and his army once again waged war against them, moving Judea toward political independence. Judas even sent a delegation to Rome in hopes of establishing an alliance against the Seleucids (1 Macc. 8). In 160 BCE, Judas was finally killed in battle at Elasa.

A figure of pronounced military prowess, Judas Maccabeus has become an icon of resistance and faith. Early literary references to Judas can be found in Dante's *The Divine Comedy* (Paradiso Canto 18), where he is listed among several great 'warriors' of God including Joshua and Charlemagne, and in Shakespeare's *Love's Labour's Lost* in which he is counted among the 'nine worthies'. In 1872 Henry Wadsworth Longfellow composed a five-verse tragedy entitled *Judas Maccabaeus*. The story of Judas and his military success was also the subject of a three-act oratorio by George Frideric Handel in 1746 to honor England's success against the Jacobite Rising at the Battle of Culloden (1745). The grandiose oratorio, which includes the famous line 'see, the conqu'ring hero comes', is still regarded highly and is even sometimes played to celebrate Hanukkah. In the visual arts, perhaps the best known representation of Judas was produced by the famous French artist Paul Gustave Doré, who illustrated several scenes from 1 Maccabees including Judas standing before the army of Nicanor. In virtually all of these references to Judas Maccabeus, the Jewish leader's military success and nationalistic zeal are celebrated and championed.

Recommended reading. Bar-Kochva, Bezalel. *Judas Maccabaeus: The Jewish Struggle against the Seleucids*. Cambridge: Cambridge University Press, 1989.

See also MACCABEES, THE; MACCABEAN MARTYRS; HANUKKAH [DRB]

Jude, Epistle of. The author of this short epistle identifies himself as Jude, a servant of Jesus and brother of James. It is generally accepted that this Jude is the half-brother of Jesus and that he humbly omits any reference to this relationship in his salutation. Some modern scholars, however, reject this idea. The letter is dated between 62 and 85 CE and has for its focus a strong warning concerning false teachers. The material that addresses these false teachers (vv. 4-18) is strikingly similar to the material in 2 Pet. 2.1–3.3. Most assume there is a literary relationship between 2 Peter and Jude. The epistle of Jude is one of the NT's Catholic Epistles.

The writer claims that his original intentions were to write a different letter but the urgency of the situation concerning the false teachers prompted him to write and encourage the Christians to 'contend for the faith' (v. 3). In the section that follows (vv. 4-18), Jude gives three biblical examples of God's past judgment on the wicked and also refers to scoffers, a similar pattern to that found in 2 Peter. The final verses (20-25) are the main point of the text as he encourages his readers to persevere by means of prayer and to demonstrate mercy toward others as they anticipate God's mercy in their final salvation.

Interestingly, the author of this letter quotes two extra-biblical sources known as pseudepigrapha (*pseudes* 'false' *epigraphe* 'writing' or 'inscription'), documents falsely attributed to other people. In v. 9, he quotes the *Assumption of Moses* and in v. 14, he cites *1 En.* 1.9, a text from *The Book of Watchers*. This has generated considerable discussion as to how authors of the NT use sources in their writings. While some NT authors allude to, or at the least show contact with extra-biblical traditions, Jude is unique in that he uses them explicitly.

Jude's reference to the *Assumption of Moses* refers to Michael the archangel. Moreover, in v. 6 he makes reference to angels who 'left their proper dwelling', an allusion to Gen. 6.1-4 where the 'sons of God', who are thought to be angels, procreate with human women. This tradition is later developed in the *Book of Watchers* (*1 En.* 1–36) where a more detailed account of these relationships is expounded as well as an explanation of the angels' subsequent judgment. Jude demonstrates a particularly clear example of some of the traditions in the Second Temple period concerning angels.

The notion of angels having relationships with humans is portrayed in the film *City of Angels* (1998) where they desire to be human, the sin for which the angels of Jude were condemned. Western culture has a definite fascination with angels and it is readily visible. The television series *Touched by an Angel* enjoyed nine years of success and numerous books have been published on the topic of angels, particularly on how humans and angels can interact. John Travolta gives a not so flattering portrayal of Michael the archangel in *Michael* (1996), and Disney portrays them interacting with humans while playing baseball in *Angels in the Outfield* (2002).

Recommended reading. Moo, Douglas J., *2 Peter and Jude*. NIV Application Commentary. Grand Rapids, Zondervan, 1997.

See also ANGEL; PETER, EPISTLES OF; PSEUDEPIGRAPHA [MDM]

Jude Thaddeus. Judas Thaddaeus is listed among the twelve disciples in Matt. 10.3 and Mark 3.18. He is known in Luke's writings as 'Judas of James' (Luke 6.16; Acts 1.13), which can be taken to mean either 'son of James' (New International Version) or 'brother of James' (KJV). Whether this refers to James son of Alphaeus, James son of Zebedee, or some other James is unclear, although tradition identifies him as the brother of James son of Alphaeus. In the Gospel of John, Judas is once called 'Judas, not Iscariot' (John 14.22).

There were two or perhaps three Judases among the twelve apostles. Judas Iscariot is, of course, well known. Later apocryphal documents refer to Thomas as 'Judas Thomas' (literally 'Judas the Twin'). It is not surprising therefore that Judas Thaddeus is also given a byname. Thaddaeus (*Thaddai*) is possibly derived from an Aramaic root meaning 'chest' or 'nipple'. If this is the derivation of the byname, it might explain the textual variant in some manuscripts of Matt. 10.3, in which he is called 'Lebbaeus who was called Thaddeus'. Lebbaeus (*Libbai*) is related to the Aramaic word for 'heart'. Perhaps Judas was a brawny, barrel-chested man. Perhaps this was in contrast to his brother, 'James the Small'.

Some attribute the letter of Jude to him. Since this letter emphasizes perseverance in difficult circumstances, he is considered the patron saint of desperate causes. One traditional prayer addresses him as 'Saint Jude, Hope of the Hopeless'. The Saint Jude Children's Research Hospital in Memphis, Tennessee is named for him. In some ancient sources, it is claimed that Jude Thaddaeus and Simon the Zealot preached together in Persia and were martyred there. His feast day is October 28 in the West and June 19 in the East.

See also APOSTLE; JUDE, EPISTLE OF; TWELVE DISCIPLES, THE [DJP]

Judea. Judea ('land of the Jews') is the name for the former Kingdom of Judah. Sometime during the Babylonian captivity, the exiles from the Kingdom of Judah began to be called 'Jews'. After they returned to the promised land from exile, the former Kingdom of Judah was called Judea because the majority of the returnees were from the tribe of Judah. It is first mentioned in Ezra 5.8.

The Persians installed a governor of the district of Judea to rule the Jews. Usually the governor was a Jew (Hag. 1.14; 2.2). After Alexander the Great conquered the Persian Empire, he ended the Persian era of Judean history (539–331 BCE). The Greek era of Judean history (331–167 BCE) ended when Jews under the Maccabees defeated the Hellenistic Seleucids in the War of the Maccabees (1 Macc. 5.45; 7.10; 11.28, 34; 12.38). For the next one hundred years or so, Judea was an independent state ruled by the high priest.

Judea became the Roman provincial name for southern Palestine after the Romans took control. The Roman era began in 63 BCE when Pompey conquered Palestine. Roman supporter Herod the Great was made king and ruled from 37 to 4 BCE and his kingdom was divided among his sons after his death. Herod Archelaus ruled Judea from 4 BCE to 6 CE. Judea was then attached to the Roman province of Syria, but was ruled by Roman procurators appointed by the emperor until the Jewish Revolt (67–70 CE). The governors of Judea had their seat of government in Caesarea on the coast. They were supervised by the Proconsul of Syria in Antioch (Luke 3.1).

NT writers (Luke 23.5; Acts 10.37, 26.20) used the term Judea for the land of the Jews, which was wider than just Judea proper. Secular writers of the time including Philo, Strabo, and Tacitus used the term in this wider sense. Josephus also used the term Judea in its wider sense in his *Antiquities* (17.13.5; 18.1.1).

Jerusalem and Bethlehem are located in Judea as are a number of other places important in biblical history, including the life and ministry of Jesus Christ. For instance, it was to Bethlehem of Judea that the wise men went in their search for the Christ child (Luke 2.5-6; cf. Mic. 5.2). It was in Bethany near Jerusalem that Jesus raised Lazarus from the dead. Jesus lived in Galilee, which was outside of Judea; however, whenever he ministered in Judea it was under the terms of the Roman governors, the most famous of whom was Pontius Pilate (26–36 CE). It was at Jerusalem that Jesus was crucified under Pontius Pilate. The resurrection and many post-resurrection appearances, such as the walk to Emmaus, occurred in Judea.

Recommended reading. Hook, Adam. *The Forts of Judea 168 BC–AD 73: From the Maccabees to the Fall of Masada*. Oxford: Osprey Publishing, 2008. Horsley, Richard A. *Scribes, Visionaries, and the Politics of Second Temple Judea*. Louisville, KY: Westminster John Knox Press, 2007. Latimer, Elizabeth Wormeley. *Judea: From Cyrus to Titus 537 B.C. to 70 A.D*. Whitefish, MT: Kessinger Publishing Company, 2010.

See also BETHANY; BETHLEHEM; JERUSALEM; LION OF JUDAH; PERSIA; ROMAN EMPIRE [AJW]

Judges, Book of. The Book of Judges is located in the historical section of the Christian canon and the *nevi'im*, prophetic, section of the Jewish canon. It focuses on the period of settlement in the land of Canaan prior to the establishment of the monarchy. During this period the Israelites were a loose federation of tribes who came together during times of crisis under the leadership of a series of judges. A repetitive cycle occurs in the book that contains four elements: the people sin, they fall under the authority of a foreign nation, they repent and call out to God, and God raises a judge and delivers them. Another theme that runs through the text of Judges is the question of proper leadership and whether or not monarchy is desirable for the nation of Israel.

Traditionally thought to have been written by Samuel, academics now believe that the book has a complex literary history that relates it to the books of Joshua, 1–2 Samuel, and 1–2 Kings. While usually considered part of the same internal division, many have noted the contradictions between the Book of Joshua and the Book of Judges, both in their descriptions of settlement and in the finer details.

The Book of Judges has been used in many ways, including as a pick up line in the Heath Ledger movie *A Knight's Tale*. On a more serious note, John Vassar has demonstrated the parallels between Clint Eastwood's *Unforgiven* and the Book of Judges. Cecil B. DeMille also made one of his biblical epics based on the story of the last judge, Samson, and his relationship with the Philistine woman Delilah.

It has also entered the realm of popular culture with the comic book renderings of Mario Ruiz and Jerry Novick. This is not the only place that the Book of Judges has influenced modern literature; Ellie Wiesel, the famous holocaust survivor, begins his novel *The Judges* with a rabbinic quote regarding this text and intends his novel to serve as a dialogue with the biblical book.

Recommended reading. Ackerman, Susan. *Warrior, Dancer, Seductress, Queen: Women in Judges and Biblical Israel*. Anchor Bible Reference Library. New York: Doubleday, 1998. Brettler, Marc Zvi. *The Book of Judges*. Old Testament Readings. London and New York: Routledge, 2002.

See also ABIMELECH; BARAK; CALEB; DEBORAH; DELILAH; EHUD; GIDEON; JEPHTHAH; SAMSON [EW]

Judgment. In biblical literature, the judgments of God are applications of his law to human behavior. He is the supreme judge (Gen. 18.25) and his actions are fair and true (Isa. 5.16). Because God is the judge, his people may appeal to him for justice, vindication, or deliverance from evil when oppressd. To give relief from evil to his people, God judges their enemies. The OT prophets announced a 'day of Yahweh' that would be a day of national salvation and judgment for Israel (Amos 1.3; Hab. 1.5), and doom for their enemies. NT writers echo the prophetic tradition when they declare that God is impartial punishes all wickedness (e.g., Rom. 1.18; Heb. 12.23). Jesus warns against false standards of judgment and their consequences in Matt. 7.1-5. The Bible speaks of a Last Judgment, a time when evil and good will be permanently separated (Acts 17.31).

Judgment has been an important theme in Christian literature and art. Michelangelo's massive mural of the Last Judgment in the Sistine Chapel, executed near the end of his life, depicts souls rising to heaven or descending to hell in the light of Christ's judgment. The *Left Behind* books are fictional accounts about the coming judgment of God.

Recommended reading. Miller, Patrick D., Jr. *Sin and Judgment in the Prophets*. Atlanta: Society of Biblical Literature, 1982. Reiser, Marius. *Jesus and Judgment*. Minneapolis: Augsburg Fortress Press, 2003. Via, Dan Otto. *Divine Justice, Divine Judgment: Rethinking the Judgment of Nations*. Minneapolis: Augsburg Fortress Press, 2007.

See also DAY, OF JUDGMENT/OF THE LORD/OF WRATH; DEATH; ESCHATOLOGY; HEAVEN; HELL; RIGHTEOUSNESS; SIN; WICKEDNESS [AJW]

Judith, Book of. Judith is a deuterocanonical book, included in the Septuagint and therefore in the Christian OT of both Catholic and Eastern Orthodox Church, while apocryphal to the Jewish and Protestant canon.

The dating is uncertain, though many recent scholars favor the period of the Maccabees (first and second century BCE). Originally written in Hebrew, the oldest surviving versions are written in Greek. The book tells of the Assyrian's invasion into Palestine and the siege of a city called Bethulia, which holds the pass to Judaea. In an apparently desperate situation of military inferiority, Judith, a daring widow from Bethulia, goes to the camp of the enemy general, Holofernes, ensnaring him with her outstanding beauty. One night when Holofernes is excessively drunk, Judith enters his tent, decapitates him, and together with her loyal maid (who frequently is depicted in paintings along with Judith) takes his head back to Bethulia. Having lost their leader, the Assyrians disperse. Judith, as a chaste widow, remains unmarried until death, despite her many suitors.

The book's historicity has long been disputed. Some consider it the first historical novel, while others have focused on its allegorical dimension or possible copying mistakes in the manuscript tradition to even out its historical fissures. Indeed, the narrative attaches to historical facts, persons, and places rather loosely; the story is set 'in the twelfth year of the reign of Nebuchadnezzar, who reigned over the Assyrians in Nineveh' (Jdt. 1.5). In fact, Nebuchadnezzar II did conquer Judah, but he apparently was never king of Nineveh, which was destroyed shortly before he ascended the throne in 605 BCE Also, the city of Bethulia, though according to the text large and widely famous, remains obscure and much debated. Still, its historical allusions give the story an air of a meticulous report with a definite time and place, a feature it shares with, while at the same time in this aspect surpasses, those of Esther, Daniel, or Tobit.

Judith has long inspired literature and the arts, including paintings by Caravaggio, Michelangelo, and Gustav Klimt. Friedrich Hebbel's *Judith* (1841) or the silent movie *Judith of Bethulia* (1914) count among the most prominent dramatic realizations. From oratorios by Vivaldi, Mozart, or Scarlatti to an opera staged in 2007 by French composer Philippe Fénelon, Judith has constantly been present in the history of music as well. Since the Middle Ages, readers of the story suggested Holofernes attempted to rape Judith, an idea possibly hinted at in Jdt. 12.12. In this respect, a series of famous paintings that was created by Artemisia Gentileschi (d. 1653) after being raped by her teacher sheds notable light on the reinterpretation of the story.

Apart from the Book of Judith, the Hebrew name *Ju'dith* ('Jewess') is also attributed to one of Esau's wives, daughter of Beeri the Hittite (Gen. 26.34; in Gen. 36.2-14 she is called Aholibamah). The corresponding masculine form appears in Jer. 36.14, 21, 23.

Recommended reading. Stocker, Margarita. *Judith, Sexual Warrior*. New Haven: Yale University Press, 1998.

See also APOCRYPHA, DEUTEROCANONICALS AND INTERTESTAMENTALS; SEPTUAGINT [HK]

Junia. In the concluding chapter of his letter to the congregations in Rome, Paul sends greetings to 'Andronicus and Junia, my relatives who were in prison with me; they are prominent among the apostles' (Rom. 16.7 NRSV). The female name Junia occurs only here in the Bible. However, whether this name refers to a female or male person is in dispute. The controversy is best illustrated through a comparison of different Bible translations. Instead of the female name Junia, the RSV, NIV, the German Luther Bible 1984, and the French *Traduction Oecumenique* feature the male name Junias. On grammatical grounds, the Greek accusative form *Iunian* could refer to either gender since the Greek text of the NT was written without accents. But the female name Junia is attested in other sources of the NT period while the male name Junias is not. This makes the NRSV option the most likely choice. This decision is significant since Paul calls both Andronicus and Junia, who were probably a married couple, 'prominent among the apostles' (the frequent translation 'well known to the apostles' is unlikely). Hence early Christians knew a female apostle, and the Christian church later venerated the couple in the traditional feast of Saints Andronicus and Junia.

Despite the evidence of the biblical text and the weight of the church tradition, the reformer Martin Luther decided to change the female name Junia into the male Junias when translating Rom. 16.7 for his German Bible. This latter name has since been favored in other translations as well, to be reconsidered only recently. Regrettably, the editorial history of NT texts contains evidence that the names of women have often been changed or omitted, and that efforts have been made to downplay their importance (e.g., the original text of Acts 17.4 mentioned 'prominent women' among Paul's converts, but scribes changed the text to say the converts are 'wives of prominent men'; in Col. 4.15 the original text mentioned a church meeting in the home of a woman named Nympha, which scribes changed to the male form Nymphas).

Recommended reading. Brooten, Bernadette J. 'Junia ... Outstanding among the Apostles' (Romans 16:7)'. In *Women Priests: A Catholic Commentary on the Vatican Declaration.* Ed. L. and A. Swidler. Pp. 141-44. New York: Paulist Press, 1977. Jewett, Robert. *Romans: A Commentary.* Hermeneia. Minneapolis: Fortress Press, 2007.

See also PHOEBE, ROMANS, EPISTLE TO THE; SCRIBES; WOMAN [CAE]

Justice. This term translates the Hebrew *mišpāṭ* and the Greek *krisis, ekdiktēsis,* and *dikaiosunē.* This concept is common in the Bible, particularly in the HB. Often God is portrayed as the administer of justice on both Israel and her enemies. The Israelites were called to reflect this attribute of God in their dealings with others, especially those for whom justice was not easily obtained, such as the poor, orphans, and widows (Isa. 10.1-2). Justice was also seen as part of God's redemptive action on behalf of Israel, as in Isaiah where God's justice is believed to be a 'light to the nations' (51.4) and that 'Zion will be redeemed by justice' (1.27). The theme of justice was also prominent during the last centuries before the beginning of the Common Era, which can be seen by the sheer number of times it appears in the documents of this time. In the NT this theme is much less pronounced, though it is somewhat prominent in Luke, where Jesus, in 11.42, accuses the Pharisees of neglecting justice and love and, in 18.1-8, tells a parable of a judge who is reluctant to show justice to a widow. In addition, the notion of fairness is sometimes associated with justice in the Bible, such as in Lev. 19.15 where the Israelites are commanded to 'not be partial to the poor or defer to the great' but that 'with justice' they should judge their neighbors.

The issue of justice towards those with little say in this world was not ignored by the early church, though most of the efforts focused on personal, not corporate charity. During and after the Reformation many groups of Christians attempted to reform the structures of society itself in order to offer welfare to those in need. However, with the focus on individualism during the Enlightenment, personal charity again became the focus. It has not been until more recent times that the church has again made concerted efforts to live out God's justice corporately. Some of these attempts include the Social Gospel movement (led by Walter Rauschenbusch), the various incarnations of liberation theology (popular among South American and African-American churches), and justice-focused faith communities (such as the Mennonites and Quakers). For many, Martin Luther King, Jr's sermon entitled 'I Have a Dream', which is based on Amos 5.24, is a manifesto of Christian justice. Others are emboldened by politicians who promise voters and constituents that they will fight for justice while in office. Even though the predominant image of justice for many is still that of judgment, the notion of fairness has never been far behind.

See also JUSTIFICATION; RIGHTEOUSNESS [JMB]

Justification. From the Greek words *dikaiōsis, dikaiosunē,* and *dikaiōma,* it appears justification is a gift from God that is a result of his grace (Rom. 5.16-21) but according to the Apostle Paul, this gift is made available through the death and resurrection of Christ (Rom. 4.25) and not by the Law, lest Christ's sacrifice be made superfluous (Gal. 2.21). Seeing that there are many *dik*-family words in the Septuagint, which translate the Hebrew *mišpāṭ,* one could state that Paul saw the cross as the purest example of God's justice. Also related is the verb 'justify' (Greek *dikaioō*). The basic thrust of this word seems to be that one is brought into right relationship with God based not on 'works prescribed by the Law' but on faith, whether one is a Jew or a Gentile (Rom. 3.28-30). Even though it appears that Paul is saying that human faith plays a part in the justification process, he makes it clear that it is God who justifies (Rom. 8.33) through his grace (Rom. 3.24). However, there are divergent voices in the NT about justification as well. In Matt. 12.36-37, Jesus says that people will be justified by what they said and did not say, and even Paul, in Rom. 2.13, says that the doers of the Law will be justified, which seems to be in agreement with Jas 2.24.

In the early church, there was little discussion of justification apart from a few references (e.g., *1 Clem.* 32.4) but this changed with the controversy between Augustine and Pelagius. In short, Pelagius taught that humans were not born corrupted and could maintain this innocence indefinitely, while Augustine taught that humans were infected with sin from birth and were in need of God's grace in order to be justified. Augustine's view became the official view of the church, though over time certain abuses, such as indulgences, began to weaken its hold. Luther spoke of some of these abuses, arguing that humans are in need of saving and that nothing they do can bring about salvation. Calvin taught (*Institutes* 3.11.2) that through Christ's intercession humans are justified, meaning they are reckoned as righteous in God's eyes and therefore accepted as such. Catholics and Protestants still hold different conceptions of justification, though some ground has been gained, as evidenced by the 1999 document entitled 'Joint Declaration on Justification by Faith', which was written by representatives of the Lutheran World Federation and the Catholic Church.

See also GRACE; JUSTICE; LAW; RIGHTEOUSNESS; SALVATION [JMB]

K

Kenosis. The Greek word *kenosis* in Phil. 2.7 describes Christ in his incarnation as 'emptied out'. As the NRSV puts it, he 'emptied himself, taking the form of a slave, being born in human likeness' (cf. 2 Cor. 9.3). The term, then, touches on the mystery of the divine becoming human, or to use John's language, the Word (Christ) becoming flesh and dwelling among us (John 1.14).

See also PAUL, THE APOSTLE; PHILIPPIANS, EPISTLE TO THE [CDR]

Keturah. Following the death of his wife Sarah (Gen. 23.2), Abraham married Keturah who bore him several children (25.1-6). The brief account of her story in Genesis and a genealogy in 1 Chronicles (see 1.32-33) note she was Abraham's concubine, suggesting a status inferior to Sarah's. That 'Abraham gave all he had to Isaac', the son of Sarah (Gen. 25.5-6), and sent the children of his concubine away from this favored son, further supports this conclusion. The Jewish historian Josephus links Keturah's grandchildren with the region of Troglodytes, meaning areas along the coasts of the Red Sea. He also mentions the curious detail that Ophren or Epher (cf. Gen. 25.4), one of Keturah and Abraham's descendants, invaded Lybia and that Epher's grandchildren in turn named the area 'Africa' after him (Josephus, *Antiquites of the Jews* 1.15.238). No doubt influenced by Josephus's remarks, several writers in later centuries circulated theories linking the Jews with African cultures, as is the case with the eighteenth-century biblical commentator John Gill, and the nineteenth-century author Robert Benjamin Lewis, in his book *Light and Truth* (1843).

See also ABRAHAM [MJG]

Key of David. Appearing only in Isa. 22.22 and Rev. 3.7, the phrase 'key of David' refers to a certain final authority. The apocalyptic vision of John the Seer speaks of different angels attached to the seven churches in Asia Minor, and further describes the messages sent to each one. With reference to the authority of the one who was sending the message to the angel of the church in Philadelphia, the phrase key of David was used in symbolizing the ultimate power that rests with Jesus Christ.

The phrase is symbolic of the everlasting covenant made by God with the Davidic dynasty (2 Sam. 7.16). In tracing Jesus' genealogy, Matthew was sure to point out that he was a direct descendant of David (Matt. 1.1-17). The key of David also symbolizes access to the promised everlasting kingdom of David. In the context of the vision shown to John, however, the phrase speaks specifically to the understanding of the power residing with the one who is descended from David and has all authority to restore the kingdom to those who have been patient and deserving (Rev. 3.7-13; cf. Acts 1.6-7).

In contemporary Western culture, this phrase contributes to the plot of *Matrix Reloaded* (2003), the second installment of the critically acclaimed *Matrix* trilogy, written and directed by the Wachowski brothers. The movie continues the story of machines battling humans, using key words and concepts from biblical prophecy. Prominent in this sequel is the use of 'The One', a phrase similar to the description in Revelation of the person who can close doors that no one can open, and open doors no one can close (3.7). In addition, in reference to this imagery of opening and shutting doors, there is a character named the Keymaker. In the movie, the Keymaker made keys to several portals and doors that were hidden within the Matrix. Kept as prisoner, the Keymaker was rescued by Neo (anagram for One) who proceeded to use the keys to open different portals.

The underlying theme to the phrase and its occurrence in both the prophecy and the movie is the hope for renewal. A common theme in apocalyptic literature, it describes the discontent with the present world and the struggle between good and evil. Of crucial importance is the fact that power usually lies in one person, who has the key to save humans from total destruction, which in this case is the 'Key of David'.

See also DAVID; COVENANT; HOPE; REVELATION, BOOK OF; KEYS OF THE KINGDOM [GOA]

Keys of the Kingdom. The phrase originates in biblical passages referring to 'the key of the house of David' (Isa. 22.22; cf. Rev. 3.7). The familiar phrase 'keys of the kingdom' usually incorporates the idea of gaining access to heaven. These keys are entrusted to St Peter in the popular imagination—often known as the 'Golden Keys'—and as a result appear in iconography associated with the Papacy because the the Popes trace their spiritual descent from St Peter (cf. Matt. 16.18). In fact, the coat of arms of Vatican City, and the design on the Vatican flag, show two keys crossing each other, representing the Keys of the Kingdom. The Coat of Arms and the flag were formally recognized on June 7, 1929 as part of the Lateran Treaty, although the keys had been in use as a part of the design for seals and coats of arms for many Popes who lived in Rome. The term helped form the title of Sir Nicolas Cheetham's history of the popes, *The Keepers of the Keys* (1982).

The term 'The Keys of the Kingdom' also became famous with the novel of that name by the British writer A.J. Cronin, published in 1941. It told the story of a Scottish missionary priest in China and was made into a film in 1944 starring Gregory Peck.

Recommended reading. Cheetham, Nicolas. *Keepers of the Keys: The Pope in History*. London: Macdonald & Co., 1982.

See also PETER, THE APOSTLE; KEY OF DAVID   [JC]

King James Version of the Bible (KJV). The King James Version, or Authorized Version of the Bible (1611) is the translation of the Holy Scriptures authorized by James I, king of England. It was the main translation of the Bible in English for well over three centuries and has had a profound impact upon the development of the English language and its literature, not to mention the English speaking churches and their spirituality. Quite plausibly, more copies of this book have been printed than any other. Although it is now 400 years old, it continues to be printed in large quantities despite the availability of numerous other English language translations.

The KJV was as much the result of politics as religion. At the time, the most popular Bible in England was the Geneva Bible and not the Bishops Bible, which was the translation authorized by the ecclesiastical authorities of the English Church. The Calvinist Puritans were using the Geneva Bible which was the translation published by John Knox and other Marian Exiles at Geneva (1559). The Geneva Bible was accurate and had literary merit but it included numerous margin notes intended to help readers understand difficult passages. King James found a number of these notes objectionable, particularly those referring to political issues.

In 1604 the Hampton Court Conference met at the summons of King James in order to deal with matters of religious concern in the United Kingdom. He supported the suggestion that a new translation of the Scriptures be made. The new translation was prepared by three panels of scholars, numbering 47 in all. They were instructed to follow the Bishop's Bible and were not to include any margin notes. The translators worked with the Hebrew and Greek manuscripts available to them as they translated. Afterward they compared their work for style as well as accuracy with the older English translations.

Private and public reading of the KJV by English speaking Protestants influenced generations and its literary influence is inestimable. Its style, stories, images, doctrines, and other literary merits have influence poets, novelists, and many other authors, so much so that it is nearly impossible to discuss English literature without reference to the KJV. The titles of many literary works, such as William Faulkner's *Absalom, Absalom*, Ernest Hemingway's *The Sun Also Rises*, Eugene O'Neill's 'Lazarus', and literary characters such as Ishmael, Ahab, and Leviathan in *Moby Dick*, or Adam in Nathan Hawthorne's *Mosses from an Old Manse*, are drawn from the KJV.

Recommended reading. Daniell, David. *The Bible in English: Its History and Influence*. New Haven: Yale University Press, 2003. MacGrath, Alister. *In the Beginning: The Story of the King James Bible and How It Changed a Nation, a Language, and a Culture*. New York: Doubleday, 2001. Nicolson, Adam. *God's Secretaries: The Making of the King James Bible*. New York: HarperCollins, 2003.

See also BIBLE; BOOK; GREEK LANGUAGE; HEBREW LANGUAGE; SCRIPTURES   [AJW]

King of Kings. This phrase, along with the alternative Lord of Lords, is a royal title, meaning king of (or among or above) all kings, ascribed to supreme rulers in antiquity; its subsequent ascriptions to God and especially to Jesus Christ are acts of theopolitical appropriation on the part of the NT writers, forcing collisions between Christology and politics.

Classical sources attest the use of these titles, sometimes as true honorifics, but also with derision and irony. Plutarch reports that Pompey refused to address the ruler of Parthia, a rival to Rome's empire, with his customary title, king of kings; Pompey also hears the title applied mockingly, when he seems to be enjoying his martial authority rather than engaging Julius Caesar in battle, according to both Plutarch and Appian. Appian's account of Rome's Syrian War labels Tigranes II, the Armenian king, king of kings because of his successful annexation of nearby principalities—but he reigns only with the permission of Pompey and Rome.

Rulers in the biblical tradition are also addressed with the king of kings honorific. It is applied to Artaxerxes in Ezra 7.12, and to Nebuchadnezzar in Dan. 2.37 and Ezek. 26.7 (not without irony because this king of kings unwittingly acts under the lordship of Israel's God). Lord of lords is used with reference to Israel's 'God of gods' (Deut. 10.17), the deity whose lordship is again connoted by his own most frequent names, *Adonai* and YAHWEH, here and in the repeated liturgical thanksgiving of Ps. 136.1-3. The NT authors continue to foreground divine sovereignty with respect to these titles. Paul refers to God as 'the blessed and only Sovereign, the King of kings and Lord of lords' (1 Tim. 6.15), and John the Revelator twice names Christ with the combined appellation (Rev. 17.14; 19.16), implying that the titles are deserved on account of a victory already won, a victory at odds with the kind of triumphs that Rome celebrated.

Revelation's deployment of the combined titles has had an enduring effect in the Christian tradition and the Western world. The *King of Kings* title has been borrowed for two major movies, first for Cecil B. DeMille's 1927 silent film, and again in 1961. The epithet has acquired a cumulative currency, appearing as the title of songs, novels, and even video games, sometimes with only tenuous connections to its earlier monarchical and divine applications. The perennial popularity of Handel's oratorio *Messiah*, with its stirring repetition of the phrase 'King of kings, and Lord of lords' during the 'Hallelujah' chorus, ensures at least a note of continuity with Revelation's textual images.

The lasting theopolitical significance of these honorifics emerges in the imbrication of human and divine titles; once ascribed to the figure at the heart of Christianity, a title cannot be lightly reassigned to a mortal ruler. The ramifications of addressing God the Father or God the Son with superlative forms of both 'King' and 'Lord' deserve further investigation, particularly in light of the issues of state and imperial sovereignty that have dominated international relations at the dawn of the twenty-first century.

Recommended reading. Caird, G.B. *A Commentary on the Revelation of St John the Divine.* Harper's New Testament Commentaries. New York: Harper & Row, 1966. Howard-Brook, Wes, and Anthony Gwyther. *Unveiling Empire: Reading Revelation Then and Now.* Maryknoll, NY: Orbis, 1999. Schnackenburg, Rudolf. *God's Rule and Kingdom.* Trans. J. Murray. Freiburg: Herder; Montreal: Palm, 1963.

See also EMPEROR; KINGSHIP; LORD [MFL]

King of Tyre. There are two biblical figures that carry this title. The first is Hiram, king of Tyre, who supplies building materials for David's house (2 Sam. 5.11; 1 Chron. 14.1) and later for Solomon's temple (1 Kgs 5.1-12). The second is the subject of an oracle in Ezek. 28.1-19, which has produced an array of interpretations from Western readers of the Bible.

Interpreters of Ezek. 28.1-19 have often noted parallels with humanity's expulsion from Eden in the Book of Genesis (Ezek. 28.13-16; cf. Gen. 3.22-24), and have thus argued that the oracle is an indictment of human (especially royal) pride. Another interpretation is that the oracle criticizes Melqart, the chief deity of Tyre during the first millennium BCE, whose name means 'king of the city'. Ancient inscriptions refer to Melqart as the Baal ('master' or 'ruler') of Tyre, and his cult was widespread throughout the Phoenician colonies of the Mediterranean. In this line of thought, Ezekiel's collection of oracles against prideful Tyre (Ezek. 26.1–28.19) concludes with a mythical condemnation of the city's chief god. The language of Ezek. 28.1-19 is reminiscent of Ps. 82, which pronounces judgment against the divine council, and of Isa. 14.12-20, which likens the king of Babylon to a fallen celestial being. In some Christian interpretive traditions, therefore, the prince or king of Tyre has been understood as a pseudonym for Satan, whose fall from heaven is briefly mentioned in the NT (cf. Luke 10.18; Rev. 12.7-10). However, nothing in Ezekiel's oracle itself directly supports a link between the king of Tyre and the figure of Satan.

Shakespeare employs a Tyrian ruler in his play *Pericles, Prince of Tyre*, but the play's main character does not suffer the fate of Ezekiel's king; the play is a moral account of a Tyrian prince who is forced to flee his home after revealing the incestuous actions of a neighboring monarch. Shakespeare's plot is loosely based on the Medieval story 'Apollonius of Tyre', which exists in Latin and Old English versions.

See also BAAL; DIVINE COUNCIL; EZEKIEL, BOOK OF; FALLEN ANGELS; GARDEN OF EDEN; LUCIFER; SATAN [IDW]

Kingdom of God (Kingdom of Heaven). The kingdom of God was central in Jesus' proclamation. He did not invent the phrase, however. The term originates in the OT (see e.g., Pss 103.19; 145.11-13) where it means the universal sovereignty of God. It appears also in the Dead Sea Scrolls and rabbinic writings. In the Gospels, the kingdom of God or kingdom of Heaven (Matthew's favorite term) refers to a present reality (e.g., Matt. 11.1-19; Luke 11.20); a future reality (Matt. 6.10; 10.23); a commodity one must seek or possess (Mark 10.14-15; Matt. 5.3; 6.33; Luke 6.20; 12.31); and a sphere to be entered (Mark 9.47;10.23-25; Matt. 5.20; 7.21; 18.19; 23.13).

Because of the diversity of the sayings and the fact that Jesus did not explicate this term, the concept of the kingdom of God has been interpreted in many ways down the ages. Ritschl, a nineteenth-century theologian, defines the kingdom of God as a society motivated by love; Jesus teaches that love is the guiding principle for the sons and daughters of the kingdom. This view conceives the kingdom of God in social terms and as an entity that human beings can establish. Johannes Weiss in his book *Proclamation of the Kingdom* (1892) submits that Jesus was an apocalyptic figure waiting for the establishment of the kingdom on earth. He wished God would vanquish all forms of evil and his ideas were developed by Albert Schweitzer who shaped this view by saying that Jesus considered himself as a catalyst in bringing about the kingdom. He sent his disciples to go and proclaim the kingdom and even taught them to pray for the coming of the kingdom. Albert Schweitzer further contends that Jesus provoked the Romans in an attempt to compel God to intervene but was killed in the process. C.H. Dodd, in *Parables of the Kingdom* (1935), contradicts this position, arguing that the kingdom of God has come. He asserts that the Greek word *engiken* in Mark 1.15, usually translated as 'is near', should be understood as 'has arrived' (*ephthasen*) as in Matt. 12.28 and Luke 11.20. Werner G. Kümmel in his *Theology of the New Testament* (1974) rejects both the apocalyptic and realized views. In harmony with Johannes Jeremias, he subscribes to the view that the kingdom of God is both present and future—the 'yet' and 'not yet', i.e. that it is within our glimpse but will be fully consummated in future, a belief common in most Catholic and Protestant churches in the West.

See also ESCHATOLOGY; PARABLE [ET]

Kings, Books of. The Books of Kings in the HB belong together with Joshua, Judges, and the Books of Samuel as part of the Former Prophets. In the Christian canon, these books are part of the OT's historical books. They were written in Hebrew and in the beginning constituted just one book. Once translated into Greek, however, they proved to be too long for one scroll (unlike the consonantal Hebrew text) and the unified Book of Kings was divided into two parts. The content of these books is closely related to the Books of Samuel for they begin with the last moments of King David's life, the king whose life, but not death, was described in 1 and 2 Samuel. The Septuagint connects the Books of Samuel and Kings into one story by calling them 1–4 Books of Kingdoms (or Reigns). The Books of Kings begin with the strife among David's sons over the Israelite throne and the king's appointment of Solomon as his successor. After the description of Solomon's reign (1 Kgs 2–11) comes the account of the division of Israel into two kingdoms: the northern kingdom of Israel, and the southern kingdom of Judah. The narrator traces the events in both kingdoms (unlike the Chronicler) focusing more on the northern state. After the destruction of Israel by Assyria, the narrator focuses solely on Judah and the events leading to the fall of the kingdom and the exile of the nation to Babylon. The Books end with Evil-merodach, king of Babylon, releasing Jehoiachin and elevating him above other kings allowing him to dine regularly at the royal table. Thus, the Books end in a positive and hopeful note in otherwise tragic circumstances. This end, however, is not only the closure of the discussed books but also the closure of the so-called Deuteronomistic History (Deuteronomy—2 Kings, without Ruth), and of the Primary History (Genesis–2 Kings, without Ruth). The Books of Kings are not a simple record of history but rather a theological interpretation of the events described. The narrator often refers the interested readers to sources containing fuller historical accounts of reigns of the kings. The author of the Books, thus, feels free to pick and choose those stories that support his theological thesis which constitutes the purpose for which the Books were written.

Some of the Bible's most memorable characters appear in 1–2 Kings. Among those often appearing in the arts and literature are Solomon, the Queen of Sheba, Jezebel, Elijah, and Elisha.

Recommended reading. Walsh, Jerome T. *1 Kings*. Berit Olam. Collegeville, MN: Liturgical Press, 1996. Cohn, Robert L. *2 Kings*. Berit Olam. Collegeville, MN: Liturgical Press, 2000.

See also FORMER PROPHETS; CHRONICLES, BOOKS OF; SAMUEL, BOOKS OF [RJM]

Kingship. The Sumerian king list from ancient Mesopotamia states that kingship descended from heaven. Similarly, the ancient Egyptians considered their king, Pharaoh, to be a divine figure, the beloved of the gods and the giver of life. In the Bible, too, kingship has strong connections with the divine. Indeed, the biblical writers saw God, and not a human, as the ultimate king over Israel and indeed, the entire world (e.g., Num. 23.21; Judg. 8.23; Ps. 47; Isa. 44.6). In this view, which other ancient Near Eastern societies shared, the human king was merely a vassal, part of a hierarchy in which God was supreme ruler.

The HB presents the ideal king as a divine servant, as shepherd and righteous protector of God's people (e.g., 2 Sam. 5.2; 1 Chron. 11.2; Ezek. 37.24; Ps. 72). God chooses the king (and thus the dynasty), and he and his descendants must observe God's law with humility and diligence (cf. Deut. 17.14-20). The king is (one of) God's 'anointed' ('messiah'; e.g., 2 Sam. 23.1; Ps. 2.2; 2 Chron. 6.42), and even God's 'son' (e.g., 2 Sam. 7.14; Ps. 2.7), titles the NT Gospels utilize to describe Jesus (e.g., Matt. 1.1; Mark 1.1; Luke 4.41; John 20.31). Some passages in the HB, however, are wary of human kingship and rather critical of the institution, stressing God's role as the only true king (e.g., 1 Sam. 8.4-22). Other passages envision a utopian future in which an ideal Davidic king will reign for eternity (e.g., Ezek. 37.24-28). As noted, in the NT divine kingship rests upon the figure of Jesus who is a descendant of David (cf. Matt. 1.1-17) and the 'king of kings' (Rev. 19.16) that God has exalted above all others (cf. Phil. 2.9-11).

Nevertheless, in Rom. 13.1-7, Paul encourages his readers to subject themselves to earthly rulers because authority to rule on earth comes directly from God. Therefore, not surprisingly, the concepts of divinely instituted kingship and divine royal authority have had a strong impact on Western governance. From Constantine I to Charlemagne to James I of England, historical monarchs have associated their royal privilege and power with the divine. James I actually wrote on the subject in *The True Law of Free Monarchies* (1598), claiming that kings hold a special, divinely granted status among humanity, and basing his argument on biblical texts. In the book *Leviathan* (1651), the philosopher Thomas Hobbes promoted absolute sovereignty of monarchies, including ecclesiastical sovereignty. Kings and queens thus invoked various forms of divine legitimization for their absolute rule until the nineteenth century. Even today, Canadian coins carry an image of Queen Elizabeth II along with the Latin expression 'D.G. Regina' (*Dei Gratia Regina*, Queen by the grace of God). Following the American and French revolutions, however, the power of absolute monarchies began to fade in the West, as did the idea of kingship as a sacred office.

Some of the most famous works of Western art and literature depict biblical kings and the concepts associated with biblical kingship. Among these are Michelangelo's sculpture of David (1504) and Handel's choral composition, *Messiah* (1741). In the lengthy poem *Confessio Amantis*, fourteenth-century English poet John Gower—a contemporary of Chaucer—employs biblical examples to express his views on the virtues of kingship; and Milton alludes to Ps. 2 in Book V of *Paradise Lost* (1674), referring to the Son of God as the anointed king of angels.

See also CHRIST; DAVID; KING OF KINGS; KINGDOM OF GOD; SON OF GOD [IDW]

Korah. Korah is a character appearing in Num. 16 who stages a rebellion against Moses. The reason for the rebellion is ambiguous, with Korah and his compatriots chaffing under Moses's leadership for some reason. The narrative indicates that this feeling was probably widespread, in that Korah was able to recruit Dathan and Abiram, sons of Eliab, and On son of Peleth—Reubenites—as well as 250 prominent members of the assembly of Israel to join with him. This is even more significant given that Korah is a Levite, a member of the tribe responsible for the spiritual wellbeing of Israel. In effect, the rebellion is an attempt to subvert the leadership structure within the camp of Israel, since Moses and Aaron, the God appointed leaders, are also Levites. In the end, the conflict is resolved by a show of force by God: the ground opens up and swallows Korah and his family, as well as Dathan, Abiram, and On, and their families. Similarly the 250 men from the assembly are consumed by fire from before God.

Some familiar motifs appear in the narrative. God, as in so many other episodes in Numbers, desires to destroy all of Israel, but relents when Moses intercedes for the people. In the end, only the rebels and their families are destroyed, conveying the idea that those who question Moses's leadership and authority will be forcefully punished. Nevertheless, the notion of divine mercy is also demonstrated by God's turning away from destroying Israel in its entirety. However, this narrative ultimately communicates the idea that social conformity to divinely sanctioned leadership and governance structures is what is expected of the Israelites; one only engages in dissent at the risk of harsh responses from the powers that be. In other words, this episode embodies and projects social values that ensure that the established authority and governance structures remain intact. This idea is not only found in the HB, but also within some contemporary political movements. By and large political conservatives desire to maintain already established authority structures and social norms, whereas liberals and radical leftists tend to advocate the reform of these structures, or their elimination for the purposes of rebuilding society. Some political theories, such as those popularized by Slavoj Žižek and the other writers in the well-known Radical Thinkers Series tend to be of the radical leftist orientation. In contrast, theorists like Jürgen Habermas, Richard Rorty, and Charles Taylor tend to be more moderate, characterizing themselves as liberal democrats. Each of these theorists, however, would probably interpret the Korah narrative as a biblical episode depicting a quashed social revolution.

Yet the name Korah also occurs in the Book of Psalms where several psalms are attributed to the Sons of Korah. Many of these psalms are written from the perspective of an exiled people, mourning the loss of home, and expressing a complex relationship with God—God being the one who both punishes and redeems. The Sons of Korah are also credited with several psalms of celebration, where God is explicitly praised as the sovereign over Israel and the entire earth. It is unlikely that there is any connection between the Korah mentioned in Numbers and the Korah mentioned in the Book of Psalms. In evangelical Christian popular culture, a group called the Sons of Korah have set many of the psalms to music. Similarly Leonard Cohen has written a collection of poems entitled *Book of Mercy*, which explores many of the themes in the Korahite psalms.

See also MOSES; NUMBERS, BOOK OF [SL]

L

Laban. Laban is Rebekah's brother and Jacob's uncle. He gave his two daughters to Jacob in marriage. Laban's story plays a significant role in the Jacob cycle (Gen. 24.29–31.55). Laban's father is Abraham's brother (Gen. 11.27). The genealogy of the branch of Na'hor is traced in Gen. 22.20-24, bringing the family down to Rebekah, and it stops there without mentioning Laban. The text states only that among the eight sons Mil'cah bore to Na'hor it was Bethu'el who became the father of Rebekah. When Rebekah appears in the narrative (Gen. 24.15, 24), she is referred to in a way that evokes to the reader the genealogy already given (22.23); but when her brother Laban is introduced in the story, he is related to his sister by the specific announcement, 'Rebekah had a brother whose name was Laban' (24.29). Laban takes prominent part in the reception of Abraham's servant, and in arranging the marriage of Isaac and his sister Rebekah (Gen. 24). The narrative indicates the man's eager hospitality, brought about after his discovery of the gold and jewelry bestowed upon his sister on behalf of Isaac (24.29-30). Influence, greed, and egotism seem to be dominant characteristics.

Nonetheless, the most significant stories involving Laban involve his extensive interactions with Jacob. Isaac blessed Jacob and sent him to his uncle Laban who lived in Paddan-aram (28.5). Laban received him and offered his two daughters, Leah and Rachel, in marriage (Gen. 29.12-30). Jacob wanted to marry Rachel, the one he first met at the well. Laban required Jacob to serve him for seven years as bride price for Rachel. This Jacob did, but Laban deceived him into marrying Leah instead (29.26). Once Jacob realized the deception he insisted on receiving Rachel, but Laban asked him to work another seven years for her, which he did (Gen. 29.15-20, 27; 30.27-43). Jacob's wives bore him sons and a daughter in rapid succession. Meanwhile, the relation with his uncle worsened. One day, Jacob decided to return to his fatherland. Outwitted by Jacob and Rachel (Gen. 30.37-43; 31.1-21), Laban pursued them to get back his flocks and the statuettes that represented his family's spirit. He overtook them and finally made peace (Gen. 31.22-54). Nothing is said of Laban after Jacob left him. Despite the Bible's presentation of his rather harmless character (though cf. Jdt. 8.25-27), Laban is normally presented in rabbinic literature as an enemy of Jacob and Israel.

Today, Laban's story is revisited by contemporary authors whose books draw attention to the intertwined lives of four celebrated women, Rachel, Leah, Zilpah, and Bilhah, all wives of Jacob. Anita Diamant, for one, tells the story from Dinah's perspective as she whispers stories of her four mothers (*The Red Tent*, 2007). Orson Scott Card paints a vivid picture of the intertwined life of Laban's nomadic family in *Rachel and Leah* (2005).

See also REBEKAH; JACOB; WELL; LEAH; RACHEL; DINAH [DR]

Labor of Love. The expression translates the Greek words *kopos* (labor) and *agape* (love) found in 1 Thess. 1.3, where the Apostle Paul describes the Thessalonian church's 'work (*ergon*) of faith and labor (*kopos*) of love and steadfastness (*hypomones*) of hope'. In this context, these three attributes are offered as a sign of the spiritual health of the Thessalonian community. Paul frequently uses the Greek terms *ergon* and *kopos* interchangeably to describe God's work—in which he is a participant—of discipleship and church building among the Gentiles. Similar phrasing comes up elsewhere in the NT, as in Paul's reference to the one doing 'a good work' among the Philippians (Phil. 1.6). Further, Paul exhorts the Corinthians to 'be steadfast, immovable, always excelling in the work (*ergon*) of the Lord, because you know that in the Lord your labor (*kopos*) is not in vain' (see also Rev. 2.2).

While in this passage, Paul is describing labor as a metaphor for pastoral activity, he understands it in very concrete terms as well. In 2 Thessalonians, Paul commends hard work to the church as a way of providing for one's own means. He stresses in both letters to the Thessalonians that he provides the financial means for his own ministry (perhaps as a tentmaker, see Acts 18.3), 'so that we might not burden any of you' (2 Thess. 3.8; see also 1 Thess. 2.9). Following this pattern, it seems that Paul offers the two kinds of work as mutually informative. Just as he is trained for the hard work of weaving tents, so also does Christ 'equip the saints for the work of ministry, for building up the body of Christ' (Eph. 4.12). Similarly, just as tentmaking involves hard work, so too are we to strive (Greek: *spoudazontes*) with our best work to make 'every effort to maintain the unity of the Spirit in the bond of peace' (Eph. 4.3; cf. 2 Tim. 2.15; Heb. 4.11). Similarly, Paul modifies the word *agape* (love) with 'labor' in 1 Thess.

1.3 to describe a particular sort of self-giving Christian love. This is the word used in 1 Cor. 13, and Gal. 5.13, where Paul suggests that because 'you were called to freedom, brothers and sisters ... do not use your freedom as an opportunity for self-indulgence, but through love become slaves to one another'.

The phrase 'labor of love' is widely used in contemporary speech, and some of the meaning described above continues to operate in the background of modern usage. One might hear it used of any variety of carefully made projects, a meticulously restored car, a hand-built table, a carefully pieced quilt. In the 2004 film *The Notebook*, the narrator describes how James Garner's character Duke 'got the notion into his head that if he restored the old house where they had come that night, Allie would find a way to come back to him. Some called it a labor of love'. In this context, the phrase does not refer to building up a community of faith (1 Thess. 1.3) but rather resembles Paul's tentmaking language suggested in 1 Thess. 2.9. It indicates good hard work done for the benefit of others. The sense is at least partially faithful to Paul's meaning, indicating work motivated by love, not profit.

Recommended reading. Fee, Gordon D. *The First and Second Letters to the Thessalonians*. New International Commentary on the New Testament. Grand Rapids, MI: Eerdmans, 2009.

See also PAUL, THE APOSTLE; TENTMAKER; THESSALONIANS, EPISTLES TO THE [JHK]

Laborers in the vineyard. In Matt. 20.1-16, Jesus tells a parable of a landowner who hires groups of laborers at five different points in a given day to work his vineyard—at the first, third, sixth, ninth, and eleventh hour. What is shocking is that at the end of the workday each group gets paid an equal wage even though the first group to join worked eleven more hours than the last group. In response to the complaining that ensues over the unfair compensation, the landowner reminds them of the agreed upon wage, arguing that he chose to give to the last group the same as he gave to the first group. He then asks, 'Am I not allowed to do what I choose with what belongs to me? Or are you envious because I am generous?' In the end, Jesus closes the parable by stating his point that the last will be first and the first will be last.

In the early Church, the parable was most often interpreted allegorically. Irenaeus sees the various hours at which the laborers were hired as periods of history: morning included the time from Adam to Noah; the third hour included the time from Noah to Abraham; the sixth hour from Abraham to Moses; the ninth hour from Moses to Jesus; and the eleventh hour from Jesus to the end of the world (*Against Heresies* 4.36.7). Origen, by contrast, interpreted the hours to refer to different stages of human life: childhood, youth, adulthood, old age, extreme old age (*In Matthaeum*). These readings were repeated and often combined by later interpreters (e.g., St Jerome, *In Matthaeum*; St Gregory, *Hom. in Evangelia*, 19; Bede, *In Matthaei Evangelium expositio*; Thomas Aquinas, *Summa contra Gentiles*, 58.8). Moreover, the laborers were often understood as signifying the clergy and the vineyard the Church (e.g., Gregory, Bede), while the denarius, paid equally to all, was thought to signify eternal life (Tertullian, *De monogamia*; Augustine, *De sancta virginitate* and *Sermons on New Testament Lessons*), or the contemplation and enjoyment of God (Aquinas). The 'burden of the day and the scorching heat' was sometimes interpreted as an indication that God's judgment at the end of the world was still far away (Aquinas, *In Matthaeum*).

Rembrandt's painting *The Parable of the Laborers in the Vineyard*, focuses on the landowner's final payment to the group of laborers who worked the longest. In this painting the complaints are depicted with one man holding out his hand for more and another pointing back at those who worked less but got paid the same. Singing about the plight of America's dispossessed migrant workers, Bruce Springsteen's title track from *The Ghost of Tom Joad* (1995) whispers the phrase 'Waitin' for when the last shall be first and the first shall be last'. This line anticipates the day when the sort of power reversal Jesus announced will become a reality. In a hedonistic fashion, Emily Dickinson concludes from this verse: 'Had I known that the first was the last / I should have kept it longer / Had I know that the last was the first / I should have drunk it stronger' (poem 1720).

See also PARABLE [DWB]

Lake of Fire. Found in the Book of Revelation and nowhere else in the Bible, the Lake of Fire is the place of ultimate punishment for Satan, his demons, and his followers. Prior to Jesus' return, the beast and false prophet are thrown alive into the lake of fire (Rev. 19.20). A thousand years later, Satan—freed from imprisonment in the Abyss—deceives the nations and is thrown into the lake of burning sulfur where he is tormented day and night with the beast and the prophet (Rev. 20.10). Death and

Hades are thrown into the lake of fire, along with those whose names are not written in the book of life (Rev. 20.14-15).

While the Bible tells us that Satan, the beast, and the false prophet will suffer eternal torment, it does not say the same about their human followers, leading to a debate as to whether eternal punishment will be conscious suffering or annihilation. Some scholars suggest that the concept of a punishment by fire and sulfur derives from the account of Sodom and Gomorrah (Gen. 19.24-25). Certainly the concept of punishment by fire was not original with Christianity. The OT associates the penalty of fire and the unrighteous. Deuteronomy 4.24 depicts God as an all-consuming fire (see too Isa. 33.11-12). Isaiah warns that the unrighteous dead will end up in unquenchable fire (66.24). Malachi promises an all-consuming fire for those who do evil (4.1).

Jewish literature of the Second Temple period is rife with references to the fiery end of the wicked. The author of Ecclesiasticus (c. 195–171 BCE) is convinced that the end of the unrighteous will be by fire (21.9; 36.7-10). Baruch (c. 150 BCE) describes the end of Israel's enemies in everlasting fire (4.35). Judith (c. 150–125 BCE), a savior of Israel, speaks of the Lord's vengeance against her country's enemies by fire and worms, which will torment them forever (16.17).

From early times, church leaders and teachers cautioned that unbelief would lead to damnation in eternal fire. The best-known account of eternal punishment appears in Dante's *Divine Comedy*, of which *Inferno* is the first part. In *Inferno*, the poet is taken on a journey through hell, which he finds is constructed in nine concentric circles of suffering, each worse than the last. In the seventh circle, for example, blasphemers, usurers and sodomites are housed in a desert of flaming sand. And in the eighth circle, corrupt politicians are found in a lake of boiling pitch.

In recent times, the whole concept of hell—lake of fire and all—has been dismissed by liberal theologians as old-fashioned and superstitious. Conservative Christians still hold to the idea, some metaphorically, others literally. Many evangelicals, including John Stott and Clark Pinnock, have embraced the idea of annihilation in the lake of fire for unrighteous humanity. It remains a popular theme in contemporary society. In 1983, an American alternative band, the Meat Puppets, released a song entitled 'Lake of Fire', with the chorus: 'Where do bad folks go when they die? / They don't go to heaven where the angels fly / They go down to the lake of fire and fry / Won't see them again till the 4th of July'. The song's writer, Curt Kirkwood, has performed it at most of his concerts with and without the Meat Puppets. It became popular afresh when performed at MTV Nirvana Unplugged.

See also GEHENNA; HELL; JUDGEMENT; PURGATORY

[DLS]

Lamb, sacrificial. The sacrificial lamb metaphor usually refers to one that is rejected or killed as a substitute for others. The phrase is repeated in the Bible thirty-four times, with NT occurrences calling Jesus 'the lamb'. The source of the metaphor is in the OT. Jews in ancient Israel valued lambs highly as a source for food and clothing, and they figured prominently in religious life as well. Even as far back as Gen. 15, there is mention of animals slaughtered as an act of religious devotion. One of the best-known sacrificial-lamb allusions in the OT appears in Exod. 12, during Moses's attempt to free the Israelites from slavery in Egypt. The last of the ten plagues involved the death of the firstborn child in every Egyptian household as an act of judgment against the nation for enslaving his people. However, to spare the Israelites, God allowed each household to kill a lamb and spread its blood on the house's doorframe instead of receiving the judgment he had promised the Egyptians. Thus the lamb died in place of the first-born child in each Israelite household.

The above example from Exodus is one that typifies the Christian use of the term. Jesus has been worshiped as the sacrificial 'Lamb of God' in Christian circles from the first century onward because his death is seen as sparing Christians from the judgment of God. Similar to the way God passed over the homes of Israelites who had sacrificed a lamb and spread its blood on their doorposts, God passes over the believer who lays claim to the sacrifice of Jesus as a shield from divine judgment.

This sacrificial lamb motif has taken root in many parts of Western culture. In politics, a candidate may be called a sacrificial lamb if they are chosen by their political party or constituents to run in an election where the chances of victory are slim. For example, the title of a 2008 *Telegraph* article was, 'Who will be Labor's sacrificial lamb in Glasgow East?' The article summed up the point when it said, 'Steven Purcell, the leader of Glasgow Council, would be the ideal candidate, but he reckons it would be political suicide for him to do it'.

In television and movies, 'sacrificial lamb' is used to describe a character whose sole purpose is to be marginalized or die to support the protagonist or the wider events of the plot. In the HBO drama *The Wire*, actor Michael B. Jordan plays a 16-year-old drug dealer called Wallace who is tragically killed by other dealers while attempting to leave the drug trade. The American musicians Skid Row and Warren Zevon both use the sacrifical lamb motif in their songs.

Recommended reading. Witherington, III. Ben. *Revelation*. Cambridge: Cambridge University Press, 2003. Atkinson, David John. *Jesus, Lamb of God: Biblical Mediatations*. London: SPCK, 1996.

See also OFFERINGS; SACRIFICE [MB]

Lamb of God. In Greek, *ho amnos tou theou* and in Latin, *agnus dei*, the term Lamb of God appears in John 1.29 and 1.36 where John the Baptist identifies Jesus as 'the Lamb of God who takes away the sins of the world'. The Book of Revelation references the 'Lamb' 29 times, as a synonym for Jesus Christ. This term has its roots in the sacrificial system of the HB. The Lamb of God recalls the Passover lamb, the sacrificial animal associated with the Exodus (Exod. 12.4-11). 1 Corinthians 5.7 and 1 Pet. 1.19 explicitly compare Christ to the Passover lamb. This understanding of the Lamb of God connects the freedom of slaves in the Exodus with freedom from sin. Other suggestions for the source of lamb of God are: the *Tamid*, the daily sacrifice of an unblemished lamb (Exod. 29.38-42); the scapegoat (Lev. 16); the 'gentle lamb' (Jer. 11.19); the guilt offering, related to the 'the binding of Isaac' (Gen. 22.8); or the 'lamb to the slaughter' (Isa. 53.7).

Symbolically, the Lamb of God is also linked to the symbols of sheep and shepherds. For example, Martin Luther interprets Ps. 23 in light of the symbol of the Lamb of God. He argues the eucharistic elements on the table, set in the presence of the Lamb, is as a picture of Christ as the Passover Lamb of God.

According to the Venerable Bede, an eighth-century monk, modern Easter celebrations developed from the integration of the symbol of Jesus as the Lamb of God with pagan rituals of fertility associated with *Eostur* (*Eostre*, *Eastre*) of Anglo-Saxon origin. *Eoster* was a figure of spring associated with eggs and rabbits, which, like lambs, represent new life, but lambs are also connected uniquely with the symbol of the resurrection through their association with Christ as lamb.

In modern usage, the *Agnus Dei* is a formal part of a Roman Catholic mass. Many have based musical works on the *Agnus Dei*, including classical composers, Samuel Barber, Wolfgang Amadeus Mozart, Gabriel Fauré, John Rutter, J.S. Bach, and modern artists like Rufus Wainwright and Michael W. Smith. The *Agnus Dei* was an important symbol in artwork from the first century to today. Carvings of the Lamb of God are found across Europe dating back as to the first century and are found on early Christian sarcophagi, on coins, and as seals to the Templars' doorways dating to the medieval period. Woodcuts include Albrecht Dürer's *Adoration of the Lamb* and Francisco de Zurbarán's *Agnus Dei*. Paintings include *Adoration of the Lamb* by Jan van Eyck, *Agnus Dei* by Paul Myhill, and *God's Lamb* by Niko Pirosmani. The Lamb of God also figures prominently in stain glass windows.

Several movies borrow the terms Lamb of God and *agnus dei* and the concepts they suggest, among them *Agnus Dei* (the English name for *Nonneborn*) directed by Caecilia Holbeck Trier, *Agnus Dei* directed by Lucía Cedrón, and *The Lamb* directed by Regardt Van Den Bergh. Books influenced by this concept include *Lamb*, Christopher Moore's satirical novel on Jesus' childhood, and *The Blood of the Lambs: A Former Terrorist's Memoir of Death and Redemption*, Kamal Saleem's account of a Muslim terrorist turned Christian.

Recommended reading. Skinner, Christopher W. 'Another Look at "the Lamb of God."' *Bibliotheca sacra* 161 (2004) 89-104. Guthrie, Donald. 'The Lamb in the Structure of the Book of Revelation'. *Vox evangelica* 12 (1981) 64-71.

See also EXODUS; GOOD SHEPHERD; PASSOVER; SHEEP [BMS]

Lamech. This is the name of two separate individuals that appear in the primeval history of Gen. 1–11. The first Lamech mentioned is the son of Methushael, a descendant of Cain (4.18-24). He is notable in the biblical record as the first polygamist, taking two wives, Adah and Zillah. He is also known for his 'sword song' (4.23-24), one of the most ancient pieces of Hebrew poetry, possibly dating as far back as the third millennium BCE. Here Lamech seems to revel in the technological advances in weaponry brought about by his son Tubal-Cain, which appear to give him a distinct and more violent edge in the carrying out of revenge. His reference to a seventy-sevenfold vengeance for himself is a direct play on his ancestor Cain's sevenfold vengeance, and seems to represent a further stage in the deterioration of pre-deluvian humanity that would eventually culminate with the generation of Noah. Perhaps more creatively, Tertullian, in chapter four of his tractate *On Monogamy*, identifies the 'seventy-seven times' of the 'sword song' as the type of vengeance befitting those with double marriages. Josephus curiously indentifies the seventy-seven as the number of children fathered by Lamech with his two wives (*Ant.* 1.2.2).

The second Lamech mentioned in the Bible is identified as the son of Methuselah, a descendant of Seth (5.25-31). In contrast to his counterpart, this Lamech is the father of the flood hero Noah, who in some sense represents a new start from the type of violence and corruption exemplified by the Cainite Lamech. In this respect, his most notable contribution to the biblical narrative is the prophetic blessing that he bestowed upon his son: Noah would usher in a period of comfort and relief from the painful toiling of the ground that Yahweh had cursed (5.29).

With the exception of genealogies (1 Chron. 1.3; Luke 3.36), both Lamechs are notably absent from the remainder of the Bible, although it is likely that Jesus alludes to the seventy-sevenfold vengeance of the Cainite Lamech in his statement to Peter on how many times a person must forgive before extracting revenge (Matt. 18.21-22). Likewise, the Sethite Lamech does reappear in the *Genesis Apocryphon* (1QapGen), where he is noticeably bewildered by the appearance of his miraculously unique son Noah.

Recommended reading. Gervitz, S. *Patterns in the Early Poetry of Israel*. Chicago: University of Chicago Press, 1963.

See also CAIN; GENESIS, BOOK OF; METHUSELAH; NOAH [TAB]

Lamentations, Book of. Lamentations is one of the world's greatest pieces of religious literature. The original Hebrew versions of the Lamentations of Jeremiah did not have a title but later Hebrew editors added the word 'ek̲ āh ('Ah, how') as a superscription, and later talmudic and rabbinic authors called it either 'ek̲ āh or qînôt (Lamentations). The Septuagint gave Lamentations the Greek title of *Threnoi* (Wailings) and the Vulgate added a subtitle: 'It comprises the Lamentations of Jeremiah the prophet'. English translations use the title Lamentations or Lamentations of Jeremiah. It was ascribed to Jeremiah by the consensus of Jewish tradition (Targum *Baba Bathra* at Jer. 1.11), perhaps as an interpretation of 2 Chron. 35.25, which says Jeremiah wrote laments after the death of King Josiah.

The Hebrew canon puts Lamentations in a section call Ketuvim (the Writings), included among the Megillot (Rolls), which are five scrolls read at specific occasions. In Jewish practice, it was customary to read the Book of Lamentations on the ninth of Ab (mid-July) in order to remember the destruction of Jerusalem and the temple. The book explores issues touching on God's sovereignty, holiness, justice, judgment and the hope of a blessed future, responding to troubling questions. Have the promises of God failed? Was God impotent to stop the Babylonians? Is there hope for the despair of the exiles? Is there justice coming to their tormentors?

Laments are expressions of sorrow, remorse, regret and grief. Beginning with the destruction of the City of Ur, the ancient Middle East created many examples of dirge poetry. Lamentations was only the latest in a tradition of somber words about the fall of a city, in this case the fall of Jerusalem in 587 BCE. Lamentations is an expression of the national sorrow over the calamity that has befallen the Kingdom of Judah.

There are five poems in Lamentations that form the individual chapters of the book. The first four use acrostics of the 22 consonants of the Hebrew alphabet (with slight exceptions). The fifth follows the corporate lament psalmody of Pss 44 and 80. The stress and rhythm pattern of Hebrew elegiac poetry is called a *qinah* or 'dirge meter'. Some call the Book of Lamentations a form of Hebrew 'blues music'.

John Donne wrote 'The Lamentations of Jeremy, For the Most Part according to Tremelius'. It was based on a Latin text developed by the Jewish convert and scholar John Immanuel Tremelius. Tremelius came to England at the invitation of Thomas Cranmer as a Hebrew instructor at Cambridge University. Kenneth Rexroth's (1905–82) 'Wednesday of Holy Week, 1940' is based on Lam. 1.2-4. George Sandys's (1577–1644) 'Judah in Exile Wanders' is based on Lam. 1.5-22. Thomas Tallis (1505–1585), a composer and organist, wrote 'Lamentations of Jeremiah' which is still performed. Leonard Bernstein composed *Jeremiah* in 1942, which was performed in 1944 in three movements: 'Prophecy', 'Profanation', 'Lamentations'. The expression 'wormwood and gall' is taken from Lam. 3.19. It appears in Charles Dickens's *Martin Chuzzlewit*.

Recommended reading. Alter, Robert. *The Art of Hebrew Poetry*. New York: Basic Books, 1981.

See also JEREMIAH; JEREMIAH, BOOK OF [AJW]

Land of milk and honey. The term derives from Exod. 3.8 as the Lord promises to bring the Israelites out of Egypt and into a land flowing with opportunity and abundance—milk and honey. This HB expression originates in God's description of the country lying between the Mediterranean Sea and the Jordan River, namely, Canaan. It is first described as 'a good and spacious land, a land flowing with milk and honey' when God commissions Moses to lead the Israelites to it. God promised this same territory to Abraham (Gen. 12) and again to Jacob (Gen. 28).

The original Hebrew (transliterated) is *eretz zavat halav ood'vash*, literally, land flowing with milk and honey. The word translated as 'flowing' comes from the verb *zoov* that means to flow or gush. Thus, in the Hebrew, the word *zavat* suggests the idea of the land's plentiful milk and honey in a sudden and swift, abundant flow. Strangely, there is no reference to the term in the NT.

Milk and honey were among the principal products of the promised land. Both were dietary staples for the semi-nomadic Israelites of biblical times, so Palestine would indeed be a promising home, abounding in goats and swarming with bees. The soil would be extremely fertile, nourishing grapevines and date trees, whose syrup was also called honey in Hebrew. The definition of milk and honey serves as a metaphor for all good things—God's blessings. The phrase flowing with milk and honey is understood to be hyperbolically expressive of the land's fruitfulness, which explains its current use to express abundance. Despite the inference of a land that would ultimately lead to a booming economy, the Israelites would be confronted by hostile indigenous people—the Hittites, Amorites, Perizzites, Hivites, and the Jebusites.

The phrase land of milk and honey is one of the first biblical expressions to have found its way into English (c. 1000 CE), through Aelfric's exposition of Num. 16.13. The term flowing with milk and honey appeared in Wyclif's 1382 translation of Ezek. 20.6 and was entrenched in English speech by the time William Tyndale used it in translating the present passage, despite his claims that he never glanced at Wyclif or any other English version of the Bible.

In the early twentieth century, many immigrants perceived the United States as a proverbial land of milk and honey. The popular perception was that the living conditions were excellent and one could become wealthy easily. Author John Steinbeck captured the disillusionment stemming from such expectations in *The Grapes of Wrath* (1939), where a once-hopeful immigrant to California ironically observes, 'this ain't no lan' of milk an' honey like the preachers say' (chap. 20). In film, the term served as the title for a controversial documentary that chronicled the formation of the Ku Klux Klan in Pulaski, Tennessee, the town where the group was founded after the Civil War. Book titles incorporating the phrase include Norton Locke's *The Land of Milk and Honey: A Cooking Book an Epicurean Tour of Israel With a History of Foods in the Holy Land* (1991), and David Cooks's two volume set, *The Land of Milk & Honey: God Made Everything with Love* (2007).

See also CANAAN, CANAANITES; EXODUS, THE; PROMISED LAND [SNW]

Languages of the Bible. The HB is written in two languages. Most is in Hebrew, an Afro-Asiatic (formerly called Hamito-Semitic) language, and a dialect of Northwest Semitic Canaanite that developed in the area between the Jordan River and the Mediterranean Sea during the second half of the second millennium BCE. Hebrew has four periods in its development: Biblical Hebrew, including Pre-Exilic and Late Biblical (early first millennium to second century BCE), Rabbinic Hebrew (second century BCE–sixth/seventh century CE), Medieval Hebrew (sixth/seventh–nineteenth century), and Modern Hebrew (nineteenth century to present). The second language of the HB is Aramaic. Aramaic is also an Afro-Asiatic language, a dialect of Northwest Semitic closely related to Canaanite. Aramaic and Canaanite began to develop differently at the beginning of the first millennium BCE, and Aramaic became the vernacular of the Jewish people during and after their exile. Aramaic passages in the HB are Ezra 4.8-6.18; 7.12-26; Dan. 2.4–7.28; Jer. 10.11; Gen. 31.47. Aramaic has several periods of development, including Old Aramaic (925–700 BCE), Official Aramaic (700–200 BCE), Middle Aramaic (200 BCE–200 CE), and Late Aramaic (200–700 CE).

The NT is written in Greek. Greek is one of the languages descended from the western branch of Indo-European that separated around 3500 BCE. Greek spread from the Balkan region to Macedonia and into Greece, where it went through successive developments, including the Mycenean period (1600–1200 BCE), Dark Ages (1200–900 BCE), Archaic period (900–600 BCE), Classical or Dialect period (600–332 BCE), Hellenistic period (332–63 BCE), Roman period (63 BCE–fourth century CE), Byzantine period (fourth–fifteenth century), Turkish period (fifteenth–nineteenth century) and modern period (nineteenth century to the present). NT Greek is often called Koine (= common) Greek because it was the form of widely used Greek that developed from the dialect of Athens and the surrounding territory (called Great Attic) as Alexander the Great spread Greek language and culture to his conquered territories. There are also a number of Hebrew and Aramaic words cited in the NT. Though it is not clear how much Hebrew was spoken during the time of Jesus, a form of Middle Aramaic was in widespread use in Palestine during this time (for citation of Aramaic in the NT, see Mark 5.41; 7.23; 15.34// Matt. 27.46).

Languages of the Bible also include the languages into which the Bible has been translated. The first sustained translation of the HB was the Septuagint, begun in Egypt in the third century BCE. Other translations include the Aramaic versions or Targums, which began to develop around the turn of the era. The Bible has since been translated into numerous vernaculars. Ancient languages include Syriac (a development of Aramaic), Latin, Coptic, Gothic, Armenian, Georgian, Ethiopic, Arabic and Old Church Slavonic, among others. The Bible has also been translated into all major modern languages, as well as many minor ones. It has been estimated by the Ethnologue (2005) that there are 6,912 languages or dialects in the world today, and the Bible in whole or part has been translated into 2,426 of these.

Recommended reading. Fitzmyer, J.A. *A Wandering Aramean: Collected Aramaic Essays*. Chico, CA: Scholars Press, 1979. Metzger, B.M. *The Bible in Translation: Ancient and English Versions*. Grand Rapids, MI: Baker, 2001. Porter, S.E. 'Greek Language'. In *New Interpreter's Dictionary of the Bible*, II. Ed. Katherine Doob Sakenfeld. Pp. 673-81. Nashville, TN: Abingdon Press, 2007. Sáenz-Badillos, A. *A History of the Hebrew Language*. Trans. J. Elwolde. Cambridge: Cambridge University Press, 1993.

See also ARAMAIC LANGUAGE; HEBREW LANGUAGE; GREEK LANGUAGE [SEP]

Laodicea. Laodicea is a city now in ruins on the Lykos River in modern Turkey. The city of Laodicea was probably founded around 261–253 BCE by the Seleucid king Antiochus II Theos, who named it after his wife Laodike. In 220 BCE, Achaios, in rebellion against Antiochus III, became the ruler of Laodicea. Later the city became part of the Pergamene Kingdom, which, under the rule of kings of Pergamum, lasted from 283 to 133 BCE.

During Roman times, Laodicea was located in the province of Phrygia in Asia Minor. Laodicea is mentioned in two major contexts in the NT. Since Laodicea was located very close to Colossae, Paul in his letter to the Colossians also mentions the Laodiceans (Col. 2.1; 4.13; along with those in Hierapolis, another nearby city; 4.15). He also mentions a letter written to the Laodiceans, which is to be read in the Colossian church (Col. 4.16). We do not have this letter of Paul to the Laodiceans, although there is a Latin pseudepigraphal Letter to the Laodiceans (it may have originally been written in Greek), which was probably composed between the second and fourth centuries CE. It is found in a number of Latin biblical manuscripts.

The Laodiceans are also mentioned in Revelation (1.11), with a letter written to them (3.14-22). John, the author of Revelation, writing to the church in Laodicea, accuses them of being neither hot nor cold. In the ancient world, hot water was valued for its medicinal and bathing uses, and cold water was valued for its drinking and the watering of plants. Lukewarm water was considered of no value, and given to servants. The Laodiceans apparently did not have access to a usable water supply of their own, even though nearby Hierapolis had hot water and Colossae cold water. As a result, the Laodiceans brought lukewarm water, undesired by others, into the city by aqueduct (whose remains are still visible at the site). This is in contrast to the wealth of the city, which was a banking center, a medical center, and a center of the woolen industry. Strabo (*Geogr.* 12.578) notes that Laodicea had sheep known for soft, black wool, around which the textile industry developed. 'Laodicean' was a type of wool in the fourth century CE.

Laodicea reached the peak of its importance and wealth in the second century, when the Emperor Hadrian visited in 129 CE and the city fashioned itself as the 'Metropolis of Asia'. In the fourth century, perhaps sometime around 365 CE, there apparently was a Christian Council of Laodicea that was held in the city, about which little is known. This council may have produced the so-called Canons of Laodicea, which are a group of 60 canons that were incorporated in early Christian canonical law, although they may have been derived from earlier councils.

Recommended reading. Akurgal, E. *Ancient Civilizations and Ruins of Turkey*. 10th ed. Istanbul: Net Turistik Yayinlar, 2007. Cross, F.L. (ed.). *The Oxford Dictionary of the Christian Church*. London: Oxford University Press,

1958. Elliott, J.K. (ed.). *The Apocryphal New Testament*. Oxford: Clarendon Press, 1993. Porter, S.E. 'Why the Laodiceans Received Lukewarm Water (Revelation 3:15-18)'. *Tyndale Bulletin* 38 (1987) 143-49.

See also COLOSSIANS, EPISTLE TO THE; PAUL, THE APOSTLE; REVELATION, BOOK OF [SEP]

Last shall be first, the. The motif of the last being first is found throughout the HB, and is an archetype which reverses the traditional assumption of the first (or firstborn) being a privileged position. This biblical archetype of the youngest sibling being favored over the firstborn can be observed in the narratives concerning Cain and Abel, Jacob and Esau, Ephraim and Manasseh, Joseph and his brothers, Rachel and Leah, and David and his older brothers.

In the NT, the theme of the last being first is often part of a paradoxical rhetoric spoken by Jesus: 'many who are first will be last, and the last will be first' (Matt. 19.30, Mark 10.31; cf. Matt. 20.16, Mark 9.35, Luke 13.30; 22.26). This is usually interpreted as Jesus emphasizing a principle of divine judgment or preference based on just reward, as opposed to one's social or religious status in this world. In an early Christian and Medieval context, the emphasis on this theme shifted to a principle of humility; it is a principle of heaven that should be reflected in this-worldly endeavors.

The idea that the last shall be first appears throughout popular music and literature, generally echoing Jesus' teaching that one's social status in this world does not reflect one's reward in heaven. For example, the lyrics to Bruce Springsteen's song 'The Ghost of Tom Joad', which are based on John Steinbeck's award-winning novel *The Grapes of Wrath* (1939), speak of a homeless preacher who is 'Waitin' for when the last shall be first and the first shall be last, in a cardboard box 'neath the underpass'. In rap and hip hop, the phrase the last shall be first appears to be a popular album and song title, having been used by Sunz of Man (1998), The Dwellas (2000), Dynas (2005), Barnes (2006), Da Common Cauze (2006), and Ronin Ichikawa (2007).

The phrase has also taken on a prophetic quality, particularly as it has been used in reference to the renowned political career of Senator Ted Kennedy. As the story goes, on the weekend of his inauguration, eldest brother John gave youngest brother Teddy a silver cigarette case with the engraving 'And the last shall be first'. This has taken on a prophetic significance ever since.

[EJW]

Last trumpet. In the OT, the trumpet (primarily *shofar*, a ram's horn; and *khatsotserah*, a silver trumpet) is often used as a signal, warning, or summons of coming battle—sometimes literally, other times symbolically (e.g., Josh. 6.4-20; Judg. 3.27; 6.34; 1 Sam. 13.3; Isa. 18.3; 27.13; 58.1; Jer. 51.27; 4.5, 19, 21). The trumpet is notably used in the collapsing of the walls of Jericho (Josh. 6.20; cf. Judg. 7.22). In such circumstances, trumpet blasts underscore the power of God over against the immediate perception of human strength. In another important display of divine power, the trumpet is featured in a loud blast at Mount Sinai announcing the presence of God (Exod. 19.16). Trumpets are sometimes mentioned in contexts describing divine judgment, including calls to repentance (Amos 2.2; 3.6; Joel 2.1, 15; Zeph. 1.16; Hos. 5.8; 8.1).

The Greek term *salpinx* (generally made of iron or bronze) is the most frequently mentioned musical instrument in the NT. In the LXX, *salpinx* is commonly used as a translation for a variety of Hebrew instruments, including those mentioned above. Paul uses the term to make a battle analogy (1 Cor. 14.8) and Hebrews alludes to Mount Sinai (12.19), but its predominant NT usage is eschatological—relating to the 'last things' (Matt. 24.31, 1 Cor. 15.52, 1 Thess. 4.16, and often in Revelation).

Our term '*last* trumpet' is used to signal the events surrounding the second coming of Christ. The phrase comes from Paul: 'We will not all die, but we will all be changed, in a moment, in the twinkling of an eye, at the last [*eschatos*] trumpet [*salpinx*]. For the trumpet will sound, and the dead will be raised imperishable, and we will be changed' (1 Cor. 15.51-52). The Book of Revelation uses the imagery of seven trumpets to structure its visionary narrative. The seventh and final trumpet in Revelation signals, 'the mystery of God will be fulfilled' (10.7).

Western literature has frequently used the last trumpet for dramatic effect. For instance, William Shakespeare's Juliet cries, 'Is Romeo slaughtered, and is Tybalt dead? / My dearest cousin and my dearer lord? / Then, dreadful trumpet, sound the general doom!' H.G. Wells features the last trumpet in two of his short stories, 'A Vision of Judgment' (1899) and 'The Story of the Last Trump' (1905). In artwork, the last trumpet has been depicted in both epic fashion (e.g., Luca Signorelli [1445–1523], *The Resurrection of the Flesh*) and more intimately, such as in the drawings of Jacques Gamelin (1738–1803) and William Blake (1757–1827), in which a trumpet 're-animates' a single skeleton at close range.

More recently, the last trumpet image has featured in American country and folk music. Johnny Cash, for example, depicted the last trumpet in several songs, including 'When the Man Comes Around' and 'Ain't No Grave (Gonna Hold This Body Down)'. Bob Dylan wrote 'Ye Shall Be Changed' (1979), which announces 'when the last trumpet blows / The dead will arise'.

Eschatological trumpet imagery has also been invoked, often implicitly or even perhaps unconsciously, in far-ranging political rhetoric. It appears in John Knox's 1558 text, 'The First Blast of the Trumpet Against the Monstrous Regiment of Women', and in the Nazi propaganda of Alfred Frauenfeld in 1937: '[our enemy] soon thought they were hearing the shrieks of the last trumpet'. More positively, President John F. Kennedy's inaugural address of 1961 includes the words, 'Now the trumpet summons us again'.

See also APOCALYPSE, APOCALYPTIC; DAY OF THE LORD /JUDGMENT/WRATH; SEVEN SEALS, SEVEN BOWLS, SEVEN TRUMPETS; THIEF IN THE NIGHT; TRUMPET; TWINKLING OF AN EYE [PGM]

Latter Prophets. Whereas the designation Former Prophets indicates Joshua, Judges, 1–2 Samuel, and 1–2 Kings, the term Latter Prophets refers to those books named after particular prophets (Isaiah, Jeremiah, Ezekiel, etc.). Within this category, canonical arrangements distinguish between so-called Major and Minor Prophets. These terms refer to their relative size, not the quality or significance of their content. It appears Augustine was the first to use these terms (in *The City of God*).

The major prophetic books are Isaiah, Jeremiah and Ezekiel in the HB, with Daniel grouped with the Writings. The Christian OT arrangement includes Lamentations and Daniel with the Major Prophets. Roman Catholic Bibles also place the Book of Baruch with Daniel, whereas Protestants place Baruch in the Apocrypha. The twelve minor prophetic books are the same for both Jewish and Christian canons: Hosea, Joel, Amos, Obadiah, Jonah, Micah, Nahum, Habakkuk, Zephaniah, Haggai, Zechariah and Malachi.

Recommended reading. Lundbom, Jack. *The Hebrew Prophets: An Introduction*. Minneapolis: Fortress Press, 2010.

See also AMOS, BOOK OF; DANIEL, BOOK OF; EZEKIEL, BOOK OF; FORMER PROPHETS; HABAKKUK, BOOK OF; HAGGAI, BOOK OF; HOSEA, BOOK OF; ISAIAH, BOOK OF; JEREMIAH, BOOK OF; JOEL, BOOK OF; JONAH, BOOK OF; MALACHI, BOOK OF; MICAH, BOOK OF; NAHUM, BOOK OF; OBADIAH, BOOK OF; ZECHARIAH, BOOK OF; ZEPHANIAH, BOOK OF; PROPHECY; PROPHETS [AJW]

Law. The five books that introduce both the Jewish Bible—the Tanakh—and the Christian Bible are referred to as the Torah. Though the English text is translated from the identical Hebrew original, Christianity refers to Torah as Law while Judaism knows it to be Instruction. For Jewish tradition, the Torah existed before God created the world (*Talmud*, Pesahim 54a). In fact, according to Simeon the Just, the creation of the world was based on three things: on Torah, worship, and lovingkindness (*Mishnah*, Avot 1.2). From a Jewish mystical perspective, the Holy One, the Torah, and Israel are one (*Zohar*, Lev. 73b). While the NT interpretation of the Torah lends itself to supersession theology (for example, the Prologue of the Fourth Gospel boldly summarizes that 'the Law came through Moses; grace and truth came through Jesus Christ' [John 1.17]), Jewish tradition would consider such a parallel synonymous. Maimonides (*Yad*, Sabbath), for instance, explains that the purpose of Torah and its contained laws is to 'promote compassion, loving-kindness, and peace in the world'. A Christianized Western culture has more commonly played out the legal and sometimes legalistic portrait of the Torah rather than the contextual meaning of instruction as understood by the authors of its text. One of many important exceptions can be found in the title of Roberto Calasso's collection of essays, *I quarantanove gradini* (The forty-nine steps), which draws its name from a Talmudic statement that every passage of the Torah holds forty-nine degrees of meaning. Hanina ben Iddi (*Talmud*, Taanit 7a) captured the spirit of the Torah in the expression: 'As water flows to the lowest level, so Torah finds its way to the lowly of spirit'.

See also BOOK OF THE LAW; JEWS, JUDAISM; MOSES [DM]

Lazarus of Bethany. The story of Lazarus appears only in the Gospel of John (John 11.1-44). There is no connection between this story and Jesus' parable about Lazarus and the rich man (Luke 16.19-31).

At John 11.1-44, Jesus is in the region of Batanea, some 150 kilometres northeast of Jerusalem, when he receives an urgent message. Two sisters, Martha and Mary of Bethany, send word that their brother Lazarus is ill. (Mary is identified as the woman who anointed Jesus—she is not to be confused with Mary Magdalene. John tells the story of the anointing at 12.1-8). In spite of Jesus' affection for Martha, Mary, and Lazarus, he remains where he is for two days before going to Bethany, which is about two miles east of Jerusalem. By the time he arrives, Lazarus has been dead and entombed for four days.

Martha, hearing that Jesus is coming, meets him on the outskirts of town. He calls her to go beyond conventional Jewish belief to faith in himself: 'I am the resurrection and the life. Those who believe in me, even though they die, will live, and everyone who lives and believes in me will never die' (11.25-26). Martha returns home, and Mary comes out to meet Jesus. Several Jews who have come to the house to pay their respects follow her. Jesus is visibly upset. They all go to the tomb, where Jesus orders that the stone at the tomb entrance be rolled away. He shouts, 'Lazarus, come out!' and the resurrected Lazarus appears at the tomb entrance, still wrapped in the grave clothes. Jesus instructs the bystanders to untie him and let him go.

Themes of interest in this story include: Jesus as the resurrection and the life who has power even over death; Jesus' intense emotions and his solidarity with his disciples in their bereavement; Jesus' timing, guided as it is by his Father's will, not human persuasion (cf. 2.4); and the resurrection of Lazarus as foreshadow of Jesus' own resurrection (John 20.1-18). In this miracle there is also a partial fulfillment of Jesus' promise that the time is coming when all the dead will hear the voice of the Son of Man, and live (5.25).

This famous story has inspired much art, literature, and music. There are numerous paintings entitled *The Raising of Lazarus*, including those by Giotto (1304–1306; Scrovegni Chapel, Padua); Geertgen tot Sint Jens (1480s; the Louvre, Paris); Rembrandt (c. 1630; County Art Museum, Los Angeles); Sebastiano del Piomlo (1517–19; National Gallery, London); Caravaggio (1608–1609; Museo Nazionale, Messina); and Vincent van Gough (after Rembrandt; 1890). There is also Pietro Annigoni's *The Resurrection of Lazarus* (1946; the Vatican, Rome).

In literature, there is a reference to the story of Lazarus in chapter 2 of Charles Dickens's *David Copperfield* (1849–59). Other literature inspired by the Lazarus story includes Leo Tolstoy, *Resurrection* (1899); Eugene O'Neill, *Lazarus Laughed* (1927); Sylvia Plath, 'Lady Lazarus' (1962); Carol Ann Duffy, 'Mrs. Lazarus' (1999); and 'Lazarus Not Raised' by Thom Gunn (1929–2004). Composers who have written works entitled *I Am the Resurrection* include Orlando Gibbons (1583–1625), Henry Purcell (c. 1659–95), Thomas Tompkins, and Carl J. Marzocchi (1976). Gustav Mahler (1860–1911) wrote a 'Resurrection' symphony.

See also JOHN, GOSPEL OF; MIRACLES; RESURRECTION [ED]

Lazarus and the rich man, Parable of. This story is found only in Luke's Gospel (16.19-31). The story raises a number of questions because it is the only parable that names one of its characters (besides Abraham). In a third-century NT manuscript (P75), the rich man is named Neves, and a fourth-century writer names him Finees (he is sometimes called Dives, following the wording in the Latin Vulgate, but this is not a name; dives means 'rich'). This naming has suggested to some that the account is a true story involving these characters. However, most scholars believe that this is a parable, although they are divided on the type of parable.

Most scholars agree that the parable is about responsible use of wealth and care for those in need. The story also provides clues about ancient notions of post-mortem existence in Hades. There are many details that are not explicated in the parable, no doubt because Jesus told this parable not to give a full-orbed picture of life after death, but to emphasize the need for financial responsibility toward those in one's sphere of influence and concern. As a result, there is no discussion of why and on what grounds the rich man goes to Hades and Lazarus goes to the bosom of Abraham, or how it is that communication can take place or not between Abraham and the rich man. However, despite these limitations, there is no doubt the story conveys the clear message that one's earthly actions have important consequences, and that these consequences, however they may actually be realized, can be of lasting and even eternal significance.

See also LUKE, GOSPEL OF; PARABLE [SEP]

Leah. According to Gen. 29.16-30, Leah, described as having 'weak' or 'delicate' eyes, was one of the two daughters of Laban, while her younger sister, Rachel, is described as beautiful. According to a rabbinic interpretation, Leah was to marry Esau, Jacob's older brother. Rabbinic tradition juxtaposes Esau and Jacob: Esau, a hunter who indulges in killing, and Jacob, a God-fearing man. When Leah learns of her destiny, she commits herself to weeping and praying to God to change her destined mate. Leah's eyes, then, become weak and delicate from all her weeping.

Although Jacob falls in love with Rachel and works for Laban for seven years to attain Rachel's hand, through Laban's deception Leah becomes Jacob's wife. Laban explains his actions in Gen. 29.26-27, namely, that it is not customary give the younger daughter in marriage prior to the older one. He then promises Rachel to Jacob for another seven years of labor.

When the Lord sees that Jacob loved Rachel more than Leah (Gen. 29.31), he opens Leah's womb and she bears Jacob six sons (Reuben, Simeon, Levi, Judah, Issachar, and Zebulun), and a daughter (Dinah). Leah's fertility sparks the commonly known rivalry between her and her then barren sister, Rachel. Leah, along with Rachel, is acclaimed by the writer of the Book of Ruth to be one of the builders of the house of Israel. It is through Leah's descendants, especially Judah, that God fulfils his covenant to Abraham.

The story of Leah and her sister Rachel has influenced a number of artists and writers, including Dante Alighieri in the fourteenth-century *Purgatorio*, which in turn inspired Dante Gabriel Rossetti's 1899 painting, *Dante's Vision of Rachel and Leah*.

See also JACOB; RACHEL; TWELVE TRIBES OF ISRAEL [RKM]

Leaven. From the Hebrew *se'or* (leaven) and the Greek *zymē* (leaven). The authors of the HB thought this culinary agent was impure for ritual use. On the eve of the flight from Egypt, Moses and Aaron direct every Israelite family to eat a lamb with unleavened bread (Hebrew: *matsah*) and bitter herbs so that God will spare their firstborn (Exod. 12.3-8). In commemoration of this event, the Israelites were to celebrate the Feast of Unleavened Bread annually (Exod. 12.14-20). Lacking the ingredient that would make it rise, this bread reminded celebrants of the haste with which their persecuted ancestors fled Egypt (Deut. 16.3). The instructions for most rituals in the HB similarly omit leaven from bread offerings (e.g., Exod. 29.2; Lev. 2.11). There are two exceptions (Lev. 7.13; 23.17). Today, Jewish communities rid their homes of leavened dough on the eve of Passover. Likewise, some Christian communities use unleavened bread during Communion, as Jesus' Last Supper with his disciples took place during the Passover.

In the NT, leaven symbolizes the uncontrollable spread of both holy and profane movements and ideas. While this permeating effect can be positive, as it is in Jesus' teachings about the rapid spread of God's Kingdom in the world (Matt. 13.33; Luke 13.20-21), he also warns his disciples to avoid the leaven of others' teachings (Matt. 16.5-12; Mark 8.15; Luke 12.1). Paul's use of the metaphor of leaven is similarly ambiguous. He warns the Corinthians of the consequences of boasting by saying that a 'little yeast leavens the whole batch of dough' (1 Cor. 5.6), but also tells them to celebrate the Feast of Unleavened Bread 'with the unleavened bread of sincerity and truth' (1 Cor. 5.8). Whether these teachers assume their audiences are familiar with the impurity of leaven for ritual use or consider its metaphorical meaning to be more significant for their purposes, its permeating effects dominate its use in the NT.

Leaven's permeating effect has come to define its metaphorical meaning in post-NT literature as well. In the second century CE, Christian authors used the metaphor of leaven to explain the process of conversion. Ignatius of Antioch encouraged the addressees of his *Letter to the Magnesians* to lay aside the old leaven of Judaism for the new leaven that is Jesus Christ (10.2); Justin Martyr used the symbol of leaven similarly in his *Dialogue with Trypho* (14.3). In Shakespeare's *Hamlet*, the eponymous character claims that any vice can become dangerous when it 'o'erleavens' one's otherwise pleasing characteristics. Abraham Lincoln celebrates the US government's triumph over 'the leaven of treason' in newly organized territories in his 'First Annual Message to Congress' (1861). Taking its title from 1 Cor. 5.8, Robertson Davies's book *Leaven of Malice* (1952) explores the far-reaching consequences of a seemingly insignificant lie upon an entire community. Although leaven is often still seen as an impure ingredient for religious practices, its permeating nature defines its primary influence on Western Culture.

Recommended reading. Schellenberg, Ryan S. 'Kingdom as Contaminant? The Role of Repertoire in the Parables of the Mustard Seed and the Leaven'. *Catholic Biblical Quarterly* 71 (2009) 527-43.

See also BREAD; EXODUS, THE; FIRSTBORN; OFFERINGS; PASSOVER; RITUAL PURITY, IMPURITY; SACRIFICE; UNLEAVENED BREAD, FEAST OF [PMF]

Legion. This term refers to a demon confronted by Jesus in the biblical story of the Gerasene demoniac (Mark 5.1-17; Luke 8.26-37). After Jesus enters the country of the Gerasenes, he encounters a man possessed by a host of demons. Jesus commands the demon to identify its name and it responds with the utterance, 'My name is Legion', adding, 'we are many' in number (Mark 5.9; Luke 8.30). Recognizing Jesus' power to cast out unclean spirits, Legion bows to Jesus and begs not to be thrown into the abyss. Instead, Jesus casts Legion into a herd of swine, which run into a lake and are downed. Matthew also records the story (8.28-34) though the name Legion does not appear. Moreover, it speaks of two demon-possessed men rather than one.

The story of the Gadarene swine conveys Jesus' miraculous power to exorcise evil and cure the sick. Legion is destroyed and the demoniac healed. However, some biblical scholars suggest that there is more to this story than meets the eye, which is evident in topographic discontinuities between the place-names Gadara and Gerasa. They argue that the authors or redactors of this story used the casting out of Legion as a veiled message of anti-Roman resistance. Roman military legions (from Latin *legio*, 'conscription' or 'army'), consisting of several thousand soldiers, occupied the Holy Land in the first century CE. The possible inclusion of a veiled metaphor against Roman military rule in the story of Legion suggests that the writers of the Gospels may have found a safe—yet daring—way to plant the seeds of dissent. According to this hypothesis, the biblical story of the Gadarene swine offers not only a vignette into Jesus' miraculous power of exorcism and healing but also a remarkable political sub-narrative within a Gospel text. Intriguingly, one Roman legion (*Legio X Fretensis*) that occupied Jerusalem following 70 CE had a boar as one of its emblems.

The twofold association of the term legion with both armies and demonic possession continued beyond Roman times. As a result, the term continued to be used in the West either to denote a fighting force, or to imply the demonic. Western fiction abounds with a references and allusions to this story. During the Medieval and Renaissance periods, popular folklore described Legion as a hydra-headed devil. Later, in Shakespeare's *Twelfth Night*, Sir Toby says, 'if all the devils of hell be drawn in a little, and Legion himself possessed him [Malvolio], yet I'll speak to him' (3.4.94-95).

In the twentieth century, C.S. Lewis mentions Legion in his book, *Surprised by Joy* (1955). William Peter Blatty, Roger Zelazny, Sheila Martin Berry, A.N. Wilson, and Terry Pratchett all allude to Legion. Legion is also a popular motif in horror novels. The following Stephen King books all contain allusions to the story: *The Dark Tower Sage, The Strand, Black House, Dessperation, The Regulators,* and *IT*. Not surprisingly, Legion is a popular name in horror films as well, including the *Exorcist III* (1990), *The Exorcism of Emily Rose* (2005), *5ive Girls* (2006), *Ghost Rider* (2007), and *Legion* (2010). Correspondingly, the demon is mentioned in the television shows, *Storm of the Century, Angel, Millennium, Supernatural, Red Dwarf,* and *Gargoyles*. A Saturday Night Live sketch titled, 'Duluth Live' acknowledges Legion in its dialogue. Other pop-culture forums such as video games, heavy-metal music, and comic books include a tip-of-the-hat to Legion. For example, the popular X-men comic book series makes Legion the name of Professor Xavier's son.

See also GADARENE SWINE [SDD]

Lemuel. Lemuel, whose name means 'belonging to God', is a king whose mother's instructions are recorded in Prov. 31.1-9. He may have ruled over the Massaeans, an Arab tribe descended from Ishmael (cf. Gen. 25.14; 1 Chron. 1.30), though it is uncertain whether the Hebrew term *massa'* refers to this tribe or means 'oracle' as it commonly does in prophetic texts (e.g., Isa. 13.1; 14.28; 15.1; 17.1; 19.1; 21.1; 21.11; 21.13; 22.1; 23.1; 30.6; Jer. 23.33; Ezek. 12.10; Nah 1.1; Hab. 1.1; Zec 9.1; 12.1; Mal. 1.1; cf. Prov. 30.1). The Septuagint translates *massa'* as 'oracle' in Prov. 31.1, leaving Lemuel's kingdom undefined, and the NRSV follows this reading.

King Lemuel is notable for receiving and presumably heeding his mother's advice. This likely explains Lemuel's popularity as a name for males until the twentieth century, when its popularity declined sharply. Notable namesakes include Lemuel Shattuck (1783–1859), whose report to the Massachusetts Health Commission in 1850 attributed many public illnesses to poor sanitation. Shattuck revolutionized public health and vital statistics record keeping, and the Lemuel Shattuck Hospital in Boston is the only teaching hospital operated by the Massachusetts Department of Public Health. Lemuel Haynes (1753–1833) was likely the first black pastor of a white congregation in America. Haynes served congregations in Connecticut, remaining at Rutland's West Parish from 1783–1813. In literature, Lemuel Gulliver is the protagonist of Jonathan Swift's *Gulliver's Travels*. Through *Gulliver*, Swift leaves a lasting imprint on the English language, especially in the characterizations of the Lilliputians and the yahoos.

See also PROVERBS, BOOK OF [DIS]

Leopard changing his spots. In an oracle threatening Judah with Babylonian exile, the prophet

Jeremiah said, 'Can Ethiopians change their skin or leopards their spots? Then also you can do good who are accustomed to do evil' (Jer. 13.23). Jeremiah implies the inevitability of judgment due to the people's inability to overcome their wicked proclivities. The saying about leopards not changing their spots means that people cannot change their nature.

The phrase appears often. Brian Goodwin's book on natural selection is entitled, *How the Leopard Changed its Spots: The Evolution of Complexity* (1994). In Shakespeare's *Richard II*, the title character says, 'Lions make leopards tame', to which the Duke of Norfolk replies, 'Yea, but not change his spots' (1.1.174). Rudyard Kipling's South African fable 'How the Leopard Got his Spots' (1902) tells of an originally yellowish leopard and Ethiopian becoming spotted and black respectively. In *More Women than Men* (1933), English novelist Ivy Compton-Burnett writes, 'A leopard does not change his spots, or change his feeling that spots are rather a credit'. Finally, the Elvis Presley recording 'Animal Instinct' includes the phrase, 'A leopard just can't change its spots / And I'm about to lurch now'.

See also ANIMALS, SYMBOLISM OF; JEREMIAH; JEREMIAH, BOOK OF; PROPHECY; PROPHETS [JWB]

Leprosy. Leprosy (Hebrew: *tsâra'ath*, Greek: *lĕpra*), one of the great scourges of the biblical world, was a generic term used to describe a variety of skin ailments. Doubtless some of the lepers of the Bible were people who indeed suffered from actual leprosy (Hansen's Disease), but many more were people with, one supposes, skin cancer, boils, rashes, and dermatitis.

Lepers in the HB were considered physically, morally, and ritually unclean. Leviticus 13 describes how priests performed the role of diagnostician. They also prescribed the appropriate response of the community, determining whether or not lepers were to be separated from others, for how long, and what tests would determine their return to the community. Leviticus 14 describes the ritual cleansing required for lepers and their habitations. Healing was considered an act of God, sometimes performed through the actions of a prophet. For example, in 2 Kgs 5, the commander of the Syrian army Naaman sought healing from the Hebrews, and was cured of leprosy after he followed the instructions of the prophet Elisha who told him to wash seven times in the Jordan River.

In the NT, Jesus healed lepers with a mere touch (e.g., Mark 1.40-45). Luke tells the story of Jesus traveling along the border between Galilee and Samaria and meeting ten lepers who cried out for pity (17.11-19). Jesus told them to go show themselves to the priest, and soon after he spoke, they were healed. Only one of the ten, a Samaritan, returned to prostrate himself before Jesus in thanks. He told the man that his faith had healed him. Leprosy was considered contagious and unclean, but Jesus was willing to touch the sick and associate with the unclean in his healing ministry.

Recent clinical studies of leprosy, combined with a close reading of the biblical sources, has resulted in a reassessment of the ancient stories. It is now assumed that most descriptions of leprosy in the Bible relate to other skin conditions besides Hansen's Disease. Such reinterpretation, however, does not detract from the main theological ideas communicated by such stories, which often speak to the authority of God's prophets and the importance of faith.

See also PHYSICIAN; SICKNESS [RL]

Let the dead bury their dead. The injunction 'let the dead bury their dead' is found in Matt. 8.22 and Luke 9.60. It is Jesus' response to a man requesting permission to bury his father before following Jesus. Providing one's father with a proper burial was an important familial obligation attested elsewhere in ancient Jewish texts (e.g., Gen. 50.5; Lev. 21.1-3; Tob 4.3), indicating it was a reasonable request. Jesus' response, therefore, is rather unexpected since it implied the obligations of discipleship superseded familial duties (on this theme, see also Matt. 10.37-39; 12.46-49; 19.29).

Not only does Jesus' statement underscore the demands of discipleship, but it also identifies some people as the metaphorical 'dead'. Commentators often interpret this to mean those who are spiritually dead. They are the ones to remain behind to care for (i.e., bury) the literally dead, while true disciples answer their religious calling. In Jesus' reorganised scheme of life and death (cf. Matt. 10.39), these people are 'the dead' in terms of their negative or ambivalent orientation to Jesus and the kingdom of heaven.

'Let the dead bury their dead' was taken up by nineteenth-century philosophers in their discussion of the value and relevance of the past. In *The Eighteenth Brumaire of Louis Bonaparte* (1852), Karl Marx argued that the past must be abandoned since it prevents humanity from realising its future: 'The social revolution of the nineteenth century can only create its poetry from the future, not from the past. It cannot begin its own work until it has sloughed off all its superstitious regard for the past .... In order to arrive at its own content the revolution of the nineteenth century must let the dead bury their dead'. Similarly, Friedrich Nietzsche adapts this statement in *On the Use and Abuse of History for Life* (1874) to characterize the attitude of those who reject the new by appealing to the great achievements of the past: 'Whether they know it or not, they certainly act as if their motto were: let the dead [i.e., the past] bury the living [i.e., the present]'.

'Let the dead bury their dead' also appears in the American literary works of Henry Wadsworth Longfellow, Henry David Thoreau, and Harper Lee. Longfellow's poem, *A Psalm of Life* (1839), uses the statement to advocate living in the present: 'Trust no Future, howe'er pleasant! / let the dead Past bury its dead! / Act,—act in the living Present!' Thoreau uses the statement in *A Plea for Captain John Brown* (1859) to refer to those who have died without ever truly living in the fullest sense. In Lee's *To Kill a Mockingbird* (1960), Sheriff Tate employs the statement to persuade Atticus Finch to leave the matter of Bob Ewell's death undisturbed: 'There's a black boy dead for no reason, and the man responsible for it's dead. Let the dead bury the dead this time, Mr. Finch. Let the dead bury the dead'.

More recently, the statement has appeared in the lyrics of Bob Dylan's 1986 song, 'Under Your Spell'. It is also the title for Randall Kenan's 1992 collection of fictional folk stories, *Let the Dead Bury their Dead*, and the album title of Burn it Down's 2000 release.

[JRM]

Let there be light. The Bible begins with an account of the creation of the universe. God creates the heavens and the earth, but the earth is a formless void. Genesis 1.3 states: 'Then God said, 'Let there be light'; and there was light'. This begins God's creative process of bringing life to planet earth. Since it is placed in an account of creation, it may seem that the immediate meaning of the term refers to a physical light. However, it is not until v. 14 that the sun, moon and stars are created; thus, the light of v. 3 cannot be referring to light from the earth's luminary sources. Secondly, there is a clear distinction throughout the HB between the light of day and the light of the sun. In understanding light as a cosmic substance in Gen. 1.3, it is likely that the narrator is thinking existentially and theologically rather than physically. Throughout the Hebrew text, the term *'or* has a consistent theological emphasis and is regularly used in the metaphorical sense.

The phrase 'let there be light' represents the first recorded words of God in the Hebrew text. According to the Robert Alter's general principle of biblical narrative, the first reported speech of a character is a defining moment of characterization and thus, carries great significance. Here, God's first speech establishes the theme of the text and indeed, of the world God creates. By saying 'let there be light', the LORD is revealing his desire and purpose for creation. Everything about God's nature and the way he acts toward the world ultimately points toward bringing about that 'light'. This is illustrated countless times throughout the biblical text as God continually brings life, salvation and deliverance to his chosen people. In Genesis, we see that the work of God in bringing light to humanity is central from the provision of clothes for Adam and Eve that foreshadows our own redemption, through the narratives of Abraham, Hagar, Isaac, Jacob, Judah and Joseph, which all illustrate that God will bring his people into the 'light' despite their foolish, evil or rebellious acts.

The expression 'let there be light' is a familiar one in contemporary speech. Various writers make use of it, including Walter M. Miller, Jr, in his novel *A Canticle for Leibowitz* (1960), where it appears as a section title.

See also CHILDREN OF LIGHT; CREATOR, CREATION; FINGER OF GOD; GOD; LIGHT; [MHH]

Letter of the Law. The unabridged *OED* provides the following definition of the word letter: 'The precise terms of a statement; the signification that lies on the surface'. Thus the letter of a statement or enactment serves to denote its literal tenor as opposed to its 'spirit', or its 'broad or general intent or meaning'. One usually employs the idiom pejoratively. Hence, modern jargon, legal or otherwise, understands the letter of the law to indicate the strict and exact force of the language used in a statute or rule, as distinguished from the spirit, general purpose, and policy of the statute.

The biblical idiom appears in 2 Corinthians. In 3.6, Paul designates himself and those with him 'ministers of a new covenant; not of letter [Greek: *to gramma*], but of spirit [Greek: *to pneuma*]; for the letter kills, but the Spirit gives life'. This negative appraisal of the Mosaic Law appears a number of times in Paul's epistles. Paul's writings do include positive statements about the law, as in Rom. 7.12:

'the law is holy, and the commandment is holy and just and good'. Nonetheless, his primary concern is to show the salvific inadequacy of obedience to the 'old written code', as opposed to the 'new life of the Spirit' (Rom. 7.6). Put differently, circumcision does not authenticate the Jew. Rather, 'a person is a Jew who is one inwardly, and real circumcision is a matter of the heart—it is spiritual and not literal' (Rom. 2.29a)

Recently author A.J. Jacobs attempted to follow the letter of the law within the Jewish and Christian Scriptures for one year. The inevitable tension with North American culture rendered punctilious obedience quite impossible. In the end, he decides to retain certain customs that nurture his spiritual life and reject those that stifle it. An application of the letter of the law proves to be the turning point in William Shakespeare's play *The Merchant of Venice*. A semantic loophole in a contract provides the occasion of its eventual overturning. The morality of the lawsuit possesses no consequence in the decision for the defendant. Yet here an application of the letter of the law served to prevent an injustice. Nonetheless, it does not always yield such ideal results. People often express frustration over apparent injustices in our courts of law based on technicalities. It is not enough that justice be done, but that justice is perceived to be done.

Recommended reading. Jacobs, A.J. *The Year of Living Biblically: One Man's Humble Quest to Follow the Bible as Literally as Possible.* New York: *Simon & Schuster,* 2007.

See also CIRCUMCISION; JEW, JUDAISM; LAW; NEW COVENANT [NRP]

Levi. The third son of Jacob and Leah, Levi is the founder of the Israelite tribe of that name, and is recorded as having three sons: Gershon, Kohath and Merari. Levi is vengeful and involved in the destruction of the city of Shechem after the rape of Dinah (Gen. 34.1-31) but is best remembered because of the importance of his ancestors, the Levites, who fulfill various priestly duties in Israel's cultic life (e.g., Num. 1.53; 3.5-39).

[JC]

Leviathan. This Hebrew word means 'twisting one'. Leviathan is a sea monster and serpent who appears several times in the Bible and then repeatedly in English culture as a symbol of nature and politics.

The Bible depicts Leviathan in two different ways. First, Leviathan represents the forces of chaos that God defeats or controls in order to make the world habitable. God 'crushed the heads of Leviathan' (Ps. 74.14) in order to create the cosmos. At the end of time, God will 'punish Leviathan the fleeing serpent, Leviathan the twisting serpent, and he will kill the dragon that is in the sea' (Isa. 27.1). Canaanite myths from the fourteenth century BCE speak of *Lotan* or *Litan*, which is etymologically related to Leviathan, and whose description as 'the twisting ... crooked serpent' is similar to Isa. 27.1 and whose 'seven heads' explains the mention of 'heads' in Ps. 74.14.

This imagery can be identified with the spiritual forces behind natural and political powers. Ezekiel calls Egypt a 'dragon in the seas' (Ezek. 32.2). Although Leviathan is not explicitly named, the dragon in Rev. 12.3 who opposes God in the end times and is behind a succession of oppressive empires has seven heads (Rev. 12.3) and is identified in Rev. 20.2 as 'that ancient serpent, who is the Devil and Satan'.

In contrast to this first use, Leviathan may be portrayed as an accepted and even celebrated part of creation. Psalm 104.6 praises 'Leviathan who you formed to play in [the sea]' which could also be translated 'you formed to play with'. The Book of Job climaxes with two speeches from God, the second of which ends with a lengthy description of Leviathan (Job 41.1-34). By asking Job whether he can control Leviathan, God makes the point that Job does not have God's power, but God's lengthy praise of Leviathan also makes the point that, although humans may not understand it, chaos is a part of creation.

Leviathan appears many times in the history of English culture and literature, but a few examples will illustrate its use as a symbolic reflection on humanity's relation to politics and nature. Hobbes's *Leviathan* was the most significant philosophical book of the seventeenth century, is considered the beginning of political science, and is still widely appreciated for its insights. Leviathan is the state that rules on behalf of all its citizens in order to protect them from their baser instincts. Thus the meaning Hobbes gives to Leviathan is an ironic play on the biblical meanings. The classic American novel *Moby Dick* by Herman Melville repeatedly calls whales Leviathans. Captain Ahab, whose name recalls a notorious Israelite king, unsuccessfully plays the role of a god in the narrative pattern by attempting to hunt down and defeat Moby Dick. The whale functions as a symbolic representation of nature as enemy and resource. At the beginning of the *Free Willy* movies, the ship that captures Willy has the same name as Captain Ahab's ship in *Moby Dick*. In these movies, however, the 'whale' is a friend, reflecting North American society's changing view of whales and more generally nature. Thus the biblical Leviathan continues to be used in contemporary society to reflect on humanity's relationship to politics and nature.

See also ANIMALS, SYMBOLISM OF; SERPENT/SNAKE, THE [AW-J]

Levirate marriage. According to Torah (Deut. 25.5-6), if a married man dies without leaving an offspring, his brother has the right to marry the widow and their first son will be accounted to the deceased brother, preserving his lineage. This is known as a levirate marriage. Should the brother refuse to marry the widow, a special ritual is performed to nullify the levirate marriage, at which time the widow is free to marry anyone outside the family (Deut. 25.7-10).

Some stories in the HB reflect the practice of levirate marriage. In Gen. 38, for instance, God takes the life of Onan, because he married the widow of his deceased brother but refused to help preserve his brother's lineage. Also worthy of note is the Book of Ruth, which tells the story of Ruth's marriage to Boaz, a relative of her deceased husband, but not all scholars view their union as a case of levirate marriage. The Gospels (Matt. 22.23-33; Mark 12.18-27; Luke 20.27-40) report a dispute between Jesus and the Sadducees. To support their view that there is no resurrection, the Sadducees tell the story of a woman who marries seven brothers who die in succession, all in accordance to levirate marriage regulations. They observe she would then have several husbands in the afterlife, which is an absurd notion. Jesus dismisses their logic, stating there is no marriage in the afterlife. Regulations regarding levirate marriage remained a popular topic of discussion in later rabbinic Judaism, receiving extensive coverage in tractate *Yebamot* of the Mishna, Tosefta, as well as the Palestinian and Babylonian Talmuds.

The influence of levirate marriage on Western culture is evident in events leading up to the English Reformation in the sixteenth century CE. At one time, King Henry VIII was married to Catherine of Aragon, the widow of his late brother Arthur. For various reasons, the king was seeking permission from Pope Clement VII to annul the marriage on biblical grounds, as Lev. 18.16 and 20.21 strictly prohibit marriage between a brother- and sister-in-law. Unfortunately for the king, his marriage with Catherine qualified as a levirate marriage, which from the biblical perspective was perfectly legal, so the divorce he wanted was not granted. This dispute eventually resulted in the break between England and the Roman Catholic Church, which is one of the most significant events in the history of Christianity.

The concept of levirate marriage appears occasionally in contemporary culture. For example, in *The Boy Who Fell out of the Sky* (2006), Ken Dornstein describes falling in love with the girlfriend of his late brother, a victim of the Pan Am Flight 103 bombing, and explains that experience in terms of the traditions of levirate law. Another example is the CBS film *Loving Leah* (2009), which tells the story of a levirate marriage between a cardiologist and his young widowed sister-in-law.

Recommended reading. Belkin, S. 'Levirate and Agnate Marriage in Rabbinic and Cognate Literature'. *Jewish Quarterly Review* 60 (1970) 275-329. Burrows, M. 'Levirate Marriage in Israel'. *Journal of Biblical Literature* 59 (1940) 23- 33. Epstein, L.M. *Marriage Laws in the Bible and the Talmud*. Cambridge, MA: Harvard University Press, 1942.

See also DEUTERONOMY, BOOK OF; GENESIS, BOOK OF; LAW; SADDUCEES [ACKW]

Levite's concubine. Judges 19 tells of a concubine (*pilegesh*) who runs away from her Levite husband to her father's house in Bethlehem. In the HB, 'whoring' (*zanah*) is the reason for her flight; in the LXX, it is anger (*ōrgisthē*) (v. 2). After four months, the Levite travels to Judah to persuade her to return. His father-in-law welcomes him, persuading him to stay for five days. On the way back to Ephraim, they find lodging in Gibeah, a Benjaminite town. They are welcomed by an old Ephraimite man, who urges them not to spend the night outside, but to stay with him. As the man entertains the Levite, the townsmen surround the house, demanding the guest so they can have sex with him. The host begs the mob to take his virgin daughter and the concubine instead; the Levite seizes his concubine and throws her to them. The Benjaminites gang-rape her throughout the night; at dawn, they release her, and she falls down in the doorway. The Levite orders her to rise; when she doesn't, he hoists her on his donkey and returns home. There, he dismembers her into twelve pieces and sends them throughout Israel, sparking a civil war (cf. 20.4-7). The story illustrates the chaotic times 'when there was no king in Israel' (19.1; cf. 17.6; 18.1; 21.25).

The story does not appear elsewhere in the Bible. Its earliest interpreters, Josephus and Pseudo-Philo, offer different retellings. Josephus (*Antiquities* 5.136-74) portrays the woman as the Levite's beautiful and impetuous wife, whose husband is smitten by her. She leaves him in anger, even though her husband exhausts himself trying to placate her. He visits her parents, willing to meet all her demands. In Gibeah, the mob is attracted by the woman's beauty; they lust after her, not her husband; rather than being thrown out by the Levite, she is seized by the Benjaminites. Pseudo-Philo (45.1-6), in contrast, portrays the woman as an adulteress who sinned with the Amalekites, taken by force by the townsmen. Josephus sanitizes the story; Pseudo-Philo blames the Israelites for avenging the woman's slaughter while tolerating Micah's idolatry (cf. Judg. 17.1-18.31).

Early Christian and rabbinic commentators generally overlook the story. Medieval commentators sometimes resort to allegory. Some see the rape as justified by the woman's adultery, others see the offer of the women to the lustful crowd as preferable to the greater sin of homosexual rape, attitudes echoed by Reformation interpreters. An exception is Pietro Vermigli (1499–1562), who blames the old man for his willingness to prostitute his daughter and the concubine.

In Byzantine art, the concubine is depicted as a prostitute, conveying monastic disapproval of concubinage. The story is seldom depicted in western art; Jan Victors's *The Levite and his Concubine at Gibeah* (c. 1650) emphasizes the concubine's youth and vulnerability.

Feminist exegetes have emphasized the androcentric perspective of the story and its interpretation throughout history. Phyllis Trible famously interprets it as a biblical 'text of terror' where male relationships, duties and politics dictate the atrocities perpetrated on the woman.

Recommended reading. Feldman, Louis. 'Josephus' Portrayal (*Antiquities* 5.136-74) of the Benjaminite Affair of the Concubine and its Repercussions (Judges 19–21)'. *Jewish Quarterly Review* 3–4 (2000) 255-92. Meyer, Mati. 'The Levite's Concubine: Imaging the Marginal Woman in Byzantine Society'. *Studies in Iconography* 27 (2006) 45-76. Thompson, John L. *Writing the Wrongs: Women of the Old Testament among Biblical Commentators from Philo through the Reformation*. Oxford: Oxford University Press, 2001. Trible, Phyllis. *Texts of Terror: Literary-Feminist Readings of Biblical Narratives*. Philadelphia: Fortress Press, 1984.

See also CONCUBINE; JUDGES, BOOK OF; LEVITES

[MALB]

Levites. The Levites are one of the twelve tribes of Israel. When the promised land was divided among the tribes, they did not receive a territorial allotment (Josh. 18.7) but instead received forty-eight towns scattered throughout Israel (Num. 35.7). The Levites also had unique duties and privileges. Their roles centered on the tabernacle (and later the temple), and were responsible for its maintenance and protection. As the nation of Israel wandered in the desert, the Levites camped around the tabernacle to protect its sanctity (Num. 1.53). They also assisted the priests, who were themselves appointed from among the Levites.

In Israel's early history, it appears the Levites' main function was to move and carry the ark of the covenant. Once the temple was built, there was little need for this so they developed other specialized roles, such as gatekeeping (1 Chron. 26.17), baking (1 Chron. 9.31), guarding the temple treasure (Ezra 8.29), singing (Neh. 12.27), and teaching the law (2 Chron. 17.8). Levites were also called on to help the priests during Hezekiah's reform (2 Chron. 29.34). Although Levites do not appear often in the NT, one of the men who passed by the victim in Jesus' good Samaritan parable was a Levite. Paul's missionary partner Barnabas was a Levite as well (Acts 4.36).

Judg. 19–20 contains the account of a Levite whose concubine is raped and murdered by men from the tribe of Benjamin. In response, the Levite dismembered her body, sent the pieces to the twelve tribes, and initiated a civil war against the tribe of Benjamin. This account has been the source of many pieces of art, including a drawing by Rembrandt (*A Man of Gibeah Offers Hospitality to the Levite and his Concubine*), engravings by Gustave Doré (found in *La Sainte Bible*), and a painting by Jean-Jacques Henner (*The Levite of Ephraim and his Dead Wife*).

St Ambrose understands the Levites and their regulations to pertain to the Christian priesthood in *De officiis ministrorum*. William Cowper laments the loss of Israel's former glory, and acknowledges the Levites in 'Expostulation'. In his *Science and Culture*, biologist T.H. Huxley complains that advocates of a scientific education 'have been excommunicated by the classical scholars, in their capacity of Levites in charge of the ark of culture'.

See also BARNABAS; GOOD SAMARITAN; LEVITE'S CONCUBINE; TABERNACLE; TEMPLE, ISRAEL'S; TWELVE TRIBES OF ISRAEL [DP]

Leviticus, Book of. Leviticus is located in the center of the Torah, the first section of the HB. This title comes from the Latin translation of the Greek title, *Leyitikon*, meaning 'book of the Levites'. While the priestly family is from the tribe of Levi, the book itself only mentions the Levites in 25.32-34. The Hebrew title, *wayyiqrā*, meaning 'and he called', is the first word of the book.

While much of the text appears to be regulations for the priests, the book is intended for the greater Israelite community. The book is concerned with the concept of holiness and explores the implications of having been called by God to be a holy people. The first seven chapters concerning sacrifices serve as a sequel to Exodus's construction of the tabernacle, as each sacrifice served a unique purpose within the system of worship. The narrative continues the account of the Israelites' wilderness experience from Exodus. Chapters 8 through 10 narrate the first attempt of the priests to enter the presence of God and fulfill their priestly duties. This attempt ends tragically with the deaths of Aaron's sons, Nadab and Abihu. Following their deaths, the categories of ritual purity are further defined in chapters 11 through 15. Chapter 16 concludes the Priestly Code with the successful Day of Atonement. Chapters 17 through 26, known as the Holiness Code, outline the personal and communal requirements for a people deemed holy by God.

The book's emphasis on rules and rituals can appear overwhelming and irrelevant for many modern readers. However, the relevance of the book is discovered as one explores Leviticus's theme of holiness. Rules and rituals were essential for a people among whom the holy God was dwelling. Boundaries were set in place to ensure that the people guarded their relationship with God as God's presence in the camp impacted all dimensions of life.

The NT relies heavily on Leviticus. When asked to describe the most important commandment, Jesus' response concerning the second greatest commandment comes from Lev. 19.18. The dietary laws of Lev. 11-15 are reflected in Jesus' proclamation that all foods were clean (Mark 7.19) and the early Christians' struggle over the same issue in Acts 10.9-15. The Book of Hebrews picks up many of the same themes, such as the role of the high priest (now fulfilled in Christ) and the relevance of sacrifices.

In recent years, passages from Leviticus have made headlines. In debates concerning homosexuality, verses such as 18.22 and 20.13 are often referred to. Due to its emphasis on sacrifices and rituals, the Book of Leviticus has often been ignored by Christians, and therefore is often not referred to in modern culture. Leviticus was the name of a Swedish Christian metal band that played through the 1980's, as well as the name of an American gospel choir. Some concepts from Leviticus have found their way into modern language, such as scapegoat and jubilee.

Recommended reading. Douglas, Mary. *Purity and Danger: An Analysis of the Concepts of Pollution and Taboo*. London: Ark Paperbacks, 1966. Gorman, Frank H., Jr. *Leviticus: Divine Presence and Community*. Grand Rapids, MI: Wm B. Eerdmans, 1997. Milgrom, Jacob. *Leviticus: A Continental Commentary*. Minneapolis: Augsburg Fortress Press, 2004.

See also ATONEMENT, DAY OF; HOLY/HOLINESS; IMPURITY; LAW; RITUAL PURITY [DP]

Life. This word usually translates the Hebrew *chaim*, or Greek *zoe* or *bios*. The Bible references two kinds of life: temporal, earthly life, and eternal, heavenly life. In the Bible, life is seen as the ultimate reward, loss, or sacrifice (Job 2.4: 'Then Satan answered the Lord, "Skin for skin! All that people have they will give to save their lives"'). The Pentateuch, the five books of law in the HB, often employs life in legal sentences, as in the well-known 'eye-for-an-eye' passage (Exod. 21.22-25; Lev. 24.19-21; Deut. 19.21), when 'life for life' is prescribed. In the dietary restrictions of the Pentateuch, blood is the life of the animal, which is why it should not be consumed (Exod. 17.10-16; Deut. 12.23).

The concept of life is prominent in the Book of Job, in which the main character says, 'I loathe my life' (Job 7.16; 9.21; 10.1). Ecclesiastes focuses on the emptiness of life, calling it 'vanity' and finding no fulfillment in the pleasures of life such as wealth. This view of life is closely related to 'Greek pessimism', a system of thought classically expressed by the Greek tragedian Sophocles in *Oedipus at Colonus*: 'Not to be born is best, but having seen the light, the next best is to go whence one came as soon as may be'.

The NT stories of Jesus and his message focus heavily on both earthly life and 'eternal' or 'everlasting' life. In Matt. 6.25-34 and Luke 12.22-32, Jesus exhorts his followers not to worry about their life, clothes, or food, saying that God will provide. Jesus' giving up his life as a 'ransom for many' (Matt.

10.28; Mark 10.45) is a major NT theme, and the Gospel of John often touches on 'eternal life'. John 1.4 focuses on 'the Word' (Jesus) through whom life came into being. Jesus calls himself the 'bread of life' and promises eternal life to those who eat his flesh and drink his blood (John 6.35-59). Many of the best-known verses about Jesus involve the concept of life, as in John 3.16 ('everyone who believes in him may not perish but may have eternal life') and John 14.6 ('I am the way, and the truth and the life').

John 3.16 catapulted to national US attention in the 1970s and 1980s due to Rollen Stewart, or 'Rainbow Man', who donned a rainbow-colored wig and held up a placard with the verse citation at high-profile sporting events. A common image associated with the biblical concept of life is the 'tree of life' (Hebrew *etz chaim*). It appears in one Genesis account of creation (Gen. 3.22) and is often understood to be distinct from the tree of the knowledge of good and evil; it resurfaces in Rev. 2.7; 22.2; 22.19. This concept is one that is present in many cultures' mythologies where it is often styled as a 'world tree'. The 2006 Darren Aronofsky film *The Fountain* revolves around the quest for immortality granted by a Tree of Life, and 2009's James Cameron film *Avatar* places a tree of life at the center of the spiritual world of the Na'vi people, the inhabitants of the lush planet Pandora. Samuel Beckett's play *Waiting for Godot* features a single tree that is often considered to represent the tree of life.

Recommended reading. Anderson, Paul N. 'The Sitz im Leben of the Johannine Bread of Life Discourse and its Evolving Context'. In *Critical Readings of John 6*. Ed. R. Alan Culpepper. Pp. 1-59. Leiden: Brill, 1997. Watson, Paul. 'The Tree of Life'. *Restoration Quarterly* 23 (1980) 232-38. [KJV]

Light. The first reference to light in the Bible is Gen. 1.3: 'Then God said, 'Let there be light'; and there was light'. This begins God's creative process of bringing light and life to the world. Throughout the Bible, the concept of light is used both as a physical description and as a metaphor. While the references to physical luminaries is more straightforward, the metaphorical use of light in the Bible covers a wide range of meanings. The biblical text in its entirety develops a beautiful understanding of God's first words. In the OT, light is symbolic of God's provision and presence, a metaphor for the life he creates, synonymous with salvation and deliverance, a description of the promised Messiah, and a sign of the covenantal relationship of Yahweh with his people. These ideas reappear in the NT with Jesus presented as God's ultimate provision for his people, and the full embodiment of his presence. Paul understood the significance of the coming of Christ as the fulfillment of God's initial words: 'For God, who said 'Let light shine out of darkness', is the one who shined in our hearts to give us the light of the glorious knowledge of God in the face of Jesus Christ' (2 Cor. 4.4).

See also CHILDREN OF LIGHT; LET THERE BE LIGHT; LIGHT UNDER A BUSHEL [MHH]

Lilies of the field. The phrase 'lilies of the field' (Greek *ta krina tou agrou*) appears in the Sermon on the Mount as Jesus encourages his disciples not to waste time worrying over worldly things. He exhorts them to instead 'consider the lilies of the field, how they grow; they neither toil nor spin, yet I tell you, even Solomon in all his glory was not clothed like one of these' (Matt. 6.28-29). Since worry accomplishes nothing and the lilies—which cannot worry—bear finer raiment than we could ever provide for ourselves, Jesus encourages us to trust in God's provision.

The phrase appears often in literature, as in Christina Rossetti's poem 'Consider the Lilies of the Field' or Cecelia M. Caddell's hymn 'Behold the Lilies of the Field'. John Keats's use of the image is ironic in 'Ode on Indolence', with its epigraph, 'they toil not, neither do they spin'. Keats determines that the pleasures of love, ambition and poetry are all exceeded by the pleasure of leisure (the irony being that if he had followed his own advice, the poem would not exist). Oscar Wilde borrows the phrase in his poem 'Humanitad', referencing the ornamentation of the arch of the Southwell Minster chapter house in Nottinghamshire which is ordained with carvings of English foliage, including lilies. Soren Kierkegaard wrote a reflection on this passage called *The Lily in the Field and the Bird of the Air: Three Devotional Discourses*. Kierkegaard reflected on the silence of the lilies and their position before God and that in fulfilling their created role they are in perfect obedience to him. We humans must align our wills with his if we are to fulfil our created role and live well and in obedience.

In some modern works, such as Somerset Maugham's *The Narrow Corner*, the phrase is taken to illustrate class struggle: some see no need to toil because there are others to do that for them. Anthony Hecht's 'Behold the Lilies of the Field' and Jacob Friesen's 'Cloister of the Lilies' both turn the phrase into a cruel inversion of itself, telling those without hope to take no concern for tomorrow.

The phrase lilies of the field was perhaps most famously used in modern times as the title of the classic 1963 film starring Sydney Poitier. In the film, based on the novel by William Edmund Barrett, Poitier's character Homer is a travelling handyman who comes across a group of nuns struggling to set up a ministry. He builds a chapel for the nuns, and though he is not compensated financially and struggles with the Mother Superior, he stays the summer working and living among the nuns, eventually completing the chapel. For his performance in this film Poitier won an Academy Award, the first ever awarded to an African American.

See also LILY OF THE VALLEY; PARABLE; SERMON ON THE MOUNT [JIM]

Lily of the valley. The Hebrew *shoshannah 'emeq* ('lily of the valleys') appears in the Bible only at Song 2.1, and it is not certain specifically to what kind of flower the text is referring. It is certainly not the green and white *convallaria maialis*, which is the scientific designation for the flower today known as the 'lily of the valley'. Scholars have posited that the flower may be the Egyptian water lotus (*shoshen* in Coptic) or the bright red anemone, which grows in the fields of Syria-Palestine, since later in the poem lips are compared with *shoshannim* ('lilies'; Song 5.13), presumably on the basis of a similar ruddy coloring.

The Song of Songs is a love poem—or, as some argue, a collection of love poems—spoken in the alternating voices of two lovers, which both Jews and Christians have interpreted as an allegory of the relationship between God and God's people. It is clear from the sequence of the text that the woman speaks the words, 'I am a rose of Sharon / A lily of the valleys', since in the following verse the man refers to his beloved as a 'lily': 'As a lily among brambles / So is my love among maidens' (Song 2.2). Rabbinic Jewish exegesis of Song 2.1 identifies the woman as the speaker; it understands the woman to be a figure of Israel as it emerged from slavery in Egypt, blossoming as a beautiful flower. Most patristic and medieval Christian commentators, however, identified the man as the speaker, who they believed to be Jesus Christ speaking to his church. They asserted that Christ was the 'lily' and that the 'valleys' were the once-lowly nations of the Gentiles, for whose salvation he was made incarnate.

The identification of Christ as the 'lily of the valley(s)' was so pervasive that it endures to the present day, even in Protestant traditions in which the Song of Songs is no longer interpreted allegorically. This is exemplified in the hymn of William Charles Fry (1837–82), a member of the Salvation Army, entitled 'The Lily of the Valley', which says of Christ: 'He's the lily of the valley, the bright and morning star / He's the fairest of ten thousand to my soul'. The French novelist Honoré de Balzac (1799–1850) composed *Le Lys dans La Vallée* ('The Lily of the Valley'), although he means this to refer to the female protagonist of the novel, and he does not associate it with Christian symbolism.

Recommended reading. Murphy, Roland E. *The Song of Songs: A Commentary on the Book of Canticles or the Song of Songs*. Hermeneia, 22. Philadelphia: Fortress Press, 1990. Pope, Marvin H. *Song of Songs*. The Anchor Bible, 7C. Garden City, NY: Doubleday, 1977.

See also ALLEGORY; LILIES OF THE FIELD; SONG OF SOLOMON, SONGS [KAS]

Lion of Judah. 'The Lion of the tribe of Judah' is a title given to Jesus by one of the 24 elders in Rev. 5.5. John has been weeping because he fears no one will be worthy to open the scroll with the seven seals, but he is comforted with the news that 'the Lion of the tribe of Judah, the Root of David' has conquered and is therefore able to break the seals on the scroll. This image of the Messiah as conquering is significant (cf. 6.2; 17.14) because the same is also expected of those who follow him into battle against the forces of evil: those who conquer are promised blessings and become children of God (Rev. 2.7, 11, 17, 26; 3.5, 12, 21; 21.7).

The OT background for this title is found in Gen. 49.9: 'Judah is a lion's whelp … He crouches down, he stretches out like a lion, like a lioness; who dares rouse him up?' The route from here to the usage found in the Book of Revelation is via a long tradition of Jewish messianic interpretation. For example, in the intertestamental book of *4 Ezra*, the conquering lion is used as an image for the long-awaited Davidic Messiah: 'And as for the lion whom you saw rousing up out of the forest and roaring and speaking to the eagle and reproving him for his unrighteousness, and as for all his words that you have heard, this is the Messiah whom the Most High has kept until the end of days, who will arise from the offspring of David, and will come and speak with them' (*4 Ezra* 12.31-32; cf. 11.37). In this way, the use of this title for Jesus in the Book of Revelation identifies him as a descendant of King David and the rightful ruler of the tribe of Judah, and it is in this capacity as Davidic Messiah that Jesus is proclaimed worthy to open the scroll.

Within Jewish tradition the lion is a symbol for the tribe of Judah, and as such features on the flag of the city of Jerusalem the ancient capital of Judah. In Christianity, the lion is frequently used as a symbol for Jesus, something which twentieth-century author C.S. Lewis utilized in his allegorical novel *The Lion, The Witch and the Wardrobe*, in which Jesus is portrayed as Aslan the lion. The Rastafarian community use the title Lion of Judah to refer to their proclaimed messiah-figure the Emperor Heili Salassie I of Ethiopia (1892–1975), who they believe to be a descendant of King David through the union of David's son Solomon and the Queen of Sheba (cf. 1 Kgs 10.1-13). The song 'Lion of Judah' by Bob Marley is based on this belief, and in a live performance of the song Marley introduced it with the following words: 'I will say to the people, man, be still and know that His Imperial Majesty Emperor Heili Salassie I of Ethiopia is the Almighty. The Lion of Judah shall break every chain'.

Recommended reading. Boxall, Ian. *The Revelation of St John*. Black's New Testament Commentaries. London: Continuum, 2006. Kovacs, Judith L., and Christopher Rowland. *Revelation*. Blackwell Bible Commentaries. Oxford: Blackwell, 2004. Woodman, Simon. *The Book of Revelation*. SCM Core Text. London: SCM Press Ltd., 2008.

See also DAVID; QUEEN OF SHEBA; REVELATION, BOOK OF; SOLOMON [SW]

Lion lies down with the lamb. The original source for this image is a prophetic oracle in Isa. 11.1-9, which announces the future coming of an ideal Davidic ruler for the people of Israel. Having begun with an outline of the superlative attributes of this coming monarch (i.e., wisdom, understanding, counsel, might, knowledge and fear of the LORD), the oracle moves seamlessly into extolling the benefits of his rule, as they pertain to both society and nature. It is in this context that the promise is made that the king's rule will bring about a peaceable kingdom, whereby the 'lion' (in actual fact, 'wolf') will lay down with the 'lamb'. Though some scholars argue that the 'lion' and 'lamb' are allegorical figures having reference to geopolitical realities in the Ancient Near East, most agree that the oracle is a vision of pastoral tranquillity in which traditional enemies in the animal world are at peace. The point of such an idealiszed portrait is to give expression to the Hebrew longing for a world of security and safety, in which the world returns to an Edenic innocence without harm and danger. There is a similar 'new creation' oracle in Isa. 65.17-25. Such hopes are often encapsulated in the Hebrew word *shalom* (usually translated 'peace', but capable of a far greater semantic range).

Perhaps the most notable expression of this image in art comes via the prodigious output of the nineteenth-century Quaker artist Edward Hicks, whose series of works entitled *The Peaceable Kingdom* involve a creative blending of Isaianic imagery with allusions to contemporary events in American history (most notably William Penn's treaty with the Native Americans).

Due to its intriguing and fantastic nature, the hope of an 'animal peace' has also proven capable of being appropriated and recontextualized for a variety of social and political causes, including nonreligious utopianism. The image fired the imagination of such poets as Percy Bysshe Shelley, whose radical work *Queen Mab* includes a notable reference to the lion 'who forgets to thirst for blood'. Yet the natural impossibility of Isaiah's scenario has also meant that the image is frequently the object of ridicule. For example, the contemporary film director Woody Allen is credited with once quipping that 'the lion and the lamb shall lie down together, but the lamb won't get any sleep'.

Recommended reading. Clements, R.E. 'The Wolf Shall Live with the Lamb: Reading Isaiah 11:6-9 Today'. In *New Heaven and New Earth: Prophecy and the Millennium: Essays in Honour of Anthony Gelston*. Ed. P.J. Harland and R. Hayward. Pp. 83-99. Leiden: Brill, 1999. Tucker, G.M. 'The Peaceable Kingdom and a Covenant with Wild Animals'. In *God Who Creates: Essays in Honor of W. Sibley Towner*. Ed. W.P. Brown and S.D. McBride. Pp. 215-25. Grand Rapids, MI: Eerdmans, 2000.

See also NEW HEAVEN, NEW EARTH; PEACE

[MBS]

Living water. Jesus used the phrase 'living water' in a conversation with a Samaritan woman. The metaphor serves to illustrate a spiritual relationship between him and those who believe his message (John 4.10-11). The image appears again in John 7.37-39. In Jesus' day, the phrase 'living water' would have evoked an image of 'running water' like that in streams rather than 'still water' from a well. The 'running water' would be fresher and sweeter than that from a well filled with water that had seeped in from underground. Water from a well would also be exposed to a greater risk of contamination than running water aerated in a stream.

In John 7, Jesus is in Jerusalem at the Festival of the Booths. On the last day he cries out, 'Let anyone who is thirsty come to me, and let the one who believes in me drink' (7.37-38), thus alluding to words spoken by the prophet Zechariah (see Zech. 14.8). John interprets this as a reference to the Holy Spirit, which had not yet been given because Jesus had not yet been glorified (i.e., resurrected). The image of living water also appears in Revelation. There we read the Lamb will guide the vast multitude in Heaven to springs of living water (Rev. 7.17). The living water is the water of life given by God (Rev. 21.5-6), which flows from the throne of God and the Lamb (Rev. 24.1). OT writers spoke of spiritual thirst and link the living water with the Spirit of God (e.g., Isa. 49.10; Ps. 36.9). In the Dead Sea Scrolls, the *Damascus Document* refers to the Law as the 'well of living water', and the *Thankgiving Psalms* thank God for putting its author at flowing streams.

For Patristic writers, living water was often synonymous with faith. Saint Augustine described the Church as the well of living water (*Contra Faustum*). During the Middle Ages and the Reformation living water that quickened the soul in faith was symbolic of faith. John Calvin used living water for various aspects of faith. John Donne's baptismal sermon on Rev. 17.7 used the image of living water to point to both salvation and sanctification (*Sermons*, 4.98). Henry Vaughn's (1621–1695) sacred poetry used living water apocalyptically in 'Tears' and in 'Jesus Weeping'. References in Shakespeare's *The Tempest* and T.S. Eliot's 'The Waste Land' are overtly biblical.

See also ETERNAL LIFE; RIVER OF LIFE; SALVATION; SAMARITAN WOMAN; SAMARITANS; WATER

[AJW]

Loaves and fishes. The phrase comes from the Greek words for *artos* (bread) and *ichthus* (fish). The most familiar references to loaves and fishes in the Bible are the stories about Jesus feeding crowds of 5000 and 4000 people (see Matt. 14.13-21; 15.32-39; Mark 6.30-44; 8.1-10; Luke 9.10-17; John 6.1-15). Jesus multiplies a few loaves and fish to feed this hungry multitude. In related stories, Jesus tells a parable about the kingdom of heaven being a fishing net (13.47), calls his disciples to be 'fishers of people' (Matt. 4.19, Mark 1.17), and multiplies fish in a net (Luke 5.4-7; John 21.1-14), suggesting that the multiplication of fish is a symbol of the growing kingdom. Fish also play a magical role in the story of Jonah and in the Book of Tobit. The word for fish in Greek (*ichthus*) is an acronym for Jesus (*I<u>e</u>sous*), Christ (*<u>Ch</u>ristos*), of God (*<u>Th</u>eou*), son (*<u>U</u>ios*), savior *(Soter)*, and was thus used as an early Christian symbol, especially in the catacombs. The same symbol is used today to identify vehicles owned by Christians. In a similar way, bread is used as a symbol throughout the NT to represent Jesus (Matt. 26.26-29; Mark 14.22; Luke 22.19; John 6.35; 1 Cor. 10.17; 11.23-30).

See also BREAD; FISH; FEEDING THE FIVE THOUSAND (FOUR THOUSAND)

[JSW]

Locusts and wild honey. This phrase in the Koine Greek of the NT is *akridev kai meli agrion*. In the Greco-Roman world of the NT, food occupied a central place in the lives of those living within the Roman Empire. For the Jews living in Palestine the strict Levitical laws and customs governing food preparation and consumption formed a core part of Jewish religious and ethnic identity and daily life. Such food laws were supposed to promote personal devotion in one's covenant relationship with Yahweh. By the first century CE, however, some Jewish religious leaders had become wealthy and self-indulgent. They engaged in gluttony and sometimes looked for ways to minimize or skirt the effects of the food laws. In this context John the Baptist's ascetic and desert-dweller diet of 'locusts and wild honey', referred to by the Gospel writers Matthew (3.4) and Mark (1.6), sent a strong prophetic call for repentance to such leaders. By adopting such a diet and living at a subsistence level in the desert, John stood in the tradition of the OT prophet Elijah.

Throughout Christian history, John the Baptist's diet has remained a subject of fascination and debate. Some scholars have suggested that John's diet was indicative of one living out his vows as a Nazarite. Others have claimed that John became a vegetarian to rebuke those who engaged in gluttony. In medieval times, John's diet was used to justify certain hermetic and monastic practices. During the reformation John Calvin criticized those who used John the Baptist's lifestyle to legitimize the monastic system. More recent scholarship has tried to examine the diet of John the Baptist in its historical context. For example, in his wide-ranging and provocative study of the subject, James A. Kelhoffer examines the eating of locusts and wild honey in both the Semitic and Greco-Roman contexts. He argues that John could have collected and consumed enough locusts on a daily basis to get the required amount of protein for survival.

In the 1870s, the notable American author John Burroughs produced a book about the natural world entitled, *Locusts and Wild Honey*. Similarly, the famous nineteenth-century American poet, Helen Hunt Jackson, used John the Baptist's diet as the title for one her poems, which was published in 1888.

Recommended reading. Gibson, Shimon. *The Cave of John the Baptist: The Stunning Archeological Study that has Redefined Christian History,* 2004. Kelhoffer, James A. *The Diet of John the Baptist: "Locusts and Wild Honey" in Synoptic and Patristic Interpretation,* 2005. Lockwood, Jeffery A. *Locust: The Devastating Rise and Mysterious Disappearance of the Insect that Shaped the American Frontier,* 2004. Wilkins, John M., and Shaun Hill. *Food in the Ancient World,* 2006.

See also FOOD, SYMBOLISM OF; JOHN, THE BAPTIST

[PRW]

Lord. The Bible uses several Hebrew and Greek words to identify God as Lord. As the maker of heaven and earth, God has the sovereignty right to rule the world. The church uses Lord as a title for Jesus Christ. The biblical terms *Kyrios* (Greek), *Adonai* (Hebrew), *Yahweh* (Hebrew), *adon* (Hebrew), and *ba'al* (Hebrew), all identify 'the Lord' or 'lords'. *Kyrios* (supreme) can indicate a property owner (e.g., Matt. 20.8; 21.40) or function as a title of respect or honor. It refers to God in the Septuagint and Jesus in the NT. *Adonai* appears in the Pentateuch as a respectful form of address to God, and sometimes refers to human masters like Potiphar (Gen. 39.2) and Joseph (Gen. 42.30, 33).

Since written Hebrew uses consonants only, Yahweh was written as YHWH, a title known as the *Tetragrammaton* ('word having four letters'; later scribes introduced the use of various markings to represent vowel sounds to facilitate uniform pronunciation of consonantal Hebrew). As the divine name, YHWH was so revered that it was not even pronounced to avoid blasphemy. When Torah was read aloud, the vowels of the word *Adonai* were combined with the consonants of YHWH to form the artificial word 'Jehovah'. In addition, the written word 'Jehovah' (when vowel points were added) was not actually pronounced and *Adonai*, lord, was used instead. Yahweh is used in the OT in combination with other words numerous times. *Yahweh-jireh* means 'the Lord will provide' (Gen. 22.14); *Yahweh-shalom* means 'the Lord is peace' (Judg. 6.24); *Yahweh-tsebaoth* means 'the Lord of hosts' (1 Sam. 1.3); or *Yahweh Elohe Yisrael*, 'the Lord God of Israel', which is used in Isaiah, Jeremiah, and the Psalms.

The Hebrew word *adon* denotes ownership or absolute control. It is applied to God as the sovereign ruler of the creation but strictly speaking, it is not a divine title because it could apply to husbands as lords of their wives; of kings as lords of their domains; of slave owners; or as a term of respect that is equivalent to Sir. Sara used *adon* (Gen. 18.12) in speaking of her husband. The Hebrew word *ba'al* means lord. In Num. 21.28 and Isa. 16.8 it identifies the nobility of Moab or the nations. It is used of husbands or for masters of businesses. Because *Baal* was associated with heathen deities it was not used for God; in fact it was specifically rejected by Hosea (Hos. 2.16). The word *seren* is a Philistine word for lord. It is found in Joshua, Judges and 1 Samuel. The 'lords of the Philistines' (*seranim*) are named. An Aramaic word for lord, *mara'*, was applied to Christ (*maranatha*; Rev. 22.20, 'Our Lord, come'). *Beelzebub* (*ba'alzebub*) means the Lord of the flies, an expression most familiar to contemporary readers through William Golding's novel of that name.

Recommended reading. Kooten, George H. van. *The Revelation of the Name YHWH to Moses: Perspectives from Judaism, the Pagan Greco-Roman World, and Early Christianity.* New York: Brill Academic Publishers, 2006.

See also CHRIST; HEBREW LANGUAGE; YAHWEH

[AJW]

Lord's Prayer. Sometimes called the 'prayer that spans the world' or the 'Pater noster' (from the opening address of the prayer in Latin), the Lord's Prayer is one of the few shared expressions of faith and worship amongst Christians. It has been an agreed basis for inter-faith dialogue, in part because of parallels with ancient Jewish prayers (The Eighteen Benedictions, The Psalter from the Qumran Community: 11QPs[a]), and also because of the sensitivity for the human condition shown in the second half of the prayer.

There are two sections to the Lord's Prayer. In its familiar form, each section has three elements. The first section has its focus on God, addressed as 'father', accenting the recognition of God's sacredness, the desire for God's justice and peace, and the execution of God's deep purposes. The second section is focused on the human community, addressing human material needs, the necessity for the restoration of relationships between people and the desire for protection against adversity (sometimes separated into two petitions). The bridge between the two sections is provided by recognition that 'earth' is the proper setting for the prayer to be expressed.

The prayer appears with different wording and different contexts in three early Christian texts: the Gospel of Matthew (6.7-13), the Gospel of Luke (11.2-4) and the *Didache* (8.2-3). The similarity between the texts has suggested that there was an earlier form of the prayer in the hypothetical document called Q. It may have had an Aramaic origin with a particular address of peasant issues. Specific petitions of the Lord's Prayer occur in isolation in the Gospel of Mark (e.g., Mark 11.25; 14.36).

The prayer has attracted multiple variations, sometimes brought by changes that occur in translation. Sometimes the variations occur in additions to the prayer (called 'embolisms'). The most famous is the doxology ('the kingdom, the power and the glory') at the end. Another is the petition for the coming of God's Holy Spirit for cleansing, perhaps part of early baptism liturgies. A further embolism comes with the repetition of the petition for deliverance in the second half of the prayer, which is followed by an extended outlining of concerns. This addition now has a standardized wording in some church orders of worship but its origins can be traced to both public liturgies and private household devotions.

This flexibility of wording and context (often contested) has characterized the history of the use of the Lord's Prayer from its beginning in the doublet of the canonical Gospels. Parts of the prayer have been inscribed in epitaphs, have figured as protective formulae in magical amulets (not dissimilar to modern body-tattooing with the prayer) and have adorned church architecture. The prayer is still used to open public institutions (such as government legislatures, school assemblies), provides a foundation element for almost every liturgical service for Christians and, via innovative translations, has become a meditative focus in New Age practice. As shown by its frequent use at liminal moments in western cinematography, the Lord's Prayer remains one of the most recognizable features of western culture and social fabric.

Recommended reading. Charlesworth, J.H., with M. Harding and M. Kiley (ed.). *The Lord's Prayer and Other Prayer Texts from the Greco-Roman Era*. Valley Forge, PA: Trinity Press International, 1994. Dundes, A. *Holy Writ as Oral Lit: The Bible as Folklore*. Lanham, MD: Rowman & Littlefield, 1999.

See also LUKE, GOSPEL OF; MATTHEW, GOSPEL OF; MEEK SHALL INHERIT THE EARTH, THE [AHC]

Lord's Supper. The Lord's Supper is a liturgical meal celebration of high importance to all Christians. Commonly recognized by its two distinct components, bread and wine, this celebration is alternatively known in the Western world as Eucharist (Greek *eucharistia*, 'thanksgiving'; Mark 14.23), breaking of bread (Acts 2.42, 46; 20.7), (Holy) Communion (from 1 Cor. 10.16), love-feast (Jude 12), Last Supper, (holy) sacrament of the table, or (Holy) Mass.

According to the key NT Gospel texts (Matt. 26.26-29; Mark 14.22-25; Luke 22.17-20), Jesus celebrated his last meal before the crucifixion in the company of his twelve disciples. Featuring the basic elements of any ordinary meal, this celebration consisted of familiar gestures open for individual interpretation. At the same time, Jesus himself proposed specific perspectives of understanding these gestures when asking to prepare a Passover meal (Mark 14.12-16). The traditional Passover celebration periodically affirmed Judean corporate identity based on the narrated memory of Israel's salvation in the exodus. In the Passover meal celebrated by Jesus, his mission for others became the new manifestation of human salvation.

In addition, the words of institution conveyed clues of how Jesus proposed to understand this meal. Jesus took bread, gave blessings, broke it, gave it to his disciples and said, 'Take; this is my body' (Mark 14.22). After the resurrection the disciples are said to have recognized Jesus when he repeated this gesture in their presence (Luke 24.30-31). The breaking of bread also references earlier meals (Mark 2.15-17; Luke 7.36-50) and the feeding miracles (Mark 6.30-44; 8.1-9). In the Ancient Mediterranean culture, meals and feasts were important occasions for developing and cultivating fellowship. Jesus used them throughout his ministry to convey the ideal of an inclusive society based on the idea that God cares for all. The bread which Jesus shared represents his life as *pro-existence* for others.

After sharing the bread, Jesus took a cup of wine, gave thanks, and gave it to his disciples to drink. Jesus called this wine 'my blood of the covenant' (Mark 14.24), quoting from the Torah story about the covenant at Mount Sinai (Exod. 24.8) according to which Moses had sprinkled sacrificial 'blood of the covenant' onto the Israelites in order to cleanse and consecrate them. Through this quotation, Jesus indicated that those who drank the wine—a traditional substitute for blood—were likewise consecrated and their sins forgiven.

Further NT texts about the Lord's Supper include 1 Cor. 11.23-26, where Paul adds the dimension of remembering Jesus and establishes this celebration as a regular liturgical event. In 1 Cor. 10.14-22, Paul emphasizes that cup and bread indicate the participation—Greek *koinonia*—in Christ's blood and body. In the Johannine speech about the bread from heaven (John 6.35-59), the misunderstanding of Christ's opponents (v. 52) conveys that eating (or chewing, v. 54) Christ's flesh and drinking his blood does not imply actual consumption of his physical body.

Throughout the church, the Lord's Supper constitutes a climax of worship. Various denominations consider it a sacrament. The Roman Catholic and Anglican churches have claimed since medieval times that the Eucharistical elements are turned into Christ's actual flesh and blood (transubstantiation). According to Reformed doctrine, these elements symbolize Christ's presence, while Lutherans reject the transubstantiation but assume the real presence of Christ's body and blood. Because it communicates effective forgiveness of sins, the Lord's Supper is celebrated weekly in some Christian denominations, yet due to its extraordinary holiness other denominations prefer fewer celebrations. In art and iconography, hardly any topic from the Gospel stories has been depicted as frequently as the Lord's Supper.

See also ATONEMENT; BLOOD; JESUS OF NAZARETH; SACRAMENTS [CAE]

Lost coin, Parable of the. The parable of the lost coin, found in Luke 15.8-10, has no parallel in the other Synoptic Gospels or in the Gospel of John. It is situated with two other parables to form a thematic unit dealing with the justification for Jesus' ministry to those outside the scope of pious Judaism.

Like other biblical parables, a Middle Eastern context is assumed. If the coin was part of a necklace, its loss lies beyond its monetary value, as one of the woman's few personal possessions. As in the case of all three parables in the Luke 15 cluster (Lost Coin, Lost Sheep, Lost [Prodigal] Son), Kenneth Bailey (*Poet and Peasant,* 1976) notes the crucial role played by the social position of the respective participants in the parables. Such roles are rarely explained since the writer (or teller) of the parable could rely on the audience to gauge their plausibility. In this case, the sole character is a woman and is viewed positively in relation to the original questioners—a controversial choice for Jesus to make in the eyes of his listeners. The woman's role is limited to domestic life hence the assumption that the lost coin must be in the house which she sweeps. In a peasant village context, the loss of money is serious for a family. When the coin is found, it is returned to its setting in the necklace just as the lost sheep was returned to its place in the flock.

The parable therefore heightens the themes of joy and restoration by narrowing the scope of the search for the thing lost, thereby increasing the reader's sense of its value and what is at stake if it cannot be found. The parable of the lost coin concludes like the lost sheep, with joy in heaven over repentance and restoration. A common method of interpretation is to look for themes that resonate with the world of the reader and deduce some reasonable way of applying their teaching. Understanding parables in this way is popular but reduces them to mere illustrations. The parable as a vehicle for meaning then becomes dispensable and arbitrary.

However, the biblical parables are typically very carefully constructed literary pieces. Recent study of parables emphasizes the need to maintain their integrity as the primary teaching style of Jesus and the rabbis (Matt. 13.34). Reading the parables in terms of their literary structure and culture yields a better sense of their subversive character over against the idea of parables as illustrations of moral principles.

Parables such as the lost coin inspire a great deal of religious art and poetry especially, in this case, over the question of 'lostness'. Modern feminist theology has naturally been drawn to female figures and metaphors in biblical texts. The lost coin has attracted interest for its cultural and feminist dimensions through the role of its central character. Nonetheless, its incorporation in Luke 15 (with Luke 15.1-2) controls its interpretation.

Recommended reading. Beavis, Mary Ann (ed.). *The Lost Coin: Parables of Women, Work and Wisdom.* Sheffield: Sheffield Academic Press, 2002.

See also LOST SHEEP, PARABLE OF THE; LOST SON, PARABLE OF THE; PARABLE [JKS]

Lost sheep, Parable of the. The parable of the lost sheep in Luke 15 employs the pastoral images of shepherd and sheep. The parable is deliberately linked to those of the lost coin and lost (prodigal) son to form a thematic but escalating unity of 'lostness'—the sheep is one of a hundred; the coin is one of ten; the son is one of two. These parables respond to the complaint about Jesus: 'This fellow welcomes sinners and eats with them' (Luke 15.2). The same parable of the lost sheep is found in Matt. 18.10-14 (but not Mark) though placed in a different context.

In the case of Luke, the parable is a justification of Jesus' ministry which included those whose position within pious Judaism marked them as 'sinners'. As such, the parable points to a restoration of the role of the Shepherd-King in Israel embodied, by implication, in Jesus.

The images of 'shepherd' and 'sheep' are drawn from various OT texts. The image of shepherd applied both to God's rule of Israel and also to the king, as God's son. The king himself was subject to the rule of God and mediated matters of justice and equity in the land. Frequently, however, this did not happen. Israel as a people was therefore viewed as sheep whose fortunes depended greatly on the ability or willingness of the king to submit to the rule of God. Psalm 23 ('The Lord is my shepherd') reflects this. The parable in 2 Sam. 12.1-15 employs the motif of 'lamb' in the context of kingship to great effect (see also Isa. 40.11 and 44.28 where, unusually, the foreign king Cyrus the Persian acts as a shepherd for God's purposes). Similar imagery is employed in the NT. In Acts 20.28, bishops (or overseers) are told to 'shepherd' the church of God which is described as a 'flock'. The depiction of Jesus as shepherd is found throughout John's Gospel. This metaphor was used by the church as an expanded definition of Israel.

Clearly, Jesus is drawing on an extensive metaphorical tradition which was well understood. He identifies himself as the shepherd of the parable and in so doing consciously connects himself with the ancient ideals of Israelite kingship. In all three parables in Luke 15, there is a contrast between the negative response of the Pharisees to Jesus' ministry and the imagined response of joy when that which is lost is found.

Many parables are the source for contemporary sayings and maxims. To describe someone as a 'lost sheep' is to say they are easily led or confused, having the character of a sheep, and to be in need of rescue. To be a 'black sheep' in the modern proverb implies a measure of worthlessness, literally because black wool is unsuitable for dying.

Contemporary interpretation of this parable relies heavily on its narrative skill and use of stock themes and images. These constitute the assumptions of the author towards his readers. This is an important departure from the idea of parables as moral tales to that of serious theology. Writers like Kenneth Bailey (*Through Peasant Eyes,* 1980; *Poet and Peasant,* 1976), Joachim Jeremias (*Rediscovering the Parables,* 1966), and Craig Blomberg (*Interpreting the Parables,* 1990), depend heavily on this method.

See also LOST SHEEP, PARABLE OF THE; LOST SON, PARABLE OF THE; PARABLE [JKS]

Lost son, Parable of the. The parable of the lost son (Luke 15.11-32) is more commonly called the 'prodigal son' on account of the character's rebellious personality. To refer to someone as a prodigal nowadays is generally to point out their inherent failings rather than their experience of restoration. However, to name the parable as lost son is to draw attention to its relationship with the parables of the lost sheep and lost coin also found in Luke 15, which draws all three into a conceptual unity and the potential for being 'found'.

Like the lost coin, the parable of the lost son is found only in Luke reflecting Luke's special source. The parable reflects Middle Eastern patterns of family life but with some very unusual twists. There is no legal precedent for a young man demanding his share of the family property (presumably converted to money), prior to the father's death. Such a demand would be viewed with horror as shameful (Kenneth Bailey, *Poet and Peasant,* 1976). Yet the father yields to the request. The estranged son damages the family's reputation as well as his own. Following hard times, the younger son awakens to the security and benefits of home and family. He returns with the intention of pious repentance rehearsed in his mind (15.17-19) though his piety is defined by his hunger not his contrition. However, his father meets him before he arrives. Although the son does repent formally, his father appears to ignore it completely. In celebration of the young son's return, the father throws a large party to which the entire community is invited. It is an unexpected expression of grace. By contrast, the response of the elder son is one of anger. He complains the younger son receives favor when punishment is deserved. The elder son dissociates himself from his father as well as brother. By refusing to enter the celebration he himself humiliates his father publicly.

Of the three parables, the lost son is clearly the climax. Unlike the other two, this parable lacks a final pronouncement of joy deliberately leaving the reader to supply the necessary judgment about the actions of the main characters. In fact, there are really two lost sons. The younger son humiliates his father, but so does the elder son. The younger son experiences the real nature of the relationship with his father only after a startling and costly display of forgiveness—the community would not expect this from the father. The elder son, by insulting his father publicly, has revealed his own perspectives on that relationship—he also stands in need of forgiveness and grace yet fails to acknowledge this. Jesus' hearers are therefore pressed to consider their own need for restoration even as they condemn the condition of others.

The parable of the lost son is the subject of voluminous literature. Understanding the cultural norms and customs presupposed in the parable is crucial for assessing how it converges with, and subverts, reader expectations. Literary studies reveal numerous rhetorical devices and styles consistent with first-century rabbinical method. The parable also discloses the particular intellectual genius of Jesus as a narrative theologian. Many modern approaches to the parable also strongly emphasize the psychosocial aspects of character interactions which are reckoned to have archetypal significance.

See also LOST SON, PARABLE OF THE; LOST SHEEP, PARABLE OF THE; PARABLE [JKS]

Lost tribes. The term 'lost tribes' refers to the ten Israelite tribes that vanish from the biblical record after the Assyrian defeat of the northern kingdom (2 Kgs 17.6; 18.11) in 722/21 BCE. From the original twelve tribes of Israel (cf. Gen. 29.31-30.24; 35.23-26; 49.1-27; Num. 24.4-51), only Judah and Benjamin remained and are said to be the ancestors of modern day Jews. Accordingly, the quest for the ten lost tribes has been an important issue within Judaism and related religious groups for centuries and different opinions on their identity exist. The Talmud also discusses a possible future reunion of the Jewish tribes mentioned in a very early section of the Mishnah (*Sanhedrin*, 110b).

Apart from these scriptural issues within Talmudic, Christian, and other theologies, popular beliefs about the ten lost tribes have evolved into ethnological ideas that play a crucial role for the identities of various religious groups. Various groups all over the world claim or are said to be descendants of one of these tribes. In India, for example, the Bene Israel, Bene Ephraim and Bene Menashe all see their origin in different Israelite tribes. The Ethiopian Beta Israel (also known as Falashas), or the Bukharian Jews, also claim their ancestry reaches back to the northern kingdom.

Other groups do not claim links to a specific lost tribe, which is the case with the Chinese Chiang Min and Kaifeng, and the Bedul tribe of Petra. A rather prominent example, however, might be the Pashtuns in Pakistan and Afghanistan. In an article in the *Jerusalem Post* from early 2010, journalist Amir Mizroch proposed the idea that this people could be of Israelite heritage, drawing on theories that orginate in the nineteenth century and even earlier. British traveller Sir Alexander Burnes observed: 'The Afghans call themselves Bani Israel, or the children of Israel, but consider the term Yahoodi, or Jew, to be one of reproach. They say that Nebuchadnezzar, after the overthrow of Israel, transplanted them into the towns of Ghore near Bamean ... they say that they lived as Israelites till Khalid summoned them in the first century of the Muhammadans' (Alexander Burnes, *Travels into Bokhara*, 1835).

Indeed, India and Southern Asia have been and still are favorite regions for those espousing theories about the lost tribe's descendants. One of the most popular accounts was published by George Moore (*The Lost Tribes and the Saxons of the East and of the West*, 1861) who tried to identify all the lost tribes as having settled in India and its neighboring regions.

One prominent theory regarding the lost tribes is called 'Anglo-Israelism', a theory that evolved in late nineteenth century and became very popular during the twentieth century in both Great Britian and the United States. It promotes the idea that Western Europeans, especially British and Northern American people, stemmed from the deported Israelite tribes who first became the Scythians or Cimmerians and later the Celts and Anglo-Saxons of Western Europe. The *Book of Mormon* claims that members from the lost tribes of Joseph and especially Manasseh assimilated into some native American tribes.

Recommended reading. Parfitt, Tudor. *The Lost Tribes of Israel: The History of a Myth*. London: Phoenix, 2003. Freed, Irvin R. *King David's Lost Throne: Israel, the Bible, and the Lost Tribes*. New York: Vantage Press, 1994. [HK]

Lot. Epic tradition says that Abraham and Lot had so many flocks and cattle that Lot chose to settle in the Jordan Valley (Gen. 13.2, 5-6a, 7a, 8-10a, 11-12). John Milton's exposition *Tetrachordon* (1645) justifies divorce on the basis of scripture (e.g., Deut. 24.1-4; Matt. 5.31-32) with explanatory stories such as the separation of Abraham and his nephew Lot (Gen. 12.5): 'Though dear friends and brethren in a strange country', they 'chose rather to part asunder than to infect their friendship with the strife of their servants'. Abraham's negotiations with Lot to settle their disputes over grazing land supposed the bond of brotherhood found in ancient covenants or treaties. Milton argues that if family and friends, joined together by nature, thought it better to separate than to risk 'a worse division', then how can marriage, 'only a civil contract', hold together individuals where 'antipathies are invincible'.

A tale is told of three mysterious strangers who visited Abraham at Hebron and Lot at Sodom (Gen. 18–19). The guests are gods, one man is Yahweh who promises to return so that Sarah will conceive a son (18.10-15; 21.1-3). Lot protects his three visitors from the sexual advances of the men of Sodom (19.4-8) in accordance with ancient laws of hospitality, which obligate a host to put the welfare of strangers before one's family because they may be gods or goddesses (e.g., Homer's *Odyssey* 17.462-87). The mythical time of the epic perspective is captured by orator George Herbert whose poem 'Decay' (*The Temple*, 1633) is an address to God: 'Sweet were the dayes, when thou didst lodge with Lot, struggle with Jacob, sit with Gideon, advise with Abraham', meeting them at familiar places, at 'some fair oak, bush, or cave'. Later tradition identifies two of the men as angels or messengers and commends Lot for demonstrating hospitality (Gen. 18.22-33; 19.1, 15; Heb. 13.2). Lot's flight from Sodom with his wife and daughters is portrayed by Peter Paul Rubens (1577–1640), who has one angel urging Lot on his way and the other warning his wife against turning her head toward Sodom (19.15-23, 26).

Lot offered his daughters to the men of Sodom, but in the revised tale Lot becomes the sexual object after his daughters get him drunk (19.8, 30-38). In Jewish midrash, Lot's duty was to protect his family, thus he was later punished by his daughters (Tan. Wa-Yera, 12). Geoffrey Chaucer's 'The Pardoner's Tale' (*The Canterbury Tales*, 1387–1400) apologizes for Lot's incest: 'Lo, how that dronken Lot unkindely (i.e., unnaturally) lay by his doughtres two unwitingly; so dronke he was he niste (i.e., did not know) what he wroughte' (i.e., what he did; ll. 199-201). Many, if not most, paintings of Lot represent the seduction scene (Lucas van Leyden 1520; Orazio Gentileschi 1622; Francesco Hayez 1833). Jan Brueghel the Elder (1568–1625) sets the episode in a magnificent landscape of Sodom and Gomorrah ablaze at night.

Recommended reading. Rilett Wood, Joyce. 'When Gods Were Men'. In *From Babel to Babylon: Essays on Biblical History and Literature in Honour of Brian Peckham*. Ed. Joyce Rilett Wood, John E. Harvey, and Mark Leuchter. LHBOT, 455. Pp. 285-98. London: T. & T. Clark, 2006. Sölle, Dorothée (ed.). *Great Women of the Bible in Art and Literature*. Macon, GA: Mercer University Press, 1994.

See also ABRAHAM; COVENANT; GOD; LOT'S DAUGHTERS; LOT'S WIFE; NOAH; SARAH; SODOM AND GOMORRAH; STRANGER [JRW]

Lot's daughters. In Genesis, Lot is the son of Haran and thus the nephew of Abraham (Gen. 11.27). He accompanies Abraham to Canaan and eventually settles in Sodom, in the plain of Jordan (Gen. 12–13). He is taken captive by King Chedorlaomer of Elam but subsequently rescued by Abraham (14.11-16). While harboring the two angels who come to Sodom, Lot attempts to dissuade the men of the city from defiling his guests by offering his two virgin daughters instead, though this is ignored (19.1-11; cf. Judg. 19.15-26). With his wife and daughters, Lot flees to Zoar to escape the destruction of Sodom and Gomorrah, though his wife, looking back, is turned into a pillar of salt (19.12-26). Eventually, Lot and his daughters settle in a cave in the hills. Lamenting that 'there is not a man on earth to come in to us after the manner of all the world' (19.31), the daughters decide to ply Lot with wine on two consecutive nights and each have intercourse with him in order to preserve offspring. Consequently, they give birth to Moab and Ben-ammi, ancestors of the Moabites and Ammonites (19.31-38; cf. Deut. 2.9, 19; Ps. 83.8).

Lot (which in Hebrew means 'to cover') is further mentioned in connection with Sodom and Gomorrah in Sir. 16.8 and Luke 17.28-32, as well as in 2 Pet. 2.6-8 where he is described as 'a righteous man' (note also Heb. 13.2). By contrast, in the pseudepigraphal book of *Jubilees* (c. 150 BCE), Lot's incest with his daughters is considered sinful enough to warrant the eradication of all his descendants (*Jub.* 16.8-9; cf. Ps. 83). In the Qur'an, Lot (here called Lut) is regarded as a prophet and the story of his incest is omitted. Other ancient authors suggest that Lot's daughters only slept with their father because they assumed that the entire human race had been destroyed (cf. Gen. 19.31); e.g., Philo (*QG* 4.56), Josephus (*Ant.* 1.205), Irenaeus (*Haer.* 4.31.2), and Origen (*Hom. Gen.* 5.4; *Cels.* 4.45). However, according to Jerome, this still does not excuse Lot himself (*Qu. hebr. Gen.* 19.30).

In agreement with Gen. 19.33-35, in 'The Pardoner's Tale', from Geoffrey Chaucer's *The Canterbury Tales* (fourteenth century), it is noted that Lot was seemingly unaware of his daughters' actions, being intoxicated (6.485). Lot's drunkenness is also highlighted in William Langland's *Piers Plowman* (fourteenth century; B.1.27-33; C.11.176-79). In John Milton's *Tetrachordon* (1645), the separation of Lot and Abraham in Gen. 13.5-12 is used to justify divorce and the dissolution of relationships. In the twentieth century, Ward Moore's science-fiction novels *Lot* (1953) and *Lot's Daughter* (1954) retell the biblical story in a modern post-apocalyptic setting (in turn providing the inspiration for Ray Milland's film, *Panic in Year Zero!* [1962]).

The story of Lot and his daughters has been the subject-matter of numerous paintings, depicting either the departure from Sodom (e.g., Albrecht Dürer's *Lot and his Daughters Fleeing from Sodom and Gomorrah* [1498]) or the incestuous relationship that followed (e.g., Bonifazio de'Pitati's *Lot and his Daughters* [1545]). With regard to the latter, Lot has variously been portrayed as either submissive (e.g., Frans Floris's *Lot and his Daughters* [sixteenth century]) or active (e.g., Albrecht Altdorfer's *Lot and his Daughters* [1537]); an act of interpretation that serves also to pass judgment on the level of his complicity.

Recommended reading. Mellinkoff, Ruth. 'Titian's Pastoral Scene: A Unique Rendition of Lot and his Daughters'. *Renaissance Quarterly* 51 (1998) 829-63. Polhemus, Robert M. *Lot's Daughters: Sex, Redemption and Women's Quest for Authority*. Stanford, CA: Stanford University Press, 2005.

See also ABRAHAM; LOT; LOT'S WIFE; MOAB; QUR'AN, THE BIBLE IN THE; SODOM AND GOMORRAH

[MAC]

Lot's wife. In Gen. 19, two divine messengers visit the city of Sodom to warn Lot and his family of the city's impending destruction. After much delaying, Lot and his wife and his two daughters set out from Sodom with the warning that they are not to look back at the city as it is being destroyed. Lot's wife ignores the warning, however, and when she turns back she is turned into a pillar of salt. It is possible that the story is etiological and intended to account for human shaped salt formations near the Dead Sea. Lot's wife is mentioned in the NT (Luke 17.32-34), where Jesus exhorts his followers to 'remember Lot's wife' and thus not look back to their old lives during the last days.

In popular culture, Lot's wife has become a symbol of looking back and of regret. In the novel based on his experiences as an American P.O.W. during the firebombing of Dresden in World War Two, Kurt Vonnegut makes explicit use of the story: 'And Lot's wife, of course, was told not to look back, where all those people and their homes had been. But she did look back, and I love her for that, because it was so human. So she was turned into pillar of salt. So it goes…. This book is a failure but then it had to be because it was written by a pillar of salt. People aren't supposed to look back. I'm certainly not going to anymore. I've finished my war book now. The next one I write is going to be fun. This one is a failure, and it had to be, since it was written by a pillar of salt'. The Russian poet Anna Akhmatova has a poem called 'Lot's Wife' in which she laments the fate of 'her / who suffered death because she chose to turn'. Lot's wife is referred to also in popular music including Hawksley Workman's 'Safe and Sound', Coldplay's 'Viva La Vida', the Thermals' 'Pillar of Salt', and in the Tony Kushner musical *Caroline, or Change* (*Lot's Wife*).

See also GENESIS, BOOK OF; LOT'S DAUGHTERS

[JZ]

Lots, Feast of (Purim). In the HB, Purim, or the Festival of Lots, is the name of the holiday established by Queen Esther, in conjunction with her cousin Mordecai, a judge at the royal court of Shushan in the ancient Persian Empire. The festival celebrates the victory over the planned genocide of the Jews residing in the Persian Empire as proposed by the King Ahaseurus's wicked Prime Minister, Haman. As the Bible recounts this story, Queen Esther records the history of this barely averted tragedy in the Book of Esther, which mandates that the holiday of Purim be celebrated by the Jewish community through giving gifts of charity to the needy, and presents of prepared food to acquaintances.

This simple summary, based on the last chapters of Esther, neatly skirts two elements of dramatic dissonance that are given full play in the Book of Esther itself. First, the very name of the festival is an allusion to the methodology—the casting of lots—that Haman utilizes to choose the day on which to annihilate the Jewish population. As such, Esther's naming makes use of the irony and disguise with which she must navigate the Byzantine corridors of power in the Persian court. Much of the dramatic tension in the book is taken up by the wiles—sexual and otherwise—that Esther uses to approach the king uninvited, even though that lapse of court etiquette is itself punishable by death (Est. 4.11).

Importantly, Esther utilizes the very methodology proposed by the enemy of her people to best him, all the while operating in disguise: Esther 'passes' as a non-Jew (even Esther's husband, King Ahaseurus, does not know that Esther is Jewish). Closely related to this concealment is the consideration of the role of 'chance' in a world in which fate appears predetermined by social class.

A second element of dramatic dissonance in the Book of Esther is that even though Esther mimics the arch villain Haman with her political schemes, she emphatically refuses to imitate him in his reduction of the value of human life. While Haman pays the king to be able to annihilate a community within the borders of the king's empire, and holds out the bribe of unlimited spoils to those who would participate in this government-sponsored campaign of violence and mayhem, Esther refuses similar actions. She does not approve such a free-for-all regarding spoils when the Jews are finally allowed to defend themselves against the Haman-approved pogroms that still threaten to break out even after Haman himself is hung (Est. 9.10, 15, 16). Importantly, Esther, unlike Haman, proposes a view of Empire where there is room for difference, and where political hierarchy does not mean personal abnegation. Haman demands that all people demonstrate this by prostrating themselves in his presence; Mordecai's refusal to accede to this decree inspires Haman's irrevocable hatred and the violent drama of the Purim story (Est. 2.2-3; 5.9).

In the end, Purim as presented by Esther reimagines the possibility of nationhood. Instead of viewing national identity as a function of brute power (as epitomized by Haman), Esther proclaims a view of national identity that is contextualized within the practices of human connection. Caring about the needy and promoting behaviors that allow for bonding with people in one's community is part of the celebration (see Est. 9.22). That all of this takes place within the context of the word—the narrative that Esther writes—emphasizes the primacy of the text in reconceiving the possibilities of politics for all people.

See also ESTHER, BOOK OF [MIRAM]

Love. The word love is used hundreds of times in the Bible. Consequently, the Bible is not only the greatest story ever told, it is the greatest love story. In the NT, this is evident most profoundly in God's unconditional love, which is manifested in the incarnation of his Son who came to die on the cross (John 3.16). God's love in the OT is often expressed as *hesed* or as loving kindness.

The Bible defines love in various ways. For instance, God is love according to one writer (1 John 4.8, 16), and it is an essential characteristic of God according to another (Deut. 7.7-8). God's love is past understanding (Eph. 3.19), eternal (Jer. 31.3), free (Hos. 14.4), sacrificial (John 3.16), and enduring (John 13.1). Two Greek words for love figuring prominently in the NT are *agape*, which often indicates unconditional love devoid of self-interest, and *phileo*, which is an ardent affection and feeling.

Central to the teachings of Jesus are the great commandments to love God with all of one's mind, heart and soul, and one's neighbor as one's self. In the case of the former, it is a call to adore God for his own sake regardless of any benefits received. Love is central to Christian ethics. Not only are Christians to love their neighbor as themselves, they must also love their enemies (Matt. 5.43-44).

Various biblical statements on love have been important to Western culture. The love between David and Jonathan, described as 'passing the love of women' (2 Sam. 1.26), is a favorite image of male friendship. The Song of Solomon's reference to 'a love stronger than death' (Song 8.6) echoes in Shakespeare's *Romeo and Juliet* and Christina Rossetti's 'An End', and is the title of a song on The The's album *Dusk*, which also appears in the Gregg Araki movie *Nowhere* (1997).

Recommended reading. Lewis, C.S. *The Four Loves*. London: Geoffrey Bles, 1960. Nygren, Anders. *Agape and Eros*. 1939. Trans. by Philip S. Watson. New York: Harper & Row, 1963.

See also AGAPE [AJW]

Lucifer. The word Lucifer is Latin and so obviously does not originate in the Hebrew and Greek Scriptures. The adjective *lūcifer* means 'light bringing', combining the feminine noun *lūx* (light, brightness) with the verb *ferō* (to bear, carry), and is used substantivally to render the Hebrew phrase 'son of dawn' in Isa. 14.12: 'How you are fallen from heaven, O Day Star, son of Dawn!' Though the wider context of this verse refers to an earthly ruler ('you will take up this taunt against the king of Babylon' [Isa. 14.4]), Christian readers, especially since the publication of John Milton's *Paradise Lost* (1667), regularly assume the passage refers to the fall of the angel Lucifer. The name Lucifer is therefore synonymous with the Hebrew *satan* (Satan; accuser) and the Greek *diabolos* (devil).

Several biblical passages inform the popular imagination concerning the Lucifer/Satan/Devil figure. He is the adversary in the Book of Job who questions the protagonist's integrity before God (1.6–2.7) and in the NT, he tempts the fasting Jesus (Matt. 4.1-11; Mark 1.12-13; Luke 4.1-13). In the Christian Scriptures, the term devil (*diabolos*) is interchangeable with the transliterated *satan* (e.g., Matt. 4.1 cf. Matt. 4.10).

The devil's fall from heaven is mentioned in Rev. 12.9: 'The great dragon was thrown down, that ancient serpent, who is called the Devil and Satan, the deceiver of the whole world—he was thrown down to earth, and his angels were thrown down with him' (cf. Luke 10.18). Many post-biblical representations of the devil and his minions reflect the influence of Dante Alighieri (1265–1321) and John Milton (1608–1674) where passages from Scripture, including some that do not refer to a spiritual villain in the original setting (e.g., Ezek. 28.11-19), contribute to a more complete narrative about the origins and character of Lucifer.

One common element in accounts of Lucifer's fall is his destructive pride (see Isa. 14.13-15; Ezek. 28.2). Satan admits this in *Paradise Lost*, where he says, 'I fell, how glorious once above thy sphere, / Till pride and worse ambition threw me down' (4.39-40). A character named Lucy (i.e., Lucifer) appears in *Not Wanted on the Voyage*, a loose retelling the biblical flood story (Gen. 6–9) by Canadian novelist Timothy Findley. In this remarkable story, Lucy appears as a cross-dressing homosexual who marries Noah's son Ham. In order to 'survive the holocaust in heaven' (cf. Rev. 12.7-9), Lucy joins the human race, a scene anticipated by the stargazing Ham who observes, 'the morning star had fallen all the way to the earth' (cf. Job 38.6-7 with Isa. 34.4 and Rev. 12.9). The story of Lucy's fall echoes the Miltonian epic, and identifies his/her crime as a 'damned and damnable pride'.

Finding representative writers and artists throughout history who explore the Lucifer/Satan/Devil character is not difficult as he is ubiquitous in post-biblical thought. Perhaps the best known example of the late twentieth century appears in Salman Rushdie's *The Satanic Verses*, a novel in which the devil (known as Iblis or Shaitan in Islam) appears as a deceiver and sly manipulator. The band Velvet Revolver draws on traditions about Lucifer's fall for their music video 'She Builds Quick Machines' (*Libertad*, 2007). The female devil falling from the sky in this video is also the Independence Angel, El Ángel de la Independencia, the symbol of Mexico City.

Recommended reading. Kelly, Henry Ansgar. *Satan: A Biography*. Cambridge: Cambridge University Press, 2006. Wray, T.J., and Gregory Mobley. *The Birth of Satan: Tracing the Devil's Biblical Roots*. New York: Palgrave Macmillan, 2005.

See also SATAN [MJG]

Luke, Gospel of. Scholars call the Gospels Matthew, Mark, and Luke the Synoptic Gospels because the three texts share a great deal of material. Like the other canonical Gospels, the background of Luke—its author, date, and provenance—is difficult to determine because the book is anonymous. It is addressed to Theophilus (1.3), as is the Acts of the Apostles (Acts 1.1). Based upon this observation and others, scholars agree that the same author wrote both Luke and Acts. According to one theory, the author of these works is the unnamed companion of Cleopas to whom Christ appeared after his death, making the author one of the first to be an eyewitness to the resurrection (Luke 24). This view is reflected in several medieval biblical play cycles (e.g., the Chester cycles of the fifteenth century). Others suggest the author is one of Paul's companions, the physician named Luke (see e.g., Col. 4.14). Marcion, in the second century CE, names Luke as the author. Around the same time, Justin Martyr mentions that Luke, the companion of Paul, wrote a 'memoir of Jesus'.

Although it is difficult to determine who wrote the document, it is apparent that the author was educated. The author uses a variety of literary styles. For example, the opening paragraph is written in classical form, which indicates that the author was well trained. Additionally, the narrator refers to the use of sources and research in the writing process (1.1-4), which many scholars suspect includes the Gospel of Mark and perhaps the (hypothetical) sayings source known as Q.

One emphasis in this Gospel is salvation (1.77; 3.6; 19.9). The author of Luke locates the story of Jesus within a larger narrative of God's redemptive plan for the world. God brings this 'redemptive history' to completion by providing salvation from sin through faith in the Jewish Messiah, Jesus Christ (19.10). As the narrator tells the story of Jesus, from his birth to his death on a cross, there is careful attention given to the fact that Gentiles, non-Jews, are also recipients of this salvation offered in the Jewish Messiah (4.25-27; 7.1-10). Other themes in this Gospel include Jesus' compassion and concern for the outcasts of society (1.46; 6.20-23; 10.21-22; 21.1-4), and appropriate use of money (see e.g., 3.10-14; 12.13-21; 16.19-31; 19.1-10).

Recommended reading. Green, Joel B. *The Gospel of Luke*. New International Commentary on the New Testament. Grand Rapids, MI: Eerdmans Publishing, 1997.

See also JOHN, GOSPEL OF; LUKE, GOSPEL OF; MATTHEW, GOSPEL OF; Q DOCUMENT; SYNOPTIC GOSPELS; THOMAS, GOSPEL OF [JFW]

Lydia. Lydia is introduced in the Book of Acts (16.14) as a 'God fearer' and purple dealer from Thyatira. She encounters Paul at the *proseuchē*, place of prayer, outside the city of Philippi, Greece. She is the first person baptized by Paul in Greece. She and her whole household are baptized and she insists that Paul and his followers come and stay in her house. The name Lydia is an ethnonym, meaning she is called according to her country of origin. Lydia is an ancient kingdom in Western Asia Minor that incorporates Thyatira. The use of an ethnonym is common practice among slaves and often this name is retained once freed.

As a purple dealer, Lydia is described in Greek as *porphuropōlis*, combining *porphureos*, purple, with *pōleō*, seller or dealer. The Latin equivalent is *purpuraria*, which can mean both purple dyer and seller. In Rome, Latin inscriptions identifying people of the purple dye trade are explicitly ex-slaves. A Latin inscription from Philippi links with these and supports the identification of Lydia as an ex-slave or freed person.

Lydia's connection to Thyatira further consolidates her likely slave status and bonding in the dye trade. Thyatira was well known for its dye trade especially the use of Madder Root which grows abundantly there. The Madder Root produced a red-purple dye known as 'Turkey Red' that was a low end alternative to the highly prized and expensive purple dye extracted from the murex mollusk that was used for the clothes of the Emperor and his family.

Lydia, named without a husband and as head of household, is likely a widow. Her status could, however, be divorced or never married if she is able to act without guardianship under the *lex Iulia de maritandis ordinibus* (18 BCE) and the *lex Papia Poppaea* (9 CE) where freeborn women with three children or freed women with four were granted privileges including the right to make legal transactions on their own. She is the only woman designated 'God fearer' in the Book of Acts. Her association with Judaism may originate in Thyatira where a large Jewish colony significantly influenced the city.

The story of Lydia and her household frames the events in Philippi and highlight a second household conversion: that of the jailor. Female and male pairings in Luke's writings are often considered an attempt at equality of gender yet here Luke's intention appears more complex. Lydia is named and the jailor is not, affording them differing status. Lydia is noted as a God fearer and the jailor is not. Luke appears to be contrasting the new situations of bringing salvation to the Gentiles, expanding the understanding of the decrees of the Jerusalem Council and demonstrating the reality of the mission to the ends of the earth. This woman is the second in Acts to host a house church, the first being the house of Mary (12.12) where many gathered to pray for Peter.

Today at Philippi there is a modern chapel commemorating Lydia and a baptistery in the river alongside. Lydia Fellowship International networks Christian women across the world and denominations in Lydia's tradition joining in prayer and mission.

Recommended reading. Ascough, Richard S. *Lydia: Paul's Cosmopolitan Hostess*. Paul's Social Network: Brothers and Sisters in Faith. Collegeville, MN: Liturgical Press, 2009. Richter Reimer, Ivoni. *Women in the Acts of the Apostles: A Feminist Liberation Perspective*. Minneapolis: Fortress Press, 1995.

See also HOUSE; PHILIPPIANS, LETTER TO THE; SLAVE [RAHC]

M

Maccabean Martyrs. Throughout the centuries, the Maccabean martyrs have been celebrated as models of both uncompromising fidelity to God and courage under religious persecution. The first detailed account of these heroic figures is found in 2 Maccabees (c. 124 BCE), a summary of a larger work describing the Maccabean revolt against Antiochus IV. 2 Maccabees describes the events surrounding the revolt led by Judas Maccabeus in terms of retribution theology, the belief that God's people are rewarded when they obey and punished when they disobey. Accordingly, the writer indicates that Antiochus's attempt to destroy the religion of the Jews was God's punishment aroused by the unfaithful Jewish elite and the success of the subsequent Jewish Revolt was God's reward for the martyrs' obedience. Seeking to provide an example for their fellow Jews and hopeful of a resurrection, the elderly Eleazar and the mother with her seven sons withstood the brutal tortures of Antiochus IV as he urged them to eat unclean food and thus publicly deny their allegiance to Israel's God (2 Macc. 6.1–7.42).

Later Jewish groups retold the story of the martyrs' remarkable endurance and spirited disposition in the face of death. In the first-century CE philosophical treatise *4 Maccabees*, the willful suffering of Eleazar and the mother with her seven sons illustrates the work's philosophical thesis: the authority of devout reason over the emotions. More than this, in *4 Maccabees* it is the martyrs' noble endurance alone, not Judas's military leadership, which defeats the Seleucid oppressors and reestablishes the Jewish way of life. In the fifth-century midrashic text, *Lamentations Rabbah* (1.16), the mother and her sons exemplify the biblical citation 'for these things I weep'. Not only are they mentioned again in the seventh-century Babylonian Talmud (*Gittin* 57b), but the martyrs continued to provide comfort and inspiration to Jews undergoing persecution during the Middle Ages (especially the Ashkenazi Jews). While the brave heroes are often remembered in conjunction with the Jewish celebration of Hanukkah, they do not play a large role in modern Jewish remembrance of Israel's history. This is most likely because many early Christian groups quickly adopted the martyrs as their own.

The stories recorded in 2 Maccabees served as models for Christian martyrologies, and by the late fourth-century Gregory Nazianzus and John Chrysostom both wrote panegyrics to honor the heroic sufferers. Soon, Eleazar and the mother with her sons were incorporated into Christian calendars and they are still celebrated annually on August 1 by many Anglicans, Catholics and Orthodox Christians. St Augustine refers to a basilica for the Maccabean martyrs in Antioch and tradition holds that their bodily remains are preserved in St Andrew's Church in Cologne, St Peter in Chains in Rome, and the Church of Agios Georgios in Istanbul. Also, a number of modern Christian theologians have shown interest in the theology of atonement and resurrection in 2 Maccabees and *4 Maccabees*. Lastly, the martyrs have inspired paintings and illustrations by several nineteenth-century artists including Wojciech Stattler, Gustave Doré, and Antonio Ciseri. For both Jews and Christians, the Maccabean martyrs have remained stirring examples of courage, endurance, and faith.

Recommended reading. Doran, Robert. 'The Martyrs: A Synoptic View of the Mother and her Seven Sons'. In *Ideal Figures in Ancient Judaism: Profiles and Paradigms*. Ed. G.W.E. Nickelsburg and J.J. Collins. SBLSCS, 12. Pp. 189-221. Chico, CA: Scholars Press, 1980. Henten, Jan Willem van. *The Maccabean Martyrs as Saviors of the Jewish People: A Study of 2 and 4 Maccabees*. New York: Brill, 1997.

See also MACCABEES; MACCABEES, BOOKS OF; MARTYR, MARTYRDOM [JP]

Maccabees. The Maccabees were a Jewish family involved in fighting the Seleucids for control of Judea, and achieved independence from the Seleucid empire from 164 until 63 BCE. Their actions began with the Maccabean Revolt, which broke out in 167 BCE after King Antiochus IV Epiphanes outlawed the Jewish religion. Antiochus was a descendant of one of the commanders of Alexander the Great's armies, having established his rule during the Diadochoi Wars that followed the death of Alexander. Initially the area of Judea was fought over by the Seleucids and the Ptolemies of Egypt, but by the time of the revolt, Judaea was firmly in the hands of Antiochus IV. He wanted everybody to worship the Greek gods and when Mattathias and his five sons refused, a revolt started which led to a guerrilla war against the Seleucids and the emergence of the Hasmonean royal dynasty.

The story of the Maccabean Revolt and the rule of the Maccabees (a nickname meaning 'Hammer') appears in the deuterocanonical books of 1 and

2 Maccabees (cf. *4 Maccabees*); *3 Maccabees* is not directly related to their rule. Maccabean martyrs are commemorated in the Eastern Orthodox Church, and some are also venerated by Roman Catholics. The retaking of the temple by the Maccabees in 164 BCE is commemorated yearly in the Jewish festival of Hanukkah.

The nature of the revolt has lent itself to many novelizations. A range of novels are set during the time of the Maccabees, one of the earliest being *The Hammer*, by Rev. A.J. Church and R. Seeley, published in New York in 1889. In 1901, James Meeher Ludlow's novel *Deborah* (New York, 1901), also covered the Maccabean period as did the novel *My Glorious Brothers* (Boston, 1948), by American writer Howard Fast (1914–2003).

See also HANUKKAH; JUDAS MACCABEUS; MACCABEAN MARTYRS; MACCABEES, BOOKS OF [JC]

Maccabees, Books of. Four books are entitled Maccabees. 1 and 2 Maccabees are among the Roman Catholic Deuterocanonical books and the Anglican Apocryphal books. Greek and Slavonic Bibles also include *3 Maccabees*. In the early Greek codices, none of the books of Maccabees are found in Codex Vaticanus, 1 Maccabees and *4 Maccabees* are found in Sinaiticus, and 1–2 Maccabees and *3–4 Maccabees* are in Alexandrinus.

1 Maccabees, probably written in Hebrew in Palestine, is now found in Greek and Syriac and Old Latin translations. Composition probably occurred after the death of John Hyrcanus in 104 BCE and before the conquest of Jerusalem by Pompey in 63 BCE. 1 Maccabees is a chronological history of the Maccabean revolt, from the inciting events of Antiochus Epiphanes, through the rise of Mattathias and his followers, to the tenure of John Hyrcanus. It is considered to be a reliable though selective historical account, drawing upon a number of sources, such as eye-witnesses, the author's own observations, poems, and written sources including Roman sources and other records.

2 Maccabees, originally written in Greek, epitomizes or abridges an earlier source, the five-volume history of the Maccabean revolt by Jason of Cyrene, plus prefixing two letters. The date of composition is difficult to establish but is probably before 63 BCE with the coming of the Romans, but after the date of the later of the two letters, 124/123 BCE. 2 Maccabees overlaps with 1 Maccabees 1–7, though they differ in the ordering of some events. In 2 Maccabees there is a much clearer theological agenda, with beliefs indicative of later Pharisaical thought (e.g., resurrection). 2 Maccabees contains the two letters to Egypt from Judea, a preface stating that the account follows Jason of Cyrene, and then events from Jason to the governorship and then death of Nicanor.

3 Maccabees, written in Greek by a skilled author, has stylistic similarities to 2 Maccabees, and so is linked with the Maccabean literature, even though the events reported occurred fifty years before the Maccabean revolt and are located in Egypt, as well as Palestine. The work, probably written in the second half of the second century BCE, is characterized by recent scholarship as a 'historical romance', a fictionalized account written for instructive purposes and only loosely tied to history. *3 Maccabees* contains three episodes: the battle of Raphia won by Ptolemy IV Philopator; Ptolemy's visit to Jerusalem and divinely aborted attempt to enter the sanctuary of the Temple; and Ptolemy's retribution against the Jews in Egypt through persecution but whose genocidal plans are averted.

4 Maccabees, written in Greek, shows the greatest familiarity with Hellenistic thought and rhetoric. Though included with the books of Maccabees, it does not mention the Maccabee family, but attributes the defeat of Antiochus IV to the Jewish martyrs. Probably dated to the mid-first century CE, it was written in Palestine or a neighboring area, and has a definite rhetorical cast. The book offers a philosophical discussion regarding reason and the passions, and then demonstration through three sets of examples.

Recommended reading. Bartlett, J.R. *The First and Second Books of the Maccabees*. Cambridge: Cambridge University Press, 1973. DeSilva, D.A. *4 Maccabees*. Septuagint Commentary Series. Leiden: Brill, 2006.

See also ELEAZAR; MARTYRDOM; MACCABEAN MARTYRS, MACCABEES, THE [SEP]

Macedonia. There are 11 references to Macedonia in Acts, and 14 others in various letters of Paul, especially Corinthians. In all cases it refers to the ancient kingdom of that name located in northern Greece. It gained some form of autonomy in about 700 BCE, and owed its origins as a major power to Philip of Macedon (reigned 359–336 BCE), and his son Alexander the Great (reigned 336–323 BCE). It came to symbolize the power of military might, with Alexander managing, in 13 years, to create an empire that covered Greece, Asia Minor, Mesopotamia, Persia, Syria and Judaea, and Egypt. His ability to lead his soldiers in battle, and to campaign to the borders of

India, created for him a reputation that continued long after his death, although the Diadochoi Wars which followed his death did result in the empire being split between his generals. By the time of the NT, Macedonia was much smaller, but still a powerful kingdom that had, under Pyrrhus, invaded Italy in 281 BCE, and threatened Rome. It was vanquished by the Romans in 168 BCE, becoming a province of the Roman Empire.

Alexander the Great ruled Macedonia with an iron fist. He may have been responsible for the murder of his father; likewise, Ptolemy may have been involved in the murder of Alexander—political power was certainly exercised in a violent manner. Yet the glory of Macedonia is seen in the great conquests of Alexander—'Alexander of Macedon', as he is referred to in Iranian school textbooks and guidebooks. The small size of Macedonia, contrasting with the vast area they controlled, was, perhaps subconsciously, adopted by the British Empire which saw Alexander as one of their great heroes (e.g, 'Some talk of Alexander' in 'The British Grenadiers', a popular song in the late nineteenth and early twentieth centuries. Certainly there remains the image of the Macedonians as stout and brave warriors from the hills that recent films have done little to contradict. Oliver Stone's *Alexander* (2004) has Alexander referring to the Macedonians as 'free people', contrasting them with the soldiers of the Persians who had been drafted.

In about 400 CE, the Romans divided Macedonia into the provinces of Macedonia and Macedonia secunda. With the fall of the Roman Empire, it ceased to exist as a political identity, and was only restored as such in 1945 with the proclamation of the Republic of Macedonia as an integral part of the Federal Republic of Yugoslavia. When, in 1991, parts of Yugoslavia started breaking away, Macedonia also did so, but the name was challenged by Greece. This led to a stand-off, demonstrations against the use of the name Macedonia, and the compromise by which the country is known in many international bodies, such as the United Nations, as the FYROM. Former Yugoslav Republic of Macedonia. Part of this also has to do with the flag of the FYROM which had on it the Star of Vergina, an ancient Macedonian emblem, leading to further controversy with Greece, and forcing Macedonia in 1995 to change its flag to that of a radiant star. [JC]

Magi. The Magi, the wise men in Matthew's account of the birth of Jesus (2.1-12), were Zoroastrian priests or Chaldean miracle-workers who looked to the stars for indications of the future, and followed a particularly bright one to the nativity at Bethlehem. The Greek *magos* translates as sorcerer or magician, which is more literal than the traditional English translation, 'wise men'. Matthew says there was more than one magus, but how many made the journey is uncertain. Because the Magi brought three different gifts—gold, frankincense, and myrrh—to the child, tradition ascribed three to their number: in the Latin Church their names were Melchior, Caspar and Balthasar. The magi arrived at Herod's court saying the star was leading them to the Messianic king of the Jews; they met with Herod, who slyly asked them to find the messiah at Bethlehem then to report back to him. The star appeared again once they left Jerusalem, and led them to the child, whom they worshiped. A dream informed them to return by a different way than Herod's court, and they are not heard from again in the NT.

The Magi lived in lands to the east (*anatolia*), perhaps as far east as Mesopotamia and Babylon and beyond to the Iranian plateau where the star-worshipper Zoroaster lived. Some ancient sources identify the Magi as followers of Zoroaster, who taught that the deities were two primal forces of good and evil in constant combat for control over the natural and supernatural. Other sources identify the Magi as Chaldean sorcerers in Mesopotamia or even the gymnosophists of ancient India.

The Magi believed that the supernatural could interpose change and movement on the otherwise unchanging patterns of the natural. The great certainty of the patterns of the heavens and their meaning and impact on human events; numbers and their combinations found in the zodiac, on earth, and in life; latent powers in substances of the earth, air, fire and water; and hidden truths found in dreams, convinced them that astral phenomena had supernatural origins, and must not be ignored. The ancient scientist Pliny condemned the Magi for introducing magic, both white and black, to the Mediterranean world; the biographer Diogenes Laertius claimed that the Magi could see material objects that were invisible to others. And Matthew leaves little doubt that the evangelist believed that dreams and astrology foretold the future.

The story of the Magi worshiping the Christ child has been reproduced in legend, literature, art, and music, such as T.S. Eliot's poem, *The Journey of the Magi*, Bartolomé Murillo's painting, *Adoration of the Magi*, and the well-known Christmas carol,

'We Three Kings' by John Henry Hopkins, Jr. In the Christian church, the feast day of Epiphany, the twelfth day after Christmas, celebrates the visit of the Magi.

Recommended reading. Molnar, Michael R. *The Star of Bethlehem: The Legacy of the Magi.* Piscataway, NJ: Rutgers University Press, 1999.

See also HERODS, THE; MATTHEW, GOSPEL OF [RL]

Magnificat. A joyful hymn of praise also known as the Song of Mary. Like all other NT texts, it was originally written in Greek. However, in devotional books it is most written in Latin or vernacular language. Its name is derived from the opening word of the Latin version: *Magnificat anima mea Dominum* ('My soul magnifies the Lord').

The text is taken from Luke (1.46-55). In the narrative, Mary visits her cousin Elizabeth who was pregnant with the future John the Baptist. After Elizabeth praises Mary for her faith, Mary sings the Magnificat in response. The hymn is, for the most part, addressed to God indirectly in the third person.

The *Magnificat* is one of the four canticles contained in the Lukan infancy narrative and frequently sung (or spoken) liturgically in Christian church services: *Magnificat* (1.46-55), *Benedictus* (1.67-79), *Gloria in excelsis* (2.13-14), and *Nunc dimittis* (2.28-32). Liturgical significance, art, and beauty are combined in the work of relevant musicians and composers throughout the centuries; e.g., in Monteverdi's *Vespers* of 1610; Bach's *Magnificat* of 1749; Mozart's K 339 *Vespers* of 1780.

Mary's song has many parallels in the OT texts, which originates from the *anawim*, 'the poor of the Lord', described by prophet Zephaniah (Zeph. 3.11) and epitomized by two personalities in Israel's history. One is Hanna, mother of Samuel, whose song provides a framework to the *Magnificat* (1Sam. 2.1-10). The other is Judith who, after her struggles for the protection of the nation, began a song of praise that in many ways anticipates Mary's song (Jdt. 16.1-2).

In the *Magnificat*, Mary rejoices in what God had done to her personally and for the good things God had done to 'those who fear him', including what God is achieving for his people Israel by the birth of its Messiah. The reversal of Mary's condition from lowliness to exaltation (Luke 1.46-49), God's mercy for all, and past and present reversals of estate (1.50-51; cf. Luke's Beatitudes in 6.20-26), lead the reader to the sense that Mary is the personification of Israel, specifically the *anawim*. This depiction of Mary appears in the panel of the 'Annunciation' of Edward Meli, a Melanesian artist from Papua–New Guinea. The colors and graphic design with which she is painted integrate her identity fully as 'a lowly servant'.

There are many theories concerning the composition of the Magnificat. Although Mary's name is in the text, it is not agreed that she composed the canticle; but like other birth hymns is pre-Lukan and was added by the evangelist to an existing narrative frame. Related to the origin of the hymn, only Jewish-Christian circles rather than a Jewish setting alone would explain the sense that salvation is accomplished through the 'house of David' and the fulfillment of 'God's promise to Abraham' (Luke 1.54-55).

Today, many writers from different perspectives offer sustained reflection on the *Magnificat*, in the context of contemporary global inequalities. From the spiritual viewpoint, Ann Johnson makes available for modern readers a portrait of Mary with an imaginative and inspiring use of Mary's song. In 2009, the Irish rock band U2 released the album 'No Line on the Horizon', which included a song entitled 'Magnificent' inspired by the canticle.

Recommended reading. Brown, R.E. *The Birth of the Messiah: A Commentary on the Infancy Narratives.* New York: Doubleday, 1993. Johnson, Ann. *Miryam of Nazareth: Woman of Strength and Wisdom.* Notre Dame, IN: Ave Maria Press: 2005.

See also ELIZABETH; INFANCY NARRATIVES; MARY, MOTHER OF JESUS [DR]

Malachi, Book of. The last book of the OT is also the last of the Twelve Prophets or Minor Prophets (so called because the books are short). It has been identified by Jews as the 'seal of the prophets'. For Christians, it is the transitional link between the OT and NT. For Jews, Malachi is the last prophet. For Christians, he is the last prophet until John the Baptist.

Malachi means 'my messenger'. The authorship is uncertain because it is not clear if Malachi is a proper name or a title for an otherwise unknown prophet. Arguments supporting the view that Malachi is a title include the observation that it is similar to Zech. 9.1; 12.1, where the term 'oracle ('burden') of the word of the Lord' is seen by modern interpreters as a mark of anonymity; that there is no other reference in the OT, LXX or the Targum to the name Malachi suggests that it is not a proper name; that the Targum sees Malachi as a title for Ezra the Scribe;

and that Malachi may be a title for an anonymous writer identified by some Jewish scholars and early Church writers as an angel in human form. None of these arguments has proven conclusive.

Traditionally, the author is assumed to be an individual named Malachi about whom nothing else is known. This is also the case for many other biblical figures. At the very least, the name is the one that was placed at the beginning of the prophecy by the book's final editor.

The date of the book is not given in the introduction, but from internal evidence scholars conclude that it was written in the postexilic period. The reasons include the use of the Hebrew word *peha* for governor (Mal. 1.8), the same word used in Haggai to describe the rank of Zerubbabel (1.1) and in Nehemiah to describe the rank of Nehemiah (5.14). The term is rare outside the postexilic era. Attempts at specific dating beyond simply the postexilic era usually place the delivery of the prophecy before the arrival of Ezra and Nehemiah to finish the rebuilding of the Temple or afterward by several decades. These two possible dates are then before 445 BCE or after 433 BCE. From the contents of Malachi, it is most likely that the text was written in Jerusalem to Jews living in a tranquil time, which had bred religious indifference so that worship was without zeal. It was also a time in which the prophet saw dilution of religion occurring through marriages with the non-Jews of the land. Its main theme is that God still loves his people and expects them to be faithful. This is a demand made in the face of experiences that seem to suggest that God is not in control of history and that all religious activity is for naught (3.6-12).

The messianic element in Mal. 4.2a ('But unto you that fear my name shall the Sun of righteousness arise with healing in his wings', KJV) was George Herbert's (1593–1633) basis for his poem 'Easter Wings'. Malachi has inspired a number of hymns. Joseph Smith used Malachi's teachings on the blessings of tithing to make it a Mormon obligation.

Recommended reading. Craigie, Peter C. *Twelve Prophets*. The Daily Study Bible Series. 2 vols. Philadelphia: Westminster, 1984.

See also LATTER PROPHETS; PROPHECY, PROPHETS

[GDB]

Malchus. The name Malchus occurs only once in the Bible, in John 18.10. All four Gospels depict the arrest of Jesus (Matt. 26.47-56; Mark 14.43-50; Luke 22.47-53; John 18.1-11). Judas, one of Jesus' twelve disciples, brought a crowd equipped with arms to take Jesus under arrest. According to the Synoptic Gospels, one of the disciples of Jesus struck a servant (or slave) of the high priest with a sword and cut off his ear. Among these three accounts, only Luke mentions that it was the right ear that was severed and that Jesus healed the injured servant afterwards (Luke 22.50-51). The same story occurs in John, which identifies by name the characters in the story: the disciple with the sword was Simon Peter and the servant with an injured right ear was Malchus (John 18.10).

Though a very minor character within the Bible, Malchus has appeared in the works of numerous artists, such as Giovanni da Milano in the fourteenth century, Fra Angelico in the fifteenth century, Albrecht Dürer and Jacopo Bassano in the sixteenth century, and James Tissot in the nineteenth century. The scene of Peter's attack on Malchus is also depicted on the portico ceiling of St Peter's Basilica in Rome. One of the many proposed explanations of Vincent van Gogh's wounded earlobe is that in his delirium the Dutch artist self-inflicted the injury to act out the scene of Malchus and Peter.

Malchus is often portrayed in films that depict the sequence of Jesus' arrest, from the silent *From the Manger to the Cross* (1912) to the recent Hollywood blockbuster *The Passion of the Christ* (2004). In the silent film *The King of Kings* (1927), Malchus episode is turned into an entertaining brawl. In a recent novel, Michel Faber, best known for his bestseller *The Crimson Petal and the White* (2002), tells in *The Fire Gospel* (2008) a story concerning the discovery of scrolls of papyrus written in Aramaic by Malchus who became a Christian convert after Jesus' death. Malchus is also mentioned by name in the Australian metal band Paramaecium's 'Injudicial' (*Exhumed of the Earth*, 1993): 'The High Priest's servant, Malchus, his ear severed from his head by the sword of Cephas was healed instantly by the touch of Christ'.

See also JESUS OF NAZARETH; JUDAS ISCARIOT; PETER

[ACKW]

Mammon. The term 'mammon' (Matt. 6.24; Luke 16.9, 11, 13) refers to material wealth and is associated with greed, especially with the worship of money and material wealth as the ultimate goal in life, the word being derived from Aramaic meaning 'riches' and the Hebrew word for 'treasure'. As such 'mammon' is presented as a 'false god'. From the Roman point of view, 'mammon' is similar to their god Dis Pater (the Greek god Plutus) who appears in Roman literature and later in Dante's *Divine Com-*

edy. In the Middle Ages, there was condemnation of 'mammon' especially at times of great hardship such as the Black Death, when some argued that it was the lack of religiosity and the importance in society attached to material wealth that was causing problems. Thomas Aquinas saw 'mammon being carried from Hell by a wolf', which had the task of capturing the human soul to encourage greed. For this reason the English writer John Milton (1608–1674) in *Paradise Lost* (1665), included a demon called Mammon who was 'a fallen angel of sordid character'.

In architecture, certain buildings are described as 'monuments to mammon'. These are generally the large banks that tower over churches, show the importance of wealth creation, and downplay the role of spirituality. Such associations are further emphasized in the careers of wealthy figures who reject philanthropy but pursue wealth for its own sake, e.g., the fictional Gordon Gekko in the film *Wall Street* (1987) in the famous 'Greed is Good' speech, which paraphrases the real-life stockbroker Ivan Boesky (1986). Mammon is also used in some fictional works, especially works of fantasy, to describe people or beings that embody avarice and greed. James Platt (1886), Joseph Hocking (1912) and François Mauriac (1946) have all published books entitled *God and Mammon*. The term 'Mammon' has been used in the titles of countless books on banking, stock-broking and unscrupulous trading.

See also GOLD [JC]

Man. In western society the word 'man' refers to a sexually mature or adult male. In the Bible, as in the literature of western culture, men are seen through three lenses—the biological state of being male, socially constructed roles within the household (e.g., husband, father) and society (e.g., civil and religious leadership), and spiritual values.

In terms of biology, the creation accounts establish the sexual differentiation of humanity, first in terms of male (*zākār*, MT; *arsēn*, LXX) and female (*něqēbā*, MT; *thēlēs*, LXX) (Gen. 1.27), and secondly in terms of their complementary relationship as man ('*īsh*, MT; *anēr*, LXX) and woman ('*ishshā*, MT; *gynē*, LXX) (Gen. 2.22-25). This differentiation of humanity as male and female is understood to be a necessary part of creatureliness requiring each to live in harmony with the other.

Cultural constructs concerning manhood abound and include: the hardworking husband and father who provides for his family (e.g., Carl in the movie *Up*), machismo (e.g., Rambo), winning at all costs (e.g., Thomas Crown, *The Thomas Crown Affair*), heroism (e.g., Colonel Braddock, *Missing in Action* films), and, indifference to one's family (e.g., Louis XVI, *Marie Antoinette*). Frequently, these constructs suggest that ordinary life is boring when compared to the excitement that can be found when ruthlessly pursuing one's dreams. Occasionally, however, literature and cinema challenge these myths when aggressive men are shown to learn through suffering that there is more to life than taking care of one's own interests (e.g., *Lord Jim, Regarding Henry, The Doctor*).

Spiritual constructs that shape Christian understandings of manhood include the doctrines of sin, salvation, sanctification, and creation. Karl Barth observes that the male–female differentiation expresses what it means to have been created in the *imago Dei* (Man and Woman, *Church Dogmatics*, III/4). In other words, as humans experience unity of purpose and action in the midst of their gendered difference, they evidence the mystery of the unity and diversity of the Trinity. Viewed from this perspective, the fact a person is 'male' is not a point of privilege. This point is taken a step further in a letter attributed to Paul which teaches that Christian husbands dramatize the humility of Christ in the way they love their wives (Eph. 5.22-30). This is not to suggest that a Christian vision of manhood is by definition 'weak' but rather that it is driven by values different from those of mere survival (e.g., Vassili Zaitsev, *Enemy at the Gates*), machismo, winning at all costs, heroism, or indifference to one's family. Thus a Christian vision of manhood turns the cultural paradigms on their head as it asserts that those who are most 'manly' are those who consider their own honors, achievements, successes to be less important than loving and nurturing those they love and seeking their success. Viewed in this light, Sidney Carton (*Tale of Two Cities*) provides a partial picture of Christian manhood when he elects to sacrifice his life rather than preserve it so that the woman he loves will have an opportunity to enjoy a long life with Charles Darnay, the man she loves.

See also FATHER; HUMAN; IMAGE OF GOD; MARRIAGE; SALVATION; SANCTIFICATION; SIN; WOMAN [KFM]

Man of Sorrows. From the Hebrew '*esh* (man) and *mch'oth* (sorrow). This exact phrase only occurs once in the Bible, in Isa. 53.3a in a description of the Servant: 'He is despised and rejected of men; a man of sorrows, and acquainted with grief' (KJV). From the early church to the Enlightenment, Christian interpreters identified the servant ('man of sorrows') in Isa. 52.13–53.12 with Jesus. On the other hand, the rabbis have traditionally identified the man of sorrows with the nation Israel. The debate over the identity of the man of sorrows continues in biblical scholarship and interfaith dialogue today. Beyond the bounds of interpretational differences, western culture has been incredibly influenced by this short biblical phrase.

Several poets and novelists echo the phrase, either in reference to their own feelings, or the biblical character (e.g., William Butler Yeats, 'The Sad Shepherd'; William Wordsworth, 'Maternal Grief', William Blake, 'The Song of Los'; Lord George Gordon Byron, 'Stanzas to Augusta'). Interestingly, the character Ishmael in Herman Melville's 1851 *Moby Dick* denies that the man of sorrows was a real figure, but yet also says he was 'the truest of all men'. It seems that the concurrent drama and irony of the man of sorrows draws western authors back time and time again.

As popular as references to the man of sorrows are in literature, they are even more fashionable in the music industry. The term 'man of *constant* sorrow' is prominently featured in the 1913 Richard Burnett piece 'Farewell Song', which was later renamed 'The Man of Constant Sorrow', after its refrain. A version of the song became famous when it was recorded and performed by the Soggy Bottom Boys in the 2000 movie *O Brother Where Art Thou?* In the movie, the song gains extreme popularity because of its ability to express the feelings of struggling people during America's Great Depression. However, not just folk artists have homed in on the phrase. The rock band Violent Femme uses the man of sorrows as a way to describe relational pain, when they say in their 1991 hit song 'Do You Really Want to Hurt Me?': 'Man of sorrows, Word unbroken, His sweat like blood came down like tears' (cf. Bruce Dickinson, 'Man of Sorrows', 1992). More famous than the songs by the Violent Femme and Burnett is the reference to the man of sorrows in Händel's *Messiah*. Near the opening of its second part, the line 'he was despised and rejected of men, a man of sorrows and acquainted with grief' is epically sung like a long exhortation. Händel was likely drawing upon the theology of the reformers when writing his piece. Based on the popularity of the phrase, it seems that it has become more than a theological axiom; it has become a colloquialism.

See also ISAIAH, BOOK OF; SUFFERING SERVANT

[JDB]

Manasseh (see Twelve Tribes of Israel).

Manasseh, King. As narrated in 2 Kings 21, Manasseh was wickeder than any other king in Israel's history. He co-ruled with his father, Hezekiah, from age 12 to 22 after which he remained king of Judah for another 45 years, becoming its longest serving ruler. During this time, the Northern Kingdom had just been conquered by Assyria. His infamy is based partially on policies he enacted that reversed those of his father, including reestablishment of pagan altars and practices contrary to divine command and shedding innocent blood, an act God is said not to pardon (2 Kgs 24.4). His transgressions were deemed greater than those of nations that God had destroyed due to their wickedness. However, as exaggerated as his disobedience was during his lifetime, in the end Manasseh came to realize his folly and prayed for pardon to God, by whom he was forgiven (2 Chron. 13.12, 13; cf. Tob. 14.10).

The rabbis teach that while his genuine contrition extended his earthly life beyond that of his beloved and righteous father, it could not reverse the consequences of his pre-repentant actions. His son, Amon, carried on Manasseh's evil practices after his death. Only his grandson, Josiah, returned his people to practice the ways of Torah. For Judaism, Manasseh is an example of how long-suffering and merciful God is to the most sinful person. One midrash portrays God saying that every repentant sinner must receive pardon while in another midrash Manasseh has been given authority to preside over the second division of Paradise where all who truly repented in this life dwell eternally (*Sifre to Deut.* 10; 47). Although the actual prayer of repentance is neither recorded nor referred to in 2 Kings, it is referred to in the Chronicler's midrash, as well as in the apocryphal *2 Baruch* (64, 65) and *Ascension of Isaiah* (2.1-6).

More than one complete version containing alleged content of this prayer exists. 4Q380 and 4Q381 are extant among the Dead Sea Scrolls and one of the three early biblical manuscript collections (Alexandrinus) includes a prayer by the same name in a collection of odes appended to the Psalter. The LXX also contains a form of this prayer, which is included in the Greek Orthodox Bible. It is also included among the earliest of Christian writings in a second- or third-century work, the *Didaskalia*. All texts are considered to be spurious and none appear in rabbinic or post-rabbinic literature.

See also MANASSEH, PRAYER OF [DM]

Manasseh, Prayer of. The individual lament over transgressions, the so-called *Prayer of Manasseh*, was written, presumably by a Jew, before the destruction of the Second Temple (70 CE). The prayer is known only in Greek and Syriac, and the question of its original language—whether it was Semitic (Hebrew/Aramaic) or Greek—is still a matter of dispute among scholars.

Thomas Aquinas stated that the *Prayer* was a part of the book of Chronicles (*Summa Theologiae* 3.984.10). This opinion is repeated at the beginning of the twentieth century by H.H. Howorth: 'the main conclusion I would press for, therefore, is that the narrative in the Apostolical Constitutions represents a portion of true Septuagint text of 2 Chronicles xxxiii, and that it was like the rest of the true Septuagint Chronicles'. However, most likely the *Prayer of Manasseh* was never an integral part of Chronicles, but only an expansion of what had been told there about one of the wickedest kings of Judah, Manasseh, who at some stage of his life regretted his evil actions and prayed to the Lord for forgiveness. In other words, the author completed the prayer mentioned in 2 Chron. 33.12-13, 19 (an 'addition' to 2 Kgs 21.16-17). The prayer under review is similar to the prayers of Esther and Mordechai composed by a Hellenistic author and preserved in the *Additions to Esther*. The *Prayer of Manasseh* does not appear in any ancient version of the book of Chronicles.

Manasseh is also mentioned in Tobit 14.10: 'Manasseh gave alms, and escaped the snare of death which he set for him'. This reference, however, does not appear in the most original form of the text, Codex Sinaiticus.

The Hebrew fragmentary manuscript with the superscription *Tefilah leManasseh* ('Prayer of Manasseh') (4QapPs^b = 4Q381, frag. 33.8-11) was found among the non-canonical Psalms from Qumran Cave Four. There is no relation between the Qumran 'Prayer' and the Apocryphal Greek (and Syraic) one. Contrasting with the Greek prayer, it seems that the Qumran version belongs to the Manasseh tradition of 2 Chron. 33.1-19. Indeed, the only compositional link between the Qumranic fragment and the story of 2 Chron. 33.1-19 is the title.

Recommended reading. Charlesworth, J.H. 'Prayer of Manasseh'. In *The Old Testament Pseudepigrapha* II. Pp. 625-37. Garden City, NY: Doubleday, 1987. Howorth, H.H. 'Some Unconventional Views on the Text of the Bible: The Prayer of Manasseh and the Book of Esther'. *Proceedings of the Society of Biblical Archaeology* 31 (1909) 89-99. Kalimi, I. *The Retelling of Chronicles in Jewish Tradition and Literature: A Historical Journey.* Winona Lake, IN: Eisenbrauns, 2009, 76-77

See also CHRONICLES; DEAD SEA SCROLLS; ESTHER, ADDITIONS TO; MANASSEH, KING. [IK]

Manna. From the Hebrew, *man hu'*—'what is it?', the question the Israelites asked upon first seeing the odd food source, the 'bread from heaven' that God provided throughout their forty years of desert wandering (Exod. 16.1-36). Having been led out of Egyptian slavery, the Israelites were less than two full months into their journey when they began to complain against their leaders, Moses and Aaron, lamenting that at least in Egypt they had not risked death by starvation. The Lord responded to their grumblings by sending quail in the evenings to satisfy their craving for meat. In the morning they also arose to find a 'fine, flaky substance, as fine as frost on the ground'. The substance resembled 'coriander seed, white; and the taste of it was like wafers made with honey' (cf. Num. 11.8, where it is described as tasting like cakes baked with oil). The Israelites were instructed to gather the manna in the morning before it melted in the sun, and to collect only as much as could be eaten in a single day. When they gathered too much the substance turned rancid and bred worms. Only on the day before the Sabbath were they allowed to gather enough for two days. On the Sabbath they rested and the manna did not spoil. The Lord continued to rain down this heavenly food until the Israelites came to the promised land of Canaan (Ps. 78.24; Josh. 5. 12).

As a natural phenomenon, manna has been explained as lichen growing on rocks and also as tamarisk resin. The most probable naturalistic explanation is that it is the secretion of two types of desert insects. These suck the sap of plants which they then excrete in drops. This excrement changes to a sticky solid as the heat of the sun causes the liquid to evaporate. Today, the saccharine-laden exudations of a number of plants are referred to as 'manna' and are sometimes administered medicinally as a laxative.

The term 'manna' has been used through the centuries as a metaphor for that which leads to a life nourished and transformed with bounty and blessings from God. Early Palestinian Targums emphasized that God purposefully sent the miracle food at the exact time Israel needed it. The Jewish philosopher Philo related manna to Greek philosophical ideals but also identified it with the wisdom of God linked to the law given to Moses at Sinai. In John, Jesus refers to himself as the 'living bread that came down from heaven' (6.51) and who thus 'gives life to the world' (6.33). In a popular sixteenth-century satire, the term 'manna' was used polemically as a metaphor for the presence of the pure Word of God at the Calvinist Lord's Supper, a Word understood as polluted in the Roman Catholic rite. Today, the term generally conveys a sense of generosity and superior quality. Groups committed to providing housing and food for the poor, as well as flourishing upscale restaurants that bear the name 'manna', are all commonplace.

Recommended reading. Borgen, Peder. *Bread from Heaven.* Leiden: Brill, 1965. Malina, Bruce. *The Palestinian Manna Tradition.* Leiden: Brill, 1968

See also BREAD; EXODUS; MOSES [EAG]

Many are called. The full phrase, 'many are called, but few are chosen', is a saying of Jesus appearing at the conclusion of the parable of the marriage feast (Matt. 22.1-14). It is the third in a series of three parables beginning in 21.28, and contains two parts. In keeping with the other two parables of the series, the first part (vv. 1-10; cf. Luke 14.15-24; *Gospel of Thomas* 64) depicts the failure of Jesus' Jewish contemporaries at large, as represented by their leadership (cf. Matt. 21.45-46; 27.15-26), to accept the dawning of the promised kingdom of heaven/God (cf. Matt. 3.2; 4.17; 6.10; see also Rev. 19.9; Matt. 9.15) through the person and work of Jesus, 'the Messiah [or Christ], Son of the living God' (Matt. 16.15-17).

However, the second part of the parable (vv. 11-13) moves beyond this central premise of the series, indicating that would-be disciples must exhibit a righteous lifestyle characteristic of the faithful in Israel (cf. Matt. 3.1-17), and therefore of the true disciple of Jesus (cf. Matt. 5.17-20; for the metaphor of a garment to represent one's disposition in life, see Zech. 3.3-5; Rev. 3.4-5; 19.8; cf. Col. 3.12). Those who do not will be no less rejected by God (cf. Matt. 24.45-51; see also 13.41-42, 49-50).

The saying in v. 14 refers back to both parts of the parable—to the generation of Jews contemporaneous with the Jesus movement, as well as any potential disciple. The term 'many' (*polys*) should be understood here as a universalizing expression, i.e., 'everyone', that does not intend any sort of limitation (cf. Matt. 20.28). As suggested in 22.9-10, *all* are 'called' (*kaleō*) or invited into the kingdom of heaven/God inaugurated through Jesus Christ.

The universality of the gospel—its availability to all people irrespective of social class or, ultimately, ethnicity—is a central feature of Matthew (cf. 5.3-11; 9.10-13; 11.25-30; 18.1-35; 24.14; and especially 28.18-19), and is central to the NT (cf., e.g., John 3.16; Rom. 10.11-13; 1 Cor. 1.24-31; Gal. 3.26-29; Col. 3.11; Rev. 5.9-10; 9.9-10). Whether one is in the end 'chosen' (*eklektos*)—accepted by God in the final judgment—is dependent upon whether one's life has demonstrated the faithfulness concomitant with membership in the people of God (cf. Matt. 7.13-27; 24.10-13; see also 2 Pet. 1.10; Rev. 17.14). For Matthew, those who have genuinely responded to the call of God through Jesus Christ will invariably produce the sort of righteousness that this calling demands (cf. Matt. 13.18-23). Thus, the chosen or 'elect' is used synonymously for disciples of Jesus (cf. Matt. 24.22, 24, 31; see similarly Rom. 8.28-30).

The saying, 'many are called', has received a fair amount of attention from Christian theologians since the early church, especially in discussion of the doctrine of predestination (cf. Augustine, *On the Predestination of the Saints*; *On Grace and Rebuke*; see also *Sermon* 90.4-6). It has also seen some measure of secular popularity in the modern era. Perhaps most notably it was used as the title of the three-year photographic study (c. 1938–41) of unsuspecting travelers on the New York subway system by the prominent American photographer Walker Evans (1903–1975), originally published in 1966. Particularly with the addition of 'few are chosen', the saying continues, moreover, to find use for journalists and other writers, e.g., a *Los Angeles Times* review of the popular television series *American Idol* was entitled, 'Many are called, but few will survive 'Idol's' Hollywood Week'.

See also ELECTION; MARRIAGE FEAST, PARABLE OF [CZ]

Many mansions. In John 14.2, Jesus says 'in my Father's house there are many dwelling places' ('many mansions' in the KJV), referring to the afterlife. In popular parlance, the phrase refers to any institution or organization, etc., offering many options or possibilities. The Rastafarian movement refers to the 'Mansions of Rastafari' alluding to the Johannine verse .

A number of books incorporate the phrase 'many mansions' in their title. Some which refer to the differences in Christian belief include Rulon S. Howells's *His Many Mansions: A Compilation of Christian Beliefs* (1976); Harvey Cox's *Many Mansions: A Christian's Encounter with Other Faiths* (1990); and *The Republic of Many Mansions: Foundations of American Religious Thought*, by Denis Lardner Carmody and John Tully Carmody (1990). It also appears in the titles of Gina Cerminara's *Many Mansions: The Edgar Cayce Story of Reincarnation* (1967); and Robin Myers's *Children of Pride: Many Mansions* (1977). The phrase was also used by *Time Magazine* (August 21, 2008) during the 2008 US presidential election, to refer to the properties owned by candidate John McCain.

Recommended reading. Carmody, Denise Lardner, and John Tully Carmody. *The Republic of Many Mansions: Foundations of American Religious Thought*. Tulsa, OK: University of Tulsa; New York: Paragon House, 1990 [JC]

Mara. From Hebrew, meaning 'bitter', from *mar*, 'bitter, bitterness'. In the book of Ruth, when Naomi returns to Bethlehem with Ruth, the women of the city meet her and ask, 'Is this Naomi?' (1.19). Because of the hardships she faced prior to her journey home—the deaths of her husband and two sons in Moab, as well as her long sojourn in a foreign land—she replies by asking them to 'call me Mara', a name meaning 'bitter', rather than by Naomi, which means 'pleasant'. Naomi claims that 'the Almighty has dealt bitterly [Hebrew: *hemar*] with me' (1.20).

In Scottish author George Macdonald's novel *Lilith* (1895), Mara is the bitter and deadly daughter of Adam whose bitterness is rooted in her intensive will to resist a passage through death to ultimate salvation. *Mara*, published by Tova Reich in 1978, tells the story of a rabbi's daughter who rebels by marrying an Egyptian-Jewish hippie and takes up a bohemian lifestyle. This Mara, like the biblical Mara, is transformed by the events of her life.

See also NAOMI; RUTH, BOOK OF [CG]

Maranatha. *Maranatha* is more than a word, but an early Christian prayer transliterated into Greek from Aramaic. It only occurs twice in available Greek texts, in 1 Cor. 16.22 and *Didache* 10.6. *Maranatha* can be broken down into three parts: *mar* meaning 'Lord', *ana* meaning 'our', and *tha* 'come!' The full phrase can therefore be translated, 'Our Lord, come!'

Paul uses *Maranatha* in the parting words of encouragement and warning to the Corinthians: 'Let anyone be accursed who has no love for our Lord. Our *Lord, come!* The grace of the Lord Jesus be with you' (1 Cor. 16.22-23). Although the interjection—cursing those who do not love the Lord—seems harsh, Paul's correspondence with the Corinthians was one of both encouragement and stern rebuke. Many of these believers thought that the blessings of the second coming of Jesus were already theirs and allowed such teaching to fracture their community. Paul's warning is appropriate: he cautions them to let their love for Jesus be the defining mark of their community, declaring in effect, 'Jesus is yet to come, but he will indeed come!'

Didache is an abbreviation of *The Teaching of the Lord to the Gentiles by the Twelve Apostles*. Scholars date this work between the first and third centuries CE, and believe it was used by some Christian groups in their religious gatherings. The book gives extensive instruction on church practice and order, and gives believers direction on how to give thanks to God, saying, '*Maranatha*! Amen' at the end of the prayer.

Maranatha in 1 Corinthians and *Didache* closely parallels Rev. 22.20, which states in its penultimate verse 'Amen. Come, Lord Jesus!' The presence of such statements at the end of Christian prayers and letters suggests that the early Christian belief in the Second Coming of Christ was an important, if not defining, mark of what it meant to be a Christian.

The Aramaic roots of this word also have significance for understanding Christian origins. Many of the earliest Christians saw themselves as worshippers in the Jewish monotheistic tradition. *Didache* 10.6 quoted above addresses the divine as the 'God of David', indicating that these believers see themselves as continuing in the Jewish tradition, while including Jesus in their monotheistic worship. *Maranatha* is a prayer to Jesus calling for him to 'come quickly!' This term should not be understood simply as the innovation of religious upstarts in the first century, but rather as an attempt on the part of early Christians to identify their messiah and Lord, Jesus, as the fulfillment of everything that was written in the Jewish scriptures.

Despite its relatively rare usage in early Christian literature, the term is surprisingly common in popular culture. Christian music artists Sho Baraka and Michael Card both have songs entitled 'Maranatha' and a well-known Christian record label is named, Maranatha! Music. *Maranatha* is used in the name of Christian schools, Bible camps, community centers, radio stations, orphanages, food companies, tour groups, photographers, newspapers, motorcycling associations, and even kennels. The above all exemplify how certain biblical phrases or themes have become commodified since the time in which they were first used.

Recommended reading. Emerton, J.A. '*Maranatha* and *Ephphatha*'. *Journal of Theological Studies* 18 (1967) 427-31.

See also ARAMAIC LANGUAGE; PRAYER; SECOND COMING [MB]

Marduk/Merodach. Marduk was the patron deity of Babylon and has a very long history. From being an almost completely insignificant god in the third millennium BCE, he became the head of the Babylonian pantheon by the first millennium BCE. His origin, like that of Babylon itself, is nevertheless practically unknown. Nobody knows for sure what his name means and when he became the main god of Babylon. It is certain, however, that during the reign of Hammurabi (1792–1750), the sixth king of the first Babylonian dynasty, Marduk rose from obscurity to become an important god. Although Marduk, like Babylon, gained importance during the reign of Hammurabi, it took several centuries before Marduk was officially acknowledged as the supreme god in the pantheon.

Most scholars agree that the superiority and absolute theological pre-eminence of Marduk were recognized in Babylonia at the end of the second millennium. But before Marduk could become the greatest god in Mesopotamia, he had to take the place of Enlil, the Mesopotamian king of the gods since the third millennium. The Babylonian priests thus had to prove that he was worthy of this new status. This is why they wrote the *Enuma Elish*, the Babylonian creation epic, where Marduk is described as the savior of the gods and the real and only creator of heaven, earth and humanity. It was written to prove, once and for all, that the god of Babylon was the new king of the gods. On close reading, it is obvious that *Enuma Elish*, from beginning to end, exists solely to assert Marduk's headship of the pantheon.

Babylon conquered Judah at the beginning of the sixth century BCE and a good portion of its population was deported to Babylonia. In those days, Marduk was the main god of the greatest and most powerful empire in the Near East. In the OT, the Babylonian god is called 'Merodach' or 'Bel', which means 'the Lord', a name that the Babylonians themselves used to call their national god. He is only mentioned in the books of Jeremiah and Second Isaiah (Isa. 40–55), and in both books, the authors are hoping that Babylon will fall along with its god. Jeremiah, who witnessed the fall and destruction of Jerusalem, wrote: 'Declare among the nations and proclaim, set up a banner and proclaim, do not conceal it, say. Babylon is taken, Bel is put to shame, Merodach is dismayed' (Jer. 50.2). The same prophet proclaimed. 'I will punish Bel in Babylon, and make him disgorge what he has swallowed' (Jer. 51.44). Babylon was eventually conquered by the Persians in 539 and Marduk would never be an imperial god again. The deuterocanonical addition to Daniel, *Bel and the Dragon*, shows the Jewish prophet proving that Bel-Marduk is a false deity.

The great god of Babylon enjoyed an odd twist of fate in the 1990s, when his name was used by a black metal band from Sweden called 'Marduk'. Black metal is arguably the most extreme form of heavy metal music and most bands sing about Satanism and opposition to Christianity. The band has recorded several albums, with titles such as 'Opus Nocturne' and 'Heaven shall burn ... when we are gathered'. Oddly enough, they never talk about the Babylonian god!

Recommended reading. Lambert, W.G. 'Studies in Marduk'. *Bulletin of the School of Oriental and African Studies* 47 (1984) 1-9

See also BABYLON [ÉB]

Mark, Gospel of. It is impossible to exaggerate the cultural influence of Mark's story. Yet that influence has been almost entirely exercised through other, derivative narratives. Mark's influence is almost inseparable from that of its imitators and correctors, Matthew, Luke and John. Few English-speakers can hear a Markan passage without intuitively supplying content from the other Gospels. This interpretative control from other Gospels tends to reduce the intense strangeness of Mark's story and to soften his focus on characters acting on a starkly bare stage.

Papias of Hierapolis attributed authorship to John Mark, associate of the apostle Simon Peter (see Acts 12.12, 25; 15.37-39; 1 Pet. 5.13; cf. Eusebius, *Church History* 3.39). Christian tradition usually located the book's composition in Rome around the time of Peter's martyrdom, making Mark somehow dependent on some version of Matthew. Mark may well incorporate prior written sources, especially an earlier narrative of Jesus' last days. The gospel, however, gives no clues to its authorship; the storyteller artfully hides the authorial voice behind Jesus' narrated actions and voice. Mark's unflattering portrayal of Peter and the other disciples makes it difficult to regard the writer as Peter's literary agent. Moreover, despite a strikingly plain style, Mark's narrative is, against Papias, carefully and subtly developed at many levels: Mark presents its naiveté with great sophistication.

Since the nineteenth century, most scholarship has seen Mark as the first, experimental, attempt to write the 'good news' (*euangelion*, 'gospel') of Jesus as the story of his appearance in Galilee and death in Jerusalem. Mark was not only the major source for the narratives of other gospels; Mark modeled a new genre of 'passion-gospel' for all narratives in which martyrdom is given an extended introduction designed to frame execution as redemptive 'good news'. Mark describes his protagonist as a 'teacher', yet, unlike the other NT Gospels and gospel genres, Mark's Jesus' rarely speaks at length and never moralizes. Instead Jesus' uncanny behavior and oracular, parabolic speech constitute the message of this introduction (*archē*, 'beginning') to the gospel. Jesus repeatedly meets ordinary, often anonymous and socially marginal characters, sometimes calling them to become disciples, sometimes performing peremptory, magical acts of grace. Mark's Jesus draws opposition from legitimate authorities, while his intimates display incompetence and petty rivalry. Three times in the central chapters of the gospel, Jesus prophesies his coming abandonment, torture, death—and resurrection. The book, but not the 'gospel', ends suspensefully, with Jesus' resurrection only hinted at, an encounter more in the reader's future than in the disciples' past (16.5-8). The resurrection narrative in Mark 16.9-20, though canonical and ancient, is a later compilation reflecting ancient readers' discomfort with the intensity of Mark's non-ending.

In the twentieth century, Jorge Luis Borges's horror story 'The Gospel according to Mark' (1970) captures the strangeness of the Second Gospel. A more recent attempt to capture Mark's peculiarities is the graphic novel *Marked* by Steve Ross, where the bare-bones composition and surreal images highlight Mark's bizarre occurrences, while the contemporary, urban setting creates new meanings out of the ancient narrative. While direct references to Markan scenes in popular culture are sparse, Mark's wording is frequently borrowed. The haunting phrase, 'my name is Legion; for we are many' (5.9), is used frequently in science-fiction and horror television shows, movies, and novels, e.g., the television series *Angel*, Stephen King's novels, etc. The television series *The X-Files* features an entire episode, titled and based on the Markan phrase *Talitha Cumi* (5.41).

Recommended reading. Schildgen, Brenda Deen. *Power and Prejudice: Reception of the Gospel of Mark*. Detroit: Wayne State University Press, 1999

See also GOSPEL; LEGION; Q; THOMAS, GOSPEL OF

[IHH & MW]

Mark of the Beast (see 666).

Mark of Cain (see Cain).

Marriage. The formal union between a man and a woman describing both the ritual by which two individuals become a socially recognized couple and the ongoing condition of relatedness. The first marriage in scripture (Gen. 1.27-28; 2.18-25) finds its meaning and significance because God creates the first man and the woman for each other, sanctions the relationship by declaring it good, and grants the couple the tasks of subduing creation and bearing children. Elsewhere in scripture, marriages are blessed by the wife's family (e.g., Gen. 24.1-4) and/or affirmed by the community (e.g., Gen. 29.27; John 2.1-11), both indicators that the validity of a marriage was established by the couple's social network.

While the OT creation passages indicate that the divine pattern for marriage is a monogamous union, other forms of marriage—polygyny (Gen. 4.19), concubinage (Gen. 36.12; 2 Sam. 5.13), and levirate marriage (Gen. 38.8; Deut. 25.5-6)—figure in the OT accounts and are regulated by Torah. The OT practice of marrying within the tribe or covenant community (Gen. 28.1; Deut. 7.3) was reflected in American miscegenation laws, the last of which was repealed in 1967, and ecclesiastical prohibitions against interfaith marriage. Additionally, Levitical limitations on consanguinity within marriage (Lev. 18) continue to shape marriage law in western democracies.

Three theological themes—covenant, personal purity, and, the *imago Dei* ('image of God')—have traditionally shaped Christian views on marriage. As a covenant, marriage is expected to be a committed and exclusive lifelong relationship, not simply a contract between two persons, and reflects God's covenant relationship with humanity (Eph. 5.32), expressing what it means to be a follower of Christ. Consequently, men are to be selfless in their love for their wives (Eph. 5.25-30). The second theme, personal purity, usually relates to the exercise of one's sexuality (1 Cor. 7.1-9). Thus Augustine, in *On the Good of Marriage,* identifies that marriage results in children, chastity, and companionship. Finally, interpretations of the *imago Dei* shape Christian views on marriage. Augustine employs a functional view of the *imago Dei* when he emphasizes the importance of childbearing (e.g., Gen. 1.28). Karl Barth, on the other hand, embraces a relational understanding of the *imago Dei* when he observes that marriage meets the innate human need for companionship, a theme which is seen in romantic literature and film where one person finds their deepest longings and needs are met in another.

While the biblical covenants and biblical social ethics provide a theological framework for establishing the legitimacy of appropriately sanctioned marriage, the concept of civil marriage is largely absent from the scriptures. Signs of the convergence of civil and religious interests are evident, however, in civil and canon law codes such as the *Codex Justinianus* and *Codex Juris Ecclesiastici Anglicani.* Indeed, the Church's views on marriage, both Catholic and Protestant, shaped Western civil marriage laws until the twentieth century when western democracies began to disengage marriage laws from the theological traditions on which they had been based. Thus, in the US, even though religious and secular interests may be included within a single wedding ceremony, the state's interests rather than the church's defines the nature of marriage and marriage law. Meanwhile, in the Netherlands couples are required by law to have a civil marriage ceremony that is separate while religiously oriented marriage ceremonies are considered optional.

Recommended reading. Bromiley, Geoffrey W. *God and Marriage.* Grand Rapids, MI: Eerdmans, 1980. Hunter, David G. (ed). *Marriage in the Early Church.* Minneapolis: Fortress Press, 1992

See also COVENANT; DIVORCE; IMAGE OF GOD; LEVIRATE MARRIAGE [KFM]

Marriage Feast, parable. This parable (Matt. 22.1-14) is one of the so-called controversy stories in Matt. 21.23–23.36 involving interaction between Jesus and Jewish leaders. The section is framed by the stories of the Cursing of the Fig Tree (21.18-22) and Jesus' Lament over Jerusalem (23.37-39). The parable has parallels in Luke 14.15-24 and *Gospel of Thomas* 64. The Lukan version occurs in the Travel Narrative (9.51–19.27) and is not framed by other controversy stories as in Matthew.

Source critics are divided because there is little overlapping vocabulary and several differences in content between Matthew's and Luke's versions. Some argue that the evangelists derived the story from Q, but that Matthew edited it more than Luke; others maintain that these versions were two independent stories told by Jesus on separate occasions. The *Gospel of Thomas* version is closer to Luke's version than to Matthew's.

In Matthew, a king sends two invitations to potential guests to attend the marriage feast of his son, but both times the guests reject the invitation. As a result, the king burns their city and invites 'outcasts' to the feast. Because this parable is about the kingdom of heaven, the king most likely represents God, and his son stands for Jesus. In the Matthean context the guests invited first represent Jewish leaders or even the whole nation of Israel (cf. 21.41, 43); the burning of the city refers to the destruction of Jerusalem in 70 CE; the guests invited next represent either Jewish outcasts or Gentiles or both; and the king's servants are Jewish prophets or Christian messengers. Verses 11-13 may be a Matthean addition to the parable, drawn from another parable. The man is cast out from the feast because he has not made appropriate preparations to attend.

In Luke's version, a householder sends an invitation by his servant to potential guests to attend a great banquet, but the guests refuse to come, resulting in 'outcasts' being invited in two consecutive invitations. In the Lukan context it is quite obvious that the banquet typifies the eschatological/messianic banquet (e.g., Luke 14.15; Isa. 25.6-9; 1 *Esd.* 2.38; 1QSa 2.11-22); the householder is God; the guests invited first represent the Jewish elite; the guests invited next symbolize Jewish outcasts and probably Gentiles; and the servant may represent Jesus.

The theme has been a relatively popular subject for artists. In addition to numerous Christian and Jewish songs about the messianic banquet, several Bible illustrators have also chosen the messianic banquet as a painting subject. Probably the most famous is the British illustrator Harold Copping (1863–1932), whose biblical illustrations, including 'The Parable of the Great Supper', are found in *The Copping Bible* (1910). Other artists who have immortalized the theme are the Swiss engraver Matthäus Merian the Elder (1593–1650; 'The Unwelcome Wedding Guest', 'The Parable of the Wedding Banquet'), the Italian painter Bernardo Cavallino (1616–56; 'The Parable of the Wedding Guest'), and the British painter John Everett Millais (1829–96; 'The Marriage Feast'). The most famous movie based on the imagery of the messianic banquet may be *Babette's Feast*, the 1987 Academy Award winner for Best Foreign Language Film.

See also MANY ARE CALLED; PARABLE [KT]

Martha (see Mary and Martha of Bethany).

Martyr, Martyrdom. Martyrdom refers to the death of a person for his or her religious beliefs or for other principles. This idea, coupled with beliefs about the efficacy of a voluntary death had profound effects on Christian, Jewish and Islamic traditions. While the vocabulary of martyrdom is post-biblical, first occurring in the *Martyrdom of Polycarp* (c. 150 CE), the concept has ancient roots. In Greco-Roman literature, the concepts of 'noble' (being freely accepted for principle or belief) and 'effective' (as providing sacral or political benefit to others) death pervade the tragedies of Euripides, Diogenes Laertius's *Lives of the Philosophers*, and Livy's *Histories*. Socrates' death in Plato's dialogues (*Apology, Crito, Phaedo*) became the paradigm for noble death. The religious concept of martyrdom reaches a climactic pitch in the Jewish stories of the Maccabean martyrs, who are explicitly portrayed as both exemplars and sacrifices propitiating God's anger and turning his wrath to mercy. The characters of Eleazar and the mother with her seven sons (2 Macc. 6–7) became synonymous with martyrdom in both rabbinic and Christian traditions and their stories offered the primary source-material for Christian theology.

Although never explicitly discussed in the NT, it is likely that the Maccabean martyr stories helped interpret the death of Jesus for both Paul and the evangelists. Jesus voluntarily accepted his death rather than faltering in his perceived purpose (e.g., John 12.27) and was not only personally vindicated in resurrection but effected a profound change in the human relationship to God (e.g., Rom. 3.23-24). Apart from implicit use, 'noble' or 'effective' death is not prominent in the NT. The word *martys*, martyr, retains its original designation of 'court witness' or simply 'witness'. Witness applies to the disciples (Luke 24.48), to the good report received by those living by faith (Heb. 11.2), and, in Revelation, to the 'blood of the witnesses' (17.6). Such usages, however, coupled with the Maccabean literature, prepared the way for later Christian development of 'witness' to describe those Christians who, by voluntarily accepting a death in imitation of Jesus, proclaim his death as well as the depth and potency of their faith.

Martyrdom profoundly influenced Christian thought. Although Roman persecutions were fitful and rarely widespread, the threat of persecution and its lasting memory in the *Acts of the Martyrs* dominated soteriology and the ethics of Christian life. Martyrs, for example, were believed to become perfect through dying. Since the martyr was Christ's soldier in cosmic battle and his athlete in the cosmic arena, martyrdom required training in both doctrinal knowledge and ethical fortitude. After Christianity was legalized, martyrdom became a thing of the past. The incipient ascetic movement and, later, monasticism replaced it.

Since martyrdom seems to belong to another age, it is unsurprising that the west has generally lost a vocabulary of martyrdom. 'Martyr' now refers negatively to passive-aggressive behavior. Nevertheless, Western culture lauds various forms of self-sacrifice and 'effective' death—for example, the Secret Service agent 'taking a bullet for' the President, and films like *Armageddon* and *Braveheart*. In recent times, Islamic concepts of martyrdom, particularly when predicated of soldiers fighting *jihad* (or suicide bombers called 'martyr brigades'), have forced recognition of different, sometimes contradictory, perspectives on what martyrdom might mean. Christian theologians are increasingly engaging these and other concepts of martyrdom as continuing globalization amplifies current ideological conflicts.

Recommended reading. de Ste. Croix, G.E.B., *Christian Persecution, Martyrdom, and Orthodoxy*. Ed. Michael Whitby and Joseph Streeter. Oxford: University Press, 2006. Frend, W.H.C. *Martyrdom and Persecution in the Early Church*. Oxford: Blackwell, 1965

See also MACCABEAN MARTYRS; PERSECUTION; SACRIFICE [JLZ]

Mary and Martha of Bethany. From the Greek *Mariam* (Mary), *Martha*, and *Bēthania* (Bethany). These sisters are mentioned three times in the NT. In the most familiar story, Martha welcomes Jesus into her home, but becomes distracted by many tasks. She complains to Jesus and asks him to command Mary to help her. Jesus tells Martha that she is 'worried and distracted by many things' and has 'need of only one thing'; Mary, who sits and listens, has chosen 'the better part' (Luke 10.38-42).

The second story of Mary and Martha, John 11, recounts the death and resurrection of Lazarus, their brother. When Jesus arrives four days too late, the sisters both claim that Jesus could have saved their brother. Even so, Martha identifies Jesus as the messiah (cf. Mark 8.29). The sisters receive little cultural attention in this story.

In the third story, Mary and Martha give a supper in Jesus' honor (John 12.1-8). As in Luke, Martha serves (*diēkonein*, cognate of *deacon*), but in textual silence. When Mary anoints Jesus' feet with perfume and wipes them with her hair, Judas criticizes her extravagance, but Jesus defends the gesture, saying it anticipates his death. Similar stories in the Synoptic Gospels (Mark 14.3-9; Matt. 26.6-13; Luke 7.37-38) led to confusion and conflation of the anointing woman with Mary. Gregory the Great (540–604), for example, declared that Mary of Bethany and Mary Magdalene were one woman: Mary Magdalene. Multiple paintings thus show 'Mary Magdalene' anointing Jesus' head 'in Bethany' or Mary 'washing his feet'. Mary of Bethany disappears from this story and Martha is forgotten.

This biblical polarization of sisters' and women's roles is unique, and thus wields significant influence. In traditional Protestant discourse, Martha is characterized as legalistic, nagging, and complaining; she represents Judaism, 'justification by works', the 'active Christian', and Catholicism. In contrast, Mary is peaceful and passive; she represents Christianity, 'justification by faith', the 'contemplative life' (e.g., *The Cloud of Unknowing* 17-24, c. 1350), and Protestantism. As an archetypal story, some welcome the 'permission' to study theology; others hear the rebuke to 'sit down and be silent'; others appreciate the nod to domestic drudgery. Some interpreters, such as John Chrysostom, Augustine of Hippo, and John Calvin, have urged balance between action and contemplation. Elisabeth Schüssler Fiorenza more recently pointed out that Martha's service (from Greek *diakonia*, cognate of *deacon*) could have referred to her *ministry*, not just domestic service; thus, Luke attempted to curtail women's leadership in the church.

The contrast between the sisters continues in art. Joachim Beuckelaer's sixteenth-century genre painting presents a vibrant Martha plucking a chicken in the foreground, with Jesus and Mary looking on from the washed-out background. Velazquez's painting (1618) depicts an older woman teaching a sour young girl by pointing to a painting of the two sisters. Henry Moore's twentieth-century abstract painting best captures Martha's surprised confusion at Jesus' rebuke.

Martha and Mary give their names to numerous health care facilities, convents, women's organizations, and housewives' blogs around the world. The *Martha Movement* promotes social action and trains women to use their political rights. In film, *Mostly Martha* (2001) features a chef; *In her Shoes* (2005) compares the life choices of two sisters, one sober and industrious, the other hedonistic. Martha Stewart built an empire on her namesake's association with homemaking.

Recommended reading. Ernst, Allie M. *Martha from the Margins: The Authority of Martha in Early Christian Tradition.* Leiden: Brill, 2009. Peters, Diane E. *The Many Faces of Martha of Bethany.* Ottawa: Novalis, 2008

See also LAZARUS; MARY MAGDALENE [JSW]

Mary, Childhood of. In the Gospels, the Virgin Mary's biography does not start before the Annunciation (Luke 1.26-38); hence her childhood does not play a role there. Nonetheless, this motif is outstandingly vivid in both Christian textual tradition and Christian art.

The most important source of this tradition is the apocryphal Gospel of James, written in the second century CE. More than a hundred early Greek manuscripts have survived of this Gospel that both show its extreme popularity and explain the wide distribution of the narratives it contains. Even the Qur'an (surah 3.35-37) gives a short account of Mary's youth (where she is connected with Mirjam, the sister of Moses and Aaron), probably inspired by the Gospel of James. The first eight chapters tell of Mary's birth and childhood, including her assignment to the temple, while the following eight chapters deal with her adolescence until her betrothal to Joseph. Roughly, the story goes as follows: Already before her birth, Mary is devoted to a life in the temple by her mother Anna. After her birth, however, she and her husband, Joachim, delay bringing her to the temple. Depictions of these early childhood days, showing Anna instructing her daughter (mostly in reading), are quite common in both the Middle Ages and the Renaissance. At the age of three, Mary climbs the steps to the temple without assistance and so symbolically chooses a life devoted to God. This is the second motif frequently depicted, especially in Renaissance art. While in the temple, Mary is nourished by an angel. At the age of twelve, she is released from the temple at the command of that angel to be married to Joseph, who is chosen among all Israelite widowers by a miraculous judgment of God.

Already in the early Middle Ages, motifs from the Gospel of James were modeled into books purporting to recount the life of Mary, such as the *Book of Legends*, written by Hrotsvith of Gandersheim, ca. 950/960. One of the most detailed, ornamented, and influential of these elaborations from the Middle Ages, however, is the *Legenda aurea* ('Golden Legend') by Jacobus de Voragine, written ca. 1263/1273, which survived in hundreds of manuscripts and many regionally differing versions throughout Europe. From there, the narrative spread into innumerable works of both popular and academic religious writing and of Christian art. The rising devotion to the Virgin Mary, noticeable in western Christianity since at least 1200, would both fertilize this process and be inspired by it. During the following centuries, Mary's parents, Anna and Joachim, became increasingly popular, especially in pictorial and sculptural arts. The 14th to 16th centuries were the high period of this interest.

During the early modern period, while Mary was still the object of great devotion, interest in Mary's youth seems to decrease markedly. Only few painting, such as Dante Gabriel Rossetti's *Infanzia di Maria Vergine* ('The Youth of Virgin Mary', 1849), still depict her as a child or together with her mother, Anna. Modern representations are remarkably rare. Anne-Marie Miéville, however, has devoted the film *Le livre de Marie* ('The Book of Mary', 1985) to Mary's parents, her childhood and adolescence, which functions as a prologue to Jean-Luc Godard's 1984 art-house film *Je vous salue, Marie* ('Hail Mary'). Both Godard and Miéville transfer the narrative to modern times: young Marie is found frequently citing Baudelaire's *Flowers of Evil* and discussing Mahler and Chopin.

[CC]

Mary, Mother of Jesus/Mary, the Virgin. Though a minor biblical character (Matt. 1–2; 12.46-50; 13.54-58; Mark 3.31-35; 6.1-6; Luke 1–2; 8.19-21; 11.27-28; John 2.1-12; 19.25-27; Acts 1.14; Gal. 4.4 and possibly Rev. 12.1-6, 13-17), Mary has fired the western imagination from the second century to today.

The earliest NT documents (Paul's letters and Mark) say little. Mark presents Mary as one of Jesus' opponents (3.31-35). The Nativity is found only in Matthew and Luke. In John, Mary is a symbol for the corporate faithful at the Cana wedding (2.1-12) and the cross (19.25-27). Though modern commentators disagree over the identity of the woman of Rev. 12.1-6, pious Catholic readings see Mary there.

The trend to exaltation in the NT continues in post-biblical theology and piety. The title *theotokos* (God-bearer), defined at the Council of Ephesus (431), soon gave rise to the Eastern image of Mary as a Byzantine empress and the Western one of the queen at court. As Queen Mother, she commanded God's attention. Increasing attention was also paid to her purity. This is epitomized in the title *aiparthenos*, ever-virgin, confessed since the early second century; it is fully expressed in the dogmas of Immaculate Conception (that Mary was from her conception preserved from sin) and Bodily Assumption (that Mary was taken body and soul to heaven). Though officially defined by the Catholic Church respectively in 1854 and 1950, these dogmas reflect ancient patterns of belief and devotion.

The move from simplicity to exaltation is also found in western art. Depictions from Roman catacombs portray biblical themes—e.g., the visitation of the Magi (Matt. 2.1-12)—or show Mary at prayer. After the fifth century, the image of Mary as Virgin Queen begins to control painting and sculpture. Majesty continues through the late Middle Ages and Renaissance, though displays of maternal tenderness at the crèche and the cross soften it. In Catholic art from the seventeenth century, dogmatic concerns are foregrounded in the light of the Reformation. Western art has produced many Marys ranging from humble handmaid to heavenly queen.

A survey of films in the second half of the twentieth century demonstrates continued diversity. Nicholas Ray's *King of Kings* (1961) and George Stevens's *The Greatest Story Ever Told* (1965) show a Western-looking adult Mary. Pier Paolo Passolini's *The Gospel according to Matthew* (1964) and Franco Zeffirelli's *Jesus of Nazareth* (1977) try to combine greater historical awareness with cultural-religious sensibilities. Mary has been presented in modern dress (Jean-Luc Goddard's *Je vous salue, Marie* [1984], Denys Arcand's *Jesus of Montreal* [1989] and against the biblical grain (Martin Scorsese's *The Last Temptation of Christ* [1988]). It was a film labeled by many as anti-Semitic that was the first to present Mary as Jewish: Mel Gibson's *The Passion of the Christ* (2004).

Why are there so many Marys? On the one hand, there is very little material to work with. If there is insufficient material in the Gospels to prepare a biography of Jesus, how much more so with Mary! On the other hand, because of her status as mother of Jesus, she continues to invite retellings of her story.

Recommended reading. Boss, Sarah Jane (ed.). *Mary: The Complete Resource*. London: Oxford University Press, 2007. Pelikan, Jarolsav. *Mary through the Centuries: Her Place in the History of Culture*. New Haven: Yale University Press, 1998. Perry, Tim. *Mary for Evangelicals. Toward an Understanding of the Mother of our Lord*. Downers Grove, IL: InterVarsity Academic, 2006

See also MARY, CHILDHOOD OF; NATIVITY; VIRGIN/VIRGIN BIRTH [TP]

Mary Clopas. According to John 19.25, the women at the foot of the cross were 'his mother, his mother's sister, Mary the wife of Clopas, and Mary Magdalene'. The text may refer to either three women (Jesus' mother, her sister, also named Mary, and Mary Magdalene) or four (Jesus' mother, her unnamed sister, Mary Clopas, and Mary Magdalene). If the reference is to three women, then Mary Clopas would be Jesus' maternal aunt (although it seems unlikely that two sisters would have the same name). The designation *Maria tēn tou Klōpa* (literally, 'Mary, the one of Clopas') probably means that she was Clopas's wife, but it could also refer to a mother–son relationship.

Mary Clopas is not mentioned elsewhere in the NT, although there are references to Marys in the synoptic passion narratives (Matt. 27.56, 61; 28.1; Mark 15.40, 47; 16.1; Luke 24.10) who may be identified with her. In the famous story of the encounter between the risen Jesus and the two disciples on the road to Emmaus (Luke 24.13-49), one of the disciples is named Cleopas (vv. 13, 18), giving rise to speculation that the other, unnamed disciple was his wife, Mary. Contemporary artistic portrayals of the Emmaus story sometimes depict the unnamed disciple as female.

The Johannine scene of the women at the cross has often been portrayed in western art. In Orthodox iconography, Mary Clopas is included among the myrrh-bearing women at the tomb on Easter morning. In Orthodox churches, the third Sunday after Easter is celebrated as the Sunday of the Holy Myrrhbearers, followed by a week dedicated to them. In the west, medieval legend conflated her with the 'Mary Salome' who accompanied Mary Magdalene, Mary mother of James and Lazarus by sea to the southern shore of Gaul after the crucifixion; the traditional location of their arrival is currently called Saintes-Maries-sur-le-Mer. In the Roman Catholic church, the feast day of St Mary Clopas is April 9.

See also EMMAUS ROAD; LAZARUS; MARY MAGDALENE [MALB]

Mary Magdalene is mentioned twelve times in the Gospels (Matt. 27.56, 61; 28.1; Mark 15.40, 47; 16.1; Luke 8.2, 24.10; John 19.25; 20.1, 10, 18), and Mark's secondary ending (16.9), the most frequently mentioned NT woman. Unlike some NT women (e.g., Mary Clopas), she is not identified by her relationship to a man, but by her hometown, Magdala (Migdal), a fishing village on the western shore of Lake Tiberias. She is always mentioned first in lists of women disciples who supported Jesus (Mark 15.41; Luke 8.1). The Gospels agree she was the first witness to the empty tomb; Matthew, Mark and John portray her as first witness to the resurrection. Luke mentions that Mary was healed of evil spirits and infirmities (8.2); Mark 16.9 says Jesus cast seven demons from her (16.9).

Before the sixth century, Mary is not described as anything but a disciple, 'apostle to the apostles'. The *Didascalia* (third century) calls her a deaconess. Some Gnostic documents say she had an intimate relationship with Jesus, e.g., the *Gospel of Philip* says Mary was Jesus' 'companion' whom he loved more than the other disciples, and whom he often kissed. Here, kissing signifies a spiritual, rather than a sexual relationship (contra *The Da Vinci Code*). In the *Gospel of Mary*, she encourages the male disciples with teachings revealed by the risen savior. Here, Mary symbolizes gnostic Christianity, while Peter represents proto-orthodox Christianity.

The idea that Mary was a prostitute seems to result from the conflation of narratives where a woman anoints Jesus (Mark 14.3-9; Matt. 26.6-13; John 12.1-8). In Mark and Matthew, the anointing takes place in Bethany, the woman is not named, and she anoints Jesus' head, anticipating his burial. In John, the woman is Mary of Bethany, sister of Martha and Lazarus, and she anoints Jesus' feet, a prophetic act foreshadowing his burial. Luke 7.36-50 has a very different story, with Jesus dining in a Pharisee's house. An unnamed 'sinful' woman enters and weeping, pours a jar of ointment on his feet. Eventually, all these stories merged into one in which a sinful 'Mary' anoints Jesus and is forgiven (cf. Luke 7.48). Mary Magdalene is not mentioned in any of these stories, but she was confused with Mary of Bethany and the sinner. In a homily delivered in 591, Gregory the Great stated that the two Marys and Luke's sinner were all one, that the 'seven devils' of Mark 16.9 were vices, and the ointment had been used 'to perfume her flesh in forbidden acts'. By repenting at Jesus' feet, Mary transformed her crimes to virtues, devoting her life to penance.

Subsequently, Mary was portrayed as a repentant prostitute, the archetype of the penitent sinner. The word 'maudlin' ('tearful, sentimental') derives from her name. This image has been perpetuated in prayer, music and art. She is the patron of prostitutes, penitents, hairdressers, perfumers and apothecaries. The Catholic church officially ruled that she was not a prostitute in 1969.

Western legend says Mary traveled to Provence, France after the resurrection, where she preached, led a life of penance, and was buried in a local church. Her symbols include the color red, an alabaster jar, a skull, a mirror, and long red hair.

In the East, the two Marys and Luke's sinner were never confused. Mary is said to have traveled as a missionary to Rome, and then joined Jesus' mother in Ephesus, where both were buried. In Orthodox icons, she is often shown holding a red egg, symbolizing the resurrection.

Recommended reading. Bellevie, Lisa. *The Complete Idiot's Guide to Mary Magdalene.* New York: Alpha, 2005

See also MARY AND MARTHA OF BETHANY

[MALB]

Mashal (see Parable).

Massacre of the Innocents. The phrase (also 'slaughter of the innocents') describes an alleged episode of infanticide by Herod the Great, client king of Judea under the Romans. The incident is recorded in Matthew's infancy narrative. According to the account, oriental magi appear in Herod's court enquiring, 'Where is the child who has been born king of the Jews?' (Matt. 2.3). Fearful of losing his throne, Herod instructs them to report to him once they have found the child. The magi, however, are warned in a dream of Herod's malicious intent and do not return (2.12). In a fit of tyrannical rage, Herod then orders the slaughter of all male children two years of age and younger in Bethlehem and the surrounding region so as to ensure the elimination of his potential rival (2.16-18).

The historicity of this incident is contested. Neither the first-century Jewish historian Josephus nor the other canonical gospels mention it. Some scholars have suggested that the account is a theological construction intended to recall events from the life of Moses as recorded in the OT (i.e., Pharaoh's slaughter of male Hebrew infants, Exod. 1.15-22). On the other hand, Herod's notoriety for ruthlessness and violent paranoia suggests that a massacre of innocent infants would not have been inconsistent with his character. In any case, the account serves its purpose in the narrative: the impending massacre prompts Joseph to flee to Egypt with Mary and Jesus until Herod's death; thus, their return is seen as a fulfillment of the OT prophecy, 'Out of Egypt I have called my son' (Matt. 2.15; cf. Hos. 11.1).

The theme of the 'massacre of the innocents' has appeared repeatedly in Western art, literature and film. The Renaissance in particular saw a great number of paintings by this title; some of the most famous include those by Cornelius van Haarlem (1590), now housed at the Rijksmuseum Amsterdam; Guido Reni (1611), now at Bologna; and Nicholas Poussin (1629), now at the Musée Condé in Chantilly, France. In literature, the massacre has appeared in such famous works as Shakespeare's *Henry V*, in which King Henry threatens to have the civilians' 'naked infants spitted upon pikes' as did 'Herod's bloody-hunting slaughtermen'. The horror of the massacre is lost in comic allusion in Mark Twain's *The Adventures of Tom Sawyer* (1876) when Tom, after persuading Ben to whitewash the fence, 'sat on a barrel in the shade close by, dangled his legs, munched his apple, and planned the slaughter of more innocents'. In Albert Camus's philosophical novel *The Fall* (1956), the incident's horror is recovered. The main character, Jean-Baptiste Clamence, argues that the massacre of the innocent infants is the reason why Jesus allowed himself to be crucified—for, Clamence reasons, 'why did they die if not because of him?' The incident is also the opening scene in the 2006 movie *The Nativity Story*.

The Christian commemoration of the reputedly massacred infant boys as martyrs and saints is reported as early as the fifth century. Today, many Christians still observe the Feast of the Holy Innocents every December 29.

Recommended reading. Brown, Raymond E. *The Birth of the Messiah: A Commentary on the Infancy Narratives in Matthew and Luke.* London: Geoffrey Chapman, 1977

See also HERODS, THE; INFANCY NARRATIVES; MAGI; MATTHEW, GOSPEL OF [BRO]

Massah and Meribah. Hebrew for 'to test' and 'to contend/strive'. In Exod. 17.1-7, the Israelites camp at Rephidim, and they complain to Moses that they have no water to drink. In answer, Moses asks them why they quarrel with him (*meribah*) and put him to the test (*massah*). Afraid that the people will stone him, Moses prays to God, and is divinely enabled to bring water from a rock at Mount Horeb. The site is named *Massah and Meribah* after the Israelites' quarrelsome behavior.

A similar tradition, which mentions only Meribah, is found in Num. 20.1-13. The Israelites are in the desert of Zin, and again they are quarrelling with Moses over their lack of water. Once again, Moses, this time with his brother Aaron, is divinely enabled to bring water out of the rock in accordance with God's command. However, because of the brothers' failure to uphold the divine honor, God pronounces that neither of them will enter the land of promise. The water from the rock is dubbed *meribah*, commemorating Israel's quarrel with Yahweh. Psalm 81.7 briefly alludes to the incident: 'In distress you called, and I rescued you; I answered you in the secret place of thunder; I tested you at the waters of Meribah'. Psalm 95.8 urges Israel not to test God as their ancestors did at Massah and Meribah. In the NT, the author of Hebrews (3.8) warns his readers against hardening their hearts as the Israelites did when they were 'tested' in the desert.

The song of Moses in Deut. 33.8-11 relates a different tradition where God's faithful servant Levi is tested at Meribah and is rewarded with the Urim and Thummim.

Western art features many scenes of Moses striking the rock and water gushing forth. The concurrence of the death of Miriam and the incident at Meribah in Numbers 20 may account for the legend of Miriam's miraculous well, which accompanied the Israelites during their wilderness wandering but temporarily dried up after she died. In the Roman Catholic liturgy, the Responsorial Psalm for the fourth Sunday in ordinary time (Year B) is Psalm 95, includes the line 'So not harden your hearts as at Meribah, as on the day at Massah in the wilderness'.

See also MIRIAM; URIM AND THUMMIM [MALB]

Mattathias (see Maccabees).

Matthew, Gospel of. As with the other evangelists, the author of Matthew remains anonymous. Dated between 70 and 100 CE, the Gospel receives its title from Jesus' tax-collector disciple, Matthew (Matt. 9.9; 10.33), to whom the Gospel was attributed by Irenaeus (c. 185) and others. Like the other NT writings, Matthew was originally written in Greek (not Hebrew as once believed). Along with Mark and Luke, Matthew is considered one of the 'synoptic' Gospels. Some passages identified with Matthew include a large portion of the Sermon on the Mount (Matt. 5–7) and many eschatological passages (e.g., 25.31-46). Matthew is also the only source to contain an account of Herod's massacre of Bethlehem's infants (2.16-17).

Matthew has been called both the 'most Jewish' and the most 'anti-Jewish' Gospel. The former description is due to its emphasis on the quotation and fulfillment of the Hebrew scriptures, the apparent depiction of Jesus as a 'new Moses', and its consonance with small details of 1st-century Jewish life, e.g., the term 'kingdom of heaven' appears 32 times in Matthew, but not in the other Gospels. 'Heaven' here serves as a Jewish circumlocution for 'God'.

The 'anti-Jewish' description comes from apparent hostility towards Judean authorities in the Gospel (e.g., calling them a 'brood of vipers'; 12.33; 23.33). Matthew's hostile depiction of the Pharisees has given that title a long polemical tradition, e.g., the adjective 'pharisaic' to mean 'rigidly legalistic'. The saying, 'His blood be on us and on our children' (27.25), has fuelled anti-Semitic thought throughout the centuries, culminating in Hitler's extermination of millions of Jews in Nazi Germany.

Various Christian movements have located their foundational texts in Matthew. Matthew contains the text historically used to support papal authority: the commission of Peter (16.17-20). The sixteenth-century Anabaptists believed that the Sermon on the Mount should be reflected in the lives of all believers. Their understanding of 'the ban' stems from Matt. 18.15-17. For Mennonites and Quakers, Matt. 5.33-37 ('Do not swear at all') is a literal commandment not to take any sort of oaths, including in court. Matthew's 'turn the other cheek' (5.39) is the guiding principle behind Christian pacifism—and personally transformational for Russian novelist Leo Tolstoy (1828–1910). Christian Science holds the story of Jesus' healing of the paralytic (Matt. 9.2-7) as foundational. Mary Baker Eddy (1821–1910) claims she was suddenly cured of an untreatable disease when she read the passage.

Matthew has also inspired innumerable artistic expressions, including J.S. Bach's *St Matthew Passion* (1727). More recently, Johnny Cash used Matthew's apocalyptic symbolism in his song, 'Matthew 24 (Is Knocking at the Door)' (1982). The Marxist, atheist Italian director, Pier Paolo Pasolini, created the 1964 film *Il vangelo secondo Matteo* ('The Gospel according to St Matthew') based upon Matthew alone rather than a Gospel harmonization. The musical *Godspell* (1970) also claims to follow Matthew.

In 1887, Scottish author Robert Louis Stevenson noted that Matthew was one of the greatest literary influences upon him: 'I believe it would startle and move any one if they could make a certain effort of imagination and read it freshly like a book, not droningly and dully like a portion of the Bible'.

Recommended reading. Clarke, Howard W. *The Gospel of Matthew and its Readers: A Historical Introduction to the First Gospel*. Bloomington, IN: Indiana University Press, 2003. Luz, Ulrich. *Matthew in History: Interpretation, Influence, and Effects*. Minneapolis: Fortress Press, 1994

See also BRIDEGROOM; CHURCH; KEYS OF THE KINGDOM; GENEALOGY; SHEEP AND THE GOATS, PARABLE OF THE; PEARL OF GREAT PRICE; PETER; SERMON ON THE MOUNT; SYNOPTIC GOSPELS; TAX COLLECTOR; TURN THE OTHER CHEEK; WHEAT AND TARES, PARABLE OF THE [PGM]

Matthias. Matthias was the apostle chosen to replace Judas Iscariot following his death his betrayal of Jesus (Acts 1.23). The same verse notes that Matthias was one of the men who had followed Jesus, but he is not mentioned elsewhere in the NT. However, he does appear in some work by early Christian writers, and the lost apocryphal *Gospel of Matthias* is attributed to him, although this is believed to be fictitious.

Although nothing is known for certain about his later career, there are many traditions associated with his life. One which appears in Greek literature was that he went to Cappadocia, in modern-day Turkey, and introduced Christianity there. A similar tradition has him associated with going to preach the Gospel in a place called Aethiopia, now believed to be modern-day Georgia, not Ethiopia.

There are also several traditions about his death. Those that claim that he was crucified are now believed to result from writers confusing him with Matthew. Others have him martyred at Colchis in western Georgia, or stoned by the Jews in Jerusalem, then beheaded, or even that he died of old age in Jerusalem. The Georgian tradition has him buried at the Roman castle of Gonio-Apsaros in Colchis, on the Black Sea, and there is a sign there claiming to mark his burial. However the versions of his life which have him dying in Jerusalem recount that his remains were brought to Germany by Helena, the mother of Emperor Constantine, and that they were reinterred at the Abbey of St Matthias at Trier, the city where she lived for some of her life. There is a terracotta relief of Matthias by Luca della Robbia (1400–1482) at the Church di Santa Croce in Florence.

See also JUDAS ISCARIOT [JC]

Medea. Medea, and its inhabitants, the Medes, are mentioned 15 times in the OT, mainly in connection with the Persians, most famously with King Darius 'the Mede'. Today, the name the country is often spelled 'Media'; it covered parts of NW Iran and modern Azerbaijan, first appearing under this name in the texts from the reign of Shalmaneser III of Assyria (reigned 858–824 BCE), although Herodotus dates the creation of the kingdom to c. 715 BCE, and historians believe that the kingdom came together a hundred years later.

The Medes became subjects of the Persians after Cyrus II ('The Great') defeated them in 550 BCE, but the term 'Medes' was still used in many instances in the Bible to refer to these people, especially with Darius—although he was not a Mede. The historically inaccurate connection is best-remembered in the song 'Daniel' by Vachel Lindsay: 'Darius the Mede was a king and a wonder, his eye was proud and his voice thunder'.

Recommended reading. Culican, W. *The Medes and the Persians*. London: Thames & Hudson, 1965

See also DARIUS [JC]

Mediator. A mediator in the OT is either a judge or one who intervenes or intercedes on behalf of another (rare *palal*). In great concern for his sons, Eli grappled with the consequences of his lineage's promiscuous acts, 'If one person sins against another, someone can intercede (*palal*) for the sinner with the LORD; but if someone sins against the LORD, who can make intercession (*palal*)?' (1 Sam. 2.25). In a word of judgment, Ezekiel proclaims that Jerusalem's sin is so bad that it provided justification for its sister city Samaria, 'Bear your disgrace, for you have furnished some justification (*palal*) for your sisters. Because your sins were more vile than theirs, they appear more righteous than you' (Ezek. 16.52). Characters in the OT often act as mediators often by praying to God (Exod. 8.28, 32.30; Pss 72.15, 138.8; 1 Sam. 7.5; Jer. 7.16, 21.2).

Mediation between God and humanity is a central theme of the Bible. Moses mediates with God on behalf of the Israelites and brings them out of the confines of Egypt (Exodus; Philo, *Life of Moses* 2). Once out of Egypt, Moses established the Levites as the high priests, who acted as continual mediators on behalf of Israel (Lev. 6.15). After the Roman invasion and occupation, the high priesthood remained, but held a more political than spiritual role. According to the Christian tradition, the coming of Jesus superseded the requirements to fulfill the law (Gal. 3.19) and established a permanent priesthood that will forever mediate (*mesitēs*) and intervene on behalf of humanity (1 Tim. 2.5; Heb. 8.6, 9.15, 12.24). While the Gospel narratives do not use the specific language of mediation, they often ascribe acts of mediation between God and humanity to Jesus (John 14.6). The sacrificial priest motif in the book of Hebrews was influential on later Christian theology, beginning with Anslem of Canterbury's theory of substitutionary atonement, which explained that Christ's sacrifice satisfied God's need to avenge sin.

The biblical notion of mediator permeates western culture and literature. The Roman court upheld convictions made by mediators and today, divorce judges are often given the title of mediator. Spiritualists are sometimes referred to as mediators who speak with the dead. Meg Cabot's *The Mediator* series tells a fictional story about a teenage girl who mediates between the world of the dead and the living. In other literature, a mediator could be the main character of a plot (usually the protagonist) who forfeits her or his life on behalf of another. In Otis Turner's black-and-white movie *The Mediator* (1916), Lish Henley (George Walsh) works as a mediator during the California Gold rush and ultimately, intercedes with a sidearm. In the 1983 film *Return of the Jedi*, Luke Skywalker (Mark Hamill) forfeits his life to his father and in doing so, awakens Darth Vader's sense of justice, ending the cosmic war and Luke's inner turmoil. Neo (Keanu Reeves) fights for the lives of all human beings in the S-F series *The Matrix* (1999, 2003), only to defeat the robots by sacrificing himself. In James Cameron's epic *Avatar* (2009), Jake Sully (Sam Worthington) is hired to mediate between the military and the Na'vi, the natives of Pandora, for privileges to mine a rare mineral. Sully's forces win the battle only by their willingness to sacrifice themselves and all that they have for freedom of the Na'vi.

See also ATONEMENT; HIGH PRIEST; MOSES [JS]

Meek shall inherit the earth. The phrase 'the meek shall inherit the earth' gained its popularity because of its place in the Sermon on the Mount (Matt. 5.5) as the third beatitude; however, it ultimately derives from Ps. 37.11: 'But the meek shall inherit the land, and delight themselves in abundant property'. The phrase represents unconventional wisdom that inverts conventional assumptions. In this vein, it is not normally the meek but the powerful who end up dominating the world. As Mark Twain once commented: 'The English are mentioned in the Bible. Blessed are the meek, for they shall inherit the earth.'

Determining the original meaning of the phrase primarily depends on how the term 'meek' (*praus*) is translated, an issue heavily debated in scholarly circles, as well as throughout the history of reflection on the text. Although English Bibles predominately translate it as 'meek', other alternatives have been used, such as 'gentle' (NASB) and 'humble' (NLT). These three translations directly correspond to the range of meanings when the term is translated in its two other occurrences in Matthew. In Matt. 11.29 Jesus uses the word to describe the kindness he himself represents 'Take my yoke upon you, and learn from me; for I am *gentle* and humble in heart, and you will find rest for your souls. For my yoke is easy, and my burden is light'. In 21.5, Jesus quotes from Zechariah with reference to himself with overtones of nonviolence: 'Tell the daughter of Zion, Look, your king is coming to you, *humble*, and mounted on a donkey'. Other translations have included 'kind', 'friendly' and 'mild'. The main translation problem is in finding an English equivalent that holds together the ideas of gentleness with the potential of strength. Chromatius (fifth century) reminds his audience that not only Jesus, but also Moses and David are described in scripture as being meek: 'Moses found the greatest favor with God because he was meek. It was written about him: "And Moses was the meekest of all people on earth. (Num. 12.3)" Furthermore, we read in David's psalm. "Be mindful, O Lord, of David and his great meekness (Ps. 132.1 [131.1 LXX])"' (*Tractate on Matthew* 17.4.1-2).

Concerning the promise of inheriting the land, Chrysostom writes, 'Tell me, what kind of earth is referred to here? Some say a figurative earth, but this is not what he is talking about. For nowhere in Scripture do we find any mention of an earth that is merely figurative. But what can this Beatitude mean? Jesus holds out a prize perceptible to the senses, even as Paul also does. For even when Moses had said, 'Honor your father and your mother', he added, 'For so shall you live long upon the earth'. And Jesus himself says again to the thief, 'Today you shall be with me in paradise'. Today! In this way he does not speak only of future blessings but also of present ones' (*The Gospel of Matthew, Homily* 15.3).

Many spin-offs of this phrase are used to support various causes, e.g., 'the weeds shall inherit the earth', 'the geeks shall inherit the earth', the robots shall inherit the earth', and 'the gadgets shall inherit the earth'.

See also BEATITUDES; SERMON ON THE MOUNT

[DB]

Megiddo. An important city state in ancient Israel, Megiddo was located on a hill where archaeologists have found the remains of 26 layers of ruins on the strategic hill which commands the head of the pass through the Carmel Ridge and overlooks the western part of the Valley of Jezreel. In the ancient world it was undoubtedly on one of the major trade routes between Egypt and Assyria and was clearly inhabited from between 7000 and 500 BCE.

The ancient Egyptians mention Megiddo and indeed the Pharaoh Thutmose III fought a war against the city in the fifteenth century BCE, described on the walls of his temple in Upper Egypt. It was during this battle that Thutmose led his forces against the king of Kadesh who had formed a large military coalition. In some chronologies, the battle is described as taking place on April 16, 1457 BCE, although others place it in 1482, 1479 or 1478. The reason for the Egyptian soldiers moving so far into Canaan was because of a Canaanite revolt led by the king of Kadesh. This led Thutmose to gather together an army of some 10,000 men, infantry and charioteers. They marched towards Megiddo and there they set up camp and decided on a quick attack on the town of Megiddo. The idea was to surprise the forces of Kadesh before the king could rally an even larger military force. The plan worked, with the Pharaoh leading his army into the attack, and many of the Canaanites fleeing to safety in Megiddo, including the kings of Kadesh and Megiddo who escaped in the confusion that followed the Egyptians sacking the baggage train. The Egyptians surrounded and lay siege to Megiddo, the siege lasting possible for seven months.

Another battle of Megiddo was fought in 609 BCE when the Egyptians again attacked and this time defeated King Josiah of Judah, where Josiah was killed (2 Kgs 23.29). As it was the location of two great battles in biblical times, it was said to be the place where Armageddon would take place—the battle between the forces of good and evil at the end of the world (Rev. 16.16).

A twentieth-century battle was fought at Megiddo on September 19–23, 1918, between the Allied soldiers of General Edmund Allenby and the Ottoman army. By that time some of the region had been excavated by the archaeologist Gottlieb Schumacher, with work starting again there in 1925 financed by John D. Rockefeller, Jr. Many of the remains found there are held in the Rockefeller Museum in Jerusalem and at the Oriental Institute of the University of Chicago. The Israeli archaeologist Yigael Yadin dug there in the 1960s, with smaller digs there since 1994 by the Megiddo Expedition of Tel Aviv University.

Recommended reading. Gale, General Sir Richard. *Great Battles of Biblical History*. London: Hutchinson, 1968. Herzog, Chaim, and Mordechai Gichon. *Battles of the Bible*. London: Weidenfeld & Nicolson, 1978. Redford, Donald B. *Wars in Syria and Palestine of Thutmose III*. Leiden: E.J. Brill, 2003

See also ARMAGEDDON; JOSIAH [JC]

Melchizedek. Melchizedek, 'king of righteousness', is the king of Salem and a priest of El Elyon. In Genesis 14, he blesses Abram after a battle for five Jordan Valley cities. Abraham presents him with gifts; this traditionally implies that the gift receiver is greater than the gift giver. Psalm 110.4 is the first biblical reference to 'a priest according to the order of Melchizedek'. This verse is quoted in Heb. 5.6 and applied to Jesus. This reflects a tradition that attempts to separate Jesus' priesthood from the genetic line of the Levites. In other words, the priesthood of Christ is wholly other than the Israelite priesthood. The ambiguity in Heb. 7.3 about the genealogy and lifecycle of Melchizedek has led to interpretations that he was immortal. This can be related to the tradition found at Qumran in the scroll known as 11QMelchizedek. This fragmented literary reference appears to ascribe divine attributes to Melchizedek. 2 *Enoch* 69–74, known as the 'Exaltation of Melchizedek', contains an account of his miraculous birth and the origins of his priesthood.

In the Gnostic texts of Nag Hammadi, a document known as *Melchizedek* equates him with Jesus Christ. This tractate prophesies that he will return as king and judge in addition to his priestly role.

Rabbinic traditions associated Melchizedek with

Shem the son of Noah. He plays an important role in rabbinic writings is said to have been the Torah teacher of Abraham.

Because Melchizedek is not an Israelite but is accepted and respected in the biblical tradition, some Christians have developed a theology called the 'Melchizedek factor'. This states that despite the Christian belief that Jesus is the only way to salvation, those who have not been able to learn about Jesus may be saved through interaction with nature which points to God.

On July 30th, the Armenian Apostolic Church commemorates Melchizedek in the Calendar of Saints.

The Church of Jesus Christ of Latter Day Saints in the Book of Mormon states that Salem was an evil city but Melchizedek was righteous and through his righteousness was able to save his city (Alma 13.17-18). They also believe that he is descended from Noah.

Recommended reading. Kobelski, Paul J. *Melchizedek and Melchireša*. Washington, DC: Catholic Biblical Association of America, 1981. Mason, Eric Farrel. *'You are a priest forever': Second Temple Jewish Messianism and the Priestly Christology of the Epistle to the Hebrews*. Leiden: Brill, 2008

See also ABRAHAM; GENESIS, BOOK OF; GNOSTICISM; HEBREWS, EPISTLE TO THE; PRIESTHOOD; QUMRAN; SHEM [EW]

Mene, mene, tekel, parsin (see **Handwriting on the wall**).

Mephibosheth. Mephibosheth ('from the mouth of shame' or 'from the mouth of [the god] Bashtu') was the name of one of King Saul's sons by his concubine Rizpah. It was also the name of the youngest son of Jonathan, son of Saul, and it is with him that the name is most frequently connected. He also was apparently known as Merib-baal ('beloved of Baal'). He was a young child when his father Jonathan died on the battlefield at Mount Gilboa. Apparently the child's nurse fled with the child but in the process, he was injured so that he was crippled in both feet. Mephibosheth was permanently disabled and grew up in obscurity in a place called Lodebar. Once David was established as king, he recalled the oath that he had made to his friend Jonathan to care for his family (1 Sam. 20.42). He inquired after any survivors of Jonathan to whom he could show kindness in accordance with that oath and was informed by Ziba, a servant of Saul, about Mephibosheth.

David summoned Mephibosheth, spoke kindly to him, bestowed upon him the former properties of Saul's house, and commanded Ziba to tend those lands for him. Mephibosheth was appointed to serve as a valued counselor to David.

When David fled in the face of his son Absalom's rebellion, Mephibosheth was not able to go with him because of his lameness. Ziba met David with provisions for his escape and reported that his master rejoiced in David's trouble and saw it as an opportune time to regain his place of power (2 Sam. 16.1-4). David then stripped Mephibosheth of his possessions and bestowed them upon Ziba, for what appeared to be his loyalty and Mephibosheth's betrayal. The report however was malicious. Mephibosheth was betrayed by Ziba who misrepresented him to David. When David did return to Jerusalem, he was met by Mephibosheth who had been in mourning, evidenced by his failure to care for his hygiene since the day of David's departure. David then restored half of his estate to him, an act that seems unjust in light of Ziba's evil misrepresentation. Mephibosheth however was undisturbed by all of this, simply rejoicing that David was safely restored to his rightful position as king (2 Sam. 19.24-28).

In the biblical text, Mephibosheth is an object of unconditional love. Little is made of Mephibosheth in western cultural sources though his name is used for some characters in fiction (e.g., *The Mephibosheth Stepsure Letters* by Thomas McCulloch, a work considered to be one of the first in Canadian fiction). More recently Mephibosheth has figured in some research work around the theme of disability in the Bible.

See also DAVID; JONATHAN; RIZPAH; SAUL [BW]

Merab (see Rizpah).

Mercy. Hebrew: *ḥesed*; Greek: *eleos*. This is a common relational term. Early, it was used for the assistance that one person gave to another in need. Accordingly, mercy overlapped use with *compassion* and *grace*. Within a relationship, mercy often demonstrated loyalty and faithfulness. Sometimes, an authority gave mercy or pardon to another who has committed an offense and deserved punishment.

In scripture, God is merciful. 'Merciful and gracious' are divine qualities that identify and characterize God (Exod. 34.6-7; Ps. 103.8). Likewise, Christ is a 'merciful and faithful high priest' (Heb. 2.17). God shows mercy by saving people from disaster (Ps. 94.17-18), like the time God saved Lot in Sodom (Gen. 19.19). God pardons those who deserve wrath (Mic. 7.18; Lam. 3.31-32). Knowing that God's mercy is abundant both now and forever (Ps. 33.5; 103.11; Jer. 31.3; Isa. 54.10) motivated people to cry for deliverance (Neh. 13.22; Ps. 44.26; 109.21). Frequently, God's people celebrated together, 'his steadfast love endures forever!' (Ps. 118; 136). In the NT, it was God's mercy that motivated him to save people from their transgressions through Christ (Eph. 1.4-5). God shares his mercy through Christ with disobedient people in order to make known his great honor (Rom. 9.15-17, 23).

Since mercy is important to God (Hos. 6.6), he expects his people to show mercy to each other (Luke 6.36). Frequently, God's mercy motivates someone to show mercy to another in need (Matt. 5.7; Rom. 12.1). The Good Samaritan exemplifies God's mercy (Luke 10.25-37). In contrast, God-haters are 'heartless and ruthless' (Rom. 1.29-32). There is great punishment for the servant who receives a priceless pardon and then does not pardon other debtors (Matt. 18.23-35).

Popular western culture continues to use mercy in the context of willing choice and pardon. From a voluntary act, President Gerald Ford pardoned Richard Nixon after Watergate and showed amnesty toward draft evaders.

In past decades, philosophers raised difficult ethical questions about mercy within retributive (past action) and reformative (future correction) theories of punishment. When and why should criminals be pardoned from their punishment? Is mercy deserved or is it a gift? How much mercy should be given? Does unequal treatment destroy justice?

In many humanitarian stories, mercy is identical with compassion. People show care for those hurting by trying to alleviate their pain and troubles. These acts of mercy include sheltering the homeless, prostitutes and drug addicts or administering aid to disaster victims. This same humanitarian spirit has been idealized since early western culture, shown in many works of art including Caravaggio (*The Seven Works of Mercy*, 1607) and Montallier (*The Works of Mercy*, 1680). Similarly, Mary has often been depicted as the mother of mercy.

The ethical tension over the right to die adopted the technical term, 'mercy killings', or the legal right to end life. The 2005 Academy award winning film *Million Dollar Baby* exposed the issue to a much larger audience. The film dramatizes a boxer's struggle through emotional and physical suffering after her debilitating spinal cord injury. Though many objected euthanasia, in the end, she convinced her friend to end her suffering through lethal injection.

See also GOODNESS; GRACE; JUSTICE; LOVE [SP]

Mercy Seat. 'Mercy-Seat' is not a direct translation of either the Hebrew *kappōret* ('place of atonement') or the Greek *hilastērion* (LXX). In his German NT, Martin Luther translated *kappōret/hilastērion* with the phrase *Gnadenstuhl* ('seat of grace'), which William Tyndale translated into English as 'Mercy Seat'. Working backwards, then, 'Mercy-Seat' refers to the *kappōret/hilastērion*, the gold slab on top of the Ark of the Covenant that was kept in the Holy of Holies and above which God promised to reside (Exod. 25.17-22). Annually, on Yom Kippur ('Day of Atonement'), the High Priest would enter this inner sanctum and sprinkle the blood of a sacrificed bull and goat on the Mercy Seat to atone for the sins of the people (Lev. 16.14-16). Thus, as the Hebrew *kappōret* indicates, the Mercy Seat is properly understood as the place where atonement takes place. This is the meaning the Greek *hilastērion* has in at least one of its two occurrences in the NT. Hebrews 9.5 refers to the 'Mercy-Seat' as part of a description of the events related to Yom Kippur which the author claims were a 'shadow of the things to come' (Heb. 10.1). The meaning of *hilastērion* in the other NT occurrence, Rom. 3.25, is a topic of continued debate. Paul says that 'God put [Jesus] forward as a *hilastērion*'. For many scholars, it seems unlikely that Paul would refer to Jesus as the 'place of atonement' and they therefore argue that the reference is to an 'atoning sacrifice'. This latter meaning is used, for example, in relation to the death of the Maccabean martyrs (*4 Macc.* 17.22). Others, however, are happy to translate *hilastērion* as 'Mercy Seat', suggesting that for Paul, as for the author of Hebrews, Jesus is both the sacrifice of atonement and the place where atonement takes place.

While 'Mercy Seat' tends to appear in the western cultural tradition as part of a broader reference to the Ark of the Covenant (e.g., Milton's *Paradise Lost*, Dickens's *David Copperfield*, and Spielberg's *Raiders of the Lost Ark*), there are a few instances in which Mercy Seat has had an allusive life of its own. Nick

Cave composed a song entitled 'Mercy Seat', later covered by Johnny Cash, that tells of the redemptive afterlife expectations of a death row convict. Neil LaBute's play *Mercy Seat* describes the avoidance of the September 11 attacks by a man who cheated death by visiting his mistress. Norman Dubie penned a collection of poems that he titled *Mercy Seat* that reflect honestly about the horror and beauty of life. '123' by the Indigo Girls offers something of an admonition with the words: 'Young children of authority, now how long can you be agile? Dancing between the altar and the mercy seat; yeah now here's a chance to make a choice, are you aware of the fire beneath your feet?' The artistic tradition tends to depict the Mercy Seat as a divine throne of sorts, picking up the theme from Exod. 25.22 of God's majestic presence. Representative of this motif is Richard Fields's painting *The Ark of the Covenant* which portrays God as the cosmic king who rules the universe from between the cherubim affixed to the 'Mercy-Seat'.

See also ARK OF THE COVENANT; DAY OF ATONEMENT [JAL]

Meribah (see Massah and Meribah).

Merodach (see Marduk).

Meshach (see Shadrach, Meshach and Abednego).

Mesopotamia. The 'land between the rivers' Tigris and Euphrates, Mesopotamia is now known as one of the 'Cradles of Civilization', where the Sumerian civilization—and some of the first cities in the world—began as early as the fifth millennium BCE, followed by the Babylonian and later Assyrian Empires. Because of the location between two major rivers, the soil was fertile, and it was possible to get high yields from crops, and this surplus helped them establish a demand for luxury goods. After Assyria, the land was a part of the Empire of Achaemenian Persia, and then the land conquered by Alexander the Great. After the Diadochoi Wars (323–280 BCE), it became a part of Seleucid Mesopotamia, and then was controlled by the Parthians and later by the Romans. It was later occupied by the Sassanids, followed by the forces of Islam.

In biblical terms, Mesopotamia is the traditional site of the Garden of Eden (Gen. 12.13-15), the ancestral homeland of Abraham (Gen. 12.4), and the site of Babylon (first mentioned in Gen. 10.10). Deuteronomy 26.5 recalls the Mesopotamia roots of Israel with the confession 'A wandering Aramean was my ancestor'.

The name Mesopotamia was used to describe the area around the Tigris and the Euphrates—not just the land between the rivers—until the early twentieth century. During World War I, the fighting there was known by the British as the Mesopotamia Campaign, and with the defeat of the Ottoman Empire in World War I, the British scholar Gertrude Bell suggested the creation of a country called Mesopotamia; it was eventually created but called Iraq.

The term Mesopotamia has also become the name of a northeastern part of Argentina situated between the Rio Parana'a and Rio Paraguay; and also some land in Oxford, England, between two rivers in the Oxford University Parks.

Recommended reading. Lloyd, Seton. *Twin Rivers: A Brief History of Iraq from the Earliest Times to the Present Day.* Oxford: Oxford University Press, 1961

See also EUPHRATES; RIVERS OF BABYLON; TIGRIS [JC]

Mess of pottage. The phrase 'mess of pottage' typically refers to trading something of great value for something relatively valueless. It comes from Gen. 25.29-34, in which Esau trades his birthright to his younger brother, Jacob, for a bowl of red lentil stew (KJV: 'mess of pottage', i.e., a portion of stew). After coming home from hunting exhausted, Esau is so hungry that he trades his birthright for the bowl of Jacob's stew.

In Genesis, Jacob and Esau, the twin sons of Isaac and Rebekah, are involved in sibling rivalry even from the womb, with the two brothers wrestling before birth and Jacob grasping Esau's heel when they are born (Gen. 25.21-26). While Jacob is portrayed as cunning and intelligent, Esau is capricious and violent (although both characters undergo significant character development before the end of their lives). Jacob also outsmarts Esau a second time in Gen. 27.1-29, tricking his aged and blind father into giving him Esau's blessing.

In the NT, this episode is remembered by the author of Hebrews, who deplores Esau's action: 'See to it that no one becomes like Esau, an immoral and godless person, who sold his birthright for a single meal' (12.16).

The phrase 'mess of pottage' is not an actual translation from the Hebrew text but has come to be associated with the biblical episode in English usage. A famous example of this phrase comes from

Henry David Thoreau's essay 'Life Without Principle' (1863): 'If I should sell both my forenoons and afternoons to society, as most appear to do, I am sure that for me there would be nothing left worth living for. I trust that I shall never thus sell my birthright for a mess of pottage'.

Recommended reading. Ahroni, Reuben. 'Why Did Esau Spurn the Birthright? A Study in Biblical Interpretation'. *Judaism* 29 (Summer 1980) 323-31. Spero, Shubert. 'Jacob and Esau: The Relationship Reconsidered'. *Jewish Biblical Quarterly* 32 (2004) 245-50

See also BIRTHRIGHT; ESAU; JACOB   [MH]

Messiah (see Christ).

Methuselah. The etymology of this Hebrew name is uncertain. Methuselah is the seventh descendant of Adam's line according to the genealogy found in Gen. 5. He was the son of Enoch, the father of Lamech, and the grandfather of Noah. We know little about this man apart from his name but because of a brief comment in Gen. 5.27, his place in the popular imagination is secure; he lived to be 969 years old, the oldest man that has ever lived (according to the Bible).

Early Jewish writings do not add much information about Methuselah beyond what Genesis offers. Josephus includes the Genesis genealogy with his name in *Jewish Antiquities* 3.79. Methuselah also appears in various pseudepigraphal texts, adding little information. Most often, these writers mention Methuselah in relation to his more famous father, Enoch.

The name Methuselah is usually synonymous with longevity in modern parlance. Uses of the name in literature include a set of plays by George Bernard Shaw entitled *Back to Methuselah*, and stories by Robert A. Heinlein and Vernon Eric Bridges, *Methuselah's Children* and *The Methuselah Factor* respectively. There is also a popular Methuselah comedy routine by Carl Reiner and Mel Brooks entitled, '2000 Year Old Man', and an episode of Star Trek with the title 'Requiem for Methuselah' (February 14, 1969). In the field of science, the Methuselah Foundation awards the Methuselah Mouse Prize to outstanding anti-aging research.

See also ADAM; ENOCH; GENEALOGY; GENESIS   [RKM]

Micah, Book of. Micah is one of the longer of the minor ('Latter') prophetic books and is placed sixth in the collection of the Twelve Prophets in the OT. The editorial introduction announces four things: the source of the oracles (Yahweh), the identity of the prophet, the time period of his ministry and the scope of the revelation.

Micah is an abbreviated form of Micaiah, 'who is like Yahweh?' He is from Moresheth, thought to be Moresheth-gath, a small village in the coastal lowlands about 20 miles SW of Jerusalem (now Tell ej-Judeideh). He is not the same Micaiah who prophesied the death of Ahab (1 Kgs 22.8-9). He lived during 'the days of Jotham [750–735], Ahaz [735–715] and Hezekiah [715–687], all kings of Judah', but his prophecies were about both the Northern and Southern Kingdoms.

The book is written in Hebrew poetic style, using parallelism to express its thoughts. Chapters 1–3 are an indictment of the people (especially the elites) of both the Northern and Southern Kingdoms for conduct that is unjust economically, politically and legally. Chapters 4–5 look to the future, to the 'latter days'. Chapter 6 returns to the indictment and chapter 7 is like a personal lament.

Micah is cited in Jer. 26.18 and his prophecy is recalled as one delivered during the time of King Hezekiah. The prophecy of Micah cited (3.12) is not favorable. In the context of Jeremiah, it is cited to defend Jeremiah's prophetic freedom because Micah was not put to death for preaching divine punishment because the people's repentance moved God to spare the kingdom.

The standard of behavior that Micah sets is not understood in terms of ritual sacrifices, for even if these included sacrificing one's first born it is not religious practice that pleases God (6.6-7). What is pleasing to the living God is righteous behavior following the standard to 'do justice, and to love kindness and to walk humbly with your God'. The gross failure to live up to this standard had evoked judgment that would be administered by pagans for the hypocrisy and corruption of the people.

It is the living God for whom Micah speaks. He says of his consciousness of God: 'I am filed with the spirit of the LORD, and with justice ad might to declare to Jacob his transgression and to Israel his sin' (3.8).

Micah's words about justice are often quoted. In 1959, the officially atheist government of the Soviet Union gave to the United Nations a bronze sculpture inscribed with the words from Micah (4.3) and Isaiah (2.4) 'they shall beat their swords into ploughshares'. In 1979, Jimmy Carter took the oath of office as president with his hand placed on a Bible open to Mic. 6.8.

In Matt. 2.6, Mic. 5.2 is cited as proof to the Magi that Bethlehem will be the birth place of the messiah. Phillips Brooks's hymn 'O Little Town of Bethlehem' uses Mic. 5.2 as do other hymns such as 'O God of Every Nation' (William W. Reid, Jr). Thomas Hardy's 'A Dream Question' is based upon Mic. 3.1-7.

Recommended reading. Allen, Leslie C. *The Books of Joel, Obadiah, Jonah and Micah*. NICOT. Grand Rapids, MI. William B. Eerdmans, 1976

See also FORMER PROPHETS; HUMBLE; HUMILITY; JEREMIAH; JUDGMENT; JUSTICE; LATTER PROPHETS; MERCY; PROPHECY; PROPHETS; SWORDS INTO PLOUGHSHARES [AJW]

Michael, the angel. 'Michael' means 'Who is like God?', the name of ten different men in the OT; most famously, the name of a principal angel. Although Michael appears rarely in the Bible (Dan. 10.13-21; 12.1; Jude 9; Rev. 12.7-9), he has received considerable attention. The intense reflection and speculation on the role of angels and archangels that is evident in Jewish and Christian tradition outside the Bible has meant that many of the general biblical materials about angels have been applied to Michael.

Michael is given the epithet of 'Prince' in Daniel (10.13, 21; 12.1); he is close to God, commands the forces of heaven, and acts as patron and defender of Israel both in the present and the last days, just as other 'chief princes' act similarly for other nations. Thus there is a cosmic mirroring of earthly conflicts. Michael is the bearer of revelation, is terrifying in appearance yet restores the fainting courage of human beings. His later association with the bearing of the deceased to heaven appears to be derived from the Epistle of Jude where Michael contends with the devil in a legal dispute over the body of Moses, a story associated with the apocryphal *Assumption of Moses*. In Jude 9, Michael's deference to God contrasts with the antagonistic independence of the devil. This battle of Michael and the forces of light against the devil (blended with the dragon, the old serpent, Satan) and his destructive forces is played out in numerous permutations from the Dead Sea Scrolls document, the *War of the Sons of Light against the Sons of Darkness* to the Apocalypse (Rev. 12.7-9) and beyond. Here, Michael's functions blur with those of the Messiah.

In other Jewish traditions, Michael becomes the angel that contended with Jacob at the river Jabbok (*Targum Pseudo-Jonathan to Genesis* 32.25; *Pirke R. El*. 36), the one who accompanied the people of Israel through their passage through the Red Sea and their desert wanderings (*Exodus Rabbah* 18.5), and the bearer of the law to Moses (*Jubilees* 1.27; 2.1). He becomes both Prince of fiery flames (symbolized by his fiery sword) and the Prince of waters (at Chonae in Phrygia) in developing Christian tradition; in Catholic and Orthodox traditions he is not just an angelic warrior and protector but the provider and patron of healing sites, such as the spring at Chonae (Colossae) in SW Turkey and the mountain at Gargano in Italy.

The dramatic brilliance of Michael's appearance and his heroic actions combined with the obscurity and indirection of his description have made him a constant favorite for literary, artistic and cinematic embellishment, from Milton's *Paradise Lost* to television appearances in the series *Xena: Warrior Princess*. His image is ubiquitous in Orthodox iconography. By contrast, the film *Michael* starring John Travolta (1995) says more about the popular association of the name with a beneficent angel than any connection with characteristics of the biblical archangel; the third volume of Philip Pullman's *His Dark Materials* darkens the figure of Michael under one of his traditional names, Metratron (*Yebamot* 16b), in a striking re-conception of the war in heaven. The Australian film *Gabriel* (2007) depicts Michael as an archangel sent to battle evil in purgatory, but who turns to the dark side himself and transforms purgatory into his own kingdom until he is confronted by Gabriel.

See also ANGEL; DANIEL, BOOK OF; DRAGON; GABRIEL, THE ANGEL; JUDE, EPISTLE OF; REVELATION, BOOK OF [AHC]

Micaiah. Seven individuals with this name are passingly mentioned in the Hebrew Bible: the mother of Judahite king Abijah (2 Chron. 13.2; contrast 1 Kgs 15.2); the son of Judean king Jehoshaphat (2 Chron. 17.7); a Levite (Neh. 11.17, 22; 12.35); a priest (Neh. 12.41); an official of Judahite king Josiah (2 Kgs 22.12; 2 Chron. 34.20); and the son of the scribe named Gemariah (Jer. 36.11, 13).

The most prominent Micaiah, ben Imlah, grants a glimpse into the life of court prophecy in the northern kingdom of Israel (1 Kgs 22; 2 Chron. 18). Prophets had access to the kings of Israel and Judah from the advent of the kingship under Saul, a phenomenon attested in other ancient Near Eastern cultures, most notably at Mari (in modern day Syria) in the eighteenth century BCE. These prophets behaved ecstatically, in that the deity in question spoke through the individual. The verb describing the actions of the court prophets is *nitrabbi'*, meaning to 'prophesy repeatedly', indicating a frenzied action. These responses are not to be confused with the actions of priests, in which a question is put to them, and a 'yes' or 'no' answer is delivered by means of divination, in Israel by means of the *urim* and *thummim*.

The reaction of Jehoshaphat to the court prophets of Ahab is instructive. After witnessing the 400 affirmatives, he wanted another opinion, even if it were but one more. The precise source of his unease is not made explicit as to whether court prophets in general aroused his suspicions, or if he found Ahab unscrupulous, or if he found something amiss in the way that these particular prophets behaved; perhaps they said nothing about how Jehoshaphat would fare personally. Clearly, prophets were considered malleable, given the exchange between Ahab's official and Micaiah, though Micaiah lets him know he will only say what God has him say (22.13). It is not clear how Ahab knows that Micaiah is being disingenuous with him initially. His pair of disastrous visions validates Ahab's mistrust.

It is interesting that God claims through the second vision that it is he who is enticing Ahab to his death. The court prophets are not labeled false, but as prophets forced to lie by a spirit sent by God. The implication is that this group is usually open to the spirit of truth. Further, Micaiah's response to Ahab's sentence is in accord with the test for a true prophet found in Deut. 18.21-22.

Jehoshaphat's response is particularly intriguing. He not only agrees to engage in a battle that a prophet he deems comparatively trustworthy announces will be a rout, but agrees to dress the part of Ahab. One must wonder if he wanted Ahab, his powerful neighbor to the north, dead, and trusted that God would announce if a similar fate awaited himself.

Ahab was certain enough of the likelihood of Micaiah's prophecy that he disguised himself, to no avail. His death fulfilled the prophecy of Elijah concerning his punishment for compliancy in the murder of Naboth (1 Kgs 21.17-29). The reader fully expects the prophet that Ahab hates to be Elijah, as the unexpected entrance of Micaiah provides a twist to the Ahab narratives.

Apart from artistic depictions of Micaiah's prophecy against Ahab, the prophet does not figure prominently in western culture, the prophet's depiction of the heavenly court is one of the earliest in the Bible (2 Kgs 22.19-22). The tactical role-playing video game *Fire Emblem*, features an heroic a female character named Micaiah.

See also AHAB; JEHOSHAPHAT; LATTER PROPHETS; PROPHETS; URIM AND THUMMIM [MAP]

Michal. Michal is the only biblical woman said to have loved a man (1 Sam. 18.20). She is one of the daughters of Saul and becomes David's first wife and is often referred to in the OT by her relationship to one of these men. It costs David 100 Philistine foreskins to marry Michal (1 Sam. 18.27; 2 Sam. 3.14). Saul desires David's death and Michal intervenes to save David's life by helping David escape through the window of his bedroom. At this point it seems that the marriage between Michal and David is over. She is given to Palti son of Laish and David marries Abigail and Ahinoam. However, after David's forces defeat Saul, he requires that Michal be given back to him. The text does not say how Michal felt about being taken from her new husband and returned to David but it does say that Paltiel followed behind her weeping (2 Sam. 3.16).

Michal only appears once more in the Bible (2 Sam. 6.16-23; cf. 1 Chron. 15.29). In this chapter the ark of the covenant has just been returned to Israel after its capture by the Philistines and David takes to the streets dancing and rejoicing. Michal is said to have been watching from the window and that she despised him. The couple meets in front of their household and Michal condemns the king's behavior. He promptly dismisses her and her concerns. The last thing the reader is told about Michal is that she remained childless until her death. Subsequent interpreters often posit that her connection with Saul is to blame for her barrenness, as God promised to eliminate the line of Saul and replace it with the line of David. In this way, Michal becomes an example of God's will triumphing over circumstance.

The rabbis argue over whether David married only Michal, or both Michal and her older sister Merab (*T Sotah* 11.18; *BT Sanhedrin* 19b). She is represented as so beautiful that every man lusted after her (*BT Megillah* 15a). In Christianity, she has typically been interpreted in a negative light. This is exemplified in Archbishop Heath's 1559 *Speech*

Against the Royal Supremacy. Her connection to Saul, who has been viewed as the yin to David's yang, her use of the *teraphim* (1 Sam. 19.13), household idols, in helping David escape, and her public insult to him all contribute to the judgment that has historically been passed on Michal. Her barrenness has been viewed as fitting punishment for her bad behavior, as bearing royal children was the highest status level that a woman of that time could hope to achieve. This prevailing view of Michal through the ages has been changing in the academic community that has dismissed the charge of idolatry and asserts that her charges against David were legally and morally correct, and in popular fiction such as *Queenmaker* (2002), a novel by India Edghill that tells the story from Michal's perspective. A striking scene in the movie *King David* (1995) portrays the bitter confrontation between Michal and David with sympathy for the queen.

Recommended reading. Clines, David J.A., and Tamara C. Eskenazi (eds.). *Telling Queen Michal's Story: An Experiment in Comparative Interpretation.* Sheffield: Sheffield Academic Press, 1992. White, Ellen. 'Michal the Misinterpreted'. *Journal for the Study of the Old Testament* 31 (2007) 451-64

See also DAVID; RACHEL; SAMUEL, BOOK OF; SAUL

[EW]

Midian. After Abraham's wife, Sarah, died, he took a concubine, Keturah (Gen. 25.1-6) who bore him six sons, one named Midian, fathered of four sons (1 Chron. 1.33). Abraham sent the children of Midian to the 'country of the east' (Gen. 25.6).

Midian's descendants roamed the desert lands of Midian east of the Jordan River and the Dead Sea. They also held territory in the southern and eastern parts of the Sinai Peninsula where they grew in numbers. Exodus and Numbers call them Midianites, while in Judg. 6.3, 33 they are called the 'people of the east'.

The Midianites and the Ishmaelites were at times identified (Gen. 37.28; Judg. 8.24). They were in the caravan that bought Joseph when he was sold in to Egyptian slavery by his brothers (Gen. 37.25-36).

When Moses fled Egypt he went to the land of Midian where he married into a Midianite family (Exod. 2.15). His Midianite wife, Zipporah, was the daughter of Jethro who served as a priest for his clan of Kenites. The Kenites were afterward closely associated with the Hebrews and their Israelite descendants. However, they never gave up their nomadic ways. Except for the Kenites, the Midianites were enemies of the Israelites.

From the time of the wilderness wanderings the Midianites are portrayed as the enemies of Israel. When the Moabites decided to fight the Israelites, the Midianites joined them, contributing to the hire of Balaam to curse Israel (Num. 22.4, 7). While in Moab, Midianite women were able to lead some of the Israelites into idolatrous practices which evoked God's wrath upon his people. Moses and the elders stopped the plague by executing everyone who had sinned with the Midianites. Thereafter God commanded Moses to harass the Midianites for seducing them with wiles (Num. 25.16-17). Shortly before his death, Moses obeyed the divine command to avenge the people of Israel for the deaths caused by the Midianites. The subsequent campaign killed five kings of Midian and all their people except for the young virgins (Num. 31.1-20).

In the time of the Judges (chs. 6–8), the Midianites rode camels, a new innovation at the time, and plundered Israelite crops and livestock. However, God raised Gideon up as a judge of Israel. In a surprise night attack Gideon, a reluctant warrior, scattered the Midianites. He enlisted the Ephraimites to help with the destruction of the Midianite army and capture four Midianite kings.

In Ps. 83.9, 11, the story of Gideon illustrates how God delivered Israel from oppression (Ps. 83.9 and 11). Isaiah declares that the people who have walked in darkness have seen a great light because God has broken the yoke of the oppressor as happened on the day of Midian (Isa. 9.2, 4). Isaiah also prophesies that Yahweh will destroy the enemies of his people (Assyrians and Egyptians) as he did Midian at the rock of Oreb (Isa. 10.26).

In 1883, Samuel Judah published a play called *The Maid of Midian*. Several novels featuring the Zipporah as the main character have been published, e.g., Lois Erickson's *Zipporah* (1989) and Marek Halter's *Zipporah, Wife of Moses* (2006). Stefan Wolpe composed a string quartet piece called 'The Man from Midian' (1942). Zipporah and her Midianite family play a significant role in the Spielberg film *The Prince of Egypt* (1998).

Recommended reading. Burton, Richard Francis. *The Land of Midian (Revisited).* Cambridge: Oleander Press, 1979. Philby, H. St John. *The Land of Midian.* London: Benn, 1957

See also BAALAM; GIDEON; KENITE; MOSES; ZIPPORAH

[AJW]

Midwife. From the Hebrew *hameyaledet,* meaning 'woman assisting at childbirth'. With only three occurrences (all in the Pentateuch), midwifery is not a major biblical concept.

In Gen. 35.17, a midwife is present at the birth of Benjamin, son of Rachel and the patriarch Jacob. Rachel dies during the birth after the midwife tells her the baby is a boy. In Gen. 38.28, a midwife delivers Tamar's twins, Perez and Zerah, tying a red string around the hand that popped out of Tamar first, to be sure which twin was firstborn. The most sustained reference is in Exod. 1.15-21. Here, the Pharaoh, fearing the strength of his slaves, tells the midwives to kill all baby Hebrew boys. However, the midwives (named Shiphrah and Puah) disobey because they 'fear God', concocting an explanation. 'Hebrew women ... are vigorous and give birth before the midwife comes'. God rewards the midwives' behavior.

The Bible's three mentions of midwives are brief but positive. The first two depict midwives as present at births as a matter of course, as though midwifery was commonly employed and accepted; the midwife holds authority, e.g., declaring the child's sex or witnessing who is firstborn. In Exodus, midwives not only merit proper names, but are depicted as bravely defying the king, escaping intelligently, and reaping divine rewards. American poet Celia Gilbert recently drew inspiration from these OT birth-assistants in her poem 'the Midwives'.

Although absent in the NT, midwives are mentioned in other depictions of Jesus' birth; in Orthodox iconography, they are often shown bathing the baby Jesus. Extracanonical gospels such as James (c. 150 CE) and Pseudo-Matthew (eighth century) include a certain Salome as a witness to the postpartum virginity of Mary; in the story, she disbelieves another midwife's declaration that Mary has remained a virgin, and examines Mary for herself. God punishes her by withering her hand, after which she believes. By the Middle Ages, Salome the midwife is associated with the Salome mentioned in Mark as a follower of Jesus (15.40; 16.1). Salome appears widely in artistic depictions of the nativity, including those by Giotto (c. 1300), Duccio (c. 1300), the Master of Flémalle (1420), and Pellegrino Aretusi (c. 1500). She remains a standard presence in Orthodox iconography today.

Biblical midwives played little role in western Christianity until the 1960s, when theologians began re-examining the Bible in search of woman-friendly passages. New references to midwifery have since been uncovered in verses like Ps. 22.9 ('it was you [God] who took me from the womb; you kept me safe on my mother's breast'), and other such passages (e.g., Ps. 71.6; Isa. 66.9). These verses portray God as divine midwife, and are useful for envisioning the female divine.

Recommended reading. Claassens, L. Juliana M. 'Rupturing God-language: The Metaphor of God as Midwife in Psalm 22'. In *Engaging the Bible in a Gendered World: An Introduction to Feminist Biblical Interpretation in Honor of Katharine Doob Sakenfeld.* Pp. 166-75. Ed. Linda Day and Carolyn Pressler. Louisville, KY: Westminster John Knox Press, 2006

See also INFANCY NARRATIVES; SALOME; SHIPHRAH AND PUAH; VIRGIN/VIRGIN BIRTH [SPR]

Millennium. From the Greek *chilioi* (thousand). The millennium refers to the future thousand-year reign of Jesus before the final judgment of humanity. There are three major views of the millennium in contemporary Christianity. First, premillennialism advocates that Jesus will return to earth before the millennium in order to establish a literal thousand-year kingdom. Second, postmillennialism holds that the millennial kingdom will be initiated through the witness of the church, and that Christ will return at the close of this period of time, usually interpreted figuratively. Third is what might be labeled amillennialism, which denies a future millennial reign of Jesus, and interprets biblical references to a millennial reign in some other way. Premillennialism is most common among Christian fundamentalists, while postmillennialism and amillennialism are most common among mainline and liberal Christian denominations.

Early Christian writers appropriated the idea of the millennium from Jewish apocalyptic writings such as 2 *Baruch*, 1 *Enoch*, and 2 *Esdras*, and especially from Revelation, the only NT book to explicitly mention a future thousand-year reign (20.2-7). The idea of a literal thousand-year reign of Christ was quite prominent within the first century of the church, and was espoused by the early Christian writers Papias, Justin Martyr, Irenaeus and Lactantius. Towards the end of the second century, however, premillennial interpretation was seriously challenged, and largely abandoned in favor of an allegorical or figurative interpretation of the millennial kingdom advocated by Origen, Jerome and Augustine, that today would be understood as more postmillennial or amillennial in nature. By the middle of the fifth century, Augustine's position had won the day, and the belief in a future literal thousand-year reign of Jesus was declared a heresy at the Council of Ephesus (431).

Despite periodic instances of the resurgence of millennialism in the middle ages, e.g., the interest sparked by the twelfth-century mystic, Joachim of Fiore, millennial speculation was not a major part of Christian theological reflection for the thousand years following Augustine's death. This all changed with the Reformation, when the idea of the millennium attracted a renewed interest among Protestants who came to view their struggle against Rome as an important phase in God's providential plan for human history. In Europe, Thomas Münster, Thomas Brightman, John Owen, Johann Heinrich Alsted, and Joseph Mede all showed a renewed interest in the millennium, and through the influence of the Puritans, New Englanders like Jonathan Edwards and Isaac Backus inculcated American Christianity with a decidedly millennial character. Nineteenth century American Christianity was markedly postmillennial in nature, and it was understood that it was the responsibility of the church, not Jesus, to usher in the millennial kingdom of God through the salvation of both the individual soul and human society. The late nineteenth and early twentieth century realization of the 'myth of progress', however, cast suspicion on human ability to initiate the millennial kingdom, particularly among conservative Protestants. This resulted in a return to the idea that only Jesus is capable of initiating the millennial kingdom, causing premillennialism to become the dominant understanding of the millennium within much of conservative evangelicalism.

Recommended reading. Grenz, Stanley J. *The Millennial Maze: Sorting out Evangelical Options*. Downers Grove, IL. Intervarsity, 1993. Hunt, Stephen J. *Christian Millenarianism: From the Early Church to Waco*. Bloomington, IN. Indiana University Press, 2001

See also ESCHATOLOGY; RAPTURE; REVELATION; TRIBULATION [AS]

Millstone. Heavy stone(s) used for grinding grain, often wheat, mentioned several times in the Bible both literally (Deut. 24.6; Judg. 9.53; 2 Sam. 11.21) and metaphorically (Job 41.24; Matt. 18.6; Mark 9.42; Luke 17.2; Rev. 18.21-22). The centrality of the millstone to life and work in the ANE is underlined by the text of Deut. 24.6, which forbids the taking of an upper millstone as collateral, because this would be tantamount to taking their life in pledge. Similarly, milling grain was an essential activity in daily life, as affirmed in Jer. 25.10 and Rev. 18.22, where the comforting sound of milling is described as a sign of peaceful domestic life (cf. Num. 11.8; Matt. 24.40-41).

Hebrew and Greek each have a variety of words which are translated 'millstone' in English. This is in part because the ancient milling apparatus involved two millstones, each with a different function. Because the lower millstone (Hebrew: *pelaḥ taḥtît,* Greek: *akmōn)* had to bear the weight of the one on top, it was particularly hard. This hardness functions as a positive metaphor for the hard (meaning undaunted) heart of the creature Leviathan (Job 41.24). The upper millstone (Hebrew: *pelaḥ rekeb,* Greek: *epimylion)* was known for its heaviness, and functions in Judg. 9.53 as the weapon that kills Abimelech. Millstones came in various sizes, as attested by the Greek language *mylos onikos* (literally, donkey-millstone) used in the Gospel occurrences of the term (Mark 9.42; (Matt. 18.6; Luke 17.2). Some of Jesus' harshest words include punishment by millstone: 'If any of you put a stumbling-block before one of these little ones who believe in me, it would be better for you if a great millstone were hung around your neck and you were thrown into the sea' (Mark 9.42). This industrial-sized donkey-millstone could be 4–5 feet in diameter and exceedingly heavy (perhaps the sort of apparatus Samson was yoked to in Judg. 16.21). Revelation 18.21-24 also draws on the heavy-millstone metaphor, depicting the destruction of Babylon as thrown into the sea like a great millstone.

Millstones are used in a wide variety of metaphors in later Christian reflection. In some cases, these draw on specific biblical texts, and in others millstones are used generically. This is not surprising, given the extent to which milling and millstones were a common element of daily domestic life. To demonstrate the range of this usage, several examples suffice. One of the first depictions can be found in the words of Ignatius at his martyrdom, 'I am the wheat of Christ, and am ground by the teeth of the wild beasts, that I may be found the pure bread of God' (*Ignatius* 4). Millstones functioned as the instrument of martyrdom of the early Christian Saints Christine and Florian. The latter is depicted by Albrecht Altdorfer's *The Martyrdom of St Florian* (c. 1530).

Use of 'millstone' as a metaphor in later theological writing is also various. In discussing temperance in his commentary on Gal. 5.25, Luther suggests, 'we need a millstone around our neck to keep us humble'. In *Pilgrim's Progress*, John Bunyan uses the millstone as a general metaphor for hardness (ch. 3) and weight (ch. 13). Isaac Watts draws on the Rev. 18.21-24 mention of 'millstone' in his hymn, 'Babylon Fallen'.

See also ABIMELECH [JHK]

Miracles. The Bible depicts the occurrence of miracles, if by that one means that events occur that either appear to contradict the laws of nature or, perhaps better, seem to follow a different set of natural laws than those by which the world as we know it normally functions, such as the parting of the Red Sea (Exod. 14.21-31), the manna in the wilderness (Exod. 16.1-35), and the miracles of Elijah and Elisha (1–2 Kgs). In the NT, Jesus is clearly depicted as a miracle worker. Over 30 miracles are related in the Gospels, including some miracles that are narrated in all three of the synoptic Gospels, some in one or two of the Gospels, and one that is depicted in all four of the Gospels (the feeding of the 5000). These miracles include a variety of types of actions. Some concern natural phenomena, such as the calming of the storm on the sea of Galilee (Matt. 8.23-27; Mark 4.37-41; Luke 8.22-25), a large number depict the healings of individuals from various maladies, such as the woman who had been bleeding for numerous years (Matt. 9.20-22; Mark 5.25-29; Luke 8.43-48), and a few even depict the dead being raised back to life, such as Lazarus (John 11.1-44). There are other miracles as well, such as the feeding miracles (Matt. 14.15-21; 15.32-38; Mark 6.35-44; 8.1-9; Luke 9.12-17; John 6.5-13).

In the first few centuries of the Christian church, miracles served as a major evidential support in Christians' apologetic battles with others, providing a strong claim to the truthfulness of Christianity on the basis of the spectacular events that surrounded its inception. Nevertheless, early on various figures of the church, such as Augustine and Aquinas, felt compelled to provide further explanations and justifications for the miracles that went beyond straightforward acceptance for apologetic value. The Enlightenment, however, brought widespread questioning regarding the occurrence of miracles. The rise of rationalism brought with it skepticism, which in many ways reached its peak in the arguments of the Scottish philosopher David Hume. Hume's contention was that miracles, as a violation of natural law, simply cannot occur. Further, he did not believe that empirical evidence, even that found in the Bible, could prove that miracles actually took place.

There have been many responses to Hume's work, including noting that he does not exclude the notion of miracles but says that by definition they cannot occur. His limited definition of a miracle as a violation of natural law is also thought by some to be overly restrictive. Even so, from the time of Hume, there has been growing skepticism of the occurrence of miracles, although there have always been those who have come to the defense of the historical veracity of miracles and their evidential value, however they are defined. In the course of discussion and debate, a number of explanations of miracles have been posited. Several of the most well known in contemporary thinking are worth noting. The history of religions school proposed that miracles were secondary accounts drawn from a variety of available religious sources marshaled in defense of the Bible's religious narrative. Rudolf Bultmann's demythologization argued that the biblical text is to be seen as a witness to individuals' existential encounter with God, not as an historical account of what actually happened in the physical world. Lastly, there have been various naturalistic explanations of the miracles that have eliminated the need for the divine element by consideration of the workings of nature itself.

Recommended reading. Brown, Colin. *Miracles and the Critical Mind*. Grand Rapids, MI: Eerdmans, 1984

See also ELIJAH; ELISHA; MANNA [SEP]

Miriam. The sister of Moses and Aaron (Exod. 15.20; Num. 26.59; 1 Chron. 6.3). She is unnamed in the birth story of Moses but plays an instrumental role (Exod. 2.1-10). She stands at a distance and watches over the baby left near the river bank while Pharaoh's daughter comes down to bathe, discovers the floating basket, and sends one of her maids to fetch it. Miriam negotiates a Hebrew nurse for Moses and returns with his mother. This scene is represented in the *Golden Haggadah*, in mediaeval manuscript painting from Barcelona (1320–1333). Deviating from the biblical tale, a shrouded and solicitous Miriam sits on a hillock, as three nude females walk through the waters; the Egyptian princess in front of her maids opens the casket to find the child wrapped in swaddling clothes (cf. Exod. 2.3-6).

In her most famous role, Miriam is the prophet who sang the Song of the Sea to celebrate Israel's defeat of the Egyptians at the Sea of Reeds (Exod. 15.20-21). All the women of Israel join her in a victory dance with timbrels (cf. Judg. 11.34; 1 Sam. 18.6, 21.11, 29.5). Historical tradition remembers that women played a part in the poetry of the prophets, and that music and song helped convey the prophetic word (Isa. 5; Amos 6.5; Hos. 2; Mic. 1.6-7, 13; Jer. 4.30-31). Miriam is viewed as the counterpart of Moses, but her song is significantly shorter than his (Exod. 15.1-18; Mic. 6.4). Another historian rejected Miriam's prophetic status to emphasize Moses as prophet (Num. 12).

Artistic representations of Miriam's performance are numerous. In the *Golden Haggadah* Miriam drums on a rectangular tambourine, in company with six dancers who play tambourines, lute and percussion instruments. In a painting from the fourteenth-century *Sarajevo Haggadah*, five women hold hands in a dance-line, while Miriam stands apart as the sole musician. Sir Edward Poynter's relief print on *Miriam* (1864) is a fine portrait of the heroine raising her tambourine and swirling in dance. Sir Edward Burne-Jones portrays his mistress as *Miriam* (1872) dancing with cymbals on a stained-glass window in St Michael and All Angels Church, Hertfordshire. Marc Chagall's colourful lithograph *Dance of Miriam* (1966) depicts her semi-nude, shaking tambourines in a lively dance with three women.

Protestant and Jewish American women of the nineteenth century reinterpreted the figure of Miriam as a way of asserting their right to speak on political and religious issues. Commenting on the American institution of slavery, Harriet Beecher Stowe (*Women in Sacred History*, 1873) reveres Miriam as a brave leader for an oppressed people. Written before the Civil War Penina Moïse's poem 'Miriam' (1833) esteems the heroine as 'the bright star/enlightener of the sea' who, in company with Moses, 'sets the nation free'. Today Jewish women place Miriam's goblet beside the wine cup of Elijah on Seder tables. Her cup is filled with water to symbolize the 'miraculous well' given to her by God to quench the people's thirst during the wilderness journey, according to midrash on Num. 21.16-18, depicted as early as 244–245 CE on the synagogue wall at Dura-Europos in Syria.

Recommended reading. Meyers, Carol. 'Miriam, Music, and Miracles'. In *Mariam, the Magdalen, and the Mother*. Ed. Deidre Good. Bloomington/Indianapolis: Indiana University Press, 2005. Trible, Phyllis. 'Bringing Miriam out of the Shadows'. *Bible Review* 5 (1989) 14-25.

See also EXODUS, BOOK OF; MOSES [JRW]

Mishael (see Shadrach, Meshach and Abednego).

Mizpah (see Watchman/Watchtower).

Moab. Moab (Hebrew: *mo'av*) was the name given by the elder daughter of Lot to her son. He was born in a cave at Zahor near the Dead Sea where Lot and his two daughters had fled following the destruction of Sodom and Gomorrah. Thinking that they were the last people left on earth, the girls had sex with their father in order to repopulate the earth. The Bible names Moab as the ancestor of the Moabites. The name in Hebrew means 'of my father', and portrays Moab as the offspring of an incestuous union (Gen. 19.37).

The Moabite territory was on the Transjordanian plateau where plains stretch eastward about thirty miles to the Arabian Desert. On the south its boundary was with Edom at 'the brook of Zered' (Deut. 2.13), probably the Wadi el-Hesa. In the north, the deep Arnon gorge (modern Wadi el-Mojib) separated it from Ammon.

The Moabites engaged in pastoral activities, some farming and trading because the King's Highway, a trade route between Arabia and Syria, passed through their land. By 2500 BCE, there were agricultural settlements that developed into a number of fortified cities by 1500 BCE. The fortifications were needed as protection from marauding nomads and from the advancing Amorites who took part of their territory.

When the Hebrews arrived, Moses requested permission for peaceful passage through Moab but was refused. As a consequence, the Hebrews took the Desert Highway around Moab on the east. Israelite defeats of the Amorites under Sihon and Og of Bashan terrified Balak, king of Moab. He hired Balaam the prophet to curse the Israelites, but the attempt backfired (Num. 22–24). Moab was viewed as the enemy of the Israel for most of their history together because they were the 'people of Chemosh' (Num. 21.29). Deuteronomy 23.3 forbids the entry of a Moabite or Ammonite into the assembly of Israel 'even in the tenth generation'. Moses saw the

Promised Land from Mount Nebo (Num. 27.12-23) in Moab and under Joshua the Israelites crossed the Jordan River from NW Moab (Josh. 3.1).

In the time of David and Solomon, the Moabites were vassals of Israel. Solomon had Moabite wives he pleased by building an altar to Chemosh, 'the abomination of Moab' (1 Kgs 11.7). This was part of the reason for the division of the kingdom after his death.

During the time of the divided monarchy, the Moabites were able to regain their independence. The Moabite Stone erected by King Mesha of Moab tells of the sacrifice of thousands of Israelites in celebration of the victory. The language and script of the Moabite Stone are very similar to Hebrew. In the early 700s BCE the Moabites became the vassals of the Assyrians and later of the Chaldeans. They had disappeared from history by the Roman era, replaced by Arabs.

The Book of Ruth tells the story of the conversion of a Moabite woman to the God of Israel through her devotion to her Israelite mother-in-law, Naomi. The genealogy of King David cites Ruth as his great-grandmother (1 Chron. 2.12-14; cf. Matt. 1.5).

The Moabit area of Berlin is thought to have acquired its name from Huguenot refugees. Moab, Utah was given its name by early Mormon settlers. The US Air Force has named its Massive Ordinance Air Blast Bomb, MOAB. Its nickname is the Mother of All Bombs (MOAB).

Recommended reading. Routledge, Bruce. *Moab in the Iron Age: Hegemony, Polity, Archaeology.* Philadelphia: University of Pennsylvania Press, 2004

See also BALAAM; BALAK; LOT; MOSES; NEBO; RUTH, BOOK OF [AJW]

Molock, Molech. A Canaanite-Israelite deity, Molock in the LXX and Molech in the Hebrew, whose name links it to notions of kingship as they share the same Hebrew root *mlk*. The deity has been associated with the underworld and is considered to be the god of child sacrifice. Molech is been associated with the phrase 'pass through fire' and the Tophet (furnace-like altar), an indication that the child sacrifice would take the form of burning the body. It is unknown whether the child sacrifice was used only in crisis situations or was part of a regular liturgical calendar. Some scholars believe that as Israelite religion developed Molech worship was subsumed into Yahwistic worship and that the sacrifice of the firstborn (cf. Gen. 22; Exod. 13; Ezek. 20; Mic. 6) has roots here.

Among academics, there has been some controversy as to whether or not this biblical character is a god or a sacrifice. Many of the occurrences of the term could be read either way. However, as pointed out by John Day, Leviticus 20.5 states that the Israelites went whoring after Molech, and one does not go whoring after a sacrifice but rather a God. This not only establishes the nature of Molech as a deity but also furthers the metaphor of idolatry as adultery.

During the medieval period, Molech was considered to be one of the princes of hell particularly known for stealing babies, evidently an expansion of his connection to child sacrifice. Molech also appears in Milton's *Paradise Lost*, where he calls for immediate action to be taken in the war against God and is one of Satan's chief officials. Flaubert's fictional reconstruction of the religion at Carthage, *Salammbô*, characterizes Molech based on rabbinic traditions. This book was released as a movie, *Cabiria*, by director Giovanni Pastrone. Based on Flaubert, Elizabeth Dilling wrote the anti-Semitic *The Plot against Christianity* and *The Jewish Religion: Its Influence Today*.

In modern English, the word 'moloch' is used to express any action that requires sacrifice. Entertainment industry icon Joss Whedon used this deity as the basis for a character in episode 8, 'I Robot ... You Jane', of season one of *Buffy the Vampire Slayer*. However, while gruesome, Whedon's Molech does most of his own killing and child sacrifice does not come into play. Alan Ginsberg used Molech as a metaphor in his work *Howl*. In this piece, Molech is used to embody the city and demonize McCarthyism. The use of Molech to make a political observation has been embraced by the American anti-abortion movement. For example, Steve Hickey recently published as *Molech in America: Bloodguilt and the Spiritual Dynamics behind Abortion* (2006). Hickey parallels the child sacrifice associated with Molech to American abortion laws.

Recommended reading. Day, John. *Molech: A God of Human Sacrifice in the Old Testament.* Cambridge: Cambridge University Press, 1989. Heider, G.C. *The Cult of Molek.* JSOTSup, 43. Sheffield: Sheffield Academic Press, 1985.

See also POLYTHEISM; SACRIFICE

[EW]

Money. In the ancient world money took a variety of forms. In ancient Israel, money was measured in terms of land, property, or weights of precious goods. For most people barter was the usual means of monetary exchange (1 Sam. 8.15; 1 Kgs 5.11; Ezek. 45.13-16). This involved trading one item, often a herd animal, for another item of approximately equal value. The use of cattle as monetary units is demonstrated by the similar Hebrew terms *miqneh* and *miqnâ* which respectively mean 'cattle' and 'something purchased' (Gen. 13.2; 17.12-13). Grains, oil, and wine were also bartered.

Quantities of precious metals were frequently used as monetary units. In the OT, the Hebrew word *kesep*, which literally means 'silver', is most commonly translated into English as 'money'. Gold, silver, copper, and iron were shaped into pieces of standard weight and used for commerce. Common weights in ancient Israel included the gerah, half-shekel, shekel, mina, and talent (Gen. 24.22; Exod. 30.13; Lev. 27.25; Exod. 38.25-26). The talent was equal to 60 minas, and the mina was equivalent to 50 shekels (60 shekels in Ezek. 45.12). The gerah was the smallest unit, equal to 1/20 of a shekel. A shekel of gold was equivalent to about 15 shekels of silver.

Coins were first minted during the seventh or sixth centuries BCE in western Asia Minor (modern Turkey). The use of coinage was then propagated by the Greeks and the Persian Empire. The first mention of coins in the Bible is in Ezra 2.69. In NT times, coins were the standard form of money. Each nation or independent city usually minted its own coins. The Jews were only able to mint coins during the brief periods in which they were independent from the Greeks or Romans. Common coins included the lepton (Mark 12.42), Roman denarius (Mark 6.34; 14.5), Tyrian shekel (Matt. 26.15), Greek drachma (Luke 15.8-9), and didrachma or half-shekel (Matt. 17.24-27). One denarius was roughly equivalent to one drachma, and both had the value of one day's pay for a common male laborer (Matt. 20.9-10, 13); two days' pay for a woman. The shekel weighed about 8.5 grams and was equal to four denarii. The mina and talent were also still used for larger sums of money.

Money often has a negative image in the Bible, especially in the NT. Jesus states that one 'cannot serve God and wealth' (Matt. 6.24). Jesus also claimed that 'it is easier for a camel to go through the eye of a needle than for someone who is rich to enter the kingdom of God' (Mark 10.24). The author of 1 Timothy warns that 'the love of money is the root of all kinds of evil' (6.10).

Recommended reading. Reifenberg, Adolf. *Israel's History in Coins from the Maccabees to the Roman Conquest*. London: East and West Library, 1953. Safrai, Zeev. *The Economy of Roman Palestine*. London: Routledge, 1994

See also ANANIAS AND SAPPHIRA; CAMEL THROUGH A NEEDLE'S EYE; CLEANSING OF THE TEMPLE; FILTHY LUCRE; MAMMON; PARABLE OF THE RICH FOOL; RICH MAN AND LAZARUS; THIRTY PIECES OF SILVER; WEALTH; WIDOW'S MITE [EM]

Mordecai. The character of Mordecai plays a central role in the Book of Esther. He is portrayed as a prominent Jew in the Persian court, Esther's elder kinsman, surrogate father and advisor. In the story's key plot movement he is the one who hears of Haman's plot to exterminate the Jews from Persia and thus, appeals to his cousin, the Queen, on their behalf. His initiative, coupled with Esther's action, results in the salvation of his people and the demise of Haman. At the conclusion of the story, in a dramatic reversal, he rises to the position of vice-regent over Persia.

Mordecai is depicted as an ideal figure, a flawless example of how Jews living in the Diaspora should conduct themselves. In many ways, Mordecai is the predominant figure in the book that has been named after his younger cousin. He is introduced before her (2.5), and is the focus of the second half of the story including a final affirmation of his life and impeccable character at the book's end (10.2-3). He is regarded as an exemplary character in his wisdom, courage, devotion to his people, and personal piety.

Mordecai can be understood as a type of character in story telling that is known as a noble champion who is tenacious, relentless and who always sticks up for the underdog. He is guided by his conscience even if it means going against the rules. He is an honorable champion of a people who are facing dire circumstances. The Talmud portrays both Mordecai and Esther as prophets. Rabbi Jose the Galilean attributed the Hallel psalms to Mordecai and Esther, which they sang after being delivered from Haman (*Pes.* 117a).

See also DIASPORA; ESTHER, BOOK OF; HAMAN; PURIM [LB]

Morning Star. The 'morning star' is the planet Venus whose light often appears brightest as dawn approaches. However, the growing light from the sun soon renders Venus invisible to the human eye. In the ancient world, astrological events were understood to reflect the activities of the gods (cf. Job 38.7), and in Ugaritic mythology the god Helel, symbolized by the morning star, is cast from the heavens by the supreme god Elyon, symbolized by the sun. Isaiah utilizes this myth in his oracle against the Babylonian king (Isa. 14.10-15), identifying the king as the morning star whose glory will fade before the greater light the Lord.

In the Latin Vulgate translation of Isa. 14.12, the Hebrew *Hēlēl*, 'morning star', is rendered as *lucifer* (from *lux* 'light' and *-fer* 'bearing'). In the Christian tradition, this latinism combined with other traditions of an angel of light cast from the heavens (Luke 10.18-19; 2 Cor. 11.14; Rev. 12.7-9, 13), to become an alternate name for Satan, the one cast out of heaven.

Within the NT, it is Jesus who is described as the 'morning star' (2 Pet. 1.19; Rev. 2.28; 22.16), in messianic fulfillment of the prophecy spoken by Balaam that, 'a star shall come out of Jacob' (Num. 24.17). In popular culture, 'Morning Star' has assumed a significance far beyond denoting the planet Venus, having variously been used to denote the Virgin Mary, John Wycliffe, Lucifer, Satan, and a British communist daily newspaper.

See also Isaiah; Lucifer; Revelation, Book of; Satan [SW]

Moses. In Judaism, the supreme prophet, lawgiver and leader of Israel; in the NT, a type of Jesus Christ, especially in the Gospel of Matthew. The hero of the books Exodus through Deuteronomy, Moses is portrayed as an Egyptian of Hebrew descent, abandoned in a reed basket to escape Pharaoh's harsh decree that every male Hebrew newborn must be murdered. His daughter discovered baby Moses while bathing in the Nile. Adopting Moses as her own, she sought a Hebrew nurse to care for the child. Moses's birth-mother was summoned by her daughter, watching nearby, and commissioned to raise her own son. A fabled life followed, summarized by the traditional American spiritual 'Little Moses'. Bob Dylan's 'Thunder on the Mountain' memorializes Moses on Mount Sinai receiving the Ten Commandments.

Jewish mythology captures the spirit of this biblical legend in a number of texts covering several centuries from the early to medieval CE. Moses's parents, Amram and Jochebed, conceived Moses despite Pharaoh's attempts to separate Hebrew men and women. Pilti, one of Pharaoh's sorcerers, learned from the Book of Signs that a Hebrew child would lead his people to the destruction of Egypt (*Sefer Ha-Yashar* 67). Moses was this redeemer, leading the Hebrews out of Egypt following a series of signs and wonders (*Exodus Rabbah* 5.13-14). Joseph's granddaughter, Serah bat Asher, a prophetess, appeared to Rabbi Yochanan (late second–early third century) and his students, telling them that the walls of the Red Sea separated and became as mirrors, reflecting every Jewish man, woman and child, past, present and future, indicating that the present redemption from Egyptian bondage was an archetype of redemption for the entire Hebrew people (*Pesikta de-Rav Kahana* 11.13). But how was Moses, a mere mortal, able to survive forty days and nights without food or drink while on Sinai receiving the commands of God? Moses was uniquely transformed into the exalted form of an angel and therefore required no sustenance during this experience (*Makhon Siftei Tzaddikim* on Gen. 1.16). Forty years of wilderness wanderings were equally wrought with miracles for Moses and the Israelites. How were they able to endure the scorching desert heat, the danger of scorpions and venomous serpents, hail and rainfall that intermittently ravages this desolate region? Seven clouds of glory accompanied them under Moses's direction—one on each side, one in front and behind, one above and below, and a seventh proceeding ahead of them to level mountains and valleys, making their journey effortless (*Targum Pseudo-Jonathan* on Exod. 12.37). Moses delivered his people to the borders of the promised land. His last request—that the heavens open so that all his people would see there is no God but the God of Abraham, Isaac, and Jacob, and that the glory of the Lord be permanently embedded in their minds and the hearts—was fulfilled by God, and the people cried out in one voice, 'Hear O Israel, the Lord our God is One!' (*Deuteronomy Rabbah* 11). Then God cast a deep sleep over him; he remains in exile with the Shekinah, tasked to keep his people and the Shekinah out of exile. Moses will eventually return to lead his people into God's glorious final redemption (*Bavli, Sota* 13b; *Sifrei on Deuteronomy* 357).

The towering figure of Moses has been commemorated in countless works of Christian art, music and literature. Zorah Neil Hurston's novel *Moses, Man of the Mountain* (1939), portrays the biblical figure in the light of African-American folklore and music. Two twentieth-century films, *The Ten Command-*

ments (1956) and *Prince of Egypt* (1998) vividly portray his career.

See also EXODUS; LAW; PHARAOH; SHEKINAH; SINAI; MOUNT [DM]

Mote and beam. While traditionally translated as 'mote', the Greek word (*karphos*) simply refers to 'any small dry body', and thus can also be translated as 'speck' or 'twig'; the Greek word for 'beam (of wood)' (*dokos*) can also be translated as 'log'. Although the exact translation is flexible, the juxtaposition created by these terms is fixed: the mote, or speck, is to be understood as a much smaller object in comparison to the beam, or log.

The Parable of the Mote and Beam, attributed to Jesus, helps to form the foundation of Christian moral teachings concerning hypocrisy, and is thought to have roots in Jewish and Arab proverbs. This parable is found twice in the NT: in Matthew's Sermon on the Mount (7.3-5), and the parallel passage in Luke (6.41-42). It is also preserved in the non-canonical *Gospel of Thomas* (26). The parable states that one cannot remove a much smaller object (mote) from another's eye, while a larger one (beam) remains in one's own. The moral lesson is quite simple: that the greater flaw lies in the person who finds faults in others, while blind to their own.

The parable is literally interpreted by Italian Baroque painter Domenico Fetti in his oil painting 'The Parable of the Mote and Beam' (c. 1619), which portrays a conspicuous but seemingly unnoticed log near the face an older man, who is seated superiorly and pointing at a small twig near a younger man's eye.

The allegory of the mote and beam has also been adopted in literature, as a way of indicating hypocrisy. Early examples of this can be found in Chaucer's *Canterbury Tales* in the Reeve's introduction to *The Miller's Tale* (1.3918-20), as well as in Shakespeare's *Love's Labours Lost* (4.3.156-59). It has also often been misapplied, as in Charles Lamb's essay 'Poor Relations' in *The Last Essays of Elia* (1833), where he uses 'a mote in your eye' to describe a needy relative. More recently, the parable has served as inspiration for the title of the acclaimed science fiction novel *The Mote in God's Eye* (1974), in which humans come into contact with the 'Moties', an alien species from a star called 'the Mote'. *Mote and the Beam* (1913) is also the title of an obscure movie, directed by Lawrence B. McGill.

The band Sonic Youth includes a song called 'Mote' in their album *Goo* (1990), with the line 'I'm island-bound, a mote inside my eye'. The song is supposedly named after the Sylvia Plath poem 'The Eye-mote' (1959), which recounts a story about a splinter in her eye: 'Neither tears nor the easing flush / Of eyebaths can unseat the speck / … blind to what will be and what was'.

See also HYPOCRITE; PARABLE; SERMON ON THE MOUNT [EJW]

Mount Carmel. From the Hebrew *har hakkarmel*, actually a mountain range in current day Haifa, Israel, overlooking the Bay of Haifa. Use of these mountains began early as archaeologists have uncovered prehistoric caves in the mountain with ancient burial sites from Paleolithic period. The name *karmel* is Hebrew for 'orchard', likely reflecting the positive weather conditions at this location for producing wine and other produce in ancient and modern times. The Egyptians and Mesopotamians knew of this location and it may have been an area of land dispute between Israel and its neighbors.

There may be some polemic of ownership in the famous biblical event set on Mount Carmel. God's power is displayed on Carmel in the battle between the prophets of Baal and the prophet Elijah (1 Kgs 18). Elijah, as prophet of Yahweh, is addressing religious syncretism between Baal and Yahweh. He calls on the people to choose between Yahweh and Baal. Elijah calls for a sacrifice to be set on wood and for the prophets of Baal to pray for their god to ignite it. When they are unable, Elijah sets up his sacrifice, pours water on it and then successfully calls on God to set it aflame. Then he commands the Yahwists to kill the prophets of Baal. It is significant here that God uses what is likely lightening to start the fire, showing he is greater than the storm god Baal, supposed to be in command of such forces. Mount Carmel remains a holy spot in the narratives of Elisha, Elijah's disciple, who resides there (2 Kgs 4.25). Beyond Elijah and Elisha, the mountain is given no other significance or reference in the rest of the Hebrew Bible.

Mount Carmel received some attention as a temple of Zeus in classical records. In the Christian period it became a monastic site. Early Christians attempted to follow the example of Elijah and live a solitary lifestyle on Mount Carmel near a place identified by tradition as 'Elijah's well'. Today an order of Catholic monks called Carmelites trace their origins back to Mount Carmel and form part of their mission around the work of Elijah. In the Carmelite crest, they utilize the imagery of a traveling monk (as a star) going up Mount Carmel.

Themes that are associated with Mount Carmel have also appeared in literature.

A character in Thomas Carlyle's *Sartor Resartus* (2.9.154) refers to the true versus false priests, the false being Baal-priests. Bernard Shaw refers to the contest on Carmel in preface to *Back to Methuselah: A Metabiological Pentateuch* (1921). Shaw compares the event on Carmel to a similar debate over the existence of God he had experienced at a bachelor party. In a contemporary story by William Hoffman, 'The Question of Rain' (*God Stories*, 1998), a pastor organizes a day of prayer for rain. The story deals with the struggles between requests of the deity and proper worship. In contemporary children's film, Nest Family Entertainment's *Animated Stories From the Bible* (using an advisory board of biblical scholars) likewise explores the event on Mount Carmel, interestingly demonizing the Baal worshippers in an extreme manner. Thus, preservation and reference to Mount Carmel in literature and film has been mediated through biblical story and the events in 1 Kings 18.

See also BAAL; ELIJAH; FIRE; MOUNTAIN [SWF]

Mount of Olives. A mountain ridge to the east of Jerusalem that was once covered in olive groves and that plays an important part in the OT and NT. Its first mention in the Bible is when David flees from Absalom (2 Sam. 15.30), and the sacred nature of the mount is mentioned in Ezek. 11.23, although the mountain itself is not named. It is clear that it was imbued with symbolism by the time of Solomon because he built altars on the southern peaks for the gods worshiped by some of his wives (2 Kgs 23.13). Zechariah 14.4 prophesies that the dead would be resurrected on the slopes of the Mount of Olives with the arrival of the messiah.

In the NT, the Mount of Olives is where Jesus stood and wept as he looked over Jerusalem (Matt. 26.76; Mark 14.72; 11.35); he also spoke to his disciples on the mountain, returning there and spending the night in the Garden of Gethsemane on the night of his betrayal and arrest (Matt. 26.36; Mark 14.32). It is for this reason that it is presumed that the Garden of Gethsemane was the location of a large orchard of olive trees.

Since ancient times, Jews have been buried on the Mount of Olives; some scholars estimate that there are as many as 150,000 graves there. The region was controlled by Jordan from 1948 until 1967, with Jewish burials beginning there after 1967. This practice continues with many senior Israeli and Jewish figures buried there including the former Israeli Prime Minister Menachem Begin (1913–1992), the British newspaper owner Robert Maxwell (1923–1991), Immanuel Jakobovits (1921–1999), the Chief Rabbi of Great Britain and the Commonwealth, and many famous rabbis. Princess Alice of Battenberg (1885–1969), the mother of Prince Philip, Duke of Edinburgh, is also buried there. As a result the Mount of Olives is the largest and oldest Jewish cemetery.

The Mount of Olives appears in many paintings including a famous scene by Caravaggio, and *Christ on the Mount of Olives* was an oratorio composed by Ludwig van Beethoven. *Mountolive* (1958) was also the name of the fourth book in the 'Alexandria Quartet' by British writer Lawrence Durrell (1912–1990).

See also GARDEN OF GETHSEMANE; MOUNTAIN

[JC]

Mountain. Mountains (Hebrew: *har*; Greek: *oros*) have always awed humans, inspiring legends about the divine and tempting humans to ascend them in body and mind to achieve personal and collective knowledge. Mountains played an important role in the Bible as places sacred to God where spiritual enlightenment could be achieved. On mountains, God appeared to Moses and Jesus was transfigured.

Mountains fascinated the ancient peoples of Asia and Africa, who typically considered such high places as the abodes of gods. The ancient Mesopotamians considered their gods, such as the king of the gods Enlil, to live upon mountains. Likewise the ancient Hebrews conceived of their one god, Yahweh, as abiding upon a mountain. Mount Sinai, on the Sinai Peninsula, exhibited terrifying 'thunders and lightnings', according to the book of Exodus, 'and a thick cloud upon the mount, and the voice of the trumpet was exceeding loud; so that all the people who were in the camp trembled' (Exod. 19.16). Moses, who had fled Egypt and dwelt in the Sinai Peninsula, saw a constantly burning phenomenon on the heights of Mount Sinai (also called Horeb), and ascended the mountain, where he approached the holy ground, discovering the presence of Yahweh in the burning bush (Exod. 3.2). On the mountain, the God of Abraham introduced himself to Moses as Yahweh, 'I am who I am', and commanded Moses to return to Egypt to free the children of Israel. After this, Moses led the Hebrews back to Sinai, where on the same mountain, he received the Law from Yahweh.

Mountains are also sacred in the NT, mirroring the contemporary Greco-Roman culture of the Mediterranean, which had long been fascinated by mountains, imagining such mountains as Olympus as being home to the gods. Jesus often prayed and fasted in the mountain wilderness of Samaria and Judaea. In the synoptic gospels, he takes Peter, James, and John and they ascended a high mountain, perhaps Mount Tabor or Mount Hermon, where Jesus was transfigured, metamorphosed before them. His clothes became preternaturally white, the figures of Elijah and Moses appeared, and a dense cloud overshadowed them, from which they heard a voice saying,: 'This is my son the beloved, hear him!' (Mark 9.7). The cloud dissipated and the prophets vanished, leaving Jesus and the disciples. They descended the mountain, and Jesus requested that they not make known the event until after his death (Mark 9.2-8; Matt. 17.1-9; Luke 9.28-36).

Western artists have frequently portrayed the biblical scenes of Moses on Mount Sinai and the Transfiguration; Raphael's *Transfiguration* (1520) is one of the most beautiful and well known of these art works.

Mountaineering is a comparatively modern practice, and increasingly in the past few centuries adventurers have found mountains as places of spiritual transformation. What some people take to be the biblical Mount Sinai (St Catherine's, Sinai Peninsula) continues to be a place of spiritual transformation for those who climb the rugged mountain to its peak, and spend time in the Greek Orthodox chapel at the summit.

See also MOSES; MOUNT CARMEL; MOUNT OF OLIVES; SINAI/HOREB; TRANSFIGURATION [RL]

Mourning. From the Hebrew term *'ebel* (grief) and the Greek *penthos*, *kopetos*, and *odyrmos*, terms which occur over a hundred times in the Bible. In modern English, 'mourning' is defined as the harboring and expression of sorrow over another's death. Grief and sadness are often conflated with mourning, as the intention of the word is to convey an intensity of experience unmatched by other human feelings. Mourning is a unique experience comprised of a variety of emotions including, but not limited to, grief, sadness, anger, resentment, shame, and perhaps even gratitude. Individuals are typically characterized as being *in* mourning, which underscores the profound internality and longevity of the experience. In the Jewish tradition, mourning is observed for thirty days after the death of a loved one. This custom is paralleled, though in different ways, in other cultures around the world. Mourning is the coming to terms with death. When observed by a religious believer, mourning is often an opportunity for the bereaved to receive consolation from God (Ps. 30.11; Isa. 60.20). Also typical of Jewish observances is the emphasis on collective mourning, which reminds the mourner that their grief need not carry them into isolation. Jewish mourners adorn themselves with customary ornaments and clothe themselves in either sackcloth or, more recently, in black garments (2 Sam 14.2). Symbolism pervades the experience in a way that reminds each mourner of the fragility and unpredictability of life and of life's unrelenting cycle, where life is born from death and death brings to an end an earthly life.

Though the experience of mourning remains unchanged and largely universal, contemporary rituals associated with mourning have changed a great deal. The level of mourning one experiences often depends on the depth of attachment one shares with the deceased; the closer the relation, the deeper and more intense the mourning. It is common for mourners to experience mourning in waves, as memories ignite the affections that were once associated with the living member, and thus communication with others about the personal significance of the deceased is often therapeutic in this regard. Mourning itself is also communicative, informing others by dress, posture, disposition, word, and emotion that the deceased was appreciated, loved, and respected. The mourning process communicates so much, in fact, that if one is seen to be without grief or unmoved to mourn, then that person is assumed either not to have cared for the dead, or is considered decidedly stoic in the face of mortality. Mourning is a staunch reminder that death is a permanent fixture in the world, and it comes upon all regardless of preparation.

Contemporary society tends to focus on how one copes with mourning. Where once a priest or pastor was sought for consolation in the face of tragedy or death, it is now equally common for mourners to consult a certified counsellor trained in the psychological impacts and consequences of mourning. In recent decades, western culture has construed aging and physical death as something to be avoided at all costs. The secondary consequences of this cultural force to prolong one's life has intensified the fear of death and corroded emotional competency related thereto. Frequently, especially among men, mourning is an indicative sign of weakness. Also culturally relevant is the artistic depiction of mourning, most commonly expressed in painting and photography. In popular culture, the rock band Tantric has produced a song entitled 'Mourning'.

See also LAMENTATIONS, BOOK OF [MA]

Music. Music has played a major role in the Bible and western culture from the OT period to the present. The OT records that music, both vocal and instrumental, was a part of ancient Israelite society, and probably played a major role in temple worship. Music in the NT is more difficult to define, but Paul (or Deutero-Paul) implored the Ephesians and Colossians to use 'psalms, hymns and spiritual songs' in their worship (Eph. 5.19; Col. 3.16). Some think that the music of the early Christian church was highly dependent upon synagogue worship, while others believe that there was greater Greco-Roman influence. In any case, most think that the singing was unison on the same note, while the use of musical instruments has been highly debated.

The influence of the Bible on the development of western music has been profound. The earliest Christian hymn with musical notation is dated to the third century (*Papyrus Oxyrhynchus* 1786) and, while not the setting of a biblical text, it has imagery redolent of biblical themes and ideas, such as creation, the trinity, and God as the bestower of good gifts. Within both Judaism and developing Christianity, music continued to play a role in worship, with manuscripts of various types being annotated with forms of notation to indicate how these documents were to be intoned within worship contexts. In early Christianity, the biblical manuscripts themselves were often annotated in this way for public worship. The Bible became the single most important text for musical invention from medieval times to the present. Various types of chant in the medieval period took as their inspiration biblical and related texts. During the Reformation, the church became a hotbed of controversy over musical forms and conventions, with the Bible continuing to serve an important role in musical development. Various biblical texts were set to music in diverse ways. John 1.1 ('in the beginning was the word, and the word was with God, and the word was God') and 1.14 ('the word became flesh'), among others, became important texts for the expansion of musical forms that the Reformation encouraged. Johann Sebastian Bach probably stands as the greatest single musical figure who utilized the biblical text for his exceptionally broad range of musical compositions, including cantatas, masses, chorales, motets, and passions. Well known and still sung regularly are his *St Matthew Passion* and *St John Passion*.

The influence of the Bible on music has not diminished since the time of Bach, even if it has never excelled beyond his great works. Händel wrote numerous biblically based oratorios, with the best known being his *Messiah*. The setting of the mass was a common musical form utilized by many of the greatest composers, including Mozart, Beethoven and Brahms, among others. Modern and contemporary composers have continued to find inspiration from the Bible, including those in the classical style such as François Poulenc, Igor Stravinsky and John Rutter. Music of the church today within the contemporary idiom is also highly influenced by the Bible, with some contemporary worship songs providing musical settings of key biblical passages. The Bible has had an important and continuing influence upon the development of music over the last several millennia.

See also PSALMS, BOOK OF [SEP & WJP]

Mustard Seed, Parable of the. The mustard seed is one of Jesus' parables about the kingdom of God, and it has become a metaphor for powerful changes wrought by a little faith. In Matt. 13.32, Jesus describes the mustard seed as 'the smallest of all the seeds, but when it has grown it is the greatest of shrubs and becomes a tree, so that the birds of the air come and make nests in its branches'. This is one of several Matthean parables to use planting and reaping as metaphors for the spread of the kingdom of God. Mark 4.30-32 and Luke 13.18-19 also relate this parable, emphasizing the great tree that grows from the small seed.

Jesus uses the metaphor of the power of faith the size of the mustard seed twice more in conversations with his disciples. In Matt. 17.20, Jesus has exorcized a boy who suffers from epilepsy. When the disciples question why they could not drive the demon out, he replies, 'Because of your little faith. For truly I tell you, if you have faith the size of a mustard seed, you will say to this mountain, 'Move from here to there', and it will move; and nothing will be impossible for you'. In Luke 17.6, Jesus uses a similar image of a mulberry tree planting itself in the ocean based on the power of faith the size of a mustard seed when the disciples ask him to increase their faith.

As today, mustard was a common condiment in Jesus' time. The term mustard is a contraction of the Latin *mustum ardens* ('burning wine'), and the practice was to mix crushed seeds with wine to make paste very similar to today's mustard. Both the leaves and seeds of the mustard plant are edible, and Romans would crush the seeds on their plates to consume with their food.

Contemporary use of the mustard seed in the arts remains true to the original lesson that a little bit of burning faith can improve desperate circumstances. In the stage version of Tyler Perry's *Madea: Diary of a Mad Black Woman* (2001), the main character's mother refers to having the faith of a mustard seed in a song about having the courage to face up to marital difficulties. Brooks Haxton pairs the power of the mustard seed with resurrection images in 'The Body of my Brother Osiris Is in the Mustard Seed' (1995), a poem about a child falling into a rushing river.

Of the three types of mustard plants, only one grows 15 feet tall or taller; most mustard plants only achieve a height of approximately four feet. Denise Levertov comments on the scarcity of mustard trees and the rarity of true faith in her poem, 'On the Parables of the Mustard Seed'. Le Wilhelm's one-act play 'Mustard Seed' (2003) emphasizes the need to think small when faced with overwhelming life circumstances as Donna, one of the two main characters, does when she is caught on top of a train heading towards a low tunnel.

Other poets find the fiery characteristic of the mustard seed an apt metaphor for the turbulence of the 1960s social and political revolutions. May Sarton's collection of poetry about the violence of the 1960s is called *A Grain of Mustard Seed*, and Nikki Giovanni aligns the power of the poetry written during the Black Rights Movement to the faith of the mustard seed in *Blues: For All the Changes*.

See also KINGDOM OF GOD; PARABLE, PLANTS, SYMBOLISM OF [KAM]

My brother's keeper. From the Hebrew *ach* (my brother's) *shamar* (keeper). The story of Cain and Abel is recorded in Gen. 4.1-16. Taking place outside of the Garden of Eden, it is the account of Adam and Eve's two sons, one a farmer (Cain) and the other a shepherd (Abel), and the series of events that follows the presentation of their respective offerings before God: 'The Lord had regard for Abel and his offering, but for Cain and his offering He had no regard (Gen. 4.4-5)'. Rejected by God, 'Cain was very angry, and his countenance fell' (Gen. 4.6). Spurning the warnings of God, Cain lured his brother Abel out into the field and murdered him. Upon being questioned by the Lord about where his brother was, Cain responded, 'I do not know; am I *my brother's keeper?*' (Gen. 4.9).

The animosity between brothers first evidenced in the relationship between Cain and Abel ends with Cain murdering his brother and concocting a lie to deny his culpability. The theme of strife between brothers is found in other Genesis narratives: Ishmael vs. Isaac, Jacob vs. Esau, Joseph vs. his brothers.

Similar narratives are recorded in the Qur'an (Sura 5.26-31) and the Mormon Pearl of Great Price (*Moses* 5.16-41), while many of the details differ from the biblical account in that the phrase 'my brother's keeper' is not attributed to Cain. Rather Cain acknowledges his culpability (Sura 5.29) and accepts the punishment that rightly belongs to him (Moses 5.39).

The phrase 'my brother's keeper' and the story of Cain's murderous ways have been employed in paintings such as *Cain Leads Abel to Death* by James Tissot (nineteenth century); literary masterpieces such as Dante's *Inferno* and John Steinbeck's *East of Eden*; and the 1985 mini-series *Kane and Abel*.

Even the computer game industry has tipped its hat to the story of Cain and Abel. In the popular computer game *Command and Conquer*, one of the central figures is Kane, who is noted to be the leader of the Brotherhood of Nod. Seth (Gen. 5.3) is a subordinate who is tasked with following the commands of Kane. Moreover, Kane is the owner of a sarcophagus with the name Abel etched upon it.

Given the plethora of references to the story of Cain and Abel it is no wonder that the phrase 'my brother's keeper' has come to serve as an ever-present reminder that as human beings we are responsible for one another's well-being. It has been the driving idea behind popular songs such as 'We Are the World', fundraising concerts such as Live Aid, and outpourings of benevolence such as those that were seen after the January 2010 devastation of Haiti by a massive earthquake.

See also ABEL; CAIN [JNR]

My yoke is easy. A yoke, usually a wooden bar, is used to bind animals to a load. The technology was adapted for human use, primarily for the purpose of carrying water, but also to control and discipline prisoners. The Bible contains more than 50 references to yokes, a few to literal yokes, but most metaphorical, to represent service, bondage, subjection or oppression. Conversely, freedom from imposed control is often portrayed as breaking free from a yoke (Gen. 27.40; Lev. 26.13; Isa. 14.25). Frequently, the OT symbol represents oppression or slavery to a foreign king (Deut. 28.48; Jer. 27.8-12).

The image of the yoke has retained this symbolic meaning. In recent times, people have referred to the 'yoke of oppression', or the 'yoke of subjugation', often with reference to overbearing or corrupt governments or systemic evils, such as slavery (Frederick Douglass, *Narrative of the life of Frederick Douglass An American Slave*, 1881), poverty or even marriage (Richard le Gallienne, *The Quest of the Golden Girl*, 1896).

The Pharisees used the term 'yoke' to describe a willing and faithful adherence to the Torah. They put great emphasis on the yoke (obedience to the Law), and to further ensure one did not violate the Law, they developed an additional Oral Law, designed to serve as a boundary of protection around it.

As portrayed in the NT, Jesus taught a message in opposition to the heavy yoke of the Pharisees. He encouraged all who would listen to instead 'take my yoke upon you ... and you will find rest for your souls ... for my yoke is easy, and my burden is light' (Matt. 11.29-30). Some alternately translate 'my yoke is kind'. Quite noticeably, Jesus did not remove the yoke, but instead invited people to follow his teaching on Torah, which would not drag them down as if they were carrying a heavy burden, but make them feel easy and light. In *Anna Karenina,* Tolstoy's characters pontificate on Christ's easy yoke to comfort themselves.

See also PHARISEES [KK]

Mystery. In Judaism, *mystērion* and its Hebrew equivalent *raz* (borrowed from Persian) refer to the hidden plans of God regarding the climax of salvation history. Occurrences of *mystērion* in the LXX appear in canonical Daniel and the Deuterocanonical books of Tobit, Wisdom, Sirach and 2 Maccabees. In pseudepigraphal writings, 'mystery' appears in 1, 3 *Enoch*, 2 *Baruch, Jubilees* and 4 *Esdras*. The term *raz* (cognates: *sôd*; *nistarot*) recur in the DSS, especially in eschatological contexts. In most cases, God reveals the *mystērion* to the faithful through revelation by the divine spirit.

While appearing in Matthew (13.11), Mark (4.11), Luke (8.10) and Revelation (1.20; 10.7; 17.5, 7), *mystērion/mystēria* in the NT primarily occurs in writings attributed to Paul (e.g., Rom. 11.25; 16.25; 1 Cor. 2.7; 15.50-51; cf. Eph. 3.3-4; Col. 1.26-27). Despite this imbalance, the meaning remains faithful to Jewish eschatology—albeit slightly modified. In the Gospels, *mystērion* refers to God's kingdom breaking into the world through the person of Jesus. In Paul, *mystērion* often defines the nature of the cross as the means of cosmic redemption. In light of this, Paul also speaks of God's spirit as the means through which believers can know the saving power of the cross by which they are perfected. Furthermore, Paul employs *mystērion* eschatologically to speak of Christ's final return and associated events.

Mystērion also occurs in various religions and philosophies. Ancient religions used *mystērion* to define the will or ways of the gods who were the sole proprietors of *mystērion*. Initiatory rituals were established through which a person obtained access to the *mystērion*— typically associated with ideas of salvation, becoming a deity and eternal life. Only those initiated via the rituals obtain knowledge of the *mystērion* and its rewards. Once initiated, the devotee had to remain silent about the ritual and the knowledge gained thereby.

In Platonism and early Neo-Platonism, *mystērion* is the unseen cosmic order of the universe; it also marked the distinction between actual truth and perceived truth. Accordingly, knowing what is actual and unseen becomes the pursuit of those desiring to be truly wise or perfect. Thus, only the wise have access to and can know the *mystērion*. Similar to the religious connotations just mentioned, the philosophical *mystērion* cannot be fully revealed—some things simply cannot be known. Moreover, ways of knowing the *mystērion* must remain secret among the elite who know them.

Gnosticism blends philosophical and religious (especially Christian) nuances. For the Gnostics, the hidden cosmic order was disrupted, creating a conflict between the (good) spiritual and (evil) physical worlds. Human existence reflects this tension: the spirit is good; the flesh is evil. A redeemer-like figure comes to earth to disclose (secretly) how one can free the good spirit from the evil fleshly prison, thus allowing the spirit to return to perfect harmony with the divine. This freeing and returning is contingent upon the individual having the knowledge (*gnōsis*) that was otherwise hidden (*mystērion*). As before, only those privy to such knowledge have access to the divine.

The modern literary genre of mystery fiction bears striking similarities to the general nature of *mystērion*. Throughout the narrative, conflict between good and evil pervades and only at the climax is the tension usually resolved. Moreover, the author is the originator of the final outcome and the reader is the one permitted to see the story from the author's perspective.

Recommended reading. Brown, Raymond E. *The Semitic Background of the Term 'Mystery' in the New Testament.* Philadelphia: Fortress Press, 1968

See also KINGDOM OF GOD [CSS]

N

Naaman. The story of Naaman occurs in 2 Kings 5. He was a general for the king of Aram and he had a terrible skin disease, leprosy. An Israelite slave girl told his wife about a prophet in Israel, Elisha, who might be able to cure his disease. He traveled to Israel with diplomatic support but when he arrived Elisha would not come to meet him. Instead he sent a servant to tell him to bathe seven times in the Jordan River. He got angry and threatened to leave but a servant convinced him to try it and he did and he was healed. In response, Naaman converted to the worship of Yahweh and sought pre-emptive forgiveness for any appearance of worship of another deity when assisting his master kneeling in worship. Naaman tried to present Elisha with expensive gifts but the prophet refused to accept them; however, his servant, Gehazi, thought this was foolish and he went after Naaman and took several gifts from him. When he returned to Elisha, the prophet knew what he had done and cursed him with Naaman's leprosy.

Rabbinic tradition associates Naaman with the bowman who shot Saul with an arrow and with Moab in Ps. 60.8. There are two explanations as to why Naaman contracted leprosy: the first is that he was a haughty person whose temperament deserved it; the second is that he contracted it as a punishment for having an Israelite slave. In the tradition, he is not considered to be the ideal convert but maintains a status higher than Jethro.

In the fourteenth and fifteenth centuries, the scene with Naaman dipping into the Jordan was a popular biblical theme for painters, including several beautiful anonymous artworks. The scene is captured in a copper piece by Luiken Caspar (1672–1708) and a 1695 woodcutting by Johann Christoph Weigel. The scene of Elisha refusing Naaman's gifts was depicted by the seventeenth-century Dutch painter Pieter de Grebber. In the painting, Elisha is actually turned completely away from Naaman in order to represent total rejection of the rich goods that he is being offered.

In contemporary times, the story was turned into a children's play to be performed in churches entitled 'Everyone Calls Him Sir'.

Recommended reading. Cohn, Robert L. 'Form and Perspective in 2 Kings 5'. *Vetus Testamentum* 33 (1983) 171-84.

See also ARAM; ELISHA; KINGS, BOOKS OF; LEPROSY [EW]

Nabal (see Abigail).

Naboth. According to 1 Kings 21, Naboth was the owner of a portion of land on the eastern slope of the hill of Jezreel, and on it he grew a small vineyard. As the land is close to the palace of King Ahab, the king indicated that he wanted to take it over. Naboth, however, told Ahab that because he had inherited the land from his father, he felt duty bound to look after it according to Israelite law and traditions. Ahab became angry and returned to his palace, later telling his wife Jezebel. Jezebel suggested charging Naboth with treason and blasphemy, and Ahab then took over the land. The prophet Elijah later visited Ahab and prophesied his death.

Three major novels featuring Naboth are Frank G. Slaughter, *The Curse of Jezebel: A Novel of the Biblical Queen of Evil* (1961); Dorothy Clarke Wilson, *Jezebel* (1955); and Olga Hesky, *The Painted Queen* (1961), the latter portraying Jezebel more favorably.

The phrase 'coveting Naboth's vineyard' is now used to describe envy. It has been used by William Winwood Reade in reference to Kansas when he stated that 'the Southerners coveted this Naboth's vineyard' in their attempt to get Kansas to become a slave state in 1854–1860, the fighting there leading to what became known as 'Bleeding Kansas'. Also Roger Williams (1603–1683), the founder of the American colony of Rhode Island and co-founder of the First Baptist Church in America, described Naboth in his book *The Bloudy Tenet of Persecution for Cause of Conscience* in which he urged that Christians not to resort to government power to enforce religious structures.

See also AHAB; ELIJAH; JEZEBEL; JEZREEL [JC]

Nag Hammadi. Nag Hammadi is the location in Egypt where a number of important papyrus codices were uncovered in 1945. The name Nag Hammadi has attached itself to and become synonymous with these texts, which are generally called the Nag Hammadi codices, and sometimes the Nag Hammadi Library or Nag Hammadi Scriptures. This collection of writings has greatly impacted scholars understanding of the NT and early Christianity in general.

The thirteen Nag Hammadi codices—a codex is a bound collection of writings—comprise some 52 tractates, with 46 different individual texts. Examples include *The Gospel of Thomas*, *The Apocry-*

phon of John, *The Letter of Peter to Philip*, *The Gospel of Truth*, and *The Gospel of Mary*. They appear in Coptic, a late form of the Egyptian language that employs Greek letters, but many assume they are copies of originally Greek texts. Scholars have confidently dated these writings to the fourth century CE, but there is still much debate concerning the date of composition for their Greek originals.

The Nag Hammadi texts represent a wide range of theological positions and a variety of beliefs regarding the creation of the world, the nature of God, and the character of Jesus. Earlier scholarship tended to treat the collection as a cohesive whole, classifying the texts as examples of heretical Gnosticism. More recently, scholars have begun to emphasize the diversity of beliefs contained in the collection, and now examine each tractate individually for its unique perspective. There is also some question as to whether each text contains elements of Gnostic ideas, or if only some of them are Gnostic in nature. A degree of variation exists even among those writings that clearly adhere to a Gnostic cosmology. Scholars often differentiate the different tractates in the Nag Hammadi library as Sethian or Valentinian, according to how closely they follow one tradition of teachings or the other.

The importance of the Nag Hammadi library for understanding the NT and early Christianity is immense. Until their discovery, students of the Bible had only descriptions of these writings, briefly mentioned by early Christian writers. The Nag Hammadi codices clearly demonstrate the fact that the four traditional gospels of the NT only represent a small selection of the many early Christian traditions. Whence these fascinating documents came is uncertain, but already by the mid-second-century Irenaeus of Lyon and his Roman contemporary, Hippolytus, could discuss passages from *The Apocryphon of John* and quote lines from *The Gospel of Thomas*. That the church fathers denounced these texts as heretical does not mean other Christians viewed them as such. Thus, the Nag Hammadi codices provide insight into the diversity of Christian groups as early as the second century and possibly earlier—several scholars have noted the similarities between *The Gospel of Thomas* and the hypothetical Q document.

Since its discovery, the Nag Hammadi library has been a source of inspiration for its many readers. Several Gnostic churches and communities exist today, including the Ecclesia Gnostica and The Gnostic Society. These groups draw spiritual guidance from the Nag Hammadi texts, and incorporate them into the more traditional Christian canon. The Nag Hammadi library has even made its way into mainstream media. A reading of *Thunder Perfect Mind*, set to jazz, formed the background of a Prada advertisement in 2005. Angelene Grace's album *Magdalene* (2007) is based on the *Gospel of Mary*.

Recommended reading. Meyer, Marvin (ed.). *The Nag Hammadi Scriptures*. New York: HarperOne, 2007. Pagels, Elaine. *The Gnostic Gospels*. New York: Random House, 1979. Robinson, James M. (ed.). *The Nag Hammadi Library*. 3rd edn. San Francisco: HarperSanFrancisco, 1990.

See also CODEX; GNOSTICISM; Q DOCUMENT

[NB]

Nahum, Book of. The Book of Nahum is found in the Minor Prophets/Book of the Twelve. Nahum's message is one of justice. Little is known about Nahum the Elokoshite. His name only appears in the Christian canon in Luke's genealogy (Luke 3.25). Nahum received an oracle from Yahweh concerning the nation of Assyria. The date can be determined from the text itself as sometime between 652 and 612 BCE. According to the prophet, Assyria, known for brutality in warfare, had been divinely utilized to judge the northern kingdom of Israel, destroyed and exiled in 721 BCE. While God had used Assyria to judge his own people, he would not forget their cruelty. He would vindicate his people and justly punish Assyria for all their sins (3.19).

Nahum's oracle begins with an acrostic describing God as 'jealous' and 'vengeful' (1.2-8). This opening contains typical theophany or 'Day of the Lord' language. The whole world is pictured as quaking and melting before the presence of God as he comes in judgment. The rhetorical question is asked, 'Who can stand before his indignation?' (1.6; cf. Rev. 6.17). God's judgment of Assyria is portrayed as a military defeat by an army that will ride straight through their capital of Nineveh. Short phrases quicken the pace of the oracle adding to the immediacy and violence of the battle.

Unlike the earlier prophetic work of Jonah, which demonstrated God's great capacity for compassion toward even the vilest of nations, Nahum's oracle does not function as a call to repent. The oracle of Nahum is not a warning. It is a death sentence. The last verse is indicative of this, 'There is no relief for your breakdown, Your wound is incurable. All who hear about you will clap their hands over you, For on whom has not your evil passed continually?' (3.19). While the oracle functioned as a death sentence on a nation that probably never heard it coming, it also functions as an epitaph. The oracle of Nahum is a promise and a warning. The promise is that God will bring justice to the world and that he will vindicate his name and his people. It is a warning to all those who oppose him that 'he is a jealous and avenging God' (1.2) and 'he is against you' (2.13).

The imagery of the Day of the Lord is common throughout the OT prophetic literature, in Revelation, and in the Gospel accounts of Jesus' death, interpreted as partial fulfillment of this Day.

The name and message of Nahum receive little mention in western culture, although the Day of the Lord or Armageddon is often used. This is not surprising as Nahum's oracle receives little attention in the church. Perhaps this is due to its unpopular images of God as vengeful and violent. Yet Nahum remains influential as a prophetic voice warning the world that God will 'pursue his enemies into darkness' (1.8).

See also ARMAGEDDON; ASSYRIA; DAY OF THE LORD; JONAH; NINEVEH; PROPHECY; PROPHETS [KB]

Name. Unlike today, when names mean little to parents naming their children (often after some celebrity they idolize, or a concocted name because 'it's different'), the ancients believed that a name reflected the nature and personality of its bearer. Persons or deities were what their names described. The OT writers agreed with that concept. God's name, therefore, is what he has revealed of his character and personality to humanity. Moreover, when God reveals his name, he is offering a personal relationship: where God's name is, there God is.

Initially in the Bible, the divine name was generalized. The broad term was *El*, which might have had its root in *Uhl*, the head ram of the flock, or guide, or more likely from *Al*, the binding power or one who holds all things together. *Elohim*, the common title for God in the OT, was a plural. Some scholars have claimed that it suggested the polytheistic background of Semitic peoples; others, as simply a plural of majesty, indicating the limitless power and glory of God. Some conservative Christians hold it to be descriptive of the Trinity, the personal intercommunication within the Godhead: 'Let us make humankind in our image' (Gen. 1.26).

As Israel's understanding of God developed, names compounded with *El* grew out of particular historic events during the ancestral era. They represented how various people experienced God's activity in particular situations, which reflected the divine nature. These included. *El-Elyon*, 'God Most High' (Gen. 14.18-22); *El-Olam*, 'Everlasting God' (Gen. 21.33); and *El-Shaddai*, 'God Almighty' (Exod. 6.3).

God disclosed his covenant name to Moses at the burning bush (Exod. 3). *Yahweh* ('Yahweh'): 'I am' (Exod. 3.14). Because of the sacredness of this name, it was generally not used except on the Day of Atonement, and then only by the high priest. Instead, Israelites used *Adonai*, 'My Lord'. Greek Jews also used 'Lord' (*kyrios*) as a substitute.

The reverence for the concept of 'name' carried over to the NT writers. John applied the covenantal name 'I am' to Jesus. In John 6.20, when his disciples thought he was a spirit as he walked on the Sea of Galilee, Jesus calmed them, 'It is I (literally, 'I am'); do not be afraid'. In John 8.58, he declared to the Jewish leaders, 'before Abraham was, I am', which they took as a statement of his deity.

Throughout the NT, 'name' as associated with Jesus, conveys the person, presence, or authority of Jesus. The idea of being baptized 'in Jesus' name' (1 Cor. 1.13-15; cf. Matt. 28.19) means that the person baptized now bears that name, belongs to Jesus, and is under his protection.

In the early church, when people became Christian believers they would take (or, in some instances be given) new names denoting that they now belonged to Christ and had left their former life. The practice was perpetuated in Roman Catholicism, particularly in the novitiate, where fledgling nuns would adopt the name of their patron saint as their own.

In western society today, the power and significance of names is found largely in mystical cult practices. For example, those who practice Kabbalah (originally a Jewish mystical offshoot) in a New Age context stress the need for names based on Kabbalistic numerology that will allow the bearer to attain and retain health, wealth, harmony, and happiness.

See also ELOHIM; GOD; I AM; LORD; TRINITY; YAHWEH [DSS]

Naming of the Animals. In the earliest Hebrew epic, God formed the first human being (*adam*) and the animals out of the dust of the ground. God created the animals as the human's counterpart, to be the human's companion, 'a sustainer beside him', and gave Adam the task of giving names to the different species of cattle, birds and wild beasts (Gen. 2.7-8, 18-20). This idea of peaceful co-existence and partnership with the animal kingdom is based on the Babylonian *Epic of Gilgamesh* in which the mountain man Enkidu lives with the animals, eats vegetation with gazelles, and drinks water with cattle and wild beasts (Tablets I-II). Inspired by both epics, the Priestly writer depicts God as blessing the animals, including fish and sea-monsters (Gen. 1.20-25). A pair of every species was saved during the flood (6.19-21; 7.13-16a; 8.1, 17-19). Afterwards God's everlasting covenant is made with human beings and animals, so both are vegetarians (1.29-30; 9.1, 9-17). A later writer, concerned with the origin of worship, discusses altars and animal sacrifice (4.2-5; 7.2-3, 8-9, 8.20-22; 9.2-8).

In a seventeenth-century Italian drama titled *L'Adamo, sacra raprasentatione* (1617), Giovanni Battista Andreini portrays Adam naming the animals at the entrance to the Garden. Just as every biblical book names some animal (e.g., antelope in Deut. 14.5; ape in 1 Kgs 10.22; donkey in Isa. 1.3), so in the visual arts the viewer names the creatures. In Jacopo Tintoretto's *The Creation of the Animals* (1550), the horse and other land animals run freely behind God as he pursues geese and other birds darting through the sky, while swarms of fish move through the sea. Among the animals named by Adam are sheep, a chicken, rabbit, ram and peacock in Jacopo Bassano's *Adam and Eve in the Garden* (1570–1575). In a panel-painting *Paradise* (1530), Lucas Cranach the Elder presents a dog lying beside Adam and Eve as they converse with God, while in the background two bears play together. Mediaeval artistic representations often show wild animals living in harmony with domesticated ones, as in Jan Brueghel the Elder's *The Garden of Eden* (1610) and Domenichino's *The Reproach of Adam and Eve* (1623–1625) where a lion lies beside a stag or a lamb respectively (Isa. 11.6-8). In Aloïs Benes's *Adam and Eve in Paradise* (1903–1985), a bearded Adam pets a white bear, and a snake nestles its head against Eve's leg.

John Milton's *Paradise Lost* (1674) speaks of 'great whales' and playful dolphins, eagle and crane, 'tawny lion' and 'scaly crocodile' (7.387-504). The libretto for Joseph Haydn's oratorio *Die Schöpfung/ The Creation*, Part Two (1794–1798), based on Milton's text, describes the appearance of perfect fully grown animals—'flexible tiger', 'nimble stag', 'noble steed'. Christopher Smart's *Jubilate Agno/ Rejoice in the Lamb* (1758–1763) is the poetry and title of Benjamin Britten's Festival Cantata (1943) in which every creature—Nimrod's leopard, Ishmael's tiger, Balaam's ass, Daniel's lion, David's bear and the poet's cat Jeoffrey appear before God and together magnify his name, as in Rembrandt's *The Holy Family with a Cat*, 1646. The soprano soloist sings of Jeoffrey (cf. Bar. 6.22), 'surpassing in beauty, from whom I take occasion to bless Almighty God'.

See also ADAM; BALAAM; COVENANT; CREATION; DANIEL; DAVID; EVE; FLOOD; GOD; ISHMAEL [JRW]

Naomi. From Hebrew, meaning 'my delight'. Derives from *no'am* meaning 'pleasantness, delightfulness', from the stem *na'em* 'was pleasant, was lovely'.

Naomi is the dominant character in the Book of Ruth and is the wife of Elimelech, mother of Mahlon and Chilion, and mother-in-law to Ruth. During a period of famine, Naomi accompanies her husband and sons into the land of Moab, where Elimelech dies and Naomi's two sons marry Moabite women—Mahlon to Ruth and Chilion to Oprah. After dwelling there for 10 years, both sons die, and Naomi sets out to return to Judah where the famine is said to have subsided. Naomi implores both of her daughters-in-law to return to their families, but Ruth refuses to leave Naomi's side. The impoverished two return to Bethlehem where those who once knew Naomi exclaimed 'Is this Naomi?' to which she answers that she should be called Mara, from the Hebrew for bitter, because the Lord has dealt bitterly with her. Naomi assists in bringing about the marriage of Boaz—a relative of her dead husband—to Ruth, and she later becomes the nurse of their child.

Some scholars argue that Naomi's insistence that her daughters-in-law remain in Moab while she returns to Judah was a test of the girls' sincerity in maintaining an Israelite life. However, it is still debated as to whether Ruth and Oprah converted prior to their marriages or if Ruth alone chose to convert upon accompanying Naomi back to Israel. The image of Naomi and the departure of her daughters-in-law, as well as Ruth pleading with Naomi, have appeared in works by many artists, including Rembrandt, William Blake, Marc Chagall, William Blake and Gustave Doré.

Recent scholarship has centered on the possibility that Naomi and Ruth were engaged in a romantic relationship, citing Ruth 1.14 in that 'Ruth clung to [Naomi]'. The use of the Hebrew verb 'to cling' (*dabaq*) is significant in that it is also found in Gen. 2.24 to describe the relationship of Adam and Eve: 'Therefore a man leaves his father and his mother and clings to his wife, and they become one flesh'.

Recommended reading. Jennings, Theodore W. *Jacob's Wound: Homoerotic Narrative in the Literature of Ancient Israel.* New York: Continuum, 2005

See also BOAZ; RUTH, BOOK OF; MARA [CE]

Naphthali (see Twelve Tribes of Israel).

Nathan. The prophet Nathan lived at the time of King David and was the man who reprimanded the king who had committed adultery with Bathsheba, the wife of Uriah the Hittite (2 Sam. 12.1-12). Interestingly the son of David mentioned in the genealogy of Jesus in Luke 3.31, is also called Nathan (cf. 2 Sam. 5.14). The prophet Nathan appears in the books of Samuel, Kings and Chronicles, and although very little is known about him except for his ministrations with King David; the fact that he was able to criticize the king has tended to make historians see him was a 'wise man' or 'sage', and he is usually portrayed as much older than King David, as in the painting by Matthias Scheits (1672).

There are many novels covering the life of King David, and Nathan makes appearances in many of them such as Ari Ibu-Sahav's *David and Bathsheba* (1951), Frank Slaughter's *David, Warrior and King* (1961), and Torgny Lindgren's *Bathsheba* (1989). However, he is better remembered in film. Albert Price played him in the 1924 film *David, or The Seventh Commandment*; with Olaf Hytten as Nathan in *The Great Commandment* (1939). In 1951, Raymond Massey played Nathan in the famous film by Henry King, *David and Bathsheba*, which had Gregory Peck as David and Susan Hayward as Bathsheba. Since then he has been played by William Devlin in *Solomon and Sheba* (1959), by David Collings in the television series *The Story of David* (1976), by Niall Buggy in *King David* (1985), and by the famous Italian actor Franco Nero in the television series *David* (1997). In 2005, the African American actor Ernie Hudson starred as Nathan in *Bathsheba* (2005).

Nathan is commemorated as a saint by the Eastern Orthodox Church, his feast day being the Sunday of the Holy Fathers which is the Sunday before Christmas. Nathan is a common Jewish surname, and also a first name.

See also BATHSHEBA; DAVID [JC]

Nathanael. The name of a disciple mentioned in John 1.45. Nathanael is usually assumed to be the same as the Bartholomew of the Synoptic Gospels since both are linked to the apostle Philip, and Bartholomew is never named in John. In either case, Nathanael is named among the apostles and in John 21.2 as a witness to the Resurrection.

The only narrative that expresses the personality of Nathanael is found in John 1.43-51. Nathanael's declaration, 'Rabbi, you are the Son of God!' (John 1.49) parallels Peter's declaration in the synoptics, 'You are the Messiah' (Mark 8.29 and par.; cf. John 11.27; 4.42). The traditional reading of John's narrative discourse considers the transformation of Nathanael's skepticism about Jesus to be inspired. It thus serves as the vehicle for further declarations by Jesus about himself and his divine identity and prepares the reader to understand the rest of the Gospel. While such a reading is plausible, the account seems contrived despite clear historical referents to place and situation. A more speculative reading suggests that Nathanael's response, 'You are the King of Israel!' (John 1.49) is more consistent with his earlier, 'Can anything good come out of Nazareth?' (John 1.45), understood as an example of Johannine sarcasm. The reader must then realize that while Nathanael has spoken through the usual patterns of human skepticism, he unwittingly gives voice to a divine wisdom without which the true significance of Jesus cannot be grasped. A similar sentiment is found in Matt. 16.17 in response to Peter's disclosure, 'flesh and blood has not revealed this to you, but my Father in heaven'.

This sort of analysis reveals a typical narrative technique in John where apparently mundane events, conflicts or discourse become vehicles for the development and escalation of key themes such as death/resurrection, flesh/spirit, kingdom of God/ kingdom of human society.

The place of Nathanael in western culture is best seen in Michelangelo's (1475–1564) *The Last Judgment*, a mural painted on the ceiling of the Sistine Chapel. The mural depicts the early tradition of Bartholomew's martyrdom—being flayed alive. In the mural he holds his own skin in one hand and a knife in the other. The face observable on the skin is reckoned to be that of Michelangelo himself, satirically representing his experience of the controversy surrounding the authentic anatomical details of his work.

Various early church traditions associate Nathanael (Bartholomew) with missionary ventures in India. This is mentioned by Eusebius (263–339). In general however, many such traditions cannot be verified though there may be truth to them. Special days are set aside to commemorate the apostles' witness to Christ and activity in the emergence of the church. In the western church, St Bartholomew's day is August 24.

The play *Bartholomew Fair* by Ben Jonson (1572–1637) takes its name from the London fair which began August 24 and which provides the backdrop for the storyline of the play, its social observations and commentary. Any association with the apostle is of course limited to the use if his name.

See also APOSTLE; BARTHOLOMEW; SYNOPTIC GOSPELS [JKS]

Nativity (see Infancy Narratives).

Nazarene. In 1962, excavations in Caesarea showed that the word Nazareth has its root meaning in the Hebrew *netzer*, describing the future royal 'branch' from the house of David (Is 11.1). In the DSS, this 'branch' is associated with the branch (*tzamah*) of Zechariah named as the builder of a future temple: 'Thus says the LORD of hosts, "Behold, the man whose name is the Branch (*tzamah*): for he shall grow up in his place, and he shall build the temple of the LORD"' (6.12).

While the two terms for 'Branch' (*netzer/tzamah*) are not identical, in first-century rabbinic exegesis it was acceptable to link equivalent terms. Evidence from the DSS supports this. The DSS look to a future son of David, and apply to him the term 'Branch', but use Zechariah's expression *tzamah* rather than Isaiah's *netzer*: 'Yahweh declares to you that he will build you a house. I will raise up your seed after you and establish the throne of his kingdom forever. I will be a father to him and he will be a son to me. This refers to the Branch (*tzamah*) of David' (4QFlor col 1, 11; commenting on 2 Sam. 7.11; see also 4QpGen. col 5, 3-4). Even more striking is the commentary on Isa. 11.1-5 where, following the quotation from Isaiah which uses the term *netzer*, the explanation substitutes *tzamah* from Zech. 6.12. These texts show that in the Scrolls the two terms *tzamah* and *netzer* are synonymous. The man named 'Branch' who will build the temple (Zech. 6.13) is identified as the messianic branch of David (Isa. 11.1).

In Matthew (2.23) and John (18.5, 7; 19.19), when Jesus is called *the Nazarene*, it is thus possible that this is more than the identity of his hometown, but a Messianic title based in the *netzer* from Isaiah. In John, *the Nazarene* is a title (*titlon*; 19.19) found only in the Passion referring to Jesus' messianic role as the builder of the eschatological temple. Jesus is condemned and dies under two titles: the Nazarene (the temple-builder), the King of the Jews (INRI) (19.19). As his body is raised on the cross, his earlier words are fulfilled. 'Destroy this Temple and in three days I will raise it up' (2.19). The temple of his body (see John 2.21) is destroyed, but as '*the Nazarene*' he is raising a new temple.

Early Christians are described as Nazarenes (Acts 24.5) and believers from the Jewish tradition continued to be referred to as 'Nazarenes' within Syrian, Persian and Armenian communities. At some stage, Matthew was translated and expanded from Greek into Aramaic or Syriac. This document, which no longer exists except in fragments, was known as the *Gospel of the Nazoreans*.

'The Nazarene' was used as a title of Jesus by Julian the Apostate (361–363), the half-brother of Emperor Constantine. Although educated in Christianity, when Julian became Emperor he restored pagan worship and revoked the rights bestowed on Christians by Constantine.

In a poem 'St Patrick's Easter Fire', by Eliza Downs the Druid priest speaks to King Leoghire of Ireland referring to Patrick as 'The Priest of the pale Nazarene'.

In 1895, the Church of the Nazarene was founded based on Wesleyan-Methodist traditions. Since that time, a number of mergers with other groups has formed one of the world's largest evangelical Christian churches with a strong missionary outreach.

Recommended reading. Coloe, Mary L. 'The Nazarene King: Pilate's Title as the Key to John's Crucifixion'. In *The Death of Jesus in the Fourth Gospel*. Ed. G. van Belle. Pp. 839-48. BETL, 200. Leuven: Leuven University Press, 2007

See also CHRIST; DEAD SEA SCROLLS; NAZARETH [MLC]

Nazareth. In biblical times, Nazareth was a small agricultural village where the climate and rainfall were favorable to vegetation and a variety of fruits. The main trade road that connected Egypt and the interior of Asia passed near Nazareth. It is situated in the southern hills of Lebanon, about 24 km from the Sea of Galilee in the east and 32 km from the Mediterranean Sea in the west.

Nazareth is never mentioned in the OT or in any pre-Christian Jewish writings. Such an irrelevant town was too small to be noted in the list of settlements of Zebulon's tribe (Josh. 19.10-16). The reference to it in John 'Can anything good come out of Nazareth?' (1.46) underscores its insignificance and disrepute, probably because it is said that the people of Galilee were largely influenced by Gentiles. It was not expected that a prophet would ever arise from Nazareth of Galilee (John 7.41-42).

The first information about Nazareth in the Gospels is found in the Infancy Narratives. For Matthew, Joseph and Mary's hometown was Bethlehem (2.11), thus the evangelist explains why they moved to Nazareth. Jesus' designation as a *Nazorean* underscored his status as the messianic *Nezer* (Branch) as prophesied by Isaiah (Matt. 2.13-23; Isa. 11.1).

Luke portrays Nazareth as the hometown of Joseph and Mary (Luke 2.39), where the Annunciation of Jesus' birth took place (Luke 1.26-38); hence the explanation is centered on why they moved to Bethlehem (Luke 2.1-5). Luke establishes Nazareth as Jesus' native place as opposed to his birthplace; the evangelist calls Nazareth the town where Jesus grew up (Luke 4.16).

Many references say that Jesus came from Nazareth (Matt. 21.11; Acts 10.38), that he remained associated with it until his death (John 19.19), and that he was called Jesus of Nazareth or 'the Nazarene' (Mark 1.24; 10.47; 14.67; 16.6; Matt. 26.71; Luke 4.34; 18.37; 24.19; John 18.5-7; Acts 2.22; 3.6; 6.14; 22.8; 24.5; 26.9), later applied to his followers (Acts 24.5). *Jesus of Nazareth* was the title chosen by Franco Zeffirelli for his classic film.

Nazareth always remains as Jesus' native place. Both apocryphal infancy gospels and modern novels have gravitated to the so-called 'hidden years' of Jesus' life in Nazareth, giving free rein to their fantasies. The story of Jesus' rejection by the people of Nazareth is found in the synoptics (Mark 6.1-6; Matt. 13.53-58; Luke 4.16-30); Luke makes his theological point by placing it at the beginning of Jesus' ministry and recalling his eminent declaration that no prophet is accepted in his own country.

In the first centuries CE, Nazareth was populated by Jews, but with the spread of the Roman Empire, the number of Christian residents there grew. From Constantine's times (324–337 CE) and onwards, the place became a shrine, a major destination for Christian pilgrimages, and churches were built on sites which related to the Holy Family. The present Basilica of the Annunciation, designed by the Italian architect Giovanni Muzio, is a modern structure built between 1955 and 1969 above the ruins of Byzantine and Crusader. Today Nazareth is home to numerous churches, and monasteries, convents, schools, hostels and hospitals; its population is a mixture of Christians of various denominations, Muslims and Jews. The richness of its history and traditions make of Nazareth an historic site.

See also BETHLEHEM; INFANCY NARRATIVES; NAZARENE [DR]

Nazirite. According to Nazirite law (Num. 6.1-21), persons who separated themselves for God (from the Hebrew verb *nazar* 'to separate' or 'consecrate') for a specified time-period were bound to renounce wine and strong drink, grow hair long and uncut, and avoid contact with the dead. Samuel had a Nazirite vocation (1 Sam. 1.11, 20-21). John the Baptist observed the Nazirite vow against drinking in contrast to Jesus, 'a glutton and a drunkard' (Matt. 11.18-19). Paul broke his Nazirite vow when he cut his hair (Acts 18.18; cf. 21.23-25).

Samson self-identifies as a Nazirite and tells Delilah that no razor shall come upon his head (Judg. 16.17; 13.4-7). As he sleeps on her lap, she has an unnamed man, presumably a Philistine servant, shave his head (16.19). Western art widely represents the cutting of Samson's hair, thus the breaking of the Nazirite vow. Artists developed the sense of the biblical episode by depicting Samson in post-coital slumber. The couple often appears semi-nude. Even Delilah appears drowsy with eyelids half-closed, while a male servant cuts off Samson's locks in Peter Paul Rubens's 1609 painting. Both Rubens and Christian van Couvenbergh (*The Capture of Samson,* 1604–1667) faithfully follow Judges 16. They portray the barber as a young person, while Anthony van Dyck (1559–1641) depicts him as elderly.

Many other artists deviate from the biblical story by presenting Delilah as Samson's hairdresser, often with enormous scissors. Examples include paintings by Lucas Cranach the Elder (1472–1553), Matthias Stomer (1630) and Adriaen van der Werff (1659–1722). The visual representations of Delilah cutting Samson's hair reinforce her role as antagonist, and they also show the influence of classical literature on Western art. The Nazirite vow in the Hebrew tale is combined with ancient Greek legendary lore in which a famous man loses his strength once a woman cuts off his locks while he sleeps (e.g., Heracles' stepfather Amphitryon; Judg. 16.6, 15-22).

Rembrandt's paintings of the Samson story (1628–1642) develop the biblical theme of co-conspiracy (Judg. 16.5, 8, 18, 21). His first painting involves both Delilah and the Philistines in the breaking of the Nazirite vow—Delilah lifts a lock of Samson's long curls, while one Philistine soldier sneaks into the room with shears. A gilded pitcher of wine on a stand hints that Samson is intoxicated and thus has broken another Nazirite vow. This detail is absent from Judges 16, but vessels of wine do appear in paintings of Samson with Delilah (e.g., Rubens,

1609). Rembrandt's *The Wedding of Samson* (1638) depicts a party where the guests gather over food and cups, a golden pitcher of wine in the foreground. The scene makes explicit what is implied in the earlier story of his marriage to a Philistine woman that he drank wine at a feast in disregard of his Nazirite consecration (Judg. 14.10-18).

See also DELILAH; SAMSON; WINE   [JRW]

Nebo. There are four types of reference to 'Nebo' in the Bible. The most important is to Mount Nebo where Moses went to see the Promised Land before he died (Deut. 34.1-4). The site is most likely modern Jebel Neba, opposite Jericho. From its summit, Mount Pisgah (mountain slope) (Deut. 34.1), most of the Holy Land can be seen on a clear day. According to Deut. 32.49, Moses went up from the plateau where the land of Moab was to see the Promised Land. He was buried nearby valley opposite Bethpeor (Deut. 34.6).

The location of Mount Nebo has also been identified with Khibeth el-Mekhaiyet. Nebo is in the Abarim range (Num. 33.47) which runs along the escarpment of the Jordan Rift Valley. It is eight miles (12.9 km) east of the Jordan River and 4,030 feet (1282.34 meters) above the Dead Sea's NE corner which can be seen below. The Byzantines built churches and other installations on the location. The site today is called Ras es-Siyaghah. In 2008, it was being excavated by archeologists directed by Franciscan monks.

Emily Dickinson's 'It Always Felt to Me—A Wrong' expresses her feelings that it was wrong for Moses to be given only the sight of the Holy Land from atop Mount Pisgah (Deut. 34.1-4). Other poems associated with the death of Moses at Mount Nebo include 'When Israel out of Egypt Came' (A.E. Houseman), ' Weep, Children of Israel' (Thomas Moore), 'The Death of Moses' (George Eliot) and 'Pisgah Sights I & II' (Robert Browning). The title of Browning's poem is important because it refers to the projects undertaken by humans that are greater than one lifetime can accomplish.

Christian tradition has interpreted the Pisgah-sights of Moses as seeing afar through the eyes of faith the advent of the Messiah as the fulfillment of the divine plan of history in the resurrection. Funeral sermons or hymns (Isaac Watts's 'There is a Land of Pure Delight') may refer to the death of believers as seeing in Christ their Pisgah-sight.

Nebo also refers to two towns: one in Judah (Ezra 2.29; Neh. 7.33), the other in Moab, part of the kingdom of Sihon (Num. 21.26-30). It was captured by the tribes of Gad and Rueben (Num. 32.3, 38) and rebuilt. It was captured again by the Moabites under King Mesha around 850 BCE and is mentioned in the Moabite Stone. Both Isaiah (15.2) and Jeremiah (48.1, 22) prophesied the destruction of Nebo as a part of God's judgment of Moab. Nebo was probably located at modern Khirbet Mehayyet, about five miles SW of Hesban.

When the Jews returned from the Babylonian Exile, there were 52 two descendants of an ancestor called Nebo. Seven of these were to divorce their foreign wives in response to the preaching of Ezra the Scribe (Ezra 10.43).

Finally, Nebo refers to a Babylonian god (Isa. 46.1). Called Nabu in Akkadian, he was considered the son of Marduk. He was originally the local god of Borsippa but rose in importance with the rise of the Babylonian Empire. He was the object of Isaiah's taunting ridicule because he could not prevent his own deportation into captivity (Isa. 46.1). The Babylonian kings Nabopolassar, Nebuchadnezzar and Nabonidus bore his name.

Recommended reading. Saller, Sylvester J., and Bellamino Bagatti. *The Town of Nebo (Khirbet el-Mekhayyat): With a Brief Survey of Other Ancient Christian Monuments in Transjordan.* Jerusalem: Franciscan Press, 1949

See also MOSES; MOUNTAIN; PISGAH   [AJW]

Nebuchadnezzar. Nebuchadnezzar (Nebuchadrezzar) was the name of several Babylonian or Chaldean kings. Nebuchadnezzar II (reigned 605–562 BCE) was the most famous. He is first mentioned in 2 Kings 24–25 as the Chaldean king who conquered the Southern Kingdom of Judah and either killed or deported most of its people. He destroyed the City of Jerusalem, the Temple of Solomon and took king Jehoiakim in chains to Babylon. Jeremiah (25.8-14) and Ezra (5.12) saw him as the instrument of God for punishing Judah.

Nebuchadnessar figures prominently in the Book of Daniel. In Daniel 2, the Jewish courtier Daniel is told Nebuchadnezzar's dream and interprets its meaning. The dream was of a great statute with a head of gold, chest and arms of silver, belly and thighs of bronze, legs of iron and feet of a mixture of iron and clay. Daniel's interpretation was of kingdoms and empires to come that would end with the fall of the earthly kingdoms. Then God would set up a new kingdom that would never be destroyed. In Christian interpretation, the kingdom that will never lack for people nor ever be destroyed is the kingdom of Christ.

In Daniel 3, Daniel's Jewish friends Shadrach, Meshach and Abednego are thrown into a fiery furnace for refusing to worship a golden idol set up by Nebuchadnezzar, and are rescued by an angel of the Lord. The awed Nebuchadnezzar issues a decree glorifying the God of the Jews. Henry Colman's 'On the Three Children in the Fiery Furnace' is a poem about the youths' disobedience of unholy human commands. This has been the subject of many comments by political theorists as a problem of political obligation.

Daniel 4 interprets a frightening dream of Nebuchadnezzar. Daniel informs the king that he will be insane for a season and wander about as a wild animal apart from human society unless he repents of his sins. Within twelve months Nebuchadnezzar, in a moment of enormous pride over his accomplishments, is bereft of his reason for 'seven times' that pass over him. After his reason returns, he praises God as the King of Heaven. The insanity of Nebuchadnezzar was used in medieval literature to identify him with the devil or as an archetype of madness. Shakespeare's reference to the insane Nebuchadnezzar's eating grass is one of many in literature such as John Donne ('The Liar'), Lord Byron ('Don Juan'), John Ruskin (*Works*) and Herman Melville ('Omoo'). Emerson compared the madness of slavery to Nebuchadnezzar's insanity.

Some interpreters have viewed insane Nebuchadnezzar's physical condition of long hair and uncut nails as a literal transformation into a beast. Saul Bellow used Nebuchadnezzar's transformation into a beast in *Henderson the Rain King* (1959).

In Chaucer's *Canterbury Tales*, the Monk's Tale identifies Nebuchadnezzar with presumptuous divine pretentions. Edmund Spencer made reference to Nebuchadnezzar's pride. Nebuchadnezzar's dreams have been the subject of poems such as Elinor Wylie's 'Nebuchadnezzar' and John Keats's 'Nebuchadnezzar's Dream'.

In Jewish legend and tradition, Nebuchadnezzar has been the great enemy (*par excellence*) of the people of God. He has been seen as a blasphemer who engages in self-deification. In Judith (1.1), he is called the 'king of Assyria', a sign of evil character. This Nebuchadnezzar is a fictional character who is different from the Nebuchadnezzar of history.

Recommended reading. Doob, Penelope B.R. *Nebuchadnezzar's Children: Conventions of Madness in Middle English Literature*. New Haven, CT: Yale University Press, 1974. Sack, Ronald H. *Images of Nebuchadnezzar: The Emergence of a Legend*. Cranbury, NJ: Associated University Presses, 1991. Wiseman, D.J. *Nebuchadrezzar and Babylon*. New York: Oxford University Press, 1985

See also BABYLON; DANIEL, BOOK OF; JUDITH, BOOK OF [AJW]

Nehemiah, Book of. The book begins with Nehemiah, a cupbearer in the court of the King Artaxerxes I of Persia (465–425 BCE), hearing a report detailing the wall of Jerusalem's state of disrepair (Neh. 1). Nehemiah is overwhelmed with grief, and is permitted by Artaxerxes to return to Judah in order to oversee the reconstruction of Jerusalem (1.4–2.8). Nehemiah then travels to Judah, inspects the walls and gates of Jerusalem, and begins to rally the people to rebuild the dilapidated structures (2.9–3.32). Once word of the Israelites' attempt to rebuild their defenses reached their enemies, plans to attack Jerusalem (ch. 4), a plot to kill Nehemiah (6.1-4), and a conspiracy to label him as a rebel (6.5-14), threatened to stop the work. Nehemiah and the Judeans, however, persevered and finished building the wall (6.15–7.4). The rest of the book largely describes Nehemiah's activities as the governor of Judah, such as conducting a census (7.5-65), in addition to moral and religious reforms led by both Nehemiah and Ezra, including the reading of the law (8.1-8), the celebration of the feast of booths (8.13-18), the confession of sins (9), the establishment of a covenant with God (9.38–10.39), and the dedication of the wall (12.27-47).

Until the third century in Christianity, and the fifteenth century in Judaism, the books of Ezra and Nehemiah formed a single and cohesive work. While the two books definitely contain distinctive characteristics, they should be read with attentiveness toward their original narrative unity. Unlike the book of Ezra, Nehemiah has generally enjoyed a favorable interpretation among Christian scholars. Ezra was often viewed as the one responsible for establishing an inferior form of Judaism, but Christian interpreters often portrayed Nehemiah as a humble and committed servant who abdicated his life of comfort and prestige in the Persian court only to put himself in harm's way in order to rebuild Jerusalem. The evangelical scholar, Edwin M. Yamauchi's assessment is typical of many conservative Protestant interpreters who continue to see Nehemiah as an example of the ideal leader. He characterizes Nehemiah as a man of: (1) responsibility, (2) vision, (3) prayer, (4) action and cooperation, (5) compassion, (6) who triumphed over opposition, and possessed (7) right motivation.

The central theological motif in the book of Nehemiah requires that one understand the book as part of a greater work that includes the book of Ezra. Nehemiah's reconstruction of the walls of Jerusalem (Neh. 1–7) should be seen as a continuation of the reforms initiated by Ezra, and the celebration and consecration that occurs toward the end of Nehemiah (Neh. 8-12) should be viewed as the culmination of all that is accomplished by the Israelites in both Ezra and Nehemiah. With this narrative unity of the two books in place, the theological message of the book of Nehemiah, not dissimilar from that of Ezra, is clearly the idea that God is at work for the betterment of the nation of Israel regardless of temporary setbacks.

See also BABYLONIAN CAPTIVITY; EZRA, BOOK OF; HAGGAI, BOOK OF; TEMPLE; ZECHARIAH, BOOK OF [AS]

Neighbor. The foundation of scripture, according to Jesus, boils down to: (1) an unqualified commitment to God, and (2) an almost equal commitment to one's neighbor (Matt. 22.37-40; Mark 12.29-31). Jesus was not offering anything new but was quoting from the Law of Moses (Deut. 6.5; Lev. 19.18), and indeed love for God and neighbor each sum up the two parts of the Decalogue. On the basis of God's love for his people the commandments establish the key characteristics of the good neighbor and the good neighborhood.

'Who is my neighbor?' This question induced Jesus to tell the Parable of the Good Samaritan (Luke 10.25-37). In the OT, the most common word for neighbor is *rēʿ*, and it appears throughout the OT (Exod. 22.7; Lev. 6.2; Deut. 15.2; Josh. 20.5; 1 Kgs. 8.31; Job 31.8; Ps. 12.2; Prov. 6.1; Isa. 3.5; Jer. 9.4). *Rēʿ* seems to refer exclusively to relationships within the covenant community, a context which is established on love (compassion, loyalty, impartiality, etc.) for one's neighbor. Jesus' teaching universalized the command to love so that one's 'neighbor' is not limited to an ethnic or religious group but extends to all types of people and relationships, even one's most bitter enemy. Even so, this conception of neighbor implies a degree of geographical proximity; one's neighbor is part of a local community however defined. The Synoptics, John, Paul, and James all pick up on this central teaching of Jesus (Mark 12.28-34; John 13.34; Rom. 13.9; Gal. 5.14; Jas. 2.8). The overall biblical concept of neighborly love is much more radical than simply doing to others what you would have done to you, but requires an active perusal of the neighbor's welfare.

Mark Twain identified the sad irony that Christians have often failed to honor the command to love their neighbors. 'Man ... is the only animal that loves his neighbor as himself, and cuts his throat if his theology isn't straight' (*Letters from the Earth*). However, the biblical ideal of neighborly love has motivated countless acts and ministries of compassion throughout history. The life of Mother Teresa is an exemplar of the selfless neighborly love, which the Bible endorses, and she spoke of the commandment to love your neighbor in her Nobel Peace Prize lecture in 1979.

The concept of self-sacrificial neighborly love overcoming extreme difference is an almost universally held ideal, which has influenced societies, policies, and religions, and which literature and film have repeatedly explored. For example, the famous philosopher John Locke wrote '[T]hat we should love our neighbor as ourselves, is such a fundamental truth for regulating human society, that, I think, by that alone, one might without difficulty determine all the cases and doubts in social morality' (*Essays Concerning Human Understanding*). In 1933, US president Franklin Roosevelt inaugurated the Good Neighbor Policy, designed to smooth relations between the US and Latin America. The principle of the policy was clearly based in scripture as Roosevelt rooted the respect of other nations in a nation's own self-respect ('First Inaugural Address'). The award-winning 2008 Clint Eastwood film *Gran Torino* poignantly depicts neighborly love as against all odds. The bigoted war vet Walt Kowalski befriends and eventually makes the ultimate sacrifice for his neighbor Thao, a young Asian boy.

Recommended reading. Miller, Patrick D. 'The Good Neighborhood: Identity and Community through the Commandments'. In his *The Way of the Lord: Essays in Old Testament Theology*. Pp. 51-67. Grand Rapids, MI: Eerdmans, 2007

See also GOOD SAMARITAN; LOVE YOUR ENEMIES; TEN COMMANDMENTS [DJHB]

Nero, the Emperor. Lucius Domitius Ahenobarbus was born at Antium (modern Anzio), December 15, 37 CE. His mother, Agrippina, was banished from Rome by Caligula in 40 CE, but then recalled by Claudius. Thanks to an act by the Senate, Claudius was allowed to marry her (his niece) in the year 49. He adopted young Lucius as Nero Claudius Drusus Germanicus, making him his eldest son (replacing his biological son Britannicus), and next in line to rule Rome. He was raised in the court, with the Stoic philosopher Seneca as his tutor. He married Claudius's daughter Octavia in 53.

He was not quite 17 when Claudius died (54). His mother struggled mightily against the tandem of Seneca and the Praetorian Prefect Burrus for control of Nero's public policy. She lost, was banished to a nearby palace, and murdered in 59.

Nero is credited by both Tacitus and Dio Cassius as having a period early in his reign, which was perhaps the best of any emperor. He was conscientious about legal decisions, tried to combat forgery, reformed the treasury, and improved public safety and order. The masses loved him.

Burrus died in 62, and Seneca soon retired, finding that he could not work with the new Praetorian Prefect, Tigellinus. Nero became more despotic after the departure of Seneca, beginning with the exile and murder of Octavia, his first wife.

In 64, he could no longer keep his passion for the arts—acting, singing, lyre playing, poetry and dancing—private, as he had been encouraged by Seneca and Burrus. He publicly performed on stage at the ethnically Greek city of Neapolis (Naples) in Italy. A year later, he was performing in Rome. He happily played any role, including women, a penchant best remembered by his portrayal of the character Canace giving birth. The pinnacle of his performing days was his tour of Greece in 66, where he was awarded 1808 first prizes, a generosity he reciprocates by declaring Greece 'free', interpreted to mean tax exempt.

As his performance schedule grew, so did his paranoia. The year 66 held no less than four suspected conspiracies, all of which entailed a purge of potential enemies. His transformation from teenage Stoic who abhorred execution to despot quick to kill was complete.

His loss of conscience was manifested in 64 in what became the first persecution of Christians. A fire destroyed three of 14 districts in Rome and heavily damaged another eight, conveniently clearing an area for him to build his massive monument, the Golden House. When fingers were pointed towards him, he blamed the Christians, a sect both powerless and hated. His blame resounded with the Romans, as they all were aware of a thwarted plot to burn Rome by another foreign cult, the Bacchanalian Conspiracy (186 BCE).

It is possible that Peter and/or Paul died in the aftermath of this incident. There are conflicting traditions and a host of other interpretational issues. Both may well have died during Nero's reign. The persecution of Christians was an especially ugly one. Nero is credited with making those convicted of Christianity into human torches, which elicited sympathy even for this hated minority.

The Roman general, later to be emperor, Vespasian, was a member of Nero's entourage to Greece in 66 when he was dispatched to take care of the Jewish Revolt. Nero lost all support in Rome, and committed suicide in 68.

Recommended reading. Griffin, M.T. *Nero. The End of a Dynasty*. London: Routledge, 1984. Malitz, J. *Nero*. Oxford: Wiley–Blackwell, 2005

See also EMPEROR; MARTYR, MARTYRDOM; ROME [MAP]

New Covenant. The metaphor of 'covenant' entails a binding agreement between two parties, used to describe God's relationship with Israel. Reference to a 'new covenant' (or 'renewed covenant') between God and Israel appears in Jeremiah. The context for this notion is the understanding that Israel had failed to abide by the covenant God had first made with them through Moses, following the exodus from Egypt (Exod. 19.1-6; Deut. 27–30; Lev. 26; see also Jer. 7.1–8.3; 11.1-21). Jeremiah, prophesying exile from the promised land, proclaims that there would come a time when God would make a new covenant with his people (31.31-34; cf. 32.39-40). Accordingly, God would restore Israel's fortunes, forgiving their sins, and inscribe God's law on their hearts in the land that God had promised them.

Though explicitly appearing only in Jeremiah, the basic substance of the new covenant is found in other of the prophetic books, as well as in the Pentateuch (cf. Deut. 30.1-6). Additional features of it are found in Ezekiel and Isaiah, where the agency of God's spirit is seen as instrumental in the transformation of God's people, resulting in a new capacity for obedience (cf. Ezek. 11.19-20; 36.1-7; 39.29; Isa. 59.21; see also Isa. 32.15; 44.3; Joel 2.28; Zech. 12.10). A further aspect of this covenant is for Ezekiel both a new Davidic king who would rule justly over the re-gathered and reunited people in the land (see also Isa. 9.6-7; 11.1-12), as well as a new temple (cf. 34.25-31; 37.15-28; 38.20; 44.28).

The fundamental claim of the NT (the name for which derives from the Latin *testamentum*, meaning 'covenant') is that the prophesied new covenant of the Hebrew scriptures has been inaugurated through the person and work of Jesus Christ. This pronouncement is made by Jesus himself, as recounted in the synoptic gospels (cf. Matt. 26.26-29; Mark 14.22-25; Luke 22.14-20). Explicit mention of the new covenant also appears in both of Paul's letters to the church in Corinth (1 Cor. 11.25; 2 Cor. 3.6), and it would seem that his theology and apostolic mission was thoroughly informed by the notion (e.g., Rom. 2.12-15; 8.1-6.; 11.13-27; 1 Cor. 2.12-13).

Hebrews, more extensively than any other NT text, similarly asserts the fulfillment of Jer. 31.31-34 by virtue of the sacrificial death and subsequent resurrection of Jesus Christ (cf. 8.8-13). As such, Christ is presented as the 'mediator' of the new covenant through which 'those who are called may receive the promised eternal inheritance' (8.15). Importantly, the NT claims not only the inauguration of the new covenant through Christ, but also that it has been universalized—inclusive of Jews and gentiles, and predicating not merely the land of Israel as an eternal possession for God's people, but the whole world.

The notion of a new covenant has seen uses outside of its biblical context. In 1992, then presidential candidate Bill Clinton characterized his political agenda by this term, relating it to his vision of the proper relationship of the US federal government to the citizenry. However, the term's primary usage and significance has remained firmly within the religious sphere into the contemporary era. To ostensibly capture their Christian character, numerous churches and other religious organizations have adorned the name 'new covenant'.

See also COVENANT; HEBREWS; JEREMIAH; NEW TESTAMENT [CZ]

New heaven, new earth. In Rev. 21.1, the prophet John has a vision of 'a new heaven and a new earth' that replaces the first creation, which passes away. God rules there eternally from the New Jerusalem (21.2-27), constructed of gold and precious stones. It is a place where mourning and pain are abolished, and immorality and impurity are banished. The new earth/new Jerusalem of Revelation echo the Genesis creation narratives. The holy city needs no sun or moon, since it is illumined by the primal light of God (21.22; 22.5; cf. Gen. 1.3); on either side of the river that flows from the throne of God is the tree of life (Rev. 22.2); the marriage of the Bride and the Lamb (19.7, 9) echoes the marriage of the first couple (Gen. 2.24).

The prophecy of Revelation echoes God's promises of 'new heavens and a new earth' in Isaiah (65.17; 66.22), referring to the postexilic restoration of Israel. In the NT, 2 Pet. 3.10, 13 use similar imagery of an eschatological 'new heavens and new earth' thought by some scholars to be influenced by Stoic thought (cf. Heb. 12.26-28). Similar imagery is found in the Jewish apocalyptic *1 En.* 91.6.

Christian beliefs about eschatology and the afterlife have been heavily influenced by Revelation's depiction of the new heaven and new earth. Christopher Columbus and other explorers saw the conquest of North America as the fulfillment of John's prophecy. John's vision was interpreted politically by British utopians of the seventeenth century who immigrated to the New World. Captain Edward Johnson wrote: 'this is the place where the Lord will create a New Heaven and a New Earth in, new Churches, and a new Commonwealth together' (*Wonder-Working Providence*, 1653). The modern revolutionary notion that immoral institutions must be abolished if social justice is to prevail is reminiscent of the utopian climax of the Apocalypse. In literature, John's vision of the New Jerusalem (cf. Ezek. 40–48; Zech. 2.4-5; 4Q554; 4 *Ezra* 10.28-59) has inspired authors as diverse as the anonymous Pearl poet, Edmund Spenser (*Faerie Queene*), John Bunyan (*Pilgrim's Progress*), William Blake (Preface to *Milton: A Poem*), Percy Bysshe Shelley (*Prometheus Unbound*), and e.e. cummings (*The Enormous Room*). Many Christian hymns echo the imagery of the final chapters of Revelation, e.g., the medieval *Chorus novae Jerusalem*, the Victorian anthem 'The Holy City' (1992), and the American hymn 'Shall We Gather at the River?' (1864), arranged by composers Aaron Copland (*Old American Songs*) and Charles Ives. Artistic works inspired by this imagery were particularly popular in the nineteenth century, e.g., Julius Schnorr von Carelsfeld's engraving *The New Jerusalem Descending from Heaven* (1851–60) and Gustav Doré's illustration *The New Jerusalem*; a stained glass window in Christ Church, Chelsea illustrating Rev. 21.1 includes the anti-slavery activist William Wilberforce, and the philanthropist Earl of Shaftsbury, along with Christ and other biblical figures

See also BOOK OF LIFE; GARDEN OF EDEN; JERUSALEM; LAMB; NEW JERUSALEM; REVELATION; RIVER OF LIFE [MALB]

New Jerusalem. (See New Heaven, New Earth).

New Testament. (Also Christian Testament and Second Testament). The collection of 27 Greek documents written by followers of Jesus, mostly in the first century. It was later named as part of the canon of Christianity. The term is equivalent to the term 'new covenant', a concept with roots in Jer. 31.31-34. The passage speaks of when God will make a 'new covenant' with his people. The term is associated with Jesus' last supper: 'This cup is the new covenant in my blood' (1 Cor. 11.25).

The earliest extant writing with a complete list of documents in the NT canon is the list Athanasius of Alexandria (367). This list includes five 'historical' books (four Gospels and the Book of Acts), 21 letters (Pauline epistles, Hebrews, and the Catholic Epistles), and Revelation. Though no ecclesiastical council attempted to define the NT canon, the councils of Hippo (393) and Carthage (397) name the 27 books in our present canon.

Around the time of the Reformation, the concept of an accessible text of the Bible for the popular masses gained prominence. William Tyndale was the first person to translate the Bible into English from Hebrew and Greek. Such a translation was forbidden in England, forcing Tyndale work discreetly in Germany and Belgium. Copies of his English translation of the NT were printed (1525 and 1534) and smuggled into England. Before Tyndale could complete his OT translation, he was arrested, imprisoned, strangled and burned (1536). The translators of the King James ('Authorized') Version of the Bible (1611) drew heavily from Tyndale's translation work.

In Western culture, the NT has played an important role as a valued and sacred piece of literature by itself. Charles Dickens once begged preachers to preach the stories of the NT alone: 'In the New Testament there is the most beautiful and affecting history conceivable by man, and there are the terse models for all prayer and for all preaching' (*The Uncommercial Traveller*, 1860–1869). Here, Dickens contrasts reading the NT by itself with modern philosophies, favoring the former in preaching. The character Tom from Harriet Beecher Stowe's *Uncle Tom's Cabin* (1852) is described as 'being a poor ignorant fellow, whose reading had been confined entirely to the New Testament'. Both authors reflect the idea that the NT is accessible even to the uneducated.

In the tradition of Tyndale and others, it is common practice for Bible publishers to publish a stand-alone NT, sometimes accompanied by Proverbs and Psalms. In Dostoyevsky's *Crime and Punishment* (1866), e.g., Sonja owns a leather-bound Russian NT that plays a symbolic role in the narrative. Its description is reminiscent of Dostoyevsky's own well-used NT.

Several Christian movements have claimed to be closer to the 'New Testament church', a view called biblical primitivism or restorationism. These movements purport to model elements of the NT church, particularly in Acts. Such groups have typically protested against more established church structures. Though understandings vary, some emphases have been the rejection of infant baptism, the need for immersion baptism, communal sharing of goods, and fewer institutional structures. These groups include the sixteenth-century Anabaptists, many Baptist groups, and various revivalist and 'holiness' movements (e.g., Methodism). Some primitivist groups have even adopted a denominational title that includes 'New Testament' (e.g., the New Testament Church of God).

Recommended reading. Kling, David W. *The Bible in History: How the Texts Have Shaped the Times*. New York: Oxford University Press, 2004. Metzger, Bruce M. *The Canon of the New Testament: Its Origin, Development, and Significance.* New York: Oxford University Press, 1997

See also CANON; NEW COVENANT; OLD TESTAMENT; OLD TESTAMENT, USE IN THE NEW TESTAMENT OF THE [PGM]

Nicodemus. Nicodemus appears only in the Gospel of John (3.1-21; 7.50-52; 19.39-42). In 3.1-21 he comes to Jesus at night; he has seen Jesus' miracles, and wants to know more. As a leading member of the Jewish council it is his duty to investigate claims of miracles. He sees Jesus as 'a teacher come from God' (3.3), i.e., a prophet, but no more. But he is genuinely open to believing in Jesus, even though he does not fully understand what Jesus says about rebirth by water and the Spirit, or about the contrast between Spirit and flesh. Part of his difficulty may lie in the fact that he is a Pharisee, a member of a Jewish sect who were strict observers of the written Jewish law. The darkness of night is a metaphor for Nicodemus's misunderstanding. But night does not last forever.

At 7.50-52 the authorities attempt to arrest Jesus; they ridicule Nicodemus when he reminds them that the law does not allow them to convict a man without a hearing. Here he is not standing up for Jesus so much as for proper procedure. At 19.39-42 Nicodemus accompanies Joseph of Arimathea to Jesus' tomb. Until this point, Nicodemus and Joseph have been 'closet disciples'. Here, as the other disciples go into hiding, these two come forward to give Jesus an honorable burial. For John, being a 'closet Christian' is not enough. Jesus' disciples must be prepared to take a public stand for him.

Nicodemus, like Pilate, is a man of high status who may lose his place in society if he becomes a disciple of Jesus. But fence-sitting is not an option (an important theme in the Gospel of John is that everyone who encounters Jesus must choose for him or against him). If he is hesitant at first, by the end of the Gospel Nicodemus has chosen to stand with Jesus.

The story of Nicodemus inspired William T. Sleeper's hymn 'A ruler once came to Jesus by night'. In art, the story of Nicodemus inspired several paintings, including Michaelangelo, *Christ Crucified between the Virgin and Nicodemus*, c. 1552–54 (the Louvre, Paris); William Holman Hunt, *The Light of the World*, 1853 (Keble College, Oxford); and John la Farge, *The Visit of Nicodemus to Christ*, 1880 (Smithsonian American Art Museum).

In literature, the mediaeval Gospel of Nicodemus had much influence upon mediaeval English literature, including the Towneley cycle play *The Deliverance of Souls* and *Piers Plowman*. In Charles Dickens's *Our Mutual Friend* (1865), a character named Nicodemus Boffin asks a string of appropriate questions.

John 3 has been very important in the evangelical preaching of the past century. This has inspired several dramatizations, including Katherine Lee Bates's *Pharisees* (1926), which features Nicodemus and a rabbi; and Perry J. Stackhouse's *The Disciple of the Night* (1926). P.E. Osgoode's *The Fears of Nicodemus* (1928) is a dramatic dialogue between Nicodemus and Joseph of Arimathea. The title poem of Edwin Arlington Robinson's *Nicodemus* (1932) is a dialogue between Nicodemus and Caiaphas. Sholem Asch's novel *The Nazarene* (1939) features a rabbi named Nicodemon. Howard Nemerov's poem 'Nicodemus' (1939) is a meditations on Nicodemus's questions.

Recommending reading. Carson, D.A. *The Gospel according to John*. Grand Rapids, MI: Eerdmans, and Leicester: Inter-Varsity Press, 1991

See also JOHN, GOSPEL OF; PHARISEE [ED]

Nile. The River Nile in Egypt is the longest in the world. The Nile and its tributaries are now located in ten African countries, but it is always most identified with Egypt and Sudan. Coming from the White Nile and the Blue Nile, the river is the source of fertility in Egypt and hence the reason for the location of the civilization of ancient Egypt. In the Bible it is an important part of the story of the captivity of the Hebrews in Egypt.

The spiritual dimension of the Nile was that the annual flooding or inundation of the Nile valley each year was so important in the life of Egyptians that the God Hapi was associated with the river, and Hapi and the ruling pharaoh combined to bring fertility to the soil. The east bank of the Nile came to represent birth and life, with the west bank representing death and the afterlife; for this reason, the Valley of the Kings and most of the tombs in Ancient Egypt are located west of the river.

The most important biblical story that focuses on the Nile was the abandoning of the baby Moses in a reed boat on the river where he is found by Egyptians and raised by the daughter of the pharaoh. It was this part of the story that has led to some authors to associate the story of his early life with that of the Pharaoh Akhenaten (d. c. 1336 BCE). The story of an abandoned baby brought up by others also forms a part of the fictional *The Egyptian* (1949) by the Finnish writer Mika Waltari (1908–1979); the hero of the story is Sinuhe, abandoned in a reed boat and found by a doctor who brings him up as his son.

Because of its mention in the Bible, and also in the works of Herodotus and later historians, and its association with the life of Alexander the Great and Cleopatra, many Europeans have been fascinated by the river and the search for its source. The oldest account of this quest is by the Jesuit Pedro Pa'aez (1564–1622), but his complete account was not published until a Portuguese language edition in 1945, and as a result many books still credit the Scottish explorer James Bruce (1730–1794) with being the first European to visit the headwaters which he records in his book *Travels to Discover the Source of the Nile* (1790). Napoleon Bonaparte's expedition to Egypt in 1798 saw his navy defeated by the British in the Battle of the Nile, and in 1858 the British explorer John Hanning Speke (1827–1864), who had travelled with Richard F. Burton (1821–1890), came across Lake Victoria, the source of the Nile. Mention should also be made of the adventurer and keen biblical scholar General Charles G. Gordon (1833–1885), killed at Khartoum at the confluence of the Blue Nile and the White Nile. With interest in Egyptology, and the advent of tourism, many North Americans and Europeans, and later people from all around the world, started embarking on Nile cruises. Agatha Christie's *Death on the Nile* (1937) being a famous detective story was made into a film in 1974.

Recommended reading. Ludwig, Emil. *The Nile: The Life-Story of a River*. New York: The Viking Press, 1937. Moorehead, Alan. *The White Nile*. London: Hamish Hamilton, 1960. Moorehead, Alan. *The Blue Nile*. London: Hamish Hamilton, 1962

See also EGYPT; MOSES [JC]

Nimrod. The biblical warrior Nimrod, great-grandson of Noah and king of Sinhar, 'the first on earth to become a mighty warrior' (Gen. 10.8-10; 1 Chron. 1.10), is credited with building the great Assyrian city of Nineveh. Some scholars associate Nimrod with the Mesopotamian hero Gilgamesh. Nimrod, is a slayer of wild beasts and a brave warrior, reputed to be one of the great warriors of the ancient world. In ancient art, there are several representations of Nimrod as an older man with a large head and carefully trimmed beard.

The figure of Nimrod led to the naming of the great Assyrian city of Nimrud; there, colossal winged and human-headed lions were found and transported to the British Museum in London. They now are among the most well-known images of the Assyrian Empire. From 1229, there was a 'Castle of the Large Cliff' on what is now the Golan Heights (Israel), known in Hebrew as the 'Nimrod Fortress'. It is close to Nimrod Village established there in 1982. Further afield, there is a Nimrod Province in south-west Afghanistan, Nimrod, Minnesota, Nimrod, Oregon, named after the Nimrod Inn that opened there in the early twentieth century. The fleet-of-foot reputation of Nimrod led to a number of racehorses being named after him, including the runner-up to the Grand National Steeplechase in 1843.

The British championed the concept of Nimrod, and in November 1799 when a French sloop *Eole* was captured in the West Indies, it was renamed the HMS *Nimrod*, finally sold off in 1811. In the following year a Brig-sloop *Nimrod* was built in Ipswich, remaining in service until 1827. To replace it, the *Andromeda* was renamed *Nimrod*, which remained in service until 1907; the destroyer *Nimrod* of the Royal Navy served from 1915 until 1926. An Indian gunboat *Nimrod* was built in 1839 in Scotland, and refitted in the following year at Basra (Iraq); and a gun vessel *Nimrod* operated from 1856 until 1865. Ernest Shackleton was the leader of the British Antarctic Nimrod Expedition in 1907–1908, using a ship called *Nimrod*, leading to the naming of Mount Nimrod in Ross Dependency, Antarctica. Two cutters called *Nimrod* operated during the Napoleonic Wars.

The warlike nature of Nimrod led to the British building a Hawker Nimrod in the 1930s, and later the Hawker Siddeley Nimrod, built by British Aerospace as an early-warning aircraft which used heavily in the Falklands War (1982) and later conflicts. During World War II, the Nimrod was an anti-aircraft tank devised by the Hungarians. Recently, the Israelis named an anti-tank guided missile after Nimrod, developed by Israel Aerospace Industries.

In literature, 'Nimrod Wildfire' was a fictional representation of Davy Crockett in James Henry Hackett's play *Lion of the West* (1830), and Nimrod Gaunt was a character in Philip B. Kerr's *Children of the Lamp* (2004). The *Nimrod International Journal of Prose and Poetry* published by the University of Tulsa, Oklahoma.

As well as a fighter, Nimrod can represent something evil, with Nimrod as a villain in the *Doctor Who* series, another Nimrod is a robot mutant in Marvel Comics' *Uncanny X-Men*, and another is a vampire in *Dracula Lives!*, another Marvel Comics series. Mention should also be made of the Nimrod Theatre Company in Sydney, Australia, founded in 1970, named after Nimrod Street in the suburb of King's Cross. The Nimrod synchrotron operated at the Rutherford Appleton Laboratory near Oxford, England, until 1978.

In popular culture, the term 'Nimrod' can also mean a foolish or silly person, possibly because of its use in a Bugs Bunny episode to refer to the bumbling hunter Elmer Fudd.

See also ASSYRIA; NINEVEH [JC]

Nineveh. The great capital city of the Assyrians, mentioned 24 times in the Bible. Its building is mentioned in Genesis (10.11); in Jonah, it is the city where God sends the reluctant prophet; the prophet Nahum prophesies its fall. It is mentioned only twice in the NT, with similar references in Matthew and Luke: 'The people of Nineveh will rise up at the judgment with this generation and condemn it, because they repented at the proclamation of Jonah, and see, something greater than Jonah is here!' (Matt. 12.41; cf. Luke 11.32).

Except for the references in the Bible, little was known about Nineveh until the 1840s, when the British archaeologist Austen Henry Layard went to the region and uncovered the remains of one of its greatest cities. This led to widespread interest in Nineveh, with Layard taking many of the smaller remains back with him to London where they form a central part of the Assyrian Rooms in the British

Museum. As a result, Nineveh came to represent the power of the Assyrians who were seen to be a cruel, ruthless warrior people whose empire was built by aggression and fear from subject races, especially through some of the tablets found at Nineveh from the reign of the Emperor Ashurbanipal (reigned 668–627 BCE). Some of the famous battle scenes and bas reliefs showing lion hunting have become world-famous.

The ancient city of Nineveh features in a number of novels including Josiah M. Ward's *Come with me into Babylon: A Story of the Fall of Nineveh* (1902). Ancient Nineveh also appears in Desmond Varaday's *Dove of Ishtar: The Story of Semiramis* (1967), and Nicholas Guild, *The Assyrian* (1988). The Australian writer Mary Kent Hughes's novel *Dust of Nineveh* (1946) is about British nurses in Iraq; and Nineveh also appears in the title of Craig Alexander's thriller, *The Nineveh Project*. However Nineveh is best-known in the title used by Allen Drury in his account of the presidency of the fictional US politician Edward M. Jason. *Come Nineveh, Come Tyre* (1973) portrays the naïve Jason allowing his government to be overthrown by a Communist conspiracy, after which he commits suicide.

There are five places in the world called Nineveh, two in the northern part of the county of Worcestershire, in the west of England. There is also a place in Pennsylvania, an unincorporated township in Johnson County, Indiana, and an unincorporated hamlet on the banks of the Susquehanna River in New York State. Overseas, Nineveh has become the symbol of the Assyrian community around the world, and there is a Nineveh Cup for soccer organized by the Assyrian Nineveh Association in Aarhus City, Denmark.

See also ASSYRIA; JONAH, BOOK OF [JC]

No respecter of persons. The phrase 'no respecter of persons' in Rom. 2.11 is one among other similar verses that speak of God as a righteous judge. In some translations, Paul says that 'God is no respecter of persons'. Some versions translate the verse, 'For God shows no partiality'. The words mean that God does not have regard for people because he is the judge of his creation. V. 11 occurs in the middle of Paul's discussion of sin, the law and God's judgment. Paul discusses the Law of Moses that defines sin and condemns those who break the law.

In Deut. 10.7, Moses preaches to the people of God: 'For the Lord your God is God of gods and Lord of lords, the great God, mighty and awesome, who is not partial and takes no bribe'. Proverbs 24.23 says the wise know that 'partiality in judging is not good'. With human nature in mind, the author of Proverbs teaches, 'To show partiality is not good—yet for a piece of bread a person may do wrong' (28.21). The message is that people will trade fairness to gain something of personal interest.

The word 'partial' is translated as 'regardeth' or 'regards' in older English translations. It comes from the same Hebrew root as the word for respect. In 2 Chron. 19.7, the writer says in a warning, 'Now, let the fear of the Lord be upon you; take care what you do, for there is not perversion of justice with the Lord our God, or partiality, or taking of bribes'.

In the NT, Jesus is addressed by the Pharisees and Herodians as someone who has no regard for status, so they say, 'Teacher, we know that you are sincere, and teach the way of God in accordance with truth, and show deference to no one; for you do not regard people with partiality' (Matt. 22.16). Their words are an appeal to vanity to trap Jesus in his own words on paying taxes to Caesar.

1 Peter 1.17 instructs believers to fear and obey God: 'If you invoke as Father the one who judges all people impartially according to their deeds, live in reverent fear during the time of your exile'. The verse makes it plain that the impartiality of God is focused upon his judging of the deeds of people.

In some passages, God's words or actions do seem to show partiality. For example, God says 'Esau have I hated and Jacob have I loved' (Rom. 9.13). The very choice of Abraham as ancestor of the chosen people implies partiality. In Zech. 2.8, God calls Israel 'the apple of my eye' so woe betide anyone who touches them. This is not partiality in judging but in faithful caring for those who have been divinely elected for service.

That God does not play favorites is also expressed in verses that say that God causes the rain to fall upon the just and the unjust alike (Matt. 5.45; cf. Luke 6.35; Acts 14.17). These verses speak of God's common grace for all.

See also ELECTION; JUDGMENT; PREDESTINATION [AJW]

Noadiah. In the Persian period, after the Judeans returned from exile (sixth century BCE), during Ezra's priestly leadership and Nehemiah's governorship in Judea (fifth century BCE), there appear brief references to two figures named Noadiah in the books of Nehemiah and Ezra. The Noadiah who received more attention is a woman prophet (Neh.

6.14). She is fleetingly alluded to by Nehemiah in his prayer asking God to remember his enemies—she, the prophetess (*nevi'ah*), and two other men already named, and 'the rest of the prophets who wanted to make me afraid'. Nehemiah felt they had been expressing disagreement or antagonism toward him and his wall-building enterprise. While there were women prophets in ancient Israel and in the early church, the number of individual women identified and remembered by the Bible is few—eleven, plus reference to groups of women prophets in OT and NT. Of these women prophets, only five of their names were remembered in the Bible, like Noadiah. The dominant patriarchal perspective of biblical authors and editors meant that rarely were women's prophetic words or extensive activities conveyed in the Bible, as is the case here with Noadiah. We cannot be sure what the details of the debate were in Nehemiah's context. Another Noadiah figure is briefly referred to in this period, in Ezra 8.33; no information of him is given, except that he is male, son of Binnui and a Levite.

Recommended reading. Gafney, Wilda C. *Daughters of Miriam: Women Prophets in Ancient Israel.* Minneapolis: Fortress Press, 2008)

See also EZRA; NEHEMIAH; PROPHECY, PROPHETS
[NCL]

Noah. In Genesis, son of Lamech (5.29), hero of the flood narrative (7.1–8.22). Noah means 'rest'; at his birth, his father proclaims that he will 'bring us relief from our work and from the toil of our hands' (5.29). In Noah's time, the earth is corrupt, and Noah, the only God-fearing and blameless man (6.9), is warned by God that he is determined to destroy his creation, and instructed to build an ark so that he and his family can escape the deluge, along with breeding pairs of 'every living thing' (6.19). Noah obeys, and he and his family are saved when God causes it to rain for forty days and forty nights (6.12), flooding the entire earth. After 150 days on the ark, the waters begin to abate, and after coming to rest on Mount Ararat, Noah sends a raven and a dove to seek dry land. When inhabitants of the ark finally disembark, Noah makes a great sacrifice of one of each of the ritually clean animals that survived the flood, and God promises never to destroy the earth by water again (8.20-22; 9.1-17), setting the rainbow in the sky as a sign of the covenant. Noah is similar to the heroes of other ancient flood legends, notably the Mesopotamian Utnapishtim and the Greek Deucalion.

The story continues with a lesser-known tale where Noah, the first viticulturist, is found lying drunk and naked in his tent by his son Ham (9.20-22), who tells his two brothers, Shem and Japheth. The two brothers bring a garment to cover their father, turning away so as not to see his nakedness. When Noah awakes and discovers Ham's disrespect, he curses Ham's son Canaan and blesses the sons of Shem and Japheth (9.24-27). Noah dies at the age of 950.

A lost extrabiblical 'Book of Noah' was known by early Jewish writers (*1 En.* 6–11; 39.1-2a; 54.7–55.2; 60; 65.1–69.25; 106–107; *Jubilees* 20.13, 21.10; *Testament of Levi* 18.2; 1*QNoah*). While rabbinic commentators were divided on the righteousness of Noah, blaming Noah's curse for bringing slavery into the world, early Christian interpreters portray him variously as a new Adam, example of obedience, and archetype of Christ. Noah's wife, called Naamah in a medieval midrash, rises to prominence in the Gnostic *Book of Norea* (fourth century). Noah is mentioned frequently in the Qur'an, where he is considered a prophet.

Noah figures in countless works of western literature, including Chaucer's *Miller's Tale*, Shakespeare's *Twelfth Night* and Milton's *Paradise Lost*. More recent literary retellings, such as Timothy Findley's *Not Wanted on the Voyage* (1984) and Anne Prevoost's *In the Shadow of the Ark* (2004) are critical of the patriarch who self-servingly allows 'all flesh' to perish. In western art, Noah frequently appears in scenes of the building of the ark, the gathering of the animals, the sending of the raven and the dove, the post-flood sacrifice, and the scene of his drunkenness. Cinematic retellings of the Noah story include the TV movie *Noah's Ark* (1999), starring Jon Voight, the comedy *Evan Almighty* (2007), where the Noah figure is played by Steve Carell, and the animated film *Noah's Ark: The New Beginning* (2012). Ironically, cheerful scenes of Noah and his ark are a favorite motif of baby furnishings and children's toys.

The search for the remains of Noah's ark is popular tabloid fodder, documented in the Mysteries of the Bible video *Noah and the Flood* (1994).

Recommended reading. Lewis, J.P. *A Study of the Interpretation of Noah and the Flood in Jewish and Christian Literature.* Leiden: Brill, 1968

See also COVENANT; FLOOD; HAM; JAPHETH; NOAH'S ARK; SHEM
[MALB]

Noah's Ark. The vehicle of salvation which enabled Noah, his family, and breeding pairs of all non-aquatic creatures to endure the cataclysmic events of the biblical flood in relative safety. A popular subject for children's books and Sunday school lessons, it has also been the inspiration behind numerous unsuccessful search expeditions to virtually every location identified with the ark's final resting place, the mountains of Ararat (Gen. 8.4).

The simplistic construction blueprint for the vessel is set out in Gen. 6.14-16: in terms of layout, it is to consist of three separate levels; in terms of dimensions, it is to measure 300 cubits long by 50 cubits wide by 30 cubits high; and, in terms of materials, it is to be constructed out of cypress wood and made water-tight by a coating of pitch on the interior and exterior. Based on this description, the ark does not appear to have been seaworthy, and many have likewise doubted the vessel's capacity to house multiple specimens of each of the world's aerial and land-dwelling creatures for a time-span of just over a year. These issues, however, were most likely of little concern for the biblical writer, who appears to have fashioned his description of the ark according to the pattern of the Jerusalem Temple which, with its tripartite layout and approximate dimensions of 100 cubits by 50 cubits by 30 cubits, can be seen to share a significant degree of congruity with the ark in terms of both physical description and salvific function.

Outside of the Genesis flood narrative, the ark would become a symbol of great appeal to a number of early Christian writers. Among these is 1 Pet. 3.19-22 which sees the ark and the church as correlating symbols of salvation over and against the chaotic waters of human corruption. Similarly, Pseudo-Cyprian's *Treatise against Novatian* also presents a typology between the flood and the ark and the church and persecution: 'That ark bore the figure of the church ... which was stricken hither and thither to such a degree by the tumultuous waters. Therefore that deluge which happened under Noah showed forth the figure of the persecution which was poured forth over the whole world' (2-5).

Beyond its symbolic appeal in the Jewish and Christian worlds, interest in Noah's ark also appears to have filtered it way into certain segments of Greco-Roman society, as suggested by a series of imperial coins struck and issued in the late second and early third centuries CE in the city of Apamea that bear images of Noah and his wife aboard and disembarking from the ark, along with the characteristic symbols of the raven and the dove bearing the olive branch. In this respect, we may also note the interesting twist that occurs in the radically reworked (gnostic) flood story found in the *Paraphrase of Shem*, where salvation from the flood occurs not by means of the construction and boarding of an ark, but in the erection of a tower that transcends the chaotic waters (25.15-35).

Recommended reading. Garcia Martinez, Florentino, and Gerard P. Luttikhuizen (eds.). *Interpretations of the Flood.* Leiden: Brill, 1998. Holloway, S.W. 'What Ship Goes There: The Flood Narratives in the Gilgamesh Epic and Genesis Considered in Light of Ancient Near Eastern Temple Ideology', *Zeitschrift für die alttestamentliche Wissenschaft* 103 (1991) 328-55. Lewis, Jack P. *A Study of the Interpretation of Noah and the Flood in Jewish and Christian Literature.* Leiden: Brill, 1968

See also FLOOD; NOAH [TB]

Noonday Demon. Found only in Ps. 91.6, as *qeṭeb yāšûd ṣāhŏrāyim* ('destruction that wastes at noonday'), in the LXX, *daimoniou mesēmbrinou* ('noonday demon'). Although the word typically means 'plague' or 'pestilence', most scholars agree that *qeteb* originally is likely a reference to a local Canaanite deity or demon, possibly Mot or Nergal, and that this is reflected in the LXX translation.

Early Christian writers disagreed over the interpretation of this phrase. Augustine suggests the noonday demon represents the temptations that all Christians must face. Jerome upholds an older interpretation that sees the midday demon as heresies and false doctrines. However, the interpretation of Evagrius Ponticus that connected the midday demon with *acedia*, or demonic thoughts toward spiritual lethargy or boredom, gained the most influence. Due largely to Evagrius's works, in the late sixth century *acedia* found its way into Gregory the Great's list of seven deadly or cardinal sins.

Thomas Aquinas refined *acedia* to mean *sloth*, a spiritual malaise as well as despair, but the practical explanations of the seven deadly sins that grew in popular medieval culture were less cerebral and more visceral. Chief among these is Dante's *Divine Comedy*, which graphically portrays the punishments of the slothful, trapped beneath of slime of the river Styx, and whose penance could only be running continuously as fast as possible. Marlowe, in *The Tragical History of Doctor Faustus*, describes the sin of sloth as a sleepy mute born on a sunny riverbank. In *The Canterbury Tales*, Chaucer's Parson preaches that sloth—which he also calls *accidie*—is born of anger and envy and that it prevents good works because it causes despair of God's mercy.

Heironymus Bosch's painting, *The Seven Deadly Sins and the Four Last Things*, depicts this spiritual lethargy literally with the image of a man asleep at his prayers, who in the Final Judgement is too lazy to resist the torments of the devils.

In the modernist period, we find Aldous Huxley's essay *Accidie*, which traces the historical development of the term, and suggests that it may also represent an *ennui*—a feeling of discontent or disillusionment and weariness with life—birthed during the Industrial Revolution and typified by the horrors of the First World War. Another modernist, the poet T.S. Eliot, gives voice to this same ennui in works such as 'The Marina' and 'The Rock'. At the close of the twentieth century, attention shifted from the mediaeval notions of sloth and the modernist ennui to the larger psychological disorder of depression, a transition catalogued in Andrew Solomon's Pulitzer-winning work on the subject of clinical depression: *The Noonday Demon: An Atlas of Depression*.

In popular media, the seven deadly sins have been represented by each character in Sherwood Schwartz's famous television series *Gilligan's Island*, acedia/sloth represented by the character of Gilligan (*Inside Gilligan's Island*, 1994). More graphically, acedia and the other sins are depicted in David Fincher's 1995 horror/thriller *Se7en*.

See also DEMON; SIN [RLM]

Not peace but a sword. A controversial passage in the NT that raises questions about the legitimacy of violence among Christian disciples. Although the NT alludes to Jesus as the 'Prince of Peace' (Eph. 2.14; cf. Isa. 9.6), whose pacifistic stance is epitomized by the Sermon on the Mount's dictum 'turn the other cheek', several NT passages ambivalently depict Jesus employing martial metaphors in his solemn instructions about the kingdom of God. In particular, Jesus warns his disciples: 'Do not think that I have come to bring peace to the earth; I have not come to bring peace, but a sword. For I have come to set a man against his father, and a daughter against her mother, and a daughter-in-law against her mother-in-law' (Matt. 10.34-35; cf. Luke 12.51-53). Additionally, he instructs his followers to go and buy a sword if they do not have one (Luke 22.36).

Ostensibly, such biblical passages appear to promote violence under Jesus authority; however, this interpretation is not widely endorsed in Christian exegesis. Since Jesus' instructions are in the context of missionary work to the lost sheep of Israel, it is therefore typical to see Jesus' words here as warnings to his disciples that they will encounter hostility from strangers and family members who resent or reject Jesus' teachings. Thus, the verses are not endorsing physical violence but preparing disciples to equip themselves with the armor of God, especially the 'sword' of the spirit, in their inevitable missionary struggles. The didactic message is clear: commitment to Jesus necessitates suffering, including estranged family relationships.

Furthermore, the passage seems to allude to the importance of making wise distinctions between earthy and heavenly treasures: it echoes Jesus' jarring words spoken in Matt. 12.46-50 where, in response to the news that his family is waiting for him outside, Jesus replies 'who is my real family?', thereby creating a disjunction between those of his own flesh and blood and his heavenly father. Likewise, Jesus' disciples should transcend ordinary filial loyalties by embracing God.

Augustine provided an early allegorical interpretation of the passage when he equated the sword with the Word of Jesus, which some will obey but others will repudiate (*Enarr. in Ps.* 45.10; 68.5; 97.7). His interpretation was followed by many other Christian writers including the later Reformers such as John Calvin.

Several works of western fiction employ the saying such as: W. Somerset Maugham's book *Catalina* (1948), which states 'He had brought not peace to the city, but a sword'; Howard Nemerov's poem 'Morning Sun' (1952); and Montague's *A Hind Let Loose* (1910). Notably, Swinburne's 'Hymn of Man' (1869) ironically reverses the biblical verse as a warning about the excesses of organized religion, which thrusts discord and strife into the world like a sword.

This seemingly militant passage from the Bible has been cited by both religious and secular authorities to justify episodes of holy war and or/just warfare. For instance, during the Second World War, the National Film Board of Canada produced a 1940 Allied propaganda film entitled, *Not Peace but a Sword* (directed by Ross McLean).

Recommended reading. Sim, D.C. 'The Sword Motif in Matthew 10:34'. *HTS Teologiese Studies/Theological Studies* 56 (2000) 84-104

See also SWORD; PEACE; SERMON ON THE MOUNT; ARMOR OF GOD [SDD]

Nothing new under the sun. The expression 'nothing new' (*'en kol-hadash*) arises from Eccl. 1.9: 'What has been is what will be, and what has been done is what will be done; there is nothing new under the sun'. The work of Ecclesiastes generally is concerned with discovering how to make a 'gain' (*yitron*, 1.3) 'under the sun' (*tahat hashemesh*, i.e., the sphere of human activity), and the declaration that there is 'nothing new' at the beginning of the work sets a pessimistic note to the search. It is unclear, however, whether the 'nothing new' refers only to nature (1.4-7) or whether it also encompasses human activity. In non-biblical usage, it generally carries the second meaning.

The phrase is unique to Ecclesiastes in scripture, and other portions of the Bible express greater hope in the newness of God's work. Isaiah 55.10 depicts each new rain as bringing about new growth. Other passages in Isaiah (42.9; 43.19; 48.6; 65.17, 22), Ezekiel (11.19; 36.26), 2 Corinthians (5.17), and Revelation (21.1, 2) also provide vivid depictions of newness.

Temporally, the use of the 'nothing new' in speech and writing can either refer to the situation of the moment (e.g., 'What's going on?' Answer: 'Nothing new' (from the last time we spoke), or frequently is a way of expressing one's present outlook on life. It expresses a lack of progress or that life is repetitious.

Rhetorically, the phrase occurs either as a statement of one's own opinion, or as a statement to be contradicted. So one finds in Austin Dobson's 1913 poem *A Tale of Polypheme* that the poet believes that even his own poem does not and cannot contribute anything new. On the other hand, it often occurs in contexts where users argue against, or at least question, the statement. In jest, Samuel Bishop suggests 'nothing new' is incorrect, for there are always new taxes to pay (Epigram CI). Similarly, Oliver Wendell Holmes in his poem about life and death asks 'What next? we ask; and is it true; The sunshine falls on nothing new; As Israel's king declared?' ('In the Twilight'). One can find it used similarly in popular works such as newspaper and journal articles where authors seek to defend or defeat the notion that there is 'nothing new'.

One can carry the same sentiment in different expressions such as the Canadian music group's tune 'It's All Been Done' (Barenaked Ladies), the line 'same old song in Kansas' 'Dust in the Wind', or the slogan 'Same [stuff], different day' from Stephen King's novel *Dreamcatcher*. Similarly, the U2 song 'New Year's Day' has Bono repeat 'Nothing changes on New Year's Day'.

Recommended reading. Fox, Michael V. *A Time to Tear Down and A Time to Build Up: A Rereading of Ecclesiastes*. Grand Rapids, MI: Eerdmans, 1999

See also ECCLESIASTES; NEW HEAVEN; NEW EARTH; WISDOM LITERATURE [SHW]

Number of the Beast (see 666).

Numbers, Book of. Numbers is the fourth book of the Bible. It Greek name in the LXX is *Arithmoi*; its Latin name in the Vulgate is *Numeri*. These names are derived from the two censuses of the Israelites described in chs. 1–4, 26. Its Hebrew name *bemidbar* ('in the desert') comes from Num. 1.1. *Bemidbar* is quite descriptive because much of the action occurs during the 40 years of desert wandering of the tribes of Israel. Numbers tells (incompletely) the middle of the story of the Hebrews' journey from Egypt to the Promised Land of Canaan.

Among the themes discussed in the book are God's nature, divine leadership, human rebellion and spiritual disobedience. These are given intense theological scrutiny as Moses and the Israelites are divinely tested and guided. The message of the book is that their disobedience and failures do not in the end frustrate the purposes of their sovereign God who is creating a people for himself.

The first part of Numbers (1.1–10.10) describes the tribes at Mount Sinai, the census, the camp assignments, gifts for the Tabernacle, treatment of lepers and wives and other matters. The second part (10.11–22.1) records events during the wilderness journey; however, chs. 15 and 18–19 interrupt the narrative with cultic legislation. Repeated grumblings against God and Moses because of the hardships of the journey result in Miriam contracting leprosy; Korah's rebellion; the people's rebellion after spies are sent to Canaan to report on conditions there; venomous serpents being sent as punishment (21.6-9); and the faithlessness of Aaron and Moses, which is punished by denial of their entry into the Promised Land. Rebellion condemns the people to wandering in the wilderness for 40 years (14.28-35). Eventually of all those who left Egypt die in the desert except for Moses, Caleb and Joshua. The final portion of this section describes the victory of the Hebrews over the Amorites and Moabites in the Transjordan.

The third section of Numbers (22.2–36.13) places the Hebrews on the plains of Moab poised to enter the Promised Land. In this section, the episode with Balaam and his talking donkey occurs (22–24). Much of the section is concerned with priestly legislation. Those who remain are the new generations born in the desert, hardened and disciplined to follow God and their leaders in the hard battle to take the land of Canaan.

English poetry has been enriched by poems based on texts in Numbers. George Herbert's 'The Bunch of Grapes' is based on the story of the spies' report (13.17-21); similarly, Anna (Anne) Killigrew's 'Death' (13.28–14.2); John Hall's 'Numeri XIII' (14.13-16); Norman MacCaig's 'Golden Calf' (14.28-35); and William Cowper's 'Lines Written under the Influence of Delirium' (1–33). The story of Balaam (22.1-30) inspired Francis Quarles's 'On Balaam's Ass' and Abraham Crowley's 'from Davideis, Book I'. Edward Taylor's 'Meditation Twenty-Five' and Thomas Merton's poems 'Place Names' were inspired by Num. 28.10 and 32.39-42 respectively.

The story of Balaam, son of Beor, an Amorite soothsayer, hired to curse the Hebrews has been described as harmonizing theology and art. Balaam's talking ass (22.1-35) is an element of the story that has been the source of many allusions including 2 Pet. 2.15-16, Thomas Nashe (*Anatomie of Absurditie*), Boethius (*Consolation of Philosophy*), Chaucer (*Boece*), Erasmus (*In Praise of Folly*), Sheridan (*Persius* 1.23), and Shakespeare (*A Midsummer Night's Dream*).

Recommended reading. Ashley, Timothy R. *The Book of Numbers*. Grand Rapids, MI: Eerdmans, 1993. Riggans, Walter. *Numbers*. Philadelphia: Westminster, 1983

See also BALAAM; SWORD [AJW]

Numbers, Symbolism of. The repeated use of many numbers throughout the Bible, notably in Revelation, has led to the prominence of number symbolism, underscored by Wisdom 11.21, God 'ordered all things in measure and number and weight'. Writers who further developed Christian number symbolism include Augustine, Isidore of Seville, Hugh of St Victor and Boethius. Dante's *Divine Comedy* and Milton's *Paradise Lost* employ symbolic numbers derived from biblical sources.

One signifies unity, while two emphasizes the dual nature of Christ, and the notion of balance. The number three indicates totality; it is the number of the Trinity (Father, Son and Holy Spirit). Abraham entertained three visitors (Gen. 18.2) and sacrifices son Isaac on the third day (Gen. 22.4). Jonah spent three days and nights in the belly of the great fish (Jon 2.1), prefiguring the three days Jesus spent entombed before the resurrection (Matt. 12.40; 27.63). Four is the number of rivers (Gen. 2.10-14), beasts (Dan. 7.3-7), evangelists, and horsemen (Rev. 6.1-8).

The number six alone is not unusually important, although it is associated with perfection, as the world was created in six days (Gen. 1). 666 is the 'number of the beast' (Rev. 13.18). The satanic aspects of this number have been linked to the heavy-metal band Iron Maiden and the horror film *The Omen* (1976, 2006).

Seven may be the most significant symbolic number. It is a number associated with entirety and completeness; festivals such as Passover last seven days. Christians recognize seven gifts of the Holy Spirit, sacraments, acts of mercy, virtues and vices, and joys and sorrows of the Virgin. Joseph interpreted Pharoah's dreams of seven years of plenty followed by seven years of famine (Gen. 41.25-30). Proverbs 9.1 speaks of seven Pillars of Wisdom, a title adapted by T.E. Lawrence for his autobiography. The seven last words of Christ are reported in the gospels (Matt. 27.46; Mark 15.34; Luke 23.34-46; John 19.26-30); they are the subject of a musical composition by Joseph Hayden, and figure in Joyce's *Portrait of the Artist as a Young Man*. The prophetic visions of Revelation speak of seven churches, spirits, lamp-stands, stars, angels, flaming lamps, seals, horns, eyes, trumpets, thunderclaps, heads, plagues, golden bowls and hills. Many filmmakers have sought the symbolic power of seven, notably in the apocalyptic films *The Seventh Seal* (1957) and *The Seventh Sign* (1988), and in *Se7en* (1995), which associated murders with the seven deadly sins. Jesus tells Peter that he must forgive a wrong 'not seven … but seventy-seven times' (Matt. 18.22). Seventy times seven refers to an indefinite period of time; the phrase is used in this sense by Nelly in Bronte's *Wuthering Heights*.

Jacob's twelve sons became the twelve tribes of Israel (Gen. 49.28). 12,000 from each of the twelve tribes are sealed (Rev. 7.3-8) to make 144,000. This number has been interpreted as that of the elect; Jehovah's Witnesses believe that specifically 144,000 people will rise to heaven. Christ had twelve disciples (Matt. 10.1). Forty is a number connected to a period of denial or exile. The flood lasted forty days and nights (Gen. 7.12). Moses (Exod. 34.28), Elijah (1 Kgs 19.8) and Jesus (Matt. 4.2) endured forty-day trials; Christians today observe 40 days of Lent.

Recommended reading. Bullinger, E.W. *Number in Scripture: Its Supernatural Design and Spiritual Significance*. Grand Rapids, MI: Kregel Publications, 2003

See also SEVEN CHURCHES OF REVELATION; SEVEN LAST WORDS OF CHRIST; SEVEN SEALS, SEVEN BOWLS, SEVEN TRUMPETS; SEVEN YEARS OF PLENTY, FAMINE; SEVENTY TIMES SEVEN; 666; TWELVE DISCIPLES; TWELVE TRIBES OF ISRAEL [ACF]

Nunc dimittis. From the Latin *nunc* (now, at the present time, at this time) *dimittis* (dismiss, are dismissing). Also known as the Song of Simeon and the Canticle of Simeon, the *Nunc dimittis* is the third of the last great canticles of the NT. Its name is derived from the opening words of a song of salvation uttered by the righteous and devout Simeon who was anxiously awaiting the consolation of Israel (Luke 2.5). Having received a promise from the Holy Spirit that he would not taste death before seeing for himself the promised Messiah and savior, Simeon was moved by the Spirit and went into the temple courts (Luke 2.27). As he stood there, Simeon met Mary, Joseph, and the infant Jesus. The Spirit's promise to Simeon was fulfilled. Taking the infant into his arms, Simeon subsequently offered God a song of praise (Luke 2.29-32), extolling God's glorious plan of salvation and its scope.

Simeon's song, although rather brief, has become beloved among Christians. In monastic traditions the *Nunc dimittis* serves as the gospel canticle for Compline, the final hour of the Divine Office. In the Anglican tradition, it serves as the gospel song for Evensong (Evening Prayer). Eastern Orthodox Churches often include the *Nunc dimittis* as a part of the daily Vespers service. In many Lutheran churches, it is sung or recited before the receiving of the bread and wine of the eucharist. In contrast, the *Nunc dimittis* has been largely absent from the liturgy and worship of congregational, Pentecostal, and non-denominational churches.

Throughout history, the words of the *Nunc dimittis* have most often been set to music. Composers frequently couple Simeon's song with the Magnificat to form beautiful choral pieces that have enriched the life and worship of the church.

In contemporary culture, the anxious Simeon who is awaiting the arrival of a promised hope and future has his story recounted in poetic and extended form in the poem by T.S. Eliot, 'A Song for Simeon' (1928). The poem presents its readers with an old man in the twilight of his life, looking eagerly to the future and the hope that it holds.

Karel Capek's play *R.U.R.* (1923) also makes use of the hope and promise of Simeon's song. The play chronicles the rise of a society that is in need of and dependent upon robots. It is eventually recognized that the robots present a threat to humankind. By the third act humanity is on the brink of extinction. Everyone except for Alquist (the clerk at the robot factory) has been killed. Recognizing that two robots, Helena and Primus, are the only hope for a new humanity, Alquist sends them out into the world. The play ends with the prophetic and hopeful words of the *Nunc dimittis* being voiced in the background.

More recently, the Showtime drama, *The Hunger*, aired an episode entitled '*Nunc Dimittis*' (October 10, 1999). Princess Dracula's friend and companion is dying. The episode focuses on the attempt by Princess Dracula's companion to achieve his dying wish (to find his successor) so that he might die at peace.

Recommended reading. Cantalamessa, Raniero. *The Mystery of Christmas: A Comment on the Magnificat, Gloria, Nunc dimittis*. Collegeville, MN: Liturgical Press, 1998. McMinkle, Marvin. 'The Lord Is Come! The Song of Simeon'. *Preaching* 14/3 (1998) 19-23.

See also LUKE, GOSPEL OF; MAGNIFICAT; SIMEON [JNR]

O

Obadiah, Book of. One of two the writing prophets who are not identified with a reference to his father, family, hometown, place of prophesying, time period of prophesying, or to some combination of these. Obadiah means 'servant of Yahweh', so this may be his role and not his actual name. There are a dozen individuals named Obadiah in OT. None of these seem to have been the one who wrote the smallest book in the OT. Attempts to identify several of these individuals (e.g., 1 Kgs 18.3-16) as the author of the book have all failed to date. As a consequence all that is known about the prophet is his name.

The dating of the book is unknown. Some commentators have argued that it was written as early as the ninth century BCE, while others have suggested dates shortly after the fall of Jerusalem 586 BCE. Others have argued for a date during the time of the Babylonian Exile or for a date shortly after the return from Babylon, as late as 400 BCE. The clues in the book are the most commonly used guides for its dating. The clues refer to the times of contact between Israel and Edom. The most likely datings are before the Exile when the Edomites, vassals of the Assyrians, first resisted Babylonian tutelage after their conquest of the western regions of the Assyrian Empire, but then abandoned Judah to Babylonian conquest, or shortly after the destruction of Jerusalem by Nebuchadnezzar.

Obadiah opens with the statement that it is a direct revelation from the Lord. The burden of the prophet's message is against Edom specifically: God will to destroy Edom as punishment for treachery toward Israel (cf. Ps. 137.7). Some scholars believe that Obadiah took an older prophetic message (Jer. 49.14-19) and applied it to a new situation (Obad 1-5). Others believe that its material was drawn from a book of prophecies against foreign nations.

The book has two parts: Oracles against Edom (1-14) and Oracles on the Day of the Lord (15-21). The Oracles against Edom begin with v. 2 and after describing how thorough will be the destruction of Edom state that the message is the 'oracle of Yahweh'. The completeness of Edom's destruction is described in vv. 5 and 6.

V. 7 describes the treachery with which Edom's allies will treat her. Vv. 8-9 describe the loss of both warriors and wisdom. The reference to Teman in v. 9 is a reference to the reputation that Edom had for wisdom. One of the friends of Job who came to visit him, Eliphaz the Temanite (Job 2.11) is identified with the town of Teman. Located in northeast Edom, it was named after a grandson of Esau. Its people were famous for their wisdom.

Vv. 10-14 are a catalogue of the evils foreign armies will visit upon Edom. These and other verses express the theological view that God is the Lord who works through human history. All nations are accountable and those committing evil acts are subject to divine judgment in the Day of the Lord.

Jewish tradition identifies Obadiah as an Edomite convert to Judaism, descended from Job's friend Eliphaz, and as the servant of Ahab and Jezebel who received his prophetic gifts for hiding 128 prophets from Jezebel (1 Kgs 18.3-4; cf. *Sanhedrin* 8.16.2; *Exodus Rabbah* 31.3). He is regarded as a saint by Orthodox and Byzantine rite churches.

See also EDOM; ESAU; LATTER PROPHETS; PROPHECY, PROPHETS [AJW]

Obedience. The biblical concept of obedience has a complex etymological history. In the OT, there are at least three different words relating to the concept. The root *yqh* (to be obedient) is rare and is primarily used to describe the commitment to a leader or parental figure (Gen. 49.10, Prov. 30.17). *Shamar* (to keep, watch, or preserve) is used most commonly to describe obedience to God and Torah. The root *yd'* (to know) is used often to describe one living in relationship with God or a ruler (Exod. 6.7, 10.2; 1 Kgs 20.13). As with other ancient Near Eastern cultures, the Israelites described the concept of obedience in covenantal language (Gen. 18.19). The *Shema* prayer (Deut. 6.4-6) concisely declares this fundamental commitment, 'The Lord is our God, the Lord alone ... Keep these words in your heart'. God called Israel to absolute obedience through the Decalogue (Exod. 20.1-18); as God's people, they were to live and worship in obedience to God's statutes (Exod. 21.1–34.18; Jer. 11.7).

As NT authors considered Christianity's relationship with the law, the concept of obedience became differently nuanced. In the light of Jesus, Christians were called to be obedient to the law of *faith* rather than Torah (Rom. 1.4, 6.16–17.2; 1 Cor. 10.7; Phil. 2.1; Gal. 3.2, 19). The language of obedience was used to describe Christ's work and sacrifice (*hypakoē*; Rom. 5.18; Heb. 5.7-8). Jesus and the early church often described themselves as obedient servants or slaves of God (*doulos*; Matt. 6.24; Acts 16.17; Phil. 2.6-8; Tit. 1.1). The call to obedience affected every aspect of the believer's life. The tension inherent in obedience to law after the coming of Christ is explicitly found in Matthew and Galatians.

Western culture has adapted the biblical language of obedience in different ways. Martin Luther claimed that God does not require works but obedience. Philip Melanchthon and John Calvin formalized three different Christian understandings of the law. Anabaptist and later Evangelicals took up the third understanding as a primary tenet of faith. Sixteenth- and seventeenth-century literature also drew on the conflicts of obedience. Shakespeare makes light of obedience and authority between genders in *The Taming of the Shrew*. In *Othello*, Iago undercuts the suffering obedience of Desdemona. John Milton (d. 1674), in *De Doctrina Christiana*, used the theme of obedience to invigorate readers to moral action.

The US has assimilated a secular form of obedience into political and popular culture. Benjamin Franklin stated, in the *Poor Richard's Almanack*, 'He that cannot obey, cannot command'. In the famous 1974 Stanford Experiment, Stanley Milgram tested subjects' willingness to follow orders to intentionally inflict pain on others. This experiment was later made into the movie *Obedience* (2000). In *The Fugitive* (1993), Dr Richard Kimble (Harrison Ford) runs from law enforcement officials because he is obedient to the intention of the law of the land to enact justice. The main characters in both *Driving Miss Daisy* (1989) and *Man of Fire* (2004) demonstrate that living obediently to someone else forms an unbreakable, mutually fulfilling relationship. *Cider House Rules* (1999) attempts to portray the complexity of obedience to the 'letter of the law' in one's home community. The CBS primetime show *The Unit* (2006–2009) demonstrated the fierce tension that arises when individuals are required to be obedient to their country, their spouses, and to justice.

See also LAW; COVENANT; NEW COVENANT; SHEMA [JS]

Offering. A ritualized act of giving to God motivated by the anticipation of reciprocal receiving. Every ritual sacrifice, therefore, is an offering. The basic sacrificial laws in Leviticus 1–7 distinguish between five different rituals (the following list includes variations of English translations): burnt offering (Lev. 1); cereal/grain offering (Lev. 2); peace/fellowship/communion/well-being offering (Lev. 3); sin/purification offering (Lev. 4.1–5.13), and guilt/reparation offering (Lev. 5.14–6.7 ET; 7.1-7). During these five rituals, burning the entire sacrifice (Lev. 1.9, 13, 17) or certain parts of it (Lev. 2.2, 9; 3.5, 11; 4.8-10, 19-20) on the 'altar of burnt offering' effects a 'pleasing odor' for God. The offerings made by humans are thus transformed and transported to God in the smoke rising to heaven. These dynamics toward God are captured by the comprehensive Hebrew term for offering, *qorban*, which means literally 'brought near (to God)'. The term *qorban* is applied to all five types of offering (Lev. 1.2, 3, 10; 2.1, 4; 3.1; 4.23, 28, 32; 5.11; 7.38). In contrast, rituals lacking the burning rite on the main altar did not count as *qorban*. Therefore the Passover (Exod. 12.1-28), an apotropaic ritual, or the scapegoat (Lev. 16.10, 20-22), an elimination ritual, were not considered as sacrifice or offering.

A term that is older than *qorban* but appears as its equivalent is the Hebrew term *minhah* (Gen. 4.3-5; Num. 16.15; 1 Sam. 2.17). It can also mean 'tribute' paid in homage of a superior party, or 'present' (Gen. 32.20 ET; 43.11-15; 2 Kgs 20.12). In cult contexts, it specifically conveys that humans owe God the sacrifice and implies the status difference between humans and God. Yet in general the motivation for offering sacrifices may vary between veneration, anticipation of divine blessings, or solicitation of God's forgiveness (atonement). Further comprehensive terms for sacrificial offerings are 'fire offering(s)' (Exod. 30.20; Lev. 22.22, 27; Num. 28.3, 19) and 'food' (Num. 28.2, 24).

The term 'offering' is equivalent to 'oblation' which is derived from the same Latin root, *offerre*. The modern English language is somewhat misleading when it comes to the precise understanding of sacrifice and offering. On the one hand, a distinction is suggested: according to general parlance and certain scholarly definitions, a sacrifice is any offering that involves some form of killing. An offering therefore consists of a nonliving object in contrast to an animal sacrifice. On the other hand, this distinction is denied when, according to common parlance, a sacrifice is 'offered'. Only this second understanding suits the HB texts in which the Hebrew terms for offering, *qorban* or *minhah*, function as comprehensive categories that comprise different types of sacrifice regardless of whether an animal or cereal is being offered.

In western churches, the term offering is frequently used for the collection of money and donations during Sunday worship. The custom of bringing the collection to, and even placing it upon the altar in order to dedicate it to the church, clearly continues the practice of sacrificial offerings as described in the HB. In the east, the Chaldean and Syriac Christian churches call the Eucharistic liturgy *Qurbanah Qadishah* ('holy offering').

Recommended reading. Eberhart, Christian A. 'A Neglected Feature of Sacrifice in the Hebrew Bible'. *Harvard Theological Review* 97 (2004) 485-93. ———. *Studien zur Bedeutung der Opfer im Alten Testament*. WMANT, 94. Neukirchen–Vluyn: Neukirchener Verlag, 2002. Marx, Alfred. 'The Theology of the Sacrifice according to Leviticus 1–7'. *The Book of Leviticus*. Ed. R.A. Kugler and R. Rendtorff. Pp. 103-20. Leiden/Boston: Brill, 2003.

See also ALTAR; ATONEMENT; FIRE; SACRIFICE

[CAE]

Og of Bashan. Hebrew *'og* is perhaps related to South Semitic *ġwg* ('man', 'man of valor'), although the etymology is uncertain. Bashan (Hauran) is located in the northern Transjordan, extending from Mount Hermon in the north to the Yarmuk River in the south. The area is renowned in biblical texts for its fertile volcanic soil, tall forests, and well-fed cattle (Ezek. 39.18; Amos 4.1).

In the biblical accounts of the Israelite conquest, Og is king of Bashan, and reigns in the twin capital cities of Ashtaroth and Edrei (Josh. 12.4; 13.12). He is identified as the last survivor of the *Rephaim* (Deut. 3.11; Josh. 12.4; 13.12), a legendary race of ancient giants and warriors (Deut. 2.20-21). A remarkably similar description appears in an Ugaritic text from c. 1200 BCE that refers to a legendary king who reigns in these same two cities, and who is also identified as one of the *Rāpi'ūma*—a term broadly equivalent to the Hebrew *Repha'im*. Og's prodigious stature is further emphasized by the account of his giant bed (or perhaps his sarcophagus, depending on one's interpretation of Deut. 3.11), measuring an imposing 9 x 4 cubits (13.5 x 6 feet). Israel's victory over Og is frequently paired with her victory over King Sihon as the two major victories in Israel's Transjordan campaign (e.g., Josh. 2.10; Ps. 135.11). The portrayal of Israel's subjugation of even the legendary might of Og provides a theological argument for the superiority of Israel's God (Num. 21.33-35; Deut. 3.1-13).

Rabbinic literature reconciles the death of the giants in the flood (Gen. 6.4-5) with the later appearance of the giant Og at the Israelite conquest in different ways, ranging from the explanation that Og had clung onto the roof of Noah's ark throughout the duration of the flood (*Genesis Rabbah* 31.13) to the explanation that Og was so tall the flood waters only came up to his ankles (*Midrash Petirat Mosheh* 1.128). Og is confused with Gog in several Greek manuscripts of the Bible, including *Codex Vaticanus* (Deut. 3.1, 13; 4.47). This confusion leads to Gog (or 'Gogmagog') also being identified as a giant in medieval works such as Geoffrey of Monmouth's *History of the Kings of Britain* (c. 1136). A 5000-year-old monolithic structure in Hauran (SW Syria), the *Rujm-el-Hiri* circle, is colloquially known today as 'Og's circle'.

In John Dryden's satire, *Absalom and Achitophel* (1681), his rotund literary opponent Thomas Shadwell is parodied as Og, exploiting the reputation of giants as large, foolish, and immoral. 'For ev'ry inch that is not Fool is Rogue. A Monstrous mass of foul corrupted matter'. The caricature of giants as vain and power-hungry is likewise exploited in Herman Melville's poem *Bridegroom Dick* (1876), where the 'giant' Captain Turret is described as 'A reeling King Ogg, delirious in power'. In *The Mill on the Floss* (1860), George Eliot reverses such popular caricatures of giants, by adapting the Christian legend of the giant St Christopher who compassionately carried Christ across a river, ascribing similar actions to 'St Ogg'. Eliot's adapted legend is a microcosm of the themes of compassion and this-worldliness which are developed in the novel. In the *Harry Potter* novels (1997–2007) by J.K. Rowling, Hagrid the half-giant's predecessor at Hogwarts is named Ogg, while his giant pet spider is named Aragog (a conflation of the Latin term for spider, *aranea*, with Gog).

Recommended reading. Noegel, Scott. 'The Aegean Ogygos of Boeotia and the Biblical Og of Bashan: Reflections of the Same Myth'. *Zeitschrift für die alttestamentliche Wissenschaft* 110 (1998) 411-26

See also FLOOD; GIANTS; GOG AND MAGOG [DG]

Oholah and Oholibah. Also spelled Aholah and Aholibah, the names are derived from the Hebrew *ohel* ('tent'), signifying God's presence. Ezekiel 23.1-48 contains an allegory of two sisters, named Oholah and Oholibah, identified in the texts as Samaria (the northern kingdom of Israel) and Judah (v. 4), presented as the wives of Yahweh. They both commit adultery against their divine husband in Egypt. Oholah's lovers are the Assyrians, who ravish and disgrace her, symbolizing the Assyrian defeat of Israel in 721 BCE. Nonetheless, Oholibah lusts after her lovers the Chaldeans, who defile the second sister, symbolizing the Babylonian defeat of

Judah in 586 BCE. The message of the prophetic oracle is that as their divine husband forsook Oholah and Oholibah for their adultery, God has forsaken Israel and Judah on account of their idolatry. The devastation of the two kingdoms is the penalty for their unfaithfulness to God (v. 48).

Despite the transparent symbolism of the prophetic text, Christian interpreters have further allegorized the parable, e.g., Gregory the Great (sixth century), who interpreted the sisters' Egyptian whoredoms as a symbol of succumbing to carnal desire; John Milton interpreted them in terms of 'the Jews', who whored 'after the heathens' inventions', a thinly veiled reference to Roman pomp and display (*Apology for Smectymnuus*). The heroine of Thomas Hardy's *Tess of the D'Urbervilles* views her rape as worthy of punishment in the light of the biblical tale of the two sisters.

See also ADULTERY; EZEKIEL; IDOLATRY   [MALB]

Oil. Oil was an essential part of life in the ancient world, used for food, toiletries, cleanliness, adornment, medicine, and ceremonies and rituals. In the Bible, oil (Hebrew *shemen*, Greek *ĕlaiōn*) featured prominently in the civic, medicinal, and religious lives of Jews and Christians. Of utmost importance were oils made from the fruit of the olive tree and sap from the myrrh tree.

Olive oil was the most commonly used oil in the ancient world. Once ripe olives were collected from trees, people used their feet, stone and mortar, or oil presses to separate the oil from the fruit. They stored the oil in stone or clay jars; olive oil keeps for a long time, and was considered such a valuable commodity that it was used in trade. Oil was an important part of food preparation. People used oil to anoint their bodies, to bring moisture to dry flesh. In Ps. 23.5, the psalmist proclaimed the goodness of God: 'thou anointest my head with oil'. Exodus 30.23-24 describes the preparation of holy oil to anoint priests as well as the altar; the oil combined myrrh, olive oil, and other spices. Exodus 27.20 indicates that lamps used to illuminate the altar in the tabernacle were fueled by oil. Olive oil, myrrh and oil of hyssop were ingredients used in Hebrew medicine. Olive oil was useful for sore throat, and as a comforting salve for wounds. In general, oil was used as an antiseptic, astringent and anti-inflammatory.

In the NT, the use of oil was part of the ministry of Jesus and his disciples. Mark 6.13 describes how Jesus ordered his disciples to go out among the people, casting out demons and healing people by anointing them with oil. Luke 7.46, indicates that anointing a guest with oil was an act of hospitality. A well-known description of the use of oil comes from Luke 10.34, in which Jesus tells the story of the good Samaritan, who stopped to help an injured man by the side of the road, ministering to his needs by pouring oil and wine on his wounds and bandaging them. Oil of myrrh was used to prepare bodies for burial. John 19.39 describes how after Jesus was crucified, Nicodemus brought 'a hundred pounds' weight' of 'a mixture of myrrh and aloes' with which to anoint his body.

In subsequent centuries, oil continued to play a role in the sacraments of the Christian church. For centuries the newly baptized and confirmed have been anointed with chrism, holy oil. Priests also anoint the sick and dying in services of healing and Holy Unction. Anointing with oil among Christians has been and continues to be symbolic of anointing with the Holy Spirit.

See also ANOINT; BALM OF GILEAD; OLIVE, OLIVE BRANCH   [RL]

Old men shall dream dreams. In the book of Joel, which is in the second division of the biblical Hebrew canon (*Nevi'im*) and the Minor Prophets portion of the Christian OT, the author interprets a devastating plague of locusts ravaging the land of Judah as the judgment of God. The second portion of the book, however, depicts the restoration of God's people (2.18–3.21). In 2.28 the author states, 'Then afterward I will pour out my spirit on all flesh; your sons and your daughters shall prophesy, your old men shall dream dreams, and your young men shall see visions'. The writer does not explicitly reveal the content of these dreams, but implies that the dreams and visions will bring unity to God's people by including both old men and young men, and that these dreams will involve some level of personal interaction between God and humanity, compared to the distance between God and humanity experienced during the perceived judgment. The writer perhaps envisions a time in which the people of God are closely attuned to God's will, receiving direct inspiration from dreams and visions.

In the NT, this phrase is quoted by Peter in Acts 2.17. While many Jews had gathered in Jerusalem to celebrate the feast of Pentecost, the writer describes the descent of the Holy Spirit upon the followers of Jesus. As many of them begin speaking foreign languages, the crowd is amazed and demands an explanation. Peter offers an interpretation of Joel 2.28, stating that this is the event of which Joel spoke, and that the death and resurrection of Jesus has inaugurated these phenomena. Peter uses this to convert many of the Jewish witnesses to faith in Jesus as the Messiah.

This phrase is often used to justify the experience of visions and dreams in modern contexts. The main goal of such proponents is usually to encourage those who experience dreams and visions to strengthen their personal faith and seek out application and interpretation of the events they contain. Whether or not these dreams are experienced in a Christian worldview, the general goal of bettering oneself or the world by applying the dreams' lessons is common.

Kansas native Esther Hill appropriated this phrase into the title of her poem, 'And Your Old Men Shall Dream Dreams', which speaks of elderly men dozing by a fire and remembering more exciting days in their dreams. Hill interprets this phrase as a general promise of peace and rest in old age rather than conveying closeness to God. In John Dryden's satirical poem 'Absalom and Achitophel', King David's advisor Achitophel anachronistically applies the words of Joel to Absalom in order to convince him to rebel against his father, stating that for the nation he is 'The young men's vision, and the old men's dream'. Washington Irving describes the effects of lingering in a legendary valley in *The Legend of Sleepy Hollow* as bewitching, causing people 'to dream dreams and see apparitions'. In contemporary culture, the dreams referred to by the use of this phrase may focus on the desire for personal wealth or success, or opportunities for such gains that have been lost in the past.

See also DREAMS; JOEL, BOOK OF; PENTECOST; PROPHECY [CEM]

Old Testament. The Old Testament (OT; also known as the Hebrew Bible, the Jewish Bible, or the First Testament) forms the first of two parts of the Christian Bible (for Jews, it is the complete Bible, called the Tanak). Christians refer to it as the 'Old' Testament to distinguish it from the 'New' covenant/testament promised by the prophets and instituted by Jesus (Luke 22.20). The Protestant OT contains 39 books (Roman Catholic: 46; Orthodox: 46+) and is comprised of several literary genres including prophecy, law, history, and wisdom. Written originally in Hebrew (for the most part), the OT was translated into Greek and later into many other languages, including early Anglo–Saxon in the tenth century CE.

Genesis, the first book of the OT, explains the origin of the universe, including animals and the human race. The laws of God are given within the first five books, called the 'Law', 'Torah', or the 'Pentateuch'. OT books including Joshua, Judges, and 1 and 2 Samuel contain stories of conquest, failure, and bravery. The book of Job offers encouragement during suffering. The Psalms and Proverbs provide devotional material for readers. The prophets give both a history of God's dealings with humanity and a preview of things to come, including the appearance of the messiah.

Many governments throughout the world have made use of the OT laws in their constitutions. Cities of refuge mentioned in the OT have also been utilized within western judicial systems whereby criminals may receive a lesser penalty for an accidental killing ('manslaughter'). Since Genesis explains that humanity is an image–bearer of God, philosophers and politicians alike have encouraged the dignity and protection of human life.

The arts show tremendous influence from the OT. Michelangelo's Sistine Chapel paintings contain numerous scenes from the OT. He also created the famous sculpture of King David. Films revealing OT influence include *The Ten Commandments* (Cecil B. DeMille, 1956), *Noah's Ark* (John Irvin, 1999), and *Esther* (Raffaele Mertes, 1999). Perhaps the most famous is *Raiders of the Lost Ark* (Steven Spielberg, 1981), featuring the ark of the covenant mentioned so often in the Torah. Modern songs borrowing from the OT include words from the psalms, prophecies, and spirituals. For instance, the pathos of the exodus of the Jews from slavery (Exodus) has been the subject of African–American gospel songs. These songs are applied to the plight of slaves in the western world.

Sectarian groups also find affinities or roots in the OT. The Rastafarians incorporate OT themes including Zion, the twelve tribes, and Babylon. Additionally, Judaism, Christianity and Islam trace their beginnings to the patriarch Abraham of Genesis. Furthermore, the Genesis narrative of Sodom and Gomorrah finds its way into contemporary discussions about homosexuality while that of David and Goliath finds its way into modern parlance when one is referring to someone larger bullying someone much smaller.

Archaeology takes great interest in the OT. The archaeologist's spade has unearthed the cities of Hazor, Jericho, Megiddo, Capernaum, and parts of Jerusalem. The city of Jerusalem that so often figures in the news, has from OT times been embroiled in controversy between the descendants of ancient Near Eastern peoples.

The OT influences those nations that provide hospitals, orphanages, soup kitchens, and other ministries. Additionally, many religious people through the centuries have found their solace in the OT. The OT most certainly will continue to be the subject of films, paintings, and historical investigations for years to come.

See also APOCRYPHA; BIBLICAL ARCHAEOLOGY; CITIES OF REFUGE; DEUTEROCANONICALS; INTERTESTAMENTALS; BIBLE; OLD TESTAMENT, USE IN THE NEW TESTAMENT; NEW TESTAMENT; SEPTUAGINT [MBW]

Old Testament, Use in the New Testament. That the Bible is referred to in the singular, as in the 'Good Book', belies the fact that it is composed of two major and very different parts: the 'Old' and 'New' Testaments. The question of their relationship is multifaceted and cannot be sufficiently comprehended by a temporal approach that sees the NT as the sequel, so to speak, of the OT. Indeed, though there have been Christian persons and groups throughout history that have fully rejected the OT as Christian scripture (such as the second–century writer Marcion), the NT itself presupposes the stories and history of the OT, and the two were canonized together as a double witness to the message of the gospel.

The NT writers, most of whom were Jews, made use of the OT in a number of ways. At the most basic level, the idiom of the NT is scriptural. Indeed, these writers' minds were so soaked in scripture (and especially the LXX) that it became the master–fund of word–pictures and the origin for the construct of their symbolic universe. This can also be expressed narratologically, for the 'story' of Jesus and the Christian church, which is 'told' in the NT presupposed and proceeded from the OT as its final and climactic sequences (see Acts 7). Related to the narrative dynamics of the Bible is the manner in which the NT depicts the messianic advent, death and resurrection of Jesus (the Messiah) as the 'fulfillment' of what was prophesied in the OT (e.g., Matt. 26.54–56). This can also be seen in the typological comparison made in the NT where certain patterns are not just repeated, but intensified and perfected such as Christ's appearance as the 'last Adam' (1 Cor. 15.45) or the recurring theme of a 'new creation' (2 Cor. 5.17).

The apparent continuity between the OT and NT should not obscure the fact that the Christ–event took most Jews by surprise as an act of God where he apocalyptically rent the heavens and sent his son to redeem the world and end the sinful plight of Israel and humanity. Thus, the cataclysmic actions of Christ became not just a sequential completion of the OT story, but also a hermeneutical key to re–read the chronicle of the history of fall and redemption, exile and restoration.

How western society has been impacted by a Christian reading of the OT is a question that can be dealt with in a number of ways. For instance, it is quite well known that the Ten Commandments undergird American civil law and it was the Christian founding fathers that built Jewish morality into the substructure of their legislature. However, on the level of law and punishment, it is also Christian advocacy groups that have been the most strongly opposed to the death penalty—a punishment advocated in the OT. Some Christian opponents of capital punishment read Jesus' command to 'turn the other cheek' (Matt. 5.39) as more normative. This modern tension in the relationship between the Testaments demonstrates their fundamental connectedness in Christian theology, but also the enigmatic complexity inherent in their union in the Christian Bible.

Recommended reading. Carson, D.A., and H.G.M. Williamson (eds.). *It is Written: Scripture Citing Scripture*. Cambridge: Cambridge University Press, 1988. Moyise, S. *The Old Testament in the New*. London: T. & T. Clark, 2001

See also ALLEGORY; HERMENEUTICS; NEW TESTAMENT; OLD TESTAMENT; QUR'AN, THE BIBLE IN THE; TYPOLOGY [NKG]

Olive, olive branch. There are 37 references to olives, olive trees, olive yards and olive branches (and the Mount of Olives) in the Bible, from the first mention in Genesis (8.11) through to the Apocalypse (Rev. 11.4; 18.13). Olive oil was used in cooking and for medicinal purposes, and the olive branch became seen as a peaceful gesture—indeed that is the allusion in Gen. 8.11, where a dove brings an olive branch to Noah, signifying the end of the flood. There is also a view that children were similar to olive branches (Ps. 128.3), quoted in the *Book of Common Prayer*: 'children like the olive–branches about thy table' (78.3 KJV).

In Greek mythology, the staff of Hermes, the messenger of the gods, was made from an olive tree, with two shoots forming the caduceus, the symbol for medicine, although the medical profession today uses the staff of Asclepius the Healer with a serpent entwined around the olive branch. The Greeks also had a ceremony for Apollo Ismenius with a boy representing the god, and another preceding him waving an olive branch. The Roman goddess Concordia who sought to restore peace (or 'Concord') between people, especially different classes in Roman society, is often pictured carrying an olive branch. Mention should also be made of the Roman writer Pliny who noted 'there are two liquids that are agreeable to the human body: inwardly wine, outwardly oil, both coming from trees, but oil the more necessary'.

The term 'Olive Branch' also had other uses. A British ship called *Olive Branch* sank off the coast of Panama in 1699. In the nineteenth century, a Boston literary magazine called the *Boston Olive Branch* which published the first poem by Elizabeth Allen, then aged fifteen, in 1851; and the first woman newspaper columnist in the United States, Sara Payson Willis Parton, often used the pen–name 'Olive Branch'.

In the twentieth century, the olive branch continued to be recognized as a symbol of peace. In 1936 the Greek runner Louis Spyridon (1873–1940) offered Adolf Hitler an olive branch at the start of the Berlin Olympics. Eleven years later, the United Nations flag was adopted showing the world surrounded by a wreath of olive branches.

Recommended reading. St Barbe Baker, Richard. *Famous Trees of Bible Lands*. London: H.H. Greaves, 1974

See also GREAT PHYSICIAN; OIL; OLIVES, MOUNT OF; PLANTS, SYMBOLISM OF; TREE [JC]

Olivet Discourse. Jesus' discourse recorded in Matt. 24.1-36, Mark 13.1-37 and Luke 21.5-36 is often also called the Apocalyptic or Eschatological Discourse. It was delivered on the Mount of Olives east of Jerusalem, opposite the ancient temple of Jerusalem. The place is also eschatologically significant in OT writings (Ezek. 11.23; 43.2-7; Zech. 14.1-9).

The episode begins with Jesus' prediction of the destruction of the temple and the disciples' questions about when this will happen, what will be the presiding sign of the event (Mark, Luke), and what will be the sign of Jesus' second coming (Matthew). The question is followed by Jesus' lengthy response.

The authenticity and interpretation of the Discourse is disputed. Some reject its authenticity altogether arguing that it is a Jewish or Jewish-Christian apocalypse assigned to Jesus, while most believe it is at least a partly authentic speech of the historical Jesus. The following four examples give a glimpse of the diversity of interpretation of the prophecy:

(1) Brant Pitre (2005) argues that the prophecy has two eschatological stages: the tribulation described in Mark 13.5-13 and the great tribulation in vv. 14-27. The tribulation begins with the death of John the Baptist, and the great tribulation begins at the eve of the destruction of Jerusalem and its temple. Jesus assumes that his second coming will happen soon after the destruction of the temple and terminate the great tribulation. In his coming, the lost ten tribes of Israel will be gathered back to Israel from exile. According to Pitre, the latter part of the prophecy failed.

(2) N.T. Wright (1992) interprets the coming of the son of man in Mark 13 metaphorically. Jesus was vindicated as a true prophet when his prophecy of the destruction of the temple was fulfilled.

(3) Traditional dispensationalist interpreters argue that Mark 13.5-27 refers to the last seven-year period preceding the coming of the son of man (Dan. 9.27), when the temple will be rebuilt and defiled. The text is divided in the following way: vv. 5-13 refer to the first half of the seven years, vv. 14-17 the middle of the period, vv. 18-23 refer to the second half of the seven years, also called the great tribulation, and vv. 24-27 speak of the coming of the son of man.

(4) Many interpreters maintain that Mark 13 describes two distinct but similar periods of great distress: the period preceding the destruction of the temple and the period preceding the coming of the son of man at the end. According to M.J. Lagrange (1906), vv. 6-18, 28-31 refer to the first period, and vv. 19-27, 32-37 to the second.

The destruction of Jerusalem and its temple in 70 CE are depicted by Josephus (*Jewish War*) and Sulpcius Severus (*Chronicle* 30). The Romans erected the Arch of Titus to commemorate it. The event has inspired many painters, including N. Poussin (1637), W. von Kaulbach (1846), D. Roberts (1850), and F. Hayez (1867).

Apocalyptism has fascinated Judeo-Christian culture, especially after World War II. A growing number of books (e.g., the *Left Behind* series), movies (e.g., *Independence Day*, *Armageddon*, the *Matrix* series, *2012*), and even video games dealing with the topic (e.g., the *Fallout* series, *The Secret World*) have entered the market.

Recommended reading. Adams, Edward. *The Stars Will Fall From Heaven: Cosmic Catastrophe in the New Testament and its World*. New York. T. & T. Clark, 2007.

Walliss, John, and Kenneth G.C. Newport (eds.). *The End All around Us: Apocalyptic Texts and Popular Culture*. London: Equinox, 2009.

See also APOCALYPSE; APOCALYPTIC; TEMPLE, ISRAEL'S [KT]

Omri. Omri was a significant historical figure but a relatively minor biblical character. He founded the first dynasty of the Northern Kingdom of Israel and moved its capital from Tirzah to Samaria, which he purchased to be his own personal property thus alleviating any tribal claims to the capital. In the OT he is only allotted ten verses (1 Kgs 16.16-17, 21-29) and he is pronounced to be worse than all the kings to came before him. However, from the archaeological data that remains it is known that Omri was a great diplomat and builder and that the nation of Israel was known in other nations as 'the House of Omri' until it was destroyed by the Assyrians. Even the biblical text leaves a small clue that Omri was considered a great king when it tells the reader that they can look in the Book of the Annals of the Kings of Israel in order to learn about 'the power he showed' (1 Kgs 16.27). This also explains the difference between the account in the Deuteronomistic History and the archaeological record. The author of Kings had particular theological point to make through the use of historical material, but his purpose was not to present a detailed history as a mere record of events; therefore many details about the life of Omri, particularly his successes, are omitted from this narrative.

In 2005, a group of rabbis published a list of names that should be banned from Jewish families and Omri topped the list. The rabbis even encouraged parents who had named their children Omri to change their names. The idea is that Omri was an evil king and using his name would open the children up to sharing in his evil and being associated with the king.

See also AHAB; KINGS, BOOK OF; JEHU [EW]

Onan, onanism. Onan was the second son of Judah and Bath-shua. He is briefly mentioned in three OT genealogies (Gen. 46.12; Num. 26.19; 1 Chron. 2.3), but most of our information about him comes from Gen. 38.1-10. There we read that God killed Onan's older brother Er before he was able to impregnate his wife, Tamar. Judah, the father of Er and Onan, then instructed Onan to take Tamar as a wife and 'perform the duty of a brother-in-law to her, and raise up off-spring for your brother' (38.8). This is a reference to the practice of Levirate marriage, which calls on a brother to impregnate his widowed sister-in-law and to raise the child in the name of his dead brother (Deut. 25.5-10). Onan did not want to give offspring to Er, perhaps so there would not be another male heir with whom he would need to share his inheritance. To avoid this, he 'spilled his semen on the ground' during intercourse with Tamar (38.9), most likely a reference to *coitus interruptus*. This displeased God, who killed him. The refusal of Onan to provide an heir for his brother and his ensuing death is a pivotal point in the Genesis narrative as it sets the stage for the Judah–Tamar incident.

Many modern scholars believe that Onan's offense in Genesis 38 was his selfish refusal to provide his brother with an heir and his sexual exploitation of Tamar, not the act of spilling semen itself. However, Christian interpreters since antiquity have drawn from this story broader principles regarding human sexuality. Augustine considered Onan an example of the sinfulness of engaging in any non-procreative sexual behavior, an opinion many have repeated throughout Christian history. The modern anti-masturbation movements that began in the late seventeenth and early eighteenth century used the story of Onan to support their arguments about the religious and medical hazards of masturbating. The strong connection between the figure of Onan and discussions of masturbation and contraceptive sexual practices led to the use of the term 'onanism' to describe masturbation and *coitus interruptus*.

Jewish interpreters of the Bible have also used the Onan story to condemn a variety of sexual practices, but they have generally been more cautious than Christian interpreters when it comes to drawing universal sexual principles from the Onan incident. The early rabbis disagreed over the exact nature of Onan's sexual act, with some reading it as *coitus interruptus*, others as masturbation, and still others as some form of 'unnatural' sex.

Brief allusions to Onan appear throughout modern English literature. A particularly interesting example is found in the chapter 'Unsummoned Guests' in Izaak Mansk's *Emil Brut*, where the story of Onan is retold using sacrificial imagery.

Recommended reading. Feldman, David. *Birth Control in Jewish Law*. New York: New York University Press, 1968.

See also GENESIS; JUDAH; TAMAR; LEVIRATE MARRIAGE [JRH]

Onesimus (see Philemon).

One thing is needful (see Mary and Martha of Bethany).

Ophir. A port mentioned in the OT, from which King Solomon is said to have taken delivery of 420 talents of gold (1 Kgs 9.28), 450 talents of gold (2 Chron. 8.18), and later algum wood (2 Chron. 9.10). It was also a source of silver, precious stones, ivory, apes and peacocks, the journeys being made every three years. Ophir is mentioned in Gen. 10.29 as one of the nations from where the people were descended from the sons of Joktan. Obviously Ophir was a center of great wealth, and trade was presumably through the Red Sea, the equivalent of land of Punt for the Egyptians.

There has been some debate over the exact location of the place described as Ophir. It is believed to be in south Sinai, but Tomé Lopes, a companion of Vasco da Gama (ca.1460–1524), believed that it might have some connection with the land ruled by the Queen of Sheba. Ophir is mentioned by the English writer John Milton (1608–1674) in *Paradise Lost* (11.99-401), and by John Masefield (1878–1967) in *Cargoes* (1934) mentions 'distant Ophir'. During the 1970s, an Israeli settlement in Sinai was called Ophira, but it was evacuated in 1982 under the terms of the Israeli–Egyptian Peace Treaty.

Subsequently, some people felt that Ophir might have been much further from the Holy Land. The German Orientalist Max Müller (1823–1900) identified Ophir as the settlement called Abhira which was located near the mouth of the Indus River. The Norwegian adventurer Thor Heyerdahl (1914–2002) managed to show that a voyage of this distance was possible in his Tigris expedition (1979)—Masefield, after all did cite the journey to Ophir as being from Nineveh along the River Tigris.

There are different theories about Ophir, with some suggesting that it might be much further away, possibly in Asia, and David Hatcher Childress (b. 1957) has even argued that it could have been located in Australia, with the sandalwood and peacocks collected by the traders on their journeys to the Red Sea from Ophir.

The port of Ophir appears in many novels, the most famous of which, *King Solomon's Mines* (1885) by H. Rider Haggard locates it in southern Africa; some of the Tarzan novels by Edgar Rice Burroughs feature a lost city called Opar in the African jungles(*The Return of Tarzan* [1913], *Tarzan and the Jewels of Opar* [1916], *Tarzan and the Golden Lion* [1923], and *Tarzan the Invincible* [1930]). The story was taken up by science fiction writer Philip José Farmer in his *Hadon of Ancient Opar* (1974) and *Flight to Opar* (1976). The African theme was continued by the South African writer Wilbur Smith (b. 1933) in *The Sunbird* (1972). Robert Howard (1906–1936) mentions a kingdom called Ophir in *Conan the Barbarian* (1932).

See also GOLD; QUEEN OF SHEBA; SOLOMON   [JC]

Original sin (see Sin).

Orphan (see Widows and Orphans).

Our daily bread (see Lord's Prayer).

P

Pagan. Pagans in the Bible are portrayed as Gentiles or non-Christians who were polytheistic idolaters practicing unclean, immoral habits and rituals. The literal term 'pagan' (Latin: *paganus*, 'rustic') is not found in the Bible, although the English word is used in some translations (e.g., Lev. 25.44; 1 Cor. 12.2, NASV). Rather, OT Hebrew and NT Greek used terms such as foreigners, foreign nations, heathens, idolaters, Gentiles, and the unclean to refer to what came to connote the pagan.

In the OT, the monotheistic Israelites were in constant confrontation with polytheistic peoples, many of whom worshiped a pantheon of nature deities, the most important of which, at least among Canaanite peoples, was Baal, the god of storms. The children of Israel under Moses committed apostasy against Yahweh by worshiping the gods of foreign nations (Num. 25). After the establishment of the kingdoms of Judah and Israel, Manasseh, king of Judah, introduced the worship of the Canaanite mother goddess Asherah and practiced soothsaying, child sacrifice, and other idolatrous practices (2 Kgs 21). The prophet Isaiah (ch. 2) condemned the 'house of Jacob' for embracing divination, soothsaying, and other ways of foreigners. The author of Lamentations bewailed the fact that heathen nations had occupied Jerusalem. Amos (7.17) referred to the lands of Gentiles as 'unclean'. Zephaniah proclaimed that God would destroy Jerusalem for embracing the worship of Baal and allowing 'idolatrous priests' such sway in the city. Clearly, Gentile pagans had no place in the monotheistic worship of Yahweh.

The writers of the NT, the gospels as well as the letters, continued the condemnation of pagan practices of polytheism and immorality. The Greek word for Gentiles and nations, in Matthew and Luke, are *ethnikoi* and *ethnē*. Jesus told his disciples at the end of the Sermon on the Mount (Matthew 5) that they must not only love their neighbors but their enemies as well, to separate themselves from the Gentiles, who at the very least love their neighbors. Moreover, his followers must not worry about the material conditions of life, which are the concerns of the Gentiles (6.32). Paul's letters condemned the ways of Gentiles, who practice fornication and commit many pagan practices such as sacrifice to idols, and railed against Christians, like those at Corinth, who embraced such ways (1 Cor. 5.1; 10.7, 20; 12.2). Paul, the great missionary to the Gentiles, waged a constant battle against his followers returning to the old ways of reliance upon the Greco-Roman nature deities who demanded little of their worshipers save animal sacrifice.

Paganism as a way of life and belief system has persisted throughout time in human society, and can refer to any polytheistic or pantheistic belief system. Neopaganism is a modern belief system in which devotees practice their beliefs of pantheism and animism in a variety of countries throughout the world.

See also ASHERAH; BAAL; GENTILE; IDOLS/IDOLATRY [RL]

Palestine. The term Palestine designates the land occupied by the Philistines, derived from Philistia. In the KVJ, the Song of Moses refers to Palestine (Exod. 15.14); newer translations have Philistia (similarly Isa. 14.29, 31). The Romans designated southern Syria (which included much of the Holy Land) as Syria Palaestina. Indeed Syria Palaestina included Jerusalem, Gaza and Caesarea, going as far north as Tyrus (Tyre, in modern-day Lebanon). St Theodosius of Palestine, a proponent of orthodoxy against the Eutychian heresy (a variant of Monophysitism, the doctrine that Christ had only one, divine nature), died in 529 near Jerusalem, hence his title.

After the Arab capture of Jerusalem in 637, the term Palestine was no longer a political designation, but it continued to be used by many travelers to the region, and also by Christian pilgrims. Countless books had Palestine in their title, such as Rev. John Lamond, *Modern Palestine, or the need for a new crusade* (London 1896), A. Goodrich-Freer, *Things Seen in Palestine* (London, 1914), and Alfred Forder, *In and about Palestine* (London, 1919). In *Everyman's Atlas of Ancient and Classical Geography*, first published in 1907, the maps of the Holy Land are titled 'Palestine —Old Testament' and 'Palestine—New Testament'. The Palestine Exploration Fund was established in 1865 to help with archaeology in the Holy Land. During World War I, the British and Australian soldiers who fought in the region called it the Palestine Campaign, which was used as the title for the history by Colonel (later General) A.G. Wavell; the term 'Palestine' appears on war memorials throughout Britain and Australia.

After the end of World War I, with the defeat of the Ottoman Empire, the British Mandated territory was called Palestine, and the term Palestine appeared on postage stamps, banknotes and on the symbols of British rule such as the Palestine Police. During the 1930s, people from the Mandated territory, including Jews, competed as members of the Palestine team at Chess Olympiads and other international competitions. The British Mandate ended in 1948, and the State of Israel was proclaimed. Ongoing disputes between Israelis and Palestinians (Arabic-speaking people of Palestinian origin) ensued. The Palestine Liberation Organization was established in 1964, and the Palestinian Authority being established in 1995 as a non-contiguous territory covering parts of the West Bank and the Gaza Strip.

Recommended reading. Anati, Emmanuel. *Palestine before the Hebrews*. London: Jonathan Cape, 1963.

See also ISRAEL; PHILISTINES [JC]

Parable. Hebrew: *mashal* (be like); Greek: *parabolē* (comparison), interchangeable with other comparative speech forms, e.g., proverb, allegory; a short story confronting the listener with the question, 'what say you?' In stating judgment, listeners judge themselves. Parables contain characters (a certain man, a Pharisee), setting (a field, a vineyard), plot and action, making them less aphoristic and more like fable or allegory.

The best known OT parable, the Ewe Lamb (2 Sam. 12.1-4), illustrates how a parable operates. The prophet Nathan tells David of a rich man who, rather than slaughter his own sheep, takes the only lamb from a poor man to whom it was 'like a daughter'. The king's indignation at the injustice judges himself, and Nathan points out the parallel. David committed the selfsame sin in taking Uriah's wife Bathsheba for himself, then arranging Uriah's death in battle. Other OT parables include, e.g., the Tekoan woman (2 Sam. 14.4-8); the lost prisoner (1 Kgs 20.38-42); and the vineyard (Isa. 5.1-7; cf. Isa. 28.23-29; Eccl. 9.14-15; Jer. 18.1-10; 13.1-11). Most commentators list 39 NT parables, all of Jesus, referring to kingdom of God, the attributes of a good disciple (sometimes by contrast, e.g., the dishonest steward, Luke 16.1-8), and the eschaton. Jesus' imagery is unique: describing God as a housewife searching for a coin (Luke 15.8-10) or the kingdom as a mustard plant (Matt. 13.31-32; Mark 4.30-32; Luke 13.18-19).

In the Middle Ages, four parables figure popularly in art and mystery plays: Good Samaritan, Prodigal Son, Ten Virgins and Lazarus. This last was so popular that the rich man was named Dives. These parables were popular topics for Medieval and early Renaissance paintings. Rembrandt painted the Prodigal Son both in his prodigality and upon his return. The fourteenth-century English poem *Pearl* cites both the Pearl of Great Price and the parable of the Vineyard. Musical settings include the oratorio *The Prodigal Son* (1869), and hymns like 'Rejoice, Rejoice, Believers!', 'I've Found the Pearl of Greatest Price', and 'Mankind is Searching Every Day'. Lazarus figures in both an English folksong and American spiritual ('Poor Man Lazarus'). The Prodigal Son figures in many songs, from the repentant son in 'That Silver Haired Daddy of Mine', to the ironic inversion of 'A Boy Named Sue'.

Writers whose works are compared to parables include Chaucer, Blake, Dickens, Kafka, Kerouac, Flannery O'Connor, Salinger and Kierkegaard. Filmed parables or references to parables include D.W Griffith's *The Modern Prodigal* (1910), *David and Bathsheba* (1951), *The Prodigal Son* (1982), *King George and the Ducky* (2000), and *Modern Parables* (2008). Avant-garde filmmakers such as David Lynch, Spike Jonze and the Wachowski Brothers are said to make existential parables. Steinbeck's *The Pearl* (1947) and O'Dell's *The Black Pearl* (1967) recall the Pearl of Great Price.

Some parables have become figures of speech: a Good Samaritan is one who does a good deed without seeking reward; a Mustard Seed means something insignificant that grows great. Pearl of Great Price, Lamp under a Bushel, Sheep and Goats and Prodigal Son are instantly recognized. Good Samaritan laws protect people who help in emergencies; charity hospitals are sometimes named Good Samaritan. Self-help, financial and management books often use parable in the title, e.g., *As Many Miles to Go: A Modern Parable for Business* (2003) and *Miller's Bolt: A Modern Business Parable* (1997).

Recommended reading. Bailey, Kenneth E. *Jesus through Middle Eastern Eyes: Cultural Studies in the Gospels*. London: Intervarsity, 1988. Snodgrass, Klyne. *Stories with Intent: A Comprehensive Guide to the Parables of Jesus*. Grand Rapids, MI: Eerdmans, 1988.

See also GOOD SAMARITAN; PEARL OF GREAT PRICE; PRODIGAL SON; RICH MAN AND LAZARUS; TEN VIRGINS [STS]

Paraclete The word 'Paraclete' is a literal rendering of the Greek word *paraklētos*, found in the NT. Its main use is in John, where it is present only in the Farewell Discourse (13.31–16.33). Here, in Jesus' long concluding address to his disciples following the Last Supper and immediately before his arrest, he employs the term to describe the Holy Spirit. John speaks elsewhere of the Holy Spirit in his Gospel but nowhere else does he employ that title. There are four occasions that make reference to the Paraclete in the Farewell Discourse. In the first passage, Jesus speaks of the Spirit as 'another Paraclete', implying that he himself is the original Paraclete (John 14.16-17). Here the Paraclete represents the personal presence of Jesus for the believing community in Jesus' absence. This usage is echoed in 1 John, which identifies the Paraclete as 'Jesus Christ the righteous one' (1 John 2.1). The second occurrence in the Farewell Discourse sees the Paraclete as the teacher, reminding the community of Jesus' words and their meaning, and echoing Jesus' own role in the Gospel (14.26). In the third case, the Paraclete plays a forensic role, bearing witness to the Johannine Father and Son, uttering divine truth just as Jesus has (15.26-27). In the last passage, the Paraclete acts as judge, not only defending the disciples, but exposing their accusers and detractors (16.7-11). In each case, the Paraclete is sent from heaven to replace the absent Jesus, continuing his role and ministry in the world. The 'Paraclete' thus plays a particular and distinctive role in relation to the Johannine Jesus, as against the 'Holy Spirit' who has a wider function.

The unusual nature of the role of the Paraclete makes translation into English difficult. The NRSV uses 'Advocate' on the basis of the literal meaning of *paraklētos*, which suggests someone who is summoned to stand 'alongside' another in the role of defense or advocacy. Certainly this translation covers the forensic functions of the Farewell Discourse. The KJV has 'Comforter', while the NRV has 'Counsellor'. Interestingly, the NJB has chosen to stay with the English word 'Paraclete', along with a footnote to explain its diverse and complex meanings (the Latin translation of the Greek being *Paraclitus*).

Some early Christian movements identified the Paraclete as a specific person, such as Montanus in the second century or Mani in the third. These groups were later considered heretical by the Christian church. Some Islamic scholars have identified the Paraclete with the Prophet Muhammad himself. In mainstream Christian tradition, however, Paraclete is a reference to the divine Spirit and not identified with any particular individual, apart from Jesus himself. English hymns have occasionally used 'Paraclete', but 'Comforter' is more common in musical and liturgical usage.

See also HOLY SPIRIT [DL]

Paradise (see Garden of Eden).

PARDES. Spelled PaRDeS, this Hebrew acronym reminds a Jewish mind of the term PaRaDiSe. The majuscule letters represent each of four standard interpretive methods established by early rabbinic sages. According to Jewish tradition, 'Torah has seventy faces' (*Shev'im Panim leTorah*)—every scripture has seventy valid levels of interpretation. Jewish hermeneutics considers these four methods of exegesis to be essential to understand scripture.

Peshat ('simple') considers a basic level of understanding, otherwise expressed as a literal reading of the text. *Remez* ('hint') explores implied meaning within a given text. *Derash* ('search') is best understood in terms of application of a text: whether applied allegorically, homiletically, or typologically, the derived meaning of any text may depart from but not contradict its simple meaning. *Sod* ('hidden') seeks to perceive mystical, esoteric, or secretive meanings in texts. These four interpretive methods overlap with each other in that each one considers an extended meaning of the text in question.

A reading of the first word of the Torah (Gen. 1.1)—'In the beginning, God created the heavens and the earth'—illustrates this approach. *Peshat*: In the beginning of the creation of the heaven and the earth, the earth was without form and void. The first word, *bereishit*, literally means 'in the beginning of' and must apply to the following words in v. 2. *Remez*: All commands in the Torah are hinted at in the first word of the Torah. When the word '*bereishit*' is considered as an acronym, it can mean *ben rishon acharei shloshim yom tifdeh*—'the first-born you shall redeem after thirty days', thus alluding to the biblical principle of *Pidyon Haben* (redemption of the first-born). *Derash*: Jewish tradition teaches that both Torah and the Jewish people are considered *reishit* ('a beginning'); as such they are each considered first with respect to the centrality of the scriptures and the purpose of creation. *Sod*: In order for the Mishnah to be correct when it states that the world was created in ten utterances (*Pirke Avot* 5.1) when in fact we can only count nine statements in the Genesis account, the rabbis included the word *bereishit* to indicate the first statement of creation. In effect, it represents the creation of time, a central dimension of the physical world. Similarily, God as *HaMakom*, 'the Place', represents the very framework of reality as we know it ('in God we live and move and have our being'). Thus the dimension of

Time and Nature's laws came into being as part of the original plan of Creation.

One can read NT passages in a similar way, e.g., when considering the phrase 'son of God': *Peshat*: As Son of God, Jesus is God the Son (John 1.1 according to the Nicene Council); *Remez*: As Son of God, Jesus had no parents or genealogy—no beginning or end (Heb. 7.1, according to the *Gospel of Barnabas*); *Derash*: Accused of blasphemy for claiming to be Son of God, Jesus recalled Ps. 2.7 that identifies all humans as sons of God, an idea further advanced by Paul when combined with faith in Jesus as Son of God (Rom. 8.19; Gal. 3.6; see also Augustine's Commentary on Ps. 121); and *Sod*: While Jesus as Son of God, having no parents or genealogy, is an example of a mystical or esoteric application, an equally clear example is identification of the title Son of God with 'Messiah' in Christian apocryphal and pseudepigraphal literature (e.g., 4 *Esdras* 7.28, 29; 13.32, 37, 52; 14.9; *1 En.* 105.2) in which esoteric conflation of the two terms is established.

See also ALLEGORY; HERMENEUTICS; TYPOLOGY

[DM]

Parousia. (See Second Coming)

Passion Narrative. From the Latin *passio* and Greek *paschein*, both meaning 'to suffer'. The term refers to the period of Jesus' greatest suffering: from the Garden of Gethsemane until his death and burial by Joseph of Arimathea (Mark 14.32–15.47 and par.). It is difficult to overstate the centrality of these accounts to the Gospels, where the theology of each evangelist is quite evident; similarly, much NT epistolary literature functions as commentary on the significance of Jesus' death. It is therefore understandable that films such as *The Passion of the Christ* (2004) and *The Last Temptation of Christ* (1988) place a heavy emphasis on so brief a period of Jesus' life. The historical accuracy of these sections of the Gospels is a contentious matter due to the high incidence of OT fulfillment citations and references (e.g., Isa. 52.13–53.12; Zech. 11.13; Ps. 22).

The relationship between the passion narrative and Christian anti-Judaism is even more controversial. Though scholars generally doubt that the evangelists had such intentions (since the Gospel authors may well have been Jews themselves), their subsequent influence on Christianity in such a way is incontestable. Passion plays from medieval times until the mid-twentieth century are particularly notorious examples, though the charges of Jewish deicide in German political writings through the Third Reich proved most devastating in the utilization of the biblical story.

The passion narrative was not initially a widespread matter of visual depiction. The oldest surviving portrayals date to the fifth century, though the passion narrative achieved considerable popularity in Renaissance art. The themes developed in any depiction of Jesus' death were largely contingent upon the painter's location and time; for example, the use of emotion, suffering, and divine prowess deviate significantly between Masaccio's *Crucifixion* (1426), Perugino's *Crucifixion with Saints* (1481), and Mantegna's *Crucifix* (1456–1459), which are nonetheless representative of their respective regions of fifteenth-century Italy. The passion narrative's portrayal of unjust humiliation has particularly resonated with subaltern artists of the late twentieth century, variously portraying Jesus as a prototypical proletarian, African, Native American, etc.

It is in a similar regard that the passion narrative has borne its most pervasive influence on Western culture; that is, the construction of exemplary suffering. The Gospels portray Jesus' execution as an honorable death (cf. 2 Macc. 6–7; *4 Macc.* 7; Plato's *Phaedo*), which ultimately acquired an unparalleled role in literary and visual representations of physical anguish. The passion narrative continues to exert a major influence in literature through the commonplace of the Christ figure's benevolent and redemptive suffering on behalf of a community to which one does not belong.

Much foreign policy has also been framed around this concept of 'unique power exhibited through suffering and purity of motivation' that prevails in popular readings of Mark's Gospel. Unsuccessful or difficult military conflicts are frequently understood as the self-sacrificial suffering of an altruistic and chosen nation. Abraham Lincoln thus alluded to Matt. 26.39 in his second inaugural address (1865): 'Fondly do we hope, fervently do we pray, that this mighty scourge of war may speedily pass away. Yet, if God wills that it continue … so it must be'.

Recommended reading. Brown, Raymond E. *The Death of the Messiah: From Gethsemane to the Grave. A Commentary on the Passion Narrative in the Four Gospels.* New York: Doubleday, 1994. Crossan, John D. *Who Killed Jesus? Exposing the Roots of Anti-Semitism in the Gospel Story of the Death of Jesus.* San Francisco: HarperSanFrancisco, 1996

See also CALVARY; CHRIST FIGURE; CROSS; DOCETISM; GARDEN OF GETHSEMANE; GOLGOTHA; PONTIUS PILATE; SUFFERING SERVANT; TRIAL OF JESUS
[CBZ]

Passover. In Hebrew, *Pesach* (Greek, *Pascha*), one of the three pilgrimage festivals that Jews are commanded by Torah to celebrate annually (along with Sukkot and Shavuot) in Jerusalem, the biblical term applied to the liberation of the Hebrew people from Egyptian bondage (Exod. 12–13). According to Philip Sydney Bernstein (*What the Jews Believe*, 1951), it is the exodus (Greek, 'the way out') of the Israelites that sets Judaism apart from all other religions as a people and nation: 'Out of a mass of slaves, Moses fashioned a nation and gave them faith. From that day to this, Jews have never ceased to be a people'. Passover affirms the great truth that liberty is the inalienable right of every human being (see Morris Joseph, *Judaism as Creed and Life*, 1903).

In the NT, the Last Supper is portrayed as a Passover meal (Matt. 26.18-19; Mark 14.12-16; Luke 22.7-15). As a result, according to early Christian replacement theology, 'Today the sacred Passover is made manifest to us, the new and holy Passover, the mystic Passover, the Passover worthy of all honor, the Passover which is Christ the Redeemer, the spotless Passover, the mighty Passover, the Passover of the faithful, the Passover that opens unto us the gates of Paradise, the Passover that sanctifies all the faithful' (*Byzantine Pentekostarion*, 'Sticheron', at Matins, c. sixth–eighth century). For Christians, Christ has become the Passover Lamb that delivers the world from the bondage of sin (John 1.29, 36) — a holy drama commemorated at Easter.

For Judaism, Passover continues as a yearly celebration of the strong hand of God who delivered his chosen people, Israel, out of Egyptian servitude and guided them into a land of promise. As Jews throughout the world celebrate Pesach, their annual festive Seder meal acts out the drama of redemption that calls every Jew to confess 'God delivered me, not only them, but me'— thus appropriating the promises and blessings of the distant past in present time and space. In film, the Passover is famously depicted in DeMille's *The Ten Commandments* (1923, 1956) and, more recently, in Spielberg's *Prince of Egypt* (1998).

See also EASTER; EGYPT; EXODUS; LAMB; LAST SUPPER; TYPOLOGY [DM]

Pastoral Epistles. Within the Pauline corpus three letters, 1–2 Timothy and Titus, named after the letters' recipients (1 Tim. 1.2; 2 Tim. 1.2; Tit 1.4), are referred to as the 'Pastoral Epistles', based on their pastoral content. This designation dates as far back as the eighteenth century. Their status has varied throughout their history, mainly because their Pauline authorship is questioned. They are missing from the early papyrus manuscript P^{46}; Marcion does not include them in his canon. However, they do appear in the Muratorian Canon, and it is evident from the historical record that these letters were accepted as canonical as early as the second century. Early witnesses including Polycarp, Tertullian and Irenaeus quote from them as authoritative and accept them as Pauline. They bear Paul's name and share some stylistic characteristics with Paul's authentic letters.

1 Timothy and Titus deal primarily with the oversight of the Christian congregations; 2 Timothy deals chiefly with sound doctrine. 1 Timothy begins with an order for Timothy to remain in Ephesus and 'instruct certain people not to teach any different doctrine' (1.4). Next, the writer instructs Timothy on church conduct, prayer and worship (2.1-15), church leadership of bishops and deacons (3.1-13), and Timothy's responsibility in the church (3.14-16). Chapter 4 deals with apostasy and instruction on how to deal with it. The topics of ministering to widows (5.3-16), elders (5.17-25), and slaves (6.1-2) follow. The writer concludes with two primary exhortations to Timothy, to 'pursue righteousness, godliness, faith, love, endurance, gentleness' (6.11); and to the rich 'not to be haughty, or to set their hopes on the uncertainty of riches, but rather on God who richly provides us with everything for our enjoyment' (6.17).

Titus begins with a greeting and an address to Titus on the isle of Crete (1.1-4). The first item addressed is instructions on the qualifications for bishops (1.5-9) and how to deal with false teachers (1.10–2.1). The author moves to congregational supervision and its theological basis (2.2-15). This leads to the issue of the believer's responsibilities in the areas of civil life and false teachers (3.1-11). The writer concludes this letter with a repeated admonition and a benediction (3.12-15).

2 Timothy begins with a greeting (1.1-5). An appeal is made to Timothy to witness faithfully in the face of false teachings (1.6–2.13), followed by a lengthy discussion of false teachers (2.14–4.5), concluding with an exhortation to faithful ministry (4.1-5). Paul's relationship to Timothy is discussed

next (4.6-18) and the letter concludes with a greeting and benediction (4.19-22).

In the twentieth century, the Pastoral Epistles were at the center of the debate over women's ordination. Some argue that these letters strictly forbid women from holding the office of bishop, priest or deacon. This view is known as 'complementarianism' because men and women's roles are understood as 'equal but different' and complementary. Those who hold this view would cite 1 Tim. 3.2, 11 and Tit. 1.6 as evidence. Others argue that these passages, and ones like them, do not forbid a woman from holding any church offices, arguing that passages like Gal. 3.27-28 teach that, in Christ, men and women's roles are identical. This position is known as 'egalitarianism' because the roles of men and women are understood to be the same or equal.

Recommended reading. Fee, Gordon D. *The Pastoral Epistles*. Peabody, MA: Hendrickson, 1988

See also CANON; EPISTLE; PAUL [JFW]

Pater Noster (see Lord's Prayer).

Patmos. Patmos is one of the Sporades Islands in the Aegean Sea. John the apostle was on this island when he received his revelation of the end times (Rev. 1.9). His open letters to the seven churches in Asia Minor were probably composed on this island as well. It is possible that John was banished to this island by the emperor Domitian (c. 95 CE) 'for the sake of the gospel'. According to Pliny's *Natural History* (4.69-70), political prisoners were banished to three of the Sporades Islands at the time.

Still inhabited today, the island is home to two World Heritage Sites, the Monastery of Saint John the Theologian, and the Cave of the Apocalypse. Patmos is mentioned only once in the Bible and its significance is strictly the presence of John on this Greek island when he received his apocalyptic visions. While pilgrims visit the 'Cave of the Apocalypse' each year, not much reference is made to the island in contemporary culture.

See also APOCALYPSE; JOHN; REVELATION [GOA]

Patriarchs and Matriarchs. A person may be a patriarch or matriarch either by virtue of their position or role within a clan or the legacy of their influence on a group of people. Patriarchy and matriarchy, on the other hand, refer to the locus of power within a clan or society and require that someone exercise authority over others. This is the sense in which the word patriarch is used (a) in the LXX as the equivalent of the head of the father's house or in the broad sense of a religious or civil official (1 Chron. 24.31, 27.22), and (b) by the Orthodox churches and the Church of Jesus Christ of the Latter Day Saints to refer to a religious official.

In contrast, patriarchs and matriarchs may occupy a position of significance within the history and psyche of a community without being the current locus of power within that community. It is in this sense that Abraham, Isaac, and Jacob along with Sarah, Rebekah, Leah and Rachel are considered the patriarchs and matriarchs of Judaism on account of God's covenant promises (Gen. 12.1-7; Exod. 6.3-5). Within western culture we find depictions of the patriarchs and matriarchs of Israel in the works of Donatello, Doré, Michaelangelo, and Rembrandt. Similarly, references to patriarchs and matriarchs appear in both classical literature (e.g., Milton, *Paradise Lost*, Books III and XII) and contemporary literature (e.g., Diamant, *The Red Tent*). Major film references to the lives of the patriarchs and matriarchs include *The Green Pastures* (1936), *Jacob, The Man Who Fought With God* (1963), *Abraham* (1994) and *Jacob* (1994). Mention also needs to be made of Alburger's opera *Sex and the Bible (Part I)*.

Although there is agreement as to the importance of these patriarchs and matriarchs, there is some fluidity as to who may also be considered a patriarch or matriarch of the OT community of faith. For example, a case may be made that, because of their role in the biblical narrative, Adam, Seth, Enos, Cainan, Mahalaleel, Jared, Enoch, Methuselah, Lamech, and Noah may be considered patriarchs (Gen. 4.17-18; 5.3-31). The NT identifies both King David, the first of Israel's kings, and the twelve sons of Jacob, the ancestors of the tribes of Israel, as patriarchs (Acts 2.29; 7.8-9). Hebrews 11 recognizes the faith of Abraham, Isaac, Jacob and Sarah, but it does not differentiate between their faith and that of Abel, Enoch, Noah, Joseph, David and a host of other men and women, suggesting that all of these OT saints may be considered patriarchs and matriarchs of faith.

Finally, it may be asked whether anyone may be considered a patriarch or matriarch of the church? Calvin, based on the NT portrayal of the relationship of the apostles to the church (cf. Matt. 16.17-19; Eph. 2.19-22), refers to the apostles as patriarchs of the church (*Harmony of the Evangelists*, comment on Luke 10.1-12). In addition to the apostles, other disciples, both men and women, have left a legacy of faith (cf. Acts 1.12-14; 18;

1 Cor. 15.3-8). In recognition of this, some late twentieth- and twenty-first-century writers explore the legacy of women in the apostolic and patristic eras of the church.

Recommended reading. Westermann, Claus. *The Promises to the Fathers: Studies on the Patriarchal Narrative.* Philadelphia: Fortress Press, 1980

See also ABRAHAM; ISAAC; JACOB; LEAH; RACHEL; REBEKAH; SARAH [KFM]

Paul, the Apostle. The preeminent proclaimer of the early Jesus movement used both Greek (Paulos) and Hebrew (Shaul) names (Acts 13.9). Named as the author of 13 NT letters, Paul was a Jew who was a vehement persecutor of the church, but became a believer in Jesus as messiah and son of God because of a revelation of the resurrected Jesus (Gal. 1.1, 13-17). Acts describes the encounter occurring as Paul travelled to Damascus to persecute believers (9.1-21; 22.1-16; 26.2-20). His 'Damascus Road experience' moved him to a reversal from persecutor to proclaimer. Paul dedicated his life to trust in Christ and the righteousness provided in Christ (Phil. 3.4-14). Paul was probably born during the first decade CE and died c. 64 in Rome.

Paul was a missionary preacher who travelled through the eastern and northeastern Mediterranean, preaching to people who had not previously heard about Christ (Rom. 15.18-20). He considered himself to be apostle to the Gentiles, whose primary task was preaching and establishing churches among them (Rom. 1.5; 15.16, 18; Gal. 2.2, 8-9; cf. Eph. 3.8). His proclamation focused on Jesus Christ who 'died for our sins' and was raised in triumph over death (cf. 1 Cor. 2.1-2; 15.3-9). His letters addressed both churches and individuals. They speak with apostolic authority about faith in and faithfulness to Jesus Christ. Some churches had serious problems (e.g., 1 Cor) that Paul aimed to correct. All of the letters indicate Paul's focus on Christ as the savior of humanity. Salvation is always understood in the letters to be given by God's grace.

Paul has been the subject of many artistic works. His image appears in the Catacombs of Praetextus near Rome (fourth century), on icons, and in many famous paintings including Conversions of St Paul by Michelangelo (1542–1545), Caravaggio (1600–1601), Pieter Bruegel the Elder (1567). Rembrandt painted *The Apostle Paul* (c. 1657), *St Paul in Prison* (1627), and *Self Portrait as the Apostle Paul* (1661). Many images of Paul appear in stained glass windows and illuminated manuscripts.

Paul's life and language figure strongly in literature and popular usage. The term 'Damascus Road experience' is frequently used as a metaphor for life-changing incidents. The description of love found in 1 Corinthians 13 is regularly employed in wedding ceremonies ('Love is patient; love is kind; love is not envious ... Love never ends'). The famous statement (and variations) attributed to Paul that 'the love of money is the root of all evil' (1 Tim. 6.10), recurs often in literature, film, television, music, and everyday speech. Many more Pauline expressions are well known ('I can do all things through Christ who strengthens me' [Phil. 4.13]; 'the wages of sin is death' [Rom. 6.13]; 'by the grace of God I am what I am' [1 Cor. 15.10]; 'all things work together for good' [Rom. 8.28]).

Paul is often branded a misogynist because of statements such as 'women should be silent in the churches' (1 Cor. 14.34); 'Wives, be subject to your husbands' (Col. 3.18; cf. Eph. 5.22); and 'Let a woman learn in silence with full submission; I permit no woman to teach or to have authority over a man' (1 Tim. 2.11). All of these are subject to interpretation; with the exception of 1 Corinthians, all the letters in which these teachings occur are considered to be Deutero-Pauline by many scholars.

Recommended reading. Cousar, Charles B. *The Letters of Paul.* Nashville, TN: Abingdon Press, 1996. Harink, Douglas. *Paul among the Postliberals.* Grand Rapids, MI: Brazos, 2003

See also APOSTLE; DAMASCUS ROAD; EPISTLE; GENTILE [RRJ]

Peace. The predominant use of peace in the Bible finds its meaning in the Hebrew concept of *shalom*. In Greek thought, peace (*eirēnē*) is best defined negatively as the absence of conflict. Though including that sense, *shalom* also carries positive connotations relating to general well-being, prosperity, good health, and an anticipated future age characterized by these things. In the LXX, *eirēnē* was usually used to translate *shalom*, and thus generally adopted its meaning within the Jewish community. Likewise, the rich sense of *shalom* is present in the NT use of *eirēnē*.

Throughout history, Christian writers and thinkers continued to use the concept of peace in similar ways, consistent with the broad range of possible meaning in the Bible. Augustine made a few notable comments on peace. In *City of God*, he describes the eternal, eschatological peace (ch. 11), the desire for all humans to want peace (ch. 12), and the different types of peace (such as civil peace, peace among people, peace between God and humans, etc.; chap. 13). In the *Enchiridion* (ch. 63), he expounds on the peace of God that 'passes all understanding'. Martin Luther's use of the phrase 'peace of conscience' throughout his writings reflects his personal experience and certain of his theological tendencies. It may also participate in the shifting emphasis toward individualism in his time. Jeremiah criticized the false prophets who declared, '"Peace, peace," when there is no peace' (6.14), and that phrase has been employed in contemporary critiques of certain social or political situations (e.g., Desmond Tutu's Nobel Lecture, December 11, 1984).

Although the rich concept of *shalom* is sometimes present in Christian discourse on the topic of peace today, in broader culture the term usually connotes a freedom from disturbance (small scale or personal) and/or an absence of violence or war (large scale). Out of the anti-war movement in the 1960s, new sets of associations and images for understanding the term 'peace' developed, which all still resonate very loudly today. The idea of personal peace or tranquility in present culture can also trigger eastern religious associations that have become increasingly popular in the west. Thus, 'peace' in contemporary western culture finds many sources of influence, with the Bible being one of them. A major way that the biblical concept of peace made its way directly into western culture is through Christmas traditions. Through hymns, carols, decorations, media, and so on, 'peace' language is frequently invoked—though, to varying degrees, it would be detached from its original meaning even by some who value the traditions.

Recommended reading. Brueggemann, Walter. *Peace.* Understanding Biblical Themes. St Louis: Chalice Press, 2001.

See also DOVE; INFANCY NARRATIVES; NOT PEACE BUT A SWORD; OLIVE, OLIVE BRANCH   [BJL]

Pearl of Great Price. Matthew 13.45-46 contains a brief parable that compares the kingdom of God to a merchant who finds a 'pearl of great price' (KJV) and sells all he has in order to possess it. Thus, the kingdom is compared to a jewel that signifies beauty and value in the biblical tradition (cf. Job 28.18; Rev. 21.21).

In popular speech, a 'pearl of great price' is something of great importance or worth, e.g., Hester Prynne christens her daughter Pearl, the product of an adulterous affair with the Reverend Dimmesdale, 'as being of great price,—purchased with all she had' (chap. 6). The Gnostic *Hymn of the Pearl* (part of the *Acts of Thomas*, third century) is an allegory of the quest of the soul for enlightenment. Augustine is one of many Christian writers who compared the pearl to Christ himself (*Confessions* 8.1.2). The fourteenth-century *Pearl Poem* portrays the poet's beloved, who wears the pearl of great price, as residing in the city of God. George Herbert's 'The Pearl: Matt. 13.45' (1633) identifies divine love as the longed-for pearl. John Steinbeck's novella *The Pearl* (1947) gives the subject a more sinister interpretation, in which a valuable pearl discovered by a poor fisherman brings disillusionment and disaster to his family and neighbors.

In Mormonism, *The Pearl of Great Price* is a selection of sacred literature first published in 1851. Christian hymns such as 'Oh That Pearl of Great Price' and 'I've Found the Pearl of Greatest Price' cite the parable, as does the 1991 album *Pearl of Great Price* by the industrial music band Will.

See also PARABLE; PEARLS BEFORE SWINE   [MALB]

Pearls before Swine. In the Sermon on the Mount, Jesus teaches 'Give not that which is holy unto the dogs, neither cast ye your pearls before swine, lest they trample them under their feet, and turn again and rend you' (Matt. 7.6, KJV). In context, the reference is to the great worth of the gospel, which should not be squandered on hostile audiences. As a figure of speech, the phrase refers to something valuable in the hands of persons who cannot appreciate it, e.g., in 'Sonnet 12', John Milton uses it to describe hostility to his progressive views on divorce: 'But this is got by casting Pearl to Hoggs'.

As a title, the phrase has found many expressions in secular culture, e.g., Pearls Before Swine was the name of an American psychedelic folk band that released five albums between 1965 and 1972. *Pearls Before Swine* is the subtitle of Kurt Vonnegut's novel *God Bless You, Mr. Rosewater* (1965). In the twenty-first century, the irreverent comic strip *Pearls Before Swine*, first published in 2000, is published internationally in more than 500 newspapers.

See also PEARL OF GREAT PRICE; SERMON ON THE MOUNT   [MALB]

Penninah (see Hannah).

Pentateuch. Derived from the Greek *pente* (five) and *teuchos* (scroll or book), the designation Pentateuch refers to the first section of the OT (also known as the Torah) comprised of the books Genesis, Exodus, Leviticus, Numbers and Deuteronomy. The collection traces the flow of a narrative spanning from the creation of the world and humankind until Israel is on the brink of possessing the Promised Land. Interspersed throughout is a compendium of detailed legal material intended to govern Israel's religious and national livelihood. In this way the Pentateuch conveys its theological message through God's interaction with the human race and Israel.

A prominent issue in Pentateuchal studies over the past two centuries pertains to authorship issues and the origins of the collection. While traditionally authorship is attributed to Moses, critical scholarship has offered other theories regarding the Pentateuch's literary history. Most influential among such theories is the Documentary Hypothesis, in large part developed by J. Wellhausen (1844–1918). This view proposes that the Pentateuch's composition was the result of the contributions of multiple authors that were combined, edited and coalesced into their present form. While the Documentary Hypothesis served as the basis for much of twentieth-century scholarship, recent decades have given rise to more vocal critiques and reevaluations concerning the feasibility of some of the theory's presuppositions. At present, what can be said affirmatively is that the Pentateuch represents a collage of literary and editorial activity that likely took place over a long period of time.

In terms of the organization of biblical material, it has been observed that the fivefold division of the book of Psalms potentially mirrors the five books of the Pentateuch. Similarly, the Gospel of Matthew's structure, largely framed by five distinct sermons of Jesus, may have been cast in light of a Pentateuchal pattern. While the significance of such correspondences remains an issue of debate, the influence of the Pentateuchal material on subsequent biblical authors is undeniable.

This influence extends significantly beyond the shaping of the written scriptures within the Jewish tradition as reverence for the Torah is evidenced by a vibrant liturgical system centered on to books of the Pentateuch. An early precedent for regular public Torah readings is seen in literature of the first century CE (Acts 15.21; Josephus *Against Apion* 2.175; Philo *On Dreams* 2.127). However, the universal custom of a fixed annual Torah reading cycle did not emerge until the twelfth century. In modern congregations this liturgical system is embedded within numerous traditions surrounding the actual reading of the Torah. Prior to public reading, the Torah scroll is carried in procession from an ark during which time congregants stand and kiss the scroll as it passes by. While the congregation stands during certain climactic portions such as the Song of Moses (Exod. 15.1-21), other portions dealing with instances of Israel's relapses are read with solemnity (e.g., Num. 11). Such reverence for the Torah witnesses to the integral role the Pentateuch played in the Jewish tradition as it traversed from the ancient world to the core of modern Jewish religious life and practice.

Recommended reading. Hamilton, Victor P. *Handbook on the Pentateuch: Genesis, Exodus, Leviticus, Numbers, Deuteronomy*. Grand Rapids, MI: Baker Academic, 2005.

See also LAW; GENESIS, BOOK OF; EXODUS, BOOK OF; LEVITICUS, BOOK OF; NUMBERS, BOOK OF; DEUTERONOMY, BOOK OF [ABP]

Pentecost. This is one of the three pilgrim festivals in Israel and it is known as the Feast of the Harvest (Exod. 23.16), the Feast of Weeks (Deut. 16.10), the day of the First Fruits (Num. 28.26; Exod. 23.16; 34.22; Lev. 23.17) and in the Greek OT as Pentecost (Tob. 2.1; 12.32). The Festival occurs seven weeks (50 days) after Passover (Deut. 16.9-10). In its origins, it was simply a harvest festival of thanksgiving for God's care and bounty in the harvest. In response to God's gifts of the grain, the people brought offerings of their first fruits. For most of the OT period, there is no indication that this is linked to an event in Israel's history, but by the time of *Jubilees* (c. 150 BCE), First Fruits is associated with a series of covenant rituals (Noah, *Jubilees* 6.1, 18; Abraham, *Jubilees* 6.19), and particularly the Sinai covenant (*Jubilees* 15.1; 6.11). While the temple existed, the major ritual of this festival was the bringing of two wheat loaves as the first fruits of the harvest. The Feast lasted only 1 day, but pigrims were allowed to bring their offerings for the following 6 days. Following the destruction of the temple in 70 CE, the rabbis shifted the focus from the celebration of the covenants to the celebration of the gift of the Law on Sinai, since the Torah was the 'first fruit' of the Exodus. The earliest reference to this association with Torah is attributed to Rabbi El'azar ben Pedath (c. 270).

The early Jesus movement drew on its Jewish heritage to interpret the meaning of the crucifixion and resurrection of Jesus. They came to believe that this event marked the beginning of the 'end times' since this was when they believed God would raise the dead. The second sign that they were living in the end times was the experience of God's Spirit. Paul called this experience of the Spirit, the 'first fruits' (Rom. 8.23). Just as the first fruits indicate that the harvest is ripening, the Spirit is the first sign of an 'end-time' process that has already started. Luke draws on this Pauline theology of the Spirit as the first fruits of the resurrection, when he dramatically describes the outpouring of the Spirit on the disciples and places this event during the Jewish Festival of First Fruits/Pentecost. This is Luke's particular theology of the Spirit. In John, the 'hour' of Jesus is the single act of his death, return to the Father and gift of the Spirit.

The major symbols of Pentecost are the powerful wind and tongues as of fire. The particular word used for wind (*pnoē*) is used almost exclusively of God's life-giving breath (Gen. 2.7; 7.2; Job 32.8); this is a divine wind. The gift of tongues enables the disciples to speak and to be understood by people of many lands, reversing what happened at the Tower of Babel (Gen. 11) when the people were dispersed and their language or tongue confused.

Recommended reading. Coloe, M.L. 'The Johannine Pentecost: John 1.19–2.12'. *Australian Biblical Review* 55 (2007) 41-56.

See also BOOTHS, FEAST OF; FESTIVALS; HOLY SPIRIT; PASSOVER [MLC]

Persia. Persia today is known by its native name as Iran. Biblical Persia was a world empire that rose to power in 539 BCE. It was destroyed by the Greeks under Alexander the Great in 331 BCE. The homeland of the Persians (Parsa) was the Iranian Plateau, which stretched from the Hindu Kush in the east to the Zagros Mountains in the west.

The Persians probably came from a tribe that flourished in the steppes of Russia as early as 2000 BCE. They settled east of the Zagros Mountains (named after the Zagarthian people), which stretch from the Straits of Hormuz to the border with modern Iraq. The first historic mention of them was made by the Assyrian king Shalmaneser III (858–824 BCE).

The Persians and the Medes (Arnadia) emerged into history with the establishment of a small kingdom at Parsumash in the early 700s by king Achaemene. His dynasty was named the Achaemenid dynasty after him. Teispes (675–640), Achaemene's successor, joined with the Medes and the Babylonians to overthrow Assyria, destroying Nineveh in 612 BCE.

Cyrus II (Cyrus the Great) founded the Persian Empire. He had ascended the Persian throne at Anshan in 559 BCE. He revolted against Media and in a short war killed the Median king Astyages. He conquered the kingdom of Lydia around 546. The biblical figure Daniel (5.28) prophesied that the Babylonian kingdom (Belshazzar's kingdom) would be given to the 'Medes and the Persians' when he read the handwriting on the wall. Babylon fell on October 13, 539 BCE.

The kings of the Persian Empire were Cyrus II, 'the Great' (c. 560–530); Cambyses (530–522); Darius I (522–486); Xerxes I (486–465); Artaxerxes I (465–424); Xerxes II (424); Sogdianos (424–423); Darius II (423–405/4); Artaxerxes II (423–359/8); Artaxerxes III (338/7–336); and Darius III (336–330).

Cyrus the Great's rule is viewed biblically as a result of the sovereignty of God using him as 'my shepherd' (Isa. 44.28) and his 'anointed' (45.1). His spirit was stirred up by the Lord to issue the decree restoring the Jews to their homeland following their long period of captivity by the Babylonians (2 Chron. 36.22-23; Ezra 1.1-4). Cyrus's decree authorized the first return of the Jews to Jerusalem. There were two other decrees that authorized additional groups to return.

References to Persian places, or, people associated with the Persians can be found in the books of 2 Chronicles, Ezra, Nehemiah, Esther, Isaiah, Ezekiel and Daniel, Haggai and Zechariah. Nehemiah begins in Susa, the Persian capital, in the very throne room of the Persian king Artaxerxes where Nehemiah is his cup bearer. The book of Esther says she was a Jew who was chosen as queen of the Persian Empire by Ahasuerus (Xerxes). Daniel is said to have served in the time of Cyrus the Persian (Dan. 1.21; 6.28; 10.1).

There are no references to Persia in the NT. However, the Wise Men who came from the east seeking the one born king of the Jews (Matt. 2.1-12) are called Magi (*magoi*) in Greek and may have been connected with the Magi (priests) of the Persians.

Recommended reading. Cook, J.M. *The Persian Empire*. London: J.M. Dent & Sons, 1983. Sam, Amini. *Pictorial History of Ancient Persia*. Bloomington, IN: Authorhouse, 2006. Yamauchi, E.M. *Persia and the Bible*. Grand Rapids, MI: Baker Book House, 1990.

See also 2 CHRONICLES; DANIEL, BOOK OF; EZRA, BOOK OF; ESTHER, BOOK OF; EZEKIEL; HAGGAI, BOOK OF; MAGI; MAJOR PROPHETS; MINOR PROPHETS; NEHEMIAH, BOOK OF; XERXES; ZECHARIAH, BOOK OF [AJW]

Pesach (see Passover).

Peter. One of the twelve apostles, mentioned about 165 times in the NT; also known as Simon and Cephas. Peter is a disciple to whom Jesus revealed himself specially. Among the first disciples chosen (Matt. 4.18; Mark 1.16; John 1.40-41), he is renamed from Simon to Peter (Matt. 10.2; Mark 3.16; Luke 6.14; John 1.42, where Simon is named Cephas, Aramaic for 'rock', translated into Greek as Peter), Peter's mother-in-law is healed by Jesus (Mark 1.30-31; Luke 4.38-39), Peter takes responsibility for Jesus (Mark 1.35-38), Jesus enters his boat when the disciples catch an abundance of fish and he recognizes who Jesus is (Luke 5.3-11), he accompanies Jesus when healing Jairus's daughter (Mark 5.37; Luke 8.51), tries walking on water (Matt. 14.28-29), asks for interpretation of a parable (Matt. 15.15), in Caesarea Philippi declares that Jesus is the Christ (Matt. 16.16; Mark 8.29; Luke 9.20; cf. John 6.68) and is instructed to found the church (Matt. 16.17-19), speaks at the transfiguration (Matt. 17.1, 4; Mark 9.2, 5; Luke 9.28, 33), is approached by those with questions for Jesus (Matt. 17.24), questions Jesus privately regarding future events (Mark 13.3), helps prepare for Passover (Luke 22.8), questions Jesus' washing his feet (John 13.6-9), enquires regarding Jesus' betrayer (John 13.24), asks where Jesus is going (John 13.36-37), Jesus foretells that Peter will deny him thrice (Matt. 26.33, 35, 69-75; Mark 14.26, 31, 66-72; Luke 22.31-34, 55-62; John 18.25-27), he is spoken to by Jesus in the garden (Matt. 26.40; Mark 14.37), defends Jesus (John 18.10-11), follows Jesus into the high priest's courtyard (Matt. 26.58; Mark 14.54; Luke 22.54; John 18.15-18), hears of Jesus' resurrection (Mark 16.7), is one of the first two of the twelve to see the empty tomb (Luke 24.12; John 20.2-6), leads the disciples fishing post-resurrection (John 21.2-3), jumps in the sea to get to Jesus (John 21.7), draws in the load of fish (John 21.11), is told to feed Jesus' sheep (John 21.15, 17), and enquires about the future (John 21.20-21). Acts includes episodes featuring Peter. He instigates finding Judas's replacement (Acts 1.15), speaks on Pentecost (Acts 2.14-39), with John he heals a lame man and responds to the crowd (Acts 3.1-26), with John, is arrested and responds to accusers (Acts 4.8-20), Peter interrogates Ananias and Sapphira (Acts 5.3-9), is thought to have healing powers (Acts 15.19), is singled out in the apostles' response to the Sanhedrin's questioning (Acts 5.29), goes with John to Samaritans and others (Acts 8.14, 20; 9.32, 34), restores Tabitha to life (Acts 9.38-43), visits Cornelius (Acts 10.5-48), is accused of consorting with the uncircumcised (Acts 11.2, 4), is imprisoned but miraculously released (Acts 12.3-17), and defends Paul's Gentile mission (Acts 15.7-11). Paul accuses Cephas/Peter of opposing communion with Gentile believers (Gal. 2.7-14). Peter apparently had followers in other congregations (1 Cor. 1.12).

Some see Peter's primacy established in the NT; others interpret these episodes—where Peter functions alongside and for other disciples—as portraying Peter as first among equals. 1–2 Peter are attributed to him; he is traditionally seen as the source behind Mark. Traditionally, Peter was put to death under Nero c. 64 CE in Rome. Many apocrypha grew up around Peter, e.g., the *Preaching of Peter* and the *Gospel of Peter* (both possibly second century), later, the *Acts of Peter*, and other apocryphal acts. Symbolically, Peter represents the disciple who acts before he thinks, transformed by meeting the risen Jesus. The biblical stories about him have been portrayed extensively in Christian art.

Recommended reading. Brown, Raymond E., et al. *Peter in the New Testament.* Philadelphia: Fortress Press, 1973.

See also APOSTLE; DISCIPLE; PETER, EPISTLES OF

[SEP]

Peter, Epistles of. The Epistles of Peter are so-called due to their claim of authorship by 'Peter, an apostle' in 1 Peter and 'Simeon Peter, a slave and apostle' in 2 Peter. The different name given in the latter, as well as other literary features, has caused many to question the Petrine authorship of 2 Peter, making it one of the most disputed letters in the NT. The letters are categorized as part of the Catholic or General Epistles. 1 Peter is generally dated in the early 60s CE, while 2 Peter is dated between 67 and 150 CE, depending on one's view of authorship

1 Peter focuses on the issue of Christian suffering. The author uses the Greek term *paschō* (to suffer) 12 times, while there are only 11 occurrences collectively in the remaining NT epistles. As the people of God, the readers are encouraged to live holy lives as obedient children (2.11-17). Instruction is given for proper conduct regarding relationships between slaves and masters (2.19-20), husbands and wives (3.1-7), and the elders of the church with their congregations (5.1-3). The letter presents the readers' present suffering as something to be expected (4.12-13). Jesus is portrayed as the ultimate expression of the just suffering for the unjust and is pre-

sented as the example for how Christians should react amid their suffering (2.21-25; 4.1-2). It is generally agreed that the suffering described is most likely verbal abuse and not physical persecution (2.1, 12, 15, 22-23; 3.1, 9-10, 15-16; 4.4, 11, 14). The letter concludes with a warning for Christians to resist their enemy the devil and associates their suffering with his prowling around like a 'roaring' lion, another possible reference to verbal abuse.

Most recently, the theme of Jesus' suffering is graphically represented in Mel Gibson's *The Passion of the Christ* (2004). An example of the innocent suffering unjustly from popular culture is the film *The Green Mile* (1999) where John Coffey (J.C., a Christ figure), who has the ability to heal and possesses uncommon spiritual insight, is wrongfully put to death.

2 Peter paints a bleak picture of the church both from within and without. First, false teachers will rise up in the midst of the congregation, specifically those who engage in a lifestyle of greed and sexual immorality (2.1-22). Second, 'scoffers' will question the reliability of the promise of Jesus' return (3.3-4). This perversion of truth ultimately leads to the destruction of the false teachers (2.1-10). Yet the writer highlights the reality of coming destruction by using the example of God's previous judgments in the Flood and Sodom and Gomorrah (2.4-10), although the expected destruction will be one in which the heavens and the earth will melt away by means of a burning fire (3.7-12).

Although 2 Peter contains apocalyptic ideas such as those seen in *The Day After* (1983), its focus on false teachers is better represented in *Leap of Faith* (1992) where Steve Martin plays a supposed Christian faith healer who swindles people out of their money. Other examples include modern-day false teachers like Jim Jones and David Koresh, who deceived many people through teachings that ultimately led to their deaths and the deaths of many others.

Recommended reading. Achtemeier, Paul J. *1 Peter: A Commentary on First Peter*. Hermeneia. Minneapolis: Augsburg Fortress Press, 1996. Moo, Douglas J. *2 Peter and Jude*. Grand Rapids, MI: MI: Zondervan, 1997.

See also CHRIST FIGURE; EPISTLE; FALSE PROPHET; PETER; SUFFERING; TRIALS AND TRIBULATIONS [MDM]

Pharaoh. In Hebrew, *far'oh* is an Egyptian loanword that means 'the great house' and later became a designation for the king himself. While the Pharaoh was the sole ruler, there is a common misconception that the living Pharaoh was a god. According to Egyptologists, the king only became a god after his death.

The most famous material artifacts of the Pharaohs are the pyramids. These began as simple mounds (mastabas) over a dead body of the Pharaoh, later built into the first step pyramid (referred to as the 'stairway to heaven' in Pyramid Text Spell 267) at Sakkara (2700 BCE). Later the step pyramid was covered (2640 BCE) and this design became perfected in the three large pyramids at Giza; the largest of these being the pyramid of Kufu with a 210 M base and 49 storeys high. The pyramid and its complex served as a mortuary temple sustaining and serving the Pharaoh in the afterlife. But they also served an economic function since sustaining their lands and crops provided employment sometimes up to 100 years after the Pharaoh had died. Later in Egyptian history, the Pharaohs moved their tombs from pyramids to the Valley of the Kings to avoid looting.

The use of 'Pharaoh' in the Hebrew Bible presents a problem for dating since they are never named (Exod. 5.1). But there are intersections between the king in Egypt and kings in the OT. As the Psalms are attributed to David, Pharaoh Akhenaten is said to have composed a hymn to Re (the sun god). Not only is the authorship parallel, but the connections between the 'Hymn to Re' and Psalm 104 are striking. Likewise, during an annual Sed festival the Egyptian king would have to prove his kingship in an elaborate cultic ceremony. In a similar way, events described in the OT, as in Psalm 2, describe the enthronement of the Davidic king.

The Bible's vision of Pharaoh has likely had some influence on the perception of Egyptians as ruthless leaders. *The Simpsons* ('The Simpsons' Bible Stories, 1999) recounts the Exodus and shares in the Bible's imagery of Millhouse as a ruthless Pharaoh. However, academic studies of Egyptology have shown the various sides to Pharaohs as competent leaders. Sometimes Egyptian art represents them as concerned and worried for their people. Thus, the image of a shepherd is common for the Pharaoh in Egyptian literature and likely a source of the biblical image of God as shepherd.

Contemporary expressions of Pharaoh such as the heavy metal band Cradle of Filth consider a pro-Pharaoh perspective in Pharaoh's battle with Moses in the song 'Doberman Pharaoh' (2003). In film, the Pharaoh of Exodus has been portrayed negatively in *The Ten Commandments* (1923, 1956) and *Prince of*

Egypt (1998). A looser connection of film's use of the biblical Pharaoh could be in *Planet of the Apes* (2001). Denzey and Gray in *Teaching the Bible through Popular Culture and the Arts* (2007) suggest that this film is essentially a deliverance story with the main human character as Moses and the leader of the apes as Pharaoh. More recently, the deposed Egyptian president Hosni Mubarak has been portrayed as a despotic Pharaoh by the media. Thus, the Bible's vision of a ruthless Pharaoh has dominated western imagination despite the complexity of the Pharaohs illuminated by Egyptology.

Recommended reading. Redford, Donald B. *Egypt, Canaan and Israel in Ancient Times.* Princeton: Princeton University Press, 1992.

See also EGYPT; EXODUS; KINGSHIP [SWF]

Pharisees. The Pharisees were a prominent religious group within early Judaism. The name 'Pharisee' (Greek: *pharisaios*) derives from the Hebrew verb *parash*, which means 'to separate' or 'to distinguish'. The significance of the name is up for debate, since the exact circumstances of their origins are unknown; there is no consensus from what or whom the Pharisees separated. They likely originated in the second century BCE, promoting strict adherence to Torah. The major ancient sources that describe the Pharisees are Josephus, the NT, and rabbinic literature. Each of these sources has its own theological bias, which makes it difficult to draw an accurate portrait of this group.

Josephus, who wrote in the first century CE, numbers the Pharisees among the four schools of thought (or philosophies), which also included the Essenes, the Sadducees, and the 'Fourth Philosophy' (*Antiquities* 18.11-25). Josephus states that the Pharisees were a leading Jewish group and the most accurate interpreters of the laws; they believe that fate works in cooperation with human action, and the soul is imperishable (*Jewish War* 2.162-63). He also reports that they numbered more than 6,000 (*Antiquities* 17.41).

The NT mentions the Pharisees in the four Gospels, Acts, and Philippians. The Gospels typically present the Pharisees in a negative light. They oppose Jesus' teaching about the Sabbath and washings, despise his association with sinners, conspire against his ministry, and are portrayed as hypocrites. Yet there are some positive NT accounts of Pharisees. In Luke, Pharisees warn Jesus that Herod wanted to kill him (13.31). In John, the Pharisee Nicodemus is receptive to Jesus' message (3.1-21; 19.39).

In Acts, the Pharisee Gamaliel withholds judgment on the nascent church (5.33-39) and some believers in the Jerusalem church are identified as Pharisees (15.5). Paul refers to himself as a Pharisee (Phil. 3.5). In Acts, when Paul is examined by the council of Pharisees and Sadducees, he appeals to this Pharisaic background by claiming that he was on trial for believing in the resurrection. This leads the Pharisees in the crowd to exonerate him (Acts 23.1-10).

After the Jewish War and the destruction of the temple (66–70 CE), the face of early Judaism changed dramatically. Jewish sectarianism faded and the legacy of the Pharisees became rabbinic Judaism. Rabbinic literature shows that the Pharisees had special interest in Sabbath observance, purity rules, and tithing.

The NT's treatment of the Pharisees has influenced their portrait in western culture. The term Pharisee often describes hypocritical, self-righteous or legalistic qualities. Allusions to the Pharisees are made in English literature as early as Chaucer. Milton responds to a proposal to accept 'papists in our churches' by saying that it 'was pharisaical, and vain-glorious, a greedy desire to win proselytes' (*Animadversions*). Bunyan's *Pilgrim's Progress* characterizes the Pharisees as hypocritical, pretentious, and having ulterior motives (pt. 1; chap. 7). Emily Brontë's *Wuthering Heights* refers to Joseph, the servant, as 'most likely, the wearisomest, self-righteous pharisee that ever ransacked a Bible to rake the promises to himself and fling the curses on his neighbors' (ch. 4). In *Billy Budd*, Melville writes the following about Claggart: 'The Pharisee is the Guy Fawkes prowling in the hid chambers underlying some natures like Claggart's' (ch. 13).

Recommended reading. Saldarini, Anthony J.J., and James C. VanderKam. *Pharisees, Scribes and Sadducees in Palestinian Society.* Grand Rapids, MI: Eerdmans, 2001.

See also ESSENES, GAMALIEL, PAUL, SADDUCEES [BCW]

Philemon, Epistle to. The Letter to Philemon is one of the shortest writings in the NT, and in spite of its intended reading to the church that meets in Philemon's house, it is focused on a domestic issue in which the apostle Paul, in prison (Phlm. 1.1, 9, 10, 13), has become involved. Yet, Paul's letter to Philemon has generated one of the most protracted and voluble debates in the history of western society—the justification or repudiation of slavery from a Christian perspective.

The prominent concern of the letter addresses the reconciliation of Onesimus (whose name means 'useful'), possibly a runaway slave known to Paul, and Philemon, his master. Various interpretations have been offered as to the situation that has given rise to the need for reconciliation: the common patristic and medieval interpretation was to interpret the 'useless' epithet (1.11) as a literal description of the waywardness of the slave, Onesimus, whom Paul corrected, returning the reformed, forgiven fugitive to his master. Others have tipped the scales and seen Philemon as the culpable master with Paul engineering a reconciliation that brought about his repentance. Some have pushed this line towards an expectation of Paul that Philemon would manumit Onesimus. A few have tried to sideline the slavery frame and seen the reconciliation as between two brothers, taking the call to brotherly address and treatment in v. 16 literally, or as Paul seeking to gain Philemon's formal release of Onesimus so that he can extend his support for Paul's work. Whatever the merits of these variations, the general acceptance remains that Onesimus is a slave and Philemon his master, and that Paul, through the use of his own position and authority and the reconceptualization of attitudes to Onesimus, brokers a harmonious relationship between the two, though probably without affecting the master–slave relationship.

Onesimus is considered to be a saint in Orthodox churches; an early Bishop of Ephesus by that name is sometimes identified with the biblical figure. Medieval and renaissance paintings frequently capture the moment that Onesimus returns humbly to his receptive master, Paul's epistle in hand, and with his hair cropped in the standard stigmatic mark of the slave (though sometimes more in the style of a tonsured monk).

The letter became the flashpoint of debate (and war) about slavery in eighteenth- and nineteenth-century Europe and America, and the polemics about whether Paul was recommending for or against slavery continue to the present. This is complicated by Paul's frequent self-designation 'slave of God/Christ', though this phrase is tellingly absent from his letter to Philemon, being replaced by the more oblique though empathetic reference to his own imprisonment. The debate has broadened in the west as, firstly, identity markers of slavery (lack of independent movement, bodily vulnerability, hard labor, minimal remuneration) have begun to be applied to sweat-shop workers; secondly, as the change of church attitudes to slavery has become a template and warrant for other liberationist movements (women's ordination, gay rights), and thirdly, as the total structure of families and households become reconsidered given that slavery was a key component of first-century households, including Christian ones (e.g., Col. 3.18–4.1; Eph. 6.5-9).

Recommended reading. Byron, J. 'Paul and the Background of Slavery: The Status Quaestonis in New Testament Scholarship'. *Currents in Biblical Research* 3 (2004) 116-39. Patterson, O. 'Paul, Slavery and Freedom: Personal and Socio-historical Reflections'. In *Slavery in Text and Interpretation.* Semeia 83–84. Pp. 263-79. Atlanta: Society of Biblical Literature, 1998. Thompson, M.A. *Colossians and Philemon.* Grand Rapids, MI: Eerdmans, 2005.

See also COLOSSIANS, EPISTLE TO THE; PAUL, THE APOSTLE; SLAVE [AHC]

Philip. One of the 12 apostles (Mark 3.18; Luke 6.14; Acts 1.13); in John, he is said to be from Bethsaida, and he calls Nathaniel to 'come and see' Jesus (1.44-48), and figures prominently in several incidents (6.5, 7; 12.21, 22; 14.8, 9). In Acts, another Philip was one of the seven chosen to assist the apostles by tending to the needs of the Greek-speaking widows in the Jerusalem church. By so doing, these ministers freed the apostles to devote their time to the ministries of prayer and teaching. This is traditionally thought to be the beginning of the office of deacon, but the Bible does not use this term in referring to the seven.

Two of these seven figure prominently in the history of the early church. One was Stephen, who became the first Christian martyr. The other was Philip, whose story is recounted in Acts 8.5-40 and 21.8-9.

After the death of Stephen, there was a general persecution of the Jerusalem church, and in particular of its Hellenistic Jewish members. Many of these Christians fled the city to escape persecution. Philip fled to Samaria, where he became the first preacher to the Samaritans. They eagerly received his message, and Peter and John later visited Samaria to bless the new converts and impart to them the Holy Spirit. Philip was so successful in his preaching that he was later called 'the Evangelist' (Acts 21.8).

On the heels of his great success in Samaria, God sent Philip to the desert road between Jerusalem and Gaza, where he met a eunuch in the service of the queen of Ethiopia (Acts 8.26-40). This royal official was reading from the book of Isaiah, and Philip helped him to understand that the passage he was reading spoke of Jesus.

After baptizing the Ethiopian eunuch, Philip preached in the coastal cities before finding his way to Caesarea, where he made his home. Years later, Paul stayed in his house while on his final trip to Jerusalem. At that time, Acts tells us, Philip had four unmarried daughters who had the gift of prophecy (21.9).

Philip the Deacon should not be confused with Philip the Apostle. It is clear from Acts 6 that the seven chosen to care for the widows were different from the twelve who had already been set apart as apostles.

According to a Greek tradition, Philip eventually became the bishop of Tralles in Lydia, Asia Minor. The gnostic *Gospel of Philip* was written in his name; there is also an apocryphal *Acts of Philip*. His feast day differs according to the traditions of the various communions from January 4 (Eastern Orthodox) to June 6 (Roman Catholic) to October 11 (Lutheran—Missouri Synod).

See also DAUGHTERS OF PHILIP; DEACON/DEACONESS; SAMARITANS; STEPHEN; TWELVE APOSTLES, THE

[DJP]

Philip, Daughters of (see Daughters of Philip).

Philippians, Letter to the. A Pauline letter to a church located in a city named after Alexander the Great's father in the eastern part of the Roman province of Macedonia. A church at Philippi was founded by Paul on his first visit there during his second missionary journey (Acts 16.11-40), including the conversion of Lydia (Acts 16.11-15). Paul probably visited Philippi twice more on his third missionary journey (Acts 20.1-2, 6), when he went through Macedonia on his way to and from Greece.

Philippians is a very positive and encouraging letter, offering joyful thanks to God for the Philippians because of their spiritual maturity. The body of the letter develops the idea of living the example set by Christ. In chap. 2, Paul offers Christ as the consummate example of how to live this way. In the paraenetic section, Paul characterizes some false teachers as 'dogs' involved in 'false circumcision'. Paul says he counts everything as loss compared to knowing Christ Jesus. He encourages the Philippians toward unity and to rejoice in the Lord, and he thanks them for their support.

Pauline authorship is not disputed, but two questions are prominent in the scholarly literature. One concerns place of composition (and hence date of composition) and the other, literary integrity. There are three major views on the place from which Paul wrote his imprisonment letters, of which Philippians is one. If written while imprisoned in Ephesus, the letter would probably date to Paul's second visit to Ephesus, from 53 to 55 CE. If written while imprisoned in Caesarea, the letter would date to 57–60 CE. However, a Roman imprisonment is most likely. In the letter, Paul refers to a praetorian guard (Phil. 1.13), those of Caesar's household (4.22), and his expectation of release (1.7, 19-27; 2.24), all of which indicate a Roman imprisonment, around 61–62 CE.

Regarding literary integrity, there have been over 20 different proposals for Philippians being a composite of multiple letters. The major proposals contend that Philippians was originally either two or three letters. Despite the arguments against unity, there is no external textual evidence of multiple letters to the Philippians, and each of the objections has been plausibly countered. Most scholars continue to endorse the unity of Philippians.

Determining the occasion for writing Philippians has proved difficult, because the letter does not appear to be written to oppose strong and specific opposition. There are two major reasons suggested for Paul's writing. The first is that Paul writes to give an assessment of his current situation. He is in prison and suffering but he is still expecting release. Nevertheless, he remains joyful in the midst of adversity (1.12-26; 2.24). The second possible reason is that Paul may be warning the Philippians of Judaizers (3.2-6), who are offering to the gentile Christians in Philippi a way to become Jews while remaining Christians. They would then be able to resist some of the pressures of the emperor cult in the city, because of special privileges the Jews enjoyed. Paul reminds the Philippians that their position is based on their spiritual status as citizens of heaven (3.20).

Philippians contains a possibly pre-Pauline hymn (2.5-11) which provides insight into early Christian worship. Famous expressions from Philippians include 'Rejoice in the Lord always; again I say rejoice' (4.5), 'the peace of God that passes all understanding' (4.7a), 'I can do all things in him who strengthens me' (4.13), and 'work out your own salvation with fear and trembling' (2.12a).

Recommended reading. McDonald, L.M., and S.E. Porter. *Early Christianity and its Sacred Literature*. Pp. 461-70. Peabody, MA: Hendrickson, 2000.

See also LYDIA; PAUL, THE APOSTLE; PRISON EPISTLES

[SEP]

Philistines. From the Hebrew word *Pelishtim* referring to the occupants of Canaan's coastal plain.

There are over 250 OT references to the Philistines. The first is found in the 'Table of Nations' (Gen. 10.14) which notes that the Philistines originated in Egypt. This may well be a reference to the fact that the Philistines settled in Egypt after their defeat at the hands of Rameses III (c. 1190 BCE). These 'sea peoples' who settled in Canaan around 1200 BCE are portrayed in the OT as an arch-enemy of Israel. From the time of the Judges through the reign of David the Philistines remained a threat to Israel's existence and territorial sovereignty (see Judg. 3.31, 13.1; 1 Sam. 7.2-17). The ongoing fight for control of Palestine ('land of the Philistines') was far more than simply a war over territory. The biblical narratives continually stress that this was a clash between the Hebrew God, Yahweh, and the head of the Philistine pantheon, Dagon and other Philistine gods (see 1 Sam. 5.1-12). From a biblical standpoint, the contacts, conflicts and compromises between the Israelites and the Philistines represented the greater competition between monotheism and polytheism, the people of the covenant ('circumcised') and those living outside the covenant ('uncircumcised'), and those who were pure and righteous in the sight of Yahweh and those who were impure and unrighteous.

The exact origin of the Philistines is still a matter of considerable historical debate. Two historical theories have predominated. The more commonly held view argues that literary and archeological sources point to an Aegean origin. This theory holds that Illyria or Crete was the Philistine homeland, and that eventually the Philistines migrated to the islands of the Aegean and then on to Egypt and Canaan. A second theory, based primarily on linguistic evidence, contends that the Philistines were of Anatolian origin. This view locates the Philistine homeland in western Cilicia on the banks of the Calycadnus River.

The Philistine Pentapolis of five city-states (Ekron, Gath, Gaza, Ashkelon and Ashdod) was located on the southern shore of the Mediterranean where they effectively controlled the main trade routes (the highways of the time) from Arabia and Egypt that supplied Palestine with a variety of goods. The Philistines were known for their brutality, and their early use of iron gave them a distinct technological advantage over their adversaries. These people were far more than simply bloodthirsty warriors, however. The available historical evidence points to a well-organized society ruled by a military aristocracy that protected and spread a flourishing culture. In fact, the Philistines produced some of the most beautiful pottery, ivory and metal objects in the Ancient Near East. The Philistines were able to maintain their territorial and cultural independence until they were conquered by the Assyrians in eighth century BCE.

Two famous biblical villains are the Philistines Delilah (Judg. 16.1-18) and Goliath (1 Sam. 17.1-51). The term 'Philistine' remains in use today, used in a derogatory manner to describe one who displays an extraordinarily high level of social crassness or cultural crudity, commonness, ignorance and/or indifference. The application of the term varies widely in its usage. For excellent visual presentations about the Philistines, see the A&E series *Mysteries of the Bible—Arch-Enemy: The Philistines* and the episode entitled *Delilah's People* in the Vision TV series *The Naked Archeologist*.

Recommended reading. Dothan, Trude. *The Philistines and their Material Culture*. New Haven and London: Yale University Press, 1982. Dothan, Trude and M. Dothan. *People of the Sea: The Search for the Philistines*. New York: Scribner, 1992.

See also DELILAH; DAGON; GOLIATH; PALESTINE

[PRW]

Phoebe. Paul begins an extended chapter of personal greetings in Romans 16 with a recommendation of Phoebe. This Greek name, which in the Bible occurs only in Rom. 16.1, means 'radiant' and is a surname of the goddess Artemis (Phoebus being the solar epithet of Artemis's brother Apollo). In the context of Romans, the name Phoebe belonged to a woman whom some identify as a freed slave. As 'our sister' she was introduced as a close associate of Paul. The recommendation continued with two further credentials: (1) Phoebe was 'also a deacon of the church at Cenchreae' (Rom. 16.1; the Greek language of the time did not distinguish between 'deacon' and 'deaconess'). The Greek term *diakonos* could have designated an official or even the leader of the congregation at Cenchreae, the eastern port for the city of Corinth where Paul dictated his letter to the Romans. Yet in many English Bible translations, this high status is obscured by rendering the term *diakonos* as 'servant' (KJV, NASB), 'helper' (NCV), or 'who serves' (GNT). Since in antiquity it was customary to mention and recommend the carrier of a letter, Phoebe might have been the person who delivered Paul's letter to Rome where she probably also read it aloud to the audience; (2) Phoebe was a 'benefactor' or 'patroness' of Paul and many others (Rom. 16.2), suggesting a person of considerable status and wealth. However, the text's editorial history shows that some scribes have changed the word 'patroness' to 'helper' in efforts to downplay Phoebe's influential position. As Paul's patroness, however, Phoebe appeared as an important authority in the proclamation of the gospel; hence Paul asked that she be met with special hospitality.

St Phoebe the Deaconess is considered to be a saint by Catholic and Orthodox Christians; her feast day is September 3. According to *Butler's Lives of the Saints* (2000, 24), some scholars concluded from remarks of Clement of Alexandria and Ignatius of Antioch that Phoebe had been Paul's wife who ministered to him as a 'sister' after his conversion.

Recommended reading. Schulz, Ray R. 'A Case for 'President' Phoebe in Romans 16.2'. *Lutheran Theological Journal* 24 (1990) 124-27.

See also DEACON/DEACONESS; PAUL; ROMANS; WOMAN [CAE]

Photini (see Samaritan Woman).

Phylactery. Derived from the Greek *phylaktērion*, 'phylactery' occurs only once in the NT during a diatribe against the religious practice of the Pharisees (Matt. 23.5). Though predominantly referred to as phylacteries in contemporary secular and Christian circles, the preferred term in Jewish contexts is *tefillin* (etymology debated). In orthodox Jewish practice phylacteries are two black leather boxes encasing select scriptural passages that are bound to the head and left hand by black leather straps during daily morning services except on Sabbaths and festival days. Each box contains four biblical passages serving as the scriptural basis for the practice (Exod. 13.1-10, 11-16; Deut. 6.4-9, 13-21). Each individual passage refers or alludes to affixing 'these words' on the head and hand as a 'sign' of what God accomplished for the nation of Israel in the exodus from Egypt. While the hand phylactery contains a single piece of parchment with all of the above passages written in their biblical sequence, the head phylactery is comprised of four separate compartments in which individual inscribed rolls of parchment are placed. Due to the influence of Kabbalah, the head phylactery is embossed on the left and right exterior with the letter shin representative of the first letter of the Hebrew word *Shaddai* ('almighty').

Though it is clear that the apparent scriptural precedent for phylacteries is expressed in the passages encased therein, the precise origin of the practice and development of prescriptions determining phylactery use is unknown. Talmudic literature expresses that within the Hebrew Bible no distinctly legal instructions are provided and as such designates the growth of the tradition to analogous oral law. The earliest known literary references to phylacteries appear in the *Letter of Aristeas* (§1959) and Josephus's *Antiquities* (4.213). Discovered along with the Dead Sea Scrolls were a small collection of phylacteries, some of which contained the Ten Commandments (Deut. 5.6-21) alongside the text of Deut. 6.4-9. Collectively this evidence is generally accepted as indicating the origin of the practice between 250 and 100 BCE.

In some contemporary Jewish circles, phylactery use is still encouraged and remains a vibrant tradition. Today, appropriately and ceremonially donning phylacteries is simplified through the assistance of dozens of animated and live user-friendly tutorials on YouTube.com. One such tutorial is provided by the world famous Tefillin Booth located near the Western Wall in Jerusalem. The Booth opened the first day tourists and Israeli citizens were granted access to the Wall after the Six Day War in 1967. Employing a multi-lingual staff, the Booth provides phylacteries and services to thousands of visitors daily traversing to the Western Wall.

Recommended reading. Vermes, Geza. 'Pre-Mishnaic Jewish Worship and the Phylacteries from the Dead Sea'. *Vetus Testamentum* 9 (1959) 65-72.

See also JEW/JUDAISM; PHARISEES [ABP]

Physician. Writers of the Bible generally viewed physicians with suspicion, as charlatans who charged fees to the sick for cures that rarely worked. Healing came through the agency of God and his priests and prophets rather than through physicians. During Jesus's time, Greco-Roman physicians developed fairly advanced medical practices based on the Hippocratic approach. With the exception of the evangelist Luke, a physician traditionally from Antioch, healing in the NT occurs not by means of physicians but by Jesus and his disciples.

The OT rarely refers to the physician *(raphah)*; the few examples include 2 Chron. 16.12, when the King of Judah, Asa, sought the help of physicians for his diseased feet. Jeremiah (8.22) cried out for a physician to apply the Balm of Gilead to the children of Israel to heal them from their sins. A positive appraisal of physicians is found in the deuterocanonical book of Sirach (10.12; 38.1, 3, 11, 15), written by a second-century BCE hellenized Jew, who praised physicians as being agents of God's healing deserving of respect.

Typically, however, the role of healer in Israelite culture was held by the priest. Leviticus provides the most extensive discussion of the diagnosis of disease and the behavioral response by the sick person and the community. Priests diagnosed diseases such as leprosy according to a complicated set of rules of observation, then determined whether or not the leper would be able to continue as a part of the community or be exiled until cured. Becoming sick and being cured were entirely in the hands of God. In Isaiah 38, King Hezekiah was dying of an abscess, but God determined that he should be granted more years; the prophet Isaiah prescribed a poultice made of a cake of figs applied to the abscess.

During the time in which the NT was written, the corpus of knowledge of Mediterranean-world physicians extended to dentistry, urology, obstetrics, ophthalmology, anesthesia, plastic surgery, and diseases of the ears and throat. Physicians practiced venesection (bloodletting), which was often considered the only remedy available when all else failed. Writers of the NT, however, rarely referred to the physician, *iatros*, as a medical practitioner except to criticize. An example is Mark 5.25-34, in which a woman suffering from a hemorrhage, who had been ill for twelve years and whom no physician had been able to help, is cured merely by touching the hem of Jesus's garment.

Luke, called in Col. 4.14 'the beloved physician', provides little in the gospel attributed to him to indicate proof or support of his profession. If he was trained in the Greek city of Antioch, he would have learned the Hippocratic ways focusing on scientific observation and a practical, common-sense approach to health. Luke's gospel, however, focuses on healing brought about by faith and love.

Indeed, the theme of the NT is that Jesus is the only true 'physician' and that medicines, salves, and baths will not heal where there is not prayer, faith and forgiveness. The concept of Christ as the 'great physician' has found many outlets in art and culture. An example is the hymn, by Barney Warren, 'Christ, the Great Physician'.

Recommended reading. Lawson, Russell M. *Science in the Ancient World: An Encyclopedia.* Santa Barbara, CA: ABC Clio, 2004.

Rosner, Fred. *Encyclopedia of Medicine in the Bible and the Talmud.* Lanham, MD: Jason Aronson, 2000.

See also BALM OF GILEAD; HEM OF HIS GARMENT; LEPROSY; SICKNESS [RML]

Pilate's Wife. There is one mention of the wife of Pontius Pilate in the Bible (Matt. 27.19), where she is unnamed, her role being to ask her husband to 'have nothing to do with that innocent man, for today I have suffered a great deal because of a dream about him'. A tradition dating back to Origen (c. 185–254) holds that she became a Christian, and she is mentioned in the apocryphal *Gospel of Nicodemus*, probably written in the eighth century, which expanded on the story and made her the grand-daughter of the Emperor Augustus, influenced by Judaism. A translated version of it gave her the name Procula, and she was also given the name Claudia—a name being mentioned once in the Bible (2 Tim. 4.21). She was to emerge as a saint in the Eastern Orthodox Church and the Ethiopian Orthodox Church. An apocryphal letter attributed to her was published in England in 1929.

In Christian art, Pilate's wife sometimes appears in images of Pilate meeting with Jesus, often behind her husband, sometimes whispering in his ear. Charlotte Brontë wrote a poem in 1846 called 'Pilate's Wife's Dream', and she been given many roles and connections which have no basis in history. When the Swedish actress Viveca Lindfors played her in the 1961 film *King of Kings*, she was portrayed as the daughter of the Emperor Tiberius. In film, she has been played by Majel Coleman in DeMille's *The King of Kings* (1927), Barbara Billingsley in *Day of Triumph* (1954), Jeanne Crain in *Ponzio Pilato* (1962), Angela Lansbury in *The Greatest Story Ever Told* (1965), Claudia Gerini in *The Passion of the Christ* (2004), and Esther Hall in *The Passion* (2008).

As well as appearing in many books and stories about Jesus, Pilate's wife has also been the subject of novels including Esther Kellner's *The Bride of Pilate* (1959), Deborah Mann's *Pilate's Wife* (1976); Hilda Doolittle's *Pilate's Wife* (2000); and Antoinette May's *Pilate's Wife: A Novel of the Roman Empire* (2006), as well as of plays, such as Wilhelm Molitor's *Claudia Procula* (1867) and Curt M. Joseph's play of the same name.

See also PONTIUS PILATE [JC]

Pillar of Cloud, Pillar of Fire. According to Exodus, God is said to have guided the Hebrews out of Egypt as a pillar of cloud by day and as a pillar of fire by night (13.21-22). When the Pharaoh subsequently attacked the Hebrews with his mighty army, it is said that God blocked the Pharaoh's soldiers with the pillar of cloud until the sea was parted and the Hebrews escaped (Exod. 14.19-25). Thereafter, the presence of the marvelous pillar became a daily part of the life for the migrants during their exodus through the wilderness to the Promised Land (Exod. 40.38).

God's divine presence as a pillar of cloud also plays an important role in accounts of the Tabernacle in the wilderness. 'When Moses entered the tent [of meeting], the pillar of cloud would descend and stand at the entrance of the tent, and the Lord would speak with Moses. When all the people saw the pillar of cloud standing at the entrance of the tent, all the people would rise and bow down, all of them, at the entrance of their tent. Thus the Lord used to speak to Moses face to face, as one speaks to a friend' (Exod. 33.9-11; cf. 40.34-38).

The biblical representation of God as a pillar of cloud and fire reflects a common motif in antiquity of associating divinity with light and harkens to ancient associations of heavenly power with awesome and frightening natural events.

Historians searching for plausible natural explanations for these events have speculated that the Bible's 'pillar of smoke' during the day and a 'pillar of fire' at night refers to volcanic eruptions during the events of the time of the Exodus. A 1963 scientific report by Neumann van Padang in the Catalog of Active Volcanoes of the World suggests that 'the Israelite account in Exod. 19.16-18 might refer to an eruption from Harrat ar Rahah' in Saudi Arabia. Others have suggested that the volcanic eruption on the island of Thera (modern Santorini) in the Aegean Sea, around 1600 BCE, may have been the natural event that caused the pillar of smoke or fire to appear during the exodus. Moreover, such a volcanic eruption was allegedly consistent with the other alarming events described in Exodus such as water appearing to be 'blood' (possibly 'red tide',) darkening of the sky (possibly caused by a volcanic ashes), and violent hail (possibly material ejected from the volcano).

In western art and literature, the 'Pillar of Fire' was adopted as the title for an Antony Tudor ballet (1942) as well as a Ray Bradbury science-fiction novel (1948). American artist Barnett Newman produced *Onement I* (1948), a painting that depicts a bold stripe of yellow evoking the biblical pillar of fire. His later work, 'Voice of Fire' (1967)—a solid red stripe on a navy blue background—was purchased by the National Gallery of Canada in 1989 at a cost of $1.8 million, which created its own clouds of controversy.

In modern cinema, the pillar of cloud or smoke and fire has been depicted in Hollywood films such as 'The Ten Commandments' (1956), 'The Prince of Egypt' (1998), and in the popular TV series LOST (2004–2010), where the pillar of smoke symbolized evil rather than goodness.

See also EXODUS; PHARAOH; EGYPT; MOSES; FIRE; TENT OF MEETING [SDD]

Pillar of Salt (see Lot's Wife).

Pisgah. (Etymology uncertain), the proper name for a mountaintop with an expansive view of the ancient lands of the Moabites and Amorites. Mentioned nine times in the Bible, this mountaintop played a crucial role in the exodus of the Israelites into the Promised Land. The exact location is uncertain; references describe it as overlooking the plains of Moab (Deut. 32.49; 34.1). Some scholars have suggested that the exact location is modern day Ras-es-Siyaghah. The Bible does not give a specific location, except that is was near Arabah.

From the biblical accounts, Pisgah seems to be the peak of Mount Nebo. Described as the slopes of Pisgah on certain occasions (Josh. 12.3; 13.2), it is also referred to as a cliff. It was part of the land allocated to the tribes of Reuben and Gad by Moses (Deut. 3.16-17). More significantly, it pertains to Moses's journey to the Promised Land.

Having led the Israelites from Egypt through the wilderness, Moses was not allowed to enter the Promised Land (Deut. 3.23-27). He was instead asked to prepare his servant Joshua to lead the people. The reason given for God's harshness to Moses is disobedience to God's instructions. Moses was told to command a rock to give water to the Israelites. Instead, Moses angrily struck the rock twice at Meribah. This incident led to God's decision not to allow either Moses or Aaron to enter the Promised Land (Num. 20.1-13). However, Moses was allowed to view the land of Canaan from the top of Pisgah (Deut. 34.1).

Less well known, Pisgah also played host to another important event in the exodus narrative. The Moabite king Balak had invited the prophet Balaam (of talking donkey fame) to curse the Israelites. Due to its height and panoramic view, Pisgah was the second place Balak asked Balaam to view and curse the Israelites (Num. 22.2–24.25). However, on all three occasions, Balaam blessed rather than cursed the Israelites.

In recent history, different establishments and public spaces alike have been named Pisgah, especially in the US From the Pisgah National Forest to Pisgah Astronomical Research Institute, to Pisgah Inn (Waynesville), all in North Carolina.

In Christian circles, Pisgah remains a symbolic connotation of things to come. Following the example of Moses viewing the Promised Land from Pisgah, sermons refer to certain points in our lives where we view the promised paradise, a new beginning, or the New Jerusalem. The words of the classic hymn 'Sweet Hour of Prayer' (1842) by William Walford, a blind lay preacher, expresses this very idea: 'Sweet hour of prayer, sweet hour of prayer, may I thy consolation share, till from Mount Pisgah's lofty height I view my home and take my flight'. The home referred to in this line is most assuredly the promise of rapture and ascension to heaven, a prominent feature in evangelical circles.

Literary works also use Pisgah as an allusion to a promised future. Most prominent is Milton's use of Pisgah in his classic work *Paradise Lost*. In the chapter 'Adam's Pisgah Vision', God shows Adam a vision of the future. The ascent to Mount Pisgah whether literally or metaphorically is often a spiritual journey or future aspirations, mostly initiated by God. While the negative reason for Moses being on the mount is often ignored, Pisgah continues to be used in connection with God's promises for believers.

See also BALAK; BALAAM; MOUNT NEBO   [GA]

Plagues. The plagues of the Bible—the 'Biblical Plagues' or the 'Ten Plagues' which strike the people of Egypt in Exodus (chs. 7–12) are sent by God to persuade the Pharaoh to allow the Hebrew slaves to leave Egypt. Many scientists have studied the various plagues and believe that these could actually have happened, although the biblical interpretations did not happen as written. The first plague, for instance, in which the water turns to blood, results in many of the fish dying. This has often been explained by the silt from volcanic activity such as the eruption of Santorini. This, or heavy rains in Lake Victoria where there is red soil, could have led to the Nile, on occasion, giving the impression of being a murky red color. The toxins would have killed the fish in the river, and this might also have led to the emergence of frogs from the river. Certainly the other plagues, such as the livestock suffering from disease, the invasion of locusts, and the like, can be explained with modern knowledge of disease.

The American archaeologist William F. Albright (1891–1971) uncovered a water trough in Egypt at El Arish with an inscription that referred to a period of darkness; the Ipuwer papyrus describes some of plague-like diseases. The writer Immanuel Velikovsky (1895–1979), author of the best-selling *Worlds in Collision* (1950), whose work has been heavily criticized, felt that the conventional chronologies of Egypt were in error, and therefore the accounts in the Ipuwer papyrus were actually referring to events several hundred years before the events of Exodus.

In the NT, the plagues of Revelation 15–16 are modeled on the plagues of Exodus. The images of the plagues were portrayed in many mediaeval illuminations and were used to explain the Black Death in the 1340s. In Cecil B. DeMille's famous film *The Ten Commandments* (1956), a number of the plagues are included, three are alluded to, but the other four are omitted; the 1998 animated feature *The Prince of Egypt* similarly abbreviates the plagues. The heavy metal group Metallica mentions some of the plagues in their songs; the punk band Lars Frederiksen and the Bastards has a song called 'Ten Plagues of Egypt'.

Recommended reading. Trevisanato, Siro Igino. *The Plagues of Egypt: Archaeology, History, and Science Look at the Bible*. Piscataway, NJ: Gorgias Press, 2005.

See also EGYPT; EXODUS; MOSES; NILE; PHARAOH   [JC]

Plants, Symbolism of. Plants in the Bible generally signify life, nature and organic things. The restorative ability of God is compared to a flower in Isa. 35.1-2. Allusions to fruitfulness and abundance can be found in Ezek. 47.12; Deut. 8.7-8; and Pss. 128.3; 144.12. Plants may also symbolize life's transience (Pss 37.2; 90.5-6; 103.15-16) and are employed to contrast extremes (Ps. 1.3-4; Isa. 40.6-8). Although not abundant, there are also plants with negative aspects, such as hemlock, thorns, thistles and prickly plants, first mentioned in Gen. 3.18.

Lilies and roses are the most frequently named flowers; however, flower names are often used interchangeably. They convey beauty and love, but also fragility, transience and pride. The poetry of the Song of Songs describes love with floral references, 'I am a rose of Sharon, a lily of the valleys' (Song 2.1). Both roses (signifying beauty) and lilies (representing purity) became associated with the Virgin Mary, largely through the writings of Bernard of Clairvaux, who described her as 'a rose without thorns'. The Marian poems of Gerard Manley Hopkins, especially *Rosa Mystica* continue this metaphor, as does the tradition of the rosary. The lily is particularly connected to the Annunciation; in paintings of this subject one is held by Gabriel.

The mustard seed, one of the smallest that can be planted, is compared to the kingdom of God (Mark 4.30-32), and used as an exhortation to have faith (Matt. 17.20). The mandrake is considered a plant that aids fertility; it figures in the story of Rachel and Leah (Gen. 30.14-16). Machiavelli's play *La Mandragola* revolves around the use of the plant as an aphrodisiac. Mandrakes also appear in *Harry Potter and the Chamber of Secrets*, as a cure for those petrified by a basilisk.

Trees appear throughout the Bible, from the Tree of Life and the Tree of Knowledge named in the Garden of Eden (Gen. 2.9) to many generic references. The cross of Christ is traditionally made from the wood of the Tree of Life, a symbol of renewal and hope for the future (cf. Rev. 2. 7; 22.2, 14.). In the arid land of Israel, olive trees were the most common; the person who trusts in God is compared to one (Ps. 52.8). Palm trees thrived in an oasis and thus were associated with fertility amidst wilderness (Exod. 15.27). Psalm 92.12 says 'the righteous flourish like the palm tree'. Palm fronds are associated with the Feast of Tabernacles and Jesus' Entry into Jerusalem (John 12.13) on what has become known as Palm Sunday. The fig tree was a very significant domesticated plant in Palestine, appreciated for both shade and fruit. There are many passages that connect it to a pleasurable, settled life, as it took years to cultivate (Mic. 4.4; Isa. 36.17). Fig leaves play a role in the Fall narrative of Genesis (3.7).

The grapevine is a symbol of the House of Israel (Ps. 80.8) and also of the Eucharist. Jesus says, 'I am the true vine' (John 15.1) and equates his blood with the wine at the Last Supper (Luke 22.20). In the Eucharistic context, grapevine imagery appears frequently in early Christian art; the mosaics at Santa Costanza in Rome are an excellent example.

Recommended reading. Musselman, Lytton. *Figs, Dates, Laurel, and Myrrh: Plants of the Bible and the Quran.* Portland, OR: Timber Press, 2007. Swenson, Allen. *The Plants of the Bible and How to Grow Them.* New York: Citadel, 2000.

See also BURNING BUSH; LILIES OF THE FIELD; LILY OF THE VALLEY; OLIVE, OLIVE BRANCH; ROSE OF SHARON; SOUR GRAPES; TREE; TREE OF JESSE; TREE OF KNOWLEDGE, TREE OF LIFE; VINE, VINEYARD

[ACF]

Pomegranate. In Hebrew, *rimmōn*, one of the 'seven species' of the land of promise enumerated in Deut. 8.8. Pomegranates appear on hems the robes of the priests of Israel (Exod. 28.33, 34; 39.24, 25, 26), and they decorate the temple of Solomon (1 Kgs 7.18, 20, 42; 2 Chron. 3.16; 4.13). Pomegranates figure prominently in the sensual imagery of the Song of Songs (4.3, 13; 6.7, 11; 7.12; 8.2), perhaps echoing the association of the fruit with ancient goddesses of love and fertility (Astarte, Persephone, Aphrodite, Juno). Coins featuring the pomegranate motif were minted in Judea during the reign of Alexander Jannaeus (107-76 BCE).

Its many seeds made the pomegranate an apt symbol of fertility. In Jewish tradition, the pomegranate symbolizes righteousness, because it is thought to have 613 seeds, the number of commandments in Torah. Thus pomegranates are traditionally eaten on the second night of Rosh Hashanah, the Jewish New Year. In Christianity, the many seeds enclosed in a single fruit symbolize the many members of the one church; the red juice of the pomegranate symbolizes the blood of the martyrs. Because of its role in the myth of Persephone, who descends to the underworld in winter and rises again in spring, in Christian art the pomegranate also conveys the hope of resurrection. In Renaissance art, paintings of the Madonna and child holding a pomegranate symbolize the Passion, e.g., Botticelli's *Madonna of the Magnificat* (1480-81) and *Madonna of the Pomegranate* (1487), Lorenzo di Credi's *Madonna and Child with a Pomegranate* (1475-80); however, in Piermatteo Amelia's *Madonna and Child* (1481), the child Jesus offering a pomegranate seed to his mother symbolizes Christian unity. The pomegranate has a very different meaning in Albrecht Dürer's *The Four Witches* (1497), where it reverts to the pagan symbolism of fertility (and possibly, in view of the Devil's presence in the scene, to the underworld). Contemporary author Sue Monk Kidd's memoir, *Travelling with Pomegranates* (2010), capitalizes on the multi-layered symbolism of the fruit.

See also FORBIDDEN FRUIT; PLANTS, SYMBOLISM OF; RIMMON; SONG OF SOLOMON, SONGS [MALB]

Pontius Pilate. Prefect of the Roman province of Judea, 26-39 CE. In all four Gospels, the person who, reluctantly, ordered the crucifixion of Jesus (Mark 15.1-15; Matt. 27.11-26; Luke 23.1-23; John 18.28-40). The Gospels have different versions of the story, e.g., Matthew records that Pilate washed his hands of Jesus, while Luke states that Pilate agreed that Jesus had not conspired against Rome; in John, Jesus makes no claim to be the Messiah. Pilate also allows Joseph of Arimathea to take the body of Jesus after the crucifixion (Mark 15.43; Matt. 27.58; Luke 23.51; John 19.38). Other than Gospels and early Christian tradition, there is little independent confirmation of his existence; however, in 1961 archaeologists found a limestone block inscribed with a dedication to Tiberius, mentioning Pilate as 'Prefect of Judaea'. He is referred to by Josephus in the *Antiquities of the Jews* and *The Jewish War*.

Nothing is known for certain about Pilate's birthplace or birth date. Possibly, his name indicates descent from the Samnites, possibly from the Samnite general Gaius Pontius (fl. 321 BCE). Birth traditions have arisen in Fortingall, Perthshire, Scotland; Tarragona, Spain; and Forchheim, southern Germany. To reach the status of prefect, he would have been involved in Roman administration, and probably served as a soldier for a time, like most Roman politicians. Mentions of Pilate in other works, such as those of Philo of Alexandria, state that he was the center of controversy on a few occasions. One involved the display of gilded shields at the palace of Herod Antipas. Another involved Pilate using the money from Herod's Temple to build an aqueduct. Luke 13.1 mentions an incident where Pilate mixed the blood of some Galileans with their sacrifices.

Many traditions have grown up around Pontius Pilate and his wife. The apocryphal *Acts of Pilate* (fourth century) was popular in medieval Europe because of its vivid details about the trial of Jesus. Pilate's wife became known as Claudia (or Procula), canonized as a saint in the Greek Orthodox Church. She is often associated with urging Pilate not to be involved in the crucifixion of Jesus (Matt. 27.19). It is believed that Pilate was banished to Gaul during Caligula's reign (37-41 CE). Local tradition has him committing suicide at Vienne in SE France.

In paintings, the Swiss artist Antonio Ciseri in *Ecce Homo* shows Pilate—albeit only his back—showing Jesus to the people of Jerusalem after the scourging. The Hungarian artist Mihály Munkácsy, in *Christ Before Pilate*, represents Pilate sitting in judgment trying to remain calm despite the raucous crowds around him.

Pilate appears in many fictional works. French writer Anatole France, in *The Procurator of Judaea* (1902), has Pilate retiring to the life of a gentleman farmer in Sicily; Simon Vestdijk, a Dutch writer, completed *De nadagan van Pilatus* ('The Last Days of Pilate') in 1938. Charles Dunscomb's *Bond and the Free* (1955) is a novel about Pilate's niece visiting her uncle in Jerusalem at the time of the trial; and Paul L. Maier's *Pontius Pilate* (1968) covers the trial from Pilate's viewpoint. Pilate was portrayed in the film *Ben Hur* (1959) by Frank Thring, and Roger Caillois wrote a novel *Pontius Pilate* (1961) portraying Pilate as an indecisive Roman administrator. He was played by Robert Hardy in the original television play of Dennis Potter's *Son of Man* (1969), and portrayed in Andrew Lloyd Webber's *Jesus Christ Superstar* (1970).

Recommended reading. Bond, Helen Katharine. *Pontius Pilate in History and Interpretation*. SNTSMS, 100. Cambridge: Cambridge University Press, 1998. Carter, Warren. *Pontius Pilate: Portraits of a Roman Governor*. Collegeville, MN: Liturgical Press, 2003.

See also PASSION NARRATIVE; PILATE'S WIFE   [JC]

Poor, Poverty. The rural poor in antiquity were exposed to the harsh realities of violence, perpetrated by invaders, bandits and tax collectors. They faced harvest failures (cf. Acts 11.28) and natural disasters. The support networks of the family, village or town of the rural poor offset these. Villagers benefited from distributions of money (Dio Chrysostom, *Orations* 7.49) or from a benefactor's offer of grain, either at reduced prices or gratis during times of famine.

However, the extremes of poverty of the rural poor should not be underestimated. An Egyptian relief from Memphis depicts starving nomads in a time of famine, their emaciated bodies revealing the outline of their rib cages. At the bottom lower left of the relief a woman picks vermin from her hair with her left hand and conveys the morsels to her mouth with her right hand. The urban poor faced dangers from the rich and powerful. In Juvenal, *Satires* 3.282-301, a poor man, returning home with the light of a single candle is despised, mocked, and beaten up by a rich thug and his attendants. Jesus, too, underscores the plight of the urban poor (Luke 16.19-31; cf. Acts 3.2-3, 6, 10).

The social stigma of poverty meant that the poor were not only seen as a threat to the social and political order but also to the divine order. A Pompeian graffito expresses contempt towards the poor. 'I hate poor people. If anyone wants something for nothing he is a fool. He should pay for it' (*CIL* IV 9839b). Juvenal (*Satires* 3.145) believed that if a poor man swore by the altars in Samothrace, his oath was fraudulent. With nothing to lose, he held the gods' punishments in contempt. In a Jewish context, Sirach's description of the 'beggar' as the 'abomination to the rich' captures the social dishonor of the pauper (Sir. 13.20; cf. 40.28).

However, the Jewish legal, prophetic, and wisdom texts highlight God's mercy towards the poor (Exod. 23.3, 6; Lev. 19.10, 15; Isa. 11.4; Zech. 7.10; Ps. 34.6; 68.10; Prov. 14.31; 19.17), and the priority of beneficence towards the destitute (e.g., *Pseudo-Phocylides* 22–24; CD 14.12-17). Jesus' call to surrender one's possessions and to give alms is relentless (Mark 10.17-22; Luke 5.11, 28; 14.3; 12.33; 16.1-13; 18.18-23; 19.1-10; 21.1-4), influencing the early church (Acts 20.33-35. cf. 2.41-47; 4.32-39; 4.36–5.11; 6.1-7; 11.12-30; 24.17). In response to Christ's self-impoverishment, Paul organizes the Jerusalem collection for the poor (Rom. 15.25-27; 1 Cor. 16.1-4; 2 Cor. 8.1-9.4; Gal. 2.10).

Bypassing the wealthy benefactors, Jesus praises an impoverished widow for her pious benefaction (Mark 12.41-44). This upends the Jewish tradition of the wealthy caring for the poor (e.g., Exod. 23.11; Lev. 19.10; 23.22; Ruth 2; Tob.1.17; Sir. 34.21, 25). Jesus establishes a counter-cultural community of 'servant-benefactors' (Luke 22.26-27) who invite the socially and economically marginalized to the eschatological banquet, with no expectation of return (Luke 14.12-14). This was the beginning of Christian charity that changed the western world through its care for the destitute, epitomized in Mother Theresa of Calcutta. Social justice advocates challenge western Christians to consider how their affluence is at the expense of 'third world' countries.

Recommended reading. Atkins, M. and Osborne, R. (eds.). *Poverty in the Roman World*. Cambridge: Cambridge University Press, 2006. Hamel, G.H. *Poverty and Charity in Roman Palestine, First Three Centuries* CE. Berkeley and Los Angeles: University of California Press, 1989. Stegemann, E.W., and W. Stegemann. *The Jesus Movement: A Social History of its First Century*. Edinburgh: T. & T. Clark, 1999.

See also FILTHY LUCRE; MAMMON RICH MAN AND LAZARUS; PARABLE; WIDOWS AND ORPHANS [JRHA]

Potiphar/Potiphar's Wife. Potiphar (Potifar), from Egyptian *p-di-p-r* ('he whom the sun god Ra has given'; Greek *Petephrēs*), and his anonymous wife, are figures in Genesis. Potiphar is the officer of Pharaoh who purchases Joseph from the Ishmaelites (Gen. 37.36).

Potiphar appreciates Joseph's piety and puts him in charge of his house. While Potiphar is away, his wife repeatedly attempts to seduce Joseph. Joseph refuses her out of respect for Potiphar. In a desperate play for attention, she ambushes Joseph while he is working and grabs his clothing. Joseph flees, leaving a piece of his garment in her hands (Gen. 39.7-12). Going to the other members of the house and eventually her husband, she claims that Joseph made sexual advances toward her and fled after she cried out. She uses the shred of Joseph's garment as evidence. Enraged, Potiphar has Joseph imprisoned (39.13-20).

Jewish and Muslim traditions debate Joseph's degree of complicity in the encounter with Photiphar's wife (Zuleika in Islam). St Jerome uses the incident to bolster Paul's admonition that it is good for a man not to touch a woman (1 Cor. 17.1). When distinguishing various forms of temptation in *De sermone Domini in Monte*, Augustine concedes that Joseph was tempted by Potiphar's wife but praises him for not being drawn further into sin. Similarly, in his *Commentary on Genesis*, Calvin praises Joseph for his good conscience before God during the incident.

In *The Divine Comedy* (1308–1321), Dante sees Potiphar's wife in the eighth circle of Hell, condemned alongside all other perjurers. Bunyan includes Potiphar's wife in *Pilgrim's Progress* as the character Wanton, who tries to seduce Christian's companion Faithful and in the process becomes a vivid example of hypocrisy. Byron alludes to her in his epic poem *Don Juan*, and in his poem 'On Fame' Keats compares her with celebrity on account of their shared fickleness. Thomas Mann dedicates the third volume of *Joseph and his Brothers* (1933–1942) to Joseph's stewardship under Potiphar and his subsequent dealings with Potiphar's wife. Potiphar and his wife appear in Andrew Lloyd Webber's musical *Joseph and the Amazing Technicolor Dreamcoat*, the former a capitalist tycoon and the latter a seductive vamp, both of whom feature in the song 'Potiphar'. The story of Potiphar and his wife is also depicted in a number of famous works of art, e.g., Guido Reni's *Joseph and Potiphar's Wife* (1631) and Rembrandt's *Joseph Accused by Potiphar's Wife* (1655).

Potiphar and his wife are noteworthy not so much for their maliciousness but more for the purpose of making Joseph look heroic. Nonetheless, Potiphar's wife has become synonymous with the seductress, as well as the negative foreign woman. Thus, this story seems to play on folk motifs in which the seemingly destructive acts of a woman engender the positive transformations of a male. Feminist interpretations of the story have not been so optimistic. In her book *Against our Will* (1975), Susan Brownmiller identifies the story of Potiphar and his wife as one of the crucial Western roots of the myth that women commonly resort to accusations of rape when rejected by a potential male partner. Notably absent is any consideration of Joseph's plight as a sexually victimized slave.

Recommended reading. Gregg, Robert C. 'Joseph with Potiphar's Wife: Early Christian Commentary Seen against the Backdrop of Jewish and Muslim Interpretations'. In *Papers Presented at the Thirteenth International Conference on Patristic Studies, Oxford 1999.* Ed. Maurice Wiles, *et al.* Pp. 326-46. Leuven: Peeters, 1997. Hollis, Susan Tower. 'The Woman in Ancient Examples of the Potiphar's Wife Motif, K2111'. In *Gender and Difference in Ancient Israel.* Ed. Peggy L. Day. Pp. 28-42. Minneapolis: Fortress Press, 1990.

See also JOSEPH [DD]

Potter's Field (see Field of Blood).

Praise. Hebrew: *halal*; Greek: *doxa*. Conceived throughout the Bible as the proper response of humanity to God, the semantic field of praise includes such terms as thanksgiving, blessing, magnifying, glorifying, and singing. The Hebrew name of the Book of Psalms, *Tehillim*, means 'laudations' or 'praises'. The most prominent English translation of the Bible, the KJV, contains 259 usages of the term, mostly in the context of praising God.

The Hebrew term *hallelujah* literally means 'praise God'. The Hallel (Pss 113–118) is a Jewish prayer of praise recited on holy days; in addition, Psalm 136, the 'Great Hallel', is recited at at Passover meal. In Islam, one of the 99 attributes of Allah is 'The Praiseworthy' (Qur'an 42.28; 59.22) Countless Christian hymns express the biblical theme of praise to God ('doxology'), e.g., 'Praise to the Lord, the Almighty' (Joachim Neander), 'Praise, My Soul, the King of Heaven' (Henry F. Lyte), and 'Praise the Lord, You Heav'ns, Adore Him' (Edward Osler). The BBC television series *Songs of Praise*, which features congregations from various parts of Britain singing traditional hymns, has been on the air since 1961.

See also HALLELUJAH; PSALMS, BOOK OF; WORSHIP [MALB]

Prayer. Communication with God (or gods) that assumes both attentiveness and a sense of distance from the divine. The latter element distinguishes prayer from conversation between God and humans.

The most basic form of prayer consists of a cry or groaning under some form of hardship, to which God frequently responds: see Abel's blood (Gen. 4.10), Israel in Egypt (Exod. 2.24), and even creation (Rom. 8.22). Similarly, the Hebrew term often translated as 'prayer' (*tefillah*) represents a lament in which one calls on God to 'listen' and rectify a bad situation. Prayers range from individual to communal, voicing distress to offering thanks, spontaneous to ceremonial.

While silent prayer is common today, in the Bible prayer is generally said aloud and thus has the possibility of being overheard. In one striking example, Eli accuses Hannah of being drunk because she prays 'in her heart/mind' without her words being audible (1 Sam. 1.14). The oral characteristic of prayer broadens its potential audience beyond speech to God to include other humans as well.

In the NT, Jesus teaches his disciples the 'Lord's Prayer' (Matt. 6.5-14; Luke 11.1-13). Such explicit teaching of prayer proves unique and articulates both the identity and purpose of the Jesus movement. In effect, the disciples knew how John the Baptist prayed and asked Jesus how they should be distinct, both in how they address God and how they should be overheard by others. In contrast to the preceding counsel to pray 'in secret', the Lord's Prayer itself is a communal prayer that uses first person plural language throughout (our, us) to articulate an alternative loyalty to the reign of God using thoroughly political language.

In addition to being a spiritual discipline practiced in religious communities, prayer has become embedded in our popular culture: movie and TV characters bargain with and make promises to God in language similar to biblical laments: 'if only you get me out of this ...', baseball players cross themselves as they come up to bat and football players go down on one knee after scoring a touchdown. Such public displays transmitted through the mass media have an analogy in the overheard nature of biblical prayer. The language of prayer has even entered the description of sporting events, where commentators refer to Hail Mary passes in football and describe desperate shot attempts as 'throwing up a prayer' in basketball. These popularized expressions reflect the biblical depiction of praying under duress in the hope of receiving a favorable divine response.

Recommended reading. Balentine, Samuel E. *Prayer in the Hebrew Bible: The Drama of Divine–Human Dialogue.* Minneapolis: Fortress Press, 1993. Longenecker, Richard N. (ed.). *Into God's Presence: Prayer in the New Testament.* Grand Rapids, MI: Wm. B. Eerdmans, 2001. Greenberg, Moshe. *Biblical Prose Prayer as a Window to the Popular Religion of Ancient Israel.* Berkeley, Los

Angeles and London: University of California Press, 1983.

See also HANNAH; LORD'S PRAYER; PRAYER OF AZARIAH; PSALMS, BOOK OF [WDS]

Prayer of Azariah. The Prayer of Azariah is one of the deuterocanonical books found in the Catholic and Eastern Orthodox canons. It is the prayer of Azariah (Abednego) while he and his friends are in the fiery furnace. Azariah, a Hebrew name meaning 'Yahu/Jehovah has helped' was one of the three Hebrew boys who refused to bow down to the golden statue erected by King Nebuchadnezzar (Dan. 3). The king commanded them to be thrown into the fiery furnace for this disobedience, but they were protected from harm by an angel.

Although the Hebrew-Aramaic version does not have this text, the Greek translation of the OT inserts this prayer, along with the *Song of the Three Young Men*, in between Dan. 3.23 and 3.24. It is mostly a prayer of penitence, praise and deliverance. The prayer spans 21 verses, followed by the narration of the king's servants stoking the furnace and descriptions of the Chaldeans near the furnace being burnt to death.

Due to the obscure nature of the text, not much reference is made to the prayer in contemporary culture. Catholics, Eastern Orthodox and other churches use this prayer in their liturgies, especially the hymn of praise in Dan. 3.29-68. Essentially a prayer of deliverance, its content is not much debated; rather there is debate as to its originality and authorship. Not much has been written on the prayer, as it only elucidates on the silence in the Hebrew text of Dan. 3.23-24.

See also DANIEL, BOOK OF; FIERY FURNACE; SONG OF THE THREE YOUNG MEN [GOA]

Preaching. Greek, *kērygma, kēryssō*; generally, the act of proclaiming a message through an authenticated messenger. Its formal study is called homiletics. It is commonly described in the NT, although its motivation can be traced at various stages through the OT. Preaching is an activity that typically involves verbal proclamation of a message either opportunistically or as a formal presentation. Preaching and teaching share certain features in the Bible—what is proclaimed must also be explained or taught. OT writers do not use the word 'preaching' yet nonetheless assume its existence. The Levites in Israel have this role and include the major personality of Ezra. Israel's prophets were also the nation's preachers, sometimes as part of the royal administration but often by those informally or charismatically inspired to proclaim a particular message.

The NT contains many examples of preaching and its content and purpose. Early Christian preaching is built around key themes that arise from the church's understanding of Jesus' identity, actions and teaching, principally his death and resurrection. The claim that the Messiah is Jesus is also central to Christian preaching (Acts 17.3; Mark 8.27-30). Thus the authority for Christian preaching resides not simply in the church and its motives, but with reference to Jesus himself. This happens because Jesus preached and is understood to have transmitted his authority to his closest disciples—the Twelve (Matt. 10.12). Authentic preaching is therefore typically measured by its commitment to the apostolic tradition, in other words, the NT.

The NT considers preaching to be central to the church's life (1 Cor. 9.16). It does not assume that everyone will preach but places it among the indispensable gifts by which it carries out its ministry (Eph. 4.11). This high view of preaching comes from the belief that the Christian message is the result of divine disclosure whose central truths were, despite controversy, held in common by the church. Nonetheless, that same content was proclaimed with great creativity according to the needs of the listeners. This can be seen in Paul's visit to Athens (Acts 17.16-32). Nor was it assumed that everyone who heard the Christian message would accept it (Matt. 10.32f). This however, did not diminish the imperative of preaching, often in very hostile circumstances. The early sermons of Peter and Stephen in Acts include motifs of prophetic judgment (Acts 3.11-26; 6.8–8.1).

The period of the sixteenth-century Reformation saw a remarkable flourishing of the printed sermon following the invention of the Gutenberg printing press in 1453. Preaching has long been associated with periods of religious revival. The preaching of John Wesley (1703–1791) was central to the Methodist revival in the eighteenth century. Wesley's characteristic style was the extension of preaching beyond the prescribed limits of church buildings, a considerable departure from his Anglican tradition. The vocational and theological convictions of those who preach make it comparatively easy to adapt preaching to the use of modern media such as radio, TV, and the internet. Ancient preaching used well-established methods of rhetorical persuasion. However, modern practitioners of homiletical theory enlarge upon this by recognizing how different kinds of sermons serve different purposes. This involves an appreciation for modern communication theory resulting, potentially, in more dynamic involvement between preacher and audience. Paul Scott Wilson (*Preaching and Homiletical Theory,* 2004), and David Buttrick (*Homiletic: Moves and Structures,* 1987) represent contemporary scholarship in the field.

Recommended reading. Dodd, C.H. *The Apostolic Preaching and its Developments.* San Francisco: Harper & Row, 1964.

See also APOSTLES; LEVITES; PROPHECY; PROPHETS; SERMON ON THE MOUNT; SERMON ON THE PLAIN [JKS]

Predestination. Predestination is the doctrine that God is the sovereign ruler of the universe who decides the issue of salvation for every human being, each of whom however, still possesses the free will to choose. The word predestination (destiny) does not appear in the Bible, but a word form of it does appear in Romans and Galatians as the Greek word *proorizō* (Vulgate, *praedestino*), which means to mark off something in advance or beforehand.

In Romans Paul writes, 'For those whom he foreknew he also predestined to be conformed to the image of his Son, in order that he might be the firstborn within a large family. And those whom he predestined, he also called; and those whom he called he also justified; and those whom he justified he also glorified (8.29-30). According to Eph. 1.5, '[God] destined us for adoption ..., according to the good pleasure of his will'; cf. 'In Christ we have also obtained an inheritance having been destined according to the purpose of him who accomplishes all things according to his counsel and will' (Eph. 1.11).

'Predestined' in Romans and Ephesians and other passages that speak of the foreknowledge of God means that God has a definite plan (Acts 2.23), made before the creation of the world (1 Pet. 1.20), that is being fulfilled in its specific parts in the fullness of time (Eph. 1.10). The plan is being worked out by God in order to adopt as his children the saints (Eph. 1. 5). The plan is the product of the free will of God and is motivated by his good pleasure (Eph. 1.5). The plan makes Christ foreordained (KJV) or chosen (NIV) or destined (NRSV) to be the savior.

As the absolute Lord of all creation God controls all things and directs them according to the ends he has chosen in his eternal plan for all of humanity. The accomplishment of God's plan matches his own counsel and will (Eph. 1.11). However, human beings are responsible for their own actions in accomplishing any part of the plan (Acts 2.23). Salvation is by God's mercy, not by human will or exertion (Rom. 9.16).

Narrowly, predestination is about the eternal destiny of every person. Roman Catholic theologians have generally seen predestination as the effect of God's foreknowledge of those will have faith and who will reject it.

The Protestant theologian Jerome Zanchius (1516–1590) taught double predestination, that is, God predestines everyone to heaven or hell before birth. Augustine, Martin Luther and John Calvin taught that God absolutely chooses (predestines) the elect; however, the destiny of the reprobate is merely 'ordained' ('foreordained or 'appointed'). In contrast, Jacobus Arminius (1559–1609) and John Wesley taught that the death of Christ provided the opportunity for people to accept the gift of salvation by exercising their own free will. The theologians at the Synod of Dort (1618–1619) debated this as the Five Points of Calvinism versus Arminianism.

Predestination has been a theme in literature, e.g., Shakespeare's Cassio (*Othello*), Thomas Hobbes's *Leviathan* and Herman Melville's *Moby-Dick*. Some see it as anti-human and others as a joyful affirmation of grace.

Recommended reading. Boettner, Loraine. *The Reformed Doctrine of Predestination.* Philadelphia: The Presbyterian and Reformed Publishing House, 1966. Calvin, John. *Concerning the Eternal Predestination of God.* Louisville, KY: Westminster John Knox Press, 1997. Sigman, Earl H. *Predestination: Coincidence, Chance, Luck.* Bloomington, IN: Authorhouse, 2005.

See also ADOPTION; ELECTION; FREEDOM; GOD; PROVIDENCE; REDEMPTION; SALVATION [AJW]

Prepare the way of the Lord. Latin: *parate viam Domini.* The source of this directive is the essential content of the commission of Second Isaiah. 'Prepare the way of the Lord, make straight in the desert a highway for our God' (40.3b). This passage reflects an Ancient Near Eastern custom: a king *en route* would send a herald before him through his land to announce his coming. His subjects would clear roads of obstacles, level hills and make causeways over valleys (Isa. 40.4). Thereby they were 'rolling out the red carpet' for an august visitor as is done today. Similarly, great fanfare would accompany the glorious self-revelation of the Lord to all humanity

(Isa. 40.5) and the repatriation of his people from their Babylonian exile.

All three synoptic evangelists cite the text.: 'Prepare the way of the Lord, make his paths straight' (Mark 1.3b; Matt. 3.3c; Luke 3.4c; cf. John 1.23b). However, they omit the phrase 'in the desert' in the second clause, following the LXX. Substitution of the phrase 'his paths' for 'a highway for our God' in the second clause facilitates re-identification of 'the Lord' with Jesus. However, a conflation of Exod. 23.20 and Mal. 3.1 immediately precedes the text in Mark: 'See, I am sending my messenger ahead of you, Who will prepare your way' (1.2b, c). The resultant inaccuracy of the introductory formula (Mark 1.2a) precipitated a relocation of the Matthean/Lukan version of the conflated citation into Jesus' laudatory assessment of the Baptist (Matt. 11.10b = Luke 11.27b add the phrase 'before you').

God had promised an angel for protection during the exodus (Exod. 23.10) and now promises a messenger in advance of his coming (Mal. 3.1). Similarly, a forerunner would precede the coming of the Messiah. Jewish religious authorities came to identify this messenger with Elijah *redivivus*, the early church, or John the Baptist (Mark 9.11-13). The visitation of the Lord/the Messiah demanded moral purification as fitting preparation (see Mal. 3.2-4; Matt. 3.7-10; Luke 3.7-14).

The expression 'prepare the way' (for somebody or something) and such variants as 'pave the way', etc., denote the creation of an opportunity for something to happen. American philosopher Henry David Thoreau employs the idiom in his essay *Civil Disobedience* (1849): '[A] State at last ... which even would not think it inconsistent with its own repose if a few were to live aloof from it, not meddling with it, nor embraced by it ... would *prepare the way* for a still more perfect and glorious State, which I have also imagined, but not yet anywhere seen' (italics added).

The musical score of Händel's *Messiah* features a tenor recitative, tenor aria and chorus based on Isa. 40.1-5. More recently, Stephen Schwartz and John-Michael Tebelak composed a song entitled *Prepare Ye the Way of the Lord* in their 1970 rock opera *Godspell*.

See also JOHN THE BAPTIST; VOICE CRYING IN THE WILDERNESS; WILDERNESS. [NRP]

Presence of God. Were one to ask, according to the Bible, 'Where is God found?', the answer would not be a simple one. It depends, in fact, on three interrelated questions: in what manner, in what form, and at what phase in history? Perhaps, in the most basic sense, Jews and Christians agree that God is not limited to one place (e.g., Ps. 139.7-10). However, because God is transcendent, that is, beyond the intellectual and physical grasp of the mortal realm, God is known to reside in the supra-physical realm — heaven (e.g., Deut. 26.15; Matt. 23.22).

There are a number of ways and places, especially in certain periods of biblical history, in which God is understood to be manifest among his people. Jews would recognize that God came to the rescue of the children of Israel in the exodus from Egypt and guided them to the Promised Land. A major expression of divine commitment to be present with Israel is the Mosaic covenant where God proclaims that he will 'dwell' among them, 'walk' among them, and that he will be their God and they his people (Lev. 26.11-12). Jews would attest that the prime expression of divine immanence was the erection of the tabernacle or temple. If Israelites wanted to seek after their God, they would naturally approach him in his 'house' (Ps. 27.4). So, in the tent of meeting, Moses would converse with God 'face to face, as one speaks to a friend' (Exod. 33.11). God, of course, could communicate with his people through messengers, especially angels. In fact, though it is not entirely clear, the 'angel of the Lord' may be identified directly with God himself as in Genesis where the angel speaks to Hagar in first person ('I will surely multiply your offspring', 16.10).

In the NT, the presence of God is marked in a new way by the incarnation of Jesus. This is clearest in John where Jesus' entrance into the world is described as his dwelling or 'tabernacling' (*skēnoō*) with humanity; this language would have conjured up images of the OT tabernacle (cf. 2.21). In a complementary way, God is also said to be present through the Holy Spirit. Thus Paul can refer to the individual Christian's body as the 'temple of the Holy Spirit' which is from God (1 Cor. 6.19; cf. Ps. 51.11).

The Bible also represents the presence of God via symbols, particularly natural ones, such as light (Ps. 18.28), water/rain (Isa. 44.3), fire (Exod. 3.1-12; Acts 2.3), and wind (Ezek. 37.9-14; Acts 2.2). These symbols are pervade western culture especially in art, as in Carravagio's distinct use of light to signal divine intervention, e.g., his famous *Conversion on the Way to Damascus*, where the fallen Pharisee Saul is jarred by the blinding light above. It is also interesting to note that several eminent American universities (including Yale) carry as their motto the Latin phrase *lux et veritas* (light and truth), a rough translation of the Hebrew Urim and Thummim. This was a device consulted by the Israelite high priest to determine God's will. The Latin *lux et veritas* is a translation based on the supposition that Urim and Thummim means something like 'lights and perfections'. Such institutions, often founded on Christian principles, associated (true) knowledge with the presence of God.

Recommended reading. Fee, Gordon D. *Paul, the Spirit, and the People of God.* Peabody, MA: Hendrickson, 1996.

See also HEAVEN; HOLY SPIRIT; LIGHT; PILLAR OF FIRE, PILLAR OF CLOUD; SHEKINAH; TABERNACLE; TEMPLE; URIM AND THUMMIM   [NKG]

Priest. Priests are mentioned numerous times in the Bible. They were the official representatives of the people before God. The Hebrew *kohen* was used to denote someone who served in a religious center, usually a temple, who performed religious rituals that included sacrifices. The same word was used for priest in Ugaritic, Punic, Arabic, Aramaic and Phoenician. It does not have a feminine form in Hebrew, although it does in other languages.

Non-Israelite priests include Melchizedek, was the first priest named in the Bible. He is identified as king of Salem (Gen. 14.18). Joseph married Asenath, the daughter of an Egyptian priest (Gen. 41.45). The non-Israelite priests of Baal are deplored by the biblical authors (e.g., 2 Kgs 10.19-20). Zechariah 1.4 uses *kemarim* to designate idolatrous priests.

Priests are linked to the idea of sin as persons who mediate between the penitent and the divine through sacrifices. Sin makes approaching the power above dangerous, and calls for intervention by someone who can intercede. The priest can offer sacrifices, prayers, thanksgiving, as the people's representative. In turn, priests represent God to humanity.

Biblically, prior to the installation of the Aaronic priesthood, the head of the family served as priest. The patriarchs built altars and offered sacrifices (e.g., Gen. 8.20; 22.13). Some priests were also political leaders. Melchizedek was both priest and king (Gen. 14.18). Reuel (Exod. 2.18), Moses's father-in-law, was both a priest of Midian and a political leader implied in the name Jethro (Exod. 2.16; 3.1).

Aaron was appointed the first High Priest (Num. 25.10-13), formally establishing the Aaronic priesthood. Other members of the tribe of Levi were the second rank of priests who assisted the Aaronids. Priesthood was hereditary, with job specific job assignments. Levites were caretakers of tabernacle and temple. They performed music, prepared sacrifices and served as doorkeepers. All wore special vestments, underwent purification rituals and were ordained in special ceremonies.

The priests served as 'messengers of God' (Mal. 2.7). They were responsible for teaching the people the Law (Deut. 31.9-13). They also were responsible for teaching the people how to distinguish between the holy and the unholy or the clean and the unclean (Lev. 10.10). They also served as judges (Deut. 17.8-13) and on occasion declared the will of God on some issue through divination (e.g., Num. 5.12-31; 1 Sam. 28.6).

In the NT, 'chief priests' are represented as opposed to the ministry of Jesus and even engineering his execution (e.g., Matt. 26.59-68). According to Hebrews, Jesus fulfilled the office of priest (*archiereus*) to become the priest, prophet and king of his people.

Since NT times rabbis and Christian ministers have performed many of the non-sacrificial functions of OT priests when teaching, counseling and leading in worship.

In modern popular culture, priests have been depicted in films and on TV series as both villains and/or champions of goodness (e.g., *The Exorcist* (1973), *The Mission* (1986), *Romero* (1989), *Doubt* (2008), and more recently, *V* (2009) and *Priest* (2011).

Recommended reading. Brutti, Maria. *The Development of the High Priesthood during the Pre-Hasmonean Period: History, Ideology, Theology.* New York: Brill, 2006. Rooke, Deborah. *Zadok's Heirs: The Role and Development of the High Priesthood in Ancient Israel.* New York: Oxford University Press, 2000. VanderKam, James. *From Joshua to Caiaphas: High Priests after the Exile.* Minneapolis: Augsburg Fortress Press, 2004.

See also AARON; CAIAPHIAS; CHIEF PRIESTS; HIGH PRIEST; LEVITES; LEVITICUS, BOOK OF; SANCTUARY; SIN; TABERNACLE; TEMPLE, ISRAEL'S; URIM AND THUMMIM   [AJW]

Principalities and Powers. The Pauline concept of principalities and powers (Greek: *archai, archontes, exousiai, dynameis, kyriotētes, thronoi, kosmokratores tou skotous toutou*, etc.) appears most prominently in Colossians (1.16; 2.10; 2.15) and Ephesians (1.21; 2.2; 3.10; 6.12), although related ideas are also found elsewhere (cf. Rom. 8.38, 13.3; 1 Cor. 2.6-8, 15.24). The principalities and powers were created by Christ (Col. 1.16), but some or all of them rebelled against God and became opposed to his purposes (Eph. 6.12). Christ's work on the cross defeated the powers in some way (Col. 2.15), and upon his return to earth he will reconcile them to himself (Col. 1.20). Meanwhile, the church is to make God's wisdom known to the powers (Eph. 3.10), and battle against them (Eph. 6.12). The concept of principalities and powers probably developed out of the Jewish understanding that God had assigned angels (or in older Israelite mythology, lesser deities under Yahweh) with the task of overseeing different territories or nations (Deut. 32.8), although some scholars argue that Paul was not using the language to refer to angelic beings (see below).

Early Christian theologians typically used the idea of principalities and powers in reference to heavenly, angelic beings, sometimes noting their territorial role (e.g., John Cassian, *Conferences*, 8.14). Believing that heaven consists of seven strata, the apocalyptic *Testament of Levi* places 'thrones' and 'dominions' in a stratum just below angels in the presence of God. Particularly influential on subsequent angelology was Pseudo-Dionysius's *Celestial Hierarchy* (late fifth century), which places the principalities and powers within nine angelic ranks. Principalities, powers, and other related terms appear in Milton's *Paradise Lost* in ways that are generally consistent with prior uses (6.199, 447; 11.221; 12.590). With some variation in names and details, interpreters have consistently understood the powers to be faithful or apostate heavenly beings in a hierarchical order, assigned to various tasks by God.

There are two main contemporary theological interpretations. The first understands the principalities and powers to be (usually fallen) spiritual beings. That is, they are seen as demons against which Christians are called to battle in the spiritual realm. How this is practiced varies considerably, but there is a common understanding that demons—beings who actively try to frustrate the work of God and attack his people—must be stopped through prayer, exorcisms, and/or other related means. This view draws heavily from the battle imagery in Ephesians 6.

A second interpretation (developed in the 1950s) is that the principalities and powers are referring to the socioeconomic forces and power structures that function as part of society. Some advocates for this view hold that Paul was referring to demons, but that his understanding should be demythologized for contemporary application; others argue that Paul had in mind those societal forces and/or actual human rulers. However, there is a common understanding that the powers may be used to refer to governments or the forces behind governments, political ideologies, capitalism, consumerism, media, and many other elements of society that can act as a corrupting force on humans. This view has stimulated considerable discussion both in academia and at a popular level, especially relating to Christian ethics and church–state relations.

Recommended reading. Arnold, Clinton E. *Powers of Darkness: Principalities and Powers in Paul's Letters*. Leicester: InterVarsity Press, 1992. Caird, George B. *Principalities and Powers: A Study in Pauline Theology*. Eoxf: Clarendon Press, 1956.

See also ANGEL; ARMOR OF GOD; CHILDREN OF LIGHT; COLOSSIANS; CROSS; DEMON; EPHESIANS; FALLEN ANGELS; SATAN [BJL]

Priscilla and Aquila. Priscilla is introduced in Acts 18.2 as the wife of Aquila, a Judean from Pontus. They leave Rome at the order of Claudius who decreed that all Judeans be expelled from that city. They meet Paul in Corinth as they share the same trade of tent making. They work alongside him in the trade and in the synagogue. When Paul leaves Corinth they travel with him and stay in Ephesus while he continues to Syria. Aquila is always mentioned with Priscilla who is known in Paul's letters as Prisca (Priscilla is a diminuitive of that name). Prisca is often mentioned first, possibly signifying that the tent trade belongs to her family and that she is a major benefactor of Paul. In Ephesus (Acts 18.26) Prisca and Aquila take Apollos aside and correct his teaching, indicating that Prisca is actively involved in the teaching.

Writing to the Corinthians, Paul sends greetings from Aquila and Prisca and the assembly or church in their house in Ephesus (1 Cor. 16.19). Prisca and Aquila share the leadership of this assembly. In Rom. 16.5, Prisca and Aquila are the leadership of the household and also noted as working with Paul and risking their lives for him.

Priscilla as co-host of a house church and collaborator of Paul has a public role in a cultural world and time where the public sphere was mostly a male domain. Her ability to work alongside Aquila suggests a development of opportunity for women in leadership in the early church.

Priscilla and Aquila are considered to be saints in the Roman Catholic church; their feast day is July 8. Priscilla is the patron saint of good marriages.

The model of mutual collaboration in leadership epitomized by Priscilla and Aquila continues to be nurtured today by the Christians for Biblical Equity who name their journal *Priscilla Papers*. This journal creates a forum for scholarly exchange in the field of biblical interpretation, theology and church history that promotes mutual service of women and men in the church, in the home and in the world. Priscilla and Aquila continue to inspire individuals such as Gretchen and Errol Mannon who set up the Global Church Planting Mission in Colorado Springs in 1996. They dedicated their home as the Priscilla and Aquila House as the center of their mission to the world.

Recommended reading. Osiek, Carolyn. 'Women in House Churches'. In *Common Life in the Early Church: Essays Honoring Graydon F. Snyder.* Ed. Julian V. Hills. Harrisburg, PA: Trinity Press International, 1998.

See also APOLLOS; PAUL [RAHC]

Procula (see Pilate's Wife).

Prodigal Son (see Lost Son, Parable of the).

Profane/Profanation. The Hebrew word for profane is *halal* which means to give open access to something in the sense of making it cheap, common or polluted. This defiles or treats with disrespect what is holy. The Greek word is *bebeloō* and carries a similar meaning.

The OT addressed the many things that could be profaned. These included God's laws (Isa. 56.6), the temple (Acts 24.6), the covenant (Mal. 2.10) and God's name (Exod. 19.22). The bulk of the biblical references to profanation are in Leviticus and Ezekiel.

The temples were so holy they were not open to the people. The word profane therefore literally meant that which was 'before the temple' and therefore outside of the sacred ground. Profaning violates or debases the sacred. It can be accidentally or deliberately done. The deliberate profaning of something sacred means to have irreverence or contempt for holy things. Destruction or abuse of the temple was profanation (Ps. 74.7; Dan. 11.31). 2 Maccabees (8.2) called the pollution of the temple a profanation.

Leviticus required that sacrifices be eaten on the day of the sacrifice or on the next day. To eat leftover sacrifice on the third day was a profanation of what is holy to God. Such offenders were to be cut off from the people (Lev. 19.8). Persons could also profane themselves by their actions. Leviticus 21.9 mandates execution by burning any daughter of a priest who profanes herself through prostitution.

Priests were consecrated men (Lev. 21.4, 9) who could diminish the spiritual power of a place or ritual by treating it in a profane manner. People could also profane themselves in other ways. Esau was a profane person because he despised or desecrated his birthright (Heb. 12.16). His profane character has been variously translated into English as immoral, defiled and godless. His profane behavior made him a foolish and irresponsible man.

The Sabbath was not to be profaned because it was a holy day. Those who profaned the Sabbath were to be put to death (Exod. 32.14). Some forms of legitimate 'profanation' (*hll*) were recognized. For example, a vineyard was no longer holy after its first fruits had been given to the Lord (Deut. 20.6; Jer. 31.5). This is similar to the burial of the worn out scrolls by synagogue personnel. It is also similar to the burning of a retired national flag.

The OT is focused on the pollution of persons, places and things. In contrast, the NT *bebeloō* is used to describe behavior that is lawless, disobedient or godless (e.g., 1 Tim. 1.9; 4.7; 6.20; 2 Tim. 2.16; Heb. 12.16). In both, however, the profanation of the name of God is treated as something that damages the divine reputation among the gentiles.

In modern times the word secular can mean that something is worldly or nonreligious. Because something is not consecrated it is profane and may not be fit for religious use. Many taboos (e.g., Polynesian) warn against profanation. Where there is a sense of the sacred there is often a sense of taboo and a consciousness that warns against breaking it. The American mountain man Jeremiah Johnson became famous for profaning a Crow Indian burial ground and then fighting for his life as the Crows tried to purify the offense by killing him.

Recommended reading. Barney, Steve. *The Sacred and the Profane.* Longwood, FL: Xulon Press, 2009. Douglas, Mary. *Purity and Danger: An Analysis of Concepts of Pollution and Taboo.* New York: Praeger, 1966. O'Connor, Patrick. *Derrida: Profanations.* New York: Continuum International, 2010.

See also BLASPHEMY; RITUAL PURITY, IMPURITY [AJW]

Promised Land. The term 'land of promise' is used in the Bible to designate Canaan, the land promised to Abraham and his descendants (e.g., Gen. 24.7; 28.15; 50.24). This, together with God's commitment to make him a great nation and to bless him so that he could be a blessing, formed the heart of the covenant with Abraham. However, he and his immediate descendants, though living in Canaan, occupied and owned little of it. The subsequent story of Israel is that of land occupation and loss. Some 400 years after Abraham, when Israel had become a large nation, God used Moses to lead Israel out of Egyptian slavery to go to the Promised Land (e.g., Exod. 3.17; 12.25; 13.11). The books of Exodus, Leviticus, and Numbers record their journey towards it. Finally, under Joshua, Moses's successor, Israel entered the land that God had appointed for their possession.

The books of Joshua and Judges describe Israel's initial conquest and subsequent struggle to gain control of the land (cf. Josh. 5.6; 22.4). 1–2 Samuel recount how Israel eventually found rest in the land under King David, while 1–2 Kings describe Israel's apostasy and exile from land. 1–2 Chronicles retell the story for a later generation to demonstrate how important temple worship and covenant faithfulness were to any hope of future restoration. Ezra and Nehemiah show how the prophetic pronouncements about return are partially fulfilled. The expectation of the restoration of a literal land located in Israel/Palestine is still very much part of some Christian eschatological doctrines. It is also a mainstay of orthodox Jewish teaching, providing justification for a Jewish homeland in Palestine.

But 'promised land' points beyond real estate in the Middle East. The idea is rooted in the biblical concept of Eden, God's paradise for the first couple, Adam and Eve. Because of their rebellion against God by eating the forbidden fruit, they were expelled from this garden and condemned to dwell outside its life-giving borders. The story of Israel is a paradigm of God's redemption of his people, restoring them to paradise. In the NT, the idea is expanded in two ways. First, the land theme is replaced with the kingdom of God which is the realm of harmony and fruitfulness. Second, the land becomes the 'new heavens and the new earth' in the eternal future where the faithful dwell with God.

Western culture has adopted the notion to represent a place or future of hope, prosperity and harmony. African American slaves used it in many of their spirituals to describe their release from bondage at death (e.g., 'Free at Last'; 'Swing Low Sweet Chariot'). The Puritans saw America as 'the promised land' (e.g., Melville's *Moby Dick*), and the romantic poets borrowed the image (e.g., Lord Tennyson in 'Lovers' Tale'). Other authors, such as O. Henry and John Steinbeck (*Grapes of Wrath*), scoffed at the notion of America as the 'promised land'. Modern culture still uses the concept too. Bruce Springsteen released a song entitled 'Promised Land', and a number of movies (Hoffman 1987 and Gitai 1996) over the last few decades have been called *Promised Land*. Perhaps all of this suggests the continuing human aspiration for a better world.

Recommended reading. Beavis, Mary Ann. *Jesus and Utopia: Looking for the Kingdom of God in the Roman World*. Minneapolis: Fortress Press, 2006. Brueggemann, Walter. *The Land, Place as Gift, Promise, and Challenge in Biblical Faith*. Philadelphia: Fortress Press, 1977

See also CANAAN, CANAANITES; COVENANT; GARDEN OF EDEN; JOSHUA, BOOK OF; JUDGES, BOOK OF; PROMISE TO ABRAHAM; PALESTINE [BW]

Prophecy. The term 'prophecy' comes from the Greek *prophēteia*, and it essentially means 'foretelling', although the term is used in a considerably wider sense in connection with biblical prophecy, since most biblical prophecies contain relatively little in the way of actual foretelling. Biblical prophecy is just as often a message of admonition. Thus, it is more accurate to call it 'forth-telling' than 'fore-telling', so long as the superhuman aspect of its agency is also emphasized.

Prophecy is the principal medium through which God speaks to the people throughout scripture. The term 'prophecy' stands for any communication of God to the people through the mouth of a human being, but the term includes a broad spectrum of phenomena. Sometimes the prophet's message consists of his or her relating the content of a dream or vision (some prophets were called 'seers'), but the classic model of prophecy is that which is presented in the books of the so-called writing prophets (Isaiah being the most meaningful for the early church). Prophecy can be recognized, in many cases, by the use of the formula 'Thus says the Lord' which typically preceded the oracles that the OT prophets pronounced. The one so speaking was considered to be representing God's very words, and so anyone who lightly dismissed what the prophet was saying stood in danger of God's judgment.

Although prophecy is usually supposed to represent the very words of God, Paul seems to acknowledge that the prophetic message can be tainted by the understanding of the one actually speaking. For this reason, and because prophecies can simply be false, he warns the Thessalonians to be neither uncritical nor dismissive of prophecies spoken in their midst

(1 Thess. 5.20). The gradual canonization of the NT scriptures eventually led many to believe that genuine prophecies were no longer being spoken; as scripture was held by many to contain all the prophecy that was 'sufficient', many Christians held the notion of continuing prophecy to be crowded out by the place now occupied by Scripture.

The idea of prophecy is found throughout the literature of the west, although the models and terminology of this idea sometimes recall specifically Greco-Roman culture rather than the biblical heritage. Most often, the term 'prophecy' is used in a neutral sense, as in the title of William Blake's poem collection, *America, A Prophecy* (1793), or it might be used in a more pagan way, as in Blake's poem 'The Four Zoas' (part of an unfinished work, dated 1797–1804).

Recommended reading. Aune, David E. *Prophecy in Early Christianity and the Ancient Mediterranean World.* Grand Rapids, MI: Eerdmans, 1983. Clements, Ronald E. *Old Testament Prophecy: From Oracles to Canon.* Louisville, KY: Westminster John Knox Press, 1996. Robeck, Cecil M., Jr. *Prophecy in Carthage: Perpetua, Tertullian, and Cyprian.* Cleveland, OH: Pilgrim Press, 1992.

See also PROPHETS [JCP]

Prophets. In biblical perspective, the prophets spoke the divinely revealed word of God. Most were men, but a few were women (e.g., Miriam, Deborah, Huldah, Anna). Israel was sometimes so hostile to the prophetic message against sinful behavior that the messengers were abused or killed (cf. 1 Kgs 18.4; Neh. 9.26; Matt. 23.27; Luke 11.47).

Hebrew prophets were initially called 'seers' (Isa. 30.10, *chozeh*), later prophets (*nabi'im*) (1 Sam. 9.9). The seer was someone who had the gift of clairvoyance which enabled them to see things, even if blind like the prophet Ahijah (1 Kgs 14). The other source of development of the office of prophet was ecstasy (1 Sam. 1.13). Bizarre behavior was also associated with ecstatic experiences that signified the presence of the spirit of God (e.g., 2 Kgs 9.11; Jer. 29.26).

Some prophets were non-professionals like Amos, a shepherd (Amos 1.1), herdsman (Amos 7.14) and sycamore fig cultivator (Amos 7.14). The prophet Deborah was also a judge in Israel (Judg. 4.4). Some were loosely organized into bands or guilds like the 'sons of the prophets' (2 Kgs 4.38). Some may have had marks of identification such as a shaven head or distinctive clothing.

In pre-monarchical Israel, cult prophets were associated with certain local shrines. Even before the temple was built, prophets served the king as did Gad, 'David's seer' (2 Sam. 24.11); later, others became court prophets (e.g., Nathan, Huldah).

The prophetic call may be exemplified by Isaiah's experience in the temple where he has a vision of God, hears angels crying 'Holy' and experiences the sensation of cleansing when a coal is touched to his lips (Isa. 6.6-7). The prophetic call narrative (e.g., 1 Sam. 3.2-14; Jer. 1.3-17; Isa. 6.1-13) emphasizes the origin (God) and content of their oracles (God's word). False prophets could have ecstatic experiences, others foresaw events, but only the true prophets could receive a divine call and message. Isaiah, Amos, Jeremiah and the other prophets were distinctive in the ANE because of the spiritual and moral messages they conveyed to an unfaithful people.

In the NT, the prophets (*prophētēs, prophētai*) are seen as witness to God's plan to send a messianic deliverer (e.g., Matt. 2.23; 5.17; Mark 1.2; Luke 1.70). Early Christian prophets are recognized in the NT (e.g., 1 Cor. 12.28-29; 14.29, 32; Eph. 4.11); in post-apostolic times prophecy becomes associated with preaching, although early Christian sects such as the Montanists (the New Prophecy) emphasized prophetic activity.

There is a long literary tradition of understanding poets as seers who are successors to the prophets. John Milton calls upon the heavenly muse for inspiration to write *Paradise Lost* (1667). Walt Whitman says *Leaves of Grass* (1855) was written after carefully reading the Bible. However, Emerson finds biblical inspiration an uneasy match for a modern theory of poetic inspiration.

Recommended reading. Clements, R.E. *Prophecy and Tradition.* Atlanta: John Knox Press, 1975. Heschel, Abraham J. *The Prophets: An Introduction.* 2 vols. New York: Harper & Row, 1962. Scott, R.B. *The Relevance of the Prophets: An Introduction to the Old Testament Prophets and their Message.* New York: Macmillan, 1968.

See also AMOS, BOOK OF; DANIEL, BOOK OF; DEBORAH; ELIJAH; ELISHA; EZEKIEL, BOOK OF; EZEKIEL; PROPHET; FALSE PROPHET; FORMER PROPHETS; HABAKKUK, BOOK OF; HAGGAI, BOOK OF; HOSEA, BOOK OF; HULDAH; ISAIAH, BOOK OF; JEREMIAH, BOOK OF; JOEL, BOOK OF; JONAH, BOOK OF; LATTER PROPHETS; MALACHI, BOOK OF; MICAH, BOOK OF; NAHUM, BOOK OF; MIRIAM; NATHAN; NOADIAH; OBADIAH, BOOK OF; PROPHECY; SIMEON; PROPHET; WEEPING PROPHET (SEE JEREMIAH); ZECHARIAH, BOOK OF; ZEPHANIAH, BOOK OF [AJW]

Proverbs, Book of. The book of Proverbs (*Mishle*) is part of the third division of the Hebrew Bible known as the Writings (*Ketubim*). The word 'proverb' has a wide semantic field but generally means 'a wise or pithy saying' or aphorism. The term also refers to figures of speech such as irony, sarcasm, or dark sayings, which require special insight. These often have a particular name. For example, a 'riddle' is a *ḥîdâ*, meaning 'an ambiguous saying'. This is the intended meaning of the word in Judg. 14.17. The Book of Proverbs belongs to the genre of Wisdom Literature. 'Wisdom' was an international phenomenon and numerous texts throughout the ANE exhibit the stock language and ideas inherent in such material. Wisdom literature is deeply concerned about the experience of humankind when faced with uncertainty, pain, and the apparent arbitrariness of life despite the best of human efforts to control life's outcomes. It describes the universal search for understanding that permits people to live wisely under such circumstances, with 'situational awareness' as we might now say.

The ancient Israelites also inquired about the best way to live—that is, to maximise life's opportunities, live in harmony with one's environment, and with God. In order to do this, Israel, like its neighboring cultures, needed a template—precepts for living that were tried and tested over time and therefore reliable. A person could build their life knowing the choices they made were sound because they had been built on Wisdom. Proverbs instructs the reader in the ways of prudence—in family life, the royal court, attitudes towards the poor, relatives, and so on. The repeated theme of sexual restraint is a paradigm for prudence. The close proximity of chaos is exemplified by the imagery of death (4.15-23; 8.34-36). In Proverbs, the primary reason to live prudently is rooted in Israel's concept of covenant. Thus, the reader finds, 'The fear of the Lord is the beginning of knowledge; fools despise wisdom and instruction' (1.7). This is an important statement because it situates Proverbs theologically, not merely as an expedient way to live.

Modern interpreters of Proverbs make use of the poetic structure of individual proverbs and note their strong aesthetic appeal. The distinctive features of proverbial wisdom (as received wisdom), is best seen in relation to other biblical wisdom texts such as Job and Ecclesiastes where the limits of such wisdom become apparent. Proverbs' theological stance is closely linked to that of Deuteronomy which assumes a divinely ordered world where correct choices result in positive outcomes. The value of the book of Proverbs can be recognised by its pervasive influence. Paul draws on Prov. 20.22 when he writes in Rom. 13.17, 'Do not repay anyone evil for evil'. The well-known prologue to John uses images and allusions from Prov. 8.22-31. Many English proverbs such as 'Pride goes before a fall' (Prov. 16.8) are derived from the Bible (e.g., Prov. 13.24; 15.1; 16.8; 26.11; cf. Eccl. 1.9; Isa. 48.22; Mark 14.38; Luke 6.31; 1 Tim. 6.10). Contemporary authors using motifs from Proverbs include, David Curzon, *Proverbs 6.6*, and Delmore Schwartz, *Do the Others Speak of Me Mockingly, Maliciously?*

Recommended reading. Crenshaw, James L. *Old Testament Wisdom: An Introduction.* Louisville, KY: Westminster John Knox, 1998. Williams, James G. *Those Who Ponder Proverbs: Aphoristic Thinking and Biblical Literature.* Sheffield: Almond Press, 1981.

See also COVENANT; ECCLESIASTES; FEAR OF THE LORD; JOB; SIRACH; WISDOM; WISDOM OF SOLOMON

[JKS]

Providence. Providence is God's activity in the world to carry out the divine plan. This is presupposed throughout the Bible (e.g., Isa. 43.15; Job 1.10, 12; 2.6; Ps. 139.16; Prov. 16.4; Eccl. 5.5; Neh. 9.6-38; Wis. 14.3; Jdt. 9.5; John 19.11; Matt. 6.25-34; Rom. 8.28; Eph. 1.11). In the history of Christian theology, four views of divine providence have emerged: Calvinism, Arminianism, Molinism and Open Theism.

Calvinism is named after the famous reformer John Calvin. Calvinism was the predominant view of the Reformers, which lost some momentum moving into the twentieth century, However, in recent decades, Calvinist theology has seen a revival within the western church. The Calvinist view of providence insists that God sovereignly plans and brings about all that occurs based upon his predetermined decree. Nothing is left up to chance.

Another theologian, Jacob Arminius, was not impressed with Calvin's idea and insisted upon the opposite view. As with his view of election, Arminius affirmed that God's providence simply involved his looking into the future and ordaining what he saw that all people would choose in his foreknowledge. God's intervention and decree will not violate human freedom, as Arminius defined it.

Molinism is named after the medieval theologian Louis de Molina. This view has recently become popular among some philosophers, but has not trickled down into the church in any serious way. Molina thought that God saw in his foreknowledge all the possible outcomes (worlds) that he could create, given human freedom, and then chose the one that most suited his purposes for the actual world. God's predestination is his actualization of the possible world that is the actual world.

Finally, open theism, an increasingly popular view today, affirms that there is no future since God is in time, just like his creation, and since people have the kind of freedom that always allows them to choose otherwise than what they chose. Since God is in time, the future is yet to be made, so God cannot know it exhaustively. God can know some things about the future, but not all of it. The open theist also thinks that God limits his ability to control his creation. He will not interfere with a person's ability to choose otherwise than what they chose. God's control or providence is limited to those things that lie outside of the domain of human freedom, defined in this sense.

Providence infiltrates western culture in interesting ways. Most prayers probably assume some form of Calvinism since people often ask God to adjust things in such a way that would require intervention within the free activity (defined as the ability to choose otherwise) of other people, such as praying for God to help doctors (guide their hands, for example) heal a sick relative. Perhaps this is why numerous hospitals are named Providence Hospital. Calvinism is also apparent in common phrases such as 'it was meant to be'. In decision making, people probably operate from a more Molinistic view, often reflecting on how things would be had they made a different choice in a particular situation. And yet we often speak as though open theism is true, as though the future remains open.

In popular culture, perhaps the most famous evocation of Calvinism is in the comic strip *Calvin and Hobbes* (1985–1995), in which the six-year-old hero, named after the theologian John Calvin, is paired with his toy tiger, named after the seventeenth-century materialist philosopher Thomas Hobbes.

Recommended reading. Tiessen, Terrance. *Providence and Prayer: How Does God Work in the World?* Downers Grove, IL: InterVarsity, 2000.

See also ELECTION; PREDESTINATION [AWP]

Psalm/Psalmist/Psalms, Book of/Psalter. From the Greek *psalmos*, itself a translation of *mizmor* (Hebrew) meaning song or instrumental music, psalm refers to the poems themselves, psalmist to those who initially spoke or wrote them, and the book to the collection of Psalms (or Psalter) as a whole.

Psalms reflect patterned language that fall into various types such as lament psalms which cry out for deliverance from sickness or the persecution of enemies and thanksgiving psalms that thank God for deliverance already experienced. Other psalms reflect communal worship, meditate on law (*Torah*), and recount biblical events. Psalms reflect the full range of human emotion and experience, which in part accounts for their ongoing significance and popularity.

Brief headings appear prominently atop individual psalms, many of which provide links to David. Whether or not these imply authorship has been debated for more than a hundred years. While the LXX witness and internal linguistic data reflecting later time periods suggest that the psalms do not derive from the historical David, the Psalter's traditional association with this figure remains significant since it links David with ritual, worship, and music as Moses is linked to the law (*Torah*) and Solomon to wisdom. It appears that the difficulty lies more with our contemporary understanding of authorship than with the documents themselves.

The book of Psalms, entitled the 'Book of Praises' (*Tehillim*) in Hebrew, reflects purposeful organization. The first two and last five psalms appropriately introduce and conclude the book, while a repeated formula (*amen* and *amen*) divides it into five sections, moving thematically from lament to thanksgiving. While the book as it stands emerged after the exile it reflects a long compositional history and includes material from a thousand year range.

The Psalms have been treasured by Jews and Christians for millennia. Psalm scrolls were found among the Dead Sea Scrolls and Psalms was one of the most referenced scriptural books in the NT (Isaiah being the other). Psalms have enjoyed continued use to the present, and can even be found, with Proverbs, as an OT book included in some editions of the NT.

While both Jewish and Christian traditions have linked some psalms to the messiah, significant distinctions remain. Some Psalms that Christians understand as referring to Jesus in light of the NT are not recognized as messianic by Jews (e.g., Pss 22, 69), and in those that both traditions commonly interpret messianically, disagreement remains over the identity of the messiah (e.g., Ps. 2).

The Psalms have functioned as prayer and hymn books for both church and synagogue. In addition to devotional use, they have played a significant role in religious education; memorizing psalms has been part of rabbinic training while reciting, chanting and reflecting on the psalms has been a significant part of monastic life in the Christian tradition.

The Psalms have provided a wealth of imagery employed in hymnody and literature over many centuries, including the description of God as rock, fortress, redeemer, midwife, refuge, and mother eagle, among others. The psalms have often been set to music, from Luther's majestic hymn 'A Mighty Fortress is our God' to Handel's *Messiah* and U2's 'Forty' to name a few.

Recommended reading. Bono, 'Introduction'. *Selections from the Book of Psalms*. New York: Grove Press, 1999. Brueggemann, Walter. *Praying the Psalms*. Eugene, OR: Cascade Books, 2007. Witvliet, Jonathan. *The Biblical Psalms in Christian Worship: A Brief Introduction and Guide to Resources*. Grand Rapids, MI: Eerdmans, 2007.

See also MESSIAH; PRAISE; PRAYER; SEPTUAGINT; SHEPHERD PSALM [WDS]

Pseudepigrapha. A term frequently used to designate a specific group of writings, related to the texts and traditions of the OT, with origins in the period between 200 BCE and 200 CE.

Literally, the term *pseudepigrapha* (the transliteration of a Greek plural noun) carries with it the connotation of writings 'with false superscription'—that is, writings attributed to someone other than their author. Although this designation may incline one to approach these texts with a degree of suspicion, pseudepigraphy was a common literary device in the ancient world that served to give credibility to a text that might not otherwise gain a hearing by attributing it to a credible figure of the past. Thus among the OT Pseudepigrapha we have books (written in a variety of genres that espouse a variety of worldviews) that come to be associated with ideal figures of Israel's past like Adam, Enoch, Moses, Isaiah, Baruch, and Solomon. In this sense, the writers were not unlike female writers of previous centuries who employed a male penname, or a high-profile politician who recites the words of his little-known speechwriter.

The term was brought into popular usage in the eighteenth century by J.A. Fabricus who published a collection of texts under the title *Codex pseudepigraphus veteris testamenti*. In the English-speaking world, the first collection of 17 OT Pseudepigrapha was published by R.H. Charles in 1913 in volume two of his *Apocrypha and Pseudepigrapha of the Old Testament*. More recently, J.H. Charlesworth has published a more extensive collection, albeit with different criteria, of 52 *Old Testament Pseudepigrapha*.

Although the boundaries of the corpus of material that falls under the title of Pseudepigrapha remains fluid and elusive, a number of texts are universally recognized, including: *1–2 Enoch, Sibylline Oracles, Testament of the Twelve Patriarchs, Jubilees, 4 Ezra, 2 and 3 Baruch, Ascension of Isaiah, Psalms of Solomon, Life of Adam and Eve*, and *Letter of Aristeas*.

Despite the Jewish origins of the majority of these texts, their greatest appeal seems to have been among the early Christians who preserved and redacted them, translated them into a variety of languages, and consulted them to bring clarity to scriptural ambiguities and doctrinal disputes. Some Christian groups, such as the Ethiopian and Coptic churches, even included a few of them in their canons. Eventually these texts would furnish the basis for much of the legendary material and apocalyptic speculation that thrived during the medieval period—the culmination of which can be seen in the creative genius of Dante's *Divine Comedy*.

For contemporary students of biblical literature, Second Temple Judaism, and Christian origins the value of these texts cannot be underestimated. First, their re-articulation and rewriting of the formative events and sacred traditions of Israel provide critical insight pertaining to how the scriptures were interpreted during the periods of Second Temple Judaism and early Christianity. Second, they provide a large amount of the literary context surrounding the writing of the NT, and are thus critical for its interpretation. In fact, a number of the NT writers either cite or allude to pseudepigraphical texts—the most notable of which is Jude's citation of *1 En.* 1.9 in vv. 14-15. Finally, the varied ideological and religious views expressed in these texts contribute to a more accurate and complete understanding of Second Temple Judaism and early Christianity by displacing any misconceptions of a normative Judaism or a monolithic Christianity.

Recommended reading. Charles, R.H. (ed.). *The Apocrypha and Pseudepigrapha of the Old Testament*. Oxford: Clarendon Press, 1913. Charlesworth, J.H. (ed.). *The Old Testament Pseudepigrapha*. 2 vols. Garden City: Doubleday, 1983–1985.

See also APOCRYPHA, DEUTEROCANONICALS AND INTERTESTAMENTALS; CANON [TB]

Ptolemy. Greek *Ptolemaios*, 'warlike'; a popular Greek name from the fourth century BCE onwards.

It was the name borne by all male members of the Macedonian dynasty who ruled Egypt from 323 to 30 BCE. Its founder, Ptolemy I, had been one of the generals of Alexander the Great, taking over the rule of Egypt and adjoining territories upon the latter's death. Traditionally, the early Ptolemaic kings are viewed as benevolent rulers who made their capital, Alexandria, into the new intellectual and cultural center of the Greek world, while their increasingly decadent scions struggled to maintain control.

As they vied with their Seleucid rivals for domination over Palestine, the Ptolemies of Egypt became involved in Jewish history. One of the prophetic visions ascribed to Daniel (Dan. 11) is actually a veiled description of the strife between the Ptolemaic and Seleucid empires. 1 Maccabees refers more openly to the dynastic conflict between the brothers Ptolemy VI and Ptolemy VIII, as well as to their dealings with the Seleucids (1 Macc. 1.17-19; 11.1-19).

Other Jewish writings of the time are more concerned with propaganda than with history. *3 Maccabees* imagines the Jews of Alexandria being miraculously saved from a pogrom under Ptolemy IV. By contrast, Ptolemy II as portrayed in the *Letter of Aristeas* (probably second century BCE) is a respectful and pious monarch who has the Law of Moses translated from Hebrew into Greek at his expense.

Although they strove to maintain the colonial dominance of Greek culture, numerous coins, statues and relief carvings depict the Ptolemies adopting traditional Egyptian iconography. To most later observers they blended with the legacy of Egypt as a whole. Consequently, explicit references to the Ptolemies in literature and art are very rare, their fortunes eclipsed by those of Alexander, their predecessor, and Cleopatra, the last of their line. Only the story told in the *Letter of Aristeas* has had constant resonance through the ages, even if only for what it says on the origin of the Greek OT.

Recommended reading. Bowman, A.K. *Egypt after the Pharaohs 332 BC–AD 642: From Alexander to the Arab Conquest.* Oxford: Oxford University Press, 1990. Fraser, P.M. *Ptolemaic Alexandria.* 3 vols. Oxford: Clarendon Press, 1972. Wasserstein, A., and D.J. Wasserstein. *The Legend of the Septuagint from Classical Antiquity to Today.* New York: Cambridge University Press, 2006.

See also ANTIOCHUS IV EPIPHANES; EGYPT; MACCABEES; SEPTUAGINT [DDC]

Puah (see Shiprah and Puah).

Publican (see Tax Collector).

Pure in heart (see Beatitudes).

Purgatory. From the Latin *purgare*, 'to cleanse'. In Catholic doctrine, purgatory is a stage in the afterlife where believers who have died in a state of grace are cleansed from their venial ('forgiveable') sins before being admitted into the divine presence. Rather than a punishment, it is conceived as a process of purification.

Although the state of purgatory is not referred to in the Bible, its existence has been inferred from passages such as 2 Maccabees 12.39-45, which speaks of prayers being offered on behalf of Jewish soldiers killed in battle, Matt. 12.31-32, where a reference to a sin that will not be forgiven in this world or the world to come implies that some sins can be forgiven posthumously, and 1 Cor. 3.12-15, where Paul speaks of human work being tested 'as by fire' on judgment day, providing the image of a fiery trial that has come to be associated with purgatory.

Many early Christian writings contain references that have been marshaled to uphold the doctrine (e.g., *Martyrdom of Perpetua and Felicity* 2.3-4; Tertullian, *The Crown* 3.3; *On Monogamy* 10.1-2; John Chrysostom, *Homilies on First Corinthians* 41.5; *Homilies on Philippians* 3.9-10), of which Augustine of Hippo was a proponent (*Sermon* 159.1; 172.2; *City of God* 21.13; *Handbook on Faith, Hope and Charity* 18.69; 19.109). Belief in an intermediate state between life and heaven is found in Jewish tradition, where the ancient rabbis differed concerning the length of time of the cleansing the souls of the dead before they proceeded to paradise; the practice of saying *kaddish*, the Jewish prayer for the dead, for 11 months after the dead of a loved one, reflects this notion. In Islamic belief, some souls are destined for eternal punishment in hell, whereas for others, hell is a temporary state of cleansing before admission to paradise.

The most influential literary account of purgatory is in part two of Dante's *Divine Comedy* (fourteenth century), where *Purgatorio* is envisioned as a seven-tiered mountain, with each level representing one of the seven deadly sins. The poet ascends each level to the Earthly Paradise at its summit, and proceeds from there to heaven and the beatific vision.

See also HEAVEN; HELL; MOURNING; PRAYER; PURIFICATION; SIN [MALB]

Purification. In the OT, purification took three primary forms. First, ritual purity generally required one who was unclean to be washed with water and separated for a period of time before restoration of fellowship with God was possible; ceremonial uncleanness could be incurred through sexual functions (menstruation, child birth, bodily discharges), contact with death (a dead human body, the corpse of an unclean animal, or a clean animal improperly slain), and skin disease. Second, purification could be procured through blood; as the writer of Hebrews asserted, 'under the law almost everything is purified with blood' (9.22). For example, Moses purified the altar by anointing it with the blood of a sin offering (Lev. 8.15). Third, purification from sin—much like the consecration of the altar in the above example—also required the spilling of blood of a sin offering. Ritual purity was not, however, equivalent to moral purity (Job 9.30-31; Jer. 2.22).

According to NT writers, purification for the Christian is no longer achieved through physical washing or sin offerings, as the atoning sacrifice of Jesus on the cross provides a purification superior to that of the Mosaic covenant: 'For if the blood of goats and bulls, with the sprinkling of the ashes of a heifer, sanctifies those who have been defiled so that their flesh is purified, how much more will the blood of Christ, who through the eternal Spirit offered himself without blemish to God, purify our conscience from dead works to worship the living God' (Heb. 9.13-14). Purification under the new covenant is not only achieved at the time of regeneration when one is cleansed by the blood of Christ (1 John 1.7), but in an ongoing process the soul of the believer is also purified through obedience to the truth of the gospel (1 Pet. 1.22; Eph. 5.26); this model parallels Jesus' teaching regarding bathing and foot-washing in John 13.

According to Roman Catholic teaching, a final purification of the souls of the elect is applied in Purgatory, prior to final judgment. This purification is achieved through cleansing fire and its purpose is deliverance from sin.

Purification is a theme repeated in various ways in western culture, though certainly not all purification ritual is tied to a biblical antecedent. In Händel's *Messiah*, the words of Mal. 3.3 (in which God 'will sit as a refiner and purifier of silver, and he will purify the descendants of Levi and refine them like gold and silver') inspired the work 'And He Shall Purify'. The anonymous 'Gawain poet' of the late fourteenth century composed the alliterative homiletic poem—editorially referred to as *Purity* or *Cleanness*—in which biblical imagery is used to warn against uncleanness and praise the virtues of purity. *The Purification of the Temple* by Jacob Jordaens is one of many paintings that depicts the story of Jesus making a whip of cords and driving money changers and traders from the Temple; this form of 'purification' is also depicted by El Greco, Giotto, Jan Sanders van Hemessen, and Rembrandt. In the theatre, an example of purification through ritual bathing is demonstrated by Blanche DuBois in the 1947 Tennessee Williams play *A Streetcar Named Desire*; Blanche, who drifts between reality and illusion, frequently bathes in a symbolic act of washing away her unsavory past.

Recommended reading. Klawans, Jonathan. *Impurity and Sin in Ancient Judaism*. Oxford: Oxford University Press, 2000. Klawans, Jonathan. *Purity, Sacrifice and the Temple: Symbolism and Supersessionism in the Study of Ancient Judaism*. Oxford: Oxford University Press, 2006.

See also LAW; PURGATORY; SACRIFICE; SANCTIFICATION; WASHING [WAS]

Purim. In the Hebrew Bible, 'Purim' (Festival of Lots), is the name of the holiday established by Queen Esther (with her kinsman Mordecai, a judge at the royal court of Shushan in the ancient Persian Empire) to celebrate the victory over the proposed genocide of the Jews of the Persian Empire plotted by King Ahasuerus's wicked Prime Minister, Haman (Est. 9.29-32). The Book of Esther commemorates this barely averted tragedy by the Queen's mandate that the holiday of Purim be celebrated by Jews throughout the world by giving charity to the needy, and presents of prepared food to acquaintances.

This summary, based on the last chapters of the Book of Esther, neatly skirts two elements of dramatic dissonance given full play in the Esther narrative itself. First, the very name of the festival of Purim is itself an allusion to the methodology—the casting of lots (3.7)—that Haman uses to choose the day on which to massacre the Persian Jews. Thus, Esther's naming of the festival uses the irony and discretion with which she must navigate the corridors of power in the Persian court. Much of the dramatic tension in the Book of Esther is taken up by the wiles—feminine and otherwise—that Esther uses to approach the king uninvited, even though that lapse of court etiquette is itself punishable by death (Est. 4.11).

Importantly, Esther utilizes the very methodology proposed by the enemy of her people to best him, all the while operating in disguise. Esther 'passes' as a non-Jew (even Esther's husband does not know she is Jewish). Closely related to the concealment, the hallmark of the Book of Esther, is the consideration of the role of 'chance' in a world where fate appears predetermined by social class and ethnicity.

A second element of dramatic dissonance in Esther is that even though Esther seems to mimic the archvillain Haman with her political schemes, she emphatically refuses to imitate him in his reduction of human life to a mere function of cash and violence. While Haman pays the king so he can annihilate a community within the borders of the Persian empire, offering the bribe of unlimited spoils to those who would participate in his campaign of violence and mayhem, Esther steadfastly refuses to approve a similar free-for-all when the Jews are finally allowed to defend themselves against the pogroms that threaten to break out even after Haman is hung (Est. 9.10, 15, 16). Unlike Haman, Esther proposes a view of empire where there is room for difference, and where political hierarchy does not imply personal abnegation (cf. Est. 2.2-3; 5.9).

Purim as presented by Esther reimagines the possibility of nationhood. Instead of national identity being viewed as a function of might and brute power (as epitomized by Haman), Esther proclaims a national identity contextualized within practices of human connection. Caring about the needy, and promoting behaviors that allow for bonding with people in one's community (Est. 9.22), both provide material ways of building society that emphasize the human dimensions and connections that are the glue of all polities. That all of this takes place within the context of the word—Esther's narrative—emphasizes the primacy of the text in reconceiving the possibilities of politics for all people.

The festival of Purim is celebrated annually on 14 Adar (or on 14 Adar II during leap years of the Jewish calendar). This holiday includes public reading of the scroll of Esther, sending gifts of food to friends and neighbors, donations of charity to the needy, and a festive meal. Masquerades and conviviality are also hallmarks of this day.

See also ESTHER, BOOK OF; HAMAN; MORDECHAI

[MM]

Q

Q document. 'Q' is the name most commonly given to the hypothetical source used by the writers of Matthew and Luke. Its name likely derives from the German *Quelle*, 'source'. NT scholars largely agree that the gospel of Mark was used by the writers of Matthew and Luke. A problem arises, however, in accounting for approximately 230 verses of material that is sometimes identical in Matthew and Luke but absent from Mark. Q is proposed as the solution to that problem. Q is largely sayings of Jesus, therefore giving the appearance that Matthew and Luke independently used Mark as a narrative source and spliced the sayings of Jesus derived from Q into that narrative framework. This view of how the gospels were composed is known as the Two Document Hypothesis (also called Two Source Hypothesis and/or Four Source Hypothesis). It bears repeating that Q is a hypothetical source; a text of Q has never been found. There are critics of the hypothesis.

Q contains some of the most famous early Christian material. the Lord's Prayer (Matt. 6.9-13 // Luke 11.1-4); the Beatitudes (Matt. 5.3-12 //Luke 6.20b-23); the longer temptation of Jesus (Matt. 4.1-11 // Luke 4.1-13); parables of the Leaven (Matt. 13.33 // Luke 13.20-21); the Lost Sheep and Coin (Matt. 18.12-13 // Luke 15.4-10); and the Entrusted Money (Matt. 25.14-30 // Luke 19.12-26); and almost all of the Sermon on the Mount/Plain (Matt. 5-7 // Luke 6.20-39).

John S. Kloppenborg pioneered the idea that Q was composed in three stages. At its earliest stage, Q contained wisdom sayings (witty, often surprising, sometimes humorous counter-cultural observations on right living). Examples would include the surprising claim that one who looks at a woman with lust has already committed adultery in his heart (Matt. 5.28). Later material was added that was 'prophetic', e.g., harsh judgments and threats of the Jerusalem elite and the temple. In its final stage of editing, the temptation narrative was added, the only narrative present in Q.

Kloppenborg's work on stratification has been pushed in new directions by many historical Jesus scholars, who argue that Q's earliest layer must reflect sayings of the historical Jesus. This assumption is evident in portraits of the historical Jesus that come from the Jesus Seminar as a whole and from many of its individual members (J.D. Crossan, Robert Funk, Marcus Borg, Leif Vaage). These portraits tend to draw parallels between the historical Jesus and the Cynics, a popular Greek philosophical movement.

Q has made a number of appearances in modern murder-mysteries, most famously in Dan Brown's *The DaVinci Code*. Part of the conspiracy theory that drives this novel is that there are secret documents that the Vatican is hiding because they tell 'the other side of the story', one that strongly challenges the traditional Catholic portrayal of Jesus. Brown describes Q creatively as 'a book of Jesus' teachings, possibly written in his own hand'. Less well known, but interesting nonetheless, is a 'pulp fiction' murder-mystery actually called *The Q Document* by James Hall Roberts (1979) which not only features Q and a Vatican cover-up, but has a character named James M. Robinson, who has been among the most influential scholars of Q in the last one hundred years.

Recommended reading. Goodacre, Mark. *The Case against Q: Studies in Markan Priority and the Synoptic Problem.* Harrisburg, PA: Trinity Press International, 2002. Kloppenborg, John S. *Q Parallels: Synopsis, Critical Notes, and Concordance.* Sonoma, CA: Polebridge Press, 1988. Robinson, James M. *Jesus according to the Earliest Witnesses.* Minneapolis: Fortress Press, 2007.

See also MATTHEW, GOSPEL OF; LUKE, GOSPEL OF; SYNOPTIC GOSPELS; TEMPTATIONS OF JESUS [ZAC]

Quadriga. Literally the 'four-horse chariot', the *quadriga* was a method of biblical interpretation that developed in the Middle Ages. It invites the reader to explore four possible layers of meaning in the text: literal, allegorical, moral, and anagogical. A thirteenth-century verse encapsulates the method:

Littera gesta docet,	The literal (sense) teaches facts,
Quid credas allegoria,	The allegorical what you should believe,
Moralis quid agas,	The moral what you should do,
Quo tendas anagogia.	The anagogical where you should direct your course.

The *quadriga* has roots in Jewish and patristic biblical interpretation. Traditional Jewish *midrash* is noted for drawing careful attention to text and asking questions about anything that seems unusual:

apparent contradictions (e.g., of history or morality), repetitions, etc., seeking to find a deeper internal coherence. It commonly draws conclusions from the etymology of words, gematria (assigning numerical values to words and letters), and other minute details.

Early Christianity was not opposed to finding 'spiritual' meanings in the Bible ('the letter kills, the Spirit gives life', 2 Cor. 3.6). Up to around 200 CE, there was little or no full-blown allegorical interpretation, but the Bible was read in christological or typological terms. OT texts were read through the lens of the Christ event, looking for anticipations of Jesus' ministry, so that the Bible's references to Christ become explicit.

A NT example would be the treatment of Melchizedek (Gen. 14.17-20) in Hebrews. In Heb. 7.1-4, the author interpreted the obscure passage from Genesis that spoke of Melchizedek in a christological manner, allowing the details of the Genesis text (titles, etymologies of Hebrew words, etc.) to point to the great high priesthood of Christ. Later exegetes would mine additional details. In particular, the detail that Melchizedek provided 'bread and wine' was interpreted as a foreshadowing of the Eucharist.

Origen (d. 254 CE) is considered the father of the allegorical method, teaching that scripture has both a face-value meaning and a deeper, spiritual meaning (some argue that Origen conceived of three senses, literal, moral, and allegorical, but in practice he actually worked with only two possible layers of meaning). By the time of John Cassian (d. c. 435), Christians asserted that scripture's spiritual meaning itself had three senses, the moral, the allegorical, and the anagogical.

Cassian's fourfold sense of Scripture (the literal plus the three spiritual senses) reflected the four modes of discourse Paul noted in 1 Cor. 14.6: 'revelation', 'knowledge', 'prophecy', and 'teaching'. Others connected the three spiritual senses to the three Christian virtues: faith, hope, and love. Combining this conceptualization with Cassian's, we arrive at the following synopsis:

1. The *literal* sense ('revelation'): a face-value reading of the text.
2. The *allegorical* sense ('knowledge'): statements of doctrine in the form of an allegory, corresponding to *faith*.
3. The *moral* sense ('teaching'): ethical guidance, corresponding to *love*.
4. The *anagogical* sense ('prophecy'): pointers to the promised future consummation, corresponding to *hope*.

Recommended reading. Mayeski, Mary A. 'Early Medieval Exegesis: Gregory I to the Twelfth Century'. In *A History of Biblical Interpretation*. II. *The Medieval through the Reformation Periods*. Ed. Alan J. Hauser and Duane F. Watson. Grand Rapids. Eerdmans, 2009. Young, Frances. 'Alexandrian and Antiochene Exegesis'. In *A History of Biblical Interpretation*. II. *The Medieval through the Reformation Periods*. Ed. Alan J. Hauser and Duane F. Watson. Grand Rapids. Eerdmans, 2009

See also ALLEGORY; HERMENEUTICS; MELCHIZEDEK; PARDES; TYPOLOGY [DJP]

Qoheleth (see Ecclesiastes, Book of).

Quick and the dead, the. The term 'quick and the dead' is mentioned three times in the NT (Acts 10.42, 2 Tim. 4.1, and 1 Pet. 4.5) in connection with judging people, with the phrase appearing in the KJV but being changed to the 'living and the dead' in the NRSV.

Alfred Edward John, the Bishop of Derby (UK) wrote a pamphlet published in 1916 entitled *Quick and Dead*; thirty years later, Gilbert F. Cope from the Society of Socialist Clergy and Ministers wrote *Quick or dead: an open letter to the British Council of Churches concerning the era of atomic power*. It was also used, in a totally different context by William Arthur Waterton for his book *The Quick and the Dead* (1956) about life as a test pilot. In yet another context, Deanna Petherbridge and Ludmilla Jordanova wrote their book *The Quick and the Dead: Artists and Anatomy*, published in 1997. The writer of cowboy fiction, Louis L'Amour, used the phrase as the title of a book published in New York in 1974 about the hero and villain in the story being able to draw their guns quickly. It was also used as the title of a book by Gamaliel Bradford, published in Boston in 1931; a novel by Thomas Wiseman, published in London in 1968; a novel by Pamela Bennetts, published in London in 1980; a book by Judy Gardiner, published in 1981; and a book by Jack Curtis, published in London in 1995, based on a screenplay by Simon Moore.

See also LAST JUDGMENT [JC]

Qur'an, the Bible in the. The Muslim scripture, containing the divine revelations believed to have been given to the prophet Muhammad (d. 632 CE), is full of material that is familiar to the reader of the Bible. The Qur'an explicitly mentions Adam, Noah, Abraham, Lot, Ishmael, Isaac, Jacob, Joseph, Moses, Aaron, Pharoah, Korah, King Saul, David, Goliath, Solomon, the Queen of Sheba, Elijah, Job, Jonah, Zechariah, John the Baptist, Gabriel, Michael, Mary, Jesus, and Satan; with possible references to Enoch, Eber, Jethro, Elisha, Ezekiel, Ezra and Haman. Unnamed biblical characters include Cain, Abel and Samuel, and women such as the wives of Adam, Abraham, Lot, Pharoah, Potiphar (called al-'Azīz) and Amran, and Moses' mother and sister. The Qur'an also acknowledges parts of the Bible such as the Torah, the Psalms, and the Gospel.

The Qur'an often only mentions biblical characters, but sometimes also narrates stories about them. With the exception of the story of Joseph, narrated fully in the Qur'an's twelfth chapter (*surah*), these stories tend to be laconic and fragmentary compared to the biblical versions, as if the audience already knows the stories and the Qur'an's purpose is to draw out a particular lesson from them. For example, the Qur'an tells the stories of the first murder (Gen. 4/Qur'an 5.27-32) and of Abraham's near sacrifice of his son (Gen. 22/Qur'an 37.100-13) with a minimum of detail, omitting even the names of important characters, and focusing instead on the moral. The story of Noah and the Flood is told over ten times in different parts of the Qur'an, always somewhat differently, but the Flood itself is barely mentioned, the focus being on Noah's preaching.

The Qur'an thus does not simply literally reflect biblical stories, but transposes, reworks, inverts, and, in some cases, eliminates or ignores them. The Qur'an incorporates not only canonical biblical material but also the ancient generative and interpretive tradition surrounding the biblical material, mediated by oral and liturgical traditions of Jews, Christians and 'pagans' in seventh-century Arabia, e.g., the annunciation of Jesus' birth to Mary, narrated twice in the Qur'an (3.42-49; 19.17-21), bears affinities not only with Luke but also with Christian traditions preserved in the *Infancy Gospel of James*. The story of the first murder (Qur'an 5.27-32) incorporates rabbinic tradition also found in the Talmud.

Biblical readers tend to expect the Qur'an to be structured like the Bible. However, the Qur'an does not, like the Bible, narrate a linear series of events beginning with creation, but rather consists of a series of orally composed speech performances characterized by dialogues, ruptures, abrupt changes in voice and much repetition. From the perspective of its biblical intertexts, the Qur'an jumps around a fair bit such that parallels to biblical material are often multiple and scattered. Moreover, unlike most of the Bible, the Qur'an is explicitly aware of itself as scripture defining itself against competing scriptures by absorbing, transforming and re-amalgamating them.

Much scholarship on the Bible in the Qur'an still presumes a Jewish and/or Christian framework into which the Qur'an is forced so that it tends to be perceived as an inferior derivation, a tendency heightened by polemical works between Christians and Muslims. Work is proceeding towards a truly objective synopsis of 'the Bible in the Qur'an'—most recently, by Marlies ter Borg.

Recommended reading. Reeve, John C. (ed.). *Bible and Qur'ān: Essays in Scriptural Intertextuality*. Atlanta: Society of Biblical Literature, 2003. Borg, Marlies ter. *Sharing Mary: Bible and Qur'an Side by Side*. Scotts Valley, CA: CreateSpace, 2010. Totolli, Robert. *Biblical Prophets in the Qur'ān and Muslim Literature*. Richmond, Surrey: Curzon, 2002

See also OLD TESTAMENT, USE IN THE NEW TESTAMENT [FVG]

Queen of Heaven. Jeremiah gave this title to a goddess worshiped by the Judeans in the late seventh–sixth centuries BCE by the offering of beverages and cakes (7.18; 44.17-19, 25). The Hebrew word for 'offerings' in the text is associated with the burning of incense to deities. Jeremiah's rebuke specifically targets women, described as making the food offerings with other household members. This may suggest a private, household-based cult, dedicated to a fertility goddess, in which women played a prominent role. The goddess's identity is unclear, but she is commonly identified with the Mesopotamian Ishtar or the Phoenician Ashtoreth (Astarte, Asherah). Ancient Ashtoreth worshippers also often venerated Baal, and honored a sacred tree or pole. Israel's prophets considered veneration of such goddesses as direct challenges to Yahweh's rule over Israel.

Milton depicted her as a demon in *Paradise Lost*: 'With these in troop / Came Astoreth, whom the Phoenicians call'd / Astarte, Queen of Heav'n, with crescent Horns; / to whose bright Image by the Moon / Sidonian Virgins paid their Vows and Songs, / In Sion also not unsung, where stood / Her Temple on th'offensive Mountain, built / by that Uxorious King, whose heart though large, / Beguil'd by fair Idolatresses, fell / To Idols foul'. (1.437-46) In her poem, 'Cakes for the Queen of Heaven', Kathleen Norris explored the appeal a woman might have found in worshiping a cosmic mother. The emergence of Israelite monotheism in the midst of Canaanite polytheism offered occasion for many prophetic denunciations in the OT in addition to Jeremiah's. Television's *Battlestar Galactica* (2003) evoked a similar tension as its polytheistic human protagonists fled the homicidal Cylons, a robotic race that was developing its own cult of a 'one true God'.

Christians began applying the title to Mary, the Mother of Jesus by the end of the twelfth century; it became commonplace by the fifteenth century. The earliest depiction of Mary as the Queen of Heaven in western art is found in the *Winchester Psalter*, created in England in the first half of the twelfth century. A later mediaeval depiction can be found in *Mary, Queen of Heaven*, ca.1485, painted by the Master of the Legend of Saint Lucy. Mediaeval Catholic piety honored the Queenship of Mary in four Latin hymns used in the Liturgy of the Hours, the daily prayer services used by priests and vowed religious: *Salve Regina, Ave Regina Caelorum, Alma Redemptris Mater*, and *Regina Coeli*. T.S. Eliot would quote the *Salve Regina* in 'Ash Wednesday', describing the cultural upheaval that followed the First World War: 'and after this, our exile'. Pope Pius XII made this a formal title of Mary in 1954's *Ad Caeli Reginam*. The encyclical asserts that Mary participated in the redemption of the world by giving birth to Christ, paralleling Eve's participation in the Fall. Since Christ is King because of his work of redemption, so Mary should be considered Queen because she shared in that work. The Coronation of the Blessed Virgin Mary is the final 'glorious mystery' of the Rosary, a popular devotional practice for Catholic Christians. Contemporary feminist thought draws upon Mary's title as a source of strength for women, as in Charlene Spretnak's *Missing Mary*.

Recommended reading. Ackerman, Susan. '"And the women knead dough": The Worship of the Queen of Heaven in Sixth-Century Judah'. In *Gender and Difference in Ancient Israel*. Ed. Peggy L. Day. Pp. 109-24. Minneapolis: Fortress Press, 1989. Pelikan, Jaroslav. *Mary through the Centuries: Her Place in the History of Culture*. New Haven: Yale University Press, 1996

See also BAAL; IDOLATRY; ASHERAH; MARY, MOTHER OF JESUS [KDP]

Queen of Sheba. The Queen of Sheba is described in 1 Kgs 10.1-13 (2 Chron. 9.1-2; cf. Matt. 12.42; Luke 11.31) as a wealthy monarch who travels to Jerusalem to test Solomon's reputed wisdom. She is so impressed by his understanding that she bestows many valuable gifts, and he in turn sends her back to her realm laden with riches.

Tradition has the Queen coming from ancient Ethiopia, and this is linked with the story that Solomon and the Queen of Sheba were romantically attached, that she returned to Sheba where their son was born, the first of the Ethiopian dynasty which ruled the Kingdom of Axum; his descendants, through various dynasties, continued to rule Ethiopia until the overthrow of Emperor Haile Selassie in 1974. This story therefore links the early Jewish (and later Christian) traditions in Ethiopia to the Hebrews—there is a common belief that the Ark of the Covenant was taken there, where it is allegedly still located. It also helps explain the later stories surrounding the legendary Emperor Prester John, the leader of an indigenous African Christian kingdom that would become an ally of Christian Europe against the Muslim Ottoman Empire.

As well as possible connections with Ethiopia, there are stories which link the Queen of Sheba to Nubia, and her visit with the various Egyptian trading missions either to Nubia, or to the land of Punt, variously located by scholars as being on the east coast of Africa between modern-day Djibouti and Mombasa. Indeed some commentators place the location of the kingdom of the Queen of Sheba much further south than Ethiopia. The much later discovery of the ruins of Great Zimbabwe led some archaeologists there to believe that Zimbabwe might have been the location of the palace of the Queen of Sheba, although these views have generally been discredited by historians.

The images of the Queen of Sheba—especially her arrival in the Holy Land, and her meeting with King Solomon—appear in many Renaissance works of art. This includes the relief on the gate of the Baptistry in Florence, which was the work of Lorenzo Ghiberti (1378–1455). The grand departure of the Queen of Sheba was captured in the painting *The Embarkation of the Queen of Sheba* by Claude Lorrain (c. 1600–1682). Händel composed 'The Arrival of the Queen of Sheba'; and she appears in numerous works of fiction such as in Czenzi Ormonde's *Solomon and the Queen of Sheba* (New York 1954) and Jay Williams's *Solomon and Sheba* (New York, 1959). There are also many films which feature actresses playing the Queen of Sheba such as Betty Blythe in *The Queen of Sheba* (1921); Gina Lollobrigida in *Solomon and Sheba* (1959); Winifred

Bryan in *The Queen of Sheba Meets the Atom Man* (1963); Halle Berry in *Solomon and Sheba* (1995); Vivica Fox in *Solomon* (1997); and Helena Bergström in *The Queen of Sheba's Pearls* (2004).

Recommended reading. Clapp, Nicholas. *Sheba: Through the Desert in Search of the Legendary Queen.* Boston: Houghton Mifflin, 2001. Simpson, St John (ed.). *Queen of Sheba: Treasures from Ancient Yemen.* London: British Museum Press, 2002. Ullendorff, Edward. *Ethiopia and the Bible.* London: Oxford University Press, 1968

See also OPHIR; SOLOMON; WISDOM [JC]

Quo vadis? The earliest version of this story appears in the apocryphal NT *Acts of Peter*, later retold by Jacobus da Voragine in the thirteenth-century *Golden Legend*. Peter leaves Rome, prompted by fellow Christians during the persecutions of Nero. Walking south out of the city on the Appian Way he sees Christ walking towards him, and asks '*Domine, quo vadis?*' (Lord, where are you going?). Christ replies '*Eo Romam iterum crucifigi*' (I go to Rome to be crucified again). Peter takes this as a sign and returns to Rome himself, where he is crucified. The location of the event on the Via Appia Antica, near the St Sebastian Gate, has been commemorated at least since the ninth century by the small church called Chiesa del Domine Quo Vadis.

The interaction references a conversation that took place after the Last Supper. Peter asked Christ where he was going, and Christ replied, 'Where I am going, you cannot follow me now; but you will follow afterwards' (John 13.36). The scene also evokes the words of Mark 8.34: 'If any want to become my followers, let them deny themselves and take up their cross and follow me'.

The Quo Vadis story is most commonly depicted in Roman art, as the story is so strongly connected to the city of Rome and the importance of Peter as the founder of the Christian community there (and the first Pope). The best example of this is Annibale Carracci's panel painting *Domine quo vadis* (1601–1602), commissioned by Cardinal Pietro Aldobrandini, now in the National Gallery in London. Carracci's oil shows St Peter recoiling, in shock at encountering Christ, who forcefully and dramatically directs him back towards the city with a sweeping arm.

The story was the topic of an historical novel by Polish writer Henryk Sienkiewicz, *Quo Vadis: A Narrative of the Time of Nero*, published at the end of the nineteenth century. The novel mixes fictional and historical characters, setting Nero's persecutions of Christians amidst a love story between a Roman patrician and a Christian woman. The novel has been the basis for at least four films and two television mini-series. The most notable was the 1951 MGM film, titled simply *Quo Vadis*, starring Robert Taylor, Deborah Kerr, Finlay Currie and Peter Ustinov, nominated for eight Academy Awards.

More recently, the phrase was used for a book of collected essays concerning the current evangelical movement. *Quo Vadis, Evangelicalism? Perspectives on the Past, Direction for the Future: Nine Presidential Addresses from the First Fifty Years of the Journal of the Evangelical Theological Society* (ed. Andreas Köstenberger, Crossway Books, 2007). This reflects a trend, across many disciplines, of using the phrase in titles of books that reflect on future directions.

See also APOCRYPHA; CROSS/CRUCIFIXION OF CHRIST; MARTYR; NERO, EMPEROR; PETER [ACF]

Qumran. Kihrbet Qumran is an ancient Jewish site 8.5 miles south of Jericho that was occupied as early as the eighth century BCE, and is the proposed location of the community that produced the Dead Sea Scrolls. Roman soldiers captured the city in 68 CE, and Jewish rebels used the site under Bar Kokhba against the Romans (132–135 CE), which could explain the large cemetery of nearly 1100 tombs. The identity of the inhabitants has been debated exhaustively. Some scholars argue that the Essenes, a Jewish-Messianic-Apocalyptic sect, were the community that wrote the DSS, and given the close vicinity of Khirbet Qumran to the cave that the DSS were discovered, they must have inhabited the site during the last stages of its existence. Theories include a scriptorium, a fortress, a villa built for a wealthy family, a pottery factory, or simply a non-sectarian settlement. The Qumran texts confirmed the accuracy of a host of the medieval manuscripts of the OT, especially Isaiah.

The archaeological finds at Qumran have influenced nearly every modern day archaeologist. The magnitude of the findings at Qumran is extensive enough, yet the discovery of the DSS changed the face of archaeology. The 1975 cult-film *Monty Python and the Holy Grail* gave rise to the adventure that an archaeologist undertakes to discover and debunk the ancient myths and legends. The trilogy known as *The Adventures of Indiana Jones* was inspired by the discoveries at Qumran, as well as the recent trilogies, *The Mummy* and *Lora Croft: Tomb Raider*.

Archaeological sites such as Qumran have sparked a renewed interest the ancient world. This fascination with the ancient ruins has instigated many movies (adventure and horror), hundreds of documentary films, and the fact that the History Channel's most popular program is the archaeological *Digging for Truth*. Qumran even gave James Cameron inspiration to produce a 2007 documentary about the hunt for the tomb of Jesus Christ in *The Lost Tomb of Jesus*.

Recommended reading. Hirschfeld, Yizhar. *Qumran in Context: Reassessing the Archaeological Evidence*. Peabody, MA: Hendrickson Publishers, 2004. Magness, Jodi. *The Archaeology of Qumran and the Dead Sea Scrolls*. Grand Rapids, MI: Eerdmans, 2003

See also BIBLICAL ARCHAEOLOGY; DEAD SEA SCROLLS; ESSENES [CHB]

R

Rabbi. A title used of Jewish religious leaders, this word is derived from the Hebrew word *rab* along with its Aramaic cognate, both of which mean 'great'. In the Bible, the word is used more precisely as a title that literally means 'Great One' or 'My Great One'. Even though 'Rabbi' is derived from a Hebrew root, the title does not appear in the OT. The NT, however, witnesses 16 uses of the word. In each case, 'Rabbi' is a Greek transliteration from Hebrew. The Aramaic cognate, 'Rabboni', is also used twice in the NT and is synonymous with the Hebrew 'Rabbi'.

All but three of the uses in the Bible are references to Jesus. Two of the exceptions are found in Matt. 23.7 when Jesus uses 'Rabbi' as a title for scribes and Pharisees. In the context of Matthew 23, Jesus instructs his disciples not to appropriate the title 'Rabbi', exhorting them to pursue humility over recognition (23.8). Ironically, Jesus allowed others to call him 'Rabbi'. This ostensible double standard suggests that Jesus perceived a distinction between himself and his followers.

John's Gospel provides unique biblical testimony concerning this word. First, John 1.38 offers an explicit definition of the term when the author explains that 'Rabbi' means 'Teacher'. The explanation is informative, as the author does not use the literal meaning of the Hebrew root, 'Great One'. Instead, John translates the word as 'Teacher' indicating that, as a title, 'Rabbi' refers specifically to religious teachers. Consequently, in the Jewish religious setting of Jesus' day, teachers were particularly revered as leaders. Conversely, religious leaders were regarded as teachers. John also contains the only verse in the Bible that applies this title to an individual other than Jesus (as opposed to a group). In John 3.26, John the Baptist's disciples refer to him as 'Rabbi'.

The use of the title fell out of favor among Christians in the early church, most likely a result of Jesus' condemnation of the word in Matt. 23.7. However, 'Rabbi' remains a prominent title in Judaism, common since the time of Jesus' death. 'Rabbi' is currently an official designation for leaders and teachers in the Jewish community, and its meaning has not strayed from the biblical meaning of 'teacher'. Consequently, this title appears frequently in Jewish and Rabbinic religious literature.

Comparatively, there are few examples of rabbis as prominent characters in Western art and literature. The 1979 movie *The Frisco Kid*, however, features Gene Wilder as a Polish Rabbi traveling to San Francisco. There are also a small number of examples of Rabbis as main characters in novels. In 1964, Harry Kemelman wrote *Friday the Rabbi Slept Late*, which is the first volume in a series of mystery novels featuring a rabbi as the principal character. In 1977, Kemelman's novels were adapted to a short-lived television series entitled *Lanigan's Rabbi*. In the late 1960s, American Rabbi and author Chaim Potok wrote *The Chosen* and *The Promise*, which extensively examine Jewish and rabbinical life. Many stories, plays, and movies feature rabbis as minor characters, including the musical *Fiddler on the Roof*, the television shows *The Simpsons* and *Seventh Heaven*, and the movie *Robin Hood: Men in Tights*.

See also JOHN THE BAPTIST [JMK]

Rachel. In Gen. 29–35, Rachel is the daughter of Laban, the younger sister of Leah, and the second but preferred wife of Jacob/Israel. Jacob, fleeing from the wrath of his brother Esau, comes to dwell in the home of Laban where he falls in love with the beautiful Rachel. He consents to work for seven years in exchange for her hand in marriage; however, upon completion of the labor, Laban deceives Jacob by marrying him to his older daughter, Leah. Jacob agrees to another seven years of work in order to marry Rachel, but this time he insists that the marriages takes place prior to the labor. As time goes by, the threesome decides to separate from the home of Laban. Yet, Rachel steals her father's *teraphim*, household gods, which causes him to chase after the family and threaten violence. Rachel hides the figures by sitting on them and survives her father's search by claiming women's troubles as her reason for not standing. Unknowingly, Jacob curses her and it seems that this curse is actually punishing Rachel for her actions because as Leah gives birth to multiple sons, Rachel appears to be barren. However, God's promise to Jacob/Israel trumps Jacob's curse of Rachel and she gives birth to Jacob's two favored sons, Joseph and Benjamin. This is a reverse parallel of the narration regarding Michal in the Book of Kings.

Considered to be a biblical matriarch (cf. Ruth 4.11), she becomes an image of lamentation in Jeremiah, who uses the image of Rachel weeping for her children, the tribes of Ephraim and Manasseh, descendants of Joseph (Jer. 31.5; cf. Matt. 2.18). Her tomb, in modern-day Bethlehem (Gen. 35.19-20; cf. 1 Sam. 10.2), is the third holiest shrine in Israel.

The meeting of Jacob and Rachel has been a popular subject for artists, such as Raphael, Marc Chagall, and Johann Christoph Weigel, throughout the ages. Rachel has also played a role in the literary arts. Fictional recreations of her life have been published by writers such as Orson Scott Card's 2004 book, entitled *Rachel and Leah* and *Water from the Well: Sarah, Rebekah, Rachel,* and *Leah* by Anne Roiphe.

Recommended reading. Frymer-Kensky, Tikva Simone. *Reading the Women of the Bible.* New York: Schocken, 2002

See also GENESIS, BOOK OF; JACOB/ISRAEL; LEAH; RAMAH [EW]

Rahab. Hebrew: *rachab*, 'broad', a prostitute in fortified Jericho, who helped Israelite spies and joined Israel. As a Canaanite, she was marked for destruction by Israelite armies (Josh. 6.17-21; cf. Deut. 7.1-6; 20.16-18). Yet, when Joshua's spies enter her establishment, she hides them and misdirects her own country's pursuing soldiers. Her motives are revealed when she surprisingly says that Yahweh has given the Israelites the land and defeated enemy armies, showing himself God of heaven and earth. She initiates with the spies a covenant of mutual kindness (Josh. 6.12), using the word *chesed* (covenant loyalty), central to Israelite religion. Some scholars find her creed improbably orthodox (cf. Deut. 26.5-9; 6.21-23), yet it provides a motivation for her helping Israel and converting, and encourages Joshua's own ideology (Josh. 2.23-24; 24.2-13). Rahab lowers the spies to freedom over the city wall where her house is built. She hangs out a scarlet cord, the sign of their covenant, and Joshua's armies destroy Jericho but save Rahab and her household (Josh. 6.17-25).

Jewish tradition compliments this proselyte, a Gentile who joined the covenant community (cf. Gen. 38.2; 41.45; Exod. 2.21). The Haggadah calls her one of the four most beautiful women in the world—bedded and informed by great men—who married Joshua and was ancestor of eight prophets including Jeremiah and Huldah (*b.Meg* 15a). Josephus sanitizes Rahab from the designation of prostitute (Hebrew: *zonah*) to innkeeper (*zun,* 'to feed'). The flax drying on her roof (Josh. 2.6) grew near Jericho and was processed into fine linen for trade; perhaps Rahab planned to change businesses.

The NT has Rahab marrying Salmon and among only five women in the genealogy of David and Jesus (Matt. 1.5). Jerome comments: 'none of the holy women are included, only those whom the scriptures blame ... that He who came in behalf of sinners, being Himself born of sinners, might destroy the sins of all'. Rahab is an example of salvation by faith (Heb. 11.31), and good works (Jas 2.25).

Early church theologians read the story as allegory. Rahab's house is the church where the doomed are invited for safety, the red cord is the blood of Christ and Joshua is Christ returning in judgment.

Popular narrative enjoys the 'tart with a heart': Bianca (*Othello*), Belle (*Gone with the Wind*), Fantine (*Les Miserable*), Nicole Kidman's Satine (*Moulin Rouge*), Julia Roberts's Vivian (*Pretty Woman*) and Luenell (*Borat*).

Scharlaken Koord (*Scarlet Cord*) is a Christian aid organisation for prostitutes in Amsterdam, offering support to those trapped by pimps or indebted or foreigners lacking friends.

See also HARLOT; JERICHO; JOSHUA

2. A mythical sea-monster symbolizing chaos, whose defeat by the gods, in Babylonian and Canaanite myths, allowed the creation of an ordered world. The Bible alludes to these myths in speaking of God in creation or in defeat of his enemies. Rahab parallels Tannin the dragon (Isa. 51.9), Leviathan (Job 3.8; Ps. 74.14) and Tiamat.

Rahab comes to mean pride or arrogance (Job 9.13; 26.12), or noisy tumult. It is also a symbol of Egypt as the boastful enemy God defeated in the Exodus (Isa. 30.7; 51.9-11; Ps. 87.4; 89.10). The Talmud calls Rahab the guardian angel of Egypt (*Baba Bathra 74b*).

Rahab is an underwater monster in *Soul Reaver* games for Playstation, and *Castlevania* for Nintendo.

Recommended reading. Bird, P.A. 'The Harlot as Heroine'. *Semeia* 46 (1989) 119-39. Day, John. *God's Conflict with the Dragon and the Sea.* Cambridge: Cambridge University Press, 1985. Sherwood, Aaron. 'A Leader's Misleading and a Prostitute's Profession: A Re-examination of Joshua 2'. *Journal for the Study of the Old Testament* 31 (2006) 43-61.

See also BEHEMOTH; LEVIATHAN [GK]

Rainbow. A phenomenon of color and beauty from the natural world, the rainbow would come to be used most prominently in the Hebrew Bible as a symbol and reminder of God's post-diluvian covenant with Noah, his descendants, and all living creatures, never again to destroy the earth and its inhabitants by flood (9.8-17).

It is noteworthy that the Hebrew word is simply 'bow' (i.e., a weapon), a symbol that many have suggested is indicative of God's mythical struggle against the primordial waters of chaos. Thus, the import of the image of God hanging his bow in the clouds is to suggest that this struggle has now been resolved, once again assuring creation of its freedom to flourish in peace and security. This motif is later picked up in *Sibylline Oracle* 1.307-23, where the Noachic covenant is invoked as the reason why a second great deluge was quenched in its initial stages and prevented from unleashing its destruction upon the earth.

In other biblical usage the image of the rainbow appears primarily in descriptions of God and other heavenly beings. Thus in Ezekiel the splendor of the rainbow's colors is used to describe the glory of Yahweh (1.28). In similar fashion, Revelation envisions a spectacular rainbow that surrounds the one seated on the heavenly throne (4.3), and another that covers the head of the mighty angel who stands on the boundary between land and sea (10.1).

In the post-biblical period, the sign of the rainbow has often been used in anticipation of social change. Notable in this respect is its usage during the German Peasants' War (1524–1525), where a flag bearing the colors of the rainbow and a peasant's boot was flown in anticipation of a new era of political, economic and religious reform. An important voice in this struggle, Thomas Müntzer (1488–1525), is accordingly depicted as bearing this flag by a statue in Stolberg, Germany. The phrase 'Rainbow Coalition' (or a variant of such) has been used to describe several political movements of the twentieth century.

The power of this symbol inspired a wealth of early nineteenth-century art including Joseph Anton Koch's *Noah's Thanksgiving*, Daniel Maclise's *Noah's Sacrifice*, and William Blake's *Noah and the Rainbow*. In recent years, allusion to the rainbow as a symbol of hope can even be heard in the lyrics of the U2 song *Beautiful Day*.

See also FLOOD; NOAH [TB]

Ramah. From the Hebrew root *rûm*, 'be high, lifted up'. The geographic designation Ramah (or variants of the name) appears around 40 times in the OT and once in the NT. Ramah often designates a town in the ancient tribal territory of Benjamin located about 10 km north of Jerusalem and 10 km west of Jericho. The modern location of Er-Ram is often identified with this Ramah, though the West Bank Palestinian city of Ramallah (approximately 12 km north of Jerusalem) is also a possibility. The father of the prophet Samuel, Elkhanah, hailed from Ramah (called Ramathaim in 1 Sam. 1.1), and Samuel made his home in the same place; the town stood as one of a number of locations on Samuel's routine circuit of prophetic ministry (1 Sam. 7.15-17) and apparently served as an important cultic center at that time. In Jer. 40.1, the Babylonians assembled the Israelite exiles at this Ramah just after destroying Jerusalem and the temple. Besides this location just north of Jerusalem, several other places called Ramah appear in the Bible, e.g., Ramah 'in the hill country of Ephraim' (Judg. 4.5) and 'Ramah/Ramoth of the Negeb' (Josh. 19.8; cf. 1 Sam. 30.27), and a Ramah in the north in Josh. 19.29, 19.36 (the Ramah here is often identified with Khirbet Zeitûn er-Râmeh in the Galilee; see also 1 Sam. 30.27; 2 Kgs 8.28-29, etc.).

The most famous reference to Ramah in the Bible occurs in Jeremiah (31.15): 'Thus says the LORD: A voice is heard in Ramah, lamentation and bitter weeping. Rachel is weeping for her children; she refuses to be comforted for her children, because they are no more'. The tradition of Rachel's weeping is probably related to Gen. 35.16-21, where Rachel, wife of Jacob, died in childbirth and was buried somewhere beside the road near Bethlehem (this same burial site is said to be near Ramah in 1 Sam. 10.2). Jeremiah transformed Rachel's tragic death into an image of the matriarch weeping for her 'children', i.e., the exiled and abandoned people of Israel.

The NT author of Matt. 2.18 quotes this passage as evidence that prophecy had been fulfilled; Jeremiah's words here were taken to refer to Herod's attempt to kill all male children two years old and under to eradicate the putative threat to his kingship over Palestine by Jesus (who was a baby at the time). Thus, Rachel's 'wailing and loud lamentation' in Matt. 2.18 refers to this incident of mass infanticide. Traditional Jewish interpretation has taken the reference to Rachel's children in Jer. 31.15 as an image of the population of Jewish exiles driven from the land after the destruction of Jerusalem in 586 BCE, all of whom would be restored to their home by God based on the intercession of Rachel's weeping. Opponents of the practice of abortion in the modern west (primarily American fundamentalist and evangelical Christians) have sometimes taken up as a motto the motif of 'Rachel weeping for her children', with its

Rape

connection to the killing of infants in Matt. 2.18, as a lament for what they see as the murder of children.

See also JEREMIAH; JEREMIAH; BOOK OF; MASSACRE OF THE INNOCENTS; RACHEL [BRD]

Rape. Latin *rapere* (to seize). In the OT, a rape context is indicated by the succession and combination of several Hebrew verbs; *'anah* (to afflict), *shakab* (to have sexual intercourse), *laqah* (to take) and *hazaq* (to seize). There are several narratives about rape in the OT, but none occur in the NT.

Dinah, daughter of Jacob and Leah, is raped by Prince Shechem. Outraged at her abuse, Dinah's brothers kill all the men of Shechem while they are healing from being circumcised (Gen. 34). Genesis 39 relates the story of Joseph, Dinah's half-brother, who faces the false charge of rape when he spurns the advances of his Egyptian master's wife. In Judges 19, a scene of hospitality and honor soon turns into horror when a Levite's concubine is gang-raped and left for dead. 2 Samuel 13 introduces us to Tamar, the daughter of King David, raped by her half-brother Amnon whose so-called love for her turns into hatred afterwards.

Rape is denounced in the Bible. Compared to murder, the penalty for raping a betrothed woman was death (Deut. 22.25-26). If the young woman was not betrothed, the rapist was compelled to marry and never divorce her (Deut. 22.28-29). Rape is said to be disgraceful and foolish, something that should not happen in Israel (2 Sam. 13.12-13).

In the twentieth and twenty-first centuries, rape has been categorised to bring awareness of the various ways and settings in which it occurs. Statutory rape is sexual activity, consensual or forced, with a legally classified minor. Date or acquaintance-rape refers to forced sexual activity between people with a prior social relationship. On college campuses and other social environments, date-rape may involve the use of alcohol and drugs to weaken the resistance of the victim. Marital or spousal rape is a recognised type of domestic abuse. When two or more perpetrators rape one victim it is classified as gang or group-rape. Recently, more research is being done on male-rape, men as victims of rape by women or other men. The history of rape gives evidence that it has been used in war contexts as a way of humiliating and instilling fear in civilians.

Popular culture has dealt with the subject of rape in art, literature and film. Anita Diamant's historical novel *The Red Tent* (1997) retells Dinah's story in Genesis 34. Diamant's interpretation is that Dinah was not raped but in love and more than willing to marry the prince. Contemporary films have attempted to treat the horrific and enduring effects of rape. Alex Haley's famous television series *Roots* (1977) traced the abuse and torture of a family of slaves fighting for freedom. *The Color Purple* (1985) gives voice to a young woman who is raped repeatedly by her step-father. Attitudes about gang-rape and women victims are conveyed in *The Accused* (1988), based on a real-life story. Rape in war is depicted in the drama *Casualties of War* (1989). The highly acclaimed film *Human Trafficking* (2005) shocked audiences with the tragic and appalling reality that women across the world are being bought and sold as sex slaves.

Rape is never depicted as honorable sexual behavior in the Bible. Significantly, all reputable literature and film in contemporary culture mirrors, directly or indirectly, this disapproval of rape.

See also DINAH; LEVITE'S CONCUBINE; POTIPHAR; POTIPHAR'S WIFE; TAMAR [JPD-W]

Raphael, the angel. A prominent angelic figure in the Book of Tobit. A combination of *rp'* ('heal') and *'l* (the divine suffix typical of angelic names), the name perhaps means 'God healed'. Raphael also appears in 1 *Enoch* (influential in earliest Christianity and canonical for the Ethiopian Church) as the archangel who battles fallen Watchers and binds and buries Azaz'el in the desert (*1 En.* 10.4-8; cf. Lev. 16.8-10). Raphael may also be the angel who stirs the healing waters at the pool of Siloam according to a textual variant in John 5.3-4.

Western representations of Raphael have been heavily influenced by Tobit. Tobit, an exiled Jew in Nineveh, is accidentally blinded by bird droppings. In Medea, Sarah is plagued by Asmodeus, a demon who has killed her seven husbands on their wedding nights. Both cry out in prayer and God sends Raphael to help them. When Tobit's son Tobias goes to collect money left in Medea, Raphael accompanies him disguised as a distant relative named Azarias. En route, Raphael/Azarias encourages Tobias to catch a fish from the Tigris and to extract its heart, liver, and gall-bladder. He guides Tobias to Sarah's house and tells him to marry her. Following his instructions, Tobias drives Asmodeus away on their wedding night by burning the fish's liver and heart. Subsequently the angel binds the demon in Egypt.

Returning to Nineveh, Tobias again follows Raphael's instructions, using the fish's gall-bladder to heal his father's blindness. When they try to pay the angel, Raphael reveals that it was he who brought the prayers of Tobit and Sarah into God's presence as 'one of the seven angels who stand ready and enter before the glory of the Lord' (12.15). After ordering them to write an account, Raphael ascends.

Raphael stands alongside two other named angels—Michael and Gabriel (with whom our angel shares a feast day, September 29)—both of whom overshadow Raphael, not only receiving more biblical mentions (Dan. 8.16, 9.21, 10.13,21, 12.1; Luke 1.14-27; Jude 1.9; Rev. 12.7), but also more appearances in literature, art, and film.

However, the traits that mark Raphael in Tobit have kept this angelic figure alive in western culture. With exceptions—e.g., Jan Havicksz Steen's (reconstructed) *Tobias' and Sara's Wedding Night* (seventeenth century)—Raphael is typically rendered as a kind, gentle angel; compare, e.g., Spanish painter Bartolomé Esteban Murillo's *Archangel Raphael with Bishop Domonte* (n.d.) with his *Archangel Michael Victorious over Satan* (c. 1665). Raphael's artist namesake produced an altarpiece entitled *Madonna of the Fish* (c. 1513) where Tobias presents the Madonna and child with a fish under Raphael's direction while Jerome, Tobit's translator, looks on. Rembrandt was particularly taken with Tobit, producing numerous works on the subject, including multiple versions of Raphael's departure (e.g., *The Archangel Leaving Tobias* [1637]).

In literature, Raphael receives no greater accolade than his role as narrator and instructor in *Paradise Lost*, notably written *after* Milton had lost his sight. Appearing in Books 4–8, Raphael is called 'the sociable Spirit' (5.221) and 'affable' (7.41). More recently, Raphael played a major role in R.A. MacAvoy's *The Damiano Trilogy* where he added 'lute instructor' to his resume, before becoming the final volume's title character (1984). The statue of the angel in the Venetian Church of the Archangel Raphael figures prominently in Salley Vickers's novel *Miss Garnet's Angel* (2002).

Recommended reading. Moore, Carey A. *Tobit: A New Translation with Introduction and Commentary*. New York: Doubleday, 1996.

See also ANGEL; GABRIEL, THE ANGEL; MICHAEL, THE ANGEL; TOBIT, BOOK OF [AR]

Rapture, the. From the Greek *harpazō* ('caught up'). The rapture is the term used among premillennial dispensationalist Christians to describe the future eschatological event when the Church is 'raptured', or caught up, to meet Jesus in the sky to live with him forever in heaven. Generally, this event is understood to be distinct from the second coming of Jesus, which is believed to occur later at the end of the tribulation in order to establish the millennial kingdom. Belief in the rapture is based on various NT passages including 1 Thess. 4.16-17: 'For the Lord himself, with a cry of command, with the archangel's call and with the sound of God's trumpet, will descend from heaven, and the dead in Christ will rise first. Then we who are alive, who are left, will be caught up in the clouds together with them to meet the Lord in the air; and so we will be with the Lord for ever'.

The idea of the rapture became prominent in the late nineteenth century among conservative evangelicals in Anglo-America along with the rise of the premillennial dispensationalist system developed by the British theologian, John Nelson Darby (1800–1882). Belief in the rapture was further popularized by the *Scofield Reference Bible* compiled by C.I. Scofield (1843–1921), first published by Oxford University Press in 1909. This Bible was a favorite among premillennial dispensationalist Christians because it included headings and marginal notes that helped to explain central prophetic passages according to Darby's premillennial dispensationalist scheme. As their name suggests, premillennial dispensationalists generally agree that the rapture, the seven years of tribulation, and the second coming of Christ, all take place before the millennial reign of Jesus. There are, however, four major chronological variations of the rapture among premillennial dispensationalists. First, and most common, is the pre-tribulation perspective in which Jesus raptures the church before the tribulation. Second, is the mid-tribulation perspective, in which Jesus raptures the church part way through the tribulation. Third, is the post-tribulation perspective, in which Jesus raptures the church after the tribulation. Finally, and least common, is the partial tribulation perspective, in which Jesus only raptures those who are spiritually prepared, occurring at various times throughout the tribulation. The vast majority of premillennial dispensationalists believe that Jesus will spare the church from the suffering of the tribulation based on their interpretation of a few NT texts such as Rev. 3.10: 'Because you have kept my word of patient endurance, I will keep you from the hour of trial that is coming on the whole world to test the inhabitants of the earth'.

In recent decades the idea of the rapture has found its way into several mainline Christian denominations, largely through the preaching of televangelists Jerry Falwell, John Hagee, Chuck Missler, Pat Robertson, and Jack Van Impe, as well as popular books such as Hal Lindsey's, *The Late Great Planet Earth* (1970), Edgar Whisenant's, *88 Reasons Why the Rapture Will Happen in 1988* (1988), and Tim LaHaye and Jerry Jenkins's, *Left Behind* series of novels and films (1995–2007). References to the rapture have been made in numerous movies, video games, and popular music, and in such television shows as *Aqua Teen Hunger Force*, *Six Feet Under*, *The Simpsons*, and *The Big Bang Theory*.

Recommended reading. Frykholm, Amy Johnson. *Rapture Culture: Left Behind in Evangelical America*. New York: Oxford University Press, 2004.

See also ESCHATOLOGY; MILLENNIUM; TRIBULATION; REVELATION [AS]

Rebekah (Rebecca in NT). Rebekah is the matriarch of the second cycle in the Founding Families narrative of the Book of Genesis (ch. 24). Rebekah is an active character who marries Isaac the son of Sarah and Abraham. Rebekah's active role is evident from the very beginning of her narrative as she is asked for her consent to the marriage with Isaac (Gen. 24.57), which goes against the cultural norm of the time period. In addition to this, God reveals his choice for chosen son to Rebekah and not to Isaac (Gen. 25.23). This results in Isaac's preference for his older son Esau and his assumption that Esau will inherit his wealth and blessing. It also leads to Rebekah's actions of deception in order to acquire the desired blessing for Jacob (Gen. 27.5-17) and thus fulfill the divine word.

The meeting between Rebekah and Abraham's servant Eliezer at a well (Gen. 25.15-27) has frequently been portrayed in western art (e.g., Bray, 1660; Castiglione, c. 1640; Coypel, 1701; Grassi, c. 1720; Tiepolo 1751; Ramboux, 1819). The basis of the strong Jewish female character Rebecca in Sir Walter Scott's famous book *Ivanhoe* is the biblical Rebekah. However, Rebekah has served as more than just inspiration for literary characters. Orson Scott Card wrote a fictionalized account of her life in 2001.

Recommended reading. Frymer-Kensky, Tikva Simone. *Reading the Women of the Bible*. New York: Schocken, 2002.

See also ISAAC; JACOB/ISRAEL; ESAU; GENESIS, BOOK OF; PATRIARCHS AND MATRIARCHS [EW]

Rechabites. In Jer. 35.1-19, the descendants of Jonadab son of Rechab, refugees in Jerusalem for fear of the Babylonian army, are brought before Jeremiah. They refuse to drink wine placed before them because of the command of their ancestor not to drink wine, build houses, sow seed or plant vineyards, but to live in tents so that they will enjoy longevity in the land. Jeremiah contrasts the Rechabites, faithful to their ancestor's command, with the Judeans, who persistently disobey God, and utters a prophecy that the line of Jonadab will never fail.

The Rechabites are not mentioned elsewhere in the Bible, but they figure in a document titled the *History of the Rechabites/Apocalypse of Zosimus*. The text narrates the adventures of Zosimus, an ascetic miraculously transported to a paradisical island where the inhabitants are naked and live blessed lives of virtue and austerity. They are the Rechabites, supernaturally translated to the island after the death of Josiah to protect them from the new king's wrath at their refusal to forsake their ancestral customs. Scholarly opinion differs as to the date and provenance of the text; Charlesworth regards it as fundamentally Jewish with Christian interpolations, with a core dating as early as pre-70 CE; Nikosky regards it as a fourth-century Christian ascetic text; Knights speculates that it could date from as late as the seventh century. The text is extant in medieval Greek, Syriac, Ethiopic, Arabic, Karshuni, Slavonic and Armenian manuscripts, attesting to its wide dissemination. In the nineteenth century, Jer. 35.6-8 provided the inspiration for the Independent Order of the Rechabites, a British temperance society that spread overseas and endured into the first half of the twentieth century.

Recommended reading. Charlesworth, James H. 'History of the Rechabites'. In *The Old Testament Pseudepigrapha*. Ed. James H. Charlesworth. II. Pp. 443-63. New York: Doubleday, 1985. Knights, Chris. 'Rechabites Ancient and Modern: A Study in the Use of Scripture'. *Expository Times* 113 (2002) 333-37. Nikosky, Ronit. 'The *History of the Rechabites* and the Jeremiah Literature'. *Journal for the Study of the Pseudepigrapha* 13 (2002) 185-207.

See also JEREMIAH [MALB]

Red Sea. The Red Sea is the sea between Africa and Asia, and the water is not red, in spite of its name. It is thought that the name might have come from red-colored plants which bloom near the surface of the water, but other scholars see it merely as a description for 'south' in the same way as the Black Sea uses 'black' to designate 'north'.

For the Egyptians, the Red Sea had long been an important waterway, using it to get to the fabled Land of Punt. The Bible mentions the Red Sea more than 50 times, all but three of these in the OT. In most of these (and in all of the NT references), the Red Sea is referred to in connection with the Hebrews crossing it when they left the captivity in Egypt for the Promised Land. However, later scholars have pointed out that the description in Hebrew is of *Yam Suf*, meaning Sea of Reeds which might actually refer to somewhere else in spite of the popular association of the Hebrews crossing of the Red Sea.

The scene of the Hebrews crossing the sea—the waters parting for them—and then the waters drowning the Egyptians has been captured in all the films about the Exodus. The scene is probably most dramatic in Cecil B. DeMille's *The Ten Commandments* (1956) with Charlton Heston playing Moses and Yul Brynner as Pharaoh. It was actually filmed in the Red Sea at Abu Ruwash. The Hebrews and the Egyptians rushed across at Abu Ruwash, with the waves drowning the Egyptians added later in Hollywood. The animated feature *Price of Egypt* (1998) also contains a memorable crossing scene. Mention should also be made of the other great story concerning the Red Sea with Lawrence of Arabia's capture of the port of Aqaba (now Eilat in Israel, filmed in Spain.

See also Exodus; Moses; Pillar of Cloud, Pillar of Fire [JC]

Redeemer. The 'redeemer' is a figure that is primarily related to the broader concept of salvation. The word is a translation from the Hebrew *ga'al* from the OT (e.g., Lev. 25.25; Ruth 3.9, 12; Job 19.25; Ps. 78.35; Isa. 41.14; 44.6) and the Greek *lytrōtēs* (Acts 7.35). It is a particularly OT concept picked up in Acts 7. The redeemer was one aspect of an OT figure known as the 'kinsman–redeemer–avenger'. This person is not known in other ancient legal systems, and in Israel, this figure was a close blood relative and always male. His duty was to protect weaker relatives, redeem property that belonged to relatives if they sold it (cf. Lev. 25.23–25), redeem the relatives if they sold themselves into slavery (cf. Lev. 25.47-55), or even avenge the killing of one of their relatives.

One OT book where this figure plays a prominent role is Ruth, in the character of Boaz. Ruth, a widow, is married to Boaz who acts as her kinsman–redeemer, and the son born out of this union is Obed, grandfather of the famous Israelite king David. In the NT, Jesus, as the great David's greater son, is viewed as the redeemer figure who has paid the penalty on behalf of sinful human beings. Therefore, by the time of the writing of the NT, the kinsman–redeemer figure has taken on a sacrificial and spiritual dimension.

This motif of redeemer and redemption is a poignant theme that pervades music, literature, and film throughout the western world. John Coltrane, a saxophone legend, recorded *A Love Supreme* (1964), which is hailed as one of the greatest jazz albums of all time. In it, Coltrane expresses gratitude to God for his redeeming act and his grace. In Victor Hugo's *Les Miserables*, Monseigneur Bienvenu is a redeemer figure who 'saves' Jean Valjean, as he tells Valjean. 'Jean Valjean, my brother: you no longer belong to evil, but to good. It is your soul that I buy from you; I withdraw it from black thoughts and the spirit of perdition, and I give it to God'. It is a powerful image of redemption wrought by the merciful action of the bishop.

In popular film, there are various figures that represent this Christ-like figure. Two well-known movies, *Braveheart* (1995) and *The Matrix* (1999) show Mel Gibson and Keanu Reeves displaying characteristics of this biblical imagery of the redeemer: whether to provide hope in their sacrificial death (*Braveheart*) or to free others from the oppression of others (*The Matrix*). In the animated film, *The Lion King* (1994), Mufasa sacrifices himself on behalf of Simba, and subsequently becomes a source of inspiration and transformation during Simba's adulthood. In the comic book series (1982–89) and film, *V for Vendetta* (2005), V personifies the avenger–redeemer figure, as he works to free the British masses from the tyranny of a totalitarian government while losing his own life in the process.

Although the 'kinsman' aspect of the OT 'kinsman–redeemer–avenger' is often jettisoned in modern interpretations of the redeemer figure, it is clear that the biblical imagery of the Christ-like redeemer figure continues to provide the inspiration for protagonists in modern storylines today.

See also Freedom; Levirate Marriage; Redemption; Ruth, Book of; Sacrifice; Salvation [MKWS]

Redemption. The word redemption is the accepted translation of the Hebrew roots *g'l* and *pdh*, both of which refer to the legal sense of redeeming as buying property or setting someone free from bondage, as the Israelites are set free from Egypt. The NT verbs *agorazō* and *exagorazō* also incorporate this legal sense but also become metaphorical in such passages as Rom. 3.24-25. Paul sees redemption (*apolytrōsis*) as having a dogmatic and a salvific meaning, often defined as deliverance (Rom. 8.23; 1 Cor. 1.30), and secondly as a ransom-price referring especially to Jesus' death (Rom. 3.24-25; 1 Cor. 6.20; Gal. 3.13).

Since redemption presumes knowledge of the meaning and consequence of sin, the process of redemption begins with repentance, something described by the Psalmist as a 'broken and contrite heart' (Ps. 51.19). The identity of the redeemed is often a point of contention. Who is truly right with God? On one end of the spectrum are those who maintain that very few find favor in his eyes, which is the case with Christian fundamentalists. Others suggest that everyone will enjoy redemption, even Satan, according to Origen's (c. 185–254) version of universalism.

The notion of redemption is everywhere in western art. Dante Alighieri's *The Divine Comedy* (1308–1321) relates a journey through *Inferno* where inhabitants long for redemption. Harriet Beecher Stowe's *Uncle Tom's Cabin* (1852) is not just an account of the mistreatment of slaves but also a theodicy based on redemptive love. Redemption figures prominently in George MacDonald's *Phantastes* (1858) and *Lilith* (1895).

In his album *The Last Temptation* (1994), Alice Cooper explores a Christian understanding of redemption, surprising audiences in the process not accustomed to the king of shock-rock dabbling in religious content. Pink Floyd's *The Wall* (1979) is a story of Pink and his disillusionment and altered consciousness. Pink punishes himself for living inside a Wall he configures by the way he perceives the circumstances of his life (bricks in the wall); ironically, razing the Wall is Pink's redemption.

On television, the continual fall and redemption of Gregory House in *House* (2004–) is an excellent example of a character struggling repeatedly for renewal. *Stargate-SG1* (7 and 14 June, 2002), *24* (23 November, 2008), and *Heroes* (season 5: 21 September, 2009–8 Feb., 2010) all have episodes named 'Redemption'.

Recommended reading. Gaffin, Richard B. *Resurrection and Redemption: A Study in Paul's Soteriology*. Phillipsburg, NJ: P. & R. Publishing, 1978.

See also FORGIVENESS; REDEEMER; SALVATION; SIN

[HP]

Rehoboam. Son of Solomon and Naamah, an Ammonite royal wife (1 Kgs 14.21, 31). He inherited a fragmented kingdom, which dissolved at his ascension into the independent kingdoms of Judah and Israel.

The scene at Shechem related in 1 Kings 12 and 2 Chronicles 10 is a remarkable point in the history of Israel. The locale was in the heart of the northern hill country. It was the site of the covenant renewal under Joshua, likely the symbolic backdrop of the meeting.

Rehoboam's counselors consisted of two groups, the older advisors who served his father, and the group of comparatively younger advisors who were his contemporaries. Rehoboam was 41, meaning his age peers were also in their forties, in the prime of maturity. Both groups of advisors understood completely what was at stake.

Solomon had wrought incredible and quick transformation to Israelite society. Israel had passed from a tribal confederation, to a chiefdom (under Saul and David), to a bureaucratic state. Solomon had greatly reduced the power of the tribes by introducing district governors, loyal to him alone, ruling territories which were not restricted to tribal areas. His offices were filled by men who were not close kin (kin office holders is a mark of chiefdoms). The kinship power structures throughout society were becoming politically obsolete.

It is remarkable is that the northern tribal leaders at Shechem were willing to accept their diminished political role in exchange for concessions, agreeing to acquiesce to the existence of a bureaucratic state at their expense. This trade seemed reasonable to Solomon's advisors, many of whom remembered the struggles of trying to centrally organize a tribal chiefdom. That the tribal leaders were accepting of the circumstances was a victory in itself.

The new group of advisors, however, was acutely aware that to legitimize the power of the tribal leaders was to deny the power of the central government over the old system. Though the responses of both groups are encapsulated in a couple of sentences, Rehoboam took three days to formulate his response, fully weighing the implications of his statement. He chose poorly, in retrospect.

The stated complaints of the tribes centered on Solomon's policies of forced labor and increased taxation. Doubtless an undercurrent of the complaints focused on the fact that most of the labor was directed towards building projects in Judah, the building of the palace and temple complex and the establishment of the port at Elath. Northerners were contributing much more than they were getting in return.

The split was rendered irrevocable by the will of Yahweh, expressed by the word of God coming from the mouth of Shemaiah (1 Kgs 12.22-24). Though continuous tension and limited warfare occurred throughout his reign, Rehoboam never tried to reconsolidate the kingdoms again.

Two notable events occurred during his reign. The first was the raid of Shishak, the founder of the 22nd (Libyan) Dynasty of Egypt. Some commentators hold that he must have taken some Judean territory in the south and southwest, owing to no mentioning of fortifications being erected in the list found in 2 Chronicles 11. Jerusalem was spared by bribery, allowing him to clean out most of the temple treasures.

Second, Jeroboam, king of Israel, expelled all of the Levites from his kingdom. The arrival of the priesthood delayed the apostasy of Rehoboam for a time (2 Chron. 11.13-17), though ultimately his reign was found wanting in the eyes of God.

Recommended reading. Weinfeld, M. 'The Counsel of the 'Elders' to Rehoboam and its Implications'. *Maarav* 3/1 (1982) 27-53.

See also JEROBOAM; SOLOMON [MAP]

Remnant. The concept of 'remnant' is expressed through different terms in the OT (especially *se'ar* and *se'erit*) to describe three minority groups. First, the concept is applied to the survivors that have escaped hardships and disasters, such as the Jews who returned from Babylon to Palestine and survived the exile (Hag. 1.12-14; Zech. 8.6, 11, 12; cf. Deut. 28.62; Lev. 26.36). A second use describes the faithful people of Israel who overcame apostasy and were preserved by God for carrying out his mission (1 Kgs 19.18; Ezek. 6.8-9, Isa. 10.20, Zeph. 3.13). During the period of the exile the concept of remnant consolidated this theological meaning. The prophets announced that 'A remnant shall return' (Isa. 10.21) so that Israel, as symbol of the people of God, will never be totally destroyed (Isa. 46.3-4).

In the postexilic period, when the temple was rebuilt by those who returned to Jerusalem, the concept of the remnant was enlarged to include believers from all nations, giving to the remnant concept a new eschatological meaning (Amos 9.11-12; cf. Isa. 45.20). The Qumran community saw itself as the promised 'holy remnant' (*Damascus Document* 1.4). Similarly, the Pharisees attempted, by their faithful observance of the Torah, to set themselves up as the announced remnant.

In the NT, the specific noun remnant (*leimma*) is found only in Rom. 11.5, but the remnant concept is largely debated (see especially Rom. 9–11). The promised remnant is understood as the people whom God calls together from Israel and the nations to constitute the church of Christ (cf. Acts 15.13-18).

The Book of Revelation expresses the notion of remnant by the adjective *loipoi* used in its plural form (from the verb *leipō*, to 'leave remaining' [Rev. 11.13; 19.21]) to describe the faithful followers of the messiah at the time of the end (cf. Rev. 12.17). This 'rest' is constituted by God's faithful followers (*ecclesiola in ecclesia*), emerging from a generalized apostasy and described as 'those who keep the commandments of God and bear testimony to Jesus' (Rev. 14.12).

In Christian history, several reform movements have seen themselves as representing 'the remnant' of God. This theological concept may be found among Waldenses, Moravian Brethren, Mennonites, Puritans, Pietists, Methodists, Millerites and Adventists, among others.

The notion that only a small group might survive from this world, and that they have the mission to bring salvation to all of humankind is particularly frequent in literature and movies dealing with the end of the world. This notion is central to the series of seven fantasy novels for children by C.S. Lewis, *The Chronicles of Narnia* (1950–1956), to volume II of J.R.R. Tolkien's high fantasy novel *The Lord of the Rings: The Two Towers* (1954) and its cinema version by Peter Jackson (2002). It inspired novels such as *Fahrenheit 451* by Ray Bradbury (1953) and even the comic-book series *V for Vendetta* by Alan Moore and David Lloyd (1982–1999). It permeates science fiction films such as *Outbreak* (1995), *Independence Day* (1996), *Armageddon* (1998), *The Day after Tomorrow* (2004) and *Avatar* (2009). The film *300* (2007) is an adaptation of the novel with the same name by Frank Mille, a retelling of the historical battle of Thermopylae (480 BCE), where a group of Greek soldiers stopped the first Persian invasion of Greece.

See also APOCALYPTIC; APOSTASY; ELECTION; PREDESTINATION; RAPTURE [RB]

Render unto Caesar. Few isolated Christian texts have entered into the common currency of western political discourse. The pronouncement of Jesus to his sly interrogators in the temple precincts (Mark 12.17 and par.: Matt. 22.21, Luke 20.25) is a notable exception and is usually construed in such discourse as a reinforcement of the separation of church and state with a Christian obligated to obedience to both (cf. Rom. 13.1-7).

The pronouncement comes as the decisive moment in a verbal trap laid for Jesus by religious and political authorities (Mark 12.13-17 // Matt. 22.15-22; Luke 20.20-26). The test seems designed either to bring down the wrath of Rome if Jesus repudiates the payment of the poll tax or to damage his popular credibility if he advocates obedience to the oppressive Roman taxation law. At this level, Jesus' reply has been taken as endorsing the authority of the state not only to tax its citizens but as a general authorization of the exercise of temporal power by whatever state is in control, including the power of the state to use its financial resources to support one particular denomination or religion (as in Germany and England).

The spatial setting is critical, however (as throughout Mark's gospel), and governs the context for Jesus' request that his opponents find a particular coin, a denarius, and name both its inscription and its image. They identify Caesar and in that moment are exposed as willing to compromise their own adherence to the law against images (Exod. 20.4-5) by bringing into the confines of God's temple a propaganda piece imaging and inscribing the 'divine father, Caesar'. Jesus' words then become an indictment of their duplicity and hypocrisy rather than a general recommendation of submissive behavior towards the state. Some extend Jesus' words to be a sharp reminder that all authority and power belongs to God, which, in the context, places a choice before his opponents to admit where *their* allegiance lies.

This tension between unqualified endorsement of the authority of the state and obedience to God has marked the use of this passage in infra-ecclesial debates, where some Christian groups have charged others with apostatizing complicity in the oppression of the state. Conversely, others have charged any Christian resistance to government law and practice as itself a form of apostasy. The conflicting perspectives of 'terrorist' versus 'freedom fighter' hang in large measure for the Christian on the conflict over the interpretation of Jesus' words 'Render unto Caesar'. Iconic names of the twentieth century become key figures in this debate: Dietrich Bonhoeffer, Oscar Romero, the Sojourners' Community, Daniel Berrigan, Dorothy Day, Martin Luther King, Mahatma Ghandi and Nelson Mandela. The tension is played out in such cultural artifacts as James Joyce's novel *Ulysses* (through the character Stephen), the novels of Kurt Vonnegut and Alan Paton, the pro-resistance 1943 war film *The Land is Mine* starring Charles Laughton and *Missing* (1982) starring Jack Lemmon.

Recommended reading. Bryan, C. *Render to Caesar: Jesus, the Early Church, and the Roman Superpower*. Oxford and New York: Oxford University Press, 2005. Cadwallader, A. 'In Go(l)d We Trust: Literary and Economic Exchange in the Debate over Caesar's Coin (Mk 12:13-17)'. *Biblical Interpretation* 14 (2006) 486-507. Horsley, R.A. *Jesus and Empire: The Kingdom of God and the New World Disorder*. Minneapolis: Fortress Press, 2003.

See also EMPEROR; MAMMON; MONEY; ROME; TEMPLE; ISRAEL'S; MARK; GOSPEL OF   [AHC]

Repentance. Biblically, repentance is one's initial response to the call of God—a turning from sinful living to obedience and faith in him. The OT does not use the Hebrew word much. When it does, it is mainly in connection with either a human or God changing a decision, e.g., 1 Sam. 15.35: 'And the Lord was sorry he had made Saul king over Israel'. The Hebrew word more clearly associated with the Christian concept of repentance is *shub*, 'to turn' or 'turn back'. It is used of rebellious subjects returning to their rightful ruler, or of a faithless spouse returning to her husband. It is used particularly of idolatrous Jews abandoning their worship of false gods to return to Yahweh. In these cases, it involved not only a change of mind, but a complete reversal of direction (or behavior) and character. It requires a rejection of sin and a wholehearted embrace of righteousness.

The NT word translating *shub* is *metanoeō* (together with its noun form *metanoia*). This term occurs 56X. It means to 'change one's mind or attitude'. At Jesus' time, repentance was often expressed by ritual cleansings (excavations of the Mount of Olives have unearthed large baths for the purpose of cleansing before entering the temple. Jesus taught that both repentance and belief were necessary. In fact, these are his central theme, 'repent and believe in the good news' (Mark 1.15). The earliest preaching of the apostles emphasized repentance, without which faith—and therefore salvation—is impossible.

Some early Christians held that, after conversion and baptism, one could not sin and repent more than once (e.g., Heb. 6.6; *Shepherd of Hermas*, Mandate 4.3). In repenting of post-baptismal sin, a rigorous system of penance was required, whereby the sinner demonstrated a true repentance through action. This included the prohibition of marriage to those who were still unwed and difficult or loathsome tasks designed to induce humility. As barbarian hoards entered the church's membership, these regulations were softened. By the Middle Ages, the Church had decreed penance compulsory on an annual basis from 1215. The Council of Trent established the Sacrament of Penance, which declared that the punishment of the post-baptismal sin in Purgatory might be lessened by certain acts of contrition, such as gifts to the poor, Masses, and the purchase of indulgences.

The Reformation leaders rejected such a system as unbiblical, averring that what is required after sin is not penance but penitence or fresh repentance. This quickly became the standard in Protestantism, and is still held by Protestant churches today.

Judaism sees repentance now to be obtained by individuals through prayer and acts of charity (Hos. 6.6). Contemporary society has softened the Christian view of repentance to one of mild regret for what one has done, with the expectation that such an attitude should please any God who might exist. This concept is exemplified in the song 'Repentance', written by Mike Portnoy, a member of the progressive metal band Dream Theater, released on June 2007 as part of the album *Systematic Chaos*. 'Repentance' is the fourth part of a Twelve-Step suite, and depicts Steps 8 and 9 in Portnoy's journey through Alcoholics Anonymous. While expressing regret for hurting friends, the artist maintains, in the chorus: 'Sometimes you've got to be wrong / Learn the hard way / Sometimes you've got to be strong / When you think it's too late'. He sees wrongdoing as a street to salvation and success.

Recommended reading. Roberts, Richard Owen. *Repentance: The First Word of the Gospel*. Wheaton, IL: Crossway, 2002.

See also FORGIVENESS, PURGATORY; SALVATION; SIN [DLS]

Resurrection. The conception of post-mortem immortality in terms of resurrection held by some Second Temple Jews (e.g., Dan. 12.2; 2 Macc. 7.9, 11, 14; 12.24-43; 14.46; *1 En.* 91.10; 2 Esdras 7.32, 37), including the Pharisees. The term (Greek: *anastasis*) marks the credo of Christian faith and refers to God's act of bringing Jesus to life following his crucifixion. Resurrection is often confused with resuscitation. In the Gospels, e.g., the raising of Jairus's daughter and Lazarus are often understood as resuscitations. Resurrection is not resuscitation in that resuscitation is only possible when all the essential body parts are in place, but resurrection is a recreation by God. The key text in understanding this concept is 1 Cor. 15.3-12: Jesus Christ *was* raised (Greek: *egēgertai*) from the dead meaning that God recreated him. Unlike a resuscitated body, a resurrected body becomes eternal and spiritual. The NT writers present a resurrected Christ as the same person but with a transformed, physical-spiritual body. Consequently, the 'resurrections' of Jairus's daughter and Lazarus are resuscitations; both eventually died, but the resurrected Christ, according to Christians, is alive today.

The historicity of the resurrection has been disputed on grounds that there are divergent reports in the Gospels; resurrection narratives are not in harmony with similar NT and other accounts; and that resurrection is peculiar to Christianity—all religious leaders from Moses to the Confucius are dead. Resurrection narratives are therefore viewed as post-Easter confessions meant to elevate Christianity. It is therefore suggested: (a) That resurrection narratives were influenced by Greek mythology, e.g., the dying and raising of Attis, Adonis, Osiris, Dionysus, etc. However, this point is disputed on grounds that Greek myths evolved over centuries. It is unlikely that the primitive church would create myths about Jesus in the presence of eyewitnesses; also, the revivification of the Greek gods was seasonal, not once-for-all; (b) Paulus suggested that Jesus resuscitated in the coolness of the grave and he went into hiding. *Prima facie*, this theory seems convincing but it is difficult to sustain in the face of agreement in the Gospels that Jesus died on the cross. More importantly, nothing of this nature has happened in history; (c) The disciples stole Jesus' body. Again this conjecture is redundant when we read about Jesus' followers being martyred for professing the resurrection, and it is unlikely that the disciples were prepared to die in protection of an invented belief. The subsequent growth of Christianity argues against this point; and (d) Speculation that the women went to the wrong tomb could have been challenged by identifying the right tomb.

Biblically, the evidence of the resurrection consists of Jesus' post-resurrection appearances (Mark 16.1-8; Matt. 28.1-11; Luke 24; John 20; 1 Cor. 15), according to which Jesus revealed himself alive to the female and male disciples and to over 500 believers. Christophanies— the self-revelations of the risen Jesus—are subjective proofs of the resurrection. The empty tomb does not prove the resurrection but is confirmatory.

The Shroud of Turin (the cloth, supposedly bearing an image of Christ, which some Catholics believe was rescued from the tomb) has proven to be a hoax through carbon-dating. Many western artists have portrayed the resurrection, e.g., Fra Angelico (1440–42), Albrecht Altdorfer (c. 1516), and Hans Memling (1490s). Mahler's *Resurrection* (Symphony #2, 1888–94) is perhaps the most famous musical work inspired by the theme. Films such as *The Passion of the Christ* (2004) and *Road Warrior* (1981) continue to reflect on the last days of Jesus.

Recommended reading. Brown, R.E. *The Virginal Conception and Bodily Resurrection of Jesus.* Mahwah, NJ: Paulist Press, 1972.

See also IMMORTALITY; PASSION NARRATIVE; PHARISEES [ET]

Retribution. From late Latin *retributio* meaning 'assigned again', from the verb *retribuere*; re- 'back' and *tribuere* 'assign'. Viewed as a form of justice, the essence of retribution is the assignment of punishment against one perceived or proven as the perpetrator of evil. The perpetrator merits the act(s) assigned to them as a form of justice. The idea is derived from social and intrapersonal values and morals as a framework for understanding the world, good, and especially evil. A person apportions blame for harm committed and seeks some form of justice via some form of suffering.

The OT offers insight into biblical, historical, and present understandings of retribution through payment, 'life for life' (Exod. 21.23-24). OT law views retribution as restoration of goods lost, or reciprocation of wrongs. However, God demonstrates justice outside societal understandings of the law, such as with David's acts related to Bathsheba (cf. 2 Sam. 11.3–12.24). Wrongful acts and retaliation not only affect individuals, but the entire community, tribe, kingdom, and nation.

The NT offers different concepts of retribution with Jesus' teaching of 'turn the other cheek' when encountering an 'evil person' (Matt. 5.38). The crucifixion is theologically interpreted in terms of God's justice and penalty for sin. Christian theologies discuss the nature of Christ losing his life so that humanity could gain life eternal as a means of atonement. Apocalyptic notions of retribution prevail when vengeance and judgment are declared to be God's (cf. Deut. 32.35; Heb. 10.30; Rev. 6.10).

Examples of proportionate exchange for injustice exist in Greek and Mesopotamian writings, especially in understandings of right and wrong, popularized by movies such as *Troy* (2004), where Achilles seeks revenge for the death of Patroclus. Religious examples of retribution, both historical and modern, are exampled by the Crusades, portrayed dramatically in *Kingdom of Heaven* (2005) as well as in present-day conflicts between Christians and Muslims; each religion views the other as committing religious injustices. Other examples include the burning or beheading of early American settlers for violation of state or religious law during the Revolutionary War and the Salem witch trials. Death to those supporting Jews during World War II as depicted in *The Diary of Anne Frank,* and the horrific retaliatory exterminations of people in Rwanda display the personal, present nature of what some consider justified acts of retribution. Historical and modern examples of retributive symbols include the gallows, humans shackled and displayed in public, the electric chair, chemical injections for capital punishment, or music videos that display self-inflicted harm like Marilyn Manson's *The Beautiful People* (2004).

Western understandings of retribution are not limited to physical injury, but also mental, emotional, and spiritual damage. It is understood as a repayment for wrongful acts consisting of probation, civil penalties, or prison sentences that may include capital punishment enforced by the state. The need for equal reciprocation and punishment is contrasted with stories such as the people of Le Chambon harboring Jews at the risk of losing their lives, and the pacifist acts of retaliation by Martin Luther King, Jr through boycotting in the American civil rights movement.

The psychology of retribution has been studied through administration of shocks to participants, demonstrating that the degree of punishment is based upon the perceived significance and damages of harm committed. The degree of justice or injustice is both an individual and societal perception and determination.

Recommended readings. Hallie, Phillip. *Lest Innocent Blood Be Shed.* New York: Harper Perennial, 1994. Wright, N.T. *Evil and the Justice of God.* Downers Grove, IL: InterVarsity Press, 2006.

See also ATONEMENT; JUDGE; JUDGMENT; JUSTICE; KINSMEN; LAW; REDEEMER; VENGEANCE IS MINE [PN]

Reuben (See Twelve Tribes of Israel)

Reuel (see Jethro).

Revelation, Book of. The book of Revelation is an apocalypse, a term which comes from the Greek word for 'revealing'. Apocalyptic was a type of Jewish literature in which heavenly mysteries are revealed through visionary activity. What is revealed relates directly to the context of the recipients; providing the 'heavenly perspective' on their earthly situation. The author of Revelation is identified as 'John', traditionally John the apostle although this view is not widely held by contemporary scholars. The most likely date for composition is either early in the reign of Vespasian (early 70s CE) or late in the reign of Domitian (early 90s CE). The dating issue turns on which context best accounts for the expectation within the text of renewed persecution.

The recipients are the seven congregations of Asia Minor named in the letters of chs. 2–3. The body of Revelation consists of a sequence of vivid images, which come fast upon each other, structured around repeating patterns of seven, the Jewish number of perfection. Through these images, John invites his recipients imaginatively to enter into his visionary representation of their world. As they gain this divine perspective, it directly challenges the dominant ideology of their time, with Rome becoming Babylon the great prostitute and beast, terrorising and corrupting the world in its idolatrous quest to secure the worship of all nations through the enforced practice of the imperial cult. The people of God are thus repeatedly encouraged to remain steadfast in resistance through persecution and difficulty. Revelation speaks of the Judgement of God, hopefully articulating the punishment of evil and the vindication of the righteous. The closing image presents a direct challenge to the claims of Rome: those who follow Christ are seen to have their true citizenship not in Babylon but in 'new Jerusalem', the holy city.

1.1-11	Opening greeting and prayers
1.12-20	One like a son of man
2.1–3.22	Seven letters to seven congregations
4.1-11	The heavenly throne
5.1–6.17	Seals 1–6
7.1-17	Interlude: The people of God are numbered
8.1	Seal 7
8.2–9.21	Trumpets 1–6
10.1-11	Interlude: John eats the scroll
11.1-14	Interlude: The two witnesses
11.15-18	Trumpet 7
11.19–15.4	7 Visions
15.5–16.21	7 Bowl-plagues
17.1–19.10	Babylon's destruction
19.11–21.8	7 Visions
21.9–22.21	The new Jerusalem

The metaphorical and visionary nature of Revelation has made it a favorite of interpreters down the centuries. Many have sought to find predictions of events either from their own time or relating to their immediate future, while others have assumed that John's images provide a literal description of the events that will immediately precede the end of the world. In contemporary western culture an 'apocalypse' has become synonymous with a world-ending scenario, with apocalyptic imagery from Revelation found in films as diverse as *Apocalypse Now*, *Pale Rider*, *Waterworld*, *Independence Day*, *Twelve Monkeys*, *Terminator* and *Ghostbusters*. Imagery from Revelation crops up in both expected and unexpected places, from Dürer's medieval woodcut *The Whore of Babylon* to the Johnny Cash song 'The man comes around'. Some religious groups have focused on particular images, for example the Jehovah's Witnesses see the 144,000 as a literal number to be fulfilled from their ranks. A different approach to the imagery of Revelation is to be found in the contemporary application of its economic and political critique of empire, treating it as a piece of subversive resistance literature which deconstructs all attempts to centralize power and wealth through systems of empire.

Recommended reading. Boxall, Ian. *The Revelation of St John*. Black's New Testament Commentaries; London: Continuum, 2006. Woodman, Simon. *The Book of Revelation*. London: SCM Press, 2008.

See also APOCALYPSE; APOCALYPTIC; JOHN OF PATMOS [SW]

Rich Fool, the Parable of. Luke's Gospel is known for its emphasis on the poor and economic justice (1.52-53; 6.24). These motifs are spelled out in the parable of the Rich Fool (12.16-21), which is the first of three 'rich man' parables in Luke (the other two are the Dishonest Steward, 16.1-9; and the Rich Man and Lazarus, 16.19-31). The parable occurs in Luke's travel narrative, the section of the Gospel depicting Jesus' journey to Jerusalem (9.51–19.27), and functions as a commentary on Jesus' polemic against greed in Luke 12.15. The parable is unique to Luke, but has a strong parallel in the apocryphal *Gospel of Thomas* (63).

In the context of an agrarian society—that is, an economy dependent on agricultural business—the rich fool serves as an exemplar of greed. By building larger storage barns for surplus crops rather than investing the crops in the local markets, the rich man is able to secure his future at the expense of the local peasant community whose subsistence is dependent on farmer's business. The Rich Fool's self-centeredness becomes more acute by Luke's use of the literary convention known as soliloquy, or 'self-talk'. Rather than consult with God about surplus wealth, the rich fool engages in self-talk with his own soul: 'Soul, you have ample goods laid up for many years; relax, eat, drink, be merry' (v. 19 KJV). The Fool's hedonistic plans, according to the early church father Ambrose, fail to recognize that there is already 'plenty of storage in the mouths of the needy' (*De Nabuthe Jezraelita* 7).

The Rich Fool's building project is a symbol of excessive pride in the economy of Jesus and the kingdom of God. To be sure, this is the only parable in the NT where God functions as an actor in the story. God shows up to reprimand the Fool: 'You fool! This very night your life is being demanded of you. And the things you have prepared, whose will they be?' (v. 20). The farmer's accumulation of wealth for future security becomes irrelevant in the face of death; consequently, the parable reminds readers that what counts in life is not 'storing up treasures', but being 'rich toward God' (v. 21).

The parable of the Rich Fool has obvious overlap in the history of western culture—a culture with a pervasive addiction to possessions. The word Luke employs for greed (*pleonexia*) in Luke 12.15 has a rich history in the Greco-Roman world; for example, the Roman scholar Plutarch in the first century says, 'Neither silver nor gold abates the love of money, nor does greed (*pleonexia*) cease with the purchase of something new' (*Moralia* 7 523.E). The word *pleonexia* also occurs in several lists of vices in early Christian literature both inside and outside the canon (Rom. 1.29; Col. 3.5; 1 *Clement* 35.5; *Polycarp to the Philippians* 2.2; *Didache* 5.1).

Around 1627, Rembrandt painted a portrait of the Rich Fool (Gemäldegalerie, Berlin). The literary structure of the parable also influenced the popular medieval English morality play, *Everyman*. The phrase 'eat, drink and be merry' has become shorthand for having a good time and is quoted by Dave Matthews in the song, 'Tripping Billies'. Perhaps the most lucid image of the Rich Fool in contemporary culture is the modern notion that one needs to invest in their retirement rather than divest their surplus resources to the poor.

See also DISHONEST STEWARD, PARABLE OF THE; LAZARUS AND THE RICH MAN, PARABLE OF; PARABLE; LUKE, GOSPEL OF; MAMMON; WEALTH [DJS]

Rich Man and Lazarus (see Lazarus and the Rich Man, Parable of).

Riddle. The unabridged OED offers the following definition of riddle: 'A question or statement intentionally worked in a dark or puzzling manner, and propounded in order that it may be guessed or answered, esp. as a form of pastime; an enigma; a dark saying'. A classic example of a riddle in the former sense is Samson's riddle to the Philistines about the honey in the lion (Judg. 14.12-14a [5-9, 14b-18]). Examples of the latter application of riddle include Num. 12.8; Ps. 49.4; Prov. 1.6; and Hab. 2.6. The Hebrew noun *ḥidah* underlies NRSV translations of the foregoing. Indeed, the NRSV does not render the noun as riddle in every case. Nonetheless, the word *ḥidah* in such instances still denotes a hard question or oblique speech (1 Kgs 10.1; 2 Chron. 9.1; Ps. 78.2; Ezek. 17.2—here an allegory [vv. 3-10]; cf.; Dan. 8.23 [underhand plot]).

By extension, a riddle can denote '[s]omething which puzzles or perplexes; a difficult or insoluble problem; a mystery', or again '[a] person or being whose nature or conduct is enigmatical'. As a verb, riddle can mean 'to speak in riddles', or 'to propound riddles', 'to interpret or solve (a riddle or question)', 'to be a riddle to (a person)', or less frequently 'to puzzle'. Thus a team in professional sports can suffer a decimation in ranks in consequence of injuries to key players. Such a team is said to be 'riddled with injuries'.

The Markan exclusion formula (4.11-12; cf. Isa. 6.9-10) has long intrigued NT scholars—i.e., 'parable' (Greek: *parabolē*) in parallel with 'mystery' (Greek: *mystērion*). Here Mark represents the dominical parables as intentionally riddling speech. The word *parabolē* is the Septuagint rendition of the Hebrew *mashal*—without exception. Indeed *mashal* often denotes a simile, similitude or a parable, and somewhat less often a proverb or a ruling saying; nonetheless it can also bear a less-than-obvious significance. The incomprehension of the addressees of Jesus' parables finds its source in moral obduracy. We encounter this motif frequently in the OT. Accordingly Jesus' listeners must interpret his teaching 'spiritually'. Matthew and Luke mute the Markan presentation significantly, but one can detect remnants of it in Matt. 11.25-26, for example. John also associates figurative utterance (Greek: *paroimia*l John 16.25, 29) with Jesus. Here moral obduracy in the form of spiritual blindness is the source of incomprehension (9.39-41). Thus Mark and John both regard the addressee's comprehension as criterion for inclusion in the believing community.

The riddle has long infiltrated the parlance of western culture. The court jesters of mediaeval times often intimated profound insight in the form of riddling discourse (e.g., *King Lear*'s 'fool' in William Shakespeare's tragedy). The Cheshire cat of Lewis Carroll's *Alice in Wonderland* is continually vexing the young Alice with his riddling speech. Thus an amused individual appears to 'smile like a Cheshire Cat'. Riddling drama continues to delight audiences—e.g., those of Samuel Beckett or Franz Kafka.

See also ALLEGORY; KINGDOM OF GOD (KINGDOM OF HEAVEN); MYSTERY; PARABLE [NRP]

Righteousness. From the Hebrew words *ṣĕdāqāh* and *ṣedeq* and the Greek word *dikaiosynē*. In the Bible this term has many different uses and meanings. Included in these connotations are the following: a quality that God reckons to those who have faith (Gen. 15.6; Rom. 4.3-9; Gal. 3.6; Jas 2.23), a quality that can be 'put on' or with which one can be 'clothed' (Job 29.14; Ps. 132.9; 61.10; Eph. 6.14), a characteristic that one acts out in obedience to God (Gen. 18.19; 1 Sam. 26.23; Prov. 11.6; Prov. 21.3; Matt. 5.20; Phil. 3.6; 2 Tim. 2.22), a criterion for God's judgment (Ps. 7.8; Isa. 11.4; Acts 17.31; Rev. 19.11), a quality that God possesses and/or exhibits (Job 37.23; Ps. 7.17; Isa. 42.21; Jer. 9.24; Matt. 6.33; Rom. 1.17), a quality sought after for the poor, orphans, and widows (Amos 5.24), the state of affairs when the Day of the Lord dawns (Isa. 61.11; Jer. 23.5; 2 Pet. 3.13), and a 'way' which can be followed (Prov. 8.20; Matt. 21.32; 2 Pet. 2.21). Even though this term has a wide range of nuances, it seems that its meaning is rooted in God's character and is closely related to 'justice'. However, those who believe in God are asked to emulate this characteristic of God in their lives and in their communities. 'Righteousness' is also closely related to 'justification' and God's saving work in Christ that has sparked much debate about whether righteousness is primarily a characteristic of God or something which God gives to those who believe.

In the early church, the varieties of meanings of 'righteousness' were also apparent, though seeing it as action in obedience to God was popular, as is seen in Polycarp, *To the Philippians* 3.1–10.3 and Hermas, *Mandate* 35.2. This trend of viewing righteousness as human action, especially as expressed in charitable deeds, remains popular in the church. Augustine and others, however, also taught that righteousness was in some way given by God to his followers. The Roman Catholic Church has maintained this interpretive tradition by teaching that righteousness is slowly infused into a believer over time through participation in the sacraments. The Protestant response to this, rooted in the teachings of Luther and Calvin, has been that righteousness is imparted or imputed to the believer in one lump sum at the first moment of belief. This debate continues today, though some ground has been gained, as evidenced by the 1999 document entitled 'Joint Declaration on Justification by Faith', written by representatives of the Lutheran World Federation and the Catholic Church.

'Righteousness' and words related to it have found their way into popular western culture as well. One example is the common phrase is 'self-righteousness', which means that someone has a high sense of self that others can easily spot. In the early twentieth century, a kind of unpremeditated and unrehearsed music performed by small bands called 'righteous jazz' became popular. Later in the same century, 'righteous' came to be synonymous with 'cool' or 'awesome' in certain regional jargons, as popularized in the films *Bill and Ted's Excellent Adventure* (1989) and *Bill and Ted's Bogus Journey* (1991).

See also ESCHATOLOGY; JUSTICE; JUSTIFICATION; LAW [JMB]

Right hand of God. Possibly originating from the Hebrew name Benjamin, the right hand of God is an idiom that is used to describe both a place of blessing and honor and the power of God. Shortly after God assured Jacob that the Abrahamic promise would continue through his lineage, Rachel gave birth to Jacob's tenth son (Gen. 35). In her last moments before passing away, Rachel named the infant *Benoni* ('son of mourning': *ben-oni*), but Jacob renamed him Benjamin ('son of the right hand' or 'son of the south': *bin-yamin*). This narrative explains the death of Rachel and it also designates Benjamin as the beloved son, who later became the patriarch of the tribe of Benjamin. There are many prominent descendants of the tribe of Benjamin, such as Saul (1 Sam. 9.1-2), his son Jonathan (1 Sam. 13.2), Ehud (Judg. 3.15), and the apostle Paul (Phil. 3.5). On multiple occasions, God delivers Israel from conquest with the right hand (Exod. 15.6; Pss 20.6; 44.3; 98.1). To be at God's right hand guarantees victory (Ps. 110.1). The biblical narrative states that Jesus, after his death, was raised and seated at the right hand of God (*dexia tou theou*) to remain humanity's advocate (Mark 16.19; Acts 7.55; Rom. 8.34) 'with angels, authorities, and powers made subject to him' (1 Pet. 3.22). The promise that one will sit at the right hand of God signifies that he or she will be in a position of mutual power and authority with God.

Western culture frequently assimilates the right hand idiom into religious imagery. The right hand of God or *manus Dei* in Latin, became a popular way of artistically depicting God's blessings. The Dura-Europos Synagogue, dated to roughly the third century CE, used the hand of God motif in several frescos to represent God's prevailing power. The fresco in Sant Climent de Taüll (Catalonia, Spain), dedicated in the eleventh century, portrays Christ giving a blessing with his right hand. Today priests and pastors often use their right hand to signify a blessing during the invocation and benediction in Christian worship services.

Other works have adapted the hand of God motif as a sign or judgment or blessing. Shakespeare used the hand of God in *Richard II* (iii.3) and in *Henry V* (ii.2) as a sign of judgment. The hand of God motif is used in the 2006 video game, *Legend: Hand of God* to describe the single player, first person character as God's retribution on earth. In the song 'Hand of God', the band Fall Out Boy described their hand as a means of executing judgment upon one's self. The hand of God is also seen as a means of blessing, as in the movie *Left Hand of God* (1955), which portrays a troubled priest who confronted the Chinese war world in 1947 on behalf of the people. The Italian movie *The Hand of God* (2007) described the life of former football star Diego Armando Maradona, who recovered from a heart attack to go as one of the most successful football players in Italy. Rap artists Maino sang of desperation and the need for the salvific hand of God in his 2008 song 'Hand of God'.

See also BENJAMIN [JS]

Rimmon. In Hebrew, *rimmon* means 'pomegranate'. The plural form *rimmonim* is used to describe the ornament of the Torah Scroll. It was used in the OT as the name for several cities, a rock, a Syrian god and as a proper name. Rimmon Parez, a camp site between Rithman and Libnah (Num. 33.19-20), is named as the fifteenth station for the Hebrew Children after they left Egypt or the fourth in Sinai.

In Josh. 15.32, Um-er-Rumamim was the name of a city in as group of 29 in the territory assigned to the tribe of Judah. It was located in the extreme south close to the border with Edom. This city is included in the prophetic vision of Zechariah (14.10). The land will be turned into a plain from Geba to Rimmon on the day when the Lord becomes king over all of the earth.

Judges (20.45, 47; 21.13) describes a terrible battle between the tribe of Benjamin and the other tribes of Israel. The Benjaminites were almost annihilated. Some 600 survivors fled toward the wilderness to the rock of Rimmon where they stayed for the next four months. The rock of Rimmon is identified as the site of the modern village of Rammun, on the edge of the hill country with a precipitous descent toward the Jordan Valley. The site is identified as a possible location for the town of Ai.

2 Samuel (4.2, 5, 9) nam6]es two captains of raiding bands, Baanah and Rechab, as sons of Rimmon, a man of Benjamin from Beeroth. They were Beerothites who had fled from Bittaim and had sojourned at Rimmon. Vv. 5 to 12 describe their plot against King Saul's son, Ishbosheth, its execution and their presentation of Ishbosheth's head to King David as a reward. However, he sentences them to death for murder.

Naaman, a leper and the commander of the Syrian army, is described as a worshiper of the Syrian storm god, Hadad (2 Kgs 5.18). However, having been cured of leprosy by the God of Israel, he petitions the prophet Elisha for forgiveness for accompanying the Syrian king and bowing with him in the house of Rimmon. Stringfellow Barr raised pointed questions about the ethical nature of this request for prior forgiveness in *An Ethic for Strangers in a Strange Land*.

1 Chronicles mentions Ain ('spring') and Rimmon separately (4.32). However, this could be combination, because Ain-Rimmon means pomegranate spring. It is named as a city of the sons of Simeon (1 Chron. 4.24). 1 Chronicles also mentions a Levitical city in the territory of Zebulun (6.77), a city called Rimmono which had pasture lands. It was allotted to the Merarites clan of Zebulun.

Moses de Leon (c. 1250–1305) is called Moshe ben Shem-Tov in Hebrew. He was born in Guadalajara, Spain and worked as a rabbi and Kabbalist, author of the mystical *Book of the Pomegranate* (*Sefer Ha-Rimmon*). John Milton in *Paradise Lost* names Rimmon's seat as being at fair Damascus (Book 1). Mary Jean Hickling Gwynne Kernahan published a novel entitled *The House of Rimmon: A Black Country Story of South Staffordshire* (1885). In 1923, Henry Van Dyke wrote a four act drama about Naaman and the House of Rimmon.

See also POMEGRANATE [AJW]

Ritual Purity, Impurity. Concepts of ritual purity and impurity were of fundamental importance in most ancient Near Eastern cultures. Permeating the lives of people, regulations on purity and removal of impurity communicated important knowledge about sanitation and health, and served to categorize perceptions of reality. According to the HB, impurity was caused by particular incidents which were not necessarily avoidable or the result of sin. Impurity was considered contagious: impure people or objects could render pure people and objects impure through physical contact (Hag. 2.12-13). Since entrance into the sanctuary and the right to participate in worship were restricted to the ritually pure, Torah features an elaborate list of what causes impurity, or who and what is considered impure (Lev. 11–15): various types of animals prohibited for human consumption (Lev. 11; cf. Gen. 7.2); women after childbirth (Lev. 12) and during menstruation (Lev. 15.19-24); 'leprous persons and houses' (Lev. 13–14; the term 'leprous' designates various skin diseases and is not necessarily identical with Hansen's Disease); men after nightly discharges (Lev. 15.1-18). Further Torah regulations include adultery (Lev. 18.20; Num. 5.13), incest (Lev. 18.6-18), and physical contact with a corpse, skeleton, or tomb (Lev. 21.1-4; Num. 19.11, 16). According to other HB texts, sexual intercourse may render humans impure (1 Sam. 21.5-6); foreign nations (Ezek. 4.13; Hos. 9.3-4) or the 'uncircumcised' (Isa. 52.1; Ezra 6.21) are generally considered impure.

To restore a person or object to purity, the impurity had to be removed through ablutions (Lev. 11.32; 15.7), fire (Num. 31.23), or blood (Lev. 8.15, 30; 14.25). In addition a waiting period (Lev. 12.4f.; 15.5-11) and the offering of sacrifices (Lev. 12.6-8) could be prescribed. According to Torah, however, human impurity (and sin) also defiled the land (Lev. 18.27-28) and God's sanctuary (Lev. 15.31; 16.16). The latter needed to be cleansed on the Day of Atonement (Lev. 16).

In contrast to these definitions of ritual purity, the prophetic books of the HB and the Psalms put more emphasis on ethical behavior. Thus Isaiah urged that people not only wash themselves but stop evil actions (1.16; cf. Jer. 33.8). In some cases, such exhortations could go to the extreme of an outright rejection of the temple cult (Isa. 1.10-15; Ps. 40.6 ET; 51.16 ET).

The NT depicts Jesus as questioning Torah purity concepts which, by his time, the Pharisees had developed into a complex system called 'tradition of the elders' (Mark 7.3-4). The critical attitude of Jesus is manifest in his frequent contact with people considered impure because of diseases, nationality, religious affiliation, social status, or gender (e.g., leper, Mark 1.40-44; tax collector, Mark 2.13-17; haemorrhaging woman, Mark 5.25-34; Samaritan woman, John 4.1-42). Within his Jewish context, Jesus ignited a reform movement conveying the ideal of an inclusive society across traditional boundaries. His claim that not food consumption but words and actions would render humans impure (Mark 7.17-23) is similar to Peter's vision in which a divine voice challenged the apostle to touch and eat unclean animals (Acts 10.9-16). Paul captured this new attitude in the motto: 'nothing is unclean in itself; but it is unclean for anyone who thinks it unclean' (Rom. 14.14).

In subsequent centuries, Rabbinic Judaism continued to develop the Torah regulations on purity. Mishnah and Tosefta have dedicated twelve tracts to this topic, and the Talmud features extensive discussions that nowadays regulate the lives of orthodox Jews.

Recommended reading. Betz, Hans Dieter. 'Jesus and the Purity of the Temple (Mark 11.15-18)'. *Journal of Biblical Literature* 116 (1997) 455-72. Douglas, Mary. *Purity and Danger.* London: Routledge & Kegan Paul, 1966.

See also ATONEMENT; BLOOD; SACRIFICE [CAE]

River. Hebrew *nāhār*. For the peoples of the ancient Near East, rivers were sources of life and death. Rivers provided the water necessary for drinking, agriculture, and religious ritual. Conversely, the rivers of Mesopotamia were known to flood without warning, causing havoc and destruction.

In the OT rivers, *nāhārîm*, are also closely associated with life and death. The first occurrence of *nāhār* is Gen. 2.10 were a river flows out of Eden to water the garden, sustaining the place were life was conceived. This river divides into the four well-known rivers: the Pishon, the Gihon to water the whole land of Cush or the South, the Tigris to water Assyria or the East, and the Euphrates for the North. Similarly, in the NT a river, Greek *potamos*, flows from the throne of God through the new earth sustaining the tree of life and brining life to all who wish to drink from it (Rev. 22.1, 17).

Israel was not like other nations whose main cities remained by rivers. As a land of mountains, hills, and valleys, the people were dependent upon the seasonal rains that would cause rivers to run down the mountains. Thus rivers became a symbol of peace and renewal (Isa. 41.18; 48.18), with all forms of running water becoming closely associated the ability to sustain life (Ps. 104.10-11). Negatively, rivers could become dangerous torrents and flood unexpectedly. Consequently, they were also symbols of judgment (Isa. 59.19).

Because of their connection with life and death, rivers were closely associated with the divine. As a result, they became localities for prayer (Ps. 137.1-3; Ezek. 3.15) and encounters with divine beings (Gen. 32.22-32). In addition, God's control over rivers and waters was a demonstration of his sovereignty (Ps. 74.15, 107.33; Isa. 19.5). The same is true in the NT. In the Roman city of Philippi, the local river was a place of prayer on the Sabbath (Acts 16.13). Upon coming up from the water of the river Jordan after his baptism, Jesus' identity is confirmed by a voice from heaven saying, 'This is my beloved Son, with whom I am well pleased' (Matt. 3.17 ESV).

Rivers continue to capture the imagination of modern peoples. The French impressionist Cladue Monet (1840–1926) continuously painted rivers including his works *Poplars on the Banks of the River Epte* and *Bridge at Giverny*. The American artist Georgia O'Keeffe (1887–1986) also captured the beauty of rivers in her paintings *From the River* and *Blue River*. The words of Psalm 137 have continued to inspire later artists. Psalm 137 relates the story of the Israeli exiles grieving for the destruction of Jerusalem by the river of Babylon, 'By the rivers of Babylon, there we sat and we wept as we remembered Zion' (137.1). It is the subject of a collagraph by modern Israeli artist Lika Tov, *By the Rivers of Babylon II*, as well as the song 'By the Rivers Dark' by Canadian artist Leonard Cohen. Further, many songs carry the title 'Rivers of Babylon', including songs by the alternative group Sublime, the disco era group Boney M., artist and producer Jimmy Cliff, and New Orleans' funk group the Neville Brothers.

See also EUPHRATES; JORDAN; LIVING WATER; NILE; RIVER OF LIVE; RIVERS OF BABYLON; TIGRIS [CLH]

River of Life. Mentioned only once in Rev. 22.1, where an angel shows the visionary 'the river of the water of life, bright as crystal, flowing from the throne of God and of the lamb' through the streets of the New Jerusalem. The image is derived from the Garden of Eden (Gen. 2.10) and from Ezek. 47.1-12, where the prophet envisions water flowing from the eschatological temple in the four directions (cf. Zech. 14.8; Ps. 46.4). The river partakes in all of the positive attributes of water, such as life, fertility and joyfulness.

The fourteenth-century English poem *The Pearl* relates a dream in which the poet falls asleep and sees his lost love, now a bride of Christ, standing across a stream. The Pearl-Maiden instructs him in the way of salvation and shows him a hill from which he can view the holy city with its crystal river. Although the Maiden instructs the lover that he must die before he can cross the river, he plunges in, and the poem ends. In Bunyan's *Pilgrim's Progress* (1678), the river is bitter, and symbolizes death.

In Christianity, the river of life figures prominently in such hymns as 'Like a River Glorious' (Frances R. Havergal, 1876), 'Shall We Gather at the River' (Robert Lowry, 1864) and 'I've Got Peace like a River' (traditional American). The lyrics of Canadian rock group The Band's 'River Hymn' (Robertson, 1971) evoke the biblical river: 'Son, you ain't never seen yourself, No crystal mirror can make it clear, Son, you ain't ever eased yourself, Til you laid down in a river bed'.

See also LIVING WATER; NEW HEAVEN, NEW EARTH; REVELATION; BOOK OF; WATER [MALB]

Rivers of Babylon. In spite of the common term 'Rivers of Babylon', the ancient city of Babylon was built on the Euphrates River, although the Tigris River is not far away. Although much of the land there is now parched, in ancient times it is believed to have been very different, with the region becoming known as the 'fertile crescent' on account of the crops grown there. This led to Babylon being associated with fertile land and wealth, best encapsulated in its famous Hanging Gardens, which was one of the Seven Wonders of the Ancient World.

In the Bible, Psalm 137 begins with the line 'By the rivers of Babylon, There we sat down, yea we wept when we remembered Zion' (KJV). Most famously in the twentieth century, the Psalm inspired the pop song 'By the Rivers of Babylon' (1978) by the German disco band Boney M., Number 1 on the British pop charts for five weeks. A remix was released in 1998. The phrase has figured in the titles of novels, e.g., by Robert Liddell (London in 1959); and by the Slovak writer Peter Pistanek (ET: 2007). The thriller *By the Rivers of Babylon* by Nelson DeMille (1978) involves two planeloads of Israeli officials heading to a UN conference crash-landing and having to fend off Palestinian commandos while Israeli special forces launch a rescue bid.

See also BABYLON; EXILE; RIVER [JC]

Rizpah. The daughter of Aiah (2 Sam. 3.7), one of the concubines of Saul (1 Sam. 21.8); her name means 'a hot stone'. She survived Saul and was involved in a quarrel between Saul's general Abner and his son IsOTosheth that resulted in Abner changing his allegiance to David (2 Sam. 3.6-8). During a famine in the reign of King David, the two children of Saul and Rizpah, Armoni and Mephibosheth, along with five sons of Saul's daughter Merab, are put to death to assuage the anger of the Gibeonites (2 Sam. 21). The bodies of all seven were exposed. Rizpah watched over the seven bodies until David eventually agreed that they should receive an honorable burial.

Although a minor character in the Bible, Rizpah owes her prominence in history largely to being the central character in the Canadian writer Charles E. Israel's novel *Rizpah* (1961). It was inspired by his teaching at Hebrew Union College in Cincinnati, and the book portrays Rizpah as the heroine who uses her wit, charm and her 'gift for loving' to help herself and family in turbulent times. Adopted by book clubs, the novel sold well around the world.

Recommended reading. Brenner, Athalya. *I Am: Biblical Women Tell their Own Stories.* Pp. 120-31. Minneapolis: Fortress Press, 2005.

See also DAVID; MICHAL; SAUL [JC]

Rock. Both rock and stone have symbolic connections to ideas including strength, stability, and firmness. The Bible usually makes the distinction between 'rock' (Hebrew: *tsur, sela'*; Greek: *petra*), part of a natural rock formation, and 'stone' (Hebrew: *'even*; Greek: *lithos*), which is not. The terms are rarely found together, but an exception can be found in the phrase, 'a stone of stumbling and a rock of offense' (Isa. 8.14). God is frequently called a rock (Deut. 32.15; Pss 18.2; 28.1; 95.15; Hab. 1.12). Such references to God invoke a number of images, including, but not limited to the strength, power, and majesty of God and God as a refuge for humanity. God as rock conveys God's salvation and protection of the people.

While the Israelites wander in the wilderness, they complain to Moses at Rephidim about a lack of water. God instructs Moses, 'Strike the rock (*tsur*), and water will come out of it, so that the people may drink' (Exod. 17.6). In Numbers, when the Israelites, now in Kadesh, complain to Moses about a lack of water, God again commands him to strike a rock (Num. 20.1-13). Paul references these stories of Israel's history in 1 Corinthians 10. Following Jewish traditions (e.g., *Targum Onqelos Num.* 21.16-20) that explain the presence of both stories by means of a wandering rock, Paul identifies Christ as the spiritual rock (*petra*) that followed the Israelites in the wilderness (1 Cor. 10.4). This striking identification imagines a preexistent Christ ministering to the Israelites who partook in both baptism and the eucharist.

The rock also appears in Peter's confession of Jesus as the messiah. Jesus responds, 'And I tell you, you are Peter (*Petros*), and on this rock (*petra*) I will build my church' (Matt. 16.18). This statement appeals to the rock as prime material for the foundation of a building and reshapes it into a prime material upon which to build the church (Matt. 7.25; Luke 6.48).

Western culture utilizes the image of the rock in ways similar to those of the biblical authors. F.W. Fraser, in 'The Shadow of the Rock' references 1 Cor. 10, saying, 'The Rock moves ever at thy side, / pausing to welcome thee at eventide'. Augustus Toplady's hymn, 'Rock of Ages', draws both on traditions of Jesus as the rock and the rock as a place of refuge. The 'Rock of Ages' can also be seen in terms of the cross, where the blow to the rock is the death of Christ.

In the late twentieth and early twenty-first centuries, the image of the rock emerges in such places as the television series *Arrested Development* (2003–2006), where the Bluth Company adapts the slogan 'Solid as a Rock'. The slogan appeals to biblical notions of the rock as an ideal foundation for building and a place of safety. Dwayne Johnson adopted the name 'The Rock' in his professional wrestling career, evoking similar images of strength, power, and immovability. An interesting twist on the rock as a place of refuge is made in the film *The Rock* (1996). San Francisco's notorious prison, Alcatraz, to which the film's title refers, is not a place of refuge, but one of nearly inescapable confinement.

Recommended reading. Luz, Ulrich. 'The Primacy Saying of Matthew 16.17-19 from the Perspective of its Effective History'. *Studies in Matthew*. Pp. 165-82. Grand Rapids, MI: Eerdmans, 2005. Terrien, Samuel L. 'The

Metaphor of the Rock in Biblical Theology'. In *God in the Fray*. Ed. T. Linafelt and T.K. Beal. Pp. 157-71. Minneapolis: Fortress Press, 1998.

See also PETER; STONE [PKH]

Romans, Epistle to the. Paul wrote this influential letter from Corinth to Christians in Rome c. 57 CE. The most probable reason for writing was to prepare the Roman Christians for the arrival of Phoebe, Paul's fellow worker. Phoebe (16.1-2) was to make arrangements for Paul to stay in Rome for a short time while they gathered resources for a missionary trip to Spain. The contents of the letter summarize Paul's understanding of the gospel and its implications for the church and the world so that the Roman Christians would be willing to send him to the ends of the earth with this message.

Romans begins with a lengthy introduction that foreshadows the contents of the letter (1.1-17). Paul declares that the gospel was promised by the prophets and concerns God's son, Jesus the Messiah. Paul is the herald of this gospel to the Gentiles, which will bring the salvation of God to all nations without distinction. In 1.18–3.20, Paul demonstrates by various proofs that all of humanity without distinction is captive to sin. In 3.21–4.25, Paul proclaims that God has provided righteousness through the sacrifice of Jesus Christ for everyone who follows Abraham's example of faith. Romans 5 provides a transition to the implications of the gospel. Justification by faith brings reconciliation with God.

As Romans 3–5 deals with sin as a forensic problem, Romans 6–8 deals with sin as a personal moral problem. Although the justification of humanity by faith in the sacrifice of Christ brings reconciliation with God, sin remains a force in the believer's life, causing an inconsistency between righteous desires and unrighteous actions. The solution is God's Spirit who leads, empowers, and encourages the believer. Romans 8 ends with one of the greatest passages on the love of God in Christian literature. Nothing can separate the believer from God's love.

Romans 9–11 highlights the relationship of Israel and the nations. God has so worked that Israel, even in its disobedience to God, brought forth salvation for the nations, and through the salvation of the nations, God will work to bring about the salvation of Israel, so that 'all Israel' made up of Jews and Gentiles, will be saved. The function of Romans 9–11 in the context of Romans is debated. It seems that one of the main ideas is that God has a place for both Israel and the nations, which leads to Romans 12–16 in which Jews and Gentiles are encouraged to get along with each other in the church. There may be differences of religious practice among believers, but Christians need to imitate the attitude of Christ who did not put his own interests above those for whom he died. As God's grace brings salvation to humans without distinction, so Christians should display grace to all without prejudice.

Romans has had a profound impact on the western church. One of its greatest theologians, Augustine, seems to have based a large part of his theology on Romans. The Augustinian monk, Martin Luther, was highly influenced by Romans, having lectured on the Epistle before and after the beginning of the Reformation. John Wesley, the founder of Methodism, was influenced by Luther's commentary on Romans. Karl Barth, one of the greatest theologians of the twentieth century, wrote a commentary on Romans that virtually changed the theological direction of Protestantism. Romans still attracts the attention of the major NT scholars of the present.

Recommended reading. Bryan, Christopher. *A Preface to Romans: Notes on the Epistle in its Literary and Cultural Setting*. New York: Oxford University Press, 2000.

See also FAITH; JUSTIFICATION; PAUL, THE APOSTLE; PHOEBE; ROME [DHJ]

Roman Empire. The Roman Empire was the dominant government of the Mediterranean world during the NT period. Originally republican, Rome's civil wars in the late first century BCE mark its transition to the *Imperium Romanorum*, or in transliterated Greek, the *Basileia Romaiōn*. Historians ancient and modern have debated the timing and nature of Rome's rebirth as an empire; Virgil's epic poetry functions as propaganda, neatly sanctioning the imperial reign of Augustus through Jupiter's pledge (*Aeneid* 12.739) to forge a new people, surpassing the gods themselves in loyalty, from the refugees of legendary Troy. Rome's rise and fall have become paradigms for modern storytelling, too, discernible in science fiction author Isaac Asimov's *Foundation* series and George Lucas's *Star Wars* film saga.

The scope and significance of the Empire's role in the Bible have been disputed, especially over the past decade. Certainly NT authors adapt terms originally used to advance imperial theology: *euangelion* ('gospel') originally connoted the 'good news' of a royal birth or military victory; *basileia*, conventionally rendered as 'kingdom', and *basileus*, 'king', can be justifiably translated as 'empire' and 'emperor', respectively; and the acclamation of Jesus as *kyrios* and *sōtēr*, 'lord:' and 'savior', would seem in direct conflict with Caesar's claim to supremacy. Even the words used to indicate Rome, *Roma* and *oikoumenē* (the inhabited, civilized world, often translated as 'empire' even where the latter term is not explicitly present, as in Luke 2.1) were understood to refer not just to locations but to divine personifications of Rome and her territory. The question is how closely early Christianity's claims rivaled those of the Empire. If the church was to survive and continue to benefit from Rome's trade routes and imposed order, it would have needed carefully to manage the political tensions inherent in its terminology.

These tensions carry serious implications for the reading of imperially charged texts. Does the affirmation of Jesus as *Emmanuel*, 'God is with us' (Matt. 1.23) eclipse Rome's claim that its emperor acts as the gods' earthly agent? When the Gerasene demoniac names himself 'Legion' (Mark 5.9), is this reference to a Roman combat unit intended to challenge the harsh imperial military? How do the ethics of God's 'empire' compare with the ways of Rome, especially in difficult parables like Luke 19.11-27? Why does Christ relinquish his 'kingdom' to the Father in 1 Cor. 15.24, in a direct reversal of the way in which control of Rome's empire was ceded?

Similarly problematic are the ramifications for negotiating modern imperial contexts. Rome's sociopolitical dominance so imprinted western society that many later governments have tried to emulate it, adopting its name (the Holy Roman Empire of the early medieval period), its emblems (the eagle), and its colonization strategies. Not surprisingly, postcolonial studies have offered penetrating analyses of Rome and subsequent empires; even in situations that are not truly 'postcolonial' because the occupying force has yet to withdraw, comparison with previously documented models can illustrate the complexity and diversity entailed in living faithfully within imperial societies.

Recommended reading. Carter, Warren. *Matthew and Empire: Initial Explorations*. Harrisburg, PA: Trinity International, 2001. Cassidy, Richard J. *Christians and Roman Rule in the New Testament: New Perspectives*. Companions to the New Testament; New York: Herder & Herder/Crossroad, 2001. Santosuosso, Antonio. *Storming the Heavens: Soldiers, Emperors, and Civilians in the Roman Empire*. Boulder, CO: Westview/Perseus, 2004.

See also EMPEROR; KINGSHIP; LEGION; ROME

[MFL]

Rome. According to legend, the city of Rome was founded on April 21, 753 BCE by Romulus, the son of Mars, on the place where he and his twin brother Remus were nursed by a she-wolf. The name Rome, derived from Romulus, was finalized after a fight developed between the brothers over the name of the city, which resulted in the death of Remus.

Until c. 509 BCE and the rise of the Republic, the city of Rome and its territories comprised the extent of the monarchical government. The precise event that signalled the transition of the Roman Republic into the Roman Empire is a matter of interpretation. Historians have proposed the appointment of Julius Caesar as perpetual dictator (44 BCE), the Battle of Actium (September 2, 31 BCE), and the Roman Senate's grant of Octavian's (Augustus's) extraordinary powers under the first settlement (January 16, 27 BCE), as candidates for the defining transition.

During the first century CE and the spread of the Christian faith, arguably the primary missionary to the nations was the apostle Paul. Although not personally responsible for evangelizing the Romans, one of his most revered letters, the Epistle to the Romans, is a cornerstone of the NT canon. It is clear from the final chapter of this letter, however, that Paul knew a number of the Jewish Christians living in Rome, whom he likely met during their exile after Claudius's expulsion of the Jews from Rome c. 45–49 CE. At this time, there were approximately 40–50,000 Jews living in Rome, whose total population was nearly one million inhabitants. Additionally, the final chapter of Acts is set in Rome, where Paul is under house arrest and is awaiting his trial before Caesar (Acts 28.11-31).

In the first three centuries CE, Christians were generally persecuted in Rome, beginning with the reign of Nero (54–68 CE). However, one of the defining moments of Rome and the Roman Empire was the emperor Constantine's Edict of Milan (313 CE) which commanded official toleration of Christianity, and the eventual establishment of Christianity as the official religion of the Empire (380 CE).

Today, Rome is still considered by Catholics as a religious center because of the location of the Vatican within its city limits, whose current city-state was founded in 1929, although it had been the seat of the papacy from 1377.

Although the eras of the Roman Republic and Empire are long past, its influence and inspiration of modern art, film and literature is still strong. For instance, the TV shows *Ancient Rome: The Rise and Fall of an Empire* (2006) and *Rome* (2005–2007) are both centered on the reign of Julius Caesar. The movie *Gladiator* (2000) focused on the political intrigue of the Emperors and the gladiatorial entertainment.

In literature, ancient Rome continues to be a setting that attracts authors. Besides such well-known Shakespearean plays as *Coriolanus, Anthony and Cleopatra* and *Julius Caesar*, there are a number of other literary works based in Rome, e.g., *I, Claudius* (1934) and its sequel, *Claudius the God* (1935), by Robert Graves; *Ben-Hur: A Tale of the Christ* (1880) by Lew Wallace; and Michael Curtis Ford's *The Fall of Rome. A Novel of a World Lost* (2007).

Recommended reading. Cornell, T.J. *The Beginnings of Rome: Italy and Rome from the Bronze Age to the Punic Wars (c. 1000–264 BC)*. London: Routledge, 1995. Goodman, Martin. *The Roman World: 44 BC–AD 180*. London: Routledge, 1997.

See also AUGUSTUS; CAESAR OCTAVIANUS; NERO, THE EMPEROR; PAUL, THE APOSTLE; ROMAN EMPIRE; ROMANS, EPISTLE TO THE [SAA]

Rose of Sharon. From the Hebrew *ḥăbaṣṣelet*, meaning 'coastal crocus' or 'splendid bulb'; a flower that blooms along the Sharon plain on the Mediterranean coast. Famously mentioned in the Song of Solomon, the flower becomes a symbol of the bride who says: 'I am the Rose of Sharon, a lily of the valleys' (Song 2.1). Originally interpreted to denote love, sensuality, and eroticism, this redolent symbol in the Song of Solomon, with the rise of Christianity, was reinterpreted as a metaphor for the longing of the church for the return of Christ, in which the Rose of Sharon symbolized Christ.

The type of flower represented by the Rose of Sharon is not clear. It has been equated with the autumn crocus, asphodel, tulip, narcissus, or sea daffodil (*Pancratium maritimum*), all of which bloom in the region. The English word 'rose' is likely a misnomer given that other indigenous species of flowering plants are more common to the area. Nevertheless, roses were a fragrant symbol of love and beauty in the ancient world, especially associated with goddess worship such as the Greek Aphrodite/Roman Venus (both of whom were Goddesses of Love). By the Middle Ages, the rose was again equated with another prominent female archetype—the Virgin Mary. Medieval monks such as St Bernard of Clairvaux and St Anthony of Padua specifically identified the Rose of Sharon with the Virgin Mary.

In modern literature, Sir Walter Scott cites the Rose of Sharon in his novel *Ivanhoe* where Prior Aymer concurs that Rebecca's beauty is evocative of the 'Rose of Sharon', but adds 'your Grace must remember that she is still but a Jewess' (Sir Walter Scott, *Ivanhoe,* 1819, chap. 7). John Steinbeck's award winning novel, *The Grapes of Wrath* (1939), includes a character named 'Rose of Sharon' who is related to Tom Joad. As an important character in the book, her pregnancy holds the promise of renewal, which is lost when she delivers a stillborn baby. Another literary nod to the Rose of Sharon appears in the writing of the American poet and pastor Edward Taylor who in his *Poems and Sacramental Mediations* (1939) compares Jesus' sacrifice to the fragrance of the rose.

More recently, the Rose of Sharon has been the subject of florid lyrics in western popular music. The opening verse of Bob Dylan's 1985 song 'Caribbean Wind' chimes: 'She was the rose of Sharon from paradise lost. From the city of seven hills near the place of the cross'. Other artists' songs that directly or indirectly acknowledge the Rose of Sharon include Kate Bush's recording, 'The Song of Solomon' (from her 1993 album *The Red Shoes*); Killswitch Engage's 'Rose of Sharyn' (from their 2003 album *The End of Heartache);* and Sting's 1999 popular hit, *Desert Rose,* which contains language evocative of the Song of Solomon.

In these ways, references to the Rose of Sharon have appeared throughout western culture like a garland of fragrant memories. The enduring literary scent of the Rose of Sharon still evokes beauty, sensuality, longing, and mystery in the mediums of literature, poetry and music.

See also MARY, MOTHER OF JESUS; PLANTS, SYMBOLISM OF; SONG OF SOLOMON, SONGS [SDD]

Ruth, Book of. Often cited as an idyllic romance, the biblical book of Ruth is nevertheless set by the author 'in the days when the judges ruled' (1.1). In contrast to the increasing lawlessness and violence that marks the Judges narrative, the story of Ruth describes how Naomi moves from emptiness to fullness through the faithful loving kindness (*ḥesed*) of her Moabite daughter-in-law Ruth.

Famine drives Naomi, her husband Elimelech and their two sons from Bethlehem ('house of bread') and they settle in Moab. Elimelech dies here. The dangers of living in a patriarchal culture are mitigated for Naomi when her sons Mahlon and Chilion marry two Moabite women. When her two sons also die, Naomi is bereft and so when she hears that the famine in Israel is over, she decides to return home, advising her daughters-in-law to stay with their own people and remarry. Ruth refuses to leave Naomi. Her initial pledge to Naomi on the road to Bethlehem—'where you go I will go, and where you lodge I will lodge; your people shall be my people, and your God my God' (or 'your gods my gods'; 1.16)—is often repeated in Christian weddings and associated with vows of marital faithfulness. Naomi and Ruth return to Israel during the barley harvest, and Ruth finds safety gleaning in the fields belonging to Boaz who has remained faithful to the laws of Sabbath and Jubilee meant sheltered those most vulnerable in Israel (Deut. 24.19-22; Lev. 19.9-10; 25; Exod. 23.10-11). When the harvest is over, it is Naomi who devises a bold plan that leads to Ruth's and Boaz's marriage. Ruth bears a son, Obed, and in the final scene we hear the women of Bethlehem address Naomi as his mother. In the same chorus the women also praise Ruth 'who loves you, who is more to you than seven sons' (4.15b).

Feminist theologian Phyllis Trible reads the story of Ruth as a human comedy that highlights women who are 'working out their own salvation with fear and trembling, for God is at work in' them (Phil. 2.12). However, Boaz also participates in this work through his loving obedience as he practices the laws of Jubilee and Sabbath.

In the broad scope of the biblical narrative, the story of Ruth is cited as a chapter in salvation history. Ruth's pledge to leave all behind to journey with Naomi recalls Abraham's sojourn. Aptly, in Jewish tradition, this story is read on the harvest feast of Pentecost. The Book of Ruth also holds rumors of the NT Pentecost when the Holy Spirit is given to any who would leave all that is familiar behind to follow the map of God's *ḥesed* in this world. A genealogy links Obed to David at the end of Ruth (4.21-22) and is followed by Matthew's genealogy that links Ruth and Boaz to Jesus Christ (1.5).

In November 1996, ArcOTishop Desmond Tutu cited the laws that sheltered Ruth in Boaz's fields, when Tutu challenged the International Monetary Fund and the World Bank to forge a contemporary jubilee law for the African nations crippled by their debt to wealthier western nations. U2's lead singer Bono joined in this 'Jubilee 2000' initiative, and traced the Jubilee tradition to Jesus Christ's ministry in his 2006 address at the annual national US President's Prayer Breakfast.

Recommended reading. Kates, Judith A. and Gail Twersky Reimer (ed.). *Reading Ruth: Contemporary Women Reclaim a Sacred Story.* New York: Random House, 1994. Trible, Phyllis. *God and the Rhetoric of Sexuality*, 166-99. Philadelphia: Fortress Press, 1978.

See also BOAZ; JUBILEE; JUDGES; MOAB; NAOMI

[AK-H]

S

Sabbath. A season of rest; one day in seven appointed for rest and worship, the observance of which was undertaken by the Israelites in the Decalogue, continues in Judaism, and has been adapted by the Christian Church with a transference of the day observed from the last to the first of the week, commonly referred to as the Lord's Day. Sabbath in Hebrew (*shabat*), literally means 'cease' or 'rest'. In Greek (*sabbaton*) and Latin (*sabbatum*), the term is defined as 'the seventh day of the week for rest and worship'.

The first reference to the Sabbath appears in Gen. 2.2-3. The creation narrative includes six days of God's creative activity followed by a seventh in which God 'stopped' all his work (Gen. 2.2-3). The Genesis model of resting after a period of labor is not given primarily for the purpose of self-recuperation or restoration, but rather as a means of maintaining the proper perspective on work and creation. In the contexts of the various versions of the Decalogue (Exod. 20.2-17; Deut. 5.6-21), it is not common work that is seen as necessitating the Sabbath, but instead, it is oppressive labor that is presented as the catalyst requiring periodic rest. The Sabbath commandment perpetually reminded the Israelites of their redemption from enslavement in Egypt. Throughout their history, observance of the Sabbath functioned as a sign of the covenant and that Israel is set aside as a special people (Exod. 31.13,16-17; Ezek. 20.12, 20).

In the NT, Jesus' words and actions are at the core of several controversies surrounding the nature of the Sabbath. Of the six Gospel passages in which Jesus' (non)observance of the Sabbath is explicitly stated, one has to do with the disciples eating food (Mark 2.23-28), and the other five are instances in which he healed someone whom the Pharisees would or could not heal (Mark 3.1-6; Luke 13.10-17, 14.1-6; John 5.1-18, 9.1-34). In each instance, it was the Pharisees who demanded Jesus' inactivity in order to meet certain legal demands. However, on each occasion, Jesus intervened on behalf of those in need.

Associated symbols include: the Garden of Eden as symbol of God's creativity and a place of rest and heaven as a place of never-ending Sabbath. In Jewish culture, during the Sabbath meal, the lighting of candles and the flames are symbolic of God's life-giving power. The loaf of white bread (*challah*), serves as a symbol of the blessing of food, which God provided for the Israelites in the wilderness. Finally, the goblet containing wine is symbolic of a 'double blessing' of goodness and gladness.

Sabbath in contemporary culture is frequently associated with a day for dispensing with the rigors of work, a time to relax and play, and a period of worship and reverence for God. The ideas of Sabbath time, Sabbath rest, Sabbath year, and sabbatical are all derivatives of the Sabbath Commandment. Several authors have written excellent books that provide a practical explanation of the Sabbath commandment and how to live the Sabbath life. Tilden Edwards's *Sabbath Time* and Donna Shepers's *Sabbath Sense: A Spiritual Antidote for the Overworked*. In music, the term Sabbath was popularized by the British heavy metal rock band Black Sabbath.

See also REST; TEN COMMANDMENTS [SNW]

Sackcloth and ashes. From the Hebrew *saq* (sackcloth) and *aphar* (ash or dust). The word ashes is literally an image of complete waste. It is also used as a metaphor for weakness, fleetingness and emptiness (Job 13.12; also Ps. 142.6; Isa. 44.20). Thus the use of ashes to express grief and loss would reflect on that literal image and metaphor. The Israelites and their neighbors would use ashes, either with sackcloth (a coarse cloth) or alone, to outwardly express a deep form of penitence (Job 42.6), grief (Job 30.18), humiliation (1 Kgs 21.27-29), and social protest (Est. 4.1-4). On one occasion even animals are said to have worn sackcloth the day Nineveh repented (Jon 3.7). People would either sprinkle ashes on their heads (2 Sam. 3.31; Lam. 2.10), sit in them (Jon 3.6), they would lie on them (Est. 4.3), or even roll in them (Jer. 6.26; Mic. 1.10).

Sackcloth and ashes often appear together (Est. 4.1, 3; Isa. 58.5; Jer. 6.26; Dan. 9.3; Jon 3.6; Neh. 9.1; Job 16.15; Lam. 2.10; Matt. 11.21; Luke 10.13). In association with their use, a fast could be imposed for a period of time (1 Kgs 21.27; Neh. 9.1; Est. 4.3; Ps. 35.13; Isa. 58.5; Dan. 9.3; Jon 3.5, 7). The rending of clothes after an unfortunate event, such as death, was also associated with the use of sackcloth as distressed people replaced their clothes as part of the mourning process or rage (Gen. 37.34; 2 Sam. 3.31; 1 Kgs 21.27; 2 Kgs 6.30; 19.1). However Isa. 58.5-9 clearly states that God is more pleased by works of justice than by people merely wearing sackcloth and ashes.

People were still wearing sackcloth and ashes in the Roman church of the fourth century, but they would perform works of justice as well (Jerome, *Epistle* 77). In medieval times, sackcloth became a 'hair shirt' that was worn under the outer clothes and next to the skin. This was enough to make a person experience discomfort for their wrongdoings. Later in the Middle Ages, however, people would voluntarily endure 'hair shirts' in order to discipline the body and their appetites (e.g., St Catherine of Siena). The hair shirt, sometimes referred to as a cilice, is mentioned in Dan Brown's *The Da Vinci Code*. One of his characters, Silas, an albino monk, wears one.

In Shakespeare's *King Henry IV*, Falstaff talks briefly about Prince Hal with the Lord Chief Justice. 'I have checked him for it, and the young lion repents. Marry, not in ashes and sackcloth, but in new silk and old sack (1.2.197-200)'. Nathaniel Hawthorne's character Catherine in *The Gentle Boy* is described as wearing a shapeless robe of sackcloth around her waist with a knotted cord, and her raven hair streaked pale with ashes.

In contemporary culture, observing Lent is the closest that many Christian get to the older tradition. On Ash Wednesday, the first day of Lent, Christians of several denominations worldwide receive a cross of ashes drawn by a priest or minister. Some observe that solemn day by fasting and also by abstaining from meat. This allows people to outwardly express their penitence not unlike that of the ancient Near Eastern tradition.

See also FAST; MOURNING; REPENTANCE [ED]

Sacraments. Properly speaking, there is no NT collective term for ritual acts such as baptism and the Lord's Supper. Even so, the ancient church understood that its members were being gradually transformed into the likeness of Christ (2 Cor. 3.13-18) and that part of this transformation was understood to take place in the various sacred acts of Christian worship. These rites and ceremonies were understood to reveal what was once unclear, and therefore the Greek-speaking church came to call them *mystēria* ('mysteries').

The Western church did not have a comparable term. Jerome (c. 400) adopted the Latin word *sacramentum*, originally used for the loyalty oath of a Roman soldier, as a similar process of transformation. The military *sacramentum* was a physical religious act that transformed the inductee's legal status. In Christian usage, it came to mean a sacred act that symbolizes (or effects) a spiritual transformation. The classic definition comes from Augustine (d. 430), who defined a sacrament as 'an outward and visible sign of an inward and invisible grace'.

At first, the church did not have such a definitive list of sacraments. Many early writers spoke of many sacraments including foot-washing, fasting, martyrdom, the Creed, the Lord's Prayer, scripture, and even the incarnation of Jesus.

As time progressed, writers devised various lists of sacraments. Pseudo-Dionysius (c. 500) listed six sacraments: baptism, the eucharist, anointing, ordination, monastic consecration, and the rites connected with burial. Peter Damian (d. 1072) argued for 12, and Hugh of St Victor (d. 1141) named nearly 30 divided into three classes.

It was Peter Lombard (d. 1160), bishop of Paris, who popularized the conception that there were seven sacraments. His *Sentences* became the principal manual of theology among Western Christians for four hundred years, and his theory about the number of the sacraments was generally accepted. In Roman Catholicism, the seven sacraments are: (1) Baptism; (2) Confirmation; (3) Reconciliation (formerly 'Penance'); (4) The Eucharist; (5) Anointing of the Sick (formerly 'Extreme Unction'); (6) Holy Matrimony; (7) Holy Orders (i.e., ordination).

To this day, Eastern Orthodox Christians maintain a more fluid definition of 'sacrament' than has been the case in the west. At the other extreme, Protestants generally limit the number of sacraments to those sacred acts with clear precedent in the ministry of Jesus: baptism and the Lord's Supper, although Martin Luther allowed for a sacrament of penance in at least some of his writings. Furthermore, some Protestants, especially in free-church traditions such as Baptist and Church of Christ, hesitate to use the word 'sacrament' at all, preferring to use terminology such as 'ordinance' in order to distance themselves from what they perceive as an over-emphasis on the transforming power of these rites.

Several controversies surround the sacraments. Christians are divided over whether these sacred acts are merely symbolic of God's transforming power or whether they are in themselves 'means of grace' that produce the spiritual results they symbolize.

In church history, some early writers challenged the Gnostics, who taught that material existence was an unmitigated evil, by appealing to the tangible and this-worldly nature of the Christian sacraments. Later, the Donatists of North Africa rejected the validity of sacraments performed by clergy who had previously renounced their faith under persecution. The wider church concluded, however, that the sacraments owed their validity to Christ and not to the person performing them.

Recommended reading. Barrett, C.K. *Church, Ministry, and Sacraments in the New Testament*. Grand Rapids, MI: Eerdmans, 1985. Martimort, Aimé Georges. *Signs of the Covenant*. St Paul, MN: Liturgical Press, 1963.

See also BAPTISM; COMMUNION; FOOD, SYMBOLISM OF; GNOSTIC, GNOSTICISM; GRACE; LORD'S SUPPER; MYSTERY [DJP]

Sacrifice. In the HB, 'sacrifice' usually refers to the material of an offering to God and the subsequent ritual that is part of worship. Sacrificial rituals are performed at a sacred site (altar or sanctuary) where God is thought to be present (Lev. 9.22-24). The basic laws of sacrifice in Leviticus 1–7 specify five different types. They determine which animals or vegetable materials may be offered. They also describe how lay persons and/or priests should perform the ritual, and which 'effects' various ritual actions have: sacrificial blood, applied to the 'altar of burnt offering' or various parts of the sanctuary (Lev. 4; 16.14-19), effects forgiveness and atonement; burning the entire sacrifice (Lev. 1.9, 13, 17) or parts of it (Lev. 2.2, 9; 3.5, 11; 4.8-10, 19-20) on the 'altar of burnt offering' effects the 'pleasing odor' for God as well as atonement. While blood application rites occur only in the sin offering ritual, the burning rite is part of all five types of sacrifice. Transformed through the altar fire, the sacrifice is transported to God in the smoke. These dynamics toward God are captured by the Hebrew term *qorban*, offering.

Today Israel's sacrificial cult is often misinterpreted as an institution bent on the annihilation of life. Yet the cereal offering (Lev. 2; it can substitute for the sin offering animal, see Lev. 5.11-13) demonstrates that a cultic sacrifice does not require a victim. Likewise, the temple cult in the Judean colony of Elephantine consisted exclusively of cereal offerings and burning frankincense. Pertinent archaeological evidence shows that objects like weapons, jewelry, and other valued items were offered to God at ancient Palestinian sanctuaries.

The term sacrifice occurs, moreover, as a metaphor in both HB and NT: righteous behavior and prayer can be called 'sacrifice' since, like ritual sacrifices, they are an expression of worship and directed to God (Ps. 50.14; 51.17 ET; 119.108; Sir. 35.1-3; Heb. 13.15-16). The term sacrifice is sometimes used in NT christological contexts. In Eph. 5.2, Jesus is called 'offering and sacrifice for God as a pleasing odor', conveying that his entire life, including his death, demonstrated exemplary love and was acceptable to God. Hebrews combined the motifs of sacrifice and consecration through blood to suggest that Christ's blood obtained eternal forgiveness of sins. Hebrews thus claimed that Christ's sacrifice superseded the HB sacrifices (Heb. 7.27; 9.14, 26; 10.10). Overall, however, the sacrifice motif is rare in NT contexts; in Rom. 3.25 and 1 John 2.2; 4.10, the translation 'sacrifice of atonement' or 'atoning sacrifice' (NRSV, NIV) is incorrect (see Atonement).

In modern western culture, the term sacrifice is mostly used metaphorically. It has been emptied of any specific notion of the addressee to whom the sacrificial act was directed. Reduced instead to material loss and failure, the term has mainly negative connotations. Thus *sacrificium intellectus* currently denotes the willingness to surrender one's intellect; soldiers killed in wars are praised for having 'sacrificed' their lives for their countries or political ideals. However, the term sacrifice is derived from Latin *sacrificium* which is composed of *sacrum facere*—'to make holy' or 'to dedicate'. Etymologically, therefore, this term does not connote aspects of killing or annihilation. The modern metaphorical use of sacrifice is thus inappropriate for understanding Israelite sacrifice.

Recommended reading. Eberhart, Christian A. 'Characteristics of Sacrificial Metaphors in Hebrews'. In *Hebrews*. Ed. Gabriella Gelardini. Pp. 37-65. Leiden and Boston: Brill, 2005. ———. 'The Term 'Sacrifice' and the Problem of Theological Abstraction'. In *The Multivalence of Biblical Texts and Theological Meanings*. Ed. Christine Helmer. Pp. 47-66. Atlanta: Society of Biblical Literature, 2006. McClymond, Kathryn. *Beyond Sacred Violence*. Baltimore: Johns Hopkins University Press, 2008.

See also ATONEMENT; BLOOD; FIRE; OFFERING; SACRIFICE, HUMAN [CAE]

Sacrifice, Human. The mindset in the ANE was that the deity who provides also has the right to require a percentage of that provision be returned via sacrifice. Phoenician and Punic texts confirm that child sacrifice was practiced in order to ensure continued fertility. It has been suggested that in reviewing Abraham's behavior in Genesis 22, he was not only familiar with the practice of child sacrifice, but he was not surprised that Yahweh would require it of him. A key passage for understanding and interpreting the element of human sacrifice is Exod. 22.28-

29. This passage requires that the firstborn is to be given back to God. It is important to note that this sacrifice can be satisfied by the substitution of a lamb or two young pigeons (Exod. 34.20; 13.13; Lev. 12.6-8).

The sacrifice of the firstborn was an existing practice in the ANE. It was performed by King Mesha of Moab to the god Chemosh (2 Kgs 3.26-27), Ammonites to Molech (Lev. 18.21; 20.2), Sepharvaim Aramaeens to Adram-melech and Ana-melech. Child sacrifice has been associated with 'passing through fire' and the *tophet* (Jer. 7 and 2 Kgs 23.10).

Also the Israelite kings Ahaz and Manasseh (2 Kgs 16.2; 21.6), and potentially Saul with Jonathan (1 Sam. 14.43-46) are connected to human sacrifice. Parallels are often drawn between this narrative and the story of Jephthah's daughter (Judg. 11.29-40). In this case, Jephthah promises God that he would sacrifice the first living thing to greet him upon returning home as a tribute to God. It turns out to be his daughter, his only child, who greets him and the sacrifice is performed.

Immanuel Kant takes issue with the positive view of Genesis 22 that most in the history of interpretation have taken. His view is that God is the moral law and therefore cannot command something or someone to break the moral law and therefore anything that suggests that the moral law should be broken cannot be of God. He suggests that Abraham should have denied that the command given was actually from God and refused to consider the sacrifice. This passage is also addressed in Søren Kierkegaard's *Fear and Trembling*, where he uses the passage to address moral theology in relationship to the philosophy of religion.

The theme of human sacrifice in the form of the *tophet* is found in the literature of Browning, Carlyle, Hawthorne, Melville, Hardy, Kipling, and Machen.

Recommended reading. Chilton, Bruce. *Abraham's Curse: Child Sacrifice in the Legacies of the West*. New York: Doubleday, 2008. Finsterbusch, Karin. *Human Sacrifice in Jewish and Christian Tradition*. Leiden: Brill, 2007.

See also ABRAHAM; AQEDAH; CHEMOSH; GENESIS, BOOK OF; ISAAC; JEPHTHAH; JUDGES, BOOK OF; MOLOCK, MOLECH; SACRIFICE; TOPHET   [EW]

Sadducees. One of the three main sects of Judaism in the late Second Temple period (c. 150 BCE–70 CE). The other two were the Pharisees and Essenes. The name Sadducee is thought to have derived from the Hebrew name Zadok, the high priest who served during the reign of King David. During the late Second Temple period, the Sadducees ran the temple, consisting of the 'priestly', and therefore elite, class. According to the historian Josephus, the Sadducees did not believe in the afterlife and emphasized the here and now (*Antiquities* 13.5.9; 10.6.2; 18.1.4-5; *Jewish War* 2.8.14; cf. Acts 23.8). The Sadducees also did not accept the oral Torah, to which the Pharisees subscribed and which later became the basis for Rabbinic Judaism.

The Sadducees are not mentioned in the Torah itself, and their mention in the NT, where they are usually portrayed as opponents of Jesus, is brief (Matt. 3.7; 16.1, 5-6; 16.11-12; 22.23, 34; Mark 12.18; Luke 20.27; Acts 4.1; 5.17; 23.6-10). They disappear from the record around the time the second temple was destroyed; after 70 CE, we hear little to nothing about the Sadducees, except in rabbinic texts mentioning the second temple period.

Recommended reading. Nickelsburg, George W.E., and Michael E. Stone. *Faith and Piety in Early Judaism*. Philadelphia: Trinity Press International, 1991. Cohen, Shaye J.D. *From the Maccabees to the Mishnah*. Philadelphia: Westminster Press, 1987. Schiffman, Lawrence. *From Text to Tradition: A History of Judaism in Second Temple and Rabbinic Times*. Hoboken, NJ: Ktav Publishing House, 1991.

See also ESSENES; PHARISEES   [SS]

Saints. Saints are persons or groups of people who are considered by God to be holy (set apart), in close relationship with God. In the OT, sainthood is not explicitly developed (though featuring occasionally in the Psalms), and relates to substantive uses of certain nouns and adjectives. There is evidence to suggest the term relates to one who is a recipient of God's *ḥesed* ('steadfast-love', 'kindness'), though it primarily relates to the Hebrew root *qdsh*, 'holy'. The concept involves imitating God's holiness, which is his distinctness and moral perfection. Practically, this imitation of God's holiness took the form of following God's commands as depicted in the Law, including both prescriptions for certain behaviors and restrictions. 'Saints' is primarily applied to God's people as a whole in the OT rather than a particular person.

This basic understanding progresses through the NT. 'Saint' develops as a substantive use of the Greek adjective *hagios*, 'holy'. However, it soon becomes the most common title for Christians in general as they find their identity in the death and resurrection of Christ and the impartation of the Holy Spirit rather than in the Law of Moses. Sainthood is simultaneously an identity and an aspiration; in Romans (1.7) and 1 Corinthians (1.2), for instance, Paul identifies his audiences as those 'called to be saints', while also referring to various groups of Christians as already being saints (such as in Ephesians and Philippians). In Revelation (e.g., 11.18; 13.7, 10), the saints form an almost political body in contrast with the forces that persecute and martyr Christians; it is the goal of those Christians alive in the times depicted to resist the temptation to forsake their faith in order to join the company of Christians who have already died.

In post-apostolic times, sainthood became much more individual in identification, leading in later eras to a large body of individuals formally recognised by the church (usually Catholic or Orthodox) as exceptional individuals who fully embodied the life of Christ. Groups such as The Church of Jesus Christ of Latter-day Saints and the Branch Davidians have taken up the description since they consider themselves the heirs of the ancient church.

Sainthood permeates western culture, in both positive and negative senses. To be called a 'saint' can be derogatory when referring to a person's excessive piety; on the other hand, there are many who reject the appellation in ordinary parlance even though their behavior is upstanding and may indeed be Christ-like. However, it is not unusual for a person who sees one's action as 'saintly', holy, or sacrificial to accept the epithet, whether it is indeed Christ-like or not. This is depicted in media such as the crime thriller film *The Boondock Saints* (in which two Irish-Catholic brothers seek to rid their home city of Boston of crime), the series of novels (and later television series and film) by Leslie Charteris depicting the thief Simon Templar as 'the Saint', and the street gang depicted in the popular video game franchise *Saints Row*.

In popular western culture, often nothing of the original meaning is implied. This is most prominent with the popularity of the saint as a mascot for sports teams, such as the New Orleans Saints of the US National Football League and the St Kilda Saints of the Australian Football League.

See also FAITH; HOLY/HOLINESS; MARTYR/MARTYRDOM; OBEDIENCE [CEM]

Salem. Salem (*slm*) is a common Hebrew root incorporated into many place names such as Jerusalem, and it is believed to be from the Canaanite God of the Dusk, Shalem whose twin brother, Shahar, is the God of Dawn. It is the city of Melchizedek (Gen. 14.18; cf. Heb. 7.1-2).

Other than Jerusalem (cf. Ps. 76.2), many places around the world are called Salem, or incorporate the word, the most well-known being Salem, Massachusetts, scene of the Salem Witch Trials of 1692, made famous in Arthur Miller's play, *The Crucible* (1953). Salem is also the capital of the state of Oregon, and there are places called Salem in Alabama, Arkansas (two), Connecticut, Florida, Georgia, Idaho, Illinois, Indiana (two), Iowa, Kansas, Kentucky, Maine, Maryland, Michigan, Mississippi, Missouri, Montana, Nebraska, New Hampshire, New Jersey, New Mexico, New York, North Carolina, Ohio, Oklahoma, Pennsylvania, South Carolina, South Dakota, Utah, Virginia (two), West Virginia, and Wisconsin (two). There are also places called Salem in Canada, Germany, India (Salem being the capital of the state of Tamil Nadu, with a population of 700,000), Indonesia, Montserrat, the Palestinian National Authority, Spain, Sweden (two) and the United Kingdom (two).

There have also been a number of people named Salem: Peter Salem, an African-American slave during the American War of Independence, and Salem Poor, an African-American soldier in the Battle of Bunker Hill in 1775. The Greek Jewish mathematician Raphaël Salem (1898–1963) was the eponym of the Salem Numbers which conjugate roots which have an absolute value no greater than 1, and the Salem Prize. Mamdouh Salem was the Prime Minister of Egypt from 1975 until 1978 under Anwar el-Sadat. There is also the Salem Castle School in Germany which includes the Salem International College; it gained prominence because of the traditions inculcated by its founder Kurt Hahn who later founded Gordonstown, a school in Scotland, and the United World Colleges.

There are many other uses of the name Salem, including for an Israeli extreme medal band; the Salem Stampede, a team in the International Basketball League; and the supertanker *Salem* which was involved in illegally selling oil to South Africa in 1980, and was then scuttled to claim insurance. There have also been three ships in the US Navy called the USS *Salem,* the earliest being a scout cruiser commissioned in 1908, the second a minelayer in 1942, and the third a heavy cruiser which was in service from 1949 until 1959. Stephen King wrote a horror novel *Salem's Lot* (1975); the original title was 'Jerusalem's Lot', was changed by the publisher because they felt it made the book seem like a religious work.

See also JERUSALEM; MELCHIZEDEK [JC]

Salome. Hellenized, abbreviated form of Hebrew s*helamzion*, (peace of Zion) from Hebrew *shalom* (peace) and *siyyon* (Zion). The only Salome named in the Bible is a follower of Jesus (Mark 15.40; 16.1), but the name is popularly associated with the daughter of Herodias in the story of the beheading of John the Baptist (Mark 6.17-28; Matt. 14.1-11; Luke 3.19-20). She is known as the daughter, who prompted by her mother, asks for the head the Baptist after dancing before Herod Antipas.

Many early writers assumed that Herodias was the name of both the mother and the daughter in the tale (Mark 6.22 can be translated 'his daughter Herodias ... danced'). Josephus names her Salome, followed by Isidore of Seville (c. 560–636).

This story is historically suspect for many reasons: it contradicts Josephus's account of John's death (*Antiquities* 18.5.2); it resembles an earlier Roman story about Lucius Quinctius Flaminius, who allegedly beheaded a man at a dinner party at the request of a courtesan; and it is questionable whether Salome would at that time have been of an age to have performed such a dance.

The historical Salome's first husband, Philip, died. She then married her cousin Aristobulus, King of Armenia, with whom she had three children. She is shown as Queen of Chalcis on a coin dating from 54 CE.

In Syrian legend, she is called Boziya; after the beheading, she runs with the head on a plate to a frozen pond where she dances. She is then beheaded, and her head is taken to her mother who goes blind. A medieval Flemish legend names her Pharaildis. She is enamored of John, her father has him decapitated, and John's head blows at her, causing her to drift through the air ceaselessly. Medieval art follows the biblical story, often depicting a youthful Salome dancing before an entranced Herod and her mother. She is also depicted carrying the bloodied head of John on a platter.

Nineteenth-century literature and art include Mallarmé's tragedy *Hérodiade* (1864), depicting the conflicts of the girl Herodiade who has her beloved killed. Heine's *Romancero* (1851) portrays a young dancer who renders Herod mad. Flaubert's *Hérodias* (1877) contrasts the prophet's voice from the dungeon with the bewitching dance of Salome above. In Huysmans's novel *A Rebours* (1884) Salome is the ultimate 'femme fatale'. Massenet's opera *Érodiada* (1881) has Salome and Jokanna bound together in mystical eroticism. In Moreau's painting *Salomé Dancing Before Herod* (1876), an abstract Salome becomes a symbol of the Orient served up for the western viewer's consumption. Other works include *Salome Dancing before Herod* (so-called *Salome Tattooed*) (1874) and *The Apparition* (1876).

Decadent art and literature greatly influenced Oscar Wilde's play *Salome* (1891), where Salome appears as the incarnation of seductive purity and power. Aubrey Beardsley's illustrations for Salome (1872–1898) ironically appropriate the decadent theme of the evil, emasculating woman. Richard Strauss's opera *Salome* (1905) based on Wilde's play, created a scandal, with its exotic orchestral colors and v violent, hypnotic harmonies. Atom Egoyan's Toronto production of *Salome* (1996, 2002) portrays Salome as an exploited, sexually abused victim of a genetically debased bloodline.

America's first art film was *Salome* (1923; dir. Charles Bryant), starring Alla Nazimova. *Salome* is the role that Norma Desmond sought to use as a vehicle to make her cinematic comeback in Billy Wilder's *Sunset Boulevard* (1950). William Deiterle's *Salome* (1953) starred a young Rita Hayworth whose innocence transformed the famous dance for King Herod into a plea to spare John's life. Clive Barker's horror film *Salome and the Forbidden* (1973) offers another perspective.

See also HEROD; HERODIAS; JOHN THE BAPTIST [EG]

Salt of the Earth. Jesus describes his followers in Matt. 5.13 as 'the salt of the earth' (Greek: *to halas tēs gēs*). This strikes us as an odd phrase. It brings to mind another saying. 'sowing salt into the earth', which means to render something barren. Of course, Jesus meant nothing like this. The salt of the earth is that which gives it flavor; and Jesus is telling his followers that they must be goodness and (in the next sentence) light to the world. Salt, of course, adds savor to our food, but it was of great value in the ancient world; people were even paid in salt, hence our English word salary.

Salt was also used as a preservative in antiquity, and it may be that Jesus had this in mind and that he was saying that his followers would preserve the earth from rot and decay. He nevertheless goes on to say that if salt loses its flavor it is useless, 'no longer good for anything, but is thrown out and trampled under foot' (Matt. 5.13b). If salt no longer has the properties of salt, it is no different than dirt and would be treated as such.

Early Christians tended to emphasize the metaphor of salt as a preservative. Augustine certainly read this passage in these terms, understanding the 'salt' to be the ministers of the gospel and the 'earth' to be the people of the world in need of purification and preservation from sin.

The phrase appears in Chaucer's *The Summoner's Tale* as the lord tries to appease the friar saying 'ye been the salt of the erthe and the savour / for goddes love youre patience ye holde!' By Chaucer's time the phrase had, become closely associated with the role of the clergy. The Protestant Reformers later accused the Roman church of losing its flavor.

Various authors have employed the term. Algernon Swinburne's poem 'The Salt of the Earth' uses the phrase to illustrate the joy and wonder of childhood. In D.H. Lawrence's poem 'Salt of the Earth', salt is the work and words of the wise and great among us; in his novel *Aaron's Rod* we read (with a whiff of irony) that 'the flower of civilization and the salt of the earth [are], namely, young, well-to-do Englishmen' (ch. 15).

In modern colloquial terms the phrase 'salt of the earth' normally refers to the honest and humble, hardworking and trustworthy. It has a folksy connotation to it, and this is reflected in its popular use, such as in country singer Ricky Skaggs's song and album 'Salt of the Earth'. The phrase as an expression has become proverbial and stands alone quite apart from Jesus' original teaching and its spiritual meaning.

In popular culture, 'Salt of the Earth' is the name of a Rolling Stones song featured on their 1968 album *Beggars Banquet.* It is also the title of a controversial 1954 film directed by Herbert J. Biberman, which was censored by the American authorities due to its strong socialist message.

See also LIGHT UNDER A BUSHEL; PARABLE; SERMON ON THE MOUNT [JIM]

Salvation. From the Latin *salvare* 'to save' and *salus* 'health' or 'help', translated from the Hebrew *yeshua* and the Greek *sotēria*. Salvation is the result of rescue from oppression, danger or illness, suggesting restoration to health and safety.

One of the basic assumptions of the Bible is that humanity is in desperate need of help. The original 'very good' that God pronounced on the first humans was soon stained by selfishness and shame and the whole creation became warped by sin. From there on the Bible is in essence the story of God's progressively unfolding plan to save Israel or the world.

That God is separate from creation and intervenes to rescue people was a novel religious idea in ancient times. The early stories of the Bible—like God's saving of Noah and his family from the flood—show God's determination to save his world. He then resolutely sets out to 'bless all nations' through the lineage of Abraham—the Hebrew people (Gen. 12.2, 3).

One of the greatest pictures of salvation in the Bible is God's liberation of the Hebrew slaves from Egypt and their dramatic entrance into the Promised Land (Exod. 14). When the Hebrews establish themselves as the kingdom of Israel, they fail to live out their salvation; that is to say, in spite of prophetic warnings, they fail to become a nation of justice and peace, and are exiled from their homeland until the return from Babylonia exile (532 BCE).

The NT presents Jesus, as Messiah and New Israel, as demonstrating God's intended salvation: a kingdom of healing for the sick, release for the captive, and good news for the poor (Luke 4). This salvation culminates in his sacrificial death on the cross, which opens God's love and rescue to the whole world (John 3.16). In the future, Jesus Christ will return, and the whole of creation will be saved from its bondage to sin and death (Rom. 8.22-25).

Salvation is one of the main themes of the western cultural tradition. The early church fathers championed the gospel as what saved them from pagan religion and demonic powers. The Reformation held up the Bible's good news that the grace of God alone justifies the faithful sinner. African-American slaves expressed their deep longing for God's rescue in spirituals like 'Swing Low, Sweet Chariot'. Roman Catholic liberation theology, peaking in the 1960s and 1970s in Latin America, emphasized God's promise to alleviate the oppression of the poor. Finally, evangelical global mission has proclaimed for over two centuries that being 'saved' by a personal encounter with God is the beginning of the Christian life.

Novels like C.S. Lewis's *The Lion, the Witch and the Wardrobe* (1950) and John Irving's *A Prayer for Owen Meany* (1989) both offer obvious salvation themes, with Lewis's tale allegorizing the story of Christ's death and resurrection.

Hollywood films convey salvation themes, often with a more humanistic focus. War films by Jewish director Steven Spielberg like *Schindler's List* (1993) and *Saving Private Ryan* (1998) offer vivid pictures of people being saved from immanent death through the daring sacrifice of heroic individuals. The suspenseful prison break *The Shawshank Redemption* (1994) and the Christian high school satire *Saved!* (2004) show salvation as rescue from unjust or unhealthy institutions.

Recommended reading. Newbigin, Leslie. *Sin and Salvation*. London: SCM Press, 2009. Okholm, Dennis L., and Timothy R. Phillips (eds.). *Four Views on Salvation in a Pluralistic World*. Grand Rapids, MI: Zondervan, 1996. Wright, Christopher J.H. *Salvation Belongs to our God: Celebrating the Bible's Central Story*. Downers Grove, IL: IVP Academic, 2008.

See also JUSTIFICATION; LIBERATION; JUSTIFICATION; SAVIOR; SIN [PS]

Samaria. Hebrew *šōměrôn*, refers to both a geographical region and a city. 1 Kings 16.21-25 details how Omri triumphed over his competitor to become sovereign of the northern kingdom of Israel. During his reign (876–864 BCE), Omri purchased a hill located NW of the ancient city of Shechem, fortifying the settlement and naming it after its previous owner, Shemer. What began as his private estate flourished and grew to be his kingdom's capital. Omri's son Ahab built a temple to the pagan god Ba'al in Samaria (1 Kgs 16.32).

The prophetic books denounced Samaria for preoccupation with wealth, abandonment of the poor, and worship of gods other than or alongside of Yahweh (See Amos 3.9, 4.1; Hos. 10.5; Isa. 8.4). In 722 BCE, destruction by the Assyrian army fell upon the city, deporting leading citizens, resettling other people groups in their place, and ending the independence of the northern kingdom of Israel. After, the Assyrians, and later the Persians, utilized Samaria as a provincial seat for governing the larger surrounding district Samerine.

Scholars debate the cause of the Samaria's demolition during the reign of Alexander the Great; however, the city was rebuilt, becoming an affluent Hellenistic municipality complete with fortification walls. Later, the Hasmonean John Hyrcanus destroyed the city, including a temple built to Yahweh by the local people.

Rome's control of the area began with Pompey in 63 BCE. Samaria was revived, and under the auspices of Herod the Great, built into a fantastic Roman metropolis. All expected features of a Greco-Roman city could now found in Samaria including a cardo, hippodrome, amphitheater, temple to Zeus–Jupiter, and protective walls. Herod renamed the city Sebaste, after the Greek title for the Roman emperor Augustus.

Luke and John state that Jesus passed through Samaria (Luke 17.11; John 4.7). In Acts, Jesus' parting words to his disciples before his ascension promised that when the Holy Spirit came upon the disciples, they would become Jesus' witness in 'all Judea, and Samaria, and to the ends of the earth' (1.8). Indeed, in Acts 8, persecution in Jerusalem causes some disciples to flee to Samaria where they teach about Jesus. In later centuries, the city became a seat for Christian bishops.

Today, the term Samaria is used by some to refer to the northern part of the West Bank, located above Jerusalem. The region has figured prominently in modern politics and warfare. Jordan controlled the region after the 1948 War of Independence, and Israel has retained control over the province since the 1968 Six Day War. As of 2011, debates over the territory continue to occur including issues related to Israeli settlements and Palestine rites.

The modern village of Sebastia is located just below the ancient site of Samaria–Sebaste. Both ancient Samaria–Sebaste and the surrounding area have been continually excavated resulting in numerous significant archeological finds including. the traces of an estate from c. eleventh–ninth centuries BCE, Roman ruins, the Samaria Ostraca (a collection of 63 inscribed potsherds), and the Wadi Daliye papyri.

Recommended reading. Bright, John. *A History of Israel*. 4th edn. Louisville, KY: Westminster John Knox, 2000. Cross, F.M. 'Aspects of Samaritan and Jewish History in Late Persian and Hellenistic Times'. *Harvard Theological Review* 59 (1966) 201-11. Crown, A.D. (ed.). *The Samaritans*. Tübingen: J.C.B. Mohr, 1989.

See also AHAB; ASSYRIA; OMRI; ISRAEL; SAMARITAN WOMAN; SAMARITANS; SHECHEM [CH]

Samaritan woman. The narrative of Jesus' dialogue with the Samaritan woman in John 4.1-42 has been dynamically interpreted through time. The Samaritan woman is generally positively related to the five senses, the symbol of the living water, and as a model convert in patristic, medieval and reformed theology as seen in the interpretations of Origen, Augustine, Gregory Nazianzen, Ambrose and Aquinas. Luther refers to her as a 'good' Samaritan woman, a model of receptive convert and faithful witness. In contrast, Jerome underlines her immorality and Calvin regards her as impertinent and saucy, maybe 'a prostitute' but one elected for salvation and commendable for her religious zeal. In the eastern church, the positive appreciation of the woman at the well gained her the title 'saint' and the name 'Photini', meaning 'bright', 'shining', 'radiant'. Her feast falls on February 26 and on the fourth Sunday of Easter.

Modern interpreters characterize the Samaritan woman differently. Some consider her as one who crosses ethnic and social boundaries, as a representative figure of the entire Samaritan people, and even as a missionary who brings people to Jesus. Others compare her with Nathanael whose experience of Jesus' knowledge of what is in a person leads to the recognition of who Jesus truly is (John 1.43-51), or contrast her with Nicodemus (John 3.1-21, man// woman, named//anonymous, Pharisee//Samaritan, visited Jesus at night// approached by Jesus at noon, disappearance at night//brought many Samaritans to Jesus). While some scholars read John 4.1-42 as a marriage metaphor between God (through Jesus) and the Samaritans, there are those who interpret it sensually and sexually. Feminist scholars underline her role as a witness for Jesus, as a 'Christian Disciple–Apostle', or as a depiction of 'Wisdom Woman'.

Visual representations also portray her constructively as a young woman who intently learns from Jesus and zealous in her mission. Paintings from Dura Europos, Syria and the catacombs in Rome picture her in simple and archaic ways. Byzantine arts contemporize her by way of her dress, watchful eye, and fixed and frontal facial expression. Paintings in late Middle Ages depict her with more sensitivity and realism as the *Maestá* by Duccio (1311) illustrate. Renaissance arts paint her with more gesture, costume and expression as evidenced by the works of Filippino Lippi (ca.1500) and Jan Joest Von Kalkar (1505–1508). Though some of the paintings of Paolo Veronese (1560, 1580–1582) during the Reformation hint at her licentiousness through her dress, most seventeenth–nineteenth-century paintings reflect otherwise, as seen in the works of Rembrandt (1655,1659), Guercino (1621, 1640–41), Champaigne (seventeenth century), Mignard (1690), Ricci (1718, 1920s) and Dyce (1833). Twentieth-century representations of the Samaritan woman reflect postmodernity and the social location of the artists as seen in the works of Edouard von Gebhardt (1914, Germany), Hatigammana Uttarananda (1980, Sri Lanka), and Olivia Silva (1981/82, Nicaragua).

A more negative perception of the Samaritan woman—as an immoral woman, prostitute or social outcast—is seen in how some English-speaking writers characterize her like Chaucer's 'Wife of Bath' in *The Canterbury Tales* (c. 1405–1410), Edmond Rostand's *The Samaritan Woman* (1921) and Margaret Hebblethwaite's 'The Story of Photina of Samaria' in *Six New Gospels: New Testament Women Tell their Stories* (1994). In the two latter stories, the status of the Samaritan woman is redeemed by her being a witness to Jesus' identity as the messiah and her subsequent missionary work.

Recommended reading. Day, Janeth Norfleete. *The Woman at the Well: Interpretation of John 4:1-42 in Retrospect and Prospect.* Biblical Interpretation Series. Leiden: Brill, 2002. Getty-Sullivan, Mary Ann. *Women in the New Testament.* Collegeville, MN: Liturgical Press, 2001.

See also JOHN, GOSPEL OF; SAMARIA; SAMARITANS

[MARICELSI]

Samaritans. In Luke 10.25-37, Jesus told a parable about a Samaritan who helped a robbery victim a priest and a Levite had ignored. Ever since, helpful strangers have been dubbed 'Good Samaritans'. 'Good Samaritan laws' protect people from lawsuits when their good intentions lead to unintended harm, and 'Samaritan's Purse' is the name of a prominent Christian charitable organization. The parable was popular in medieval art, with Jesus himself often identified as the central figure. Thus we may not realize that, in biblical terms, a 'Samaritan' would rarely be called 'good'.

The inhabitants of Samaria referred to themselves as *Shamerim*, 'keepers' (i.e., of Torah), rather than *Shomronim*, 'inhabitants of Samaria'. By NT times, Samaritans and Jews looked on each other with equal disdain (see Luke 17.18; John 4.7-9).

One cannot pinpoint a single event that marked the definitive break between Jews and Samaritans. There are signs of friction between the northern and southern tribes as far back as the early years of David's reign. Undoubtedly, the breakup of the United Monarchy (c. 922 BCE) both reflected and contributed to the animosity between the two groups. No doubt there was a gradual drifting apart, probably with as much to do with politics and economics as religion.

In the NT, therefore, Samaritans are often cast as outsiders in stories that challenge prevailing attitudes toward 'the enemy'. It was meant to be shocking that a Samaritan was the hero of Jesus' parable. (How would readers today respond to 'the Good Lesbian'?—or 'the Good Fundamentalist'?). The theme of learning to accept a presumed enemy or outsider is common in literature. In John Ball's novel *In the Heat of the Night*, a white Southern police chief overcomes his racial prejudice to team up with an African American detective from Philadelphia to solve a murder mystery. Harper Lee's *To Kill a Mockingbird* explores similar themes.

As a religious sect, the Samaritans emerged in the postexilic period out of the same matrix that produced other Jewish sects such as the Pharisees and Sadducees. The earliest references to a rival religious community based on Mount Gerizim (see John 4.20) are from the second century BCE (Sir. 50.25-26; 2 Macc. 5–6; *Jubilees* 30). The Samaritans still exist today as a tiny minority in Israel and the West Bank.

Most Samaritan literature is late, but it describes a people who were scrupulously Torah-observant. Like their Jewish neighbors, they believed in and worshiped one God, avoided images, observed the Sabbath rigidly, circumcised their male children, and kept the festivals described in the Pentateuch.

Even in their points of sectarian emphasis there is nothing other Jewish sects did not echo. Like the sectarians of Qumran, they rejected the Jerusalem temple, having set up a rival sanctuary on Mount Gerizim (John 4.20) in the time of Alexander the Great—which was destroyed under John Hyrcanus (c. 128 BCE). They also maintained a rival priesthood traced through Eleazar.

Like the Sadducees, Samaritans accepted only the Pentateuch as authoritative. They maintained their own text, the Samaritan Pentateuch, which highlights Samaritan theological slants, but also preserves some good textual readings. Also like the Sadducees, they rejected the idea of resurrection.

Like many Jews of the Second Temple period, Samaritans espoused expectations of a future redeemer. They hoped for the *Taheb* ('restorer'), who would come as a 'prophet like Moses' (Deut. 18.18). This expectation is reflected in Jesus' encounter with a Samaritan woman in John 4.25-26.

Recommended reading. Brindle, Wayne A. 'The Origin and History of the Samaritans'. *Grace Theological Journal* 5 (1984) 47-75.

See also GOOD SAMARITAN; SAMARIA; SAMARITAN WOMAN [DJP]

Samson. Judges 13–16 contains the extended narrative or saga of Samson, the book's last judge. Samson, from the Hebrew word for 'sun', does not have many similarities with the other deliverers in Judges. Instead, he breaks a divine vow, marries non-Israelite women, participates in trickery, performs superhuman feats of strength, and spends significant time in Philistia, outside of Israel. In addition, much of Samson's story focuses on his relationship with women: his barren mother is visited by an angel who reveals his Nazirite status; he takes, marries, and abandons a woman from Timnah; he sleeps with a prostitute from Gaza; Delilah betrays him. All of these characteristics and actions make him a very curious judge. Parallels between Samson and Hercules have often been made.

One story out of several that exemplifies the unusual quality of the Samson saga occurs in Judges 14. Samson sees and immediately wants a Philistine as his wife. On his way to get her, a lion approaches and Samson tears him apart. This experience leads Samson to tell a riddle to his friends, a riddle that is too obscure to solve. However, Samson's new wife coaxes the riddle out of him and betrays him to his friends, foreshadowing the episode to follow with Delilah. This betrayal incites Samson to kill thirty men and subsequently to set afire the Philistine's grain.

Interestingly, although Samson is not portrayed in an entirely positive light in the book of Judges, Christians—ancient and modern—often see him allegorically as a prefiguration of Christ. For example, Augustine draws out the parallels between the two figures in his *Sermo de Samsone*, and George Herbert's (1593–1633) poem 'Sunday' uses the image of Samson tearing down the gates of the city in comparison with Christ's resurrection.

Samson and his companion, Delilah, have been subjects of many musical pieces. The tragic story also inspired French composer, Camille Saint-Saëns (1835–1921) to write the noted opera *Samson et Dalila*. In popular culture, the Grateful Dead sang about the couple with the following line: 'If I had my way, I would tear this whole building down'. Neil Sedaka performed 'Run Samson Run', which included this advice: 'Run Samson run, on your mark you better start. I'd sooner trust a hungry lion than a gal with a cheatin' heart'. The Tom Jones hit 'Delilah' is sung in the person of a modern-day Samson.

Literary figures also drew from the story of Samson. John Milton's drama *Samson Agonistes* (1671) portrays the fallen hero in a tragic mode. Henry Wadsworth Longfellow (1807–1882) used Samson in his anti-slavery poem *The Warning*. The last stanza reads: 'There is a poor, blind Samson in this land, Shorn of his strength, and bound in bonds of steel, Who may, in some grim revel, raise his hand, And shake the pillars of this Commonweal, Till the vast temple of our liberties A shapeless mass of wreck and rubbish lies'. seventeenth-century English poet Francis Quarles used the judge as inspiration for 3468 lines of rhyming couplets, a poem entitled *The History of Samson*.

Finally, movie directors enjoy retelling the tale of Samson and Delilah: Cecil B. DeMille (Paramount Pictures, 1949), Lee Philips (Comworld, 1984), William Hanna and Joseph Barbera (Turner Home Entertainment, 1986), and Nicolas Roeg (Turner Home Entertainment, 1996).

Recommended reading. Cohen, G.C. 'Samson and Hercules'. *Evangelical Quarterly* 42 (1970) 131-41. Crenshaw, James L. *Samson: A Secret Betrayed, a Vow Ignored*. Atlanta: John Knox Press, 1978.

See also DELILAH; JUDGES; BOOK OF; NAZIRITE; PHILISTINES; RIDDLE [TM]

Samuel. His story is told in 1 Samuel 1–12; two books of the OT are named after him. Miraculously born to the barren Hannah, raised at Shiloh by the priest Eli, prophet and judge of Israel, one of the most important leaders of Israel, who anointed the first two kings of Israel, Saul and David. After gathering the tribes at Mizpah, he readies them for battle against the Philistines who are subsequently slaughtered. After the Israelite victory, he retires. When Samuel dies, King Saul is so distraught that he resorts to a spirit medium to raise his ghost (1 Sam. 28.3-25). Samuel is remembered as a hero and prophet in both OT and NT (1 Chron. 9.22; 11.3; 26.28; 29.29; 35.18; Ps. 99.6; Jer. 15.1; Acts 3.24; 13.20; Heb. 32).

Samuel's feast day in the Orthodox liturgical calendar is August 20; the Armenian Apostolic Church commemorates him on July 30. He is a revered prophet in the Qur'an. The Tomb of Samuel is located in present-day Israel, where it is visited by Jews, Christians and Muslims.

Several artists since the Renaissance have portrayed Samuel. The Italian baroque artist Salvator Rosa in a 1668 painting shows a bearded and heavily cloaked apparition of the spirit of Samuel raised by the Medium of Endor. Samuel also appears in several novels including Buford M. Johnson's *Priest of Dagon* (1952) and Shirley Watkins's *The Prophet and the King* (New York, 1956). Samuel was played by Paul Newlan in *David and Bathsheba* (1951), with Gregory Peck as King David, and by Denis Quilley in *King David* (1995), starring Richard Gere.

See also DAVID; ELI; HANNAH; SAMUEL, BOOKS OF; SAUL; WITCH OF ENDOR [JC]

Samuel, Books of. 1–2 Samuel recount a pivotal point in the biblical drama. Named after the prophet and judge of Israel, Samuel, they describe the rise of monarchy in Israel. The laws regarding kings in Deuteronomy anticipate this era in Israel's history (17.14-20). Judges seems to suggest that the answer to Israel's apostasy and rebellion might be kingship (17.5; 18.1; 19.1; 21.25); the Book of Ruth culminates in the birth of a boy, the grandfather of Israel's greatest king, David (4.13-22). Although the end of 2 Samuel reports 'the last words of David' (2 Sam. 23.1-7), the final chapter of David's life plays out at the beginning of 1 Kings, yet his legacy and influence extend far beyond these pages. David's reign becomes a standard for the succession of Israelite monarchs in 1–2 Kings (1 Kgs. 3.14; 11.6; 15.3, 11; 2 Kgs. 14.3; 16.2; 18.3; 22.2). David's reputation as Israel's preeminent poet and composer (1 Sam. 16.18, 23; 18.10; 2 Sam. 22.1-51; 23.1-7) is supported by superscriptions ascribing countless psalms to David, some referring to specific events in 1–2 Samuel (Pss. 3; 7; 18; 34; 51; 52; 54; 56; 57; 59; 60; 63; 142). The Samuel narratives are taken up and recast for the purposes of a later audience in 1–2 Chronicles. Links exist between 1–2 Samuel and other parts of the canon. These books (particularly God's covenant with David in 2 Sam. 7) provide the seeds for Israel's messianic hope for a Davidic descendant to inaugurate an era of peace and justice. This hope emerges in the prophets and is fulfilled in Jesus, Son of David and triumphant Lamb (see Rev. 5).

1–2 Samuel chronicle: (1) Samuel's life as prophet and Israel's last judge (1 Sam. 1–7); (2) the rise and fall of Saul as Israel's king (1 Sam. 8–31); (3) the reign of David (2 Sam. 1–24), a man after God's heart. The books communicate the reign of Yahweh, and the need for Israel's rulers to exercise leadership in submission to God and in obedience to his prophetic word. The narratives reflect a mastery of literary art, depicting poignantly and honestly the range of human experience and emotion (e.g., Hannah's shame and heartache over her childlessness, the turmoil of Saul's apparent schizophrenia, David's guilt over his sin with Bathsheba and his pain and sorrow over its consequences, his grief over the demise of his family, etc.). Many of these narratives reflect universal truths which resound today (appearances can deceive, the danger of forbidden fruit, the value of loving one's enemies, the cost of real friendship, the consequences of indulgent parenting, etc.).

The narratives and characters of 1–2 Samuel have been portrayed in well-known artworks, literature, film and music; perhaps the most notable contemporary example is Leonard Cohen's song, 'Hallelujah', popularized through cover versions by John Cale in *Shrek* (2001), Jeff Buckley, Rufus Wainwright, K.D. Lang (at the opening ceremonies of 2010 Winter Olympics in Vancouver), and Alexandra Burke's stunning performance on Britain's hit reality program *The X Factor*.

The enduring significance of 1–2 Samuel is by no means limited to art and popular culture. Though medieval and early modern Christian thinkers tended to (mis)use these books to garner uncritical support for 'Christian' monarchy, the Samuel narratives have much to offer Christian reflection, both positively and negatively, on political theology (e.g., God's intention for just and equitable governance according to the divine created order).

Recommended reading. Alter, R. *The David Story: A Translation with Commentary of 1 and 2 Samuel*. New York: Norton, 1999. Arnold, B.T. *1 and 2 Samuel*. Grand Rapids, MI: Zondervan, 2003.

See also BATHSHEBA; HANNAH; DAVID; SAMUEL; SAUL [DJHB]

Sanctification. To 'make holy' (Latin: *sanctificare*); the process of connecting some person, place or thing with God through grace. Sanctified persons are set apart from sin in order to be dedicated to God's righteousness. In some Christian theologies, believers are sanctified by the atoning death of Christ. Churches, cemeteries, liturgical vessels, furniture (e.g., communion tables) are among places and things sanctified because their use is dedicated to God as separated from profane use.

A requirement of God for people is for them to be holy if they are to be in communion with him. The people of God were called to be holy just as God is holy (Lev. 19.2; 20.26). However, the holiness of humans is never that of the attribute of God. In the OT the people were called upon to consecrate themselves before they approached the Lord (Exod. 19.22-24). Persons, places and things were sanctified by the sprinkling of blood or water (Num. 19.9-22).

Time is also to be sanctified. The Sabbath is a holy day; sanctified and not to be profaned (Ezek. 20.12-24). Behavior is to be sanctified by holy obedience, living according to the Torah. Such obedience keeps God's name holy and sanctified the people (Lev. 22.31-32).

The biblical writers interpret the Babylonian exile and its wake in terms of the habitual sinfulness of people, which profaned God's name. In response there arose an eschatological vision of the purification of the people (Dan. 7.18-22; Ps. 34.10). God himself would sanctify the people and thereby hallow his name. Ezekiel (36.22-27) describes the sanctification as a three-step process in which the people are sanctified by the sprinkling of water in order to purify them from sinfulness. They are then to be sanctified with a 'new heart' (Ezek. 11.19; Jer. 31.31-34). Finally the spirit of the Lord would be put into the human heart. The end result is a new person freed from the inclination of the human heart to do evil; instead the person is freed to be obedient to God.

In the NT disciples are called to be holy (1 Pet. 1.15-16) and to manifest divine perfection (Matt. 5.48). The sanctification of Christians is eschatological and accomplished by the salvation received in Christ (2 Thess. 2.13) through his atoning sacrificial death. The individual Christian is a sanctified temple of the Lord as are Christian communities (1 Cor. 6.11; Eph. 2.21; 1 Pet. 2.9). Christians are 'made holy' by anointing (1 Cor. 1.30; Eph. 5.26; 1 John 2.20), which is a benefit of the sacrificial death of Jesus Christ affecting the soul of the believer and not just externals (Heb. 9.11-14).

Sanctification can also mean consecration to a specific mission or service. Prophets were sanctified (Jer. 1.5; Eccl. 49.7). The holiness of Christians is not a passive gift of sanctification that exhibits what they have received. It is a call to active obedience that reflects what they have received (Rom. 6.19; 1 Thess. 4.3, 7; 1 Tim. 2.15; Heb. 12.14).

In Christian terms, sanctification is a process of growth in holiness. The believer accepts by faith that he or she is justified as righteous by God because of the sacrifice of Christ. Accepting Christ as Savior begins a lifelong process of growing in grace (sanctification) so that the holiness of believer is a growing identification with God. The term is especially associated with the holiness movement, which emerged from the Methodist church in the mid-nineteenth century.

Recommended reading. Ferguson, Sinclair B., and Gerhard O. Forde. *Christian Spirituality: Five Views of Sanctification*. Downers Grove, IL: Intervarsity Press, 1989.

See also ATONEMENT; CHRIST; FAITH; GRACE; HOLY/HOLINESS; JUSTIFICATION; REDEEMER; SACRIFICE; SALVATION [AJW]

Sanctuary. Hebrew: *Miqdash*, 'sanctuary, sacred place'. The root *qdš* is a common Semitic stem with a range of meanings (clean, holy, sacred, set apart, consecrated) connected to the idea of holiness. The form of the word with a prefixed *m-* can indicate location or place; the sanctuary is the holy place where, on certain occasions, ritual acts were performed by authorized personnel. The term was also used to refer to consecrated offerings given to the Levites, the sacred vessels of the tabernacle, the Holy of Holies or inner sanctuary of the temple, or all holy things associated with the temple (*miqdashim*, 'holy things'). In late biblical Hebrew, the term is combined with *beth* forming the construct *beth miqdash*, 'house of the holy place' or 'house of the sanctuary' (NRSV, 2 Chron. 36.17; see Haran, 14-15).

The term first appears in the Song of Moses (Exod. 15.17), but sanctuaries or holy sites (whether altars or established holy sites) are also mentioned or alluded to in Genesis (see Gen. 8.20-21; 12.6-9; 13.3-4, 18; 14.13, 18; 18.1; 21.33; 22.1-14; 23.17; 25.9-10; 26.23-25; 28.10-22; 31.13, 43-54; 33.20; 35.1-15, 27; 38.12-23; 41.45; 46.1; 48.3; 49.29-30; 50.13). On special occasions relating to the cycles of life and nature, sanctuary patrons came to participate in various forms of worship such as offering sacrifice and participating in sacred feasts. The role of the sanctuary was to facilitate such acts of worship, providing a place, both in Israel and elsewhere in the ANE, for worshippers to commune with a deity.

In the ANE (especially Canaan), sanctuaries share several important features with the sanctuaries described in the Bible. In Ugarit the sanctuaries of *b'l* and *dgn* were situated near the city center (indicating political and economic status). There is a pervasive idea that the deity transmitted the architectural design to the king or the architect (in Ugarit, *Kôtaru*, the divine architect outlines the plan of the heavenly sanctuary; thus, the earthly sanctuary is a model of the heavenly). This idea is still present in western religious traditions due to its preservation in both the OT and NT (Exod. 35; Isa. 6; Ezek. 39–47; Heb. 9; Rev. 21). Special feasts or banquets for the guests of the deity took place at the *b'l* sanctuary in Ugarit (*Keilalphabetische Texte aus Ugarit* [KTU] 1.4; 1.7; 1 Sam. 9.11-13, 19, 23-25).

In Exodus–2 Kings, the sanctuary appears in three prominent forms. First, the *mishkan* ('tabernacle'), covered by the *'ohel moed* ('tent of assembly') that Moses was commanded to construct (Exod. 25–31). The *mishkan* and *'ohel moed* constituted a portable sanctuary and some scholars have argued that similar structures are alluded to in texts from Ugarit and Mari. Second, Solomon's Temple (see 2 Sam. 7.1-17; 1 Kg 4.2; 1 Kg 5–9), destroyed after the Babylonian Invasion. Third, the Second Temple, whose initial construction and foundations appear to have been initiated by Sheshbazzar (Ezra 5.16; cf. Ezra 3–6; also Haggai and Zechariah [especially Zech. 6, 8]). In the NT, the sanctuary (*naos*) is distinguished from the temple (*hieron*) in many passages (e.g., Matt. 23.16; Acts 17.24; 1 Cor. 3.16; Eph. 2.21; 2 Thess. 2.4; Rev. 3.12; 21.22).

Important concepts surrounding the function of ANE and biblical sanctuaries continue to influence modern notions of sacred space. Mosques, churches, synagogues, and other 'holy' places bear some important similarities to ancient sanctuaries and are a clear indication that western architectural and ideological traditions were heavily influenced by the traditions of the ancient Mediterranean, Levant and Mesopotamia. This can be seen in the similarities and differences in the western architectural and functional terms employed to describe the holy space and holy objects within that space (e.g., altar, ark, congregation, etc.).

Recommended reading. Haran, M. *Temples and Temple-Service in Ancient Israel*. Winona Lake, IN: Eisenbrauns, 1985.

See also HOLY/HOLINESS; HOLY OF HOLIES; TABERNACLE; TEMPLE; TENT OF MEETING [CHB]

Sanhedrin. An English term derived from the Greek word *synhedrion*, meaning 'sitting together', 'council' or 'assembly'. During the time of Jesus, the Sanhedrin was the highest Jewish court of appeal (e.g., Mark 14.55; Matt. 26.59; Luke 12.66; John 11.47; Acts 4.15; 5.21; 24.20). In the Gospels and Acts, the Sanhedrin is referred to as 'the elders', or the 'chief' or 'high priests' (Luke 22.66; Acts 5.21; 22.5).

The development of this body in Jewish history is shrouded in mystery. Some think that it evolved around the third-second centuries BCE, during the reign of Antiochus III. This position remains conjectural; some trace it back to the wilderness wanderings when Moses appointed the 70 elders (Num. 6.16-24). According to Josephus, the Sanhedrin was both a judicial and political council under the patronage of the high priest or king. Rabbinic sources speak of two Sanhedrins: the Great Sanhedrin consisting of 71 members convened in the Hall of Gazit ('hewn stones') in the temple, and the Lesser Sanhedrin of 23 members, which convened in small towns to preside over matters of lesser gravity. This view seems attractive because $3 \times 23 = 69$, close to the 71 or 72 figure constituting the full Sanhedrin.

Regarding the duties and responsibilities of this body, the NT presents a picture of both secular and religious powers. It had the powers to arrest, incarcerate (e.g., Mark 14.43; Matt. 26.47; Acts 9.2) and examine those who infringed the law in general (Acts 4, 8), but it had no prerogative to impose the death penalty (John 18.31); this was imposed by the Roman rulers. Consequently, the Sanhedrin had full jurisdiction over religious matters though they had limited civic responsibilities such as tax collection. This explains why Jesus was charged with blasphemy and poisoning hearers with false teaching when he was brought before the tribunal (e.g., Matt. 26.57). Paul was charged with violating the laws of Moses (Acts 23.1-10), a case in which the Sanhedrin could exercise its authority without restraint.

According to the rabbinic literature, the Sanhedrin exercised its powers within the confines of a constitution which proscribed trials at night, on the Sabbath or festive days; conflicting statements by the witnesses; passing a verdict of condemnation on the same day as a trial (the verdict was to wait until the next day, following a two-thirds majority vote); and cross-examining the accused that could lead to self-incrimination. That is, by later, rabbinic standards, the picture presented in the Gospels is that in the trial of Jesus, the Sanhedrin violated its own laws. The venue of the trials, the house of the high priest (Mark 14.55) was inappropriate and those who attended did not constitute the required quorum for a trial.

In western art, scenes of Jesus' trial before the Sanhedrin are plentiful, e.g., Giotto (thirteenth century), Duccio di Buoninsegna (1308–11), Fra Angelico (1447–49), Donatello (1460s), Albrecht Dürer (1504, 1511, 1512). Scenes of this famous trial are standard in Jesus movies from *The King of Kings* (1927) to *Jesus of Nazareth* (1977) to *The Passion of the Christ* (2006).

Recommended reading. Mantel, Hugo. *Studies in the History of the Sanhedrin*. Cambridge, MA: Harvard University Press, 1965.

See also CAIAPHAS; PASSION NARRATIVE [ET]

Sapphira (see Ananias and Sapphira).

Sarah. Sarai or as she is renamed Sarah (both meaning 'Princess'), is the matriarch of the first cycle in the Founding Families narratives found in the book of Genesis (11.29–13.1; 16.1–18.15; 20.2-21.12; 23.1-2, 19; 24.36; 25.10, 12; 49.31). She is the first wife of Abraham (formerly Abram) of Ur and the owner of Hagar the Egyptian; twice, Abraham claims that she is his sister because he fears that foreign kings (Pharaoh, Abimelech) will kill him so they can marry her (Gen. 12, 20); Gen. 20.12 confirms that she is indeed her husband's half-sister, the daughter of Terah, Abraham's father, by another mother. Believing that she was barren, Sarah gives her maid Hagar to her husband as a wife in order to have a child through her. This was a common practice in these ancestral narratives. Hagar does conceive with Abraham and gives birth to Ishmael; however, Sarah, after a word from God, also gives birth to a son, Isaac. Due to difficulties between the boys, Sarah with God's consent has Hagar expelled from the household. Hagar and Ishmael leave and Isaac becomes the sole inheritor, who is even referred to by God as Abraham's only son (Gen. 22.2). The burial of Sarah at Hebron is recounted in Genesis 23; the site is the traditional location of the Tomb of the Patriarchs and Matriarchs, a Jewish pilgrimage site. She is remembered as an ancestor of Israel in Isa. 51.2.

Jewish and Christian receptions of Sarah have been mixed. In the NT, she is portrayed as an ancestor in faith (Heb. 11.11), and an obedient wife (1 Pet. 3.6), the freewoman who bore the legitimate son of Abraham (Gal. 4.22, 23, 30, 31), ancestor of the children of faith. In rabbinic tradition, she is counted as one of the seven women prophets of Israel.

Nineteenth-century women who embraced the Cult of Domesticity tended to view Sarah as a model of hospitality and proper womanhood. Other groups, such as the twentieth-century womanist movement, view her as the oppressor of slaves as evidenced by her use and dismissal of Hagar.

Traditional views of Sarah have tended to be negative because when she heard that she would give birth after turning 90 she laughed (18.12). This has been seen as a lack of faith and used as a warning to young women not to doubt God's promises, as is evidenced by the hundreds of websites that cite this story. However, it should be noted that Gen. 17.17 portrays Abraham's laughter when God promises him a son by Sarah.

The biblical stories of Sarah have often been portrayed by western artists, e.g., Jan Provost's *Abraham, Sarah and the Angel* (1520s), Adrien van der Werff's *Sarah Bringing Hagar to Abraham* (1696), and Guercino's *Abraham Casting out Hagar and Ishmael* (1657), with Sarah turning her back on the pitiable scene. Sarah has played a literary role in both the academic and popular literature, *Daughters of Sarah* was a feminist newsletter published from 1974 to 1995. The life of Sarah has been fictionalized in Orson Scott Card's *Sarah* (2000) and Marek Halter's *Sarah* (2004).

Recommended reading. Schneider, Tammi J. *Sarah: Mother of Nations.* New York: Continuum, 2004. Taylor, Marion Annual, and Heather E. Weir. *Let Her Speak for Herself: Nineteenth-Century Women's Writing on Genesis.* Waco, TX: Baylor, 2006.

See also ABRAM/ABRAHAM; GENESIS, BOOK OF; HAGAR; ISAAC; ISHMAEL; PATRIARCHS AND MATRIARCHS [EW]

Satan. A celestial *satan* ('adversary') appears in three OT books (Job 1–2; Zech. 3; 1 Chron. 21.1); the common noun occurs an additional 12X. In Job and Zechariah, *the satan* in the divine council questions the piety of human beings. Here, *the satan* is a title not a personal name, representing his role as accuser. Similarly, in 1 Chronicles, *a satan* (possibly a human being) provokes David to take a census of Israel, thus bringing pestilence on the land.

This character also appears in the NT with 36 references to *ho satanas*, a character associated with *ho diabolos*, the Greek translation of the Hebrew (cf. Rev. 12.9). The popularity of this character grew during the Second Temple period, but the job of *the satan* in both Testaments is to test human piety.

The understanding of Satan has developed throughout history. In the early church, authors like Justin Martyr, Tertullian, Ireneaus, and Origen conflated other biblical characters with Satan (e.g., the serpent of Genesis 3; the defeated 'morning star' of Isaiah 14; the disgraced king of Tyre of Ezekiel 28); these passages are now more closely associated with Satan than the actual celestial *satan* passages. His identification as the serpent associates Satan with original sin; Isa. 14.12 is where the nickname 'Lucifer' originates (cf. Rev. 22.16). The idea that Satan led a revolution in heaven before the creation of humanity (or as a result of that creation due to his jealousy) is a Christian myth derived from the biblical Satan character conflated with Isa. 14.12, Ezek. 28.12-19 and Luke 10.18.

The Faust legend, famously associated with the poets Marlowe and Goethe and the composer Gounod, contributed the idea that an ambitious person can make a 'deal with the devil' to achieve success despite the moral repercussions. This can be interpreted as a fictional working out of the debate between science (Satan) and faith (morality).

Other literary works have also contributed to modern views of Satan. Dante's *Divine Comedy* (1308–1321) depicts Satan as large and frightful, but impotent. In contrast, Milton's *Paradise Lost* (1667) created a new era in the development of Satan. Milton gives Satan a heroic and sympathetic reading despite casting him as the incarnation of evil whose agenda is to overthrow God. While Milton may have been portrayed Satan as a flawed hero in order to highlight the grandeur of God's victory over him, many of readers have been inspired by the Satan figure, including Shelley, Blake, and Churchill.

Satan has now gained his own following, which includes Satanic churches and a Bible (written in 1969 by Anton LaVey). Aleister Crowley and the Society of the Golden Dawn, the Ophite Cultus Satanas, and even versions of Wicca (e.g., Lady of Endor Coven, Toledo, OH) all have promoted veneration of Satan. However, not all modern Satanists believe in God, or even in Satan as a supernatural entity; e.g., the Church of Satan, which sees Satan as symbolizing certain values and qualities.

The modern media boasts many Satan depictions, especially in film. *The Exorcist, Rosemary's Baby, The Last Temptation of Christ, The Witches of Eastwick, The Devil's Advocate, The Omen,* and *The Passion of the Christ* demonstrate the range of presentations found in film. In television, Satan has been used (*South Park, Family Guy, the Simpsons, Supernatural, Doctor Who, Torchwood, Angel,* and *Reaper*) as everything from a smooth talking business man to the traditional red, horned devil.

Recommended reading. Kelly, Henry Ansgar. *Satan, A Biography.* Oxford: Oxford University Press, 2006. Pagels, Elaine. *The Origins of Satan.* New York: Vintage, 1995.

See also DEVIL; DIVINE COUNCIL; EVIL; JOB, BOOK OF; LUCIFER; SERPENT [EW]

Saul, King. Saul (Hebrew *sha'ul*), the son of Kish was chosen from the tribe of Benjamin, the smallest Israelite tribe (1 Sam. 9.21) as the first king of Israel. The initial portrayal of Saul (and kingship in general) in 1 Samuel 8–12 alternates between positive and negative depictions, but after 1 Samuel 12, the portrait of Saul is largely negative, culminating in Saul's rejection as king by God (1 Sam. 15.26).

Beginning in 1 Samuel 16, Saul's doomed reign contrasts with the rise of David, so that by the end of 1 Samuel, the trappings of kingship have all passed to David. Thus, David is anointed as the next king by the prophet Samuel (1 Sam. 16), Saul's rightful heirs acknowledge David as Saul's successor and aid him against their father (1 Sam. 17, 19, 20, 23), Saul's people praise David more than Saul (1 Sam.

17), and even Saul recognizes David as his successor (1 Sam. 24.20). Saul makes multiple attempts to kill David, but each effort is thwarted, until Saul dies in battle against the Philistines, taking his own life after receiving a mortal wound (1 Sam. 31).

The story of Saul is greatly abbreviated in 1 Chron. 10.1-14, emphasizing Saul's consultation with the medium of Endor as the cause of his demise, while the superscription of a number of psalms refer to Saul's conflict with David (Pss 18, 52, 52, 57, 59), implicitly contrasting David's close connection to God with God's absence in Saul's life.

Saul has often been understood as a tragic figure, so that Lord Byron's *Hebrew Melodies*, and Browning's *Saul* depict Saul as resolutely marching towards his fate, joining a poetic rendition by Rainer Maria Rilke and the dramatic works of authors like Jean de la Taille, Pierre du Ryer, Vittorio Alfieri, Voltaire, Alphonse de Lemartine and André Gide, and Thomas Hardy's novel, *The Mayor of Casterbridge*. These retellings emphasize Saul's 'madness' and his conflicts with those around him, although God, who figures prominently in the biblical narrative, often remains in the background. By contrast, G.F. Händel and C. Jennens's oratorio, *Saul*, emphasizes God and his freedom to choose or reject.

Saul has also inspired a variety of visual representations of his life and death. Rembrandt depicts David playing the harp before Saul not once but twice, first spotlighting Saul as a strong, brooding figure ready to strike his rival, then as careworn and weary. Most modern visual retellings of Saul's story enfold him into David's story, such as in films as diverse as *King David* (1985) to the children's Veggie Tales video, *Dave and Giant Pickle* (1996). The figure of Denethor in J.R.R. Tolkien's *Lord of the Rings* trilogy, the brooding, temporary ruler of Gondor who realizes that his days are numbered yet feebly attempts to retain his power, and whose children aid the interests of the future king (Aragorn) before Denethor kills himself, may also serve as a tragic Saul-like figure.

Recommended reading. Ehrlich, Carl S., and Marsha C. White (eds.). *Saul in Story and Tradition*. FAT, 47; Tübingen: Mohr Siebeck, 2006.

See also DAVID; KINGSHIP; SAMUEL, BOOKS OF; SAMUEL; WITCH OF ENDOR [GO]

Saul, of Tarsus (see Paul, the apostle)

Savior is a divine predicate, used in biblical texts to express God's saving activity on behalf of his people. *Sōtēr*, the term used in the LXX and the NT, builds upon a rich foundation of Jewish and Greco-Roman concepts. Savior (Hebrew: *moshia*) is relatively uncommon in the OT, appearing rarely in the historical books but somewhat more often in the Psalter, as God receives praise and hears urgent cries for help; moreso in Isaiah, where the title conveys God's exclusive prerogative to redeem Israel (as in Isa. 43.11: 'I am the Lord, and besides me there is no savior', NRSV). Even when the term is absent, the sense of God's saving action is not. His steadfast, covenantal love (*ḥesed*) operates even when the covenant has been broken, or in situations where no one else is able or willing to render aid.

In the NT's social context, savior figures abounded, so clarifying Jesus' status as savior became a priority for early Christian witness. Like the patron gods of Rome's cities, a savior would descend from heaven to rescue his citizen-clients, but the savior whose epiphanic appearance Paul expected was the crucified, resurrected and glorified Lord, Jesus Christ (Phil. 3.20-21; Tit 2.13). Like the apotheosized emperors, the ascended Christ could be proclaimed as savior and prince, or ruler—yet he was exalted to grant amnesty and repentance for sin (Acts 5.31). Even in the imperial milieu, the Jewish heritage remains evident. In Tit. 2.11-14, only the author's identification of the *sōtēr* figure with Jesus distinguishes his hopes from those of hellenistic Judaism; in 2 Tim. 1.9-10, a fragment preserved from the early church's liturgical life, the community's worship is focused in a manner similar to Israel's, offering praise to a savior who dismantles death itself. The biblical community expresses its thanks to its only savior for past, present, and future rescue.

Today, the savior title and salvation language reappear in new liturgical additions, whether in the church ('My Jesus, my Savior, Lord, there is none like you', from Darlene Zschech's 1994 song 'Shout to the Lord') or in concert venues (Starfield's 2010 songs 'The Saving One' and 'No Other Savior'). In popular culture, figures explicitly labeled as saviors are harder to locate, but they continue to appear in the form of superheroes, such as the perpetually popular Superman (who argues, in the 2006 film *Superman Returns*, that the world still cries out for a savior), or Captain America, the messianic paragon who brings salvific, American muscle to save the world.

Recommended reading. Jewett, Robert and John Shelton Lawrence. *Captain America and the Crusade* *against Evil: The Dilemma of Religious Nationalism.* Grand Rapids, MI: Eerdmans, 2003. Placher, William C. *Jesus the Savior: The Meaning of Jesus Christ for Christian Faith.* Louisville. Westminster John Knox, 2001. Wieland, George M. *The Significance of Salvation: A Study of Salvation Language in the Pastoral Epistles.* Carlisle: Paternoster, 2006.

See also CHRIST; DELIVERANCE; REDEEMER; REDEMPTION; SALVATION [MFL]

Scales. In English Bibles, used in two different and unrelated senses: (a) the covering of a reptile, Hebrew *qasqeseth* (fish scales), and *maghen* (crocodile scales—same as the word for shield), Greek *lepis* (scales of fish), only mentioned in the NT by Saint Paul in Acts 9.18; and (b) a balance for weighing, Hebrew *mo'znayim* (from the root to weigh, test, prove), *peles* (balance or scale), *qaneh* (scales), and *'eben* (originally a stone). Greek *zygos/zugon* (balance) is mentioned only in Rev. 6.5.

In the first sense, *qasqeseth* is used literally of certain types of fish allowed for eating (Lev. 11.9. 'Everything in the waters that has fins and scales'); the same word is used for Goliath's protective 'coat of mail' (1 Sam. 17.5).

Maghen, meaning shield, also is used of the scales of a crocodile (Job 41.15, in Hebrew v. 7). Another closely related word *meghinnah* has the sense of 'covering' or 'blindness', found only in Lamentations 3.65 (although the NRSV translates this as 'anguish'). This would relate to the only NT example, below.

The NT *lepis* only occurs in Acts 9.18, where it is said of St Paul that 'immediately something like scales fell from his eyes', i.e., not literal scales. Hence, the modern English idiom, 'the scales fell from my eyes' in the sense 'I realized the truth'.

In the second sense, all four Hebrew words (*mo'znayim, qaneh, peles,* and *'eben*) are used for weighing literally (and translated 'weight', 'balance', 'scales') as in the weighing of food or other commodities, but with the exhortation to be honest with one's dealings; see Lev. 19.36 ('you shall have honest balances, honest weights'); cf. Prov. 16.11. Because such weighing was subject to abuse and deception (e.g. putting one's finger on the scales), the figurative use evolved and is also frequent in the OT: the idea of 'wicked balances' as a sign of fraud, e.g., Mic. 6.11: 'Can I [God] tolerate wicked scales and a bag of dishonest weights?' This sense is particularly frequent in the Minor Prophets such as Hosea and Amos, where the abuse of social justice is frequently criticized, e.g., Hos. 12.7: 'A trader, in whose hands are false balances'; and Amos 8.5: to 'practice deceit with false balances'.

In a passage that demonstrates God's incomparable power, Isa. 40.12 asks rhetorically: 'Who has ... weighed the mountains in scales and the hills in a balance?' This in contrast to the insignificance of nations (v. 15) who 'are accounted as dust on the scales'. In a famous passage, Daniel (5.27) describes how the Babylonian king Belshazzar was 'weighed on the scales and found wanting' immediately prior to his overthrow.

In Homer's *Iliad* and Virgil's *Aeneid*, Zeus/Jupiter holds up scales at points when a significant figure (Hector in the *Iliad*, Turnus in the *Aeneid*) is about to die, thus showing at least in part the tenuous nature of human life, as well as the predetermined fate of the hero in question.

The Roman goddess Justitia or Lady Justice is sometimes depicted in painting and sculpture as a young woman holding a sword in one hand and scales in the other (sometimes with a blindfold to portray the impartiality of true justice). Examples of statues are located at the 'Old Bailey' Central Criminal Court in London (no blindfold) and the Well of Justice in Bern, Switzerland (with blindfold).

'Scales of Justice' also refers to several TV and radio shows as well as novels.

See also SCALES FELL FROM HIS EYES [GDB]

Scales fell from his eyes. 'And immediately scales fell from his eyes, and he could see again' (Acts 9.18). Paul's conversion, during which he was blinded then made to see again, is described in Acts 9. It is a dramatic story of the Pharisee Saul, a relentless persecutor of Christians, being stunned by a bright light and divine voice on the road to Damascus. Paul, after experiencing the risen Christ, neither ate nor drank, and his vision was obscured. The Book of Acts describes how the Holy Spirit came to a Christian named Ananias in Damascus, who was bidden to go to the house where Paul was staying, where he was to lay his hands on him to restore his sight. Ananias went to the house of a man named Judas, where he found the emaciated, blind Paul, who was praying to God, no doubt for salvation and direction. Ananias laid his hands on Paul in an act of receiving him into the Christian fold, and conveying to him through Christ the Holy Spirit. The Spirit entered Paul and a flaky substance like scales (Greek *lepides*) fell from his eyes, and his vision was restored. Then Ananias baptized Paul, who now took food and drink.

Saul, the persecuting Pharisee who was blind, became Paul the disciple of Christ who could see. Pietro da Corona painted *Ananias Restoring the Sight of Saint Paul* in 1631. Curious tourists in Damascus are still shown a house reputedly belonging to St Ananias.

See also BLINDNESS; PAUL, THE APOSTLE; SCALES
[RL]

Scapegoat. The scapegoat was a goat driven off into the wilderness as part of the ritual of Yom Kippur, the Day of Atonement. Leviticus 16 describes the ritual. The priest cast lots for two goats. One of the goats was sacrificed as a sin offering to God. The other goat was driven out into the wilderness after the priest laid his hands on it and confessed over it the sins of the Israelite people.

The word 'scapegoat' was invented by William Tyndale as he translated the Bible into English in the 1520s. Tyndale was challenged by the Hebrew 'for *Azazel*'. He was not certain if the term referred to the wilderness where the goat was sent or to a supernatural power that resided in the wilderness, a desert demon or the Devil. Tyndale interpreted *Azazel* as *ez ozel*, 'the goat that departs' or the 'goat that escapes'. The second goat certainly could not have been offered to the Lord because that sacrificial goat had to have no defect. The sins of the Israelites were conferred on the second goat so it had to be sent away.

Hebrews 13.11-13 draws a connection between the sacrifice of animals on the Day of Atonement and the death of Christ. The early Church Fathers described both goats as prefiguring Christ's sacrifice. Cyril of Alexandria and Theodoret identified the goats as representing Christ in both his natures: his human nature dying in the flesh as the Son of Man and the scapegoat seen as the Son of God escaping death through his resurrection. Christ-as-scapegoat carries away the sins of the world.

By the Victorian era, scapegoat had lost most of its biblical connotations. It became a metaphor for someone or some group selected to bear the blame for calamity, trouble, or bad times. The verb, scapegoating, is the act of holding a person, group of people, or thing responsible for a multitude of problems.

The most famous example of scapegoating in modern history is the Nazi Party's propaganda blaming the Jews for Germany's post-World War I economic woes and political collapse. Scapegoating usually is applied to a minority group less able to defend itself. The process also may be applied to organizations, such as governments, corporations, or various political groups. In the first decade of the twenty-first century, illegal immigrants in the United States were regularly blamed for such social and political problems as the high cost of health care, electoral fraud, and rising tuition at state universities. Oil speculators were the scapegoats in the rapid increase in gasoline prices the United States and other countries experienced during the spring and summer of 2008.

Scapegoating is particularly prevalent in sports. Bill Buckner, first baseman for the Boston Red Sox, was blamed for losing the 1986 World Series because of an error. Scott Norwood, the kicker for the National Football League's Buffalo Bills, became the scapegoat in Super Bowl XXV when he missed the probable game-winning field goal. Some sports scapegoats pay the ultimate sacrifice for their blunders. Andres Escobar, a Columbian soccer player, was shot and killed after he scored a goal on his own net knocking his team out of the 1994 World Cup.

Recommended reading. Douglas, Tom. *Scapegoats: Transferring Blame*. London: Routledge, 1995. Eberstadt, Mary. 'The Scapegoats among Us'. *Policy Review* (December 2006–January 2007) 25-46.

See also ANIMALS, SYMBOLISM; ATONEMENT, DAY OF; SACRIFICE; WILDERNESS
[JDR]

Scribes. While generally portrayed in the NT as part of the villainous conspiracy that opposed and wished to kill Jesus (Matt. 20.18; Mark 2.16), the role and function of scribes in antiquity is more accurately portrayed in the OT (such as Ezra 7.1-28), where they are shown to be part of the Jewish religious and political elite, serving as both arbiters of the Law and important political functionaries. To fully understand the importance and function of scribes in antiquity, one must realize that they were not limited to Judaism and/or Christianity or even the biblical texts. Scribes as portrayed in the Bible were part of a wider, international 'scribal class' that could be found in the service of the various kingdoms of the ANE from approximately the sixth century BCE onward, where they played a key role in the administration of the various kingdoms.

While these various scribes were in the service of individual kingdoms, because of the cosmopolitan nature of their 'Wisdom Schools'—the intellectual centers that produced and shared common scribal myths, techniques and hermeneutics—they facilitated a cross-cultural flow of wisdom, law, medicines, astrology, divination, magic and language, which were in turn disseminated throughout the various royal courts of the ANE. As a result, despite the fact that each scribe functioned in the service of an individual state, evidence of basic scribal wisdom tropes—such as the Creation–Flood story—can be found in many different 'religions' with only minor modification depending on each tradition. It should be noted, however, that this preponderance of shared mythic tropes was not simply the reinvention or recycling of mythic or textual sources. In their role as both religious and political specialists, the labor of the scribe had a specific purpose tied to the maintenance and continuity of the position of the 'sacred' king who, as the 'son (or agent) of the god', ruled and held court in a manner which reflected the status and position of the national god who in turn reigned in heaven (1 Chron. 17.12-13; Mark 1.1). Considering the importance of this task, it is unsurprising, then, that many scribal groups—including Jewish and Christian scribes—projected their position onto an anthropomorphic figure of divine Wisdom, who revealed the beginning and the end of the universe as mediated by a god who held court in heaven and who created through the use of divine law and according to a divine, written plan (*1 En.* 42.1-3; Prov. 1–8; Wis. 6.12–11.1; Rev. 10.7–11.8).

Recommended reading. Schiffman, Lawrence H. *Reclaiming the Dead Sea Scrolls*. Philadelphia: Jewish Publication Society, 1994. Smith, Jonathan Z. 'Wisdom and Apocalyptic'. In *Visionaries and their Apocalypses*. Ed. Paul D. Hanson. Pp. 101-20. Philadelphia: Fortress, 1983.

See also WISDOM [GK-F]

Scriptures. The term 'scripture' denotes a writing or corpus of writings that is religiously authoritative, usually in the sense of being foundational for a religion's self-understanding and core doctrines. Early Jewish writers in Hebrew referred to their scripture as *mikra* (= reading [text]), while Christian and Jewish writers in Greek called it *graphē* (= writing), a word appearing in the NT. In the earliest period, however, the Jewish Bible was more often referred to in terms of its component parts. Thus it was called 'the Law and Prophets' or 'the Law, Prophets, and Writings', with the latter being the basis for the Hebrew acronym *tanakh* (still used by Jews today). The English word 'Bible' (= book), which also derives from Greek (*biblion*), represents a subsequent development, as do the terms 'Old Testament' and 'New Testament'.

A religion may have other writings to which it looks for guidance, but which are denied the status of 'scripture' *per se* on the grounds of their subordination to some other writing. What lends authority to 'scripture' can differ from one religion to another, and can even be a matter of great controversy within a given religion. Ever since the Reformation, for example, the dominant understanding of the so-called 'scripture principle' in Christianity has turned on the notion of divine authorship and/or verbal inspiration. For the first few centuries of the Church, however, scripture's authority derived simply from the fact that it preserved the testimony of the apostles regarding Christ's redemptive act. The notion of scripture as a text with its identity grounded in itself was not to appear until sometime after the extent of scripture had been effectively settled, and it is not until the time of Gregory the Great that God is called the *auctor* (author) of scripture.

There have been a number of poems dedicated to the beauty or sacredness of scripture, including Francis Quarles's 'On the Holy Scriptures', Emily Dickinson's 'The Bible is an Antique Volume', and Stevie Smith's 'Magnificent Words'.

In western culture, the idea of a writing possessing foundational authority has often been wrested from its religious context and used to denote important works in non-religious realms. In this way, a given writing might be dubbed 'the Bible of such-and-such', as in Vera Brittain's reference to Olive Schreiner's *Woman and Labour* (1911) as the 'Bible of the Women's Movement'.

Recommended reading. Barton, John. *Holy Writings, Sacred Text: The Canon in Early Christianity*. Louisville, KY: Westminster John Knox, 1997. Trebolle Barrera, Julio. *The Jewish Bible and the Christian Bible: An Introduction to the History of the Bible*. Leiden: Brill, 1998.

See also APOCRYPHA/DEUTEROCANONICALS/INTERTESTAMENTALS; BIBLE; BOOK; CANON; NEW TESTAMENT; OLD TESTAMENT; SCROLL [JCP]

Scroll. Scrolls are books that can be made compact by rolling them into rolls. Around the world scrolls have been used in China, Japan, India and elsewhere. The writing material composing them have included slits of bamboo, palm leaves, the skins of animals, paper and papyrus.

There are a number of references to books and writing in the Bible. All of these references are to books in the form of scrolls (Deut. 28.58; Josh. 1.8;

Ps. 45.1; Isa. 8.1; Jer. 8.8, 25.13; Ezek. 2.9-10; Rev. 5.1). Biblical books (*mᵉgillot*) were scrolls made of papyrus, sheep skin, goat skin or calf skin.

In the OT era, scrolls were usually made of papyrus paper made from papyrus reeds grown along the Nile. The Phoenician city of Gebal (earlier Gubla) was called Byblos by the Greeks is now modern Jbeil in Lebanon. In biblical times it was a center of papyrus manufacturing and is mentioned also as source of builders for Solomon's temple (I Kgs 5.18).

Papyrus paper forms a thick writing surface somewhat like modern paper. To make a papyrus scroll, thin strips of the pith of the papyrus plant would be arranged side-by-side. A second layer would be placed on top of the first layer crosswise. This would form the front and the back side of the sheet of papyrus paper. Water and pressure by squeezing or pounding would then be applied to bond the strips into a single sheet. The sheets would be dried and then smoothed with rubbing stones or shells. They would then be sown into long strips to form the roll that would become a scroll.

Scribes wrote on papyrus on the side where the papyrus strips ran horizontally which thus became the inside (*recto*) of the book. Scrolls were usually written within (*recto*) and if necessary continued on the outside (*verso*) of the book. Rarely a book would be written on the outside (*verso*). Ezekiel 2.9-10 and Revelation 5.1 both refer to a book written on both recto and verso sides, which is technically known as an opistograph.

Papyrus was used in Egypt and in the Mediterranean area as early as 3000 BCE. The development of papyrus scrolls represents a technological advance in the manufacturing of books because scrolls while bulky are much more compact and can hold more information in a smaller and lighter book than an equivalent number of clay tablets.

The use of leather may have replaced earlier scrolls written on papyrus. Some were written as books, but letters were also written as small scrolls as well. The 'sands of Egypt' have revealed many scrolls as archeology has progressed in Egypt where worn out scrolls were used as packing around mummies in their sarcophagus.

Tanned skins of animals were instead of papyrus because vellum was stronger and more durable outside of Egypt, which found papyrus cheaper. Using leather for scrolls became a rabbinic tradition that has continued until modern times in synagogues.

Edward Taylor in 'Meditation Seven' is based on Ps. 45.1-2 and its reference to writing. The most famous scrolls related to the Bible are the Dead Sea Scrolls. Modern literature abounds in references to biblical scrolls.

Recommended reading. Greenlee, J. Harold. *Scribes, Scrolls and Scripture: A Student's Guide to New Testament Criticism.* Grand Rapids, MI: Eerdmans, 1985. Miller, Stephen M., and Robert V. Huber. *The Bible: A History, the Making and Impact of the Bible.* Intercourse, PA: Good Books, 2004.

See also BOOK; DEAD SEA SCROLLS; SCRIPTURES

[AJW]

Sea. In the Bible the word 'sea' (Hebrew *yām*; Greek *thalassa*) is used hundreds of times to refer to bodies of waters of various sizes. Four bodies of water are frequently referred to in the Bible as seas. The first is the Mediterranean Sea, which is usually called the Great Sea or the Western Sea (Judg. 5.17; Josh. 1.4; Deut. 11.24). The second is the Red Sea, or Sea of Reeds, the main body of water in the Exodus story (Exod. 10.19; 15.4). Third is the Sea of Galilee, also called the Sea of Tiberias or the Sea/Lake of Chinnereth (Num. 34.11; Luke 5.1; John 6.1). Finally, the Dead Sea is often referred to as the Sea of Salt, Sea of the Plain, or Eastern Sea (Gen. 14.3; Deut. 3;17; Ezek. 47.18).

The other sea which was of extreme importance to the ancient Israelites was the cosmic sea (Gen. 49.25; Deut. 33.13; Ps. 135.6). People in the ANE believed that the earth was a flat disc covered by a dome (the sky) which was surrounded by a vast universal ocean. The Israelites often referred to this cosmic sea as 'the deep' (Hebrew *tĕhôm*; see Gen. 1.2).

In the pre-modern world, the sea was one of the most awesome forces known to humanity. It was wild and chaotic, a place of violent power and ferocious creatures (Ps. 74.13-14; 93.3-4). The sea symbolized the chaotic forces of the world, which were opposed to human and divine order. In a number of biblical passages God is portrayed as being in conflict with the sea (Exod. 15.1-18; Job 26.12; 38.8-11; Isa. 27). In Revelation, the seven-headed beast that represents evil earthly powers emerges out of the sea (13.1-10; see also Dan. 7). At the end of Revelation God creates a new heaven and new earth for humanity to live on, but notably 'the sea was no more' (Rev. 21.1). Many scholars have speculated that the sea is abolished in Revelation 21 because the sea was associated with the evil, chaotic forces at war with God.

The Israelites were not alone in viewing the sea as a place of danger and chaotic power. Similar ideology is present in other ancient texts, such as the Babylonian poem known as *Enuma Elish* and Homer's *Odyssey*. In modern times the sea still retains some of the mystery, majesty, and power, which it had in the ancient world. This can be seen in modern stories and myths based on the sea, such as Davy Jones, *Moby-Dick*, Sebastian Junger's book, *The Perfect Storm* (1997), and the Disney film *Oceans* (2010).

Recommended reading. Day, John. *God's Conflict with the Dragon and the Sea: Echoes of a Canaanite Myth in the Old Testament.* Cambridge: Cambridge University Press, 1985. Kloos, Carola. *Yhwh's Combat with the Sea: A Canaanite Tradition in the Religion of Ancient Israel.* Leiden: Brill, 1986.

See also BOAT; DEAD SEA; LEVIATHAN; FLOOD; SEA OF GALILEE; RED SEA; WALKING ON WATER [EM]

Second Adam. From the Greek *deuteros anthrōpos* (second man) in 1 Cor. 15.47, in addition to *eschatos Adam* (last Adam) in 1 Cor. 15.45. As the first human, Adam's life is recorded in Genesis 1–5, but several Jewish writings, such as the *Life of Adam and Eve* (*Apocalypse of Moses*), also explore Adam's life closely and even distinguish between two Adams (cf. Philo's *Allegory of the Law* 1.31-32; *On the Creation of the World* 46). In the Pauline literature, soteriological associations are made both directly and indirectly between Christ and Adam through (1) (re-)creation motifs (Rom. 5.12-21; 8.18-30; 1 Cor. 15.21-22, 44-49); (2) image language (Rom. 8.29-30; 1 Cor. 15.49; 2 Cor. 4.4; Col. 1.15); and (3) the use of 'man' (*anthrōpos*) language (1 Cor. 15.45; Col. 3.9-11). In both 1 Corinthians 15 and Romans 5, Paul makes extended comparisons of Christ to Adam, primarily focusing on life and death.

In 1 Corinthians 15, Paul argues for the eschatological reality of human resurrection after the manner of Christ's resurrection. When comparing Adam and Christ, he first contrasts the death that comes from Adam with the life that comes from Christ (1 Cor. 15.21-22). Paul later discusses the nature of the resurrection body, describing a distinction between the physical (or natural) body and the spiritual body. Based upon Gen. 2.7 (LXX), he contrasts the first Adam who became a 'living being' with the last Adam who became a 'life-giving spirit'. Paul furthers the comparison with a distinction between the first man as 'earthly' and the second man as 'heavenly' (1 Cor. 15.47).

In Romans 5, Paul does not call Christ the 'last' or 'second' Adam as in 1 Corinthians 15, but he does call Adam a 'type' (or 'pattern') of Christ (Rom. 5.14). Paul describes death and condemnation as the result of Adam's sin, whereas Christ brings righteousness and life-giving grace through his obedience. Particularly important is the 'if Adam ..., how much more Christ ..'. comparison that Paul uses numerous times.

Early Christian authors emphasize the Adam–Christ dialectic, especially within the context of the image of God. They employ it to highlight the continuity between God's work in Adam and the restoration of humanity in Christ as new creation, rather than seeing physical creation as bad. Irenaeus, in particular, uses this connection to refute dualists like the Valentinians.

The nudity of Christ in Michelangelo's sculpture *Risen Christ* leads many to associate the return to the original state of Adam in the garden. While Rodin's *Adam* sculpture focuses on the first Adam, art historians note aspects that point to Christ. In literary works, the connections between Adam and Christ are more explicit. In particular, Milton's *Paradise Lost* explores in detail the story of Adam and Eve in the garden, with connections to Christ throughout. These connections are more specifically engaged in Milton's sequel *Paradise Regained*. Dante's *Divine Comedy* also links Adam and Christ. For instance, Dante details the connection between the tree of knowledge (Gen. 2.17) and the cross in *Purgaturio*, Canto 32 (see also *Paradiso*, Canto 13). Piero della Francesca (d. 1492), in his fresco cycle 'The Story of the True Cross' in the church of San Francesco in Arezzo, Italy, also portrays this connection between the cross and the tree in the garden.

Recommended reading. Scroggs, Robin. *The Last Adam.* Oxford: Basil Blackwell, 1966. Kreitzer, Larry J. 'Christ as Second Adam in Paul'. *Communio viatorum* 32 (1989) 55-101. O'Collins, Gerald. 'The Second Adam'. *America: The National Catholic Weekly* 190 (12 April 2004). http.//www.americamagazine.org/content/article. cfm?article_id=3540.

See also ADAM; CHRIST; EDEN [BCB]

Second Coming. Many NT writings presuppose that the resurrected and exalted Jesus, the son of man, will ultimately return from heaven to judge humanity, defeat the powers of evil, and establish his messianic kingdom on earth (e.g., Matt. 16.27; 1 Thess. 1.10; 2 Thess. 1.7-10; Rev. 27.1-7; cf. Mark 13.26; Matt. 24.30; Acts 1.11; 2 Thess. 2.8; Rev. 1.7), an outgrowth of Hebrew prophetic proclamations of God's arrival to pass judgment on Israel and its enemies (e.g., Isa. 13.9; Amos 8.9, 10; Joel 1.15; 5.20; cf. Dan. 7.13-14). In some passages, the Greek term *parousia* ('arrival', 'presence'), denoting the visit of a distinguished personage or the manifestation of a god, is used in this eschatological context to denote the second coming of Christ (e.g., 1 Cor. 15.23; 1 Thess. 2.19). Contemporary scholars sometimes use the term 'parousia delay' to refer to Christian efforts, beginning in the NT, to explain the lengthy gap between the ascension and the second coming (e.g., 2 Pet. 3.4-9).

While orthodox Christianity has consistently confessed that Jesus Christ 'will come again to judge the living and the dead, and his kingdom will have no end' (Nicene Creed), belief in a literal parousia, and speculations as to its actual date, have waxed and waned throughout Christian history, from the Montanists (second century) to medieval apocalypticists like Joachim of Fiore (d. 1202), to the Reformers, the Puritans, and the nineteenth-century Millerites, precursors to the Seventh-Day Adventist Church.

Christian hymnody traditionally correlates Advent and the Second Coming in works such as 'Lo! He comes with clouds descending' (John Cennick, 1752), 'Come thou long-expected Jesus' (Charles Wesley, 1744), and 'The King shall come when morning dawns' (trans. John Brownlie, 1907). The famous *Dies Irae* ('Day of Wrath'), historically part of the Roman Catholic Requiem Mass, describing the judgment of humanity by Christ at his coming, has been set to music by many composers, including Mozart, Verdi, Fauré and Andrew Lloyd Webber. The American 'Battle-hymn of the Republic' (Julia Ward Howe, 1862) draws its inspiration from biblical depictions of the parousia ('Mine eyes have seen the glory of the coming of the Lord'). In twentieth-century literature, its most famous evocation is the poem 'The Second Coming' by William Butler Yeats, written after the end of World War I: 'Surely some revelation is at hand; Surely the Second Coming is at hand. The Second Coming!' (1919).

Popular culture, both religious and secular, remains fascinated by speculations about the timing, scope and events surrounding the Second Coming, as evidenced by the many books, graphic novels, films, video games and musical works that evoke it, notably the 2004 British TV miniseries, *The Second Coming*, in which a video store worker (played by Christopher Eccleston) becomes convinced that he is the son of God who has returned to judge the world in the near future.

Recommended reading. PBS Home Video. *Frontline: Apocalypse!* VHS, 1999. Wojcik, Daniel. *The End of the World as We Know It: Faith, Fatalism, and Apocalypse in America.* New York: New York University Press, 1997.

See also APOCALYPSE; APOCALYPTIC; ASCENSION; HEAVEN; JUDGMENT; KINGDOM OF GOD; MILLENNIUM; RAPTURE; REVELATION, BOOK OF; SON OF MAN
[MALB]

Seek and you shall find. From Genesis to Revelation, the Bible is a book dedicated to searching and finding. This 'seek and find' imagery is applied to both the physical world (looking for people, property, food, etc.), as well as taking on a moral or religious quality: seeking God or his kingdom, one's own spirit, meaning or satisfaction in life, and wisdom or understanding in general.

In the OT, God himself is credited with the declaration that whoever seeks God shall find him (Jer. 29.13; cf. Deut. 4.29; 1 Chron. 28.29). In the NT, the phrase 'seek and you shall find' is attributed to Jesus, part of a longer monologue concerning continual asking, seeking and knocking. Matthew includes this speech in Jesus' Sermon on the Mount (7.7-11), while in Luke it occurs during his regular ministerial activity (11.9-13). Augustine interpreted this teaching of Jesus as referring to the finding of truth (*De sermone Domini in Monte*, 2.21.71), which brings to mind the Gnostic belief that salvation comes from *gnosis*, or secret knowledge. Thus, as we can see in the *Gospel of Thomas* (2; cf. 92, 94), the charge to 'seek and find' encourages the reader to seek truth from Jesus, with a promise that he who seeks this truth will find eternal rest. This sentiment is echoed in other apocryphal texts, including *The Gospel of the Hebrews* and *Thomas the Contender*.

In modern literature, the motif of 'seeking and finding' is used much as it was in biblical literature, concerning both physical and spiritual quests. The phrase is also at times directly quoted: for example, the traditional KJV rendering of the phrase is spoken by Porfiry, in Dostoevsky's *Crime and Punishment* (1866). In an attempt to both arrest Raskolnikov, as well as convince him that life is still worth living, he declares: 'What sort of prophet are you, do you know much about it [life]? Seek and ye shall find. This may be God's means for bringing you to Him. And it's not for ever, the bondage ...'

The phrase 'seek and you shall/will find' is also frequently used as a song title, or in lyrics. While at times found in a more religious context, like in 'Under the Rose' by KISS, some of the most famous examples refer to something else entirely: the search for love. One song which provides such a romantic context is 'Someone to Watch over Me', composed by George Gershwin for the musical *Oh, Kay!* (1926), since performed by countless artists including Sting, Amy Winehouse and Lady Gaga. As the song goes: 'There's a saying old, says that love is blind / Still we're often told, "seek and ye shall find" / So I'm going to seek a certain lad I've had in mind'. Along the same lines, the Isley Brothers' song 'Seek and You Shall Find' speaks about the trials of finding true love: 'The years have passed / I'm still all alone / but no longer do I ask / I place my faith in five little words / from somewhere in the past / those words were seek and you shall find'.

'Seek and Ye Shall Find' was also the title of an episode of the television series *Touched by an Angel* (April 5, 1998).

See also GNOSTIC, GNOSTICISM; SERMON ON THE MOUNT, PLAIN [EJW]

Sennacherib. Sennacherib was king of Assyria from 705 to 681 BCE, preceded by Sargon II and succeeded by Esar-haddon (cf. 2 Kgs 18–19; Isa. 36–37; 2 Chron. 32.1-23). After Sennacherib came to rule, Hezekiah began preparing for a revolt against Assyria, with support from Egypt. In 701, Sennacherib moved toward Jerusalem to quell the anti-Assyrian coalition led by Hezekiah. Even after demanding a tribute from Hezekiah (2 Kgs 18.14-16), Sennacherib proceeded with his attack. The Annals of Sennacherib claim that he overtook 45 fortified cities in Judah, along with countless other towns, and had the capital under siege.

For reasons that are not entirely certain, Sennacherib was unable to penetrate Jerusalem. In his annals, he boasts that he shut Hezekiah up in Jerusalem 'like a caged bird', but does not indicate that he actually overtook it. According to the biblical account, Hezekiah pled to Yahweh that he should save them to demonstrate his own greatness in the face of Sennacherib's arrogant slander and blasphemy (2 Kgs 19.14-19). Isaiah gave Hezekiah a positive message from God (2 Kgs 19.20-34), and that night 'the angel of Yahweh' struck down 185,000 Assyrian soldiers (2 Kgs 19.35).

Herodotus records a story about the Assyrian army entering Egypt for battle, which has been noted for its similarities to Sennacherib's defeat at Jerusalem. The night before the battle, field mice ate the quivers and bowstrings of the Assyrian army, causing them to be slaughtered the following day (*Histories* 2.141). The extraordinary defeat in both cases has led some scholars to suggest that the two stories are related. Whatever prevented Sennacherib from conquering Jerusalem, he eventually left and returned to Nineveh (2 Kgs 19.36). Some time after his return, two of his sons killed him while he was worshiping in the temple of Nisroch, his god. The irony in the biblical portrayal of Sennacherib is that the angel of Yahweh was able to defeat his army overnight when Hezekiah invoked Yahweh, while Nisroch was unable to protect Sennacherib from his own sons, even when he was worshiping Nisroch in the temple.

Sennacherib is best remembered in western culture for what has been recorded in the Bible. The most prevalent uses of Sennacherib (historically and contemporarily) relate to his prideful arrogance, the miraculous defeat at Jerusalem, and/or the murder by his own sons in the temple of Nisroch. Sennacherib has been used for illustrative purposes in homilies and devotions, both currently and by writers in the past. The romantic George Byron composed a poem entitled 'The Destruction of Sennacherib', which describes Sennacherib's attack on Jerusalem and subsequent defeat by the 'Angel of Death'. Published in 1815, it was consistent with the romantic preoccupation with ancient history. The content of the poem may have parallel themes with Napoleon, who was defeated at Waterloo the same year as the poem's publication. Mussorgsky composed a piece of music of the same title inspired by Byron's poem (1867).

Although there are not too many unique examples of how Sennacherib has been used in western culture, he is commonly remembered as the antagonist of a definitive story in Jewish history. The story of Sennacherib has challenged communities of faith to trust Yahweh, be humble, and stand in awe of his sovereignty.

Recommended reading. Grabbe, Lester L. (ed.). *'Like a bird in a cage': The Invasion of Sennacherib in 701 BCE*. London: Sheffield Academic Press, 2003. Luckenbill, Daniel D. *The Annals of Sennacherib*. Chicago: University of Chicago Press, 1924.

See also ASSYRIA; HEZEKIAH; JERUSALEM [BJL]

Septuagint. From Lat. *septuaginta*, 'seventy'; commonly abbreviated LXX) is a collection of Jewish writings in the Greek language. It mostly consists of translations from the Hebrew scriptures, supplemented with original compositions in Greek and translations of Hebrew/Aramaic books not included in the Hebrew canon. Although the LXX was originally an exclusively Jewish collection, it was quickly adopted by early Christianity, and thus became the Greek OT. This in turn was translated into Latin and numerous other languages besides. For Christians, the LXX remained the authoritative version of the OT until Jerome (fourth century CE) returned to the Hebrew original to prepare his Vulgate translation (although the Vulgate retained writings outside the Jewish canon).

According to the so-called *Letter of Aristeas* (second century BCE), the first Greek translations were made by 72 two Jewish elders, who translated the five Books of Moses (Pentateuch) for Ptolemy II Philadelphus in the early third century BCE. Eventually, the name 'Septuagint' or 'translation of the seventy(-two)' was applied to all other books beside the Pentateuch. In fact, there is no such thing as *the* Septuagint—the translations were made by a variety of translators working over several centuries and adopting different methods, ranging from extreme formalism to creative rewriting.

The LXX is an important source for the study of the OT, especially for textual criticism. Apart from the Dead Sea Scrolls, the oldest extant manuscripts of the Hebrew scriptures date to the tenth–eleventh centuries CE (the so-called Masoretic text), while the LXX translations derive from originals that are up to 13 centuries older. Combined with the evidence from the DSS, the LXX gives access to the textual form of the OT between the third century BCE and the first century CE. However, assessing the relations between the (translated) LXX text and its (non-extant) source text poses problems of its own. Being a translation, the Septuagint may also in certain places reveal how OT texts were interpreted around the turn of the era. This is of special importance to OT quotations in the NT, which are often taken from the Septuagint rather than from the Hebrew text.

Recommended reading. Jobes, K.H.. and M. Silva. *Invitation to the Septuagint*. Grand Rapids, MI: Baker Academic, 2000. Marcos, N. Fernández. *The Septuagint in Context: Introduction to the Greek Version of the Bible.* Leiden, Boston, Köln: Brill, 2000. Pietersma, A., and B.G. Wright (eds.). *A New English Translation of the Septuagint and the Other Greek Translations Traditionally Included under That Title.* New York and Oxford: Oxford University Press, 2007.

See also APOCRYPHA/DEUTEROCANONICALS/INTERTESTAMENTALS; CANON; OLD TESTAMENT, OLD TESTAMENT, USE IN THE NEW TESTAMENT; VULGATE   [DDC]

Sermon on the Mount. The Sermon on the Mount is the traditional name for a speech attributed to Jesus in Matthew (5.3–7.27). In the sermon, Jesus instructs his disciples to lead the way of life God demands if they are to enter the Kingdom of Heaven in the end time (5.20, 7.1; cf. 25.1-13). The sermon offers chiefly ethical instructions for right conduct among people and towards God.   Matthew probably composed the sermon by expanding upon a sermon in the sayings gospel Q (6.20-49). As with most of Q, Matthew has redacted its sermon to conform to his own theological concerns. While some sayings approximate sayings of the historical Jesus, most come from Matthew or early church traditions.

The sermon's ethical instructions are rigorous. For Matthew, these instructions constitute the Law in its true or perfect form (5.17), the standards of which are much higher than in the Law as written in the OT. Ethical instruction occurs from the start: in the first section, Jesus blesses situations including oppression and humility, some of which God will remove or reciprocate (5.3-12). Ethical teaching becomes more explicit in the next section, where Jesus demands adherence to the Law's 'perfect' standards (5.48) for forgiveness, marital fidelity and magnanimity (5.17-48). In a third section, Jesus admonishes his disciples to pray, to be charitable and to fast in a way that is genuine (6.1-18). Following further sections that among other things discourage collection of wealth (6.19-34), Jesus closes by urging adherence to his instructions in an unmistakably foreboding tone (7.13-27).

As part of Matthew, the sermon seeks to an extent to define and legitimate Matthew's Jewish-Christian community *vis-à-vis* a larger and in some cases hostile Jewish populace. Written probably during the 80s CE in Syria, the sermon tries to characterize Jesus and his community as distinct (5.21-48) and to justify itself before Pharisaic Jews (5.10, 5.20).

In western culture, the position of the Sermon on the Mount, or at least of passages in it, has been profound but mixed. The west has upheld and emulated the sermon, but has also found it problematic. This has proven to be the case in both Christian and secular culture. In Christian culture, the sermon has remained a popular source of moral instruction. Augustine (354–430) greatly admired it, and its teachings have found continuing influence through the twentieth century. The best-selling *Sermon on the Mount* by Emmet Fox (1934) draws upon the text, which has also appeared in numerous edifying films and stage-works (including N. Ray's *King of*

Kings [1961] and S. Schwartz's *Godspell* [1970]). By the same token, the sermon's demand for moral 'perfection' has often been a source of unease for theologians including Martin Luther (1483–1546), for whom the sermon stood in tension with notions of salvation by faith alone.

In a more secular context, the sermon has similarly provoked approval and discomfort. Leo Tolstoy and Mohandas Gandhi have found the sermon a powerful source of pacifism (see Matt. 6.38-40, 43-44; 7.12), and the pacifist movement proved influential during the twentieth century. Yet at the same time, the sermon has provoked unease. At least since the Renaissance, many scholars and artists have been troubled about humanistic studies, especially Classics, given the belief of Jerome (c. 347–420) that in a dream, God quoted Matt. 6.21 to discourage him from philology.

Recommended reading. Luz, U. *Matthew*. Hermeneia. Minneapolis: Fortress Press, 2001–2007. Stanton, G.N. (ed.). *The Interpretation of Matthew*. 2nd edn. London: SPCK, 1995 (1983).

See also LAW; MATTHEW, GOSPEL OF; PHARISEES; Q; SERMON ON THE PLAIN [AD]

Sermon on the Plain. 'Sermon on the Plain' is a name used for the collection of teachings given by Jesus in Luke 6.17-49. It parallels a generally better-known account in Matthew 5–7, known as the Sermon on the Mount. Luke's account is shorter; commentators note that most of the changes are the lack of Matthew's material about the Law, which would not have been of as great interest to Luke's Gentile audience. Commentators differ on whether the two accounts represent the same event, as well as whether either or both are a summary, or a typical set of teachings that Jesus may have repeated in different locations.

Luke sets the sermon in a section dealing with the ministry of Jesus in Galilee (4.14–9.50). This section opens with a pair of healings, moves into debates about fasting and the Sabbath, and then relates the call of the apostles to ministry. After the sermon, Luke relates more healings. Each of these events has a messianic aspect that portrays Jesus as one who surpassed the greatest prophets.

The body of the sermon in begins with the Beatitudes (6.20-26), which name particular groups outside the social mainstream and then pronounce divine blessings upon them. Luke's account adds four parallel 'woes' addressed to those who are well-off. This pattern continues a theme of the Gospel: the divine reversal of earthly standards of well-being that began with Mary's Magnificat at the Annunciation. This theme continues in Jesus' first sermon (4.16-30) and throughout the gospel.

The second section of the sermon (6.27-36) contains a number of aphorisms that have become catch-phrases in western cultures. It begins with the command 'love your enemies'. As the section continues, examples of sharing freely and of practical expression of love include 'if anyone strikes you on the cheek, offer the other also'. Jesus also states the Golden Rule, 'do to others as you would have them do to you'. The section concludes with a series of illustrations demonstrating that anyone can be kind to those who are kind to them, but the follower of God must go beyond that.

A third section also contains many memorable phrases. It begins with the admonition not to judge, but forgive (6.37-38). This is illustrated with a series of parables (6.39-49) showing the application of the principles of the sermon in a life of discipleship. These parables use figures of the blind leading the blind, removing the log in one's own eye, bearing fruit from a good heart, and building a solid foundation as the basis of faithful life.

Interpretation of the sermon produces a variety of disputes. These center on whether the teachings are intended to be real-life guides, or if followers should view them as a purely spiritual goal. Some commentators see Matthew's lengthier version of the sermon as such spiritualization.

See also ANNUNCIATION; BEATITUDES; GALILEE; GOLDEN RULE; MAGNIFICAT; SERMON ON THE MOUNT [TV]

Seraphim (see Cherubim and Seraphim).

Serpent/Snake. Hebrew and Greek have a number of words for snakes and serpents. The most common are Hebrew, *naḥash*, and Greek *ophis*, which may be translated either 'serpent' or 'snake'.

The biblical story of the serpent in the Garden of Eden is one of the most widely recognized and influential biblical stories. The serpent tells Eve that, if humans eat the fruit of the tree, they 'will not die; for God knows that when you eat of it your eyes will be opened, and you will be like God, knowing good and evil' (Gen. 3.4-5). Later Christian tradition identified the serpent with Satan and the eating of the fruit as the original sin that caused the Fall. This interpretation has had an immense influence on western culture. The story is frequently alluded to and its influence is a major reason for the frequent use of snakes and serpents to represent evil, as in the Harry Potter books and movies. It has even become part of the English language in expressions like 'snake in the grass' for a treacherous person. Augustine interpreted the story as an allegory about temptation with the snake representing sensuality. This has remained a major association in western culture. James Joyce, in *A Portrait of the Artist as a Young Man*, for instance, has Stephen describe his captivity to his sexual organ as 'the serpent, the most subtle beast of the field' (ch. 3).

Some poets, however, have interpreted the story much differently. Byron's *Cain*, for instance, says 'The snake spoke the truth; it was the tree of knowledge; It was the tree of life; knowledge is good, And life is good; and how can both be evil?' (*Cain*, 1.36-38). Pedrini and Pedrini think some English Romantic poets reversed the negative interpretation of serpent imagery in order to express their faith in a better world. Thus Shelley in the *Revolt of Islam* portrays 'the great Spirit of Good' as a serpent rejected by humans because they did not know 'good from evil' (I, xxviii, 373-76). These literary interpretations anticipate contemporary ecofeminist interpretations of the story. Eve takes the initiative through her relationship with nature (represented by the serpent and tree) in gaining the ability to think critically that makes humans fully human, yet has consequences both good and bad.

Karen Joines shows that in the ancient Near East serpents can represent not only chaos, but also youthfulness, life, immortality, and wisdom. These associations are present in other biblical passages that have influenced western literature and art. In the Book of Numbers, Moses raises a bronze serpent on a pole, so that people who have been bitten by venomous snakes can be healed (21.8). The Gospel of John compares Jesus to the serpent that Moses raised up in the wilderness (3.14). Another influential reference is Jesus' direction to be 'wise as serpents and innocent as doves' (Matt. 10.16). William Blake makes extensive use of serpent imagery that freely combines all these biblical references in order to represent, among other things, immortality and human imagination.

Recommended reading. Joines, K.R. *Serpent Symbolism in the Old Testament: A Linguistic, Archaeological, and Literary Study*. Haddonfield, NJ: Haddonfield House, 1974. Pedrini, L.N., and D.T. Pedrini. *Serpent Imagery and Symbolism: A Study of the Major English Romantic Poets*. New Haven, CT: College & University Press, 1966.

Walker-Jones, A. 'Eden for Cyborgs: Ecocriticism and Genesis 2–3'. *Biblica* 16 (2008) 263-93.

See also ANIMALS, SYMBOLISM OF; DRAGON; FALL; GARDEN OF EDEN; LEVIATHAN; SATAN [AW-J]

Servant (see Slave).

Servant of the Lord (see Suffering Servant).

Seth. Two different figures named Seth relate to the OT. The first is the third son of Adam and Eve. Since the other sons Cain and Abel dominate most of the narrative with the first biblical murder, Seth is given little attention in Genesis and throughout the OT. Often this makes such figures good candidates for elaboration in later myth. Thus, Josephus's *Antiquities* represents the descendants of Seth setting up pillars inscribed with secrets of geometry and science. Likewise, the pseudepigraphal *Testament of Adam* (first–fifth century CE) narrates Seth's return to Eden at the command of his father Adam. He returns with three seeds from the tree of life that he buries with his father. These later grow into three trees used for the wood of the three crosses of Jesus' crucifixion.

An ancient Christian Gnostic sect, the Sethians, traced its genealogy back to the offspring of Seth. Likely due to the minimal role Seth plays in the OT, he is given no attention in contemporary sources.

The second figure, while not mentioned in the OT, has an interesting relation to it. The Egyptian god Seth defends the boat of the sun god Re from the sea monster Apophis. There are possible connections with Yahweh commanding the seas (Exod. 15.8) and commanding sea monsters (Gen. 1.21; Ps. 148.7; Sir. 43.26). In later Egyptian myth, Seth is the god who battles for kingship with Horus (compare Yahweh's battle with Pharaoh in Exod. 15.18). Subsequently, Egypt demonizes Seth for trying to upset the divine council decision of Horus as king. Such negative representation leads Seth to be associated with outsiders, the desert and the copper trade of Syria-Palestine (Israel). While Baal is most likely influential on various expressions of Yahweh, Seth is a potential candidate. Representations of Yahweh controlling the sea, or Yahweh and his place as king, could have been influenced by Seth, if not indirectly through Baal due to the Seth–Baal connection.

In science fiction, Seth is one of the Goa'uld system lords in the television series *Stargate SG–1* (1997–2007). In season 3, Seth begins a cult on earth. The military finds the cult in its compound and attempt to free the followers from Seth's mind-control. The plot functions as an interesting commentary on the rise of cults in North America; in particular the details echo the cult of David Koresh (d. 1993) in Waco, Texas. Some even note that the actor who portrays Seth (Robert Duncan) was chosen for his resemblance to David Koresh.

Also in the science fiction genre, *Doctor Who* ('Pyramids of Mars', 1975) has an Oxford archaeologist discover Seth beneath a pyramid after his defeat by Horus. Seth is a boss (final character of a level in a video-game) in *Tomb Raider 4*. Seth also appears in Marvel Comics (first appearance in *X-Men #100*). In Marvel Universe, Seth is a green god of death but is syncretized with multiple mythologies and becomes the serpent he fought in Egyptian myth.

Contemporary usages of Seth have been influenced directly by contemporary interest in Egyptian religion. Some have effectively used the Seth myth for contemporary social commentary. Most positive attributes of Seth from early Egyptian religion are not maintained. Further, all possible connection of Seth with Yahweh of the OT seems to be lost in contemporary consciousness.

Recommended reading. Klijn, Albertus Frederik Johannes. *Seth in Jewish, Christian and Gnostic Literature*. Leiden: Brill, 1977. Velde, Herman te. *Seth: God of Confusion: A Study of his Role in Egyptian Mythology and Religion*. Probleme der Ägyptologie. Leiden: Brill, 1967.

See also BAAL; EGYPT; GOD [SWF]

Seven Churches of Revelation. The visionary book of Revelation is a circular letter sent to seven churches in seven different cities in the Roman province of Asia, which is in western Asia Minor (modern-day Turkey): Ephesus, Smyrna, Thyatira, Pergamum, Sardis, Philadelphia, and Laodicea. These seven cities lie within a roughly circular pattern, each being separated by about 50 miles. As such, they were ideally situated as centers of communication for John, Revelation's author, and for the apostle Paul, who founded the churches in Asia (cf. Acts 18.18–19.41). Each of the instructions to the seven churches (Rev. 2.1–3.22) follows a similar pattern. The One addressing each church (1) identifies himself ('These are the words of'); (2) gives the command to write; (3) pronounces his evaluation of their faithfulness ('I know') through praises, exhortations, complaints, threats, acknowledgments, and advice; and (4) concludes each pronouncement both with a command ('listen to what the Spirit is saying'), and with a promise to the one 'who conquers'.

The historical backgrounds of each church are helpfully clarified by Colin Hemer (1986), who updates the groundbreaking work of Sir William Ramsay (1904). But the question that has engaged commentators throughout the ages is the interpretive significance of the seven churches beyond their first-century context. Two approaches in particular have gained currency: the typological or spiritual, and the salvation-historical.

The typological approach sees the seven churches of Revelation as representative of seven types of churches that exist in any time or place and which each exhibit characteristics similar to one of the churches in Revelation. Following on from Victorinus (Bishop of Pettau, third century), Matthew Henry's influential commentary (1721) went beyond historical analysis to also encourage the reader to apply the spiritual instructions of the seven letters to their particular church contexts.

The salvation-historical approach divides church history into seven epochs from the first century up until the return of Christ, with each epoch being characteristic of the qualities and conditions of one of the seven churches. This view was systematically elaborated first by English Franciscan Henry of Cossey (fourteenth century) in his commentary *Super Apocalypsim*. Thus, for example, the church of Sardis became predictive of the period beginning with Charlemagne (768–814) and ending with Joachim of Fiore (1132–1202), whose era concludes with the Turkish ruler Saladin taking Jerusalem from the Crusaders (1187) (Saladin's siege is powerfully depicted in the movie, *The Kingdom of Heaven* [2005], starring Orlando Bloom). This sevenfold schema was reclaimed in modernity in England (the Plymouth Brethren, twentieth century) and in America (Miller's Adventism, nineteenth century; the dispensationalism of Scofield's famous KJV notes [1909], where Sardis represents the Protestant Reformation).

Englishman John Foxe, author of the famous *Foxe's Book of Martyrs*, followed Henry's lead, but centered his sevenfold interpretation of Revelation around the 'persecution' motif (*Actes and Monuments* [1583 ed.]; *Eicasmi* [1587]). Puritan John Brightman (*A Revelation of the Revelation* [1607]) integrated Foxe's persecution motif while updating Henry's sevenfold historical schema to include Brightman's era, and then reinterpreted each age religiously. Thus, 'hypocritical' Sardis came to represent the German Reformation under Luther, while 'godly' Philadelphia was the Genevan Reformation under Calvin, and the Church of England was the 'lukewarm' Laodicean church.

Recommended reading. Hemer, Colin J. *The Letters to the Seven Churches of Asia in their Local Setting.* Grand Rapids, MI: Eerdmans, 1986. ——. 'Seven Churches'. In *A Dictionary of Biblical Tradition in English Literature*. Ed. David Lyle Jeffrey. Pp. 696-98. Grand Rapids, MI: Eerdmans, 1992. Kovacs, Judith, and Christopher Rowland. *Revelation*. Blackwell Bible Commentaries; Oxford: Blackwell, 2004.

See also ALLEGORY; HERMENEUTICS; NUMBERS, SYMBOLISM OF; REVELATION, BOOK OF [RJK]

Seven Last Words of Christ. The 'seven last words' refer to seven phrases that the Gospels attribute to Jesus on the cross. The phrases vary in each Gospel, and none has all of them. The phrases are usually combined for devotional purposes during Lent and for Good Friday observances:

'Father, forgive them, for they do not know what they are doing' (Luke 23.34). According to Luke, Jesus speaks the first phrase at the start of the crucifixion. Luke states that as people stood by, leaders and soldiers mocked Jesus, concluding with 'save yourself'.

'I tell you the truth, today you will be with me in paradise' (Luke 23.43). The Gospels record that two other criminals were crucified with Jesus. The account relates that one mocked him, but the other recognized his wrongdoing and asked Jesus to remember him, to which Jesus replied with the second phrase. Tradition identifies him as Dismas. This name is used by a Roman Catholic outreach to inmates and others affected by crime.

To his mother, 'Dear woman, here is your son', and to a disciple, 'Here is your mother' (John 19.26-27). The disciple then takes Mary into his home. He is identified as the one whom Jesus loved, a title which appears several times in John, but the person is never named (traditionally, the apostle John). To Roman Catholics, this phrase indicates Mary's primacy in the church, but many Protestants interpret it as indicating faithful care as being the mark of the church.

'Eloi, Eloi, lama sabachthani?'—which means, 'My God, my God, why have you forsaken me?' (Matt. 27.46; Mark 15.34). The only phrase to appear in two Gospels, it seems to be a quotation of the first line of Psalm 22. Some among the witnesses took it as a cry for Elijah (Eli). Scholars disagree as to whether the quotation should be read as a cry of abandonment or a reference to the entire Psalm, which expresses faith in God's coming vindication.

'I am thirsty' (John 19.28). All four gospels record that Jesus was offered a wetted sponge, but only John records that Jesus expressed thirst. The gospel prefaces that this occurred in order to fulfill scripture, alluding to Ps. 69.21.

'It is finished' (John 19.30), indicating the completion of his work.

'Father, into your hands I commit my spirit' (Luke 23.46), possibly a quotation of Ps. 31.5. The death of Jesus, portrayed as a voluntary handing over of his spirit, then follows, at which point the leader of the soldiers expresses awe (although some read it as further mocking).

There are several musical settings of the Seven Last Words. Among the best-known, Franz Joseph Haydn composed a series of orchestral pieces to be played in between liturgical readings, first performed in 1787. He also arranged it for string quartet and for piano solo. In 1796, he recast it as an oratorio. Theodore DuBois composed an 1867 oratorio that is popular with church choirs. A band describing itself as 'Christian hardcore death metal' uses the name Seven Last Words of Christ, citing Matt. 7.23 as seven words it wants to prevent anyone from hearing.

See also PASSION [TV]

Seven Seals, Seven Bowls, Seven Trumpets. These three symbolic images in Revelation introduce and structure three separate sequences of seven end-time events described in chs. 5-16. They are woven into the complex literary unity of the book based on the number seven (*hepta* in Greek), signifying completeness. The three series may not signify 21 different events, but a threefold retelling of the fullness of human destiny. Furthermore, the number seven harks back to the seven days of creation in Gen. 1.1–2.3. The seventh seal, trumpet and bowl are climactic, like the seventh day.

In Rev. 5.1, John sees a scroll in the hand of the enthroned God sealed with seven seals (*sphragis*). Only one person, Jesus—the Lion of Judah and the Lamb—is worthy to open the kingly seals and disclose the contents. The Lamb opens the seals one at a time, each revealing an episode of human destiny (6.1–8.5). At the opening of the first four seals, the four horsemen are released onto the earth.

The sequence of the seven angels blowing the seven trumpets (*salpingx*) spans 8.6–11.9. The instrument symbolizes public proclamation, and in the NT it usually announces the end-time coming of

Jesus for judgment. The first six trumpets announce disasters and conflicts, and the seventh introduces the enthronement of Christ. The sequence of the seven bowls covers chap. 16. In v. 1, a loud voice tells the seven angels, 'Go and pour out on the earth the seven bowls (*phialē* in Greek; 'vials' in the KJV) of the wrath of God'. The bowls symbolize overflowing fullness, and in this chapter a series of worldwide disasters hit those within humanity who have refused to give glory to God.

While in the earliest church these images were understood to denote immediate events preceding the imminent second coming, by the fifth century less literal interpretations had arisen. For Augustine (354–430), Revelation points to the perpetual conflict between the church and the world and not to sequences of events. In the late Middle Ages, a strong interest in periodization of Christian history arose. Exegetes such as Joachim of Fiore (second half of the twelfth century) used the sevenfold sequences to work out periods in which God accomplishes his purposes for the world through the church.

The Reformation period witnessed considerable historicizing of these sequences for the purpose of inter-church polemics, and this excess contributed to a progressive reluctance to identify historical correspondences. Nonetheless, counterexamples exist today. Sizable pockets of evangelical Christianity gravitate toward historicist renderings of the seven seals, trumpets and bowls, due to the influence of *The Scofield Reference Bible* (1909) and its seven divine dispensations. David Koresh taught the Branch Davidians that his own divine role was determined by the 'Seven Seals'.

By and large, contemporary interpreters lean toward poetic and existential understandings. Ingmar Bergman's movie *The Seventh Seal* (1958) uses the symbol not as a cypher for a historical event but as an evocation of something all humans must face: death. Works as diverse as Franz Schmidt's Oratorio *The Book with Seven Seals* (1937) and Avenged Sevenfold's 2001 heavy metal album *Sounding the Seventh Trumpet* witness to the fact that these dramatic symbols continue to stimulate artistic imagination.

See also ANGEL; APOCALYPSE, APOCALYPTIC; FOUR HORSEMEN; LAMB OF GOD; NUMBERS, SYMBOLISM OF; REVELATION, BOOK OF; SEVEN CHURCHES OF REVELATION; TRUMPET [MD]

Seven years of plenty, famine. Part of the Joseph cycle, Gen. 41.1-57 recounts the tale of the Pharaoh's dreams of seven fat cows devoured by seven gaunt cows, and seven plump ears of grain swallowed by seven blighted ears. The Pharaoh is troubled by these dreams which none of his magicians and sages can explain, so his chief butler, recently released from prison, suggests the convict Joseph, whom he knows to be able to interpret prophetic dreams. When Joseph is brought before the king, he explains that the dream is God's way of warning Pharaoh that Egypt will suffer seven years of plenty, followed by seven years of famine (41.29-31). The doubling of the dream indicates that God's will is unchangeable. Joseph advises the king to select a wise administrator to ensure that sufficient produce from the prosperous years will be saved to sustain the nation through the famine, and Pharaoh appoints Joseph to the task.

In the Jewish lectionary sequence, this story is part of the weekly Torah reading *Miketz* (Gen. 41.1–44.17); it is also read at Hanukkah. In western culture, 'seven years of plenty/famine' refers to any period of prosperity followed by leaner times. The phrase figures in the titles of many books of widely different genres, e.g., Ben Thompson's *Seven Years of Plenty*, published in 1998, charting the development of pop music, Virginia Haggard's memoir *My Life with Chagall: Seven Years of Plenty with the Master as Told by the Woman Who Shared Them* (1986) and the recently published *Seven Years of Plenty Cookbook*.

See also DREAM; EGYPT; HANUKKAH; JOSEPH; NUMBERS, SYMBOLISM OF; PHARAOH [MALB]

Seventy times Seven. The phrase 'seventy times seven' comes from Matt. 18.21-22, in which Peter asks Jesus how often he should forgive a church member: 'As many as seven times?' Peter asks. Jesus replies, 'Not seven times, but, I tell you, seventy-seven times' (NRSV). Other versions—including KJV, NAB, ESV, and *The Message*—have 'seventy times seven', leading to the use of this phrase as a synonym for unconditional forgiveness in contemporary culture.

The Greek term behind this phrase in Matthew is *hebdomēkontakis hepta*, which translates literally to 'seventy times [and] seven'. The twist in the translation confuses 'times' (occurrences, which is the meaning of the Greek) with 'times' (multiplied by) in English such that 'seventy times seven' is misunderstood to mean 490 times. In actuality, the number signified by the Greek words is seventy-seven.

In Luke, Jesus' command to forgive appears in a different context and takes a different form, while still containing a doubling of sevens. 'If the same person sins against you seven times a day, and turns back to you seven times and says, 'I repent,' you must forgive' (17.4). Here Jesus makes forgiveness conditional on repentance, whereas in Matthew's version of the command—the one that is most often quoted—forgiveness appears to be unconditional.

The number seven has typological significance throughout the Bible. Seven is used to indicate completeness or totality. The work of creation was completed in seven days. A doubling of the number seven occurs early in Genesis when Lamech, who has killed a man, laments, 'If Cain is avenged seven-fold, truly Lamech seventy-seven fold' (4.24). Here, the sevens point to an infinite expanse of vengeance, as opposed to the boundless forgiveness found in Matt. 18.22.

The symbolic significance of the number seven continues in the NT: there are seven last sayings of Jesus on the cross, seven loaves multiplied, and seven spirits cast out of Mary Magdalene. In the Book of Revelation, there are numerous heptads (groups of seven): spirits of God, churches, stars, seals, last plagues, bowls or vials, and thunders. The number seventy-seven only emphasizes this by symbolizing infinite and limitless fullness, as in Luke's genealogy where Jesus stands as the seventy-seventh generation of human history (3.23-38).

In popular culture, 'seventy times seven' has become shorthand for an ideal of Christian forgiveness, i.e., forgiveness without bound. 70x7 is a contemporary Christian rock band that claims the name as 'synonymous with God's eternal forgiveness'. On the group's website they explain the meaning of the number. 'Jesus is telling us we should *always* forgive our brothers when they have sinned against us'. In addition to this band, a number of Christian musical groups have adopted 'seventy times seven' as a band name, album name, or song title.

'Seventy times seven' has graced a number of book titles, from novels and self-help books to theology and religious-studies titles. A few of these include, *Seventy Times Seven: The Power of Forgiveness*, by Johann Christoph Arnold; *Seventy Times Seven: A Novel of Trial and Triumph in Old Philadelphia*, by Sandi Z. Rebert; *Seventy Times Seven: Forgiveness and Peacemaking,* by Doris Donnelly; and *Seventy Times Seven: Sin, Judgment, and Forgiveness in Matthew*, by Thomas W. Buckley.

See also FORGIVENESS; NUMBERS, SYMBOLISM OF

[MM]

Sex, Sexuality. Whereas sex refers to both the anatomical differentiation of males and females as well as the sexual act, sexuality refers to a person's pattern of life through which one engages in sexual activity. Sexual practices among humans produce significant physiological, emotional, psycho-social and spiritual effects. These effects may be characterized as positive, as might occur within a mutually consensual relationship, or negative, as occurs when an individual is sexually violated (e.g., rape of Tamar; 2 Sam. 13).

In the OT creation accounts we note the divine differentiation of humans as male and female as well as the assertion that the normative context and purpose for expressing human sexuality are within marriage and for conceiving children (Gen. 1.27-28; 2.7, 18-25). For many Jews and Christians, the creation accounts place a high value on human sexuality, calling the people of God to look beyond self-pleasure and to consider sexuality in the light of God's act of creation and his covenant with his people. Thus, the Torah code of conduct for the community of faith censures sexual practices which violate either the marital covenant (Exod. 20.14; Lev. 18.18); the sanctity of the covenant community (Exod. 20.14; Lev. 18.6-17, 20-21); or, the order of creation (Lev. 18.19, 22-23). This perspective also appears in the NT (e.g., Matt. 5.27-32; 1 Thess. 4.3-7; Heb. 13.4) where we note the emergence of two additional themes relating to human sexuality—the role of marital sexuality as a possible hedge against sexual immorality (1 Cor. 7.1-9) and the introduction of celibacy as the only Christian alternative to marriage for exercising one's sexuality (Matt. 19.10-12; 1 Cor. 7.7-8).

While the biblical ideals concerning sexuality did much to shape civil law in western Europe, history tells of the mistresses of the nobility (e.g., Henry VIII) and some church leaders (e.g., Pope Alexander VI), the widespread practice of prostitution (e.g., story of Jack the Ripper), the sexual exploitation of children (cf. William T. Stead, 'Maiden Tribute of Modern Babylon', *Pall Mall Gazette*, July 1885), and those who engaged in same-sex sexual behavior (e.g., Marquis de Sade, Oscar Wilde). While W.T. Stead was motivated by a concern for exploited children, the life and writings of the Marquis de Sade foreshadow the sexual revolution of the 1960s which introduced an ethos of open sex in and outside of marriage (e.g., *Sex and the City*), public nudity, gay liberation (which gained strength following the Stonewall riots in

New York city) and the normalization of pornography (e.g., *Penthouse*).

In the wake of this liberalization of sexual attitudes a number of writers have reflected on the value of abstinence (Lauren Winner, *Real Sex*; Dawn Eden, *The Thrill of the Chaste*) and monogamy (Dr Pat Love, *Hot Monogamy*) as legitimate expressions of a person's sexuality. In contrast to the writings of the early church which tended to view celibacy as a higher calling than marriage (Augustine, *On Holy Virginity*), much of the recent interest in abstinence, celibacy and monogamy is motivated by a desire to elevate human sexuality by reserving it for heterosexual marriages in which mutually respectful sex between consenting adults serves unitive, procreative, and sacramental functions. Both Jewish and Christian theologians have reflected on the legitimacy of committed same-sex relationships within their respective religious traditions.

Recommended reading. Balswick, Jack K., and Judith O. Balswick. *Authentic Human Sexuality*. Downers Grove, IL: InterVarsity, 2006. Hasbany, Richard L. *Homosexuality and Religion*. London: Routledge, 1990. Winner, Lauren. *Real Sex: The Naked Truth about Chastity*. Grand Rapids, MI: Brazos, 2005.

See also ADULTERY; DIVORCE; FAMILY; GNOSTICISM; MAN; MARRIAGE; WOMAN [KFM]

Shadrach, Meshach and Abednego. The names of Daniel's three Hebrew friends (Dan. 1.7). Shadrach is the Chaldean name given to Hananiah, whose Hebrew name means, 'Yahu has been gracious' or, 'Jehovah gives'. Meshach is the Chaldean name given to Mishael, and though the etymology for Mishael is uncertain, it has been suggested that it could mean, 'who is what El (God) is?' or, 'Who is like God?' Abednego is the Chaldean name given to Azariah, whose Hebrew name means, 'Yahweh has helped'. The etymology for the Chaldean names seem uncertain, but some scholars have suggested that Abednego could mean, 'servant of Nebo/Nabu', arguing that *nego* is a Chaldean derivative of the Hebrew word Nebo.

Probably of royal blood or just Jewish nobility (Dan. 1.3-4), these three defied king Nebuchadnezzar's decree to worship his golden statue (Dan. 3). All three preferred to be thrown into the fiery furnace than to bow down to Nebuchadnezzar's idol, and in essence disobey God's law of worshiping no other gods. Following the theme of Yahweh's sovereignty over all places and events, the three found themselves unharmed, aided by an angel with them in the furnace. The king is amazed, and subsequently, all three are promoted (Dan. 3.24-30; cf. Dan. 6).

These stories are both referred to in Bob Marley's song *Survival* (1979). Marley's use of both stories in his song is not coincidental. Like African-American slaves, the Hebrew boys were under servitude and oppression in a country that was not theirs and asked to worship a god foreign to them. In the song, the survival of Shadrach, Meshach and Abednego meant something important to the reggae artist, whose songs of freedom catapulted him into fame in the 1970s.

One of the deuterocanonical books of the Hebrew scripture is named after Abednego. The *Prayer of Azariah* is an addition to the book of Daniel, and details the prayer of Azariah in the furnace. Traditionally inserted between Dan. 3.23 and 3.24, the prayer consists of praise, penitence and request for deliverance. Also, following this is another section called the *Song of the Three*, obviously named after them. According to tradition, this was the song the boys sang while they were in the furnace. Both prayer and songs are used liturgically in Catholic and Orthodox churches.

Other cultural references include Johnny Cash's song *The Fourth Man in the Fire* (1969). Authors like Herman Melville, in his book *Moby Dick* (1851), have made comparisons to the story of the boys in the fire. Harper Lee's *To Kill a Mockingbird* (1960) portrays characters reenacting the faith of the boys (chapter 12).

Evangelical Christians often misinterpret the faith of Shadrach, Meshach and Abednego. Their faith is usually interpreted as trusting in God to protect them, whereas, the boys had insisted, 'If our God whom we serve is able to deliver us from the furnace of blazing fire and out of your hand, O king, let him deliver us. But if not, be it known to you, O king, that we will not serve your gods and we will not worship the golden statue that you have set up' (Dan. 3.17-18). For the boys, there was no compromise even if God decided not to protect them. For this, the boys feature prominently in Hebrews' chapter on faith (11.34).

Recommended reading. Beaulieu, Paul-Alain. 'The Babylonian Background of the Motif of the Fiery Furnace in Daniel 3'. *Journal of Biblical Literature* 128 (2009) 273-90.

See also DANIEL, BOOK OF; PRAYER OF AZARIAH; SONG OF THE THREE [GOA]

Shalom (see Peace).

Sheep. In Hebrew *tzo'n* and in Greek *probaton,* the concept of sheep is closely related to other terms including ewes, flocks, lambs, goats, and rams. Referenced over 500 times in the Bible, sheep represent one of the most important animals both economically and symbolically in the agrarian society of ancient Israel. In the Bible, sheep represent a source of food and wool (1 Sam. 14.32; Isa. 7.21-22; Lev. 13.47), a commodity (2 Kgs 3.4), and are central to the sacrificial system (Exod. 12.3-6). Conventional uses of the metaphor in scripture (Pss 23; 119.176; Isa. 53.6; Jer. 50.6; Ezek. 34.11-23; Matt. 10.6; 15.24; John 10; Luke 15.1-8) equate people with sheep and persons in authority (kings, leaders, or God) with shepherds as caretakers of the people as sheep. Thus, God's people are associated with the characteristics of sheep as docile and easily led (or misled). Lambs are also associated with sacrificial victims dying in place of another. Meanwhile, the caretakers of the sheep may be positive (e.g., John 10) or negative figures (e.g., Ezekiel 34). In the NT, parables portraying sheep comment on the role of God as leader of his people and on the characteristics of God's people in response to him. Symbolically, sheep are related to other images such as the Good Shepherd, the Lamb of God, the sacrificial lamb, and the Passover lamb.

In early Christianity, references to sheep were popular particularly in the third–fifth century (e.g., art in the catacombs, on sarcophagi, and small statuettes). Reformers Luther and Calvin point to the dependent relationship between the shepherd and the sheep in passages like Psalm 23, while Augustine recommended Psalm 23 for those facing martyrdom.

Two significant Jewish resistance movements used the phrase 'like sheep to the slaughter' to describe martyrdom. In the closing years of the Second Temple period, Romans persecuted the Jewish people; a groups of rabbis called the Ten Martyrs stood in defiance of a Roman ban on studying the Torah and paid with their lives. These Ten Martyrs are commemorated in the liturgies of Yom Kippur and Tisha B'Av. Maimonides praises these Ten Martyrs, describing them going 'like sheep to the slaughter' (in *Yesodei HaTorah* 5.4). Similarly in 1942, Abba Kovner used this phrase to rouse Jewish resistance fighters against the Nazis. Today, some Holocaust scholars have argued against using the phrase in describing Holocaust victims because of its dehumanizing effect and potential misrepresentation of Jewish resistance movements at the time of the Holocaust. Nevertheless, many Holocaust victims have used such animalistic phrases as part of their self-description of their experiences.

Literary and artistic references to the biblical metaphor of sheep include Spenser's *Shepheardes Calendar,* Milton's *Lysidas,* Bunyan's *Pilgrim's Progress,* Händel's *Messiah*'s song 'He shall feed his flock', Murillo's *The Good Shepherd,* and the ongoing literary fascination with Psalm 23. Modern interpretations of the sheep metaphor are equally profuse and frequently pejorative, at times focusing on the dehumanizing and collective quality of sheep, as shown in films such as *Modern Times* (1936) and *About a Boy* (2002). The phrase 'don't be a sheep' has been used for anti-smoking campaigns and political and consumerism critique. Andrew Napolitano's *Nation of Sheep* uses the sheep/shepherd metaphor pejoratively to critique political leaders. In a more positive use, in Catholicism, papal addresses have linked the shepherd/sheep metaphor to papal governance.

See also GOOD SHEPHERD; LAMB, SACRIFICIAL; LAMB OF GOD; LOST SHEEP, PARABLE OF THE; SHEEP AND THE GOATS, PARABLE OF THE; SHEPHERD PSALM; ANIMALS, SYMBOLISM OF [BMS]

Sheep and the goats, Parable of the. Found only in Matt. 25.31-46, the passage is not considered a parable by most interpreters because there is no conventional narrative, but it is considered a parabolic statement with expansion and application by Jesus. The purported parable is part of the last of Jesus' five Matthean discourses, at the end of the eschatological discourse and parables of Matthew 24–25. Despite its placement, some scholars question its authenticity to Jesus. However, reference to the son of man and his judging point to its authenticity.

Although referred to as the parable of the sheep and goats, these animals are relatively insignificant to this parable. Their use probably refers to the practice of shepherding at that time, in which sheep and goats were herded together until they needed to be segregated for a purpose, e.g., sheering. The Greek papyri from Egypt frequently refer to sheep and goats together, but there is no sense that one is better than the other. The larger parable, however, is not about shepherding, but about the coming judgment of the son of man, who comes as a divine figure to judge the nations. The image then shifts to a king, equated with the son of man as sovereign and judge. He speaks to the nations who have been segregated like the sheep and the goats, some to the right and others to the left. The right side signifies positive judgment, and the left negative. The king ushers those on the right into the kingdom, for they have compassionately offered services to him, such as giving food, drink, hospitality, clothing, comfort, and aid while imprisoned. Those on the left are cursed for their failure to render such aid. Neither side remembers or recognizes when they gave or denied such aid to the Lord. The major critical question of this parable is focused upon who are the 'least of the brethren' for whom the nations do or do not perform their good deeds.

Scholars have proposed three major interpretations. Most agree that the parable concerns the last judgment before the divine throne, but where scholars vary is the basis of the judgment. One popular contemporary alternative is that the 'least of the brethren' are those mentioned later in the parable, the hungry, thirsty, disenfranchised, unclothed, ill, and imprisoned. Judgment is rendered on the basis of how one has treated those in need. A second alternative is that the standard for judgment is how people have treated Jesus' followers, that is, his brothers (and sisters). A third choice is that the 'least of the brethren' are Christian missionaries, and judgment is rendered according to how they have been treated by the world. In a contemporary context, one might wish to argue for the first position and advocate for good deeds to be done for those in need and judgment for those who do not. However, the likelihood is that Jesus addressed this parable to the situation of how his followers, as his representatives, were to be treated by the surrounding world. The parable indicates judgment for those who mistreat Jesus' followers, and reward for those who minister to their needs. This parable is not endorsing a works-righteousness in which one earns favor simply by performing these fundamental acts of good will, but it does seem to advocate that treatment of Jesus' followers sets the standard against which humans are judged.

Recommended reading. Hultgren, Arland J. *The Parables of Jesus: A Commentary*. Pp. 309-30. Grand Rapids, MI: Eerdmans, 2000. Snodgrass, Klyne R. *Stories with Intent: A Comprehensive Guide to the Parables of Jesus*. Pp. 543-63. Grand Rapids, MI: Eerdmans, 2008.

See also ANIMALS, SYMBOLISM; PARABLE; SHEEP

[SEP]

Shield. Generally a noun, but also frequently used as a verb; the English word goes back to the Old English poem *Beowulf* (in the form *scield* or *scyld*), illustrating that in English literature also, warfare has a long history.

In the OT, there are two main Hebrew words: *tsinnah* (root 'to preserve or keep') for the larger shield (covering the whole body), and *maghen* (root 'to cover'; same root as *gan*, garden) for the smaller. Sometimes both are used together in the same verse, for example Ps. 35.2 ('shield and buckler').

In a literal sense, the shield is the chief defensive weapon of a soldier, and is usually listed along with other weapons, e.g., 2 Chron. 26.14 ('shields, spears, helmets, coats of mail, bows, and stones for slinging'). The OT shield was generally made out of wood and leather, and could be anointed with oil, presumably as a symbol of the soldier's consecration for battle (e.g., 2 Sam. 1.21). The Philistine warrior Goliath had another soldier carrying his shield for him (1 Sam. 17.7), perhaps as a way of emphasizing his size and importance. There are also examples of shields made out of gold (e.g.,1 Kgs 10.17), apparently for ceremonial rather than defensive purposes; the softness of gold would render it useless for protection against spears and swords (as well as being an extremely wasteful use of the precious metal).

In a figurative sense, just as the soldier's shield protects him against the arrows and spears of the enemy, so God is described as the 'help and shield' of the House of Israel (Ps. 115.9), indicating God's role in protecting the faithful from the spiritual—and at times physical— attacks of the enemy. Indeed the first use of the word in the OT occurs in Gen. 15.1, when God says to Abram. 'Do not be afraid, Abram, I am your shield; your reward shall be very great'.

The NT contains the only example of the Greek word *thyreos* (from the word *thyra*, a door, since this type of shield resembled a door in shape): 'taking the shield of faith', again indicating, explicitly here, the protection against, and indeed quenching of, the 'flaming arrows of the evil one' (Eph. 6.16).

In classical literature, Homer and Virgil each describe a famous shield, using an extended ecphrasis (a detailed poetic description of what is on the shield). In the former (*Iliad* 18) the Shield of Achilles depicts, among other things, a City at War and a City at Peace (an oblique reference to Troy); it is also referred to by the twentieth-century poet W.H. Auden in his poem 'The Shield of Achilles' in which he evokes scenes from World War II as well as the crucifixion of Christ. In the latter (*Aeneid* 8), the Shield of Aeneas alludes to the victory of the future Roman Emperor Augustus over Anthony and Cleopatra in the battle of Actium (31 BCE). In a myth recorded in Ovid's *Metamorphoses* (4) the hero Perseus beheads the hideous Medusa while observing her reflection in a polished shield, rather than looking directly at her.

In modern times, the American TV series *The Shield*, depicting interactions between corrupt police officers and LA street gangs, played for several seasons before ending in late 2008. The acronym S.H.I.E.L.D. was introduced in the 1960s by Marvel Comics, and used in the 2008 Marvel Studios films *Iron Man* and *The Incredible Hulk*, standing for 'Strategic Homeland Intervention, Enforcement and Logistics Division'.

See also ARMOR OF GOD; SWORD; SWORDS INTO PLOUGHSHARES [GDB]

Shekinah. Popularly referred to as Holy Spirit, the term Shekinah ('dwelling') is commonly referred to in Judaism as 'the Divine Presence' (Eliezar ben Shammua, *Midrash Tehillim* 32); 'the King' (Eliezer ben Isaac, *Orhot Hayyim*), and 'the great King' (Maimonides, *Guide for the Perplexed*). The term is not found in the Hebrew Bible, wherein *Ruach HaKodesh* is the Hebrew expression for 'Holy Spirit'. A derivative of the verb 'to dwell/to rest' (*lishkan*), it shares association with other derivatives of the same verb which do appear in the Tanak. The cloud of Divine Presence that led the children of Israel throughout the wilderness wanderings is said to have rested (*shakhan*) upon the Tabernacle when not journeying. The term for Tabernacle (*Mishkan*) is a substantival derivative. Kabbalah (mystical Judaism) identifies Shekinah as the tenth transmigration (*Sefirah*) of the Holy One (also referred to as *Malkut*, 'Kingdom') to humanity. At the level of Shekinah all humans can experience God. The Torah is a vestment to the Shekinah (*Zohar*, Gen. 23ab). In Aggadic Midrash, one day the Shekinah will fill the world from end to end (*Midrash Esther Rabbah* 1.4). In present times, the Shekinah is present in a Beth Midrash (house of study, synagogue) even when only one person is there (*Mekilta* to Exod. 20.21).

Due to its feminine grammatical form, 'Shekinah' as an epithet for the divine presence has become an emblem for contemporary Christian and Jewish feminist movements. Some retreat centers focusing on spiritual exercises have also adopted the name, emphasizing inspiration, relaxation, and recreation in a natural setting designed to experience the presence and glory of God.

Recommended reading. Patai, Raphael. *The Hebrew Goddess*. Pp. 202-20. Detroit: Wayne State University Press, 1990.

See also HOLY SPIRIT; TABERNACLE; WISDOM [DM]

Shem was Noah's first son, who survived the flood with his entire family (Gen. 6–9), according to the Priestly (P) version of the story. P lists the nations originating from Shem: Elam (Persia), Asshur (Assyria), Arpachshad (Babylonia), and Aram (Syria; Gen. 10.1, 22-23; cf. 1 Chron. 1.4, 17-27). P makes Abraham a descendant of Shem, enumerating nine generations or three millennia separating Shem from Abraham (11.10-28, 31-32). A later list establishes the Hebrew ancestry of Abraham (10.21, 24-31): Shem is the father of Semitic peoples (derived from *Shem*), *the children of Eber* or all Hebrews, including those who became Israel. Inserted towards the end of P's flood narrative (Gen. 9.1, 9-17, 28-29) is an intrusive tale about Noah planting a vineyard, drinking wine and becoming inebriated. His son Ham 'saw his nakedness', but Shem and Japheth walked backwards to cover Noah with a garment. When Noah awakens from his stupor, he curses Canaan, Ham's son, and bestows a blessing on Shem (Gen. 9.18-27).

Postbiblical Jewish writers commend Shem and Japheth for their respectful behavior, but Shem deserves the greater praise because he was the first to cover Noah. Without discussing Ham, Josephus (first century CE) simply reports that Noah 'prayed for prosperity to his other sons' (*Antiquities* 1.6.3). In some rabbinic storytelling, the heavenly academy of Shem and Eber is the place of study for Abraham. Medieval interpreters (c. 1100) found in Genesis 9 the division of humanity into three estates: free men (Shem), soldiers (Japheth) and servants (Ham). Reformation leader Martin Luther regarded Shem and Japheth as models of piety for owing reverence to their father, as stipulated by the fifth commandment (Exod. 20.12; Deut. 5.16). Honor of parents dominated Protestant interpretation of Genesis 9 (e.g., The Church of England's *Bishops Bible* 1568) and became a popular theme in assessing Noah's sons (e.g., British exegete Adam Clarke, 1817; proslavery American writer Josiah Priest, 1843). In an address *Our Historic Mission* (1858) Benjamin Palmer, influential Presbyterian Pastor in New Orleans, identified three races, Shem (Asia), Japheth (Europe/America), and Ham (Africa): Shem transmits religion and worship, Japheth cultivates the intellect, and Ham drives the sensual appetites. In Palmer's reading of world history, Japheth was destined to dominate Shem and Ham.

In the visual arts, a Noah window in Chartres Cathedral, France (1235–1240) depicts Shem as the forerunner of prayerful priests. Bernardino Luini's painting *The Mocking of Ham* (1510–1515) depicts Noah unconscious under a grape-laden tree, while Shem and Japheth make a concerted effort to cover Noah with a cloak without glancing at his nudity. Similarly, a woodcut illustration appearing in the 1535 Coverdale Bible represents Shem and Japheth walking backwards to place a cloak over Noah's exposed genitals. By contrast, woodcut illustrations from the Cologne and Lübeck Bibles (1469/1494) and from Luther's *Deutsch Catechismus* (1531) represent only one brother covering Noah. In light of the mimetic theory of René Girard, Stephen Haynes proposes that 'the doubling' conduct of Shem and Japheth suggests sibling rivalry and victimization of Ham.

Recommended reading. Haynes, Stephen R. *Noah's Curse: The Biblical Justification of American Slavery*. Oxford: Oxford University Press, 2002. Whitford, David M. *The Curse of Ham in the Early Modern Era: The Bible and the Justifications for Slavery*. Burlington, VT: Ashgate, 2009. Zuffi, Stefano. *Old Testament Figures in Art*. Trans. Thomas Michael Hartman. Los Angeles: Getty Museum, 2003.

See also CANAAN; FLOOD; HAM; JAPHETH; NOAH
[JRW]

Shema. From the Hebrew verb *shema'*, 'to hear;' the first word of Deut. 6.4: 'Hear, O Israel. The Lord is our God, the Lord alone'. Throughout the OT and NT, authors often allude to Deut. 6.4-5 to express the fundamentals of Israel's religion: the oneness of Israel's God, and Israel's duty to love God. Isaiah, for example, declares: 'Thus says the Lord, the King of Israel, and his Redeemer, the Lord of hosts. I am the first and I am the last; besides me there is no god' (44.6; see also Jer. 32.39-41; Ps. 50.7; Zech. 14.9; John 10.30; 1 Cor. 8.6). When asked to identify the 'most important' of all commandments, Jesus recites Deut. 6.4-5 (Mark 12.29-30).

In Judaism, Deut. 6.4-9 (together with Deut. 11.13-21), and Num. 15.37-41 are joined to form a daily liturgy, the *Keri'at Shema'* ('the reading of the Shema'), recited as part of the morning and evening service in the synagogue. The standard Shema liturgy today is comprised of blessings that encapsulate the biblical passages. In the morning, two blessings are said before the Shema, 'Who forms light and creates darkness (*Yotzer 'Or*)', 'With Abounding Love (*Ahavah Rabbah*)'. One blessing is said after, 'True and Certain (*Emet Ve-Yaziv*)'. The evening Shema contains the preceding blessings 'Who at Thy word brings on the evening twilight' (*Ma'ariv Aravim*), and 'With everlasting love, (*Ahavat Olam*)'. 'True and trustworthy' (*Emet ve-Emunah*), and 'Cause us to lie down in peace' (*Hashkivenu*) are the two blessings recited after.

The literary form and structure of the Shema liturgy, with its biblical portions and blessings, is arranged to evoke God's sovereignty, affirm the unity of God, and transmit the biblical narrative of creation, revelation, and redemption. As a confession of faith, the Shema is often referred to as 'the acceptance of the yoke of the Kingdom of Heaven' (cf. *b. Ber.* 13a-b, 14b). In the late antique period the Shema came to be understood as having the power to protect against ones enemies (*b. Sotah* 42a); in *Midrash on Psalms* 4.9, the recitation of the Shema upon retiring to bed is said to protect one from demons of the night.

Canadian poet A.M. Klein reworks themes of the Shema in his poem, 'Stance of the Amidah'.

Thyself do utter the Shema! Sound the great horn of freedom, and gather from the four corners of the earth as we do gather the four fringes to kiss them, Thy people, Thy folk, rejected Thine elect.

The poem urges God, not the congregation, to recite the Shema, to gather the dispersed Jews from the corners of the earth like the fringes of the prayer shawl. This image recalls the last section of the liturgy, when the worshipper gathers these fringes from the four corners of the prayer shawl and kisses them as a sign of devotion.

Recommended reading. Kimelman, Reuven. 'The Shema Liturgy: From Covenant Ceremony to Coronation'. In *Kenishta: Studies of the Synagogue World*. Ed. J. Tabory. Pp. 9-105. Ramat-Gan: Bar-Ilan University Press, 2001.

See also BLESSED/BLESSING; WORSHIP [JP]

Sheol. The proper Hebrew noun Sheol (*sh'wl/sh'l*; etymology uncertain) occurs 67 times throughout the OT referring to the underworld inhabited by the deceased. Though the OT does not present a formal doctrine concerning the fate and destination of the dead, Sheol is described through various metaphors and images reflecting the Israelite belief concerning what existence beyond the grave entailed. Characteristically Sheol, is presented as a pit (Isa. 14.15; Ezek. 31.16), a deep abyss shrouded in darkness (Job 14.13; 17.13) and a realm of destitution (Prov. 30.16) in which the dead remained in a shadowy existence. Sheol is predominantly personified as possessing an insatiable appetite (Prov. 27.20; Isa. 5.14) with a broad throat (Hab. 2.5) and open mouth

(Ps. 141.7), capable of consuming those in the land of the living (Ps. 49.14; Prov. 1.12; Job 24.19). Figuratively, the living often refer to the 'cords of Sheol' (Ps. 18.5; 116.3; 2 Sam. 22.6) or drawing near to Sheol (Ps. 88.3) when facing impending death. Sheol is as inescapable as death itself (Ps. 89.48) and is a fate even envisaged by the righteous (Isa. 38.9-11; Job 17.13-16). Though the abode is repeatedly associated with sorrow and grief (Gen. 37.35; 42.38; 44.29, 31) nowhere in the OT is the notion of post-mortem punishment conveyed or developed. Despite its often distant and otherworldly presentation Sheol remained within the reaches of God's divine dominion (1 Sam. 2.6; Ps. 139.8).

The ambiguity and complex connotations associated with the realm of Sheol in the OT are evident in the spectrum of translation values attributed to the term in English Bibles. A potentially complicating factor for effective interpretation and accurate translation of 'Sheol' is the fact that in the LXX Sheol was translated as Hades (*hadēs*) thereby associating the foggy Hebrew conception of the underworld with the analogous yet markedly different Greek notion of the abode of the dead. While NASB and NRSV consistently utilize the transliteration 'Sheol', NIV alternatively opts for 'grave' or 'the depths', NLT-SE idiomatically renders 'the place of the deceased' and KJV most often equates the term with 'Hell'.

In many cases, popular culture has capitalized on the dark and shadowy nature of the realm of Sheol. In Anne Rice's *New York Times* bestselling novel *Memnoch the Devil* (1995), Sheol is the destination of the souls of the deceased deemed unworthy for admittance into heaven. In the science fiction novel *Starship Troopers* (1959) by Robert A. Heinlein, later expanded into an Oscar nominated motion picture by Director Paul Verhoeven (1997), Sheol is the name of a colony planet inhabited by a dangerous breed of insect-like aliens. In the comic series *Hellboy*, Hellboy's father is intriguingly designated as a 'Prince of Sheol'. Finally, in 2003 the Swedish metal band Naglfar released an album simply entitled *Sheol*.

Recommended reading. Alexander, T.D. 'The Old Testament View of Life after Death'. *Themelios* 11 (1986) 41-46. Johnston, Philip S. *Shades of Sheol: Death and the Afterlife in the Old Testament*. Downers Grove, IL: InterVarsity Press, 2002. Segal, Alan F. *Life after Death: A History of the Afterlife in the Religions of the West*. New York: Doubleday, 2004

See also GEHENNA; HADES; HELL [ABP]

Shepherd. From the Hebrew, *rō'eh*, and the Greek, *poimēn* or *poimainō*. As an agrarian society, shepherding was a prominent occupation in ancient Israel. Many people in Israel's history were shepherds, e.g., Abel (Gen. 4.2) and Jacob (Gen. 30.29-31). Two of Israel's most important leaders, Moses and David, were shepherds prior to assuming leadership of the nation (Exod. 3.1; 1 Sam. 17.14-15).

'Shepherd' as a metaphor came to symbolize Israel's leaders: pre-monarchical rulers like Moses and Joshua (Num. 27.17); Jewish monarchs like David and Ahab (2 Sam. 5.2; 1 Kgs 22.17); and members of the nation's non-monarchical leadership (e.g., Jer. 2.8; Zech 10.2-3). Similarly, the biblical authors appropriate the metaphor for Gentile monarchs like Nebuchadnezzar (Jer. 43.12) and Cyrus (Isa. 44.28), as well as for military commanders (e.g., Mic. 5.5-6). Israel's God is regularly viewed as a shepherd to his people, because he delivers them from dangers (e.g., Ezek. 34.11-13) and provides for their needs (e.g., Ps. 23; Jer. 31.9-10). He is explicitly called 'Shepherd' in Gen. 49.24; Ps. 23.1; 80.1, and Eccl. 12.11.

This pattern of using 'shepherd' as a metaphor for earthly rulers and for God continues in Second Temple Jewish writings. Philo of Alexandra implicitly appropriates the metaphor for Moses (*Virtues* 58); King David is compared with a shepherd in the DSS (5Q504; 1Q34). The metaphor is applied to God in describing his mercy (4Q509; cf. Ben Sira 18.13-14), and his ruling power (e.g., *1 En.* 89–90). *Psalms of Solomon* 17.40 uses the term in relation to the Davidic messiah. Of particular note during this period is the extension of the symbolism of the metaphor beyond ruling to include teaching (*2 Baruch* 77.13-16; cf. Damascus Document 13.7-12).

The NT authors appropriate the metaphor for Jesus: he is the Good Shepherd (John 10.11-18; cf. Heb. 13.20; 1 Pet. 2.25; Rev. 7.17), who provides for the needs of the people of Israel (Mark 6.34-44), and who, like God according to Ezekiel 34, heals Israel of their sicknesses (Matt. 9.35-36). The image of Jesus as the Good Shepherd of his people is subsequently taken up, especially in the third and early fourth centuries, by ancient painters and sculptors, who often depict Jesus in shepherd's garb carrying a lamb on his shoulders. More recently, the scriptural title, *The Good Shepherd*, was used for the title of a 2006 action-thriller film depicting the birth of the CIA. A character named 'Jack Shephard' was also the main hero of the popular TV series *LOST* (2004–2010).

NT authors also employ the metaphor for assembly leaders, who are responsible for watching over Christ-believers (John 21.15-17; 1 Pet. 5.2-4)—something they accomplish in part through their teaching (Act 20.28-31; Eph. 4.11). This idea of assembly leaders as 'shepherds' is reflected in contemporary Christianity. The leaders of local churches are often called 'Pastors'—the transliteration of the Latin term for 'shepherd', *pastor*; further, in some circles, 'Pastors' are called 'Shepherds'.

Despite the immense significance of the shepherd as a metaphor in the Bible, one of the most endearing of legacies of 'shepherd' are the numerous Christmas carols that speak of the literal shepherds who witnessed the birth of Jesus (Luke 2.8-20), e.g., 'Shepherds in the fields abiding, watching over your flocks by night' (*Angels from the Realms of Glory*), 'While shepherds kept their watching over silent flocks by night' (*Go Tell it on the Mountain*), and *While Shepherds Watched their Flocks by Night*.

See also LAMB; LAMB OF GOD; SHEEP; SHEPHERD PSALM [WB]

Shepherd Psalm. Psalm 23 (LXX 22), beginning with the phrase 'The Lord is my shepherd, I shall not want' (KJV) is perhaps the most beloved and well known in the Psalter. The comforting image of God as a shepherd caring for his people is traditionally held to be grounded in David the Psalmist's youthful occupation. Every verse of the Psalm is replete with familiar phases, e.g., 'green pastures', 'still waters', 'paths of righteousness', 'the valley of the shadow of death', 'I will fear no evil', 'in the presence of mine enemies', 'my cup runneth over', 'surely goodness and mercy shall follow me', 'I will dwell in the house of the Lord forever'. In Christianity, the metaphor of God as shepherd merges with the image of Christ the Good Shepherd (John 10.11).

In Judaism, Psalm 23 is traditionally sung at the third Sabbath meal and as part of the funeral service. Orthodox Christians pray the Psalm in preparation for the eucharist. The Psalm has been set to music by many composers (e.g., Bach, Schubert, Vaughan Williams, McFerrin), and it forms the basis of many traditional hymns, e.g., 'The Lord's My Shepherd, I'll Not Want', 'The King of Love My Shepherd Is', 'Green Pastures', 'My Shepherd Will Supply My Need'.

See also DAVID; PSALM/PSALMIST/PSALMS, BOOK OF; SHEEP; SHEPHERD [MALB]

Shibboleth. In Judg. 12.1-7, the warrior Jephthah leads the men of Gilead in a battle against the men of Ephraim. The Gileadites take control of the fords of the Jordan River leading to Ephraim, and use the Hebrew word *shibboleth*, which the Ephraimites pronounce differently as *sibboleth*, as a way to identify their Ephraimite enemies. The Gileadites kill 42,000 men of Ephraim by the use of this test.

In Hebrew, the word *shibboleth* means 'ear of grain' or 'torrent'. Due to the biblical story, it has come to refer to a watchword, a generally accepted precept, or a mode of behavior or dress that identifies a person as belonging to a certain social class or group. For example, in the TV series *The West Wing*, episode 30, titled 'Shibboleth', President Bartlett is convinced of a Chinese Christian refugee leader's sincerity when he uses the phrase 'faith is the true Shibboleth' to make his case for admission to the US.

See also GILEAD; JEPHTHAH [MALB]

Shiloh. A major Israelite sanctuary before the establishment of the temple in Jerusalem, located between two other major sanctuaries, Shechem and Bethel. Archaeological excavation of Shiloh has uncovered evidence of Canaanite or Israelite presence. Biblical accounts say that Shiloh was an organized cultic center that held the Ark of the Covenant (1 Sam. 4.4). It is where the barren Hannah prayed to Yahweh for a son (1 Sam. 1.9); when the prayer was answered she sent her son Samuel to study under the high priest Eli at Shiloh. Before the establishment of the main temple in Jerusalem by David, Shiloh held a place in Israelite religion as one of the main sanctuaries. Biblical tradition tells that due to the Israelites' sin, the Philistines destroyed Shiloh and carried off the ark of the covenant (1 Sam. 4). The Bible interprets this event as Yahweh leaving Israel (1 Sam. 4.22). After the ark was recovered, it and cultic worship were moved to Jerusalem.

Since Shiloh was a place where Yahweh chose to place the ark and set up a legitimate cultic center, it competes with Jerusalem temple on some levels as the proper site of Yahweh's dwelling. Thus there are two competing biblical traditions regarding Shiloh, one positive (Josh. 18.1-10; 19.51; 22.9-34) and one negative (e.g., Gen. 49.10-12; Ps. 78.60-72; Jer. 7.12-15). The compilers or writers of the OT, advocating a pro-Jerusalem stance, demonstrated Jerusalem's position by emphasizing that Shiloh was a tent shrine while Jerusalem was a proper temple (Ps. 78). This seems to be successful since Jerusalem as cultic center and Zion theology dominate the OT and remains an important expression in Judaism today. Shiloh is rarely mentioned after David sets up his house and temple in Jerusalem. Jeremiah uses God's abandonment of Shiloh (in the leaving of the ark) as a warning against sin and the same fate for Jerusalem (7.8-14). After Jeremiah, no other reference is made to Shiloh in the Bible. However, one passage of the OT that may refer to Shiloh as a person (Gen. 49.10) has been given some attention for its messianic implications.

Jerome knows Shiloh in a letter to colleagues. Mosques and a Christian church have been discovered there. Shiloh is also located on an ancient mosaic map of Madaba (sixth century), although its mislocation on the map could be an indication of its lack of importance at that time.

Shiloh has been used as a name for various towns in the US, and for many churches. It is sometimes used as a personal name, most recently as name of the child of actors Angelina Jolie and Brad Pitt. It is also the title of a Neil Diamond song 'Shilo' (1967) about an imaginary friend. Finally, it is the title (1998) of a novel by Phyllis Naylor about a dog named Shiloh and a young boy trying to protect the dog, later turned into a movie. Thus, in western culture Shiloh only remains as a name. It seems that biblical associations of Shiloh have had little impact on contemporary usages of the term, perhaps since the editors of the OT successfully supplanted Shiloh with Jerusalem. Thus Shiloh has not become part of Jewish expression nor a significant element in literature or film.

Recommended reading. Schley, Donald G. *Shiloh: A Biblical City in History and Tradition.* Sheffield: JSOT Press, 1989.

See also HIGH PRIEST; JERUSALEM; JEREMIAH; MOUNTAIN; TABERNACLE; TEMPLE. ISRAEL'S [SWF]

Ship. (See Boat).

Shiprah and Puah. Shiphrah ('clear skies', 'beautiful') and Puah ('fragrant blossom', 'young girl') are two midwives in the Exodus story who refused Pharaoh's order to kill Hebrew male babies at birth.

In the narrative of Exodus 1, Pharaoh felt threatened by rapid population growth among the children of Israel, and aroused fear of them rebelling or leaving his land. That propaganda seemed to justify his first plan: to conscript them to labor on large public works without payment. Yet they only grew in number. Next, he introduced crushing workloads, including work on agriculture. Then, he gives orders to the midwives to kill their own people, hoping they were demoralized enough to commit infanticide. Though Pharaoh's subjects feared him, the midwives actively oppose this genocide because they believe in Yahweh God of Israel. They acted secretly but Pharaoh found out and summoned them to his court to overawe them. It is a scene full of contrasts: a powerful male king whose word is law versus powerless females, probably slaves without any voice. Yet they speak, claiming that Hebrew slave women are stronger than Egyptians, which taps into Pharaoh's racist fears. They claim that Hebrew women deliver their own babies without help, too quickly for midwives to kill them. Even if their story stretches the truth, the midwives are immortalized as heroines of resistance against an oppressive, genocidal regime. Because of their belief in God, the writer says God gives them families of their own—so personally as well as professionally they help their people survive and thrive. The writer does not record Pharaoh's reply, nor even his name. His final move is to order his own people to throw Hebrew babies into the Nile. One of the babies born in that generation is Moses, who is put into the river, but in a basket. Eventually he leads the Hebrews to freedom. Some Jewish legends identify Shiphrah with Jochebed, the mother of Moses (Exod. 1.6-21).

Until this point God has not been mentioned in Exodus, and seems absent during his people's suffering. Yet the midwives believe in God, and God acts on their behalf. This picks up on some of the overall themes of the Pentateuch, namely God's command to Adam and Eve to be fruitful and multiply (Gen. 1.28), and the covenant promise that Abraham would be the father of many people, and would bless many nations, and would have a promised land (Gen. 12.1-3; 15.5, 13-14). In Exodus, we see progress towards at least two of these goals.

Shiphrah and Puah's title can be translated as 'Hebrew midwives' or 'midwives of the Hebrews', so some have suggested they may even be Egyptian, yet their names seem Semitic (the later name Sapphira in Acts 5.1 comes from the same Semitic root at Shiphrah.) Since only two midwives could perhaps not attend to such a large and active population, it may be that they were the heads of the guild of midwives.

They are remembered by midwives as examples of the sacred trust of healers, and of a commitment to follow their consciences over propaganda and threatening power.

See also COVENANT; EXODUS; MOSES; PHARAOH [GK]

Shofar. 'Ram's horn', derived from a Semitic root (Akkadian *sapparum*, 'wild sheep' or 'goat'). *Shofar* is found 72 times in the OT. Its earliest appearance is in Exodus (19.16, 19.19, 20.15), at Sinai just prior to the receiving of the commandments. Here, the *shofar*'s blast invokes a sense of awe and mystery. The word appears twice in one verse in Leviticus (25.9) where it announces the new month, the forerunner of Rosh Hashanna and Yom Kippur, as well as the 'release' of the Jubilee year.

It next appears in Joshua (6.4-6, 8-9, 13, 16, 20); the priests march around the city walls seven times, continually blowing the *shofar*. This depicts a ritualistic use of the *shofar*; God gave the command to blow it and the players were priests. The *shofar* has a primitive and almost animalistic sound, but it does not have the power or volume of a trumpet. This is the only place where priests are the ones playing the *shofar*; generally their role is to play the trumpet.

The *shofar* appears again Judges (6.34, 7.8, 16, 18-20, 22). In 6.34, the *shofar* is sounded as a rallying call to battle. In chap. 7, 300 men blow the *shofar* and in addition to being a war cry, this has the mysterious effect on the enemy camp of causing men to turn against one another. For those familiar with the sound of the *shofar*, 300 *shofarot* blasted simultaneously would be both eerie and intimidating.

Other instances of the *shofar*'s use as a herald are in the books of Samuel (1 Sam. 13.3; 2 Sam. 2.28, 6.15, 15.10, 18.16, 20.1, 22) and Kings (1 Kgs 1.34, 39, 41; 2 Kgs 9.13). The use in these passages encompasses proclamations of battle, victory, and kingship.

The *shofar* also appears in several prophetic texts (Isa. 18.3, 27.13, 58.1; Jer. 4.5, 19, 21, 6.1, 17, 42.14, 51.27; Ezek. 33.3-6; Hos. 5.8, 8.1; Joel 2.1-2, 15; Amos 3.6; Zeph. 1.16, Zech. 9.14). Its use there is usually symbolic or metaphoric; in one case God himself blows the horn (Zech. 9.14). The *shofar* is understood, in these texts, to represent an important signal. The word has a similar metaphoric or symbolic meaning in several Psalms (47.6, 81.4, 98.6, 150.3).

The *shofar* can be seen as a symbol of Judaism in the archeological record of the early centuries CE (for example, the Capernaum synagogue of the first century CE; Ephesus of the second–third centuries; Rome, second–fifth centuries). Because of its importance in ritual life, the *shofar* has been a popular motif in Jewish ceremonial and decorative art of every era. The roles of the *shofar* and trumpet seem to have become reversed at some point; the Talmud says 'what was called a trumpet has become a Shofar, and what was called a Shofar has become a trumpet' (*Shabbat* 36a). The *shofar* eventually took on the ceremonial function originally performed by the trumpet. Only after the *shofar* was taken into the service of the Second Temple did its sound assume spiritual significance. It retains that significance up to the present: its evocative sound during services for Rosh Hashanna and at the conclusion of Yom Kippur are the only living echo of ancient Israel. The *shofar* has never been modified; the instrument used today is unchanged from its biblical progenitor.

Composer George Crumb (1929–) included a shofar in his song setting of 'Joshua Fit de Battle of Jerico', found in Vol. 2 of *Selections from American Songbooks* for baritone, amplified piano, and percussion (2003). This is probably the only place the shofar is blown in a non-liturgical setting.

See also TRUMPET [HL]

Shulamite. From the Hebrew *haššûllammît*, 'the Shulammite' or 'the Shulamite'. This appellation refers to the anonymous woman in Song 6.13–7.9 in most English translations which follow the LXX chapter and verse division. In the Masoretic Text, the standard edition of the Hebrew Bible, this section begins a new chapter and comprises Song 7.1-10.

Four suggestions have been made as to the puzzling identity of the Shulammite: (1) as a feminine version of Solomon, which is used to refer to the man in Song 1.5; 3.7, 9, 11; 8.11, 12; (2) as a variant of *šûnammît,* the people of Shunem in the Jezreel plain, and especially in relation with Abishag, the beautiful Shunammite who ministered to King David in his old age (1 Kgs 1.1-4, 15; 2.12-25); (3) as a conflation of the name of the war goddess '*Shulmânîtu*' (Ishtar) and the '*Shunammite*'; and (4) as a noun derived from the root *šlm,* meaning 'the perfect one' or 'the peaceable one'. Since there is no consensus yet on this debate, other scholars prefer to transliterate the term rather than translate it.

As part of the Song of Songs, this text has been interpreted allegorically in medieval times. For instance, the Jewish commentator Rashi (1040–1105) understands *haššûllammît* in cultic and didactic ways; the Christian theologian Honorius of Autun (d. 1151) regards the woman as the primitive church and also relates her to Mary, the mother of Jesus; and Nicolas of Lyra (1270–1349), a Franciscan, associates the Shulammite with both the church and Christ. Modern interpretations have also looked at *haššûllamît* from literary, ANE, social science, psychological, political, and feminist perspectives. For example, Carol Meyer highlights the empowerment of the woman by investigating its faunal, military and agricultural imageries, while Athalya Brenner compares the *šûllammît* realistically to a woman who is considered a 'mixed bag', one who dances suggestively but not necessarily aesthetically captivating.

The rich imagery that portrays the Shulammite has also widely influenced literature, music, arts and liturgy. Examples of these are Abraham Goldfaden's Yiddish operetta, *Shulamit* (1880); Julius Zeyer's Czech drama *Sulamit* (1883); Alexander Ivanovich Kuprin's Russian romance, *Sulamif* (1923), and Arturo Capdevila's Argentinian play, *La Sulamita* (1916). Visual representations of the Shulammite include paintings by Albert Joseph Moore (1864) and Marc Chagall (1965–1966) as well as illustrations by Zeev Rabban in the book *Song of Songs* (1923). Because *Song of Songs* is deemed as an allegory of God's love for Israel, Sephardic and Mizrahi Jews read the book on Sabbath eve. Most traditional Jews also read it on the Sabbath of Chol HaMoed during Passover, or on the seventh day of the holiday, as a remembrance of their 'romance' with God which began in the Exodus story.

Recommended reading. Black, Fiona C. 'Unlikely Bedfellows: Allegorical and Feminist Readings of Song of Songs 7:1-8'. In *Song of Songs*. Feminist Companion to the Bible (Second Series). Ed. Athalya Brenner and Carole R. Fontaine. Pp. 104-29. Sheffield: Sheffield Academic Press, 2000. Exum, J. Cheryl. *Song of Songs*. Old Testament Library. Louisville, KY: Westminster John Knox, 2005.

See also SABBATH; SEPTUAGINT; SONG OF SOLOMON, SONGS [MARICELSI]

Shroud. The Shroud of Jesus was the burial cloth in which his body was wrapped after the crucifixion, after which it was taken to the tomb, and remained there until the resurrection. The existence of the Shroud is mentioned in all four Gospels (Matt. 27.59, Mark 16.46, Luke 23.53, and John 19.40), which refer to a 'linen cloth', with Matthew adding that the cloth was 'clean', and John mentioning 'cloths' (plural). John also notes an important extra piece of information that when Simon Peter and another disciple entered the empty tomb after the resurrection, they saw 'the linen wrappings lying there. And the napkin that was about his head, not lying with the linen clothes, but wrapped together in a place by itself' (20.6-7).

It appears that in about 1355, a nobleman in southern France, Geoffrey de Charny, publically displayed when he claimed was the Shroud of Jesus. He had taken part in a Crusade in 1345, and spent some years as a prisoner in England, before returning to his estates and being killed at the Battle of Poitiers in 1356. His widow subsequently displayed the Shroud, and it was shown on a number of later documented occasions, being moved to Turin in 1578 and was later owned by the House of Savoy, who became Kings of Italy. Because it has been held in Turin, it is often known as the Turin Shroud. In 1898, when Secondo Pia photographed the Shroud, he saw on the negatives the image of a head, and this has led to much speculation about the cloth.

There has been a vast body of books, magazine and newspaper articles about the validity of the Turin Shroud, with the historian Ian Wilson being able to argue persuasively that the Shroud might have been the Mandylion (a miraculous image of the face of Jesus associated with Abgar the Black of Edessa), which was held in Constantinople prior to its sacking in 1204. There was an attempt to disprove the Shroud with radio-carbon dating, but this method of testing was shown to have had major flaws by writers Holger Kersten and Elmar R. Gruber. Lynn Picknett and Clive Prince, in their book *Turin Shroud—In Whose Image?* (1994) claimed that the image on the Shroud was made by a photographic process by Leonardo da Vinci, but that it might have the face of Jesus, his head having possibly been preserved by the Knights Templar.

Whatever the truth or otherwise of these many theories over the Turin Shroud, the Mandylion and the Shroud have both hugely influenced our view of Jesus. Whereas some very early representations of Jesus had him clean-shaven, and very 'Roman' in his appearance, the finding of the Mandylion led to the portrayal of Jesus as tall and bearded, and this has come to represent the image of Jesus that has appeared in most books and paintings since medieval times.

See also PASSION [JC]

Sickness. Although the Bible mentions a wide variety of sicknesses, few are described in detail, and many illnesses are categorized under generic terms such as leprosy. Illnesses described range from acute sicknesses such as fever, abscesses, diarrhea, and stroke to chronic sicknesses such as cancer, gout, menstrual bleeding, scurvy, paralysis, blindness, deafness, and leprosy and other ailments of the skin. A theme in both the OT and NT is that sickness is brought upon the sinner, hence healing can only come from God responding to true repentance. Faith in God's healing power is the means by which mental illness, brought about by demons, is eradicated.

In the OT, illness is not only a product of life and age but of sin as well. The Hebrew word for sickness is *machalah*. In Exodus 15, God promises to keep sicknesses from the children of Israel as long as they abide by the covenant. In 2 Chronicles, God smote King Jehoram with a disease of the bowels. With God's permission, Satan brought about a variety of plagues, including skin sores, upon Job as a means to test his faith. Indeed, sores, abscesses, and other skin diseases figure prominently in the OT; Jewish law required quarantining the person with such skin sicknesses, and prayers for healing. In Leviticus, where leprosy and skin ailments are described in detail, few remedies, save folk remedies, are provided for the disease. Although the OT emphasizes that healing is in God's hands, some cures or treatments are briefly described. For example, when King Hezekiah was dying of an abscess (Isaiah 38), Isaiah prescribed a poultice made of a cake of figs. Barley was also used in poultices. Skin ailments were treated with olive oil, balsam and balm of Gilead. One treatment for fever was fasting; another was sweating.

Sicknesses in the NT are similarly described as the result of human frailty or sin, and very few cures are offered. The Greek word for sickness is *astheneia*; another word used to describe sickness is *nosos*, literally 'malady'. Most often in the NT, Jesus or his disciples heal the sick through prayer or miracles; in Luke 10.9, Jesus commands his disciples to heal the sick when they evangelize from town to town. Jesus himself drew huge crowds to hear him preach and to have their sicknesses healed by his words or touch. The people healed by Jesus felt his power (e.g., Mark 3.15; 5.30; Matt. 10.1; Luke 5.17; 8.46; 9.1), the power of God's grace and love, coming into them; if physical healing occurred, so did spiritual and emotional healing.

Sickness as a result of sin and the inadequacy of physician's remedies is the theme of Christian Science, founded by Mary Baker Eddy in 1875.

Recommended reading. Rosner, Fred. *Encyclopedia of Medicine in the Bible and the Talmud.* Lanham, MD: Jason Aronson, 2000.

See also BALM OF GILEAD; LEPROSY; OIL; PHYSICIAN; SICKNESS UNTO DEATH [RL]

Sickness unto death. The phrase 'sickness unto death' comes from the KJV. It is a fairly literal translation of words Jesus addresses to his disciples in John when he first hears of the illness of his friend, Lazarus (11.4). The Greek words are: *hautē hē astheneia ouk estin,* 'this illness is not towards death'. The problem is that, in the narrative, Lazarus literally does die, as Jesus informs his disciples two days later (11.11-13). When he arrives at Bethany, near Jerusalem, Jesus finds that Lazarus has been buried for four days. Despite this, he commands the tomb to be opened and calls Lazarus forth to life (11.38-44).

In this sense, the phrase is an ambiguous one. What is the meaning of Jesus' statement that Lazarus's sickness is not 'unto death'? A clue lies in other language and imagery that the Johannine Jesus uses in the same context. Twice in the story Jesus speaks of Lazarus's illness and death as revealing the glory of God, once at the beginning of the story and once towards the end (11.4, 40). In John's language, 'glory' means the radiance of God's life-giving presence. In this story, Jesus shows himself to be 'the resurrection and the life' (11.25-26); not just a healer but one who possesses divine authority over life and death. In this way, for John, God's glory shines forth in Jesus raising Lazarus to life. Death may seem at first to take Lazarus, but the grip of death is reversed. Of course, John is aware that Lazarus is still mortal, as is apparent in the later plot of the authorities to kill him (12.9-11). In this sense, 'death' perhaps also a symbolic meaning in this context. Lazarus's ultimate destiny is life, which has the last word in this Gospel. For John, the raising of Lazarus is thus a sign pointing to the theme of life which is bound up in Jesus' identity in this Gospel.

Writing on this passage, the early theologians of the church argue that God does not cause Lazarus's illness in order to make a display of divine power. Rather, God turns natural causes into an expression of glory by reversing death and bringing life from death.

The phrase 'sickness unto death' is also the title of a book written by Danish philosopher Søren Kierkegaard (1849). Kierkegaard interprets the phrase metaphorically as referring to original sin rather than literal death. For him, sin is the failure to become a true individual, a view that influenced later existentialist philosophers. For Kierkegaard, the ultimate manifestation of such failure is despair. Thus, for him, the 'sickness unto death', to be avoided above all else, is the sin of despair, a condition from which only genuine religious faith can protect.

The phrase 'sickness unto death' is no longer used in modern translations of the Bible and is generally seen as archaic, although it was the translation adopted by the RSV as late as 1952. One modern translation suggests, 'This illness isn't fatal' (Common English Bible, New Testament, 2010), which obliterates some of the ambiguity of 'sickness unto death'. The NRSV translates the same words as 'This illness does not lead to death', a translation that sufficiently captures the meaning of the Greek, but perhaps loses some of the ambiguity in the Johannine text.

See also LAZARUS; SICKNESS [DL]

Sidon (see Tyre and Sidon).

Sign. A sign points to or represents something, usually much larger and more important than itself. Biblical signs often point to the wondrous acts of God.

At least seven Hebrew words for sign are used in the OT. They have many meanings referring to marks of identity, statements, warnings, omens, proofs, lessons, testimonies, and assurances.

In general, the words for sign point to the mighty acts of God such as the miracles by which God delivered the Hebrews from bondage in Egypt (Exod. 7.3) The blood on the lintels of houses of the Hebrews was a sign a sign of God's mercy to the Israelites. The rainbow was set as a sign of assurance that the world would not be destroyed by flood again (Gen. 9.12-12). Circumcision was given as a divine sign.

The world *oth* ('appointed') is used of signs that have been appointed to a certain task. It is the most common Hebrew word for sign. In Gen. 1.14, God appointed lights in the sky for signs and for seasons. The word *debar* ('word') is used in Ps. 105.27 for the subject matter of a sign.

Daniel uses the word *athin* ('signs') three times (4.2-3; 6.27) to denote the signs and wonders done by God. The word *mopheth* ('wonders') is translated as sign in 1 Kgs 12.3, 5 and elsewhere for the visible manifestation of the work that God is doing.

Numbers 26.20 uses the Hebrew word *nes* for a banner or ensign. Jeremiah 6.1 uses the word *maseth* for a signal. Ezekiel 39.15 uses the word *tsiyyun* for a monument that functions as a sign.

NT Greek uses *sēmeion* to denote a sign, a mark, a signal. Many of the references to sign in the Gospels are to the signs sought by a wicked and perverse generation (Matt. 12.38-39; 16.1, 3-4; Mark 8.12-13; Luke 11.16, 29-30). Jesus found those who were seeking signs to be lacking in faith. Signs and wonders done by false prophets and deceivers are also cited and denounced.

False signs include those denounced as lying wonders or spectacles, e.g., the marvels of the Egyptian priests in competition with Moses. Warnings are given against false messiahs who show great signs and wonders (Matt. 24.24). The 'lawless one' is also to be accompanied by signs that are lying wonders who will deceive people into believing what is false (2 Thess. 2.7-12). Revelation refers to 'signs', miraculous and astral, portending the last things (12.1, 3; 13.13, 14; 15.1; 16.14; 19.20).

Jesus' miracles in John were signs of divine presence and aids to those with faith. Peter in his Pentecost sermon uses *sēmeion* for the signs and wonders prophesied by Joel (Acts 2.19). The word is also used of the signs and wonders done by the apostles (Acts 4.30).

Within the church, baptism is seen as an outward sign of the inward work of regenerating grace by the Holy Spirit. The Lord's Supper is also a sign of the Lord's death until his return.

The phrase 'signs and wonders' has been used frequently in literature. Its medieval use as the Christian marvelous was diminished in the modern era, but it is still used eschatologically to refer as a sign of the times that refers to the end of the age.

Recommended reading. Aichele, George. *Sign, Text, Scripture: Semiotics and the Bible*. New York: Continuum, 1997. Connelly, Douglas. *Miracles: Signs of God's Glory*. Downers Grove, IL: InterVarsity, 1999. Exum, J. Cheryl. *Signs and Wonders: Biblical Texts in Literary Focus*. Atlanta: Scholars Press, 1989.

See also APOCALYPSE/APOCALYPTIC; JOHN, GOSPEL OF; MIRACLES; SIGNS OF THE TIMES; SIGNS AND WONDERS [AJW]

Signs of the Times. The exact phrase *ta sēmeia tōn kairōn* appears only in Matt. 16.3, while variations and implications of the phrase appear elsewhere. The Matt. 16.3 reference is somewhat unique in that it speaks primarily to Jesus' earthly ministry as God's messiah, whereas the focus elsewhere is on the final return of Christ. Accordingly, the variations and implications of this phrase appear in prophecies or general statements about the events surrounding that final return.

In Matthew 24, Jesus responds to his disciples who ask, 'what will be the sign of your coming and of the end of the age?' (24.3) with an apparent list of 'signs'—e.g., false messiahs, national conflicts, famines, earthquakes, rampant lawlessness. In 1 Thessalonians, Paul refers to various 'times and seasons' (5.1) related to the return of Christ, although he does not elaborate on what these entail. However, he does mention the events that immediately precede the final return of Christ—i.e., a divine shout, the archangel's call, blasting of God's trumpet, Christ's descent from heaven, resurrection of the dead, the (so-called) rapture, and being with Jesus for eternity (1 Thess. 4.16-17). The point of this description shows the rapid speed with which the events occur, which fits well with the statement that 'the day of the Lord will be like a thief in the night' (1 Thess. 5.2; cf. 1 Cor. 15.50-53).

The details of 2 Thess. 2.1-12 could be read as fleshing out Paul's obscure 'times and seasons' comment in 1 Thess. 5.1. In 2 Thessalonians 2, the description includes: massive apostasy, emergence of the man of lawlessness, defilement of the temple, the lawless one's delusions of grandeur, victorious return of Christ, defeat of Satan, etc.

Given this meaning and usage, it is no wonder that the phrase in modern culture often appears in many 'doom and gloom' predictions about the world. Various forms of media are available that speak to the general notion of 'signs of the times' or particular 'signs' that suggest the imminent end of the world. The widely sold book by Hal Lindsay, *The Late Great Planet Earth* (1970), the recent award-winning film, *2012* (2009), the rather humorous book by Patricia Carlin, *How to Tell If Your Boyfriend Is the Antichrist: And If He Is, Should You Break Up With Him?* (2007), and websites devoted to predicting the timing of the rapture based on current world events (www.raptureready.com) are examples of this availability. All of these 'doom and gloom' predictions related to the 'signs of the times' seem to miss the fundamental meaning to the biblical concept. The 'signs' are largely general in nature and not specific to a particular place, time or event. Moreover, the 'signs' are meant to bring hope and not despair. A central function of the 'signs' is to remind believers that even though such evil and painful and destructive times exist now, there will come a time when such things will no longer exist. More generally, in secular speech, the phrase refers to anything expressive of contemporary attitudes, events, etc.

See also APOCALYPTIC; RAPTURE; SIGNS; SIGNS AND WONDERS [CSS]

Signs and wonders. Originating in the OT and usually preceded by the descriptor 'miraculous' the idiom 'signs and wonders' was generally associated with the events relating to the Exodus from Egypt (Exod. 7.3; Deut. 4.34; 6.22; Neh. 9.10; Ps. 135.9). In the NT, Jesus is credited once with pejoratively using the phrase as an indication of someone with a weaker faith (John 4.48). But its current popular appeal is attributed to the four references in the book of Acts (Acts 4.30, 5.12, 14.3, 15.12). While the Bible is vague in explaining their nature contextually they authenticate the work of the disciples as a testimony to the divinity of Christ. It is generally believed that these signs and wonders included but were not limited to things such as speaking in tongues, healing, prophecy, miracles of nature and the discernment of spirits.

By the fourth century, attention to signs and wonders waned by attempts to solidify church orthodoxy. Under the reign of Constantine the Great, Christianity was legalized. No longer a faith on the move with the possibility of reinventing itself, it defined itself with formal creeds. Similarly, the canonization of the NT further diminished the need for extracurricular spiritual activity. In time, many would argue that Paul had this in mind when he foretold that when the 'complete comes, the partial will come to an end' (1 Cor. 13.8-10)—where 'partial' refers to signs and wonders.

The fourth century also witnessed the first notable Christian execution by Christians for wrong belief and practice. The issues leading to the death of Priscillian of Avila are not important here, but the chilling effect that it had on any openness to signs and wonders was substantial.

Things remained relatively unchanged until the early part of the twentieth century when a group self-identified as Pentecostals revived the concept of signs and wonders. Equating them with the charismatic gifts in 1 Corinthians 12–14 these religious enthusiasts renewed world-wide attention to the idea of miraculous signs and wonders in particular speaking in other tongues and gifts of healing.

By the middle of the twentieth century, it was not long before this enthusiasm spread into long established church organizations and many 'Charismatic' Catholics, Lutherans and Anglicans joined the parade and began extolling the virtues of signs and wonders even if the majority continued to be resistant to the new Pentecostal emphasis.

In 1982, John Wimber, a conservative evangelical, began teaching a course entitled, 'Signs and Wonders' at the prestigious Fuller Theological Seminary. The course quickly became the most popular, and the most controversial course offered on campus, because Wimber actively pursued in class the demonstration of signs and wonders. In a short time, the course spilled outside the classroom and Wimber found himself at the head of a new and growing denomination called Vineyard, with signs and wonders as its flagship identity.

In 1995, signs and wonders gained international attention when a Vineyard church in Toronto (Toronto Airport Christian Fellowship, TACF) experienced as part of their worship a range of spiritual manifestations that while not completely novel, stretched the limits of what even Wimber had envisioned. Followers were seen falling, weeping, laughing, grunting all in the name of the SW. Wimber eventually withdrew their membership status in Vineyard but the Toronto experience continues to dominate as a leading edge in identification with the phenomenon.

See also SIGNS; SPIRITUAL GIFTS; TONGUES, SPEAKING IN [RFH]

Silas. The person known as Silas first appears in the book of Acts. The intention of the author is to continue the narrative begun in Luke, this time following the disciples of Jesus as they spread the message of his resurrection to all of Judea and beyond into the wider Greco-Roman world. Silas is present in the narrative from Acts 15.22–18.15.

In Acts 15, many of the leaders of the nascent church have met to discuss the issue of non-Jews joining their gatherings. Silas and other 'leading men among the brothers' are selected to carry a letter of instruction and goodwill to the church in the city of Antioch. Acts 15.32 states that Silas was a prophet who encouraged and strengthened the Antiochene congregation. The tradition of Silas as a prophet is reiterated in Eusebius's (c. 260–341 CE) *Church History* 5; 17.3.

Silas then accompanies Paul, also called Saul, as he revisits churches in what is now modern Turkey (Asia Minor) and Greece. In Philippi, a leading Roman city, both are arrested and beaten. Upon their release, they demand an apology for their shameful treatment, claiming to be Roman citizens.

In the NT letters 2 Corinthians (1.19), 1 and 2 Thessalonians (1 Thess. 1.1; 2 Thess. 1.1), and 1 Peter (5.12), reference is made to 'Silvanus', a companion of Paul and amanuensis for Peter. Today, many assume that Silas and Silvanus are one in the same. The difference in name is thought to be related to hellenization or latinization of an Aramaic or Hebrew name, a theory possibly traced to Jerome (c. 347–420). However, Pseudo-Hippolytus (*On the Apostles and Disciples*) says that Silas became the bishop of Corinth and Silvanus bishop of Thessalonica.

It is the story of Paul and Silas's prison stay in Acts 16 that is evoked by modern artists. After the angry crowd and soldiers beat and arrest them in Philippi, Paul and Silas are chained in the inner jail. At about midnight, the other prisoners hear them praying and singing hymns to God. Although a sudden earthquake causes the prison doors to open and their chains to unfasten, the prisoners remain in their places, preventing the required death of the jailer. Overwhelmed, the jailer falls before Paul and Silas, requesting their counsel for conversion.

The pericope is the subject of a nineteenth-century painting by American artist Washington Allston, Victorian era illustrator William Hatherell, and English painter James Thornhill. Additionally, it is the subject of a short poem by the nineteenth-century American poet Emily Dickinson, and a song entitled 'Paul and Silas' by the modern rock band Phish.

Silas is the subject of religious fiction books *The Scribe: Silas* by Francine Rivers and *The Silas Diary* by Gene Edwards. In the popular novel *The DaVinci Code* by Dan Brown, Silas is the name of the albino, masochistic monk who commits several murders in the story.

See also ACTS OF THE APOSTLES; PAUL; PHILIPPI [CH]

Siloam. Hebrew *šilōaḥ*; Greek *silōam*, refers to a location at the southern end of the old City of David (the earliest section of Jerusalem). In the Bible, there are a number of references to this location which was primarily known for its water storage reservoirs. Before the time of King Hezekiah water from the Gihon spring (1 Kgs 1.33, 38, 45) in the Kidron valley was brought to Siloam by a series of channels and aqueducts (Neh. 3.15; Isa. 8.6; 22.11). Hezekiah renovated this system by digging a tunnel through the hillside from the Gihon on the east side of Jerusalem to Siloam on the south side (2 Kgs 20.20; 2 Chron. 32.30). Once completed, water flowed from the Gihon spring through the hill until it emerged and flowed into the reservoirs at Siloam. In 1880, archaeologists discovered an inscription inside Hezekiah's tunnel written in an archaic form of

Hebrew which dates to the eighth century BCE. This inscription, called the Siloam Inscription, records how the tunnel was carved by workers digging at either end until they met in the middle.

In the Gospels, Siloam is mentioned twice. In Luke 13.4, Jesus refers to an incident where 18 people are killed when 'the tower of Siloam fell on them'. Since Luke tells us nothing more it is impossible to determine the location and nature of this tower. The tower referred to may have been a columbarium—a dovecote used for raising pigeons. The second reference to Siloam is in John 9.1-12. In this passage Jesus meets a man who was born blind. He tells the man to wash in the pool of Siloam and then he will be able to see. As with Luke, John assumes that the reader is familiar with this location and does not describe it any further.

In 333 CE, a Christian pilgrim from Bordeaux traveled to Jerusalem and reported seeing a four-sided colonnade around the pool of Siloam. For centuries the location of the Siloam pool was usually associated with a small reservoir near a fifth-century church in southern Jerusalem. In June 2004, during some construction work on a modern water pipe, archaeologists discovered the remains of a large stepped pool dating from the first century CE. This massive pool is 225 feet long and is located a short distance southeast of the traditional site of the Siloam Pool. Scholars now believe that this newly discovered pool is the authentic Pool of Siloam where Jesus is said to have healed the blind man.

Siloam has been mentioned a number of times in western literature. Augustine used the pool as an analogy to describe the commissioning of Christian apostles (*Sermo*, 135.1-2). John Milton also refers to 'Siloa's Brook' in connection with the oracle of God at the beginning of *Paradise Lost* (1.10-13). Bishop Reginald Heber spoke of the peace of Siloam in his 1811 hymn, 'By Cool Siloam's Shady Rill'. Finally, John Greenleaf Whittier used the imagery of Siloam in several of his poems, including 'To the Memory of Thomas Shipley' and 'The Preacher', which was dedicated to the famous eighteenth-century evangelist, George Whitefield.

Recommended reading. Elitzur, Yoel. 'The Siloam Pool—'Solomon's Pool'—Was a Swimming Pool'. *Palestine Exploration Quarterly* 140 (2008) 17-25. Shanks, Hershel. 'The Siloam Pool: Where Jesus Cured the Blind Man'. *Biblical Archaeology Review* (September–October 2005) 16-23.

See also HEZEKIAH; JERUSALEM; WATER; WELL

[EM]

Simeon (see Twelve Tribes of Israel).

Simeon, prophet. Simeon is a significant religious figure found only in Luke (2.25-35). He is not named as a prophet or a priest of the Jerusalem temple, although in Luke's description of him he acts characteristically as both priest and prophet. Simeon circumcises the infant Jesus and is described as righteous, devout and anticipating the divine liberation of Israel from Rome (v. 25). Luke describes Simeon as filled with the Holy Spirit and similarly identifies Jesus as a divine sign (vv. 26-27, 34). This is Luke's way of consolidating the reader's understanding that Jesus is the Christ—divinely appointed from the beginning, the infancy narratives and early childhood anticipating the nature and extent of his ministry. That Jesus is brought to the temple in conformity with the Torah is a telling observation from Luke who is concerned to situate Jesus as the Messiah who fulfils Jewish hopes and is also the means of universal Gentile inclusion.

Whereas Matthew expresses Jewish hope in terms of OT prophecy, Luke does so by means of canticles more accessible to a Gentile readership—songs of praise not taken directly from scripture but composed of biblical themes pointing again to Luke's comprehensive understanding of salvation which includes Jews and Gentiles, men and women, without regard—'all peoples' (Luke 2.31-32).

Although Jesus is presented in the temple by both his mother and father, Joseph is a secondary figure for Luke. Mary is the dominant personality in the narrative. Simeon blesses the parents but addresses himself to Mary in the second prophetic utterance (2.33-35). In contrast to the first prophecy (2.29-32), which expresses Simeon's praise, the second is more ominous. Accordingly, the infant Jesus will mature and bring to light the true condition of people, something not welcomed by everyone—in effect, the messianic age will result in 'the falling and rising of many' (2.34). It will also be costly, in that Mary will experience the pain of loss in her motherhood—'and a sword will pierce your own soul too' (2.35). This is generally understood to foreshadow Jesus' crucifixion.

The unique prophetic role assigned to Simeon is a favorite subject of among early modern and Renaissance painters such as Rembrandt, Raphael, Aert de Gelder, Fabriano, and Hans Holbein. The Orthodox Church with its culture of iconography sees in Simeon the 'receiver of God' since Simeon holds Jesus during the Temple scene. Contemporary artists such as Ron DiCianni and Carolyn Sylvester are more apt to explore the psychological dimensions of the encounter with Simeon. This involves reading Simeon's reactions to the infant Jesus in terms of emotional joy and celebration rather than the religiously contemplative tone of Renaissance art.

The liturgy of the Anglican Church (and others), uses the words of Simeon in Evening Prayer in the *Nunc Dimittis*. Simeon is also a model of contemporary poetic contemplation. T.S. Eliot (quoting almost verbatim from Lancelot Andrewes's *Christmas Sermon*) in *A Song for Simeon* declares:

> Let the Infant, the still unspeaking and unspoken Word,
> Grant Israel's consolation
> To one who has eighty years and no to-morrow.

Similarly, the English divine, John Donne (1626, *Sermon IV*) expresses the idea of Simeon as prophetic archetype who sees beyond the moment to the fulfillment of God's kingdom. Simeon becomes the model believer whose destiny is shaped by Christ, and understands the significance of God's deliverance yet without laying claim to absolute knowledge of final things.

See also LUKE, GOSPEL OF; MARY, MOTHER OF JESUS; NUNC DIMITTIS; PROPHECY, PROPHET [JKS]

Simon Peter (see Peter).

Simon of Cyrene. The character Simon of Cyrene appears in the synoptic Gospels (Matt. 27.32; Mark 15.21; Luke 23.21) where he is pressed into bearing the cross of Jesus on the way to the crucifixion. This has become the first stop in the Catholic Lenten observance of the Stations of the Cross, and is an important element in the Gospel passion narratives. In many accounts of the crucifixion, Simon is portrayed as a black African—Cyrene being a Mediterranean port located on in modern-day Libya, east of Benghazi and west of Tobruk. However some scholars have suggested that he may not have been African as there was a large Jewish community in the port, with many settling there during the reign of Ptolemy Soter (reigned 323–285 BCE). The Cyrenians had their own synagogue in Jerusalem, and it is quite possible that Simon was visiting Jerusalem for the Passover because of his Jewish ancestry. The name Simon does not necessarily prove that the man was Jewish, as it could have easily been a name he used in Jerusalem or given to him by the writers of the Gospels. It is not clear whether Simon was given the job of helping Jesus with the cross because he was a sympathizer, or whether, as seems more probable, he was a bystander. There are also Gnostic traditions which that Simon crucified instead of Jesus (e.g., the *Second Treatise of the Great Seth*).

Mark states that Simon was the 'father of Alexander and Rufus' (15.21), and some have sought to identify one of his sons as the Rufus mentioned by Paul in Rom. 16.13, or have made a connection with the 'men of Cyrene' who preached Christianity to the Greeks in Acts (11.20). By tradition, Rufus and Alexander, the sons of Simon, became missionaries and the fact that they are referred to in Mark suggests that they might have been well known to Christians in Rome. In 1941 in the Kidron Valley, archaeologists located a burial cave which had an ossuary dated to before 70 CE with the Greek inscription 'Alexander, son of Simon'. Both names are common, but some speculated that it might be the tomb of the son of Simon of Cyrene.

Simon of Cyrene has appeared in most of the films about Jesus; he was played by William Boyd in *The King of Kings* (1927). He was played by Rafael Luis Calvo in *King of Kings* (1961); by Sidney Poitier in *The Greatest Story Ever Told* (1965), and by Jarreth J. Merz in *The Passion of the Christ* (2004). The New York poet Ridgely Torrence wrote a play called *Simon the Cyrenian* (1917), with the African American singer and actor Paul Robeson playing him in the 1920 YWCA production directed by Dora Cole, sister of Bob Cole. He also appears on a postage stamp issued by Jordan in 1966 where he resembles a medieval farmer rather than an African or North African Jew. Mention should also be made of the Cyrenian (or Simonian) movement established in the British Isles that worked to help the homeless and other disadvantaged on the principle of sharing the burdens of the unfortunate.

See also CROSS/CRUCIFIXION OF CHRIST; PASSION NARRATIVE [JC]

Simon Magus. A revered traveling magician of the first century CE affectionately known by the people of Samaria as 'the Great Power'.

The earliest extant witness to Simon Magus is found in Acts 8.4-25, where he appears to represent the first great obstacle to the spreading of the apostolic message beyond the boundaries of Jerusalem. There is little agreement among scholars regarding the creative liberties the Lukan author has taken with his source material in the composition of this narrative; however, in its final form the narrative, although initially beginning with a recap of Philip's successful missionary exploits to Samaria, eventually climaxes in what amounts to a conflict between two Simons—Simon Magus (the Great Power) and Simon Peter (the super-apostle who had walked with Jesus).

The main source of tension occurs when the magician, impressed by the miraculous demonstrations of the apostles, sought to buy the power of the Holy Spirit. Enraged by this first act of 'simony' (the term used to describe the sale of ecclesiastical offices), Peter then harshly rebuked his opponent for what he perceived to be his inherent wickedness. In this respect, the account of Simon Magus is the first of many related accounts in Acts that clearly differentiate between magic (a commercial enterprise) and the power of the Holy Spirit (see also the episodes of Elymas (13.4-12), the fortune-telling slave-girl (16.16-24), and the sons of Sceva (19.11-20).

Though the figure of Simon the Magician appears only briefly in the book of Acts, the description of his character and activities was greatly expanded (and darkened) by a number of early Christian writers such as Justin, Irenaeus, Hippolytus, and Epiphanius who consistently branded him as a charlatan and a heretic, and his followers as a serious threat to genuine Christianity. In addition to these, the rivalry between Peter and Simon is renewed and expanded in legendary form in the *Acts of Peter*, which culminates in the depiction of Simon Magus falling to his dishonorable death after a botched attempt to mimic the ascension of Christ. A similar version of his death is depicted in the *Acts of Peter and Paul*, captured in a painting by Felippion Lippi in the church of Santa Maria del Carmine in Florence.

In recent years, the image of Simon has been recast or alluded to in a number of audio-visual and literary projects that include: the 1954 movie, *The Silver Chalice*; a series of Simon Magus short stories written by R.L. Tremblay and published in 1997 under the title of *Scroll of Thoth: Simon Magus and the Great Old Ones*; Lynn Pickett and Clive Prince's pseudo-historical book *The Templar Revelation: Secret Guardians of the True Identity of Christ*, which presents Simon as the successor to John the Baptist; and a 1999 film by Ben Hopkins that bears the title *Simon Magus*.

Recommended reading. Haar, Stephen. *Simon Magus: The First Gnostic?* Berlin: Walter de Gruyter, 2003.

See also GNOSTIC; GNOSTICISM; WITCHCRAFT [TB]

Simon the Zealot. Perhaps the most obscure of Jesus' disciples is Simon the 'zealot'. Referred to as a 'zealot' (*zēlotēs*: Luke 6.15; Acts 1.13), Simon is also called *kananaios* (Matt. 10.4; Mark 3.18). Ancient commentators and modern translators have mistakenly translated *kananaios* as 'Canaanite'. Both titles, *zēlotēs* and *kananaios*, stem from the Hebrew word *qana*, meaning 'zealous'. What, then, did Simon's 'zeal' consist in?

Certain scholars postulate that Simon belonged to the 'revolutionary party' (i.e., Josephus's 'Fourth Philosophy': *Jewish War* 2.117-18; *Antiquities* 18.1-10, 23-25). This movement, of which Josephus was critical, comprised two groups who opposed Roman rule in Judea. First, the *sicarii* (or 'dagger-men') assassinated or kidnapped the Jewish ruling elite who cooperated with the Romans, plundering their property (Josephus, *Jewish War* 2.254-57, 264-66; *Antiquities* 20.172, 208-209). Second, the 'zealots' led the Jewish uprising against Rome from the winter of 67-68 CE until their defeat at the siege of Masada in 73 (*Jewish War* 4.135, 138-41; 7.268-70). In Josephus's opinion, this group of 'hotheads' precipitated the tragedy in 70 CE culminating in the Roman destruction of the Jerusalem temple.

Scholars debate whether a 'party' of zealots ever existed at the time of Jesus. Josephus uses the word *zēlotēs* of those who rebelled against Rome from 67/68 CE onwards. Some scholars conclude from this that Simon did not belong to any 'official' revolutionary party — since none existed until 67/68 CE— but simply supported the rising anti-Roman fervor in the early first century.

Other scholars argue that a 'revolutionary party' existed from the time of Judas the Galilean onwards (Josephus, *Antiquities* 18.3-9, 6 CE) until the demise of the movement in 73. These scholars conclude that Simon was a member of this party with strong revolutionary sympathies before his conversion, only to join Jesus' disciples later on. Ironically for Simon, among this group was Matthew the 'tax collector' (Matt. 9.9; 10.3), a hated collaborator with Rome.

However, possibly scholars have drawn the wrong conclusion regarding the meaning of *zēlotēs* in regards to Simon. Simon, the 'zealous one' could just have been 'zealous for the Law'. In other words, he belonged to the 'zeal' tradition of Phinehas (Num. 25.6-13) and the Maccabees (1 Macc. 2.27; cf. 2.24; 26, 50), a tradition with which Paul the Pharisee was intimately familiar (Gal. 1.14; Phil. 3.6).

A second-century church tradition lists Simon among the apostles writing the so-called *Epistula*

Apostolorum ('Epistle of the Apostles'). Later, Isodore, archbishop of Seville (560–636 CE), collected apocryphal anecdotes about Simon in *De Vita et Morte* 5.5 ('Concerning Life and Death'). This is expanded in the legendary work, c. 1260 CE, called *The Golden Legend: The Lives of Saint Simon and Jude*. This purports to describe Simon's evangelism in Egypt and his missionary outreach, accompanied by Jude, in Persia and Armenia, where both were supposedly martyred.

Finally, 'zeal' traditions are still present in the world today. Terrorist movements impose their will upon their enemies through violence and suicide bombings, whereas the 'religious right', with evangelical zeal, attempts to influence governmental policy through various political lobby-groups. The zealot's willingness to go outside the law was well depicted on the screen in Sylvester Stallone's *Rambo* series and, in real life, by the career officer and bureaucrat, Oliver North.

Recommended reading. Horsley, R.A. *Bandits, Prophets, and Messiahs: Popular Movements at the Time of Jesus.* New York: Harper & Row, 1985. Hengel, M. *The Zealots: Investigations into the Jewish Freedom Movement in the Period from Herod I until 70 AD*. Edinburgh: T. & T. Clark, 1989.

See also MACCABEAN MARTYRS; MACCABEES; TAX COLLECTOR; ZEALOTS [JRHA]

Sin. Hebrew, *hata*; Greek, *hamartia*, both connoting missing or failing to hit a target; related are the Hebrew terms *pasha*, 'rebellion', and *avōn*, referring either to an offense, the guilt resulting from it, or its punishment. Generally, biblical language of sin refers to offences against God and against other human beings.

Sin in the OT is conceived in terms of offences against the commandments of Torah that can be rectified through repentance and ritual means, notably the sin offering (Lev. 4.1–6.13; 9.7-11, 22-24; 12.6-8; 15.2, 14, 25-30; 14.19, 31; Num. 6.10-14), especially on the Day of Atonement (Lev. 16); also at annual festivals and priestly consecrations (Num. 28, 29; Exod. 29). In the NT, while sin retains the meaning of offending against God (e.g., Luke 11.3; cf. Matt. 6.12), Jesus' teaching in Mark 7.1-23 portrays sinning as a kind of moral impurity emanating from within the human being that is far more serious than ritual impurity.

In Romans 5–7, Paul portrays sin as a personified force of evil, which, along with death, is an overwhelming power to which all people are vulnerable due to Adam's transgression; Torah cannot permanently rectify sin, but rather convicts human beings of their inability to live up to it. For Paul, only Jesus Christ has the power to liberate humanity from sin's power (Rom. 8.1). For Paul, human acts of righteousness, including Torah obedience, are insufficient to deal with sin; only faith in Christ's ultimate righteousness can justify the believer before God (Rom. 4.5). James 2.14-26 famously takes issue with a simplistic notion of justification by faith, noting that righteous works must complement faith.

Paul's writings provide the scriptural basis for Augustine's doctrine of original sin, meaning a hereditary pollution shared by all human beings after the Fall. Although this doctrine was vigorously opposed by some of Augustine's contemporaries, who held that Adam's sin affected only himself, not all humanity (e.g., Theodore of Mopsuestia, Celestius, Pelagius), the notion of original sin became dominant in western Christianity. Famously, Martin Luther's despair over the impossibility of achieving righteousness before God led him to explicate the doctrine of justification by faith alone through the grace of God. For Luther, human efforts, and especially the sacraments of the church, were insufficient to overcome sin; only faith in the efficacy of Christ's sacrificial death could justify the believer. In modern times, the doctrine of original sin finds a musical retelling in the Eurythmics' song 'Missionary Man' (1986) sung by Annie Lennox.

Catholic teaching has traditionally distinguished between mortal and venial sins. The former are serious sins which, if unrepented, lead to eternal estrangement from God; the latter are 'forgivable', lesser sins which do not lead to damnation. The Catholic Sacrament of Reconciliation (Confession, Penance) provides an opportunity for penitents to confess their sins to a priest, who recommends a penance (including reparations of wrongs committed) and absolves them from their sins. For Protestants, sin is traditionally a personal matter between the believer and God, unmediated by sacramental rites.

In 1999, the Vatican and the Lutheran World Federation adopted a joint statement on justification, bringing Catholic and Lutheran teachings on the efficacy of faith to remedy sin closer. Other Protestant denominations have subsequently followed suit.

Recommended reading. Wyschogrod, Michael. 'Sin and Atonement in Judaism'. In his *Abraham's Promise: Judaism and Jewish–Christian Relations*. Ed. R. Kendall Soulen. Pp. 53-74. Grand Rapids, MI: Eerdmans.

See also ATONEMENT; ATONEMENT, DAY OF; FAITH; FALL, THE; JUSTIFICATION; PURGATORY; REPENTANCE; SIN AGAINST THE HOLY SPIRIT; SIN WILL FIND YOU OUT; SINS OF THE FATHERS [MALB]

Sin against the Holy Spirit. In the synoptic Gospels, Jesus warns of blaspheming against the Holy Spirit. He cautions that although all other sins may be forgiven, the sin against the Spirit is uniquely unforgivable. In Mark (3.22-30) and Matthew (12.22-32), Jesus' warning is addressed to the scribes and Pharisees who reject his miracles, plot to kill him, and accuse him of being empowered by Satan. Placed in the context of Jesus' ministry and miracles, the sin against the Holy Spirit here appears to consist of attributing Jesus' works to the power of evil rather than to the power of the Spirit of God. This sin is unforgivable because it not only rejects the divine nature of Jesus' works but it also aligns God's Spirit with Satan.

Luke 12.4-12 places Jesus' admonition in a different context. It is directed toward Jesus' disciples rather than his opponents, is immediately followed by a prohibition against worry in the face of persecution, and is united with its surrounding verses by a common theme: confession of the divine agents before others (vv. 8, 10-12). The significance of this setting, and especially the fact that Jesus' warning in v. 10 is followed by his words in vv. 11-12, suggests that readers are to interpret the sin against the Spirit in relation to confession and persecution. In this context the blasphemy against the Spirit is best understood as an inadequate response to Christian persecution. It consists of believers renouncing Jesus, and by implication, renouncing the Spirit who empowers him. The seriousness of this act is implied by Jesus' words in v. 4: if believers deny Jesus and the Spirit before others, then Jesus may deny them salvation from the one who has authority to cast them into hell.

The sin against the Holy Spirit has proven somewhat enigmatic to interpreters of scripture. Some interpreters have connected it with the 'sin that is mortal' in 1 John 5.16-17, suggesting that this 'mortal sin' refers to the blasphemy against the Spirit. The *Didache*, an early second-century treatise on Christian teaching, applies this blasphemy to those who reject the authentic prophesies of some traveling prophets (*Did* 11.7). Later interpreters have understood the sin in various ways, including: apostasy, murder, suicide, and the rejection of the Holy Spirit's divinity.

The concept of an unforgivable sin remains a part of western culture. The controversial practice of capital punishment in parts of the United States, for example, suggests that some people believe there are certain crimes that cannot be pardoned. This concept also frequently appears in literature and popular culture, although here it is often employed metaphorically and in ways foreign to the biblical meaning. For example, in *Gone With the Wind* protagonist Scarlett O'Hara is said to have committed 'the one unforgivable sin' in her society: succeeding at business without the help of men. Metaphorical uses such as this indicate that, although the biblical meaning has been lost, the idea of an unforgivable sin possesses such dramatic weight and symbolic flexibility that it has become a staple in Western thought and expression.

Recommended reading. Tipson, Baird'.A Dark Side of Seventeenth-Century English Protestantism: The Sin against the Holy Spirit'. *Harvard Theological Review* 77 (1984) 301-30.

See also BLASPHEMY; HOLY SPIRIT; SATAN; SIN [KDH]

Sin will find you out. This biblical figure of speech connotes the seriousness of sin and its inevitable ramifications. In its original context in Num. 32.23, the sons of Reuben and Gad request the land of Gilead, east of the Jordan, as their homeland, but promise to remain faithful to Israel and to participate in the conquest of Canaan. Moses agrees, but warns that if they do not do as they have promised, they will have sinned against Yahweh, and this sin will surely 'find them out'. More generally, this biblical expression is closely linked to God's warnings related to his peoples' propensity to disobey. Contextually, the biblical narrative recounts God's nature as consistent with his words and he thus requires the same consistency for his people. It is significant that this idiom seems particularly related to sins committed after making a thoughtful affirmation to do otherwise. The literary rhythm of the whole of Numbers 32 finds closure in God's command warning his people to 'do what you have promised' (v. 24).

Other religious traditions express similar concepts. Commonly referred to as karma, both Hinduism and Buddhism maintain an aspect of reciprocity related to wrongdoing, acknowledging the reality that committing a wrongful act, especially when having affirmed otherwise, carries spiritual implications.

In 2006, pop sensation Justin Timberlake released his long awaited album *FutureSex/LoveSounds*. One song on that album which captured the vividness of this biblical expression was 'What Goes Around ... Comes Around'. The lyrics paint a common picture of love gone wrong when one person decides that their promise to be faithful is quickly forgotten for more pleasurable options. At the core of the refrain is a haunting reminder that when you decide to hurt someone that you need to prepare, in due time, to be visited with the same pain since your sin will find you out.

See also RETRIBUTION; SIN; SINS OF THE FATHERS
[DR]

Sinai, Mount. Sinai is used two ways in the OT, either as the desert region of Sinai between Egypt and Syria-Palestine (Israel), or more popularly as the mountain of God at which Moses encounters God in the burning bush and receives the first set of ten commandments while Israel is in the desert on their way to the promised land after their escape from Egypt. As a mountain, in some traditions it is called Sinai while in others it is referred to as Horeb (e.g., Exod. 17.6).

The location of the mountain has always been a matter of dispute and little progress has been made determining its location. The mountain of Sinai functions in biblical tradition as a place of theophany (divine appearance) to establish a covenant with Israel and make it into a 'kingdom of priests, a holy nation' (Exod. 19.6). Thus, like many temples of the ancient world, Sinai is a meeting place between heaven and earth. Accordingly it is referred to as 'holy ground' (Exod. 3.5) on which Moses removes his sandals.

Likely the writers who composed the narratives about Sinai were writing long after the time of the exodus, so elements surrounding Sinai reflect the theology of the temple (Ps. 68.18). The image of Yahweh coming down to the mountain in a cloud is reminiscent of images in Ezekiel. Later, the OT legitimates the call of Elijah by setting him in a similar theophany on Horeb and thus increasing the importance of Moses's call (1 Kgs 19.11-12); this is reinforced by the NT as Moses appears with Elijah in the transfiguration of Jesus (Mark 9.4). The events at Sinai also function as a typological scene of the call of the prophet. Thus, Jesus is cast as fulfilling the prophetic office and delivering commandments, the beatitudes, on another mount, like Moses. Both the transfiguration and beatitudes are said to take place on raised places (*oros*). Besides the above, specific reference to Sinai in the NT is limited and demonstrates no development from the OT (Acts 7.38; Gal. 4.24-25).

Contemporary usage of Sinai is limited, although the association with spiritual experiences on raised places like mountains remains in human consciousness. The classical music of C.P.E. Bach has a score of *Israelites in the Wilderness*. Most famous is the representation of Sinai in Cecil B. DeMille's *The Ten Commandments* (1956) as a fiery mountain of God after which Moses sees the burning bush, comes down from the mountain starkly changed in physical appearance. Contemporary film representations of the biblical events often beg the question of how an image motivated genre tries to communicate a narrative based one. There are several hospitals named after Mount Sinai in e.g., New York City, Chicago, Toronto and Montreal.

Mount Sinai (Jebel Musa) in present-day Egypt, the site of St Catherine's Monastery, is a popular pilgrimage site and tourist attraction. Other suggested locations include mountains in Edom/Nabatea or Arabia, or Har Korkom in the Negev.

See also BEATITUDES; COVENANT; ELIJAH; EXODUS, BOOK OF; GOD; JERUSALEM; MOUNTAIN; SERMON ON THE MOUNT; TRANSFIGURATION
[SWF]

Sins of the fathers. The reference to 'the sins of the fathers' is found in Exodus 20 when God gives the Ten Commandments to Moses and the Hebrews recently freed from slavery in Egypt. In the second commandment, God says, 'Do not bow down to any idol and worship it, because I am the Lord your God and I tolerate no rivals. I bring punishment on those who hate me and on their descendants down to the third or fourth generation' (v. 6). Stories of the burden placed on a child, especially following a child into adulthood, to correct or pay for a parent's mistakes continue to proliferate throughout popular culture, although in contemporary references, the parental conflict rarely refers to idolatry or blasphemy. The term 'sins of the fathers' covers a range of family issues from alcoholism and drug abuse, sexually transmitted diseases, domestic violence, treason and murder.

Sins of the Father is the title of the 2002 made-for-TV movie based on historical events. In this film, a grown son decides to reveal his father's complicity in a 1965 Baptist church bombing in Alabama which killed four African-American girls. The crime had remained unsolved, and the father's role in it had been a well-kept family secret, until his son Tom informs the authorities about his father's true whereabouts on the night of the bombing. The theme of a son confronting his father is also found in *Shaking Dream Land* (2006). In this film, upon learning that his wife is pregnant, a man begins having nightmares rooted in his childhood memories, and he can only stop the horrible dreams by confronting his father.

Yet in many stories, 'sins of the father' defines the child facing the consequences of his family's actions without having an actual face-to-face confrontation between parent and child. In the third season of *Star Trek: The Next Generation*, Lieutenant Commander Worf faces dishonor from the Klingon High Council which is unjustly shaming Worf's father in order to bury a national scandal. In the 1993 video game *Gabriel Knight: Sins of the Father*, the main character is trying to solve a series of voodoo-based murders and discovers that he is part of a long-time voodoo curse. *Sins of the Fathers* is also the title of a 2004 film, the final movie in a trilogy, about a movie actor whose family was murdered by a serial killer.

The term can be found among entertainment for young adults as well. It is the title of a 1996 animated Spider Man adventure and is the title of the tenth novel in a series by Rob Kidd based on *The Pirates of the Caribbean*.

See also SIN; SIN AGAINST THE HOLY SPIRIT; SIN WILL FIND YOU OUT; SOUR GRAPES [KAM]

Sirach (Ecclesiasticus). This work forms part of the Deuterocanonical/Apocryphal section of the biblical canon, and, like Proverbs, is wisdom literature. The 51 chapters are the composition of Jesus son of Eleazar, son of Sirach of Jerusalem (Sir. 50.27) around 180 BCE. Originally composed in Hebrew, the author's grandson translated it into Greek in Egypt sometime after 132 BCE. The Greek version often forms the basis for modern translations, such as the NRSV. Hebrew versions were considered lost until their rediscovery first with four manuscripts from the Cairo Geniza between 1896 and 1900, and then further manuscripts and fragments in subsequent decades. Hebrew fragments were also discovered at Qumran.

The existence of the work in different languages has led to multiple names. Greek manuscripts identify the title as *Sophia Iēsou huiou Sirach* ('the wisdom of Jesus son of Sirach'), commonly known as Sirach. No extant Hebrew copy bears a title, though commonly one uses 'Ben Sira' to refer to the Hebrew text. The Latin tradition identifies the book as 'the church book' (*Ecclesiasticus*), which is the name commonly used in English Bibles.

Like Proverbs, Sirach covers a wide range of topics with adages that present themselves as universal truths. Unlike Proverbs, however, Sirach makes more frequent reference to specific Israelite traditions (e.g., the list of valiant men in 44.1–50.24). One significant contribution is the equation of Wisdom with Torah (Law), so that Sirach stands between an earlier emphasis on experiential wisdom (Proverbs) and the later emphasis upon Torah study in rabbinic Judaism (Sir. 24, esp. v. 23). The work also contains in 50.25-26 one of the earliest references to the religion of the Samaritans, who figure in several of Jesus' encounters (e.g., Luke 10.25-37; 17.11-19; John 4).

Besides its direct contribution as a wisdom book, Sirach contributes to our understanding of the development of the OT canon. The grandson's prologue makes one of the earliest references to the tripartite division of the Hebrew Bible (Law, Prophets, Writings). The content of these divisions is not specified, though Sirach himself makes mention of the twelve prophets (49.10).

Allusions to Sirach in the NT may include, for example, the image of dethroning rulers in Sir. 10.14 and Luke 1.52, the evidence of action in Sir. 27.6 and Matt. 7.16, and the image of the yoke in Sir. 51.26-27 and Matt. 11.28-29. In some cases, there are also connections with Jewish liturgical texts, such as the use of 'shield of Abraham' in the Amidah, which elsewhere only occurs in the Hebrew text of Ben Sira (51.12).

Sirach's ongoing influence can be detected in classical music, such as Mendelssohn's *Elijah*, which, although concerned with the character from 1 Kings, draws directly upon Sir. 48.1-12 in the final section of the oratory. Bach also famously utilized Sir. 51.27, 'See with your own eyes that I have labored but little and found for myself much serenity', in the fifth movement of his *Ein deutsches Requiem*.

Proverbs from Sirach have also entered into common usage. One can find 'Whoever touches pitch gets dirty' (13.1) or 'Have regard for your name, since it will outlive you longer than a thousand hoards of gold' (41.12) in a selection of books, journals, and magazine articles.

Recommended reading. Dell, Katharine. *'Get Wisdom, Get Insight'. An Introduction to Israel's Wisdom Literature*. London: Darton Longman & Todd, 2000.

See also APOCRYPHA/DEUTEROCANONICALS/INTERTESTAMENTALS; PROVERBS; WISDOM [SHW]

Sisera (see Jael).

666. In Revelation, humanity is divided into two groups: Those marked with the name of God (7.3; 14.1), and those marked with the name of the beast from the earth (13.16-17; 14.9-11). Both these marks are symbols of ownership, received on the forehead or hand as public symbols of allegiance. John sets the interpretation of the mark of the beast as a riddle for his readers, saying: 'This calls for wisdom: let anyone with understanding calculate the number of the beast, for it is the number of a person. Its number is six hundred sixty-six' (Rev. 13.18).

John is here utilising the Jewish system of *gematria*, which was the practice of equating letters with numbers, and then adding those numbers together to find the numerical value of a person's name. An example of this is a piece of graffiti from Pompeii which reads 'I love the girl whose number is 545'. The most widely accepted explanation for John's riddle is that 666 (six hundred and sixty-six) represents Nero Caesar.

Greek	ν	ε	ρ	ω	ν
Hebrew	נ		ר	ו	ן
Number	50		200	6	50

Greek	κ	α	ι	σ	α	ρ
Hebrew	ק			ס		ר
Number	100			60		200

It is interesting to note that 666 is also the result if the same process is applied to the Greek word for 'beast'.

Greek	θ	η	ρ	ι	o	ν
Hebrew	ת		ר	י	ו	ן
Number	400		200	10	6	50

A modern-day equivalent to this process is the reduction of words to numbers when typing using predictive text on a mobile telephone. For example the name Simon, in 'predictive text' numbering, becomes 7–4–666. The *gematria*-based identification of Nero with the beast from the earth strengthens the economic and political critique of Rome, which runs throughout Revelation, but it is possible that John is making a further point as well. In Jewish numerology, the number seven represented perfection, and the number of the beast is a thrice-repeated falling short of divine perfection.

Contrary to popular belief, the number is not associated with the Antichrist in Revelation, or in any other biblical writing. Many interpreters throughout the centuries have sought to locate the answer to John's riddle within their own context, rather than that of the original recipients of the letter. The 'number of the beast' has been variously used to identify the Pope, all Roman Catholics, French kings named Louis, Hitler, the contemporary global political system, the period of Saracen rule (635–1300 CE), the year of the beginning of Muslim political expansionism (666 CE), the period between the execution of Charles I of England and the expected overthrow of Parliament, Ronald Wilson Reagan, a tattoo on the forehead, and barcodes. Even a cursory search of the internet reveals that the process of seeking a contemporary answer to this ancient riddle is alive and active. In film, the number 666 is often used to denote the presence of evil, as is seen in the movie *The Omen: 666* (2006). In a clever marketing ploy, the film was released at 06:06:06 in the morning of the June 6, 2006 (6/6/06).

The number 666 also features in the lyrics of 'The Number of the Beast' (1982), a song by the heavy metal band Iron Maiden.

See also ANTICHRIST; BEAST; NERO; NUMBERS, SYMBOLISM OF; REVELATION, BOOK OF [SW]

Slaughter of the Innocents (see Massacre of the Innocents).

Slave. A person subjected to servitude through violent domination, natal alienation, and personal dishonor. Whereas slavery in recent history targeted particular ethnicities, slavery in the ancient world was not racially based. A slave was considered property (Lev. 25.45-46), an animated tool, could be purchased and sold (Lev. 25.44-45), inherited (Lev. 25.46), freed (1 Cor. 7.21), promoted (Gen. 39.3-4; Matt. 25.20-23), and punished (Matt. 25.30) at the discretion of his or her master.

In the OT, the slave (*'ebed*) often appears in legal and proverbial literature without drawing much attention to his or her identity or economic and political significance. Notable Hebrew slaves were Hagar and Joseph. Israelite slaves were primarily acquired through debt-bondage (Exod. 21; Lev. 25; Deut. 15) and as war captives (1 Kgs 9.21). Because the Israelites belonged to God, who had redeemed them from Egyptian bondage (Exod. 5.1-23; Lev. 25.42-43), those who purchased fellow Israelites were mandated to treat their slaves modestly, without harshness, and to free them every year of Jubilee, or the nation would be punished (Jer. 34.8-22). Slaves could, however, choose to continue to serve their human masters for life (Exod. 21.5-6; Deut. 15.16-17). The Torah permitted Israelites to own slaves from foreign nations, whether captives or aliens (Lev. 25.44-45), and many were employed in both private and national service (1 Sam. 8.10-18; 1 Kgs 10.2-5).

In the NT, the slave (*doulos*, *pais*, *oiketēs*) is a ubiquitous term appearing both literally and figuratively in all literary genres. Slaves are commonly the beneficiaries of the ministries of Jesus and his followers (Matt. 8.5-13; Acts 8.27-39). Paul wrote an entire letter to Philemon to secure the slave Onesimus as a partner in Christian service (Phlm. 10-21). However, slavery is never prohibited in the NT. Paul encourages slaves who can receive manumission to do so if possible (1 Cor. 7.21). However, throughout the NT slaves are repeatedly encouraged to obey their earthly masters (*kyrios*) as if their masters were the heavenly Lord (*kyrios*), despite any maltreatment slaves might receive (Eph. 6.5-8; Col. 3.22-24). Slavery language is also used figuratively in the NT to articulate one's devotion to spiritual forces, such as evil spirits and sin (John 8.34-36; Gal. 4.1-9) and God and righteousness (Rom. 1.1; 6–8; Gal. 1.10; Rev. 1.1). Furthermore, slavery figuratively depicts the servile and sacrificial nature of Christian ministry (Mark 10.42-45; 1 Cor. 9.19; Phil. 2.7).

Slavery has for centuries been a sad reality in western society. It is in some countries still a very real problem, especially in the form of sweatshops and human trafficking. Slavery was perhaps most memorably and shamefully realized in its American form when until the Civil War Black Africans, and occasionally Native Americans, were subjected to forced labor, for instance on the tobacco and cotton farms of the antebellum South. Interestingly, the Bible was used both to promote and combat the abolition of slavery in the events leading up to the Emancipation Proclamation. Many important novels involve slavery, including Harriet Beecher Stowe's *Uncle Tom's Cabin* (1852), Toni Morrison's *Beloved* (1987), Barry Unsworth's *Sacred Hunger* (1992), and Edward P. Jones's *The Known World* (2003). The television miniseries *Roots* (1977) along with the popular films *Glory* (1989), *Amistad* (1997), and *Amazing Grace* (2006) also portray the circumstances surrounding western slavery and its abolition.

Recommended reading. Harrill, Albert J. *Slavery in the New Testament: Literary, Social and Moral Dimensions*. Minneapolis: Fortress Press, 2005. Harris, Murray J. *Slave of Christ: A New Testament Metaphor of Total Devotion to Christ*. New Studies in Biblical Theology; Downers Grove, IL: InterVarsity, 1999. Chirichigno, G.C. *Debt-Slavery in Israel and the Ancient Near East*. Sheffield: Sheffield Academic Press, 1993.

See also BOOK OF THE LAW; FREEDOM; LORD; OBEDIENCE; PHILEMON; SERVANT; STEWARD [JKG]

Snare. In Hebrew, *pach* (an animal trap) and in Greek *pagida* (snare or trap). A snare is a type of hidden baited animal trap constructed by tying a self-securing slip knot into a piece of rope or thin metal with tension delivered from a bent branch or stick, or in modern times, an alternative tension mechanism. When triggered, the snare tightens around the animal's head or appendage from which it is unable to loosen itself or break the snare free from the natural anchor, normally a rock or tree that fastens the snare down. The imprecision and unpredictability of snares as hunting instruments—responsible for killing too many animals too violently—has led to bans in many western countries.

Use of the term in both the OT and NT is in every instance allegorical. 'Snare' is never intended to describe the actual trapping of animals but always to a uniquely moral trapping of human beings. What changes in many appearances of the term is the subject or object doing the snaring or being ensnared: one can become a snare to another person (Exod. 10.7; Judg. 8.27); idolatry or sin can ensnare a person or community (Exod. 23.33; Deut. 7.25; Ps. 141.9; Prov. 18.7; 1 Tim. 6.9); in the NT, the deceptions of Satan are considered especially snaring (1 Tim. 3.7; 2 Tim. 2.26).

Accompanying references to snares in both Testaments is a warning or exhortation to avoid snares of sin and evil. The imagery is brimming with moral insight. Humanity resembles an animal enticed by some object it desires so deeply it is willing to risk the unknown in order to taste it. Once tasted the snare tightens and is set; the more it is resisted the more bound the ensnared becomes. Bondage can become so great, in fact, that the life of the trapped ends in violent thrashing against its meagre but unrelenting adversary. Yet, the snare is also cast in positive terms. For example, God is sometimes described as laying snares for the wicked (Ps. 9.16, 11.6). The snare is therefore referred to both as a morally tenuous trap for humans to avoid and a means for catching and extinguishing problems that do not belong where they are.

In contemporary western societies, snare can refer either to a thin-cord noose trap for larger animals like rabbits, foxes or coyotes, or it can also refer to a type of wood and wire framed drum that stands centerpiece in common drum sets. The former, not the latter, has biblical roots. Many countries, including the whole of the European Union, have banned the use of snares for what are viewed as 'inhumane' methods of trapping. Malfunction, neglect, and accidental violence to unsought animals are the principal reasons offered for the continued regulation of snare traps. Morally speaking, the term snare still enjoys random incarnations, especially in preaching, describing fruitfully the means sin or evil use to latch onto the inattentive or unreflective person and the potential consequences that result. Legally, snare is synonymous with entrapment, where an individual is persuaded or encouraged by law enforcement to commit a crime for which they are subsequently charged. *Snare* is also the title of a science fiction novel by Katherine Kerr, as well as the name of a character in the Transformers series.

See also ALLEGORY; SIN [MA]

Sodom and Gomorrah are referred to in Gen. 10.19, among the 'cities of the plain' (Gen. 10.19; 13.10, 12-13; 19.13, 24-26) that border Canaan, the home of Noah's cursed son Ham's descendants (9.22-27). When Abraham receives God's contingent promise of relationship, descendants, and the land of Canaan in Gen. 12.1-3, 7, he departs Haran, taking along his barren wife, Sarah, and his nephew and heir, Lot (Gen. 12.4; cf. 11.27-30). Following a dispute, Lot rejects Canaan (13.8-9), leaving for the cities of the plain (13.12). Asides about those cities' wickedness (13.13) and destruction (13.10) emphasise his poor choice. He is not forgotten, however. When Sodom is captured by foreign kings (14.1-13), Abraham rescues him (14.14-24), freeing him to return there.

Following a visit by three men who promise him a son by Sarah (18.1-16), Abraham is told of the impending divine investigation of Sodom and Gomorrah (18.17-19). This echoes earlier investigations of humanity (Gen. 4–11) and will show his descendants, Israel, how God will respond to nations—themselves included (e.g., Exod. 32.10; Num. 14.12)—that choose violence over righteousness (18.19). Told to be a blessing to the nations in 12.1-3, the patriarch intervenes, seeking justice from the 'Judge of all the Earth' (18.25), but offering no consistent argument for what he wants. When the bargaining ends at ten righteous men, God departs.

When two angels (or messengers) arrive in Sodom, Lot offers them hospitality (19.3). When the city's men come to molest his guests (19.4-5), however, he offers them his two daughters (19.8), arguably indicating a lack of righteousness. Unplacated, the mob is blinded and judged (19.11-13). For the 'remembrance of Abraham' (19.29), Lot is dragged from the doomed city (19.16), finally recognizing God for himself (19.18). At his request, Lot goes to Zoar (19.18-23), and then to the hills with his daughters (19.30), his wife turning to salt as she looks back (19.26). Finally, the incestuous origins of Israel's neighbors, Moab and Ammon, are narrated, as Lot's daughters lie with their drunken father (19.30-38).

The story of Sodom and Gomorrah proved popular (Deut. 29.23; 32.32; Isa. 1.9-10; 3.9; 13.19; Jer. 23.15; 49.18; 50.40; Lam. 4.6; Ezek. 16.46-56; Amos 4.11; Zeph. 2.9; Matt. 10.15; 11.23-24; Luke 10.12; 17.28-32; Rom. 9.29; 1 Tim. 1.10; 2 Pet. 2.6; Jude 7; Rev. 11.8). Central to its afterlife was speculation about its sin(s), whether sexual (e.g., lust [Philo, *Abraham* 134-45], fornication [*Jubilees* 16.5-6], sex with prostitutes [*Testament of Levi* 14.6], unnatural sex [*Testament of Naphali* 3.4], sex between males [Augustine, *City of God*, 16.30], and licentiousness [2 Pet. 2.7]) or not (e.g., arrogance [Sir. 16.8], xenophobia [Josephus, *Antiquities* 1.194-95], greed [*b. Sanh.* 109a; *m. Ab.* 5.10], and either failure [Matt. 10.14-15] or refusal to be hospitable [Wis. 19.14]). Indeed everything 'wicked', the western tradition concluded, happened in Sodom, making it home to every 'contemporary' sin.

Artistic representations abound: e.g., Abraham with angels (Chagall), pleading for Sodom (Guisto), Lot with angels (Blake), the Sodomites (Rembrandt), Lot fleeing (Raphael), Sodom's destruction (Turner), Lot's wife (Maître), and his seduction (Velázquez). A 1963 Robert Aldrich epic film, *Sodom and Gomorrah*, starred Stewart Granger, and De Sade's libertine *120 days of Sodom* was filmed by Pasolini (1976). Modern musical representations include Jerry Garcia's *Gomorrah*, Mind Eclipse's *Live in Sodom*, and the thrash metal of German band, Sodom.

Recommended reading. Carden, Michael. *Sodomy: A History of a Christian Biblical Myth*. London: Equinox, 2004. Lyons, William J. *Canon and Exegesis: Canonical Praxis and the Sodom Narrative*. Sheffield: Sheffield Academic Press, 2002. Fields, Weston W. *Sodom and Gomorrah: History and Motif in Biblical Narrative*. Sheffield: Sheffield Academic Press, 1997.

See also GENESIS; ABRAHAM; LOT; LOT'S WIFE; PROMISE [WJL]

Solomon. The tenth of David's 17 (2 Sam. 3.2-6; 5.14-16) or 19 (1 Chron. 3.1-8) sons; the second son of Bathsheba (2 Sam. 11.3; cf. 1 Chron. 3.5), hence the name Solomon, literally 'replacement'.

Solomon's rise concludes the portion of the Bible known as the Succession Narrative, in which the successor to David is revealed (2 Sam. 13–1 Kgs 2). His half-brother Adonijah has a private coronation outside Jerusalem. David's public support of Solomon ends Adonijah's claim, witnessed publicly by the masses.

Solomon initiates a brief bloodbath to consolidate his throne, killing Adonijah, the Saulide Shemei, and Joab. He builds the temple and palace complex in Jerusalem, finishing David's centralization of religion program. Comparing the lists of officials of David's and Solomon's officials, one notices the de-emphasis of military in favor of administrative officials in Solomon's realm.

Solomon's building projects cemented an economic relationship with Hiram of Tyre, the leading economic power in the ANE. That Solomon had a trade deficit requiring the secession of 20 northern cities to Tyre is hardly surprising. Nor is a joint Tyrian–Israelite port on the Red Sea, as the Tyrians would show profits regardless of the detail of the arrangement by cutting out middlemen in the Red Sea trade. Aside from maritime access, overland transport and storage, Israel likely contributed little to the venture.

To accomplish his construction projects, a state instituted corvée was necessary. The organization of this massive labor project may have been the genesis of Solomon's recreation of the internal division of Israel. Under David, the land was organized tribally (1 Chron. 27.16-24). Solomon's districts did not correspond with tribal areas, and was administered by officials appointed by and answerable only to him. This move towards political centralization and the establishment of a central bureaucracy marks an emergent preindustrial state. Israel had developed from a loose tribal confederacy before Saul to a chiefdom (in which kin groups surrender some authority to a leader whose close kin control key resources) under Saul and David to Solomon's state.

The corvée and the imbalance of the disbursement of the new wealth pouring into the nation disproportionately spent in Judah alienated the northern tribes (David had more kinship and economic ties with the south). Doubtless, the declining power of tribal kin groups also troubled the northern groups. The Ephraimite Jeroboam led an abortive rebellion, laying the groundwork for the division of the kingdom after Solomon's death. Solomon's economic power is evidenced by his foreign wives, and in particular his Egyptian wife. Though this era was a comparative down one for Egypt, the practice of Egyptian princesses leaving Egypt is only attested on one other occasion. 1 Kings 11.42 attributes him with a 40-year reign (cf. 2 Chron. 9.30).

Despite his mixed record as a ruler, Solomon is remembered in western culture for his surpassing wisdom (e.g., 1 Kgs 4.19; 34; 10.23; 2 Chron. 1.11; 9.22; Matt. 12.42; Luke 11.31); his wealth (e.g., H. Rider Haggard's adventure novel *King Solomon's Mines* [1885], made into a movie in 1950); and the grandeur of his kingdom (Matt. 6.29). The Book of Proverbs is attributed to him; as are the Song of Songs and the Book of Wisdom. The Jewish midrashic tradition associates him with magic and supernatural powers. The Talmud lists him as one of 48 prophets. The Qur'an portrays him as a worshipper of Allah. His encounter with the Queen of Sheba has been celebrated in art, literature, music and film.

Recommended reading. Handy, L.K. (ed.). *The Age of Solomon*. Leiden: Brill: 1997.

See also PROVERBS; QUEEN OF SHEBA; SONG OF SOLOMON, SONGS; TEMPLE, ISRAEL'S; WISDOM [MAP]

Song of Solomon, Songs. A book of the OT. In the Christian tradition it is counted among the wisdom or poetical books, while in the Jewish tradition it is one of the five *megilloth* ('scrolls'), closely associated with the Passover liturgy. 'Song of Songs' literally translates the Hebrew *shir hashirim* ('the loveliest song'), whereas 'Song of Solomon' underlines the traditional authorship of King Solomon. Both denominations derive from the book's title verse (1.1), although the verse may be variously translated as 'the song of songs, which is of/for/concerning Solomon'.

Judgments on the book's date of composition range from the tenth century BCE to hellenistic times. This is not helped by the fact that its poetic language combines archaisms with very late features. The Song appears as a collection of songs and poems of varying length and diverse content, taken from different poetical traditions and combined into a single composition. However, biblical scholars are not agreed upon the structure and unity of the book as a whole.

The Song is subject to various interpretations, which may be roughly divided into either 'literal' or 'allegorical' readings. Its earliest commentators read it as a dramatic composition, recounting a three-way love affair between King Solomon, one of his harem girls and a poor shepherd boy. Though this was the dominant interpretation up until nineteenth-century criticism, it is only rarely encountered nowadays. Others read the Song simply as a sublime poetic composition, stressing the links with love poetry from the Arabian, Egyptian and Sumerian traditions. Some critics further develop the interpretation of the Song as love poetry, assuming an erotic or even pornographic subtext. At the other end of the spectrum are the mystical and/or ecclesiological interpretations, which read the Song as an allegory of the relationship between God and Israel, Christ and the Church, Christ and the individual soul, or Christ and the Holy Virgin.

The influence of the Song on various aspects of western culture can hardly be overestimated. Its allegorical dimensions have inspired various Christian authors, as well as the Jewish kabbalistic tradition. Both the mystical writings of Bernard of Clairvaux (twelfth century) and John of the Cross's *Spiritual Canticle* (sixteenth century) were heavily influenced by the Song of Songs. The Song is central to the adoration of the Holy Virgin, from whence it inspired numerous pieces of sacred music. Important examples are Giovanni Pierluigi da Palestrina's *Motets from the Song of Songs*, Claudio Monteverdi's *Vespro della Beata Vergine* and Johann Sebastian Bach's cantata *Wachet auf, ruft uns die Stimme* (BWV 140). The same verses greatly influenced visual representations of the Holy Virgin. An overview of the various links between the Song of Songs and the Virgin may be found in the illuminated manuscript known as the *Grimani Breviary* (c. 1520).

The literal interpretations of the Song of Songs are not without a rich tradition of their own. Works of literature referencing the Song of Songs as an instance of sublime love poetry include Geoffrey Chaucer's *Canterbury Tales* (fourteenth century), John Steinbeck's *Grapes of Wrath* (1939) and Umberto Eco's *The Name of the Rose* (1980). A group of paintings by Jewish–Russian painter Marc Chagall depicts scenes from the Song of Songs. In the musical area one may cite Ralph Vaughn Williams's *Flos Campi* (1925).

Recommended reading. Exum, J. Cheryl. *Song of Songs: A Commentary*. Louisville, KY: Westminster John Knox Press, 2005. Pope, M.H. *Song of Songs: A New Translation with Introduction and Commentary*. Anchor Bible, 7C; Garden City, NY: Doubleday, 1977.

See also ALLEGORY; SOLOMON [DDC]

Song of the Three. The *Song of the Three Young Jews* is also called the *Song of the Three Young Men* or the *Song of the Three Children* in English versions of the Bible. The *Song* and the *Prayer of Azariah* which precedes it are often treated as a single unit. They are one of three additions to the Greek version of Daniel.

The *Prayer of Azariah* and the *Song of the Three Young Jews* are not in any of the ancient Hebrew–Aramaic manuscripts; however, they do appear in the early editions of the LXX. They are accepted as canonical by the Roman Catholic and Orthodox Churches.

The Daniel 3 tells the story of the refusal of Shadrach, Meshach and Abednego to worship the idol set up by King Nebuchadnezzar. For their righteous disobedience of the unholy order of King Nebuchadnezzar they are thrown bound into fiery furnace. The 'Prayer of Azariah' and the 'Song of the Three Young Jews' are 68 additional verses inserted in between Dan. 3.23 and 3.24.

In Dan. 1.7, the three young Jews, Hananiah (Ananias), Mishael and Azariah of the tribe of Judah are given the Babylonian names Shadrach, Meshach and Abednego. However, after they are thrown into the fiery furnace they are called by their Hebrew names. Azariah in vv. 24-45 prays as the three are walking in the flames of the furnace. The prayer begins with praise, moves to confession for themselves and the Jewish nation and finally petitions God for mercy and deliverance of his people according to his promises. They make a sacrifice of a contrite heart. The final plea is for God to confound the unrighteous and to hallow his name before the unbelievers. The prayer is similar in form and content to many of the Psalms.

Verses 46-48 are a transition reporting the flames breaking forth to kill some of the Chaldeans stoking the fire. Verses 49-50 introduce the Angel of the Lord who shields the three youths from the deadly heat of the flames in the furnace.

Verses 51-90 are the verses of the *Song of the Three Young Jews*. They with one voice sing in praise of God. Their praise in vv. 52 to 87 is a powerful song of adoration that calls upon angels, beasts, aspects of nature and the people of Israel including their priests to give praise to God (cf. Ps. 148) for the wonders wrought by God. Then vv. 88-89 are words of praise giving thanks as the three express their gratitude for their delivery from death.

The *Prayer of Azariah*, as deuterocanonical, is not canonical for Protestants and Jews. However, because it closely resembles Daniel's prayer (9.3-19), and some of the psalms (e.g., Ps. 31; 51), it is a good model for biblical prayer.

In the Orthodox tradition, the three youths are alluded to in matins service music performed on December 17, their feast day. The Orthodox also remember them on the last two Sundays of Advent. Their story is read on Holy Saturday, and they are commemorated as prophets in the Lutheran Church on December 17.

Early Quakers made political use of the three youths by refusing to remove their hats in court. Book Six of the 1998 novel, *The Poisonwood Bible* by Barbara Kingsolver, is entitled 'The Song of the Three Children'.

See also APOCRYPHA, DEUTEROCANONICALS AND INTERTESTAMENTALS; DANIEL, BOOK OF; PRAYER OF AZARIAH; SHADRACH, MESHACH AND ABEDNEGO   [AJW]

Son of God. Greek: *huios tou theou*. Biblically, this expression is an appellative of one chosen by God to accomplish a task, corporately used of Israel (Hebrew: *benei elohim*; e.g., Exod. 4.22; Isa. 1.2; Jer. 3.22; cf. Deut. 32.6; Jer. 31.9), individually used as adoptive sonship and a royal title for the king on David's throne (e.g., 2 Sam. 7.14; 1 Chron. 17.13; cf. Ps. 2.7), heavenly beings (e.g., Job 1.6; Ps. 82.6; Dan. 3.25), and in the NT, messianically and divinely attributed to Jesus (e.g., Matt. 3.17; Mark 1.11; Luke 3.22; Acts 13.33; Rom. 1.4; Heb. 1.5; Rev. 2.18). The devil and demons use it with reference to Jesus, the former in the temptation sequence (Luke 4.3, 9), and the latter in a miracle scene where Jesus healed many of diseases (Luke 4.41). Jewish officials plotted the death of Jesus because they deduced his claim to be that he was the 'Son of God' (John 19.7). This expression signifies Jesus' claim that he was as divine as God, begging the question of whether or not he was of the same substance (the Trinity).

Jewish apocryphal literature ascribes this appellation to heavenly beings (Wis. 5.5) and the suffering righteous man (Wis. 2.16-18; Sir. 4.10). Qumran texts, such as 4Q246, messianically refer to the 'son of God' (cf. also 4QFlor I.11ff; 1QSa II.11-12).

This expression finds its roots in ancient Egypt and in the hellenization project of Alexander the Great, the 'son of Zeus'. This was representative of Greco-Roman mythology where the gods would mate with a human. Greco-Roman Caesars were called divine 'sons of God', and accepted worship as such. The NT use of the 'son of God' is antithetical to these as it claims there is only one son. Arius of Alexandria in the fourth century CE denied that the phrase claimed that Jesus was divine.

There is a modern distinction between humanity and the Son of God. This was the inspiration of G.F. Händel's line in *The Messiah*, 'Unto Which of the Angels Said He at Any Time'. Bruce Springsteen appeals to the human thoughts of his own children in the 2005 song, *Jesus Was an Only Son*. Lawrence Ferlinghetti's poem entitled, *Christ Climbed Down*', tells a compassionate story of how Jesus willingly descended as the Son of God into a forgetful world who would rather forget him for Christmas 'tinsel'. Bruce Cockburn's song, *Cry of a Tiny Babe*, makes the Son of God a humanitarian. Joan Osborne imparts vivid imagery about what the Son of God would look like and act like if placed in modernity in her 1995 song, *One of Us*. One of the main heroes in Milton's *Paradise Lost* and *Paradise Regained* is the Son of God because he is not just a man. Juxtaposed between God the Father giving humankind free will and the rationality of the Son of God in the novel, *The Brothers Karamazov* by Fyodor Dostoyevsky, Ivan narrates Jesus' temptation and the Devil's claim that he was the Son of God.

Post-Enlightenment scholars of the historical Jesus shed doubt upon the claim to divine sonship. In the 1965 film, *The Greatest Story Ever Told*, Jesus' divine claim lacks miracles to validate his claim of divinity. *The Da Vinci Code* (2006) proposes the idea that 'maybe, human is divine'.

Recommended reading. Collins, Adela Yarbro, and John Joseph Collins. *King and Messiah as Son of God*. Grand Rapids, MI: Eerdmans, 2008. Hengel, Martin. *The Son of God*. Philadelphia: Fortress Press, 1976.

See also CHRIST; INCARNATION; JESUS OF NAZARETH; SON OF MAN; SONS OF GOD   [CHB]

Son of Man. Hebrew: *ben-ādām*, an ancient Semitic expression used in the OT exclusively in poetic and ceremonial literature to denote a human being, individually or corporately (e.g., 2 Sam. 7.14; Isa. 56.2; Ezek. 31.14; Dan. 2.38; Joel 1.12), to differentiate between a human being and God (e.g., Num. 23.19; Job 25.6; Ps. 8.4; Isa. 51.12), or a title God gives to Ezekiel (e.g., Ezek. 2.1, 3, 6, 8). Jewish Aramaic Targums (paraphrases) from the early Christian era interpret the Aramaic (*bar ᵉnāš*) usage in Dan. 7.13 as an appellation of the messiah. In the NT ([*ho* *huios [tou] anthrōpou*), it is used exclusively in the Gospels by Jesus, in the third person, as his favored self-designation to claim the parallel messianic sentiment found in Dan. 7.13-14 upon himself. He uses it prophetically and messianically to describe the functionality of his life and ministry (e.g., Matt. 13.37; Mark 2.10; Luke 7.34), his death (e.g., Matt. 8.31; Luke 17.25), and the age to come (e.g., Matt. 19.28; Mark 8.38; Luke 21.36). Exception to this is only found in Mark (e.g., 8.31; 9.9), and when a crowd in Jerusalem fails to comprehend Jesus' messianic claim (John 12.34). Apart from the Gospels, it functions as an appellation for Jesus (Acts 7.56; Heb. 2.6) and is descriptive of heavenly beings (Rev. 1.13; 14.14).

Although this expression was not used often in early Christian writers, they attributed it to Christ's humanity describing the two natures of Christ, one human and one divine in one being. In Gnostic Christian literature, its usage departs from the NT as it is used for the son of the first man, who is actually the highest god.

Some modern interpretation rejects the notion that Jesus uses this expression as self-designative. Some scholars argue that it may to a heavenly being that is to come. Jesus' use is not self-referential, but refers to humanity in general. Some Jewish scholars maintain that the expression as used by the historical Jesus differs from the Gospel usages, and therefore should be translated as 'man' or 'one'.

In contemporary culture, this expression has been used apothegmatically. William Blake morphed it into an impersonal function or principle in the poem *Milton: A Poem*. Nobel Prize winning T.S. Eliot alluded to Ezek. 2.1 in *The Waste Land*, and describes a bleak desperate debauchery of tradition as he masterfully writes, 'Son of man, / You cannot say, or guess, for you know only / A heap of broken images' (19b-22). Phil Collins's optimistic approach in his song entitled, 'Son of Man', encapsulates maturity. The surrealist painter René Magritte's self-portrait, *The Son of Man*, strayed from the biblical definition and articulated the human condition. Magritte played on the meaning of God hidden/Son revealed juxtaposed with the human psyche as he said that 'we always want to see what is hidden by what we see ... a sort of conflict ... between the visible that is hidden and the visible that is present'.

Some have reinterpreted the expression to justify heinous crimes such as the father/son allusion of the chosen name for serial killer David Berkowitz a.k.a. 'Son of Sam'. Tupac and Outlawz's rap song, *Black Jesuz* and Johnny Cash's country song, *If Jesus Ever Loved a Woman* have taken it and contemporized Jesus' humanity.

Recommended reading. Lindars, Barnabas. *Jesus Son of Man*. Grand Rapids, MI: Eerdmans, 1983. Müller, Mogens. *The Expression 'Son of Man' and the Development of Christology: A History of Interpretation*. London: Equinox, 2008.

See also CHRIST; SECOND ADAM; SECOND COMING; SON OF GOD; SONS OF GOD [CHB]

Sons of God. In Hebrew, 'the sons of God' is *bene (ha) elohim*. This or a derivative of the phrase can be found in Genesis (6.1, 4), Psalms (29.1; 82.6), and Job (1.6; 2.1; 38.7), as well as in a fragment of Deut. 32.8 found among the DSS. Waltke and O'Connor demonstrate that the adjectival genitive form of *bene* paired with a noun can be used to represent a particular class of that noun. For example, in Deut. 2.19 when the text refers to the 'sons of Ammon' it is really speaking about the Ammonites and in Ezek. 2.1 when it says 'son of man', it is really saying human being. Therefore, the sons of God should be taken to mean divine beings or gods.

The sons of God usually appear in texts in order to set the scene in the divine realm, such as in Job 1–2 and Psalm 82. Yet, in Genesis 6 the sons of God are said to have had mated with the daughters of Adam in order to create the Nephilim, giants. There have been numerous studies and hypotheses about the identity of these sons in this passage both from the academic realm and in theological speculation. For example, Milton portrays these characters in *Paradise Lost* and *Paradise Regained*. In the Second Temple literature, the sons of god are associated with the watchers in Enoch (especially in 1 *Enoch*).

In the Latter Rain movement, the Sons of God represent a new type of Christian who have supernatural powers and will bring about a transformation on the earth; they are also called Joel's army.

The sons of God have been used in many different ways, including having a motorcycle club and a band named after them. Carolyn Carpenter's *Sons of God* is a 2004 movie in which the characters of biblical heaven interact with the love affair of a modern human couple. Danielle Trussoni's *Angelology* (2010) is based on the premise that malevolent Nephilim still inhabit the earth.

See also ELOHIM; GIANTS (NEPHILIM) [EW]

Sons of Thunder (see Boanerges).

Sophia (see Wisdom).

Soul. The essential statement is found in Gen. 2.7: 'Then the Lord God formed man from the dust of the ground, and breathed into his nostrils the breath of life; and the man became a living being'. The KJV renders the last phrase, 'man became a living soul'. The word 'living being' or 'soul' is the Hebrew *nephesh*, 'principle of life'. All creatures have *nephesh*, because all have life. In ancient Israel, people did not *have* a soul; each *was* a soul. We would say today that every person is a 'self'.

The NT combines the Hebrew notion of soul with ancient Greek concepts of the soul (*psychē*) as the life principle. Revelation on one occasion uses 'soul' for the human spirit (6.9-11). Paul uses body, soul, and spirit together as an expression of human holism (1 Thess. 5.23).

Greek philosophy led many early theologians down diverse paths. Irenaeus, influenced by Stoicism, envisioned the soul as an ethereal substance created by God but separate from the body. Platonism influenced Origen, who believed the soul was pre-existent, separated from God by sin. As it sought union with God, it inhabited a newborn. On the death of the body it inhabited, it would seek a new host.

During Augustine's time (third–fourth centuries), there was debate whether the soul was directly created by God, or the result of procreation. Tertullian upheld procreation; Augustine wavered. Thomas Aquinas (thirteenth century) pronounced those who held to procreation of the soul heretics. Present-day theologians are divided.

Much confusion as to the soul results from the misunderstanding of the biblical concept, fostered by Greek philosophy. Since biblically the soul is the self, when one dies, the soul dies. Thus, there is no 'immortal soul'. The Bible teaches that the spirit (*ruach* or *neshamah*) returns to God who gave it (Eccl. 3.20-21; 12.7). Only God is immortal. All life—temporal or eternal—is conditional on God's granting it.

The late twentieth century brought fresh interest in the soul through Eastern religions, most of which have some important life force at their core. Buddhism holds to *anatta*, which is an incorporeal mental component of living things that transcends death and is born anew in a new being. Hindus believe that *atman* is a part of the Supreme Mind, which never dies, migrating from body to body. Taking cues from the OT, the Qur'an speaks of God breathing the soul into humankind. Originally good and pure, the soul develops over the life of the person in whom it resides for better or worse. At death it sleeps until Judgment, when the person is rewarded or punished, according to one's obedience to Allah.

That a segment of *The Simpsons* was devoted to the soul in 1995 and turned out to be one of its most popular shows is an indication of current interest about this matter. An unbelieving Bart sells his soul to Milhouse for $5, only to discover that his existence has been compromised. Bart begins to suspect that his soul really does exist, and goes through many difficult moments until his sister, Lisa, retrieves it for him.

The idea of soul reincarnation is still popular today. In her book *Soul Survivor: The Reincarnation of a World War II Fighter Pilot* (2009), Andrea Leininger tells the story of her son, James, who from the age of two had nightmares about his need to escape from a burning plane. An investigation showed he was reliving the life of a WW II fighter pilot, James Huston. She concluded that he possessed the soul of this dead aviator.

See also HOLY SPIRIT; LIFE [DLS]

Sour grapes. Grapes were the major fruit in the diet of ancient Israelites. Early grapes started to ripen in June and July, but the harvest occurred in August and September. The vintage was celebrated with wine, song and dance around the vineyards (Judg. 9.27; Isa. 16.10). If eaten too early, grapes were sour and had a bad taste. Isaiah sang a drinking song the people enjoyed about a poor yield having a bitter taste: 'My beloved had a vineyard on a fertile ridge. He hoped it would yield grapes, but it yielded wild grapes' (Isa. 5). Inspired by Isaiah's song Jeremiah speaks of Israel as a choice vine that became a wild vine (Jer. 2.20-21; Isa. 5.2). These references anticipate the popular proverbial saying of the exilic–postexilic periods: 'The fathers have eaten *sour grapes*, and the children's teeth are set on edge' (Ezek. 18.1-2; Jer. 31.29). The people are complaining that they are unjustly paying for the sins of their ancestors (Lam. 5.7). The metaphor of sour grapes is tied to the epic covenant and its stipulation that Yahweh will visit 'the iniquity of the fathers upon the children and the children's children, to the third and fourth generation' (Exod. 34.6-7). Ezekiel based his alternative interpretation of the righteous person on the Exodus law code with its concern for justice and innocence (Ezek. 18.5-9; Exod. 23.6-8). He and other writers develop the argument that all persons, both ancestors and descendants, are responsible for their own sins (Ezek. 18.4, 20; Deut. 24.16; Jer. 31.30). The important question is the relation of individuals to society, the ethical obligations they share for the well-being and honor of the whole community.

The unabridged OED offers the following definition of sour grapes: it is a proverbial expression 'said … with allusion to Aesop's fable of 'The Fox and the Grapes'—a fox cannot reach some grapes so he decides that they are not ready to eat, i.e., sour—when a person is heard to disparage something which it is suspected he would be glad to possess if he could;' hence '*sour-grapeism*, the action or practice of disparaging something because it is out of reach', and the adjectival modifier '*sour-grapey*'. A well-known example is the reaction of a young man to a girl who rebuffs him. Needless to say, he initially found her quite desirable, but her rejection has wounded his pride and undermined his self-esteem. Forced to admit his failure to a friend, the young man nonetheless tries to save face by rationalizing that she was not exactly 'God's gift to men' after all, and delivers a litany of her alleged shortcomings. The friend responds, 'Sounds to me like *sour grapes*'.

The question, of course, is whether the Bible or the Greek fabulist Aesop (c. 560–500 BCE) has directly influenced current western parlance. *Prima facie* it appears to be the latter. Nonetheless, *sour grapes* would have been a familiar life-experience in the Greco-Roman world. Socio-rhetorical critic Vernon K. Robbins has recently demonstrated the degree to which ancient Jewish, early Christian and Mediterranean writings have influenced one another.

See also HARVEST; PLANTS, SYMBOLISM OF; VINE; VINEYARD; WINE [NRP & JRW]

Sower, Parable of the. The parable of the Sower is found in all three synoptic Gospels, with many variations (Matt. 13.1-9, 18-23; Mark 4.1-9, 13-20; Luke 8.4-15), as well as in the *Gospel of Thomas* 9 and 1 *Clement* 24.5. The parable tries to account for both rejection and acceptance in those hearing the preaching of the kingdom of God by Jesus and his disciples. Parable scholars distinguish between the parable proper ((Matt. 13.3-9; Mark 4.3-9; Luke 8.5-8) and the allegorical interpretation appended to it. However, as an allegory, the metaphors of 'seed', 'birds', 'soil', and 'harvest', utilize familiar Middle Eastern agricultural terms. These are identified with the internal condition of the listeners (good soil, poor soil, harvest), the preached word (seed), and the conditions which compete with the proclamation (rocky soil, birds, weeds). The harvest (salvation), has been thought by some to be so remarkably large that an eschatological focus in the parable must be in view. More recent consensus concludes the harvest (thirty, sixty, hundred fold) should be regarded as a normal yield.

The OT furnished the basic images for the parable, cf. Isa. 55.10-11, and perhaps Jer. 4.3. The parable is consistent with the themes of these texts but they are developed along midrashic lines by Jesus. This process contributed to the obscurity of some parables and the failure of the disciples and others to grasp their significance in relation to Jesus' ministry, as noted in Matt. 13.10.17 and parallels. The receptivity of the listeners is therefore not simply equated with their moral disposition—it reflects their capacity to appreciate Jesus' radical break from Israelite expectations of the Kingdom. Jesus' proclamation also raises questions about his own identity in relation to the tradition of Israel's prophets as is apparent from Matt. 13.17. This builds on Matthew's stress on Jesus as the one who fulfils Jewish eschatological hopes.

The agricultural background of the parable represents an easily recognised theme for many people, even those with no rural background. Such recognition does not require a detailed understanding of Middle Eastern farming practices, which Joachim Jeremias suggested was quite different from present methods, i.e., seed was scattered broadcast, *then* the soil turned over. This seeding method afforded relatively few controls over the outcome of the harvest and may be reflected in the parable itself; however, this reconstruction of ancient agriculture has been questioned.

The parable was clearly in wide circulation in the early church. The imagery of the parable has inspired numerous literary and artistic projects. *The Sower and the Sheaf* by Vincent van Gogh (1853–1890) was painted at a time where awareness of the laboring class and its economic plight was emerging in western culture generally. Van Gogh was himself inspired by earlier artists of this theme. The artistic mood is vigorous and assertive in its physical portrayal of the Sower. There is no necessary theological link to the original parable—its motifs are built on thematic association. The sixteenth-century Dutch painter Pieter Brueghel the Elder (1525–1569) was similarly inspired by the agricultural and folk culture aspects of the parable. His *Parable of the Sower* celebrates peasant toil and life. Octavia E. Butler uses themes of the Sower explicitly in her science fiction/horror novel, *Parable of the Sower* (2000). The novel depicts a post-apocalyptic scenario in which a new society rises tentatively to replace one collapsed under social degradation. These examples illustrate the manner in which parables can evoke interpretations that depend less on original historical or cultural context than on single dissociated themes.

Recommended reading. White, K.D. 'The Parable of the Sower'. *Journal of Theological Studies* 15 (1964) 301-307.

See also ALLEGORY; PARABLE [JKS]

Spare the Rod. Disciplining children by inflicting pain with a rod (or strap/belt) was once a common parenting strategy to reprimand misbehaving children. The Bible was often cited to justify this practice as Prov. 13.24 states: 'Those who spare the rod hate their children, but those who love them are diligent to discipline them'. Similarly, Prov. 23.13-14 instructs: 'Do not withhold discipline from your children; if you beat them with a rod, they will not die. If you beat them with the rod, you will save their lives from Sheol'.

Supporters of corporal punishment still turn to these passages to condone their view that physically disciplining children is an appropriate and necessary tactic in child rearing; others, however, decry such behavior as child abuse, which they argue is contrary to Jesus' own empathy for children (e.g., Mark 10.13-14; Matt. 19.14; Luke 18.16). Advocates of corporal punishment contend that Proverbs offers a strong message to take discipline seriously in order to teach children how to behave in this world. They argue that parents need to set their children straight to cultivate character formation, even if this involves force. Parents who refuse to physically punish their offspring allegedly produce children who will misbehave as adults. Such parents are supposedly shirking their biblical responsibility of child rearing.

Although this thinking prevailed for generations, it is an attitude that has been largely abandoned in contemporary western societies where hitting children is a criminal offense. In almost all western countries, violence against children, including spanking, is illegal. Sociologists and psychologists have shown that spanking leads to many problems later in life, which manifest themselves in other ways. Thus, spanking is typically viewed today as counterproductive and ultimately ineffectual, for producing healthy functioning members of society.

Nonetheless, Proverbs's influence continues to be felt in modern renditions of the biblical verse, e.g., as evidenced by Samuel Butler's poem *Hudibras*, which offers the most famous paraphrase of this biblical verse in western literature: 'Spare the rod and spoil the child' (2.1.843). This variant was further popularized by Mark Twain's *The Adventures of Tom Sawyer* (1876), who has Aunt Polly erroneously quote Butler's version as the actual biblical text, stating: 'I ain't doing my duty by that boy, and that's the Lord's truth, goodness. Spare the rod and spile the child, as the Good Book says' (ch. 1). Correspondingly, Ichabod Crane praises Butler's well-known saying as a 'golden maxim' (Washington Irving, *Legend of Sleepy Hollow*, 1820). Additionally, Butler's work, *The Way of All Flesh* (1903) refers to the biblical passages (ch. 5).

Another noteworthy reference to the biblical saying in literature is Nathaniel Hawthorne's *The Scarlet Letter* (1850), which comments that corporeal punishment was once commonplace: '[T]he frequent application of the rod, enjoined with Scriptural authority, were used, not merely in the way of a punishment for actual offenses, but as a wholesome regimen for the growth and promotion of all childish virtues' (ch. 6).

It is evident from the above that western literature took a biblical passage and gave it a robust life of its own. In many cases, the modified version became even more popular than the original text, robustly influencing western views of child rearing. Even today, some evangelical Christian writings such as James Dobson's *The New Dare to Discipline* (1996), still firmly advocate corporal punishment.

See also BEATITUDES, THE; BLESSED; CHILD; CHILDREN OF GOD; SUFFER THE LITTLE CHILDREN [SDD]

Sparrow's Fall. When Jesus instructed his apostles to go out and spread the good news, he warned them of the trials that they would endure on his behalf, but added that they should not be afraid because God vigilantly watches over them. This notion is encapsulated in the idea that even a sparrow's fall is observed by God: 'Are not two sparrows sold for a penny? Yet not one of them will fall to the ground apart from your Father. And even the hairs on your head are all counted. So do not be afraid; you are more value than many sparrows' (Matt. 10.29-31). A variant of the story occurs Luke 12.6-7, which substitutes 'five sparrows sold for two pennies'. Both Gospels make it clear that the apostles were esteemed much more than sparrows and that God would be watching over them in their travels.

Throughout history, these biblical verses about sparrows have generated a variety of interpretations in western culture and theological reflection.

The predominant view has been to see the story as indicative of God's omniscience. This understanding, popular among early church theologians, claims that even seemingly trivial events are not outside God's knowledge for God sees everything.

A second viewpoint is to see the above passages as indicative of God's providence and control over the events of history. This view is particularly prominent among Calvinists for whom the underlying message is to trust in God's provident care.

Others have seen the image as either a justification of human superiority over the animal world, or alternatively, an instance of God's compassion for his creatures (*Anathemata* 8.240).

In western literature, the image of the fallen sparrow appears in Shakespeare's *Hamlet,* Alexander Pope's *Essay on Man*, Mark Twain's *The Mysterious Stranger*, and in Emily Dickinson's poem, 'Mama Never Forgets her Birds'. More recently, the story inspired Mary Doria Russell's award-winning science fiction novel, *The Sparrow* (1996).

Among the aforementioned authors, Shakespeare parodies the belief in predestination when he writes, 'Not a whit, we defy augury [the practice of divining from the flight of birds]: there's a special providence in the fall of a sparrow. If it be now, 'tis not to come; if it be not to come, it will be now; if it be not now, yet it will come' (*Hamlet* 5.2.221-24).

The 2006 Hollywood film, *Pirates of the Caribbean: Dead Man's Chest*, portrays Captain Jack Sparrow falling into the Davy Jones's Locker (the monstrous grave of the sea); coincidentally, the real poet David Jones's work *Anathemata* alludes to the biblical context in his verse: 'They say he cared / when sparrows fall' (8.240).

See also BIRDS, SYMBOLISM OF; DOVE; PROVIDENCE; PREDESTINATION [SDD]

Spirit (see Holy Spirit).

Spiritual Gifts. Spiritual gifts (*charismata*) are mainly discussed in the letters of Paul. They may be defined as divine empowerments given by God so that believers may perform effective ministry. They are understood in 1 Cor. 2.4-5 and 12.7 as manifestations of the presence and power of God, intended to serve the common good of the church.

There are four principal lists of spiritual gifts in the NT: Rom. 12.6-8; 1 Cor. 12.8-10; 1 Cor. 12.28-30; and Eph. 4.11. These cite a great diversity of ministries or activities, including prophecy, teaching, leadership, giving, mercy, and tongues. Since these lists are different from each other, most agree they are not meant to provide a comprehensive summary of every possible gift but merely to suggest the great variety of spiritual manifestations through which God is at work in the church.

In Pauline theology, spiritual gifts function as indicators of the purpose for which Christians were created and the means by which they bring glory to God. A similar theme is developed in *Chariots of Fire* when Olympic runner and future missionary Eric Liddell states, 'I believe God made me for a purpose, but he also made me fast. And when I run I feel his pleasure'.

Spiritual gifts are consistently discussed in the context of the church as the body of Christ (Rom. 12.4-5; 1 Cor. 12.14-26; Eph. 4.12, 15-16). This is what is meant when the NT speaks of membership in the church: one is a 'member' of the church in the same way that a hand or a foot is a 'member' of one's body. In this light, 1 Pet. 4.11 speaks of gifts in terms of stewardship or the proper allocation of resources within a household. Rather than exalting the possessor, the NT speaks of God giving gifts for the benefit of all. Spider-Man's moral guidepost, 'With great power comes great responsibility', is an apt summary of Paul's teachings about the proper use of gifts in 1 Corinthians 12–14.

The exercise of spiritual gifts has often been a source of controversy. The early church struggled to balance the spontaneous 'charismatic' impulses of groups like the Montanists, who emphasized the immediacy of the Spirit, against the legitimate institutional need for stability and order. The result was an increasingly hierarchical church where access to the Spirit became confined to what the church provided through the sacraments. Even so, reform movements persisted in highlighting the possibility of unmediated encounters with God.

Certain gifts have provoked theological as well as institutional controversies. Since the early twentieth century, Pentecostals have taught that all the gifts described in the NT, particularly in Acts, should be operative in the church today. The charismatic movement brought this theology into churches not historically affiliated with Pentecostalism. Thus, one can speak of 'charismatic Baptists' or 'charismatic Catholics' who maintain ties to their churches of origin but also speak in tongues, pray for divine healing, etc. Other Christians, however, have argued that the more dramatic manifestations such as healings and tongues were limited to the apostolic age. Thus, the more controversial gifts were not meant for today, and contemporary manifestations must be understood as something other than the work of God.

Recommended reading. Dunn, James D.G. *Jesus and the Spirit.* Grand Rapids, MI: Eerdmans, 1997. Fee, Gordon D. *Paul, the Spirit, and the People of God.* Peabody, MA: Hendrickson, 1996. Kelsey, Morton. *Encounter with God: A Theology of Christian Experience.* Mahwah, NJ: Paulist Press, 1988.

See also ACTS, BOOK OF; HOLY SPIRIT; PENTECOST; PROPHETS; TONGUES, SPEAKING IN [DJP]

Spy (Spies). Direct and indirect references to spies figure in both OT and NT. The Hebrew words for spying were derived from the verb *ra'ah* (to see), *ragal* (to use the feet) and *tur* (to go about, to trade). The words indicate that the job of a spy was to go into enemy territory and reconnoiter their strength.

The explicit story of spies in the history of Israel begins with the 12 spies sent out by Moses in Num. 13.1-20. The idea for the mission was due to the people according to Deuteronomy (1.22). One man was selected from each of the 12 tribes. Their mission was to spy out the land in order to determine its geographic characteristics, its productivity (economic strength), the numbers of the people and their strength, their cities and their defenses (military strength). The reconnaissance team was to begin in the Sinai where the Hebrews were camped, to work its way north through the Negev, and then through the hill country. Their intelligence report was to be backed by real evidence of the fruits of the land.

When the spies returned, their majority report was contradicted by the minority report of Joshua and Caleb, urging invasion. The majority report spread disinformation to discourage the invasion; while the minority urged it. The majority prevailed and sparked a popular uprising against Moses. However, the Lord condemned that generation to wander in the wilderness for its faithlessness. The history of the failed spy mission is recounted in Deut. 1.22-45.

Thirty-nine years later in the year or so before the beginning of the conquest of Canaan, Moses sent spies to the Amorite city of Jazer (Num. 21.28). Their reports were apparently useful in the successful battle that expelled the Amorites from Jazer.

Joshua (ch. 2) secretly sent two spies sent to Jericho. They were saved from the city guardians by Rahab, a prostitute to whose house they had gone. She helped the spies to escape from the city by climbing down a rope from a window in her house which was built into the city wall. When Jericho was taken, Rahab and her family were spared (Josh. 6.22-25). According Matthew's genealogy (1.5), she married and had descendants that included King David and Jesus.

During the period of the Judges, the Danites send five spies to find for them a place to settle. They came upon a place called Laish in a quiet valley. The intelligence they gather is used to destroy the people in a surprise attack so that they can take the place for the Tribe of Dan.

During King David's reign, his envoy to the Ammonites is humiliated while on a peaceful mission (2 Sam. 10.1-3; 1 Chron. 19.1-3). The reason for the vile treatment of the ambassador was the suspicion of the Ammonites that he was actually a spy seeking a pretext for war.

In Gal. 2.4, Paul refers to spies (*kataskopeō*) as false believers inserted into the Christian community. Apparently their role was to be disruptive agents who would teach falsely or contradict sound teaching.

Indirect references to spies are found elsewhere in the NT. King Herod, the Pharisees, and the Chief Priest also sent agents to gather information about the public ministry of Jesus (e.g., Mark 6. 14-16; Matt. 22.16; Mark 3.6; 12.13). Herod's wife knew about the message John the Baptist was preaching about her incestuous marriage (Mark 6.17).

Recommended reading. Sheldon, Rose Mary. *Spies of the Bible: Espionage in Israel from the Exodus to the Bar Kokhba Revolt.* St Paul, MN: MBI Publishing, 2007.

See also CALEB; JOSHUA; RAHAB [AJW]

Star (see Magi).

Stars in their Courses. From the Song of Deborah in Judges. A prophet and one of Israel's great judges, Deborah guided the Israelites out of a period of unrest, which began with Ehud's death, the fall of the Hittites, and Rameses II's death. For 20 years, the Israelites had been 'cruelly oppressed' by the Canaanite commander Sisera, but Deborah prophesied that the Israelite general Barak should summon ten thousand men to take position on Mount Tabor in order to conquer Sisera (Judg. 4.3, 6-7). She also prophesied that Barak would not be the one to kill Sisera, but that God would deliver him into the hands of a woman. At Barak's request, Deborah accompanied him and his warriors up to Mount Tabor, and on the appointed day, she ordered the men into battle. Sisera's army was massacred, and although he initially escaped on foot, he was later killed by Jael, the wife of Heber. Thus, Deborah's prophecy was fulfilled. Eventually, the Israelites also destroyed King Jabin of Canaan, and then Deborah and Barak recount the ordeal in a song of victory in Judges 5.

This Song of Deborah indicates that God himself fought on behalf of the Israelites, sending torrential rains and flash floods to help defeat Sisera. 'The stars fought from heaven, / from their courses they fought / against Sisera. / The torrent Kishon swept them away, / the onrushing torrent, / the torrent Kishon' (Judg. 5.20-21). Some scholars also interpret this passage to mean that the Israelites were influenced by the stars, or astronomically guided.

Predictably, this phrase appears often in well-known hymns. For instance, songwriter and Christian worship leader Simon Brading has a song called 'Stars in their Courses Above'. And Thomas A. Chisolm wrote in 1923 a hymn entitled 'Great Is Thy Faithfulness', in which the second verse proclaims 'Summer and winter, and springtime and harvest, / Sun, moon and stars in their courses above, / Join with all nature in manifold witness / To Thy great faithfulness, mercy and love'. In more secular popular culture realms, however, the phrase has served as a title for a number of books on everything from United States Civil War history to astronomy. Historical romance novelist Gilbert Morris has a book titled *Stars in their Courses* (1995), Book 8 in his Appomattox Saga. Historian and novelist Shelby Foote released in 1994 a non-fiction military history of the Gettysburg Campaign entitled *Stars in the Courses: The Gettysburg Campaign*. Isaac Asimov, prolific science fiction author, wrote *The Stars in their Courses* (1971), a collection of seventeen non-fiction essays about astronomy, physics, chemistry, and sociology. In 1960, Harry Brown released a novel titled *The Stars in their Courses*, which retells the story of *The Iliad* in 1870s Colorado. The movie *El Dorado* (1966), directed by Howard Hawks, is loosely based on Brown's novel. And Sir James Jeans's *The Stars in their Courses* (1931) attempts to introduce laymen readers to what Jeans calls 'the most poetical of the sciences', astronomy.

With such powerful symbolism behind it, this phrase will likely continue to appear in songs, books, movies, and games of the future.

See also DEBORAH; JUDGES; BARAK; JAEL; SISERA
[DN]

Stephen. All that is known about Stephen is found in Acts 6–7. He was selected by the church in Jerusalem to attend to the needs of its Greek-speaking widows and he holds the honor of being the first Christian martyr. In Eastern Christianity, he is designated the 'Protomartyr'.

Stephen's name was Greek, suggesting that he was a hellenistic Jew, born in some foreign land and only later immigrating to Jerusalem. The time of his conversion to Christianity is unclear. One early tradition claims that he was one of the 70 disciples that Jesus sent out in Luke 10, but this is purely speculation.

Stephen first enters the scene during a time of dissatisfaction in the church with respect to its ministry to Greek-speaking widows. The early church, like the synagogue, had programs of assistance for needy widows, and some of the Greek-speaking Jews in the Jerusalem congregation complained that their widows were being neglected. The apostles addressed the issue by appointing seven men, including Stephen, to oversee the matter. These are traditionally understood to be the first deacons, although Scripture does not use that term to describe them.

The Bible notes Stephen's exemplary character. He had a good reputation and was 'full of the Spirit and of wisdom' (Acts 6.3), 'full of faith and the Holy Spirit' (Acts 6.5), and 'full of grace and power' (Acts 6.8). Although chosen to 'wait on tables', Stephen soon distinguished himself as a worker of miracles and a powerful, provocative speaker.

Stephen's blunt declarations that the temple was no longer the means by which to seek reconciliation with God enraged the people and the Jewish leadership. As such, Stephen stands in a long line of figures from history and literature who ran afoul of those in power because they spoke a truthful but unwelcome message. One thinks of such figures as Thomas Becket (whose story is told in T.S. Eliot's *Murder in the Cathedral*) and Martin Luther King, Jr in this regard. Eliot's work can be taken as a call to oppose the fascism in the 1930s. Two decades later, Arthur Miller's *The Crucible* was inspired by the anti-Communist paranoia of the 1950s. Both works explore the dynamic by which powerful people suppress a message they prefer not to hear.

Stephen's opponents brought false witnesses who claimed he had blasphemed against Moses and God. In his defense before the Sanhedrin, Stephen recounted the history of God's saving acts and how God is in no way bound to earthly structures or institutions in completing his work. This speech so enraged Stephen's audience that they immediately rushed at him and took him out to stone him. Like Jesus, people tried to kill him because of his message (Luke 4.28-30). And like Jesus, he died praying for the forgiveness of his killers (Luke 22.34; Acts 7.56).

Luke notes that Saul of Tarsus took an active part in Stephen's death (Acts 8.1). Saul later became the renowned apostle Paul, and some theorize that the experience of Stephen's martyrdom opened the way for his eventual conversion.

The feast of Saint Stephen is celebrated on December 26 in the Western Church. Hence the song that begins 'Good King Wenceslas looked out on the feast of Stephen' describes an action of the king on the day after Christmas. He is the patron saint of deacons, headaches, horses, coffin makers, and stonemasons. Scenes of the Stoning of Stephen are a commonplace of western art (e.g., Fra Angelico, 1447–49; Paolo Uccello, c. 1435; Vittore Carpaccio, 1520; Pietro da Cortona, c. 1660).

See also Deacon/Deaconess; Martyr; Martyrdom; Stoning [DJP]

Steward. Normally, a slave or free financial administrator of a household or kingdom. A steward, although subordinate to the householder, functioned as his or her manager and representative. He therefore possessed considerable authority and responsibility. Although stewards typically functioned with some degree of autonomy, they were also required to obey the instructions of their masters for fear of pending judgment. In the OT, stewards are often identified as 'the one over the house' (*'asher 'al-habbayit*) of a particular householder or king. Joseph, for instance, was placed 'over the house' of Potiphar (Gen. 39.4) and following his imprisonment was promoted 'over the house' of Pharaoh (Gen. 41.40). Obadiah (1 Kgs 18.3) and several minor biblical characters were also placed 'over the palaces' of Israel and Judah.

In the NT, the steward (*oikonomos*) and stewardship (*oikonomia*) appear figuratively for Christians entrusted with great responsibility. Some stewards are praised as wise, good, and faithful while others are assessed as shrewd, wicked, and lazy. In the parables of Jesus, a steward in one instance is a free business manager (Luke 16.1-13) and in another a highly trusted household slave (Luke 12.42-48// Matt. 24.45-51; cf. Luke 19.11-27//Matt. 25.14-30). The Pauline letters periodically employ stewards and stewardship metaphorically for church leaders and leadership appointments (1 Cor. 4.1-2; 9.17; Col. 1.25; Eph. 3.2; Tit. 1.7), as did Ignatius, the late first-century bishop of Antioch, in his letter to Polycarp (6.1). 1 Peter identifies all spiritually gifted Christians as 'good stewards of the manifold grace of God' (4.10). Hebrews even implies that Christ was entrusted a stewardship, stating that he was 'faithful over God's house' (3.6). Erastus was also introduced by Paul as Corinth's city steward, or treasurer (*oikonomos tēs poleōs*, Rom. 16.23), although there is much debate surrounding his social and political status.

In modern western culture, stewards are typically conceived of in two ways. As in antiquity, a steward or stewardess can refer to a position of service in a domestic or commercial context. In this sense the term is synonymous with a butler or flight attendant. In western culture, the quintessential butler is a snooty, serious, expressionless, and aged male who speaks with a British accent, much like Geoffrey, the Banks family butler from the early 1990s television sitcom *The Fresh Prince of Bel Air*, and Alfred, the butler of Bruce Wayne in the *Batman* comic series. By contrast, the stereotypical 'stewardess' is young, beautiful, cheerful, and female. A steward can also refer to a trustee who lacks any formal obligations or servile connotations. In this sense a 'good steward' is simply one of cares for his or her belongings, whether money or perhaps the environment, and therefore treats and spends them responsibly, especially in an ecclesiastical context. Surprisingly, stewards have not previously occupied the attention of many artists. Johann Christoph Weigel produced a woodcut of the *Dishonest Steward* (1695) from Luke 16.1-8, but not many others have treated the subject in a noteworthy manner.

Recommended reading. Layton, Scott C. 'The Steward in Ancient Israel: A Study of Hebrew (*'ašer*) *'al-habbayit* in its Near Eastern Setting'. *JBL* 109 (1990) 633-49. Reumann, John. *Stewardship and the Economy of God*. Grand Rapids, MI: Eerdmans, 1992. Williams, Ritva H. *Stewards, Prophets, Keepers of the Word: Leadership in the Early Church*. Peabody, MA: Hendrickson, 2006.

See also Joseph; Son of Jacob; Servant; Slave; Talents, parable; Unjust Steward, parable [JKG]

Stigmata. From the plural of the Greek *stigma* (mark or brand). The wounds in the hands and feet corresponding to the marks Christ received when nailed to the cross, and the wound in his side from being stabbed with the spear are considered the marks of the stigmata. Some stigmatics have also exhibited wounds on the forehead or back, corresponding respectively to the marks from the Crown of Thorns or the scourging.

When Jesus appeared to the disciples after his resurrection, Thomas was absent and stated 'unless I see the mark of the nails in his hands, and put my finger in the mark of the nails and my hand in his side, I will not believe' (John 20.25). A week later Jesus reappeared and said to Thomas, 'Put your finger here and see my hands. Reach out your hand and put it in my side. Do not doubt but believe' (John 20.27). Thomas put his finger into the hole in his side and was convinced, thus, the wounds of Christ, later manifest on Christians, have come to signify the power of belief. The stigmata are referred to by Paul at the end of Galatians (6.17) where he says, 'I carry the marks of Jesus branded on my body'. Scholars have debated whether this was intended to be a literal or figurative remark.

The marks of the stigmata have been exhibited by various people throughout history. The first documented stigmatic was St Francis of Assisi, whose experience took place on the mountaintop at La Verna in 1224. Many artistic representations of Francis receiving the stigmata were painted between the thirteenth and seventeenth centuries, notably by Giotto and Ghirlandaio. Through the twentieth century, over 300 people have exhibited signs of stigmata. Other significant stigmatics include Blessed Angela of Foligno (thirteenth century), St Christina of Stommeln (1268), St Catherine of Siena (1375), St Veronica Giuliani (1697), and Padre Pio (1918). The variety of people—lay and religious, yet predominantly female—who have experienced stigmata is exemplified in popular literature. Jodi Picoult's *Keeping Faith* (2006) features a young girl who exhibits stigmata, while the stigmatic in Ron Hansen's *Mariette in Ecstasy* (1992) is a nun. That the stigmata stands in for the wounds of Christ is the concept behind the 'anti-novel' *The Stigmata Proxy* by Jason Rogers (2005), billed as a psychological experiment in bringing on stigmata. Phyllis Alesia Perry's 1999 novel *Stigmata* also evokes the proxy concept, with a modern protagonist suffering physical manifestations of the wounds endured by her enslaved ancestors.

Films that focus on a stigmatic include *The Exorcism of Emily Rose* (2005) and *Stigmata* (1999). In the latter, a Vatican priest (Gabriel Byrne) travels around verifying miracles, including investigating an American woman (Patricia Arquette), who is exhibiting signs of stigmata. This references the Vatican's Congregation for the Doctrine of the Faith, which validates miraculous events. Substantiation of stigmata is a tricky endeavor, again reflected by the 'false stigmatics' in Carl Hiassen's 1997 novel *Lucky You* and the film *The Butterfly Effect* (2004). A number of contemporary television shows, including *The X-Files*, *House*, *The Simpsons*, *Judging Amy*, *Picket Fences*, and *Nip/Tuck*, have featured purported stigmatics in episodes that deal with issues of their authentication and acceptance.

Recommended reading. Freeze, Mike. *They Bore the Wounds of Christ: The Mystery of the Sacred Stigmata.* Huntington, IN: Our Sunday Visitor, 1989. Harrison, Ted. *Stigmata: A Medieval Mystery in a Modern Age.* New York: St Martin's Press, 1994.

See also CROSS/CRUCIFIXION OF CHRIST; CROWN OF THORNS; MAN OF SORROWS; THOMAS, DOUBTING [ACF]

Still small voice. Elijah, the most commanding of the former prophets, ministered during the reign of King Ahab and his wife Jezebel, who promoted the worship of Baal and Asherah and killed the prophets of God. The story of Elijah's consequential visit to Ahab is told in 1 Kings 17–19. The prophet announce that God was sending punishment—a three year drought. Elijah's authority is not his own because he is from obscure origins. The authority for his prophetic announcement is God's word.

After the prophecy, Elijah goes into hiding first at the Brook of Cherith where he is fed by ravens. He goes next to the home of a widow in Zarephath in Sidon (outside Ahab's jurisdiction) where he lives for awhile. During the third year of the drought Elijah is commanded to return and to confront Ahab, which he does. A contest is then arranged between Elijah and the 450 prophets of Baal. They fail to bring rain, but Elijah's prayer effects the fiery consumption of the sacrifice on the altar he had built, followed by major storm. Before it breaks, the prophets of Baal are killed and Elijah outruns Ahab's chariot to Jezreel.

When Ahab tells Jezebel what happened, she sends Elijah a death threat, which completely unnerves him. He flees for his life first to Beersheba and then a day's journey into the wilderness gripped by depression and fear. His despairing prayer for God to take his life is like Jonah's following his preaching (Jon 4.3). Instead of dying, he is divinely provided with food, and then goes to Mount Horeb (Sinai) where he lodges in a cave.

After 40 days and nights, the word of the Lord comes to him, saying 'What are you doing here, Elijah?' The question is rhetorical. It is saying, who gave you permission to get into a despairing funk? He replies, expressing the depths of his self-pity, saying that he has been very jealous for the Lord, yet all of the faithful are dead and he alone is left. In reply God tells Elijah to stand at the mouth of the cave. He then experiences a violent whirlwind, a terrible earthquake and a fire, but the Lord was in none of these. Traditional heralds of God (Pss 18.7-10; 29.3-9) they are here a form of *via negativa* theological statement describing God by what is not.

When Elijah hears the 'small still voice' (1 Kgs 19.13 KJV, AV) he covers his face in reverence and repeats his claim to the last remaining faithful servant. God says he has 7000 men with knee unbowed to Baal. He commissions Elijah to anoint Hazael to be king of Syria, Jehu son of Nimshi king of Israel and Elisha as his successor.

God's presence is thus often described as known through a 'small still voice'. Some describe it as a silent whisper where the 'hearer' is confronted by the divine in quietness. It has been the claim of many spiritual people that in times of peace and silence they have heard it as an audible silence necessary for communion with God as expressed by David Schubert in his poem 'A Successful Summer'.

Recommended reading. Jacobs, Michael. *Still Small Voice*. London: SPCK Publishing, 1993. Simmons, Shirley D. *A Still Small Voice*. Parker, CO: Outskirts Press, 2005.

See also AHAB; BAAL; ELIJAH; ELISHA; FORMER PROPHETS; HOREB, MOUNT; JEZEBEL; JEZREEL; JONAH; MOUNT CARMEL; PROPHETS; SINAI, MOUNT; STRANGE WOMAN; WIDOW OF ZAREPHATH [AJW]

Stone. Biblical Hebrew has a several words for a common rock or stone (*eben*; Exod. 15.5). A rugged stone or cliff was a *sela*, the name given to Petra the mountain city of the Edomites. In contrast a sharp stone was a *tsur* (Job 41.30).

In the NT, Greek words for stone are used a number of times. The general word was *lithos*, but a small stone was a *petros* after which Peter was named. Verb forms of stone usually applied to stoning (*saqal*, Deut. 13.10). Collecting stones for stoning was a separate word *ragam*, Lev. 20.2). The NT term for stoning is a Greek form of *lithos*. Other words were used for rock.

More important than stoning and the varied uses of stones as markers, weapons or for other uses is the theological use of the word stone. It is used metaphorically in Isaiah (8.14). The prophet is told the Lord of Hosts will become a stone of stumbling for the Houses of Israel. 'He' will be 'a stone one strikes against ... He will be a stone where many will stumble, fall and be broken'. In Isa. 28.16, God tells the prophet that he will lay in 'Zion a foundation stone, a tested stone, a precious cornerstone, a sure foundation'. This is spoken in response to scoffers in Jerusalem who have made a pact with death; who tell each other not to worry because that they shall take refuge in lies (Isa. 28.14-15).

When Nebuchadnezzar has a troubling dream, Daniel interprets it for him saying that the king saw a stone not cut by human hands, which destroyed a colossal statue. He interprets the stone as a symbolizing God's creation of an everlasting kingdom that will put down all other kingdoms (Dan. 2.44-45).

The Psalmist writes that the 'stone which the builders reject has become the chief corner stone'. This event is 'the Lord's doing' (118.23). The appropriate response is to declare: 'This is the day the Lord has made; let us rejoice and be glad in it'. The cause of joy is the stone which is the chief cornerstone.

The Gospels identify Jesus with the stone of Ps. 118.22 (Mark 12.10; Luke 20.18; Matt. 21.42). He was the stone which the builders (the chief priests) had rejected. He was the foundation, the cornerstone of the church binding the whole building together.

In Romans, Paul discussed the rejection of Jesus by the Jewish leadership and others in terms of the rejected stone (9.30-33). He combines quotes from Isa. 8.14 and 28.16 to say that the rejection was a rejection of God's gift of salvation.

The image of Christ as the stone of stumbling which is the stone of foundation is found in Acts 4.11, Eph. 2.20 and 1 Pet. 2.4-6. The message is that Jesus is a sure foundation for those who trust in him, but becomes condemnation for who reject him.

The picture of the mysterious stone has been used for many theological purposes. In 1492 James Ryman wrote a carol, 'The Sone of God in thron' using the image. The rejected stone has also figured in T.S. Elliot's 'The Rock' and in Somerset Maugham's *Catalina*.

See also CHRIST; PETER; ROCK; STONES CRY OUT; STONING [AJW]

Stone that the builders rejected. (See Stone).

Stones cry out. There are two references to the 'stones cry out' in the Bible (Hab. 2.11 and Luke 19.40). In Habakkuk, people are told that if they gained their house by evil means, 'the very stones will cry out from the wall'; in Luke, Jesus uses the phrase against the Pharisees after being told that the disciples should stop preaching, to which he said: 'I tell you, if these were silent, the stones would shout out' ('shout' replacing 'cry' in the NRSV). The implication is that if something bad is done, or something good is not done, and no one says anything, then the stones, regarded as silent, would emit a positive or negative energy. In many ways, it is associated with the idea of 'good vibes' or 'bad vibes' from when somebody first meets another person, or visits somebody's house.

The term has also been used by some Asian writers. The Japanese writer Hikaru Okuizmi won the Akutagawa Prize in 1994 for his novel *Ishi no Raieki*, translated into English as *The Stones Cry out*. The Cambodian, Molyda Szymusiak used the title *The Stones Cry out* (originally *Les pierres crieront* in French) as the title of her autobiography of the terrible time she faced in Cambodia under the Communist Khmer Rouge from 1975 until 1979. With nobody to speak out against the atrocities by the Communists, it was only the stones which were able to bear witness to the misery and terror. Indeed for this very reason, some people do not like to visit former concentration camps, prisons or sites of execution, because the stones bear witness to what has happened there.

See also ROCK; STONE [JC]

Stoning. A form of corporate, capital punishment found throughout the HB/OT, NT and classical literature. Since everyone in the community could participate, no individual was responsible for the execution. The offender would stand before a crowd, who would hurl stones at him or her until he or she died. Mishnah *Sanhedrin* 6.4 recounts that stoning would involve dropping a victim from a height and pushing stones onto him or her. A person cannot be stoned on the evidence of one witness and the witnesses are the first to throw stones (Deut. 17.6-7).

Sometimes stoning occurred outside the town, at the front gate, or in the case of a new husband, at the adulteress's father's house, for being a harlot in her father's house. Stoning was considered the harshest form of execution, worse than burning, decapitation or strangulation. Stoning could be the result of different sins: blasphemy (Lev. 24.13-16; 23); worshiping Molech (Lev. 20.2; Deut. 13.7-12; 17.2-7); divination or witchcraft (Lev. 20.27); violating Sabbath (Num. 15.35-36); the rebellious son (Deut. 21.18-21); and sexual indiscretion (Deut. 22.13-21; cf. John 8.7). Additionally, people and animals could also be stoned for coming too near Mount Sinai (Exod. 19.13); an ox that killed a person could be stoned, along with its owner, under certain conditions (Exod. 21.29-33).

Stoning narratives are: of the blasphemer in the camp (Lev. 24.13-16); the man gathering sticks on the Sabbath (Num. 15.35-36); Achan for taking plunder from enemies in violation of God's instructions (Josh. 7.25); Naboth for blaspheming (1 Kgs 21.13); the priest-prophet Zechariah (2 Chron. 24.20-22); Stephen (Acts 7.58-60); and an adulteress (John 8.2-7). Several persons are stoned or nearly stoned by angry mobs, e.g., Rehoboam's taskmaster Adoram (1 Kgs 12.18), Moses (Exod. 17.4; Num. 14.10), Joshua and Caleb (Num. 14.10), and David before the inhabitants of Ziklag (1 Sam. 30.6). Jesus and his apostles were often in danger of being stoned by crowds for blasphemy (John 10.31-33; 11.8; Acts 5.26; 14.5, 19). Offenses stipulated in Torah for an unspecified death penalty were considered to be stoning offences by the rabbis.

Acts narrates the martyrdom of Stephen, who rebuked his people with a long speech and was stoned to death, due to false witnesses (6.8–7.60). Like the case of Zechariah, apparently Stephen also was blamed for blasphemy (6.11), and punished according to the precedent setting story and law such as in the Pentateuch (Lev. 24.11-16, 23).

Stoning was usual punishment in the Greco-Roman world, alluded to as early as the *Iliad* (*Iliad* 3.56). In Greece, stoning was likely never a typical sentence, and would have been reserved for specific crimes. By Roman times the practice had become more arbitrary, and not necessarily associated with particular crimes.

The Muslim Hajj contains a ritual 'stoning of the devil', where stones are thrown at columns or a wall to represent Abraham's stoning Satan. Stoning as a capital punishment has remained in parts of the Islamic world through modern times. Stoning remains a legally acceptable punishment in Indonesia, Iran, and Afghanistan (by the Taliban). Stoning was also practiced in pre-modern Japan.

Recommended reading. Goldin, H.E. *Hebrew Criminal Law and Procedure*. Pp. 131-40. New York: Twayne, 1952. Hirzel, R. *Die Strafe der Steinigung*. Darmstadt: Wissenschaftliche Buchgesellschaft, 1967. Kalimi, I. *The Retelling of Chronicles in Jewish Tradition and Literature: A Historical Journey*. Winona Lake, IN: Eisenbrauns, 2009, 40-43. Pease, A.S. 'Notes on Stoning among the Greeks and Romans'. *Transactions and Proceedings of the American Philological Association* 38 (1907) 1-18.

See also STEPHEN; STONE [IK]

Strait and narrow. These two words, from the Greek *stenē* (strait) and *tethlimmenē* (narrow), appear together in Matt. 7.14: 'For the gate is narrow and the road is hard that leads to life, and there are few who find it'. This text belongs to the last part of Jesus' 'Sermon on the Mount' (Matt. 7.1-29).

This phrase evokes the image of an athlete's hard training in preparation for a difficult race. On several occasions, Jesus pointed out the necessity of discipline, submission to God, and perseverance in reaching the ultimate goals of life (Matt. 5.1-12; Luke 13.24; 18.22-30). Only those who are able to renounce what is superfluous and what is useful but not indispensable, and endure the difficulties of the way will be able to travel the hard path of life until the end.

Conventional thinking views *narrow* as a negative concept, while *wide*, its antithesis, is perceived as positive (cf. Josh. 17.15 and Isa. 8.20). However, Jesus reverses this imagery in this famous aphorism. He invites his followers to enter through the narrow gate, and depart from the wide road that leads to nothingness (Matt. 7.13-14; Luke 13.24). This metaphor refers both to the difficulties of a life of submission to God, and to the relatively small number of those who renounce the easy life of self-indulgence.

Many great ascetics and mystics of Christianity, such as St Benedict and St Augustine, correlated the concept of the strait and narrow with obedience to God, and juxtaposed this with the wide road followed by the rest of the world (*De Sermone Domini in Monte* 2.33.77). The pre-reformer Wyclif defined the narrow way as the faithful keeping of God's commandments, and the strait gate as the fear of God which leads to an abandonment of sin. Reformers such as Calvin identified the wide gate as a worldly life, and the narrow gate as restrictions in lifestyle for committed believers. The Puritans related entering the narrow gate with adult conversion.

The famous Presbyterian Matthew Henry associated the narrow gate and the less frequented path with conversion and regeneration (*Commentary* 5.92-93). For the founder of Methodism, John Wesley, the narrow way refers to the necessity to strive for a 'separated' life from the world. The narrow path metaphor also inspired the seminal book *The Way* (1939), by José Maria Escriva de Balaguer (1902–1975), founder of Opus Dei, a lay Catholic movement committed to a sanctified life through secular work and mortification.

On this theme, John Bunyan (1628–1688) wrote the allegorical novel *The Pilgrim's Progress: From This World to That Which Is to Come* (1678), one of the most influential books in English literature. After a dangerous journey through ways 'Crooked and Wide', Christian arrives at the 'Wicket-gate' (a small door set within a larger one). After repenting from his sins, he is able to set upon the 'narrow way … as straight as a Rule can make it', that leads to his final destination, the Celestial City (cf. Rev. 22.14). The theme of this famous book is alluded to in many works, including the video game *Deus Ex: Invisible War* (2003). In contemporary culture, the topic of a hard journey that leads to salvation appears in novels such as *The Road*, by Cormac McCarthy (2006), and in the film of the same name (2009).

See also Deep; Discipline; Harlot; Sermon on the Mount; Wide [DAVS]

Strange woman. In Proverbs, the 'strange woman' (*issha zara, nokriyya*) is the opposite of the good wife and mother, a figure to be scrupulously avoided by the sage (5.20). She is characterized as a flatterer (2.16; 5.36; 6.24; 7.5), an evil, predatory creature, who lies in wait for young men as if they were quarry (23.26-28). Synonymous with the prostitute, the adulteress and the foolish woman (cf. 7.1-27), she is portrayed misogynistically and xenophobically, contrasting with the exaltatation of Lady Wisdom (e.g., 1.20-33; 8.1-36; 9.1-6; Rev. 2.20-25). Although not necessarily described as such, throughout the Bible, strange/foreign/loose women are portrayed as both powerful and deadly (e.g., Delilah, Jezebel, the Whore of Babylon), and closely aligned with idolatry (e.g., Num. 25.1-9; 1 Kgs 11.1-13; Hos. 1–3; Ezra 10.2). In the DSS, the strange woman of Proverbs becomes generally symbolic of evil (4Q184).

Western culture is replete with stereotypical 'wicked women', from the archetypal 'woman' railed against by early Christian 'fathers' such as Tertullian and Jerome to the femme fatale of film noir (including 1946's *The Strange Woman*, with the title character played by Hedy Lamarr). In popular culture, songs about dangerous and deceitful women who destroy men through their sexual treachery are particularly prevalent, e.g., the Electric Light Orchestra's 'Evil Woman' (1975), Foreigner's 'Cold as Ice' (1977), Hall and Oates's 'Maneater' (1982), Bon Jovi's 'You Give Love a Bad Name' (1986), and Kiss's 'Modern-Day Delilah' (2009).

Recommended reading. Aguiar, Sarah Appleton. *The Bitch Is Back: Wicked Women in Literature*. Carbondale/Edwardsville: Southern Illinois University Press, 2001. Camp, Claudia V. *Wise, Strange and Holy: The Strange Woman and the Making of the Bible*. Gender, Culture, Theory 9; JSOTSup, 320. Sheffield: Sheffield Academic Press, 2000. Golf, Matthew. 'Hellish Females: The Strange Woman of Septuagint Proverbs and 4QWiles of the Wicked Woman (4Q184)'. *Journal for the Study of Judaism* 39 (2008) 20-45.

See also DELILAH; HARLOT; JEZEBEL; PROVERBS; WISDOM [MALB]

Stranger. Variously translated from the Hebrew *ger* and *toshab*, and the Greek *paroikos*, as stranger, foreigner, resident alien and sojourner. While the first sojourner is Cain, Abraham is also a stranger and a sojourner (Gen. 23.4), paradigmatic of the Hebrew experience that colors biblical narrative and Law: 'You shall not oppress a resident alien; you know the heart of an alien, for you were aliens in Egypt' (Exod. 23.9).

Hospitality figures strongly in the Bible. Abraham and Lot hurry to welcome divine strangers, but Lot's neighbors in Sodom invite divine destruction for mistreating the guests. Job champions 'the cause of the stranger' (Job 29.16), and among the traits that separate sheep from goats in Matthew is the willingness to welcome strangers (25.31-46). Jesus is a stranger in John's Gospel, unrecognized by his own (1.11), but recognized as the mysterious gardener at the tomb (20.10-18) and the unknown stranger on the shore (21.1-13).

Exile from the Promised Land makes God's people strangers. It is an alienating experience: 'How can we sing the song of the Lord in a foreign land?' (Ps. 137.4). The 'other' for Israel is the Gentile, who is integrated in Isaiah 40–66 and the NT, but the Psalmists also struggle with a kind of spiritual alienation as strangers to God (e.g., Ps. 39). Moreover, there is a sense that the Christian is forever a stranger and sojourner here (Heb. 11.13; 1 Pet. 2.11).

Artists use the biblical theme diversely. 'The Wandering Jew' trope becomes stereotypical in European folklore, where the Jew is the eternally cursed exile. The wayfarer in Chagall's painting, *The Wandering Jew*, travels past a distant, uninviting village where the church figures prominently, next to a picture of a single goat, symbolic of the eternally rejected (Matt. 25.31-46).

English writers capture the Wayfarer in the character of Everyman, who, in Bosch's (1450–1516) *Haywain Triptych*, walks 'The Path of Life', a Prodigal Son surrounded by greed and violence. Famously, Christian from Bunyan's *Pilgrim's Progress* encounters strangers upon his way. Some impede his progress, like Mr. Worldly Wiseman; but others help, including Good Will, a hidden Jesus. Christ as wayfaring stranger occurs in popular art, even as late as Joan Osborne's 'One of Us', where God may be 'Just a stranger on a bus' returning home.

The mysterious stranger may be an opportunity to entertain angels (Heb. 13.2). However, the stranger could just as likely be evil, ambivalence displayed variously from the tall, handsome, dark stranger in romantic lore to Satan in Twain's *The Mysterious Stranger*. Clint Eastwood captures the malevolent hero who rides into town as the Stranger in *High Plains Drifter*, and the Man With No Name in The Dollars Trilogy. Even in popular music, where 'Strangers in the Night' exchange glances, there is also the one night stand of Supertramp's 'Goodbye Stranger' or cold betrayal in Hillary Duff's 'The Stranger'.

Camus's novel *L'Étranger* suggests images like 'foreigner', 'stranger', 'outsider', and even 'disconnected'. The alienation is both socio-economic—the French protagonist kills a colonial Arab—and personal, themes also hinted at in Hinton's novel and film *The Outsiders*. With recent American immigration, themes of the stranger have re-emerged. Lazarus's 'Mother of Exiles', Lady Liberty, inviting the tired, poor, and huddled masses who yearn freedom is a stark contrast to the Wall of Mexico stemming the tide of northbound migration. This tension is caught in films like *Spanglish* and *Crash*, but less ostensibly in alien invasion pieces like *Men in Black* and *Alien*, and in *Planet 51* and *Avatar*, where the stranger roles are reversed.

See also ABRAHAM; GOD; GOOD SAMARITAN, PARABLE OF; JOSHUA; LOT; NEIGHBOR; STRANGER IN A STRANGE LAND [BDGD]

Stranger in a strange land. This phrase is found in Exod. 2.22 and resonates deeply with those who know what it means to live in new surroundings or who are immigrants. Contemporary cultural depictions of the immigrant experience (e.g., music: *Immigrant*; film: *Fiddler on the Roof, Journey of Hope*; TV: *Once Upon a Time in Toronto*; literature: *America and I* [Anzia Yezierska], *Stranger in a Strange Land* [Robert Heinlein]) explore this subject from a different perspective than the scriptures. Indeed, a Christian reflection on the immigrant experience moves beyond the existential and socio-political factors that inform secular perspectives and incorporates important biblical and theological truths.

In the OT the terms alien, foreigner, and sojourner (Hebrew: *gēr*, *tôšāḇ*, *zār*, *nēkār*, *nokrî*) describe two distinct but related sets of circumstances, the experience of the people of God living in Egypt (Exod. 22.21) and non-Jews who lived within Israel. With respect to the second group, the foreigner living in Israel was to be loved rather than oppressed (Exod. 23.9; Lev. 19.33-34; Deut. 10.19), permitted to rest on the Sabbath (Exod. 23.12), allowed to glean the fields and vineyards (Lev. 19.10, Ruth 2) and permitted access to the cities of refuge (Num. 35.15). The theological basis of Israel's obligation to treat strangers well is their experience of God's act of redemption from the mistreatment they experienced in Egypt. Balanced against these benefits, the sojourner was to abstain from blasphemy (Lev. 24.16), eating blood (Lev. 17.10, 13), and immorality (Lev. 18.26). The stranger was to also respect the worship of Israel, e.g., abstain from leavened bread during Passover (Exod. 12.19), refrain from idolatry (Lev. 20.2), and not work on either the Sabbath or the Day of Atonement (Exod. 20.10, Lev. 16.29). Finally, if sojourners wished to participate in the Passover it was necessary that the males be circumcised (Exod. 12.48).

In the NT, the people of God are described as sojourners living in a foreign land (Eph. 2.19; 1 Pet. 1.1, 17, 2.11), a description which invites Christ-followers to understand that, as with the immigrant, their sense of identity is defined by a perspective and values which lie outside their physical and social context. In addition, the Christian's response to those who are outsiders is understood to reflect the extent to which that person's attitudes and lifestyle are shaped by the gospel (Matt. 25.35, 38, 43-44).

Evidence that this theological perspective on the sojourner has influenced western culture may be seen in the emergence of the field of social work in the nineteenth-century which, among other things, sought to address the social and health needs created by waves of immigration. Similarly, J.S. Woodsworth (*Strangers within our Gates*) and others within the Social Gospel Movement employed theological values to shape their response to the needs of immigrants. Finally, the group *Christians for Comprehensive Immigration Reform* has recently (a) affirmed that shared moral and theological principles compel Christians to care for and seek justice for the stranger, and (b) called for fair and humane immigration reform within the United States.

Recommended reading. Soerens, Matthew, and Jenny Hwang. *Welcoming the Stranger: Justice, Compassion and Truth in the Immigration Debate*. Downers Grove, IL: InterVarsity, 2009.

See also EXILE; STRANGER [KFM]

Suffer fools gladly. The word 'suffer' in the expression 'suffer fools gladly' denotes abstinence from judgment on those who manifest annoying or unpleasant behavior. Thus, to suffer fools gladly is to exhibit patience with those whom one considers less intelligent than oneself.

The origin of this expression is 2 Corinthians 11.19 (KJV): 'For ye suffer fools (Greek: *aphronōn*; cf. 16, 17) gladly, seeing ye yourselves are wise (Greek: *phronimoi*)'. Evidently, tolerance of the unwise is deemed a mark of wisdom, otherwise we miss the biting irony of Paul's subsequent remarks. Moreover, widespread ignorance of the second clause serves to reverse the original sense of the verse in modern parlance. Consider such statements as the following. 'John always gives the other fellow a fair hearing, but he will not suffer fools gladly'. Here, by implication, John is considered a discerning individual. However, literary critic, the late H. Northrop Frye, once said this of 'silly reviews' about himself. '[W]hat is important about free speech in a democracy is not only that everyone has a right to express an opinion, however ill-considered, but that fools should have full liberty to speak so that they can be recognized to be fools'.

Indeed Paul labelled boasting (Greek: *kauchaomai* and cognates) as one form of foolishness (Greek: *aphrosynē*) (vv. 16-19; cf. 21b-33). Proponents of 'another gospel' had visited the Corinthian church. So-called 'super-apostles' were preaching salvation by works in lieu of faith in Christ (vv. 4-5). One occasion of their boasting is their self-authenticating Jewish pedigree (v. 22). Judaizing Christians had caused similar difficulties for Paul in Galatia (see Gal. 1.6-9; 3.1-5) and he issues a warning about the problem to the church at Philippi (Phil. 3.2-3).

A lack of wisdom or manifestation of foolishness connotes impiety for OT writers. We note such statements as the following: 'The fool [*aphrōn*] has said in his heart, there is no God' (Ps. 13.1a = 52.1a LXX); 'The fear of the Lord is the beginning of wisdom [*sophia*], and all that act accordingly have good understanding' (Ps. 110.10a = Prov. 1.7a LXX). Paul was a Jew, and this understanding of wisdom and foolishness would have represented an element of his conceptual background. Yet the word fool does not always connote a negative significance. For example, the court jester in Shakespeare's play *King Lear* was called a fool. Such people not only provided entertainment but quite often spoke truths that others dared not express. Hence the maxim 'Many a truth is told in jest'.

See also FOOL, FOOLISHNESS; FREEDOM; PAUL, THE APOSTLE; WISDOM [NRP]

Suffer the Little Children. Mark 10.13-16, Matt. 19.13-15 and Luke 18.15-17 tell a similar story of people who bring children so that Jesus 'might touch them'. The disciples 'rebuked' those who brought the children (Mark 10.13). When Jesus saw the actions of the disciples, he told them to 'Suffer the little children to come unto me, and forbid them not: for of such is the kingdom of God' (Mark 10.14, KJV). Then Jesus blesses the children (Mark 10.16; Matt. 19.15). This story suggests that children were not generally well-received in adult contexts, yet Jesus welcomes them.

Only Mark's account emphasizes Jesus' emotions: he 'embraces' the children and is 'indignant' with the disciples. Matthew's Jesus is more noble and refined; he 'lays his hands on the children' and prays (19.13). In Luke, Jesus is more active: he touches, not children, but 'infants', and 'calls out' to them; Luke does not mention a blessing (18.15-16). Some think that Luke may have been addressing questions about infant baptism in the first century.

Whereas the Gospel uses 'suffer the little children' to encourage inclusion, popular culture uses the phrase to point to children who actually suffer. Some examples include book titles: Donna Leon's novel by that name describes an illegal adoption ring; Barbara Davis's true crime story describes a man who raped and murdered a little girl after he killed her mother; and Mary Raftery's exposé (with Eoin O'Sullivan) reveals the brutal abuse of 100,000 children in Irish state-sponsored Catholic schools from 1868 to 1969. Steven King's short story horror film describes a Miss Sibley who must 'suffer' the transformation of her school children into aliens. In an *ER* episode with this title, a heroin addict steals her baby's methadone and abandons the newborn at the hospital; in a *Deadwood* episode, a desperate young woman becomes a prostitute in order to survive on the frontier. The Pat Benatar song, 'Suffer the Little Children', refers to 'Melissa' who unexpectedly passed away; The Smiths sang of the 1960 'Moor Murders' of several children in Manchester, England. Ironically, most of the art work on this phrase depicts Jesus with happy children.

See also CHILD; CHILDREN OF GOD; SPARE THE ROD [CF]

Suffering Servant. The Suffering Servant is the Servant of the Lord, a figure described in the fourth of four Servant Songs. The first of the Songs (Isa. 42.1-4) deals with the call of the Servant. He will bring justice to the Gentiles and for the earth. The second Song (Isa. 49.1-6) contains the commission of the Servant. He will be a 'light to the Gentiles'. The third Song presents the commitment of the Servant (Isa. 50.4-9). His commitment to being God's servant is so strong that he will endure all manner of suffering no matter how humiliating, including being spat upon. The fourth Song contains the consummation of the Servant (Isa. 52.13–53.12). He will be the suffering servant who bears the sins of his people and gives his life for their redemption.

The Suffering Servant Song (Isa. 52.13–53.12) has five parts: the Servant Exalted (Isa. 52.13-15) summaries the whole prophecy of the servant; the Servant Despised (Isa. 53.1-3) is recognized by Israel as the one rejected; the Servant Wounded suffers for the sins of his people (Isa. 53.4-6); the Servant Cut Off is killed for their sins and is entombed with the wicked and a rich man (Isa. 53. 53.7-9); and the Servant Satisfied declares that he who bore the sins of many will see the fruit of his work and be satisfied (Isa. 53.10-12).

The identity of the Servant in the Servant Songs is not given in Isaiah. There have been three main interpretations of the Servant's identity. The collective identity sees the Servant as all of Israel. Critics of this view point out that Isaiah is preaching to a people under God's chastisement who are therefore missing the messianic element of the Servant. The remnant interpretation identifies the Servant as the remnant of Israel who returned from exile. A few have identified the Servant with Cyrus the Great or with other individuals such as Zerubbabel, Moses and others. For the NT writers, the Servant Songs are theological utterances that apply to Jesus the messiah. They are in agreement that the Servant of the Lord would have to suffer in order to fulfill his mission. His suffering would be redemptive because it would be the means by which he would give his life as a ransom for others. About 40 NT references to Isaiah are to the Suffering Servant Song (Isa. 52.13–53.12). One or more of these verses are quoted in Matt. 8.17, John 12.38, Mark 15.28, Luke 22.37, Rom. 10.16 and 15.21 and 1 Pet. 2.22-25.

The passion narrative in the Gospels and the Book of Acts stress the suffering and hostility inflicted onto the messiah who is referred to as 'his Servant Jesus' (Acts 3.13 26) and as 'Your Servant Jesus' (Acts 4.27, 30) suffering as Isaiah had prophesied. In Acts (8.35) Philip interpreted the Suffering Servant (Isa. 53.7-8) for the Ethiopian treasurer as Jesus Christ.

From the beginning of the church, Christ has been identified as the sinless Suffering Servant. Many works of literature have used the Servant Songs and the Suffering Servant both directly and indirectly. Frequently the Suffering Servant in English literature is described as the Man of Sorrows (Isa. 53.3).

Recommended reading. Baron, David. *Servant of Jehovah: The Sufferings of the Messiah and the Glory That Should Follow: An Exposition of Isaiah 53*. London: Morgan & Scott, 1922. North, Christopher R. *The Suffering Servant in Deutero-Isaiah: An Historical and Critical Study*. London: Oxford University Press, 1956.

See also CYRUS; ECCE HOMO; LAMB OF GOD; LAMB, SACRIFICIAL; MAN OF SORROWS; MESSIAH; PASSION NARRATIVE; SLAVE [AJW]

Sufficient unto the day. This phrase comes from Matt. 6.34, 'Take therefore no thought for the morrow: for the morrow shall take thought for the things of itself. Sufficient unto the day is the evil thereof' (KJV); the idea is 'Take the trouble of the day as it comes' (*Bible in Basic English*) or 'Have no anxiety about tomorrow' (People's NT). This practical principle summarizes the second part of the Sermon on the Mount (Matt. 6.25-34). It reminds believers that it is useless to worry about things that might—or might not—happen in the future, and invites them to trust in God's providence. Since every day brings its own cares, to anticipate them would only double them. Instead of accumulating burdens and anticipating trouble, we are invited to consider that each day brings its own measure of toil. Wise is the person who learns not to try to bear tomorrow's burdens today.

This advice from Jesus echoes other Bible passages, such as 'Eat and drink, for tomorrow we die', etc. (Isa. 22.13, Eccl. 9.7-9; cf. 1 Cor. 15.32). It responds to the rabbinic question. 'And if not now, when?' (*Pikei Avot*, 1.14) and rejoins the famous classical existential caution, *carpe diem* ('Seize the day') from the Latin poet Horace (*Odes* 1.11.8, 'To Leuconoe').

The theme of the shortness of life (*De Brevitate Vitae*) and the advantages of enjoying the present has marked the western culture from ancient times. The phrase *Carpe diem* may be found throughout the centuries on countless sundials. It is the theme of the most ancient and popular European academic song, *Gaudeamus Igitur*, often sung during graduation ceremonies in universities around the world.

The theme 'Enjoy the present, life is short, and time is fleeting' has been explored by many artists throughout history. It inspired the poem 'To the virgins, to make much of time' (1648) by Robert Herrick (1591–1674), which begins, 'Gather ye rosebuds while ye may / old time is still a-flying'. From there, the pre-Raphaelite painter John William Waterhouse (1849–1917) took the title for his famous painting *Gather Ye Rosebuds while Ye May* (1909).

The theme 'seize the day' has been the title of novels (Saul Bellow, 1956), of a radical English band (1997) specialized in protest songs; of folk music albums (Damien Dempsey, 2003) and of many songs (Avenged Sevenfold, 2005). The same theme has inspired the gospel song 'One day at a time, Sweet Jesus' (Marijohn Wilkins and Kris Kristofferson). *One Day at a Time* is the title of Joan Baez's most personal album (1970), including the song 'I live one day at a time' (Willie Nelson); *One day at a time* was also the name of an American TV comedy series created by Whitney Blake and Allan Manings, shown on CBS from 1975 to 1984. Using other words, the theme is present in many songs such as 'Don't worry, be happy!' (Bobby McFerrin, 1988).

The importance of fully living the present is a recurrent theme in the work of Paulo Coelho. It has been underlined in films such as *Dead Poets Society* (1989), *Groundhog Day* (1993), *The Bridges of Madison County* (1995), *The Bucket List* (2007) or the series *Prison Break* (2005–2009).

Recommended reading. Galloway, Lincoln E., "Consider the lilies of the field ...': A Sociorhetorical Analysis of Matthew 6.25-34'. In *Multivalence of Biblical Texts and Theological Meanings*. Ed. Christine Helmer and Charlene T. Higbe. Pp. 67-82. Atlanta: Society of Biblical Literature, 2006. Macaskill, Grant. 'Matthew 6.19-34: The Kingdom, the World and the Ethics of Anxiety'. *Scottish Bulletin of Evangelical Theology* 23 (2005) 18-29.

See also PROVIDENCE; SERMON ON THE MOUNT [RB]

Sun. Biblical references to the sun are linked with solar imagery in the ANE. Since ancient worship regarded the celestial bodies as deities, the sun often took a place as the head deity. This is the case with the head sun god Shamash in Mesopotamian iconography. Likewise, in Egyptian religion the sun played an important role in the religious expression of Pharaoh Akhenaten, where the sun god Aten was elevated to a supreme status during his reign.

Given the widespread worship of the sun as a deity in the ANE, it not surprising that solar imagery is used of Yahweh in the OT. Some of the earliest passages refer to Yahweh as shining (Deut. 33.2; Num. 6.25). Personal names also incorporated an understanding of Yahweh associated with the sun (*Zerakhyah*: 'Yah shines forth'; 1 Chron. 5.32). Yahweh as 'Lord of Hosts' could imply military command over the celestial bodies that signify other deities or angels. Most strikingly, Psalm 104 resembles an Egyptian hymn to the solar deity (*The Great Hymn to Aten*). Scholarly debate has revolved around to what extent Yahwism was a solar religion in its earliest forms. Archaeological evidence seems to support some type of solar dimension to Yahwism such as the solar orientation of temples. The solar dimension of Yahwism seems to be passed on to humans affected by God's presence; Moses's face becomes radiant after his encounter with God on Sinai (Exod. 34.29-30). Since the later editors of the OT were operating from a monotheistic perspective, some of the solar imagery of Yahweh is only now recognizable in the background of the text.

The association of shining or the sun with holiness (Matt. 13.43) and the deity would continue in the NT, e.g., in the portrayal of Jesus in the Transfiguration (Matt. 17.1-9; Mark 9.2-8; Luke 9.28-36), and perhaps the resurrection narratives. The image of light may have roots in solar expressions of Yahweh and thus became part of later Christian expression of Jesus as 'the light of the world' (John 8.12).

Religious art continues to represent holiness with light, albeit rarely the sun. Solar imagery in western culture seems to be taken more from Aztec or Egyptian influences rather than biblical ones. The imagery of the sun on US dollar bill with the illuminated all-seeing eye above the pyramid in its capstone was created by secretary of the Second Continental Congress (1782), Charles Thompson. He seems to mix Egyptian imagery with the Christian and political leanings of the Congress. Theories about such symbolism have been the subject of many recent popular movies like *National Treasure* (2004), *Laura Croft: Tomb Raider* (2001). Thus, while solar imagery has made its way into western culture, it seems to be less a product of biblical influence and more of other religious influences.

Recommended reading. Taylor, J. Glen. *Yahweh and the Sun: Biblical and Archaeological Evidence for Sun Worship in Ancient Israel*. JSOTSup, 111: Sheffield: JSOT Press, 1993.

See also DEITY; TRANSFIGURATION; YAHWEH [SWF]

Susanna. The first of three apocryphal additions to Daniel, traditionally placed at the beginning of the book because Daniel is still young in this story. It can stand on its own as a folktale but also reinforces a legal principle: the two witnesses required for condemnation in biblical law must be questioned separately.

Susanna is an Israelite woman with pious parents and a wealthy husband. He is the most distinguished man in Babylon, and the two elders appointed as judges frequently hear cases in his house. They both lust after Susanna and discuss their passion with one another. One hot day, they follow her into the garden and hide while she bathes. After she sends away her maids to fetch oil, the men approach and tell her they want to lie with her. They threaten to accuse her of adultery with a youth if she refuses. Groaning, Susanna states that she would rather refuse and fall in their hands, risking death, than face certain death if she agrees. She screams, the servants rush in and the elders tell their lie.

At a trial the next day before Susanna's entire family, everyone believes the elders because they are judges, and she is condemned to death. When she cries out to God, the 'holy spirit' of a young Daniel is stirred. He berates the people for accepting the elders' account without examination. He cross-examines them separately, and when asked under which tree they had spied Susanna, their answers conflict. Proven to have lied, they are condemned to death. The conclusion states that Daniel had a great reputation from that day on.

Susanna's screaming in the garden and crying out to God at her trial show her to be not only a passive bystander in her own story, yet she is primarily seen as an object of either lust or scorn. She vanishes from the story once Daniel appears.

This 64-verse story had an impact on western culture out of proportion to its length. There are hundreds of paintings called 'Susanna and the Elders', in which Susanna is beautiful, naked, and vulnerable and the elders usually leering and grotesque. Numerous plays and poems of the past few centuries are based on *Susanna*. Shakespeare knew the story, since in the court scene (Act 4) of *Merchant of*

Venice, Portia is called a 'wise' and 'second' Daniel. Händel wrote an oratorio based on the story in 1749.

An interesting re-telling of the story is the 1949 American opera *Susannah* by Carlisle Floyd. The setting is a small Tennessee town. Susannah is seen bathing naked on her farm by the Elders, who blame her for inciting their lust. A 15-year-old boy tells her she was seen, and that the Elders also forced him to say publicly that she would let him 'love her up'. Sam, her brother, urges Susannah to go to church and confess to preacher Olin Blitch, but she cannot do it. Blitch comes to her farm and tells her to pray with him. She refuses to confess to anything, and Blitch seduces her. The next day he pleads with the community to forgive Susannah, but they refuse; and Susannah refuses to forgive Blitch. When Sam hears what happened, he kills Blitch. At the end, Susannah pulls a gun on the mob when they come for Sam. Standing defiantly in the doorway, she is 'an inviolably strong and inexorably lonely figure in self-imposed exile' (from the libretto). In this true twentieth-century retelling, the emphasis has shifted completely to Susanna, with no Daniel or God figure to save her.

See also APOCRYPHA/DEUTEROCANONICALS/INTERTESTAMENTALS; DANIEL, BOOK OF [HL]

Sweat of Your Brow. One consequence of Adam and Eve's disobedience was the cursing of the ground. Thorns and thistles would thrive with the result that food production would be toilsome, i.e., 'by the sweat of your brow' (Gen. 3.19). The curse of the ground has lasting implications for human labor. However, the distinction between the value of work and the Fall's effect on work is vital. Sweat-inducing work and not work itself is a punishment for sin. As divine image-bearers, humans, already in Eden, were to work ('fill the earth and subdue it'; Gen. 1.28), and Adam's naming of the animals is an early example of human labor (Gen. 2.19-20). So humanity's tilling and cultivating the earth is held out as the creational norm.

Because of the Fall, the ground no longer yields its fruit without human effort, as the unfolding story of scripture reveals. Cain and Abel both work but each had different motivations for offering the fruit of their labor to God. Similarly, human craftsmanship went into the golden calf (Exod. 32.4), the tabernacle and the ark (Exod. 35.30–40.33)—the result of the former was the alienation of God and his people (32.7-10) and of the latter was God's presence with his people (40.34-38). The Preacher in Ecclesiastes knows that work is a gift of God (2.24; 3.13; etc.) but struggles at times to find meaning in work amid life's enigmas. The NT also affirms the goodness of work (e.g., Paul warns against idleness, urges slaves to work with integrity, and stresses the importance of work for sustenance).

Attitudes toward work have been varied in the history of western civilization. For the Greeks and Romans (with the exception of the Stoics) work was an evil to be avoided at all costs. A similar attitude toward work continued into the medieval period. Theologians polarized the sacred and the secular so that vocations in the church were idealized and those of 'mundane' life were disparaged. However, in the religious orders manual labor and spiritual disciplines came together, constituting a rhythm for life. Furthermore, medieval guilds insured a high standard of craftsmanship, and membership in a guild was an honor. In the Renaissance work represented human freedom and creativity. The Reformation marks a shift as Tyndale, Luther and Calvin, among others, rightfully stressed that all forms of work (washing dishes, laboring in a workshop, farming, etc.) are equally valid and ought to be done in service to God. Abraham Kuyper and his followers have thoughtfully explored the implications of this view of work. The Reformation restored the biblical dignity of work, but it also played a role in the development of industrialization (where labor was a commodity to be exploited), capitalism, and the kind of workaholism typical in the west today. Marxism, on the other hand, holds that humans reach their full potential by engaging in free productive activity. It seems, however, that manual labor has once again fallen on hard times. Recently Mathew Crawford argues that today westerners value jobs in which theoretical knowledge is most important with the result that manual labor is devalued. Christian attitudes toward work are improving as theologians are constructing a biblical view of human labor.

Recommended reading. Crawford, M.B. *Shop Class as Soulcraft: An Inquiry into the Value of Work*. New York: Penguin, 2009. Hardy, L. *The Fabric of This World: Inquiries into Calling, Career Choice, and the Design of Human Work*. Grand Rapids, MI: Eerdmans, 1990. Meilaender, G. *Working: Its Meaning and its Limits*. Notre Dame, IN: University of Notre Dame Press, 2000.

See also FALL, THE [DJHB]

Sword. The most important weapon of war in antiquity, thus a symbol of warfare, bloodshed and strife. Biblical history writing flows with blood when Israelites, enemies and prophets die by the sword (Josh. 10.28-37; Judg. 20; 1 Kgs 19.1-17). Ehud thrusts a short sword into the belly of the Moabite king as he sits in his privy (Judg. 3.15-23). Fearing death by the sword, Adonijah and Joab escape to altars of refuge (1 Kgs 1.50-52; 2.28-32). God kills by the sword (Exod. 5.3; 22.24; Jer. 12.12), but God also breaks the sword and abolishes war (Hos. 1.7b; 2.18b). The peaceful image is of swords being beaten into ploughshares (Mic. 4.3). Used as a positive metaphor, God's word is sharper than a two-edged sword (Heb. 4.12) or called 'the sword of the Spirit' (Eph. 6.17). In Matt. 26.52, Jesus warns that 'they that take the sword shall perish with the sword' (KJV).

In *The Suicide of Saul* (1562), Pieter Brueghel the Elder depicts the bloody death-scene of the first king of Israel (1 Sam. 31). When Philistine archers badly wound Saul, he falls upon his sword, his armor-bearer following suit (31.1a, 2-3, 4b-6). In a later storyline, Saul fears humiliation by the enemy but his armor-bearer refuses to run him through with the sword (31.1b, 4a, 7-13). Brueghel's Saul appears as a crowned king and heroic warrior, a striking contrast with his sad fate—his throat pierced with a sword, his mouth hanging open. As the enemy patrol approaches with spears and swords, we watch the armor-bearer throw himself on his sword.

Western artists represent two different versions of the fight between David and Goliath. David struck down the Philistine with a stone, after which David took his sword and beheaded his opponent (1 Sam. 17.40-41, 48-49, 51). An 1123 fresco from a Barcelona Church shows a fallen Goliath, his sword still in its sheath. With one hand David seizes Goliath by the hair, and with the other he raises his sword to cut off his head. Michiel Coxcie (1499–1592), Michelangelo (1509) and Daniele da Volterra (1509–1566) depict the fallen champion face downward (17.49b), David striding over him with a sword, while terrified Goliath awaits decapitation (17.51). A parenthetical insertion adds the contradictory interpretation that David killed Goliath with only a sling and a stone. David carried neither sword nor spear because Yahweh delivered him (1 Sam. 17.37-39, 45-47; cf. Exod. 18.4; Josh. 24.12). Iconography shows David carrying a shepherd's staff, shoulder bag, sling and Goliath's head, as in Hebrew mediaeval manuscripts and portrayals by Francesco Pesellino (1450), Lorenzo Lotto (1526), and Thomas Flatman (1637–1688). In such scene-representations the dead giant is decapitated by his own huge sword.

Western artists capture the humor of the folktale of the prophet *Balaam and his Ass* (Num. 22.21-35), e.g., Pieter Lastman (1622) and Jacopo Vignali (1640). Three times on a journey a donkey sees an angel carrying a sword, swerves from the path and stops only to be flogged by Balaam. The point is that a jackass can be a better visionary than a prophet. Since Rembrandt (1626) places the angel behind the animal, the ass cannot see the sword. Rembrandt captures the action at its climax when Balaam threatens, 'I wish I had a sword to kill you', and the ass speaks.

See also ARMOR OF GOD; BALAAM; EHUD; DAVID; GOLIATH; NOT PEACE BUT A SWORD; SAUL; SWORDS INTO PLOUGHSHARES [JRW]

Swords into ploughshares. 'Swords into ploughshares' is a phrase that comes from two Hebrew prophets: Isa. 2.4 and Mic. 4.3. The complete passage, 'they shall beat their swords into ploughshares, and their spears into pruning hooks, nation shall not lift up sword against nation, neither shall they learn war any more' appears identically in both. There are only minor variations in the introduction to each. Commentators disagree as whether Isaiah or Micah first used the phrase, or whether it might be a quotation from some other source. The latter is the more common view.

Micah and Isaiah were contemporaries in eighth-century BCE Judah. At this time, the kingdom was prospering due to control of major trade routes and territorial expansion. As time progressed, however, Tiglath-pileser III came to power in Assyria, and became an increasing threat, resulting in a time of turmoil. In the light of this turmoil, Isaiah announced judgment and redemption to Judah. The passages promise a future age, marked by peace and destruction of weapons, when all peoples of the earth will go to Zion and learn from Yahweh.

Micah's words appear to be those of a rural villager on behalf of his fellows, who were suffering exploitation and injustice perpetrated by the wealthy. In Micah, the phrase is about halfway through the book, where the promise of peace follows Yahweh's threats of punishment against those who abuse the poor and deny social justice.

In an apocalyptic section of the book of Joel (3.10), the phrase is reversed: 'beat your ploughshares into swords, and your pruning hooks into spears', in a portrayal of the battle that would precede the reign of God. The two original passages, along with Joel's reversal, have contributed to a strain of interpretation that views the prophets as announcing the future coming of a Messiah who would end war. Some who follow this interpretation expect a reign of God, inaugurated through Jesus Christ, could become reality in the world through cooperation, while others await a great battle between good and evil, such as Armageddon, to take place first.

In his 1961 farewell address, American President Dwight D. Eisenhower alluded to the phrase, saying that those who make ploughshares could at one time make swords as needed, but world politics had changed, and that while a permanent military–industrial complex was necessary, it held great dangers.

The phrase is often found in anti-war or social protest songs and slogans. Examples include Michael Jackson's 'Heal the World' (1991), the finale of the musical *Les Misérables* (1980), and the US veterans' assistance group Swords to Plowshares.

See also APOCALYPSE; APOCALYPTIC; ARMAGEDDON; ASSYRIA; ISAIAH; JESUS OF NAZARETH; JOEL; JUDAH; MESSIAH; MICAH; PROPHETS [TV]

Synagogue. The English word 'synagogue' is a transliterated derivative of the Greek verb *synagogein*, 'to gather together with [others]'. Archaeological evidence indicates that synagogues may have existed in the Land of Israel (Gamla, Herodium, Masada, Capernaum, Chorazin) and in Diaspora (Ostia, Delos) as early as the end of the late Second Temple era. Synagogues are not mentioned in the OT but appear commonly in the NT. In the latter context, they are often pejoratively portrayed (e.g., Matt. 6.5, 6, where hypocritical Jews 'love to pray standing in the synagogues and the streets' and Rev. 2.9, where there are 'those who say they are Jews but are not, who are from the synagogue of Satan'). Influenced by such ascriptions, from Constantine the Great on the Church followed suit with prohibitions against Jews enlarging, beautifying, or otherwise elevating their synagogues (these terms express the ban of Alfonso X, 1261). In Christian art, images of Ecclesia (Church) and Synagoga (Synagogue), personified as women, one crowned and bearing the cross and chalice, the other blindfolded and carrying a broken staff and Torah scroll slipping from her hand, portray the dominance of Christianity over Judaism. For rabbinic Judaism, however, the synagogue has from its beginnings been a Beth Midrash (House of Study) wherein the Oral Torah (*Talmud*) and Written Torah (*Tanakh*) provide a context for community worship, thus fulfilling covenantal commitment to God. Traditionally, in order to establish a Beth Midrash ten men (Minyan) are required to be living in community.

Recommended reading. Runesson, Anders, Donald D. Binder and Birger Olsson. *The Ancient Synagogue from its Origins to 200 CE*. Leiden: Brill, 2008.

See also CHURCH; TEMPLE, ISRAEL'S; WORSHIP [DM]

Synoptic Gospels. The synoptic gospels are Matthew, Mark and Luke, which have an apparent 'same view' of the ministry and teaching of Jesus of Nazareth. The synoptics are often printed in a book called a synopsis so that readers can appreciate the literary relationships between various portions of these three gospels. E.g., by using a synopsis one can see which episodes appear in which gospels, including which pericopes or units of material are found in Mark and one or both of the other gospels, or in Matthew and Luke but not in Mark, or in one of the Gospels alone.

Such findings have prompted questions regarding synoptic relationships. The similarities and differences among the three accounts—which were recognized in the early church—have prompted development of at least four major theories regarding synoptic relationships. One of these, which includes John, is that there may be four gospels, but each is a part of a larger account of the entire ministry and teaching of Jesus. Tatian's *Diatessaron*, produced in the last half of the second century, harmonized all four gospels into a single account. It was so popular that it appears to have been the gospel of choice for several centuries in certain Christian communities, such as the Syriac church, in the Syriac language into which the *Diatessaron* was either written or translated early on. Such harmonies are still produced, such as the *Reader's Digest New Testament*. A second theory is that the synoptics have a common basis in shared tradition. This theory has taken various forms through the years. Some have argued that the commonalities among the synoptic Gospels go back to a body of oral tradition that was remembered by Jesus' earliest followers and then written down. Jesus' followers may have been functioning like disciples of other Jewish teachers of the time in remembering their teacher's words. Others have contended that Jesus' earliest followers may have written down accounts of his actions and words. A third theory is that there is a distinct literary relationship among the synoptics in which Matthew was written first, and then Mark used Matthew and Luke used both of them. This so-called

Griesbach hypothesis, named after the eighteenth-century scholar Jacob Griesbach, continues to be promoted by some scholars. The traditional ordering of the gospels with Matthew first reflects belief in the early church that Matthew was the first and most important gospel, and hence placed first in canonical order. A fourth theory is that Mark was the first, and Matthew and Luke used it and a common source of sayings material (usually called Q, from the German *Quelle*, source). This two-source document hypothesis has several variations. One is that Matthew and Luke also had access to their own unique material, so that each of the evangelists had access to four sources—hence the four-source hypothesis. A growing number of scholars have difficulty with the Q hypothesis—which has grown in some circles from a posited body of tradition to a written document with various editorial layers and its own theology—and believe that they can 'dispense with Q' in their analysis of synoptic relations.

Recommended reading. Streeter, B.H. *The Four Gospels: A Study of Origins, Treating of the Manuscript Tradition, Sources, Authorship, and Dates.* London: Macmillan, 1924. Stein, Robert H. *The Synoptic Problem: An Introduction.* Grand Rapids, MI: Baker Books, 1987.

See also GOSPELS; LUKE; MARK; MATTHEW; Q

[SEP]

Syrophoenician Woman. Mark's story of the Syrophoenician woman (7.24-30) is paralleled in Matthew with that of the Canaanite woman (15.21-28). Matthew's story has long controlled the history of interpretation. The 'Sunday of the Canaanitess' is a fixed day in the Orthodox liturgical calendar and is celebrated with an accent on the transition of the gospel from its Jewish roots into Gentile reception.

The story features a woman of foreign ethnicity and without embedding in a male guardian. She approaches the Jewish healer, Jesus of Nazareth, seeking the healing of her possessed daughter, only to receive a strong rebuff. However, she refuses to accept the rejection and delivers an answer that is praised as an example of great faith in Matthew's telling and as a healing word in Mark. The conclusion of both stories accents the restoration of the daughter.

By naming the woman as Canaanite, Matthew's version evokes the long traditions of enmity with Jews. Her presence testifies against the thorough execution of the Joshua pogrom on the earlier inhabitants of the land (Josh. 11.20) and her liturgical language in her plea to Jesus ('Have mercy on me, Lord, son of David') lays claim to the temple worship from which her race is banned (Zech. 14.21). Her answer to Jesus' ethnocentric rebuttal wrings the breakthrough of healing for foreign women by the exercise of faith (cf. Matt. 8.5-13) and is taken as indicating the breakthrough of the early Jesus movement into Gentile acceptance and even as the model of humble, acquiescent piety, especially in earlier interpretations.

By contrast, the Markan story accents the triumph of the word, not the faith, of a woman —'for saying that' (v. 29). The contest between the words of Jesus and the words of the woman has dominated the history of interpretation in the last two centuries. A barely hidden apologetic exoneration of Jesus' harsh words has been sought through postulating a humorous or ironic by-play, the non-committed use of a Jewish proverb antipathetic to dogs, the pedagogical cultivation of the woman's faith or the development of the historical Jesus' awareness of his mission. Conversely, especially among feminist and two-thirds-world interpreters, the word of the woman has been prized as the voice of women in the shaping of the gospel, as the vanguard of the Gentile mission, as the resistance of a dominated group against a colonizing master, as a preservation of the integrity of local culture as a shaper of the Christian message, even as a Cynic philosopher's wit that subverts conventional perspectives.

Usually overlooked is the importance of the Syrophoenician's daughter, who not only repeatedly anchors the flow of the narrative and exchange of dialogue but who provides the culminating point of the story. The household of two women, mother and daughter, becomes the final repudiation of any patriarchal necessity for the appropriation of the gospel (cf. Mark 10.30 with the omission of 'fathers' in the household of the reign of God). More significantly, this aspect of the story lays the foundation for the dramatic privileging of children in and for the reign of God (Mark 9.36-37; 10.13-16).

Recommended reading. Cadwallader, A.. *Beyond the Word of a Woman: Recovering the Bodies of the Syrophoenician Women.* Adelaide: ATF Press, 2008. Jackson, G. *'Have mercy on me': The Story of the Canaaanite Woman in Matthew 15.21-28.* London: Sheffield Academic Press, 2002. Schüssler Fiorenza, Elisabeth. *But She Said: Feminist Practices of Biblical Interpretation.* Boston: Beacon Press, 1992.

See also CANAAN; CHILD; GENTILES; MARK, GOSPEL OF; MATTHEW; GOSPEL OF, WOMAN

[AHC]

T

Tabernacle. The portable religious shrine during Israel's wilderness wandering. The word 'tabernacle' stands for several Hebrew and Greek words. In Hebrew, *'ohel* ('tent'), *mishkan* ('residence') and *sukka* ('hut or booth') are used for tabernacle. The Greek word is *skēnē* (any habitation made of greenery, skins, cloth, or other material; e.g., Matt. 17.4; Mark 5.9; Heb. 11.9) or *skēnōma* (2 Pet. 1.13, 14; Acts 7.46).

The basic biblical sources for information about the tabernacle are Exodus 25–28 (construction) and 35–40 (priestly work). Other aids include details of the Temple of Solomon (1 Kgs 6; 2 Chron. 3–4; and Ezekiel's vision (Ezek. 40–43).

The OT mentions three tabernacles. The first was a provisional tabernacle established after the sin of the Golden Calf. This was a tent erected outside the camp. The 'Tent of Meeting' was where people could go as if going to an oracle (Exod. 33.7). The second was the Sinaitic Tabernacle built according to the plan revealed to Moses. The third was the Davidic Tabernacle erected by David in Jerusalem as a dwelling place for the Ark of the Covenant (2 Sam. 6.12, 17).

Following the intercession of Moses after the Golden Calf episode, a new copy of the law was given as God renewed his covenant with Israel. They were then invited to contribute to the construction of the Tabernacle and did so exceeding the resources needed (Exod. 36.5-6). The construction proceeded under the direction of Bezalel and Oholiab (Exod. 35.30; 36.2). It was completed on the first day of the first month (Nisan) of the second year after the Exodus from Egypt. The services were then begun (Exod. 40).

The Sinaitic Tabernacle was placed at the center of the camp rather than outside like the Tent of Meeting. The tribes were camped around it with three tribes of the twelve on the north, south, east and west. The Levites camped by families on each of the four sides of the Tabernacle. When the Israelites marched they moved as an army with the Levites carrying the portable Tabernacle in the middle of the army. It was God's dwelling place at the center of the whole people and it was portable because God is a universal and not a local deity.

According to Judges (18.1) the Tabernacle remained at Shiloh. A Danish archeological expedition excavated Shiloh and concluded that it was destroyed around 1050 BCE, probably by the Philistines after the Battle of Ebenezer. Following this defeat, Samuel established worship at Mizpah and elsewhere. During David's lifetime the bread of the Presence was kept at Nob (21.1-6) and some of the furniture was at the high place of Gibeon. The last mention of the Tabernacle is 1 Kings 8.4 (cf. 2 Chron. 24.6). David brought the Ark of the Covenant to a tent he had erected on Mount Zion (1 Chron. 15.1; 16.1-2; 2 Sam. 6.17).

In the NT, 'tabernacle' is sometimes used figuratively, referring to the perishable human body (2 Cor. 5.1, 4; 2 Pet. 1.3, 14), and to the imperishable sanctuary in the heavens, especially in Hebrews (e.g., 8.2; 9.11; cf. Rev. 13.6; 15.5), contrasted with the transitory one human-built built one (Heb. 8.5; 9.2, 3, 6, 8; 13.10). In John's vision, God's presence with humanity is portrayed as an eschatological tabernacle (Rev. 21.3)

Tabernacle has been used for the name of worship centers and by musical groups such as the Mormon Tabernacle Choir. In the Roman Catholic church, a 'tabernacle' is a receptacle for storing the consecrated host.

See also ARK OF THE COVENANT; HIGH PRIEST; LEVITES; PRIEST; SACRIFICE; SANCTUARY; TEMPLE, ISRAEL'S; TENT OF MEETING [AJW]

Tabernacles, Feast of (see Booths, Feast of, Succot).

Talents, Parable of the. About diligence and stewardship, the parable appears in Matt. 25.14-30. The lesson is the importance of nurturing one's 'talents' because one does not know exactly when the master will return and demand an accounting of their management. The first and second servants, who doubled the amounts their master trusted them to invest, received more rewards. But the servant who fearfully did nothing with his lost all resources and was thrown into darkness. The parable measures growth by individual responsibility for developing one's gifts. Faith must be active, not passive.

The word 'talent' originates in the Greek *talanton*, a variable unit of weight or money referring to a talent-weight, approximately 75 pounds, of gold or silver. Although the Bible does not reveal an exact monetary value, a talent exceeds many years of labor; because the servants are trusted with the amounts of five, two and one, managing such tremendous sums indicates the duty's importance. The meaning of 'talent' as an inclination or will entered English from medieval Latin *talenta*. Matthew's parable extends the word to its modern sense of aptitude or skill, particularly a gift from God.

Another version appears in Luke 19.12-27, the parable of the *minas* (traditionally translated 'pounds'). In Matthew, the third servant buries the talent, a safe disposition which did not increase the value, but in Luke, wrapping the talent in cloth does not secure it at all. The monetary amounts are much smaller in Luke (cf. Mark 13.33-37). If Jesus' parables can be categorized as those for recruiting followers and those for maintaining discipline among leaders, then the talents parable would be geared to leaders.

An alternate interpretation sees the third servant as bravely speaking truth to power and getting punished for it. So the parable endorses what the third servant says and does in seeking to shame the master for insufficient faith and for exploiting people by reaping where others have sown. A whistle-blower, the third servant pays a hard price for honesty. In this interpretation, the master does not necessarily symbolize God.

The most essential literary connection with the parable of the talent is John Milton's sonnet 'When I Consider How My Light Is Spent'. Written c. 1655, after Milton lost his sight, the sonnet expresses the speaker's considering 'That one talent which is death to hide / Lodged within me useless'. Milton's allusion evokes the meaning of 'talent' as skill and the perception that God requires people to use their gifts and work to their potential. Like the third servant, this speaker wonders whether he can meet God's expectations. Yet Patience comforts him that God expects people to bear their burdens, and 'they also serve who only stand and wait'. The poem suggests a challenge of Providence and demonstrates Milton's reconciling to the fact of blindness while still proving productive with his writing.

Recent cultural references to the parable of the talents include a two-book series by African American science fiction writer Octavia Butler: *The Parable of the Sower* (1994) and *The Parable of the Talents* (1999). The dystopian novels describe Earthseed, a new religion created in a near-future, crumbling society. Visual artist Ian Pollock made forty paintings about the parables of Jesus; his *Talents* (2000) depicts a suited Caucasian man juggling three men with different racial features, raising questions about whether the master is good and how the parable could be used to justify financial profit despite injustices such as slavery and other human exploitation.

See also PARABLE; PROVIDENCE; SOWER, PARABLE; STEWARD; UNJUST JUDGE, PARABLE [AC]

Tamar (Genesis). The story of Tamar (Hebrew: 'date palm') in Genesis 38 illustrates a number of institutions that become part of Israelite society. The story takes place in a context where women belonged to male households. It was within that household that they found protection and economic purpose. Without male protection, women were potential victims. The economic roles of women in most ancient Near Eastern societies were extremely limited outside the household. The options for most widows were concubinage, slavery, prostitution, or subsistence gathering after harvest.

Er, the eldest son of the patriarch Judah, died childless, meaning his estate would return to his father's, leaving his wife Tamar. Upon Judah's death, there was no guarantee she would be allowed to remain as part of that estate.

To reduce this circumstance, Israelites (like many other societies) employed levirate marriage, in which a woman is to be impregnated by the closest male relative of the childless deceased, so that the child would legally the heir of the deceased, who would inherit her dead husband's estate.

However, another social institution came into play. Israelites practiced primogeniture, where the eldest son received an extra share of the father's estate. If Tamar married the second son, Onan, and bore an heir for Er, then there would again be three sons of Judah, meaning the estate would be divided into four shares, with Er's fictive son receiving half, and his brothers Onan and Shelah each receiving a quarter. However, if Er had no offspring by Tamar, then there would be two sons surviving after Judah's death, meaning there would be three shares of land. Onan would receive two thirds, and Shelah would receive a third. Onan dutifully has sex with Tamar, but rather than risking a pregnancy that will reduce his inheritance, he practices *coitus interruptus*. Onan's disobedience angered God, who killedhim. Judah, alarmed, decided to not risk the life of his youngest son by pairing him with Tamar, thus ensuring that she would not gain an estate for Er.

Tamar's plan was both desperate and ingenious. Sheep shearing time was an event in which one's annual wealth hinged upon and a place where debts were settled. Visiting a prostitute was something of an insurance policy, as the ritual act of fertilization was symbolic of fertility. Tamar disguises herself as a prostitute, realizing that this added motive would attract Judah, just as she realized that finding him on the way to the shearing meant he would have to pay her in kind before he had a more portable (and less identifiable) form of wealth. She negotiated for his staff and ring, indisputable evidence of their sexual encounter.

Judah was eager to kill Tamar when it was discovered that she was pregnant, thus ensuring that his last son would not die in an encounter with her. However, the magnitude of his sin in not allowing her to produce an heir is proclaimed when she produces the evidence that he was the father of the child, and Judah proclaims her righteous (Gen. 38.26). Tamar's twin sons are able to inherit two thirds of Judah's estate upon his death, as Onan had hoped to do. Through her son Perez, Tamar becomes the ancestor of King David.

Matthew 1.3 lists Tamar as one of the ancestors of Jesus. Scenes of the lascivious encounter between Judah and Tamar are a frequent theme of western art (e.g., Arent de Gelder, 1667; Jan van Noort, seventeenth century; Vernet, 1840; Chagall, 1950).

See also JUDAH; LEVIRATE MARRIAGE; ONAN, ONANISM [MAP]

Tamar (2 Samuel). Like her ancestor of Genesis 38, her name means 'date palm'. Tamar's story is told in 2 Sam. 13.1-21, where she is the beautiful daughter of King David, sister of Absalom. Her half-brother Amnon becomes sexually obsessed with her, and he conspires with his cousin Jonadab to trap her into sleeping with him. Amnon feigns illness, and tells the king that he would like his sister to visit him and prepare him some food. When Tamar presents him with the bread she has made, Amnon commands everyone in the room to leave, and he rapes her, despite her pleas and warnings. Amnon's 'love' for Tamar turns to hatred, and he has her turned out of the house, where she tears her royal robe, puts ashes on her head, and leaves, weeping loudly (cf. Deut. 22.23-24). The king is angry over the rape, but does nothing to punish Amnon; Absalom comforts his sister, and two years later has Amnon assassinated by his men in revenge for the shaming of Tamar (13.22-24). Absalom flees Israel, and later leads a rebellion against David that almost costs him the throne. 2 Samuel 14.27 notes that Absalom had one daughter whom he named Tamar (2 Sam. 14.27).

In western culture, the tragic rebellion of Absalom is given much more attention than the disaster that befalls his sister, who disappears from the biblical text after the rape story. However, scenes of the rape of Tamar are frequently portrayed in western art, e.g., Eustache le Sueur's *Rape of Tamar* (c. 1640), Guercino's *Amnon and Tamar* (1649–50), Jan Steen's *Amnon and Tamar* (seventeenth century) and Philip Santvoort's *Rape of Tamar* (c. 1718). The biblical novel *The Rape of Tamar* by Dan Jacobson was published in 1970; more recently, the Jewish feminist novelist Naomi Ragen wrote *The Sacrifice of Tamar* (2001), the story of a young New York Orthodox woman who is raped by a stranger.

Feminist interpreter Phyllis Trible's groundbreaking book *Texts of Terror* includes a chapter on 'Tamar: The Royal Rape of Wisdom', contrasting Tamar's wisdom and Amnon's foolishness (cf. 2 Sam. 13.12-13). Tamar's House in Saskatoon, Canada, named after the biblical Tamar, victim of an incestuous rape, was a community-based agency providing services to adult female survivors of sexual abuse.

Recommended reading. Trible, Phyllis. *Texts of Terror: Literary-Feminist Readings of Biblical Narratives.* Pp. 37-64. Philadelphia: Fortress Press, 1984.

See also ABSALOM; AMNON [MALB]

Tanakh. The term Tanakh is an acronym comprising the first letter from each of the three sections of the Hebrew Bible: *Torah* (Instruction), *Nevi'im* (Prophets), and *Ketuvim* (Writings). For Judaism, the entire collection of books is known as the Written Torah, whereas the Talmud is the Oral Torah. This collection of sacred writings is identical to the Protestant Christian OT in its Hebrew original. The Tanakh numbers and orders its individual texts differently than does the OT, arriving at a count of 24 books. What Christianity refers to as the Minor Prophets is viewed as a single book entitled the Book of the Twelve; the books of Samuel, Kings, and Chronicles number three and not six; Ezra–Nehemiah forms a single literary work; Daniel is included in the last section, as it emerged in the Persian period of history when the Writings were collected.

For Judaism, there is nothing 'Old' about the covenants contained therein. According to Sigmund Freud (*Moses and Monotheism* [1939]), 'it was (this) Holy Book, and the study of it, that kept the scattered people together'. So influential has the Tanakh become that Ralph Waldo Emerson declared, 'Our Jewish Bible has implanted itself in the table-talk and household life of every man and woman in European and American nations' (*Representative Man: Plato* [1845]).

See also CANON; OLD TESTAMENT [DM]

Tarshish. 1. Tarshish was a city region, best known perhaps as the exotic location to which the prophet Jonah tried to escape by boat.

Scholars have suggested various sites, including Tyrseni of the Etruscans in Italy, Carthage in North Africa, Tarsus in Cilicia near the Mediterranean coast of Turkey, and Great Britain or specifically Cornwall. The best accepted site is Tartessos in SW Spain, in the Guadalquivir Valley. Colonized by the Phoenicians, and a recognized source of metals and precious stones, it was called Tartessus by classical writers like Strabo (*Geography* 3.2.11) and Pliny (*Natural History* 37.43). Herodotus (*History* 4.152) places it 'beyond the Pillars of Hercules' or Straits of Gibraltar. Popularly, Tarshish was thought of as an exotic, distant location and a source of many luxuries.

William Albright suggests the name comes from the Akkadian *rashashu*, 'to be smelted', and *tarshishu* might mean a refinery. This could explain connections to more than one location. Ezekiel identifies Tarshish as a source of silver, iron, tin and lead (Ezek. 27.12), the tin a component of bronze in the Bronze Age.

Ships of Tarshish, or Tarshish-class ships, were probably large vessels 'heavily laden' (Isa. 2.16) with ore or refined metal. Wiseman alternately suggests the name may be linked to Greek *tarsos*, 'oar'. Tarshish ships are rowed (Ezek. 27.25-26; Jon 1.13). With help from the small maritime nation of Tyre, Solomon had a fleet of Tarshish-ships, probably in the Mediterranean (1 Kgs 10.22; 2 Chron. 9.21), and also at Ezion-Geba in the Gulf of Aqabah (2 Chron. 8.17-18), with its links to Arabian, African and Indian trade. Later, King Jehoshaphat tried the same strategy but suffered shipwreck (2 Chron. 20.36-37).

In prophetic rhetoric, Tarshish and its Phoenician trading partners are targets of God's judgment on arrogance (Isa. 2.12-17; 23.1-14; cf. Ps. 48.7). The Messiah, symbolized by Solomon, will receive tributes from Tarshish, among other islands and faraway places (Ps. 72.1, 10). In a passage describing Israel's future glory, Tarshish ships bring back exiles to build up Israel, with wealth and foreign workers (Isa. 60.9; 66.15-21).

Tarshish was proverbially faraway and exotic, something like Timbuktu in eighteenth-century English imagination; or Shangri-La, subject of a novel but jokingly named by US President Roosevelt as the base for the first bombing of Tokyo; or even Katmandu in twentieth-century pop music.

2. Tarshish is also the name of a yellow precious stone, variously translated as beryl, yellow jasper, chrysolite (see Exod. 28.20; 39.13; Ezek. 1.6; 28.13; Dan. 10.6; Song 5.14).

3. Probably linked to the gem is the personal name Tarshish belonging to Noah's great-grandson (Gen. 10.4; 1 Chron. 1.7); a descendant of Benjamin (1 Chron. 7.10); and a Persian nobleman (Est. 1.14).

Recommended reading. Bright, John. *A History of Israel*. Louisville, KY: Westminster John Knox Press, 2000.

See also JONAH; SOLOMON; TYRE [GK]

Tarsus. Tarsus, according to Strabo (c. 64/63 BCE –21 CE) the geographer, our best ancient source for the city (*Geography* 16.5.12-15), was situated on a plain inland from the coast of the Mediterranean Sea, with the Cydnus river running through it.

According to ancient mythology, the city was founded by Greeks from Argos who traveled with Triptolemus in his quest for Io. In Roman times, the city was in the Roman province of Cilicia in Asia Minor, modern day Turkey. Strabo notes that the city was known in particular for its study of philosophy, but also for all of the areas of learning, to the point of surpassing such intellectual centers as Athens and Alexandria. What was different about Tarsus was that those who studied there, unlike in other centers of learning, were natives of the city. Foreigners apparently did not travel to Tarsus to study as they did to other cities of repute, and even its own students moved on to other cities for further study and usually did not return. Stoic philosophers were especially well known in Tarsus, including the teacher of Caesar Augustus, but other philosophical schools were also to be found, such as those who followed in the line of Plato's Academy and Neo-Pythagoreans like Apollonius of Tyana (according to Philostratus in *Life of Apollonius* 1.7). There were also grammarians and writers of tragedy who lived in Tarsus. The city was visited by Mark Antony, who promised to build a gymnasium, and who met Cleopatra there. The city was also given to a variety of political scandals in the years leading up to the first century CE.

In western culture, the best known person to come from Tarsus is 'Saul of Tarsus', or Paul the Apostle. In Acts, he refers to himself as a citizen of Tarsus, which was then, according to Luke, 'no insignificant city' (Acts 21.39), and says he was born there, and possibly educated there as well (22.3). There has been much discussion of Acts 22.3 and whether it indicates that Paul was educated in Tarsus or in Jerusalem under Gamaliel. The Greek phrasing can be interpreted in different ways. Most scholars believe that this verse indicates that Paul was educated in Jerusalem, but it is at least arguable that this verse indicates that Paul received his grammar school education in Tarsus—a city known for its educational system, which would account for the level of his literary skills—before going to Jerusalem for his rabbinical education.

There have been a few important archaeological finds made at the site of ancient Tarsus, although the remains from the Hellenistic and Roman periods are buried beneath the modern city. Two significant artifacts are a first-century CE inscription honoring Caesar Augustus that refers to him as 'son of God', and a sarcophagus from the third century CE built in the Greek style with depictions of figures from Homer's *Iliad*. There are also some remains from prehistoric times and the Hittite period.

Recommended reading. Akurgal, Ekrem. *Ancient Civilizations and Ruins of Turkey*. Trans. John Whybrow. 10th edn. Istanbul: Net Turistik Yayinlar San, 2007.

[SEP]

Tax Collector. Greek *telōnēs*. Due to militaristic expansion, the Roman Republic eventually no longer needed to tax its Italian citizens. Rather, it looked exclusively to the provinces for revenues. Accurate census-taking, however, was an administrative headache. To simplify matters, taxes were assessed on entire communities rather than individuals.

Taxes were collected by *publicani*, tax farmers. Periodically, the *publicani* bid for the right to collect taxes in particular regions, paying the state in advance, i.e., the *publicani* made loans to the state that Rome was required to pay back with interest. The *publicani* kept anything in excess of their original bid, and the interest due from the treasury. They nonetheless ran the risk that they might not be able to collect as much as their original bid.

The process was highly corrupt, e.g., tax farmers could use their profits to collude with local officials and landholders to purchase grain at low prices to hold until times of shortage. Tax farmers were also the bankers of the ancient world, lending cash at exorbitant interest rates of 4% per month or more. The ancients lumped publicans together with beggars, thieves and robbers. In occupied Judea, tax collectors were seen as Roman collaborators and perhaps religiously suspect.

Jesus' opponents were scandalized that he had 'sinners and tax collectors' among his followers (Matt. 9.11). Surprisingly, Jesus is recorded using 'tax collector' as a term of opprobrium (Matt. 18.17). Matthew—a tax collector—is the traditional author of the Gospel, and possibly the saying is ironic. Jesus elsewhere tells a parable in which a repentant tax collector is favorably compared to a self-righteous Pharisee (Luke 18.9-14).

Augustus (31 BCE–14 CE), abolished the tax farming system amid complaints from the provinces and large, unpayable provincial debts. The system was gradually replaced by direct taxation through paid civil servants. Each province was required to pay a wealth tax of about 1% and a poll tax on each adult. This new procedure required regular census-taking to evaluate the taxable number of people and their economic status. Taxation switched mainly from owned property and wealth to an income tax. Thus, revenues varied greatly based on economic conditions. Theoretically, the system was fairer and more resistant to corruption.

In NT times Rome collected both direct and indirect taxes, and the indirect taxes—customs, tolls, fees for pasture rights on public land, etc.—were still subcontracted to *publicani*. Matthew's job (Matt. 9.9) was therefore probably closer to that of a 'customs agent' or 'rent collector'. Most of Matthew's profits would have wound up in the hands of a wealthy 'chief tax collector' like Zacchaeus (Luke 19.2).

The stereotype of tax collectors as greedy and dishonest makes them excellent illustrations of penitence. Two Gospel stories of repentant tax collectors stand out: the story of Zacchaeus and Jesus' parable of the Pharisee and the tax collector (Luke 18.9-14). Both passages are prominent in Eastern Orthodox spirituality and are read on the eleventh and the tenth Sundays before Easter. Early interpreters sometimes appealed to Zacchaeus (whose name means 'pure' or 'innocent') as an illustration of Jesus' saying, 'Blessed are the pure in heart, for they shall see God' (Matt. 5.8). Zacchaeus in his tree has been taken as a symbol of being crucified with Christ.

In *The Tax Collector*, a 1543 painting by Paul Vos, the tax collector sits amid his records, assessing the tax burden of two beleaguered taxpayers. Centuries later, the Beatles sang 'Taxman' to protest the taxing away of most of their earnings.

See also RENDER UNTO CAESAR; ROMAN EMPIRE

[DJP]

Tekoa (see Amos, Book of).

Temple, Israel's. In ancient agricultural societies, temples were loaded with meaning and significance, edifices around which artistic, social, religious, economic, and political activity revolved. Here was the dwelling place of heaven, where humans could exercise their technologies of sacrifice to harness celestial power for earthly purpose. Temples were the intersections where earth met heaven, where gods engaged humans.

The temple around which much of the Bible gravitates was in Jerusalem, located on a bluff called Mount Zion. According to biblical historiography, Jerusalem's first temple was built by Solomon in the tenth century BCE (1 Kgs 5–8). That magnificent example of ancient architecture was destroyed by the Babylonians in 586 BCE (2 Kgs 24–25), then rebuilt to a smaller scale by Jews returning from exile in 515 BCE (Neh. 2; Hag. 1, 12). In 20 BCE, this postexilic second temple underwent extensive refurbishment under the direction of Herod the Great, in an effort to provide the Romans with a showcase example of Greco-Roman architecture in the hinterland of Palestine. The grandest temple the ancient world had ever seen, it was also the shortest lived. In 70 CE, the Romans destroyed the second temple and the surrounding city, bringing under imperial control the brooding riotous elements of Judea. The famous 'Wailing Wall' that stands in Jerusalem today is the only remnant of Herod's grand architectural venture.

Although Jerusalem's temple has lain in ruin far longer than it ever stood operational, it nevertheless has captivated western religious imagination for two millennia. The Jewish fast day of *Tisha B'Av* (ninth of *Av*) commemorates the fall of the first and second temples. In rabbinic Judaism, wedding ceremonies feature the crushing of a glass underfoot in mournful memory of the glory of Solomon's temple, while burial practices orient the feet of the entombed toward Jerusalem so that upon resurrection, they might stand up and walk towards the Holy City. The Talmud records the *Even Shetiyah* legend that mythologizes a foundation stone deep beneath the temple site, upon which God stood when he created the cosmos. Christians spiritualize a 'Jerusalem above' made with divine hands, shelved high above any earthly corruption (cf. Rev. 14.15, 17; 15.5, 6, 8; 16.1, 17), while at the same time engaging their earth-bound feet in pilgrimages to the earthly Jerusalem below. In the NT, the body of Jesus (John 2.21), the believer (1 Cor. 3.15-17), or the church (e.g., 2 Cor. 6.16, 19; Eph. 2.21) is identified with the temple. The Islamic legend of the *Journey in the Night* says that Muhammad was transported to the Temple Mount in Jerusalem, and, upon arrival, ascended through the cosmos to the highest heaven. As cornerstone to Muhammad's journey, 'Abd al-Malik built the magnificent Dome of the Rock in 691, still glistening at the center of modern Jerusalem.

Far from the Middle East, Mormons built many American temples, each with the Solomonic inscription 'Holiness to the Lord' inscribed on its wall. The Mormon temple in Cardston, Alberta, built in 1913, was constructed from white hand-hewn granite quarried offsite in Nelson, British Columbia. Near the geographical center of the North American continent stands the legislature of Manitoba, which according to researcher Frank Albo, was built by Freemasons in 1920 to the exact specifications in the Bible's description of Solomon's edifice. Jerusalem also finds its way into the modern virtual worlds of the cinema, with a refuge dubbed Zion in the Hollywood blockbuster *The Matrix*.

Recommended reading. Schmidt, Francis. *How the Temple Thinks: Identity and Social Cohesion in Ancient Judaism.* Sheffield: Sheffield Academic Press, 2002.

See also DAVID; EXILE; JERUSALEM; SOLOMON; TABERNACLE; TEMPE OF THE HOLY SPIRIT; ZION [DAB]

Temple of the Holy Spirit. The image of the temple of the Holy Spirit occurs four times in the NT (1 Cor. 3.16-17; 1 Cor. 6.19-20; 2 Cor. 6.16–7.1; Eph. 2.19-22). This imagery is applied to the church three times. In 1 Corinthians 3.16-17, Paul uses the image to support his argument against division in the church at Corinth. He argues that the Corinthian congregation should not be divided according to its various ministers but united by the one God who dwells in the church by his Spirit. Those who attempt to fracture the community place themselves in danger of divine judgment because the church is not merely an assembly of worshippers but the very temple of God, graced with God's presence by the Holy Spirit. Paul uses the image similarly in 2 Cor. 6.16–7.1. Here the image serves as the basis for Paul's ethical instructions. Paul reminds the Corinthian church that it is the temple of God and that as such its members should avoid all ungodly behaviors. Ephesians 2.19-22 describes the Ephesian church as members being built together into a holy temple of God. The reference to the Spirit in v. 22 is ambiguous, and it may be translated as 'spiritually', or 'in the spirit'. It may also modify the verb 'built together' or the phrase 'into a dwelling place for God' which precedes it in the Greek. Given the word order, and the Pauline tendency to describe the Spirit as the means by which God dwells among his people, this verse may be translated 'in whom you also are built together into a dwelling place for God in the Spirit'. Therefore, the temple imagery declares the reality of God's presence in the church by his Spirit.

Paul also applies the image of the temple of the Spirit to the bodies of individual Christians. In 1 Cor. 6.19-20, Paul opposes the licentious behavior of some believers. He instructs his audience to avoid fornication because their bodies, like the church itself, are indwelt by the Holy Spirit.

The image of the human body as a temple of the sacred remains a part of Western culture. Icons and portraits of the Madonna as pure and holy often illustrated the cultural ideals for the female body. Walt Whitman responded to the common Christian stress on the spirit over the body by reversing the emphasis. In his 1885 poem, 'I Sing the Body Electric', he declares, 'If anything is sacred the human body is sacred'. In the 1960s, the phrase 'my body is a temple' gained favor among some female supporters of the feminist movement. The sentiment was later satirized in episode GABF08 of *The Simpsons*, in which Homer Simpson says his body is a temple. The sanctity of the body has also become a common theme in New Age spirituality.

Recommended reading. Fee, Gordon D. *God's Empowering Presence: The Holy Spirit in the Letters of Paul*. Peabody, MA: Hendrickson, 1994.

See also CHURCH; HOLY SPIRIT; TEMPLE; ISRAEL'S
[KDH]

Temptation. From the Greek *peirazō* and the Hebrew *nasah*, both meaning 'test'. This theme pervades biblical literature, from humanity's creation through the struggles of the early church. Ancients used temptation synonymously with 'testing', denoting a character assessment of faithfulness, devoid of any sinful connotations (e.g., Exod. 15.25; Isa. 7.12; Matt. 4.1; Gal. 6.1). Skepticism of one's reliability motivated the examiner, rather than a desire to lead the tested into wrongdoing. Biblical texts therefore have more in common with the amoral loyalty tests of *The Departed* (2006) than Satan's offer of sexual intercourse in *The Last Temptation of Christ* (1960). Testers differed, usually God or a human, but the serpent (Gen. 3.1-6) and Satan (Job 1–2; Matt. 4.1-11) also performed this duty. Many attributed such ordeals to supernatural figures other than God, including James 1.13 and various heterodox Christian and Jewish sects.

In contemporary usage, temptation is a subset of the larger category 'testing', also incorporating the previously unrelated concept of 'enticement'. It applies to instances where a possible misdeed would bring about immoral self-gratification. Tempters never force a decision, but offer an opportunity to display the tempted's adherence to ethical principles. Although God tested Israel's faithfulness and vice versa in the Bible, one cannot label these 'temptations' in the modern sense of the word. Biblical tales that might fall under this modern rubric include the episodes of Potiphar's wife (Gen. 39), Achan (Josh. 7), and Delilah (Judg. 16). However, words meaning 'test' are entirely absent. Modern readers interpret many other biblical narratives through this lens of sinful desire.

One cannot easily overstate the importance of temptation in western culture. It thematically unifies Milton's *Paradise Lost* and *Paradise Regained* and much of Shakespeare's corpus. Chaucer employed it humorously in 'Miller's Tale' and with more gravity in 'Wife of Bath's Tale'. Temptation also functions as a widespread method for establishing a character's heroic qualities. Contemporary temptations typically mimic biblical options of earthly pleasures vs. transcendent or heavenly principles. This commonly takes the form of sexual renunciation via self-sacrifice, lately by Bruce Wayne of Rachel Dawes in *Batman Begins* (2005) and in the allegory of teen lust from the *Twilight* saga (2005–2008). Resistance to the lure of wealth and power is a similarly frequent motif, as with Darth Vader's offer of imperial rule to Luke Skywalker in *The Empire Strikes Back* (1980). These instances may recall Delilah's seduction of Samson (Judg. 16) and Satan's offer of earthly dominion to Jesus (Matt. 4.8-10). However, contemporary instances frame moral uprightness against hedonism or corruption from earthly excess, whereas biblical texts often evince anti-idolatrous interests.

The forbidden fruit commonly symbolizes temptation. Cartoonists also combined Freud's work on the id, ego and superego with religious imagery to form the trope of a miniature angel and devil whispering into the protagonist's ear. Wilderness is prevalent as a symbolic setting, shared by both Testaments and subsequent writings. To this effect, rules did not apply in the forest for much medieval literature. Visual depictions of biblical tests were rare until the eleventh century. More licentious narratives, such as the episodes featuring Potiphar's wife and Delilah, are entirely absent for several more centuries. Abraham's binding of Isaac (Gen. 22) received extensive attention in medieval and Renaissance art, in addition to subsequent philosophy, notably in Søren Kierkegaard's *Fear and Trembling* (1843).

Recommended reading. Gibson, Jeffrey B. *The Temptations of Jesus in Early Christianity*. Sheffield: Sheffield Academic Press, 1995. Grayston, Kenneth. 'The Decline of Temptation—and the Lord's Prayer'. *Scottish Journal of Theology* 46 (1993) 279-96.

See also AGONY IN THE GARDEN; FORBIDDEN FRUIT; SERPENT, SNAKE; TEMPTATIONS OF JESUS; WILDERNESS

[CBZ]

Temptations of Jesus. From the Greek *peirazō* (test) and *Iēsous* (Jesus). The story of Jesus spending 40 days in the wilderness is recorded in Matt. 4.1-11, Mark 1.12-13 and Luke 4.1-13. During, or at the end of, the 40 days, Jesus is tempted by Satan, or the devil. The account in Mark does not provide details about the actual temptations of Jesus, but Matthew and Luke both state that Jesus fasted during his time in the wilderness and was tempted three times. The three temptations can be summarized as follows: (1) 'command these stones to become loaves of bread'; (2) 'throw yourself down' from this temple mount for you will be saved; and (3) I will give you 'all the kingdoms of the world and their glory' if you worship me. Jesus overcomes each temptation by quoting scriptures back to the devil (who quotes scripture himself).

Medieval Italian painter Duccio di Buoninsegna (1250/60–1318) vividly depicts the 'kingdoms of the world' temptation with Jesus standing on a hill in the midst of several small cities (representing the kingdoms), confronting a bat-winged black tempter with an accusatory pointed finger. Fra Angelico's Roman-garbed Jesus stoically stands in opposition to a bat-winged, sharp-jawed Satan, who has bird's feet (c. 1450). Botticelli (c. 1445–1510) portrays all three temptations of Christ, and the ministering spirits, as peripheral scenes in a Renaissance-style Italian city. Flemish painter Simon Bening (1483–1561) gives us a more subdued Christ politely refusing to turn a stone into bread for Satan, here an old man with pointed ears and bird's feet (cf. Juan de Flandes). Gustave Doré (1832–1883), like Duccio, shows Jesus as resolute, refusing to even look at the kingdoms of the world as Satan desperately kneels and tugs at his arm, begging him to give in. In his 1854 painting, Ary Scheffer shows a naked and swarthy tempter with black wings engaged in heated debate with a contemplative but firm Christ, dressed in clean robes. Ivan Kramskoy's 1872 depiction of a very human *Christ in the Wilderness* stands in contrast, showing a bedraggled Christ sitting alone in a barren and stony wilderness, locked in a posture of intense prayer and concentration, possibly encountering the only spiritually present Satan.

Several films have been directly influenced by this story, including a dramatic scene in the 1921 Denmark film, *Blade af Satans bog* ('Leaves from Satan's Book'), inspired by a novel by Marie Corelli. *The Last Temptation of Christ*, a 1988 film based on the novel by Nikos Kazantzakis, draws its title from the name of this pericope. There is even a non-fiction collection of essays that evaluates the message of the novel and film, called *Scandalizing Jesus?: Kazantzakis's The Last Temptation of Christ Fifty Years On* (2005). In 1989, Peter Gabriel released his album, *Passion: Music for The Last Temptation of Christ*.

The story of Jesus being tempted in the wilderness is a source of relate-ability and profundity, perhaps because it inspires many to know that he 'was tested by what he suffered' and is thus 'able to help those who are being tested' (Heb. 2.18).

See also JESUS OF NAZARETH; SATAN; SON OF GOD

[JDB]

Ten Commandments. Also called 'Decalogue' (Greek: *deka* = ten; *logos* = word) and in the OT referred to as 'the ten words' (Hebrew: *'aseret haddevarim*, e.g., Exod. 34.28). A designation for the set of precepts, revealed by God to Moses on Mount Sinai (Exod. 20.2-17)/Mount Horeb (Deut. 5.6-21). There are no major differences between the two accounts, except for the reason to remember the Sabbath. The Jewish holiday *Shavuot* or the 'Festival of Weeks' (Pentecost) commemorates the moment God gave the Ten Commandments to his people.

Some scholars assume that early in the transmission history of the text, the Decalogue was a collection of ten stereotypical, short formulas that can still be found in Exod. 20.13-16 or Deut. 5.17-20. Strictly speaking, the Decalogue consists mostly of prohibitions ('You shall not') instead of *commandments*. Only the precepts to remember the Sabbath and to honor one's parents are formulated positively.

According to the biblical account, the precepts were engraved on two stone tablets. The Ten Commandments are often presented as such in visual arts, e.g., the lithographs *Drawings for the Bible* (1960) of Mark Chagall or Gustave Doré's *Moses Showing the Ten Commandments* (engraving, 1865). Rembrandt van Rijn's *Moses Smashing the Tables of the Law* (oil on canvas, 1659) shows the breaking of the tablets by Moses when he is confronted with the idolatry committed by the Israelites in his absence.

A numerical division into ten separate commandments is absent in the biblical accounts. Hence, it differs according to the religious tradition. Only Judaism considers Exod. 20.2 ('I am the Lord your God') as the first precept and not as an introductory address. Following Augustine (*Questions of Exodus*, 71)—and later stipulations by the Council of Trent—Roman Catholics and most Lutherans regard Exod. 20.3-6 as only one and Exod. 20.17 as two commandments. Eastern, Anglican and Calvinist Christians on the other hand adopted the division made by Philo (*On the Decalogue*), Flavius Josephus (*Antiquities* III.91), Origen (*Homilies on Exodus*) and others whereby Exod. 20.3-6, instead of Exod. 20.17, is split into two commandments.

An important reference in the NT can be found in Matthew 5 where Jesus reinterprets the Jewish law. More literal quotations are present in Matt. 19.18; Mark 10.10; Luke 18.20 and Rom. 13.9, where the order of the commandments differs.

In popular culture, Cecil B. De Mille's *The Ten Commandments* (1923/1956) and the mini-series *The Ten Commandments: A Grand Retelling of the Epic Story of Moses* (2005), produced by ABC are well known retellings. In 1988, Krzysztof Kieślowski produced his *The Decalogue*, a series of ten short movies initially made for Polish television with a modern interpretation of the individual commandments.

In American society, the Decalogue causes many debates. For instance, R. Aderholt introduced the *Ten Commandments Defense Act* (2003), which was meant to protect the authority of states to display the 'Ten Commandments' in public places. The discussion is based on the question whether the Decalogue is part of the legal history of the country or rather intrinsically religious and as such—when present in public buildings—a violation of the separation of church and state.

Recommended reading. Segal, Ben-Zion, and Levi, Gershon. *The Ten Commandments in History and Tradition*. Jerusalem: Magnes Press, 1985. Thum, Veronika. *Zehn Gebote für die ungelehrten Leute. Der Dekalog in der Graphik des späten Mittelalters und der frühen Neuzeit*. Kunstwissenschaftliche Studien, 136; München: Deutscher Kunstverlag, 2006.

See also ARK OF THE COVENANT; COVENANT; EXODUS; BOOK OF GOLDEN CALF; HOREB; SERMON ON THE MOUNT [EV]

Tender mercies. From the Hebrew *racham* (tender love, compassion) and the Greek *splagchnon* (bowels; the inward parts) and *eleos* (mercy; pity; compassion). The Hebrew word *racham* translated as 'tender mercies' in the KJV, NKJV, ASV, DBT, and ESV is employed in such OT passages as Pss. 25.6, 40.11, 69.16, 79.8; Prov. 12.10; Dan. 9.8; and Jer. 16.5. Similarly, these translations render the Greek phrase *splagchnon eleos* as 'tender mercies' in passages such as Luke 1.78; Phil. 1.8; and Col. 3.12. By contrast, the more literal translations of the NASB, NRSV, and HCSB often employ the words 'mercy', 'compassion', and 'affection' when these Hebrew and Greek phrases are used.

Whether one is speaking about 'tender mercy', 'mercy', 'compassion', 'affection', or 'lovingkindness', the underlying premise remains the same. Bound up within these words are what the biblical writers believe to be some of the foundational attributes of God's character. God is infinitely patient and loving, even when those whom God loves present themselves as less than lovable. The 'tender mercies' of God are seen most clearly in the fact that God would: (1) lovingly provide and sustain a weak and vulnerable creation and, (2) graciously provide for the salvation and forgiveness of sins for a wayward and sinful humanity.

The motif of God's 'tender mercies' has found its way into the collective consciousness of western culture. For the Scottish churchman and practical philosopher Thomas Dick it was of great importance that one could look at the world and the whole of creation and see that God's 'tender mercies are displayed over all his works'. Because of this, Dick held that one could rightly reconcile the Christian faith and science.

Numerous authors have utilized the imagery of a long-suffering and patient God whose 'tender mercies' abound in some of their greatest works. One such example is John Bunyan's famous *The Pilgrim's Progress* in which the protagonist, Christian, is on a journey from the City of Destruction to the Celestial City. Along the course of his journey, Christian becomes sidetracked, lost, etc. God, in tender mercy and love, sends people such as 'Evangelist', 'Faithful', and the gatekeeper 'Good Will' to help and guide him on his journey, so that he may eventually reach the Celestial City.

Western films have also employed the imagery of patience, longsuffering, and compassion both with regard to the relationships between one human being and another, as well as between humanity and the divine. An example of this would be the Hollywood production *Tender Mercies* (1983), starring Robert Duvall as down-and-out country singer Mac Sledge. A drunk who has reached rock bottom, Mac is graciously given a job working at a budget motel in exchange for a place to stay. Rosa Lee, the hotel owner, gives him the room on the condition that he quit drinking. Eventually the two wed, attend a small church, and end up being baptized after receiving the gift of salvation. The premise of the movie is that redemption can come, and often does, as a result of God's tender mercies.

See also AGAPE; HOPE; LOVE; MERCY [JNR]

Tent of Meeting. The OT mentions three tabernacles (Latin for 'tent'). The first mention was a provisional Tabernacle described in Exodus 33. This account of the Tent of Meeting follows the story of the sin of the Golden Calf. This was a tent erected outside of the camp by Moses. It was some distance away from the camp and was called the Tent of Meeting by Moses. It is also translated the Tabernacle of Meeting or the Tabernacle of the Congregation.

The type of tent that Moses erected is not described in Exodus; however, it was probably a typical ancient middle eastern tent, in Hebrew '*ohel*. Middle Eastern nomads have used tents since time immemorial as movable habitations. The tents were made of poles covered with cloths or curtains that provided shelter from the wind and sun as well as from the rain and cold. The cloths covering the poles were usually of woven goat hair, which is usually tight enough to keep out the heaviest of rains. Ropes attached to tent pegs driven into the ground at the bottom and tied to the top of the tent kept the poles in place. Called *amud* ('column') in Hebrew, they usually numbered nine.

From before the Golden Calf event, the Tent of Meeting outside the camp was a place to which the Hebrew people could go to inquire of God. The people would go there as if going to an oracle (Exod. 33.7). When Moses went to the Tent of Meeting (*'ohel mo'ed*) the people would stand at the doors of their tents to watch. They would see the pillar of cloud descending to stay at the entrance of the Tent of Meeting while the Lord spoke with Moses. In response, the people would worship the Lord. When Moses left the Tent of Meeting Joshua the son of Nun, the young *aide-de-camp* of Moses, remained behind in the tent.

After the Sinaitic Tabernacle was erected it was sometimes called the 'tent of meeting' (Exod. 38.8). A bronze altar was made from the mirrors of the women who served at the entrance of the Tabernacle or 'Tent of Meeting'. The name in all cases signified a place of the people for meeting God. It was also where Aaron and his sons were ordained to their priestly ministry, but instead of Tabernacle the Sinaitic Tabernacle is often translated as 'Tent of Meeting' (Lev. 8.3). In Lev. 8.31, they are commanded to be at the 'Tent of Meeting' for seven days, until the days of their ordination are completed. Other references to the Sinaitic Tabernacle as the Tent of Meeting include Lev. 24.3, Num. 3.25, 4.1, 27.2 and other texts. The use of the term is favored by some translations and not by others.

In the history of American revivalism, tent meetings have been a frequent feature. People have been invited to come to the tent revival to meet God. Movies such as *Elmer Gantry* (1960), *The Apostle* (1997) and *Blues Brothers* (2000) have used tent revivals as part of the settings for the story. Tent revivals have also been used by missionaries in the field.

Recommended reading. Menken, John. *The Tent of Meeting: Texts*. Santa Fe, NM: Tent of Meeting, 1985. Colton, G. Woolworth. *The Sanctuary or Tent of Meeting, Usually Called the Tabernacle: A Short Study of its Forms, Materials, etc.* New York: G.W. & C.B. Colton, 1895.

See also AARON; LEVITES; MOSES; PRIEST; TABERNACLE; PILLAR OF CLOUD, PILLAR OF FIRE [AJW]

Tentmaker. Acts 18.3 refers to Paul as a tentmaker (*skēnopoios*), who meets with the Jewish couple Priscilla (Prisca) and Aquila in Corinth, followers of the same trade, and with whom he stays and works during the day, spending the evenings in the synagogue, debating with both Jews and Greeks. Although Paul's letters do not specifically mention tentmaking, he does emphasize his practice of self-support for his missionary endeavors by the work of his own hands (e.g., 1 Cor. 4.12; 9.12; cf. 1 Thess. 4.11; 2 Thess. 2.10). 1 Thessalonians 2.9 states 'we worked night and day, so that we might not burden any of you while we proclaimed to you the gospel of God'. Similarly, several ancient rabbis are said to have supported themselves through manual labor, e.g., the elder Hillel, a wood-cutter; Shammai, a builder (*Midrash Shabbat* 31); R. Joshua, a blacksmith (*Midrash Berakot* 28a); and R. Jose, a tanner (*Midrash Shabbat* 49b). Ronald F. Hock (1980) develops the theme of Paul as an artisan-missionary.

The apostle's methodology was certainly not the dominant one of the day. Many other religious leaders depended on support from wealthy individuals and the religiously devout. In fact, when Jesus sent his disciples out he commanded them to 'remain in the same house, eating and drinking whatever they provide, for the laborer deserves to be paid'. Paul himself did not argue against this practice. He argues in 1 Cor. 9.3-14 that an apostle is entitled to a material harvest for the planting of spiritual seed, and Pseudo-Paul reminds his protégé Timothy, that a laborer deserves to be paid (1 Tim. 5.18).

Since that time others have followed and continue to follow Paul's example. William Carey (1761–1831), considered the father of modern evangelical missions, worked as a factory owner and professor to support his missions work abroad. At present, tentmaking also allows missionaries access into countries which are closed to Christian influences. Here working professionals accept secular employment which both funds and veils missionary activity.

Recommended reading. Hock, Ronald F. *The Social Context of Paul's Ministry: Apostleship and Tentmaking*. Philadelphia: Augsburg Fortress Press, 1980.

See also PRISCILLA AND AQUILA [DC]

Thaddeus (see Jude Thaddeus).

Theological Virtues. From the Latin *virtus* and the Greek *aretē*, virtue has a long history in western thought. A virtue is a disposition or excellence of character that directs behavior towards good ends. The expression 'theological virtues' designates three such qualities (faith, hope and love/charity). These are called *theological* virtues because in Christian theology their object is God.

While ancient Greek and Roman literature did not use virtue terminology in an exclusively moral sense (e.g., Homer, *Iliad* 15.642), reflection upon moral virtues was an important aspect of the ethical tradition into the present era (Plato, *Meno* 77a-b; Aristotle, *Nichomachean Ethics* 1144a-b). Broadly speaking, this tradition identified four chief (cardinal) virtues—prudence, self-control, courage and justice. These are usually regarded as midpoints between contrasting vices and are *acquired* by training. To these, Christian theology added the three theological virtues (e.g., Thomas, *Summa Theologiae* 1–2.61-62).

In the biblical tradition, there is a close correlation between wisdom and virtue. Like virtue, wisdom is acquired by training, particularly in Torah (Ps. 119.11-12; Prov. 2.1-15). It is associated with the qualities of prudence, righteousness (justice), and fidelity to God's commandments (Deut. 6.1-9). There are relatively few formal virtue lists in the OT or the Apocrypha, and those that do exist tend to be found in the Wisdom literature (e.g., Wisdom 8.7). The NT contains fourteen virtue lists (1 Cor. 13.13; 2 Cor. 6.6-8; Gal. 5.22-23; Eph. 4.32; 5.9; Phil. 4.8; Col. 3.12; 1 Tim. 4.12; 6.11; 2 Tim. 2.22; 3.10; Jas 3.17; 1 Pet. 3.8; 2 Pet. 1.5-7).

Common to both canonical divisions is the notion of love as the principal theological virtue (Deut. 6.5; Matt. 23.34-40). The triad of faith, hope and love is derived from 1 Cor. 13.13, although a similar triad appears in the Vulgate version of Sir. 2.8-10. Three characteristics differentiate the theological virtues from the other virtues: first, they are received from God's Spirit and not acquired by training (cf. Gal. 5.22-23); second, since their object is God, they do not lie between two extremes; one cannot have them in excess; and third, because they are directed towards an ultimate object, they are everlasting; they persist into the eschatological age. This final point is likely to be what Paul has in mind when he states that these three 'remain' (1 Cor. 13.13).

Representations of the theological virtues occur often in western art. Raphael's fresco of the virtues in the *Stanza della Segnatura* (1511) is notable for its personification of the theological virtues as cherubs. More frequently, faith, hope and love are represented as women. Notable works include Vermeer's *Allegory of Faith* (c. 1670–72) and Baglione's *Charity and Justice Reconciled* (1622). Charity is often portrayed as a breastfeeding mother, as in Blanchard's *Allegory of Charity* (ca.1636–37). The link between charity and lactation derives mainly but not exclusively from Marian imagery, as David's *Rest on the Flight to Egypt* (ca.1510) illuminates. The classical tale of Pero breastfeeding the elderly Cimon was also the subject of several artworks devoted to *Roman Charity* (e.g., Reubens, 1612), and it reappears as a motif in Steinbeck's novel *The Grapes of Wrath* (1939).

See also AGAPE; FAITH; HOPE; LOVE; TORAH; WISDOM [MJL]

Thessalonians, Epistles to the. The two Thessalonian letters are among the letters attributed to the Apostle Paul.

At some point around 50 CE, Paul and his fellow missionaries, Silvanus (Silas) and Timothy, came to the city of Thessalonica in the Roman province of Macedonia. There they worked as laborers or artisans and taught their 'gospel', the message of salvation from sin through Jesus in his death and resurrection. Teaching in the synagogue, the city marketplaces, and private homes, they quickly developed a small following of believers. Initially these were Jews or others sympathetic to Judaism from the synagogue (Acts 17.1-4), but eventually most of these followers came from Gentile backgrounds, turning from the polytheism of their civic and family religions to the monotheistic worship of the Jewish God through belief in Jesus (1 Thess. 1.9-10). However, the missionaries and their followers experienced significant opposition from others in Thessalonica on religious, social, and political grounds, and Paul and Silvanus were forced to leave the city (1 Thess. 2; Acts 17.4-10).

This sudden departure left Paul with concerns for the wellbeing of the Thessalonian believers, so Paul sent Timothy back to Thessalonica to check on the young church. Timothy returned with the news that the Thessalonian believers were continuing in their 'faith' and 'love', believing in the one true God and the gospel message and meeting the social and practical needs of their fellow believers (1 Thess. 3.1-6). However, their 'hope' for divine blessing at Jesus' future return from heaven was diminished in the face of the death of one or more of their fellow believers (1 Thess. 4.13). Thus, Paul and his fellow missionaries wrote 1 Thessalonians to encourage the Thessalonian believers to continue in their faith in God and love for one another, and to rebuild their hope for the future grounded in the gospel.

Many scholars doubt the authenticity of 2 Thessalonians. However, if the letter was indeed personally authorized by Paul, it likely reflects circumstances immediately subsequent to those recounted above. Most significantly, the Thessalonian believers had somehow been led to believe that the final 'day of the Lord' had already occurred and that they had missed out on the divine blessings at Jesus' future return (2 Thess. 2.1-2). Thus, Paul, Silas, and Timothy wrote 2 Thessalonians for much the same reasons as 1 Thessalonians, but with a more detailed description of some events they believed must happen prior to Jesus' return (2 Thess. 2.1-12).

As arguably the earliest extant Christian writings, the Thessalonian Epistles have great historical significance for understanding the beliefs and practices of earliest Christianity. In addition, several specific passages and themes from the letters have received special attention in the history of interpretation. For example, Paul's description of 'the Jews' killing Jesus, opposing God's messengers, and thus receiving God's wrath (1 Thess. 2.14-16), has played a significant role in Jewish–Christian dialogue and discussions regarding alleged anti-Semitism in Christianity. Also, the descriptions of living believers being 'caught up' to the sky at Jesus' future return (popularly the 'rapture'; 1 Thess. 4.17) and of the 'lawless one' opposing God and deceiving the world prior to Jesus' return (popularly the 'antichrist'; 2 Thess. 2.3-12) have fueled much speculation among many conservative western Christians especially since the early nineteenth century regarding such 'end-time' events.

Recommended reading. Malherbe, Abraham J. *The Letters to the Thessalonians.* Anchor Bible, 32B. New York: Doubleday, 2000. Fee, Gordon D. *The First and Second Letters to the Thessalonians.* New International Commentary on the New Testament. Rev. edn. Grand Rapids, MI: Eerdmans, 2009.

See also ANTICHRIST; GOSPEL; PAUL, THE APOSTLE; RAPTURE, THE [MWP]

Thief in the night. The expression 'thief in the night' is found twice in the NT in 1 Thess. 5.2 and 1 Pet. 3.10 (cf. Matt. 24.43; 12.39). Both refer to the Second Coming that will take the world by so much surprise so that its arrival will be like a thief striking when least expected. The expression was obviously one used at the time to refer to someone coming and going silently, and some scholars have seen the message as suggesting that Jesus will surprise sinners and bring them the offer of salvation just before the Second Coming, with others arguing that he will come to take back his church.

Although the expression is often used as a term of abuse, it has been relatively little used in literature. However, *A Thief in the Night* was the title of a 1972 film produced by Russell S. Doughten and Donald W. Thompson (who was also the director), the first of four about a young woman, Patty, who dismisses the Gospels but gradually comes to believe them; after her husband disappears in the Rapture, she recognizes that she should not have rejected Christianity. The film remains well known largely because it includes 'I Wish We'd All Been Ready', a Christian rock song by Larry Norman. *A Thief in the Night* is also the title of John Cornwell's book, published in 1989, about the death of Pope John Paul I in 1978, refuting the allegations made by David Yallop's *In God's Name*, published five years earlier. Yallop had claimed that John Paul I was murdered and as a result Cornwell was called to the Vatican and asked to investigate the death himself. While Yallop answers the question 'Why?', Cornwell asks 'How?' and comes to the quite different conclusion that Pope John Paul I died day before the official date, discovered on the floor after a heart attack, put to bed, and found the next morning so that he could be remembered as dying with dignity. It is not clear whether Cornwell was referring to death coming like the 'thief in the night' or whether it was a reference to the neglect of the Pope's health and disregard of his worsening physical condition that led directly to his death, such that some of the perpetrators were the proverbial 'thieves'.

See also RAPTURE; SECOND COMING [JC]

Third Heaven. In 2 Cor. 12.2-4, Paul reports that he had experienced a heavenly ascent to the 'third heaven'. Paul's reference belongs to his 'Fool's Speech' (2 Cor. 11.1–12.18). He is responding there to the threat posed by the 'false' apostles (2 Cor. 11.13). They boasted in their superior charismatic gifts and Jewish ancestry, highlighting their 'visions and revelations' (12.1). What was Paul's response to these 'super-apostles' (2 Cor. 11.5; 12.11) who claimed to be superior 'visionaries'?

First, Paul boasts in his weaknesses because God's power was demonstrated in the weakness of the cross and not in visionary transports (2 Cor. 11.30; 12.7b-10; 13.4). Second, Paul recounts his heavenly ascent with grim humor to show the Corinthians the foolishness of boasting. Paul is uncertain whether the vision of Paradise was 'in body' or 'out of body' (2 Cor. 12.2b, 3b), a fatal admission because Jewish heavenly ascent accounts were usually clear on the issue (e.g., *1 En.* 71.1, 5). Here Paul mocks himself as a rank amateur on the apocalyptic stage. Worse, although Paul heard 'unutterable words' in his vision of Paradise (2 Cor. 12.4), causing him elation (12.7a), God had refused his apostle the opportunity to express what he heard (12.4b). Again, Paul spoofs the opponents' boasting culture by portraying himself as a 'visionless visionary'.

But what do we know about other visionary ascents like Paul's? Apart from the OT ascents (Gen. 5.24; 2 Kgs 2.2-15), the genre of apocalyptic literature in Second Temple Judaism recounts visionary experiences of the heavens and their inhabitants. Apocalyptic literature is pseudonymous, written in the name of a famous figure transported to heaven (e.g., Enoch, *1 En.* 14, 37, 71), or another OT character (e.g., Moses, Abraham, Isaiah). Apocalyptic visions describe the heavenly throne room, the angelic liturgy, the heavenly tablets, and calendrical and cosmological matters. Sometimes these visions were induced by ascetic methods (*Testament of Isaac* 4.1-7, 12, 43-48, 49-50). But Paul's description of the ascent (2 Cor. 12.2: 'was caught up') underscores God's work in effecting it. The Jewish apocalypses disagree regarding the number of heavens (thee, five, seven, or ten?). But, from the parallelism of 2 Cor. 12.2b and 12.4b, Paul clearly considers 'Paradise' to be in the 'third heaven'.

Heavenly ascents were known in the Greco-Roman world (Apuleius, *Metamorphoses* 11.23; Livy, 1.16; Lucian, *Icarus* 22; Ovid, *Metamorphoses* 14.805-852; Plutarch, *Sera* 23-24). In subsequent centuries, Christian writers authored two apocalypses of Paul, each based on 2 Cor. 12.2-4, to justify orthodox doctrine (*Vision of Paul*) or Gnostic teaching (*Apocalypse of Paul*). There is also an Islamic legend that Muhammad's journey to Paradise included entry into the 'third heaven' and that Joseph greeted him there on arrival. Last century, James Hampton claimed that God and his angels had visited him not in dreams but in physical form and had spoken to him. In response, from 1950 to 1964 in his Washington garage, Hampton produced 180 glittering objects for his *The Throne of the Third Heaven of the Nations' Millennium General Assembly* project. Modern charismatic believers also claim to have had 'third heaven' visionary experiences which, unlike Paul, they describe in detail. Whatever the status of these claims to heavenly visions might be, they indicate a cross-cultural preoccupation with the 'third heaven'.

Recommended reading. Harrison, J.R. 'In Quest of the Third Heaven: Paul and his Apocalyptic Imitators'. *Vigiliae Christianae* 58 (2004) 24-55. Gooder, P.R. *Only the Third Heaven: 2 Corinthians 12.1-10 and Heavenly Ascent.* Edinburgh: T. & T. Clark, 2006.

See also APOCALYPSE; APOCALYPTIC; CHERUBIM AND SERAPHIM; GARDEN OF EDEN; HEAVEN [JRHA]

Thirst. Themes of desire, yearning and longing are widespread in the scriptures. Thirst is employed in physical sense expressing, both the need to quench physical thirst (Exod. 17.3; Judg. 15.18; Matt. 25.35;

John 4.13; 19.28; Rom. 12.20; cf. Prov. 25.21), and severe privations (Ps. 107.5; 1 Cor. 4.11). Symbolically the word indicates a strong desire for something, e.g., 'hunger and thirst for righteousness' (Matt. 5.6; 1Pet. 2.2; cf. Sir. 51.24; Plato, *Republic* 8) and for God, 'I thirst for God' (Ps. 42.2; 63.1; 143.6; see Dave Branon, *My Soul Thirsts for God*, 2009).

A metaphorical sense is already present in the OT, based on the physical experience of Israel in the wilderness, where Moses struck the rock at Meribah and water came out (Exod. 17; Num. 20.1-13). For the prophets, thirst is the beginning of conversion. It is God's invitation to abundant life: 'Everyone who thirsts come to the waters; and you that have no money, come, buy (without price) and eat!' (Isa. 55.1). Amos speaks of a thirst not for water but for 'hearing the words of the Lord' (8.11). Proverbs metaphorically evokes things that are never satisfied: 'Sheol, the barren womb, the earth ever thirsty for water and the fire that never says, 'Enough'' (30.16).

Several prominent accounts involving thirst with theological and spiritual senses are found in the Gospel of John. The story of the Samaritan woman (4.1-42) embodies spiritual yearning and its fulfillment. Material water is a daily physical necessity. As Jesus says, 'Everyone who drinks of this water will thirst again' (4.13), but the water that Jesus gives ultimately slakes all thirst (4.14). The symbol of water as thirst-quenching indicates Jesus' invitation to come to him (6.35) and the capacity to respond to humanity's deep longing. The same invitation is issued at large to the crowd in Jerusalem and denoted that living water, which is the gift of the Spirit, is for all (7.37). On the cross, Jesus utters the one word, 'I thirst' (*dipsō*; 19.28), to express his desire not just for physical water but for the will of God (see 4.34; 5.30; 19.29), thus the scripture might be perfect completed (19.30; cf. Ps. 69.21). Jesus expresses his 'thirst' now to 'drink' the 'cup' of suffering and death that the Father has given him to drink (18.11).

Ultimately, the living water represents the fulfillment of God's promise: 'to the thirsty I will give water as a gift' (Rev. 21.6; 22.17). The liturgy of the Feast of All Saints evokes the day when believers can be with them experiencing the same total happiness when 'they will hunger no more, and thirst no more' (Rev. 7.16-17; cf. Isa. 49.10).

People everywhere are hungry and thirsty, insatiably longing and seeking. Most cannot explain their emptiness in words; everyone experiences it. Is water a human right for all people? Many communities in the world are asking this fundamental question (*Thirst*, film by Alan Snitow & Deborah Kaufman, 2003). People today express their yearning and curiosity by seeking in the Internet for persons, electronic marketing, books, pictures and games (Ken Kalfus, *Thirst*, 1999). Yet, thirst also symbolizes prayer; the more one prays the more one desire to spend more time with God; the only one who can fill endless yearnings. Augustine puts it in his classic prayer: 'You have made us for yourself, O Lord, and our hearts are restless until they rest in you' (cf. *Confessions*).

See also LIVING WATER; SAMARITAN WOMAN; WATER; WELL [DR]

Thirty pieces of silver. Judas Iscariot is described in the Bible as being paid 'Thirty Pieces of Silver' to betray Jesus (Matt. 27.3), the number 30 representing a significant amount of money, but payment made in silver rather than gold, undoubtedly so that Judas would have been able to spend the money without provoking any suspicion. In films, this is shown by Judas receiving a small bag of coins—enough to jingle, but not too many so that they cannot be quickly concealed. Matthew 27.3 claims that Judas felt remorse for his betrayal of Jesus, returned the money to the chief priests and hanged himself (27.5). According to the Lucan author, the unrepentant Judas used the money to buy a field, where he burst asunder and died (Acts 1.16-20).

In Taylor Caldwell's and Jess Stearn's novel *I, Judas* (1977), Judas attempts to return the money to Caiaphas who refuses to accept it shouting that 'this money shall never go back to the treasury. For it is blood money, and it is not lawful to keep this reminder of your perfidy'. There are also mentions of it in books such as Bertram Brooker, *The Robber* (1949), and LeGette Blythe, *Tear for Judas* (1951). The term has since become recognized as a payment made for betrayal—blood money—the recipient often being known as a 'Judas', the name used as a term of denigration.

The phrase has also been used as the title of a number of books including those by Clarence Budington Kelland (1913), Andrew Soutar (1931), Charles Stewart Black (1934), John MacBeath (1936), Erica Reiner (1980), and the passion play by Maud Dorothy Reed, published in 1944, as well as the play by Howard Fast, published in 1954.

See also JUDAS ISCARIOT; TREASURE [JC]

Thomas, Doubting. The name traditionally ascribed to one of Jesus' disciples in the Gospel of

John. John's brief narrative of Thomas (20.24-29), part of his resurrection account, does not in fact apply this label to Thomas, and the narrative aims chiefly to portray Thomas's *progression* from doubt in Jesus' resurrection to belief (Greek: *pisteuō*) in it. According to the story, Thomas hears from the other disciples that Jesus has been resurrected and has appeared to them, but he demands physical evidence as verification. Shortly thereafter, Jesus appears to Thomas and offers, by his appearance and his invitation to touch his wound, just the verification that Thomas required. By Jesus' appearance (Thomas never touches Jesus' wound), Thomas comes to belief in the resurrection with the expression 'My Lord and my God!' (20.28). At the same time, John's Jesus implies that readers are perfectly capable of belief without such an experience as Thomas has (20.29). Most scholars agree that the Thomas narrative marks the original end of John's gospel.

By portraying Thomas's progression to belief, John 20.24-29 seeks to achieve broader theological and narrative aims. Foremost among these is to encourage readers to emulate Thomas's belief (part and parcel of belief that Jesus is the Christ [1.12; 3.16]) and to emphasize John's portrayal of Jesus as God by closing the gospel with the same equation that opens it (cf. John 1.1). These aims imply, however, that the Thomas narrative is less than historically plausible. While most critics agree that one of Jesus' disciples was named Thomas, few find credibility in John's account in 20.24-29.

Broadly speaking, the western tradition has prioritized various elements of the doubting Thomas story. On the one hand, some Christians, including those of south India, have upheld Thomas as a paradigm of discipleship and belief, a fact evident in the grand painting of John 20.27-28 that marks the entrance to Thomas's alleged tomb in the Santhome Cathedral, Chennai. On the other hand, many people have highlighted Thomas's doubt, so that while Thomas himself is a holy individual and saint, he remains a paradigm of uncertainty. This view has influenced medieval Christian art (including works by Mariotto di Nardo and Marco Pino), and poetry, such as Dante's description of viewing the Veil of Veronica in the *Divine Comedy* (*Paradiso*, canto 31). This view has also been the basis for the mildly pejorative phrase 'doubting Thomas', probably first used in the seventeenth century, to describe sceptics or people who demand verification. American President Abraham Lincoln used the phrase in this sense to characterize his experimental approach to work, and the term has similarly been applied in media that include film (for instance, in the 1935 comedy *Doubting Thomas*, starring Will Rogers). Intriguingly, Glenn Most has argued that while John does not intend to portray Thomas touching Jesus, western tradition has ironically tended to portray precisely this, not only because people have inaccurately read John 20, but also because of a need to argue for the bodily existence of the risen Christ, and the desire in artistic works to show 'recompenses for the melancholy of Jesus' refusal of Mary's desire' to touch him (20.17), often portrayed in medieval artistic scenes of John's passion narrative.

Recommended reading. Bonney, William. *Caused to Believe: The Doubting Thomas Story as the Climax of John's Christological Narrative*. Biblical Interpretation Series, 62; Leiden: Brill, 2002. Most, Glenn W. *Doubting Thomas*. Cambridge, MA: Harvard University Press, 2005.

See also JOHN, GOSPEL OF [AD]

Thomas, Gospel of. There are two books called the *Gospel of Thomas*. One of these is better called the *Infancy Gospel of Thomas* because it claims to report deeds of the boy Jesus. The other *Gospel of Thomas* is a Gnostic writing that was recovered by archaeologists in 1945 near the village of Nag Hammadi in Upper Egypt. The latter was one of a collection of Gnostic books in Coptic translations of Greek originals.

In the infancy gospel, Jesus performs a series of childhood miracles. It is extant in four versions—two in Greek (one much longer than the other), one in Latin, and one in Syriac. These stories are about the miraculous power and divine wisdom of the boy Jesus. However, almost all of the miracles are destructive, with four at most being beneficial. The stories tell of Jesus pronouncing a curse upon another boy after the latter has spoiled some pools made by Jesus. Another story says that a boy was running, unintentionally ran into Jesus and then fell down dead. In another story a teacher who swatted Jesus on the head was cursed and then fell to the ground.

There are many other tales, with one of Jesus making twelve live sparrows out of clay being included in the Qur'an. The *Infancy Gospel of Thomas* was considered heretical by orthodox Christians.

The Coptic *Gospel of Thomas* found at Nag Hammadi in 1945 is a Gnostic book composed of 114 sayings attributed to Jesus. In 1898 and in 1903, Greek fragments of the book were discovered at

Oxyrhynchus in Egypt; however, they were not well understood until after the full Coptic version was discovered.

The prologue says that the book contains 'the secret sayings' that Jesus dictated to Judas Thomas the Twin (Didymus). However, the Coptic *Gospel of Thomas* is not a gospel in the genre of NT Gospels. While the latter have sayings, they are connected by a narrative that relates the ministry of Jesus. In contrast, the sayings in the *Gospel of Thomas* at best resemble the 'Q Source' believed by scholars to have been used by Matthew and Luke in writing their gospels. 'Q' is German for Quellen which means 'source'. The sayings in the *Gospel of Thomas* are believed to be similar to Q, believed to have been a similar collection of sayings.

Scholars believe that the *Gospel of Thomas* was composed in Syria between the end of the first century and the end of the second. Because it claims Judas Thomas to be its scribe, it is thought to have been produced by someone associated with the ascetic Encratite sect of Gnostics.

Most of the sayings are introduced with the formula 'Jesus said'. Saying 1 promises deliverance from death to those who find illumination in the sayings; they will gain understanding of the true self (Saying 2). The theme is esoteric wisdom that will provide a return to the spiritual realm. Salvation comes from the secret *gnosis* (knowledge), not from the justifying and sanctifying deeds of the dying and rising Christ.

Recommended reading. Doresse, Jean. *The Secret Books of the Egyptian Gnostics*. New York: Viking, 1959. Meyer, Marvin W. *The Secret Teachings of Jesus: Four Gnostic Gospels*. New York: Random House, 1984. Robinson, James M. *The Nag Hammadi Library in English*. Rev. edn. New York: HarperCollins, 1990.

See also GNOSTIC; GNOSTICISM; GOSPEL; HERESY; JESUS; CHILDHOOD OF; MIRACLES; Q; WISDOM [AJW]

Thorn in the Flesh. From 2 Cor. 12.7, where Paul boasts about his mystical experiences: 'Therefore, to keep me from being too elated, a thorn was given me in the flesh, a messenger of Satan to torment me, to keep me from being too elated'.

The troubled, misshapen or wounded hero is a staple of western culture: from the deranged but noble Don Quixote to the grotesque Phantom, who haunts the Opera in Gaston Leroux's 1909 novel and its more famous remakes. This paradigm seems to include few if any women, a comment on the paradigm rather than the women. There are, however, innumerable troubled males: short, weak and uncertain Frodo in *The Lord of the Rings*, the haunted crusader *Batman* (like most comic book heroes, a cowboy figure), bumbling Charlie Chaplin and Shakespeare's vacillating *Hamlet*. Other examples include Dr Jekyll (whose thorn is Mr. Hyde*)* through *Beauty and the Beast* to the opium-addicted Sherlock Holmes. The orphaned (i.e., permanently wounded) Luke Skywalker resembles the alcoholic cowboy anti-hero played by Clint Eastwood in the movie *Unforgiven* (1992) or the alcoholic priest of Graham Greene's 1940 novel *The Power and the Glory*. But it is Odysseus, who makes man's imperfection the essence of his tirades against the gods, who is the prototypical protagonist of the western canon. Paul, whose faults have always troubled his readers, is perhaps better suited to be a misfit anti-hero than any in the early Christian pantheon.

As a Jew steeped in the scriptures, Paul's unusual repetition of the words 'To keep me from being too elated' may also serve to link his 'thorn' to the sufferings of the righteous but tormented Job. More attention should also be given to Paul's place in and his self-identification with the Hebrew prophetic tradition, where complaints similar to his are well known (e.g., Jeremiah whose fault was that he was too young). The thorn may also represent Paul's opponents, sent by Satan to keep him from rejoicing in his missionary successes. It is possible that Paul is obliquely referring to the thorn of derision of Ezek. 28.24. However, most commentators believe that the thorn refers to some personal ailment or weakness. Building precariously from scattered hints in his letters, would-be Pauline biographers have suggested everything from a hare-lip or chronic depression to the possibility that Paul was effeminate and, despite—or perhaps because of—his anti-homosexual rhetoric in Romans, latently gay. The imaginative fourth-century descriptions of the apostle have him as slight, small man with a high, balding forehead—as Donald Harman Akenson has noted, something of 'an early version of Lenin'. The second-century apocryphal *Acts of Paul and Thecla* describes Paul as 'baldheaded, bowlegged ... with meeting eyebrows and a slightly hooked nose'. Paul was never remembered as a Hellenistic poster-boy.

The expression 'thorn in the flesh' evolved in idiomatic English to having a 'thorn in one's side', meaning bearing with a persistent difficulty or annoyance (cf. the whole genre of 'sidekick' movies from *Some Like It Hot* and *The Odd Couple* through *Shanghai Noon* to *Planes, Trains and Automobiles* or *Shrek*). Surprisingly, redemption often results. Luther, whose fear had him shaking as a new priest at the altar, challenged half of Europe in the Reformation. The recently published diaries of Mother Theresa revealed her incredible charity to have been built on a personal and persistent questioning of God's love. That (human) weakness shows (God's) strength is the essence of Paul's sometimes tortuous arguments. It is an argument he lived out. Like Aesop's famous lion, the apostle was both humbled and oddly enough, humanized, by whatever thorn brought him such undefined pain.

See also PAUL, THE APOSTLE; PLANTS, SYMBOLISM OF [MA]

Thou art the man. Following David's plot to have Uriah the Hittite killed, the prophet Nathan tells David a parable about a rich man stealing from a poor man. When an outraged David pronounces a harsh punishment on the rich man, Nathan unveils his critique of David's actions, telling David, 'You are the man!' (2 Sam. 12.7). Realizing his abuse of power and moral failure, David responds, 'I have sinned against the Lord' (2 Sam. 12.13).

The line in King James's English has appeared in literature as the title of a short story by Edgar Allen Poe and a novel by Mary Elizabeth Braddon. In Poe's *Thou Art the Man* (1850), a corpse names his murderer (via ventriloquism) by gasping the title phrase. The plot of Braddon's *Thou Art the Man* (1894) is likewise driven by a mysterious murder's effects on estranged lovers.

The triangular relationship between David, Nathan and Bathsheba is also characteristic of *film noir*, a popular American cinematic genre in its heyday during the 1940s and 1950s. *Films noir* are often characterized by the interplay between a lone male figure, a *femme fatale*, and some version of corrupt society, usually in the form of organized crime or a case a detective is called on to solve. In classic detective movies like *The Big Sleep* (1946), the final resolution comes when the private investigator (Humphrey Bogart) has solved the mystery and explained to the criminal (John Ridgely) how his crimes were foiled. Drawing on these cinematic conventions, spoofs like *Austin Powers: International Man of Mystery* (1997) include climactic scenes of confrontation between Powers (Mike Myers) and Dr Evil (also played by Myers) that illicit a sense of remorse over the villain's criminal past.

The Bathsheba incident does not end with David's concealed sin but with David's angst following Nathan's indictment. David seeks penance through prayer for himself (see Ps. 51) and his dying infant son (2 Sam. 12.15-19). Similarly, in *The Apostle* (1997), Euliss 'Sonny' Dewey (Robert Duvall) is a womanizer turned Pentecostal preacher after assaulting his wife's boyfriend. Seeking his own salvation by saving others through energetic evangelism, Dewey dubs himself Apostle E.F. as he flees his past. The film's climax shows E.F. preaching his final sermon while the police wait outside the church building to arrest him. E.F. is willingly arrested and the film ends with E.F. working in a chain gang—his past having finally caught up with him.

Many painters have portrayed Nathan's confrontation of David. Notable works include Rembrandt's two sketches of *Nathan Admonishing David* (1652–53); Peter Roethermel's *Thou Art the Man* (1884); and Julius Schnorr von Carolsfeld's engraving *Nathan Confronts David* (1851–60).

See also BATHSHEBA; DAVID; URIAH [DIS]

Though he slay me. This phrase refers to Job 13.15 in which the central character, following considerable misfortune, declares of God, 'Though he slay me, yet will I trust in him' (KJV). The translation of this verse presents significant difficulties. The Hebrew text contains the word for 'no, not' while ancient notes in the text's margin suggest this should be read as the word for 'to him, in him'. While phonetically insignificant, this ambiguity means that the verse can be translated in two quite different ways. Following the marginal note (known traditionally as the *Qere*) renders the verse, 'Though he slay me, yet will I trust in him'. In contrast, the written Hebrew (known traditionally as the *Ketiv*) results in the more negative, 'See, he slays me; I have no hope'.

The more positive *Qere* has had greater impact upon western culture. It is attested to in ancient Greek translation, in Jerome's fifth-century Latin Vulgate, and in the English King James Version. Job's trust in God in the face of suffering has made these sentiments a paragon of piety for commentators such as Gregory the Great and John Calvin in the sixth and sixteenth centuries respectively. In Elizabeth Gaskell's mid-nineteenth-century novel *Cranford*, Miss Jessie Brown utters Job's words of trust in response to the death of her father and illness of her sister.

While Jewish reception as a rule largely favors the *Qere* in biblical interpretation (the *Qere* traditionally directing a verse's oral delivery) in the Mishnah, originating from around the second century CE, the ancient rabbis acknowledge the difficulty of interpreting this verse, suggesting that 'the matter rests in doubt'. Modern translations have begun to reflect this also, with the NIV and NRSV taking different routes (following the *Qere* and *Ketiv* respectively). Several commentators have even spoken positively of the ambiguity of Job's words. In a 2003 article in the Catholic newspaper *The Tablet*, the Jewish scholar Edward Kessler approvingly cited the tension between the two meanings of the verse, suggesting that such tension creates room for appreciating the ambiguities of the Bible and the consequent diversity of Jewish and Christian biblical interpretation.

See also JOB [DCT]

Throne. From the Greek *thronos* (Hebrew: *kisse'*), a seat that signifies authority and honor, particularly that of royalty. The Hebrew term is used in a variety of contexts to refer to the chairs of distinguished persons, including governors (Neh. 3.7), priests (1 Sam. 4.13, 18), and most notably kings (for foreign kings, see Exod. 11.5; Jer. 43.10; Jonah 3.6; for Solomon's throne, see 1 Kgs 10.18-20). The throne is most fundamentally a symbol and representation of the power of the one seated in it. Even mere proximity to the throne can designate power (1 Kgs 2.19).

Of earthly thrones in the Bible, the throne of David is the most commonly referred to and important. God establishes the throne along with the Davidic covenant, the promise that David and his descendants will rule over his kingdom for all time (2 Sam. 7.13-16). After its creation, the throne of David is mentioned numerously throughout the OT, often in prophetic and messianic contexts (Isa. 9.7; 16.5; Jer. 13.13; 22.4, 30; 29.16; 33.17, 21). The OT also employs the imagery of the throne to symbolize God's power and sovereignty. Prophetic and apocalyptic visions repeatedly portray God as a king seated on a throne. The throne of God is said to be in the heavens, with the earth as a footstool (Isa. 66.1; Ezek. 1.26), indicating God's authority over all nations. The features of God's throne are described differently, but the descriptions invariably emphasize its majesty and glory, and hence the majesty and glory of God (cf. Dan. 7.9-10; Ezek. 1.26).

The biblical imagery of God's heavenly throne has had a powerful influence on Jewish mystics for thousands of years. Ezekiel's description of the heavenly throne is a central motif in the literature of Merkabah mysticism, the goal of which is the attainment of a vision of God seated on the heavenly throne. The throne of God is not always imagined as heavenly, though. The ark of the covenant is sometimes imagined as the throne of God (Exod. 25.20-22). Jeremiah refers to Jerusalem as the 'throne of the Lord' (3.17), and Isaiah closely associates the temple in Jerusalem with God's throne (6.1).

The NT takes up both the imagery of the Davidic throne and that of God's throne, often with messianic overtones. The angel Gabriel informs Mary that Jesus, as messiah, will assume the throne of David (Luke 1.32). In Revelation, Jesus sits with God on God's throne (Rev. 2.22). The throne is the seat of final judgment, conducted either by God (Rev. 20.11-12), or by Jesus and his disciples, each with their own throne (Matt. 19.28). It is possible that Revelation also depicts the disciples sitting on their own thrones at the judgment, as it describes 24 thrones around God's, occupied by 24 elders (Rev. 4.4). These elders might represent the 12 tribes of Israel, along with the 12 disciples. As with Jewish mystics, biblical descriptions of God's throne have impacted Christian mystics. Revelation, with its rendition of the heavenly throne, can itself be read as an example of early Christian mysticism. Christian art often portrays God or Christ seated on a heavenly throne, and Christian hymns often cite the divine throne (e.g., 'God is Still on the Throne'; 'Before the Throne of God'; 'Around the Throne of God Above'; 'Christ Returned to Claim his Throne').

Recommended reading. Eskola, Timo. *Messiah and the Throne: Jewish Merkabah Mysticism and Early Christian Exaltation Discourse*. Tübingen: Mohr Siebeck, 2001.

See also ARK; COVENANT; REVELATION; TEMPLE [NB]

Throne of Grace. This phrase is found only once in the Bible, Heb. 4.16: 'Let us therefore come boldly unto the throne of grace (*tō thronō tēs charitos*), that we may obtain mercy, and find grace to help in time of need' (KJV). The expression is a typical Jewish circumlocution for 'throne of God', expressing the divine attributes of kindness, favor and loyalty. In its context in Hebrews, the phrase refers to Jesus' role as both high priest and sacrifices who enables believers to approach the divine throne, the seat of God's power, justice and mercy (e.g., Ps. 9.4, 7; 11.4; 45.6, 8; 93.2; ; 97.2; 103.19; Isa. 6.1; 66.1; Jer. 3.17; Lam. 5.19; Ezek. 1.26; 10.1; 43.7; Dan. 7.9; Matt. 5.34; 23.22; Acts 7.49; Heb. 1.8; 8.1; 12.2; Rev. 1.4; 4.2-11). Possibly an early expression of Jewish *merkabah* ('throne') mysticism, the image figures in the

Christian mediaeval trinitarian motif of the 'throne of mercy' with God enthroned, holding Christ on the cross, with a dove, representing the Holy Spirit, descending (e.g., Nicolò di Pietro Gerini, *The Trinity*, c. 1400). The phrase is common in English literature, e.g., 'We must all come to the throne of Grace at last, Mr. Casslilis' (Robert Louis Stevenson, *New Arabian Nights*, 1882). The image is also a favorite of Christian hymnody (e.g., 'Behold the Throne of Grace', 'O Come to the Throne of Grace', 'Come Boldly to the Throne of Grace').

See also GRACE; HEBREWS, EPISTLE TO THE; MERCY SEAT; THRONE [MALB]

Tiberius. Tiberius Claudius Nero was the second emperor of Rome. He was the son of Augustus's wife Livia and ruled from the death of Augustus in 14 CE until his own death in 37 CE. Despite his prowess as a general, Tiberius was adopted as the son and heir of Augustus only after all other options were exhausted. Tiberius was forced to divorce his wife Vipsania, whom he loved dearly, and marry Julia, the promiscuous daughter of Augustus. The ancient sources describe Tiberius as an unhappy and moody man who retired from the public life of Rome in 26 CE. Tiberius spent much of his retirement on the island of Capri where ruins of his palace can still be reached by the ambitious tourist. Tiberius's time away from Rome allowed Sejanus, the praetorian prefect, to increase his power and terrorize Rome until his death in 31 CE.

Tiberius is only mentioned once by name in the NT (Luke 3.1). However, in many other Gospel passages, the title Caesar refers to Tiberius. While Tiberius plays a small role in the NT, Luke 3.1 is critical because it establishes a date for the beginning of Jesus' ministry, the fifteenth year of the reign of Tiberius, 29 CE.

Later Christian writers such as Tertullian and Eusebius claim that Pontius Pilate recounted the supernatural deeds and resurrection of Jesus to Tiberius, who brought them to the attention of the Roman senate. Eusebius and Tertullian further claim that although the senate rejected Jesus' status as a God, Tiberius provided some level of protection for Christians.

In western culture, Tiberius has often been overlooked. He is in the shadows of the pivotal Augustus who ruled before him and the cruel and salacious stories of Caligula who succeeded him. However, Tiberius does appear in many books and films about the Roman Empire such as *I Claudius* (1976), *Ben Hur* (1959) and *Caligula* (1979).

The city Tiberias, on the Sea of Galilee, was founded by Herod Antipas in 20 CE in honor of Tiberius. Much of the Jerusalem Talmud was compiled in Tiberias and despite a major earthquake in 1837, Tiberias continues to be a thriving resort city.

Recommended reading. Levick, Barbara. *Tiberius the Politician*. London: Routledge, 1999. Seager, Robin. *Tiberius*. Malden, MA: Blackwell Publishing, 2005.

See also AUGUSTUS, CAESAR OCTAVIANUS; CAESAR; EMPEROR; ROMAN EMPIRE; AND ROME [KS]

Tigris. One of the main rivers in Mesopotamia—the Euphrates is the other—mentioned twice in the Bible: Gen. 2.14, in a description of the Garden of Eden, as being on the eastern side of Assyria; and Dan. 10.4, where the prophet is on the river's bank. In Hebrew, it was known as the *Hiddeqel*.

The source of the river is in the Taurus Mountains in eastern Asia Minor (Turkey); the river flows to the Shatt-al-Arab, through the marshes, into the Persian Gulf. There are many tributaries, e.g., the Great and the Little Zab, and the Diyala, originating in the Zagros Mountains. Altogether, the Tigris is 1,150 miles (1,850 km) long, and it was one of the main transportation routes through Mesopotamia. Aerial photography in the twentieth century confirmed the large number of ancient irrigation canals in the region, showing that the water from the Tigris was used to sustain city life and agriculture. In biblical times, many of the great cities were located on the banks of the Tigris: Nineveh, Ctesiphon and Seleucia, as well as Baghdad and Mosul. The southern part of the river also represented the eastern boundary of the kingdom of Babylonia, and the western boundary of the land of the Elamites; the northern part was Assyrian-controlled.

The Tigris and the Euphrates are two of the best-known rivers in the ancient Middle East, and in fighting in Mesopotamia from then, through the time of Alexander the Great, the Crusades, World War I, and in until modern times (with the invasion of Iraq in 2003), there are many references to armies 'crossing the Tigris'. The capture of the city of Kut-el-Amara, on the river's banks, by the British in September 1915, and the subsequent surrender on April 29, 1916, became major events in the Mesopotamia Campaign of WW I, which led to the founding of modern Iraq. The tiles which marked the German Consulate visible from the river are now in the Imperial War Museum in London.

Iraq became known as the land between two rivers, Tigris and Euphrates, the phrase forming the title of Seton Lloyd's history of the country. One of the first Iraqi stamps, issued in 1923, showed small boats called *gufas* on the Tigris. In 1959, when escaping after the failure of the assassination attempt on Prime Minister Qassim, the young Saddam Hussein swam across the Tigris, and after becoming President in 1979, he made swimming at Salahuddin, near Tikrit in the Tigris an annual event in which he would show his strength and relive the escape. He became popular with many of the local landowners, and in 2004 when escaping the US soldiers, he hid on a farm near Salahuddin where he was captured on December 13, 2004.

The southern part of the Tigris River was largely marsh and swamp, made famous by studies of the Marsh Arabs living there. Wilfred Thesiger's *The Marsh Arabs* (1954) and Gavin Maxwell's *A Reed Shaken by the Wind* (1957) are the most famous. In 1977, the Norwegian adventurer Thor Heyerdahl, aiming to show that ancient Sumerians could spread their culture throughout the region, built a reed boat on the banks of the river. The boat was called *Tigris* and Heyerdahl recorded this in his book *The Tigris Expedition* (1979). In the 1980s, the draining of the marshes to allow Iraq to have more farmland was an environmental (and social) disaster. The draining of the marshlands, however, was celebrated by Saddam Hussein's government, with postage stamps issued on April 28, 1999, to commemorate the opening of the 'Great Dam' on the river.

See also EUPHRATES; MESOPOTAMIA; RIVER [JC]

Timothy, 1–2 (see Pastoral Epistles).

Titulus Crucis. In the crucifixion story, the wooden notice affixed to the headboard of the cross noting the crime of the person being executed. The inscription on the headboard of Jesus is noted in all four gospels with slight variations: 'This is Jesus, the King of the Jews' (Matt. 27.37); 'The King of the Jews' (Mark 15.26); 'This is the King of the Jews' (Luke 23.38); and 'Jesus of Nazareth, King of the Jews' (John 19.19). John records a dispute between Pontius Pilate and the chief priest over the inscription, and records that the inscription was 'in Hebrew, in Latin, and in Greek' (19.20); Luke also says it was written in three languages.

The inscription became abbreviated as INRI, the Latin initials for *Iesus nazarenus, Rex Iudaeorum* ('Jesus of Nazareth, King of the Jews'), possibly influenced by the Roman usage of abbreviations such as 'S.P.Q.R'. ('the Senate and the People of Rome'). Indeed both abbreviations appear on the painting *Crucifixion*, attributed to Marco da Pino (1525–1567/8), at the Escorial Palace in Spain, and over time some painters and sculptors have included the complete inscription, some the abbreviated version. El Greco and Francisco de Goya both used the full inscription, with Anton van Dyck's *Christ on the Cross* (1627) showing the headboard on a piece of paper attached to the cross.

The headboard has long fascinated some historians, and Helena, the mother of the Emperor Constantine, was given a piece of wood with an inscription on it, which has been venerated since the fourth century, held at the Church of Santa Croce in Gerusalemme, Rome. Curiously, this relic has the inscription running from right to left, as though a Hebrew scribe wrote in Hebrew first, from right to left, and then continued with the Greek and the Latin. Luke's statement that the inscription was 'in *letters* of Greek and Latin and Hebrew' (KJV; author's italics) has been taken to indicate a problem with the inscription itself, such as the writing in Greek and Latin being back-to-front. Pilate's refusal to change the wording (John 19.21) hints that writing the headboard must have taken some time, and he did not want to delay proceedings any further. This suggests to some that the *Titulus Crucis* in Rome is possibly authentic, as any later writer would have forged it with the writing from left to right.

See also CROSS/CRUCIFIXION OF CHRIST; PONTIUS PILATE [JC]

To everything there is a season. The beginning and thesis of Eccl. 3.1-8, a poem asserting that there is a set time for every activity in human life. In the NRSV, the poem starts: 'For everything there is a season, and a time for every matter under heaven: a time to be born, and a time to die; a time to plant, and a time to pluck up what is planted'. The text includes 14 sets of antithetical statements called merisms (e.g., a time to love, and a time to hate); both the number 14 (7 x 2) and the opposites in juxtaposition suggest that this poem addresses the whole spectrum of human activity.

This passage has functioned both as a source of comfort and despair for its readers. Because the poem itself never mentions God, some interpreters find in it a detached determinism; others see an attentive God who is in control of all aspects of human activity (cf. 3.11). Either way, the author (Qoheleth) asserts that these events occur at times outside the realm of human control.

The repetition, style, and message of the passage set it apart in the OT, and as a consequence it has played a prominent role in the English Bible's reception history. At least from Chaucer's time, the text appears in numerous major literary works. In Chaucer's *The Canterbury Tales*, the host implores the Oxford Clerk to tell a tale. 'I trowe ye studie aboute som sophyme, / But Salomon seith, 'every thing hath tyme.' / For Goddes sake, as beth of bettre chere. / It is no tyme for to studien here' (4.5-9). Antipholus of Syracuse tells Dromio of Syracuse in Shakespeare's *Comedy of Errors*: 'Learn to jest in good time, there's a time for all things' (2.2.65). Paula employs the quotation of Eccl. 3.1 to reject Somerset's kiss in Thomas Hardy's *A Laodicean*. 'To everything there is a season, and the season for this is not just now'. T.S. Eliot's poetry also alludes to this passage in 'The Love Song of J. Alfred Prufrock' and the first two pieces of *The Four Quartets*.

The text of Ecclesiastes 3 has also been popularized through music. In 1954, Pete Seeger wrote *Turn! Turn! Turn! (To Everything There Is a Season)*, which the folk-rock band The Byrds popularized in 1965. The song reproduces the entire text of Eccl. 3.1-8 except for the phrase: 'A time for war'. Although written in the 1950s, the Byrds's recording found favor with those who opposed the Vietnam War given the song's conclusion: 'A time for peace, I swear it's not too late'. The Byrds's recording later appeared in the 1994 *Forrest Gump* soundtrack. Additionally, the Sugar Hill Gang's 1979 single *Rapper's Delight* adapted the words of Eccl. 3.2-8. 'Now there's a time to laugh, a time to cry / A time to live, and a time to die / A time to break and a time to chill / To act civilized or act real ill'. Stevie Wonder's 2005 album *A Time to Love* featured a song by the same name, which includes a number of allusions to Eccl. 3.

Countless other speeches, books, films, and television programs make use of phrases from this poem as well, further showing the prominent role of this biblical passage in western culture today.

Recommended reading. Christianson, Eric S. *Ecclesiastes through the Centuries*. Malden, MA: Blackwell, 2007. Limburg, James. *Encountering Ecclesiastes: A Book for our Time*. Grand Rapids, MI. Eerdmans, 2006.

See also ECCLESIASTES [BCW]

Tobias (see Tobit, Book of).

Tobit, Book of. One of the deuterocanonical books, written probably around 200 BCE. It is a short story in the genre of the edifying novel or Jewish romance that was popular in postexilic literature, another example of which is Judith. Its original language was probably Aramaic. It survives in Hebrew and Aramaic fragments found as part of the DSS. Three Greek recensions have also been preserved, containing Aramaisms.

Tobit is a tale about a pious man who is a captive from northern Israel in the time of the Assyrian captivity. Persecuted because he has given aid and comfort to fellow Israelites, he is blinded accidentally and is forced by circumstances to bear the shame of being supported by his wife. So great is his shame that he prays that he might die. Prayer is also offered for a young Jewish maiden, Sarah, in Ecbatana because she is haunted by the demon Asmodeus. The demon has killed seven suitors who came seeking her hand in marriage. Each died on their wedding night before consummating the marriage. She too is despondent and wishes for death.

Tobit wants to send Tobias, his son, to Rages in Media to collect ten silver talents that he had left there, but is afraid for the youth's safety. Tobias fortuitously meets the angel Raphael who has been sent to heal Tobias and free Sarah. Having assumed the guise of a man named Azariah, Raphael becomes the hired traveling companion of Tobias, who brings along his dog. At the Tigris River they catch a fish. Azariah tells Tobias to preserve its heart, liver and gall which he carefully does. They continue their journey to Ecbatana where Tobias becomes betrothed to Sarah, who turns out to be a kinswoman.

On their wedding night, on the angel's instructions, Tobias burns the heart and liver of the fish. The stench drives the demon away to Egypt to which Raphael quickly journeys. There he binds the demon hand and foot. Tobias and Sarah, now happily married travel, back home where he is now believed to be lost because he is long overdue. There, he uses the fish gall to anoint his father's eyes, restoring his eyesight. The angel reveals his identity, and departs.

Scholars believe that the fictional nature of the story is demonstrated by the numerous historical and geographical errors it contains (wrong names, dates, events and locations). In addition it contains numerous symbolic names and other features of an idealized story.

The story is written in the style of an historical narrative to tell of a pious individual who keeps the law, is wise, devoted, compassionate and courageous. This type of individual exhibits the piety a person of

God should have. Commitment to the law is commitment to the God who stands behind the covenant and protects his people. Who will be healed and triumph while disaster befalls those who disobey the law.

Scenes from Tobit have been frequently portrayed by western artists; the most commonly depicted scene portrays Tobias and the angel, accompanied by a dog. Raphael is one of the three archangels (with Gabriel and Michael) in Christian tradition. Salley Vickers's novel *Miss Garnet's Angel* (2002) is a contemporary retelling of the tale that has inspired readers to seek out the Venetian sites referred to in the novel.

Recommended reading. Moore, Carey A. *Tobit: A New Translation with Introduction and Commentary.* Anchor Bible; New York: Doubleday, 1996.

See also APOCRYPHA, DEUTEROCANONICALS AND INTERTESTAMENTALS; ASMODEUS; DEMON; FISH, FISHER, FISHING; INTERTESTAMENTALS (*see* APOCRYPHA); RAPHAEL, THE ANGEL   [AJW]

Tobias (see Tobit, Book of).

Tomb of Jesus. The newly carved and previously unused tomb that Joseph of Arimathea had built for himself and in which Jesus was inhumed, after his crucifixion, is mentioned in the four Gospels: Matt. 27.57–28.10; Mark 15.42–16.10; Luke 23.50–24.24; John 19.38–20.18. These texts describe the funerary monument as the site of three major and consecutive moments of Jesus' story. He was buried in a rock-cut tomb after the authorization given by the Roman prefect Pontius Pilate to take his body down from the cross and before the Sabbath in accordance with Jewish law. The women intending to complete his embalming discovered his empty opened grave three days later. Then, through angels or Christ's appearances, the particular women received the announcement of his resurrection.

These biblical events made Jesus' tomb a symbol of resurrection, the foundation of the Christian faith. As such, the theme spread widely, mostly in accordance with the scriptures, such as in motifs of European art showing the Entombment, the Holy women at the tomb and the appearance of the risen Jesus to Mary Magdalene called *Noli me tangere*. But non-biblical interpretations exist: some musical compositions named *Sepolcri* that were performed during Holy Week in the seventeenth and eighteenth centuries, display fictive meetings between characters of the OT and NT at Christ's sepulcher.

From topographical references, a garden near Golgotha outside the walls of Jerusalem (John 19.41), the Bible contributed to the search for the material remains of the site of the resurrection, from antiquity up to the contemporary period. The *Life of Constantine* by Eusebius of Caesarea describes the unearthing of a tomb of Jesus, around 325 CE, which the Roman emperor ordered to be sheltered with a basilica, the present Church of the Holy Sepulchre in Jerusalem. The site soon became an important object of devotion for Christians: Pope Urban II started the First Crusade in 1095, offering as a pretext the deliverance of the Holy Sepulchre from Muslim authority and threats to pilgrimage. Worshippers still visit the holy place: even Homer, in *The Simpsons* television show, disrespectfully falls asleep on the cenotaph during a church trip to Israel (2010). The authenticity of this traditional site is disputed. In 1883, the British General Charles Gordon rather proposed an area located in the north of Jerusalem, outside the Damascus Gate, named the Garden Tomb. Director Simcha Jacobovici claimed, in the documentary film *The Lost Tomb of Jesus* (2007), that archaeologists had found Christ's ossuary in his family tomb in Talpiot, suggesting his followers secretly removed his body from the initial tomb (Matt. 27.62-66; 28.11-15).

Contemporary fiction often links the discovery of Christ's grave with conspiracies. In the adult comic book *Jacula* by the Italian studio Giolitti (1968–1982), Satan organizes the quest for Jesus' remains to convince humans that his resurrection is a myth. *The Body* (dir. Jonas McCord, 2001) recounts the Vatican's plans to silence the archaeological finding in Jerusalem of a skeleton showing marks of crucifixion, in order to preserve Christianity. Forensic anthropologist Temperance Brennan, in the novel *Cross Bones* by Kathy Reichs (2005), suspects alternately Jewish, Christian and Muslim extremists to be involved in the murder case of the trafficker of the contents of a possible sepulcher of Jesus.

Recommended reading. Bahat, Dan. 'Does the Holy Sepulcher Church Mark the Burial of Jesus?' *Biblical Archaeology Review* 22,3 (1986) 26-45. Meyers, Eric M. 'The Jesus Tomb Controversy: An Overview'. *Near Eastern Archaeology* 69/3–4 (2006) 116-18.

See also GOLGOTHA; JERUSALEM; RESURRECTION; SHROUD   [CD]

Tongues, Speaking in. By some accounts, there are 35 biblical references to *glossolalia* (literally 'to speak in, with or by') in the NT. Generally occurring in the plural *glossais lalein*, 'tongues' is mentioned in Mark (16.17), Acts (2.4, *et al.*) and 1 Corinthians 12–14. Sometimes described as a known foreign language but unknown to the speaker (Acts 2.2-8), sometimes the language of angels, sounding like strings of syllables that seem to come together more or less haphazardly (1 Cor. 13.1), and sometimes a prayer language (1 Cor. 14.14), 'tongues' mystified and sometimes confused (Acts 2.6) onlookers wherever it was practiced. The only common denominator seemed to be a clear ascription to the work of God's Spirit as the originator.

A precedent for this connection between the work of the Spirit and tongues is found in the tradition of OT ecstatic prophecy. The author of Acts affirms this precedent by including a modified Joel 2.28-32 in Acts 2.17-21 announcing the work of the Spirit being mediated through dreams, visions and possibly other forms of abnormal behavior.

From the first century to the present, the history of tongues-speech is spotty. After Montanus revived the practice in the second century, Augustine (fourth century) relegated it to an apostolic phenomenon. Tongues-speech then remained largely dormant until the early part of the nineteenth century where it resurfaced among Shakers, followers of the Presbyterian Edward Irving, and the Latter Day Saints of Jesus Christ.

Then, on April 18, 1906 in Los Angeles, at a small mission church on Azusa Street, tongues-speech experienced a resurrection of sorts and reasserted its presence into the life of the church. Proclaiming 'this is that' which happened to the early church, apologists for this manifestation soon organized themselves denominationally.

Today, Pentecostalism, the twentieth-century global church sect spawned by this manifestation, accounts for 27% of Christendom. Parodied as an extreme form of religious expression, it has been featured in the religious satires, *Leap of Faith* (1992), *Saved* (1996), and *Borat: Cultural Learnings of America for Make Benefit Glorious Nation of Kazakhstan* (2006) and *The Simpson's Movie* (2007). Robert Duvall portrays a more sympathetic cinematic view of Pentecostalism in *The Apostle* (1997). Here the protagonist, Sonny, is a morally ambiguous revival-style Pentecostal preacher. Surprisingly, while the film presents a certain slice of Pentecostal worship it stops short of exhibiting actual tongues-speech. Doubtless this was done for fear that any such acting might give an unwanted satirical slant.

Musically, *Speaking in Tongues* is the title of at least two critically acclaimed albums, by the Talking Heads (1983), and Desperate Measures (2007). In both cases, while the lyrics do not occasion the actual religious practice of Tongues-Speech, the titles are used metaphorically to describe life in an incoherent world where solutions often sound like babble.

Tongues-speech also makes an appearance in Grant Morrison's subversive DC comic series *The Invisibles*. The comic series features the head of John the Baptist as a 'glossolalic speaking head'. (*The Invisibles: Arcadia Part IV*, DC Comics, April 1995). Reflecting a postmodern message, the head is the voice of the Baptist's subconscious mind that is capable of being interpreted by the unconscious minds of others allowing everyone to make their own interpretation of the vocalizations.

See also HOLY SPIRIT; SPIRITUAL GIFTS [RFH]

Torah (see Law).

Tower of Babel (see Babel, Tower of).

Transfiguration, Mount of. The story of the Transfiguration of Jesus occurs four times in the NT, in each of the three Synoptic Gospels (Mark 9.2-13//Matt. 17.1-13//Luke 9.28-36) and once in the Epistles (2 Pet. 1.16-18). It tells of Jesus' ascent of the mountain in the company of three apostles—Peter, James and John—the transfiguring (changing) of his clothing, the appearance of Moses and Elijah, the divine voice from the cloud confirming Jesus as the divine Son, and the fearful, uncomprehending response of the disciples.

In the OT, as in the classical world, mountains are associated with divine revelation. Both Moses and Elijah are associated with experiences of revelation on Mount Sinai/Horeb. In the Transfiguration story, Jesus on the mountaintop stands on the boundary between heaven and earth, belonging equally in both domains, surrounded by his disciples on the one hand and with the two greatest of the prophets, on the other: citizens of both earth and heaven. The radiant clothing (and face), the cloud and the voice, are all revelatory, attesting to Jesus' identity, and preparing the way for his journey to the cross.

Traditionally, the Transfiguration has been associated with Mount Tabor, located in southern Galilee. Strong as this tradition is in the early centuries of the church, it also has problems. Mount Tabor is not much more than a hill and could hardly be described as 'a high mountain' (Mark 9.2); and in the first century CE there was a Roman fortification on the top. Other possible locations have been suggested, e.g., Mount Hermon, a very high mountain in northern Galilee, also the source of the Jordan River; local pagan traditions thought that the chasm on one side of Hermon led down into the underworld. However, biblical language is not always literal, and it may be that Tabor is still the likeliest place for the mysterious event that took place in the presence of the three disciples.

Given that the NT gives no specific location for this event, it is probably not of great importance to situate it with any precision. What is important is the symbolic and theological meaning of the Transfiguration: its presentation of Jesus as the one who bridges the gulf between heaven and earth, who holds both in his embrace, and who points to God's future and its promise of transformation for all. In the synoptic gospels, Jesus is the one who scales the cosmic depths and heights, in his baptism, transfiguration, and crucifixion/resurrection/ascension, all of which are theologically linked in relation to salvation. The transfiguring of human disfigurement is what the story of the Transfiguration seeks to address.

In western art, scenes of the Transfiguration are commonplace, e.g., Fra Angelico (1440–42); Boticelli (c. 1500), Veronese (1555–56). It is also a typical scene in Orthodox iconography. Many churches celebrate the Feast of the Transfiguration on August 6, and there are many churches, monasteries and basilicas named after the biblical event.

Recommended reading. Lee, Dorothy. *Transfiguration*. London and NewYork: Continuum, 2004.

See also ELIJAH; HOREB; MOUNT; JAMES, THE APOSTLE; JOHN, THE APOSTLE; MOSES; PETER; SINAI; MOUNT
[DL]

Treasure. (Greek: *thesauros*). The Bible treats 'treasure' as both a verb and a noun. Treasure as an object is often equated with earthly success, as when Prov. 15.6 says, 'In the house of the righteous there is much treasure, but trouble befalls the income of the wicked'. The concept of earthly treasure is not often favorable, however. The author of Ecclesiastes notes that the accumulation of treasure does not atone for the fact that life is vanity (2.8). The prophetic books use this trope to denote both punishment and reward mediated by God (see Isa. 45.3; Jer. 15.13; 17.3; 20.5). A number of NT sayings of Jesus involve treasure, as when he preaches a parable about the kingdom of Heaven being like a treasure in a field (Matt. 13.44, 13.51), one of the earliest literary references to 'buried treasure'. The synoptic gospels relate the story of the rich man who asks Jesus what he should do to inherit eternal life, to which Jesus responds that he should sell his possessions and give the money to the poor, after which he will have 'treasure in heaven' (Matt. 19.21//Mark 10.21//Luke 18.22). Jesus again exhorts his followers to store treasures in heaven in Matt. 6.19-21// Luke 12.33-34, noting, 'For where your treasure is, there your heart will be also'. Paul, too, highlights the importance of heavenly treasure, writing of the power of God, 'We have this treasure in clay jars...' where the 'clay jars' are typically interpreted to refer to the human body (2 Cor. 4.7).

Treasure takes on a different dimension in each of the two narratives of the birth and childhood of Jesus. In Matthew, the magi bring Jesus treasures of gold, frankincense, and myrrh (2.11). In Luke, Jesus' mother, Mary, 'treasures' (KJV) the amazing things that happened at the birth of her son, and also his teaching in the temple at age 12 (2.19, 2.51).

Since biblical times, the idea of buried treasure has developed in western culture. The Copper Scroll, found among the Dead Sea Scrolls at Qumran in the mid-twentieth century, purports to be a map directing the reader to the hidden locations of (yet undiscovered, if the references are indeed literal) hordes of precious metals. Robert Louis Stevenson penned the wildly popular *Treasure Island* in 1883; the basic storyline of hidden treasure has formed the basis for many popular films, including *Treasure of the Sierra Madre* (1948), the Indiana Jones series, *National Treasure* and its sequel (2004, 2007), and the *Pirates of the Caribbean* franchise. Las Vegas is home to popular pirate-themed casino Treasure Island Casino and Resort. Christian crossover alternative band Jars of Clay took their name from 2 Cor. 4.7.

See also PARABLE; WISDOM
[KJV]

Tree. Many varieties of trees are mentioned in the Bible, some of which are actual trees, while others are representations such as family trees, or symbols of steadfastness. These vary from the Tree of Life in the Garden of Eden, through to the Tree of Jesse, from which traditionally the cross was made for the crucifixion of Jesus (cf. Isa. 11.1-3).

Richard St Barbe Baker made a detailed study of the trees in the Bible, and located references to the olive, oak, tamarisk, almond, chestnut, shittah, fig, pomegranate, palm, algum, cedar, cypress, fir, myrtle, apple, willow, poplar, sycamore, and vine. Of these, the cedar is one of the best known, and indeed is incorporated on the flag of Lebanon. Such trees were mentioned in the *Epic of Gilgamesh*, and by the 1970s, there were only five large cedars surviving which could date from biblical times.

There is also a 'Tree of Knowledge' in Quma, in modern-day Iraq, purported to be the original tree in the Garden of Eden. It was reported to have died in 1946, although ten years later when King Faisal II visited the region, he was shown another tree, possibly grown from seeds from the first.

Recommended reading. St Barbe Baker, Richard. *Famous Trees of Bible Lands*. London: H.H. Greaves, 1974.

See also OLIVE, OLIVE BRANCHES; PLANTS, SYMBOLISM OF; POMEGRANATE; TREE OF JESSE; TREE OF KNOWLEDGE, TREE OF LIFE [JC]

Tree of Jesse. The family line of Jesse, father of King David. The tree is referred to in Isaiah (11.1-3) and has come to represent the family tree or ancestry of Jesus. The lineage of Jesus is also mentioned in Matthew and Luke, with Matthew (1.1-17) tracing his ancestry back to Abraham and Luke (3.23-38) back to Adam. This genealogy showing a royal ancestry for Jesus became important in medieval Europe where heredity was important, especially links to royal and noble lines. This led to the depiction of the Tree of Jesse in illuminated manuscripts, stained glass windows, embroidery and wall paintings, mainly in England and France. In most cases, the representation is that of a stylized family tree, with the earliest surviving version being in the Vysehrad Codex of 1086, a series of Coronation Gospels presented to Vratislav II, the first King of Bohemia. The Lambeth Palace Bible, held in London, dates from between 1140 and 1150 and also shows the Tree of Jesse.

The most famous image of the Tree of Jesse is that on the stained glass windows at Chartres Cathedral in northern France. Made between 1140 and 1150, it is composed of eight square central panels, and seven rectangular ones on each side. There are also stained glass windows depicting it in the Saint-Denis Basilica in Paris, at York Minster (ca.1150), and at Canterbury Cathedral (c. 1200) that were probably also made in France. Mention should also be made of the stained glass windows at St Kunibert, Cologne (1220–1235). Other examples can be found at Sainte-Chapelle in Paris (1247), and the Cathedral of Le Mans (thirteenth century). There are also several late medieval and early modern stained glass windows in little-known religious buildings such as at Dorchester Abbey, Oxfordshire, England; St Leonard's Church, Leverington, Cambridgeshire; Holy Well and St Dyfnog Church, Llanrheadr, Denbighshire, Wales; and in France at Saint-Étienne Church, Beauvais; and at the Cathédrale Notre-Dame, Moulins.

Many early Bible manuscripts such as the Saint-Bénigne Bible and the Capuchin's Bible at the Bibliothèque Nationale de France also have elaborate Trees of Jesse, as does the Macclesfield Psalter (c. 1330), now at the Fitzwilliam Museum, Cambridge, and the Psalter and Hours of John, Duke of Bedford (c. 1420–23), held at the British Library. Michelangelo in his painting on the ceiling of the Sistine Chapel, chose to represent the ancestry of Jesus in another form without showing the symbolic tree.

Other images of the Tree of Jesse have been found on an ivory comb from Bavaria; and carved near the entrances to numbers of religious buildings, including at the entrance to the Cathedral of Santiago de Compostela, Spain; at Amiens Cathedral, France, at Notre-Dame de Paris; and at the Cathedral of St Peter, Worms, Germany. There is also a mosaic representation of the tree at St Mark's Basilica, in Venice. With the Gothic revival in the late nineteenth century, a number of stained glass windows started to be added to parish churches in England at St George's Church, Slough, Berkshire; Hove and Stonegate, East Sussex; Froyle, Hampshire; St Matthew's Church, Newcastle, Northumberland; Rogate, West Sussex; and Claines, Worcestershire.

See also PLANTS, SYMBOLISM OF; TREE [JC]

Tree of Knowledge, Tree of Life. Supernatural trees described in Gen. 2.9 as being placed with Adam and Eve in the Garden of Eden. Adam is warned that he is not to eat the fruit of the tree of knowledge (Hebrew: *Es hadda at tob wara*) or he will die. We should note that for the Hebrews the word 'knowledge' connoted more than mere cognition; it implied intimate and physical experience. To know one's wife implies sexual knowledge and to know the Lord is to live according to his precepts. The tree of knowledge of good and evil then implies a change not only in the mind of those who eat of it, but in their very nature. It represents the entire moral realm; to eat of it is to become a moral being. The tree is also an important symbol for the reality of choice and possibility of sin and disobedience.

Although the tree of knowledge appears to be unique to Hebrew culture, a tree of life is found in many cultures throughout the world, including others in the ANE. Babylonian mythology held that two trees guarded heaven: the tree of truth and the tree of life. The Tree of Life was not included in the prohibition delivered to Adam, yet it is mentioned in Gen. 3.22 as a further temptation to humanity from which they need to be protected. From the passage, it appears as though the tree of life was supposed to bestow eternal life upon those who ate of its fruit, and thus we can infer that Adam and Eve were not supposed to have eaten of it while in the garden.

The trees of life and knowledge have both featured prominently in our cultural heritage. Many myths and legends exist about both trees. Early Christian legends link the Tree of Life with the cross upon which Jesus was crucified. John Milton's *Paradise Lost* has had a profound impact on the way the trees have been interpreted, in Book VI Milton describes how God created many trees 'and all amid them stood the tree of life / High eminent, blooming ambrosial fruit / of vegetable gold; and next to life / Our death, the tree of knowledge grew fast by / Knowledge of good bought dear by knowing ill'. Byron's play *Cain* features a conversation in which Cain scandalizes Adam and Eve by saying that 'the serpent spoke *truth;* it *was* the tree of knowledge, it *was* the tree of life: knowledge is good, life is good. How can both be evil?' Modern authors who have employed the trees and their imagery include Yeats, whose poem 'The Two Trees' paints a haunting and mysterious portrait of the two trees, and C.S. Lewis, whose Narnia series feature the symbolism of the trees.

Both the tree of knowledge and the tree of life have been frequently depicted in visual arts. Paintings of the creation story and the Garden of Eden and Adam and Eve often feature one or both of the trees. Among the most iconic are Lucas Cranach the Elder's series of sixteenth-century paintings of Adam and Eve, Michelangelo's fresco in the Sistine chapel and many examples of Celtic art which frequently features the tree of life as a vine motif.

The 2006 film *The Fountain* starring Hugh Jackman explores mortality and employs the Tree of Life as a symbol. In modern use the term 'tree of life' sometimes refers to a person's familial heritage or the evolutionary past of earth's organisms, as coined by Charles Darwin.

See also ADAM; APPLE; EVE; FALL, THE; GARDEN OF EDEN; TREE [JIM]

Trial of Jesus. According to the Gospels, after his seizure at Gethsemane (Mount of Olives), Jesus was tried by the Sanhedrin and then handed over to Pontius Pilate for his execution by the Romans. The trial of Jesus is described in all the Gospels as beginning on Thursday night and continuing until Friday morning, after which Jesus was handed over to the Romans (Mark 14.53–15.15; Matt. 26.57–27.26; Luke 22.66–23.12; John 18.19-24, 28-30). According to Luke, there was a third trial, before Herod Antipas. Pilate offers to release either Jesus or Barabbas as a Passover boon, but the crowd ask for Barabbas to be freed (Mark 15.15; Matt. 27.26; Luke 23.18).

In historiographical terms, the trial of Jesus has been used in Europe as an excuse for anti-Semitism as it links leaders of the Jewish community directly to the sentencing of Jesus for heresy, although it was actually the Romans who imposed the death sentence. As the Gospels do have a detailed account of the trial, it seems likely that supporters of Jesus such as Joseph of Arimathea or Nicodemus, might have been present, or alternatively people who were there later told the early Christians what transpired.

The scene of the trial of Jesus is a popular subject in art. The Florentine painter Giotto di Bondone (d. 1337) depicted the scene, as did Fra Angelico in *Jesus before Caiaphas*. The trial also appears in many novels including Robert Graves's *King Jesus* (New York, 1946); Bertram Brooker's *The Robber* (Des Moines, 1949); Charles Dunscomb's *Bond and the Free* (New York 1955); Taylor Caldwell's *I, Judas* (New York, 1977), and many other books. In films, it is portrayed in a variety of ways, usually following the accounts in the Gospels whereby it is more show than trial, where the guilt of Jesus is assumed, and Caiaphas and others are anxious to manipulate Jesus into admitting blasphemy.

Recommended reading. Bammel, Ernst (ed.). *The Trial of Jesus*. London: SCM Press. Brown, Raymond E. *The Death of the Messiah: From Gethsemane to the Grave*. New York: Doubleday, 1999. Juel, Donald. *Messiah and Temple: The Trial of Jesus in the Gospel of Mark*. Society of Biblical Literature Monograph Series, 31. Missoula, MT: Scholars Press, 1977.

See also BARABBAS; CAIAPHAS; PASSION NARRATIVE; PILATE [JC]

Trials and Tribulations. From the Greek *peirasmos* (trial) and *thlipsis* (tribulation). The phrase 'trials and tribulations' is a common expression for suffering in Christian and non-Christian vernacular. The phrase does not occur in the Bible, yet its meaning is influenced by the occurrence of the individual words 'trial' and 'tribulation' within their respective biblical contexts.

The word trial means to suffer from temptation or testing (Deut. 7.19; Luke 4.13; Jas 1.2) and is well known from the Lord's Prayer: 'And do not bring us to the time of trial (*peirasmos*)' (Matt. 6.13). The word tribulation, on the other hand, refers to affliction or suffering caused by persecution (Mark 4.17; Acts 11.19). In Daniel, the word tribulation takes on apocalyptic significance to characterize the suffering that will take place as a prelude to the end of history (12.1). Daniel's apocalyptic use of tribulation profoundly influenced the eschatology of the NT. In Mark, Jesus teaches that a period of tribulation will occur prior to his return (13.19; Matt. 24.21), and Revelation, also from Daniel, teaches that a 'great tribulation' will occur in the last days (Rev. 7.14).

It is difficult to say who coined the phrase 'trials and tribulations'. John Chrysostom (347–407 CE), an early church father, is most likely the first to juxtapose the words, although they read in inverse order. 'But whoever is in affliction (*thlipsis*) and temptation (*peirasmos*), this person stands near to him, whoever is journeying on the narrow way' (*Homily* 1.5 on 2 Cor). Over time, the phrase became an important way of speaking about suffering of various types. The German novelist Theodor Fontane wrote a romantic novel about a couple who slowly breaks up, appropriately titled, *Irrungen Wirrungen* (*Trials and Tribulations*, 1888).

In contemporary culture, the phrase is used in a variety of contexts. Martin Luther King, Jr, in his speech, 'I Have a Dream' (1963), quotes the phrase in the context of African American's struggle for civil rights. 'I am not unmindful that some of you come here out of excessive trials and tribulations'. Don Evans, the noted African American playwright, wrote a play titled *The Trials and Tribulations of Staggerlee Booker T. Brown* (1985); the phrase is quoted during a prayer in the film *Light of Day* with Michael J. Fox (1987).

In conservative Christian circles, the phrase trials and tribulations is used apocalyptically despite the absence of the exact phrase in the Bible. In the bestselling *Left Behind* series, authors Tim Lahaye and Jerry Jenkins speak of the 'trials and tribulations' of unbelievers left behind on earth during the rapture (*Tribulation Force* 1996, 64).

See also APOCALYPTIC; ESCHATOLOGY; RAPTURE; TRIBULATION [DJS]

Tribulation, The. From the Greek *thlipsis* (suffering). Tribulation is a term used among premillennial dispensationalist Christians to describe a future seven-year period of catastrophic suffering usually following the rapture, and preceding the second coming of Jesus and the establishment of his millennial kingdom. The idea of a distinct period known as the tribulation is derived from a particular interpretation of various biblical passages that mention a future time of great suffering, often, but not always, translated as 'tribulation' in the King James Version of the Bible. 'For at that time there will be great suffering, such as has not been from the beginning of the world until now, no, and never will be' (Matt. 24.21). Most contemporary translations of the Bible, such as the New Revised Standard Version, translate the word *thlipsis* as suffering or affliction rather than tribulation, and even the more conservative New International Version uses the word tribulation only once (Rev. 7.15).

An understanding of the tribulation hinges on a complex interpretation of Daniel 9, in which Daniel makes a prophecy concerning seventy weeks of Israel's history, a day in this book representing a year, thus, translating into four hundred and ninety years. Premillennial dispensationalists believe that the first sixty-nine weeks (or four-hundred and eighty-three years), of Daniel's prophecy, refers to the period of Israel's history from the rebuilding of Jerusalem in the books of Ezra and Nehemiah, to the crucifixion of Jesus. They argue that because the Jewish people did not accept Jesus as their Messiah (as, they believe, was intended), that God was forced to initiate a new 'dispensation' known as the church dispensation, or the age of grace, that came between Daniel's sixty-ninth and seventieth 'week' of Israel's history, and, consequently halted the progression of God's prophetic programme. This pause in God's prophetic plan, they argue, was intended to allow humanity, and specifically the Jewish people, another opportunity to accept the Christian gospel. The age of grace, however, will be brought to an abrupt end by the rapture at an undetermined time, at which point Jesus will carry away his Church into heaven, initiating the seven years of suffering known as the tribulation. The tribulation will mark the emergence of the 'anti-Christ' (a false religious leader), and 'the Beast' (a tyrannical political leader), as well as a whole host of natural disasters and persecutions that those unbelievers who are 'left behind' on earth following the rapture will suffer through. Premillennial dispensationalist Christians believe that the tribulation will culminate in the second coming of Jesus, when he will do battle with the forces of the anti-Christ and the Beast at Armageddon, and establish his millennial kingdom on earth. Similar to the premillennial dispensationalist idea of the rapture, the tribulation is not an official teaching within the vast majority of Christianity, and is limited to those denominations with historical or theological ties to the development of nineteenth and twentieth-century Christian fundamentalism. Despite the fact that most Christian denominations consider the idea of the tribulation as heterodox, the preaching of several televangelists, and, more importantly, the best-selling books *The Late Great Planet Earth* (1970) by Hal Lindsey, and the *Left Behind* series (1995–2007) by Tim LaHaye and Jerry Jenkins, have made the ideas of the rapture and the tribulation mainstays of Anglo-American Christianity and popular culture.

Recommended reading. Boyer, Paul. *When Time Shall Be No More: Prophecy Belief in Modern American Culture.* Cambridge, MA: Belknap Press, 1994.

See also APOCALYPTIC; ARMAGEDDON; DANIEL; ESCHATOLOGY; MILLENNIUM; RAPTURE; REVELATION; TRIALS AND TRIBULATIONS [AS]

Trinity. The term used to name the three members of the Godhead (divine nature or essence)— Father, Son and Holy Spirit. The Father is without origin, the Son is eternally begotten and the Holy Spirit proceeds from both Father and the Son (*filioque*) in Western Christianity; for Eastern Orthodoxy, the Spirit proceeds only from the Father. The term (from Latin: *trinitas*) does not appear in the Bible, but foundational teachings do.

OT and NT passages from which the Trinity has been adduced include Psalm 110 'The Lord said to my Lord' and others that imply conversation between divine persons. God the Father is revealed as the Lord and maker of heaven and earth (John 5.26; 1 Cor. 8.6; Eph. 3.14-15). The Son is declared to be the image of the invisible God, the exact representation of God's being and nature and the Messiah–Redeemer (John 1.1-18). The Spirit is God's active power, invisibly influencing, inspiring, regenerating, guiding and filling the creation (John 14.26; 15.26; Gal. 4.6; Eph. 2.18).

The three persons of the Trinity live and work together as one (John 16.13-15). They are three in one and one in three, all of whom are equal; hence, the Trinity is a tri-unity. In the plurality of the Trinity there is self-knowledge because only the Father knows the Son and only the Son knows the Father (Matt. 11.27).

The Trinitarian formula of 'Father, Son and Holy Spirit' is found twice in the Bible: in Matt. 28.19, Jesus commands his disciples to make and baptize others in the name of the Father, the Son and the Holy Spirit. The formula is also found in the benediction concluding 2 Corinthians (13.14).

Historically, the doctrine of the Trinity has been held to be a great mystery because pertains to the nature of the unknowable God, known only by his own self-revelation. The Trinity as a part of God self-revelation is only a partial revelation, but it is still sufficient for apprehending the mystery.

The development of the doctrine of the Trinity began in the early Church and is still ongoing. From the beginning, Christians have rejected the charge that the Trinity is 'tri-theism' because there is only one God. Nor have Christians understood the Trinity to be 'tri-modalism', the idea that there is one God who appears in three modes as does water (vapor, liquid and solid). Rather, the Church has always taught that God is one and is yet three persons (*personae*) who are distinct members of the one Godhead.

The Trinity has been the subject of many treatises, liturgical expressions, hymns and other works. It is point of discussion in Langland's *Piers Plowman*, John Donne's *The Litanie*. In the Calendar of the Christian Year, Trinity Sunday is the Sunday after Pentecost Sunday about which Herbert wrote two poems, 'Trinity Sunday' as did John Keble's *The Christian Year* (1827). In western religious art, the trinity is often portrayed as a scene of the Father enthroned as an old man accompanied by his Son, Jesus, with the Holy Spirit in dove form hovering over them.

In popular films, in the *Matrix* science fiction trilogy (1999, 2003, 2003) featured an important character named Trinity.

Recommended reading. Dünzl, Franz. *A Brief History of the Doctrine of the Trinity in the Early Church.* London: T. & T. Clark, 2007. Erickson, Millard J. *Making Sense of the Trinity: 3 Crucial Questions.* Grand Rapids, MI: Baker, 2000. Letham, Robert. *The Holy Trinity: In Scripture, History, Theology, and Worship.* Phillipsburg, NJ: P & R Publishing, 2004.

See also CHRIST; FATHER; GOD; HOLY SPIRIT; JESUS OF NAZARETH; SON OF GOD; SON OF MAN [AJW]

Troubling the waters. The phrase 'troubling the waters' comes from a miracle story in John 5. The verse containing the phrase (John 5.4) is generally omitted or placed in footnotes in recent translations because it is not in the oldest manuscripts. It appears to be a later addition, offered to explain the background of the tale.

In this story, Jesus was in Jerusalem for a festival. He went to a pool, Bethzatha, where people with various afflictions waited for an angel to 'trouble' or 'stir up' the water. The first to enter the pool afterward was cured. At the pool, Jesus met a man who had attempted to find relief for his ailment for 38 years. Having no assistant, he was never successful. After a short conversation, Jesus cured the man by telling him to get up and walk.

The cure is the prologue to a longer story, in which we learn that the incident took place on the Sabbath. The Jewish authorities claimed that both the man carrying his mat and Jesus' action of cure were work, forbidden on the Sabbath. The gospel notes Jesus' response to this claim as the basis of the first rejection of him by the Jewish authorities.

The story is notable for its statements that have often been used to claim that sin causes illness or disability, for Jesus later told the man, 'Do not sin any more, so that nothing worse happens to you' (v. 14) . However, the text makes no claim about why the man was ill in the first place. To most commentators, it seems to be an eschatological statement calling for continued repentance.

Water appears frequently in the Bible as a symbol of God's action. Thus, later writings often link various passages involving water. This is the case in two American slave songs. 'Let God's Saints Come In' prays 'Come down, angel, and trouble the water', so that the saints may enter 'Canaan land', coupling this story with the Exodus. 'Wade in the Water' urges preparation, for 'God's gonna trouble the water'. It then retells the story of the Exodus. Some have interpreted these as escape instructions: by wading through waterways, pursuit dogs would be thrown off-track. Others interpret them as a prayer for divine intervention.

'Wade in the Water' appears in two episodes of *The Fresh Prince of Bel-Air*, an American television comedy (1990–1996) about a Philadelphia teenager from a troubled neigborhood who went to live with relatives in a well-off California suburb. Two 2008 movies, *Wade in the Water* and *Trouble the Water*, document life in New Orleans, Louisiana after the Katrina hurricane.

See also Exodus; Miracles; Sabbath; Water

[TV]

Trumpet. The word in the OT is represented by two different Hebrew words standing for entirely different instruments: *shofar* and *chatzotzrah*. Yet both are almost always both translated as 'trumpet' in English-language Christian Bibles. The *shofar*, a ram's horn, was never a real instrument since it can only play very few notes. It is still used today in High Holiday synagogue services—the only live sound preserved from ancient Israel. The *chatzotzrah* was the forerunner of the modern trumpet and is the modern Hebrew word for trumpet. The modern 'folded' trumpet (as opposed to a long straight tube) was created around 1400 CE. Trumpets have been commonplace in symphony orchestras since the nineteenth century.

The *shofar* and *chatzotzrah* are two distinct entities with different functions.

Shofar is translated in Jewish Bibles as either 'horn' or 'ram's horn', while in Christian Bibles it is almost always 'trumpet' (the sole exceptions are Joshua 6, where *shofar* is variably translated 'trumpet of ram's horn' or simply 'trumpet;' Psa. 98.6 and Hos. 5.8, where *shofar* and *chatzotzrot* appear in the same verse and *shofar* is translated as 'horn'). The only exception in Jewish Bibles is the JPS translation of *shofar* in Job 39.24-25 and Neh. 4.12, 13: uniquely there it is translated 'trumpet'. The word is found 72 times in the OT. Its most well-known appearance is in Joshua (6.4, 5, 6, 8, 9, 13, 16, 20), where the priests march around the walls of Jericho seven times, continually blowing the *shofar*. The common image most people have of the trumpets' blasts blowing down the walls is completely mistaken. The *shofar* was more likely used as a signaling instrument to call the army.

Trumpets trace their roots back as far as 1500 BCE. Bronze and silver trumpets were found in Egyptian tombs. In their earliest form they were used for communication: mustering or cheering signals during a battle, announcing arrivals and coronations. These usages continued through the centuries in the form of military taps or its associations with pomp and pageantry in the Middle Ages.

The earliest physical representations of the two kinds of trumpet referred to in the Bible are found in two places: short and broad military trumpets can be seen on Bar Kokhba coins minted during the revolt with Rome (132–136 CE). Silver temple trumpets, long and conical with a broadened bell, are visible on the Arch of Titus relief in Rome, part of the spoil taken from Jerusalem (the victory was in 70 CE; the arch was dedicated in 85 CE).

Chatzotzrah (plural *chatzotzrot*) is found 28 times in the OT (only once in the singular form, in Hos. 5.8). It first appears in Numbers (10.2, 8-10; 31.6), where God commands that two silver trumpets be made and blown by the priests at war time and for sacred occasions. In later texts, the trumpets usually serve one of these functions (Ezra 3.10; Neh. 12.35, 41; 1 Chron. 15.24; 16.6; 2 Chron. 13.12, 14; 29.26-28). The only later mention of *silver* trumpets is in 2 Kgs 12.14. The word *chatzotzrot* occurs frequently in verses that include other instruments in musical celebrations (Ps. 98.5-6; 1 Chron. 13.8; 15.28; 16.42; 2 Chron. 5.12-13; 20.28; 23.13). The *shofar* is never included in such lists.

Most occurrences of the word trumpet (Greek: *salpynx*) in the NT are found in Revelation, where seven angels blow their trumpets. Other occurrences are in Matthew (6.2; 24.31), 1 Corinthians (15.51), 1 Thessalonians (4.16), and Hebrews (12.19). There is virtually no correlation to the significance of the word in the OT.

See also SHOFAR; TRUMPETS, FEAST OF [HL]

Trumpets, Feast of. From the Hebrew *zikhron/ yom teru'ah* ('memorial/day of trumpet blasts'). Celebrated on the first day of the seventh month in the Hebrew calendar, the Feast of Trumpets was the first of the Israelites' autumnal harvest festivals. The Bible provides brief descriptions of the celebration of this holiday: the Israelites observed it as a Sabbath, made additional sacrifices, assembled a holy convocation, and sounded trumpets (Lev. 23.24-25; Num. 29.1-6). This feast's celebration during the harvest and its characteristic trumpets shaped the two themes that came to be associated with it. Harvest festivals were not only times of uneasiness about the success of the next planting season but also celebrations for the provisions already received. Trumpets likewise emphasize the themes of fear and celebration, as they can signify the uncertainty of war (Ezek. 33.1-6) and call people to rejoice (Num. 10.10; Ps. 150.3).

Ancient and contemporary interpretations of the Feast of Trumpets mark it as a day of judgment and as a new beginning. Biblical texts witness to the rising importance of this feast, as their authors locate important events on the first day of the seventh month (Ezra 7.73b–8.2; Ezek. 45.20). Likewise, the author of the second-century BCE book of *Jubilees* associates this date with the abatement of the waters of judgment during Noah's time and God's promise to bless Abraham and his descendants (6.26, 12.16-24). By the fifth century CE, this feast was known as Rosh Hashanah, the beginning of the year, which coincided with God's judgment of humanity. One of the liturgical readings for Rosh Hashanah today combines the themes of fear and celebration: in the story of Abraham's near-sacrifice of Isaac (Gen. 22.1-19), the planned sacrifice threatens God's promise to Abraham but the provision of a lamb highlights God's faithfulness to the promise. Through the celebration of Rosh Hashanah, the Feast of Trumpets continues to influence spiritual practice in Western culture today.

The Feast of Trumpets has also influenced Western culture by providing a foundation for the combination of the themes of trepidation and celebration. As in the Feast of Trumpets, harvest festivals today celebrate the previous year but also encourage solemn reflection. For example, when Abraham Lincoln established the date for the celebration of Thanksgiving in the US, he encouraged participants to give thanks to God for their blessings and to be penitent for their nation's perversity and disobedience. In the movie *Pieces of April* (2003), the struggle of preparing Thanksgiving dinner in an inadequate apartment teaches the titular character to appreciate her own dysfunctional family, despite what little hope the family has for complete reconciliation. Trumpets, the other distinguishing feature of this feast, became associated with apocalyptic literature. Apocalyptic literature likewise exhibits the themes of celebration and fear, as shown by the book of Revelation in which six trumpets herald devastation (8.6–9.21) and a single trumpet ushers in the kingdom of the Messiah (11.15). More recent apocalyptic literature also shows these two themes, as in H.G. Wells's apocalyptic book *The War of the Worlds* (1898) in which the promise of a new future comes only after the near destruction of humanity.

Recommended reading. Reich, Eli. 'God of Judgment, God of Compassion: A Reading of the Rosh Hashanah Service'. *Judaism* 46 (1997) 259-69.

See also APOCALYPSE, APOCALYPTIC; AQEDAH; ESCHATOLOGY; HOLIDAYS, FEASTS, FESTIVALS; LAST TRUMPET; SEVEN SEALS, SEVEN BOWLS, SEVEN TRUMPETS; TRUMPET [PMF]

Tubal Cain. A member of the eighth generation of humans, a direct descendant of Cain. The etymology of his name is uncertain, possibly from the roots *yabal* (bringer-forth, or brought forth of) and *Qayin* (Cain). Third son of Lamech and only son of Lamech's second wife Zillah, Tubal-Cain had a sister Naamah. Not much is known about Tubal-Cain besides the fact that he made all kinds of bronze and iron tools (Gen. 4.22).

In western culture, Tubal-Cain is not a common name. However, among secret societies and religious orders, Tubal-Cain is often used symbolically. Stemming from his association with being an artificer of bronze and iron tools, Tubal-Cain is seen among the Freemasons as he who gives the mind the dual powers of spreading out consciousness and of gaining sharpness and acuity, tempering the mind so that it becomes active, reliable and intelligent, in order to fight the battles of the Inner King.

Tubal-Cain is also the symbolical level or stage a student of Freemasonry achieves towards becoming a Master Mason. This level is considered to be the letting go of the ego so that the self spreads out to become one with the all.

The British witch Robert Cochrane, a blacksmith, named his coven the 'Clan of Tubal-Cain'. The reason for this choice is unknown. However, the horned god worshiped by Cochrane and members of his coven was sometimes referred to as Tubal-Cain.

Not to be confused with his half-brothers Jabal and Jubal who were pioneers in their fields (Gen. 4.20-21), we were only told that Tubal-Cain made tools. Whether he was a pioneer in his chosen field cannot be ascertained. In spite of this lack of information, Tubal-Cain however persists in the western world as the first blacksmith.

See also JABAL; JUBAL; NAAMAH [GA]

Turn the other cheek. This phrase originates in Matt. 5.38-39 in the Sermon on the Mount. In a subsection of teaching on retaliation, Jesus says, 'You have heard that it was said, 'An eye for an eye and a tooth for a tooth'. But I say to you, Do not resist an evildoer. But if anyone strikes you on the right cheek, turn the other also' (cf. Luke 6.27-31). One of several reversals in the discourse of commonly accepted practices, turning the other cheek involves not allowing one's feelings concerning some personal wrong sustained to control one's reactions. Such seemingly illogical action identifies one with the 'good news of the kingdom' Jesus spreads while teaching throughout the region. Through this teaching Jesus seems to be attempting to correct the interpretation of the Jewish law (cf. Exod. 21.23-27; Deut. 19.21; Lev. 24.20) by contemporary religious leaders that transformed a typical ancient Near Eastern judicial provision for self-defense into an allowance for revenge.

Although allowing love of one's enemy to override feelings of personal vengeance was not uncommon in the OT (cf. Lev. 19.18; Lam. 3.30), Jesus' teachings emphasize the shortfalls of a system of proportionate punishment.

One of the main dividing points in the interpretation of this statement is whether or not it is to be taken literally. Many Christians throughout history, such as Augustine, have ruled that Jesus simply speaks against excess retaliation, and that personal defense is allowed (although not exacting revenge is viewed as a great mercy by Augustine). Dietrich Bonhoeffer, like others reacting against Hitler's Nazi regime, understood this teaching as not applying literally in matters of great injustice.

Others have interpreted this teaching as a call to non-violent resistance, prohibiting not only proactive physical force, but also reactive physical force. Among notable proponents of this ideology in western culture are Henry David Thoreau, who suggested in *Walden* that this teaching of Jesus had become more fashionable in his time with humanists and not just Christians. However, it is clear that carrying through with such an ideology proves difficult, as Mark Twain remarks in *The Innocents Abroad*: 'I know it is my duty 'to pray for them that despitefully use me', and therefore, hard as it is, I shall still try to pray for those fumigating, macaroni-stuffing organ grinders'. A rare practical illustration of Jesus' command comes in H.G. Wells's *Tono-Bungay*, as one character is shocked by another's non-violent response to being slapped.

Often the demonstration of this command is linked to a person or group enduring hardship without fighting back. The non-violent demonstrations associated with the Civil Rights movement in the southern US, with Martin Luther King, Jr at the forefront, are a prominent example. In the biopic *The Jackie Robinson Story*, African-American baseball star Jackie Robinson is portrayed as a person who constantly 'turned the other cheek' despite racist threats against his life.

Very few have taken the ideology of pacifism to its extreme conclusion. The Mennonite religious community remains an outspoken advocate of non-violence. More extreme groups call for 'Christian anarchy', basing its denial of the authority of governments that resort to physical violence to enforce laws on Leo Tolstoy's *The Kingdom of God is within You*.

Recommended reading. Brown, Douglas E. 'Turn the other cheek'. *Restoration Quarterly* 31/2 (1989) 65-74.

See also EYE FOR AN EYE, TOOTH FOR A TOOTH; LEX TALIONIS; PEACE; SERMON ON THE MOUNT; SERMON ON THE PLAIN [CEM]

Twelve Apostles, the. The 12 apostles represent the inner circle of the many followers of Jesus during his ministry. The list of the twelve varies among the Gospels with the following nine named each time: Peter, Andrew, James (son of Zebedee), John (brother of James), Philip, Bartholomew, Matthew, Thomas, and James (son of Alphaeus). Mark and Matthew also include Thaddeus, Simon the Cananean, and Judas Iscariot, whereas Luke (6.13-16) names Simon the Zealot, Judas the son of James, and Judas Iscariot. Acts 1.13, however, provides the same list as Luke's Gospel with the exception of Judas Iscariot, since subsequent to Judas Iscariot's defection, the now eleven disciples were forced to select another to replace him, which they did in choosing Matthias (1.15-26).

The term 'the twelve' (*hoi dōdeka*) is found in all four canonical Gospels (e.g., Matt. 10.1; Mark 3.14; Luke 8.1; John 20.24), where their significance is twofold: in one sense they serve as models of faithful disciples for followers of Jesus. They also represent Jesus' eschatological re-gathering of the twelve tribes of Israel (Matt. 19.28; Luke 22.30). In John, the twelve disciples seem to be of less importance in comparison to the 'beloved disciple' (e.g., John 13.21-25). Elsewhere in the NT, Paul significantly testifies to the continuing importance of 'the twelve' as witnesses to the post-resurrection appearances of Jesus (1 Cor. 15.5). Finally, in Revelation the names of the twelve apostles are found on the twelve foundations of the wall of the holy city (Rev. 21.12-14).

Representations of the twelve in the visual arts tend to focus on Jesus' calling of his disciples. For example, see Domenico Ghirlandaio's 1481 fresco 'Calling of the First Apostles' and Caravaggio's 'The Calling of Saints Peter and Andrew' (1603–1606). However, the most famous work of art featuring the 12 apostles is undoubtedly Leonardo da Vinci's 'The Last Supper' (1498), which recently received a resurgence in interest due to Dan Brown's bestselling novel, *The Da Vinci Code* (2003), which, along with its big screen adaptation (2006), sensationally suggested that the disciple to the right of Jesus in da Vinci's work was not in fact John but Mary Magdalene, whom Jesus secretly married and with whom he had a child before his death.

The number of disciples is the subject of dispute in the satirical film *Dogma* (1999) in which the character Rufus (Chris Rock) claims to be the thirteenth apostle (cf. Mark 15.21; Rom. 16.13) who was left off the list because he is black.

In 1903, the English composer Edward Elgar wrote an oratorio entitled *The Apostles*, in which he narrates the story of the twelve apostles' experience of the ministry of Jesus. More recently, an allusion to the twelve can be found in Johnny Cash's rendition of Christopher Wren's 'Jesus was a Carpenter' (1973). 'And he found them as they wandered through the wild Judean mountains / And he found them as they pulled their nets upon the Sea of Galilee'.

In architecture, perhaps the most well-known depiction of the twelve is found on the balustrade of St Peter's Basilica in Vatican City, which includes thirteen statues: John the Baptist, Christ the Redeemer, and eleven of the disciples minus Peter, who, along with the apostle Paul, is portrayed in a more prominent statue at the entrance of the basilica.

See also APOSTLE; BELOVED DISCIPLE; DISCIPLE; PETER [DRB]

Twelve Tribes of Israel, the. The twelve tribes of Israel arise from the twelve sons of Jacob (Gen. 35.23-26). Jacob had sons with his two wives Rachel and Leah, and with their maidservants, Bilhah and Zilpah. Jacob confers his blessing on each of his sons at the end of his life (Gen. 48.9-20; 49.1-28). Jacob's blessings on his sons in Genesis and the descriptions in Joshua probably reflect characteristics associated with the tribes and their lives and history afterwards. Some variation appears after the first listing in Genesis 35 by having Joseph represented by his two sons Ephraim and Manasseh (see the confusion of the blessing with these two in Gen. 48). Other lists appear in Numbers 1 and 26 when a census of Israel is taken in each text. Moses blesses the 12 tribes in a similar way to Jacob at the end of his life in Deuteronomy 33.

A detailed account of the portions of the land allotted to each of the 12 tribes by Joshua occurs as they enter and take over Canaan (Josh. 13–22). An exception in this is the tribe of Levi, which does not receive a specific portion of the land. This particular land allotment is preceded by a similar one found in Numbers 34–35. The interesting exception of allotting land to women and not just to the sons is the episode of the Daughters of Zelophehad (Numbers 36). The tribal arrangement plays a significant role for Israel until after the reigns of David and Solomon when the 10 northern tribes separate from the two southern ones. The exile extinguishes most traces of this structure so that by NT times they are largely symbolic and traditional.

The fact that the tribal structure of Israel practically disappeared in the exilic period has given room for speculations about the connections to the lost 10 tribes in more recent times. A helpful overview of this claim can be found in the PBS special *Where Are the Ten Lost Tribes of Israel?* and in the foundational materials in *Journey to the Vanished City: The Search for a Lost Tribe of Israel*, by Tudor Parfitt (2000) and *Letters from Beyond the Sambatyon: The Myth of the Ten Lost Tribes*, edited by Simcha Shtull-Trauring (1997).

In the NT, the tribes are known mostly as a collective that signifies all Israel (Matt. 19.28; Acts 6.7). Paul can still trace, or at least name his tribal lineage in Phil. 3.5 and his reference to the Israel of God would appear to include Jews and gentiles in the churches (Gal. 6.16; see also James 1.1). The prophet Anna is said to belong to the tribe of Asher (Luke 2.36). Revelation uses the designation of the twelve tribes as symbolic of Israel before the throne of God (Rev. 7.1-8; cf. 14.1-5). The *Testament of the Twelve Patriarchs* is patterned after Jacob's blessing scene in Genesis. If it was written before the Common Era it may have influenced the theology of the early church and possibly Jesus himself. If it was written within the Common Era, possibly c. 200, then it is more a witness to the early church's ethics and theology.

Many nations still refer to their own earlier tribal organization and history. The film *Braveheart* (1997) is an example of a Scottish tribal saga. The musical *Joseph and the Amazing Technicolor-Dreamcoat* (1970) explores another side to the tribal relationship.

Recommended reading. Barmash, Pamela. 'At the Nexus of History and Memory: The Ten Lost Tribes'. *Association for Jewish Studies Review* 29 (2006) 207-36.

See also ISRAEL [DMACL]

Twinkling of an Eye. This exact phrase, *en rhipē ophthalmou*, is commonly understood as originating from Paul (1 Cor. 15.52, KJV), where it refers to the suddenness of the parousia. The phrase does appear later in the Qur'an (*Surah* 16.77; 27.40; 54.50), and in similar contexts to that of Paul, i.e., God (Allah) is about to act in the world in a powerful and definitive way. While the specific focus may vary between Paul's usage and Qur'an's, the intended meaning is the same: immediacy.

In general, the Greek term *rhipē* means 'impulse' or 'sudden' or 'immediate'. Scholars often translate the Egyptian cognate, *án-t* to mean 'a third of a second', thus providing a basic understanding for how sudden or immediate. Conceptually, *rhipē* is linked with the Hebrew term, *rega'* which also means 'sudden'. Relevant to Paul's use of *rhipē*, *rega'* occurs mostly in the prophetic writings of the OT and is often related to dramatic shifts in life and/or history wrought by God. When linked with the human eye, the term *rhipē* is often translated as 'blinking' or in the nearly archaic form, 'twinkling', thus maintaining the idea of quickness.

With regard to Paul's phrase in 1 Cor. 15.52, John Chrysostom favors the idea of blinking (*Homily on 2 Corinthians* 42.3), while Augustine suggests not blinking but the speed at which light enters the eye (*Sermon* 362.20). For Paul, however, the focus is not necessarily on the eye or the way in which the eye functions; instead, the focus is on the incalculable speed at which the events described occur. This fits well with other NT descriptions of Christ's final return (1 Thess. 5.1-2; 2 Pet. 3.10; cf. 1 Thess. 4.17). Moreover, Paul's use of *rhipē* in the context of 1 Cor. 15.52 harmonises with the OT notion of *rega'* as a dramatic shift in life and/or history.

The phrase appears in numerous classical works (e.g., Cervantes, Donne, Dostoyevsky), most often in the writings of Shakespeare, Dickens, Melville, Tolstoy, Doyle, Burroughs, and London. In such cases, the meaning of the phrase remains the same as the biblical usage — i.e., an event that is sudden or beyond calculation. Given its usual religious connotations, the phrase was favored by many early American preachers such as Charles Spurgeon, Jonathan Edwards and John Wesley, all of whom were deeply and reverently anxious about the return of Christ.

See also EYE; PAROUSIA [CSS]

Two Houses. Any great teaching undoubtedly is repeated not only by the listeners but also by the originator. Within early Jewish tradition, aggadic midrash (creative and imaginative narrative exposition of biblical ethical principle) finds multiple expressions throughout the extant Judaic literary corpus. Two separate Gospels with potentially two distinct contexts present two unique versions of a parable of the two houses or two house-builders.

Teaching one: Matt. 7.24-27 concludes the Sermon on the Mount, the first of five editorially positioned discourses intended to parallel the five books of the Torah (Genesis to Deuteronomy), with a teaching framed in Hebrew didactic structure that could very well have been entitled 'The Two Foundations'. In this account, one builder established a structure solidly on bedrock (Greek, *epi tēn petran*). Another built a structure precariously on 'sand' (Greek, *epi tēn ammon*). Rain fell, floods came, winds blew and beat upon each house.

Teaching two: Luke 6.46-49 offers a similar teaching framed in Greek didactic structure positioned at the close of a collection of related, albeit limited, themes subsequent to the call of the twelve apostles. One builder dug deep and laid a foundation solidly upon bedrock. Another built a structure, literally 'upon the land without a foundation' (Greek, *epi tēn gēn chōris themeliou*). A flood arose and a stream broke against each house.

In both teachings, the houses solidly built withstood nature's onslaught of forces while the houses precariously built collapsed.

Geographically, the settings for wise house-building correlate to Judaea and the Galilee, respectively, since the former lacks the rich topsoil that generally and generously covers the latter. Thus the need in the second account for digging to reach bedrock.

The ethical application may include political intrigue. The politics of the story may be found in the fact that Pontius Pilate was prefect for Rome over all of Judaea, but because of his widely known detestation of Jews chose to live in a Mediterranean villa he constructed at Caesarea Maritima. As recent archaeological excavation has demonstrated regarding Crusader walls along its shoreline, building along the sandy shores of the Mediterranean required constant renovation of the structures at their foundations because the water and wind continually eroded their base. In contrast, those who lived inland characteristically complained about having always to deal with rocky terrain that made their lives burdensome—the parable subverts this perspective. Having no real alternative, builders had to deal with the rock. Now they are portrayed as wise builders. Perhaps, as inserted comic relief, their nemesis and absentee landlord, Pontius Pilate, was portrayed as a foolish builder.

Application of the cultural memory of this teaching finds its way into popular song and expression, wherein 'the wise person builds on rock' alludes to strong choices people make whereas 'the foolish person builds on sand' indicates poor decision-making.

See also PARABLE; ROCK [DM]

Two Witnesses. The phrase 'two witnesses' refers, broadly, to Jewish and Christian legal and eschatological tradition, and, more specifically, to the two figures depicted in Rev. 11.3-12. In this passage, these two figures are described as prophesying for 42 months (1,260 days) in the 'holy city' and are designated as 'witnesses', 'olive trees', 'lampstands', and 'prophets'. These witnesses are described as having supernatural abilities, such as breathing fire from their mouths to devour their enemies, preventing rain from falling, turning the waters to blood, and striking the earth with various plagues (Rev. 11.5-6). Following their period of 'testifying', they are overcome by the beast, and the people of the earth rejoice over their demise (11.7-10). After three and a half days, they are raised from the dead and ascend to heaven in the sight of their enemies (11.11-12).

The designation 'witness', from the Greek *martys* (witness), is drawn from a legal context. In the biblical tradition, stress is placed on the reliance upon two or three witnesses (e.g., Num. 35.30; Deut. 17.6; 19.15). In Revelation, the theme of 'witness' is important (cf. 1.2, 5, 9; 2.13; 3.14; 6.9; 12.11, 17; 17.6; 19.10; 20.4; 22.16, 20), with the two witnesses serving as key figures. The testimony given likely carries both the sense of testifying to the truth of the Christian message and the testimony regarding the rejection of the world. The imagery in Revelation is also likely influenced by that of Zechariah 3–4, depicting the two figures of Zerubbabel and Joshua.

The two witnesses have been identified in various ways throughout history. In the early church, Enoch and Elijah were common designations (advocated by Tertullian) due to statements in Gen. 5.24 and 2 Kgs 2.11-12 about their translation to heaven. They have also been identified as pairs of OT figures such as Moses and Elijah (due to the nature of their supernatural powers) and Elijah and Jeremiah (advocated by Victorinus). They have also been identified as significant early Christian figures, such as James and John or Peter and Paul. In addition to these biblical figures, the two witnesses have also been seen as eschatological figures or as symbols of the corporate witness of the church.

In western culture, the influence of this imagery may be observed in several areas. Although the more particular connotation of a 'martyr' as one who dies for their religious faith is not likely meant by the various occurrences of *martys* in Revelation, the usage likely served an important role in the development of the technical term in Christian usage. In this way, the two witnesses may be seen as representative of this notion. Additionally, the two witnesses have also been connected with individuals and groups in church history, such as Protestants in their resistance to Roman Catholicism (e.g., the illustration in the 1534 Luther Bible, where the two witnesses preach in Wittenberg in the presence of the beast, which wears the papal crown). Interest in the two witnesses as eschatological figures has also been fuelled in recent years, particularly in the North American context, through the publication of the *Left Behind* series.

Recommended reading. Black, M. 'The 'Two Witnesses' of Rev. 11.3f. in Jewish and Christian Apocalyptic Tradition'. In *Donum gentilicium: New Testament Studies in Honour of David Daube*. Ed. C.K. Barrett, E. Bammel, and W.D. Davies. Pp. 227-37. Oxford: Clarendon Press, 1978. Considine, Joseph S. 'The Two Witnesses: Apoc. 11.3-13'. *Catholic Biblical Quarterly* (1946) 377-92. Strand, Kenneth. 'The Two Witnesses of Rev. 11.3-12'. *Andrews University Seminary Studies* 19 (1981) 127-35.

See also ANTICHRIST; APOCALYPTIC; MARTYR, MARTYRDOM; REVELATION, BOOK OF [MN]

Typology. The study of types and antitypes—events, people, places, and institutions that serve as an example or pattern for other events, people, places, and institutions—and the meaning correlations between them. Thus, typology may be regarded as a general concern of humanity as they draw connections by analogy between figures and experiences to understand and navigate the phenomena about them.

An important interpretative technique in ancient Israel and early Judaism, typology allowed for the reinterpretation of Israel's formative people (e.g., patriarchs, David) and events (e.g., creation, Egyptian captivity, exodus, wilderness experience) in new circumstances. It was later adopted by NT and other early Christian writers who searched the OT for analogies that would shed understanding on the person and work of Christ. For example, Paul describes Christ as a second, sinless Adam (Rom. 5.12-21), and Hebrews correlates the mysterious priest-king Melchizedek and Jesus the High Priest (7.1-28).

Discussion of typology in Christian theology and biblical studies has often been limited to matters of salvation history and the relationship between the Testaments. However, given that in the NT the word *typos* and its derivatives appear to be used in both technical (Acts 7.44; Rom. 5.14; 1 Cor. 10.6; Heb. 8.5; 1 Pet. 3.21) and non-technical ways (Phil. 3.17; 1 Thess. 1.7; 2 Thess. 3.9; 1 Tim. 1.16; 2 Tim. 1.13), it seems that for the biblical writers it was an interpretative technique that operated within somewhat fluid parameters.

Nonetheless, four general features guide its employment. First, the orientation of a typological correlation may be presented as either prospective, anticipating something that lies in the future (Isa. 43.18-21), or retrospective, discerned in hindsight after the emergence of the antitype (1 Cor. 5.7). Second, the typology's axis may be either vertical (spatial), describing the relationship between heavenly and earthly realities (Heb. 9.1-28), or horizontal (temporal), envisioning the relationship between earlier and later events, persons and institutions (Rom. 5.14). Third, the correlation may (Rom. 5.14) or may not (1 Cor. 10.1-11) involve a heightening between type and antitype. Fourth, the articulation of the typology may be either explicit (Matt. 12.40) or implicit (e.g., Matthew's presentation of Jesus according to the pattern of Moses).

In the patristic and medieval periods, typology as an interpretative approach was usually subordinated to its more fanciful and ambiguous counterpart, allegory. Only with the Reformation, and Luther's and Calvin's emphasis on the literal sense of scripture, did typology once again become a prominent method of biblical interpretation.

Today, typological correlations pointing back to significant biblical people and events continue to emerge in art, literature and film. Notably, Tolkien's *Lord of the Rings* offers multiple implicit typologies that point back to the life and ministry of Jesus. Examples include: the parallels between the hobbit Frodo who bears 'the ring' to Mount Doom, and Jesus who carries his cross to Golgotha—both of whom for the good of the world bear burdens that only they could bear; and, the parallels between the wizard Gandalf and Jesus—both of whom lay down their life for the good of the world, descend into the belly of the earth, and are consequently 'resurrected' to life in a new glorified state.

Recommended reading. Goppelt, Leonhard. *Typos: The Typological Interpretation of the Old Testament in the New*. Trans. Donald H. Madvig. Grand Rapids, MI: Eerdmans, 1982. Lampe, G.W.H., and K.J. Woollcombe. *Essays on Typology*. London: SCM Press, 1957. Rad, Gerhard von. 'Typological Interpretation of the Old Testament'. In *Essays on Old Testament Interpretation*. Ed. Claus Westermann. Pp. 17-39. London: SCM Press, 1963.

See also ALLEGORY; HEBREWS, EPISTLE TO THE; HERMENEUTICS [TB]

Tyre and Sidon. The two most significant Phoenician cities during the biblical period. Phoenician contact with Egypt is attested from the fourth millennium. Cedar trees were needed in Egypt as building material, and cedar resin was a component in the process of mummification.

Phoenician ships stopped throughout the Mediterranean world, as well as the Atlantic coasts of Morocco and Spain. Herodotus describes Phoenician merchants at work, selling their wares beside their beached ships. They established a number of colonies throughout the Mediterranean and Atlantic coast of Morocco. Tyre's colony of Carthage is the best known. They are known to classical authors for their dying of cloth, as metal workers, glass producers, and of course, as merchants and shippers.

The two cities are used interchangeably at times in classical, ancient Near Eastern, and biblical sources. Kings of one city are often confused with the other city, and Phoenicians in general are referred to as 'Sidonians' often.

Tyre was located on an island (originally two islands) a half mile off the coast of modern day Lebanon, selected for its defensive advantages. It had a twin city on the shore, which provided the island fortress with food and water. Phoenicia controlled the sea, meaning it was virtually impervious to siege, even when its mainland city was destroyed by invaders (e.g., Nebuchadnezzar laid siege to the island for thirteen years).

Tyre is the epitome of wealth (and arrogance) in the OT (Isa. 23; Ezek. 26–28). This imagery is by no means an exaggeration. Tyre had attested ties to both the Davidic line (2 Sam. 5; 1 Kgs 5; 9; 22) and to the Omride dynasty. The diplomatic marriage of Jezebel, a Tyrian princess (her father was a usurper, and a priest of Baal), to Ahab demonstrates the power of the new dynasty of Omri (1 Kgs 16.31-34). It also reflects the proximity of Israel to Tyre (Mount Carmel was the boundary between these lands), and the control that Israel had over land routes destined for Phoenicia from the Arabian Peninsula and Egypt. Likewise, the aid given to David and Solomon reflect this geographic reality.

The ancient Israelites and Judeans were constantly inclined to religious syncretism with Phoenician deities. In an environment in which rain-fed agriculture is the primary economic activity for the bulk of the population, farmers naturally hedged their bets by paying homage to the storm god Baal as well as Yahweh (1 Kgs 18). The disturbing practice of offering a *mulk* (or human infant sacrifice; there was no god named Moloch, as this was a mistake created when the Bible received vowel letters centuries later) is rightly condemned (e.g., Jer. 32.35).

Tyre resisted Alexander in 332. Alexander built a mole, as the island became a manmade peninsula, and Persia was stripped of its navy as this last Phoenician city fell. Both cities attained prominence during the Hellenistic period. Tyre surpassed Sidon in importance during the Roman period. Jesus spent time in Tyrian territory (e.g., Matt. 15.21), and Tyrians and Phoenicians were present when he preached (e.g., Luke 6.17).

The two greatest things the world is indebted to the Phoenicians for would be the introduction of the alphabet to the Greeks and the mythological imagery which was borrowed to describe Yahweh in psalms and poetry (e.g., Yahweh as the Rider of the Clouds, Ps. 68.5, an epithet of Baal).

Recommended reading. Lipinski, E. (ed.). *Phoenicia and the Bible*. Studia phoenicia, 9. Leuven: Peeters, 1991. Katzenstein, H.J. *The History of Tyre*. Jerusalem: Schoken, 1973. Moscati, S. (ed.). *The Phoenicians*. New York: Abbeville Press, 1988.

See also JEZEBEL; KING OF TYRE; SYROPHOENICIAN WOMAN [MAP]

U

Uncircumcised. (See Circumcision).

Unclean (see Ritual Purity, Impurity).

Unclean Spirit (see Demon).

Unforgivable Sin, the (see Sin against the Holy Spirit).

Unicorn. In western culture, unicorns are mythical beasts resembling horses, with a single horn projecting from their heads. References to unicorns in the KJV are found in verses such as Num. 23.22; 24.8 and Deut. 33.17. These emphasize the great strength of the unicorn and it usually symbolizes God's sovereign power, whose voice makes the cedars of Lebanon skip like unicorns (Ps. 29.6).

What were the biblical writers referring by the Hebrew word *rᵉ'em*? There are two likely answers. The first is to horned wild cattle known as Aurochs or *Urochs* (*Bos primigenius tarus*), believed by some to be the cattle depicted on cave paintings. Wild cattle existed in the time of Caesar's battles in Germany. They died out in Europe in the 1600s, but attempts are underway to back breed them.

The other possibility is the wild ox of the Middle East. In biblical times, kings wore helmets with wild ox horns (Ps. 92.10; 132.17-18). The horns were also used as drinking cups. Large horns could hold up to four gallons. The Assyrian kings enjoyed hunting wild oxen. This dispute aside, neither the wild ox nor the wild cattle were unicorns.

The LXX translated *rᵉ'em* as *monokeros*. This Greek translation may have been influenced by Babylonian mosaics or Egyptian paintings. The images are two-dimensional side views that show only a single horn. Tiglath-pileser I (c. 1115–1102 BCE) is known to have hunted wild oxen or cattle in the Lebanese mountains. The LXX may have identified the one-horned beast in Dan. 8.3 as a unicorn. Whether wild cattle or wild oxen, the *rᵉ'em* was a beast no one could tame (Job 39.9-10; Ps. 22.21; 92.10; Isa. 34.7). Most translations now favor 'wild ox' as found in verses like Num. 24.7 as the best translation for *rᵉ'em*.

The Talmudic rabbis wrote that the *rᵉ'em* survived the Flood by being tied to the outside of Noah's ark. Jerome's Vulgate used unicorn (*unicornis*) when following the LXX, although sometimes it used rhinoceros. Luther's German Bible also used unicorn (*Einhorn*). The KJV followed the LXX. While 'unicorn' was an unfortunate translation for the two horned wild ox which scholars now believe was the animal described in Job 9–12, its biblical and extra-biblical usages made it a fixture of biblical tradition.

During the Middle Ages a Christianized natural philosophy book, *Physiologus*, provided a major source of unicorn lore. Unicorns could be captured by a virgin; leading the animal to a wooded area where the unicorn ranges, she would seat herself and soon it would come and lay its head in her lap, making it vulnerable to capture. The scene was critical to symbolic interpretations of Christ. Writers allegorized unicorns so that they stood for hermits or other religious figures. Others used unicorns to expound courtly love. Paintings and tapestries portrayed scenes of unicorns.

Until the 1700s, many travelers' tales, natural philosophies, and encyclopedists expanded unicorn lore. However, by the 1600s doubts were being raised about the existence of unicorns in works such as *Vulgar Errors* by Thomas Browne. When William Hogarth wrote *Marriage à la mode* in 1745, a unicorn horn in a physician's shop was sufficient to identify him as a quack.

Today, stuffed toy unicorns are popular children's toys. Many Canadians fondly remember 'The Unicorn' as the theme song of *The Irish Rovers*, a popular TV series produced by the Canadian Broadcasting Corporation (1971–1975).

Recommended reading. Bright, Michael. *Beasts of the Field: The Natural History of Animals in the Bible*. London: Anova Books, 2006. White, T.H. *The Bestiary*. New York: Penguin, 1960.

See also ANIMALS, SYMBOLISM OF; FLOOD; KJV; NOAH'S ARK; SEPTUAGINT [AJW]

Unjust Judge, parable or 'parable of the importunate widow', a parable of Jesus on prayer in Luke 18.1-9, including the parable proper (vv. 2-5) and its introduction or explanation (vv. 1, 6-8). Teaching his disciples to pray persistently, Jesus tells them a parable about a judge who 'neither feared God nor had respect for people' and a widow who kept coming to him saying: 'Grant me justice against my opponent'. Jesus' characterization of the judge is against expectation. In Jewish tradition fear of the Lord is the basis of rendering wise judgment (Ps. 111.10) and the judge's attitude in the parable is in contrast with the ideal judge portrayed in Sirach

(35.12-15). Also, according to OT teaching widows were to enjoy a particular respect (Deut. 14.29; Isa. 10.2; Jer. 22.3; Zech. 7.10). Initially the judge refuses the widow's request, but he eventually gives in to her, not in fear of God nor respect for people, but because the widow kept bothering him, so that she 'may not wear him out by continually coming'. Here the parable ends and Jesus explains it to his disciples. First he contrasts the judge and God, asking the rhetorical questions: if this is what an unjust judge will do, 'will not God grant justice to his chosen ones who cry to him day and night?' and 'Will he delay long in helping them?' Jesus then answers himself: 'I tell you, he will quickly grant justice to them'. Concluding this teaching, Jesus asks one last question: 'And yet, when the Son of Man comes, will he find faith on earth?'—that is, a faith as persistent as the widow's! Linked to the previous section about the coming of God's kingdom and the son of man (Luke 17.20-37), the parable pertains to God's promise to speedily vindicate his praying people of faith.

In Dante's *Divine Comedy* (1308–1321) we find an echo of the parable in the importunate widow's plea to Emperor Trajan. Even if not the origin of the saying 'the squeaking wheel gets the most grease', the parallel is obvious. In *The Family Sabbath-Day Miscellany* (1841), author C.A. Goodrich tells the story of a group of widows in West New York who found inspiration in this parable to do something about their miserable situation. In an announcement in the *London Gazette* (1859), the famous nurse Florence Nightingale characterized herself as the importunate widow and Lord Stanley as the unjust judge. The theme of a powerful person giving in to a weaker one for selfish reasons can be seen in the movie *As Good as it Gets* (1997). Jack Nicholson plays the obsessive-compulsive writer Melvin Udall and Helen Hunt plays Carol Connelly, a single mother (a modern-day widow) of a sick child, who is the only waitress who can tolerate Udall at the restaurant where he always eats. When Carol decides to get a job closer to Brooklyn so she can spend more time with her asthmatic son, Udall arranges to pay for her son's medical expenses, albeit for his own selfish reasons.

Recommended reading. Matthews, Mary W., Carter Shelley and Barbara Scheele. 'Proclaiming the Parable of the Persistent Widow (Lk. 18.2-5)'. In *The Lost Coin: Parables of Women, Work and Wisdom*. Ed. Mary Ann Beavis. Pp. 46-70. London Press, 2002.

See also Parable; Widow [TA]

Unjust Steward, Parable of the. This parable (Luke 16.1-13, although many interpreters think the original parable went to either v. 8a or v. 9) has proved to be an enigma, because, at least on the surface of the story, a steward who has not kept his books and then falsifies his master's accounts is commended for these apparently unjust practices.

As a result, there have been numerous possible explanations of the parable. It has been proposed that: this was an allegory commending the giving of alms; the steward is commended for wisely using the present to ensure his own future; Jesus here compromises with evil; Jesus commends the clever and resolute behavior of a man threatened by an imminent crisis; Jesus does not commend the unethical behavior but the cleverness and resourcefulness of the steward when faced with difficulty; oriental customs regarding stewards and debt commend the steward for releasing the master's debtors from unfairly high interest; the master may have been unaware of the usurious interest being charged to his debtors; the parable is about the master's mercy toward his debtors; the commendatory comments in vv. 8-9 are ironic and do not encourage such behavior at all; the parable is an endorsement of sharing physical property; the parable is addressed to the master who equates wealth and social status; the parable provides an eschatological warning to the nation of Israel; the parable is autobiographical about Jesus in relation to the Jewish leaders; the story is a picaresque adventure of a man living by his wits; the parable is about social values and how they need to be rethought; the steward's actions are an attempt to forgive debt in the seventh year; or there is something textually wrong with the ending of the parable that demands emendation. At least 15 different interpretations of this parable have been offered, with no end in sight.

Several of the major issues that continue to be raised in discussion of this parable are the following: (1) How do we frame the major interpretive difficulty of the parable, that is, that the master and hence Jesus appear to praise unrighteous action on the part of the steward? (2) Where does this parable end? If it ends at the end of v. 13, then there are a number of statements regarding wealth that need to be integrated into the interpretation. If the parable ends sooner (e.g., v. 8a or at the end of v. 9), then the parable has less interpretation included in it. (3) How are the cultural and economic conditions of the parable to be understood? These may just be incidental details reflecting Jesus' life circumstances, although many of Jesus' parables seem to make much of economic issues. (4) Are Jesus' statements regarding praise of the steward related to the steward himself or his actions? (5) What exactly is the unrighteousness that the steward has done? (6) Is the 'Lord' of v. 8a the master of the servant or Jesus? (7) Who is the primary audience of the parable, the disciples or the Pharisees? Answers to these questions help to focus interpretation of the parable.

Though not as popular as other parables, the parable of the unjust steward has continued to attract occasional interpretive interest. Most noteworthy perhaps was William Tyndale's *The Parable of the Wicked Mammon*, published in 1528.

Recommended reading. Porter, S.E. 'The Parable of the Unjust Steward (Luke 16.1-13): Irony *is* the Key'. *The Bible in Three Dimensions*, 27-53. Ed. D.J.A. Clines, S.E. Fowl, and S.E. Porter. Sheffield: JSOT Press, 1990.

See also PARABLE; STEWARD   [SEP]

Unknown God. An altar inscription in Athens that Paul cites in an evangelistic speech to the Greeks on the Areopagus, also called Mars Hill (Acts 17.16-34). Using the altar inscription as a starting point, Paul begins by exploring hellenistic motifs that he and his audience hold in common: the transcendent self-sufficiency of God (v. 25); God is near, and not only transcendent (vv. 27, 28a); and 'we too are his offspring' (v. 28b), a quotation from a poem by Epimenides. In the second part of the speech (17.19-31), Paul argues for monotheism and calls his hearers to repentance in light of the divine judgment for idolatry coming through God's resurrected son, Jesus Christ (v. 31).

Did such an altar exist in Athens? Pausanius (late second century CE) in his *Description of Greece* mentions that some altars inscribed with 'unknown gods' (plural) were extant near one of Athens's harbors. But this is different from Paul's claim that the inscription was in the *singular* ('unknown god'), and also ascribed *to* that unknown god. Pieter van der Horst cites archaeological evidence that minor Hellenistic altars inscribed with 'unknown gods' (Miletus, Pergamum) or '*to* unknown gods' (northern Phrygia) were located near temples or main altars. Even though no altar with an inscription in the singular has yet been found, van der Horst suggests that, in light of the existing literary and epigraphic evidence, Paul's claim is not improbable.

What is the story behind the inscription? In his *Lives of Eminent Philosophers*, Diogenes Laertius (early third century CE) describes an Athenian attempt to deal with a severe plague (c. 580 BCE). After sacrificing to every known god, but without avail, they brought a famous religious teacher named Epimenides from Crete. This is the same Epimenides quoted in Paul's speech (17.23b; cf. Tit. 1.12). Epimenides had the Athenians offer sheep as atonement to the anonymous god responsible for the plague. The plague stopped soon thereafter. Diogenes says 'anonymous altars' were built in honor of this god that still stood in his day.

The philosophical milieu of Paul's day is not dissimilar to contemporary postmodern approaches. The 'emerging church', as somewhat of a decentralized postmodern Christian movement, prioritizes engagement with mainstream culture rather than isolation from it. Some well-known emerging churches even use 'Mars Hill' in their name (e.g., Seattle, Grandville, MI). Rob Bell (Grandville) is known for his best-selling books *Velvet Elvis* and *Sex God*, and his popular spiritual short films called NOOMA (*pneuma* is Greek for 'spirit').

The Mars Hill altar inscription is seen in mystical literary works like John Middleton Murry's, *To the Unknown God* (1924), 'Unknown God' by Irish literary renaissance poet G.W. Russell (1867–1935), and John Steinbeck's *To a God Unknown* (1933). The *New English Dictionary* (Oxford, 1888) claims that Thomas Huxley coined the term 'agnostic' from the altar inscription *agnōstō theō* ('to the unknown god'). The debate between representational and abstract art is captured in two paintings at opposite ends of the twentieth century. Henry Tonks's painting *The Unknown God* (1923) caricatures the abstract art of Post-Impressionists, including Cézanne, while James Daugherty's (1887–1974) abstract painting, *Altar to the Unknown God* (1971) hangs in the Smithsonian American Art Museum.

Recommended reading. Horst, Pieter W. van der. 'The Unknown God (Acts 17.23)'. In *Knowledge of God in the Greco-Roman World*. EPRO, 112. Ed. R. van den Broek, T. Baarda, and J. Mansfeld. Pp. 19-42. Leiden: Brill, 1988. Richardson, Don. *Eternity in their Hearts*. Ventura, CA: Regal Books, 1981.

See also AREOPAGUS   [RJK]

Unleavened Bread, Feast of. This was the first of Israel's major pilgrimage feasts. It was to take place over seven days in March–April (15–21 Nissan [*Abib*]). The feast was closely tied to the celebration of Passover marking Israel's deliverance from Egypt on 14 Nissan so that it became the foremost of the festivals. Because of the close temporal connection between Passover and the Feast of Unleavened Bread, the two feasts eventually fused in common speech, practice, and in popular writing.

The Israelites kept the feast by journeying to Jerusalem (Deut. 16.5-8). For the duration of the festival week, the people did not eat any product with yeast or leaven in it. In fact, all leaven was to be removed from their residences. The celebration included a holiday from any work for seven days and the offering of daily special sacrifices. The feast opened and closed with 'sacred assemblies'.

While the Feast of Unleavened Bread primarily celebrated God's redemption of his people from Egypt, it also marked the beginning of barley harvest, the first grain to be harvested. The celebration included the Feast of Firstfruits in which the first ears of grain harvested were offered to God.

The feast is connected to both redemption and creation. The unleavened bread pointed to Israel's redemption by reminding Israel of the haste with which they left Egypt so that their bread did not have time to rise (Exod. 12.24; Deut. 16.3). It linked Israel to creation by celebrating God's covenant love in providing for their needs and reminding them of new beginnings. In the history of Israel provided by the Chronicler, the observance of this festival served as an indicator of the faithfulness of the nation (e.g., 2 Chron. 30.21; 35.17-19).

The Feast of Unleavened Bread is mentioned several times in the NT (Matt. 27.7; Mark 14.1; 12; Luke 22.7; Acts 12.3; 20.6). Passover and the Feast of Unleavened Bread have survived in Jewish religious celebrations. The Christian sacrament of communion also arose out of particularly the Passover celebration. The bread used in the Lord's Supper was the unleavened bread (*matzah*) of the Passover and the Feast of Unleavened Bread.

See also FIRSTFRUITS; HOLIDAYS, FEASTS, FESTIVALS; PASSOVER [BW]

Upper Room. The 'upper room' (Gk. *anagaion*, 'room upstairs' in the NRSV) is where Jesus ate the Passover meal (known also as the 'Lord's Supper' or 'Last Supper') with his disciples (Mark 14.15; Luke 22.12). In the passion narrative, this is the last undisturbed gathering of Jesus with his disciples before his arrest, trial, and crucifixion. For this reason, it symbolizes intimacy and transition. The intimacy of this gathering is emphasised in John, where Jesus washes the disciples' feet, engages in a lengthy discourse, and prays for his disciples (13.1–17.26). However, neither John nor Matthew explicitly says that this meal took place in the upper room; this must be inferred from parallels with Mark and Luke. It is possible that this same upper room continued to be the main gathering place for the disciples during (and perhaps after) the period leading up to Pentecost (cf. Acts 1.13, Greek *hyperōon*).

In Catholic tradition, the upper room in which the Last Supper took place is known as the Cenacle (Latin *cenaculum*), a popular pilgrimage site in the Old City of Jerusalem since the fourth century, mentioned by the Christian pilgrim Egeria in her *Travels*. A fourteenth-century building known as the Cenacle stands over a site where early Christians apparently gathered on Mount Zion. This location eventually became identified, somewhat speculatively, with the upper room in Christian tradition.

The upper room is most famously depicted in Leonardo da Vinci's fifteenth-century painting, *The Last Supper*. This painting portrays Jesus with the twelve disciples, who are reacting to the news that one of them would betray him. More recently, the Spanish impressionist Salvador Dalí's painting, *The Sacrament of the Last Supper* (1955), renders the upper room as a nexus between inside and outside space.

Although 'the upper room' has been used as a title for several books and as the name of a British rock band, it most frequently appears in popular usage as a name for Christian churches and gatherings. Thus, it has remained a powerful Christian symbol of intimacy with Jesus. The Cenacle Sisters is a Roman Catholic religious order specializing in spiritual ministries such as retreats, spiritual direction and adult faith formation, cofounded in nineteenth-century France by Father Steven Terme and Therese Couderc (canonized in 1970). In the US, the *Upper Room* magazine has published daily devotionals inspired by biblical texts since 1935.

Recommended reading. Murphy-O'Connor, Jerome. 'The Cenacle–Topographical Setting for Acts 2:44-45'. In *The Book of Acts in its First Century Setting*. Ed. Richard Bauckham. Pp. 303-21. Grand Rapids, MI: Eerdmans, 1995.

See also LAST SUPPER [JRM]

Upright. In the Bible, the term 'upright' is most often a translation of the Hebrew *yashar* in the OT and the Greek *dikaios* in the NT; the concentration of the figurative (moral) use of the term is found in Psalms and Proverbs. In the OT, this figurative usage refers to behavior that is ethically and legally right for humankind according to Yahweh's perfect standard of righteousness; the righteous person who idiomatically does what is right (*yashar*) in the eyes of the Lord may be referred to as 'upright' or 'upright in heart', while the crooked-hearted are referred to as the treacherous or the wicked. The word 'upright' is also used to describe God, his commands, and the way in which he relates to his people; thus, 'a faithful God, without deceit, just and upright is he' (Deut. 32.4). The NT's figurative use of 'upright' is much less frequent, being used only to describe the centurion Cornelius (Acts 10.22), the Thessalonian Christians (1 Thess. 2.10), overseers of the church (Tit. 1.8), and the way in which Christians in general are instructed to live (Tit. 2.12). In both OT and NT usage, uprightness is closely associated with righteousness, and could be applied to both Jews (e.g., the Psalmist) and Gentiles (e.g., Job, who is described as upright three times) who feared God.

While use of the term 'upright' is uncommon in modern colloquial English, the idiomatic idea of being on 'the straight/strait and narrow' or being 'straight' or 'on the level' in one's dealings conveys the general idea of the term. The antonym of being crooked (i.e., dishonest or corrupt) also finds its parallel in the biblical vocabulary.

The victory of the upright and destruction of the wicked (e.g., Prov. 14.11) is depicted widely in western culture. Just as the upright are a blessing to the city (Prov. 11.11) and are hated and persecuted by the wicked (Ps. 37.14; Prov. 29.10), the American comic book superheroes that emerged after the Great Depression depicted heroes with an uncompromising moral code who would defend a helpless populace against the powerful and wicked. Comic book heroes of that period and into the 1960s—such as Superman and Spiderman—portrayed the iconic upright character who, outside of a religious context, battled for justice at great personal risk and with reluctance to kill opponents.

Analogous to the God of David who 'saves the upright in heart' (Ps. 7.10; cf. 11.7), a depersonalized protection for the upright is common in films. In movies and related media, the idea of a 'Hollywood ending' (a phrase coined in 1929) displays the public desire for entertainment to depict a positive, happy outcome to dramatic conflict—at the expense of realism, if necessary. In such movies the audience can expect the upright to suffer but ultimately flourish while the wicked are defeated or destroyed. For example, in the 1999 movie *The Mummy*, Evelyn Carnahan tells the scheming Beni precisely what the audience desires to be true. 'You know, nasty little fellows such as yourself always get their comeuppance'. At the end of this type of film, the wicked are defeated and the upright are triumphant.

See also CROOKED; JOB; JUSTICE; RIGHTEOUSNESS; STRAIT AND NARROW [WAS]

Ur. A very ancient Sumerian city located in southern Mesopotamia, in what is today the desert of southern Iraq. It was one of the largest cities in Sumer and, along with the city of Uruk, was one of the most influent cities in the ANE in the third millennium. The patron god of the city was the moon-god Nanna.

In the OT, the city of Ur is only mentioned four times (Gen. 11.28, 31; 15.7 and Neh. 9.7) and is presented as the homeland of Abraham. His father, Terah, was also born there. Ur is thus the starting point of Abraham's migration that will lead him and his family to Canaan, which will eventually become the land promised by God to his people. When Ur is mentioned in the OT, it is always followed by the expression 'of the Chaldeans', referring to a group of nomadic tribes that established themselves in the region surrounding Ur in the eleventh century BCE. They eventually became dominant in Babylonia (late seventh century BCE). The biblical expression 'Ur of the Chaldeans' is thus relatively late.

The city of Ur was rediscovered and systematically excavated from 1922 to 1934 by Sir Leonard Woolley in a joint expedition between the British Museum and the University of Pennsylvania. The discoveries made by Woolley are arguably among the most important archaeological discoveries in the Mesopotamian area. Woolley's most impressive discovery came from what he called the 'Royal Cemetery'. Some 1850 tombs, dating from the twenty-eighth to the twenty-second centuries BCE, were found. Among them were 16 that Woolley termed 'royal'. According to Woolley, it was a royal cemetery because the so-called royal tombs were filled with rich goods and surrounded by an impressive number of secondary tombs of people who were apparently ritually sacrificed in honor of the rulers at their funerals. The victims may have been sacrificed (willingly or not) to accompany their ruler in the afterlife. However, no traces of violence were found on the corpses, so, what happened? Nobody knows for certain. Even if most scholars believe that the people in the secondary tombs were sacrificed, they don't agree on the causes and circumstances surrounding this ceremony. Furthermore, there is not enough evidence to prove that it was indeed a royal cemetery. Conversely, the arguments against this theory are not totally convincing. In sum, this ancient cemetery is still clouded in mystery.

Recommended reading. Moorey, P.R.S. 'What Do We Know about the People Buried in the Royal Cemetery?' *Expedition: The University Museum Magazine* 20 (Fall 1977) 24-40. Pollock, Susan. 'Chronology of the Royal Cemetery of Ur'. *Iraq* 47 (1985) 129-58.

See also ABRAHAM; BABYLON; MESOPOTAMIA [ÉB]

Uriah. Uriah the Hittite, husband of Bathsheba, was an officer of the Israelite army, a native of Jerusalem and a faithful Yahwist. Uriah is a name meaning 'Yahweh is my light/fire'. Four other Uriahs named in the OT are either prophets or priests of Yahweh (2 Kgs 16.10-16; Jer. 26.20-23; Neh. 3.21; 8.4). Uriah the Hittite is named in the list of the thirty (2 Sam. 23.24-39), which may have been David's elite officers' corps formed during his flight from Saul. In accordance with David's plan to possess Bathsheba, Uriah was killed while fighting for Israel. In contrast to David, Uriah abides by the Torah and observes the wartime soldier's ban against conjugal relations. Despite this, the scribes did not claim Uriah as one of them, but as a 'Hittite', an outsider. Hittites were a people whose capital in central Anatolia was the center of a significant empire in the second millennium BCE. The Hittite empire eventually collapsed at the end of the Late Bronze Age at which time they populated Canaan, along with a territory to the north of Palestine. Because of Uriah's hybrid identity, the 'author' of the text gave Bathsheba a double identity, 'daughter of Eliam, the wife of Uriah the Hittite', confirming her Israelite heritage.

Uriah's story is a (con)text of struggle for identity that is all too familiar to immigrants struggling for identity. Is it possible that the Hittites, a community displaced by the Israelites, practiced ethnic 'disidentification', the act of distancing one's group from another group so as not to be mistaken and suffer the blame for the presumed misdeeds of that group? This is a strategy of survival for colonized and diasporic people, and was used frequently by Asian Americans in the US before the 1960s.

Immigrants often find themselves negotiating a complex maze of identity-formation described as (1) hybridity, a doubleness that brings together, but also maintains separation through multi-identities of members of diasporas and (2) liminality, the state of 'in-betweenness' resulting from hybridity. Hybridity allows one to move about freely in two or more cultures and highlights the 'positive' side of liminality, e.g., as long as Uriah was 'useful' to Israel, he was considered its own.

Hybridity facilitates exploration of interculturation in the postcolonial world as it lifts the veil on the lie that we are pure, pristine and singular, and allows the complex mixtures of different cultures, ethnicities and religious identities to be clearly evident. From the tension of hybridity comes new opportunities for discourse through altering the conceptualization of identity so that it no longer functions as a stable reference point. It then combines with other ideas, concepts, and beliefs resulting in new and different understandings of self, of context and of the world. Uriah's story reminds us that we live in mixed, interrelated, dynamic cultures in which hybridity and interculturation are constantly occurring. Hybridity can be a useful aid in identity-formation of oppressed peoples and an inspiration for change in society enabling different ethnicities to learn to accept, live and embrace one another.

In western culture, a 'letter of Uriah' is a treacherous one, like the missive Uriah carried from David to his general Joab to send him to the thick of battle (2 Sam. 11.15). Uriah is seldom portrayed in art; a notable exception is Rembrandt's *David and Uriah* (1665), portraying the king sending Uriah to his fate, with the prophet Nathan in the background.

Recommended reading. Kim, Uriah (Yong-Hwan). 'Uriah the Hittite: A (Con)Text of Struggle for Identity'. *Semeia* 90–91 (2002) 69, 72-75.

See also BATHSHEBA; DAVID; THOU ART THE MAN [GJSK]

Urim and Thummim. The Urim and Thummim are some of the most interesting and least understood objects mentioned in the OT. The word Urim (*urim*) is usually translated 'lights' or 'revelations' while Thummim (*tummim*) is rendered 'perfections' or 'truth'. Both words are plural in Hebrew.

The nature and function of the Urim and Thummim are unknown. In the OT they are usually associated with a priestly official. According to Exod. 28.30 and Lev. 8.8, Moses placed the Urim and Thummim in the breastplate attached to the ephod worn by the high priest Aaron. They are often thought to be stones of some kind used for the purpose of divining God's will (Num. 27.21; 1 Sam. 14.41 LXX).

Some scholars believe that the Urim and Thummim functioned like dice. A petitioner who sought God's will would ask a question of God, and then the priest would use the Urim and Thummim to receive a 'yes' or 'no' answer. This procedure can be seen in 1 Sam. 23.9-12; 30.7-8. Using the Urim and Thummim did not guarantee that God would give an answer. There are a few instances in the OT where the Urim and Thummim were consulted to no response (1 Sam. 14.36-37; 28.6). They seem to have fallen into disuse after the establishment of the Davidic monarchy. Ezra 2.63 and Neh. 7.65 mention the Urim and Thummim, but it is uncertain whether these references indicate that these objects where still in use.

The Urim and Thummim have occasionally been mentioned in modern literature. References are made in James Joyce, *Ulysses*, Paulo Coelho, *The Alchemist*, John Milton, *Paradise Lost*, and Arthur Conan Doyle's short story *The Jew's Breastplate*. The Urim and Thummim play a central role in *The Revenge of the Wizard's Ghost* by John Belliars and *The Face of God* by Bill Myers.

In the Church of Jesus Christ of Latter-day Saints, the Urim and Thummim played a significant role in the life of Joseph Smith, the founder of the church. Smith claimed to have translated the *Book of Mormon* from a set of gold plates by using a pair of spectacles which contained the Urim and Thummim. Joseph Smith also asserted that he received other divine revelations by using the Urim and Thummim.

Several universities have incorporated the Urim and Thummim as their motto. These words, in Hebrew, are written across the open book displayed on the shield of Yale University. The Latin translation, *Lux et Veritas*, is written below. Indiana University and the University of Montana also have *Lux et Veritas* as their motto.

Recommended reading. Robertson, Edward. 'The Urim and Tummim: What Were They?' *Vetus Testamentum* 14 (1964) 67-74. Van Dam, Cornelius. *The Urim and Thummim: A Means of Revelation in Ancient Israel*. Winona Lake, IN: Eisenbrauns, 1997.

See also EPHOD; HIGH PRIEST; PROPHECY [EM]

Uzziah (Azariah). *Uzziyahu (azaryah)* 'Yah is my strength', 783–742 BCE. IN 2 Kings he is called Azariah (excluding 2 Kgs 15.13, 32, 34) while the Chronicler exclusively refers to him as Uzziah. The account in 2 Kings has a positive view of Uzziah, stating that he 'did what was right in the sight of the Lord, just as his father Amaziah had done' (2 Kgs 15.3). Chronicles provides a more complex portrayal. Although 2 Kings' account is embedded in Chronicles, Chronicles emphasizes his success (political, military, and agricultural) when he followed prophetic advice. However, the king eventually falls into the classical trap of hubris, decides to claim for himself priestly roles and thus is struck with a skin disease (leprosy) which makes him ritually impure and outcast.

The name Uzziah appears three times in Isaiah (1.1; 6.1; 7.1), once in both Hosea (1.1) and Amos (1.1). The name also appears in connection with a great earthquake mentioned in the book of Zech. 14.5 (perhaps also Amos 1.1). All of these examples were used by the author(s) as a way to date the words of the prophets.

Josephus embellished the narrative of the confrontation between the hubristic king and the priests (Josephus mentions that Uzziah threatened to kill them). According to Josephus's account, at the height of the confrontation a great earthquake 'rent' the temple and the sun shone upon Uzziah's face causing his leprous condition.

The name Uzziah occurs once in the NT in Jesus' genealogy through Joseph in Matt. 1.8-9. The author names Joram as the father of Uzziah. According to 1 Chron. 3.11-12, Joram is the third great-grandfather of Azariah/Uzziah (omitting Ahaziah, Joash, and Amaziah). These were likely omitted so that Matthew's genealogy fit his numbering system of 14 generations from Abraham to David, from David to the Exile, and from the Exile to Joseph.

In early Christian literature, Uzziah's story is used as an example and warning to reverence religious leadership. The scene is recalled in the Letter/Epistle of Ignatius to the Magnesians, the first *Treatise* of Cyprian, and the *Apostolic Constitutions*. These examples also tie Uzziah's attempt to act unlawfully as a priest to the stories of Korah, Dothan and Abiram who attempted to usurp power from Moses and Aaron (see Num. 16; 26.9-10). Similary, rabbinic literature recalls Uzziah's story and ties it together with the story of the golden calf (Exod. 32.1-9; Ps. 106.16-19) and, as in early Christian literature, with the followers of Korah.

Calvin uses Uzziah's story to show the separation between the office of a king and the priest and uses the example as a comparison to Melchizedek (who he sees as a type of Jesus Christ), the only biblical character presented as both a king and a priest (Calvin, *Hebrews*, 70; *Psalms*, 165). In Calvin's *Harmony of the Law* he couples the story of Miriam's leprosy with that of Uzziah's, emphasizing, as in his other commentaries, that the office of priest, in his opinion, is to be reserved solely for those consecrated (Calvin, *Harmony of the Law,* 4.25-30).

See also KORAH [CHB]

V

Vale of Tears. The term is refers to earthly sorrows that are to be left behind when one enters heaven. It is like a 'mortal coil', a poetic term that means the troubles of daily life and the strife and suffering of the world. The term invokes an image of a suffering sojourner struggling through a valley ('vale') of troubles and sorrow. The phrase is used in the prayer *Salve Regina*: 'To you do we send up our sighs, mourning and weeping in this *vale of tears*'. The expression is akin to Ps. 23.4's reference to the valley of the shadow of death: the phrase implies that the wickedness of the world makes it dark and reprieve comes only from divine salvation. The Valley of Baca in Ps. 84.6 is referred to as a 'valley [vale] of tears'. The New Advent Bible uses the term in Ps. 84.6-7 which reads, 'Blessed is the man whose help is from you: in his heart he has disposed to ascend by steps, in the *vale of tears*, in the place which he has set'. Additionally, the Douay–Rheims translation of the Bible features the term in the same verses. The Vale of Tears symbolizes a place of spiritual sorrow and suffering that God's people will escape from in the end. The promise is that God will wipe away tears and sorrows (Isa. 25.8; Rev. 21.4).

Vale of Tears is also referred to as The Valley of Tears (Hebrew: *emek habakha*). It is the name given to an area in the Golan Heights after it became the site of a major battle in the Yom Kippur War. On October 6, 1973 the Syrian Seventh Infantry Division attacked the Israeli Seventh Armored Brigade in the area between Mount Hermonit and a southern ridge known as 'Booster' in Israel, or Tel el Mekhafi in Arabic. Allegedly, the Syrians started the offensive with an artillery barrage, but failed to move tanks across the anti-tank ditch. This encounter spanned four days with the Syrians retreating for unknown reasons.

In literature, 'Vale of Tears' was used by Henry Wadsworth Longfellow in his book *The Beleaguered City*: 'Down the broad *Vale of Tears* afar / The spectral camp is fled; / Faith shineth as a morning star, / Our ghastly fears are dead'. Scottish poet, journalist and hymnologist James Montgomery also used the phrase in his book *The Issues of Life and Death* where he penned: 'Beyond this vale of tears / There is a life above, / Unmeasured by the flight of years; / And all that life is love'.

In the contemporary media, the term was used as the title of an episode of the television series *Kung Fu: The Legend Continues* (1996), starring the late David Carradine. A 2004 Public Broadcasting Service (PBS) documentary that chronicled the plight of women in Afghanistan also used the title *Veil of Tears*. The popular social media outlet YouTube features a short film entitled *Vale of Tears* (2008) by Stephen Paulus and Michael Dennis Browne.

In popular music, the bands Organum (1994), Dream Disciples (1997) and Minneapolis based Soul Asylum have each penned songs entitled 'Vale of Tears'. Additionally, the group *Fearful Symmetry* (2008) captured the term in their 2008 compact disc entitled 'This Sad Vale of Tears'.

See also VALLEY OF THE SHADOW OF DEATH [SNW]

Valley of Dry Bones. (See Dry Bones, Valley of).

Valley of the shadow of death. From the Hebrew *gay* (valley) and *tsalmaveth* (deep darkness). 'Shadow of death' occurs 20 times in the KJV (e.g., Job 3.5; 10.21, 22; 24.17; 34.22; 38.17; Amos 5.8; Jer. 2.6; 13.16). However, its strong impact can be felt in Pss. 23.4; 107.10, and Isa. 9.2. Early translators used 'the valley of the shadow of death' for *gay tsalmaveth*. They understood the Hebrew *tsalmaveth* to be a compound of *tsal* (shadow) and *maveth* (death). So the LXX translates it as *skia thanatou* (LXX Ps. 22.4), 'shadow of death'. However *tsalmaveth* is based on the root *tslm* meaning 'deep darkness'.

Psalm 23 relies on the image of a shepherd leading sheep through a valley or gorge where not even a glimpse of light can be found and where they fear their natural predators hide. This verse is meant to comfort people who are facing troubling times. It says 'God is with you even when you are terrified'. This psalm is widely used in funeral services because of the association with death.

St Irenaeus, Bishop of Lugdunum in Gaul, wrote in *Against All the Heresies*, 'For as the Lord 'went away in the midst of the shadow of death,' where the souls of the dead were'. He was referring to Jesus whom he believed to have descended into hell for three days after he was crucified in order to release the innocent who were trapped in hell. John Calvin, a French theologian and pastor during the Protestant Reformation, had the right meaning in mind when he was writing about the 'dark valley' in his commentaries (cf. In*stitutes of the Christian Religion* 1.17.11; 3.2.21; 3.2.28; 3.13.5). Only the shepherds could keep the sheep safe from dangers surrounding it when walking through a dark valley.

Geoffrey Chaucer writes in *The Parson's Tale*, 'the lond of mysese and of derknesse, where as is the shadwe of deeth, whee as ther is noon ordre or ordinaunce, but grisly drede that evere shal laste'. *The Duchess of Malfi* by English dramatist John Webster has a scene depicting Bosola's final moments, a reflection of John Calvin's comments in the Institutes: 'O, this gloomy world! / In what a shadow, or deep pit of darkness / Doth womanish and fearful mankind live!'

Modern musicians have included this idiom in their songs as well, e.g., in the Tossers' 'The Valley of the Shadow of Death': 'though you walk ever on / through the valley of the shadow of death'. Here, the 'you' refers to an individual who has died. Other examples are Group Crew I's 'Forgive Me': 'Lord though I walk through the valley of the shadow of death / I'm not scared cause You're holding my breath / I only fear that I don't have enough time left / To tell the world that there's no time left'; and Coolio's 'Gangsta's Paradise': 'As I walk through the valley of the shadow of death / I take a look at my life and realize there's not much left'.

See also DEATH; HELL; SHEPHERD PSALM; VALE OF TEARS; DRY BONES, VALLEY OF [EID]

Vanity. From the Hebrew *hebel*; the word occurs in the OT 76 times, 38 times in Ecclesiastes, where in most cases it is translated as 'vanity' in the NRSV and many other English versions. The word opens and closes the core section of the book in 1.2 and 12.8: 'Vanity of vanities. All is vanity'. The phrases 'all is vanity' and 'this is (also) vanity' form a refrain throughout the book (1.14; 2.11, 17, 23, 26; 4.4, 16; 5.10; 6.2, 9; 7.6; 8.14; 9.2). The literal meaning of *hebel* appears to be 'breath' or 'vapor', although it is more commonly used metaphorically in the majority OT references. In Ecclesiastes, the core metaphorical meaning is uncontrollability or incomprehensibility rather than nothingness or emptiness, as the LXX might have implied. However, the precise nuance of the word must be determined contextually.

In the Vulgate, Jerome translated *hebel* as *vanitas*, a word that means in Latin 'emptiness' or 'insubstantiality'. In the arts, *vanitas* is the type of painting concerned with the fragility of human beings and their world of desires and pleasures in the face of the inevitability and finality of death. The *vanitas* tradition was a particularly important element in still-life paintings in the Netherlands and elsewhere in Europe in the sixteenth and seventeenth centuries.

In contemporary understanding, vanity is often associated with pride in oneself or one's appearance. For instance, Charles Allan Gilbert published a widely known drawing depicting a double image in which the scene of a woman admiring herself in a mirror, when viewed from another perspective, appears to be a human skull. He picked up the phrase 'All is Vanity' from Ecclesiastes and named this famous optional illusion as such.

The vanity motif has also become a cliché in western literature. For example, it appears in William Dunbar's poem 'Of the World's Vanity'. Robert Browning's bishop in 'The Bishop Orders his Tomb at St Praxed's Church' (1845) ironically commences his deathbed request for a luxurious tomb inscribed with 'Vanity, saith the preacher, vanity'. The concluding paragraph of William Makepeace Thackeray's *Vanity Fair* (1847) also quotes Eccl. 1.2, '*Ah, Vanitas vanitatem!*'

In additional to literature, the vanity theme has influenced classical music such as Granville Bantock's *Vanity of Vanities* (1914). In contemporary popular music, Pearl Jam's 'Meaningless' (1992) is perhaps also an allusion to the key term *hebel* in Ecclesiastes, as is the Kansas song 'Dust in the Wind' (1977).

Recommended reading. Christianson, Eric S. *Ecclesiastes through the Centuries*. Blackwell Bible Commentaries. Pp. 98-141. Malden, MA: Blackwell, 2007. Miller, Douglas B. 'Qohelet's Symbolic Use of *hbl*'. *Journal of Biblical Literature* 117 (1998) 437-54.

See also ECCLESIASTES [EH]

Vashti. The first Queen of Ahasuerus in the Book of Esther (1.9, 11, 12, 15, 16, 17, 19; 2.1, 4, 17). Vashti is considered to be a Persian name meaning 'the beloved', 'the desired one', or 'the best'. Her name foreshadows the events of the text. During a state festival Ahasuerus summoned Vashti in order to show off her beauty (often interpreted to mean to appear naked or to dance) to the people of his court. Vashti refused, and in consultation with his lawyers, Ahasuerus made a royal decree that banished Vashti and declared all men to be rulers in their own homes. Whether or not Vashti was divorced or executed is a matter of debate. The removal of Vashti opens the door for Esther to become Queen in her stead and save the Jewish people for imminent doom.

While modern feminist movements tend to view Vashti as a hero and a martyr for her actions, historical interpretations have not been favorable. In Jewish midrash, Vashti was seen to be deserving of her punishment due to the philosophy of measure for measure justice; since God would not allow someone who was innocent to be punished, then Vashti must have deserved the punishment she received. These interpretations claim that Vashti was the great-granddaughter of Nebuchadnezzar and therefore her death was a means of fulfilling Isa. 14.22. However, they also cast Vashti as an astute political schemer who ended up getting caught in her own political web. The early rabbis also claim that presenting herself to the king would not have been outside her character, as exhibitionism would fit with her evil nature, but that God had done something to maim her physically, such as leprosy, the addition of a tail, or even the appearance of male genitalia.

In the nineteenth century, Vashti changes from a villain to a hero. Many women authors saw Vashti as a role model. Those who followed the Cult of Domesticity applauded her refusal to prance immodestly before her husband and his guests and therefore upheld the separate status of women and their virtues despite her disobedience to her husband. This is exemplified in the work of Harper and Helen Hunt Jackson. In contrast, women of the emerging women's rights movement, such as Elizabeth Cady Stanton, Anna Howard Shaw, Ella Wheeler Wilcox and Lucinda Chandler, embraced her as one who throws off tyranny and sexual exploitation.

Modern times have seen Vashti highlighted as the leader of the first feminist revolution and she has been embraced by diverse feminist groups as a role model and ancestor in the fight for equality. This is emphasized by Hanna Kahat's religious feminist movement the Kolech. Particularly important to these groups is a desire to reverse the contrast usually made between the wanton Vashti and the sweet Esther. They view Vashti as the protector of female sexuality who refuses to comply with patriarchal society, whereas Esther is the one who uses her sexuality to function within the establishment.

This spirit has even crept into Purim celebrations with the recent production of 'Vashti was Right', a musical that dares to question the historical interpretations particularly the role of Queens.

See also ESTHER, BOOK OF; PURIM [EW]

Vaticinium ex eventu. A Latin term referring to a prophecy believed to be retrospective. That is, the critic examining a prophecy claims that it was written after events had occurred and not before, so the prophecy is a prediction after the fact.

The is usually used in religious contexts which psychology calls precognition or paranormal. There are two sides to the use of the term. The traditional Christian side does not use it in studies of the Bible. It is not a term usually found in Bible dictionaries, or in dictionaries of Christian theological terms in Latin or Greek. It is not used in evangelical theological studies or biblical studies, although it is frequently used in historical-critical biblical studies. Neither traditional Jews nor Christians believe that the prophecies in the scriptures are after the fact predictions.

The term is used most commonly by those who do not believe that prophecy of future events is possible, either because it does not conform to their understanding of the divine, or because there is no God to inspire prophecy. Modernists usually discount precognition or premonition of events as the products of hindsight bias. That is, the person making a claim to knowledge of an event before it actually occurred was actually mentally reordering the times and knowledge of the event so that the mind believed it came after the prior knowledge. In other words, sceptics reduce prophecy or any form of parapsychology to a psychological phenomenon that can be explained by ordinary psychological processes. This is not acceptable to biblical believers except in carefully defined circumstances. However, biblical believers have to beware of simply holding a noncritical bias in favor of prophecy just as modernists hold a non-critical bias in opposition to prophecy.

Both believers and non-believers agree that *vaticinia ex eventu* may be legitimately used for some non-biblical works that make predictions. The reason they can agree is because the evidence for identifying a prophecy as a *vaticinia ex eventu* is either adequate or the evidence offered makes the conclusion necessary. For example the *Aeneid* of Virgil describes events occurring in the time of the Trojan War, 1200 years earlier. Among his prophecies is the curse of Dido that is then considered predictive of the Punic Wars. The involvement of the gods and goddesses by Virgil gives the *Aeneid* a divine authority that elevates it beyond mere human history.

Other ancient retrospective prophecies include the *Uruk Prophecy* that predicts events about Nebuchadnezzar, the *Prophecy of Nefertiti* and the *Demotic Chronicle*. No modern person whether believer or non-believer would accept the prophecies in these and many other ancient works as more than *vaticinia ex eventu*. Similarly, historical-critical biblical scholars question whether prophecies such as those recorded in Mark 13 are authentic utterances of Jesus or oracles formulated after the fall of Jerusalem (70 CE).

Claims that ancient non-biblical passages are parallels to biblical prophecies and are therefore *vaticinia ex eventu* can be refuted by noting that all human thought or emotion is 'psychological' and that all literary forms are also human. To recognize common human attributes in biblical prophecies with non-biblical *vaticinia ex eventu* passages is to recognize common humanity. This does not necessarily warrant the conclusion that the biblical passages are merely human and not from a divine origin.

Recommended reading. Cook, Robert R. 'Divine Foreknowledge: Some Philosophical Issues'. *Vox evangelica* 20 (1990) 57-72. Osswald, Eva. 'Zum Problem der vaticinia ex eventu'. *Zeitschrift für die alttestamentliche Wissenschaft* 75 (1963) 27-44.

See also PROPHET, PROPHECY [AJW]

Veil. A veil is generally a covering placed over all or part of the face. They have been used since ancient times in many cultures.

Veils appear in several contexts in the Bible. Some of the Hebrew words used in the OT may also refer to a shawl, curtain, or any type of wrap. They are generally a traditional sign of modesty. Thus, the prophets frequently use the image of removing a veil, coupled with stripping of clothing and jewellery, as a symbol of shame.

Although generally associated with women, men also wear veils at times. The most notable biblical example is Moses, who, after meeting God, wore a veil when meeting the people (Exod. 34.29-35). Most commentators read the passage as stating that Moses had a shining face after the meeting, but Michelangelo's sculpture of Moses is based on an older reading of him having horns.

In the NT, 'veil' is used in the KJV for the curtain separating the inner chamber of the temple (holy of holies). Only the high priest entered this space, and that only once a year. The synoptic gospels record that this curtain tore when Jesus died.

Paul's correspondence with the church at Corinth mentions veils in several contexts. 1 Corinthians 11.6-7 states that women ought to cover their heads, while men ought not to do so. This is generally interpreted as instruction that women should wear hats, a veil, or let their hair grow long. Paul's rationale is that men are the 'image and reflection' of God, while women are the 'reflection' of men. Commentators note that the words are unclear about what kind of covering Paul specifies; the language could also refer to shawls or a plain hairstyle. Overall, it reflects a cultural attitude of the day that attached shame to women with shaved heads, resulting in frequent discussion of cultural accommodation in religious practice.

Paul also uses the veil as a figure of speech to refer to human limitation and lack of understanding. In 2 Cor. 3.14-16, he refers to the story from Exodus of Moses and his veil to argue that those who refuse to accept Jesus as the Messiah lack understanding. In 2 Cor. 4.3, he uses similar symbolism to refer to all who turn from God.

Veils often appear as symbols of the mystery of death and the afterlife. This is the case with many hymns. Similar imagery also appears in Nathaniel Hawthorne's short story 'The Minister's Black Veil' (1837) or in J.K. Rowling, in *Harry Potter and the Order of the Phoenix* (2003), where the Veil is the barrier between realms of the living and the dead.

See also HOLY OF HOLIES; PROPHETS; TEMPLE [TV]

Vengeance is Mine. From the Hebrew *li* (to me) and *naqam* (vengeance). This expression first appears in Deut. 32.35. It is used near the conclusion of the Song of Moses in a description of the superiority of the God of Israel, over against the gods of the surrounding nations. God will mete out vengeance and recompense upon the nations for their injustice toward God's people.

The expression is referred to twice in the NT. In Rom. 12.19, Paul counsels his readers, 'never avenge yourselves, but leave it to the wrath of God, for it is written, 'Vengeance is mine, I will repay, says the Lord.'' The author of Hebrews (10.30) cites the phrase as a warning to those who would turn away from God by means of their rejection of his son.

Early Christian interpretation of the phrase offers differing motivations for abstention from revenge. Origen comments on Rom. 12.19, 'For if we avenge ourselves, there is not much we can do apart from demanding an eye for an eye or a tooth for a tooth, or else insulting others as they have insulted us. But if we reserve these things to the vengeance of God, he will without doubt punish them far more severely than we ever could' (*Commentary on the Epistle to the Romans* 5.84). On the contrary, Ambrose of Milan (fourth century) writes, 'Since God said …

'Vengeance is mine, I shall repay,' he says in the Gospel that we should pray for those who harm us, in order that he who promised vengeance might not seek revenge against them. For [God] wants to forgive by your will, which is fitting according to his promise. But if you seek revenge, you have it, since the unjust man is punished more by his thoughts than by judicial severity (*Letter* 14 *Extra Coll* [63].84).

Perhaps not surprisingly, modern reflection upon this phrase has also been variegated. Twentieth-century British writer G.K. Chesterton wrote that, 'Many saints and sages have denounced violence. But they treated vengeance as something too great for man' (*George Bernard Shaw*, 56). In contrast, Irish playwright George Bernard Shaw, at least according to Chesterton, 'treats vengeance as something too small for man—a monkey trick he ought to have outlived, a childish storm of tears which he ought to be able to control' (*George Bernard Shaw*, 56). John A. Moroso, an American writer, wrote a novel entitled *Vengeance is Mine* (1917), also adapted to film.

In contemporary culture, the phrase has come to express one's justification in seeking revenge for wrongs incurred. The popular American sitcom *30 Rock* aired an episode entitled 'Vengeance is Mine'. The second season of the British television drama *Messiah* is entitled 'Messiah II: Vengeance is Mine', and deals with a serial killer who takes revenge on all those implicated in the wrongful imprisonment of his father. American rock singer Alice Cooper's eighteenth solo album, *Along Came a Spider*, includes a track entitled 'Vengeance is Mine'.

See also JUSTICE; RETRIBUTION; REVENGE

[NTB]

Vessel. Hebrew: *keli*; Greek *keramion* (a jar); also *skeuos*. This biblical term is most commonly used to denote a container made by a potter (e.g., 1 Chron. 4.23; cf. Rom. 9.21-23). Specific attention is at times given to unique vessels or containers used or related to temple worship (e.g., 1 Kgs 7.48; Heb. 9.21). Reference in the NT is famously connected to Passover preparation when Jesus tells his disciples to look for a person carrying a jar filled with water (Luke 22.10). While the implication is uncertain, there is an aspect of the unfolding of God's sovereign implied in this narrative.

In the context of relations between husbands and wives, 1 Pet. 3.7-9 admonishes the husband to treat his wife with honor as 'the weaker vessel' (*hōs asthenesterō skeuei*), traditionally taken to refer to the stereotype of women as less capable of enduring physical or emotional strain than men (cf. 1 Thess. 4.4).

In Kabbalah, the 'breaking of the vessels' is a stage in creation where the vessels (*kelim*) created by God to contain the divine light are too small, and are shattered by the light shining into them. Canadian novelist Adelen Wiseman uses this legend as the inspiration for her novel *Crackpot* (1974), the story of a young Jewish woman who prevails over a life of abuse and deprivation to repair the damage done to her in childhood.

See also EARTHEN VESSEL; WOMAN [DR]

Vine/Vineyard. From the Hebrew *gopher* and *kerem* or Greek *ampelos* and *ampelōn*. Given the abundance of vineyards in the Middle East, they are an integral part of the Bible's cultural landscape. Their first mention is in Genesis 9, when Noah plants a vineyard and later becomes intoxicated. Joseph interprets a cupbearer's dream about a vineyard (Gen. 40) and receives blessings from his father Jacob using the vine as a symbol of his future fruitfulness (Gen. 49). Prophets employ the image of Israel as a vineyard tended by God that becomes fruitless (e.g., Ps. 80; Ezek. 15, 17; Hos. 10.1; Jer. 2.21, 8.13; most notably Isa. 5.1-7, the 'Song of the Vineyard'). Elsewhere, God warns Israel that if they continue to sin, they will plant vineyards but not eat their produce (Deut. 28), but if they repent, they will enjoy the produce (Jer. 31; Amos 9.14); times of peace are rendered poetically as everyone dwelling 'under their vines and fig trees' (1 Kgs 4.25; 2 Kgs 18.31; Mic. 4.4). The Song of Songs uses the vineyard both as one of its main settings and as a description of the lovers' sexuality.

Jesus uses the vineyard as a symbol of the Kingdom of God. That this Kingdom is not limited to Israel is shown in the Matthew 20 parable about a landowner who hires men to work in his vineyard in the morning; he later hires more men and then pays the same wage to all regardless of the hours worked. Picturing his own reception in the world, Jesus tells another parable of a landowner who sends three servants to collect the produce from his vineyard; when they are all beaten and turned away, he sends his son, who is murdered (Mark 12; Luke 20). (The page heading of this 'Parable of the Vineyard' in Luke 20 was misspelled the 'Parable of the Vinegar' by printer John Baskett in 1717, causing that rare edition to be known as the 'Vinegar Bible'). In John 15, Jesus refers to himself as the 'true vine' and his followers as the branches, which speaks of the union of the believer with Christ. It further points to his sacrificial shedding of blood, symbolized in the Eucharist by drinking wine (Matt. 26). These implications are embraced by the Vineyard Church, which, founded in 1983 by John Wimber, is currently one of the fastest growing Evangelical movements in the world.

The vine and vineyard appear in several of George Herbert's poems, including 'Love-joy' and 'Good Friday' (1633). Julia Ward Howe's 'Battle Hymn of the Republic' (1861), written to encourage Union Army enlistment during the Civil War, begins with the vibrant image of God in Revelation 14 tramping out the grapes of his wrath in a wine press. In 1939, John Steinbeck used the same image in *Grapes of Wrath*, implying that the government and upper classes ignored the suffering of starving migrant families during the Great Depression. The celebrated poet of the Canadian Arctic Robert William Service wrote a short poem, 'My Vineyard' (1956), wherein the narrator acknowledges that despite the universe's vastness, God cares for him just as he cares for his vineyard.

Recommended reading. Laney, Carl. 'Abiding in John: The Analogy of the Vine in John 15:1-6'. *Biblitheca sacra* 146 (1989) 55-66. Wallace, Howard. 'Harvesting the Vineyard'. In *Seeing Signals, Reading Signs*. Ed. Mark O'Brien and Howard Wallace. Pp. 117-29. London and New York: T. & T. Clark, 2004.

See also EUCHARIST; LABORERS IN THE VINEYARD; SOUR GRAPES; WINE [KCM]

Virgin/Virgin Birth. More correctly, the 'virginal conception' (and not to be confused with the Immaculate Conception), a phrase derived from the Greek word *parthenogesis* meaning the beginning ('genesis') of life in a virgin (*parthenos*). With reference to the birth of Jesus, this term refers to the conception of Jesus without the fertilization of the egg by a male through sexual intercourse. The Gospel writers say that Jesus was conceived before Mary had slept with Joseph (Matt. 1.18; Luke 1.31).

Critical thinkers do not accept the historicity of the virginal conception of Jesus for the reason that the Gospel writers read OT prophecies out of context. Matthew, for example, imposes the virginal conception of Jesus on Isa. 7.14. The Hebrew version of Isaiah uses *almah*, which means a woman of marriageable age and not necessarily a virgin in the biological and strict sense and not the word *bethulah*, which means a woman who has not been 'deflowered'. Matthew replaces Hebrew *almah* with Greek *parthenos* to imply that Jesus was born miraculously. Isaiah's prophecy refers to an ordinary conception by a young woman; Matthew takes this prophecy to imply conception by a sexually inexperienced virgin. Traditionally, miraculous birth is often associated with great people such as politicians, philosophers, scientists, religious figures and so on. Paul, one of the greatest theologians of the NT, says that Jesus was 'born of a woman, born under the law' (Gal. 4.4) and 'was descended of David according to the flesh' (Rom. 1.3). Subsequent generations of Christians, however, hold the belief that Jesus was miraculously conceived through the work of the Holy Spirit.

Many western artists have portrayed the angelic annunciation of the miraculous birth to the Virgin Mary, e.g., Andrea del Sarto (c. 1528), Fra Angelico (1433–34, 1440–42), Giotto (1306).

Recommended reading. Brown, R.E. *The Birth of the Messiah: A Commentary on the Infancy Narratives in Matthew and Luke*. Garden City, NY: Doubleday, 1977.

See also ANNUNCIATION; HOLY SPIRIT; IMMACULATE CONCEPTION; INFANCY NARRATIVES; MARY, THE VIRGIN [ET]

Voice from the whirlwind. The Hebrew word for whirlwind is *supah* ('hurricane'; Job 37.9) with a root meaning 'to snatch away'—a violent blast of wind that sweeps away everything in its path. Whirlwinds are often used to indicate God's activity, fitting accompaniments to epiphanies, visible manifestations of God (e.g., Ezek. 1.4, Nah. 1.3; Zech. 9.14).

In the Book of Job, the voice of God answers Job from a whirlwind (38.1; 40.6). Job, a wisdom book uses the whirlwind as the vehicle for Job's epiphany. Until the voice from the whirlwind speaks to him, God has been *Deus absconditus*, hidden and unknowable to the human mind. Job who had been suffering without a clue now experiences God's presence as he had previously wanted. Perhaps accepting his friends' false idea that sin and only sin causes suffering, Job has sought God's presence in order to prove that his suffering is innocent. So God, in a series of speeches (Job 38.1–42.6), replies to Job's complaints.

Some commentators suspect that God appearing to Job as a voice from a whirlwind surprised Job more than the fact of his appearing in any form. The use of voice from the whirlwind signifies that God is not a mere storm deity. Rather, he is a power that is greater than nature and a being who is hidden and yet can still be manifest to human beings.

God accuses Job of doubting that God has a plan for the world (38.2). Doubting that there is a purpose to life is a very common suspicion when people are confronted with evil in the world. God then demands that Job answer some questions about the natural order. Many of these natural science questions put to Job can be answered today; however, vv. 12-38 show that the operations of nature are beyond human strength. Job 38.39–39.30 are questions dealing with God's care of the animal world. Job 40.1-2 finishes God's first speech and all Job can do is put his hand over his mouth for he has nothing to say.

God has more to teach Job, so once again, the voice from the whirlwind speaks. It challenges Job to control Leviathan (probably crocodile) or Behemoth (probably hippopotamus). The point is that humans (in Job's day and to the present) lack the wisdom to control things which only God can create. All this forces Job to acknowledge that the purposes of God point to the magnitude of divine power. Job replies that he has misspoken.

Voice(s) of the whirlwind is a phrase use in a number of works to refers to the 'whirlwind' of revolution, e.g., the Chinese Cultural Revolution. Some writers have used 'voice from the whirlwind' as a motif that allows people in the storms of human affairs to tell their stories. This includes books such as *The Whirlwind of War: Voices of the Storm, 1861–1865*, by Stephen B. Oates. In 1987, Walter Jon Williams published a cyberpunk science novel, *Voices of the Whirlwind*, alluding to the chaotic life of the hero. The Coen brothers' 2009 film *A Serious Man*, based on the Book of Job, ends with a scene of a menacing whirlwind approaching a school as the title character's son looks on and a teacher struggles to open the door of his school's tornado shelter.

Recommended reading. Perdue, Leo G., and W. Clark Gilpin (eds.) *Voices from the Whirlwind: Interpreting the Book of Job.* Nashville, TN: Abingdon Press, 1994. Vicchio, Stephen J. *The Voice from the Whirlwind: The Problem of Evil and the Modern World.* Eugene, OR: Wipf & Stock Publishers, 2001.

See also EVIL; GOD; JOB; WISDOM [AJW]

Voice crying in the wilderness. Latin: *vox clamantis in deserto*. The source of the metaphor of the voice crying in the wilderness is the initial words of the commission of the prophet in Second Isaiah. The latter is found at the beginning of the Book of the Consolation of Israel (Isa. 40–55) where a voice from the so-called council of heaven cries out in the wilderness (Isa. 40.3a). All four Gospels cite the text: 'the voice of one crying out in the wilderness' (Mark 1.3a; cf. Matt. 3.3b; Luke 3.4b; John 1.23a). However, two alterations are noteworthy: first, the referent of the quotation has now become John the Baptizer; second, the evangelists in accordance with the LXX, have re-associated the 'voice crying' with 'the wilderness'.

The unabridged *OED* provides the following definition of the phrase 'in the wilderness': 'unrecognized, out of favor'. Thus 'a politician, political party, etc ... out of office' can be deemed 'in the wilderness'. The earliest OT referent is the 40-year consignment of the Israelites to the wilderness for their questioning of the Lord's deliverance into the Promised Land (Num. 14.33). Hence a 'voice crying in the wilderness' in modern parlance serves to denote an individual whose warnings about the truth of a situation, or the dangers inherent in it, are unheeded. Yet the message of the Baptist would appear to have enjoyed wide acceptance (see Mark 1.5; Luke 3.7. 9, 21; Matt. 3.5, 7; John 1.19).

A classic example of a 'voice crying in the wilderness' is late British Prime Minister Sir Winston Churchill in the years prior to World War II. As early as 1930, he ascertained the threat of German aggression under Adolf Hitler and for a decade urged the nation to prepare for war. Unfortunately, his warnings fell on deaf ears. Churchill finally assumed leadership on the day of Hitler's *Blitzkrieg* advance on France—May 10, 1940. Still, lack of preparation would nearly cost Great Britain the war.

Another example would be American lawyer Ralph Nader who has invested four decades of his life to advocacy for environmental protection, consumer and automotive safety, and as a watchdog over corporate corruption. Initially his challenges to the *status quo* served to alienate him from the rest of society, but his dogged persistence and hard-won victories came to be an inspiration to like-minded others. His numerous personally funded foundations continue to represent a challenge to corporate, industrial and government policies.

See also JOHN THE BAPTIST; ISAIAH; WILDERNESS [NRP]

Voice of the turtle. The expression 'voice of the turtle' (KJV) appears in Song of Songs 2.12, as a herald of spring. The Hebrew word in this verse is *tor* which means turtledove (the species in Latin is *Streptopelia turtur*, etymologically related). The turtledove is also referred to as a herald of spring in Jer. 8.7. The Hebrew word for turtle, *tzav*, is not found here or anywhere else in the OT. Whether the translator who rendered turtledove as turtle (Old English, from Latin *turtur,* probably of imitative origin) thought it was a more poetic form of the word is unknown. There is no consistency in the KJV usage of 'turtle' in place of 'turtledove'. It uses them interchangeably when listing sacrifices; in three places (Lev. 12.8, 15.29, Num. 6.10) 'turtle' is used, while in all other such lists, 'turtledove' is found. The translation was rarely carried forth in later translations (exceptions include the English Revised Version, Webster's Bible Translation, and the Geneva Study Bible).

The expression 'voice of' occurs hundreds of times in the Bible, but only twice referring to the voice of an animal (generally the voice is God's, the people's, a person's, or heard in song). Other than the turtledove in Song of Songs 2.12, the voice of the *shakhal* (poetic word for lion) is heard in Job 4.10.

The turtle, of course, has no voice. The voice of the turtledove, also known as the mourning dove, is parodied by Chaucer in *Merchant's Tale* (part of the *Canterbury Tales*; 1380s). A popular singing group chose the name Voice of the Turtle because of its particular resonance. Their logo is an ancient lyre with a tortoise shell as its resonating box, incorporating the image in an interesting way. *Voice of the Turtle* was the title of a 1943 play by John William Van Druten; the 1947 film based on this play starred none other than Ronald Reagan. The same title was used for a 1968 album of folk music by John Fahey. *Voice of the Turtle* is the title of two anthologies: of Cuban stories by Peter R. Bush, and of American Indian Literature 1900–1970 by Paula Gunn Allen, and of a 2009 novel by Mary Mills Ullrich. A reviewer in the magazine *Science* titled his review of a new guide to sea turtles 'Marine Ecology: Voice of the Turtle' (Fredric Janzen; book is *Sea Turtles: A Complete Guide to their Biology, Behavior, and Conservation* by James R. Spotila; Johns Hopkins University Press, Baltimore, MD, 2004).

See also LYRE [HL]

Vow. Hebrew: *nadar*; Greek: *euchē*. A vow or oath is a solemn promise made to God, a person, or family. It is typically guaranteed by the integrity of the one making the promise. An object of great personal value is often part of that guarantee being forfeit in the event the vow or oath is not performed. The Bible offers many examples of the serious nature of vows. Individuals, families, and Israel itself made vows under various circumstances. God is also portrayed as one who makes and keeps vows. Invocation of the name of God as witness to the intention is characteristic of vows and marks their ultimate seriousness. This is illustrated in the account of Jephthah's daughter (Judg. 11.35) which, despite its tragic subject matter, speaks of the irrevocable character of a vow made to God. The pattern of the vow and its solemnity is communicated in a relatively predictable way, with variations. It may involve only the stated intention of the one making the vow.

There are numerous examples of vows in the Bible. Numbers records the terms of the Nazirite vow and the process by which failure of the vow can be rectified (6.1-27). The Nazirite was a visible sign within ancient Israel of their particular relationship to God. John the Baptist may have been bound by similar vows. To swear an oath often invoked the name of God for ultimate solemnity. Abraham's search for a wife for Isaac involves just such an invocation with the placement of his servant's hand under Abraham's thigh (Gen. 24.2-3). Also of note is Abraham's recollection of God's oath to him (Gen. 24.7) recalling Gen. 12.7. Jacob's vow to God at Bethel (Gen. 28.20) has no witness other than God. Jacob rehearses his vow to God before Laban (Gen. 31.13). Here, Jacob recalls that God (Gen. 28.13) renewed the Abrahamic vow, thus stressing its absolute character.

To violate a vow is to invite serious and long-term harm upon oneself. The Wisdom tradition of the OT is similarly clear that vows made to God must not be taken lightly (e.g., Eccl. 5.4-5; Prov. 20.25). Therefore, one should not be delinquent in fulfilling any vow, much less one of this kind.

Examples of vows from the NT are found at Acts 18.18; 21.23. In the first instance, Paul is described as cutting his hair because he was under a vow. This may be the conclusion of a temporary Nazirite vow, although the text is unclear. The second example involves a strategy of the Jerusalem Council to calm Jewish-Christian concerns regarding Paul's alleged disregard of Jewish law. Those under a vow are taken by Paul to the temple to perform the purification procedures required. In the event, the strategy failed. A vow may be reflected in Acts 5.1-11. Although no vow is explicitly mentioned, the deaths of Ananias and Sapphira are linked to what may have been an interior vow. Their failure to fulfil the vow is described as 'lying to God' (Acts 5.4).

The same solemnity concerning vows and oaths is found in legal systems whether made with belief in God or not. Weddings usually involve declarations made as vows of love. Installation for public office is also attended by oaths. Persons may refuse oaths on a Bible in court in which case alternate procedures apply. This is usually a matter of conscience. Rituals for making vows and oaths normally reflect their importance and gravity.

See also Ananias and Sapphira; Jephthah's daughter; Nazirite; Wisdom [JKS]

Vulgate. The Vulgate is the name commonly given to a translation of the Bible into Latin made from about 382 to 405–406 CE. The name comes from the Latin word for 'common' or 'shared', signifying its widespread use.

It is mostly the work of Jerome (Hieronymus) (c. 345–420), one of the leading scholars of his day. Jerome produced Latin translations of other works, and as a proponent of the monastic life, was engaged in several theological controversies.

As the Catholic Church replaced Greek with Latin as its official language, Pope Damasus commissioned Jerome to correct older Latin translations of the Gospels and Psalms. As the project progressed, it became a translation of the entire Bible. Previous Latin translations had been from the Greek translation known as the Septuagint, but Jerome translated the Hebrew portions from the original language.

As Jerome translated the OT, he distinguished between the books and portions written in Hebrew or Aramaic and those written in Greek. He did not regard the Greek portions as having the same authority as the Hebrew portions. He argued that these 'apocrypha' could be read for education, but not for establishing doctrine. This position was revived in the Renaissance and taken up by several of the Protestant reformers in the sixteenth century.

The Vulgate was the official Bible of the Catholic church through the medieval period. The Council of Trent, called in response to the work of the early Protestant reformers, affirmed the Vulgate, with corrections and including the deuterocanonical portions, as the authentic and standard Bible at its fourth session in 1546. Amid a multitude of versions, Clement VIII issued a corrected version in 1592. This was revised in 1907 and 1969.

Many medieval and later translations of the Bible into other languages were made using the Vulgate. The scholar Erasmus produced a Greek text in 1516. This text became the basis of many Reformation translations. Many of these translations challenged long-held theological positions, such as the sacramental system of the medieval church.

The Douay–Rheims Bible of 1582–1610, an English translation that remains the preferred version for some Roman Catholics, was made from the Vulgate. In 1966, the Jerusalem Bible broke from this tradition, being translated from the original languages, as have later Catholic translations such as the New American Bible.

The Vulgate is also important today as a basis for textual study, as it gives clues to the underlying texts used. When compared to such texts, it also gives clues to theological thought in its time. Many translators continue to use it as a reference for understanding obscure words or difficult phrases.

See also Apocrypha, Deuterocanonicals and Intertestamentals; Aramaic language; Canon; Greek language; Hebrew language; Septuagint

[TV]

W

Wages/Wages of Sin. Wages in the OT are denoted by one of several Hebrew words: *sakar* (Gen. 31.8; Exod. 2.9); *maskoret* (Gen. 29.15, 31.41; Ruth 2.12); or *pᵉulla* (Lev. 19.13; Ps. 109.20). These are translated as 'hire' or 'reward'. In the NT two Greek words are translated as 'hire' or 'reward'—*misthos* (John 4.36) and *opsonion* (Luke 3.4; 2 Cor. 11.8; Luke 6.23).

The idea of wages as something of value for work performed includes the idea that labor is the property of a worker and wages are the price paid for that property. The first biblical instance of the payment of wages is the exchange in kind between Jacob and his father-in-law, Laban (Gen. 29.15, 20; 31.7-8, 41). The payment of wages for services rendered in money developed in more urban societies, e.g., Egypt.

Wages in general are mentioned in several passages including Hag. 1.6 and Ezek. 29.18-19 in the OT and in John 4.36 in the NT. The rate of wages was cited in Matt. 20.2 (Parable of the Householder) as a denarius per day (16 cents). Unscrupulous employers could set wage rates unfairly. To meet this problem, the Mosaic Law required the prompt and fair payment of wages, especially to day laborers whose ability to eat and provide for their families was totally dependent upon their wages (Lev. 19.13). Failure by an employer to pay wages promptly was censurable behavior (Deut. 15.18). Withholding wages was denounced by prophets (Jer. 22.13; Mal. 3.5) and in the NT by James (5.4).

In the NT, workers were paid in actuality (Mark 1.20) and the principle announced that 'the laborer deserves to be paid' (Luke 10.7). Paul used this principle to make the point that those who work to earn their wages are not reciving a gift but what is legally due them. Salvation is the gift of God, but damnation is the recompense due those who work for the grim wages of sin, i.e., death (Rom. 6.23). This verse was stressed by Reformation leaders including John Calvin (*Commentary on Romans*). Matthew Tyndale in his *Obedience of a Christian Man* (1.177) says that the wages of sin are paid to the devil for partaking of the pleasures of this world. Christopher Marlowe's character Dr Faustus earns the wages of sin for deliberately misinterpreting Rom. 6.23.

John Bunyan's Christian in *Pilgrim's Progress* says that he could not live on the wages of sin. Tennyson's poem 'Wages' uses Bunyan as does Thomas Carlyle's 'The French Revolution'. Richard Wright's *Black Boy* is a commentary on the American 'gospel of success'. The term occurs in pop culture music titles and to suggest the evil nature of detective and mystery stories. It is used in titles on a range of topics, from sexually transmitted diseases (STDs), to economic issues to social problems.

This idea that labor is the property of the laborer is known as the labor theory of value, e.g., by John Locke in his *Two Treatises on Civil Government* (1689), by Adam Smith in *The Wealth of Nations*, by Karl Marx in *Das Kapital* (1867) and by other economists.

See also DEATH; FILTHY LUCRE; FRUIT OF THE SPIRIT; GRACE; MONEY; SATAN; SIN; SIN WILL FIND YOU OUT; SWEAT OF YOUR BROW   [AJW]

Walking on Water. In Mark 6.45-52 (cf. Matt. 14.22-33; John 6.15-21), the disciples are crossing the sea of Galilee at night in a boat with the wind against them, and Jesus appears to them, walking on the sea. The disciples are terrified, thinking he is a phantom, so Jesus admonishes them not to be afraid; he enters the boat, and the wind ceases. Matthew adds the detail of Peter offering to join Jesus on the water; when Jesus agrees, Peter walks on the sea, only to lose heart; he begins to sink and Jesus saves him, admonishing him for his lack of faith (14.28-30). The scene is evocative of OT passages that proclaim the power of God over the waves (e.g., Ps. 42.7-8; 65.7-8; 89.8-9; 107.23-32).

In western culture, the phrase to 'walk on water' means to do the impossible. The scene of Jesus walking on the sea is a favorite scene of devotional art, and it frequently figures in the titles of books, movies (e.g., *Walking on Water*, 2002), and popular hymns. In films, characters with godlike qualities are sometimes portrayed as walking on water, e.g., Truman Burbank in *The Truman Show* (1998), the Forest God in *Princess Mononoke* (1997); *Jesus of Montreal* (1989) introduces the Mary Magdalene character, Mireille Fontaine, in a scene evocative of the biblical episode.

See also BOAT; FAITH; PETER; SEA; WATER

[MEM]

War in Heaven. Contrary to the popular image of heaven as an abode of perpetual peace, the Bible specifically portrays heaven as a battle-arena in the protracted warfare between good and evil. Revelation (12.7-9) describes a war in heaven between Michael (and his allied angels) against the dragon

(Satan/Devil) and his minions, where the latter are defeated and cast out.

While some Christians have interpreted Revelation's 'war in heaven' as a reference to Lucifer's angelic rebellion against God resulting in the war of fallen angels prior to the fall of humankind, it is more typical, however, for Christians to read this passage as a prophecy of a future strife in the endtimes. Many Christians holding to Dispensational beliefs are convinced that the war in heaven is connected to the events of the Great Tribulation, although interpretations of the timing of events vary in Dispensational frameworks. Nonetheless, Christian theological readings often attempt to situate the violent narrative and symbolism of Revelation within a larger cosmological and/or eschatological framework.

Western culture has been fascinated by the theme of heavenly battle and spiritual combat. Hesiod's *Theogony* depicts the Olympian gods defeating the Titans and casting them down to Tartarus. Likewise, Isaiah (14.4-19) equates the *hubris* of the King of Babylon to the morning star that will be cast down from heaven to earth. Extra-canonical books such as the *Enoch* and *Jubilees* deal extensively with angelic warfare.

Depictions of celestial warfare and heavenly strife have proliferated across the canvases of western artists as evidenced in the works of Hieronymus Bosch, Albrecht Dürer and Gustave Doré, among others. The Middle Ages saw a glorification of chivalrous themes of valor and bravery in which battles with dragons (such as St George and the Dragon) became popular motifs among knights. Military prowess was stoked by the paragon of St Michael the Archangel. In the late Middle Ages, western literature saw a retelling of the 'war in heaven' account through John Milton's *Paradise Lost* (1667), which popularized the interpretation of the war as a result of Satan's rebellion *before* the Fall.

Notions of heavenly warfare remain prominent in modern cultural media including films, art, music, literature, and even theologically inspired political ideology. Celestial conflicts between good and evil have become box-office hits, with numerous movies depicting angelic warriors fighting against corrupt angels, demonic hoards, alien invaders, or, belatedly, vampires: e.g., *The Prophecy* (1995); *Gabriel* (2007); *Kingdom of Heaven* (2005); *Legion* (2010); and *Priest* (2011). The graphic novel series 'War in Heaven', by Jeff Krelitz, is planned for release as a motion picture trilogy with the first film titled: *The Truth About the War in Heaven: Declaration of War*.

Such depictions have caught the eye of computer programmers who have released a video game entitled, *The War in Heaven: A Christian Action Game* (1999), where one can virtually participate in spiritual warfare by opting to join either the heavenly or fallen angels.

The biblical 'war in heaven' continues to capture the imaginations of modern audiences; simultaneously, it functions transgressively to dislodge popular notions of heaven as a cozy abode of eternal peace. As angel Gabriel in *The Prophecy* (1995) reminds readers: angels are weapons of war—not adorable cherubim.

Recommended reading. Brakke, David. *Demons and the Making of the Monk: Spiritual Combat in Early Christianity.* Cambridge, MA: Harvard University Press, 2006. Revard, Stella Purce. *The War in Heaven: 'Paradise Lost' and the Tradition of Satan's Rebellion.* Ithaca, NY: Cornell University Press, 1980.

See also FALLEN ANGELS; FALL, THE; LUCIFER; MICHAEL, THE ANGEL; TRIBULATION, THE; WOMAN CLOTHED WITH THE SUN [SDD]

Washing. The act of washing occurs in several senses in the Bible, both literal and figurative. In its most mundane sense, it refers to cleansing of the body, typically the washing of feet after travelling. This is nothing particular to biblical literature, although Jesus' washing the feet of his disciples (John 13) turns an everyday act into a teaching point.

Under the Mosaic covenant, rules for ritual purity detailed what was 'clean' or 'unclean' and the means by which ritual purity (or cleanliness) could be maintained—which typically involved washing with water. Washing occurred in a number of contexts. A few examples include: priests washed before approaching the altar of Yahweh (e.g., Exod. 30.17-21); portions of sacrifices were washed prior to offering (e.g., Lev. 1.9); and if an Israelite became unclean through contact with unclean foods, the unclean individual could become clean again through washing with water and separation until evening (Lev. 11.24-27). Attention to ritual purity led to the development of the *miqvah*, a bath designed to immerse and wash the body for ritual cleanliness. In Second Temple Judaism, the Pharisees (and their proto-Hasidic forerunners) practiced washing that extended beyond the requirements of the Mosaic Law, and this became a source of conflict between the religious leaders and Jesus and his disciples (Mark 7.1-23).

The Bible also contains several figurative senses of washing. The biblical writers associated Christian baptism with the washing away of sins (Acts 22.16; cf. Ps. 51; Isa. 1.16; Jer. 4.14), and scripture itself is viewed as an agent of spiritual washing or cleansing (Eph. 5.26). In a related sense, the Christian believer is *spiritually* washed through the regeneration of the Holy Spirit (1 Cor. 6.9; Tit. 3.5; cf. Ezek. 36.25-27). In a different context, Pilate used the gesture of washing his hands to demonstrate his unwillingness to accept responsibility in the condemnation of Jesus (Matt. 27.24). And in a final and more general figurative sense, God used the Flood to wash away the egregious sins of the world through the destruction of most of humankind (cf. 1 Pet. 3.20-22).

The figurative connection between washing and purity remains strong in western thought. Idiomatically, one may still wash one's hands of some matter to separate oneself from responsibility or culpability (cf. Matt. 27.24). The saying 'cleanliness is next to godliness', associated with a sermon by John Wesley (although it probably predates him), is a common adage.

In the arts, washing in the different biblical senses has influenced a number of works. The most familiar image of figurative washing is from Shakespeare's *Macbeth*, in which the sleepwalking Lady Macbeth attempts to wash treacherous blood from her hands (5.1). In the 1996 film *Romeo and Juliet,* the confessions of love between Romeo and Juliet are symbolically washed into purity by transferring the balcony scene of Shakespeare's play from the Capulet orchard to a swimming pool; in the film, instead of Romeo saying, 'Call me but love, and I'll be new baptized', the lovers fall into the pool together.

Painters have depicted biblical washing in a variety of pieces, including: Piero della Francesca's *Baptism of Christ* (1448–50), Tintoretto's *Christ Washing the Feet of the Disciples* (1557) and *Baptism of Christ* (1579–81), Ford Maddox Brown's *Jesus Washing Peter's Feet at the Last Supper* (c. 1581), Piero della Carracci's *Baptism of Christ* (1584), Nicholas Poussin's *The Baptist Baptises the Crowds* (1632), Francis Danby's *The Deluge* (1840), Henri-Georges Roualt's *Baptism of Christ* (1911), Norman Adams's *The Flood* (1961), and Hans Feibusch's *The Footwashing* (1990).

See also BAPTISM; FLOOD; FOOTWASHING; PURIFICATION; RITUAL PURITY/IMPURITY; WATER   [WAS]

Watchman/Watchtower. Guards (Hebrew: *shamar*; Greek: *phylax*) appointed as lookouts were commonly stationed in strategic locations to provide assurance to a community that they would not be suddenly or unknowingly attacked. Watchmen were also commissioned by invading armies to protect the interest of the troops whose position was often more vulnerable than that of those they were attacking (see Judg. 10.11). An elevated lookout post (watchtower) was stationed at the top of a city's entrance gates (e.g., 2 Sam. 18.24) to guard the city (Song 3.3). Watchmen represented the authority of the ruler whose interests they protected (2 Sam. 18). Calling watchmen 'blind' was a serious insult, further mocking the people's trust and their ruler's real commitment to their wellbeing (Isa. 56.10).

From a biblical perspective, though watchmen kept watch day and night (Isa. 62.6), they guarded in futility unless they acknowledged the protection that their God provided them above all (Ps. 126.1). From a Jewish or Christian perspective, it is God who is the true Watchman (Ps. 12.1-8); the divine throne is his Watchtower (Jer. 31.28) and the prophet is the voice of the Watchman (Ezek. 3.17). Extended metaphorically, the psalmist appeals to God to be the Watchman of his speech (Ps. 140.3).

In contemporary culture, Bob Dylan (*John Wesley Harding*, 'All Along the Watchtower', 1967) paints a similar portrait depicting the security that citizens feel when they (falsely) take their leaders' protection for granted ('all the women came and went, barefoot servants'), when not hirelings but 'princes kept the view'. Ironically, while the eyes of the people are distracted ('businessmen they drink my wine, ploughmen till my earth'), the only word of consolation comes from a self-interested thief ("No reason to get excited,' the thief he kindly spoke'). The Watch Tower Bible and Tract Society of Pennsylvania is the official corporation of the Jehovah's Witnesses; its best-known publication is *The Watchtower* magazine.   [DM]

Water is mentioned throughout the Bible (Hebrew: *mayim*; Greek: *hydōr*). The creation account describes a canopy over the atmosphere made of water, and refers to a day when, instead of rain, a mist arose from the ground to water everything (Gen. 2.6). Water figures in a literal way throughout the OT in rituals of cleansing and the blessing of rain for crops, and metaphorically in references to the refreshment of water as symbol of God's blessing. Yet it could symbolize uncontrollability (Gen. 49.4). Water was also used (as in virtually all ancient religions) as a means of ritual purification. Its destructive side is regularly featured as well, as in the flood of Genesis 6–7, and in the drowning of the Egyptian army in Exodus 14–15. The

Gospel of John uses the symbolism of water to refer to the Holy Spirit, or to the life of Christian regeneration, and water figures in an obvious way in the Christian rite of baptism—a rite based (at least genetically) on an Israelite rite of cleansing.

Dependency on water was never far from most people's minds in biblical times, and the blessings of water (and the curse of drought) were among the people's foremost concerns. The prophets threatened the land with drought when the people did not live uprightly before the Lord (see 1 Kgs 17.1, Jer. 14.1-6; Hag. 1.10-11). For an agrarian society, with much lower yields than modern farmers are accustomed to, drought for a single season was a very serious dilemma. Conquering armies often cut off water supplies as a means of weakening a city's resistance (see 2 Kgs 2.19-25), and ownership of local well could be a cause of great contention (see Gen. 26). One of the ten plagues of Egypt turned the Nile to blood, a threat to an important staple of the Egyptian people (Exodus 7). The Israelites' thirst during the wilderness wanderings led to a standoff between the people and Moses (Exod. 17; Num. 20).

The NT rite of baptism also provides another obvious contact with water, and early (noncanonical) references to Christ purifying the water of the Jordan River at his baptism by John the Baptist seem to indicate that some baptismal theologies thought of water in more than merely symbolic terms. (The dominant early baptismal theology, found primarily in Paul's writings, viewed the baptismal waters as symbolic of the grave, but Augustine's theology of original sin [early fourth cent. CE] helped ensure the longevity of a symbolism of washing).

Water retained some of these biblical values in western literature, usually by the direct influence of the Bible. John Bunyan uses water as a symbol of death (as in the Apostle Paul's understanding of baptism) in *The Pilgrim's Progress*. Emily Dickinson recalls the notion of 'living water' in 'I know where Wells grow—Droughtless Wells'.

Recommended reading. Jones, Larry Paul. *The Symbol of Water in the Gospel of John*. Sheffield: Sheffield Academic Press, 1997. Luyster, R. 'Wind and Water: Cosmogonic Symbolism in the Old Testament'. *Zeitschrift für die alttestamentliche Wissenschaft* 93 (1981) 1-10.

See also BAPTISM; LIVING WATER; PURIFICATION; RITUAL PURITY/IMPURITY; SEA; WALKING ON WATER; WASHING; WATER OF BITTERNESS; WELL   [JCP]

Water of Bitterness. The *mê hammārîm hamĕ 'ārărîm* or Bitter Water Test, describes the trial of the suspected adulteress (*sotah*) (Num. 5.11-31). Part of the Torah, this passage describes in detail a ritual or legal procedure carried out in order to determine whether a woman accused by her husband of committing adultery is innocent or guilty. A number of important steps are taken in order to make the test valid: (1) the husband brings a grain offering to the priest; (2) the priest prepares a drink in an earthen vessel consisting of a mixture of holy water and dust from the floor of the tabernacle (cf. Exod. 32.20); (3) the accused woman is set before the Lord and instructed to drink it after taking an oath. The oath sworn by the accused brings about a curse, and places her under divine jurisdiction if she is found guilty. After drinking the mixture one of two results will follow. If she is guilty she will suffer from what appears to be a miscarriage if she is pregnant or a prolapsed uterus and bitter pain if not. If the woman is innocent then she will be immune from the curse and as added proof of her innocence will become pregnant. While the law may be initiated by the husband based on two scenarios (a man is jealous and suspicious after his wife has strayed or a man is jealous and suspicious even though his wife has not strayed), the law applies completely and solely to the suspected wife.

This ritual is often compared to a trial by ordeal, which involves determining guilt by subjecting the accused to unpleasant experiences such as drinking a potion and trusting God to determine the outcome. It also resembles purgatory oaths in which the oath-taker invites God to directly punish him or her if he or she is indeed guilty. Sometimes the purgatory oaths require only the words alone to make them valid, but they are often followed by a ritualistic or symbolic action to effectuate the oath such as the drinking of a magical liquid (e.g., Hammurabi's Laws 132). The water of bitterness is also referred to in the apocryphal *Protevangelium of James*, which describes the birth, infancy and life of the Virgin Mary. In this text, both Mary and Joseph must undergo a test in order to prove that they did not have sexual relations despite the fact that Mary is found pregnant. Specifically, Mary and Joseph are given the 'Lord's drink test' so that their sins may be revealed. The Talmudic tractate *Sotah* describes the ordeal in detail, although it had fallen into disuse by the time the tractate was written.

Trials by ordeal, oath-taking and/or the use of mystical potions for the purpose of disclosing guilt or truth have become commonplace in literature and modern entertainment. The Salem witch trials and the Spanish Inquisition often involved trials by ordeal to determine guilt. In courthouses and for federal officials sworn into office, oaths are taken while placing a hand on the Bible. It is assumed that if an oath is taken under false pretenses, the oath-taker will be judged and punished by God. Finally, mystical potions intended to reveal truth have found their way into modern children's books. In J.K. Rowling's popular Harry Potter series, Veritaserum is a powerful potion used to extract hidden truths from those who drink it.

Recommended reading. Fishbane, Michael. 'Accusations of Adultery: A Study of Law and Scribal Practice in Numbers 5:11-31'. *Hebrew Union College Annual* 45 (1974) 25-45. Frymer-Kensky, Tikva. 'The Strange Case of the Suspected Sotah: Numbers 5:11-31'. *Vigiliae christianae* 34.1 (1984) 11-26.

See also ADULTERY; WATER [LV]

Way. From Hebrew *'orach, derek,* or Greek *hodos.* Many religions use 'way' as a metaphor for the path of a person's spiritual life. Consider the ancient Chinese philosophy of the Tao (meaning the Way), Buddhism's Eightfold Path, the Japanese religion of Shinto (literally, 'Way of the Gods'), or the lengthy 'Poem of the Way' by thirteenth-century Sufi mystic Ibn al-Farid. The Jewish and Christian traditions are no exception, and make multitude references to following God's way of righteousness.

The first figurative use of way occurs in Genesis 18, when God speaks of Abraham's duty to keep to his way. During the Exodus, God guides Israel's way via a pillar of cloud by day and a pillar of fire by night. The Bible's differentiates between kings who followed their own way, and those, like David, who followed the way of the Lord. Psalms and Proverbs make over a hundred references to the paths of life people choose; Psalm 1, for example, speaks of those who follow an evil way and those who follow the way of righteousness. People are warned that some ways seem right but end in death (Prov. 14.12) and are admonished to raise their children in the way they should go (Prov. 22.6). The Jewish and Christian scriptures speak of preparing the way for the coming messiah, and the gospels claim this prophecy is fulfilled in the ministry of John the Baptist.

More fundamentally, Jesus claims that he *is* the way. In John 14, he tells the disciples that he is returning to the Father and they will follow. Thomas, understanding literally, says that they do not know the way, and Jesus says, 'I am the way, and the truth, and the life. No one comes to the Father except through me'. He teaches the difficulty of salvation in Matthew 7 by picturing the way to salvation as narrow but the way to destruction as broad. The epistles, especially those of John, admonish believers to keep the way of righteousness, and, perhaps most tellingly, the first collective name for early Christians was followers of the Way (Acts 9.2; 19.9, 22-24). In a different sense, some in the Anglican community characterize themselves as the 'via media', or 'middle way'—a bridge between the Protestant and Catholic paths of western Christianity.

Literature frequently alludes to the way to symbolize the human struggle to reach God or enlightenment. The tenth-century elegy 'The Wanderer' recounts a man's winding path that eventually finds stability in God. Likewise, John Bunyan's *Pilgrim's Progress* (1678) narrates Christian's progress on the Way to the Heavenly City despite several temporary departures. St John of the Cross, a sixteenth-century Carmelite mystic, wrote the long poem 'Dark Night of the Soul' to address the difficulty of the soul's journey to God. Robert M. Pirsig's *Zen and the Art of Motorcycle Maintenance* (1974), often called the world's bestselling philosophy text, seeks enlightenment during a motorcycle trip across the United States. Paul McCartney's ballad 'The Long and Winding Road' (1970) meditates on the difficulties of the way to finding love, and Joni Mitchell's 1969 song 'Woodstock' urges us to find our way 'back to the garden'. Jack Kerouac's Beat novel *On the Road* (1957), however, deconstructs the teleology of these other stories by ending on a note of unfulfillment and continued indirection.

Recommended reading. Bricker, Daniel. 'The Doctrine of the 'Two Ways' in Proverbs'. *Journal of the Evangelical Theological Society* 38 (1995) 501-17. Peterson, Eugene. *The Jesus Way.* Grand Rapids, MI: Eerdmans, 2007

See also JOHN THE BAPTIST; PREPARE THE WAY OF THE LORD [KCM]

Weaker vessel. (See Vessel).

Wealth. Wealth, usually represented by *hōn* in Hebrew, refers not only to money and riches, but also the assets available for people to sustain their livelihood such as livestock, land, etc., a sign of God's blessing for covenant obedience (Deut. 28.1-14). In Proverbs, the rich are encouraged to care for the poor and wealth is the result of diligence and wisdom (10.4; 11.24). In addition, warnings are given against trusting in, or pursuing after, riches

(11.28). The OT prophets are the only place we find an explicit critique of wealth. This critique relates to the mistreatment of others (Jer. 17.11; Hab. 2.5; Amos 5.10-11) and wrong attitudes about wealth such as pride (Ezek. 28.5; Hos. 12.8).

In the NT, teachings regarding wealth, *ploutos*, take a different tone. The gospels portray Jesus as explicitly stating, 'A person cannot serve God and wealth' (Matt. 6.24). In Luke's gospel, apart from his unique story of Zacchaeus, the poor are portrayed as those who respond to Jesus' message more readily than do the socially advantaged. The Deutero-Pauline letters to Timothy warn against the dangers of riches (1 Tim. 6.9-10) and James demonstrates a negative view of the rich as those who oppress the poor (Jas 2.6). Revelation takes an even more radical approach by praising poverty (Rev. 2.9) and denouncing wealth (Rev. 3.17), and appears to view participation in the Roman economy as something that is not an option for the faithful (Rev. 18.4).

While material wealth is viewed as a feature of the present age in the Deuteronomistic tradition, the NT pushes the idea of God's blessing into the future age. The present age is seen as a time where the faithful receive the spiritual blessing of salvation while looking forward to the consummation of God's kingdom. Some view this as a time of physical, material blessing (Isa. 60.5; 61.6; Rev. 20–21). This does not mean that people in the early church did not have money or were encouraged to abandon wealth. On the contrary, the biblical tradition states that there were wealthy people in the church and its members pooled their assets together and lived a somewhat sectarian lifestyle similar to what is seen in the desert communities of Qumran (cf. Acts 4.32-37). The pursuit of wealth and the love of money are what is denounced, not wealth itself.

Certainly nothing divides classes of cultural existence more than wealth and the status it provides. This is true in any society and can be seen in struggles for economic equality in certain attempts at socialist governments of the nineteenth and twentieth centuries. Hollywood also portrays the pitfalls of wealth that is gained suddenly or through unjust means in such films as *Brewster's Millions* (1985) and *Scarface* (1983). The film *Dawn of the Dead* (1978, 2004) critiques American consumerism while *It's a Wonderful Life* (1946) demonstrates how good people struggle to get by and ultimately overcome rich oppressors. In recent decades, the 'prosperity gospel' is promoted within the Christian tradition by claiming the promises of good health and material wealth found in the OT traditions. Frequently associated with televangelists in the charismatic tradition, these people propose that giving to their ministry will result in a return of God's blessing based on the amount they give.

Recommended reading. Blomberg, Craig L. *Neither Poverty nor Riches: A Biblical Theology of Possessions.* Downers Grove, IL: InterVarsity, 2001

See also GOLD; MAMMON; POOR, POVERTY [MDM]

Wedding at Cana. The account of the wedding celebration at Cana in Galilee (John 2.1-11) is found only in John's Gospel The wedding narrative is introduced by its own chronological marker, 'On the third day' (2.1), connected to its context by 'the next day' (1.29, 35, 43), and concludes (2.11) with the statement that this was the first of Jesus' signs which 'manifested his glory'. Such markers quickly connect the reader with the author's ultimate goal of presenting Jesus as the Christ (20.30-31) and with the Johannine prologue (1.1-5), signifying John's belief that Jesus was God's instrument of a new creation (Gen. 1.1-4).

The geographic, religious and cultural notes in the text (location of Cana, water for purification rites, wedding protocols) likewise help readers situate themselves in an authentic Jewish context. The narrative can be read as validating Jesus' claim to prophetic status and insight already apparent in John through the testimony of John the Baptist to Jesus, the baptism of Jesus, and the calls of Peter and Nathaniel. The reader is also offered the author's insight into the significance of these events. For example, the dialogue between Jesus and his mother becomes much more than a conversation—'my hour has not yet come' (2.4) is Jesus' enigmatic reply to Mary's comment, 'They have no wine'. (2.3). This is John's allusive introduction of a new wine which will have both an eschatological and immediate significance in relation to Jewish purification piety. This moves the reader to reflection on Jewish law and tradition (cf. John 1.17).

The plot is built around dramatic irony from both the perspective of the reader and also the servants. Each knows what other principal characters do not. The miracle of transformation of water to wine is occasioned by the crisis of the wine running out—a festive embarrassment! What may be intended is that the best wine has already been drunk with the guests not fully satisfied rather than there being no wine at all. The inferior wine, served last when guests do not know the difference, now has to be served prematurely—the guests will notice this immediately. However, the new wine, drawn from the water jars, is of such a quality as to be superior even to the best wine already served. This is the dramatic irony—the steward assumes the new (transformed) wine to be the good wine, but serving it last reverses customary expectation. However, the reader as well as the servants know the truth to which the transformation points. John understands this event to be a 'sign', the first of seven. By this he means a sign of validation that Jesus is the Christ, the central theme already disclosed; cf. 1.18, 29, 34, 41, 49; 2.11.

Biblical themes give rise to artistic interpretation. The Wedding at Cana is a favorite subject. Jan Vermyen (1500–1559), Paolo Veronese (1528–1588), Carl Heinrich Bloch (1834–1890), and Louis Kahan (1902–2002) are examples. Bloch is used by the Mormon Church to illustrate many of their publications. Veronese has received contemporary multimedia interpretation from Peter Greenaway where the massive painting is explored in detail. The wedding depicted in John provokes occasional discussion about Jesus' sexuality and familial relations—for example, that the wedding was Jesus' own. The novelist Barbara Thiering (*Jesus the Man,* 1990) speculates that Jesus was twice married. Serious scholarship rejects the view.

See also JOHN, GOSPEL OF; SIGN   [JKS]

Weeping and gnashing of teeth. From the Greek *klauthmos kai ho brygmos tōn odontōn.* A number of images describe the fate of unbelievers in the NT. The well-known images of 'outer darkness' (Matt. 8.12; 22.13; 25.30; Luke 13.25) and 'fiery furnace' (Matt. 13.42, 50) are found in conjunction with the oft-cited literary expression, 'weeping and gnashing of teeth'. This idiom is concentrated in Matthew, where it is employed six times (8.12; 13.42, 50; 22.13; 24.51; 25.30). It appears once in Luke (13.28). The expression is recorded on the lips of Jesus in descriptions of final, or eschatological, judgment.

As is common to all descriptions of the wicked, their fate stands in stark contrast to that of believers. The blessed enjoy a future without mourning or weeping (Matt. 5.4; Rev. 21.4), while the cursed anticipate unceasing anguish (Luke 6.25; *1 En.* 108.3; *2 En.* 40.12). Gnashing of teeth depicts anger and hatred (Job 16.19; Ps. 35.16, 37.12; Acts 7.54), presumably directed toward God in the contexts of Matthew and Luke. Dante's *Divine Comedy* uses the images of weeping and gnashing in describing the lots of those he encounters on his travels through hell.

The datedness of the expression has lent itself to being employed by authors in descriptions of the tirades given by hotheaded preachers. In Herman Melville's *Moby Dick* (1851), the expression is found on the lips of a preacher 'beating a book'. More generally, the expression has been used to describe the lot of those who suffer for whatever reason. Mark Twain exemplifies such a use in his *Life on the Mississippi* (1883), where the expression is utilized to depict the downcast state of fired river pilots and their crew.

In contemporary culture, the phrase can be used to communicate real anger, though it is more often employed hyperbolically to express disappointments of any kind.

See also HELL; JUDGMENT   [NTB]

Weeping Prophet (see Jeremiah).

Well. Water is scarce in many parts of Palestine from May to September, thus wells and cisterns are vital, both in rural and in populated areas. The insufficiency of springs made it necessary to collect rain-water in cisterns and pools. Water was stored in holes cut into rock or dug in soil. Before and after the conquest, wells are frequently mentioned in scripture together with field, vineyard and flock as important part of people's common assets (Num. 21.22; Deut. 6.11; 2 Chron. 26.10).

Wells and fountains were not plainly distinguished in name. It depends upon the translations of the different Hebrew words to indicate well, cistern, pit, fountain or pool. The proper words for 'well' are *bor* and *be'er*, as for Beer-sheba, 'well of the oath', the place where Abraham made a covenant with Abimelech after he complained to him about a well of water (Gen. 21.31). Yet other terms are provided in the Bible, as *'ayin*, 'fountain', e.g., referring to the spring where Abraham's servant met Rebekah, future wife of Isaac (Gen. 24.13,16,45; cf. 1 Sam. 29.1; Num. 33.9). Isaac's entire life occurs along with wells; he 'dug again the wells of water' that had been filled in by the Philistines (Gen. 26.18).

The *haberkah*, 'pool', was more elaborate water supply system developed in major cities such as Megiddo and Jerusalem. Since the spring was sometimes outside the walls, it was vulnerable in time of war (Isa. 7.3; 36.16.). In the NT 'pit' (Matt. 15.14; Luke 14.5), the 'pool of Bethesda' (John 5.2,4,7) and the 'pool of Siloam' (John 9.7,11) are also mentioned. However, the most outstanding story about a well is that of the encounter of the Samaritan woman with Jesus at Jacob's well. Jesus offers eternal well of living water (John 4.6, 14).

The well, in the past and as today, represents a center of life in the Middle East. Women gather around it following their daily duties (1 Sam. 9.11), and travelers, human and animal, come to it for refreshment. News of the vicinity and of the distant regions is carried to and from the well. It is, indeed, a prominent center of a series of distinctive biblical scenes, such as the encounter between Rebekah and the servant of Abraham (Gen. 24.11); between Jacob and Rachel (Gen. 29.1-11) and between Moses and the daughters of Jethro, including his future wife Zipporah (Exod. 2.15).

The well is also used figuratively. Jeremiah warns that idols, armies and material objects in which Israel trusted were 'broken cisterns', since the people 'has forsaken God the fountain of living water and became cracked cisterns that can hold water no more' (Jer. 2.13). Proverbs asserts that 'the mouth of the righteous is a fountain of life' (10.11), and describes 'good wives' as cisterns deserving of commitment and fidelity: 'drink water from your own cistern, flowing water from your own well' (Prov. 5.15). Recalling this passage of the scripture, a Latin-American theologian encourages Christians to be alert to God's word in the context of 'our own history'.

The well metaphor provides continual inspiration for believers. The works of Teresa of Avila and John of the Cross, evoking the 'dark night' (symbolically: God seems distant and cold) remain lucid and available in contemporary times.

See also BETHESDA; JACOB; SAMARITAN WOMAN; SILOAM; THIRST; WATER [DR]

Wheat and Tares, Parable of the. This parable is one of the kingdom of heaven parables found in Matthew 13. In addition to Matt. 13.24-30, 36-43, the parable also occurs in *Gospel of Thomas* 57. In Matthew, the parable and its interpretation are separated by two other kingdom parables. Only in two other cases does Jesus explain the meaning of his parable in detail (Matt. 13.18-23, 47-50 and parallels).

The parable has five stages: good sowing (v. 24b), hostile sowing (v. 25), growth (v. 26), first question and answer (vv. 27-28a), and second question and answer with further instructions (vv. 28b-30). The allegorical interpretation has three parts: narrative introduction (v.36), list of seven items from the parable (vv. 37-39), apocalyptic explanation (vv. 40-43).

The parable's origin and interpretation are debated. Some scholars argue that both the parable and interpretation go back to the historical Jesus. A great number of scholars disagree and maintain that only the parable itself —in whole or part—was told by the historical Jesus, whereas its interpretation was created by Matthew. Both interpretive and linguistic arguments have been presented for the latter view. For example, J. Jeremias (1952) claimed that the interpretation section has 37 Matthean terms, suggesting that the evangelist created it. However, later vocabulary analyses have reduced the number of Matthean terms to seven (M. de Goedt), two (I. Jones), or even one (R. Khatry). The claim that the parable and its interpretation cannot have the same origin because of the shift of focus from the command to let both wheat and tares grow together in the parable to the judgment in the interpretation has also been challenged. The interpretation, which underlines the judgment motif, goes beyond the parable, but the same theme is also present in the parable.

A few scholars reject both the parable and its interpretation as authentic to Jesus. The main argument for the rejection, first suggested by A. Jülicher (1910), is that the historical Jesus could not have used allegory. This argument is now widely challenged. Some of those who reject the authenticity of the parable argue that the parable is a rewritten version of the Parable of the Seed Growing Secretly (Mark 4.26-29).

The interpretation of the parable is also debated. Traditionally the parable is interpreted as a reference to the mixed character of the church: it consists of the righteous and unrighteous. However, it is better to see it as a reference to the mixed character of the world (v. 38); although the kingdom is present, the righteous and unrighteous coexist in the world until the end.

The parable has inspired a few artists. The oil painting *Landscape with the Parable of the Tares among the Wheat* painted by Abraham Bloemaert in 1624 and now exhibited at Walters Art Museum in Baltimore is probably the most famous. This painting represents the transition from mannered landscape paintings to more realistic landscape paintings. In it, the horned devil in the background is sowing tares among the wheat while naked peasants sleep in the foreground. Other famous pieces of art about this parable are *The Parable of the Tares*, a set of four engravings on laid paper, painted by the Dutch Gerald de Jode in 1568; *The Parable of vicious weed säendem* by the Italian Carracci Agostino (1557–1602); and *The Parable of the Tares* by the British John Everett Millais (1865).

Recommended reading. Snodgrass, Klyne R. *Stories with Intent: A Comprehensive Guide to the Parables of Jesus*. Grand Rapids, MI: Eerdmans, 2008.

See also ALLEGORY; KINGDOM OF GOD/HEAVEN; PARABLE; PLANTS, SYMBOLISM OF [KT]

Wheels within wheels. The prophet Ezekiel portrays a glimpse of heaven that is at once both mystical and mysterious. In the prophet's own words, 'the heavens were opened and I saw visions of God' (1.1). Gleaming amber and fire filled the seer's vision. Lightning issued forth from the fire. Ezekiel saw what he described as wheels spinning of their own accord as well as somehow spinning within each other—wheels within wheels.

This sometimes disturbing and always enigmatic imagery is unique to Ezekiel. Even when set in the initial context of the chariot throne of God, the metaphorical poetic language eludes satisfactory interpretation. A NT passage echoes such an inexplicable event wherein Paul described his own supernatural rapture into the divine domain ('whether out-of-body or not, I could not tell') as a series of dream-like sounds and images that he was neither able physically to imitate nor linguistically capable of describing (2 Cor. 12.1-4). Although Paul did not speak of wheels within wheels, the context implies a similar spiritually perceivable phenomenon.

Similar ambiguity has shrouded the lyrics of Bob Dylan. In a recent work, the modern bard elicits Ezekiel's heavenly imagery, linking mystical experience ('As I walked out tonight in the mystic garden') with terrestrial mystery ('No one on earth would ever know'), all the while framing his theophanic experience in the fantastic imagery of the prophet ('It's bright in the heavens and the wheels are flying') (Bob Dylan, 'Ain't Talkin'', *Modern Times*, 2006). Whether Ezekiel's divine revelation or Dylan's cryptic vision, what remains common is the unspeakable nature of the experience. The American folk song 'Ezekiel Saw the Wheel' ('and a wheel in a wheel whirling') alludes to Ezekiel's enigmatic vision.

In everyday speech, the expression 'wheels within wheels' refers to a set of complicated and interrelated circumstances that surreptitiously influences events, e.g., in Oscar Wilde's play *An Ideal Husband* (1895), Sir Robert Chiltern explains to his wife: 'Gertrude, truth is a very complex thing, and politics is a very complex business. There are wheels within wheels. One may be under certain obligations to people that one must pay. Sooner or later in political life one has to compromise. Everyone does'.

See also EZEKIEL; THRONE [DM]

Where two or three are gathered. This phrase comes from Matt. 18.20, 'for where two or three are gathered in my name, I am there among them'. It is the first part of a section that deals with the requirements given to the church as followers of Jesus. The section begins with a discussion about greatness in the Kingdom of God. This discussion concludes with an admonition to accept the faith like a child. The section then turns to general principles of church order, especially forgiveness and excommunication, and concludes with a parable calling on followers to imitate God's grace in practices that reach beyond the most extravagant human imagination.

The phrase 'two or three' appears frequently in scripture as a standard of trustworthiness. Deuteronomy 17.6 requires the evidence of two or three witnesses for a death sentence. Deuteronomy 19.15 extends the requirement of witnesses to any criminal charge. Immediately before this passage, Matt. 18.16 requires two or three witnesses to any extended confrontation with other members, and Matt. 18.19 states that if two agree on a matter and ask, it will be granted. Elsewhere in the NT, the phrase appears in 1 Cor. 14.27-29, which limits speaking in tongues or prophesying in worship services to two or three. Paul emphasizes this use in 2 Cor. 13.1. The use of this standard is reflected in 1 Tim. 5.19 and Heb. 10.28.

This passage has been interpreted in diverse ways. To some, it is about the authority of the church to remove or otherwise control members. To others, the statement that only two or three are required to gain the presence of Jesus is an authorization for Free Church traditions or home church practices. In a similar vein, the passage has been popular with those promoting small groups within the larger church. Among modern-day 'prosperity gospel' traditions, it is used to argue that God must honor a request for wealth when two or three ask in faith. Overall, in a variety of traditions, the statements are understood to indicate the communal nature of the church, and to remind the church of the continuing presence of Christ, along with the need to remove personal vendettas by requiring consensual judgment.

Recommended reading. Boring, Eugene M. 'The Gospel of Matthew: Introduction, Commentary, and

Reflections'. In *General Articles on the New Testament, Matthew, Mark: The New Interpreter's Bible.* VIII. Pp. 87-505. Ed. Leander E. Keck. Nashville, TN: Abingdon Press, 1995.

See also CHURCH; KINGDOM OF GOD/HEAVEN; WEALTH [TV]

Whited Sepulchre. From the Greek *koniaō* (whitened) and *taphos* (sepulchre or tomb). With the exception of Rom. 3.13, all other instances of 'sepulchre' mentioned outside Matthew use the synonym *mnēma*. This metaphor appears in Matt. 23.27, when Jesus chides the Pharisees for their hypocrisy and false piety that was concerned with outward appearances and neglected the things of the spirit. They are lazy, wear long garments to be noticed in public, take the places of honor at banquets, desire to be addressed by lofty titles, observe minute biblical commandments and yet are unjust, unmerciful, and unfaithful while hypocritically declaring they would have acted righteously where others failed.

Jesus uses two images to castigate them. He says they wash only the outside of the cup and leave the inside dirty, and that they are whited sepulchres (using the oft quoted phrasing of the KJV). Echoing the parallel image of the cup, Jesus describes the Pharisees as whitewashed and righteous in outward appearance but full of the bones of the dead and hence unclean and unrighteous in their souls. The image was drawn from the tradition of whitewashing tombs prior to Passover to avoid the ritual uncleanness spoken of in Num. 19.16. This warning is likely also the source of the Luke 11.44 account of Jesus calling the Pharisees 'concealed tombs'. Likewise, the admonition of Ps. 5.9 quoted in Rom. 3.13 is that the throats of the wicked lie like open graves, and Paul condemns High Priest Ananias in Acts 23.3 by calling him a whitewashed wall that God is going to strike.

Jesus' meaning in addressing the Pharisees as whited sepulchres is clear, and it is one that is often repeated throughout the Bible: God looks at the heart and thoughts and so knows the true nature of human beings despite what they might convince other people to think of them. Like the cup or the tomb, we are defiled by what is inside us, not by what outward customs we follow (cf. 1 Sam. 16.7; Mark 7).

'Whited sepulchres' is certainly a poignant biblical image, and in literature, it is used to its greatest effect by Joseph Conrad. In his 1902 novella *Heart of Darkness*, the city of Brussels is pictured as a whitened sepulchre by Marlow, the secondary narrator. He thus indicates that while it claims to participate in a 'civilizing mission' based on advanced ideals, it is really only interested in the Congo for reasons of profit that willfully overlook the suffering and death forced on the African population. The argument of Matthew 23 girds Jonathan Swift's poem, 'The Place of the Damned' (1731), in which people of high and honorable positions of public responsibility are indicted along with the rest as sinners despite their outward righteousness. And in James Joyce's *Ulysses* (1922), the protagonist, Leopold Bloom, attends a burial and sees a large old rat that has made its way into a tomb where Bloom imagines him feasting on corpses. Joyce alludes to the hypocritical actions of the gentlemen present at the funeral towards Bloom, whom they tacitly spurn because he is Jewish. In Eugene O'Neill's *Mourning Becomes Electra,* Christine remarks how their home always seems to her to be like the whited sepulchre of the Bible because its architecture combines paganism and Puritan ugliness.

Recommended reading. Garland, David. *The Intention of Matthew 23.* Leiden: Brill, 1979.

See also PHARISEE; RITUAL PURITY, IMPURITY [KCM]

Whole duty of man. Ecclesiastes 12.13 (KJV) says, 'Fear God, and keep his commandments; for this is the whole duty of man'. The verse continues to say that God will judge every deed, secret or open, whether good or evil.

The 'fear of God' can be understood at the beginning of wisdom. It is similar to Mic. 6.8 which asks about the religious duty of all humans—'what has the Lord required of you, but to do justice, love kindness and to walk humbly with your God'.

When asked what the greatest commandment, Jesus answered by combining two commandments. The first is that everyone should love God with all one's mind, heart and soul. The second is to love one's neighbor as one's self (Matt. 26.36-40; cf. Mark 12.28-34; Luke 10.25-28; Deut. 6.5). He added that upon these do all of the law and prophets depend. Jesus did not expressly say that the Great Commandment is the whole duty of a person but, it is implied.

The phrase 'the whole duty of man' has been used in a number of devotional, theological and legal works. In the legal area the international jurist Samuel von Pufendorf (1632–1694), a philosopher, jurist, economist, statesman and historian, published a book on law in 1673 entitled, *The Whole Duty of*

Man according to the Law of Nature. He examined duties from moral natural law built into the visible universe, knowable by reason.

Augustine commented on Eccl. 12.13 saying that it is keepers of God's commandments who have a real existence (*City of God* 20.3). The eighteenth-century German theologian Johann Arndt (1555–1621) used 'the whole duty of man' in his theological work *True Christianity: Or the Whole Economy of God towards Man and the Whole Duty of Man towards God* (1605–1610). His work, which influenced St Bernard of Clairvaux and Thomas à Kempis, sought to define true Christianity as the practice of faith.

In 1659, an English Protestant devotional book was published anonymously although it had an introduction by Henry Hammond. It was influential for the next 200 years and helped to define the Anglican tradition. It is now believed to have been written by Richard Allestree (1619–1681), who was a Royalist soldier and after the Restoration became a professor of divinity at Eton College. Allestree's *The Whole Duty of Man* has been cited approvingly in numerous works of fiction such as *The Mayor of Casterbridge* by Thomas Hardy, *The Haunted Baronet* by Sheridan Le Fanu and others. Non-fiction works such as W.E.B. DuBois's *The Souls of Black Folk* cites it as does David Hume (although critically) in *An Enquiry Concerning the Principles of Human Understanding*.

Other critics have taken Allestree to task because as a Royalist he promoted a passive duty to obey the poor in the lower orders to obey like children. John Wesley prior to his conversion held the book in high regard, but publicly denounced the book after his conversion. William Cowper described Allestree's book as self-righteous and pharisaical. Thomas Carlyle called it mere half-Christianity and the passive half at that.

See also ECCLESIASTES; BOOK OF; GREAT COMMANDMENT; JUDGEMENT; SHEMA; TEN COMMANDMENTS
[AJW]

Whore of Babylon. The city of Babylon spawned the empire that conquered Judah, ransacked the Temple in Jerusalem, and exiled much of its populace (597/586 BCE). In the first century CE, it was the Roman Empire that controlled the land of Palestine. In Revelation, John sees a 'woman sitting on a scarlet beast ... [which] had seven heads ... and on her forehead was written... 'Babylon the great, mother of whores'... [who] is the great city that rules over the kings of the earth' (17.3-5, 18).

It is easy to see why Revelation's addressees could symbolically identify 'Babylon, the great city' with Rome, and, by extension, with the entire Roman Empire. An angel tells John that 'the seven heads are seven mountains on which the woman is seated' (17.9). Rome was situated among seven hills and was personified as a woman, the goddess Roma. Roma is even pictured as sitting on seven hills in a coin struck by Vespasian in 71 CE. Early Judaism also spoke of Rome as 'Babylon' (*Sibylline Oracles* 5.143; *4 Ezra* 2.36-40).

John assures his seven churches though that Rome will fall. In fact, this integrated empire of 'church and state', so to speak, is said to self-destruct through a clash of the very religious, political and economic elements that empower her: 'the [seven-headed] beast will hate the whore ... devour her and burn her up' (17.15, 16). Revelation 18 pictures Rome's ultimate destruction: 'the kings of the earth ... see the smoke of her burning ... and say, 'Alas, alas, the great city, Babylon ... for in one hour your judgment has come'' (18.10).

Revelation's negative picture contrasts with Paul's more positive view that the Roman Empire was 'God's servant for your good' (Rom. 13.4). Paul's attitude informs the modern development of Christian political consciousness, while Revelation's portrayal is used by some radical Christian pacifists to justify a rejection of political engagement, and even of military service and public judgeship.

The Whore in Revelation has also influenced western literature. Post-reformation political commentary was engendered from the Puritan identification of the Whore with Roman Catholicism (e.g., *Geneva Bible* [1560]; cf. also, the Westminster Confession [1646] and the *Scofield Reference Bible* [1917]). In the *Faerie Queen*, Edmund Spencer's allegorical tale of struggle between Elizabethan England and Scotland, Duessa the Whore, who represents Mary Queen of Scots, is dressed in the same manner as the Whore in Rev. 17.1-3 (4.29; 8.29). Thomas Dekker's play *The Whore of Babylon* (1605) creates an allegorical kingdom where English Catholics are allied with Catholic Spain in acts of treachery against English royalty (Elizabeth I and King James I).

In the mid-1800s, American tabloid journalism used Revelation's Babylon as staple imagery for the moral decay that was rife in larger cities, particularly New York. Apocalyptic imagery also permeates popular novels of that era, like George Lippard's best-seller *The Quaker City* (200,000 copies) and Harrison Buchanan's *Asmodeus*.

Western media have also incorporated Whore of Babylon imagery. Fritz Lang's film classic, *Metropolis* (1927), features an exotic club dancer mimicking the Whore of Babylon in a climactic scene. In his well-crafted but sexless sex film, *Samson and Delilah* (1949), Cecil B. DeMille alludes to Babylon the Harlot through his portrayal of Delilah. More recently, the Megami Tensei video games, set in 1990s Tokyo, incorporated a Mother Harlot who is seated on a seven-headed demon.

See also BABYLON; HARLOT; REVELATION; ROME

[RJK]

Wicked Tenants, Parable of the. This parable is found in each of the three Synoptic Gospels (Mark 12.1-12, Matt. 21.33-43, Luke 20.9-19), as well as in the non-canonical *Gospel of Thomas* (65). It tells of a vineyard owner who leases his vineyard to some tenants. When he attempts to collect what is owed to him the tenants variously beat and kill his servants; both the number of servants sent and the way they are treated changes differs depending on which Gospel is being read. Finally the owner sends his son, whom the tenants recognize as the heir and kill in order to gain the inheritance. In *Thomas* this is where the parable ends, while in the canonical Gospels a question follows: 'what then will the owner of the vineyard do?' (Mark 12.9a and par.). In Mark and Luke, Jesus answers this question himself, saying that the owner will destroy the tenants, while in Matthew the crowd offers the same answer. In each case this answer is followed by a quotation of Ps. 118.22: 'The stone that the builders rejected has become the cornerstone'. Interestingly enough this quotation also follows the parable in the *Gospel of Thomas*, although it is presented as a separate saying.

This parable has generally been interpreted as an allegory in which the owner is God, the servants represent the prophets, the vineyard is either Jerusalem or more likely the kingdom of God, and the son is Jesus, while the tenants are typically viewed as representing the Jewish leaders. This understanding is strengthened when we realize that this parable, at least as preserved in Mark and Matthew, is built upon language borrowed from the Song of the Vineyard in Isa. 5.1-7, in which the owner of the vineyard is clearly God. Throughout the history of the church, this parable has generally been understood as telling not only of Jesus' death, and through the citation of Ps. 118.22, his ultimate triumph, but also of the passing of the kingdom of God from Israel to the church. It should be noted, however, that modern interpreters in this post-holocaust era stress that it is the leaders of Israel who are condemned, not the people as a whole.

In modern scholarship, this parable is a source of a continuing debate, with several scholars holding that the non-allegorical version of the parable found in *Thomas* represents the original, while the synoptic versions represent either a creation or at least a complete re-adaptation by the early church. Many of the arguments on both sides of the debate ultimately come down to the level of presuppositions, with neither side able to definitively make their case. If the parable is not an allegory then the story becomes one of a successful(?) murder to claim the vineyard, perhaps in an attempt to restore land to poor farmers from the hands of a wealthy landowner, a story which is certainly possible in first-century Palestine.

Throughout church history, the parable has been vulnerable to anti-Jewish interpretation, although Irenaeus used it against Marcion to demonstrate that the Jewish God was indeed the father of Jesus (*Against Heresies* 4.36). In popular culture, this parable has not received much attention outside of the church, the Christian radio program *Adventures in Odyssey* adapted the parable in Episode 141, recasting the story as a western.

Recommended reading. Hester, James D. 'Socio-Rhetorical Criticism and the Parable of the Tenants'. *Journal for the Study of the New Testament* 45 (1992) 27-57. Snodgrass, K.R. *The Parable of the Wicked Tenants*. Tübingen: J.C.B. Mohr, 1983.

See also ALLEGORY; PARABLE; STONE THAT THE BUILDERS REJECTED; VINE, VINEYARD [MP]

Widow of Nain. In Luke 7.11-17, Jesus approaches the gates of a town called Nain (a small village seven miles southeast of Nazareth), where he encounters a funeral procession for the only son of a widow who has died and is being carried out on a bier. Luke writes that Jesus has compassion for the widow and he orders her not to weep. By walking up and touching the bier he causes the crowd to stop and immediately commands the corpse to rise. As the young man sits up and begins to speak, Luke details how Jesus returns him to his mother. The emotional force of this story is the desperation that characterizes the desperate condition of the childless widow. Ancient readers especially would have understood how the death of an only son would profoundly compound the plight of a widow, adding to her already marginal status in the ancient world.

This pericope shares close parallels with the story of Elijah's raising of the widow's son in Zarephath (1 Kgs 17.17-24), recounted in Jesus' synagogue sermon in Luke 4.25-26. Parallels include encountering a widow at the entrance of a city gate, the death of the widow's only son, a resuscitated son given back to his mother, and a favorable response from those present, recognizing the healer as a prophet of God. Together with the story of the healing of a centurion's slave (Luke 7.1-10), these two stories provide the narrative upon which the subsequent discussion of Jesus' identity is based (7.18-35).

Early Christian theologian Cyril of Alexandria, in emphasizing the unity of Jesus' dual nature as human and divine, highlights how the story brings these two natures together to effect the resuscitation. Jesus speaks the divine word of God by telling the young man to get up, as well as touches the bier with his human body. Cyril asks, 'What is more powerful than the Word of God? Why then did he not work the miracle by only a word but also touched the bier? It was, my beloved, that you might learn that the holy body of Christ is productive for the salvation of man. The flesh of the almighty Word is the body of life and was clothed with his might (*Commentary on Luke, Homily* 36)'.

A selection from a poem by George MacDonald, entitled 'The Widow of Nain', focuses on the widow's silence in the story and interprets it as a sign of the overpowering emotional effect that both the grief and joy had on her, leaving her speechless. 'No word of hers hath left a trace / Of uttered joy or grief; / Her tears alone have found a place / Upon the holy leaf. / Oh, speechless sure the widow's pain, / To lose her only boy! / Speechless the flowing tides again / Of new-made mother's joy!' The silence of the widow is also emphasized in Lucas Cranach the Younger's, 1569 painting, *Auferweckung des Jünglings zu Nain*. The widow's face is covered with a niqab which depicts the silent treatment she is given in the Lukan story; a silence which has forced readers to guess at the emotions she would have felt at each stage of the story.

See also WIDOWS AND ORPHANS; WIDOW OF ZAREPHATH. [DB]

Widow of Zarephath. Zarephath was a Phoenician port city located on the Mediterranean coast between Tyre and Sidon, and thus, outside of Israel. Elijah, one of the greatest Israelite prophets, goes there during a time of physical and spiritual famine in the land (1 Kgs 17.8-24). There, he meets a widow and asks her for some water and food. There had been a drought for some time, and the widow replied that she had no food. All that remained was a little flour and oil. Her plan was to cook what remained for her and her son, and then they would eat it and die.

Elijah assures the widow that if she makes him some bread first, her flour and oil will not run out until the drought ends. The widow acts in faith and obedience to Elijah, and indeed, her food does not run out.

Some time later, the widow's son gets sick and dies. Elijah prays to God for the healing of the boy. Miraculously, God raises the child. The widow states, 'Now I know that you are a man of God, and that the word of the LORD in your mouth is truth' (1 Kgs 17.24). The widow reveals her knowledge of the LORD and recognizes Elijah as a true prophet of God.

This narrative demonstrates God's even about the plight of a poor, lowly widow. It also teaches that God is not only at work in Israel, but also in the lives of the outsiders in the surrounding nations.

The story occurs at a time portrayed as one of spiritual decline in Israel. Israel's king, Ahab, is not serving Yahweh and is adamantly antagonistic to Elijah. In light of this greater context, the faithful and obedient response of the widow is all the more magnified.

Ministry to widows is a common theme in the Bible. The OT teaches that providing for the poor and widows is an important part of one's worship of God. In the NT, Jesus and the disciples also take care to demonstrate the importance of providing for widows.

The theme of the 'outsider' (a person living outside of Israel) experiencing the salvation of God is also a major theme. The incident implies that God's deliverance is not only for Israel, but also for the surrounding nations. In the NT, Jesus is portrayed as ministering not only to the Jews, but to all people. Stories like the Widow of Zarephath help develop and illustrate these themes.

The widow's story has been portrayed by many western artists, including Bartholomeus Breenbergh (c. 1630), Bernardo Strozzi (1630s), Giovanni Lanfranco (1621–24), Pier Francesco Mola (1648/50) and John Bates Bedford (1862).

Today, ideally, government systems are set up to ensure that the poor and widows are provided for. Yet, the Bible teaches that it is still the individual responsibility of those who have much to help those who are less fortunate.

See also ELIJAH; WIDOW OF NAIN; POOR, POVERTY; WIDOWS AND ORPHANS [MHH]

Widows and Orphans. In the rules of typesetting, the terms widows and orphans are used to refer to words in a paragraph that, due to spacing issues, end at the top of a second page (widows) or begin at the end of the first page (orphans). The mnemonic designed to remember the difference between these is 'an orphan has no past and a widow has no future'. Though the Bible does portray widows and orphans as estranged from the dominant social structures of society, its relationship to this use has more to do with normalizing the conflation of these two groups and popularizing their use in western discourse. Widows and orphans are mentioned together numerous times in both the OT and NT in a series of laws describing their proper treatment as well as in multiple narratives which illustrate their dependence on the contributions of others to ensure their wellbeing (Gen. 38, Num. 27.8-11; Deut. 25.5-10, Ruth 4; Jdt. 8). Often mentioned alongside resident aliens and the poor, they are considered a category of persons living in volatile conditions and possessing marginal status in the ancient world. In order to ensure their proper treatment, the Mosaic Law threatens anyone who dares to mistreat them with God's retributive justice: 'You shall not abuse any widow or orphan. If you do abuse them, when they cry out to me, I will surely heed their cry; my wrath will burn, and I will kill you with the sword, and your wives shall become widows and your children orphans' (Exod. 22.22-24).

The early church continued to uphold these concerns even if it did change particular practices. Care of widows and orphans is placed at the center of what defines pure and undefiled religion (Jas 1.27). The early church instituted a daily distribution of bread to those widows in need (Acts 6.1) and assumed responsibility for their care (1 Tim. 5.9). 1 Timothy 5.3-16 specifically defines what constitutes identification of widows and their proper treatment. The author divides widows into two separate categories. The first class is cared for by the church and must be 60 years old or more (due to sexual security for Tertullian and Erasmus; due to not being able to participate in manual labor for Jerome and Aquinas). The second class of widows is to be taken care of by relatives or encouraged to remarry. It is in this context that the author repeatedly emphasizes the responsibility that a family has to its own widows. Modern readers, however, have expanded this decree of familial support to apply to everything from gun control the right to bear arms, to those who wish to castigate families who make women leave the house and join the workforce, to those who combat the Equal Rights Amendment to the US Constitution.

Many ancient theologians (Ignatius, Polycarp, Clement of Alexandria, Tertullian, Cyprian, *Apostolic Constitutions*) refer to an 'order of widows' that endured in the early church for several centuries. Childless widows seem to have been honored in the later church for several reasons. Chrysostom argues that by not having children they are all the more free to please God and serve others. Ambrose claims they are able to persist in prayer. Jerome states that they remember past enjoyments and called to persevere. Augustine uses widows as models or analogues of how every soul should observe its own poverty and desolation in this world, depending on God as its only defender.

Recommended reading. Thurston, Bonnie Bowman. *The Widows: A Women's Ministry in the Early Church*. Philadelphia: Fortress Press, 1989.

See also POOR, POVERTY; WIDOW OF NAIN; WIDOW OF ZAREPHATH; WIDOW'S MITE [DB]

Widow's Mite. The story of the poor widow's donation of two 'mites' (KJV) to the Jerusalem temple treasury is recounted in Mark 12.41-44 and Luke 21.1-4. In both instances, Jesus looks on as many rich people contribute large gifts to the temple offering. Both Mark and Luke specify the paltry amount the widow gives, two copper coins (*lepta duo*). The Marcan evangelist explains that the sum of the donation was one-quarter of a *quadrans*, the smallest possible coin in Roman currency.

Mark 12.43 narrates that Jesus summoned his disciples, drawing their attention to the widow's donation. Jesus praises the widow and interprets her apparently negligible gift as actually more than all the others gave, not numerically but in comparative value. The contrast described in Mark 12.44 makes all the difference in Jesus' estimation. While all the others gave from their excess, the widow gave from extreme poverty. Both Mark and Luke express that this insignificant sum of money comprised 'her whole living', that is, the widow's only resources for life.

Widows—along with orphans and foreigners—were considered among the most vulnerable and underprivileged categories of persons in the biblical tradition. Many scriptures reinforce God's special concern for widows (e.g., Deut. 10.18), commands against oppressing widows (e.g., Exod. 22.22; Matt. 23.14 = Mark 12.40 = Luke 20.47), and injunctions to care for widows (e.g., Isa. 1.17; James 1.27). The archetype for the destitute but generous widow is found in the Widow of Zarephath (1 Kings 17.8-24).

Both John Chrysostom and Augustine connect the image of the widow's mite to that of a 'cup of cold water' (Matt. 10.42) in their homilies on various biblical texts. Both images stand in as symbols for an act of generosity, almsgiving, or compassion.

The pittance the widow gives (Mark 12.42; Luke 21.2) was first termed a 'mite' in Wycliffe's fourteenth-century English translation of the NT. Although there was no 'mite' coin in England, the term may derive from the name of a medieval Flemish copper coin, or the term may be adapted from the Latin term *minuta* (in the Vulgate translation). 'Mite' came to denote something of small size, whether monetary, animal, or human.

In English poetry and literature, the 'widow's mite' is used often as a cipher for a selfless gift or to convey the 'very last penny' of a destitute person. William Blake's (1757–1827) 'Auguries of Innocence' uses the term 'mite': in a context that plays upon the contrast between apparent value and comparative worth, reminiscent of Jesus' commentary on the widow's offering: 'The poor man's farthing is worth more / Than all the gold on Afric's shore. / One mite wrung from the lab'rer's hands / Shall buy and sell the miser's lands; / Or, if protected from on high, / Does that whole nation sell and buy'. American Philip Freneau's (1752–1832) poem, 'On a Travelling Speculator' utilizes the image of the disadvantaged widow to portray the swindling speculator in a more negative light. 'He seemed a sea-hawk watching for his prey. / With soothing words the widow's mite he gained'. The whole poem 'The Widow's Mite' by Frederick Locker-Lampson (1821–95) makes use of the biblical image, but transforms the 'mite' into the widow's 'puny and decrepit son'. However it is appropriated, the *widow's mite* is a gift of great extravagance because it is all she has.

See also POOR, POVERTY; WIDOWS AND ORPHANS; WIDOW OF NAIN; WIDOW OF ZAREPHATH [KJL-P]

Wilderness. The unabridged *OED* provides the following definitions of the word *wilderness*: without the article, '[w]ild or uncultivated land'; with the article or other defining word, '[a] wild or uncultivated region or tract of land, uninhabited, or inhabited only by wild animals'. A number of words serve to denote *wilderness/desert* in the OT, but the most frequent is the Hebrew term *midbar*. The latter is rendered *erēmos* (Greek) by the LXX translators in the overwhelmingly majority of cases. NT writers also tend to employ *erēmos*—adjectivally and substantively—as well as its less frequent substantive cognate *erēmia*.

A number of momentous events in Israel's history take place within the context of wilderness. Some of these are: the call of Moses to leadership in the Exodus (Exod. 3.1–4.18); Israel's 40-year sojourn before entry into the Promised Land, including: rebellion against/testing of God (Exod. 17.1-7; Num. 20.1-13); double giving of the Law (Exod. 19.1–23.33 [1st]; 34 [2nd; cf. Deut. 5.1-33); Golden Calf incident (Exod. 32); flight of Elijah from Jezebel (1 Kings 19), including: theophany ('small voice') at Mount Horeb (vv. 4-18); and the route of repatriation of Judah/Jerusalem after exile in Babylon (Isa. 40.1-5). The NT writers also relate significant events in the wilderness: ministry of John the Baptist (Matt. 3.1-17; Mark 1.1-11; Luke 3.1-22; John 1.6-8.37; temptation of Jesus (Matt. 4.1–11; Mark 1.12-13; Luke 4.1-13); and Paul in Arabia (cf. Hebrew *arabah* [wilderness]) after conversion (Gal. 2.17).

Samuel Johnson's characterization of wilderness existence captures Mark's (1.13) description very well: 'a tract of solitude and savageness' (*Dictionary of the English Language*, 1755). Wilderness as such localizes the struggle of good vs. evil in both Testaments. It was essentially a place of grave danger.

The harnessing of the wilderness through human technology over two millennia continues to be one of the most powerful narratives in western culture's 'return to Eden'. Bernhard W. Anderson observes:

> ... in times of thanksgiving Americans affirm their belief that, despite the sordid aspects of injustice and violence, the hand of God was guiding the 'pilgrim feet ... whose stern, impassioned stress, a thoroughfare for freedom beat, across the wilderness' (so Katharine Lee Bates, *America, the Beautiful* [1895]).

However, the environmental ravages of the industrial revolution engendered a widespread reaction in the nineteenth century—Romanticism. The wilderness came to possess intrinsic value for the Romantics. No longer was it considered an object of human conquest. One example is the poetry of William Wordsworth, another the writings of philosopher Henry Thoreau. The latter recounts his reflection on wilderness experiences in such journals as *Walden Pond; or, Life in the Woods* (1854).

This attitudinal shift continues to exert its influence to this day. Indeed the love of wilderness areas has gained considerable momentum in recent decades. The intricacies of natural phenomena and the vastness of the cosmos have always provided a sobering perspective on the place of our kind within the broader scheme (cf. Ps. 8). Understandably biblical writers often employ wilderness as the theatre of divine encounters.

Recommended reading. Anderson, Bernhard W. *Understanding the Old Testament*. 4th edn. Englewood Cliffs, NJ: Prentice–Hall, 1986. Eisenberg, Evan. *The Ecology of Eden*: Toronto. Random House of Canada, 1998. Merchant, Carolyn. *Reinventing Eden: The Fate of Nature in Western Culture*. New York and London: Routledge, 2003.

See also HOREB; JORDAN; SINAI, MOUNT; VOICE CRYING IN THE WILDERNESS [NRP]

Wind bloweth where it listeth. In John 3.6-8, Jesus explains to the Pharisee Nicodemus what it means to be 'born again': 'That which is born of the flesh is flesh; and that which is born of the Spirit is spirit. Marvel not that I said unto thee, Ye must be born again. The wind bloweth where it listeth, and thou hearest the sound thereof, but canst not tell whence it cometh, and whither it goeth: so is every one that is born of the Spirit' (KJV). In the Greek of the NT, the term *pneuma* means both 'wind' and 'spirit', making the analogy between the wind and the spirit particularly apt.

In Christian theology, the passage has been interpreted in terms of the beneficent operations of divine grace since the time of Augustine (*On the Grace of Christ, and on Original Sin* 2.28), an interpretation followed by such diverse theologians as Thomas Aquinas, John Calvin and Matthew Henry. The phrase has also been secularized to refer to the freedom of the human mind or spirit, for good or for ill. It can also simply refer to the freedom to move wherever one chooses, as in this quotation from Sir Walter Scott's *Rob Roy* (1817): 'You are a happy man, Frank—you go and come, as the wind bloweth where it listeth'.

See also BORN AGAIN; HOLY SPIRIT, THE; JOHN, GOSPEL OF; NICODEMUS [MALB]

Wine. Used in both OT and NT as a symbol of blessing or curse. In a region subject to devastating droughts, wine conveyed life and health. The image is famously invoked by Psalm 23: 'You prepare a table before me in the presence of my enemies; you anoint my head with oil; my cup overflows'. Human blessings and divine covenants promised an abundance of wine (Gen. 27.26-29; Deut. 7.12-16); God punished disobedience by withholding grapes and wine (Deut. 28.39, 51; Joel 1.10). Wine was a sign of restoration, and the prophets described mountains that would drip with wine when God acted to save his people (Amos 9.13; Joel 3.18). Isaiah envisioned 'a feast of well-matured wines' on Mount Zion (Isa. 25.6). The prophets also employed God's wine as a metaphor for his judgment against his enemies, as when he offered Jeremiah a 'cup of the wine of wrath' for the nations (Jer. 25.15). This imagery is expanded to include the winepress in which God tramples his enemies (Is 63.3; Rev. 14.19-20; 19.15), alluded to in the title of John Steinbeck's *Grapes of Wrath*. In the American Civil War, Julia Ward Howe's *Battle Hymn of the Republic* saw in the progress of the Union Army, God 'trampling out the vintage where the grapes of wrath are stored'. Wine can also symbolize an overflow of sin, as in Revelation's 'Babylon the Great', offering 'the wine of the wrath of her fornication' (17.1-6).

Jesus builds upon the images of covenant-making and banquets in his celebration of the Last Supper, describing the wine cup as his blood of the covenant (Luke 22.20), a cup that he would not drink again until he drank it 'new in the Kingdom of God' (Mark 14.25). Jesus used negative imagery as well, describing his suffering in Jerusalem as drinking from a cup (Mark 10.38-39; Matt. 26.39).

While some passages caution against drunkenness (Prov. 20.1, Eph. 5.18), others praise God for giving 'wine to gladden the human heart' (Ps. 104.15; Ps. 4.7; Eccl. 9.7). A famous example is Jesus' changing water into wine at the wedding feast at Cana (John 2). Paul warned against drunkenness (Rom. 13.13; Gal. 5.21), but advised Timothy to 'take a little wine for your stomach' (1 Tim. 5.23). Characters in Ernest Hemingway's *Farewell to Arms* discuss the advice: 'We'll drink once more for your liver's sake'. 'Like Saint Paul'. 'You are inaccurate. That was wine and the stomach. Take a little wine for your stomach's sake'. 'Whatever you have in the bottle. For any sake you mention'.

American Christians have been ambivalent biblical references to wine. The Puritans valued it, but proponents of the nineteenth-century temperance movements read a 'two-wine' theory into scripture's equivocal counsel regarding alcohol. They argued that since the OT (not the NT) used two different words for wine, there were both unfermented and fermented 'wines' in the biblical narratives, the first spoken of positively, and the second negatively. They found this convincing because they believed that 'modern science' proved alcohol to be poisonous. While no biblical scholars give credence to this argument, it can still be found among supporters of temperance.

Recommended reading. Chiffolo, Anthony F., and Rayner W. Hesse. *Cooking with the Bible: Biblical Food, Feasts, and Lore.* Westport, CT: Greenwood Press, 2006. MacDonald, Nathan. *Not Bread Alone: The Uses of Food in the Old Testament.* Oxford: Oxford University Press, 2008. Merrill, John L. 'The Bible and the American Temperance Movement: Text, Context, and Pretext'. *Harvard Theological Review* 81 (1988) 145-70.

See also BANQUET; CUP; EUCHARIST; HARVEST; VINE; VINEYARD; WEDDING AT CANA [KDP]

Wings of the morning. The phrase 'wings of morning' or 'wings of dawn' comes from Ps. 139.9 (MT 139.10) and is part of a beautiful series of verses (7-12) affirming the inability of the psalmist to escape God's presence (cf. Jer. 23.24) or more positively, the continuing presence of God with the psalmist in all circumstances, locations, etc. The imagery seems to be the journey of the sun (cf. Mal. 4.2 [MT 3.20]) from its rising and setting until its ultimate settlement in the netherworld, which has affinities to the plot of the sun in Egyptian hymns.

The early church utilized this passage in three predominant ways: (1) a call to repentance and confession, (2) a warning against sinfulness, or (3) a demonstration of the connection between the members of the Trinity (e.g., Augustine). The first two relate to the psalmist's inability to flee from God, and the trinitarian interpretation comes from the relationship between God's spirit and presence in v. 7 (MT, v. 8). Theologically, it also seems to support the classical notion of God as omnipresent or at the very least, many believers, both Christian and Jewish, interpret it as such.

Surprisingly, in spite of the potency of its imagery, the phrase 'wings of morning/dawn' has not received substantial treatment in art, literature, and music until recently. In the twentieth century, several Christian groups (e.g., Mercy Me) have set Psalm 139 to music and Jewish painter Irv Davis has depicted its variegated imagery, including the wings of dawn, in one of his many Psalms paintings.

In the secular world, *Wings of Morning* is the title of a book by Thomas Childers concerning the last American bomber shot down in World War II, and this phrase is likely the inspiration behind Johnny Cash's song 'Wings in the Morning'. Thus, although 'wings of the morning' is not as well known as other imagery and metaphors from the Psalter (e.g., 'the Lord is my shepherd'), this phrase is beginning to capture the popular imagination.

Recommended reading. Allen, Leslie C. 'Faith on Trial. An Analysis of Psalm 139', *Vox evangelica* 10 (1977) 5-23.

See also BIRDS, SYMBOLISM OF; DOVE; PSALM/PSALMIST/PSALMS, BOOK OF; SUN; WINGS LIKE A DOVE [DAS]

Wings like a dove. This phrase comes from Ps. 55.6, in which the psalmist describes a condition of anguish and terror, calling out, 'O that I had wings like a dove! I would fly away and be at rest'. The image of the dove in flight has positive connotations rooted in the story of Noah and the flood (Gen. 6–9). Noah sends out a dove to find land. When the dove returns with an olive branch, he knows the water has subsided (Gen. 8.11). The next time Noah sends out the dove, it does not return, signaling that the earth is ready to receive and shelter living things (Gen. 8.12). The image of the dove is an important symbol of peace and unity.

Later in Psalm 55, the psalmist names the source of his agony: 'It is you, my equal, my companion, my familiar friend' (55.13). A number of organizations in support of victims of domestic violence (often based in religious communities) cite this passage and capitalize on the dove as a symbol of a woman fleeing an abusive situation. One particularly widespread educational video bears this title: *Wings like a Dove: Healing for the Abused Christian Woman.*

'Hear My Prayer' (German: '*Hör' mein Bitten*') is a Christian anthem for chorus and orchestra written by Felix Mendelssohn in 1844. The hymn is famous for the passage 'O for the Wings of a Dove'. The text, originally written by William Bartholomew in English, comes from Psalm 55: 'O for the wings, for the wings of a dove! Far away, far away would I rove!' This hymn was popular and the image of the dove's wings would have been a familiar literary allusion in the nineteenth century.

This image is also conjured in the 1958 bestselling country song by Bill Ferguson (recorded by Ferlin Husky), 'On the Wings of a Dove'. The song was featured in the 1983 film *Tender Mercies*. The song invokes the image of a God who does not forget his people; in the midst of hardship, God 'sends down his love, / on the wings of a dove'.

The Wings of the Dove is the title of a 1902 novel by Henry James that tells the story of Milly, a dying American heiress who is traveling in Europe and meets a couple who exploit her kindness and innocence for their own financial gain. Of the main character, James writes, 'Milly was indeed a dove; this was the figure, though it most applied to her spirit'. The deceptive character Kate continually refers to Milly as a dove, and at Milly's death invokes the image of a dove's wings spreading out and covering them all.

In 1997, Iain Softley directed *The Wings of the Dove*, the critically acclaimed film based on the book. Starring Helena Bonham Carter and Linus Roache, the film was widely hailed as the best film adaptation of James's novel. Whereas the novel portrays the characters' dark attempts to defraud the white dove that was Milly as futile, the film shows their efforts to be fruitful but fraught, at least for Roache's character, with unbearable guilt and shame. Near the end of the film, as Milly's coffin floats across the water from Venice, Roache's voice is heard off-camera speaking the words of Psalm 55, 'And I said, O that I had wings like a dove, for then I would fly away, and be at rest'.

See also BIRDS, SYMBOLISM OF; DOVE; WINGS OF THE MORNING [MM]

Wisdom, Wisdom Literature. The term 'Wisdom' (*hokmâ*, in Hebrew; *sophia* in Greek) refers to a philosophic outlook in which people inquired about the most prudent ways to live. The nature of reality and the unpredictability of life stimulated a deeply felt need to order life so that people could live within human society and the threat to order minimised. Wisdom thought recognized that life was fragile and that one should therefore make judicious and prudent life. The body of literature that grew up around this way of thinking is called 'Wisdom Literature'. It was an international phenomenon in the ancient Near East, predating and influencing the biblical books. The universal appeal of wisdom literature points to its shared human experience. Wisdom distinguishes mere prudence and the acquisition of spiritual knowledge.

Israel integrated its distinctive religious awareness with ideas of wisdom. In Proverbs it is the 'fear of the Lord' that is the source of wisdom, not empirical knowledge (1.7). Israel's motive to live prudently was not only for the sake of rational self-interest, but because of its special relationship with God: 'Do not be wise in your own eyes; fear the Lord, and turn from evil' (3.7).

The theological roots of Israelite wisdom lie in the direct relation between cause and effect found in Deuteronomy. This is conventional wisdom. However, the authors of Job and Ecclesiastes, question its absolute authority. They discovered that even correct decisions often produce undesirable results. Death itself is a participant in this situation. The proverbial methods of wisdom conclude that the search for wisdom is intrinsically worth pursuing yet inherently unstable: 'All this I have tested by wisdom; I said, 'I will be wise,' but it was far from me'. (Eccl. 7.23), and 'the righteous and the wise . . . their deeds are in the hand of God; . . . the same fate comes to all' (9.1-2).

Job expresses a similar sentiment: 'He takes the wise in their own craftiness; and the schemes of the wily are brought to a quick end' (5.13). Job despairs because a life fashioned by wisdom did not prevented personal calamity—Job therefore loathes his life. He cannot control it despite strict religious duty. 'Why did I not die at birth, come forth from the womb and expire?' (3.11). Thus, Job attempts to face the apparent contradiction of God's goodness and personal misfortune—a situation called 'theodicy'.

Proverbs uniquely personifies wisdom (Prov. 8.1–9.6) using the imagery of creation to portray its divine attributes. This picture of wisdom is conventional in its call to prudence (8.12-13) countering the threat of disorder (the adulterous woman of 7.4-5) by depicting wisdom as a wise, hospitable and beautiful woman (9.1-6).

The deuterocanonical books of Sirach and Wisdom/Wisdom of Solomon carry on the Jewish wisdom tradition in hellenistic/Greco-Roman times. NT writers use the themes of wisdom to associate individuals with divinely inspired understanding (e.g., Matt. 11.19; 12.42; Mark 6.2; 1 Cor. 2.1-16). Gnostic thought adopts the image of Sophia and some modern feminism connects Sophia with goddess worship, since divine wisdom is often personified as a woman (e.g., Prov. 8.1–9.8; Wis. 7.22–8.1).

The Puritan Anne Bradstreet wrote *The Vanity of All Worldly Things* (1650), which employs the 'vanity' motif in Ecclesiastes. William Blake's *Illustrations of the Book of Job* (1825) captures the imagined pain of Job. Rabbi Harold Kushner uses Job in *When Bad Things Happen to Good People* (1983).

Recommended reading. Johnson, Elizabeth A. *She Who Is: The Mystery of God in Feminist Theological Discourse*. New York: Crossroad, 1992. Rad, Gerhard von. *Wisdom in Israel*. New York: Continuum, 1993.

See also Ecclesiastes; Job; Proverbs; Sirach; Wisdom of Solomon; Word [JKS]

Wisdom of Solomon. Wisdom of Solomon (or simply Wisdom) is one of the Apocryphal/Deuterocanonical writings. It is found among the wisdom writings in Catholic and Orthodox Bibles, but is not considered scripture by either Protestants or Jews. An anonymous Jew living in Egypt wrote the book in Greek as late as the first century CE. While the true author is unknown to us, he or she wrote under the guise of wise King Solomon, who lived nearly a millennium before the writing of Wisdom. The first verse tells us that the book is addressed to the 'Rulers of the Earth', but it seems to be primarily written for the benefit of Jews living in Egypt. Because the author talks about the persecution of the righteous by the wicked, some scholars have suggested that the author wrote Wisdom to encourage Jews to remain faithful during a time of suffering and persecution. The book deals with diverse themes and issues, including: the nature of wisdom, the problem of suffering, death and immortality, idolatry, creation, divine mercy and justice, and Jewish history.

Wisdom consists of three major sections: chs. 1–6 contrast the ultimate fates of the wicked/foolish and the righteous/wise. While the wicked may prosper in this life and the righteous may suffer, the righteous will be vindicated and enjoy immortality in the end; chs. 7–9 autobiographically recount Solomon's quest for wisdom, and proclaim the value of seeking it. Like Proverbs, Wisdom of Solomon personifies wisdom as a woman and speaks of her in very exalted, almost divine terms; and chs. 10–19 begin with a retelling of Israel's history and the role that wisdom played in all of its major events. This retelling is followed by detailed discussions of God's mercy and justice during the Exodus from Egypt and the Conquest of the Promised Land, as well as a digression on idolatry.

Wisdom is one of our most valuable examples of how Jews living in the Greco-Roman world made sense of their sacred traditions in a new cultural context. It is deeply influenced by the Jewish scriptures, but has also been shaped by the language, philosophy, and literary techniques of the Greek-speaking culture in which it was written.

Throughout Christian history Wisdom has been one of the most popular of the deuterocanonical books. Potential allusions to it are found as early as the NT (compare Rom. 1.17-32 with Wis. 13.1-9 and Wis. 7.25-26 with Heb. 1.3), and early Christian theologians like Augustine often quoted from it. Its language is still found in Christian prayers and liturgies. Some Ash Wednesday services open with the following prayer. 'Almighty and everlasting God, you hate nothing you have made and forgive the sins of all who are penitent', an allusion to Wisd. 11.24: 'For you love all things that exist, and detest none of the things that you have made'.

Recommended reading. Winston, David. *The Wisdom of Solomon: A New Translation with Introduction and Commentary*. Anchor Bible, 43. Garden City, NY: Doubleday, 1979.

See also Apocrypha, Deuterocanonicals and Intertestamentals; Solomon; Wisdom Literature
[JRH]

Wise and Foolish Builders (see Two Houses)

Wise and Foolish Virgins. A parable found only in Matt. 25.1-13 (but cf. Luke 13.25), which likens the kingdom of heaven to ten young women (Greek *parthenoi*) who are awaiting the arrival of the bridegroom in order to accompany him to the wedding feast and whose role it is to mark his arrival with burning torches or lamps (*lampas*). Five of the young women have their lamps and oil ready and are thus named 'wise' or 'sensible' (*phronimoi*), while five of them are unprepared and thus 'foolish' (*morai*) (cf. the use of these terms in Matt. 7.24-27). As the bridegroom is delayed, all fall asleep. At midnight, when his arrival is announced, the foolish ones seek to borrow the others' oil, but the 'wise' refuse. The 'foolish' hurry to the merchants to redress their lack, and so fail to enter the feast. Arriving late, they are denied entry by the bridegroom, who announces 'I do not know you' (cf. Matt. 7.23; contrast Rev. 3.19-20). The parable is a call to live in readiness, in the face of the apparent delay of the final time of salvation.

Many aspects of the parable have been interpreted allegorically (virginity, the number five, the delay, the sleep, midnight, the merchants), but most attention has been given to the significance of the oil. Prior to the Reformation, most interpreters understood the oil as good works and almsgiving. Luther distinguished between the *lamps*, representing the outward form of the Christian life, and the *oil*, representing true faith, which by definition cannot be purchased (Sermon 52, Oct. 21, 1522). J.S. Bach's Cantata 'Wachet auf ruft uns die Stimme' (B.W.V. 140, ca.1731) incorporated Philipp Nicolai's hymn (1599), and—with its vivid imagery reminiscent of the Song of Songs and Revelation—has become the most famous cultural artifact based on this parable, shifting the parable's warning tone to one of joyful anticipation.

The readiness of the 'wise' young women and the foolishness of not being prepared are alluded to in various literary contexts, from Milton's ninth sonnet through to Faulkner's *Requiem for a Nun* (2.1). From the nineteenth century onwards, the eschatology in view has generally shifted from the 'end of the age' to the individual's own end. William Blake painted four versions of the subject in watercolor, resembling classical low-relief sculptures. However, for Blake it is those who are 'fond of Literature & Humane & polite accomplishments' who 'have their lamps burning' (Letter no. 21). 'Being prepared' became a prominent cultural value through the Scouting movement.

Most definitions of the idiom 'burning the midnight oil' are unaware of the double meaning of 'midnight oil', yet it is alluded to in William Cowper's poem 'Retirement' (1790), which contrasts temporal and spiritual concerns. A secular use of the image came to prominence in 1967 with Jim Hendrix's song 'Burning of the Midnight Lamp', and this led to the choice of 'Midnight Oil' as the name for the Australian alternative rock group in 1976.

Recommended reading. Balabanski, Vicky. 'Opening the Closed Door: A Feminist Rereading of the 'Wise and Foolish Virgins (Matt. 25.1-13)''. In *The Lost Coin: Parables of Women and Work and Wisdom*. Ed. Mary Ann Beavis. Pp. 71-97. Sheffield: Academic Press, 2002.

See also ALLEGORY; ESCHATOLOGY; PARABLE; WISDOM, WISDOM LITERATURE [VB]

Wise as serpents. Jesus said 'I am sending you out like sheep into the midst of wolves; so be wise as serpents and innocent as doves' (Matt. 10.16). Luke 10.3 keeps the sheep-among-wolves warning about persecution in the context of mission, but leaves out the wise–innocent admonition, which in the *Gospel of Thomas* is the warning to seekers to be sly as snakes and simple as doves because religious leaders take the keys of knowledge and hide them (39.3).

From Genesis to Revelation, the serpent is portrayed as an embodiment of evil. The Greek word for 'serpent' or 'snake' is *ophis*. While not always diabolical, it is usually negative. Typical of mythologies, perhaps because of its hypnotic body movement or its deadly strike, Genesis 3 pictures the serpent in Eden as shrewd and cunning (cf. 1 Cor. 11.3). The dove, by contrast, brings good news about the end of chaos (Gen. 8.8-12) and represents the witless politics of a failing state (Hos. 7.11). While the serpent is Satan (Rev. 20.2), the dove is the Holy Spirit (Matt. 3.16). Matthew 10.16 contrasts images of evil and innocence, cunning and naivety.

In Milton's *Paradise Lost*, Satan found the serpent to be the 'suttlest Beast of all the Field', a common theme. In Joyce's *A Portrait of the Artist as a Young Man*, the preacher warns about 'the devil, once a shining angel ... now a foul fiend come in the shape of a serpent, the subtlest of all beasts of the field'. It is rare in literature or film to see the combination of an innocent character who is also cunning. More commonly, the shrewd take advantage of the naïve, like the traveling doctor of Western films, selling 'snake oil' cure-alls to unsuspecting townsfolk, or Cut-me-own-Throat Dibbler in Pratchett's Discworld, purveyor of 'anything that could be sold hurriedly from an open suitcase in a busy street' (*Guards! Guards!*). The greedy TV preacher stereotype fits well with Pirelli in *Sweeney Todd*, promising to make hair re-grow, or Honest John Fox in *Pinocchio*, who consistently cheats the naïve puppet-child.

Occasionally the innocent thrive. In the 1939 film *Mr. Smith Goes to Washington*, the dirty politician's guilty confession exonerates the guileless protagonist—recaptured in *Evan Almighty* and *Legally Blond 2*. In classic lore, the proud Emperor is hustled, but the innocent child reveals the bare truth. Innocence wins, though not through cunning. It is uncertain if the shrewd–innocent character can exist without hypocrisy. 'When Angels and Serpents Dance', P.O.D. sing, 'one must lead'. In Bunyan's *Pilgrim's Progress*, Mr. By-Ends ridicules Christian for being 'for Religion when in rags and contempt', while he is religious 'when he walks in his golden slippers ... and with applause'. It is suggested that the overly religious Christian is disobeying Jesus' commandment to be wise as serpents. Harry Potter uses innocent-cunning and the gift of Parseltongue—'serpent language'—to defeat the Slytherins and the serpentine Voldemort, but Harry is touched deeply by evil and loses some innocence.

The admonition to cunning–sincerity exists. Eco writes, 'It is necessary ... to be innocent as the dove with Monsieur de Toiras, but also sly as the serpent' (*The Island of the Day Before*). Typically, however, characters get lost either in the world of the serpent or the dove, fail altogether—'with little or no sharpness of faculty or any trace of wisdom of the serpent, nor yet quite a dove' (Melville, *Billy Budd*)—or succeed only in being wise as doves and innocent as serpents.

See also ADAM; ANIMALS, SYMBOLISM OF; BIRDS, SYMBOLISM OF; DOVE; EVE; SATAN; SERPENT/SNAKE [BDGD]

Wise Men (see Magi).

Wise woman of Tekoa. A nameless woman who played a fundamental advisory role during the tumultuous reign of David (2 Sam. 14.2-20). When David refused to grant amnesty to Absalom his son for killing his brother, Joab intervened in the dispute by recruiting the wise woman of Tekoa to plead Absalom's case.

The woman was instructed by Joab to use a fictional story to convince David of the need to forgive and bring Absalom back from exile. She approached David with a story of how her two sons had been involved in a fight. One brother was killed and members of the family were demanding the death of the other, which would leave her with no heir. Convinced this was a true story, David promised the woman that anyone who tries to hurt her or her son would be brought to justice. Having secured such a verdict from the king, the woman proceeded to inform David that he was the culprit. His crime was not forgiving his son Absalom and bringing him home from exile. David discovered this was a ruse plotted by Joab, but still acquiesced to the request to bring Absalom home.

Along with prophets and priests, wise men and women occupied prominent roles in monarchical administrations in most ancient Near Eastern cultures (cf. Jer. 18.18). Part of the retinue always called upon in times of national crises, sages were usually members of the elites who were either groomed for such positions (Dan. 1.3-4), or possessed such uncommon wisdom that made them invaluable to the king and the society. Often times they were called upon to interpret the king's dream, a failure to which sometimes meant their execution (Exod. 7.11; 41.8; Dan. 2.12-14).

While several female prophets are mentioned in the Bible, only two wise women are mentioned. The only other woman classified specifically as a wise woman in the Bible is the woman who saved the city of Abel from destruction with her wise plan (2 Sam. 20.16-22). Though prophets like Huldah also played advisory roles (2 Kgs 22.14-20), she is not explicitly called a wise woman.

Modern interpretations see the wise woman of Tekoa as a political advisor. While some scholars have argued that she was just an actress relying on the wisdom of Joab, the text specifically refers to her as a wise woman (2 Sam. 14.2). Her use of satire to avert a national crisis in Israel cannot be understated (cf. 2 Sam. 12.1-23). Even though she was only relaying Joab's message, her brilliant and convincing act made it possible for David to see the wisdom of forgiving Absalom.

A prototype of the woman who has the king's ears and solves a national problem, the wise woman of Tekoa remains a symbolic portrayal of political as opposed to spiritual advisors. One particular difference is that while the priests and prophets consulted God to make decisions, the wise woman of Tekoa (and of Abel) did not need to consult God (cf. Dan. 2.12-19). They were the leaders' moral consciences, a role occupied mostly by prophets.

See also JOAB; NATHAN; PROPHET; WISDOM, WISDOM LITERATURE [GA]

Witch of Endor. A necromancer from the town of Endor near the Esdraelon Plain. She is known primarily on account of her consultation with King Saul who sought her services after he had failed to receive insight from the Lord regarding his upcoming battle with the Philistines by means of the other forms of divination (dreams, urim, prophets).

The account of this incident, found in 1 Sam. 28.3-25, is often regarded as a satire on the disoriented king. After recently undertaking to purge all mediums and wizards from Israel, a disguised Saul now crosses enemy lines by night to consult one, and in so doing violates the legislation of Deut. 18.9-14, which expressly prohibits communication with the dead, in order to speak with the recently deceased Samuel. Ironically, Samuel's words would be of little comfort to the anxious king, instead revealing only the end of his kingship and his imminent death in battle the very next day.

The encounter ends with the medium's preparation of a lavish feast for the horrified king and his men. This detail is usually understood to be an ironic act of compassion and hospitality; however, given that it was common practice in the ancient world for a king to execute a messenger who presented him with bad news, this action might more reasonably be regarded as a shrewd and desperate attempt by the medium to preserve her life from a man who would have nothing to lose by taking her life.

Outside of the biblical narrative, the evaluation of the medium appears to have been both positive and negative. Pseudo-Philo, for example, associates her with Israel's enemies by identifying her as the daughter of a Midianite diviner who had once lead Israel astray (64.3), and completely eliminates the oft regarded details of her hospitality and tenderness. Josephus, on the other hand, hesitates to say anything negative at all about her, but instead praises her character as a model for all to emulate (*Antiquities* 6.340-42).

Remarkably, the memory of this obscure biblical character has managed to transcend the ages, appearing as a focal point in notable works of art by Rembrandt in the seventeenth century, William Blake in the eighteenth century, and Gustave Doré in the nineteenth century. Subsequently, the Witch of Endor continues to live on as a character in Michael Scott's *The Alchemyst: Secrets of the Immortal Nicholas Flemel*, as the name of a Royal Navy cutter in the Horatio Hornblower novel *Flying Colours*, and in the character named Endora from the television series *Bewitched*.

Recommended reading. Reis, Pamela Tamarkin. 'Eating the Blood: Saul and the Witch of Endor'. In her *Reading the Lines: A Fresh Look at the Hebrew Bible*. Pp. 147-67. Peabody, MA: Hendrickson, 2002.

See also SAMUEL; SAUL; WITCHCRAFT [TB]

Witchcraft. Translated from several Hebrew words for necromancy, divining or sorcery; the first biblical appearance of the Hebrew *mechashefah* is Exod. 22.17: 'a woman who practices witchcraft shall not live', the only biblical condemnation of female practitioners of witchcraft. This verse was cited throughout the Middle Ages as a legal argument for burning witches.

The NT refers to witchcraft/magic (Greek *pharmakeia*) in Acts 19.17-20, where Christian converts who formerly practiced magic abandon the practice. Negative references are in Gal. 5.20, where it is lumped with indecency and debauchery; and Revelation, with fornicators and murderers (9.21; 18.23; 21.8; 22.15).

Most biblical references to witchcraft are condemnatory but are not to named persons (Lev. 19.31, 20.6). Samuel equates divination with rebellion (1 Sam. 15.23), yet is himself summoned up from the dead by Saul through the necromancer of Endor (1 Sam. 28.12). Saul is condemned for consulting a necromancer in 1 Chron. 10.13. Saul had earlier forbidden recourse to 'familiar spirits' (1 Sam. 28.3).

Josiah banishes all 'ghosts and familiar spirits' during his purification of the holy places (2 Kgs 23.24). Isaiah makes several references to the diverse practices of witchcraft (8.19; 19.3; 47.9-12; 57.3), often mockingly. Similarly, Jeremiah lumps together dreamers, diviners and sorcerers as false prophets (27.9; cf. Mal. 33.5).

Only three practitioners of witchcraft are named in the OT: Manasseh, Jezebel, and the woman of Endor. Manasseh practiced every sort of sorcery and divination, all displeasing to Yahweh (2 Chron. 33.6). In the end, he repents his ways and is forgiven (2 Chron. 33.10-17). Jezebel is described as one who 'commits both harlotry and sorcery', thereby linking the two (2 Kgs 9.22). The woman of Endor (1 Sam. 28.7) practiced necromancy, 'prediction of the future by supposedly communicating with dead people' (OED).

The Endor scene may have inspired Shakespeare to write of Macbeth's encounter with the three witches. Another playwright probably influenced was Eugene Scribe, who wrote the play on which Verdi's opera *Un Ballo in Maschera* (*A Masked Ball*, 1859) was based. In Act 2, the sorceress Ulrica predicts death for the king who comes to her in disguise.

The necromancer of Endor is represented in several musical works, invariably in unusual and foreboding music. This is particularly true of Arthur Honegger's 1921 oratorio *Le Roi David* in which the 'sorceress' is a dramatic spoken part. In Händel's 1738 oratorio *Saul*, the 'Witch of Endor' is sung by a tenor, underlining her infernal, unnatural nature. This biblical scene was clearly inspirational for every composer who set it to music.

Women are believed to have engaged in activities like sorcery and soothsaying because of their marginal position in official religion. The dominant religion officially condemned popular religion in an attempt to mute and destroy it. However, popular religious practices were secretly tolerated and flourished. This offered women possibilities to develop their abilities in ways they could not do in official religion. Women continue to act as fortunetellers in some countries. According to a 2008 *New York Times* article (July 8), lawmakers in Tajikistan banned all forms of what they label witchcraft, calling it an 'illegal and parasitical industry'. Yet soothsaying is one of the only career opportunities open to the mainly middle-aged and unmarried women who ply this trade. This echoes the situation as it was in Israel and elsewhere nearly 3000 years ago.

Recommended reading. Leneman, Helen. *Love, Lust and Lunacy: The Stories of Saul and David in Music.* Sheffield: Sheffield Phoenix Press, 2010. Russell, J.B. *A History of Witchcraft: Sorcerers, Heretics, and Pagans.* 2nd edn. London: Thames & Hudson, 2007.

See also WITCH OF ENDOR [HL]

Witness (see Martyr/Martyrdom).

Wolves in Sheep's Clothing. Among the many memorable sayings found in Jesus' Sermon on the Mount is his biting comment: 'Beware of false prophets, who come to you in sheep's clothing but inwardly are ravenous wolves' (Matt. 7.15). This laconic statement first appears in *Aesop's Fables*, whose folkloric tales predate Jesus. The saying, therefore, likely offers an instance of cross-cultural syncretism; however, biblical precursors for the idea are found in Deut. 13.1-11, which warns Israel of fraudulent prophets (*mesith*: magicians) who cunningly lead the people astray. The image of the wolf was particularly fearsome and negative in biblical texts. Wolves were seen as terrifying creatures preying on helpless victims such as children or sheep (Matt. 10.16; Luke 10.3; John 10.12; Acts 20.29). They were described as 'savage' (Acts 20.29) and 'ravenous' (Gen. 49.27; Matt. 7.15) for they would 'devour' (Gen. 49.27), 'tear' (Ezek. 22.27) and 'destroy' (Jer. 5.6) their victims.

In the gospels, Jesus has little patience for predatory or spurious religious behavior such as false religious teachers, ostentatious prayers, or greedy moneychangers. He strongly condemns all of these activities and warns his followers to avoid the syrupy sayings of religious charlatans. His stern words are directed not only toward the 'true' sheep of Israel but also toward deceptive teachers who court hellfire through their trickery. Many early church writers continued to admonish false prophets as 'wolf-like' figures who threatened the faithful (Augustine, *Sermo* 137.12; *De sermone Domini in Monte* 2.24.80; Ambrose, *De Spiritu Sancto* 2.10.108-109; Jerome, *Epistle* 22.38; 147.11). False prophets within the fold necessitated vigilance to ensure that the Christian flock was not devoured by 'spiritual predators'.

Jesus' condemnation of charlatans was an important catalyst in fuelling nascent notions of heresy and apostasy in early Christian hermeneutics. Consequently, the wolf metaphor offers interesting implications for the issues of authentic belief and intolerance in early Christian thought. Moreover, since wolves are pack animals who work together to kill their prey, the metaphor additionally implies that there is an 'alpha' male within the pack—the supreme predator, con-artist, and deceiver known as Satan.

The widespread dissemination of both *Aesop's Fables* and biblical wolf symbolism in Medieval Europe facilitated the popularity of this saying, which came to denote any deceptively sweet-sounding person of devious intent. Western literature often employed the phrase to refer to corrupt clerics and politicians (i.e., Chaucer's *Friar, Summoner, and Pardoner;*, Langland's *Piers Plowmann*; Shakespeare's *Henry VI*; and Samuel Butler's *The Way of All Flesh*). During the Middle Ages, the big, bad wolf character also became a popular theme in children's stories and fairy tales (e.g., the Grimms's *Little Red Riding Hood, The Wolf and the Seven Young Kids*, and *The Three Little Pigs*). Furthermore, wolves were associated with the uncanny ability to shapeshift to conceal their true nature and intentions—another manifestation of trickery to fool their prey. *Lycanphobia* (fear of werewolves) penetrated, like fangs, deeply into the genres of horror, fantasy, and adventure literature as well as modern role playing games and comics. Masquerading wolves also captured the imagination of Hollywood. The TV series, 'Airwolf' (1984–1987), depicted a secret helicopter whose clandestine missions were symbolized by its military logo of a wolf in sheep's clothing. A TV episode of *Zorro* (1990) was also titled 'A Wolf in Sheep's Clothing'.

The modern recognition of wolves as an endangered species has helped to rehabilitate their image in Western culture but the west's longstanding fear of wolves still resonates today like howls in the literary imagination.

Recommended reading. Mitts-Smith, Debra. *Picturing the Wolf in Children's Literature.* London: Routledge, 2009.

See also ANIMALS, SYMBOLISM OF [SDD]

Woman. In western society, the word 'woman' refers to a sexually mature female from the age of menarche through to and including menopause.

In the OT, the sexual differentiation of humanity is seen first in terms of male (*zākār*, MT; *arsēn*, LXX) and female (*něqēbā*, MT; *thēlēs*, LXX) (Gen. 1.27), and secondly in terms of their complementary relationship one to the other as man ('*īsh*, MT; *anēr*, LXX) and woman ('*ishshā*, MT; *gynē*, LXX) (Gen. 2.22-25). Furthermore, when the second creation account states God made woman out of Adam's side (see Michelangelo, *Creation of Eve*) it affirms that women are 'of the same substance' as men, that is to say they are physically of the same type (Gen. 2.21). Similarly, when Adam declares 'this is bone of my bones and flesh of my flesh' (Gen. 2.23) he also affirms the woman to be of the same 'essence' as himself. That is to say, they shared the essential characteristics that differentiate humans from the rest of the created order (cf. Gen. 2.18, 20), namely that both were created in *imago Dei* (Gen. 1.27). While the sexual differentiation of humanity requires men and women to live in harmony and does not confer privilege on either, interpreters differ as to the nature of the relationship between men and women (e.g., egalitarian, complementarian, patriarchal).

Two enduring cultural constructs concerning womanhood are the Madonna (e.g., Rafael's painting, *Sistine Madonna*) and the Magdalene. The Magdalene is portrayed variously as the sensual seductress, an archetype of repentant sinners (e.g., Antonio Canova, *The Repentant Magdalene*, Mel Gibson's, *Passion of the Christ*), and a faithful disciple (e.g., Annibale Carracci, *The Dead Christ Mourned— The Three Marys*). The Madonna archetype may be seen in the values associated with *Marianismo* (Latin America) which venerates the feminine virtues of sexual purity, moral strength, passivity and the ability to bear children. In recent years, the feminist concept of woman as a self-determining free-agent who is in all ways equal to men has emerged as a third secular construct of womanhood. This view of womanhood is, as Fox-Genovese (*Women and the Future of the Family*, 2000) observes, shaped by western views on the role of the individual.

In contrast to these constructs, the biblical concept of womanhood takes a different trajectory. There is, for example, both an acknowledgement of the equality of men and women (e.g., Gen. 1.26-30; 2.18-23; 1 Pet. 3.7) as well as the interdependence of men and women (e.g., Phil. 2.3-4) which guards against individualistic thinking. Second, while women are enjoined to cultivate the virtues of moral strength and sexual purity (e.g., 1 Pet. 3.1-6), men are also urged to cultivate these virtues (Gal. 5.22-24) as well as to honor and respect their wives (Eph. 5.25-28; 1 Pet. 3.7), thus shutting the door on *Marianismo*. Finally, the scriptures do not portray women, as a group, as temptresses but rather hold both men and women responsible for how they exercise their sexuality (e.g.,1 Thess. 4.3-7). Viewed in this light, a Christian vision of womanhood overturns cultural paradigms as it asserts that women, in their humanity, are bearers of the image of God and, in their experience of salvation, are reborn in the likeness of Christ (Rom. 8.29) and are heirs of the divine promise.

See also HUMAN; IMAGE OF GOD; MAN; MARRIAGE; MARY, MOTHER OF JESUS; MARY MAGDALENE; SALVATION; SANCTIFICATION; SEX/SEXUALITY [KFM]

Woman Caught in Adultery. The pericope of the woman caught in adultery is one of the favorites of many Christians because of the genuine humanity it brings to a story involving Jesus. This episode, found in most modern English Bibles at John 7.53–8.11, depicts the scribes and Pharisees bringing a woman caught in adultery to Jesus, who is teaching in the temple. They tell Jesus that the woman was caught in the very act of adultery and they want to know what he thinks should be done. As the narrator states, they were attempting to test him so that they could accuse him. Jesus bends down and writes something in the ground. When they persist in asking Jesus what he thinks, he says that the one who is without sin should throw the first stone at her, and then he bends down and writes again. The group of scribes and Pharisees slips away one by one, oldest to youngest, until Jesus and the woman are left alone. Jesus then rises and asks her where her accusers are and whether anyone is condemning her. She says that no one is, to which Jesus replies that he is not condemning her either, and that she should go and no longer sin.

Many questions have been raised about this episode, such as how it is that these men found this woman in the very act of adultery, whether this episode indicates that Jesus could write (there is good evidence that he could read), and what sort of knowledge Jesus had of the men so that they slipped away quietly, among others. The most important critical issue regarding this episode, however, is that it does not appear in a number of the earliest and best manuscripts. Although this episode is found at John 7.53–8.11 in some manuscripts and in a number of other places in a few other manuscripts, sometimes in later manuscripts appearing with indication that the passage was believed to be a later insertion, it is missing in a number of major early sources. These include two of the earliest and best papyrus manuscripts, the two major early codex manuscripts (Sinaiticus and Vaticanus), other major codex manuscripts including probably codex Alexandrinus, the Syriac NT tradition, some manuscripts in the Old Latin tradition, and most Coptic traditions. The only major manuscript that includes this episode is codex Bezae from the fifth century, along with the later Byzantine manuscript tradition, as well as the Latin Vulgate.

Despite this lack of evidence, the story itself seems to be relatively early, if not canonical, because it was probably known by the second-century bishop Papias, as cited by the later church historian Eusebius (*Ecclesiastical History* 3.39). The episode was apparently also found in the *Gospel of the Hebrews*, an apocryphal gospel probably from the second century. Nevertheless, the story of the woman caught in adultery is not found in the earliest manuscript tradition, and hence was probably a later tradition that was not part of the original form of John, but may have been attached to it because it seemed to be in keeping with Johannine themes and ideas (although it is found in one manuscript of Luke).

Despite its questionable canonical status, the episode of the woman caught in adultery continues to inspire powerful artistic renderings, in which the accusatory scribes and Pharisees are contrasted with the terrified woman and calm, forgiving, and confident Jesus, e.g., Tintoretto (1546–48); Guercino (1621); Poussin (1653); Rembrandt (1644); Polenov (1886–87).

See also CANON; JOHN, GOSPEL OF [SEP]

Woman Clothed with the Sun. In Rev. 12.1-17, a character who appears as a sign in heaven; she is clothed with the sun, wearing a crown of twelve stars, and the moon is under her feet. While the woman is pregnant and in labor, a red dragon with seven heads, ten horns, and seven crowns on his heads appears and stands by the woman ready to devour her child who is said to 'rule all nations with an iron rod' (12.5). However, as soon as the woman gives birth, God takes her son safely to his throne. The woman then flees to a place prepared by God and there, she is cared for.

The thwarted dragon, who proceeds to lose a battle in heaven and is cast onto earth, decides to persecute the woman, but she is rescued by the earth (*gē*) and escapes his grasp. The dragon, furious at having his destructive plans spoilt three times, takes his anger out on the woman by making war with the rest of her offspring: those who keep the commandments of God, who know and have heard the testimony of Jesus Christ.

Steeped in rich Jewish apocalyptic tradition and imagery, the woman clothed with the sun has been interpreted as representing many important biblical figures and themes: the Virgin Mary/the new Eve, the church, the nation of Israel, and the Daughter of Zion.

The maternal and birth imagery that surround the woman points to the birth of Christ by the Virgin Mary. Seen in this light, the woman's 'male child' (Rev. 12.5) is Jesus who 'rule[s] all nations with a rod of iron'. The dragon's attempt to devour the woman's child mirrors King Herod's attempt to kill the infant Jesus (Matt. 2.16). The woman is also a new Eve: the conflict between Eve, the serpent, and her unborn descendants in Gen. 3.15 echoes the scene of the woman, the serpent/dragon, and her 'male child', which is also a figure of Mary, King Herod, and the Matthean birth narrative, respectively. This Marian understanding also symbolizes the woman as the church: the mother of all followers of Christ. The woman, as well as the church, brings forth children into a world with whom the dragon/devil vows constant warfare. The woman represents the people of God by the reference to the crown of twelve stars: a figuration of the twelve tribes and the twelve apostles; thus, she is understood to be representative of Israel who brings forth the Messiah. She is also seen as the OT image of the Daughter of Zion: in a place of honor (e.g., Ps. 9.14; Isa. 62.11), yet at the same time disgraced (e.g., Isa. 1.8; Jer. 4.31; 6.2): in labor while awaiting her own death and her child's. Here, the Daughter of Zion is recast in the image of cosmic birth and apocalyptic anguish.

The best known image of the woman clothed with the sun in popular culture is a series of watercolors by the English poet and artist William Blake (*The Red Dragon Paintings*) painted between 1805 and 1810. Writers and filmmakers have used Blake's paintings as their inspiration: notably Thomas Harris's novel *Red Dragon* and its film adaptations, *Manhunter* (1986) and *Red Dragon* (2002).

See also APOCALYPSE, APOCALYPTIC; BIRTH; CHILDREN OF ISRAEL; CHURCH; DAUGHTER OF ZION; DRAGON; EVE; HERODS, THE; ISRAEL; JOHN OF PATMOS; MARY, MOTHER OF JESUS; REVELATION, BOOK OF; TWELVE TRIBES OF ISRAEL [RKM]

Womb. In the Bible, the 'womb' (Hebrew *rechem*) is referred to most often in the context of conception and birth. The OT describes the ability or inability to conceive as God's 'closing' or 'opening' of the womb, often as a form of blessing or punishment. In Genesis 30, Jacob refers to God withholding the 'fruit of the womb' from Rachel, just as later in the same story God 'opened her womb'. The Pentateuch also places a special emphasis on the firstborn human or animal (the offspring who 'opens the womb') as belonging to God. Thus, reference to God's ability to punish through the withholding of conception and children (centered on the womb) forms part of the prophetic vocabulary of condemnation and threat, often coupled with God's control over Israel's more general destiny and prosperity (cf. Hos. 9.11-16).

In the poetic and prophetic books, the womb is often used metaphorically to indicate the beginning of one's earthly existence, and is often used as a way of marking the beginning of human life. Job 10.18-19 presents the stillborn child as not having ever 'been'. More commonly, the womb is referred to as a poetic manner of saying 'lifelong', such as 'from my mother's womb I guided the widow' (Job 31.18), or 'I have been a nazirite to God from my mother's womb' (Judg. 16.17). This language occurs in the statements about birth and death in Job and Ecclesiastes, with the womb being both the point of life's origin and a sign of life's endpoint. 'Naked I came from my mother's womb, and naked shall I return there (Job 1.21), 'as they came from their mother's womb, so they shall go again, naked as they came' (Eccl. 5.15). Psalm 110.3 extends this metaphor, and makes reference to the morning dew as coming from the 'womb of the morning'.

Although exiting the womb at birth marks the beginning of life, the OT views God as active in 'shaping' the child in the womb (Ps. 139.13), a process that is viewed as rather mysterious by the Bible's (mostly male) authors (cf. Eccl. 11.5; 2 Macc. 7.22). This notion of God's role in 'shaping' the child in the womb is referred to in the prophetic books as an additional aspect of God's foreknowledge and control over human destiny. Isaiah 44 and 49 describe God's plans for his people and his prophet as preceding Isaiah's birth: 'the LORD called me before I was born, while I was in my mother's womb he named me' (Isa. 49.1). Jeremiah's call narrative moves God's plan to an earlier time yet: '*Before* I formed you in the womb I knew you, and before you were born I consecrated you; I appointed you a prophet to the nations' (Jer. 1.5). In Genesis, God's prediction of rivalry between Esau and Jacob (and their descendants the Edomites and Israelites) gives an explanation for their current unsettled relations in the womb (Gen. 25.2-23). God's compassion or mercy or love is often conveyed by the related term *racham* (Exod. 33.19; Jer. 6.23; 13.14; Ps. 18.1; 102.13).

The NT draws upon the references from the OT outlined above. Paul describes his commissioning as an apostle 'before I was born' (literally 'from my mother's womb', Gal. 1.15), echoing the language of Jeremiah and Isaiah, with God's purpose for Paul preceding his birth, even though Paul's knowledge of his true calling only arrived much later. Luke includes the story of John the Baptist 'leaping in the womb' when Mary announces her pregnancy to Elizabeth, a foreshadowing of John's prophetic role in preparing the way for the ministry of Jesus (Luke 1.44).

See also BIRTH [MWM]

Word. The Word of God is a crucial biblical category, used in a variety of ways throughout the scriptures. In the OT, word is a translation of the Hebrew *dabar*, often appearing in the construction *dabar Yahweh* (Word of God). The phrase is especially common in the prophetic writings, occurring more than 50 times in Jeremiah alone. In many instances, the word of God has the power to bless, curse, and accomplish God's purposes in the world.

In the NT, two Greek nouns are translated as word, *logos* and *rhēma*. The former occurs more than 300 times. The NT use of the term has a variety of meanings, many of them expanding on appearances of the term in the OT. The most famous instance occurs in the Prologue to John where the eternal *logos* incarnates as Jesus Christ (John 1.14). A number of scholars suspect this passage was originally a hymn to divine wisdom, and that the term 'word' was an editorial addition to the hymn. Like the *logos* of John 1, Wisdom is personified in the OT. In Prov. 8.22, 27-31, Wisdom (*Sophia*) is the co-agent in creation, something also true of the Word in John 1.1-3. Significantly, earlier writers used 'Word' and 'Wisdom' more or less interchangeably (e.g., Wis. 9.1-2; Sir. 24.3). Paul refers to Christ as 'the wisdom of God' in 1 Cor. 1.24, 30 (cf. Col. 2.2). The Word is, for Paul, God's Wisdom come among us. For Gentile Greek readers of John 1, the term *logos* would also bring to mind the reason present in the universe since the term was used by Greek philosophers to denote the rational principle of order by which the universe is sustained and held together, motifs also present in the Johannine prologue.

In the Christian theological tradition, Word of God refers not only to the incarnate son of God but also to the Bible and the act of preaching. Both Jews and Christians describe themselves as 'people of the book', and that is due to their shared belief that God speaks through the scriptures, especially when proclaimed by the rabbi or minister to the congregation.

The broader cultural relevance of the term conjures up images of divinely inspired speech. There have been many claiming to speak for God throughout western history, many of them abusing their authority at the same time. Adolf Hitler is an example of one who frequently invoked the 'Almighty's' blessing in his nationalistic speeches to the German people. This example demonstrates the extent to which the phrase Word of God can be subject to ideological distortion and why many are justifiably suspicious of anyone claiming to possess or have the inside scoop on the Word of God, precisely because they have seen how such speech can be used to control and to dehumanize.

Recommended reading. Ashton, John. 'The Transformation of Wisdom: A Study of the Prologue of John's Gospel'. *New Testament Studies* 32 (1986) 161-86.

See also CHRIST; JOHN, GOSPEL OF; WISDOM [CRJH]

Word of God, the (see Word).

Worm that does not die. From the Greek *skōlēx* meaning grub, maggot, or earthworm, etymology uncertain. The phrase 'worm dies not' appears in Mark 8.46-48 where Jesus quotes from Isa. 64.12 to admonish his disciples not to cause any children that believe in him to sin, from which point, he uses a series of analogies to illustrate the severity of judgment in the afterlife for those who choose not to obey him. Jesus' warning has dual significance: the imagery of the worm is retrospective since it references worms found in the valley of Hinnom, and it prefigures the punishment of hell written in Rev. 21.8.

In Jesus' time, residents of Jerusalem are thought to have frequented the valley of Hinnom, located southwest of the city to burn refuse, garbage, carcasses of dead animals, and sometimes, criminals. There, fires smouldered incessantly, and worms lived and bred in the putrid condition of burning flesh and bones. Centuries before, during monarchical times, some kings such as Manasseh (2 Chron. 33.6) and Solomon (1 Kgs 11.7) are said to have practiced abominable acts of worship to the pagan god Moloch by sacrificing some of their infants in the flames, an act in direct violation of one of Yahweh's specific commands (Exod. 20.3). Josiah, the last righteous king of Judah, in a religious revival, did away with the ritualistic sacrifices, and the valley of Hinnom, a place of ill-repute, became associated with judgment and punishment.

For textual reasons, some scholars believe that the phrase 'worm dies not' should not appear in vv. 44 and 46. They argue that it suffices to have the phrase in v. 48. Hence, the phrase appears once in some translations, placing less emphasis on the eternal judgment. In the KJV, however, the phrase appears in vv. 44, 46, and 48.

In the OT, one of the words for 'worm' is *rimmâh* (Exod. 16.24, Job 17.24, Job 19.26). *Sas* translates as 'worm' but refers to a moth in Isa. 51.8. The worm has sustained its disdainful image as a symbol that is associated with death, agony, torment, and filth (Acts 13.23). In later times, various genres of expression similarly associated worms with death or torture. In Edgar Allan Poe's 'Conqueror Worm', Poe masterfully employs the use of metaphor of man's life and experiences as if it were a stage of phases, only to succumb in the end of a futile life, conquered by death with the worm feasting on the dying soul. In popular culture, as portrayed in Tim Burton's *Beetlejuice* (1988) a maniacal sandworm burrows itself in sand and intermittently surfaces. At the end of the movie, the monstrous-looking worm devours the antagonist as if to rid the other characters of some evil. In the dark comedy *Tremors (*1990), worm-like creatures burst through their subterranean abode to torture and kill the human characters. Even in our postmodern electronic age, the diabolical and torturous worm reappears with a twist on a classic literary work. In the video game *Dante's Inferno Third Circle: Gluttony*, giant worms appear in a dark gastric underworld of an unknown being's organ. Its mission is to kill anyone who dares pass by.

See also ANIMALS, SYMBOLISM OF; GEHENNA; HELL; SHEOL [GM]

Wormwood. From the Hebrew *la'anah* (wormwood, bitterness) and the Greek *apsinthos* (wormwood). Wormwood is a plant with a bitter taste that is most often used as a metaphor for bitterness and sorrow (Deut. 29.18; Prov. 5.4; Jer. 9.15, 23.15; Lam. 3.15, 3.19; Amos 5.7, 6.2). The phrase 'gall and wormwood' (Lam. 3.18-19) is used this way in Anne Brontë's *Agnes Grey*: 'It was gall and wormwood to see that splendid, highly accomplished woman, once so courted and admired, transformed into an active managing housewife'. In Revelation, Wormwood is the name of the burning star that falls from heaven that embitters a third of the world's rivers and springs, rendering them undrinkable (8.11). In C.S. Lewis's *The Screwtape Letters* (1945) Wormwood is the name of the junior demon that receives letters of instruction from his uncle and senior demon, Screwtape (1945).

See also PLANTS, SYMBOLISM OF [AS]

Worship. Acts of worship have been important in human cultures since the earliest times. In the OT, worship of God takes various forms, from the personal interactions of various figures to more corporate and institutionalized forms that involve recognition of sacred sites and places, such as Mount Sinai. The ancient Israelites also developed a portable means of worship, the Ark of the Covenant, before finally constructing a temple in Jerusalem under the reign of Solomon. This provided a permanent and fixed place of worship, and served as a center of Israelite religious life until its destruction (586 BCE). It was restored after the return from exile and greatly enhanced by Herod the Great, before its destruction by the Romans in 70 CE. This became the focused center of Jewish worship. Temple worship involved various ritual acts, including music, the reading of Torah, and the offering of sacrifices. Early Christian worship reflects somewhat similar patterns, in that worship is seen first as a personal act of relationship to God/Jesus which then becomes corporate and formalized as early Christians gathered together in various groups.

Little is known about early Christian worship practice, and scholars speculate about the influence of the synagogue and Greco-Roman cultic practices. In any case, Christian worship probably involved at least the reading of scripture, celebration of the Last Supper or Eucharist, the singing of 'psalms, hymns, and spiritual songs' (Eph. 5.18-19; cf. Col. 3.16; Jas 5.13) and some form of early proclamation or preaching. Whereas Jewish worship after the destruction of the temple remained organized around synagogue worship, Christian worship took a number of different and distinct forms, often reflective of local cultural influence. In light of OT temple worship, as well as possibly the influence of various pagan religious practices, it is perhaps not surprising that Christianity also grew out of local house churches and began to develop its own buildings suitable for larger scale worship. One of the most important divides of the church, however, was over the use of the local vernacular in worship, with the western church tending toward retention of Latin and the eastern church utilizing the vernacular.

The fourth century, because of the political institutionalization of Christianity, evidenced significant developments in worship practices, including such liturgies as that of John Chrysostom, which continues to be used in the Orthodox churches. The Reformation brought a number of changes in worship practice to the church, including the use of vernacular languages for churches in the west. However, there were more fundamental developments in the liturgy as well, including the concept of the priesthood, the role of corporate worship, and the function of the sacraments or ordinances. Christian worship undertook some of its most widespread changes during the nineteenth and twentieth centuries. With the breakdown and fragmentation of much institutionalized Christianity in the west, a number of new church movements developed, along with their own worship practices. These new church groups spread throughout North America, and brought with them new conceptions of the function of the clergy, the democratization of worship practices, and the growth of a populist church tradition. This transformation of worship has continued in recent times with what has sometimes been called the 'worship wars' of Protestant and other churches, with disputes over music serving as emblematic of more fundamental conflicts over the changing ways in which worship is practiced in the contemporary church.

See also CHURCH; EUCHARIST; SACRIFICE; SYNAGOGUE; TEMPLE, ISRAEL'S [SEP & WJP]

Wrath. The wrath of God is a biblical (and anthropomorphic) term expressing the displeasure of God at sin. It may be directed at individuals, nations, or at his covenant people. In the Bible, God is portrayed as righteous, holy and perfect in all divine judgments. Consequently, sin, as rebellion against God, evokes a justifiable and righteous anger against sin. It is mentioned many times in the Bible. It is not considered to be an expression of emotion, a fit of anger, or a malicious act. Rather it is like the executing of justice upon an offender of the law by a judge. Wrath expresses the divine holiness as it comes in contact with the evils people do. It expresses the divine response to all unrighteousness (Rom. 1.18).

In the OT, the wrath of God may be manifest against humanity in general. The Flood, the destruction of Sodom and Gomorrah and the plagues of Egypt are interpreted in terms of God's wrath against sin. It may also be expressed against his disobedient covenant people because of their disbelief of the spies' report that they could enter the land of promise (Num. 13–14), which resulted in the wilderness wanderings. Elsewhere, the wrath of God against Israel's repeated disobedience, a form of disbelief, was portrayed as plague, poisonous snakes, military defeats, and other tokens of divine displeasure with Israel's sins. The prophets (e.g., Isa. 13.9, 13; Ezek. 7.12, 19; Zeph. 1.15, 19) repeatedly warned against the Day of the Lord as a Day of Wrath.

The NT has numerous warnings to escape the wrath of God. In general the wrath of God in the NT refers to the Last Judgment. Revelation presents vivid pictures of the wrath of God in the end times (e.g., 6.17). The wrath of God will be revealed, poured out and unveiled against those who reject the truth of God. The basic theme of Romans is that the Mosaic law 'worketh wrath;' however, the mercy of God as an expression of divine love, saves from wrath through the atoning death of Christ Jesus (Rom. 5.9). Rejecting the mercy of God in Jesus condemns unrepentant sinners to experience the wrath of the Lamb (Rev. 6.16).

The biblical doctrine of the wrath of God has repeatedly been questioned from before the beginning of Christianity. Philo of Alexandria, a hellenized Jew (20 BCE–50 CE), defended the doctrine against Stoic attacks. Marcion of Sinope (c. 110–160) was declared a heretic for teaching the wrath of God was the work of the evil Demiurge of the Jewish scriptures.

Nineteenth-century theologians Friedrich Schleiermacher (1768–1834) and Albrecht Ritschl (1822–1889) rejected the doctrines of divine punishment, including hell. Some Christian sectarians reject the wrath of God as a false teaching, claiming instead that there will be a universal salvation for humanity.

The Day of Wrath (*Dies Irae*) was influentially evoked in the thirteenth-century hymn by that name, used as a sequence in the Roman Catholic Requiem Mass until Vatican II; also found in Anglican missals: 'Day of wrath! O day of mourning! See fulfilled the prophets' warning, Heaven and earth in ashes burning!' (*Roman Missal*, 1962). The *Dies Irae* has been set to music many times (e.g., by Haydn, Berlioz, Mahler, Gounod), and is referred to frequently in western literature (e.g., by Macaulay, Goethe, Wilde, Eco).

Recommended reading. Nur, Amos, and Dawn Burgess. *Apocalypse: Earthquakes, Archaeology, and the Wrath of God.* Princeton, NJ: Princeton University Press, 2008.

See also ATONEMENT; CHRIST; DAY, OF JUDGMENT/ OF THE LORD /OF WRATH; GRACE; HELL; LAW; MERCY; SIN [AJW]

X

Xerxes. Greek name of the Persian king called Ahasuerus in the Bible. He figures prominently in the Book of Esther where he is called Ahasuerus in both the HB and LXX. His Persian name was Khshayarsha. English biblical translations traditionally use Ahasuerus instead of Xerxes. Scholars are not completely certain if the biblical Ahasuerus is Xerxes due to uncertainty arising from spelling variants in different languages in which it is found.

Traditionally, the biblical Ahasuerus is identified as Xerxes I (reigned 485–465 BCE), the son of Darius I and the grandson of Cyrus the Great of the Achaemenid dynasty. His name appears in three books of the Bible: Ezra, Daniel and Esther.

Ahasuerus/Xerxes is cited as a ruler in Ezra 4.6; however, the verses that follow (7-23) cite opposition during the reign of Artaxerxes I, the son of Xerxes. The citations have raised issues over the dates for the work of both Ezra and Nehemiah. In Dan. 9.1, Ahasuerus is cited as the father of the Darius who threw Daniel into a lions' den.

The Book of Esther is romantic story about the rescue of the Jewish people by Esther (Hadassah) from their enemies during the reign of Xerxes. The plot to kill Xerxes by two of his eunuchs stymied by her uncle Mordechai cited in the book is like many plots against the Persian kings known from history. The historic Xerxes died a victim of a plot executed by a eunuch and his vizier, Artabanos.

The story of Esther and Xerxes has been retold in rabbinic literature and in countless Christian sermons. The novel *Esther* (1884; republished 1938) was written by Henry Brook Adams who wrote under the pen name Frances Snow Compton. Adams's plot portrays a modernist socialite in love with an Episcopal minister as a clash between faith and reason. Other novels have been a close re-telling of the story such as Rebecca Kohn's *The Gilded Chamber: A Novel of Queen Esther* (2005). The movie, *One Night with the King* (2006) is the latest of over a dozen movies on Esther made by Hollywood since 1913 (a list which includes the Veggie Tales' *Esther: The Girl Who Became Queen*, 2004).

The historical Xerxes I began his reign by suppressing revolts in Egypt and pacifying Babylonia. He fought the Greeks who had defeated his father at the Battle of Marathon (490 BCE). In 483 BCE he began his western campaign, bridging the Hellespont on pontoons supported by a vast fleet.

Spartan King Leonidas and his 300 badly mauled Xerxes' army at the Battle of Thermopylae (August 480 BCE) before they were betrayed. The event has been portrayed in the films *The 300 Spartans* (1962) and *300* (2007). The latter was based on Frank Miller's novel. *300* was spoofed in *United 300* (2007) with the emperor Jerxes as a terrorist.

Next, Xerxes conquered Athens, but the tide turned when the Greek navy defeated the larger Persian fleet at Salamis on September 28, 480 BCE. Xerxes withdrew, and his expeditionary force was destroyed by the combined Greek armies at Plataea (479 BCE).

Gates of Fire (1998) by Stephen Pressfield interprets Xerxes trying to understand Spartan culture and prowess in battle. Xerxes is also portrayed in the historical novel, *The Dragon of the Isthar Gate* and in Gore Vidal's *Creation*. In music, he is most famously portrayed in Händel's opera *Serse* (1738), opening with the famous area *Ombra ma fù*, sung by the king.

Recommended reading. Llywelyn, Morgan. *Xerxes*. New York: Chelsea House, 1989.

See also ESTHER, BOOK OF; ESTHER, ADDITIONS TO; HAMAN; MORDECAI; PERSIA [AJW]

Y

Yahweh, YHWH. This is the divine name for the major deity of the Israelites and is sometimes referred to as the Tertragrammaton/Tetragram (from the Greek for four letters), made up of the consonants YHWH. Since Hebrew did not originally have vowels, the Masoretes (who provided the vowels on which current English translations are based) wrote the constants *Yahweh* with the vowels from *Adonai* (Lord) or *Elohim* (God; Gen. 3.14) to indicate that the holy name should not be spoken but rather read as 'Lord'. Thus 'Jehovah' pronounces the *ketib* (what is written), reading the consonants YHWH with the vowels from *Adonai* versus *qere* (what is to be read). Respect for the divine name is known in scribal practice of the DSS (200 BCE–60 CE) where the name of God is sometimes written in paleo-Hebrew (an older form of the Hebrew script). The pronunciation Yahweh is a scholarly construction based on discussions of Hebrew philology, theophoric names (personal names with divine elements in them, like Isaiah, 'Yahweh is my help') and interpretations (Exod. 3.14).

Yahweh is a prominent figure in Israelite history, with early traditions in the south (Deut. 33.1-4) of Israel. The name Yahweh is dateable and widely attested in early poetry (twelfth to tenth century BCE) of the OT (Exod. 15.1-18; Judg. 5), in extrabiblical material like the Mesha Stela/Moabite Stone (835 BCE) and in early Hebrew inscriptions (Kuntillet 'Ajrud, eighth century BCE).

Yahweh is often portrayed as a warrior ('Yahweh of hosts') and a storm deity in some of the OT's earliest poetry (Exod. 15.1-18; Deut. 33). Likely at the earliest point in Israel's history, Yahweh was one god among many who had his own place in the divine council of the gods. Like Baal, at an earlier period Yahweh was subservient to the head god El (Deut. 32.8-9). While the Canaanite god El was a part of early Israelite worship (hence the name Isra*el*), Yahweh eventually became Israel's primary deity. Later Yahweh was conceived as head of the divine council (Ps. 82) and in the exilic period Israel embraced monotheism (Isa. 43.10; 44.6-8). The name Yahweh is often an indication of the J source in the source-critical theory of JEDP.

Various literary studies have explored the name YHWH/Yahweh. Recently Harold Bloom's *Jesus and Yahweh: The Divine Names* (2005) partly examines literary characteristics of Yahweh's name and its relation to Jesus. Christians now refer to Yahweh in prayer and liturgical music, sometimes not pronouncing the name according to Jewish practice. In many current English Bibles Yahweh is translated 'Lord'. Some denominations have incorporated pop music into their liturgical celebrations that maintain the divine name as in U2's song 'Yahweh' from the album *How to Dismantle an Atomic Bomb* (2004).

In ancient Israel, knowing the names of divine beings seemed to have magical associations (Gen. 32.24-30). Likewise, invoking a name that sounds ancient seems to elicit a particular response by contemporary listeners/worshippers. On a popular level Yahweh is sometimes used as a catch-all for religion as seen in Doug Underwood's *From Yahweh to Yahoo!: The Religious Roots of the Secular Press* (2002), which explores religious tendencies in current news media.

Recommended reading. Smith, Mark S. *The Early History of God: Yahweh and Other Deities in Ancient Israel.* San Francisco: Harper & Row, 1990.

See also BAAL; CANAAN/CANAANITES; DEITY; ELOHIM; HEBREW LANGUAGE; I AM; SHEMA; SUN [SWF]

Yom Kippur (see Atonement, Day of).

Z

Zacchaeus. The name of the senior tax collector mentioned only in Luke 19.1-10 (not the traitor of 2 Macc. 10.18-22). The story comes from Luke's special source. It stresses Luke's concern to proclaim grace to those contemporary Jewish piety condemned as sinners. The story has all the characteristics of a reported event—rich in detail and direct speech. Behind the event, cultural and theological assumptions are at work. Zacchaeus is a Jewish proxy for Roman tax gathering and therefore viewed as negatively as his namesake in 2 Maccabees.

The message proclaimed by Jesus, according to Luke, raises the fundamental question of whether divine grace is defined along racial, gender, or religious lines. Zacchaeus is the sinful archetype (by the standards of Pharisaic piety)—he deserves judgment not grace. His encounter with Jesus breaks the stylized expectations of piety in which the narrative initiative belongs to Jesus despite the obvious curiosity of Zacchaeus. Jesus' surprising self-invitation to Zacchaeus' home comes as a startling rallying point in the face of Zacchaeus' popular condemnation. Jesus' might have been expected to share the hospitality of a 'righteous' man but not a sinner. Zacchaeus's repentance parallels the lavish expression of gratitude in the account of Luke 7.36-50 and concludes with a programmatic aphorism that defines the rationale for Jesus' actions.

The work of Vernon K. Robbins (*Exploring the Texture of Texts*) considers the implicit assumptions of individuals and groups in biblical narrative. Three related themes meet in this narrative. First, Zacchaeus's repentance is beyond any normal expectation. Leviticus 6.5, for example, limits the restoration required in cases of fraud. Zacchaeus offers to go far beyond the requirements of the Torah—he voluntarily relinquishes 'half of my possessions' to the poor (Luke 19.8). Second, the declaration that Zacchaeus now enjoys salvation (19.9) is the consequence, not of legal demand, but of his encounter with Jesus. Zacchaeus' actions declare his gratitude for Jesus' pronouncement of reconciliation implied in, 'because he too is a son of Abraham'. (19.9)—a view at variance with that expressed by the Pharisees in John 8.31-59. Third, the narrative ends (19.10) with a saying regarding Jesus' wider purposes found elsewhere in Luke.

The story of Zacchaeus is compelling for its theology and narrative detail. Various groups ranging from legal services, financial stewardship, to gay and lesbian transformation groups co-opt the name of Zacchaeus as a paradigm for their activities whether a good fit or not. Zacchaeus is also a popular figure in religious iconography depicting a mindset of religious curiosity, repentance and faith. Henri Nouwen's idea of hospitality to the 'other'—the marginalized, is a theme derived from Zacchaeus.

Poetically, Nannie R. Glass (*The Mountain Spring And Other Poems*, 1913) offers a traditional devotional perspective on Zacchaeus, while Joshua McKinney explores the subtle narrative notes in 'Come Down', (*Sacramento Literary Review and Calendar* 11, 5 [2005]). Depictions of the incident range from icons to modern cartoon representations (usually for the religious education of young children), though historically, numerous efforts to visualize the scene date from at least the eleventh century. The physical features of Zacchaeus's stature, his clothing, and the sycamore tree he climbed feature in ways intended to draw the observer into identification with him in relation to Jesus (as in the children's song, 'Zacchaeus was a wee little man'). Zacchaeus becomes the type for those displaced or alienated as a result of their earned reputation or by the boundaries of the community, which did not easily restore persons to full membership.

See also REPENTANCE; TAX COLLECTOR [JKS]

Zacharias. In the Gospel of Luke, the father of John the Baptist, husband of Elizabeth (Luke 1.5-80). When Zacharias, a priest, is serving in the temple, the angel Gabriel announces to him that his barren wife, Elizabeth, will become pregnant and bear a son called John. For his skepticism, he is struck dumb during the course of the pregnancy, but when Elizabeth, a kinswoman of Mary, gives birth, Zacharias is filled with the Holy Spirit and utters a prophecy that his son shall be a prophet of God (1.67-80). Luke 3.2 refers to John as the son of Zacharias.

According to the second-century *Infancy Gospel of James* (also called the *Protevangelium of James*), Zacharias was killed in the forecourt of the temple, a conflation of the father of the Baptist with a prophet named in Matt. 23.35 and Luke 11.51. A figure associated with Advent, he is mentioned in Canadian poet Margaret Avison's 'Christmas: Anticipation' ('the patient years in the appointed place brought Zacharias, dumb with unbelieving'). Contemporary Catholic composer Michael Joncas's 'Canticle of Zachary' is an Advent hymn beginning with the line

'Blest be the God of Israel, the everliving Lord' (cf. Luke 1.68).

See also ELIZABETH; GABRIEL, THE ANGEL; JOHN THE BAPTIST [MALB]

Zealots. The term 'Zealots' has been used by historians to identify Jewish revolutionary groups in the century leading up to the first Jewish revolt against Rome (66–73 CE). In the last quarter century, however, many scholars have narrowed its definition. Based on the descriptions given by the Jewish historian Josephus, the Zealots first appeared in 67 CE as one of several groups in Jerusalem involved in the revolt, comprised of mostly Jewish peasants and brigand chiefs who fled to Jerusalem from the countryside seeking refuge from the advancing Roman troops. The title of their newly formed coalition was likely inspired by the 'zeal tradition' popular in first-century Palestine. According to this tradition, pious Israelites could share God's zeal for his honor and his law and could thus join in his righteous anger and retribution. The zeal-inspired violent acts of Phinehas (Num. 25.6-13) or the prophet Elijah (1 Kgs 18) became popular features of first-century Judean literature. Although such zeal for God's law could be manifested non-violently (i.e., martyrdom), in the case of the Zealots and other Jewish groups in revolt, it fueled their revolutionary behavior. One of Jesus' disciples is called 'Simon the Zealot' in the NT (Mark 3.18; Matt. 10.4; Luke 6.15; Acts 1.13), probably not because he belonged to the Zealot movement of the 60s, but because of his zeal for the Law.

Once in Jerusalem, the Zealots usurped the local nobility's leadership and thwarted all hope of reconciliation with Rome. Rather than preparing for battle with the advancing Roman troops, the Zealots spent most of their time feuding with other Jewish groups. Only when the Roman general Titus besieged Jerusalem in the spring of 70 did the Zealots finally fight and die alongside their fellow Jews.

Another first-century revolutionary group often discussed in conjunction with the Zealots is 'the Sicarii'. This ancient network, named after their curved knives (*sicae*), appeared around 52 CE, further destabilizing the social, economic and religious situation in Judea by targeting 'compromising' Jewish elites for assassination. When their key leader, Menahem, was killed by a rival group during the early stages of the revolt, the Sicarii took control of Masada—Herod's old fortress—where they stayed until committing mass suicide in 73/74. Later in Jewish history, after the devastating results of the Bar-Kokhba revolt (132–135), the Rabbis moved away from a violent approach to zeal, choosing to either ignore or vilify the Zealots, Sicarii, and other revolutionaries of the first century.

Several literary works have been inspired by the Zealots and the Jewish revolt in general. In 1677, John Crowne wrote a drama entitled *The Destruction of Jerusalem by Titus Vespasian* and Henry Hart Milman wrote the dramatic poem *The Fall of Jerusalem* in the nineteenth century. Both dramas involve members of the Zealots as well as other Jewish revolutionaries. In 1970, Ernest Gann wrote a historical fiction about Masada called *The Antagonists*, and in 1998 Gloria Miklowitz wrote a similar book called *Masada: The Last Stand*. Both of these works celebrate the unswerving commitment shown by the Sicarii at Masada. Gann's novel was turned into a miniseries aired on ABC called *Masada* (1981). In the 1970s, the Avalon Hill Game Company even came out with a board game entitled *Siege of Jerusalem* in which the player becomes a Zealot leader. For many Jews and modern Israeli's, the fortress at Masada remains a powerful national symbol. There Israeli soldiers regularly take the oath: 'Masada shall not fall again'.

Recommended reading. Hengel, Martin. *The Zealots*. Edinburgh: T. & T. Clark, 1989.

See also FALL OF JERUSALEM, THE; ROMAN EMPIRE; SIMON THE ZEALOT [JP]

Zebulun (see Twelve Tribes of Israel).

Zechariah. *Zekharyah*, 'Yah remembered': (1) King of Israel, son of Jeroboam II (2 Kgs 14.29; 15.8; 15.11); (2) Maternal grandfather of Hezekiah, king of Judah (2 Kgs 18.2; 2 Chron. 29.1); (3) A descendant of Reuben (1 Chron. 5.1); (4) A common name among priests and levites (1 Chron. 9.21; 9.37; 15.18, 20, 24; 16.5; 24.25; 26.2, 14, 11; 2 Chron. 20.14; 24.20-21; 29.13; 34.12; Ezra 8.16; 10.24-26; Neh. 11.12; 12.16, 35, 41; 1 Esdras 1.15; 8.44); (5) Father of Iddo, chief of the tribe of Manasseh (1 Chron. 27.21); (6) Teacher commissioned by Jehoshaphat, king of Judah, to teach the law in the cities of Judah (2 Chron. 17.7-9); (7) Son of Jehoshaphat killed by his brother, Jehoram, after taking his father's throne (2 Chron. 21.12); (8) One who understood the visions of God during Uzziah's reign (KJV 2 Chron. 26.5; NRSV translates the root as *yare'* 'fear' rather than *ra'ah* 'see'); (9) Ruler of the house of God who gave freewill offerings to the priests for the Passover celebrated during Josiah's reign (2 Chron. 35.8; 1 Esdras 1.8); (10) Zechariah the prophet, the son of Berechaiah, son of Iddo (Ezra 5.1; 6.14; Zech. 1.1, 7; 7.1, 8; 1 *Esdras* 6.1; 7.3); (11) Name of two chiefs who 'went up ... from Babylon' with Ezra (Ezra 8.3, 11; 1 *Esdras* 8.30, 37); (12) Son of Elam, mentioned in a list of those who took foreign wives in the book of Ezra (Ezra 10.26; 1 Esdras 9.27); (13) One who stood with Ezra as he read from the book of the Law (Neh. 8.4; 1 Esdras 9.44); (14) Zechariah, son of Amariah, grandfather of Athaiah, a resident in Jerusalem mentioned in Nehemiah (Neh. 11.4); (15) Zechariah, son of Shiloni, the name of an ancestor of Maaseiah, also a resident in Jerusalem mentioned in Nehemiah (Neh. 11.5); (16) Son of Jeberechiah, called as a witness to the oracle given in Isa. 8.1-4. The similarities between the names Zechariah son of Berechiah and Zechariah son of Jeberechiah have caused much discussion concerning the relationship between the two names (Isa. 8.1-4; Zech. 1.1); (17) The father of Joseph who was placed (with Azariah) in charge of some of the forces of Judas Maccabeus. He was ordered by Judas to take charge of the people and not engage in battle until his return. He disobeyed and was defeated in battle. The text states that the situation occurred because he 'did not listen to Judas and his brothers' and 'did not belong to the family of those men through whom deliverance was given to Israel' (1 Macc. 5.61-62); (18) in contemporary English translations, the name Zacharias, father of John the Baptist, is often rendered as Zechariah (Luke 1.5-18; 3.2).

In the NT, Zechariah the son of Jehoida (who prophesied against the people for turning away from Yahweh and serving 'groves and idols') is confused with Zechariah the prophet. Because of the former's stance against what he perceived as forbidden forms of worship, he was stoned by the people at the command of Joash, king of Judah (2 Chron. 24). Matthew associates this tradition with Zechariah the prophet by amending the text with 'son of Barachiah' (Matt. 23.35; Zech. 1.1) while Luke (11.51) does not add 'son of Barachiah' showing that the two gospels, in their final redactional forms, understood differently Jesus' reference to Zechariah.

See also ZECHARIAH, BOOK OF; ZACHARIAS [CHB]

Zechariah, Book of. The book of Zechariah is part of the second division of the OT, the prophets (*Nevi'im*). It is the second last book of the Minor Prophets in the Christian arrangement of the OT. The book is written in the postexilic era when the exiles of Judah have returned from Babylon to Jerusalem to rebuild the temple. Traditionally, the book of Zechariah is divided into two sections. The first section (Zech. 1–8) describes a series of night visions related to the prophet by an interpreting angel, while the second section (Zech. 9–14) is composed of various oracles with apocalyptic overtones.

Early interpreters focused on the 'branch' (Zech. 3.8; 6.2) and additional oracles in Zechariah 9–14 as messianic predictions of Jesus in the NT. This is demonstrated in Matthew's reuse of Zech. 9.9, which depicts the triumphal procession of Jesus into Jerusalem on a donkey as the fulfillment of prophecy (Matt. 21.1-11). In addition, the visions and symbols in Zechariah are an important source of inspiration for the writer of the Apocalypse. This is evident in the similarities between the description of coloured horses in Zech. 1.8-12 and Rev. 6.1-8.

Zechariah and his visions have also been captured in artwork throughout the centuries. Michelangelo (1475–1564) featured the prophet Zechariah in the famous Sistine Chapel above the door in which the Pope ceremoniously enters on Palm Sunday, a testament to the enduring legacy of messianic interpretations of Zechariah. In addition, Gustave Doré (1832–1883), in a wood engraving, depicted Zechariah 6 in his *Zechariah's Vision of Four Chariots*.

In more recent times, the messianic interpretation of Zechariah has played an important role in the theology of religious groups like the Branch Davidians. Their self-appointed leader, David Koresh, saw himself as a messianic figure by drawing on allusions in Zechariah, Psalms and Revelation.

Recommended reading. Boda, Mark. *Haggai–Zechariah*. NIV Application Commentary; Grand Rapids, MI: Zondervan, 2004. Jauhiainen, Marko. *The Use of Zechariah in Revelation*. Tübingen: Mohr Siebeck, 2005.

See also BABYLONIAN EXILE; ZECHARIAH [HLM]

Zelophehad, Daughters of. The episode of the daughters of Zelophehad occurs in the narrative context of the allotment of the land in the wilderness, after the Exodus but before entry into Canaan (Num. 26.32-33; 27.1-11; 36.1-12; Josh. 17.3-6). Zelophehad and his daughters are minor characters whose story establishes precedents for inheritance by females in a society in which the male is primary and identity is established through kinship groups defined through the male line. Zelophehad, who has died, had five daughters and no sons. The daughters petition Moses to allocate them the portion of the land that would have gone to their father, so that his memory would be preserved in the association between land and name. The request is granted with divine approval on condition that they marry within their clan. In later interpretation the story has functioned: (1) as a basis for rules for inheritance (particularly in Jewish interpretation), (2) more recently, to model women asserting themselves without breaching societal boundaries in a context in which they are secondary to males, and (3) as a symbol for the provision of shelter and support to disempowered women, such as victims of domestic violence. The rabbinic *Bava Batra* 119b teaches that the daughters were Torah students, wise and righteous.

A motif of female inheritance of the father's assets appears in modern literature and film (e.g., *Lara Croft*, *The King of Texas*), usually as backstory for a plot about subsequent events. In contrast, the biblical account does not detail the subsequent life of the daughters [PT]

Zephaniah, Book of. A minor (Latter) prophetic book placed ninth in the scroll of the Twelve Prophets. The name means 'the Lord hides' (i.e., 'protects'). Three other OT figures bore this name (1 Chron. 6.36-38; Jer. 21.1; Zech. 6.10). Zephaniah has the longest genealogy of any of the prophets (cf. Jer. 36.14). He is identified (or identifies himself) as 'Zephaniah the son of Cushi son of Gedaliah son of Amariah son of Hezekiah' (1.1). Most commentators believe that the length of the genealogy is to make sure that the name Cushi would not permit anyone to dismiss his message on the grounds he was Ethiopian (or African). The reference to Hezekiah may or may not show that he is also of royal lineage. If Zephaniah does not mean King Hezekiah, then it is not clear why he went beyond the usual prophetic practice of naming only his father. All of the names in his genealogy except Cushi are a form of Yah(weh), indicating his Israelite nationality.

Zephaniah lived in Judah, possibly Jerusalem, contemporary with Jeremiah and Nahum. His prophetic message was delivered in the time of King Josiah (640–609 BCE) the son of Amon (Zeph. 1.1). Interpretation of verses in the book suggest that his message was delivered early in Josiah's reign (2 Kgs 22.1–23.30; 2 Chron. 34–35), prior to his reforms in 621 BCE. Baal worship and the syncretistic practices of its priests were abolished by Josiah. The destruction of Nineveh prophesied in Zeph. 2.13 did not occur until 612 BCE. Some date the whole book's writing between 640 and 621 (probably in the 630s); however, others place chap. 3 between 621 and 609.

The prophetic activity of Zephaniah was the first for decades. The last prophetic activity had been when Isaiah (701 BCE) prophesied against Sennacherib during the siege of Jerusalem. During the reigns of Manasseh (687–642) and Amon (642–640) the only prophetic activity had been a judgment on Manasseh's reign uttered by Yahweh's servants the prophets (2 Kgs 21.10). Following Zephaniah, a number of other prophets (e.g., Jeremiah, Obadiah, Nahum) were very active.

The book is the 'word of the Lord' to Zephaniah (1.1), organized into three parts: a universal warning of judgment; an exhortation to repentance; and the promise of salvation. Its main focus is upon the Day of the Lord which is a Day of Judgment and Wrath upon all Judah and all other nations. Other prophets had warned about the divine judgment that was being stored up to be delivered to the wicked (Obad 15; Joel 1.15; Amos 5.18-20, Isa. 13.6), but Zephaniah is focused on this theme. It will be a day in which God intervenes in history to establish his Kingdom of Righteousness.

Judgment is pronounced upon Judah and Jerusalem; upon the surrounding nations and upon the whole world. But, it is also a time of salvation because the love of God will preserve a remnant among whom the kingdom of righteousness will be established.

Zephaniah is a source for lectionary readings and for many Advent and Christmas sermons. Jonathan Swift's (1667–1745) poem 'The Day of Judgment' is based on Zeph. 1.14-18.

Recommended reading. Robertson, O. Palmer. *The Books of Nahum, Habakkuk, and Zephaniah*. The New International Commentary on the OT; Grand Rapids, MI: William B. Eerdmans, 1990.

See also BAAL; DAY, OF JUDGMENT/OF THE LORD/OF WRATH; FORMER PROPHETS; JOSIAH; LATTER PROPHETS, PROPHECY, PROPHETS; WRATH [AJW]

Zerubbabel. From Hebrew roots *zera* (seed) and *babel* (Babylon), 'seed of Babylon' (or 'seeded in Babylon'). Another possibility for the root is *zarab* ('to be burned or scorched'). Zerubbabel is the name of the governor of Judah in postexilic Israel, grandson of King Jehoiachin deposed by Nebuchadnezzar, a direct descendant of David. He is described as the son of Shealtiel (or Salathiel) in all biblical occurrences except for one (cf. 1 Chron. 3.16-19).

With the blessing of the Persian king Cyrus the Great, Zerubbabel was a key player in the rebuilding of the Second Temple in Jerusalem. Featured prominently in the postexilic prophecies of prophets Haggai and Zechariah, Zerubbabel's role in the establishment of the Second Temple's community restoration and religious practices cannot be overstated. Along with the high priest Joshua, Zerubbabel reinstituted the Levite's order, as well as built the altar and laid the foundation of the temple (Ezra 3.2-10).

Sometimes confused with Sheshbazzar, Zerubbabel seems to have been the last ruler of the Davidic dynasty. Besides his importance in the rebuilding of Jerusalem and the temple, not much is known about him and his influence in the postexilic Jerusalem. In the early Jewish 1 *Esdras* 3.1–5.6, Zerubbabel is presented as a sage who impresses the Persian king Darius with his wisdom, thus motivating the king to support his work in Jerusalem.

Among modern-day Christians, Zerubbabel symbolizes the vision/faith for restoration, renewal, and completion. Evangelicals often quote verses from Zechariah: 'Not by might, nor by power, but by my spirit, says the Lord of hosts' (4.6) and 'The hands of Zerubbabel have laid the foundation of this house; his hands shall also complete it. What are you, O great mountain? Before Zerubbabel you shall become a plain; and he shall bring out the top stone amid shouts of "Grace, grace to it!"' (4.9) Both verses are often used as prayers and sermon topics; the first to declare the sovereignty of God, and the second testifying to God's promise to sustain those he has commissioned. Similarly, another verse is used to talk about 'days of small beginnings' (4.10). Applied to the theme of obstacles faced in achieving one's dreams, the verse is usually associated with encouragement.

In context, these three verses were part of the oracle given to Zerubbabel through the prophet Zechariah. Zerubbabel had faced opposition while rebuilding the temple (Ezra 4). The work was considerably slowed down, and brought to a halt until the second year of the reign of Darius. Zerubbabel was, however, encouraged by the prophets Haggai and Zechariah (Ezra 5.1-2).

Recommended reading. Kessler, John. *The Book of Haggai: Prophecy and Society in Early Persian Yehud.* Pp. 70-80. Leiden: Brill, 2002.

See also CYRUS; EZRA; NEHEMIAH; HAGGAI; JERUSALEM; TEMPLE, ISRAEL'S; ZECHARIAH [GA]

Zilpah (see Bilhah and Zilpah).

Zion. The origin of the word is uncertain. It could be related to the Hebrew *ṣāwāh* (to erect) or *ṣāyāh* (to be dry). It may come from the Hurrian *seya* (brook), which is below the city of David, or from the Arabic *ṣāhweh* (hillcrest), which is its location or *ṣâna* (protect), because Zion was fortified on a hill.

Zion is used in four ways in the OT: It was first a place on the SE ridge of the modern-day Temple Mount where there was a Jebusite fortress which David conquered (2 Sam. 5.7, 9) and renamed Jerusalem. It then became the mount on which Solomon built his temple where Yahweh dwelt and sat enthroned (1 Kgs 8.1; Ps. 76.2; Isa. 8.18; Ps. 9.11). It was where Yahweh set his chosen Davidic king who would rule humanity forever (Isa. 28.16; Mic. 4.7; 2 Sam. 7.13; Ps. 2; 110; 132). Since Jerusalem was built around this mount, the whole city came to be known as Zion (Isa. 40.9), so much so that it could be used as a synonym for Jerusalem (Lam. 2.6-8). Finally, Zion came to refer to all of Israel, though perhaps only those who were loyal to Yahweh rather than all of those whose ancestors were Abraham, Isaac and Jacob.

Zion traditions are rarely found in the NT (cf. Matt. 21.5; John 12.15; Rom. 9.33; 11.26; 1 Pet. 2.6; Rev. 14.1) or beyond, due largely to the increasing Gentile population of the church. It is understandable that a tradition known to few outside Judaism would survive among them. So the Jewish idea of sacred space was delocalized and, instead, spiritualized (Gal. 4.22-26; Heb. 12.22). The Dome of the Rock possibly sits atop the biblical Zion.

Zion connotes joy where kings ascended and decreed the cancelations of debts or the release of prisoners. It further connotes divine election since it is where Yahweh chose his earthly dwelling place and earth's king. Lastly, Zion is understood to mean peace since it was Yahweh's earthly throne. The mountain took prominence during the monarchy as a site of pilgrimage and came to the fore after the divided kingdom (Israel and Judah) when the Judean kings were interested in centralizing sacrificial worship in Jerusalem in order to consolidate religious and political power. The term, then, was tightly associated with the temple mount and did not lose its spatial reference. The fate of the mount, the city and the people in the nation were intertwined and that is why any of them could be referred to with the same term. Israel's religious self-understanding is tied to the fate of its holy mountain.

These same connotations of joy, election, and peace are used in the films *The Matrix, The Matrix. Reloaded, and The Matrix: Revolutions.* 'Zion' in the film is a fortress in which those elected to recruit and deliver humans from the human farms hide from the Matrix. Everyone born there is considered free and anyone freed is brought there. The international Reggae star Bob Marley also capitalized on Zion's positive connotations in his music. The songs 'Iron, Lion, Zion' and 'Zion Train' sing of the invincibility of an iron lion in Zion and of the soul train coming one's way with Zion for its final destination. Lauryn Hill, Bob's daughter-in-law, sings of having found the joy of her world in Zion after experiencing overwhelming emotion during her pregnancy ('To Zion'). Likewise, Christian hymns frequently celebrate Zion (e.g., 'We're Marching to Zion'; 'Zion's Daughter'; 'Come, Ye Sons of Zion'; 'O Zion, Haste').

See also DAUGHTER OF ZION; JERUSALEM [SV]

Zipporah/Tzipporah. From Hebrew, *sippor*, meaning 'bird'. In Exodus, Tzipporah is the wife of Moses and the daughter of Jethro, a Midianite priest. After Moses flees from Egypt and Pharaoh, he settles among the Midianites, an Arab people, where he rescues the seven daughters of Jethro from the shepherds who are harassing them. In gratitude, Jethro offers Moses his daughter, Tzipporah, in marriage. The couple has two children, Gershom and Eliezer.

Tzipporah is featured in a very difficult passage of the Bible when Moses, his wife, and their sons are heading back to Egypt (Exod. 4.24-26). The family is resting overnight when God attacks Moses. It is then that Tzipporah takes a flint and cuts off her son's foreskin (though it is not known which son) and flings the foreskin at 'his' feet. However, at whose feet she threw the foreskin is a mystery to scholars— it could have been the feet of the child, Moses, or God. At any rate, her actions stop the attack. Because of this incident, the rabbis assume that Tzipporah had converted to Judaism, since she was knowledgeable about the commandment of circumcision. Later, sometime before the exodus from Egypt, Moses sends Tzipporah and the children away. After the Exodus, Jethro is going to visit Moses and he takes the family with him. Moses goes out to meet his father-in-law, but nothing is said of Tzipporah.

Interestingly, Moses's wife—albeit not by name—appears in Numbers when Miriam and Aaron launch an attack against Moses because of the 'Cushite woman' whom he married and subsequently was neglecting (Num. 12.1). The Cushites were an African ethnic group, and indeed the Midianites were a dark-skinned people often called *Kushim*, Hebrew to describe black Africans. The historian Flavius Josephus refers to the 'Kushite woman' as the wife Moses married before fleeing Egypt, during his campaign to Ethiopia as a general for the Egyptians. Some scholars agree that Moses may have had multiple wives, as was common among the patriarchs. However, there is no mention of any children by a second marriage, nor of a marriage itself. Ultimately, Jewish and Christian tradition assumes that Miriam and Aaron were referring to Tzipporah.

Tzipporah's intense loyalty to Moses, paired with her name, meaning 'bird', are reminiscent of the loyalty of the Egyptian goddess Isis, who is often portrayed as a bird of prey, to her husband Osiris. In rabbinic literature her name is explained as having been given to her because, when questioned as to who had rescued her, she flew out of the house like a bird and returned with Moses.

In the twentieth century, she has been portrayed memorably by Yvonne de Carlo in *The Ten Commandments* (1956). Actress Michelle Pfeifer gave her a voice in the 1998 DreamWorks animated film *The Prince of Egypt*, which delves into the life of Moses. The story embellishes the biblical story, suggesting that Moses and Tzipporah actually met prior to when Moses saved her and her siblings from the shepherds, and portrays her as Moses's companion and equal. She is also the subject of one of the books in Marek Halter's Canaan Trilogy. Using the biblical story, Halter imagines the life of the little-known wife of Moses in *Zipporah: Wife of Moses*.

See also AARON; MOSES; JETHRO; EXODUS, BOOK OF; MIRIAM [CG]

Zophar (see Job's Friends).

www.ingramcontent.com/pod-product-compliance
Lightning Source LLC
Chambersburg PA
CBHW080356170426
43193CB00016B/2737